MEN IN WHITE

The History of New Zealand Test Cricket

Don Neely & Francis Payne

Hodder Moa

National Library of New Zealand Cataloguing-in-Publication Data
Neely, D.O. (Donald Owen), 1935- and Payne, F.K. (Francis Keith), 1951-
Men in White : the history of New Zealand test cricket / Don Neely.
Previous ed.: Men in White, The History of New Zealand International Cricket. 1986.
ISBN 978-1-86971-095-8
1. Cricket—New Zealand—History. I. Title.
796.3580993—dc 22

A Hodder Moa Book
Published in 2008 by Hachette Livre NZ Ltd
4 Whetu Place, Mairangi Bay
Auckland, New Zealand

Text © Don Neely and Francis Payne 2008
The moral rights of the authors have been asserted.
Design and format © Hachette Livre NZ Ltd 2008

Designed and typeset by Francis Payne
Printed by Everbest Printing Co. Ltd., China

Jacket photographs
Front: Daniel Vettori, Stephen Fleming, Martin Crowe and Sir Richard Hadlee. Basin Reserve. *Photosport*.

Back – top: The 1949 New Zealand team, from left: Walter Hadlee *(captain)*, Brun Smith, Frank Mooney, Martin Donnelly, Merv Wallace, Ces Burke, Verdun Scott, John Reid, Jack Cowie, Harry Cave, Geoff Rabone, John Hayes, Bert Sutcliffe, Jack Phillipps *(manager)*. *Don Neely*. Back – bottom: The 1981 New Zealand team against India, from left: John Reid, Geoff Howarth *(captain)*, Lance Cairns, Jock Edwards, Ian Smith, Bruce Edgar, Richard Hadlee, Martin Snedden, Jeremy Coney, John Wright, Gary Troup. *Don Neely*.

Contents

For Paddianne. Without her encouragement and assistance there would be fewer works about New Zealand cricket's history – **Don Neely**

For everyone who has supported the New Zealand cricket team over the years – **Francis Payne**

Foreword

When Don Neely invited me to provide the foreword to the second edition of *Men in White*, I immediately checked to see who had written the original foreword. It was, not surprisingly, my dear friend of many years and my former captain Walter Hadlee.

He wrote that he was deeply honoured to be invited and so am I; firstly, to be writing it and secondly, to be following in Walter's footsteps. Walter's contribution was a chapter in itself of some 5,000 words; a series of wonderful reminiscences from a long and distinguished lifetime on and off the cricket field and descriptions of the deeds of so many great cricketers who played with and against him.

I could not and would not attempt to emulate him but, like him, I do have a host of wonderful memories of cricket and cricketers, many of them arising from forty years of commentating which covered some five hundred matches of one, three, four and five days' duration. Walter was something of a rarity amongst top level cricketers — he was keen about statistics and I mean statistics covering a wide range of fields (top level cricketers are usually well versed in their own facts and figures!).

As a bridge partner, he would, from time to time, interrupt the playing of a hand with a sudden question of how many times so and so had made 50 before lunch in a test match at Old Trafford or something equally obscure and irrelevant. It was no doubt introduced to divert the opposition's train of thought and could be highly disconcerting! Walter found ample material to research and reminisce about in *Men in White* as he would have done in its successor, this new edition of *Men in White*.

The new edition also differs from the original in that it is confined to official test matches, whereas its predecessor contained particulars of every match played by a New Zealand XI whether a test (official or unofficial) or a first-class match at home or abroad.

It is indeed appropriate that this history should concentrate on test cricket. It is a delight to be able to state in 2008, 22 years after the publication of *Men in White,* that test cricket has regained its status in the eyes of the public. For some years it appeared to be under threat from one-day internationals, but it seems to me that with the dramatic development of 20-over cricket here and overseas, it is the 50-over game which might well prove vulnerable.

Those of us who are octogenarians have watched developments with a degree of disbelief and, from time to time, concern so it is important that *Men in White* should make its welcome reappearance on the literary stage.

The descriptions of the test matches from 1930 to 1985 have been skilfully and sensitively edited with the result that little is lost in terms of words whilst a reduction in the number of photograph sections has been compensated for by their inclusion in each match description.

Several 'new' photographs have been included, even for matches played more than 50 years ago, and, of course, we now have colour. Every test has been illustrated with New Zealand players with 203 of the 237 test players appearing at least once in the photographs.

The coverage of each test match ends with a distinctive 'Milestones' section, which gives a clear précis of special achievements, statistical and otherwise, of certain participants, e.g., test debuts — with the Black Caps' number in brackets — record dismissals and some fascinating facts such as "the two umpires were both former New Zealand test players".

I found it fascinating indeed to read through the original description of play and players and to see the pieces eliminated or substituted by the author and editor in the new edition. This was presumably done to provide an improved commentary, some of it no doubt brought about by some 25 years of reflection.

With a brief pre-war service journalistic career and with a passion for sport in general (cricket and rugby football in particular), I have been privileged to review or write the foreword for a significant number of sporting publications but, sadly and, who knows, perhaps significantly, these have never included one of Don and Padianne Neely's books.

I am so pleased that I am now provided with the opportunity of expressing my deep appreciation of their work over many years. Skilled and experienced archivists, authors, statisticians and observers (and sportsman in the case of Don), their histories of institutions, establishments, sports and sports persons have been invaluable whether written alone or with Joseph Romanos (although I was deeply hurt that I couldn't find any reference in *Lancaster Park* to my kicking 17 points for Army in a club rugby match at Lancaster Park in 1942!).

Supported by that superb statistician Francis Payne (how I miss those days when there could be telephone calls at any hour of the day or night from Francis enquiring as to whether I knew anything about so and so who played a solitary match some time in the nineteenth century for someone or other), the second edition of *Men in White* will be warmly welcomed.

The first edition (of which I am the proud owner of two large editions and one small) was described on its original cover as "the ultimate book on New Zealand cricket" and in it the commentary, facts and figures are preceded by an introduction from the author, Don Neely, setting out in remarkable detail the origins and history of the game beyond and throughout New Zealand.

It was a comprehensive history in its own right, extending far beyond descriptions of matches, facts and figures. This edition is no different in its quality, but the material is fresh and only goes to confirm what I have believed for many years — that we have in the author an historian unsurpassed in the wonderful world of cricket.

Don Neely can be described as the ultimate 'all round' cricketer, player and captain at first-class level, historian, writer and administrator.

He is the current President of New Zealand Cricket, a role which he fills with dignity and distinction and he is, above all, a passionate lover of the game.

Iain Gallaway
Dunedin, March 2008

Introduction

When the first European settlers arrived in New Zealand in 1840, sport as we know it today was virtually non-existent, with the exception of cricket and athletics. It was said that the first settlers who went to the colonies of the British Empire – India, Australia, Canada, South Africa and New Zealand – arrived with the Bible, the musket, the oak and cricket gear; and like the oak, cricket took root and flourished. Its growth was assisted by the Duke of Wellington, who in 1841 issued an order that a cricket ground was to be made adjunct to every military barracks and this included the colonies.

In England in 1846 William Clarke gathered together "The Eleven of England", later known as the "All England Eleven", and set out with missionary zeal to take cricket throughout the countryside of England. He was assisted by the ever-increasing railway network that would take his team to new venues.

Clarke's team would play whenever a guaranteed purse was offered – wet or fine, play or no play. Like all the great advances made in cricket, entrepreneurs have provided the main impetus and professional players have always embraced them, seeking to improve their earning potential. These games not only showcased cricket and spread its popularity but also showed young men that the game could be another form of employment.

Cricket in New Zealand in 1858 was confined to clubs playing other clubs in their towns and settlements. Communication between the settlements was primitive, and

travel was mainly by river and sea. The total population in the 1858 census was just 115,462, of whom 56,049 were Maori.

Pressure by settlers for land and Maori fears that they would lose their entire economic base led to skirmishes and, later, wars in the Waikato and Taranaki. New Zealand's population was boosted with a large influx of British Army personnel. The soldiers, and crews of visiting naval ships, provided fresh opposition for the local clubs.

The population in the South Island, especially in Dunedin, also rose dramatically with the discovery of gold in Otago and the subsequent rush. The new arrivals also increased the ranks of cricketers playing the game.

The entrepreneurs in England saw the opportunity to ship their game to Canada and America in 1859 where their team, led by George Parr, played before large and fashionable crowds. According to one report, each of the tourists received £90 from the profits of the two-month venture.

The American Civil War of 1861–65 halted any further excursions to that part of the world. However, Parr and his players were enticed by Messrs Spiers and Ponds to tour Australia in 1864. Their offer, which was accepted, guaranteed to pay each player £150 and provide first-class travel to and around Australia.

Thanks to the enterprise of Shadrack Jones of Dunedin, Parr's team was also brought out to Otago and Canterbury. In a practice game before the All England XI match against an Otago XXII, a Canterbury team played the home side on

An underarm bowler is about to deliver a ball during a match at Nelson Square, Picton. Note that neither the batsmen nor the wicketkeeper is wearing pads and no one is wearing the traditional white clothing. The pitch is unprepared and the fieldsmen are very close.

27 January 1864; this match is recognised by the Association of Cricket Statisticians as the first first-class match to have been played in New Zealand.

This first visit to New Zealand by an overseas team attracted large and enthusiastic crowds. It was estimated that the tournament would have cost Jones about £3000 to stage, yet it apparently returned a profit.

In 1864 William Gilbert Grace, two days before he turned 16, made 170 and 56 not out for South Wales against the Gentlemen of Sussex at Hove. For nearly 40 years Grace bestrode the sporting world and he changed the face of cricket, particularly batting, forever.

His numerous exploits were given much publicity in England by the local press and their papers providing international coverage, making Dr W.G. Grace a world figure. In 1873 the English County Cricket Championship was inaugurated and this too was followed avidly in New Zealand.

Auckland assembled its first representative team in more than a decade in 1873/74 and ventured forth upon a national tour that was greeted as "the greatest event in New Zealand cricket". The Auckland team sailed to Otago, Canterbury, Wellington and Nelson and won all four games.

With the population of New Zealand having increased to 344,984 by the 1874 census, towns were now cities and were large enough for the players to form associations to look after their welfare. Wellington led the way in 1875 by forming the first Cricket Association. Others soon followed in each of the main centres: Otago in 1876, Canterbury in 1877 and Auckland in 1883.

Some England players contracted to tour Australia in 1876/77 and New Zealand was also involved. To cover the costs of the proposed tour, thought to be about £6000, the agents set out to arrange a series of fixtures in New Zealand. They sought guarantees of £60 a match as well as the gate takings and a proportion of the profits from liquor and the food booths at the grounds, where the agents took it upon themselves to fix the charges.

The England side, led by James Lillywhite Jr., and with 11 other professionals, played in Australia in November, December and January before sailing to New Zealand, where they played an Auckland XXII on 29 January 1877. They visited six other ports before playing their last game against a Southland XXII.

On 6 March 1877, they sailed from Bluff back to Melbourne and nine days later they played a combined Australian team, this time on even terms, 11-a-side, in the game acknowledged as the first test match.

During their time in New Zealand, large crowds attended the games and interest in cricket was heightened. The profit from the 39 days in New Zealand paid for the players' voyage to and from England.

The monetary success of the English trip through New Zealand was not lost on the Australian cricketers who had formed themselves into a company to tour England in 1878. Their tour began in Queensland early in November 1877 and they played nine matches around Australia before touring New Zealand from 9 January to 7 February 1878.

Great Australian cricketers Fred Spofforth, the demon bowler, Jack Blackham, the prince of wicketkeepers, Charlie Bannerman and Dave Gregory created a furore of excitement and their visit stimulated public interest to a higher level in this country. They returned to Australia for six more games before sailing to England, with all their travelling expenses covered by their short trip to New Zealand.

This was to be the pattern for many years to come. From Parr's visit in 1864 until 1914, England or MCC sent six teams; Australia sent 15 and Fiji one. Each time the game of cricket received a great boost.

The Premier, Julius Vogel, initiated various public work programmes in the 1870s, which led to rapid expansion of New Zealand's transport facilities. The growing network of road and rail and improved telegraphic communications enabled increased representative contests between the provinces. The game grew at a remarkable rate, but the major excitement for cricket followers in New Zealand continued to be provided by overseas teams featuring the illustrious names of the cricket world.

By the 1880s cricket was established as the premier summer sport in New Zealand. A boom in immigration from the United Kingdom had reinforced the ranks of players and all those arriving knew of Dr W.G. Grace and had lived with his image adorning all types of products, from Coleman's Mustard to porcelain ashtrays. In English-speaking countries, Grace was the most easily recognisable man in the world.

Wickets began to improve with the introduction of horse-and-hand-powered mowing machines, which also served to level the ground by trimming off bumps. Consequently, the art of batting and ground fielding improved dramatically.

Newspapers reported club matches and meetings and were especially generous in their coverage of representative games, when two full columns were often allocated to ball-by-ball summaries of the day's play.

The Canterbury Cricket Association organised a tour by a team from New South Wales in 1894. The Canterbury selector, Arthur Ollivier, chose a New Zealand team to play the visitors on 15 January. There were complaints in Wellington's *Evening Post* about Canterbury "hosting the match, picking the team and running the whole lot".

This match led indirectly to a meeting of provincial delegates on 27 December 1894. Mr Ollivier proposed the resolution that led to the formation of the New Zealand Cricket Council, whose job it was to govern New Zealand cricket, arrange tours at home and abroad and share any profits, fairly. This enlightened decision was taken 11 years before the Australian Board of Control was established.

The first New Zealand team selected under the auspices of the NZCC played New South Wales on 30, 31 December 1895 and won by 142 runs. New Zealand had put a toe into the waters of international cricket. Cricket was now the national game of New Zealand.

It was difficult to select the New Zealand side to tour Australia in 1899 as four major players were not able to obtain leave from their employers. It was a challenge playing against full-strength sides from Melbourne and elsewhere in Victoria. Even though Arthur Fisher, Alec Downes, Dan Reese and Ernie Upham, four local champions, were in the side, they were no match for their Australian counterparts, who included Victor Trumper, Monty Noble and Frank Laver.

The successful introduction of the Ranfurly Shield, presented in 1905 by the Governor of New Zealand the Earl of Ranfurly, for the best provincial rugby side was a masterstroke. The triumphant tour of the New Zealand rugby team to the British Isles, France and North America saw an explosion of rugby in all areas of New Zealand and rightfully it became the national game.

In 1906/07 the Governor-General, Lord Plunket, presented a shield for competition among the four major associations and Hawke's Bay. The shield was awarded controversially to Canterbury. The Plunket Shield was to be played in the same vein as the Ranfurly Shield, on a challenge basis. In their first defence of the Plunket Shield on 14–17 December 1907, Canterbury lost by an innings and 135 runs to Auckland.

In 1909 the Imperial Cricket Conference was constituted, with the MCC, Australia and South Africa as the original members.

After an interval of 15 years the New Zealand Cricket Council arranged for a second team to visit Australia. This time Dan Reese was not the youngest member, but the captain and best performer. Other players who had done well in New Zealand first-class cricket, such as Nessie Snedden, Billy Patrick and Don Sandman, were out of their depth against the might of New South Wales, containing such great Australians as Victor Trumper, Charlie Macartney, Warren Bardsley, Arthur Mailey and Charles Kellaway. South Australia had Clem Hill while Victoria had Warwick Armstrong and young fast bowler Ted McDonald.

In an attempt to improve the skills of the younger players following the First World War, which had eliminated five years of their apprenticeship in cricket, Australia sent two sides to New Zealand in 1920/21 and 1927/28. So did the state sides: New South Wales in 1923/24, Victoria in 1924/25 and the Melbourne Cricket Club in 1926/27.

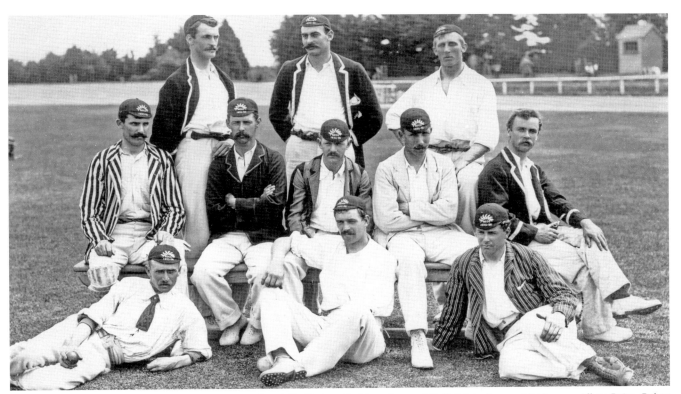

The first official New Zealand cricket team. Back row (from left): Herbert De Maus, Leonard Cuff, Edwin Pearce. Middle row: Albert Rains, Robert Blacklock, Alfred Holdship (captain), Arthur Fisher, Andrew Labatt. Front row: William Robertson, Alec Downes, Alfred Clarke.

In most cases the visitors featured players that were great, or were to become great. The likes of Vernon Ransford, Vic Richardson, Alan Kippax, Bert Oldfield, Bill Woodfull, "Stork" Hendry, Archie Jackson, Bill Ponsford and Clarrie Grimmett proved too strong but the experience did develop the quality of the local players they faced.

It could be said that the older local players, such as Syd Hiddlestone, Stan Brice, Jim Shepherd, Raoul Garrard and Bert Kortlang showed that they could have coped with international cricket. For youngsters like Roger Blunt, Stewie Dempster, Ces Dacre and Ken James, these games provided a vital finishing school in cricket.

In 1925/26, after so many visits by Australian teams over the previous seven years, the NZCC decided it was time once more to tour Australia, even though the Victorian captain, Edgar Mayne, at the end of his side's tour the previous season, had warned that few New Zealanders would be equipped with adequate technique to cope with the faster wickets. Mayne considered that more good would come if a tour went to England.

However, the trip to Australia went ahead. The team did improve during the tour and there was praise for some of the batting and fielding, but the bowling was deemed to be weak, lacking penetration. Regrettably, the tour was not a financial success.

The Imperial Cricket Conference confirmed membership on 31 May 1926 to the governing bodies of India, New Zealand and West Indies, thus opening the way for these countries to play test cricket.

A bold move was taken in October 1926 when Dan Reese, now the Chairman of the NZCC, proposed that a public company be floated to raise funds to send a cricket team to the United Kingdom. New Zealand Cricket Ltd was launched and Reese moved that the council take at least 500 of the 10,000 £1 shares. The selectors were instructed to pick players who had at least 10 years of cricket ahead of them. Thus a young and inexperienced team was announced for a 38-match tour that did not allow for any tests.

In what was termed "the wettest English summer in memory" the tourists won seven and lost five of the 26 first-class fixtures, with 14 draws. Six batsmen bettered 1000 runs in first-class matches: Stewie Dempster, Roger Blunt, Tom Lowry, Jack Mills, Curly Page and Ces Dacre. Having played only one first-class game before he left, young Bill Merritt, bowling right-arm leg-spinners, was an outstanding success with 107 first-class wickets.

The New Zealand team that visited Australia in 1925/26. Back row (from left): Rupert Worker, Cyril Crawford, Hec Gillespie, Charlie Oliver, Ray Hope, Tom Lowry, Bill Cunningham, Ken James, Arthur Alloo. Front row: Dan McBeath, Roger Blunt, Billy Patrick (captain), Frank Peake (manager), Ces Dacre, Cyril Allcott.

Ken James, the wicketkeeper, made 31 stumpings. During the tourists' second game against Essex, Canon F. Gillingham provided five-minute radio summaries of play at hourly intervals.

This was the first radio broadcast of cricket and it meant that many more people in different parts of the world were able to follow the game. Unfortunately, the shareholders in the tour did not receive any dividends.

In 1929/30 the MCC sent two teams abroad, one to New Zealand and the other to the West Indies. Part of their mission was to introduce each country to test cricket. Because of the International Date Line, New Zealand was ahead on time and thus became the fourth country to play a test match, on 10 January 1930.

With the introduction of administrative boards of control and the establishment of the Imperial Cricket Conference in 1909, entrepreneurs all but disappeared from cricket. They began to re-emerge stealthily during the Centenary Test held in Melbourne in 1977.

The proprietor of television station Channel Nine, Kerry Packer, seized on player dissatisfaction with poor payments, primitive television presentation and unimaginative marketing of the product, as well as the possibility of a viable business opportunity. The major test players in the world embraced Packer's World Series Cricket.

The revolution, driven by television, imaginative marketing and advanced technology, rejuvenated the old game and introduced it to millions of new followers in a different guise. Over time it introduced new shots, different techniques and attitudes and changed the face of test cricket for the betterment of the traditional game.

Now, as this book is going to print, entrepreneurs from India are bringing their expertise to bear on what was a simple game that originated in the peace and tranquillity of the countryside. We await the outcome of the Indian Premier League and other innovations in the knowledge that if commonsense prevails then only good will come for the game, the players, its followers and its history.

Note to readers.

Every test in this edition of *Men in White* is numbered. Every match is illustrated and 203 of the 237 Black Caps appear at least once. Each player's test debut is recorded in "Milestones" with their cap number in brackets.

1929/30 MCC in New Zealand

▌1 NEW ZEALAND v ENGLAND *(First Test)*

at Lancaster Park, Christchurch on 10, 11, 13 January, 1930
Toss : New Zealand. Umpires : W. Butler and K.H. Cave
England won by 8 wickets

An MCC side made up of six professionals and eight amateurs played 17 matches, nine resulted in handsome wins, the rest in draws. It was not a full strength England side but this historic contest was recognised as New Zealand's first official test match.

The Lancaster Park wicket proved to be fast, and the pace of the England attack troubled the New Zealanders who were soon floundering at 15-3. Moments later, New Zealand was plunged into more despair as Maurice Allom, a right-arm fast-medium bowler making his test debut, delivered an extraordinary over.

The first ball struck Roger Blunt's foot on the full and he was fortunate to survive a leg-before-wicket appeal. The batsmen scampered through for a leg-bye, but the next ball knocked back Stewie Dempster's wicket. Tom Lowry played at and missed the third ball, and was dismissed leg-before-wicket to the fourth. Ken James was caught by the keeper next ball, and Ted Badcock was bowled by the last delivery in the over.

New Zealand was 21-7, four wickets having fallen in five balls. Allom's hat trick was the 10th to occur in test matches. (Appropriately, among the spectators at Lancaster Park, was the great Australian bowler Hugh Trumble. Now aged 63, he could reflect upon his unique feat of twice taking hat tricks against England.)

Blunt had watched this dismal procession of failures from the safety of the non-striker's end and he now offered stern defence to retrieve the situation. George Dickinson, Bill Merritt and Matt Henderson assisted in taking the score to 112, leaving Blunt not out on 45.

The England openers were both dismissed by 20, but Duleepsinhji and Frank Woolley combined to add 61 and the tourists reached 147-4 at stumps on the first day. Rain prevented any play on the second day – the first Saturday in the Christchurch season to be affected by the weather.

On the third morning, Lowry showed inspired captaincy as he switched bowlers to great effect. Blunt, New Zealand's batting hero, took three wickets (two in successive balls) for eight runs in a brief spell, and both Badcock and Curly Page achieved success in their first overs. The last six England wickets fell for 34 runs.

Despite Lowry's clever leadership, the crowd was openly hostile to him, possibly because he was wearing his blue club cap rather than the New Zealand cap.

England's lead of 69 runs was not overtaken until the

home team had lost three wickets. Harry Foley and Blunt fell cheaply, but Dempster and Page cut well on the drying wicket. A fine captain's innings from Lowry, who scored 40 in an hour and a half, gave New Zealand some hope of saving the game, but he could find no support. When the last man was out at 131 England required 63 to win in the 105 minutes remaining.

Eddie Dawson and Arthur Gilligan were soon dismissed by Blunt, but Duleepsinhji and Woolley chased the runs and the game was over within 45 minutes, during which time the home team bowled 19 overs. In spite of the time lost because of rain, England won on the third day. It was the most inauspicious first step.

NEW ZEALAND

C.S.Dempster	b Allom	11	c Duleepsinhji b Allom		25
H.Foley	c Duleepsinhji b Nichols	2	c Nichols b Allom		2
A.W.Roberts	c Duleepsinhji b Nichols	3	(6) c & b Worthington		5
M.L.Page	c & b Nichols	1	st Cornford b Barratt		21
R.C.Blunt	not out	45	(3) c Legge b Woolley		7
T.C.Lowry*	lbw b Allom	0	(5) b Nichols		40
K.C.James†	c Cornford b Allom	0	lbw b Worthington		0
F.T.Badcock	b Allom	0	(9) b Nichols		0
G.R.Dickinson	b Nichols	11	(8) c Barratt b Woolley		8
W.E.Merritt	b Allom	19	b Allom		2
M.Henderson	b Worthington	6	not out		2
Extras	(b 7, lb 4, nb 3)	14	(b 9, lb 6, nb 4)		19
TOTAL	(47.1 overs)	**112**	(60.3 overs)		**131**

ENGLAND

E.W.Dawson	c Lowry b Henderson	7	lbw b Blunt		10
A.H.H.Gilligan*	c Henderson b Badcock	10	b Blunt		4
K.S.Duleepsinhji	c Dickinson b Henderson	49	not out		33
F.E.Woolley	c Merritt b Dickinson	31	not out		17
G.B.Legge	b Blunt	36			
M.S.Nichols	c Dickinson b Page	21			
T.S.Worthington	b Blunt	0			
M.J.L.Turnbull	c Merritt b Badcock	7			
F.Barratt	st James b Merritt	4			
W.L.Cornford†	c Lowry b Blunt	6			
M.J.C.Allom	not out	4			
Extras	(b 3, lb 1, nb 2)	6	(w 1, nb 1)		2
TOTAL	(63.1 overs)	**181**	(18.5 overs) (2 wkts)		**66**

Bowling	O	M	R	W	O	M	R	W
ENGLAND								
Nichols	17	5	28	4	14.3	6	23	2
Allom	19	4	38	5	15	6	17	3
Barratt	4	1	8	0	9	2	16	1
Worthington	7.1	1	24	1	13	4	19	2
Woolley					9	2	37	2
NEW ZEALAND								
Badcock	18	7	29	2				
Dickinson	11	1	40	1	2	0	4	0
Merritt	13	1	48	1	2	0	7	0
Henderson	8	1	38	2	7	2	26	0
Blunt	11.1	4	17	3	7	1	17	2
Page	2	1	3	1				
Dempster					0.5	0	10	0

Fall of Wickets	NZ	E	NZ	E
	1st	1st	2nd	2nd
1st	5	20	8	14
2nd	11	20	28	17
3rd	15	81	65	–
4th	21	113	79	–
5th	21	148	86	–
6th	21	148	86	–
7th	21	163	111	–
8th	64	168	111	–
9th	103	172	125	–
10th	112	181	131	–

MILESTONES

- Maurice Allom became the eighth player to take a hat-trick in test cricket. The Australians Hugh Trumble and Jimmy Matthews performed the feat twice.

- It was the first time in test cricket that four wickets were captured in five balls; a feat replicated in 1978 by Chris Old For England v Pakistan and in 1990/91 by Wasim Akram for Pakistan v West Indies.

- All the New Zealand team were making their test debut. Official test cap numbers are Ted Badcock (1), Roger Blunt (2), Stewie Dempster (3), George Dickinson (4), Harry Foley (5), Matt Henderson (6), Ken James (7), Tom Lowry (8), Bill Merritt (9), Curly Page (10), Alby Roberts (11).
- Allom, Tich Cornford and Arthur Gilligan were making their debut for England.
- Lancaster Park became the 17th venue to host a test match.

2   NEW ZEALAND v ENGLAND *(Second Test)*

at Basin Reserve, Wellington on 24, 25, 27 January, 1930
Toss : New Zealand. Umpires : K.H. Cave and L.T. Cobcroft
Match drawn

Foley, Roberts and Henderson were replaced in the New Zealand team by Jack Mills, Lindsay Weir (a 21-year-old Auckland batsman beginning a distinguished career for his country) and Eddie McLeod.

Morris Nichol's first over, bowled on a lively wicket and with the aid of a northerly breeze, gave Dempster and Mills a fiery welcome. The last ball reared up at Dempster and cannoned off his head for a leg-bye. The Wellington opener had been forced to retire twice in one innings when batting for his province against the visitors.

However, the New Zealand pair survived the early barrage and by lunch had reached 113. Both had completed centuries at tea, when the total was 227.

Woolley broke the partnership by bowling Mills after the New Zealand openers had compiled a stand of 276 in four and a half hours. Mills hit 13 fours in his innings of 117 and showed ability to time the hook shot to perfection.

Although Dempster hit only eight fours in his innings of 136 he was so busy scoring ones and twos that he had the honour of scoring the first century for New Zealand in the test match.

He eventually misjudged a ball from Woolley and was stumped by Tich Cornford by a substantial margin. Lowry became Woolley's third victim of the day, and the crowd departed well satisfied with New Zealand's effort of 339-3.

The following morning, Woolley's artfully flighted left-arm spinners took another four wickets, giving him his best bowling analysis in test cricket of 7-76. Apart from the excellent opening stand, Page (67) and Blunt (36) were the only other significant contributors to the final total of 440.

Spirited bowling by Ted Badcock and Dickinson had England in trouble at 149-5, but poor catching allowed the initiative to slip away from New Zealand. Mills dropped an easy chance from Nichols, and his subsequent 78 not out helped England avoid the follow-on and reach 320 on the third morning.

Dempster gave a chance off the first ball in New Zealand's second innings, but completed a fine double by scoring 80 not out before Lowry declared at 164-4. England required

The first official New Zealand test team. Back row (left to right): Ted Badcock, Alby Roberts, Harry Foley, Matt Henderson, Eddie McLeod (12th man), Bill Merritt. Front row: George Dickinson, Curly Page, Roger Blunt, Tom Lowry (captain) Stewie Dempster, Ken James.

285 to win in 110 minutes, and a draw was inevitable. The crowd was entertained by a delightful display by Duleepsinhji (56 not out) before the close of play. The gate takings of £1125 set a new record for a game in this country.

The President of the NZCC, Dan Reese, expressed the belief that the New Zealanders' inability to hold catches had cost them the chance of achieving an historic victory.

MILESTONES

- Right-hand opening batsman Stewie Dempster became the first New Zealander to score a test century.

- Left-hand opening batsman Jack Mills made a century on debut.

- Their opening partnership of 276 is the best for any wicket by New Zealand against England after 78 years and 91 tests between the two countries.

- Eddie McLeod (12), Mills (13) and Lindsay Weir (14) made their test debuts.

- Frank Woolley became the first bowler to take five or more wickets in an innings against New Zealand.

- The Basin Reserve became the 19th test match venue.

NEW ZEALAND

C.S.Dempster	st Cornford b Woolley	136	not out	80
J.E.Mills	b Woolley	117	b Nichols	7
T.C.Lowry*	c Duleepsinhji b Woolley	6		
M.L.Page	c Cornford b Allom	67	c Bowley b Woolley	32
R.C.Blunt	c Duleepsinhji b Woolley	36	b Worthington	12
E.G.McLeod	b Woolley	16	not out	2
G.L.Weir	lbw b Woolley	3	(3) c Duleepsinhji b Woolley	21
K.C.James†	c Cornford b Worthington	7		
G.R.Dickinson	c Worthington b Woolley	5		
W.E.Merritt	lbw b Worthington	0		
F.T.Badcock	not out	4		
Extras	(b 17, lb 18, nb 8)	43	(b 1, lb 2, nb 7)	10
TOTAL	(136.3 overs)	440	(53 overs) (4 wkts dec)	164

ENGLAND

E.H.Bowley	b Blunt	9	c Weir b Dickinson	2
E.W.Dawson	b Badcock	44	c Lowry b Badcock	7
K.S.Duleepsinhji	c Blunt b Badcock	40	not out	56
F.E.Woolley	c Lowry b Dickinson	6	b Merritt	23
G.B.Legge	c James b Dickinson	39	c Lowry b Weir	9
M.S.Nichols	not out	78	not out	3
T.S.Worthington	st James b Merritt	32		
A.H.H.Gilligan*	b Merritt	32		
F.Barratt	b Badcock	5		
W.L.Cornford†	c Page b Badcock	10		
M.J.C.Allom	c Lowry b Dickinson	2		
Extras	(b 11, lb 4, nb 8)	23	(b 4, lb 2, nb 1)	7
TOTAL	(107.5 overs)	320	(39 overs) (4 wkts)	107

Bowling	O	M	R	W	O	M	R	W
ENGLAND								
Nichols	20	5	66	0	9	1	22	1
Allom	28	4	73	1	6	1	21	0
Barratt	33	4	87	0				
Worthington	22	3	63	2	10	0	44	1
Bowley	5	0	32	0	5	0	19	0
Woolley	28.3	5	76	7	23	9	48	2
NEW ZEALAND								
Dickinson	19.5	3	66	3	8	0	24	1
Badcock	36	6	80	4	17	8	22	1
Blunt	14	3	44	1	3	0	12	0
Page	2	0	8	0				
Merritt	34	3	94	2	9	1	41	1
McLeod	2	0	5	0				
Weir					2	1	1	1

Fall of Wickets

	NZ	E	NZ	E
	1st	*1st*	*2nd*	*2nd*
1st	276	20	23	8
2nd	288	81	91	12
3rd	295	91	135	58
4th	385	135	155	98
5th	410	149	-	-
6th	410	219	-	-
7th	425	288	-	-
8th	431	293	-	-
9th	431	303	-	-
10th	440	320	-	-

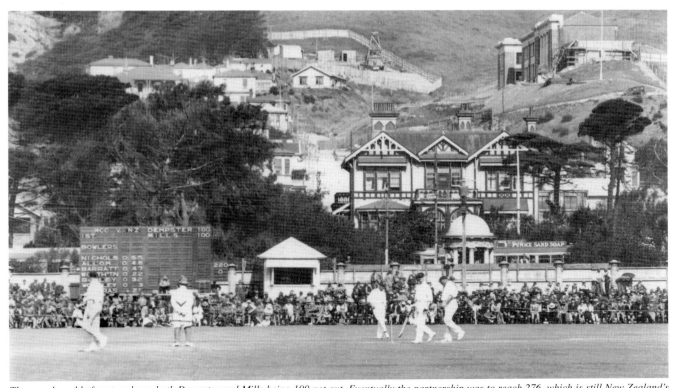

The scoreboard before tea shows both Dempster and Mills being 100 not out. Eventually the partnership was to reach 276, which is still New Zealand's highest opening partnership against England. Dempster scored the first test century for New Zealand.

3 NEW ZEALAND v ENGLAND *(Third Test)*

at Eden Park, Auckland on 14, 15, 17 February, 1930
Toss : New Zealand. Umpires : K.H. Cave and L.T. Cobcroft
Match drawn

Heartened by the advantage that they had established in Wellington, the New Zealanders approached this game with high hopes even though there had been a gap of three weeks between the tests. These were dashed when rain washed out play for the first two days. Up to 13 cm of rain fell on the first day and a steady downpour continued during the second.

The chairman of the New Zealand Cricket Council, Arthur Donnelly, proposed to Gilligan that the match be extended over Tuesday and Wednesday, making it in effect a five-day test. But the English captain objected that this would be contrary to specific instructions he had received from MCC.

However, at breakfast on Monday morning a Marconigram from England requested Gilligan to arrange an extension of play or agree to another match, at a later date. Ten minutes before play was to begin, the tourists agreed to a fourth test

at Eden Park the next weekend. Wanganui agreed to forego their fixture with England so that the game could take place.

Lowry won the toss on the last day of the test and asked England to bat in order to give the crowd the chance to see a relaxed batting exhibition from the tourists. Despite the slow wicket and outfield, 426 runs were scored during the day.

Ted Bowley, aged 39, had coached in Auckland for the last three seasons. His capabilities as a batsmen, a slow bowler and slip fieldsman were known to all the Plunket Shield players who had played against him when he was playing for Auckland. In two hours, he reached his century and then threw his wicket away.

Duleepsinhji also completed a century in two hours and together they added 111 in 63 minutes for the second wicket. Gilligan declared at tea after England had reached 330 for four in three and a half hours.

In the short time that was left Dempster continued his good form with an unbeaten half-century and concluded the game with a six off the last ball.

MILESTONES

- Cyril Allcott (15) and Herb McGirr (16) made their test debuts.
- Ted Bowley became the first batsman to score a century against New Zealand.
- Eden Park became the 21st test match venue.

The captain of the first seven tests that New Zealand played was the autocratic Tom Lowry. He played for Auckland, Wellington, Cambridge University, Somerset, MCC and the Gentlemen.

ENGLAND		
E.H.Bowley	st James b Merritt	109
E.W.Dawson	b Merritt	23
K.S.Duleepsinhji	c & b Allcott	117
F.E.Woolley	run out	59
G.B.Legge	not out	19
M.S.Nichols	not out	1
A.H.H.Gilligan*		
M.J.C.Allom		
F.Barratt		
T.S.Worthington		
W.L.Cornford†		
Extras	(lb 2)	2
TOTAL	(88 overs) (4 wkts dec)	**330**

NEW ZEALAND		
C.S.Dempster	not out	62
J.E.Mills	lbw b Barratt	3
G.L.Weir	not out	27
T.C.Lowry*		
R.C.Blunt		
M.L.Page		
K.C.James†		
C.F.W.Allcott		
H.M.McGirr		
F.T.Badcock		
W.E.Merritt		
Extras	(lb 3, nb 1)	4
TOTAL	(34 overs) (1 wkt)	**96**

Bowling	O	M	R	W
NEW ZEALAND				
McGirr	12	2	46	0
Badcock	11	2	22	0
Merritt	28	1	119	2
Blunt	6	2	16	0
Page	5	1	16	0
Weir	4	0	20	0
Allcott	22	2	89	1
ENGLAND				
Nichols	5	0	18	0
Allom	6	4	3	0
Barratt	12	3	26	1
Worthington	6	1	11	0
Legge	5	0	34	0

Fall of Wickets	E	NZ
	1st	*1st*
1st	82	27
2nd	193	-
3rd	286	-
4th	320	-
5th	-	-
6th	-	-
7th	-	-
8th	-	-
9th	-	-
10th	-	-

4 NEW ZEALAND v ENGLAND *(Fourth Test)*

at Eden Park, Auckland on 21, 22, 24 February, 1930
Toss : England. Umpires : K.H. Cave and L.T. Cobcroft
Match drawn

The Otago Cricket Association refused to extend leave for its professional Ted Badcock and Mal Matheson, a medium-pace bowler from Auckland, replaced him. Likewise, George Dickinson was also unable to get leave from his employer.

England ensured a series win by batting beyond the lunch break on the second day. A sound beginning by the top order allowed Geoffrey Legge and Morris Nichols to chase runs during the first afternoon. Legge, captain of Kent, used every ounce of his 16 stone to larrup the bowling on the following day. Apart from escaping a stumping chance when he was 47, his innings of 196, scored in 280 minutes and including 23 fours, was a faultless exhibition of powerful hitting.

England was eventually dismissed after 445 minutes for 540 runs. To avoid defeat, New Zealand needed to bat through the next five sessions. By the end of the second day, the home team had reached 171-4, Weir having batted sensibly to score 50 in two hours.

When he and Allcott were dismissed early on the last day New Zealand's position looked precarious. A century partnership between Lowry (80) and McGirr (51) used up vital time and the last wicket fell at 387 after 445 minutes, the same duration as England's first-innings.

Although New Zealand had been dismissed four runs short of the follow-on target, Gilligan decided to bat again. Three wickets fell for 22 runs, with Matheson completing his test debut by dismissing two batsmen for seven runs.

ENGLAND

E.H.Bowley	run out	42	b Matheson	6
E.W.Dawson	c Allcott b Blunt	55		
K.S.Duleepsinhji	b Allcott	63		
F.E.Woolley	b Allcott	10		
G.B.Legge	c Matheson b Weir	196	(4) b Blunt	0
M.S.Nichols	b McGirr	75	(3) not out	7
T.S.Worthington	b Merritt	0		
A.H.H.Gilligan*	b Merritt	25		
F.Barratt	c Mills b Blunt	17		
W.L.Cornford†	c Matheson b Page	18	(1) b Matheson	2
M.J.C.Allom	not out	8		
Extras	(b 19, lb 11, nb 1)	31	(b 6, lb 1)	7
TOTAL	**(171.4 overs)**	**540**	**(12.3 overs) (3 wkts)**	**22**

NEW ZEALAND

C.S.Dempster	c Cornford b Allom	27
J.E.Mills	c Duleepsinhji b Allom	12
G.L.Weir	b Barratt	63
M.L.Page	c Cornford b Woolley	25
R.C.Blunt	b Nichols	0
C.F.W.Allcott	run out	33
T.C.Lowry*	lbw b Allom	80
H.M.McGirr	st Cornford b Woolley	51
K.C.James†	lbw b Worthington	14
W.E.Merritt	not out	18
A.M.Matheson	b Allom	7
Extras	(b 31, lb 16, nb 10)	57
TOTAL	**(166.1 overs)**	**387**

Bowling	O	M	R	W	O	M	R	W
NEW ZEALAND								
McGirr	15	2	65	1	3	1	4	0
Matheson	30	6	89	0	5	2	7	2
Merritt	34	2	127	2				
Allcott	47	17	102	2				
Weir	10	1	29	1				
Blunt	21	8	61	2	3.3	2	4	1
Page	14.4	4	36	1				
Lowry					1	1	0	0
ENGLAND								
Nichols	19	4	45	1				
Barratt	37	12	60	1				
Allom	26.1	5	42	4				
Woolley	41	10	100	2				
Bowley	28	6	58	0				
Worthington	15	5	25	1				

Fall of Wickets	E	NZ	E
	1st	*1st*	*2nd*
1st	60	20	12
2nd	150	71	21
3rd	170	127	22
4th	190	131	-
5th	374	186	-
6th	375	193	-
7th	432	293	-
8th	475	349	-
9th	526	373	-
10th	540	387	-

MILESTONES

- Mal Matheson (17) made his test debut.

New Zealand's opening pair of Jack Mills, wearing only one batting glove, and Stewie Dempster. Note the fern on Mills' cap is different from the trademark symbol of today.

AVERAGES

New Zealand

BATTING	M	I	NO	Runs	HS	Ave
C.S. Dempster	4	6	2	341	136	85.25
H.M. McGirr	2	1	0	51	51	51.00
G.L. Weir	3	4	1	114	63	38.00
J.E. Mills	3	4	0	139	117	34.75
C.F.W. Allcott	2	1	0	33	33	33.00
T.C. Lowry	4	4	0	126	80	31.50
M.L. Page	4	5	0	146	67	29.20
R.C. Blunt	4	5	1	100	45*	25.00
E.G. McLeod	1	2	1	18	16	18.00
W.E. Merritt	4	4	1	39	19	13.00
G.R. Dickinson	2	3	0	24	11	8.00
M. Henderson	1	2	1	8	6	8.00
A.M. Matheson	1	1	0	7	7	7.00
K.C. James	4	4	0	21	14	5.25
A.W. Roberts	1	2	0	8	5	4.00
F.T. Badcock	3	3	1	4	4*	2.00
H. Foley	1	2	0	4	2	2.00

BOWLING	O	M	R	W	Ave
R.C. Blunt	65.4	20	171	9	19.00
F.T. Badcock	82	23	153	7	21.85
G.L. Weir	16	2	50	2	25.00
G.R. Dickinson	40.5	4	134	5	26.80
M.L. Page	23.4	6	63	2	31.50
M. Henderson	15	3	64	2	32.00
A.M. Matheson	35	8	96	2	48.00
W.E. Merritt	120	8	436	8	54.50
C.F.W. Allcott	69	19	191	3	63.66
H.M. McGirr	30	5	115	1	115.00
T.C. Lowry	1	1	0	0	-
E.G. McLeod	2	0	5	0	-
C.S. Dempster	0.5	0	10	0	-

England

BATTING	M	I	NO	Runs	HS	Ave
M.S. Nichols	4	6	4	185	78*	92.50
K.S. Duleepsinhji	4	6	2	358	117	89.50
G.B. Legge	4	6	1	299	196	59.80
E.H. Bowley	3	4	0	162	109	40.50
F.E. Woolley	4	6	1	146	59	29.20
E.W. Dawson	4	7	0	152	55	21.71
A.H.H. Gilligan	4	4	0	71	32	17.75
M.J.C. Allom	4	3	2	14	8*	14.00
T.S. Worthington	4	3	0	32	32	10.66
W.L. Cornford	4	4	0	36	18	9.00
F. Barratt	4	3	0	26	17	8.66
M.J.L. Turnbull	1	1	0	7	7	7.00

BOWLING	O	M	R	W	Ave
M.J.C. Allom	100.1	24	194	13	14.92
F.E. Woolley	101.3	26	261	13	20.07
M.S. Nichols	84.3	21	202	8	25.25
T.S. Worthington	73.1	14	186	7	26.57
F. Barratt	95	22	197	3	65.66
G.B. Legge	5	0	34	0	-
E.H. Bowley	38	6	109	0	-

1931 New Zealand in England

In 1930 New Zealand was caught in the grip of the Great Depression, and the NZCC was conscious of the heavy loss incurred by the pioneering 1927 tour. It would have been desirable to postpone the forthcoming tour but no other date was available until the mid-1930s.

Again, it was decided to float a limited liability company to finance the tour. New Zealand Cricket Limited offered the public 12,000 shares of £1. Another source of revenue was provided by an Art Union held in association with the New Zealand Football Association.

The proceeds contributed to the tourists' boat fare. There was much satisfaction when the itinerary was announced. A test would be played at Lord's and New Zealand's growing status in world cricket was confirmed by the fact that only four minor counties appeared on the fixture list.

When the Hawke's Bay earthquake occurred on 3 February 1931 questions were asked about proceeding with the tour. After much deliberation, Arthur Donnelly, the chairman of the Cricket Council, said that the tour would proceed.

Following a sensational victory over a strong MCC side in their fourth game, two additional test matches were hastily arranged. Leading into the first test match, the batting of Stewie Dempster had many English critics comparing him favourably with Don Bradman, who had broken every record for a tourist in England the previous season.

5   NEW ZEALAND v ENGLAND *(First Test)*

at Lord's on 27, 29, 30 June, 1931
Toss : New Zealand. Umpires : F. Chester and J. Hardstaff, Sr
Match drawn

Tom Lowry was reported as saying, "The English selectors have paid us a compliment by placing a very strong team in the field." He won the toss and decided to bat first.

New Zealand reached 50 within 40 minutes to set the tempo that was sustained for the rest of the game. The introduction of Ian Peebles, the right-arm leg-spinner, brought about the downfall of Mills and Weir before lunch, when the score was 132-2.

The twin attack, of two right-arm leg-spinners, Peebles and Walter Robins, saw New Zealand collapse to be all out for 224. Many of the batsmen had been reluctant to use their feet to the slow bowlers and were undone, offering tentative prods from the crease.

England's pride was dented by an inspired opening spell from Ian Cromb, who knocked the top off the home team's innings by disposing of Arnold, Bakewell and Hammond.

With England reeling at 31-3 Jardine, the England captain, the elegant Duleepsinhji, the experienced Woolley and Peebles all fell to Bill Merritt before stumps. The New

Zealanders left the field having compensated for their disappointing batting by restricting England to 190-7. The day had produced 414 runs and 17 wickets.

Any optimism entertained by the tourists proved false the next morning as Les Ames and Gubby Allen delighted the crowd of 23,000 with a new test record for an eighth-wicket partnership of 246. The pair profited from some wayward bowling and scored freely in front of the wicket.

Lowry made many bowling changes, and none had effect until the introduction of Weir, who quickly captured the three remaining wickets to finish with 3-38.

England's total of 454 set the tourists the task of bettering their previous effort simply to avoid an innings defeat. The situation looked grim when Mills was dismissed second ball. Dempster and Weir, however, began with caution and gradually the runs flowed. Weir batted on courageously, after suffering two blows on the shoulder, but was eventually foiled by a shooter from Allen after the pair had added 99.

The third day belonged entirely to New Zealand. Dempster's innings of 120 gave him a tour aggregate of over a thousand runs. Page survived a torrid time to reach his century. In the half-hour before lunch, he faced a barrage of short-pitched deliveries from Voce, bowling to a leg-side trap and was poised on 99 at the break. He was dismissed shortly after completing his century.

Roger Blunt and Lowry continued in a cavalier fashion. Blunt looked set to become New Zealand's third century-maker in the innings before Robins bowled him for 96.

The tourists had staged an extraordinary comeback and Lowry was presented with the luxury of declaring, leaving his rivals the target of 240 runs to make in 140 minutes.

England's embarrassment continued as they lost five wickets before stumps were drawn. During the three days 1,239 runs were scored, 140 overs were bowled each day and 34 wickets fell.

Accolades were heaped upon the visiting side and very quickly Surrey and Lancashire graciously consented to drop their planned fixtures, and to make The Oval and Old Trafford available for two more tests.

MILESTONES

- Stewie Dempster became the first New Zealand batsmen to score a test century overseas.

- Ian Cromb (18) and Jack Kerr (19) made their test debuts for New Zealand.

- The eighth wicket partnership of 246 between Allen and Ames remained the highest for this wicket until 1996/97 when Wasim Akram and Saqlain Mushtaq added 313 for Pakistan against Zimbabwe.

NEW ZEALAND

C.S.Dempster	lbw b Peebles	53	(2) b Hammond		120
J.E.Mills	b Peebles	34	(1) b Allen		0
G.L.Weir	lbw b Peebles	37	b Allen		40
J.L.Kerr	st Ames b Robins	2	(6) lbw b Peebles		0
R.C.Blunt	c Hammond b Robins	7	b Robins		96
M.L.Page	b Allen	23	(4) c & b Peebles		104
T.C.Lowry*	c Hammond b Robins	1	(9) b Peebles		34
I.B.Cromb	c Ames b Peebles	20	(7) c Voce b Robins		14
C.F.W.Allcott	c Hammond b Peebles	13	(10) not out		20
W.E.Merritt	c Jardine b Hammond	17	(8) b Peebles		5
K.C.James†	not out	1			
Extras	(b 2, lb 12, w 1, nb 1)	16	(b 23, lb 10, w 1, nb 2)		36
TOTAL	(74.3 overs)	224	(157.4 overs) (9 wkts dec)		469

ENGLAND

J.Arnold	c Page b Cromb	0	c & b Blunt		34
A.H.Bakewell	lbw b Cromb	9	c Blunt b Cromb		27
W.R.Hammond	b Cromb	7	run out		46
K.S.Duleepsinhji	c Kerr b Merritt	25	c James b Allcott		11
D.R.Jardine*	c Blunt b Merritt	38	(7) not out		0
F.E.Woolley	lbw b Merritt	80	(5) b Cromb		9
L.E.G.Ames†	c James b Weir	137	(6) not out		17
I.A.R.Peebles	st James b Merritt	0			
G.O.B.Allen	c Lowry b Weir	122			
R.W.V.Robins	c Lowry b Weir	12			
W.Voce	not out	1			
Extras	(b 15, lb 8)	23	(lb 2)		2
TOTAL	(134 overs)	454	(55 overs) (5 wkts)		146

Bowling ENGLAND	O	M	R	W	O	M	R	W
Voce	10	1	40	0	32	11	60	0
Allen	15	2	45	1	25	8	47	2
Hammond	10.3	5	8	1	21	2	50	1
Peebles	26	3	77	5	42.4	6	150	4
Robins	13	3	38	3	37	5	126	2
NEW ZEALAND								
Cromb	37	7	113	3	25	5	44	2
Weir	8	1	38	3	5	1	18	0
Blunt	46	9	124	0	14	5	54	1
Allcott	17	3	34	0	10	2	26	1
Merritt	23	2	104	4	1	0	2	0
Page	3	0	18	0				

Fall of Wickets		NZ	E	NZ	E
		1st	1st	2nd	2nd
1st		58	5	1	62
2nd		130	14	100	62
3rd		136	31	218	94
4th		140	62	360	105
5th		153	129	360	144
6th		161	188	389	-
7th		190	190	404	-
8th		191	436	406	-
9th		209	447	469	-
10th		224	454	-	-

6   NEW ZEALAND v ENGLAND *(Second Test)*

at The Oval on 29, 30, 31 July, 1931
Toss : England. Umpires : F. Chester and J. Hardstaff, sr
England won by an innings and 26 runs

1931 will be remembered as one of the wettest summers in the history of England. So far on tour, New Zealand had played 23 matches, but 18 had been drawn, so bad was the weather. Unfortunately for the tourists their best batsman, Dempster, was suffering from a strained leg muscle and was unable to play.

The winning of the toss was vital to the outcome of this match. The England openers began comfortably on a slow wicket, which offered little bounce or turn. The slips did not accept chances from both batsmen, and the openers looked set for a long stay. With the total at 84 Sutcliffe made a bad call, and his partner Bakewell, was run out.

A brief shower during lunch made New Zealand's task no easier. The slippery ball was difficult to grip and Sutcliffe and Duleepsinhji steadily accrued runs as the New Zealand attack wheeled up innocuous offerings. None of the New Zealand bowlers was able to exploit the helpful conditions.

Both batsmen reached centuries and then were dismissed

forcing the pace towards the end of the day. Together they added 178 runs for the second wicket in just over two hours, though both might have been caught from miscalculated strokes before they had reached 30.

Heavy rain overnight did not prevent play starting on time, with England 312-3. 104 runs were added in 50 minutes before Jardine declared at 416-4. Hammond slaughtered the bowling, moving confidently down the wicket to hammer full tosses through the covers, and raced to 100 not out (13 fours) in even time.

Mills and Weir began batting against Tate and Brown, who were soon replaced by the spinners Verity and Peebles. It was not until Allen, the fastest bowler in the England attack, was introduced that the spiteful bouncing nature of the drying wicket was revealed.

With New Zealand's score at 42, Mills was bowled off the last ball of Allen's first over. By the time he had completed eight overs, he had captured four wickets for eight runs and New Zealand's innings was in tatters. Lowry and Kerr defended stoutly, adding 65 before Lowry was dismissed.

Well aware of the advantages his bowlers had enjoyed, Jardine claimed, "Lowry's was the best innings seen at the Oval for many years, because the wicket was so troublesome." The innings quickly folded and New Zealand were forced to follow on.

There would be no remarkable recovery as at Lord's in New Zealand's second innings. The fiery Tate exploited the still dangerous wicket, as did Peebles. Mills, Blunt and Kerr provided valiant resistance, but it was Vivian, the youngster, who caught the eye. Neville Cardus wrote, "Vivian flashed his bat quite truculently and scored 51, including a great on-drive for six off Verity." His innings lasted 95 minutes.

In his *Daily Mail* column, Jack Hobbs hoped the New Zealanders would not be "downcasted by defeat". He suggested that, "had they won the toss and batted on the easy wicket the first day, they would have saved the game." He also commented that Vivian had batted beautifully and that he regarded him as a splendid player of the future.

Followers of the game in New Zealand were treated to a novel method of reporting play in this test. For the first time, the radio-telephone link between London and Wellington was used to send sporting news around the world.

Arthur Gilligan used a microphone installed in a bedroom of the Grand Central Hotel to broadcast his account of the day's play to the president of the Wellington Cricket Association, who relayed it to the radio station.

MILESTONES

- Giff Vivian (20) made his test debut, aged 18 years and 267 days.

Curly Page cuts powerfully backward of point during his second innings century watched by Les Ames the England wicketkeeper. Note the large white dustcoat worn by the umpire.

The two teams posed before the start of the second test. Back row (left to right): Roger Blunt, Gubby Allen, Jack Kerr, Walter Hammond, "Dad" Weir. Standing: Cyril Allcott, Ian Cromb, Ron Talbot, Freddie Brown, Giff Vivian, Les Ames, Jack Mills, Hedley Verity, Maurice Tate. Seated: Ken James, K.S. Duleepsinhji, Tom Lowry, Douglas Jardine, Curly Page, Herbert Sutcliffe. In front: Bill Merritt, Fred Bakewell, Ian Peebles, Bob Gregory, (England 12th man).

ENGLAND

H.Sutcliffe	st James b Vivian	117
A.H.Bakewell	run out	40
K.S.Duleepsinhji	c Weir b Allcott	109
W.R.Hammond	not out	100
L.E.G.Ames†	c James b Vivian	41
D.R.Jardine*	not out	7
F.R.Brown		
G.O.B.Allen		
M.W.Tate		
I.A.R.Peebles		
H.Verity		
Extras	(b 1, lb 1)	2
TOTAL	(131.3 overs) (4 wkts dec)	**416**

NEW ZEALAND

J.E.Mills	b Allen	27	b Brown		30
G.L.Weir	b Allen	13	b Peebles		6
R.C.Blunt	c Ames b Allen	2	(4) b Peebles		43
M.L.Page	c Peebles b Tate	12	(3) b Tate		3
H.G.Vivian	c Ames b Allen	3	c Brown b Peebles		51
T.C.Lowry*	c Jardine b Brown	62	c Duleepsinhji b Peebles		0
J.L.Kerr	c Ames b Allen	34	b Tate		28
K.C.James†	lbw b Brown	4	c Peebles b Verity		10
I.B.Cromb	c Hammond b Verity	8	not out		3
W.E.Merritt	c Hammond b Verity	8	lbw b Tate		4
C.F.W.Allcott	not out	5	c Allen b Verity		1
Extras	(b 2, lb 9, nb 4)	15	(b 6, lb 10, nb 2)		18
TOTAL	(95.1 overs)	**193**	(84.3 overs)		**197**

Bowling	O	M	R	W	O	M	R	W	Fall of Wickets			
NEW ZEALAND										NZ	E	NZ
										1st	1st	2nd
Cromb	30	5	97	0					1st	84	42	19
Allcott	44	7	108	1					2nd	262	44	38
Vivian	34.3	8	96	2					3rd	271	45	51
Weir	10	1	36	0					4th	401	53	139
Merritt	12	0	75	0					5th	-	92	143
Blunt	1	0	2	0					6th	-	157	162
ENGLAND									7th	-	167	189
Tate	18	9	15	1	21	6	22	3	8th	-	168	189
Brown	29	12	52	2	16	6	38	1	9th	-	188	196
Verity	22.1	8	52	2	12.3	4	33	2	10th	-	193	197
Peebles	12	3	35	0	22	4	63	4				
Allen	13	7	14	5	13	4	23	0				
Hammond	1	0	10	0								

7 **NEW ZEALAND v ENGLAND** *(Third Test)*

at Old Trafford, Manchester on 15, 17, 18 August, 1931
Toss : New Zealand. Umpires : F. Chester and J. Hardstaff, sr
Match drawn

The last test at Old Trafford proved a most depressing affair, no play being possible until after three o'clock on the last day. Lowry put England in, perhaps suspecting that the wicket might help his bowlers in the 195 minutes of play possible.

It may, too, have been suggested to him by New Zealand's opening batsmen that they would prefer to avoid meeting the explosive Harold Larwood until the after match-function. Whatever his motives, the 4000 loyal spectators were treated to a regal display of the arts of batting by Sutcliffe and Duleepsinhji who added 126 runs in 110 minutes.

There were suggestions that a fourth test be played in place of the traditional fixture between the champion county and the Rest of England but this did not happen. Had the match taken place it is probable that the New Zealand Cricket Council would have made a profit on the tour. The loss of the gate from the third test was a significant financial setback.

Returning home, Lowry explained "The past summer was about the wettest ever experienced in England. In all, the team was prevented from playing for 28 complete days, which meant an average of one day off in almost every match. It was necessary to attend the ground in time for the start of play and remain there until perhaps three, four or five o'clock, awaiting a possible chance of making a commencement. It was more tiring waiting about in the pavilion than it would have been if the team was actually on the field."

In naming Stewie Dempster one of its five cricketers of the year, *Wisden* stated, "In Dempster, New Zealand possessed the best batsmen that country has ever produced."

The warmth of the welcome home was cooled by news that NZCC had disqualified Merritt from representing New Zealand in future. He had signed for a Manchester club, thereby breaking an undertaking made by the tourists not to return to England as players for at least two years.

Explaining the situation on behalf of the Cricket Council, Tom Reese said, "A player has broken an agreement and the steps taken by the council will stand as a clear warning to all other cricketers."

ENGLAND

H.Sutcliffe	not out	109
E.Paynter	c James b Cromb	3
K.S.Duleepsinhji	c Allcott b Vivian	63
W.R.Hammond	c Cromb b Vivian	16
D.R.Jardine*	not out	28
L.E.G.Ames†		
G.O.B.Allen		
F.R.Brown		
H.Larwood		
I.A.R.Peebles		
H.Verity		
Extras	(b 4, nb 1)	5
TOTAL	(71 overs) (3 wkts)	**224**

NEW ZEALAND

T.C.Lowry*
C.S.Dempster
J.E.Mills
M.L.Page
G.L.Weir
K.C.James†
A.M.Matheson
I.B.Cromb
C.F.W.Allcott
H.G.Vivian
R.C.Blunt

Bowling NEW ZEALAND	O	M	R	W		Fall of Wickets E
						1st
Matheson	12	1	40	0	1st	8
Cromb	16	6	33	1	2nd	134
Allcott	27	6	75	0	3rd	166
Vivian	14	1	54	2	4th	-
Blunt	1	0	12	0	5th	-
Lowry	1	0	5	0	6th	-
					7th	-
					8th	-
					9th	-
					10th	-

AVERAGES

New Zealand

BATTING	M	I	NO	Runs	HS	Ave
C.S. Dempster	2	2	0	173	120	86.50
R.C. Blunt	3	4	0	148	96	37.00
M.L. Page	3	4	0	142	104	35.50
H.G. Vivian	2	2	0	54	51	27.00
T.C. Lowry	3	4	0	97	62	24.25
G.L. Weir	3	4	0	96	40	24.00
J.E. Mills	3	4	0	91	34	22.75
C.F.W. Allcott	3	4	2	39	20*	19.50
J.L. Kerr	2	4	0	64	34	16.00
I.B. Cromb	3	4	1	45	20	15.00
W.E. Merritt	2	4	0	34	17	8.50
K.C. James	3	3	1	15	10	7.50
A.M. Matheson	1	-	-	-	-	-

BOWLING	O	M	R	W	Ave
G.L. Weir	23	3	92	3	30.66
H.G. Vivian	48.3	9	150	4	37.50
W.E. Merritt	36	2	181	4	45.25
I.B. Cromb	108	23	287	6	47.83
C.F. W.Allcott	98	18	243	2	121.50
R.C. Blunt	62	14	192	1	192.00
T.C. Lowry	1	0	5	0	-
M.L. Page	3	0	18	0	-
A.M. Matheson	12	1	40	0	-

England

BATTING	M	I	NO	Runs	HS	Ave
H. Sutcliffe	2	2	1	226	117	226.00
G.O.B. Allen	3	1	0	122	122	122.00
L.E.G. Ames	3	3	1	195	137	97.50
D.R. Jardine	3	4	3	73	38	73.00
W.R. Hammond	3	4	1	169	100*	56.33
K.S. Duleepsinhji	3	4	0	208	109	52.00
F.E. Woolley	1	2	0	89	80	44.50
A.H. Bakewell	2	3	0	76	40	25.33
J. Arnold	1	2	0	34	34	17.00
R.W.V. Robins	1	1	0	12	12	12.00
E. Paynter	1	1	0	3	3	3.00
I.A.R. Peebles	3	1	0	0	0	0.00
W. Voce	1	1	1	1	1*	-
F.R. Brown	2	-	-	-	-	-
H. Larwood	1	-	-	-	-	-
M.W. Tate	1	-	-	-	-	-
H. Verity	2	-	-	-	-	-

BOWLING	O	M	R	W	Ave
M.W. Tate	39	15	37	4	9.25
G.O.B. Allen	66	21	129	8	16.12
H. Verity	34.4	12	85	4	21.25
I.A.R. Peebles	102.4	16	325	13	25.00
F.R. Brown	45	18	90	3	30.00
R.W.V. Robins	50	8	164	5	32.80
W.R. Hammond	32.3	7	68	2	34.00
W. Voce	42	12	100	0	-

Bill Merritt was an outstanding success as an 18-year-old leg-spinner on New Zealand's tour of England in 1927. He captured 97 wickets in 1931.

1931/32 South Africa in New Zealand

The second South African team to tour Australia played five test matches. They were badly beaten by Bradman and a strong Australian side in all five games. They extended their tour to include a brief sojourn in New Zealand, where they played Auckland and two test matches in 16 days. As Tom Lowry was unavailable for the tests, Curly Page became the second New Zealander to lead his country in a test match.

8 **NEW ZEALAND v SOUTH AFRICA** *(First Test)*
at Lancaster Park, Christchurch on 27, 29 February, 1 March, 1932
Toss : New Zealand. Umpires : W. Butler and J.T. Forrester
South Africa won by an innings and 12 runs

The relatively low standard of bowling in domestic cricket had not prepared the New Zealanders for another encounter with an international attack. On an excellent batting strip New Zealand were quickly reduced to 38-3, before Lindsay Weir and Alby Roberts settled down and put New Zealand back in the game with a fourth wicket partnership of 90.

The remaining batting was dominated by Ted Badcock, who hit three sixes in his bright innings of 64. However, the crowd of 6000, basking in perfect weather, watched a disappointing innings conclude at 293.

The pick of the visiting bowlers was Quintin McMillan. His right-arm leg-spinners worried all the batsmen. Jim Christy and Bruce Mitchell were fortunate to survive the half-hour before stumps, with Christy being dropped twice.

After the rest day, both batsmen gave early chances as they added 196 for the first wicket before Christy was run out by a superb throw from the boundary by Jack Kerr. Mitchell's 113 occupied 190 minutes.

The remaining South Africans batted in an aggressive way with Eric Dalton hitting out boldly and racing to 82 before Page, at silly mid-on, took a sensational catch to end the innings at 451.

McMillan's leg-spinners and googlies exposed a lack of technique among the batsmen in New Zealand's second innings. His five wickets for 66 runs gave him a bag of nine for the match. Only Weir showed grit and judgment as he battled on to 74 not out in a total of 146.

The South Africans' fielding was in direct contrast to the sloppy New Zealand effort, with the captain, Jock Cameron, making three smart stumpings to confirm his reputation as a great wicketkeeper.

"Dad" Weir enjoyed his best test match scoring 46 and 74 not out.

NEW ZEALAND

Batsman	Dismissal		Dismissal (2nd)	
C.S.Dempster	b McMillan	8	b Quinn	12
J.L.Kerr	b Bell	0	c Vincent b Bell	3
R.C.Blunt	run out	23	c Mitchell b Vincent	17
G.L.Weir	c Mitchell b Vincent	46	not out	74
A.W.Roberts	st Cameron b Mitchell	54	c & b McMillan	17
M.L.Page*	c Taylor b McMillan	22	st Cameron b McMillan	0
F.T.Badcock†	c Dalton b Bell	64	st Cameron b McMillan	5
K.C.James	c Cameron b McMillan	3	(9) lbw b Quinn	0
I.B.Cromb	c Morkel b McMillan	25	(8) c Vincent b McMillan	0
D.C.Cleverley	not out	10	b Quinn	7
J.Newman	c Balaskas b Mitchell	19	lbw b McMillan	4
Extras	(b 4, lb 13, nb 2)	19	(b 1, lb 5, nb 1)	7
TOTAL	(114.4 overs)	**293**	(61.5 overs)	**146**

SOUTH AFRICA

J.A.J.Christy	run out	103
B.Mitchell	c James b Cromb	113
H.W.Taylor	b Badcock	9
H.B.Cameron*†	c James b Badcock	47
X.C.Balaskas	run out	5
E.L.Dalton	c Page b Newman	82
D.P.B.Morkel	b Newman	51
C.L.Vincent	c Page b Blunt	3
Q.McMillan	c Badcock b Blunt	6
N.A.Quinn	run out	3
A.J.Bell	not out	2
Extras	(b 14, lb 10, nb 3)	27
TOTAL	(136.5 overs)	**451**

Bowling	O	M	R	W	O	M	R	W
SOUTH AFRICA								
Bell	32	8	64	2	9	3	11	1
Quinn	29	7	46	0	15	6	17	3
McMillan	19	2	61	4	20.5	4	66	5
Vincent	23	7	57	1	14	3	33	1
Mitchell	7.4	0	31	2	1	0	6	0
Balaskas	4	0	15	0				
Morkel					2	0	6	0
NEW ZEALAND								
Cleverley	22	2	79	0				
Badcock	38	8	88	2				
Newman	28.5	4	76	2				
Blunt	16	0	60	2				
Cromb	26	4	94	1				
Page	6	0	27	0				

Fall of Wickets

	NZ 1st	SA 1st	NZ 2nd
1st	1	196	16
2nd	26	227	16
3rd	38	249	41
4th	128	262	70
5th	149	299	70
6th	189	376	76
7th	198	395	94
8th	251	423	103
9th	265	432	117
10th	293	451	146

MILESTONES

- Don Cleverley (21) and Jack Newman (22) made their test debuts for New Zealand.

- Jim Christy became the first South African to score a test century against New Zealand.

- The match marked the end of the test career of South Africa's great batsman, Herbie Taylor, who had played 42 tests, scoring seven centuries and 2936 runs at 40.77.

9 NEW ZEALAND v SOUTH AFRICA *(Second Test)*

at Basin Reserve, Wellington on 4, 5, 7 March, 1932
Toss : New Zealand. Umpires : K.H. Cave and W.P. Page
South Africa won by 8 wickets

Giff Vivian, unavailable for the first test, returned at the expense of Jack Kerr, and Don Cleverley and Jack Newman made way for Cyril Allcott and George Dickinson.

In splendid conditions Stewie Dempster was in his most aggressive mood. In the space of 75 minutes he struck 10 well-timed boundaries and set the tone for an exciting day's play. At lunch, the total was 126-2, with Vivian on 30.

When New Zealand's fifth wicket fell at 158 Ted Badcock joined Vivian and, with aggressive batting, the sixth-wicket pair added 100. The left-handed Vivian continued to hit the ball with great power and his driving, hooking, and cutting were a feature of a splendid century.

He became the first New Zealander to score a century against South Africa and the youngest to score a century in test cricket. Ian Cromb's quick 51 not out was well supported by Allcott and Ken James and New Zealand's total of 364 was achieved in 315 minutes.

Quintin McMillan captured five wickets, but his bowling was treated with less reverence than in the previous test. South Africa reached 78-2 by the end of the day's play, in which 442 runs had been scored and 120 overs bowled.

An hour was lost because of rain but the visitors still ended the second day with a lead of 46 with one wicket standing thanks to positive play by Jim Christy, Ken Viljoen and Xenophon Balaskas.

Balaskas, selected mainly as a leg-spinner, was of Greek origin and was unbeaten on 122 at stumps. His innings was remarkable for its unorthodoxy. Vivian continued in a starring role, capturing 4-58 off 20 overs of clever left-arm spin bowling.

With the wicket playing easily and Vivian again batting well, a draw appeared likely when lunch was taken with New Zealand 109-3. A splendid spell of left-arm fast-medium bowling by Neville Quinn, a silly run out and weak batting saw the New Zealand innings collapse for 193. With 73 in the second innings, Vivian had an exceptional all-round game.

This left South Africa a target of 148 runs to be made in 135 minutes. Christy and Bruce Mitchell added 100 in the first hour and the victory was secured by eight wickets.

New Zealand cricket officials continued to lament the loss of players who had left to play professional cricket in England. It was estimated that with Bill Merritt and Roger Blunt each having had two tours of England and Ces Dacre and Ian Cromb one each, the cost was approximately £5000.

NEW ZEALAND					
C.S.Dempster	c Vincent b McMillan	64	c Cameron b Quinn	20
G.L.Weir	b McMillan	8	b Quinn	1
R.C.Blunt	lbw b Quinn	25	b Brown	17
H.G.Vivian	c Dalton b McMillan	100	c Vincent b Balaskas	73
A.W.Roberts	lbw b Quinn	1	b Quinn	26
M.L.Page*	c Mitchell b Brown	7	(7) c & b Balaskas	23
F.T.Badcock	c & b McMillan	53	(6) run out	0
G.R.Dickinson	st Cameron b McMillan	2	b McMillan	5
C.F.W.Allcott	c Dalton b Mitchell	26	b Quinn	15
I.B.Cromb	not out	51	c Christy b McMillan	2
K.C.James†	b Mitchell	11	not out	0
Extras	(b 12, lb 4)	16	(b 4, lb 6, nb 1)	11
TOTAL	(99.5 overs)	**364**	(72 overs)	**193**

SOUTH AFRICA					
J.A.J.Christy	c Dempster b Badcock	62	c Roberts b Badcock	53
B.Mitchell	b Cromb	0	c James b Dickinson	53
H.B.Cameron*†	c Blunt b Vivian	44	not out	22
K.G.Viljoen	b Page	81	not out	16
E.L.Dalton	c James b Dickinson	42		
X.C.Balaskas	not out	122		
Q.McMillan	c Dickinson b Allcott	1		
C.L.Vincent	c & b Vivian	33		
L.S.Brown	c Page b Vivian	7		
N.A.Quinn	b Vivian	8		
A.J.Bell	lbw b Dickinson	2		
Extras	(b 2, lb 2, w 1, nb 3)	8	(lb 6)	6
TOTAL	(141.2 overs)	**410**	(41.2 overs) (2 wkts)	**150**

Bowling	O	M	R	W	O	M	R	W	Fall of Wickets				
SOUTH AFRICA										NZ	SA	NZ	SA
										1st	1st	2nd	2nd
Bell	16	1	47	0	10	0	30	0					
Quinn	28	6	51	2	24	9	37	4	1st	42	2	14	104
Brown	14	1	59	1	10	3	30	1	2nd	79	78	23	115
McMillan	29	2	125	5	21	2	71	2	3rd	135	133	66	-
Vincent	6	1	32	0					4th	139	220	122	-
Christy	2	0	11	0					5th	158	256	122	-
Mitchell	4.5	0	23	2					6th	258	257	157	-
Balaskas					7	2	14	2	7th	269	362	171	-
NEW ZEALAND									8th	270	386	186	-
Dickinson	26.2	7	78	2	8	2	33	1	9th	339	394	192	-
Cromb	23	9	48	1	3	0	13	0	10th	364	410	193	-
Badcock	24	6	70	1	11	2	31	1					
Allcott	27	4	80	1	7	0	27	0					
Blunt	10	0	38	0	2.2	0	11	0					
Vivian	20	7	58	4	7	0	15	0					
Page	11	3	30	1	3	0	14	0					

MILESTONES

- Giff Vivian became the youngest batsman to score a century in a test match. He was 19 years and 121 days old.

Giff Vivian in the nets. Keeping wickets is Ken James.

1932/33 MCC in New Zealand

The England team, led by Douglas Jardine, arrived in New Zealand, having beaten Australia four-one in the controversial bodyline series. A barrage of short-pitched balls bowled to a packed leg field curbed the brilliance of Don Bradman. Bitter recriminations reached government level, and it appeared for a time that the tour might be abandoned. Even though it was at the height of the world depression, record crowds flocked to the test grounds in Australia, as they were to do so in New Zealand.

10 NEW ZEALAND v ENGLAND *(First Test)*

at Lancaster Park, Christchurch on 24, 25, 27 March, 1933
Toss : England. Umpires : T.W. Burgess and R.C. Torrance
Match drawn

The match began sensationally, with Herbert Sutcliffe being out in the first over. Eddie Paynter was bowled by the first ball of the second, each before he had scored, while Walter Hammond was dropped in the slips. This turned out to be a catastrophe for New Zealand as he went on to score 227.

With Les Ames, 242 were added in 145 minutes for the fifth wicket. Hammond, who many regarded as the greatest English batsmen, toyed with the unbalanced and erratic New Zealand attack, scoring boundaries with relentless ease. Ames again demonstrated his appetite for New Zealand bowling and reached his century. Bad light brought a merciful relief to the game early, with England 418-5.

Hammond was dismissed early on the second day, which allowed Bill Voce and Freddie Brown to indulge in some big hitting with 108 runs added in 45 minutes. The marathon fielding effort resulted in two casualties. Ted Badcock damaged a finger and Giff Vivian was admitted to hospital with water on the knee and took no further part in the game.

The New Zealand top order batting countered accurate pace bowling with skill and determination, but sharp catching by the visitors saw New Zealand lose their second wicket with the score at 59. Lindsay Weir and Jack Kerr, who added 94 together, consolidated the innings before Weir was dismissed shortly before stumps for a resourceful 66.

The remaining wickets fell for another 70 runs; all out 223, a deficit of 337. Jardine enforced the follow on; with nearly 3 hours of play left. A dust storm, followed by rain and bad light terminated the match in the middle of the afternoon.

ENGLAND					
H.Sutcliffe	c James b Badcock	0			
E.Paynter	b Smith	0			
W.R.Hammond	b Badcock	227			
R.E.S.Wyatt	run out	20			
D.R.Jardine*	c James b Badcock	45			
L.E.G.Ames†	b Vivian	103			
F.R.Brown	c Kerr b Page	74			
W.Voce	c Dempster b Page	66			
M.W.Tate	not out	10			
G.O.B.Allen					
H.Verity					
Extras	(b 8, lb 7)	15			
TOTAL	(147.3 overs) (8 wkts dec)	**560**			

NEW ZEALAND					
C.S.Dempster	c Wyatt b Allen	8	not out		14
P.E.Whitelaw	c Brown b Verity	30	not out		17
G.L.Weir	c Hammond b Voce	66			
J.L.Kerr	c Hammond b Brown	59			
M.L.Page*	c Voce b Allen	22			
K.C.James†	lbw b Tate	2			
H.D.Smith	b Tate	4			
J.Newman	b Voce	5			
D.L.Freeman	b Voce	1			
F.T.Badcock	not out	10			
H.G.Vivian	absent hurt				
Extras	(b 3, lb 10, nb 3)	16	(lb 1, nb 3)		4
TOTAL	(116.1 overs)	**223**	(16.1 overs) (0 wkts)		**35**

Bowling	O	M	R	W	O	M	R	W
NEW ZEALAND								
Badcock	54	11	142	3				
Smith	20	0	113	1				
Newman	25	5	91	0				
Freeman	20	2	78	0				
Vivian	19	1	72	1				
Page	2.3	0	21	2				
Weir	7	0	28	0				
ENGLAND								
Tate	37	16	42	2	3	1	5	0
Voce	17.1	3	27	3	4	0	13	0
Allen	20	5	46	2	4.1	1	5	0
Brown	19	10	34	1				
Verity	23	7	58	1	3	1	6	0
Hammond					2	0	2	0

Fall of Wickets	E	NZ	NZ
	1st	1st	2nd
1st	0	25	-
2nd	4	59	-
3rd	46	153	-
4th	133	186	-
5th	375	194	-
6th	424	205	-
7th	532	211	-
8th	560	212	-
9th	-	223	-
10th	-	-	-

The team for the first test against England contained young right-arm leg-spin bowler Doug Freeman (dark overcoat) being congratulated by Nelson coach and former New Zealand player Herb McGirr (white shirt). Also in the picture is New Zealand representative Jack Newman (tweed overcoat). The founder of Newman Transport, Thomas Newman, stands alongside his son.

MILESTONES

- Doug Freeman (23), Dennis Smith (24) and Paul Whitelaw (25) made their test debuts.

- Smith captured a wicket with his first ball in test cricket.

- Freeman became New Zealand's youngest test player aged 18 years and 197 days.

- Hammond and Ames added 242 for the fifth wicket, which was a record for test cricket for this wicket.

11 NEW ZEALAND v ENGLAND *(Second Test)*

at Eden Park, Auckland on 31 March, 1, 3 April, 1933
Toss : New Zealand. Umpires : K.H. Cave and J.T. Forrester
Match drawn

Bob Wyatt replaced the England captain Douglas Jardine, who was suffering from a bout of rheumatism. Stewie Dempster's train was late arriving in Auckland, so Jack Mills and Paul Whitelaw opened the New Zealand innings.

Gubby Allen bowled a maiden over to Whitelaw, and then Mills faced the Yorkshire fast bowler Bill Bowes. Attempting to cut the first ball he was bowled. Lindsay Weir came to the crease, played back to his first ball and was surprised to see his off stump knocked back. Dempster came in facing a hat trick, which he survived, before embarking on a one-man mission to save the innings.

Exhibiting a stubborn defence when necessary and seizing upon every opportunity to score from loose deliveries, Dempster gave one of the most gallant displays in his career. He used his feet freely to the slow bowlers, placed the ball delicately around the field and showed fine judgment in calling for singles.

Bowes continued to bowl with pace and accuracy and all six of his victims were bowled. With the exception of Dempster, who was unbeaten on 83 when the innings ended at 158, the New Zealand batsmen suffered the consequences of a timid approach. England was 127-1, with Walter Hammond looking ominously smug on 41, when the first day's play ended.

The second day belonged entirely to Hammond. The natural power and ease of his stroke play, accompanied by serene confidence, carried him to a new world test record of 336 not out.

His innings lasted 318 minutes and included 10 sixes (three off successive balls from Jack Newman) and 34 fours. His last century was scored in just 47 minutes. In the last test in Australia, Hammond had scored 101 and 75 not out, in Christchurch, 227, and now 336 not out. His last four test innings had totalled 739 runs at an average of 369.50.

Requiring almost 400 runs simply to make England bat again, New Zealand was fortuitous when rain allowed only 20 minutes play on the third day. It was to be another four years before New Zealand played another official test match.

As soon as the Auckland test finished, Stewie Dempster left on the *Tainui* to take up a business proposition with Sir Julien Cahn. Dempster would never play for his country again, a loss that was keenly felt. He continued to be a prolific scorer in English county cricket where he captained Leicestershire.

NEW ZEALAND

P.E.Whitelaw	b Bowes	12	not out	5
J.E.Mills	b Bowes	0	not out	11
G.L.Weir	b Bowes	0		
C.S.Dempster	not out	83		
J.L.Kerr	lbw b Voce	10		
M.L.Page*	st Duckworth b Mitchell	20		
F.T.Badcock	b Bowes	1		
K.C.James†	b Bowes	0		
J.A.Dunning	b Bowes	12		
J.Newman	b Voce	5		
D.L.Freeman	run out	1		
Extras	(b 9, lb 4, nb 1)	14		0
TOTAL	(56.5 overs)	**158**	(8.3 overs) (0 wkts)	**16**

ENGLAND

H.Sutcliffe	c Weir b Freeman	24
R.E.S.Wyatt*	b Dunning	60
W.R.Hammond	not out	336
E.Paynter	b Dunning	36
L.E.G.Ames	b Badcock	26
G.O.B.Allen	b Badcock	12
F.R.Brown	c Page b Weir	13
W.Voce	b Weir	16
G.Duckworth†	not out	6
W.E.Bowes		
T.B.Mitchell		
Extras	(b 7, lb 4, w 1, nb 5)	19
TOTAL	(156 overs) (7 wkts dec)	**548**

Bowling												
ENGLAND	O	M	R	W	O	M	R	W				
Allen	5	2	11	0	3	1	4	0				
Bowes	19	5	34	6	2	0	4	0				
Mitchell	18	1	49	1								
Voce	9.5	3	20	2	1.3	0	2	0				
Brown	2	0	19	0								
Hammond	3	0	11	0	2	0	6	0				

Fall of Wickets	NZ	E	NZ
	1st	*1st*	*2nd*
1st	0	56	-
2nd	0	139	-
3rd	31	288	-
4th	62	347	-
5th	98	407	-
6th	101	456	-
7th	103	500	-
8th	123	-	-
9th	149	-	-
10th	158	-	-

NEW ZEALAND	O	M	R	W
Badcock	59	16	126	2
Dunning	43	5	156	2
Freeman	20	1	91	1
Newman	17	2	87	0
Page	6	2	30	0
Weir	11	2	39	2

MILESTONES

- Jack Dunning (26) made his test debut.

- Hammond's 336 not out was the highest score in test cricket, beating Don Bradman's 334 made against England at Leeds.

- Hammond's 10 sixes in his innings was a record for test cricket.

Eden Park was the scene of carnage wrought by Walter Hammond in scoring a new test record 336 not out.

1937 New Zealand in England

The difficulty of developing talented young players fit for test cricket on a diet of three Plunket Shield fixtures a season was assisted when a touring MCC side played four unofficial tests during the 1935/36 season. It saw the introduction of some new names that were to become important in New Zealand's cricket history. Jack Cowie, Walter Hadlee and Merv Wallace.

There was pleasure among the cricket fraternity when the itinerary for New Zealand's third tour of the United Kingdom was announced. Three tests were included from the outset among the 32 designated first-class games. Along with the three previously mentioned players there was excitement at the announcement that 19-year-old Martin Donnelly and left-hand batsman Bill Carson would also make the tour.

Tom Lowry's experience in England made him ideally suited to the job of manager, and his scarcely diminished skills as a cricketer meant that he was more than a useful substitute for injured or rested players.

12 **ENGLAND v NEW ZEALAND** (*First Test*)

at Lord's on 26, 28, 29 June, 1937
Toss : England. Umpires : F. Chester and F.I. Walden
Match drawn

New Zealand's inconsistent performances leading up to the first test made selection a difficult proposition. They had won only one and lost five of 12 first-class games. Much interest was centred on the young Yorkshire batsman, Len Hutton, with centuries in each of his previous three innings.

Before a crowd of 20,000 spectators he struggled for 25 minutes before he was bowled for a duck by a ball from Jack Cowie, which cut back to find a gap between bat and pad.

Joe Hardstaff and Walter Hammond survived the quick bowlers to reach lunch at 87-2. This pair broke free from their shackles during the afternoon, and both recorded centuries in a 240-run partnership that lasted 219 minutes. It was the second time in a week that Hardstaff had made a century against New Zealand.

Once they were separated, a middle order slump brought New Zealand quick wickets and the day ended with England 370-7. The tourists' keen fielding saved many runs and the bowlers deserved praise for collecting four wickets for 36 at the end of the day.

Eddie Paynter batted defiantly with the late-order batsmen and was last out with the score at 424. Jack Cowie and Alby Roberts bowled bravely and deserved four wickets apiece.

Early in New Zealand's first-innings Jack Kerr was hit in the face pulling at a bouncer from Hammond and had to retire hurt. With the dismissals of Giff Vivian, Walter Hadlee and Curly Page, with the score at 66, he returned to the crease to

battle courageously. Merv Wallace hit two sixes and six fours in a sparkling innings of 52.

Like Hutton, Martin Donnelly departed for a duck on his test debut, and at 176-6, New Zealand was in danger of being required to follow on. However, Sonny Moloney (64) and Roberts (66 not out) combined sound defence and judicious shots to add 104 for the eighth wicket.

With a lead of 129 runs England lost both openers cheaply before Hardstaff and Charlie Barnett set about increasing England's lead with a lusty partnership of 104 runs in 52 minutes. The England captain, Walter Robins, declared at lunch, giving New Zealand a target of 356 runs to win or to bat out two sessions to save the game.

That prospect was soon under threat with Bill Voce and Alf Gover able to make their venomous deliveries rear up from a good length. Wallace was twice struck on the hand by awkward bouncers, but showed his pluck by scoring a second half-century. In one over he hit Hedley Verity to the boundary four times.

For the second time in the game Kerr batted soundly and assisted by Donnelly, enabled New Zealand to reach stumps with two wickets in hand.

ENGLAND					
L.Hutton	b Cowie	0	c Vivian b Cowie		1
J.H.Parks	b Cowie	22	b Cowie		7
J.Hardstaff jnr.	c Moloney b Roberts	114	c Tindill b Roberts		64
W.R.Hammond	c Roberts b Vivian	140			
E.Paynter	c Dunning b Roberts	74			
C.J.Barnett	b Cowie	5	(4) not out		83
L.E.G.Ames†	b Vivian	5	(5) c sub (J.R.Lamason)		
			b Roberts		20
R.W.V.Robins*	c Tindill b Roberts	18	(6) not out		38
W.Voce	c Tindill b Cowie	27			
H.Verity	c Cowie b Roberts	3			
A.R.Gover	not out	2			
Extras	(b 4, lb 9, w 1)	14	(b 5, lb 8)		13
TOTAL	(155.3 overs)	**424**	(42 overs) (4 wkts dec)		**226**
NEW ZEALAND					
H.G.Vivian	lbw b Gover	5	(7) c Verity b Voce		11
J.L.Kerr	c Ames b Robins	31	not out		38
W.A.Hadlee	c Verity b Voce	34	(1) b Voce		3
M.L.Page*	c Paynter b Robins	9	c & b Robins		13
W.M.Wallace	lbw b Parks	52	lbw b Parks		56
M.P.Donnelly	c Hammond b Robins	0	(9) c Ames b Voce		21
D.A.R.Moloney	c & b Verity	64	(3) run out		0
E.W.T.Tindill†	c Hammond b Robins	8	lbw b Voce		3
A.W.Roberts	not out	66	(6) c sub (G.E.Hart) b Gover		17
J.A.Dunning	b Gover	0			
J.Cowie	lbw b Voce	2			
Extras	(b 4, lb 18, nb 2)	24	(b 4, lb 8, w 1)		13
TOTAL	(111.2 overs)	**295**	(76.5 overs) (8 wkts)		**175**

Bowling	O	M	R	W	O	M	R	W	Fall of Wickets				
NEW ZEALAND										E	NZ	E	NZ
										1st	1st	2nd	2nd
Cowie	41	10	118	4	15	2	49	2	1st	13	9	8	15
Roberts	43.3	11	101	4	14	3	73	2	2nd	31	36	19	15
Dunning	20	3	64	0	9	0	60	0	3rd	276	66	123	15
Vivian	46	10	106	2	4	0	31	0	4th	284	131	163	85
Moloney	2	1	9	0					5th	302	131	-	87
Page	3	0	12	0					6th	307	147	-	143
ENGLAND									7th	339	176	-	146
Gover	22	8	49	2	18	7	27	1	8th	402	280	-	175
Voce	24.2	2	74	2	18.5	8	41	3	9th	415	281	-	-
Hammond	6	2	12	0					10th	424	295	-	-
Robins	21	5	58	3	16	3	51	1					
Verity	25	13	48	1	14	7	33	1					
Parks	11	3	26	2	10	6	10	1					
Hutton	2	1	4	0									

MILESTONES

- Jack Cowie (27), Martin Donnelly (28), Walter Hadlee (29), Sonny Maloney (30), Eric Tindill (31) and Merv Wallace (32) made their test debuts for New Zealand.

- Len Hutton, made his debut for England, scoring 0 and 1, scarcely a portent of the greatness that was to come. He was to play 79 tests for England.

Merv Wallace, on debut, became the first New Zealand test batsman to score in excess of 50 in both innings of a test.

13 ENGLAND v NEW ZEALAND *(Second Test)*

at Old Trafford, Manchester on 24, 26, 27 July, 1937
Toss : England. Umpires : W. Reeves and E.J. Smith
England won by 130 runs

The inability of the England bowlers to force a victory at Lord's resulted in six changes to the England side. Alby Roberts had a damaged shoulder and was replaced by Norm Gallichan in the New Zealand side.

Heavy rain before the test softened the wicket and nullified the pace of Jack Cowie, who had previously proved so troublesome to the England openers. On a cold, damp day, Len Hutton, silenced his critics with his calm and correct batting, in partnership with Charlie Barnett, whose full-blooded stroke play was the dominant factor in their partnership of exactly 100. Hutton too, reached a precise individual century before he departed after 202 minutes.

Solid contributions from Joe Hardstaff, Walter Hammond and Eddie Paynter carried England to 237-3 by tea. Cowie seemed to find extra vigour and captured three wickets for 13 in six overs immediately following the break and, with Gallichan picking off the tailenders, England had lost their last six wickets for only 56 runs. Robins declared overnight.

On another dreary morning, New Zealand lost five wickets before lunch for 144 runs with Giff Vivian batting gracefully in scoring a half-century. Walter Hadlee, whose highest score to date on tour was 64, chose the afternoon session to reveal his true talents and attacked all the English bowlers, advancing to 50 in his first hour at the crease.

Although the tempo of his innings slowed a little he continued to loft loose deliveries. Seven runs short of a century Hadlee played a strong shot to square leg, but slipped and knocked over his stumps. Facing a deficit of 77, New Zealand removed three of the English batsmen for 37 runs in the last hour of play on the second day.

When play commenced on the final morning, Cowie bowled magnificently and England was soon in trouble and were 75-7, a lead of only 152 runs. Freddie Brown, who came in at number nine, was dropped three times before he made 21, and went on to top score with 57.

Together with Les Ames 72 invaluable runs were added for the eighth wicket. England had been let off the hook and its final total of 187 meant that New Zealand faced a difficult target of 265 in four hours.

Cowie's bowling analysis of 6-67 caused Neville Cardus to write: "Cowie bowled with admirable accuracy and tenacity. He delivered scarcely one lame or harmless ball in an hour and a half. No finer exhibition of quick, reliable bowling has been seen at Old Trafford for several years."

In New Zealand's second innings, Vivian and Sonny Moloney began the chase with a lively partnership of 50, but when the latter was run out a decline set in. Although Vivian batted on serenely and completed his second half-century in the match, a disaster unfolded around him.

Tom Goddard managed to get turn out of the bowlers' footmarks and his off-spinners seemed to intimidate tentative batsmen. Donnelly refused to submit and was unbeaten on 37 when the innings ended at 134 just after tea.

In the London *Daily Telegraph* Howard Marshall suggested that poor catching had cost the tourists an historic victory: "The New Zealanders had the game safely in their hands and then let it slip through their fingers."

MILESTONES

- Jack Cowie's match analysis of 10-140 saw him become the first New Zealander to take 10 wickets in a test match.

- Norm Gallichan (33) made his test debut.

- Len Hutton scored the first of his 19 test hundreds.

ENGLAND

L.Hutton	c Dunning b Vivian	100	c Vivian b Cowie	14
C.J.Barnett	c Kerr b Cowie	62	lbw b Dunning	12
J.Hardstaff jnr.	st Tindill b Vivian	58	c Tindill b Cowie	11
W.R.Hammond	b Gallichan	33	c Moloney b Cowie	0
E.Paynter	lbw b Cowie	33	c Cowie b Vivian	7
L.E.G.Ames†	not out	16	lbw b Dunning	39
A.W.Wellard	b Cowie	5	(8) c Wallace b Vivian	0
R.W.V.Robins*	b Cowie	14	(7) c Moloney b Cowie	12
F.R.Brown	b Gallichan	1	b Cowie	57
C.I.J.Smith	c Kerr b Gallichan	21	c & b Cowie	27
T.W.J.Goddard	not out	4	not out	1
Extras	(b 4, lb 7)	11	(lb 7)	7
TOTAL	(129 overs) (9 wkts dec)	**358**	(60.5 overs)	**187**

NEW ZEALAND

H.G.Vivian	b Wellard	58	c Ames b Smith	50
D.A.R.Moloney	lbw b Smith	11	run out	20
W.M.Wallace	st Ames b Brown	23	b Goddard	5
J.L.Kerr	b Wellard	4	b Smith	3
M.P.Donnelly	lbw b Wellard	4	not out	37
W.A.Hadlee	hit wicket b Wellard	93	b Goddard	3
M.L.Page*	c Smith b Hammond	33	b Goddard	2
E.W.T.Tindill†	b Brown	6	lbw b Brown	0
N.Gallichan	c Brown b Smith	30	c Wellard b Goddard	2
J.A.Dunning	not out	4	b Goddard	3
J.Cowie	st Ames b Brown	0	c Wellard b Goddard	0
Extras	(b 4, lb 11)	15	(b 7, lb 1, nb 1)	9
TOTAL	(107.4 overs)	**281**	(53.4 overs)	**134**

Bowling	O	M	R	W	O	M	R	W
NEW ZEALAND								
Cowie	32	6	73	4	23.5	6	67	6
Dunning	28	5	84	0	12	2	35	2
Gallichan	36	7	99	3	8	4	14	0
Vivian	28	7	75	2	17	5	64	2
Page	5	0	16	0				
ENGLAND								
Smith	22	7	29	2	14	2	34	2
Wellard	30	4	81	4	14	2	30	0
Hammond	15	5	27	1	6	1	18	0
Goddard	18	5	48	0	14.4	5	29	6
Brown	22.4	4	81	3	5	0	14	1

Fall of Wickets	E 1st	NZ 1st	E 2nd	NZ 2nd
1st	100	19	17	50
2nd	228	65	29	68
3rd	231	91	29	73
4th	296	105	46	94
5th	302	119	46	102
6th	307	218	68	104
7th	327	242	75	109
8th	328	268	147	116
9th	352	280	186	134
10th	-	281	187	134

The 1937 New Zealand team. Back row (from left): Tom Lowry (player/ manager), Bill Carson, Jack Cowie, Norm Gallichan, Walter Hadlee, Jack Lamason, John Dunning, Denis Maloney, Bill Ferguson (scorer/ baggage man). Seated: Eric Tindill, Alby Roberts, Giff Vivian, Curly Page (captain), "Dad" Weir, Jack Kerr. Front: Merv Wallace, Martin Donnelly.

14 ENGLAND v NEW ZEALAND *(Third Test)*

at The Oval on 14, 16, 17 August, 1937
Toss : New Zealand. Umpires : A. Dolphin and E.J. Smith
Match drawn

To the disappointment of a 6000 strong crowd, only half an hour's play was possible on the first day. A lively wicket, and yet another silly run out, saw New Zealand collapse to 47-4 the next morning.

Sonny Maloney and Martin Donnelly stiffened the middle order with a 50-run stand, during which time the pitch dried out and became more amiable. Donnelly was in a dashing, almost audacious mood and his half-century was full of crisp shots. After lunch, Curly Page and Alby Roberts added fifties with a sensible combination of defence and confident strokes. In reply to New Zealand's total of 249 England lost three wickets for 36 runs at stumps.

On the final morning, Denis Compton and Joe Hardstaff settled in and added 125 runs for the fourth wicket before Compton was unluckily run out when a ball glanced off the bowler's hand onto the wickets. Hardstaff made his second century in the three-test series, having also scored two half-centuries.

The wicket was now responsive to spin and England applied considerable pressure. Giff Vivian stuck to his task, bringing up his third half-century of the series, but at 107-6, and Page out of action with pulled stomach muscles, New Zealand teetered on the brink of disaster. The tailenders responded bravely and remained at the wicket long enough to ensure an honourable draw.

The great English batsman, Jack Hobbs, protested that three-day tests were futile. It was absurd to bring a team halfway around the world when it was well known beforehand that the series would produce unsatisfactory draws.

Without doubt, the outstanding player in the touring party was Jack Cowie. His bag of 19 wickets in the three tests was twice that taken by any other bowler in both teams, and his 114 wickets (at an average of 19.95) in first-class matches established a record for a New Zealand tourist in England.

Wisden described Cowie, as "a player with enormous capacity for work, who seemed impervious to fatigue and was accurate in length and direction. He often bowled a vicious off-break and as he could also make the ball lift and swing away, he was the bowler to be feared. Had he been an Australian he might have been termed 'a wonder of the age'."

NEW ZEALAND

Batsman	Dismissal	R		Dismissal	R
H.G.Vivian	c Ames b Gover	13		lbw b Hammond	57
W.A.Hadlee	b Matthews	18		c Compton b Matthews	0
W.M.Wallace	run out	8		lbw b Gover	7
G.L.Weir	c Matthews b Gover	3		c Barnett b Goddard	8
M.P.Donnelly	c Hutton b Robins	58		(6) c Ames b Hammond	0
D.A.R.Moloney	b Hammond	23		(5) b Compton	38
M.L.Page*	c Washbrook b Robins	53		absent hurt	
A.W.Roberts	c Hutton b Gover	50		(7) lbw b Goddard	9
E.W.T.Tindill†	b Robins	4		(8) not out	37
J.A.Dunning	c Gover b Robins	0		(9) b Compton	19
J.Cowie	not out	4		(10) c Robins b Hutton	2
Extras	(b 2, lb 11, nb 2)	15		(b 4, lb 5, nb 1)	10
TOTAL	**(83.1 overs)**	**249**		**(68.4 overs)**	**187**

ENGLAND

Batsman	Dismissal	R		Dismissal	R
C.J.Barnett	c Hadlee b Cowie	13		c Roberts b Dunning	21
L.Hutton	c & b Vivian	12			
C.Washbrook	lbw b Vivian	9		(2) not out	8
D.C.S.Compton	run out	65			
J.Hardstaff jnr.	b Cowie	103			
W.R.Hammond	c Wallace b Cowie	31			
L.E.G.Ames†	not out	6			
R.W.V.Robins*	c & b Roberts	9			
A.D.G.Matthews	not out	2			
T.W.J.Goddard					
A.R.Gover					
Extras	(b 2, lb 1, w 1)	4		(lb 2)	2
TOTAL	**(93 overs) (7 wkts dec)**	**254**		**(9.2 overs) (1 wkt)**	**31**

Bowling

ENGLAND	O	M	R	W	O	M	R	W
Gover	28	3	85	3	12	1	42	1
Matthews	22	6	52	1	8	2	13	1
Goddard	10	2	25	0	18	8	41	2
Hammond	7	1	25	1	11	3	19	2
Robins	14.1	2	40	4	11	2	24	0
Hutton	2	0	7	0	2.4	1	4	1
Compton					6	0	34	2

NEW ZEALAND	O	M	R	W	O	M	R	W
Cowie	24	5	73	3	4	1	15	0
Roberts	15	4	26	1	4	1	9	0
Dunning	25	5	89	0	1.2	0	5	1
Vivian	29	5	62	2				

Fall of Wickets

	NZ 1st	E 1st	NZ 2nd	E 2nd
1st	22	15	4	31
2nd	36	31	19	-
3rd	42	36	46	-
4th	47	161	87	-
5th	97	222	94	-
6th	145	240	107	-
7th	222	249	150	-
8th	244	-	182	-
9th	244	-	187	-
10th	249	-	-	-

AVERAGES

New Zealand

BATTING	M	I	NO	Runs	HS	Ave
A.W. Roberts	2	4	1	142	66*	47.33
H.G. Vivian	3	6	0	194	58	32.33
D.A.R. Moloney	3	6	0	156	64	26.00
J.L. Kerr	2	4	1	76	38*	25.33
W.A. Hadlee	3	6	0	151	93	25.16
W.M. Wallace	3	6	0	151	56	25.16
M.P. Donnelly	3	6	1	120	58	24.00
M.L. Page	3	5	0	110	53	22.00
N. Gallichan	1	2	0	32	30	16.00
E.W.T. Tindill	3	6	1	58	37*	11.60
J.A. Dunning	3	5	1	26	19	6.50
G.L. Weir	1	2	0	11	8	5.50
J. Cowie	3	5	1	8	4*	2.00

BOWLING	O	M	R	W	Ave
J. Cowie	139.5	30	395	19	20.78
A.W. Roberts	76.3	19	209	7	29.85
N. Gallichan	44	11	113	3	37.66
H.G. Vivian	124	27	338	8	42.25
J.A. Dunning	95.2	15	337	3	112.33
D.A.R. Moloney	2	1	9	0	-
M.L. Page	8	0	28	0	-

England

BATTING	M	I	NO	Runs	HS	Ave
J. Hardstaff jnr.	3	5	0	350	114	70.00
D.C.S. Compton	1	1	0	65	65	65.00
W.R. Hammond	3	4	0	204	140	51.00
C.J. Barnett	3	6	1	196	83*	39.20
E. Paynter	2	3	0	114	74	38.00
F.R. Brown	1	2	0	58	57	29.00
L.E.G. Ames	3	5	2	86	39	28.66
W. Voce	1	1	0	27	27	27.00
L. Hutton	3	5	0	127	100	25.40
C.I.J. Smith	1	2	0	48	27	24.00
R.W.V. Robins	3	5	1	91	38*	22.75
C. Washbrook	1	2	1	17	9	17.00
J.H. Parks	1	2	0	29	22	14.50
H. Verity	1	1	0	3	3	3.00
A.W. Wellard	1	2	0	5	5	2.50
T.W.J. Goddard	2	2	2	5	4*	-
A.R. Gover	2	1	1	2	2*	-
A.D.G. Matthews	1	1	1	2	2*	-

BOWLING	O	M	R	W	Ave
J.H. Parks	21	9	36	3	12.00
L. Hutton	6.4	2	15	1	15.00
C.I.J. Smith	36	9	63	4	15.75
D.C.S. Compton	6	0	34	2	17.00
T.W.J. Goddard	60.4	20	143	8	17.87
R.W.V. Robins	62.1	12	173	8	21.62
W. Voce	43.1	10	115	5	23.00
F.R. Brown	27.4	4	95	4	23.75
W.R. Hammond	45	12	101	4	25.25
A.W. Wellard	44	6	111	4	27.75
A.R. Gover	80	19	203	7	29.00
A.D.G. Matthews	30	8	65	2	32.50
H. Verity	39	20	81	2	40.50

MILESTONES

- Denis Compton, at the age of 19 years and 83 days, became the youngest man selected for England in an official test. He played 78 tests for England.

- Cyril Washbrook made his debut for England. He played 37 tests and formed a notable opening partnership with Len Hutton.

After scoring 103, Joe Hardstaff was comprehensively bowled by Jack Cowie. Observing from silly-mid-on is Giff Vivian and behind him is Les Ames.

1945/46 Australia in New Zealand

After an absence of international cricket for more than six years because of World War II, a month-long tour was hastily arranged for Australia to visit New Zealand. All four major associations were played and the final game was to become the first official test between the two countries.

Because the Imperial Cricket Conference had not approved the tour, this match was not given official test status at the time. In March 1948 the tour and the test were belatedly recognised by the ICC. Many of the Australian tourists took part in the victorious Ashes series the following season.

15 NEW ZEALAND v AUSTRALIA

at Basin Reserve, Wellington on 29, 30 March, 1946
Toss : New Zealand. Umpires : H.W. Gourlay and M.F. Pengelly
Australia won by an innings and 103 runs

Heavy rain before the match damaged the prepared wicket and a substitute wicket was hastily offered. The result was that the game began on a rain-damaged, crumbling wicket that the Australian bowlers exploited to the fullest.

In the morning session four wickets fell for 37 runs. That was a mere foretaste of the disaster to follow, as Bill O'Reilly and Ernie Toshack proved to be unplayable. The last eight wickets fell for just five runs and the total of 42 was the lowest scored by a New Zealand team.

The spirits of the large crowd were lifted when Jack Cowie bowled Ken Meuleman in his first over. Any hopes of an early breakthrough vanished when Bill Brown was dropped at fine leg with his score at 13. Together with Sid Barnes 109 runs were added before the next wicket fell. Australia ended the first day on 146 with seven wickets in hand.

On the second morning, a crowd of 20,000 watched the

tourists rattle on 28 runs in the first five overs. Then Cowie discovered a spiteful patch in the wicket, and in 11 overs claimed four wickets as the Australian middle order collapsed.

Eager to see his attack operating on this wicket, Brown declared at 199-8. Cowie's six wickets for 40 off 21 overs was a fine effort against a talented batting combination.

Every vantage point around the Basin was occupied when Walter Hadlee and Mac Anderson opened New Zealand's second innings. Less than two hours later, the last wicket had fallen and the home team had suffered its second humiliation in as many days. Such was the public's interest in cricket after the lean war years that the New Zealand Cricket Council collected record gate-takings of £3000.

NEW ZEALAND					
W.A.Hadlee*	c Miller b Toshack	6	b Miller		3
W.M.Anderson	b Lindwall	4	b Lindwall		1
V.J.Scott	c Barnes b O'Reilly	14	c Tallon b Miller		4
W.M.Wallace	c Barnes b Toshack	10	run out		14
E.W.T.Tindill†	b Toshack	1	lbw b Toshack		13
C.G.Rowe	b O'Reilly	0	b O'Reilly		0
L.A.Butterfield	lbw b O'Reilly	0	lbw b O'Reilly		0
D.A.N.McRae	c Hassett b O'Reilly	0	(9) c Meuleman b McCool		8
C.Burke	lbw b Toshack	1	(8) b Toshack		3
J.Cowie	st Tallon b Toshack	2	c Toshack b O'Reilly		0
D.C.Cleverley	not out	1	not out		1
Extras	(b 3)	3	(b 5, nb 2)		7
TOTAL	(39 overs)	**42**	(32.2 overs)		**54**

AUSTRALIA		
W.A.Brown*	c Rowe b Burke	67
K.D.Meuleman	b Cowie	0
S.G.Barnes	b Cowie	54
K.R.Miller	c Hadlee b Burke	30
A.L.Hassett	c Tindill b Cowie	19
C.L.McCool	c Hadlee b Cowie	7
I.W.Johnson	not out	7
D.Tallon†	c Scott b Cowie	5
R.R.Lindwall	c Anderson b Cowie	0
W.J.O'Reilly		
E.R.H.Toshack		
Extras	(b 5, lb 3, nb 2)	10
TOTAL	(74 overs) (8 wkts dec)	**199**

Bowling	O	M	R	W	O	M	R	W
AUSTRALIA								
Lindwall	8	1	13	1	9	3	16	1
Toshack	19	13	12	4	10	5	6	2
O'Reilly	12	5	14	5	7	1	19	3
Miller					6	2	6	2
McCool					0.2	0	0	1
NEW ZEALAND								
McRae	14	3	44	0				
Cowie	21	8	40	6				
Cleverley	15	1	51	0				
Butterfield	13	6	24	0				

Fall of Wickets			
	NZ	A	NZ
	1st	*1st*	*2nd*
1st	7	9	3
2nd	15	118	5
3rd	37	142	12
4th	37	174	36
5th	37	186	37
6th	37	186	37
7th	37	196	39
8th	37	199	41
9th	40		42
10th	42		54

MILESTONES

- The first official test between New Zealand and Australia.

- Mac Anderson (34), Ces Burke (35), Len Butterfield (36), Don McRae (37), Gordon Rowe (38) and Verdun Scott (39) made their test debuts for New Zealand.

- Future great Australian cricketers, Ray Lindwall, Keith Miller and Don Tallon made their test debuts for Australia.

- Bill O'Reilly, the great Australian right-arm leg-spinner, playing in the last of his 27 tests for Australia, had match figures of eight wickets for 33 runs.

New Zealand team. Back row (from left): Gordon Rowe, Paul Whitelaw, Verdun Scott, Don McRae, Len Butterfield, Ces Burke, Mac Anderson. Front: Eric Tindill, Merv Wallace, Walter Hadlee (captain) Jack Cowie, Don Cleverley.

1946/47 MCC in New Zealand

16 NEW ZEALAND v ENGLAND

at Lancaster Park, Christchurch on 21, 22, 24, 25 March, 1947
Toss : England. Umpires : O.R. Montgomery and M.F. Pengelly
Match drawn

England had lost 3-0 to Australia before flying to New Zealand for three provincial games and one test match. Bert Sutcliffe had scored 197 and 128 for Otago against the tourists so came into his first test match in splendid form.

Opening the innings with his captain Walter Hadlee, they combined to add 133 runs for the first wicket. Hadlee went on to complete his only test century in 130 minutes of aggressive batting. When he was dismissed for 116 he had seen his team through to 195-2.

Alec Bedser and Dick Pollard then struck at the heart of New Zealand's innings. Jack Cowie and Tom Burtt resisted in the last hour, and took the score to 306-8 by stumps.

The ninth wicket partnership continued to defy the England attack the next morning until Cowie departed and Hadlee declared. Cowie made an early breakthrough to have both openers out with the score at 46.

When Walter Hammond, playing in his last test match, came to the crease the crowd of 11,000 gave this cricket legend a standing ovation. He rewarded them by playing an innings of sublime elegance, with his trademark, the cover drive, played to perfection.

His 79 was the backbone of England's 265, which they reached for the loss of seven wickets before Hammond declared at the end of the second day's play. Once again the medium fast bowling of Cowie had been outstanding, as he claimed a further six English wickets.

At this time New Zealand played three-day tests but after rain had wiped out the third day, an additional day was added during a match for the first time in 70 years of test cricket. Unfortunately, this day was also rained out.

An unusual feature of the match was that both captains, Hammond and Hadlee, had declared their first-innings closed.

Rival captains Walter Hammond, left, and Walter Hadlee had memorable games. It was Hammond's final test of an illustrious career while Hadlee scored his only test century.

NEW ZEALAND

Batsman	Dismissal	Runs
W.A.Hadlee*	c Bedser b Yardley	116
B.Sutcliffe	c Evans b Bedser	58
V.J.Scott	c Hammond b Pollard	18
W.M.Wallace	c Evans b Bedser	9
D.D.Taylor	lbw b Bedser	12
F.B.Smith	b Bedser	18
E.W.T.Tindill†	b Pollard	1
R.H.Scott	b Edrich	18
J.Cowie	b Pollard	45
T.B.Burtt	not out	24
C.A.Snedden		
Extras	(b 10, lb 11, nb 5)	26
TOTAL	(102.4 overs) (9 wkts dec)	**345**

ENGLAND

Batsman	Dismissal	Runs
C.Washbrook	c Smith b Cowie	2
N.W.D.Yardley	b Cowie	22
W.J.Edrich	c Taylor b Scott R.H.	42
D.C.S.Compton	b Cowie	38
W.R.Hammond*	c Sutcliffe b Cowie	79
J.T.Ikin	c Tindill b Cowie	45
T.G.Evans†	not out	21
T.P.B.Smith	c sub (C.Burke) b Cowie	1
A.V.Bedser	not out	8
D.V.P.Wright		
R.Pollard		
Extras	(b 5, lb 1, nb 1)	7
TOTAL	(83 overs) (7 wkts dec)	**265**

Bowling	O	M	R	W
ENGLAND				
Bedser	39	5	95	4
Pollard	29.4	8	73	3
Edrich	11	2	35	1
Wright	13	1	61	0
Smith	6	0	43	0
Yardley	4	0	12	1
NEW ZEALAND				
Cowie	30	4	83	6
Scott R.H.	23	3	74	1
Burtt	14	1	55	0
Snedden	16	5	46	0

Fall of Wickets	NZ	E
	1st	*1st*
1st	133	2
2nd	195	46
3rd	212	79
4th	212	125
5th	234	222
6th	238	241
7th	258	249
8th	281	-
9th	345	-
10th	-	-

MILESTONES

• Tom Burtt (40), Roy Scott (41), Brun Smith (42), Colin Snedden (43), Burt Sutcliffe (44) and Don Taylor (45) made their test debuts for New Zealand.

• This was Walter Hammond's 83rd and final test match. He had scored 7429 runs at an average of 58.45, with 22 centuries, and had taken 83 wickets and held 110 catches.

1949 New Zealand in England

The selection panel that chose the fourth New Zealand team to visit England comprised three men who had participated in the 1937 tour. They were Walter Hadlee, Jack Kerr and Merv Wallace. Extensive trials were held throughout the country to discover players of quality from provincial centres who were not representing the major associations.

These trial matches turned up one interesting player, Fenwick Cresswell, a slow-medium bowler from Marlborough. Cresswell had a peculiar action that brought him chest-on at the moment of delivery. He had first played for Marlborough in the 1933/34 season. The trial that he played in was his debut in first-class cricket.

There were suggestions that a precedent, set by including the expatriate Martin Donnelly in the team, should have been extended to fast-bowler Tom Pritchard. He had enjoyed two successful seasons with Warwickshire, taking 93 wickets in 1947 and 172 wickets in 1948, and his presence would have bolstered what was acknowledged to be a weak attack.

New Zealand began the tour most impressively, winning five of their first 10 games. The outstanding player at this stage was Merv Wallace, who almost scored 1000 runs before the end of May.

All the batsmen were showing appreciation of fine weather and good wickets by scoring runs in an aggressive style, all that is with the exception of Bert Sutcliffe, who was slow to find his form. The slow, left-arm deliveries of Tom Burtt had won several games.

Before the first test, English critics were of the opinion that it was unfortunate that the four tests were to be of only three days duration. It was thought that both sides possessed very strong top order batting, and there was doubt that either side could capture 20 wickets in the time allotted.

17 ENGLAND v NEW ZEALAND *(First Test)*

at Headingley, Leeds on 11, 13, 14 June, 1949
Toss : England. Umpires : W.H. Ashdown and D. Davies
Match drawn

By seven o'clock in the morning the first spectators were queuing at the Headingley Gates, through which 31,000 people would enter to watch the first day's play. At stumps, England had lost five wickets and scored 307 off 114 overs.

The two premier England batsmen of the decade, Len Hutton and Denis Compton, both scored centuries in contrasting styles. Hutton played cautiously, preferring to play the slow bowlers from the crease, whereas Compton was prepared to use his feet to try and unsettle Tom Burtt, but the left-armer continued to bowl economically.

Writing in the *Sunday Times*, Neville Cardus, expressed his disappointment: "England performed not more than moderately, occasionally a little depressingly. Only at intervals could runs be scored at a pace likely to bring victory in the three-day match."

Within an hour on the second day England had lost its remaining five batsmen for the addition of 65 runs. Burtt achieved a just reward by capturing four wickets to end with 5-97, while Cowie added another victim to end with 5-127 off 43 overs.

Opening the bowling for England, Trevor Bailey began with a lively spell and captured the first three wickets to leave New Zealand 80-4 at lunch. Martin Donnelly and Brun Smith launched a grand counter-attack, which saw 94 runs added in the next hour.

Donnelly drove and pulled with handsome power before he became Bailey's fourth victim. Smith overcame a diffident beginning and gained confidence from his aggressive partner. Swift, exciting running between the wickets was a feature of this partnership, which added 120 for the fifth wicket.

A feature of Smith's batting was the large proportion of runs that he scored with the cut shot. Defiant batting from Frank Mooney and Jack Cowie halted a mid-innings collapse, where four wickets fell for 33 runs.

The third and last day of the match began with Mooney and Cowie continuing their partnership until Bailey claimed his sixth wicket of the innings, giving England a lead of 31 runs. A pulled muscle prevented Cowie from bowling in England's second innings. In his place as opening bowler was Donnelly, but only for a short time.

Cyril Washbrook and Bill Edrich combined to score 118 runs for the second wicket after Hutton had been dismissed in Harry Cave's first over. Washbrook, batting with a runner because of a muscle strain, reached 103 in three hours before the innings was declared closed.

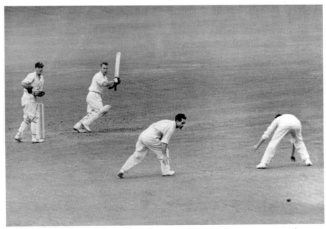

Brun Smith, playing his favourite cut shot, had an exceptional game scoring 96 and 54 not out. The wicketkeeper is Godfrey Evans.

New Zealand were left just two and a half hours in which to score 299 runs. In an hour's enterprising batting before tea, Bert Sutcliffe and Verdun Scott put on 82 runs.

After the pair had added 112 Scott was caught at extra cover. The effervescent Smith was sent in but thoughts of winning were remote and the main interest now centred on the possibility of Sutcliffe scoring a century before the close of play, but regrettably this did not occur. Smith completed an excellent double, being 54 not out at the end of play.

Writing in the *Yorkshire Post*, Jim Kilburn wrote: "Although England was given the advantage of the first innings, it was never able to dictate the course of the game and in the end was forced to confess small faith in its own bowling resources on a good wicket."

ENGLAND

L.Hutton	c Sutcliffe b Cowie	101	c Mooney b Cave	0
C.Washbrook	c Sutcliffe b Cowie	10	not out	103
W.J.Edrich	c Donnelly b Cowie	36	b Cave	70
D.C.S.Compton	st Mooney b Burtt	114	c Mooney b Cave	26
A.Wharton	lbw b Cowie	7	b Sutcliffe	13
F.G.Mann*	c Scott b Burtt	38	not out	49
T.E.Bailey	c Scott b Cowie	12		
T.G.Evans†	c Mooney b Burtt	27		
A.V.Bedser	c Donnelly b Burtt	20		
J.A.Young	st Mooney b Burtt	0		
W.E.Hollies	not out	0		
Extras	(b 3, lb 4)	7	(b 4, lb 2)	6
TOTAL	(127.3 overs)	**372**	(68 overs) (4 wkts dec)	**267**

NEW ZEALAND

B.Sutcliffe	c Evans b Young	32	c Bedser b Young	82
V.J.Scott	c Washbrook b Bailey	1	c Bedser b Young	43
W.A.Hadlee*	c Edrich b Bailey	34	(4) not out	13
W.M.Wallace	c Evans b Bailey	3		
M.P.Donnelly	c Young b Bailey	64	(3) not out	54
F.B.Smith	c Compton b Edrich	96		
G.O.Rabone	c Evans b Edrich	13		
F.L.H.Mooney†	c Edrich b Bailey	46		
T.B.Burtt	c Bedser b Compton	7		
H.B.Cave	c Edrich b Bailey	2		
J.Cowie	not out	26		
Extras	(b 2, lb 8, nb 7)	17	(b 1, lb 2)	3
TOTAL	(118.3 overs)	**341**	(49 overs) (2 wkts)	**195**

Bowling	O	M	R	W	O	M	R	W
NEW ZEALAND								
Cowie	43	6	127	5				
Cave	27	5	85	0	26	3	103	3
Rabone	18	7	56	0	17	4	56	0
Burtt	39.3	16	97	5	15	2	56	0
Donnelly					5	0	20	0
Sutcliffe					4	1	17	1
Scott					1	0	9	0
ENGLAND								
Bailey	32.3	6	118	6	9	0	51	0
Bedser	22	8	56	0	9	1	26	0
Edrich	9	2	18	2	2	0	13	0
Young	22	6	52	1	14	3	41	2
Hollies	25	6	57	0	11	3	33	0
Compton	8	2	23	1	1	0	5	0
Hutton					3	0	23	0

Fall of Wickets	E	NZ	E	NZ
	1st	1st	2nd	2nd
1st	17	4	0	112
2nd	92	64	118	147
3rd	194	69	162	-
4th	214	80	201	-
5th	273	200	-	-
6th	322	251	-	-
7th	330	254	-	-
8th	353	273	-	-
9th	367	284	-	-
10th	372	341	-	-

MILESTONES

- Harry Cave (46), Frank Mooney (47) and Geoff Rabone (48) made their test debuts.

- Trevor Bailey, who was to play 61 tests for England, made his test debut.

- Martin Donnelly and Brun Smith created a New Zealand test record of 120 for the fifth wicket.

- Frank Mooney and Jack Cowie created a New Zealand test record of 57 for the 10th wicket.

18 ENGLAND v NEW ZEALAND (*Second Test*)

at Lord's on 25, 27, 28 June, 1949
Toss : England. Umpires : W.H. Ashdown and F. Chester
Match drawn

A capacity crowd of 31,000, basking in glorious weather, watched Len Hutton and Jack Robertson proceed to 48 before Tom Burtt was introduced and bowled Hutton in his first over. By lunch three further wickets had fallen for a total of 83 runs. George Mann was bowled by Harry Cave early in the afternoon, and England looked uncomfortable at 112-5.

Although Jack Cowie and Burtt continued to bowl tightly, the lack of another top-quality bowler became apparent as Denis Compton and Trevor Bailey escaped the noose and runs flowed quickly. Their sixth-wicket stand realised 100 runs in 68 minutes and Compton achieved his second century in as many tests (and his thirteenth in test cricket) before he was caught on 116.

As so often happens at the end of a substantial partnership, Bailey (93), was immediately dismissed when a ball snicked off Geoff Rabone flew from Frank Mooney's boot into the slips. At 313-9, Mann declared leaving New Zealand to bat out the last quarter of an hour's play.

New Zealand advanced to 372-7 by stumps the next day with aggressive stroke play. Verdun Scott and Bert Sutcliffe scored 89 for the first wicket, but once this pair departed, the crafty leg spin of Hollies disposed of Walter Hadlee and Merv Wallace before lunch when New Zealand was 160-4.

Under a blazing afternoon sun Martin Donnelly reigned supreme. He was content to wait for the occasional loose ball, which he stroked away with silky power. With Rabone, 76

Martin Donnelly became the first New Zealand batsmen to score a double century in a test match. Critics raved over his skills while Godfrey Evans and Trevor Bailey admired them from close quarters.

runs were added for the sixth wicket. Mooney contributed to a stand of 78, while Donnelly brought up a century in three and a half hours and progressed to 126 by the end of the day. The tourists' lead on the first innings was the first managed by a New Zealand team against England.

The last morning added to the record book. Another 112 runs were added in 90 minutes. When he was caught by Hutton off the bowling of Jack Young, Donnelly had batted for 355 minutes and hit 26 fours. He had achieved exactly 1000 runs on tour.

Trailing by 171, England faced five hours at the crease to ensure a draw. Hutton and Robertson responded by scoring a record 143 for the first wicket against New Zealand. Even though Robertson scored 121 it would not prevent him being dropped for the third test.

Donnelly's innings was heralded as one of the greatest seen at Lord's. At cricket's headquarters he had now recorded centuries in a test, for Gentlemen v Players and in the Oxford v Cambridge match.

An editorial in the *Christchurch Star Sun* reported: "The Dominion's cricketers, by their splendid performances against England's best, have stolen the sporting thunder of 1949. The long awaited rugby tour of South Africa, the highlight of New Zealand's national game, was expected to be the big attraction, and the cricket in England a pleasant addition to the numerous international sports fixtures arranged for this year.

But as the All Blacks' progress to date has hardly justified hopes, so have the cricketers excelled themselves. The volume of cricket discussion in the Dominion at the present time is remarkable and undeniably this stimulation of public interest will be for the good of the sport."

MILESTONES

- The England captain, George Mann, became the first test captain to declare on the first day of a test match, a decision contrary to the laws applying to international cricket. He later apologised for his error.

- Martin Donnelly's innings of 206 was the highest individual score by a New Zealander in a test match.

- The New Zealand total of 484 was the highest achieved by New Zealand against England.

19 ENGLAND v NEW ZEALAND *(Third Test)*

at Old Trafford, Manchester on 23, 25, 26 July, 1949
Toss : England. Umpires : F. Chester and F.S. Lee
Match drawn

In spite of scoring 173 runs in three test innings, Brun Smith was sacrificed for the third test to make way for John Reid, whose recent batting form was impossible to ignore. The England selectors made five changes, the most notable of which was the replacement of the team's captain, George Mann, by Freddie Brown, who had played against the 1937 tourists.

Rain had fallen 36 hours before the start of this test and the outfield was damp. Brown gambled that conditions would help his bowlers. It was not, however, a lively wicket that led to New Zealand losing four wickets for 82 runs during the morning, but the penetrative bowling of Trevor Bailey.

Reid's task in his test debut was unenviable. His partner, however, was the seasoned Martin Donnelly, just the man for a crisis. The pair battled until the last over before tea, when Reid was trapped in front by Les Jackson, but not before he had completed a half-century and added 116 with Donnelly.

New Zealand ended the day at 276-8 thanks to Geoff Rabone and Tom Burtt adding 52 for the eighth wicket. Some critics suggested that New Zealand's slow run-rate was already an attempt to play for a draw.

However, Neville Cardus was more generous, saying that Donnelly "Had staked another claim to a position amongst the finest of contemporary batsmen." Reid he described as "club cricketer in excelsis. I do not mean that he is not endowed technically, but only that he combines the commonsense against a good ball and unabashed appetite for a brawny blow against a bad one."

The crowd of 38,000 on the second day was the biggest

ENGLAND					
L.Hutton	b Burtt	23	c Cave b Rabone	66
J.D.B.Robertson	c Mooney b Cowie	26	c Cave b Rabone	121
W.J.Edrich	c Donnelly b Cowie	9	c Hadlee b Burtt	31
D.C.S.Compton	c Sutcliffe b Burtt	116	b Burtt	6
A.J.Watkins	c Wallace b Burtt	6	not out	49
F.G.Mann*	b Cave	18	c Donnelly b Rabone	17
T.E.Bailey	c Sutcliffe b Rabone	93	not out	6
T.G.Evans†	b Burtt	5		
C.Gladwin	run out	5		
J.A.Young	not out	1		
W.E.Hollies				
Extras	(b 9, lb 2)	11	(b 9, lb 1)	10
TOTAL	(103.1 overs) (9 wkts dec)	**313**	(103 overs) (5 wkts)	**306**

NEW ZEALAND		
B.Sutcliffe	c Compton b Gladwin	57
V.J.Scott	c Edrich b Compton	42
W.A.Hadlee*	c Robertson b Hollies	43
W.M.Wallace	c Evans b Hollies	2
M.P.Donnelly	c Hutton b Young	206
F.B.Smith	b Hollies	23
G.O.Rabone	b Hollies	25
F.L.H.Mooney†	c Watkins b Young	33
T.B.Burtt	c Edrich b Hollies	23
H.B.Cave	c & b Young	6
J.Cowie	not out	1
Extras	(b 16, lb 3, w 3, nb 1)	23
TOTAL	(159.4 overs)	**484**

Bowling	O	M	R	W	O	M	R	W	Fall of Wickets			
NEW ZEALAND										E	NZ	E
										1st	1st	2nd
Cowie	26.1	5	64	2	14	3	39	0	1st	48	89	143
Cave	27	2	79	1	7	1	23	0	2nd	59	124	216
Rabone	14	5	56	1	28	6	116	3	3rd	72	137	226
Burtt	35	7	102	4	37	12	58	2	4th	83	160	226
Sutcliffe	1	0	1	0	16	1	55	0	5th	112	197	252
Wallace					1	0	5	0	6th	301	273	-
ENGLAND									7th	307	351	-
Bailey	33	3	136	0					8th	307	436	-
Gladwin	28	5	67	1					9th	313	464	-
Edrich	4	0	16	0					10th	-	484	-
Hollies	58	18	133	5								
Compton	7	0	33	1								
Young	26.4	4	65	3								
Watkins	3	1	11	0								

attendance for a post-war test in England. They were impatient to watch what was expected to be a cavalcade of runs from the home team. Len Hutton and Cyril Washbrook had a century partnership before Washbrook was caught behind.

The crowd was sweltering in great heat during the afternoon, and in their frustration began slow handclapping. Reg Simpson, batting at five, was slow at the start. His first 50 occupied 115 minutes, but in the last hour he began to display clean hitting and reached his century in another 28 minutes.

The limitations of New Zealand's bowling attack had been particularly apparent in the last session of play when Bailey and Simpson added 105 runs.

In an hour's batting on the last morning Bailey reached 72 not out but four quick wickets fell and Jack Cowie ended with three and Tom Burtt six.

Facing a deficit of 147, New Zealand were 109-3 as the spinners threatened to break through. If Donnelly had not survived a stumping opportunity when he was on 22, England may well have triumphed.

The two New Zealand left-handers put on 78 for the fourth wicket and Bert Sutcliffe completed his maiden test century in 170 minutes. Donnelly then figured in stands of 48 with Reid and 60 with Rabone and the game was saved.

The outstanding bowler for the 1949 touring side was Tom Burtt. In the four test matches he captured 17 wickets and ended with 129 first-class wickets for the tour.

NEW ZEALAND

Batsman	Dismissal	Runs	2nd innings	Runs
B.Sutcliffe	b Bailey	9	lbw b Compton	101
V.J.Scott	b Bailey	13	b Jackson	13
W.A.Hadlee*	b Bailey	34	c Brown b Hollies	22
W.M.Wallace	c Washbrook b Close	12	lbw b Hollies	14
M.P.Donnelly	lbw b Bailey	75	st Evans b Brown	80
J.R.Reid	lbw b Jackson	50	b Bailey	25
G.O.Rabone	c Brown b Bailey	33	not out	39
F.L.H.Mooney†	b Jackson	5	st Evans b Brown	15
T.B.Burtt	st Evans b Compton	32	not out	27
H.B.Cave	b Bailey	12		
J.Cowie	not out	3		
Extras	(b 3, lb 9, nb 3)	15	(b 2, lb 4, nb 6)	12
TOTAL	(128.2 overs)	293	(110 overs) (7 wkts)	348

ENGLAND

Batsman	Dismissal	Runs
L.Hutton	st Mooney b Burtt	73
C.Washbrook	c Mooney b Cowie	44
W.J.Edrich	c Rabone b Burtt	78
D.C.S.Compton	b Cowie	25
R.T.Simpson	c Donnelly b Burtt	103
T.E.Bailey	not out	72
F.R.Brown*	c Wallace b Burtt	22
T.G.Evans†	c Mooney b Burtt	12
D.B.Close	c Rabone b Burtt	0
W.E.Hollies	c Mooney b Cowie	0
H.L.Jackson	not out	7
Extras	(b 2, lb 2)	4
TOTAL	(128 overs) (9 wkts dec)	440

Bowling ENGLAND	O	M	R	W	O	M	R	W
Bailey	30.2	5	84	6	16	0	71	1
Jackson	27	11	47	2	12	3	25	1
Close	25	12	39	1	17	2	46	0
Hollies	18	8	29	0	26	6	52	2
Brown	18	4	43	0	21	3	71	2
Compton	6	0	28	1	8	0	28	1
Edrich	4	1	8	0	5	0	26	0
Simpson					2	1	9	0
Washbrook					2	0	8	0
Hutton					1	1	0	0
NEW ZEALAND								
Cowie	36	8	98	3				
Cave	30	4	97	0				
Burtt	45	11	162	6				
Rabone	10	0	43	0				
Sutcliffe	5	0	22	0				
Reid	2	0	14	0				

Fall of Wickets	NZ	E	NZ
	1st	1st	2nd
1st	22	103	24
2nd	23	127	58
3rd	62	172	109
4th	82	258	187
5th	198	363	235
6th	205	404	295
7th	217	419	313
8th	269	419	-
9th	288	419	-
10th	293	-	-

MILESTONES

- John Reid (49) made his test debut.

- Brian Close, a Yorkshire all-rounder aged 18 years and 149 days, became the youngest Englishman to appear in a test match.

- Freddie Brown captained England for the first time.

20 ENGLAND v NEW ZEALAND *(Fourth Test)*

at The Oval on 13, 15, 16 August, 1949
Toss : New Zealand. Umpires : D. Davies and F.S. Lee
Match drawn

New Zealand was forced to make one change in their test line-up. Frank Mooney was still nursing a swollen finger and it was decided that John Reid would keep wicket and Fen Cresswell made his test debut in the same year that he had appeared in his first first-class game.

The England selectors came up with an unbalanced attack, which included three leg-spinners (Freddie Brown, Eric Hollies and Doug Wright), two quick bowlers (Trevor Bailey and Alec Bedser) and off-spinner Jim Laker.

For the first time in the series Walter Hadlee won the toss. With an excellent wicket in their favour Bert Sutcliffe and Verdun Scott combined in yet another century partnership, scored in 80 minutes, which ended just before lunch when Scott flashed at Bailey and was caught in the slips by Bill Edrich, one of three catches he was to hold in the innings.

Sutcliffe batted in his most regal style before changing his mind and being caught off Hollies for 88. With Merv Wallace in scintillating form New Zealand were well placed at tea on 239-3.

In the first over after the break, Wallace (55) edged a ball to Edrich in the slips, a mistake emulated by Martin Donnelly in the next over. Play ended with New Zealand 320-8. England used eight different bowlers and, curiously, Laker delivered just three overs in the day.

The visitors were quickly dismissed for 345 at the start of the second day. Any thoughts that England had depleted its batting were allayed as the top order plundered 432 runs for the loss of four wickets. Len Hutton and Reg Simpson shared England's best opening stand of the series (147) in better than even time and then Edrich joined Hutton to add 218 for the second wicket.

Hutton spent 45 minutes going from 90 to his century and then embarked on his second hundred at a blistering pace. This took a mere 85 minutes and took his tally of boundaries to 25 before Geoff Rabone caught him in the slips.

Edrich, too, picked up the pace of his innings. His first 50 took two hours, the second barely an hour. Cresswell took his fourth wicket of the day, the sum of New Zealand's success.

A crowd of nearly 30,000 had been treated to a magnificent display of batting by a team supposedly overstocked with bowlers. Alex Bannister was enraptured by Hutton's exhibition: "His great, faultless double century was about the finest I have seen him play in England. In an innings which for sheer brilliance dwarfed any previous efforts by an English batsman in the series and for a scoring-rate was the complete answer to his critics."

Seeking quick runs, the remaining six England batsmen fell for 50 runs within an hour on the last morning. Cresswell, who had bowled splendidly throughout the innings, ended with six wickets for 168 off 42 overs in his test debut.

Despite Sutcliffe scoring his second half-century of the game (54), New Zealand were in some danger when the fourth wicket fell at 131 and the first-innings deficit had not yet been overtaken. Both Reid and Wallace looked most uncertain at the start of their innings on a wicket that was now taking turn.

After batting for almost two hours Wallace was deceived by Hollies and was stumped for 58. The young Reid greeted the second new ball by slamming 14 runs off Bailey's first over as he and Rabone added 88 for the sixth wicket. New Zealand had made the game safe when Reid mistimed a shot and was caught in the covers for 93, scored in 130 minutes.

An editorial writer in the *Daily Telegraph* proclaimed: "The honours, such as they are, undoubtedly go to the New Zealanders, who have met and held the full strength of English cricket as they were hardly expected to do. A rising standard in New Zealand cricket is reflected in the results of these tests."

The success of the tour to England in 1949 did for New Zealand cricket what the 1905 All Blacks had done for their game, it raised New Zealand's status in the world of cricket.

The experienced pair of Verdun Scott, left, and Bert Sutcliffe excelled with an opening partnership of 121 at the start of the fourth test.

MILESTONES

- Fen Cresswell (50) made his test debut.

- Cresswell became the first New Zealand bowler to take five or more wickets on his test debut.

- This was the first series of four tests that had not seen a finish in any game.

- Len Hutton and Bill Edrich added 218 for the second wicket, a record for England against New Zealand.

NEW ZEALAND

Batsman	1st innings		2nd innings	
B.Sutcliffe	c Bedser b Hollies	88	c Brown b Bedser	54
V.J.Scott	c Edrich b Bedser	60	c Evans b Bedser	6
J.R.Reid†	lbw b Wright	5	(5) c Wright b Laker	93
W.M.Wallace	c Edrich b Bedser	55	(6) c Brown b Bedser	58
M.P.Donnelly	c Edrich b Bailey	27	(6) c Brown b Bedser	10
W.A.Hadlee*	c Evans b Bedser	25	(3) c Edrich b Hollies	22
G.O.Rabone	c Evans b Bailey	18	lbw b Laker	20
T.B.Burtt	c Evans b Bailey	36	c Compton b Laker	6
H.B.Cave	b Compton	10	not out	14
J.Cowie	c Hutton b Bedser	1	c Wright b Laker	4
G.F.Cresswell	not out	12	not out	0
Extras	(lb 1, w 1, nb 6)	8	(b 10, lb 5, nb 6)	21
TOTAL	**(112.1 overs)**	**345**	**(97 overs) (9 wkts dec)**	**308**

ENGLAND

Batsman		Runs
L.Hutton	c Rabone b Cresswell	206
R.T.Simpson	c Donnelly b Cresswell	68
W.J.Edrich	c Cave b Cresswell	100
D.C.S.Compton	c Scott b Cresswell	13
T.E.Bailey	c Reid b Cowie	36
F.R.Brown*	c Hadlee b Cresswell	21
T.G.Evans†	c Donnelly b Cowie	17
J.C.Laker	c Scott b Cowie	0
A.V.Bedser	c Reid b Cowie	0
W.E.Hollies	not out	1
D.V.P.Wright	lbw b Cresswell	0
Extras	(b 6, lb 11, nb 3)	20
TOTAL	**(117.2 overs)**	**482**

Bowling

ENGLAND

	O	M	R	W	O	M	R	W
Bailey	26.1	7	72	3	11	1	67	0
Bedser	31	6	74	4	23	4	59	3
Edrich	3	0	16	0				
Wright	22	1	93	1	6	0	21	0
Laker	3	0	11	0	29	6	78	4
Hollies	20	7	51	1	17	6	30	2
Brown	5	1	14	0	10	0	29	0
Compton	2	0	6	1	1	0	3	0

NEW ZEALAND

	O	M	R	W
Cowie	28	1	123	4
Cresswell	41.2	6	168	6
Cave	24	4	78	0
Burtt	24	2	93	0

Fall of Wickets

	NZ	E	NZ
	1st	1st	2nd
1st	121	147	24
2nd	134	365	68
3rd	170	396	115
4th	239	401	131
5th	239	436	188
6th	272	469	276
7th	287	470	283
8th	311	472	299
9th	320	481	308
10th	345	482	-

AVERAGES

New Zealand

BATTING	M	I	NO	Runs	HS	Ave
F.B. Smith	2	3	1	173	96	86.50
M.P. Donnelly	4	6	0	462	206	77.00
B. Sutcliffe	4	7	0	423	101	60.42
J.R. Reid	2	4	0	173	93	43.25
W.A. Hadlee	4	7	1	193	43	32.16
G.O. Rabone	4	6	1	148	39*	29.60
T.B. Burtt	4	6	1	131	36	26.20
V.J. Scott	4	7	0	178	60	25.42
F.L.H. Mooney	3	4	0	99	46	24.75
W.M. Wallace	4	6	0	144	58	24.00
J. Cowie	4	5	3	35	26*	17.50
H.B. Cave	4	5	1	44	14*	11.00
G.F. Cresswell	1	2	2	12	12*	-

BOWLING	O	M	R	W	Ave
G.F. Cresswell	41.2	6	168	6	28.00
J. Cowie	147.1	23	451	14	32.21
T.B. Burtt	195.3	50	568	17	33.41
G.O. Rabone	87	22	327	4	81.75
B. Sutcliffe	26	2	95	1	95.00
H.B. Cave	141	19	465	4	116.25
W.M. Wallace	1	0	5	0	-
V.J. Scott	1	0	9	0	-
J.R. Reid	2	0	14	0	-
M.P. Donnelly	5	0	20	0	-

England

BATTING	M	I	NO	Runs	HS	Ave
R.T. Simpson	2	2	0	171	103	85.50
C. Washbrook	2	3	1	157	103*	78.50
L. Hutton	4	6	0	469	206	78.16
J.D.B. Robertson	1	2	0	147	121	73.50
T.E. Bailey	4	5	2	219	93	73.00
A.J. Watkins	1	2	1	55	49*	55.00
W.J. Edrich	4	6	0	324	100	54.00
D.C.S. Compton	4	6	0	300	116	50.00
F.G. Mann	2	4	1	122	49*	40.66
F.R. Brown	2	2	0	43	22	21.50
T.G. Evans	4	4	0	61	27	15.25
A.V. Bedser	2	2	0	20	20	10.00
A. Wharton	1	2	0	20	13	10.00
C. Gladwin	1	1	0	5	5	5.00
W.E. Hollies	4	3	2	1	1*	1.00
J.A. Young	2	2	1	1	1*	1.00
D.B. Close	1	1	0	0	0	0.00
J.C. Laker	1	1	0	0	0	0.00
D.V.P. Wright	1	1	0	0	0	0.00
H.L. Jackson	1	1	1	7	7*	-

BOWLING	O	M	R	W	Ave
J.C. Laker	32	6	89	4	22.25
H.L. Jackson	39	14	72	3	24.00
D.C.S. Compton	33	2	126	5	25.20
J.A. Young	62.4	13	158	6	26.33
A.V. Bedser	85	19	215	7	30.71
T.E. Bailey	158	22	599	16	37.43
W.E. Hollies	175	54	385	10	38.50
W.J. Edrich	27	3	97	2	48.50
C. Gladwin	28	5	67	1	67.00
F.R. Brown	54	8	157	2	78.50
D.B. Close	42	14	85	1	85.00
D.V.P. Wright	28	1	114	1	114.00
C. Washbrook	2	0	8	0	-
R.T. Simpson	2	1	9	0	-
A.J. Watkins	3	1	11	0	-
L. Hutton	4	1	23	0	-

1950/51 MCC in New Zealand

21 NEW ZEALAND v ENGLAND *(First Test)*

at Lancaster Park, Christchurch on 17, 19, 20, 21 March, 1951
Toss : New Zealand. Umpires : E.G. Brook and S.B. Tonkinson
Match drawn

Although England left Australia having lost the series four tests to one, their victory in the final test was the first achieved by England over its arch-rival since the Second World War.

A crowd of 15,000 watched Bert Sutcliffe and Verdun Scott begin batting in fine weather. The wicket offered little assistance to the quick trio of Trevor Bailey, Alec Bedser and Brian Statham but its sluggish nature inhibited free stroke making. Scott's departure brought together John Reid and Sutcliffe who proceeded to compile a New Zealand test record second-wicket partnership of 131 runs.

Sutcliffe reached his century in 226 minutes. Many of his runs were scored by turning full-length deliveries off his toes to the mid-wicket boundary. Reid's half-century was also a restrained affair. New Zealand were 247-3 at stumps.

Merv Wallace, who had rarely batted to his full potential at test level, recovered from an uncertain start and displayed more confidence on the second morning. With Walter Hadlee forcing the pace, they added 94 runs for the fourth wicket.

Frank Mooney and Tom Burtt were the only batsmen to keep pace with the clock. Their bright stand of 80 entertained the crowd and allowed Hadlee to declare at tea; 417-8, scored in nine hours.

E. W. Swanton, tour correspondent of the *Daily Telegraph* reported: "The English team was playing with a relaxed attitude, a natural reaction to the long tour of Australia ... the players could not galvanise themselves into greater effort whether bowling or fielding."

England's innings began with a curious incident, rare in test cricket. In response to the solitary appeal of Mooney, Cyril Washbrook was given out leg-before to Fen Cresswell's first delivery. Hadlee spoke to the England opener, as he walked reluctantly towards the pavilion, and then conferred with umpire Tonkinson. Washbrook was recalled, apparently having snicked the ball onto his pad.

Before stumps on the second day, Alec Moir, playing in his first test, deceived the experienced Len Hutton with a perfectly flighted leg-spinner. The wicket was now showing signs of wear, and it was suggested that Moir and Burtt could embarrass the England batsmen on the third day.

England adopted a cautious approach, with all the top order batsmen scoring slowly. Reg Simpson and Denis Compton joined in a 129-run stand for the third wicket and by stumps England was 100 runs behind, but still had six wickets in hand.

Trevor Bailey, whose dogged batting had earned him the nickname of "Barnacle", crept past 50 after 270 minutes at the crease but then added another 84 runs in half that time. Doug Wright helped Bailey add 117 for the ninth wicket.

When Moir bowled Statham, the last English batsman, he had taken six wickets for 155 off 57 overs. England's total of 550 runs had occupied more than 12 hours. A total of 35,000 people had watched four days' play, which produced gate takings of £5731.

Alex Moir, the right-arm leg-spinner from Dunedin, began his test career taking six wickets during his marathon spell of 56.3 overs.

MILESTONES

- John Hayes (51), Tony MacGibbon (52) and Alec Moir (53) made their test debuts.

- Moir became the second New Zealand bowler to take five wickets, or more, in an innings on debut.

- Brian Statham, who was to play 70 tests and take 252 test wickets, made his test debut for England.

- Bert Sutcliffe and John Reid created a New Zealand test record of 131 for the second wicket.

NEW ZEALAND

B.Sutcliffe	b Statham	116			
V.J.Scott	b Bailey	16	(5) not out		10
J.R.Reid	b Wright	50			
W.M.Wallace	c Brown b Bedser	66			
W.A.Hadlee*	c Brown b Bailey	50	(1) c Evans b Simpson		8
A.R.MacGibbon	lbw b Wright	4			
F.L.H.Mooney†	st Evans b Tattersall	39			
T.B.Burtt	b Brown	42			
A.M.Moir	not out	0	(4) not out		7
J.A.Hayes			(2) lbw b Washbrook		19
G.F.Cresswell			(3) c Evans b Simpson		2
Extras	(b 16, lb 16, w 1, nb 1)	34			0
TOTAL	(157.2 overs) (8 wkts dec)	**417**	(13 overs) (3 wkts)		**46**

ENGLAND

L.Hutton	b Moir	28
C.Washbrook	c Mooney b Hayes	58
R.T.Simpson	c Wallace b Moir	81
D.C.S.Compton	b Burtt	79
T.E.Bailey	not out	134
F.R.Brown*	c Scott b Cresswell	62
T.G.Evans†	c Hayes b Moir	19
A.V.Bedser	c Hayes b Moir	5
R.Tattersall	b Moir	2
D.V.P.Wright	c MacGibbon b Cresswell	45
J.B.Statham	b Moir	9
Extras	(b 20, lb 8)	28
TOTAL	(221.3 overs)	**550**

Bowling	O	M	R	W	O	M	R	W
ENGLAND								
Bedser	41	10	83	1				
Bailey	30	9	51	2				
Statham	24	6	47	1				
Tattersall	16	3	48	1				
Wright	27	2	99	2				
Brown	15.2	3	34	1				
Compton	4	0	21	0	2	0	10	0
Washbrook					4	0	25	1
Simpson					4	1	4	2
Hutton					3	0	7	0
NEW ZEALAND								
Hayes	43	11	85	1				
Reid	10	2	29	0				
MacGibbon	27	6	74	0				
Cresswell	34	10	75	2				
Moir	56.3	16	155	6				
Burtt	49	23	99	1				
Scott	2	0	5	0				

Fall of Wickets			
	NZ	E	NZ
	1st	2nd	2nd
1st	37	57	9
2nd	168	108	29
3rd	203	237	29
4th	297	264	-
5th	307	356	-
6th	335	388	-
7th	415	398	-
8th	417	406	-
9th	-	523	-
10th	-	550	-

22   NEW ZEALAND v ENGLAND *(Second Test)*

at Basin Reserve, Wellington on 24, 26, 27, 28 March, 1951
Toss : New Zealand. Umpires : J. McLellan and M.F. Pengelly
England won by 6 wickets

Rain prevented any play on the first day and on Easter Monday the New Zealanders began batting on a wicket affected by seepage under the covers. By the end of the day 13 wickets had fallen for 167 runs.

Doug Wright caused the home team most trouble. He had a long springy run, incorporating skips and jumps, resulting in briskly delivered leg-spinners. Figures of 5-48 in this innings gave him 100 wickets in test cricket.

Alec Moir, who had enjoyed a good debut as a bowler at Christchurch, now distinguished himself with the bat. Coming in at number seven with the score at 94, he contributed 26 not out of 31 runs before the last wicket fell at 125 after four hours of dreary batting.

England lost three cheap wickets before stumps. Had New Zealand's catching been efficient on the second day, England would not have attained a lead of 102 runs. Len Hutton gave three chances in his innings of 57 and Freddie Brown, the other major contributor with 47, was dropped before he reached double figures.

Verdun Scott pulled a tendon in his leg while fielding so Tom Burtt opened the New Zealand innings with Bert Sutcliffe. This pair made only 32 runs in the 80 minutes until stumps on the third day.

Roy Tattersall, a tall right-arm off-spinner, ran through the New Zealand top order on the final morning. He captured the first five wickets to fall at a cost of just 13 runs.

At six down for 98, the home team's chances looked bleak. Scott, normally a sedate opening bat, then embarked upon a defiantly aggressive stand with Moir, which added to 50 in even time. Of the last 105 runs, Scott, using Tony MacGibbon, as his runner, contributed 60.

The England batsmen found the medium-pace in-swingers of Fen Cresswell difficult to counter.

New Zealand's total of 189 left England the seemingly simple task of scoring 88 runs in 145 minutes. However, skilful field placings by Walter Hadlee and extremely tight bowling by Fen Cresswell and Burtt restricted the tourists to 35 in almost an hour before tea.

A curious incident occurred when Moir bowled the first over after tea. It was apparently overlooked that he had delivered the last over before the adjournment. Thirty years previously Warwick Armstrong, the Australian captain, had bowled two consecutive overs in a test in England.

At 80-4, within the last half-hour, Brown arrived at the crease, determined to avoid the lethargy that had attended his teammates. Soon a fine drive to the long-on boundary carried England to victory with 14 minutes to spare.

The tourists, having achieved England's first win over New Zealand since 1937, departed for home by flying boat. The English critics filed caustic reports of the dawdling display given by both sides in this series.

E. W. Swanton said: "If there has been any great merit, technically or tactically, in the last two days' cricket it has not been apparent."

MILESTONES

- Walter Hadlee announced his retirement from test cricket.

NEW ZEALAND

B.Sutcliffe	c & b Wright	20	b Tattersall		11
V.J.Scott	lbw b Bailey	0	(7) c Sheppard b Bedser		60
J.R.Reid	b Brown	11	b Tattersall		11
W.M.Wallace	b Wright	15	(5) c Brown b Bailey		1
W.A.Hadlee*	lbw b Wright	15	(4) c Bailey b Tattersall		9
A.R.MacGibbon	c Brown b Wright	20	lbw b Tattersall		0
F.L.H.Mooney†	c Compton b Bailey	3	(8) b Tattersall		0
T.B.Burtt	c Parkhouse b Wright	3	(2) b Tattersall		31
A.M.Moir	not out	26	c Bedser b Bailey		26
J.A.Hayes	b Tattersall	0	b Bailey		5
G.F.Cresswell	run out	0	not out		0
Extras	(b 3, lb 5, nb 4)	12	(b 30, lb 2, nb 3)		35
TOTAL	(70 overs)	125	(72.2 overs)		189

ENGLAND

L.Hutton	c Reid b Moir	57	c Hadlee b Cresswell		29
R.T.Simpson	b Moir	6	b Burtt		5
W.G.A.Parkhouse	b Burtt	2	c & b Burtt		20
D.S.Sheppard	b Hayes	3	(5) not out		4
D.C.S.Compton	b Burtt	10	(4) b Cresswell		18
F.R.Brown*	b Hayes	47	not out		10
T.E.Bailey	st Mooney b Burtt	29			
T.G.Evans†	b Cresswell	13			
A.V.Bedser	b Cresswell	28			
D.V.P.Wright	not out	9			
R.Tattersall	b Cresswell	1			
Extras	(b 11, lb 8, nb 3)	22	(b 1, lb 4)		5
TOTAL	(97 overs)	227	(45.2 overs) (4 wkts)		91

Bowling ENGLAND	O	M	R	W	O	M	R	W
Bailey	11	2	18	2	14.2	1	43	3
Bedser	19	6	21	0	24	10	34	1
Brown	6	1	10	1	1	0	1	0
Tattersall	15	9	16	1	21	6	44	6
Wright	19	3	48	5	12	2	32	0
NEW ZEALAND								
Hayes	20	2	44	2				
Cresswell	15	6	18	3	18	8	31	2
Moir	28	5	65	2	6	0	19	0
Burtt	27	14	46	3	21.2	10	36	2
MacGibbon	7	0	32	0				

Fall of Wickets	NZ 1st	E 1st	NZ 2nd	E 2nd
1st	1	10	25	16
2nd	25	31	62	56
3rd	37	40	76	60
4th	68	69	82	80
5th	69	140	82	-
6th	83	144	98	-
7th	94	173	105	-
8th	102	216	156	-
9th	105	218	187	-
10th	125	227	189	-

The New Zealand team which played in both tests. Back row (from left): Alex Moir, Tom Burtt, Frank Mooney, Johnny Hayes, Tony MacGibbon, Verdun Scott, Les Watt (twelfth man), Fen Cresswell. Front: Bert Sutcliffe, Merv Wallace, Walter Hadlee (captain), John Reid.

1951/52 West Indies in New Zealand

23 **NEW ZEALAND v WEST INDIES** *(First Test)*
at Lancaster Park, Christchurch on 8, 9, 11, 12 February, 1952
Toss : New Zealand. Umpires : M.F. Pengelly and B. Vine
West Indies won by 5 wickets

Even though the West Indies had lost 4-1 in Australia there was eager anticipation to see these exciting cricketers play in New Zealand for the first time. Before play the teams stood in the middle with heads bowed as a mark of respect to King George VI, who had died two days earlier.

After the loss of Ray Emery, Geoff Rabone and Verdun Scott proceeded cautiously on a wicket that was turning viciously. Alf Valentine, a left-arm spinner, obtained very quick spin, which bit turf out of the wicket. Sonny Ramadhin turned his deceptive finger-spinners both ways and his subtle variations of flight and pace demanded excellent defensive techniques.

After Scott was bowled by Ramadhin with New Zealand's score at 91 Rabone, John Reid and Brun Smith quickly succumbed; 115-5. Bert Sutcliffe, captaining New Zealand for the first time, decided to hit his team out of trouble in the last session. He plundered 24 off three overs from Ramadhin, but then fell to a catch off that bowler.

The spinners were now spelled after 73 overs, and Don Beard and Frank Mooney added 50 for the ninth wicket. Just before stumps, the New Zealand innings ended at 236.

A record crowd of 18,000 enjoyed a fascinating second day when Frank Worrell and Clyde Walcott entertained with sparkling batting, despite bitterly cold weather and poor light. Fortunes fluctuated throughout the day, with the bowlers seizing back the initiative with timely triumphs.

At lunch, the tourists were 72-3. Worrell (71) and Walcott (65) flourished with a 129-run partnership in even time before John Hayes bowled Walcott. The first ball in Hayes' next over bowled Worrell and Gerry Gomez was caught behind off the next. Tea was then taken with the score 189-7.

Wicketkeeper Sam Guillen, who returned to live in New Zealand after the tour, survived the hat trick and aided John Goddard in a crucial half-century stand for the eighth wicket. Half an hour before stumps, the innings ended at 287, a lead of 51. Tom Burtt's slow left-arm deliveries demanded respect and captured five wickets.

Rabone and Emery advanced the score to 44 before they were both dismissed within the space of two runs. John Reid failed again, but Sutcliffe and Scott, united this time in the middle order, carried New Zealand to 118-3.

The guileful Ramadhin now cast a web over the batsmen. After six consecutive maidens he disposed of both Scott and Sutcliffe. Smith, with Rabone as a runner, offered the only resistance later in the innings, which closed at 189. Ramadhin

had taken four wickets in 38.2 overs, conceding an average of one run an over. He had match figures of 9-125.

Requiring 139 to win, the tourists reached 24 without loss at the end of the third day. Five wickets fell for 99 before lunch on the last day, but Worrell (62 not out) and Gomez saw West Indies through to victory. The gate takings of £5900 established a record for a test in New Zealand.

NEW ZEALAND					
R.W.G.Emery	lbw b Gomez	5	c Stollmeyer b Valentine	28
G.O.Rabone	c Christiani b Ramadhin	37	lbw b Goddard	18
V.J.Scott	lbw b Ramadhin	45	b Ramadhin	29
B.Sutcliffe*	c Stollmeyer b Ramadhin	45	(5) b Ramadhin	36
J.R.Reid	b Ramadhin	0	(4) b Valentine	3
F.B.Smith	c Weekes b Valentine	9	b Gomez	37
F.L.H.Mooney†	not out	34	lbw b Gomez	1
T.B.Burtt	c Christiani b Valentine	1	(10) not out	9
A.M.Moir	c Worrell b Valentine	15	lbw b Ramadhin	5
D.D.Beard	run out	28	(8) c Christiani b Worrell	10
J.A.Hayes	st Guillen b Ramadhin	1	b Ramadhin	2
Extras	(b 15, lb 1)	16	(b 10, w 1)	11
TOTAL	(119.4 overs)	**236**	(114.2 overs)	**189**

WEST INDIES					
J.B.Stollmeyer	c Sutcliffe b Burtt	23	c Reid b Beard	13
R.E.Marshall	c Reid b Moir	16	c sub b Burtt	26
F.M.M.Worrell	b Hayes	71	not out	62
E.D.Weekes	b Burtt	7	(5) b Moir	2
C.L.Walcott	b Hayes	65	(4) lbw b Burtt	19
R.J.Christiani	c Scott b Beard	3	c Mooney b Hayes	3
J.D.C.Goddard*	c Reid b Burtt	26		
G.E.Gomez	c Mooney b Hayes	0	(7) not out	14
S.C.Guillen†	c & b Burtt	54		
S.Ramadhin	b Burtt	10		
A.L.Valentine	not out	0	(nb 3)	3
Extras	(b 2, lb 4, nb 6)	12		
TOTAL	(97.2 overs)	**287**	(59 overs) (5 wkts)	**142**

Bowling										Fall of Wickets			
WEST INDIES	O	M	R	W	O	M	R	W		NZ	WI	NZ	WI
										1st	1st	2nd	2nd
Gomez	28	12	47	1	12	3	25	2	1st	5	42	44	28
Worrell	11	3	25	0	15	6	24	1	2nd	91	42	46	48
Ramadhin	36.4	11	86	5	38.2	21	39	4	3rd	102	57	49	86
Valentine	38	15	51	3	41	19	73	2	4th	102	186	118	91
Goddard	4	1	8	0	8	3	17	1	5th	115	189	119	99
Marshall	2	1	3	0					6th	153	189	148	-
NEW ZEALAND									7th	162	189	172	-
Hayes	12	2	52	3	12	2	28	1	8th	181	240	172	-
Reid	9	2	25	0					9th	231	278	187	-
Burtt	29.2	7	69	5	16	3	37	2	10th	236	287	189	-
Moir	20	1	70	1	18	4	49	1					
Rabone	6	1	17	0									
Beard	21	5	42	1	13	4	25	1					

MILESTONES

- Bert Sutcliffe became the fourth captain of New Zealand.

- Don Beard (54) and Ray Emery (55) made their test debuts.

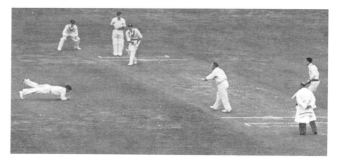

Bert Sutcliffe dives at short mid-off to catch Jeff Stollmeyer. Also in the picture is Geoff Rabone at slip and wicketkeeper Frank Mooney.

24 NEW ZEALAND v WEST INDIES *(Second Test)*

at Eden Park, Auckland on 15, 16, 18, 19 February, 1952
Toss : New Zealand. Umpires : J.C. Harris and T.M. Pearce
Match drawn

At the end of the first day, when the West Indies had scored 288 runs for the loss of just two wickets, the pundits continued to debate Bert Sutcliffe's decision to send the tourists in to bat.

Any advantage he might have sought with the new ball was negated when a shower of rain fell within half an hour of play commencing, taking the shine off the ball and making the ground conditions slippery, although the wicket continued to offer easy batting.

Soon after lunch, a generous act of sportsmanship added to New Zealand's difficulties. Allan Rae was sent back by Jeff Stollmeyer, his fellow opener, but slipped over before regaining his ground. The ball was returned to Alec Moir, who had an easy run out opportunity, but chose not to remove the bails.

At this stage, Rae had scored nine runs; but he was to add another 90 before Tom Burtt bowled him to take the first wicket at 197. Don Beard immediately dismissed Roy Marshall, but Stollmeyer (135 not out) and Everton Weekes added 86 attractive runs in the last hour.

Stollmeyer fell at 152, which included 14 boundaries, to a brilliant stumping by Frank Mooney standing up to Beard. Frank Worrell and Clyde Walcott then thrilled the crowd on the second day with an exhilarating stand of 189 runs in 138 minutes for the fifth wicket.

Both batsmen exhibited an array of exotic strokes and completed centuries before providing Ray Emery, a part-time medium-pacer, with his only two test wickets. After 504 minutes, John Goddard declared at 546-6.

Gordon Leggat was yorked by Worrell with the second ball of New Zealand's innings, and by stumps another three wickets had fallen, with only 76 runs on the board. Only Verdun Scott (41 not out) batted with any confidence.

Rain fell on the rest day but the pitch contained no vices when play began again. Scott's dedicated innings lasted 253 minutes and contributed 84 runs, more than half of the home team's total of 160. At one stage, Alf Valentine conceded one run in 13 overs; his innings return was three wickets for 29 runs off 35 overs.

New Zealand was fortunate that rain intervened to prevent what must surely have been a severe drubbing in this test. Drizzle sent the players from the field soon after the home team began its follow-on, and on resuming later an appeal against the light was upheld. Bad weather kept the players in the dressing room on the last day.

WEST INDIES		
J.B.Stollmeyer	st Mooney b Beard	152
A.F.Rae	b Burtt	99
R.E.Marshall	b Beard	0
E.D.Weekes	c Reid b Hayes	51
F.M.M.Worrell	c Sutcliffe b Emery	100
C.L.Walcott	lbw b Emery	115
D.St E.Atkinson	not out	8
J.D.C.Goddard*		
S.C.Guillen†		
S.Ramadhin		
A.L.Valentine		
Extras	(b 6, lb 10, nb 5)	21
TOTAL	(159.4 overs) (6 wkts dec)	**546**

NEW ZEALAND				
J.G.Leggat	b Worrell	0	not out	6
R.W.G.Emery	c Guillen b Atkinson	5	c Walcott b Atkinson	8
V.J.Scott	c Stollmeyer b Valentine	84		
B.Sutcliffe*	c Worrell b Ramadhin	20	(3) not out	2
J.R.Reid	st Guillen b Valentine	6		
G.O.Rabone	b Stollmeyer	9		
F.L.H.Mooney†	c Walcott b Stollmeyer	6		
A.M.Moir	b Ramadhin	20		
T.B.Burtt	c Goddard b Valentine	1		
D.D.Beard	c Weekes b Ramadhin	4		
J.A.Hayes	not out	0		
Extras	(b 4, lb 1)	5	(lb 1)	1
TOTAL	(99.4 overs)	**160**	(17 overs) (1 wkt)	**17**

Bowling	O	M	R	W	O	M	R	W
NEW ZEALAND								
Hayes	30	3	106	1				
Beard	40	8	96	2				
Reid	14	4	33	0				
Burtt	36	4	120	1				
Moir	16	2	69	0				
Rabone	15	1	48	0				
Emery	7.4	0	52	2				
Sutcliffe	1	0	1	0				
WEST INDIES								
Worrell	12	3	20	1	9	3	12	0
Atkinson	18	3	42	1	8	5	4	1
Valentine	34.4	21	29	3				
Ramadhin	25	12	41	3				
Stollmeyer	8	3	12	2				
Goddard	2	0	11	0				

Fall of Wickets	WI	NZ	NZ
	1st	1st	2nd
1st	197	0	0
2nd	202	12	-
3rd	317	50	-
4th	321	61	-
5th	510	93	-
6th	546	101	-
7th	-	155	-
8th	-	155	-
9th	-	160	-
10th	-	160	-

MILESTONES

- Gordon Leggat (56) made his test debut.

The old dressing room at Eden Park, later the headquarters of the Auckland Cricket Society, forms the backdrop of the New Zealand side for the second test. Back row (from left): Jim Everest (manager), John Reid, Gordon Leggat, Verdun Scott, Don Beard, John Hayes, Ray Emery, Frank Mooney. Front row: Alex Moir, Geoff Rabone, Bert Sutcliffe (captain), Tom Burtt, Eric Dempster.

1952/53 South Africa in New Zealand

25 **NEW ZEALAND v SOUTH AFRICA** *(First Test)*
at Basin Reserve, Wellington on 6, 7, 9, 10 March, 1953
Toss : South Africa. Umpires : R.G. Currie and J. McLellan
South Africa won by an innings and 180 runs

South Africa continued on to New Zealand after squaring the series in Australia 2-all and earning much praise for their brilliant fielding. South Africa's superiority was never in doubt in the two tests in New Zealand.

Four players made their test debuts for New Zealand and Merv Wallace, who had returned to top-level cricket, was appointed captain of the side. The first day's play was dominated by the batting of Jackie McGlew, who reached his maiden test century after 238 minutes, and was unbeaten on 151 at stumps, when the tourists were 300-6.

McGlew had stroked the ball freely and, with the New Zealanders giving a laborious display in the field, he picked up many singles from defensive pushes. Bob Blair gave the home team a brief hope by capturing three wickets for 12 runs with the second new ball.

Anton Murray proved an able partner for McGlew on the second day. They added 246 runs, a world test record for the seventh wicket, before Murray was stumped after completing his only test century. McGlew, however, survived chances at 175 and 199 and was still at the wicket on 255, a record for South Africa, when the declaration was made at 524-8.

A feature of his innings was his stamina, which allowed him to run short singles throughout his stay of 534 minutes. His innings contained 19 fours and a five. The home team's fielding had deteriorated even further, with many players seemingly unable to return the ball efficiently from the deep.

In the two hours remaining on the second day New Zealand scored 80 for the loss of Gordon Leggat's wicket.

By the end of the third day South Africa had disposed of New Zealand for 172, made in 123 overs, and captured two wickets for 58 in the follow-on.

Bert Sutcliffe (62) was the only batsman to shrug off the defensive attitude in the first innings, but both he and Wallace had been dismissed a second time by stumps.

Leggat and Ted Meuli added 63 for the third wicket, the best stand of the innings. Once these two departed New Zealand collapsed to be all out for 172, the same total achieved in the first innings.

On a wicket offering every advantage to batsmen, South Africa had bowled 109 maidens in 243 overs. The attack was steady rather than lethal, but a succession of batsmen cast away their wickets in a strangely submissive fashion.

SOUTH AFRICA		
D.J.McGlew	not out	255
J.H.B.Waite†	c Mooney b Blair	35
J.C.Watkins	c Reid b Blair	14
K.J.Funston	b Fisher	2
W.R.Endean	c Mooney b Blair	41
R.A.McLean	b Blair	5
J.E.Cheetham*	b Burtt	17
A.R.A.Murray	st Mooney b Burtt	109
P.N.F.Mansell	run out	10
H.J.Tayfield	not out	27
E.R.H.Fuller		
Extras	(b 5, lb 4)	9
TOTAL	(174 overs) (8 wkts dec)	**524**

NEW ZEALAND					
B.Sutcliffe	c McGlew b Watkins	62	b Murray		33
J.G.Leggat	c Fuller b Tayfield	22	c Endean b Watkins		47
F.E.Fisher	b Fuller	9	(9) c Waite b Watkins		14
W.M.Wallace*	c Waite b Murray	4	(3) b Tayfield		2
E.M.Meuli	c Endean b Murray	15	(4) b Fuller		23
L.S.M.Miller	c Endean b Tayfield	17	(5) c Waite b Watkins		13
J.R.Reid	b Murray	1	(6) c Waite b Murray		9
F.L.H.Mooney†	not out	27	(7) b Tayfield		9
A.M.Moir	run out	1	(8) c Fuller b Watkins		0
T.B.Burtt	lbw b Fuller	10	lbw b Tayfield		0
R.W.Blair	b Fuller	0	not out		6
Extras	(b 3, nb 1)	4	(b 16)		16
TOTAL	(123.4 overs)	**172**	(118.5 overs)		**172**

Bowling										Fall of Wickets			
NEW ZEALAND	O	M	R	W	O	M	R	W			SA	NZ	NZ
											1st	1st	2nd
Blair	36	4	98	4						1st	83	71	43
Fisher	34	6	78	1						2nd	92	91	46
Reid	24	8	36	0						3rd	177	96	109
Burtt	44	7	140	2						4th	187	98	121
Moir	35	4	159	0						5th	189	127	137
Sutcliffe	1	0	4	0						6th	238	131	141
SOUTH AFRICA										7th	484	134	142
Fuller	19.4	7	29	3	27	8	43	1		8th	494	135	162
Watkins	27	17	29	1	23.5	14	22	4		9th	-	172	162
Tayfield	38	15	53	2	32	12	42	3		10th	-	172	172
Mansell	11	3	27	0	13	2	30	0					
Murray	28	15	30	3	23	16	19	2					

More than 13,000 spectators turned the large rectangular Basin Reserve into an oval by sitting on the boundary edge. The carillon, the National Museum and Wellington Technical College can be seen above the old grandstand. Jackie McGlew completed his 255 not out on this day.

MILESTONES

- Bob Blair (57), Eric Fisher (58), Ted Meuli (59) and Lawrie Miller (60) made their test debuts.

- Jackie McGlew's 255 not out was a new individual test record for South Africa and also a record for any test at the Basin Reserve.

- The seventh wicket partnership between McGlew and Anton Murray of 246 was a world test record.

26 NEW ZEALAND v SOUTH AFRICA *(Second Test)*

at Eden Park, Auckland on 13, 14, 16, 17 March, 1953
Toss : South Africa. Umpires : J.C. Harris and T.M. Pearce
Match drawn

Five changes were made to the home side with another three debutants included. New Zealand secured the fourth South African wicket at 139 but poor catching had allowed several batsmen to survive chances offered early in their innings.

John Waite was dropped on two and went on to make 72. Russell Endean (116) and Jack Cheetham (54) added 130 for the fifth wicket, both batting into the second day. The tourists were content to wait for the occasional loose delivery and their total of 377 occupied almost eight and a half hours.

New Zealand, too, batted very slowly in its reply, and by stumps had lost Murray Chapple and Bert Sutcliffe, while scoring 74 runs at the rate of one every two minutes. Sutcliffe had taken 15 minutes to score and was just beginning to find his usual freedom when he was caught behind.

Coming in at number three, Geoff Rabone remained at the wicket for 215 minutes before he was run out; his 29 runs contained only one boundary. Matt Poore and Merv Wallace contributed usefully in the middle order without dominating.

New Zealand avoided the follow on through a stubborn ninth-wicket stand by Lawrie Miller and Eric Dempster, which boosted the score from 207 to 245. Although New Zealand trailed South Africa by 132 runs, its first innings of 245 took almost the same amount of time, over eight hours.

The start of South Africa's second innings was another painfully slow spectacle. Seven runs were scored in the first half-hour, 50 in 1½ hours and 80 for two by lunch. The pace quickened in the afternoon but Cheetham did not declare

until tea; 200-5. Some spectators expressed their resentment by booing the South African captain when he came out to bat.

New Zealand was left 90 minutes to bat, with no possible hope of reaching the 323 runs required for victory. *Wisden* commented that "The pitch was slow, low and discouraging to stroke production." An editorial in the *New Zealand Herald* took up the cause of those who were complaining about the increasingly dull nature of the game.

"During the test, we saw what was contemporary test cricket, runs scored throughout the four days at an average rate of fewer than 40 an hour, and a wicket falling about once in 50 minutes, probably when a batsman's subconscious revolted at the deadly dullness of it all."

SOUTH AFRICA

D.J.McGlew	c Chapple b Dempster	18	b Reid	50
J.H.B.Waite†	c Mooney b Blair	72	b Poore	26
J.C.Watkins	c Reid b Blair	30	c Sutcliffe b Poore	12
K.J.Funston	c Dempster b Poore	13	(5) b Rabone	17
W.R.Endean	st Mooney b Rabone	116	(6) not out	47
J.E.Cheetham*	run out	54	(7) not out	10
R.A.McLean	c Reid b Rabone	0	(4) c Rabone b MacGibbon	20
A.R.A.Murray	b Reid	6		
P.N.F.Mansell	not out	30		
H.J.Tayfield	b Rabone	9		
E.R.H.Fuller	c Mooney b Poore	17		
Extras	(b 7, lb 2, nb 3)	12	(b 6, lb 6, w 4, nb 2)	18
TOTAL	(162 overs)	**377**	(78 overs)(for 5 wkts dec)	**200**

NEW ZEALAND

B.Sutcliffe	c Waite b Tayfield	45	run out	10
M.E.Chapple	c Cheetham b Tayfield	22	c McGlew b Watkins	7
G.O.Rabone	run out	29	not out	6
M.B.Poore	b Mansell	45	not out	8
W.M.Wallace*	c Mansell b Tayfield	23		
L.S.M.Miller	c Waite b Murray	44		
F.L.H.Mooney†	c Endean b Tayfield	2		
J.R.Reid	c Waite b Watkins	7		
A.R.MacGibbon	c Murray b Watkins	2		
E.W.Dempster	c Funston b Tayfield	14		
R.W.Blair	not out	0		
Extras	(b 7, lb 5)	12		0
TOTAL	(171.2 overs)	**245**	(19.3 overs) (2 wkts)	**31**

Bowling	O	M	R	W	O	M	R	W
NEW ZEALAND								
Blair	30	6	64	2	11	3	26	0
MacGibbon	28	6	72	0	16	6	17	1
Reid	22	3	55	1	13	5	21	1
Dempster	39	9	84	1	13	4	29	0
Rabone	24	4	62	3	17	4	46	1
Poore	19	8	28	2	8	1	43	2
SOUTH AFRICA								
Fuller	37	13	60	0	8	1	14	0
Watkins	38	20	51	2	8	3	12	1
Murray	31	16	29	1				
Tayfield	46.2	19	62	5	2.3	0	5	0
Mansell	18	9	29	1	1	1	0	0
Cheetham	1	0	2	0				

Fall of Wickets	SA	NZ	SA	NZ
	1st	*1st*	*2nd*	*2nd*
1st	39	54	62	16
2nd	78	70	80	20
3rd	124	141	116	-
4th	139	152	124	-
5th	269	175	173	-
6th	274	185	-	-
7th	308	203	-	-
8th	330	207	-	-
9th	340	245	-	-
10th	377	245	-	-

MILESTONES

- Murray Chapple (61), Eric Dempster (62) and Matt Poore (63) made their test debuts.

Within a fortnight of the second test two trial matches had been played and a team of 14 players was named to tour the Union of South Africa, beginning in 228 days time. Some surprise was expressed when Geoff Rabone was announced as the touring captain.

He had previously declared himself unavailable for the tour but, when Merv Wallace declined the leadership, the selectors pleaded their case to Rabone, who agreed.

Members of the New Zealand side begin assembling in Auckland. From left, Ted Meuli, Murray Chapple, Bob Blair, Tony MacGibbon, and Matt Poore. Note the small overnight bags with boots attached to the handles.

1953/54 New Zealand in South Africa

New Zealand's itinerary for their first tour of South Africa included 17 first-class matches, with five tests and three matches against state teams in Australia on their way home.

On the boat *Arawa* Frank Mooney damaged the top joint of a finger, which was to affect his normal high quality wicketkeeping throughout the tour.

With the exception of John Reid, who was engaged in the Lancashire League, none of the New Zealanders had played cricket for seven months and were glad of three days of intensive practice before their first game in South Africa.

27 SOUTH AFRICA v NEW ZEALAND (*First Test*)

at Kingsmead, Durban on 11, 12, 14, 15 December, 1953
Toss : South Africa. Umpires : A.N. McCabe and B.V. Malan
South Africa won by an innings and 58 runs

Both John Waite and Jackie McGlew were ill at ease against the pace attack and both were dropped, depriving New Zealand of a chance of restricting the home team to a modest first-innings total. Tony MacGibbon struck twice, however, to have South Africa 143-3.

The new batsman, Roy McLean, looked uncomfortable and had managed just a single when he was dropped by Bert Sutcliffe off John Reid. McLean and Ken Funston then prospered in a 135-run partnership which carried South Africa to 278-3 by stumps.

In glorious conditions McLean was again put down by Sutcliffe (it was alleged that he asked the New Zealander what he wanted for Christmas) and was thus permitted to complete his maiden test century in 138 minutes.

Although Clive van Ryneveld had batted as high as number three in the order in previous test cricket, he now entered at number eight and compiled a cultured half-century, adding 85 with Hugh Tayfield, before Jack Cheetham declared at 437-9 after 500 minutes. The New Zealand bowlers had manfully overcome their disappointments to capture the last six wickets for 169 runs.

Faced with a target of 288 to avoid the follow-on the tourists struggled for two hours on a wearing wicket, in bad light, before an appeal was upheld. Neil Adcock had bowled at fierce pace and the ball flew about dangerously but it was Tayfield, the right-arm off-spinner, who dismissed Sutcliffe and Murray Chapple. New Zealand was 70-2 at stumps.

On the third day Geoff Rabone persevered against Tayfield while the ball spun viciously off the crumbling wicket. After six hours Rabone was eighth out for 107 (nine fours) his third century in first-class cricket and his first in test cricket.

He had added 62 runs for the fifth wicket with Matt Poore but Tayfield (6-62) triumphed and New Zealand was all out for 230.

By stumps on the third day the tourists were floundering at 22-2 in their follow-on. Funston had held two diving catches at leg-slip off John Watkins to dismiss Murray Chapple and Reid. The loss of Sutcliffe and Frank Mooney in the first 20 minutes of the fourth day effectively ended New Zealand's chances of saving the test.

The ball was leaping and skidding unpredictably off the wicket, the South Africans were swift and sure in the field and only Rabone seemed capable of defending his wicket. His defiant innings of 68, which occupied more than three hours, was the only score better than 20 as the tourists collapsed for 149. South Africa had inflicted a crushing victory with 90 minutes to spare.

A report in the *Natal Mercury* bluntly stated, "New Zealand was completely outplayed from the moment the toss was lost on Friday. The New Zealanders put up a game display, showed fine courage and plenty of fight. They were no match for the Springboks in cricket ability."

Because of the lack of a high-powered short-wave transmitter in South Africa, direct radio broadcast to New Zealand was impossible. A local commentator sent a series of coded cables to Wellington where, half an hour after they were sent 7200 miles underwater and 2700 miles overland, they were interpreted and broadcast by Lance Cross and Pat Earnshaw.

MILESTONES

• Guy Overton (64) made his test debut.

• Neil Adcock, a tall right-arm fast bowler, made his debut for South Africa. He was his country's first pace bowler to take 100 test wickets. He is ranked 12th overall in test averages for players who have taken 100 or more wickets.

The New Zealand team on the steps of Parliament Buildings. Note the dress of the day – gabardine raincoats and felt hats.
Back row (from left): Murray Chapple, Matt Poore, Bob Blair, Tony MacGibbon. Middle row: Bert Sutcliffe, Guy Overton, Lawrie Miller, Ian Leggat. Front row: Jack Kerr (manager), Bill Bell, John Beck, Frank Mooney, Eric Dempster, Geoff Rabone (captain).

- South Africa's crushing victory, by an innings and 58, was their first win at home in 23 years.

- Geoff Rabone was top scorer in both New Zealand innings. His 107 was the highest score for New Zealand against South Africa.

SOUTH AFRICA		
D.J.McGlew	b MacGibbon	84
J.H.B.Waite†	b Overton	43
W.R.Endean	b MacGibbon	6
K.J.Funston	lbw b Reid	39
R.A.McLean	c Chapple b Blair	101
J.C.Watkins	c Mooney b MacGibbon	29
J.E.Cheetham*	b Rabone	17
C.B.van Ryneveld	not out	68
H.J.Tayfield	b Overton	28
A.R.A.Murray	b Blair	0
N.A.T.Adcock		
Extras	(b 10, lb 8, w 1, nb 3)	22
TOTAL	**(115 overs) (9 wkts dec)**	**437**

NEW ZEALAND				
B.Sutcliffe	c Waite b Tayfield	20	c Endean b Tayfield	16
G.O.Rabone*	lbw b Tayfield	107	(5) b Adcock	68
M.E.Chapple	b Tayfield	1	(2) c Funston b Watkins	1
J.R.Reid	b Tayfield	6	(3) c Funston b Watkins	0
L.S.M.Miller	lbw b van Ryneveld	13	(6) lbw b Murray	18
M.B.Poore	c Cheetham b Tayfield	32	(7) st Waite b van Ryneveld	1
F.L.H.Mooney†	b Watkins	9	(4) c Waite b Adcock	7
A.R.MacGibbon	st Waite b van Ryneveld	21	c Watkins b Tayfield	19
E.W.Dempster	not out	7	c McGlew b Adcock	0
R.W.Blair	b Tayfield	2	st Waite b Tayfield	6
G.W.F.Overton	b van Ryneveld	2	not out	3
Extras	(b 9, lb 1)	10	(b 6, lb 3, nb 1)	10
TOTAL	**(105.6 overs)**	**230**	**(82.1 overs)**	**149**

Bowling	O	M	R	W	O	M	R	W
NEW ZEALAND								
Blair	22	2	104	2				
Reid	16	2	49	1				
Overton	27	8	92	2				
MacGibbon	27	4	73	3				
Poore	5	0	30	0				
Dempster	10	1	36	0				
Rabone	8	0	31	1				
SOUTH AFRICA								
Adcock	19	3	52	0	14	4	38	3
Watkins	15	5	28	1	14	7	16	2
Murray	7	5	9	0	7	4	8	1
Tayfield	36	17	62	6	26.1	12	35	3
van Ryneveld	28.6	6	69	3	21	9	42	1

Fall of Wickets	SA	NZ	NZ
	1st	1st	2nd
1st	113	39	6
2nd	140	53	15
3rd	143	75	24
4th	278	100	36
5th	294	162	85
6th	335	181	103
7th	337	215	125
8th	422	215	125
9th	437	219	146
10th	-	230	149

28 SOUTH AFRICA v NEW ZEALAND *(Second Test)*

at Ellis Park, Johannesburg on 24, 26, 28, 29 December, 1953
Toss : South Africa. Umpires : C.D. Coote and D.T. Drew
South Africa won by 132 runs

Geoff Rabone lost his sixth toss in nine matches and New Zealand took the field in brilliant sunshine before a crowd of 8000. The bowlers made the most of early life in the wicket and three of South Africa's top order were out for 43. Russell Endean and Clive van Ryneveld scored most of the 259 runs made for the loss of eight wickets by the end of the first day.

The New Zealanders celebrated Christmas Day with dinner at the Wanderers Club where John Beck, the youngest member of the team, was elected to preside over the festivities.

On Boxing Day a record crowd of 25,000 people witnessed what Bill Ferguson, who had scored in more than 200 test matches, considered the most dramatic day of cricket he had ever experienced.

Before play began news arrived from New Zealand of the Tangiwai railway disaster, in which 151 people were killed. Among the dead was the fiancée of Bob Blair. The young Wellingtonian withdrew from the match, while his grieving team-mates returned to the battle.

The last two South African wickets added 12 runs and then Neil Adcock subjected the New Zealand batsmen to a savage assault of deliveries that leapt at the body at great pace.

After New Zealand lost both openers for nine runs, Bert Sutcliffe was struck by an Adcock delivery on his left ear, the lobe of which was split, and he was taken to hospital for observation. In 25 minutes John Reid was hit five times before he was caught for three.

Far right: Before he had scored, Bert Sutcliffe received a frightening blow which split his left ear lobe and he was taken to hospital. His partner is Matt Poore.

Right: Geoff Rabone top-scored in both New Zealand innings.

Lawrie Miller received a fierce blow on the chest, staggered off, coughing blood, and was taken to hospital. Another Adcock bouncer hit Matt Poore and broke the wicket.

It is doubtful whether any player has made a test debut in such a calamitous situation as did John Beck, who came out just before lunch with the score at 35-4 with two batsmen having retired hurt and in hospital, and one having withdrawn in tragic circumstances.

The 19-year-old survived with Frank Mooney for 52 minutes, scoring 16 of 22 runs. When he was dismissed Miller returned to the crease to a loud ovation from the crowd. Later, another huge cheer erupted when Sutcliffe emerged, his head swathed in a turban of bandages.

Mooney held his end intact while Sutcliffe launched a glorious onslaught. After surviving a chance in the covers, Sutcliffe twice lofted Tayfield for six in one over and the partnership rushed to 50 in 39 minutes.

With the follow-on avoided Mooney, Tony MacGibbon and Guy Overton were dismissed and the players began to depart for the pavilion, believing Blair to be back at the hotel.

Suddenly the players stopped their walk from the middle and a buzzing crowd fell silent. From the tunnel emerged the stricken figure of Blair.

The huge crowd rose in profound silence as Sutcliffe, blood seeping through his bandage, went to meet his comrade, placed his arm around Blair's shoulders and accompanied him to the wicket.

In Tayfield's next over Sutcliffe hit three sixes into the crowd before taking a single, which left Blair to face the strike and he too swung the ball over the mid-wicket fence. 25 runs off the over and the crowd, its moment of sadness having passed, clamoured for more.

The pair added 33 runs in 10 minutes to leave New Zealand 187 all out. Although statistics took second place to the high drama of the occasion, it is interesting to note that Sutcliffe's 80 not out was made in 112 minutes, but contained only 28 scoring shots. His total of seven sixes in an innings had been bettered only once before in test cricket.

Aggressive bowling by MacGibbon and Reid, with improved catching, saw South Africa out for 148, the lowest test innings by any team against New Zealand. This left the tourists a reasonable target of 233 to win but, once again, the ferocity of Adcock and David Ironside pummelled the visitors.

The final day began with New Zealand wanting 165 runs with seven wickets in hand. The events of the preceding days had drained the New Zealanders and the last seven wickets could manage just 32 runs. The innings closed at exactly 100 and a match that had soared to the heights of classical tragedy now stumbled rather shamefacedly off the stage.

A total of 53,000 spectators, who attended the four days of the second test, was sufficient to guarantee the financial

The bandaged Sutcliffe returned with New Zealand 82-6 and immediately launched an all-out attack.

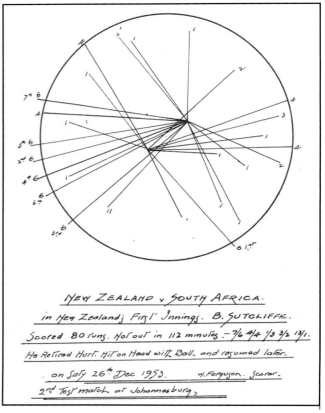

"Fergie" Ferguson's wagon-wheel of Sutcliffe's heroic innings.

success of the tour. The *Cape Times* was lavish in its praise of the New Zealanders: "All the glory was for the vanquished. Fiery bowlers on a fiery pitch failed to wither the dauntless spirit of a side of lesser cricket talent, perhaps, but not of smaller hearts. Memories of the match will not be of the runs made or of the wickets taken, but of the courage displayed."

MILESTONES

* John Beck (65) made his test debut.

SOUTH AFRICA

D.J.McGlew	c Reid b MacGibbon	13	b MacGibbon		8
A.R.A.Murray	c Chapple b Blair	7	(9) c Blair b Overton		13
W.R.Endean	c Sutcliffe b Reid	93	c sub (I.B.Leggat) b Reid		1
K.J.Funston	lbw b Overton	0	c Overton b MacGibbon		11
R.A.McLean	c Blair b Overton	27	(7) lbw b Reid		36
C.B.van Ryneveld	b Blair	65	(8) c Reid b MacGibbon		17
J.E.Cheetham*	c Mooney b MacGibbon	20	(6) c Sutcliffe b Reid		1
H.J.Tayfield	not out	20	(5) b Reid		34
J.H.B.Waite†	c Mooney b MacGibbon	0	(2) c Reid b MacGibbon		5
D.E.J.Ironside	b Reid	13	not out		11
N.A.T.Adcock	run out	0	c Poore b Overton		6
Extras	(b 3, lb 2, nb 8)	13	(lb 3, nb 2)		5
TOTAL	(80 overs)	**271**	(53.1 overs)		**148**

NEW ZEALAND

G.O.Rabone*	c Endean b Ironside	1	c van Ryneveld b Adcock		22
M.E.Chapple	b Adcock	8	c Waite b Ironside		22
M.B.Poore	b Adcock	15	b Adcock		1
B.Sutcliffe	not out	80	c Endean b Murray		10
J.R.Reid	c Endean b Adcock	3	(6) c Funston b Ironside		1
L.S.M.Miller	b Ironside	14	(7) c Waite b Adcock		0
J.E.F.Beck	c Waite b Murray	16	(8) c Endean b Ironside		7
F.L.H.Mooney†	b Ironside	35	(5) c Funston b Adcock		10
A.R.MacGibbon	c Endean b Ironside	0	not out		11
G.W.F.Overton	c Murray b Ironside	0	(11) run out		2
R.W.Blair	st Waite b Tayfield	6	(10) b Adcock		4
Extras	(b 3, lb 4, nb 2)	9	(b 3, lb 5, nb 2)		10
TOTAL	(53.2 overs)	**187**	(47.5 overs)		**100**

Bowling	O	M	R	W	O	M	R	W
NEW ZEALAND								
Blair	17	4	50	2	5	0	14	0
Reid	18	3	63	2	16	5	34	4
Overton	20	4	68	2	12.1	1	33	2
MacGibbon	22	5	61	3	20	2	62	4
Rabone	3	0	16	0				
SOUTH AFRICA								
Adcock	14	2	44	3	19	4	43	5
Ironside	19	4	51	5	20.5	10	37	3
Murray	12	3	30	1	8	3	10	1
Tayfield	8.2	2	53	1				

Fall of Wickets	SA	NZ	SA	NZ
	1st	1st	2nd	2nd
1st	13	5	11	35
2nd	37	9	13	38
3rd	43	23	24	58
4th	100	35	37	75
5th	168	59	44	76
6th	226	82	67	76
7th	244	138	112	76
8th	244	146	122	84
9th	271	154	138	89
10th	271	187	148	100

22,000 acclaim Kiwis in day of great cricket drama

THE *most wonderful and dramatic day's cricket seen in Johannesburg for 20 years. That was the verdict of the 22,000. And there's a new "King of Ellis Park"—Bert Sutcliffe.*
  NOT FOR YEARS WILL THE CROWD WHICH BASKED IN THE EMERALD ARENA FORGET THE DRAMA, THE EXCITEMENT, THE POIGNANCY AND THE THRILLS OF THIS SECOND DAY IN THE SECOND TEST. GEOFF RABONE'S NEW ZEALANDERS HAVE WON A SPECIAL PLACE IN THE HEART OF THE ELLIS PARK CROWD, A POINT PROVED EMPHATICALLY WHEN TOWARDS THE CLOSE OF THEIR INNINGS THE CROWD, PARTICULARLY THE NON-EUROPEAN SECTION, CHEERED DELIGHTEDLY AS SUTCLIFFE WAS DROPPED IN THE OUTFIELD.
  But first the details. It took Rabone's men a few minutes under half an hour to dismiss Ironside and Adcock and end the Springbok innings at 271. Two and three-quarter hours later the New Zealanders were out for 187, but in a fighting 51 minutes before the close they had sent back three Springboks for 35.

A headline summarising the dramatic events of Boxing Day.

29 SOUTH AFRICA v NEW ZEALAND *(Third Test)*

at Newlands, Cape Town on 1, 2, 4, 5 January, 1954
Toss : New Zealand. Umpires : D. Collins and S. Collins
Match drawn

The tourists had little time to lick their wounds. On New Year's Day 1954 they returned to the front-line for the third test, making three changes to their team. Geoff Rabone won his first toss of the series and eagerly anticipated use of an excellent batting strip.

With Murray Chapple as his partner, the New Zealand captain batted slowly but surely through the morning. His innings of 56 occupied four hours. Chapple was uncomfortable facing Adcock but took the long handle to Tayfield and batted for 198 minutes before he was dismissed for 76. Their partnership of 126 was the best opening stand for New Zealand in tests since 1946/47.

Although the South African bowlers wilted in the afternoon, Matt Poore (31) and Bert Sutcliffe (37) were not prepared to attack during the last session. New Zealand ended a very slow day's play at 212-2.

By the time the score reached 271 both overnight batsmen were out and this opened the way for a thrilling partnership worth 176 in 147 minutes between John Reid and John Beck. Reid, who had failed to reach double figures in his last ten test innings, took more than an hour to hit his first boundary but his fifty came up in 102 minutes and his maiden test century 57 minutes later.

After Reid was bowled for 135, Beck assumed the aggressive role and unleashed a flurry of searing cover drives and lusty hook shots. A huge cheer greeted a six by Beck, which raised the team's 500 in 635 minutes.

One short of his century, Beck was called through for a short single by Eric Dempster, keen to give his partner the strike. Dick Westcott fired in a return that broke the stumps before Beck could make his ground, thus ending a superb innings by the 19-year-old.

John Reid acknowledges his first test hundred. As his previous ten tests innings had all been single figure scores it is no wonder he is delighted. John Beck is his partner and John Waite is the South African wicketkeeper.

South Africa recommenced at five without loss on the third morning. Tony MacGibbon struck two early blows, dismissing John Waite and Westcott but Jackie McGlew and Russell Endean proved more resilient. Both eventually fell to MacGibbon and Rabone picked up three wickets at the end of the day leaving South Africa 206-7.

Jack Cheetham enjoyed a crucial stroke of luck in the second over of the last day. Rabone forced his rival captain back on his stumps and his bat touched the wicket and upset a bail which finally settled into place without falling.

With Hugh Tayfield as his companion until the last ball before lunch, Cheetham went on to reach 89, his highest score in test cricket. The last wicket fell at 326, giving Rabone his best bowling figures in tests, 6-68. Rabone was delighted to ask the South Africans to bat again for the remaining three hours left in the test.

MILESTONES

- Bill Bell (66) and Ian Leggat (67) made their test debuts.

- New Zealand exceeded 500 in an innings for the first time in test cricket.

- John Reid and John Beck shared a New Zealand fifth wicket test record partnership of 176.

- Geoff Rabone's return of 6-68 off 38.7 overs was the best by a New Zealand bowler in tests against South Africa.

- It was the first time in test cricket that New Zealand was able to enforce the follow-on.

NEW ZEALAND

G.O.Rabone*	lbw b van Ryneveld	56
M.E.Chapple	c Waite b van Ryneveld	76
M.B.Poore	c McGlew b Adcock	44
B.Sutcliffe	c Waite b Ironside	66
J.R.Reid	b Murray	135
J.E.F.Beck	run out	99
F.L.H.Mooney†	b Ironside	4
A.R.MacGibbon	c McGlew b Ironside	8
E.W.Dempster	c Endean b Ironside	0
I.B.Leggatt	c McGlew b Tayfield	0
W.Bell	not out	0
Extras	(b 14, lb 3)	17
TOTAL	(165.3 overs)	**505**

SOUTH AFRICA

D.J.McGlew	c Sutcliffe b MacGibbon	86	c Chapple b Poore	28
J.H.B.Waite†	lbw b MacGibbon	8	st Mooney b Rabone	16
R.J.Westcott	c Leggatt b MacGibbon	2	b Dempster	62
W.R.Endean	c Sutcliffe b MacGibbon	33	not out	34
R.A.McLean	c Mooney b Rabone	9	not out	18
C.B.van Ryneveld	c Mooney b Rabone	23		
J.E.Cheetham*	b Rabone	89		
A.R.A.Murray	lbw b Rabone	6		
H.J.Tayfield	c Leggatt b Rabone	34		
D.E.J.Ironside	c MacGibbon b Rabone	10		
N.A.T.Adcock	not out	8		
Extras	(b 6, lb 6, nb 6)	18	(b 1)	1
TOTAL	(127.7 overs)	**326**	(54 overs) (3 wkts)	**159**

Bowling SOUTH AFRICA	O	M	R	W	O	M	R	W
Adcock	29	3	105	1				
Ironside	46.3	16	117	4				
Murray	34	8	93	1				
Tayfield	33	10	80	1				
van Ryneveld	23	1	93	2				
NEW ZEALAND								
MacGibbon	33	13	71	4	8	4	15	0
Reid	20	7	48	0	4	1	8	0
Leggatt	3	0	6	0				
Bell	18	5	77	0	6	2	22	0
Rabone	38.7	10	68	6	10	6	16	1
Dempster	8	3	19	0	6	0	24	1
Sutcliffe	5	1	13	0	7	0	33	0
Poore	2	0	6	0	12	1	39	1
Chapple					1	0	1	0

Fall of Wickets

	NZ	SA	SA
	1st	1st	2nd
1st	126	17	26
2nd	145	23	57
3rd	239	82	139
4th	271	101	-
5th	447	172	-
6th	472	180	-
7th	490	204	-
8th	505	299	-
9th	505	313	-
10th	505	326	-

Bob Connelly, cartoonist for the Rand Daily Mail, *acknowledges New Zealand's highest score in test cricket.*

John Beck is run out for 99. His partner, Eric Dempster, hangs his head while John Waite, the South African wicketkeeper, and Clive van Ryneveld show no sign of jubilation.

30 SOUTH AFRICA v NEW ZEALAND *(Fourth Test)*

at Ellis Park, Johannesburg on 29, 30 January, 1, 2 February, 1954
Toss : New Zealand. Umpires : D.T. Drew and B.V. Malan
South Africa won by 9 wickets

In the provincial game prior to the fourth test Geoff Rabone was struck on the instep of his right foot by a full toss which broke a bone and ended his tour. Bert Sutcliffe assumed the captaincy for the rest of the tour.

The New Zealanders were disturbed to see that Ellis Park was almost as green as it had been for the fateful second test. Their confidence was shaken, too, by the discovery that water had seeped under the covers and the pitch was soft. On the eve of the game the groundsman stated that he did not believe the wicket would last for four days.

Fears about the state of the wicket prompted Sutcliffe to send South Africa in to bat when he won the toss. However, by lunch 61 runs had been scored without loss and the first wicket did not fall until 104 runs were on the board. The dismissal of Jackie McGlew, at 104, heralded a change in New Zealand's fortunes.

Four more wickets fell for 21 runs in the next hour. Thirteen deliveries from Guy Overton produced three catches. Bob Blair soon had Clive van Ryneveld caught behind and Sutcliffe threw down Jack Cheetham's wicket after chasing the ball to the boundary. 200-7 at stumps showed that the New Zealand bowlers, given good support in the field, could dominate their opponents.

John Waite had failed as an opener so far in the series but now, batting at number eight, he scored 52 to help South Africa through to 243 all out.

Hugh Tayfield celebrated his 25th birthday by winkling out six batsmen for 13 off 14 overs. The wicket was offering minimal spin and his success was achieved by subtle variation in flight and length.

Sutcliffe was given a hero's welcome and attempted to return the compliment by lofting his third ball over the long-on boundary, where Roy McLean ran in from the fence to hold a magnificent catch. John Reid played for turn that did not eventuate and succeeded only in edging a catch.

Lawrie Miller and John Beck were bowled in Tayfield's next over and, in the off-spinner's fourth over, Matt Poore

was caught and bowled to give Tayfield five wickets without conceding a run, leaving New Zealand 46-7.

Eric Dempster and Tony MacGibbon added 23 for the eighth wicket but the innings ended at 79 after three hours. Cheetham enforced the follow-on and, by stumps, New Zealand was eight for the loss of Frank Mooney's wicket.

Murray Chapple joined Dempster, who had been promoted to open the innings, in a defiant third wicket stand of 71. At one stage the pair added 44 runs in half an hour. However, rain and bad light caused frequent interruptions and, in such unsettling conditions, the tourists battled and were 148-6 in the four hours of play that was possible.

Twenty minutes after lunch on the last day the game was over and South Africa had clinched the five-match series. Neil Adcock took five wickets to end New Zealand's innings at 188 and the home team was left with only a few runs to win.

SOUTH AFRICA

D.J.McGlew	lbw b MacGibbon	61	not out		6
R.J.Westcott	c Chapple b Overton	43	lbw b MacGibbon		1
J.C.Watkins	c Mooney b MacGibbon	6			
W.R.Endean	c Sutcliffe b Overton	7			
R.A.McLean	c Sutcliffe b Overton	0			
C.B.van Ryneveld	c Mooney b Blair	11			
J.E.Cheetham*	run out	29	(3) not out		16
J.H.B.Waite†	run out	52			
H.J.Tayfield	c Reid b Blair	19			
D.E.J.Ironside	not out	3			
N.A.T.Adcock	b Blair	0			
Extras	(b 3, lb 5, nb 4)	12	(nb 2)		2
TOTAL	(98 overs)	243	(6.2 overs) (1 wkt)		25

NEW ZEALAND

F.L.H.Mooney†	run out	23	b Adcock		2
M.E.Chapple	c Waite b Ironside	4	(4) c sub (K.J.Funston) b Watkins		42
M.B.Poore	c & b Tayfield	18	c Endean b Adcock		0
B.Sutcliffe*	c McLean b Tayfield	0	(6) b Adcock		23
J.R.Reid	c Waite b Tayfield	0	c Ironside b Tayfield		26
L.S.M.Miller	b Tayfield	0	(7) c Waite b Tayfield		0
J.E.F.Beck	b Tayfield	0	(8) b Adcock		21
E.W.Dempster	not out	21	(2) c Waite b Watkins		47
A.R.MacGibbon	st Waite b Ironside	10	b Adcock		8
R.W.Blair	b Tayfield	1	not out		5
G.W.F.Overton	b Adcock	0	c van Ryneveld b Ironside		1
Extras	(lb 1, nb 1)	2	(b 5, lb 6, nb 2)		13
TOTAL	(46.3 overs)	79	(92.1 overs)		188

Bowling	O	M	R	W	O	M	R	W
NEW ZEALAND								
Blair	19	4	42	3	3	0	6	0
Reid	21	3	67	0				
MacGibbon	26	6	57	2	3	0	16	1
Overton	32	10	65	3				
Miller					0.2	0	1	0
SOUTH AFRICA								
Adcock	11.3	1	27	1	26	8	45	5
Ironside	14	5	20	2	23.1	6	50	1
Watkins	7	1	17	0	12	4	13	2
Tayfield	14	7	13	6	29	12	48	2
van Ryneveld					2	0	19	0

Fall of Wickets	SA	NZ	NZ	SA
	1st	*1st*	*2nd*	*2nd*
1st	104	14	4	4
2nd	112	34	8	-
3rd	122	34	79	-
4th	122	34	113	-
5th	125	42	139	-
6th	139	42	141	-
7th	174	46	168	-
8th	227	69	182	-
9th	243	76	183	-
10th	243	79	188	-

31 SOUTH AFRICA v NEW ZEALAND (*Fifth Test*)

at St George's Park, Port Elizabeth on 5, 6, 8, 9 February, 1954
Toss : New Zealand. Umpires : D. Collins and F.R.W. Payne
South Africa won by 5 wickets

Bert Sutcliffe again proved adept at predicting the fall of a coin and decided to bat when he won the toss. On a docile wicket the South African attack was seldom hostile but contained the openers with accurate bowling, supported by typically fine fielding.

Frank Mooney batted for more than two hours to reach 24 before Tayfield held a splendid catch. Matt Poore compiled a solid 41 and Sutcliffe's innings of 38 carried him beyond a thousand runs for the tour.

Neil Adcock and John Watkins took the new ball with the score at 135-3 and New Zealand was soon reeling at 146-6. John Beck (48) attempted to hit the team out of trouble and 40 runs were scored off Adcock's next five overs but two more wickets fell before stumps, leaving New Zealand at 218-4. A few minutes batting on the second day saw the tourists dismissed for 226.

South Africa progressed cautiously to 40 by lunch and then John Reid and Bill Bell bowled unchanged until tea, when only 67 runs were added for the loss of three wickets. Another three batsmen were dismissed before the end of a slow day's cricket; 194-6.

The tail-enders managed to edge past New Zealand's total and Mooney and Murray Chapple began the second innings facing a deficit of 11 runs. New Zealand was only six runs ahead when Sutcliffe and Poore came together to add 60 for the third wicket. Reid was at his aggressive best and contributed 41 of 55 runs scored in partnership with Sutcliffe.

On the last day Reid kept up with the clock until, at 73, he attempted a second run in order to keep the strike and was run out by Jackie McGlew. Clive van Ryneveld accounted for the tail and New Zealand was all out for 222.

Requiring 212 runs for victory in 225 minutes the South Africans had a brisk opening stand of 44 but the loss of McGlew, Dick Westcott and Ken Funston gave the tourists the advantage at three down for 81. Russell Endean responded with a match-winning innings of 87 in 93 minutes, including 13 runs plundered off one over from Eric Dempster.

An effortless sequence of cover drives and cuts resulted in 14 boundaries, and South Africa cruised to victory an hour after tea to win the series 3-1. New Zealand's most obvious weakness on tour had been the want of consistent batting.

Middle order collapses had denied the tourists any chance of contesting the test series and, combined with lamentable catching, prevented the team pressing home the advantage gained by the bowlers in provincial matches.

Only four times did New Zealand exceed 300 runs in an innings and six times they were dismissed for under 200.

The most improved player in the touring party was Tony MacGibbon. Arriving in South Africa with 49 first-class wickets at the costly average of 40.63 he cut down his long run up and developed tight control for prolonged spells.

His ability to move the ball off the seam earned him 50 wickets at 19.42 and Jack Cheetham's praise as "one of the world's greatest bowlers."

NEW ZEALAND

F.L.H.Mooney†	c Tayfield b Murray	24	c van Ryneveld b Adcock		9
M.E.Chapple	c Waite b Watkins	18	lbw b Murray		8
M.B.Poore	c Waite b Adcock	41	c Waite b van Ryneveld		18
B.Sutcliffe*	c Waite b Watkins	38	c & b van Ryneveld		52
J.R.Reid	b Adcock	19	run out		73
L.S.M.Miller	c Endean b Adcock	0	(9) c Waite b Adcock		2
J.E.F.Beck	b Adcock	48	(6) b Tayfield		12
E.W.Dempster	c & b Watkins	16	(7) st Waite b van Ryneveld		1
A.R.MacGibbon	b Watkins	7	(8) c Adcock b Watkins		14
R.W.Blair	c Murray b Tayfield	8	st Waite b van Ryneveld		8
W.Bell	not out	0	not out		21
Extras	(lb 1, w 1, nb 5)	7	(lb 3, nb 1)		4
TOTAL	(92.3 overs)	**226**	(87.6 overs)		**222**

SOUTH AFRICA

D.J.McGlew	b Bell	27	run out		38
R.J.Westcott	lbw b Reid	29	b MacGibbon		11
J.E.Cheetham*	c Sutcliffe b MacGibbon	42	(7) not out		13
K.J.Funston	lbw b Reid	10	(3) c Mooney b MacGibbon		0
W.R.Endean	c Reid b MacGibbon	32	(4) c & b Bell		87
J.C.Watkins	b Reid	13	(5) b Reid		45
C.B.van Ryneveld	lbw b Blair	40	(6) not out		10
J.H.B.Waite†	not out	20			
H.J.Tayfield	c Sutcliffe b Blair	2			
A.R.A.Murray	lbw b Reid	7			
N.A.T.Adcock	b MacGibbon	5			
Extras	(b 3, lb 1, nb 6)	10	(b 5, lb 4, nb 2)		11
TOTAL	(98.1 overs)	**237**	(47.3 overs) (5 wkts)		**215**

Bowling SOUTH AFRICA	O	M	R	W	O	M	R	W
Adcock	19	1	86	4	19	1	45	2
Watkins	16	6	34	4	14	6	21	1
Tayfield	29.3	15	35	1	17	5	51	1
van Ryneveld	7	1	15	0	20.6	7	67	4
Murray	21	4	49	1	17	7	34	1
NEW ZEALAND								
Blair	16	4	39	2	7	0	15	0
MacGibbon	22.1	2	55	3	10	0	44	2
Reid	32	16	51	4	15	2	64	1
Bell	28	6	82	1	9.3	0	54	1
Dempster					5	0	27	0
Mooney					1	1	0	0

Fall of Wickets	NZ 1st	SA 1st	NZ 2nd	SA 2nd
1st	24	40	13	44
2nd	64	69	17	46
3rd	99	89	77	81
4th	141	140	122	188
5th	146	146	161	198
6th	146	173	166	-
7th	176	207	181	-
8th	188	209	189	-
9th	226	224	193	-
10th	226	237	222	-

MILESTONES

- The South African wicketkeeper, John Waite, created a world record of 23 dismissals in a five-test series.

- Tony MacGibbon created a record for a New Zealand player in a test series by capturing 22 wickets.

AVERAGES

New Zealand

BATTING	M	I	NO	Runs	HS	Ave
G.O. Rabone	3	5	0	254	107	50.80
B. Sutcliffe	5	9	1	305	80*	38.12
J.R. Reid	5	9	0	263	135	29.22
J.E.F. Beck	4	7	0	203	99	29.00
M.E. Chapple	5	9	0	180	76	20.00
M.B. Poore	5	9	0	170	44	18.88
E.W. Dempster	4	7	2	92	47	18.40
F.L.H. Mooney	5	9	0	123	35	13.66
A.R. MacGibbon	5	9	1	98	21	12.25
L.S.M. Miller	4	8	0	47	18	5.87
R.W. Blair	4	8	1	40	8	5.71
G.W.F. Overton	3	6	1	8	3*	1.60
I.B. Leggatt	1	1	0	0	0	0.00
W. Bell	2	3	3	21	21*	-

BOWLING	O	M	R	W	Ave
G.O. Rabone	59.7	16	131	8	16.37
A.R. MacGibbon	171.1	36	454	22	20.63
G.W.F. Overton	91.1	23	258	9	28.66
R.W. Blair	89	14	270	9	30.00
J.R. Reid	142	39	384	12	32.00
M.B. Poore	19	1	75	1	75.00
E.W. Dempster	29	4	106	1	106.00
W. Bell	61.3	13	235	2	117.50
F.L.H. Mooney	1	1	0	0	-
M.E. Chapple	1	0	1	0	-
L.S.M. Miller	0.2	0	1	0	-
I.B. Leggatt	3	0	6	0	-
B. Sutcliffe	12	1	46	0	-

South Africa

BATTING	M	I	NO	Runs	HS	Ave
C.B. van Ryneveld	5	7	2	234	68*	46.80
D.J. McGlew	5	9	1	351	86	43.87
W.R. Endean	5	8	1	293	93	41.85
R.A. McLean	4	6	1	191	101	38.20
J.E. Cheetham	5	8	2	227	89	37.83
H.J. Tayfield	5	6	1	137	34	27.40
R.J. Westcott	3	6	0	148	62	24.66
J.H.B. Waite	5	7	1	144	52	24.00
J.C. Watkins	3	4	0	93	45	23.25
D.E.J. Ironside	3	4	2	37	13	18.50
K.J. Funston	3	5	0	60	39	12.00
A.R.A. Murray	4	5	0	33	13	6.60
N.A.T. Adcock	5	5	1	19	8*	4.75

BOWLING	O	M	R	W	Ave
J.C. Watkins	178	29	129	10	12.90
H.J. Tayfield	192.6	80	377	21	17.95
D.E.J. Ironside	123.2	41	275	15	18.33
N.A.T. Adcock	170.3	27	485	24	20.20
C.B. van Ryneveld	102.4	18	305	10	30.50
A.R.A. Murray	106	34	233	6	38.83

At the end of the fifth test the tourists held a party for the pressmen who had accompanied them around South Africa. Bert Sutcliffe (playing the piano) and Bill Ferguson's wife, known to all as "The Duchess" led the singing. From left: Tony MacGibbon, Bill Ferguson, Sam Mirwis, John Beck, Brian Gillespie, Jack Kerr, John Reid, Ian Leggat, Matt Poore, Dick Brittenden, Geoff Rabone and Frank Mooney.

1954/55 MCC in New Zealand

32   NEW ZEALAND v ENGLAND *(First Test)*

at Carisbrook, Dunedin on 11, 12, 14, 15, 16 March, 1955
Toss : England. Umpires : R.G. Currie and S.B. Tonkinson
England won by 8 wickets

After losing the first match of the 1954/55 Ashes series by an innings and 154 runs, Len Hutton's men triumphed in the second, third and fourth tests. England had won a series in Australia for the first time in 22 years. Much of the credit for the unexpected success was due to younger members of the team, including batsmen Colin Cowdrey and Peter May and fast bowlers Brian Statham and Frank Tyson.

New Zealand was asked to bat first on a pitch softened by recent rain. Hutton was keen to exploit any advantage, knowing that he had a very fine bowling attack, headed by the genuine pace of Statham and Tyson, with Trevor Bailey as his third medium-quick bowler before Johnny Wardle and Bob Appleyard could be called upon with top quality spin.

To compound the home team's problems, the heavy outfield was obviously going to make run-scoring difficult.

The early loss of Murray Chapple should have prepared the crowd of 8400 for the painstaking batting by Bert Sutcliffe and Geoff Rabone. Conditions were difficult and by lunch the pair had only crept to 24. Rabone's innings lasted over three hours, but his persistence allowed Sutcliffe to come to terms with the England bowlers and he brought up his 50 in 200 minutes.

Tyson blasted through the New Zealand middle order and eventually Sutcliffe found himself joined by the last batsman, Ian Colquhoun, and he attempted to salvage what he could in the last minutes of the day's play.

His desperate flurry ended when he was caught in the covers for 74 and the home team was all out for 125 at the end of a painfully slow day's batting.

New Zealand's bowlers, defending a pathetic total, won much applause from the crowd of 16,000 by restricting England to 209 for eight. All the England top order batsmen were contained by the accuracy of John Reid, Harry Cave and Tony MacGibbon.

Wardle and Tyson batted freely in the last hour, where they added 52, before Tyson was out and an appeal against the light was upheld.

Rain prevented any play on the scheduled third and fourth days, and Hutton declared before the start of play on the last day. Sutcliffe, on whom New Zealand pinned its hope to survive, batted with quiet confidence through the morning session, with the score reaching 67 for one.

As Arthur Mailey Saw It

IT WAS WITH DEEP REVERENCE THAT I RAISED MY HAT TO CARISBROOK, A GROUND ON WHICH I PLAYED MY VERY FIRST TEST WAY BACK IN 1913

SO ENTHUSIASTIC WAS I THAT, MY OLD NURSE SAID I STARTED APPEALING FOR LBW ON MY WAY TO THE GROUND

GOO

HUSH DARLING

WHAT A DIFFERENCE !!

SCORE BOARD N. ZEALAND DRELUNCH SCORE 1 FOR 25

THE BATTING HAS SLOWED DOWN SINCE I GAVE UP BOWLING

AND MR RABONE TIRED AFTER A LONG TRIP FROM AUCKLAND HAD ABOUT 3½ HOURS SLEEP AT THE WICKET

EVANS

BERT SUTCLIFFE ON A PEDESTAL FOR A FINE ALMOST LONE HANDED INNINGS

MR CHAPPLE WHO SCORED 4 AGAINST M.C.C. AT CHURCH WAS NOT SO SUCCESSFUL YESTERDAY

ANYHOW I MUST PUT

HEAVY DRAMA COULD BE TURNED INTO LIGHT COMEDY, OR VICE VERSA, SAYS MAILEY, BUT . . .

N.Z. In Bad Way At End Of First Day's Play

The Otago Daily Times *published this cartoon by former Australian great leg-spinner Arthur Mailey after a gloomy first day's play at Carisbrook.*

NEW ZEALAND

G.O.Rabone*	st Evans b Wardle	18	lbw b Wardle		7
M.E.Chapple	b Statham	0	(3) b Statham		20
B.Sutcliffe	c Statham b Bailey	74	(2) run out		35
J.R.Reid	b Statham	4	b Tyson		28
S.N.McGregor	b Tyson	2	c Cowdrey b Appleyard		8
L.Watt	b Tyson	0	b Appleyard		2
H.B.Cave	b Tyson	1	b Tyson		1
A.M.Moir	b Statham	7	(9) lbw b Tyson		10
R.W.Blair	b Statham	0	(10) b Wardle		3
A.R.MacGibbon	c Evans b Bailey	7	(8) b Tyson		0
I.A.Colquhoun†	not out	0	not out		1
Extras	(b 5, lb 4, nb 3)	12	(b 7, lb 10)		17
TOTAL	**(81.2 overs)**	**125**	**(56.3 overs)**		**132**

ENGLAND

L.Hutton*	c Colquhoun b Reid	11	c Colquhoun b Blair		3
T.W.Graveney	b Cave	41	not out		32
P.B.H.May	b MacGibbon	10	b MacGibbon		13
M.C.Cowdrey	lbw b Reid	42	not out		0
R.T.Simpson	b Cave	21			
T.E.Bailey	lbw b Reid	0			
T.G.Evans†	b Reid	0			
J.H.Wardle	not out	32			
F.H.Tyson	c McGregor b MacGibbon	16			
R.Appleyard	not out	0			
J.B.Statham					
Extras	(b 13, lb 17, nb 6)	36	(lb 1)		1
TOTAL	**(92.5 overs) (8 wkts dec)**	**209**	**(15.2 overs) (2 wkts)**		**49**

Bowling	O	M	R	W	O	M	R	W
ENGLAND								
Tyson	19	7	23	3	12	6	16	4
Statham	17	9	24	4	15	5	30	1
Bailey	12.2	6	19	2	8	4	9	0
Wardle	26	15	31	1	14.3	4	41	2
Appleyard	7	3	16	0	7	2	19	2
NEW ZEALAND								
Blair	8	1	29	0	4	0	20	1
MacGibbon	24.5	11	39	2	7.2	2	16	1
Reid	27	11	36	4	4	2	12	0
Cave	24	15	27	2				
Moir	9	1	42	0				

Fall of Wickets	NZ	E	NZ	E
	1st	1st	2nd	2nd
1st	3	60	24	22
2nd	63	71	68	47
3rd	68	101	75	-
4th	72	150	96	-
5th	76	152	98	-
6th	86	152	103	-
7th	103	156	103	-
8th	113	208	123	-
9th	122	-	126	-
10th	125	-	132	-

Immediately after the lunch break Sutcliffe set out for a second run but was beaten by a magnificent throw from May at fine leg. Reid watched the departure of Chapple, Noel McGregor and Les Watt with little advance to the score.

Tyson (4-16) then dispensed with Cave and MacGibbon, trapped Moir leg-before-wicket, and delivered the coup de grace by shattering Reid's stumps. England had plenty of time to score the 49 runs required for victory.

MILESTONES

- Ian Colquhoun (68), Noel McGregor (69) and Les Watt (70) made their test debuts.

- This was the first test played at Dunedin. Carisbrook became the world's 38th test venue.

- Five-day tests were played in New Zealand for the first time.

33 NEW ZEALAND v ENGLAND *(Second Test)*

at Eden Park, Auckland on 25, 26, 28 March, 1955
Toss : New Zealand. Umpires : J.C. Harris and J. McLellan
England won by an innings and 20 runs

The public interest in the visiting England cricket side was almost on the same scale as that reserved for leading rugby nations with 18,000 being present on the first day when Frank Tyson disposed of both Gordon Leggat and Matt Poore in his second over.

Bert Sutcliffe and John Reid were troubled by the sharp lift of the pace bowlers but any forceful shots skimmed over the very fast outfield so that New Zealand's fifty was on the board within an hour.

In the last over before lunch, Sutcliffe hooked a Statham bouncer and was caught for 49. For the first time in six tests the England bowling attack failed to gain a wicket in a session as Reid and Geoff Rabone added 66 between lunch and tea. Once Reid was dismissed the floodgates opened and the last five wickets fell for 11 runs.

Intermittent showers delayed the start of play and continued for most of the day. The crowd of 30,000 was absorbed by an enthralling struggle.

The wicket was still providing bounce and also turning a little. Peter May and Colin Cowdrey battled through until just after tea, when both departed at 112. England ended the day at 148-4 with Len Hutton, batting at five, being not out.

Hutton and his partners struggled throughout the first session, scoring only 35 runs. Alec Moir exploited conditions intelligently and it was thought that his leg-spinners would be almost unplayable in England's second innings.

When Sutcliffe and Leggat began New Zealand's second innings, to wipe off the deficit of 46, no one could have foreseen what was to occur in the next 104 disaster-strewn

minutes, where 162 balls would be bowled. Only Sutcliffe reached double figures and only Harry Cave hit a boundary. Five batsmen failed to score.

The last five wickets fell for four runs as New Zealand were dismissed for the lowest total in any test innings, 26. The New Zealand batsmen were undone by four great bowlers, all bowling superbly.

The ferocious pace of Tyson, coupled with the sustained accuracy of Brian Statham, the mesmeric off-spin of Bob Appleyard, and the variety of spin of Johnny Wardle, all supported with sharp catching, proved too much.

At the end of the game it was revealed that vandals had removed the covers off the wicket the night before this fateful day. Cliff Waters, the head groundsman, discovered this while inspecting the arena after midnight. No rain had fallen and the senseless act had no effect on the wicket.

Arthur Mailey, the Australian critic, described New Zealand's batting as: "too pathetic for words ... merely holding a negative bat at the ball is not batting at all."

This test marked the end of Len Hutton's international career, which had begun against New Zealand in 1937. In 79 tests he aggregated 6971 runs at an average of 56.67. At first-class level he had scored 129 centuries.

NEW ZEALAND

B.Sutcliffe	c Bailey b Statham	49	b Wardle		11
J.G.Leggat	lbw b Tyson	4	c Hutton b Tyson		1
M.B.Poore	c Evans b Tyson	0	b Tyson		0
J.R.Reid	c Statham b Wardle	73	b Statham		1
G.O.Rabone*	c Evans b Statham	29	(6) lbw b Statham		7
S.N.McGregor	not out	15	(5) c May b Appleyard		1
H.B.Cave	c Bailey b Appleyard	6	c Graveney b Appleyard		5
A.R.MacGibbon	b Appleyard	9	lbw b Appleyard		0
I.A.Colquhoun†	c sub (J.V.Wilson) b Appleyard	0	c Graveney b Appleyard		0
A.M.Moir	lbw b Statham	0	not out		0
J.A.Hayes	b Statham	0	b Statham		0
Extras	(b 3, lb 6, w 4, nb 2)	15			0
TOTAL	(88.4 overs)	200	(27 overs)		26

ENGLAND

R.T.Simpson	c & b Moir	23
T.W.Graveney	c Rabone b Hayes	13
P.B.H.May	b Hayes	48
M.C.Cowdrey	b Moir	22
L.Hutton*	b MacGibbon	53
T.E.Bailey	c Colquhoun b Cave	18
T.G.Evans†	c Reid b Moir	0
J.H.Wardle	c Reid b Moir	0
F.H.Tyson	not out	27
R.Appleyard	c Colquhoun b Hayes	6
J.B.Statham	c Reid b Moir	13
Extras	(b 12, lb 3, nb 8)	23
TOTAL	(119.1 overs)	246

Bowling	O	M	R	W	O	M	R	W		Fall of Wickets		
ENGLAND										NZ	E	NZ
										1st	1st	2nd
Tyson	11	2	41	2	7	2	10	2	1st	13	21	6
Statham	17.4	7	28	4	9	3	9	3	2nd	13	56	8
Bailey	13	2	34	0					3rd	76	112	9
Appleyard	16	4	38	3	6	3	7	4	4th	154	112	14
Wardle	31	19	44	1	5	5	0	1	5th	171	163	14
NEW ZEALAND									6th	189	164	22
Hayes	23	7	71	3					7th	199	164	22
MacGibbon	20	7	33	1					8th	199	201	22
Reid	25	15	28	0					9th	200	218	26
Cave	24	10	25	1					10th	200	246	26
Moir	25.1	3	62	5								
Rabone	2	0	4	0								

MILESTONES

- New Zealand's second innings score of 26 remains the lowest total in a test innings.

Peter May takes a legside catch off Bob Appleyard to dismiss Noel McGregor in New Zealand's second innings at Eden Park.

The scoreboard at Eden Park records New Zealand's innings of 26 all out, still the lowest total in test cricket. Bert Sutcliffe top scored with 11 and five batsmen failed to score.

1955/56 New Zealand in Pakistan and India

New Zealand embarked on a most arduous period of test cricket when, in October 1955, they began a tour of Pakistan and India, playing eight tests and eight first-class games. Conditions and transport in both these countries were decidedly third world and all the players contracted stomach illnesses that were with them throughout the tour and in some cases for several years.

The players quickly discovered that new techniques were required of both batsmen and bowlers on matting wickets, and that the ball would come off this surface at varying pace and height depending on how tightly the matting had been stretched over the turf and how much it had been dampened early in the morning.

34 PAKISTAN v NEW ZEALAND *(First Test)*

at National Stadium, Karachi on 13, 14, 16, 17 October, 1955
Toss : New Zealand. Umpires : Idris Beg and Shujauddin
Pakistan won by an innings and 1 run

Intense heat, and the debilitating effects of dysentery may have contributed to New Zealand's disappointing batting on the first day. Only 45 runs were scored in the first session for the loss of Bert Sutcliffe's wicket.

For the first time since Pakistan had become a test-playing nation in 1952 the slow bowlers did the bulk of the bowling and the wicket-taking. The right-arm off-spin bowler Zulfiqar Ahmed and his captain, Abdul Kardar, left-arm slow, captured 14 wickets in the course of the game.

Impatient shots proved the downfall of the New Zealand top order, and it was only the defiance from the lower batsmen, Harry Cave, Jack Alabaster and Tony MacGibbon, that saw New Zealand reach 164. In reply Pakistan struggled against tight bowling from MacGibbon and Cave, and only the wicketkeeper Imtiaz Ahmed (64) looked accomplished. The last four wickets doubled Pakistan's total to a respectable 289 and a lead of 125 runs.

Shujauddin, who had just compiled his highest test score of 47, captured the first three wickets to fall with his slow left-arm deliveries in his first three overs. On the last day Zulfiqar captured five of the six wickets to fall as New Zealand collapsed to be all out for 124, one run short of making Pakistan bat again.

Zin Harris accumulated 21 runs in three and a half hours, and the last four wickets tumbled for just six runs. Zulfiqar had match figures of 11 for 79 off 83.5 overs.

At the conclusion of the test, Kardar suggested that the New Zealanders, whom he described as "very fine sportsmen", had yet to come to terms with matting wickets.

NEW ZEALAND

J.G.Leggat	c Imtiaz b Fazal	16	lbw b Zulfiqar	39
B.Sutcliffe	c Kardar b Zulfiqar	15	b Shujauddin	17
M.B.Poore	st Imtiaz b Zulfiqar	43	b Shujauddin	0
J.R.Reid	c Khan b Kardar	10	(5) c Waqar b Zulfiqar	11
P.G.Z.Harris	c Wazir b Kardar	7	(6) run out	21
S.N.McGregor	c Alimuddin b Shujauddin	10	(4) lbw b Shujauddin	0
H.B.Cave*	b Kardar	0	c sub (Agha Saadat Ali) b Zulfiqar	21
J.C.Alabaster	c sub (Agha Saadat Ali) b Zulfiqar	14	b Zulfiqar	8
A.R.MacGibbon	b Zulfiqar	33	c Hanif b Zulfiqar	0
A.M.Moir	c Khan b Zulfiqar Ahmed	10	c Alimuddin b Zulfiqar	2
T.G.McMahon†	not out	0	not out	0
Extras	(b 4, lb 2)	6	(b 1, lb 4)	5
TOTAL	**(133.2 overs)**	**164**	**(108.3 overs)**	**124**

PAKISTAN

Hanif Mohammad	c McGregor b Cave	5
Alimuddin	c MacGibbon b Moir	28
Waqar Hassan	c McMahon b Cave	17
Maqsood Ahmed	b MacGibbon	2
Imtiaz Ahmed†	c McMahon b MacGibbon	64
A.H.Kardar*	run out	22
Wazir Mohammad	c & b Cave	43
Shujauddin	b MacGibbon	47
Zulfiqar Ahmed	b MacGibbon	10
Fazal Mahmood	not out	34
Khan Mohammad	run out	5
Extras	(b 4, lb 1, nb 7)	12
TOTAL	**(130.1 overs)**	**289**

Bowling	O	M	R	W	O	M	R	W		Fall of Wickets		
PAKISTAN										NZ	P	NZ
										1st	1st	2nd
Fazal	31	12	46	1					1st	18	5	27
Khan	23	9	27	0	13	3	33	0	2nd	50	25	27
Zulfiqar	37.2	19	37	5	46.3	21	42	6	3rd	71	32	27
Kardar	31	10	35	3	27	15	22	0	4th	95	74	79
Shujauddin	11	7	13	1	22	12	22	3	5th	95	140	79
NEW ZEALAND									6th	95	144	109
MacGibbon	37.1	8	98	4					7th	114	222	118
Cave	24	6	56	3					8th	129	240	120
Reid	30	17	34	0					9th	163	251	122
Moir	37	9	87	1					10th	164	289	124
Poore	2	0	2	0								

MILESTONES

- First test between New Zealand and Pakistan.

- Jack Alabaster (71), Zin Harris (72) and Trevor McMahon (73) made their test debuts.

- The New Zealand side became the first to travel to their destination by air.

Tony MacGibbon continued to impress at test level with his control of length and ability to move the ball either way. In oppressive conditions he was lion-hearted.

35 PAKISTAN v NEW ZEALAND *(Second Test)*

at Bagh-e-Jinnah, Lahore on 26, 27, 29, 30, 31 October, 1955
Toss : New Zealand. Umpires : Daud Khan and Idris Beg
Pakistan won by 4 wickets

New Zealand squandered the advantage of batting first on a genial turf wicket. Three of the four batsmen dismissed for 76 runs were caught hooking at the short-pitched bowling of Khan Mohammad. Noel McGregor laboured to reach his first test half-century in three hours, while his partner Noel

Harford, who was fortunate to survive an early chance, then blossomed with a series of free-flowing shots.

His 50 came up after 110 minutes, and although he had arrived at the wicket an hour and a half after McGregor he overhauled his partner before stumps, where he was 81 not out and the team's score 206-4.

Harford became Khan's fourth victim after the fourth wicket partnership had added 150 runs. At 267 McGregor was dismissed for 111 after 340 minutes of dedicated batting. The lower-order batting, led by Tony MacGibbon (61), saw the innings end at 348.

MacGibbon and John Hayes then dismissed both of Pakistan's openers cheaply. A brief revival after tea was broken by Alec Moir, who bagged three wickets for six runs in seven overs, leaving Pakistan 87-5 at stumps.

Waqar Hassan, who had been dropped in the slips late on the second day, was joined by Imtiaz Ahmed. This partnership remained intact until five minutes before stumps. They added 308 runs for the seventh wicket and Waqar established a new individual record for his country when he was caught behind for 189, including 30 boundaries and lasting 430 minutes. At stumps, Imtiaz was 158 not out.

Waqar's record was short-lived. When Imtiaz was finally dismissed, after 380 minutes, he had scored 209 and Pakistan had reached a record total of 561.

New Zealand's reply suffered a severe setback when the first three wickets fell for 60 runs. Solid efforts again by McGregor, Reid, Harford and MacGibbon saw New Zealand reach 328 midway through the afternoon of the last day.

Pakistan required 116 to win in 110 minutes. After an enthusiastic chase, victory was achieved with four wickets and 18 minutes to spare. Reid caused all the batsmen some concern, claiming four wickets with his medium-fast deliveries. The large crowd appreciated Cave's refusal to adopt negative, match-saving tactics and stood to applaud the New Zealanders off the field.

The second test between Pakistan and New Zealand was played at the Bagh-e-Jinnah Ground in Lahore.

NEW ZEALAND					
B.Sutcliffe	c Waqar b Khan	4	lbw b Shujauddin		25
M.B.Poore	c Alimuddin b Khan	6	c Imtiaz b Zulfiqar		9
P.G.Z.Harris	run out	28	b Shujauddin		11
S.N.McGregor	lbw b Kardar	111	c Imtiaz b Khan		43
J.R.Reid	c Maqsood b Khan	5	b Kardar		86
N.S.Harford	c Maqsood b Khan	93	(7) c Khan b Zulfiqar		64
A.R.MacGibbon	lbw b Zulfiqar	61	(6) c Wazir b Kardar		40
E.C.Petrie†	b Kardar	0	c Hanif b Kardar		7
H.B.Cave*	c & b Zulfiqar	14	c Alimuddin b Zulfiqar		17
A.M.Moir	b Mahmood	8	not out		11
J.A.Hayes	not out	0	lbw b Zulfiqar		0
Extras	(b 4, lb 10, nb 4)	18	(b 6, lb 5, nb 4)		15
TOTAL	(160.5 overs)	**348**	(158.2 overs)		**328**
PAKISTAN					
Hanif Mohammad	hit wicket b Hayes	10	lbw b Reid		33
Alimuddin	c Sutcliffe b MacGibbon	4	c MacGibbon b Reid		37
Shujauddin	b Moir	29	(7) not out		1
Waqar Hassan	c Petrie b MacGibbon	189	(5) c MacGibbon b Hayes		17
Wazir Mohammad	lbw b Moir	0	(8) not out		2
A.H.Kardar*	b Moir	2	c Reid b Hayes		11
Khan Mohammad	run out	10			
Imtiaz Ahmed†	b Moir	209	(3) c Cave b Reid		0
Maqsood Ahmed	c Cave b Reid	33	(4) c McGregor b Reid		8
Zulfiqar Ahmed	not out	21			
Mahmood Hussain	c MacGibbon b Sutcliffe	32			
Extras	(b 3, lb 7, nb 12)	22	(b 2, lb 4, nb 2)		8
TOTAL	(185.3 overs)	**561**	(26.5 overs) (6 wkts)		**117**

Bowling	O	M	R	W	O	M	R	W
PAKISTAN								
Khan	34	10	78	4	18	6	26	1
Mahmood	31.5	4	67	1	21	6	47	0
Shujauddin	43	11	84	0	38	12	79	2
Zulfiqar	35	13	71	2	43.2	10	114	4
Maqsood	3	1	4	0				
Kardar	14	5	26	2	38	15	47	3
NEW ZEALAND								
Hayes	37	12	107	1	8.5	2	25	2
MacGibbon	40	7	135	2	5	0	20	0
Reid	35	13	82	1	8	2	38	4
Cave	30	6	84	0	5	0	26	0
Moir	39	13	114	4				
Poore	3	0	13	0				
Sutcliffe	1.3	0	4	1				

Fall of Wickets	NZ	P	NZ	P
	1st	*1st*	*2nd*	*2nd*
1st	8	11	34	45
2nd	13	23	43	49
3rd	48	84	60	80
4th	76	84	148	93
5th	226	87	224	107
6th	267	111	237	115
7th	267	419	252	-
8th	333	482	293	-
9th	348	517	324	-
10th	348	561	328	-

MILESTONES.

- Noel Harford (74) and Eric Petrie (75) made their test debuts.

- Waqar Hassan and Imtiaz Ahmed created a new Pakistan test record for any wicket of 308.

- Imtiaz Ahmed became the first batsman to score a double century for Pakistan, and the first wicketkeeper from any country to score a test double century.

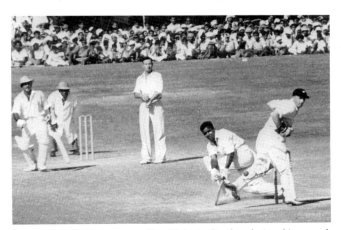

Imtiaz Ahmed (209) sweeps Alex Moir to fine-leg during his record-breaking partnership with Waqar Hassan (189) of 308 for the seventh wicket. Eric Petrie is the wicketkeeper.

36 PAKISTAN v NEW ZEALAND *(Third Test)*

at Dacca Stadium, on 7, 8, 9, 11, 12 November, 1955
Toss : New Zealand. Umpires : Daud Khan and Idris Beg
Match drawn

When the tourists left New Zealand they believed that they would be able to buy bats at Karachi. These proved to be of very poor quality, and the players were reduced to pooling their resources. An urgent order was sent to the English firm of Gunn and Moore and 14 bats were sent to Pakistan.

The shipment was then seized by officials who refused to release it until the tourists left the country. By the time of the third test, only three serviceable bats remained.

The tourists travelled almost 2000 km across India to East Pakistan (now Bangladesh) to play the third test at Dacca. Government offices were closed on the first day of the test but no play was possible for three days because of persistent rain.

When play got underway on the fourth day the New Zealand batsmen had to contend with a most unpredictable matting wicket. Some deliveries skidded through, others reared up awkwardly. To add to their problems the heavy atmosphere offered significant help to the swing bowlers.

Khan Mohammad and Fazal Mahmood demolished the top order batting. Tony MacGibbon, who was in the best batting form of the touring party at this time, struggled valiantly and he alone looked composed. New Zealand totalled a mere 70 runs. Khan exploited conditions ideal for his medium-fast bowling, and was rewarded with 6-21.

Harry Cave and John Reid found the wicket to their liking and both took two wickets to have Pakistan tottering at 55-4. The young Hanif Mohammad recovered from a let-off before he scored to reach 68 by the end of an extraordinary first day.

Pakistan advanced from 113-5, at the start of the last day, to be 195-6 when Abdul Kardar declared. Hanif combined an impregnable defence with a number of cultured strokes before he went for 103. This was the second test century by a young man who would become Pakistan's finest batsman.

New Zealand needed to bat through until lunch, 35 minutes away, and survive the afternoon to save the test. Fazal quickly disposed of Gordon Leggat, but injured a finger and could not bowl more than six overs. His team-mates accounted for another five wickets, and the tourists were in dire trouble with 45 minutes of play remaining.

Another stubborn stand by John Guy and MacGibbon defied an enthusiastic attack to carry New Zealand through to 69-6 by the end of the game. They had faced 90 overs.

When the team arrived in India, Cave said about their time in Pakistan: "The varying temperatures under which we played never allowed us to settle down. The brevity of the tour prevented us becoming acclimatised and did not allow us to study the turf and matting wickets, which varied from place to place. The crowds were lovers of cricket and extremely sporting; the umpiring was very good."

MILESTONES

• John Guy (76) made his test debut.

NEW ZEALAND

J.G.Leggat	b Khan	1	c Saadat Ali b Fazal	1
B.Sutcliffe	b Fazal	3	c Imtiaz b Khan	17
M.B.Poore	b Fazal	0	c Saadat Ali b Kardar	18
S.N.McGregor	b Khan	7	c Imtiaz b Zulfiqar	4
J.R.Reid	c Imtiaz b Khan	9	b Kardar	12
N.S.Harford	c Imtiaz b Fazal	0	c Hanif b Khan	1
J.W.Guy	st Imtiaz b Zulfiqar	11	not out	8
A.R.MacGibbon	not out	29	not out	7
E.C.Petrie†	lbw b Khan	6		
H.B.Cave*	c Saadat Ali b Khan	0		
A.M.Moir	c Shujauddin b Khan	0		
Extras	(lb 4)	4	(lb1)	1
TOTAL	**(39.2 overs)**	**70**	**(90 overs) (6 wkts)**	**69**

PAKISTAN

Alimuddin	b Reid	5
Hanif Mohammad	c Reid b Cave	103
Waqar Hassan	lbw b Reid	8
Shujauddin	c Guy b Cave	3
Imtiaz Ahmed†	b Cave	11
A.H.Kardar*	b MacGibbon	14
W.Mathias	not out	41
Agha Saadat Ali	not out	8
Fazal Mahmood		
Zulfiqar Ahmed		
Khan Mohammad		
Extras	(lb 1, nb 1)	2
TOTAL	**(76 overs) (6 wkts dec)**	**195**

Bowling	O	M	R	W	O	M	R	W
PAKISTAN								
Fazal	20	7	34	3	6	3	12	1
Khan	16.2	6	21	6	30	19	20	2
Zulfiqar	3	1	11	1	16	8	13	1
Kardar					28	17	21	2
Shujauddin					9	8	1	0
Hanif					1	0	1	0
NEW ZEALAND								
MacGibbon	20	4	64	1				
Cave	20	4	45	3				
Reid	30	10	67	2				
Moir	6	1	17	0				

Fall of Wickets			
	NZ	P	NZ
	1st	1st	2nd
1st	1	22	12
2nd	4	30	22
3rd	9	37	32
4th	15	55	51
5th	20	86	52
6th	26	182	56
7th	54	-	-
8th	64	-	-
9th	68	-	-
10th	70	-	-

Autographed caricatures of the 1955/56 tourists. Top (from left): Harry Cave, John Reid, Bert Sutcliffe, Jack Alabaster, Alex Moir. Middle: Matt Poore, Trevor McMahon, Eric Petrie, John Guy, Zin Harris. Bottom: Tony MacGibbon, John Hayes, Noel Harford, Gordon Leggat, Noel McGregor.

AVERAGES

New Zealand

BATTING	M	I	NO	Runs	HS	Ave
A.R. MacGibbon	3	6	2	170	61	42.50
N.S. Harford	2	4	0	158	93	39.50
S.N. McGregor	3	6	0	175	111	29.16
J.R. Reid	3	6	0	133	86	22.16
J.W. Guy	1	2	1	19	11	19.00
P.G.Z. Harris	2	4	0	67	28	16.75
J.G. Leggat	2	4	0	57	39	14.25
B. Sutcliffe	3	6	0	81	25	13.50
M.B. Poore	3	6	0	76	43	12.66
J.C. Alabaster	1	2	0	22	14	11.00
H.B. Cave	3	5	0	52	21	10.40
A.M. Moir	3	5	1	31	11*	7.75
E.C. Petrie	2	3	0	13	7	4.33
J.A. Hayes	1	2	1	0	0*	0.00
T.G. McMahon	1	2	2	0	0*	-

BOWLING	O	M	R	W	Ave
B. Sutcliffe	1.3	0	4	1	4.00
J.R. Reid	103	42	221	7	31.57
H.B. Cave	79	16	211	6	35.16
A.M. Moir	82	23	218	5	43.60
J.A. Hayes	45.5	14	132	3	44.00
A.R. MacGibbon	102.1	19	317	7	45.28
M.B. Poore	5	0	15	0	-

Pakistan

BATTING	M	I	NO	Runs	HS	Ave
Imtiaz Ahmed	3	4	0	284	209	71.00
Waqar Hassan	3	4	0	231	189	57.75
Hanif Mohammad	3	4	0	151	103	37.75
Mahmood Hussain	1	1	0	32	32	32.00
Zulfiqar Ahmed	3	2	1	31	21*	31.00
Shujauddin	3	4	1	80	47	26.66
Wazir Mohammad	2	3	1	45	43	22.50
Alimuddin	3	4	0	74	37	18.50
Maqsood Ahmed	2	3	0	43	33	14.33
A.H. Kardar	3	4	0	49	22	12.25
Khan Mohammad	3	2	0	15	10	7.50
W. Mathias	1	1	1	41	41*	-
Fazal Mahmood	2	1	1	34	34*	-
Agha Saadat Ali	1	1	1	8	8*	-

BOWLING	O	M	R	W	Ave
A.H. Kardar	138	62	151	10	15.10
Zulfiqar Ahmed	181.1	72	288	19	15.15
Khan Mohammad	134.2	53	205	13	15.76
Fazal Mahmood	57	22	92	5	18.40
Shujauddin	123	50	199	6	33.16
Mahmood Hussain	52.5	10	114	1	114.00
Hanif Mohammad	1	0	1	0	-
Maqsood Ahmed	3	1	4	0	-

37 INDIA v NEW ZEALAND *(First Test)*

at Lal Bahadur Shastri Stadium, Hyderabad on 19, 20, 22, 23, 24 November, 1955
Toss : India. Umpires : J.R. Patel and M.G. Vijayasarathi
Match drawn

John Hayes and Tony MacGibbon made the most of early life in the pitch by dismissing the Indian openers during the first session of play. Polly Umrigar, and Vijay Manjrekar, then batted throughout the rest of the day, adding 202 runs in even time. Both completed centuries before stumps; 250-2.

When Manjrekar was caught for 118 on the second morning, the partnership of 238 was India's best for any wicket at test level. Umrigar was majestic in attack and although he was dropped at 187 and 200, the concentration that carried him through 503 minutes at the crease had put India in an unbeatable position and taxed the New Zealand bowlers and field.

Playing in his first test, Kripal Singh became the third Indian batsmen in the innings to score a century. Fortunately for them, the tourists had time to recuperate on the rest day.

The right arm leg-spin bowler Subhash Gupte was introduced into the Indian attack early on the third morning, and his leg breaks disposed of both openers. Batting at three, left-hander John Guy countered Gupte with diligent defence, while his partner, John Reid, was more cavalier, striking nine boundaries in his score of 54. Guy was still at the wicket at stumps, having doggedly accumulated 57 runs in almost a full day's play.

On the fourth day Guy, batting with extraordinary dedication in only his second test, completed a century in 435 minutes. His extreme caution continued even after passing the hundred; in the next half-hour he added only two runs before he was caught.

Tony MacGibbon and Matt Poore struggled to avoid the follow-on and when the last wicket fell at 326, New Zealand were 23 runs short of the target. Gupte took seven wickets. Four of his victims fell to quicker deliveries, and the other three batsmen were deceived by balls tossed up to entice false shots.

Bert Sutcliffe, who had not enjoyed a good tour to date, now batted with great assurance throughout the last day. Powerful drives and forcing shots off the back foot brought him his third century in test cricket, and he was unbeaten on 137 at the close of play.

Guy again occupied the crease for 103 minutes and Reid, after taking half an hour to get off the mark, joined Sutcliffe in a delightful century partnership in the dying stages of the game. After the game the Indian captain, Ghulam Ahmed, said it was a treat to watch Sutcliffe bat.

Right: Playing in only his second test match, John Guy batted for 435 minutes and became the second-youngest player to make a century for New Zealand. It was an innings of monumental concentration.

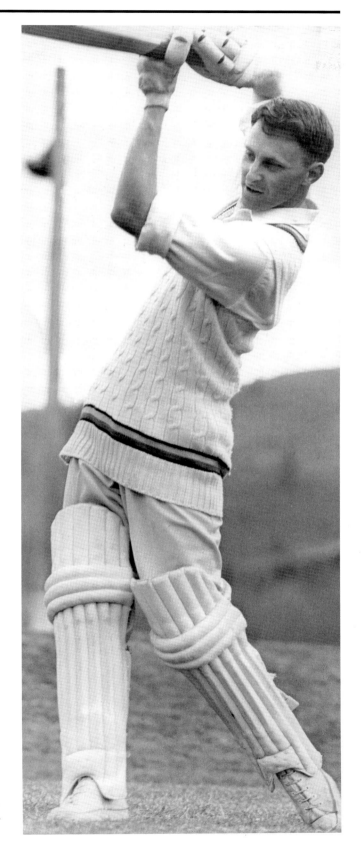

INDIA

M.H.Mankad	c Alabaster b MacGibbon	30
P.Roy	c Petrie b Hayes	0
P.R.Umrigar	c Petrie b Hayes	223
V.L.Manjrekar	c MacGibbon b Hayes	118
A.G.Kripal Singh	not out	100
G.S.Ramchand	not out	12
D.G.Phadkar		
V.N.Swamy		
N.S.Tamhane†		
S.P.Gupte		
Ghulam Ahmed*		
Extras	(b 8, lb 4, nb 3)	15
TOTAL	(175.1 overs) (4 wkts dec)	**498**

NEW ZEALAND

B.Sutcliffe	c Umrigar b Gupte	17	not out	137
E.C.Petrie†	b Gupte	15	lbw b Gupte	4
J.W.Guy	c Ghulam Ahmed b Mankad	102	c Ghulam Ahmed b Mankad	21
J.R.Reid	lbw b Ramchand	54	not out	45
S.N.McGregor	st Tamhane b Gupte	19		
N.S.Harford	lbw b Gupte	4		
A.R.MacGibbon	c Kripal Singh b Ghulam Ahmed	59		
M.B.Poore	lbw b Gupte	23		
H.B.Cave*	st Tamhane b Gupte	14		
J.C.Alabaster	lbw b Gupte	11		
J.A.Hayes	not out	1		
Extras	(b 2, lb 5)	7	(b 2, lb 2, nb 1)	5
TOTAL	(209.4 overs)	**326**	(92 overs) (2 wkts)	**212**

Bowling	O	M	R	W	O	M	R	W
NEW ZEALAND								
Hayes	26	5	91	3				
MacGibbon	43.1	15	102	1				
Reid	16	2	63	0				
Cave	41	20	59	0				
Alabaster	31	5	96	0				
Poore	9	2	36	0				
Sutcliffe	9	1	36	0				
INDIA								
Phadkar	25	11	34	0	12	5	24	0
Swamy	8	2	15	0	3	3	30	0
Gupte	76.4	35	128	7	18	7	28	1
Ghulam Ahmed	39	15	56	1	13	2	36	0
Mankad	36	16	48	1	25	7	75	1
Ramchand	20	12	33	1	14	7	14	0
Kripal Singh	1	0	5	0				
Umrigar	4	4	0	0				

Fall of Wickets	I	NZ	NZ
	1st	1st	2nd
1st	1	27	42
2nd	48	36	104
3rd	286	119	-
4th	457	154	-
5th	-	166	-
6th	-	253	-
7th	-	292	-
8th	-	305	-
9th	-	325	-
10th	-	326	-

MILESTONES

- First test between New Zealand and India.

- India's score of 498-4d was their highest in test cricket.

- Polly Umrigar's 223 was the highest individual score for India.

- Polly Umrigar and Vijay Manjrekar created a new Indian record for the second wicket of 238 runs. It was also the highest score for any wicket for India.

- John Guy became the second youngest New Zealander, at 21, to score a test century.

The venue for the first test between India and New Zealand, Fateh Maidan, Hyderabad.

38   INDIA v NEW ZEALAND *(Second Test)*

at Brabourne Stadium, Bombay on 2, 3, 4, 6, 7 December, 1955
Toss : India. Umpires : B.J. Mohoni and M.G. Vijayasarathi
India won by an innings and 27 runs

A crowd of more than 20,000 gave India's new opener, Vijay Mehra, a warm reception when he came to the wicket with Vinoo Mankad. At the age of 17 years and 265 days he was the youngest man to represent his country. He survived for an hour before being caught in the gully off John Hayes. Harry Cave captured two valuable wickets before lunch.

At 63-3 Kripal Singh joined Mankad and this pair batted serenely through the rest of the day. By stumps Mankad had contributed 132 of his team's 233 runs. Cave used his height to full advantage and bowled with great economy; his 28 overs cost only 29 runs.

Mankad continued to bat magnificently on the second day before he was dismissed for precisely the same total achieved by Polly Umrigar in the first test, 223. After a slow day's cricket, a declaration was made at 421-8 and in the 20 overs until stumps New Zealand could manage only 21-1.

On the third morning Bert Sutcliffe dominated a second wicket partnership of 73 with John Guy. He had added 60 to his overnight score of 13 when a firecracker explosion in the stands upset his concentration and he edged a ball into the slips.

The holiday crowd of 40,000 included many roisterers who created a cacophony of cheering and rhythmical clapping as the bowlers ran up to the wicket. Four times, John Reid (who had an injured ankle and was using Sutcliffe as a

In extreme heat Harry Cave bowled a Herculean 48 overs to capture three wickets.

runner) withdrew from his stance as the crowd noise rose to a crescendo.

The Indian captain Polly Umrigar appealed in vain for silence and when Reid was persuaded by the Indian players to continue batting he was given out leg-before-wicket to the next ball.

In spite of a fine innings by Tony MacGibbon, the last five wickets fell for 50 runs and New Zealand were forced to follow on. The second innings saw fine bowling by Subhash Gupte, who captured 5-45.

He exploited footmarks made by the medium-pacers with suicidal batting from the New Zealand top order Eric Petrie, Sutcliffe, Reid and MacGibbon who were all caught in the area backward of square-leg. A total of five excellent catches were held as the tourists' innings crumbled to 99-7 at stumps.

Within an hour on the last day New Zealand were dismissed for 136 and India had accomplished a convincing victory. The home team's catching was a significant factor in the outcome of this game.

The correspondent for the *Bombay Chronicle* was outraged by some of the game's events, commenting: "According to the unwritten laws of sportsmanship, the second test match is considered abandoned on 5 December 1955, two New Zealand batsmen, Sutcliffe and Reid, being out to crowd intimidation."

MILESTONES

• Vinoo Mankad equalled Polly Umrigar's record set in the first match for the highest individual innings for India in a test (223).

39 INDIA v NEW ZEALAND *(Third Test)*

at Feroz Shah Kotla, Delhi on 16, 17, 18, 20, 21 December, 1955
Toss : New Zealand. Umpires : D.D. Desai and N.D. Nagarwalla
Match drawn

For the first (and only) time in this series New Zealand won the toss and ended the first day holding the advantage over India. The wicket was lifeless, and although it gave no assistance to the bowlers, it also restricted the full range of strokes from the batsmen.

Gordon Leggat was the only wicket to fall on the first day. Bert Sutcliffe combined intense concentration and a fine appreciation of scoring possibilities. His unbeaten innings of 134 contained 19 boundaries. John Guy displayed his usual dedication and reached 44 not out in 160 minutes. The unbroken partnership was worth 120 runs; 218-1 at stumps.

INDIA

M.H.Mankad	c sub (T.G.McMahon) b Poore	223
V.L.Mehra	c Harris b Hayes	10
P.R.Umrigar*	b Cave	15
V.L.Manjrekar	c Alabaster b Cave	0
A.G.Kripal Singh	b Cave	63
G.S.Ramchand	b MacGibbon	22
N.J.Contractor	c Petrie b MacGibbon	16
D.G.Phadkar	not out	37
N.S.Tamhane†	b Poore	10
S.R.Patil	not out	14
S.P.Gupte		
Extras	(lb 3, nb 8)	11
TOTAL	**(158 overs) (8 wkts dec)**	**421**

NEW ZEALAND

B.Sutcliffe	c Gupte b Ramchand	73	c Mankad b Gupte	37
E.C.Petrie†	lbw b Gupte	4	c Gupte b Phadkar	4
J.W.Guy	c Gupte b Ramchand	23	lbw b Gupte	2
J.R.Reid	lbw b Patil	39	c Phadkar b Patil	4
P.G.Z.Harris	lbw b Gupte	19	c Tamhane b Mankad	7
A.R.MacGibbon	c Mankad b Phadkar	46	c Patil b Gupte	24
M.B.Poore	c Umrigar b Phadkar	17	b Mankad	0
H.B.Cave*	run out	12	c Umrigar b Mankad	21
A.M.Moir	lbw b Gupte	0	c Manjrekar b Gupte	28
J.C.Alabaster	b Mankad	16	b Gupte	4
J.A.Hayes	not out	0	not out	0
Extras	(b 3, lb 2, w 4)	9	(b 1, lb 4)	5
TOTAL	**(134.1 overs)**	**258**	**(77.4 overs)**	**136**

Bowling	O	M	R	W	O	M	R	W
NEW ZEALAND								
Hayes	26	4	79	1				
MacGibbon	23	6	56	2				
Cave	48	23	77	3				
Reid	3	1	6	0				
Alabaster	25	4	83	0				
Moir	12	2	51	0				
Poore	19	3	49	2				
Sutcliffe	2	0	9	0				
INDIA								
Phadkar	28	10	53	2	6	4	5	1
Patil	14	3	36	1	9	4	15	1
Gupte	51	26	83	3	32.4	19	45	5
Ramchand	31	15	48	2	6	4	9	0
Mankad	10.1	3	29	1	24	8	57	3

Fall of Wickets	I	NZ	NZ
	1st	1st	2nd
1st	36	21	13
2nd	61	94	22
3rd	63	133	33
4th	230	156	45
5th	281	166	67
6th	347	218	68
7th	365	231	86
8th	377	232	117
9th	-	258	136
10th	-	258	136

Batting first for the only time in the five test series Bert Sutcliffe and John Reid took full advantage of excellent conditions adding a record 222 for the third wicket. Sutcliffe's 230 not out was the highest score made by a New Zealand batsman in a test match.

Early on the second day Guy was caught at deep fine leg after completing a half-century. John Reid joined Sutcliffe and in the next three hours 222 runs were added before Harry Cave declared after tea at 450-2. Sutcliffe's magnificent 230 not out, a New Zealand test record, contained 30 fours and lasted nine hours. Reid's contribution of 119 not out included 10 fours and a six.

The young Indian openers, Nari Contractor and Vijay Mehra, survived 16 overs before stumps. This slow scoring-rate continued on the third day, when 163 runs were scored off 85 overs, of which 35 were maidens. Cave (18 runs off 22 overs) created difficulties for the Indian batsmen by swinging the ball both ways. Contractor was dismissed at 119-3 and Vijay Manjrekar and Kripal Singh defended solidly for the rest of the day.

India's 250 came up after eight hours but once the follow on had been averted runs began to flow more freely. By stumps on the fourth day, the home team had compiled 393-5 in 11 hours. Manjrekar had plodded through the day to be 140 not out. The *Hindu* newspaper described his innings as: "a triumph of intense application in adversity ... he forsook vain deeds and played nobly for India."

Ram Ramchand, who quickly scored 72, provided a bright interlude in another dull day's play that ended with India still trailing by 57 runs. The final day saw batsmen still dominate proceedings. Manjrekar's innings of 177 included 24 fours and lasted for nine hours. Bapu Nadkarni and Prakash Bhandari carried the score through to 531, when a declaration came.

Noel McGregor, who had sat for seven hours with his pads on waiting to bat, was asked to open the second innings and showed that he too could prosper on this featherbed wicket. In five days 1093 runs were scored for the loss of just 10 wickets.

MILESTONES

- Bert Sutcliffe's score of 230 not out was a New Zealand record for test cricket.

- Bert Sutcliffe and John Reid put on 222 unbroken, a record third wicket partnership for New Zealand.

- India's total of 531 was a record score for that country.

40 INDIA v NEW ZEALAND *(Fourth Test)*
at Eden Gardens, Calcutta on 28, 29, 31 December, 1, 2 January, 1956
Toss : India. Umpires : D.D. Desai and S.K. Ganguli
Match drawn

At this stage of the tour many of the visitors had lost up to six kilograms in weight because of the heat and attacks of sickness. In the smaller centres some of the accommodation arrangements were unusual, but a buoyant sense of humour carried the team through its tribulations.

Although the Calcutta wicket was better grassed than any other the tourists had encountered, it did not significantly help the New Zealand attack. Instead, John Hayes, Harry Cave and John Reid relied upon hostile accuracy and movement in the air to beat the Indian batsmen.

Excellent fielding aided the cause and India, a team that had scored over 400 in each of its previous three innings, was routed for 132 in three hours. New Zealand ended the first day on 35 for the loss of Gordon Leggat.

Once Bert Sutcliffe departed, to a dubious caught behind decision, a splendid third wicket partnership of 184 between Reid (120 not out, 19 boundaries) and John Guy (91) helped the tourists through to 262 by stumps on the second day, a lead of 130 runs with six wickets in hand.

Reid had been severe on persistent short-pitched bowling, cracking powerful shots off the back foot. Guy had confirmed his status as a reliable test batsman with an innings of great resolution over almost five hours. In London, the *News Chronicle* proclaimed that New Zealand were within a hand's reach of a victory that they had sought for 26 years.

A rest day intervened before the tourists could continue the fray. Unfortunately, the first ball on the resumption of play bowled Reid and the last six wickets tumbled for 74 runs with Subhash Gupte capturing six wickets in the innings.

NEW ZEALAND

J.G.Leggat	c Manjrekar b Gupte	37	not out	50
B.Sutcliffe	not out	230		
J.W.Guy	c Mehra b Sunderam	52	not out	10
J.R.Reid	not out	119		
S.N.McGregor			(2) c Tamhane b Manjrekar	49
A.R.MacGibbon				
M.B.Poore				
H.B.Cave*				
J.C.Alabaster				
T.G.McMahon†				
J.A.Hayes				
Extras (b 7, lb 5)		12	(b 3)	3
TOTAL (176 overs) (2 wkts dec)		**450**	(58 overs) (1 wkt)	**112**

INDIA

V.L.Mehra	c McMahon b Hayes	32
N.J.Contractor	b Reid	62
P.R.Umrigar*	b MacGibbon	18
V.L.Manjrekar	c McMahon b Cave	177
A.G.Kripal Singh	b Hayes	36
G.S.Ramchand	st McMahon b Poore	72
R.G.Nadkarni	not out	68
P.Bhandari	b MacGibbon	39
N.S.Tamhane†		
G.R.Sunderam		
S.P.Gupte		
Extras (b 16, lb 4, nb 7)		27
TOTAL (241.5 overs) (7 wkts dec)		**531**

Bowling	O	M	R	W	O	M	R	W
INDIA								
Sunderam	39	5	99	1	3	0	8	0
Ramchand	38	11	82	0	3	0	11	0
Gupte	39	10	98	1	6	1	22	0
Nadkarni	54	13	132	0	3	1	10	0
Bhandari	6	0	27	0	7	2	12	0
Manjrekar					20	13	16	1
Kripal Singh					7	3	10	0
Contractor					6	1	17	0
Mehra					3	0	3	0
NEW ZEALAND								
MacGibbon	59.5	16	121	2				
Cave	50	28	68	1				
Hayes	44	9	105	2				
Reid	41	14	86	1				
Alabaster	29	9	90	0				
Poore	15	4	26	1				
Sutcliffe	3	0	8	0				

Fall of Wickets	I	NZ	I
	1st	1st	2nd
1st	98	68	101
2nd	228	111	-
3rd	-	119	-
4th	-	208	-
5th	-	335	-
6th	-	458	-
7th	-	531	-
8th	-	-	-
9th	-	-	-
10th	-	-	-

At Eden Gardens, Calcutta, New Zealand dismissed India for 132 in the first innings. The players leaving the field are, from left, John Reid, Bert Sutcliffe, Noel McGregor, Trevor McMahon, Harry Cave, John Guy, John Hayes, Noel Harford, Gordon Leggat and Tony MacGibbon.

The early loss of Vinoo Mankad suggested that the home team might struggle to overhaul the 204 run deficit. But Nari Contractor and Pankaj Roy batted through the rest of the day; 107-1. Roy scored exactly 100 on the fourth day, sharing a 143-run partnership with Vijay Manjrekar. Intelligent batting from Ram Ramchand, who completed a century, enabled Polly Umrigar to declare at 438-7.

A draw seemed inevitable, with New Zealand set the impossible target of 235 in an hour and a half. Dattu Phadkar, the Indian fast bowler, quickly disposed of Leggat and Guy. After tea, Gupte and Vinoo Mankad found spots on the wearing pitch and suddenly Sutcliffe, Reid, Noel McGregor and Noel Harford were back in the pavilion.

Tony MacGibbon and Harry Cave defended grimly for the last half-hour to save the game in which New Zealand had been so handily placed at the end of the second day.

41 INDIA v NEW ZEALAND *(Fifth Test)*

at Corporation Stadium, Madras on 6, 7, 8, 10, 11 January 1956
Toss : India. Umpires : A.R. Joshi and M.G. Vijayasarathi
India won by an innings and 109 runs

The tourists arrived in Madras determined to obtain victory in the last test of the series and thus share the rubber. That possibility became more distant when Harry Cave lost the toss and faced the prospect of bowling on a pitch that was heavily weighted in favour of the batting side.

Vinoo Mankad and the bespectacled Pankaj Roy, the Indian openers, batted throughout the first day, while the New Zealand attack struggled to make the ball bounce stump high. The tourists' fielding was generally efficient, and many runs were cut off, though Roy was dropped in the slips when he was 60 and the total 126.

At stumps, India was 234 without loss, Roy 114 and Mankad 109. John Reid maintained control before bruising a heel, which prevented him bowling again in the match.

The opening partnership was broken after eight hours batting when Matt Poore bowled Roy for 173. The partnership of 413 created a new world test record for the first wicket. Mankad was dismissed shortly afterwards for 231. India declared at the end of the second day for 537 for three.

New Zealand's only option was to occupy the crease for

INDIA

M.H.Mankad	c McMahon b Reid	25	c MacGibbon b Reid	17
N.J.Contractor	b Hayes	6	b Hayes	61
Pankaj Roy	b Hayes	28	lbw b Cave	100
V.L.Manjrekar	c Reid b Cave	1	c MacGibbon b Reid	90
P.R.Umrigar*	run out	1	b MacGibbon	15
G.S.Ramchand	b Reid	1	not out	106
J.M.Ghorpade	b Alabaster	39	c Sutcliffe b Cave	4
D.G.Phadkar	run out	0	b Hayes	17
C.T.Patankar†	b Reid	13	not out	1
G.R.Sunderam	not out	3		
S.P.Gupte	b Alabaster	4		
Extras	(b 4, lb 2, nb 5)	11	(b 9, lb 10, nb 8)	27
TOTAL (59.3 overs)		**132**	(209 overs) (7 wkts dec)	**438**

NEW ZEALAND

J.G.Leggat	c Patankar b Sunderam	8	c Mankad b Phadkar	7
B.Sutcliffe	c Patankar b Ramchand	25	lbw b Gupte	5
J.W.Guy	lbw b Gupte	91	b Phadkar	0
J.R.Reid	b Sunderam	120	(5) b Mankad	5
S.N.McGregor	b Gupte	6	(4) b Mankad	29
A.R.MacGibbon	st Patankar b Gupte	23	(7) not out	21
N.S.Harford	c Mankad b Ramchand	25	(6) c Phadkar b Gupte	1
H.B.Cave*	c Umrigar b Gupte	5	not out	4
J.C.Alabaster	c Patankar b Gupte	18		
J.A.Hayes	b Gupte	1		
T.G.McMahon†	not out	1		
Extras	(b 7, lb 3, nb 3)	13	(lb 2, nb 1)	3
TOTAL	(145.5 overs)	**336**	(34 overs) (6 wkts)	**75**

Bowling	O	M	R	W	O	M	R	W		Fall of Wickets			
NEW ZEALAND											I	NZ	I	NZ
											1st	1st	2nd	
Hayes	14	3	38	2	30	4	67	2		1st	13	25	40	8
MacGibbon	13	3	27	0	43	16	92	1		2nd	41	55	119	9
Cave	14	6	29	1	57	26	85	2		3rd	42	239	262	37
Reid	16	9	19	3	45	21	87	2		4th	47	255	287	42
Alabaster	2.3	0	8	2	27	7	52	0		5th	49	262	331	47
Sutcliffe					7	0	28	0		6th	87	300	370	55
INDIA										7th	88	310	424	-
Phadkar	35	9	76	0	4	1	11	2		8th	125	318	-	-
Sunderam	21	6	46	2	3	1	13	0		9th	125	333	-	-
Gupte	33.5	7	90	6	14	7	30	2		10th	132	336	-	-
Ramchand	37	15	64	2	1	0	4	0						
Mankad	1	0	9	0	12	8	14	2						
Ghorpade	1	0	17	0										
Umrigar	17	7	21	0										

three days and hold out for a draw. Although the wicket was showing some signs of wear, Bert Sutcliffe and Gordon Leggat were not unduly troubled by the Indian attack or the ring of close fieldsmen on the morning of the third day.

Once Leggat departed at 75, Reid joined Sutcliffe to carry the score to 109 when the left-hander was dismissed for 47 after 204 minutes of unusual restraint. Subhash Gupte found a spot to his liking and engineered a middle order collapse that swept away John Guy, Noel McGregor and Tony MacGibbon and left New Zealand 156-6.

With Johnny Hayes unable to bat because of a touch of fever, New Zealand was soon dismissed for 209, with Gupte increasing his tally to five wickets in the innings. India's stranglehold on the match was obvious, half of the 132 overs in the tourists' first innings had been maidens.

Leggat and Sutcliffe shrugged off any weary spirits as they began the follow-on, with Leggat, in particular, displaying admirable concentration as he batted his way through to stumps to be 61 not out in a total of 114-1.

India's remarkable all-rounder Mankad captured four wickets with his left-arm orthodox spin to go with his record innings as a right-hand batsman. Reid continued to bat bravely and, with Harry Cave, a desperate rearguard action produced 68 runs for the eighth wicket before Gupte had the final say capturing the last two wickets to give India victory by an innings and 109 runs.

INDIA

M.H.Mankad	c Cave b Moir	231
Pankaj Roy	b Poore	173
P.R.Umrigar*	not out	79
G.S.Ramchand	lbw b MacGibbon	21
V.L.Manjrekar	not out	0
A.G.Kripal Singh		
N.J.Contractor		
D.G.Phadkar		
N.S.Tamhane†		
J.M.Patel		
S.P.Gupte		
Extras	(b 18, lb 11, nb 4)	33
TOTAL	(177 overs) (3 wkts dec)	**537**

NEW ZEALAND

J.G.Leggat	lbw b Phadkar	31	c Tamhane b Mankad	61
B.Sutcliffe	c Umrigar b Patel	47	c & b Gupte	40
J.R.Reid	b Patel	44	(4) c Umrigar b Gupte	63
J.W.Guy	c Umrigar b Gupte	3	(3) st Tamhane b Gupte	9
S.N.McGregor	c Phadkar b Gupte	10	(6) c Gupte b Mankad	12
A.R.MacGibbon	c Phadkar b Gupte	0	(7) lbw b Patel	0
M.B.Poore	lbw b Gupte	15	(5) b Mankad	1
A.M.Moir	c Umrigar b Patel	30	c Ramchand b Mankad	1
H.B.Cave*	c Roy b Gupte	9	not out	22
T.G.McMahon†	not out	4	b Gupte	0
J.A.Hayes	absent ill		absent ill	
Extras	(b 4, lb 10, nb 2)	16	(b 1, lb 8, nb 1)	10
TOTAL	(132 overs)	**209**	(130.3 overs)	**219**

Bowling	O	M	R	W	O	M	R	W		Fall of Wickets			
NEW ZEALAND											I	NZ	NZ
											1st	1st	2nd
Hayes	31	2	94	0						1st	413	75	89
MacGibbon	38	9	97	1						2nd	449	109	114
Cave	44	16	94	0						3rd	537	121	116
Reid	7	3	10	0						4th	-	141	117
Moir	26	1	114	1						5th	-	144	147
Poore	31	5	95	1						6th	-	145	148
INDIA										7th	-	190	151
Phadkar	15	4	25	1	28	13	33	0		8th	-	201	219
Ramchand	4	3	1	0	8	5	10	0		9th	-	209	219
Gupte	49	26	72	5	36.3	14	73	4		10th	-	-	-
Patel	45	23	63	3	18	7	28	1					
Mankad	19	10	32	0	40	14	65	4					

John Guy, the non-striking batsman, watches Bert Sutcliffe drive Subhash Gupte on the off-side. Fielding at leg-gully is Kripal Singh. The wicketkeeper is Narendra Tamhane who fashioned an amazing record, claiming 16 stumpings in the 21 tests that he played.

MILESTONES

- Vinoo Mankad and Pankaj Roy created a new world test record of 413 for the first wicket.

- Mankad's score of 231 was the highest made for India in a test match.

- India's total of 537 was their highest in test cricket.

- Subhash Gupte, in capturing 34 wickets, equalled the Indian record for the most wickets in a series.

- Bert Sutcliffe's series aggregate of 611 runs was a New Zealand test record.

AVERAGES

New Zealand

BATTING	M	I	NO	Runs	HS	Ave
B. Sutcliffe	5	9	2	611	230*	87.28
J.R. Reid	5	9	2	493	120	70.42
J.G. Leggat	3	6	1	194	61	38.80
J.W. Guy	5	10	1	313	102	34.77
A.R. MacGibbon	5	7	1	173	59	28.83
S.N. McGregor	4	6	0	125	49	20.83
H.B. Cave	5	7	2	87	22*	17.40
A.M. Moir	2	4	0	59	30	14.75
P.G.Z. Harris	1	2	0	26	19	13.00
J.C. Alabaster	4	4	0	49	18	12.25
M.B. Poore	4	5	0	56	23	11.20
N.S. Harford	2	3	0	30	25	10.00
E.C. Petrie	2	4	0	27	15	6.75
T.G. McMahon	3	3	2	5	4*	5.00
J.A. Hayes	5	4	3	2	1*	2.00

BOWLING	O	M	R	W	Ave
J.R. Reid	128	50	271	6	45.16
J.A. Hayes	171	27	474	10	47.40
M.B. Poore	74	14	206	4	51.50
H.B. Cave	254	119	412	7	58.85
A.R. MacGibbon	220	65	495	7	70.71
J.C. Alabaster	114.3	25	329	2	164.50
A.M. Moir	38	3	165	1	165.00
B. Sutcliffe	21	1	81	0	-

India

BATTING	M	I	NO	Runs	HS	Ave
M.H. Mankad	4	5	0	526	231	105.20
A.G. Kripal Singh	4	3	1	199	100*	99.50
V.L. Manjrekar	5	6	1	386	177	77.20
P. Roy	3	4	0	301	173	75.25
P.R. Umrigar	5	6	1	351	223	70.20
G.S. Ramchand	5	6	2	234	106*	58.50
P. Bhandari	1	1	0	39	39	39.00
N.J. Contractor	4	4	0	145	62	36.25
D.G. Phadkar	4	3	1	54	37*	27.00
J.M. Ghorpade	1	2	0	43	39	21.50
V.L. Mehra	2	2	0	42	32	21.00
C.T. Patankar	1	2	1	14	13	14.00
N.S. Tamhane	4	1	0	10	10	10.00
S.P. Gupte	5	1	0	4	4	4.00
R.G. Nadkarni	1	1	1	68	68*	-
S.R. Patil	1	1	1	14	14*	-
G.R. Sunderam	2	1	1	3	3*	-
Ghulam Ahmed	1	-	-	-	-	-
J.M. Patel	1	-	-	-	-	-
V.N. Swamy	1	-	-	-	-	-

BOWLING	O	M	R	W	Ave
V.L. Manjrekar	20	13	16	1	16.00
S.P. Gupte	356.4	152	669	34	19.67
J.M. Patel	63	30	91	4	22.75
S.R. Patil	23	7	51	2	25.50
M.H. Mankad	167.1	66	329	12	27.41
D.G. Phadkar	153	57	261	6	43.50
G.S. Ramchand	162	72	276	5	55.20
G.R. Sunderam	66	12	166	3	55.33
Ghulam Ahmed	52	17	92	1	92.00
V.L. Mehra	3	0	3	0	-
A.G. Kripal Singh	8	3	15	0	-
N.J. Contractor	6	1	17	0	-
J.M. Ghorpade	1	0	17	0	-
P.R. Umrigar	21	11	21	0	-
P. Bhandari	13	2	39	0	-
V.N. Swamy	18	5	45	0	-
R.G. Nadkarni	57	14	142	0	-

1955/56 West Indies in New Zealand

While New Zealand were playing their final games in India, the West Indies had arrived in New Zealand and before the first test had beaten Auckland, Waikato and Southland comfortably and had the better of a match against Canterbury.

42 NEW ZEALAND v WEST INDIES *(First Test)*

at Carisbrook, Dunedin on 3, 4, 6 February, 1956
Toss : New Zealand. Umpires : L.G. Clark and A.E. Jelley
West Indies won by an innings and 71 runs

The apparent good state of the Carisbrook wicket encouraged Harry Cave to bat first in fine conditions. However, at least one ball an over would scuttle through barely above ground level and the occasional delivery flew from a good length.

The left-handers, Bert Sutcliffe and John Guy, were struck on their bodies several times during a hostile spell from Frank King. The spin twins, Sonny Ramadhin and Alf Valentine, had immediate success and ran through weak New Zealand batting. Ramadhin finished with 6-23 and New Zealand's innings ended at 74, made in less than three hours.

The wicket appeared to have settled down considerably when the tourists began batting. The slow left-arm spin bowler Allen Lissette's first half-dozen overs in test cricket yielded the wicket of Allie Binns. West Indies were 72-3 when Everton Weekes and Collie Smith came together.

As the bowlers flagged the run-rate accelerated; at one stage 83 runs flowed in 45 minutes. Weekes raced to his third successive century on tour in 132 minutes. He and Smith put on 162 in 112 minutes. At stumps West Indies were 234-3.

Within quarter of an hour of the start of the second day Weekes, Smith and Denis Atkinson had departed for the addition of only two runs. Facing the second new ball, John Goddard and Ramadhin added 75 runs and the innings ended at 353. Cave was the best of the New Zealand bowlers, combining a tight line with late movement. Bob Blair was the most successful with four wickets, but he had been expensive.

West Indies' spinners were quickly introduced in New Zealand's second innings. Sutcliffe countered them with accomplished footwork and had made 48 of the opening partnership of 61 before he went. Ramadhin captured his 100th wicket in tests when he had Gordon Leggat leg-before.

In the last gloomy half-hour of a bleak day, John Beck adopted a policy of attack and chanced his arm by relying on pull shots to mid-wicket. Alec Moir, his partner, was equally belligerent and the day ended at 158 for six.

Rain delayed the start of the third day for over an hour and Beck and Moir carried their partnership to 90 runs. The match concluded with a day and a half to spare when Ramadhin captured his ninth wicket of the game.

NEW ZEALAND

B.Sutcliffe	b Valentine	9	c Binns b Valentine	48
J.G.Leggat	c Sobers b Atkinson	3	lbw b Ramadhin	17
J.W.Guy	c Goddard b Ramadhin	23	st Binns b Smith	0
J.R.Reid	b Ramadhin	10	run out	23
S.N.McGregor	run out	0	b Smith	11
J.E.F.Beck	b Valentine	7	lbw b Atkinson	66
R.W.Blair	c Binns b Ramadhin	0	c Depeiaza b Smith	0
A.M.Moir	not out	15	c Binns b Ramadhin	20
H.B.Cave*	b Ramadhin	0	c Pairaudeau b Valentine	0
T.G.McMahon†	c Binns b Ramadhin	0	b Ramadhin	2
A.F.Lissette	lbw b Ramadhin	0	not out	1
Extras	(b 5, lb 2)	7	(b 19, lb 1)	20
TOTAL	(62.2 overs)	**74**	(110.2 overs)	**208**

WEST INDIES

B.H.Pairaudeau	c Lissette b Blair	0
A.P.Binns†	b Lissette	10
G.St A.Sobers	run out	27
E.D.Weekes	c McMahon b Cave	123
O.G.Smith	b Blair	64
D.St E.Atkinson*	c McMahon b Cave	0
C.C.Depeiaza	b Lissette	14
J.D.C.Goddard	not out	48
S.Ramadhin	b Blair	44
A.L.Valentine	lbw b Blair	2
F.M.King	absent hurt	
Extras	(b 9, lb 10, nb 2)	21
TOTAL	(112.5 overs)	**353**

Bowling	O	M	R	W	O	M	R	W
WEST INDIES								
King	8	2	11	0				
Atkinson	7	5	2	1	13	5	25	1
Depeiaza	2	0	3	0	3	0	12	0
Valentine	24	13	28	2	36	17	51	2
Ramadhin	21.2	13	23	6	36.2	17	58	3
Smith					18	7	42	3
Sobers					4	4	0	0
NEW ZEALAND	O							
Blair	22.5	5	90	4				
Cave	26	12	47	2				
Reid	17	3	43	0				
Lissette	28	11	73	2				
Moir	19	3	79	0				

Fall of Wickets	NZ	WI	NZ
	1st	1st	2nd
1st	3	0	61
2nd	36	30	65
3rd	36	72	73
4th	43	234	108
5th	54	234	108
6th	54	236	108
7th	54	272	198
8th	62	347	201
9th	70	353	207
10th	74	-	208

The inventive brilliance of left-hand batsman John Beck is exhibited as he attacks the visitors' spinners, scoring 66 in 81 minutes in an entertaining end to the game.

MILESTONES

- Allen Lissette (77) made his test debut.

43 NEW ZEALAND v WEST INDIES *(Second Test)*

at Lancaster Park, Christchurch on 18, 20, 21 February, 1956
Toss : West Indies. Umpires : J. Cowie and W.J.C. Gwynne
West Indies won by an innings and 64 runs

Sam Guillen, former West Indies test wicketkeeper, had been living in New Zealand and playing for Canterbury but was some months short of the four-year residential qualification. New Zealand sought permission from the Imperial Cricket Conference and the West Indian Board to include him in their team. It was granted and he was selected for the second test. Harry Cave was incapacitated and John Reid was appointed New Zealand's captain for the first time in a test match.

A little early life in the Lancaster Park wicket saw the top order of the visitors struggling, except for Everton Weekes. His fifth century in as many first-class innings was completed in 142 minutes and included 16 boundaries. When he was dismissed for 103 his team was 169-6.

The advantage of the middle order breakthrough was squandered by some loose bowling which allowed John Goddard and Denis Atkinson to survive until tea; 203-6. The pair were severe on the new ball attack in the last session and the partnership was worth 143 before Reid held a fine caught-and-bowled chance from Atkinson; 349-7 at stumps.

Goddard was unbeaten on 83 when the last wicket fell at 386 on the second morning. Rain stopped play in the early afternoon. After an early tea the weather cleared and the spinners again mesmerised the local batsman. At stumps, New Zealand was languishing at 93-5.

The West Indian slow bowlers, Sonny Ramadhin, Collie Smith and Alf Valentine claimed 15 wickets on the third day as New Zealand was bundled out for 158 in its first innings and 164 following on. One of the few batsmen to emerge with credit was Tony MacGibbon who scored 31 not out and 34.

Calamity struck at the heart of the middle order as the score went from 115-3 to 121-8 as five wickets added only six runs. This sorry day might have concluded earlier than 4.25 pm if the West Indian wicketkeeper Clairmonte Depeiaza, had not missed several catches and stumpings.

So far in the series, the home batsmen had shown an almost complete ineptitude against spin bowling. In the first two tests, Ramadhin, Smith and Valentine had taken 35 of the 40 wickets that had fallen.

WEST INDIES

H.A.Furlonge	lbw b Blair	0
B.H.Pairaudeau	b Reid	13
G.St A.Sobers	b Lissette	25
E.D.Weekes	b Sinclair	103
O.G.Smith	c Reid b MacGibbon	11
C.C.Depeiaza†	b Reid	4
D.St E.Atkinson*	c & b Reid	85
J.D.C.Goddard	not out	83
S.Ramadhin	b MacGibbon	33
D.T.Dewdney	run out	3
A.L.Valentine	run out	1
Extras	(b 9, lb 8, w 1, nb 7)	25
TOTAL	**(136.5 overs)**	**386**

NEW ZEALAND

B.Sutcliffe	st Depeiaza b Ramadhin	26	st Depeiaza b Smith	10
S.N.McGregor	b Dewdney	19	c Depeiaza b Valentine	17
L.S.M.Miller	c Goddard b Ramadhin	7	c Weekes b Ramadhin	31
J.R.Reid*	b Valentine	28	(5) b Smith	40
J.W.Guy	c & b Ramadhin	3	(6) b Valentine	4
J.E.F.Beck	lbw b Ramadhin	4	(4) st Depeiaza b Smith	13
S.C.Guillen†	b Valentine	15	c & b Smith	0
A.R.MacGibbon	not out	31	hit wicket b Valentine	34
I.M.Sinclair	b Ramadhin	7	c Goddard b Valentine	0
R.W.Blair	b Smith	2	c Sobers b Valentine	9
A.F.Lissette	b Smith	0	not out	1
Extras	(b 14, lb 2)	16	(b 4, lb 1)	5
TOTAL	**(75.5 overs)**	**158**	**(60.4 overs)**	**164**

Bowling	O	M	R	W	O	M	R	W		Fall of Wickets			
NEW ZEALAND											WI	NZ	NZ
Blair	27	5	66	1							1st	1st	2nd
MacGibbon	33	9	81	2						1st	0	39	22
Reid	24	7	68	3						2nd	28	50	62
Lissette	20	5	51	1						3rd	72	67	62
Sinclair	30.5	9	79	1						4th	109	85	115
Sutcliffe	2	0	16	0						5th	163	90	120
WEST INDIES										6th	169	113	120
Dewdney	16	5	31	1	8	2	20	0		7th	312	121	120
Atkinson	10	3	16	0	3	0	6	0		8th	361	140	121
Ramadhin	26	10	46	5	9	1	26	1		9th	368	156	133
Valentine	22	9	48	2	22.4	11	32	5		10th	386	158	164
Smith	1.5	1	1	2	18	4	75	4					

MILESTONES

- Sam Guillen (78) and Ian Sinclair (79) made their debuts. Guillen had previously played for West Indies.

- John Reid captained New Zealand for the first time in a test.

- Sam Guillen became the eleventh player to represent two countries in test cricket.

- Everton Weekes became the third player, after Don Bradman and C.B. Fry to score five hundreds in consecutive innings.

An aerial view of Lancaster Park, the venue for the second test, with six Operation Deep Freeze Globemasters flying over. On the right are the gasworks and the railyards. The Port Hills are in the background.

44 NEW ZEALAND v WEST INDIES *(Third Test)*

at Basin Reserve, Wellington on 3, 5, 6, 7 March, 1956
Toss : West Indies. Umpires : L.G. Clark and W.J.C. Gwynne
West Indies won by 9 wickets

The New Zealand Cricket Council broke with tradition by requesting Merv Wallace to assist the team's preparation for the remaining two tests. This was the first time a coach had been appointed for a New Zealand team.

The first day of this test ended on a familiar note, with New Zealand having missed vital chances and now facing a difficult struggle just to save the game. The New Zealand bowlers were both lively and accurate, but several fielding errors frustrated their efforts. Bruce Pairaudeau and John Goddard resumed after lunch, at 96 for one, and a mix-up saw both batsmen stranded at the striker's end. Appalling fielding allowed both batsmen to survive.

Soon, three wickets fell for two runs; 119-4 and New Zealand had seized the initiative. Everton Weekes had scored three when Harry Cave induced an edge for a straightforward catch to Don Beard in the slips, who dropped it.

The West Indian captain, Denis Atkinson, added 120 with Weekes for the fifth wicket, and after he was dismissed a further run out opportunity was missed which saw Allie Binns and Weekes add another 106 in little more than an hour. For the third time in three tests Weekes was sublime in scoring another century in 133 minutes and the tourists were comfortably placed at 361-6.

The last West Indian wicket fell at 404 on the second morning. By lunch New Zealand had lost three wickets for 28 runs. When John Reid fell at the same score, the home team's chances of surviving for even three days looked forlorn. Don Taylor and John Beck carried the score to 104 before Taylor was run out.

New Zealand was all out for 208 before lunch on the third day with Beck's 55 runs in 279 minutes being unable to prevent New Zealand being asked to follow-on for the third consecutive test. Atkinson, bowling into a fresh breeze, flummoxed the home team's middle order with swing and variation of pace combined with sharp movement off the wicket.

From 141-5 overnight, New Zealand lost two more wickets while one run was scored. Taylor was ninth out for 77, scored in 155 minutes. For the second time in the game New Zealand were dismissed for 208 (the third such total achieved by New Zealand in six innings).

MILESTONES

• Trevor Barber (80) made his test debut.

• Everton Weekes broke Bert Sutcliffe's record aggregate for a New Zealand season.

WEST INDIES

Batsman	Dismissal	R	2nd innings	R
B.H.Pairaudeau	c MacGibbon b Cave	68	c Sinclair b MacGibbon	8
G.St A.Sobers	c Barber b Reid	27		
J.D.C.Goddard	c Beard b MacGibbon	16	not out	0
E.D.Weekes	c Guillen b Cave	156		
O.G.Smith	lbw b MacGibbon	1		
D.St E.Atkinson*	run out	60		
A.P.Binns†	lbw b Beard	27	(2) not out	5
S.Ramadhin	c Beard b Reid	15		
F.M.King	not out	13		
D.T.Dewdney	run out	2		
A.L.Valentine	c McGregor b Reid	2		
Extras	(b 9, lb 3, nb 5)	17		0
TOTAL	(135.5 overs)	**404**	(5.2 overs) (1 wkt)	**13**

NEW ZEALAND

Batsman	Dismissal	R	2nd innings	R
L.S.M.Miller	c & b King	16	c Binns b Dewdney	7
S.N.McGregor	c Weekes b Smith	5	c Binns b Atkinson	41
A.R.MacGibbon	c Goddard b Valentine	3	b Atkinson	36
D.D.Taylor	run out	43	c Pairaudeau b Atkinson	77
J.R.Reid*	b Ramadhin	1	b Atkinson	5
J.E.F.Beck	lbw b Sobers	55	b Smith	6
R.T.Barber	b Ramadhin	12	c Goddard b Ramadhin	5
S.C.Guillen†	b Smith	36	c Goddard b Dewdney	0
D.D.Beard	not out	17	c Binns b Atkinson	5
H.B.Cave	b Atkinson	0	c & b Sobers	5
I.M.Sinclair	lbw b Atkinson	0	not out	18
Extras	(b 11, lb 9)	20	(b 2, nb 1)	3
TOTAL	(140 overs)	**208**	(106.5 overs)	**208**

Bowling

NEW ZEALAND	O	M	R	W	O	M	R	W
MacGibbon	24	4	75	2	3	1	6	1
Cave	37	10	96	2				
Beard	34	9	90	1	2.2	0	7	0
Reid	32.5	8	85	3				
Sinclair	8	0	41	0				
WEST INDIES								
Dewdney	11	3	26	0	17	3	54	2
King	8.4	3	18	1				
Smith	29	15	27	2	14	7	23	1
Ramadhin	30	11	63	2	21	10	33	1
Valentine	35	20	31	1	15	9	18	0
Atkinson	12.2	2	20	2	31	12	66	5
Sobers	14	11	3	1	8.5	4	11	1

Fall of Wickets

	WI	NZ	NZ	WI
	1st	1st	2nd	2nd
1st	72	23	16	12
2nd	117	23	82	-
3rd	117	27	93	-
4th	119	28	99	-
5th	239	104	121	-
6th	345	116	141	-
7th	387	176	142	-
8th	387	205	180	-
9th	391	208	185	-
10th	404	208	208	-

Don Taylor hooks unsuccessfully at Tom Dewdney. John Reid, the nonstriking batsman, watches the ball sail through to Allie Binns.

45 NEW ZEALAND v WEST INDIES *(Fourth Test)*

at Eden Park, Auckland on 9, 10, 12, 13 March, 1956
Toss : New Zealand. Umpires : J.C. Harris and T.M. Pearce
New Zealand won by 190 runs

Few of the 8000 people present on the first day of this test would have harboured premonitions of history in the making as the New Zealand batsmen again struggled in the opening session.

John Reid had ended the home team's run of bad luck with the toss but Noel McGregor and Tony MacGibbon were dismissed by lunch; 48-2. John Beck and Reid came together with the score at 87-4. While the New Zealand captain was circumspect against the good ball, his quick eye allowed him to pick up loose deliveries and dispatch these with uninhibited power.

Beck had scored only a handful of runs in a cautious hour before tea but he, too, unleashed a number of free strokes as the partnership scurried along to a hundred in 121 minutes. His innings ended four runs later, when Gary Sobers brilliantly caught him. The fifth wicket stand was the best produced yet in the series by the home team. Bad light stopped play 40 minutes early; 203-6 with Reid unbeaten on 82.

Rain and bad light restricted play on the second day to a little more than four hours, during which time 148 runs were scored. Nevertheless, it was an absorbing battle. After a brief interruption because of rain, Reid played back on the damp wicket, his foot slipped, and his heel barely touched the stumps. However, the bails fell and he was out for 84. Another shower sent the players from the field, and when play resumed, Tom Dewdney captured the last three wickets to finish with 5-21 off 19.5 overs.

The home team's pace attack dominated West Indies' top order. Harry Cave's lively in-swingers and the accurate speed of Tony MacGibbon troubled all the batsmen. New Zealand enjoyed a definite advantage for the first time in the series. When MacGibbon achieved the seemingly impossible feat of finding the edge of Everton Weekes' bat, three wickets were down for 46. Hammond Furlonge played a watchful innings and was unbeaten at stumps with the score 96-5.

After the rest day rain prevented a resumption until after lunch on the third day. Slowly, West Indies carried their score to 139, when Furlonge was caught behind off Cave for 64. Following another break for a shower, Cave captured the last two wickets to end with his best figures at test level of four for 22 off 28 overs. MacGibbon also achieved his best figures at test level, with four for 44 off 21 overs.

The last five West Indies wickets had tumbled for six runs; it was the first time in many years that the New Zealand field had accepted every catch and the reward was a healthy lead of 110.

Denis Atkinson sought to restrict the New Zealand top order in the less than two hours remaining on the third day

and when Lawrie Miller was dismissed off the last ball of the day New Zealand were 61 for two. When the sixth New Zealand wicket fell at 101, Atkinson, in a single-handed attempt to save his team's honour, had captured all six for 39 runs. He had pitched the ball just short of a length and been able to cut it back sharply from the off.

The obvious policy for New Zealand was to score quick runs and set a reasonable target for the afternoon. Atkinson's tight attack had made runs difficult to come by, until Sam Guillen made 41 out of 46 in better than even time, enabling Reid to declare at 157-9 at lunch.

Set a target of 268 to win in the last two sessions the visitors were immediately placed on the defensive when Cave bowled Bruce Pairaudeau, with his first ball. Stunning catches by MacGibbon and Murray Chapple, and Collie Smith being bowled by Cave had alarm bells ringing. Sobers was run out and Alphonso Roberts was bowled by Don Beard to have the West Indies 22-6 after the innings had been in progress for 40 minutes.

In the next hour, Everton Weekes and Allie Binns put on 46 runs as the New Zealanders sought in vain for another breakthrough. The anxious spectators kept one eye on the desperate struggle taking place in the middle, and another on the threatening bank of clouds.

Leg-spinner, Jack Alabaster was now brought on. His second delivery was short and wide and Weekes swung the

NEW ZEALAND					
S.N.McGregor	c Smith b Dewdney	2	c Binns b Atkinson		5
L.S.M.Miller	c Weekes b Valentine	47	c Weekes b Atkinson		25
A.R.MacGibbon	b Smith	9	c Weekes b Atkinson		35
D.D.Taylor	lbw b Valentine	11	c Valentine b Atkinson		16
J.R.Reid*	hit wicket b Dewdney	84	c Binns b Atkinson		12
J.E.F.Beck	c Sobers b Ramadhin	38	lbw b Atkinson		2
S.C.Guillen†	run out	6	st Binns b Valentine		41
M.E.Chapple	c Atkinson b Dewdney	3	lbw b Ramadhin		1
D.D.Beard	c Binns b Dewdney	31	not out		6
H.B.Cave	c Smith b Dewdney	11	(11) not out		0
J.C.Alabaster	not out	1	(10) b Atkinson		5
Extras	(b 7, lb 5)	12	(b 4, lb 5)		9
TOTAL	(166.5 overs)	**255**	(80 overs) (9 wkts dec)		**157**

WEST INDIES				
H.A.Furlonge	c Guillen b Cave	64	c MacGibbon b Beard	3
B.H.Pairaudeau	c MacGibbon b Cave	9	b Cave	3
G.St A.Sobers	c Guillen b MacGibbon	1	(6) run out	1
E.D.Weekes	c Guillen b MacGibbon	5	c McGregor b Alabaster	31
O.G.Smith	b Beard	2	b Cave	0
D.St E.Atkinson*	b Reid	28	(3) c Chapple b Cave	10
A.T.Roberts	b MacGibbon	28	b Beard	0
A.P.Binns†	lbw b MacGibbon	0	b Alabaster	20
S.Ramadhin	b Cave	3	c Miller b Beard	0
A.L.Valentine	c Taylor b Cave	0	st Guillen b Cave	5
D.T.Dewdney	not out	0	not out	4
Extras	(b 1, lb 3, nb 1)	5		0
TOTAL	(78.3 overs)	**145**	(45.1 overs)	**77**

Bowling	O	M	R	W	O	M	R	W
NEW ZEALAND								
Dewdney	19.5	11	21	5	12	5	22	0
Atkinson	32	14	45	0	40	21	53	7
Valentine	41	20	46	2	6	0	29	1
Ramadhin	23	8	41	1	18	6	26	1
Smith	31	19	55	1	4	0	18	0
Sobers	20	7	35	0				
NEW ZEALAND								
MacGibbon	21	5	44	4	6	1	16	0
Cave	27.3	17	22	4	13.1	9	21	4
Reid	18	5	48	1	6	2	14	0
Beard	9	4	20	1	15	7	22	3
Alabaster	3	1	6	0	5	4	4	2

Fall of Wickets				
	WI	NZ	NZ	WI
	1st	1st	2nd	2nd
1st	9	25	14	4
2nd	45	32	61	16
3rd	66	46	66	16
4th	87	59	91	16
5th	191	94	100	18
6th	203	139	101	22
7th	205	140	109	68
8th	210	145	146	68
9th	250	145	155	68
10th	255	145	-	77

bat in a violent hook shot. He connected with the bottom of the bat and the ball looped lazily out to the square-leg boundary where Noel McGregor, who had suffered a wretched game as an opening batsman, redeemed himself with a vital catch; 68-7. Tea was taken with the score at 77-9.

As news of the afternoon's drama spread around Auckland people abandoned workplaces and rushed to Eden Park to what must surely be New Zealand's first test victory after 26 years of earnest, but often humiliating endeavour. The crowd seethed with excitement during the break and then settled down to watch the last rites being administered.

Beard bowled a maiden over to Dewdney then Cave's first ball tempted Valentine to stretch forward and Guillen completed a splendid stumping. The fieldsmen swooped in to souvenir the stumps. People engulfed the ground, thumping the back of the instant heroes and offering cheers for Reid and Atkinson.

Torrents of praise inundated the New Zealanders. Denis Atkinson declared his opponents "the finest bunch of fellows we have ever played against." The England captain, Peter May, was reported as saying "without being unkind to the West Indies, I am delighted. The New Zealanders have been magnificent losers, and they richly deserve their success."

Writing in the London *Daily Mail* Alex Bannister offered a toast to "those grand sportsmen – the New Zealand cricketers". Bannister wished the New Zealanders many more test successes – but not too many over England.

After the celebrations had died down Reid said it was imperative that Merv Wallace be included as a player in the team to visit England. "A team of experienced players, with the levelling of youth, should be taken on the tour." Reid added that he would be happy to serve under Wallace who had "succeeded in inspiring confidence in the players' own abilities. His knowledge of the game exceeded that of anybody else in New Zealand."

MILESTONES

- New Zealand achieved their first test victory in their 45th game.

- In his 100th first-class game John Reid not only made the highest New Zealand score of the series but became New Zealand's first captain to win a test match.

- West Indies' total of 77 was their lowest score in a test.

The moment of victory at Eden Park, 1956. Every player wants a piece of history at the fall of the last wicket. From left, John Reid, Murray Chapple, Sam Guillen and Don Taylor. The last batsman dismissed, Alf Valentine, is caught up in the joy of New Zealand's first test victory after 45 tests.

AVERAGES

New Zealand

BATTING

BATTING	M	I	NO	Runs	HS	Ave
D.D. Taylor	2	4	0	147	77	36.75
A.M. Moir	1	2	1	35	20	35.00
A.R. MacGibbon	3	6	1	148	36	29.60
D.D. Beard	2	4	2	59	31	29.50
J.R. Reid	4	8	0	203	84	25.37
J.E.F. Beck	4	8	0	191	66	23.87
B. Sutcliffe	2	4	0	93	48	23.25
L.S.M. Miller	3	6	0	133	47	22.16
S.C. Guillen	3	6	0	98	41	16.33
S.N. McGregor	4	8	0	100	41	12.50
J.G. Leggat	1	2	0	20	17	10.00
R.T. Barber	1	2	0	17	12	8.50
I.M. Sinclair	2	4	1	25	18*	8.33
J.W. Guy	2	4	0	30	23	7.50
J.C. Alabaster	1	2	1	6	5	6.00
H.B. Cave	3	6	1	16	11	3.20
R.W. Blair	2	4	0	11	9	2.75
M.E. Chapple	1	2	0	4	3	2.00
A.F. Lissette	2	4	2	2	1*	1.00
T.G. McMahon	1	2	0	2	2	1.00

BOWLING

BOWLING	O	M	R	W	Ave
J.C. Alabaster	8	5	10	2	5.00
H.B. Cave	103.4	48	186	12	15.50
A.R. MacGibbon	87	20	222	9	24.66
D.D. Beard	60.2	20	139	5	27.80
R.W. Blair	49.5	10	156	5	31.20
J.R. Reid	97.5	25	258	7	36.85
A.F. Lissette	48	16	124	3	41.33
I.M. Sinclair	38.5	9	120	1	120.00
B. Sutcliffe	2	0	16	0	-
A.M. Moir	19	3	79	0	-

West Indies

BATTING

BATTING	M	I	NO	Runs	HS	Ave
J.D.C. Goddard	3	4	3	147	83*	147.00
E.D. Weekes	4	5	0	418	156	83.60
D.St E. Atkinson	4	5	0	183	85	36.60
H.A. Furlonge	2	3	0	67	64	22.33
S. Ramadhin	4	5	0	95	44	19.00
B.H. Pairaudeau	4	6	0	101	68	16.83
G.St A. Sobers	4	5	0	81	27	16.20
O.G. Smith	4	5	0	78	64	15.60
A.P. Binns	3	5	1	62	27	15.50
A.T. Roberts	1	2	0	28	28	14.00
C.C. Depeiaza	2	2	0	18	14	9.00
D.T. Dewdney	3	4	2	9	4*	4.50
A.L. Valentine	4	5	0	10	5	2.00
F.M. King	2	1	1	13	13*	-

BOWLING

BOWLING	O	M	R	W	Ave
D.St E. Atkinson	148.2	62	233	16	14.56
S. Ramadhin	184.4	76	316	20	15.80
O.G. Smith	115.5	53	241	13	18.53
A.L. Valentine	201.4	99	283	15	18.86
D.T. Dewdney	83.5	29	174	8	21.75
G.St A. Sobers	46.5	26	49	2	24.50
F.M. King	16.4	5	29	1	29.00

The victorious 1956 New Zealand team. Back row (from left): Gordon Burgess (manager), Jack Alabaster, Harry Cave, Tony MacGibbon, Don Beard, Sam Guillen, Lawrie Miller, Merv Wallace (coach). Front: Ian Sinclair, Murray Chapple, Don Taylor, John Reid (captain), John Beck, Noel McGregor.

1958 New Zealand in England

Because of their improved performances in test cricket the fifth New Zealand team to tour England were awarded five five-day tests. Some New Zealand critics were despondent with the dismal batting and slovenly fielding that had been exhibited in the Plunket Shield series.

John Reid, the captain, suggested seasoned players such as Murray Chapple, John Guy, Noel McGregor and Don Taylor were more suitable candidates than some of the youngsters chosen for the tour. He was also upset that Merv Wallace had not been selected, either as a player or the coach.

England reigned supreme in the cricket world in the late 1950s. In the previous seven years they had won 27 of 57 tests, lost only 11 and had not been beaten in any series.

On the eve of the first test, New Zealand's tour record of six wins, three draws and a loss had been bettered only by the 1948 and 1953 Australians of the 12 teams that had visited England since the war.

New Zealand's success was largely due to its fine seam bowling attack and the all-round skills and maturing captaincy of Reid. Heavy rain in Birmingham prevented any net practice prior to the test.

46 ENGLAND v NEW ZEALAND (First Test)

at Edgbaston, Birmingham on 5, 6, 7, 9 June, 1958
Toss : England. Umpires : J.S. Buller and C.S. Elliott
England won by 205 runs

The New Zealanders surprised everyone, themselves included, by disposing of the much-vaunted England batting line-up for 221 runs before tea on the first day. Tony MacGibbon's opening delivery was a wide down the leg side, which went for four but he then dismissed both England openers, leg-before-wicket. England were 29-3 when Peter May became associated with Colin Cowdrey in restoring England's fortunes.

The previous season they had shared a world record test partnership of 411 runs against the West Indies on the same ground but this time they were restricted to 121 before May, shaping to drive a MacGibbon outswinger, only succeeded in getting an edge to be caught by Eric Petrie.

MacGibbon claimed his first five-wicket bag in test cricket while Jack Alabaster benefited from some rash shots played by the tailenders and finished with 4-46. Against the world's most potent bowling attack New Zealand ended the day 41-3.

Fred Trueman was at his best in favourable conditions the next day. Some deliveries reared up at batsmen, others shot along the ground. He kept his opponents guessing with subtle changes of pace and swing. Six wickets fell during the morning for the addition of only 32 runs.

Jack D'Arcy survived for more than two hours in scoring 19 runs. The largest partnership was worth 26 runs made by Harry Cave and John Hayes for the last wicket, which carried New Zealand beyond the follow-on threat.

Once again England lost early wickets and Peter Richardson, who had flashed dangerously at rising balls, was rather fortuitous to still be at the wicket having scored 71 of England's total of 131-3.

Between showers the biggest crowd yet on the tour, 25,000, saw Richardson dismissed for 100 while Cowdrey scored another competent 70 before May declared at 215-6, a lead of 342. MacGibbon's 3-41 gave him eight wickets for the match. New Zealand were 69-4 at the close.

The game was quickly wrapped up on the fourth day, with only MacGibbon, scoring 26 in 95 minutes, resisting the versatile attack. E. M. Wellings, correspondent for the *Evening News*, doubted that any team would have done "materially better" than the New Zealanders: "It is nothing new to see international sides tumbling before English test bowlers in conditions that cater for their exceptional skill."

ENGLAND

P.E.Richardson	lbw b MacGibbon	4	c Cave b MacGibbon	100
M.J.K.Smith	lbw b MacGibbon	0	c Petrie b MacGibbon	7
T.W.Graveney	c Alabaster b Hayes	7	c Petrie b Cave	19
P.B.H.May*	c Petrie b MacGibbon	84	c Petrie b MacGibbon	11
M.C.Cowdrey	b MacGibbon	81	c Reid b Hayes	70
T.E.Bailey	c Petrie b Alabaster	2	not out	6
T.G.Evans†	c Petrie b MacGibbon	2	c Reid b Cave	0
G.A.R.Lock	lbw b Alabaster	4		
F.S.Trueman	b Alabaster	0		
J.C.Laker	not out	11		
P.J.Loader	b Alabaster	17		
Extras	(lb 3, w 4, nb 2)	9	(b 1, lb 1)	2
TOTAL	**(75.5 overs)**	**221**	**(96.2 overs) (6 wkts dec)**	**215**

NEW ZEALAND

L.S.M.Miller	lbw b Trueman	7	b Trueman	8
J.W.D'Arcy	c Evans b Trueman	19	c Trueman b Loader	25
N.S.Harford	b Bailey	9	(4) c Graveney b Loader	23
J.R.Reid*	b Bailey	7	(6) b Bailey	13
W.R.Playle	b Trueman	4	(3) c Bailey b Loader	8
T.Meale	lbw b Trueman	7	(5) c Smith b Lock	10
A.R.MacGibbon	c Evans b Laker	5	(8) c Cowdrey b Laker	26
E.C.Petrie†	lbw b Loader	1	(10) not out	5
J.C.Alabaster	b Trueman	9	c Laker b Lock	11
H.B.Cave	not out	12	(7) b Bailey	1
J.A.Hayes	run out	14	c Bailey b Lock	5
Extras		0	(lb 1, w 1)	2
TOTAL	**(69.3 overs)**	**94**	**(77.3 overs)**	**137**

Bowling NEW ZEALAND	O	M	R	W	O	M	R	W
Hayes	15	2	57	1	20	3	51	1
MacGibbon	27	11	64	5	24	8	41	3
Cave	12	2	29	0	28.2	9	70	2
Reid	6	3	16	0	9	2	18	0
Alabaster	15.5	4	46	4	15	7	33	0
ENGLAND								
Trueman	21	8	31	5	17	5	33	1
Loader	21.3	6	37	1	23	11	40	3
Bailey	20	9	17	2	20	9	23	2
Lock	2	2	0	0	8.3	3	25	3
Laker	5	2	9	1	9	4	14	1

Fall of Wickets	E 1st	NZ 1st	E 2nd	NZ 2nd
1st	4	12	24	19
2nd	11	21	71	42
3rd	29	39	94	49
4th	150	43	198	64
5th	153	46	214	93
6th	172	54	215	94
7th	185	59	-	95
8th	191	67	-	123
9th	191	68	-	131
10th	221	94	-	137

MILESTONES

- Jack D'Arcy (81), Trevor Meale (82) and Bill Playle (83) made their test debuts.

The rain transformed a good batting wicket into a spinners' paradise. Both Jim Laker and Tony Lock were able to turn the ball considerably and the occasional delivery jumped from the wicket. New Zealand's misery began when Fred Trueman trapped Miller in front with the total at four.

England's spinners were called in after only eight overs, and although the visitors tried to carry the attack to the bowlers, too often they picked the wrong ball to attack. Laker had three victims at no cost in his first three overs. Lock ended with 5-17 and Laker 4-13.

New Zealand's total of 47 was the lowest in a test at Lord's and the lowest in any test in England since South Africa's 30 at Birmingham in 1924.

Rain between the second and third days further affected the uncovered wicket. The start was delayed for a half an hour before Jack D'Arcy and Lawrie Miller, who had survived a scoreless 10 minutes on the previous evening, were again exposed to treacherous batting conditions. D'Arcy batted for two hours to score 33, while his team-mates trudged to and from the middle in a sombre procession.

Lock captured four wickets to give him a match analysis of 9-29. New Zealand's second innings lasted three hours and totalled 74 runs. The last wicket partnership of 18 between John Hayes and Eric Petrie was the best by any New Zealand pair in either innings.

A crowd of 22,000 had watched the test reach its melancholic conclusion by mid-afternoon on the third of the

Tony MacGibbon was a big-hearted bowler who seemed inexhaustible. His lively fast-medium pace, with a command of late out-swing, deservedly captured eight wickets in the test at Edgbaston. Umpire Syd Buller watches for a no-ball. MacGibbon was to capture 20 wickets in the series.

47 ENGLAND v NEW ZEALAND *(Second Test)*

at Lord's on 19, 20, 21 June, 1958
Toss : England. Umpires : D. Davies and C.S. Elliott
England won by an innings and 148 runs

The Lord's wicket was unusually placid and gave the New Zealand bowlers no assistance. The combination of a tight line and excellent fielding restricted England to just 55 runs in the first session for the loss of Peter Richardson, well caught on the leg-side by Eric Petrie for 36.

The run-rate quickened a little after lunch, but Mike Smith (47) and Tom Graveney (37) were caught behind before the tea break. The big wicket of Peter May came first ball after tea to have England 141-4. A fifth wicket partnership between Colin Cowdrey and Trevor Bailey realised 60 runs in even time before Bailey became Petrie's fourth victim. John Hayes bowled Cowdrey in the last over of the day to give New Zealand the satisfaction of taking seven wickets for 237.

Bad weather delayed resumption until 3.20 pm on the second day when England were dismissed for 269. Both Hayes and MacGibbon finished with four wickets apiece.

ENGLAND

P.E.Richardson	c Petrie b Hayes	36
M.J.K.Smith	c Petrie b Hayes	47
T.W.Graveney	c Petrie b Alabaster	37
P.B.H.May*	c Alabaster b MacGibbon	19
M.C.Cowdrey	b Hayes	65
T.E.Bailey	c Petrie b Reid	17
T.G.Evans†	c Hayes b MacGibbon	11
G.A.R.Lock	not out	23
F.S.Trueman	b Hayes	8
J.C.Laker	c Blair b MacGibbon	1
P.J.Loader	c Playle b MacGibbon	4
Extras	(lb 1)	1
TOTAL	**(123.4 overs)**	**269**

NEW ZEALAND

L.S.M.Miller	lbw b Trueman	4	c Trueman b Loader	0
J.W.D'Arcy	c Trueman b Laker	14	c Bailey b Trueman	33
W.R.Playle	c Graveney b Laker	1	b Loader	3
N.S.Harford	c & b Laker	0	c May b Lock	3
J.R.Reid*	c Loader b Lock	6	c Cowdrey b Trueman	5
B.Sutcliffe	b Lock	18	b Bailey	0
A.R.MacGibbon	c May b Lock	2	c May b Lock	7
J.C.Alabaster	c & b Lock	0	b Laker	5
E.C.Petrie†	c Trueman b Laker	0	not out	4
R.W.Blair	not out	0	b Lock	0
J.A.Hayes	c Cowdrey b Lock	1	c & b Lock	14
Extras	(lb 1)	1		0
TOTAL	**(32.3 overs)**	**47**	**(50.3 overs)**	**74**

Bowling	O	M	R	W	O	M	R	W
NEW ZEALAND								
Hayes	22	5	36	4				
MacGibbon	36.4	11	86	4				
Blair	25	6	57	0				
Reid	24	12	41	1				
Alabaster	16	6	48	1				
ENGLAND								
Trueman	4	1	6	1	11	6	24	2
Loader	4	2	6	0	9	6	7	2
Laker	12	6	13	4	13	8	24	1
Lock	11.3	7	17	5	12.3	8	12	4
Bailey	1	0	4	0	5	1	7	1

Fall of Wickets

	E	NZ	NZ
	1st	1st	2nd
1st	54	4	11
2nd	113	12	21
3rd	139	12	34
4th	141	19	41
5th	201	25	44
6th	222	31	44
7th	237	34	56
8th	259	46	56
9th	260	46	56
10th	269	47	74

scheduled five days. These spectators were compensated by a limited overs exhibition match, in which England scored 145 in 20 overs and New Zealand was 130-5 when rain stopped play after 14 overs.

Denis Compton wrote in the *Sunday Express*: "How undeserved was this defeat. The New Zealanders dismissed the cream of English batting for a total of 237 on a perfect batting wicket on the first day. But rain came at night and for the remainder of the game they had to cope with a wicket on which the ball lifted and spun."

If the tourists hoped to bat their way into better form before the third test, two weeks away, they were thwarted by a spell of bad weather that accompanied them to the north of England. Only 11 hours play was possible in the two fixtures scheduled between the tests.

Johnny Hayes distinguished himself with this stunning catch of Godfrey Evans in the second test. He also took four wickets in England's innings. Behind the wicket Jack Alabaster, John Reid and Eric Petrie appeal enthusiastically.

48 ENGLAND v NEW ZEALAND *(Third Test)*

at Headingley, Leeds on 3, 4, 5, 7, 8 July, 1958
Toss : New Zealand. Umpires : J.S. Buller and F.S. Lee
England won by an innings and 71 runs

Play did not get under way until two o'clock on the third day. John Reid won his first toss in the test series and was faced with a difficult decision. The wicket was still very damp but seemed a better batting proposition than a drier surface with a wearing top.

Indeed, England's seamers toiled in vain for 75 minutes until Jack D'Arcy was caught off Fred Trueman with the score at 37. Jim Laker and Tony Lock were then introduced and the all too familiar rout was re-enacted as seven wickets toppled for only 12 runs. John Sparling, playing in his first test, survived for 80 minutes and was on nine when the last wicket fell at 67. Laker and Lock had combined bowling figures of 40 overs, nine wickets for 31 runs.

England opener Arthur Milton batted patiently and became the second player from Gloucestershire to compete a century in his maiden test – the first was W.G. Grace in 1880. England were 73-2 when Milton was joined by Peter May. They added 194 in 152 minutes, the time taken by May to score his century. They both hit 11 boundaries in their centuries.

New Zealand was precisely 200 runs in arrears and the only conceivable plan for the tourists was to bat through an hour and a half plus the final day. By stumps, however, they were again in deep trouble to the two mesmeric spinners as the first three batsmen were dismissed before stumps for 32.

Bert Sutcliffe was dismissed to the second ball of the last morning which brought Bill Playle to the crease to play an innings of remarkable fortitude. In 194 minutes he produced only seven scoring shots and tallied just 18 runs, but won praise for his intense concentration. Tony MacGibbon's response to the team's predicament was quite the opposite.

In 80 minutes he hit six boundaries in his 39, New Zealand's best individual score in six test innings. A valiant stand by the youngsters, Playle and Sparling, offered New Zealand the slight hope of holding out for a draw but the spinners were not to be denied with Lock taking 7-51 and England winning by an innings and 71 runs.

New Zealand had pinned their hopes for good performances on their two most experienced batsmen, Sutcliffe and Reid, but so far they had been to the crease 10 times and accumulated just 71 runs.

NEW ZEALAND

L.S.M.Miller	c Smith b Laker	26	lbw b Lock		18
J.W.D'Arcy	c Smith b Trueman	11	b Lock		6
N.S.Harford	c Cowdrey b Laker	0	lbw b Lock		0
B.Sutcliffe	b Laker	6	lbw b Lock		0
J.R.Reid*	b Lock	3	c Trueman b Laker		13
W.R.Playle	c Milton b Lock	0	b Laker		18
A.R.MacGibbon	b Laker	3	lbw b Lock		39
J.T.Sparling	not out	9	c May b Lock		18
E.C.Petrie†	c Cowdrey b Lock	5	b Lock		3
H.B.Cave	c Milton b Laker	2	c Cowdrey b Laker		2
J.A.Hayes	c Evans b Lock	1	not out		0
Extras	(lb 1)	1	(b 6, lb 6)		12
TOTAL	(59.1 overs)	**67**	(101.2 overs)		**129**

ENGLAND

M.J.K.Smith	c Reid b MacGibbon	3
C.A.Milton	not out	104
T.W.Graveney	c & b Sparling	31
P.B.H.May*	not out	113
M.C.Cowdrey		
T.E.Bailey		
T.G.Evans†		
G.A.R.Lock		
F.S.Trueman		
J.C.Laker		
P.J.Loader		
Extras	(b 5, lb 8, w 1, nb 2)	16
TOTAL	(102 overs) (2 wkts dec)	**267**

Bowling	O	M	R	W	O	M	R	W
ENGLAND								
Trueman	11	5	18	1	14	6	22	0
Loader	5	2	10	0	13	7	14	0
Bailey	3	0	7	0	3	2	3	0
Laker	22	11	17	5	36	23	27	3
Lock	18.1	13	14	4	35.2	20	51	7
NEW ZEALAND								
Hayes	13	4	30	0				
MacGibbon	27	8	47	1				
Reid	26	7	54	0				
Sparling	23	2	78	1				
Cave	13	4	42	0				

Fall of Wickets	NZ	E	NZ
	1st	1st	2nd
1st	37	7	23
2nd	37	73	23
3rd	37	-	24
4th	40	-	32
5th	46	-	42
6th	46	-	88
7th	49	-	121
8th	59	-	124
9th	66	-	129
10th	67	-	129

MILESTONES

- John Sparling (84) made his test debut.

- Both England's opening batsmen, Mike Smith and Arthur Milton, were double internationals. Smith had won a test cap for England in rugby and Milton had played soccer for England.

The 1958 tourists to England. Back row (from left): Noel Harford, Jack Alabaster, John Ward, Bill Playle, Tony MacGibbon, Trevor Meale, Jack D'Arcy, Eric Petrie, John Sparling. Front row: Lawrie Miller, Bob Blair, John Hayes, John Reid (captain), Harry Cave, Bert Sutcliffe, Alex Moir.

49 ENGLAND v NEW ZEALAND *(Fourth Test)*

at Old Trafford, Manchester on 24, 25, 26, 28, 29 July, 1958
Toss : New Zealand. Umpires : D.E. Davies and W.E. Phillipson
England won by an innings and 13 runs

The MCC touring team for Australia was to be announced on the rest day of this test and the England selectors decided to use this match as something of a trial. Of the third test team Bailey, Cowdrey, Laker, Loader, Milton and Smith were omitted, Richardson, Statham and Watson returned and three new caps were named: Ted Dexter, Ray Illingworth and Raman Subba Row.

For the first time in the series, the tourists kept England in the field all day and compiled their best tally yet – 220-6. Although the wicket was easy-paced, Brian Statham and Fred Trueman knocked the top off the New Zealand innings by lunch. Jack D'Arcy and Noel Harford were dismissed leg-before in the first half-hour and Bert Sutcliffe and John Reid carried the score to 62 before they were both dismissed on the stroke of lunch.

Bill Playle and Tony MacGibbon added 55 and when Playle was dismissed a further 49 runs were added with John Sparling until MacGibbon was caught behind on 66 – the first half-century scored by a New Zealander in the series. Sparling

celebrated his 20th birthday by batting through until stumps, when he was 45 and Eric Petrie 32.

The young Aucklander was caught behind on the second morning for 50, bringing to an end New Zealand's best partnership of the series – 61 runs. Petrie had reached 45, when a Trueman bouncer struck him on the head. The England masseur drove him to hospital in Trueman's car and it was decided that he should not take the field again until Monday, the fourth day.

Reid donned the keeper's pads for the first time since he had deputised for Frank Mooney in South Africa. It was not, however his first appearance as a test wicketkeeper – he had been selected in that role for the test at The Oval in 1949.

The England openers, Peter Richardson and Willie Watson, both left-handers, were not troubled by an accurate attack and their partnership of 126 was the first century opening by England at home in two years. It ended when Reid stumped Richardson. Bad light ended play a little early, with Tom Graveney and Peter May at the wicket and the score 192-2.

Rain, the constant companion of the tourists, prevented play until almost 3 o'clock on the third day and only 45 minutes' play was possible, with Graveney the only batsmen dismissed. Petrie was restored to fitness and soon caught Subba Row early on the fourth day.

John Sparling celebrated his 20th birthday by scoring a valiant half-century, one of only three made by New Zealand in the five-test series.

Peter May continued his superlative form with his second century, made in 153 minutes. His partnership with Dexter was highlighted by powerful drives on both sides of the wicket from both players. Reid had the rare distinction of adding three wickets as a bowler to his earlier stumping.

More rain fell overnight and a drying breeze made the wicket a spinner's dream. On a flat surface in the first innings, Tony Lock had taken 1-61 off 33 overs. Now, with conditions so much in his favour, he reaped seven victims for 35 runs off 24 overs, including his 100th in test cricket.

NEW ZEALAND					
B.Sutcliffe	b Statham	41	b Statham		28
J.W.D'Arcy	lbw b Trueman	1	c Subba Row b Lock		8
N.S.Harford	lbw b Statham	2	b Illingworth		4
J.R.Reid*	c Trueman b Lock	14	c Watson b Lock		8
W.R.Playle	lbw b Illingworth	15	lbw b Lock		1
A.R.MacGibbon	c Evans b Statham	66	lbw b Lock		1
J.T.Sparling	c Evans b Statham	50	c & b Lock		2
E.C.Petrie†	retired hurt	45	c Statham b Illingworth		9
A.M.Moir	not out	21	c Evans b Lock		12
J.A.Hayes	b Trueman	4	not out		5
R.W.Blair	b Trueman	2	b Lock		0
Extras	(b 4, lb 2)	6	(b 5, lb 2)		7
TOTAL	(128.5 overs)	267	(52 overs)		85

ENGLAND		
P.E.Richardson	st Reid b Sparling	74
W.Watson	c MacGibbon b Moir	66
T.W.Graveney	c sub (J.C.Alabaster) b MacGibbon	25
P.B.H.May*	c Playle b MacGibbon	101
R.Subba Row	c Petrie b Blair	9
E.R.Dexter	lbw b Reid	52
T.G.Evans†	c Blair b Reid	3
R.Illingworth	not out	3
G.A.R.Lock	lbw b MacGibbon	7
F.S.Trueman	b Reid	5
J.B.Statham		
Extras	(b 13, lb 4, w 1, nb 2)	20
TOTAL	(129.3 overs) (9 wkts dec)	365

Bowling ENGLAND	O	M	R	W	O	M	R	W	Fall of Wickets		NZ 1st	E 1st	NZ 2nd
Trueman	29.5	4	67	3	2	1	11	0	1st		15	126	36
Statham	33	10	71	4	9	4	12	1	2nd		22	180	36
Dexter	5	0	23	0					3rd		62	193	46
Lock	33	12	61	1	24	11	35	7	4th		62	248	49
Illingworth	28	9	39	1	17	9	20	2	5th		117	330	49
NEW ZEALAND									6th		166	337	51
Hayes	19	4	51	0					7th		227	351	60
MacGibbon	34	8	86	3					8th		257	360	78
Blair	27	5	68	1					9th		267	365	80
Moir	17	3	47	1					10th		-	-	85
Sparling	21	7	46	1									
Reid	11.3	2	47	3									

MILESTONES

- Ted Dexter, 62 tests, and Ray Illingworth, 61 tests, made their debuts for England.

50 ENGLAND v NEW ZEALAND *(Fifth Test)*

at The Oval on 21, 22, 23, 25, 26 August, 1958
Toss : New Zealand. Umpires : D.E. Davies and F.S. Lee
Match drawn

By three o'clock on the first day New Zealand had lost half its complement of wickets for a meagre 55 runs on a wicket that was in excellent order. England's cordon of fieldsmen behind the wicket aided their faster bowlers with sharp catching.

John Reid, who had excelled in the county matches, at last appeared to transport his excellent form with the bat into a test match. He combined caution with aggression for more than an hour, hitting one six and two fours before he was deceived by a slower ball from Tony Lock. Not for the first time in the series, Tony MacGibbon batted in a spirited fashion but, regrettably, only briefly.

John Sparling ducked into a short-pitched delivery from Fred Trueman that did not rise and was hit on the left ear. He was stunned by the blow and took no further part in the match. After tea, Alec Moir showed the established batsmen what could be achieved with an adventurous approach. He scored his highest total in tests, 41 not out, and the last wicket stand with Bob Blair contributed 29 to the team's total of 161.

From 11 overs before stumps Peter Richardson and Arthur Milton reached 30. Play did not resume until late on the morning of the second day when three overs were bowled, all maidens, before a deluge flooded The Oval, preventing any possibility of play on the Saturday or Monday. This typified the appalling weather that had dogged the tourists. 174 hours or 29 full playing days had been lost through rain.

For the first time in the series New Zealand had the advantage of a wicket in its favour, and MacGibbon exploited it splendidly. He bowled a long spell at lively fast-medium pace. He commanded late outswing and he moved the worn ball dangerously off the wicket. England was embarrassingly placed at 129-6 at lunch and only a rollicking innings of 39 not out by Trueman took them past 200.

Although an innings defeat seemed unlikely, with the home team leading by just 58 runs and having less than three hours in which to bowl New Zealand out, when the tourists were 21-3 a clean-sweep in the series was still possible. A sensible approach by Reid and Bert Sutcliffe denied England any further success and the game was drawn. The match had been restricted to only 12 hours play.

The dominant player of the series was the left-arm spinner Tony Lock, who captured 34 wickets at an average of 7.47 runs apiece.

MILESTONES

- This was New Zealand's 50th official test match.

- Tony MacGibbon established a new record for New Zealand in a test series against England by taking 20 wickets.

- Godfrey Evans made his 86th appearance at test level, one more than Walter Hammond, the previous record holder.

- Peter May captained England for the 25th consecutive occasion, equalling the record of Australia's Bill Woodfull.

England loses its first wicket in the fifth test as Bob Blair yorks Peter Richardson for 28. The other batsman is Arthur Milton.

NEW ZEALAND

L.S.M.Miller	c Lock b Laker	25	c Evans b Statham	4
J.W.D'Arcy	c Milton b Bailey	9	c & b Lock	10
T.Meale	c Lock b Trueman	1	c Cowdrey b Laker	3
B.Sutcliffe	c Watson b Trueman	11	not out	18
J.R.Reid*	b Lock	27	not out	51
W.R.Playle	b Statham	6		
A.R.MacGibbon	b Bailey	26		
J.T.Sparling	retired hurt	0		
E.C.Petrie†	c Milton b Lock	8		
A.M.Moir	not out	41		
R.W.Blair	run out	3		
Extras	(lb 4)	4	(b 2, lb 3)	5
TOTAL	(75 overs)	**161**	(55 overs) (3 wkts)	**91**

ENGLAND

P.E.Richardson	b Blair	28
C.A.Milton	lbw b MacGibbon	36
W.Watson	b MacGibbon	10
P.B.H.May*	c Petrie b Blair	9
M.C.Cowdrey	c Playle b Reid	25
T.E.Bailey	c Petrie b MacGibbon	14
T.G.Evans†	c Petrie b MacGibbon	12
G.A.R.Lock	c Reid b Moir	25
J.C.Laker	c Blair b Reid	15
F.S.Trueman	not out	39
J.B.Statham		
Extras	(b 2, lb 4)	6
TOTAL	(68.5 overs) (9 wkts dec)	**219**

Bowling	O	M	R	W	O	M	R	W	Fall of Wickets			
ENGLAND										NZ	E	NZ
Trueman	16	3	41	2	6	5	3	0		1st	1st	2nd
Statham	18	6	21	1	7	0	26	1	1st	19	39	9
Bailey	14	3	32	2					2nd	24	62	17
Laker	14	3	44	1	20	10	25	1	3rd	40	85	21
Lock	13	6	19	2	18	11	20	1	4th	46	87	-
Milton					4	2	12	0	5th	55	109	-
NEW ZEALAND									6th	93	125	-
Blair	26	5	85	2					7th	105	162	-
MacGibbon	27	4	65	4					8th	132	162	-
Reid	7.5	2	11	2					9th	161	219	-
Moir	8	1	52	1					10th	-	-	-

AVERAGES

New Zealand

BATTING	M	I	NO	Runs	HS	Ave
A.M. Moir	2	3	2	74	41*	74.00
J.T. Sparling	3	5	2	79	50	26.33
A.R. MacGibbon	5	9	0	175	66	19.44
B. Sutcliffe	4	8	1	122	41	17.42
J.R. Reid	5	10	1	147	51*	16.33
J.W. D'Arcy	5	10	0	136	33	13.60
E.C. Petrie	5	9	3	80	45*	13.33
L.S.M. Miller	4	8	0	92	26	11.50
J.A. Hayes	4	8	2	44	14	7.33
J.C. Alabaster	2	4	0	25	11	6.25
W.R. Playle	5	9	0	56	18	6.22
H.B. Cave	2	4	1	17	12*	5.66
T. Meale	2	4	0	21	10	5.25
N.S. Harford	4	8	0	41	23	5.12
R.W. Blair	3	5	1	5	3	1.25

BOWLING	O	M	R	W	Ave
A.R. MacGibbon	175.4	50	389	20	19.45
J.C. Alabaster	46.5	17	127	5	25.40
J.R. Reid	84.2	28	187	6	31.16
J.A. Hayes	89	18	225	6	37.50
A.M. Moir	25	4	99	2	49.50
J.T. Sparling	44	9	124	2	62.00
R.W. Blair	78	16	210	3	70.00
H.B. Cave	53.2	15	141	2	70.50

England

BATTING	M	I	NO	Runs	HS	Ave
C.A. Milton	2	2	1	140	104*	140.00
P.B.H. May	5	6	1	337	113*	67.40
M.C. Cowdrey	4	4	0	241	81	60.25
E.R. Dexter	1	1	0	52	52	52.00
P.E. Richardson	4	5	0	242	100	48.40
W. Watson	2	2	0	76	66	38.00
T.W. Graveney	4	5	0	119	37	23.80
G.A.R. Lock	5	4	1	59	25	19.66
F.S. Trueman	5	4	1	52	39*	17.33
M.J.K. Smith	3	4	0	57	47	14.25
J.C. Laker	4	3	1	27	15	13.50
T.E. Bailey	4	4	1	39	17	13.00
P.J. Loader	3	2	0	21	17	10.50
R. Subba Row	1	1	0	9	9	9.00
T.G. Evans	5	5	0	28	12	5.60
R. Illingworth	1	1	1	3	3*	-
J.B. Statham	2	-	-	-	-	-

BOWLING	O	M	R	W	Ave
G.A.R. Lock	176	93	254	34	7.47
J.C. Laker	131	67	173	17	10.17
T.E. Bailey	66	24	93	7	13.28
F.S. Trueman	131.5	44	256	15	17.06
J.B. Statham	67	20	130	7	18.57
P.J. Loader	75.3	34	114	6	19.00
R. Illingworth	45	18	59	3	19.66
C.A. Milton	4	2	12	0	-
E.R. Dexter	5	0	23	0	-

1958/59 MCC in New Zealand

51 NEW ZEALAND v ENGLAND (*First Test*)

at Lancaster Park, Christchurch on 27, 28 February, 2 March, 1959
Toss : England. Umpires : J. Cowie and E.W.T. Tindill
England won by an innings and 99 runs

180 days after of the fifth test at The Oval, New Zealand faced England in a test match in Christchurch. Only six of the team had been on the tour of England. Peter May's team left England heralded as one of the strongest sides to represent that country but was soundly and surprisingly beaten four-nil in the Ashes.

The England openers, who had consistently failed in the Ashes, were both dismissed within the first hour. Tom Graveney and May steadied proceedings before Ken Hough trapped Graveney in front for his first test wicket: 98-3. New Zealand had good reason to feel pleased when May was dismissed for 71 and England were six wickets down for 197.

However, the elegant figure of "Lord Ted" Dexter blunted the home attack with majestic drives and sweetly timed strokes square of the wicket. In the session after tea he passed beyond his first test century and, in partnership with Fred Trueman, put on 81 in an hour for the eighth wicket. At stumps, Dexter was 123 not out and England 336-8.

A record crowd for Lancaster Park of 19,000 saw John Reid wrap up the innings, taking the last two wickets to finish with three, the same as Hough. The two test debutant openers, Roger Harris and Bruce Bolton, struggled for survival against the extreme pace of Trueman and Frank Tyson. Following the lunch break, Tony Lock was introduced into the attack and wickets began tumbling as he made the ball spin prodigiously and leap viciously.

New Zealand was embarrassingly placed at 102-9 when New Zealand's last batsman, Hough, smashed 16 runs from one of Trueman's overs. He delighted the crowd, scoring 31 not out before Trueman claimed his 100th test wicket by dismissing Eric Petrie leg-before.

In Australia Lock had the paltry return of five wickets in four tests and those at an average of 75 runs a wicket. On this substandard wicket he was transformed into the demon that had devastated the New Zealanders in 1958 in England.

Facing a deficit of 232 runs Harris and Bolton survived until stumps, accounting for 28 runs. By lunch on the third day New Zealand were 101-3 with left-handed John Guy batting defiantly yet playing some cultured shots.

Lock changed ends and his first ball of the afternoon enticed a catch from Sutcliffe. The dismissal of Guy saw the innings disintegrate with the last seven wickets adding only 32 runs. Lock claimed another six wickets, taking 11-84 in the match. During the course of the game fragments of shell, small pieces of china and pebbles were picked from the pitch

– the marl used in the preparation of the wicket had been ground at a pottery factory.

ENGLAND		
P.E.Richardson	c Petrie b Blair	8
W.Watson	c Petrie b Blair	10
T.W.Graveney	lbw b Hough	42
P.B.H.May*	c Hough b Moir	71
M.C.Cowdrey	b Hough	15
E.R.Dexter	b Reid	141
J.B.Mortimore	c & b Moir	11
R.Swetman†	b Hough	9
F.S.Trueman	lbw b Reid	21
G.A.R.Lock	b Reid	15
F.H.Tyson	not out	6
Extras	(b 12, lb 13)	25
TOTAL	**(142.1 overs)**	**374**

NEW ZEALAND				
R.M.Harris	c Lock b Tyson	6	b Trueman	13
B.A.Bolton	c Swetman b Lock	33	c May b Mortimore	26
J.W.Guy	c Trueman b Lock	3	c Lock b Tyson	56
J.R.Reid*	b Tyson	40	c Cowdrey b Lock	1
B.Sutcliffe	c Lock b Tyson	0	c Trueman b Lock	12
S.N.McGregor	c Lock b Mortimore	0	lbw b Lock	6
J.T.Sparling	st Swetman b Lock	12	b Tyson	0
A.M.Moir	c Graveney b Lock	0	c Swetman b Lock	1
E.C.Petrie†	lbw b Trueman	8	not out	2
R.W.Blair	lbw b Lock	0	c Trueman b Lock	2
K.W.Hough	not out	31	b Lock	7
Extras	(b 5, lb 4)	9	(b 1, lb 5, nb 1)	7
TOTAL	**(72.5 overs)**	**142**	**(72.2 overs)**	**133**

Bowling	O	M	R	W	O	M	R	W
NEW ZEALAND								
Blair	31	5	89	2				
Hough	39	11	96	3				
Moir	36	9	83	2				
Reid	18.1	9	34	3				
Sparling	16	7	38	0				
Sutcliffe	2	0	9	0				
ENGLAND								
Trueman	10.5	3	39	1	8	2	20	1
Tyson	14	4	23	3	14	6	23	2
Lock	26	15	31	5	28.2	13	53	6
Mortimore	22	8	40	1	21	10	27	1
Dexter					1	0	3	0

Fall of Wickets	E	NZ	NZ
	1st	*1st*	*2nd*
1st	13	22	37
2nd	30	33	68
3rd	98	83	79
4th	126	83	101
5th	171	86	117
6th	197	101	119
7th	224	101	120
8th	305	102	121
9th	367	102	123
10th	374	142	133

As a boy growing up in New South Wales, Ken Hough opened the bowling for his state's colts team with the great Australian cricketer Alan Davidson. He later played soccer for both Australia and New Zealand. A large and very strong man, he bowled at fast-medium pace. At Lancaster Park he delighted the crowd by taking 16 off one over from Fred Trueman in his score of 31. From left: Tony Lock, Eric Petrie, Colin Cowdrey and wicketkeeper Roy Swetman watch another mighty heave.

MILESTONES

- Bruce Bolton (85), Roger Harris (86) and Ken Hough (87) made their test debuts.

- The two umpires, Jack Cowie and Eric Tindill, were both former New Zealand test players. Tindill completed the unique accomplishment of representing his country at test cricket and test rugby and refereeing test rugby and umpiring test cricket.

52 NEW ZEALAND v ENGLAND *(Second Test)*

at Eden Park, Auckland on 14, 16, 17, 18 March, 1959
Toss : England. Umpires : J. Cowie and R.W.R. Shortt
Match drawn

On the eve of the second test Bert Sutcliffe announced his intention to retire from international cricket. The Meteorological Service predicted that a cyclone would cross Auckland in the next few days.

Throughout the first day, gale force winds buffeted Eden Park and, despite the blustery conditions, a crowd of 17,500 enjoyed an intriguing day's play. After 15 minutes both New Zealand openers found themselves at the same end and Bruce Bolton was run out. Ted Dexter, who had not captured a wicket in his first four tests, now bowled into a fierce wind, produced late in-swing and quickly captured three wickets.

Since the battering that Bert Sutcliffe had received from Neil Adcock in South Africa five years ago, he had rarely looked comfortable against quick bowling. His approach to Fred Trueman and Frank Tyson was patient, confident and courageous before he was sixth out, with the score at 98. Valiant batting by the tailenders, with Hough again distinguishing himself with a lusty 24 not out, saw New Zealand all out for 181.

Peter Richardson and Tom Graveney put on 68 runs at a respectable rate for England's second wicket before a minor collapse saw five batsmen dismissed for 183. Peter May, displaying almost perfect technique, showed why many critics regarded him as the greatest batsman produced by England since the Second World War.

Aided firstly by Roy Swetman and then Trueman the England captain carried his team to 311-7 at stumps on the second day. May's contribution was an unbeaten 124, which took his test aggregate beyond 4000 runs. He was denied an opportunity to increase this tally when rain washed out the remaining two days.

NEW ZEALAND

B.A.Bolton	run out	0
R.M.Harris	c Swetman b Dexter	12
S.N.McGregor	hit wicket b Trueman	1
J.W.Guy	b Dexter	1
B.Sutcliffe	b Lock	61
J.R.Reid*	b Dexter	3
J.T.Sparling	c Swetman b Trueman	25
A.M.Moir	c Graveney b Trueman	10
E.C.Petrie†	c Trueman b Lock	13
R.W.Blair	c Cowdrey b Tyson	22
K.W.Hough	not out	24
Extras	(b 7, lb 1, nb 1)	9
TOTAL	**(89.3 overs)**	**181**

ENGLAND

P.E.Richardson	c Bolton b Moir	67
W.Watson	b Hough	11
T.W.Graveney	b Moir	46
P.B.H.May*	not out	124
M.C.Cowdrey	b Hough	5
E.R.Dexter	c Petrie b Moir	1
J.B.Mortimore	b Hough	9
R.Swetman†	run out	17
F.S.Trueman	not out	21
G.A.R.Lock		
F.H.Tyson		
Extras	(b 4, lb 6)	10
TOTAL	**(118 overs) (7 wkts)**	**311**

Bowling	O	M	R	W
ENGLAND				
Trueman	26	12	46	3
Tyson	20	9	50	1
Dexter	19	8	23	3
Lock	20.3	12	29	2
Mortimore	4	1	24	0
NEW ZEALAND				
Blair	27	6	69	0
Hough	38	12	79	3
Reid	4	1	19	0
Sparling	20	6	48	0
Moir	28	4	84	3
Sutcliffe	1	0	2	0

Fall of Wickets

	NZ	E
	1st	1st
1st	3	26
2nd	6	94
3rd	11	165
4th	16	182
5th	41	183
6th	98	223
7th	116	261
8th	125	-
9th	157	-
10th	181	-

The New Zealand players enter the field under the shadow of the new No.1 Stand being built on the southern side of the ground at Eden Park. From left: John Reid, John Guy, Bob Blair, Ken Hough, Noel McGregor, Alex Moir, Bruce Bolton, Bert Sutcliffe and John Sparling.

1961/62 New Zealand in South Africa

The full implications of the Afrikaner Nationalist Government's policy of apartheid was beginning to attract worldwide concern and 70 demonstrators staged a protest outside the building where the NZCC was selecting the team to visit South Africa. Within a year South Africa would declare itself a republic and be forced to withdraw from the Commonwealth. By 1970 South Africa was effectively barred from test cricket until 1992.

Two veterans from the 1953/54 team in South Africa, John Reid and Murray Chapple, were appointed captain and vice-captain. Gordon Leggat, who had also been in the earlier team, was named as manager and his man- management skills played a vital role in the success of the tour.

Prior to the first test, eight first-class games had been played and seven had been drawn. Cricket followers were delighted when it was announced that the first test would be broadcast nightly from 9.30 pm by radio telephone. This test was notable for the fact that seven new Springboks were named in the home side and four for the visitors.

53 SOUTH AFRICA v NEW ZEALAND (First Test)

at Kingsmead, Durban on 8, 9, 11, 12 December, 1961
Toss : South Africa. Umpires : W.P. Anderson and D.R. Fell
South Africa won by 30 runs

South Africa was comfortably placed after Jackie McGlew and Roy McLean had taken the score to 185-2 before Jack Alabaster bowled McLean for an entertaining 63. Alabaster (4-59) and Frank Cameron (3-60) now broke through and the last seven wickets fell for 107 runs. McGlew was unbeaten on 127, having carried his bat for over five hours. His innings combined sweetly timed leg glances and occasional flowing drives plus many defensive pushes that resulted in singles.

Although Reid had bowled 11 overs on the first day, he was suffering from influenza, which became serious enough to comfine him to his bed on the rest day. His batting was affected by the illness and he was unable to bowl in South Africa's second innings.

New Zealand struggled against the pace bowling and their best contributions came from Paul Barton (54) and Zin Harris (74). Gary Bartlett, batting at number nine, shared a record stand of 73 runs with Harris for New Zealand's eighth wicket against South Africa. In scoring 245 New Zealand trailed by 47 runs.

South Africa began the third day at 13 without loss but Dick Motz, who began with four wides, captured three quick wickets before the total reached 40. John Waite and Colin Bland added 72 for the fourth wicket before Graham Dowling, substituting for Reid, ran out Bland with a fine throw.

113-5 became 149 all out as Alabaster and Cameron again shared the last six wickets. Bartlett bowled with great pace

and accuracy but was plagued by no-balls, conceding 22 in the game.

With a day and a half to bat and requiring 197 runs, the tourists adopted an overly cautious approach in seeking to preserve their wickets rather than play shots. Noel McGregor was the exception to this defensive policy and he stroked the ball beautifully to hit six boundaries in his innings of 55.

Peter Pollock intimidated the visitors with his pace, capturing 6-38, giving him a match analysis of 9-99, the best performance by a South African fast bowler in 143 test matches. Reid's illness was a severe blow to his side considering that they lost by the narrow margin of 30 runs.

SOUTH AFRICA

D.J.McGlew*	not out	127	b Motz	5
E.J.Barlow	b Motz	15	c Dick b Motz	10
J.H.B.Waite†	c Dick b Bartlett	25	c sub (G.T.Dowling) b Cameron	63
R.A.McLean	b Alabaster	63	c Bartlett b Motz	0
K.C.Bland	c Reid b Cameron	5	run out	30
M.K.Elgie	b Motz	1	st Dick b Alabaster	0
S.O'Linn	lbw b Cameron	8	c Cameron b Alabaster	6
P.M.Pollock	c Dick b Cameron	0	c Dick b Cameron	15
G.B.Lawrence	c Sparling b Alabaster	16	lbw b Alabaster	0
K.A.Walter	c Dick b Alabaster	0	c Dick b Cameron	1
H.D.Bromfield	lbw b Alabaster	0	not out	0
Extras	(b 11, lb 6, w 1, nb 14)	32	(b 2, lb 4, w 5, nb 8)	19
TOTAL	(88.5 overs)	292	(61.2 overs)	149

NEW ZEALAND

J.W.Guy	c Walter b Pollock	8	c Bromfield b Pollock	1
J.T.Sparling	c Waite b Pollock	13	c Waite b Walter	10
P.T.Barton	c Elgie b Lawrence	54	c Waite b Pollock	23
S.N.McGregor	c Barlow b Walter	20	c Walter b Bromfield	55
J.R.Reid*	c Pollock b Lawrence	13	(6) c Waite b Pollock	16
P.G.Z.Harris	c Elgie b Walter	74	(5) lbw b Pollock	0
A.E.Dick†	c Waite b Pollock	3	c Waite b Pollock	2
R.C.Motz	c McGlew b Walter	0	(9) b Bromfield	10
G.A.Bartlett	c Pollock b Walter	40	(8) c O'Linn b Bromfield	23
J.C.Alabaster	lbw b Lawrence	2	c Bromfield b Pollock	8
F.J.Cameron	not out	0	not out	1
Extras	(b 1, lb 1, nb 16)	18	(b 1, lb 1, nb 15)	17
TOTAL	(99.3 overs)	245	(79.3 overs)	166

Bowling	O	M	R	W	O	M	R	W
NEW ZEALAND								
Motz	23	3	64	2	20	1	51	3
Bartlett	9	3	39	1	9	3	11	0
Cameron	27	5	60	3	15.2	1	32	3
Reid	11	1	38	0				
Alabaster	17.5	2	59	4	17	6	36	3
Sparling	1	1	0	0				
SOUTH AFRICA								
Pollock	22	3	61	3	20.3	8	38	6
Walter	25.3	6	63	4	16	5	34	1
Lawrence	29	6	63	3	25	8	40	0
Barlow	8	3	17	0				
Bromfield	15	5	23	0	18	4	37	3

Fall of Wickets

	SA 1st	NZ 1st	SA 2nd	NZ 2nd
1st	20	20	17	7
2nd	82	33	38	23
3rd	185	63	38	53
4th	216	89	110	53
5th	233	150	113	100
6th	253	153	129	102
7th	263	162	137	137
8th	286	235	137	150
9th	292	245	144	162
10th	292	245	149	166

MILESTONES

- Gary Bartlett (88), Paul Barton (89), Frank Cameron (90), Artie Dick (91) and Dick Motz (92) made their test debuts.

- Artie Dick set a New Zealand test wicketkeeping record of seven dismissals (six catches and a stumping) in a match.

54 SOUTH AFRICA v NEW ZEALAND *(Second Test)*

at Wanderers Stadium, Johannesburg on 26, 27, 28, 29 December, 1961
Toss : South Africa. Umpires : W.P. Anderson and H.C. Kidson
Match drawn

Despite suspicions that the wicket would be damp after showery weather, Jackie McGlew decided to bat first in the Boxing Day test. Intermittent rain saw players on and off the field and the day ended with the home side 80-1.

Dick Motz and Frank Cameron shared the first four wickets for a total of 102 runs. John Waite contributed a stylish 103 runs, with 13 boundaries, to the total of 188 when he was caught behind off Cameron. Kim Elgie led a revival in the late order batting and South Africa was dismissed for 322, the last four wickets having put on 134 runs.

Before this tour the Otago man had been regarded as a stock bowler but he now emerged as potent weapon with his ability to swing the ball both ways and obtain awkward movement off the wicket. He was the best of the bowlers, capturing five wickets.

Godfrey Lawrence, a six-foot eight-inch Rhodesian, better-known as "Goofy", was assisted by Waite, who accepted four catches as he disposed of eight batsmen for 53 runs off 31 overs. Playing in his first test Graham Dowling was the mainstay of the innings for over four hours before he was run out and the innings ended at 223 – a deficit of 99. Seeking quick runs in the last hour of the third day, Eddie Barlow and McGlew added 59 by stumps.

The next day began with wickets falling and belligerent batting from Barlow and Roy McLean enabled McGlew to declare at lunch. The target of 278 in four hours, against mainly defensive field placings, proved too great.

Dowling completed his second half-century of the match, while the New Zealand captain Reid batted freely until stumps were drawn. His aggressive attitude suggested that an exciting finish might have eventuated if most of the first day had not been lost to rain.

SOUTH AFRICA

D.J.McGlew*	lbw b Motz	5	run out		38
E.J.Barlow	c Reid b Motz	47	c Dick b Motz		45
J.H.B.Waite†	c Dick b Cameron	101	(6) c Dick b Bartlett		4
R.A.McLean	c Bartlett b Cameron	2	c & b Motz		45
K.C.Bland	c Barton b Cameron	0	c McGregor b Motz		24
S.O'Linn	b Cameron	17	(7) not out		5
M.K.Elgie	b Bartlett	56	(3) b Motz		0
P.M.Pollock	run out	37	not out		1
G.B.Lawrence	c Guy b Bartlett	22			
K.A.Walter	c Barton b Cameron	10			
H.D.Bromfield	not out	11			
Extras	(b 3, lb 9, w 1, nb 1)	14	(b 8, lb 4, nb 4)		16
TOTAL	(103.2 overs)	**322**	(43 overs) (6 wkts dec)		**178**

NEW ZEALAND

S.N.McGregor	c Walter b Lawrence	13	c Bromfield b Walter		11
G.T.Dowling	run out	74	c Waite b Pollock		58
P.T.Barton	c Waite b Lawrence	10	c Waite b Lawrence		11
J.R.Reid*	lbw b Lawrence	39	not out		75
J.W.Guy	c Waite b Lawrence	9	b Pollock		0
P.G.Z.Harris	c Elgie b Lawrence	0	not out		9
A.E.Dick†	b Bromfield	16			
G.A.Bartlett	c Waite b Lawrence	31			
R.C.Motz	c Waite b Lawrence	3			
J.C.Alabaster	c Barlow b Lawrence	17			
F.J.Cameron	not out	1	(lb 1)		1
Extras	(b 1, lb 6, nb 3)	10			
TOTAL	(92.3 overs)	**223**	(68 overs) (4 wkts)		**165**

Bowling	O	M	R	W	O	M	R	W
NEW ZEALAND								
Motz	27	4	70	2	17	2	68	4
Bartlett	21	2	82	2	13	1	44	1
Cameron	36.2	9	83	5	13	1	50	0
Reid	9	2	33	0				
Alabaster	10	2	40	0				
SOUTH AFRICA								
Pollock	20	4	49	0	14	6	18	2
Walter	23	4	62	0	18	5	38	1
Lawrence	30.3	12	53	8	22	4	45	1
Barlow	3	0	15	0	3	2	5	0
Bromfield	16	6	34	1	7	0	30	0
Elgie					4	0	28	0

Fall of Wickets	SA	NZ	SA	NZ
	1st	*1st*	*2nd*	*2nd*
1st	25	18	85	22
2nd	99	41	85	49
3rd	102	107	92	120
4th	102	132	168	124
5th	159	132	169	-
6th	188	163	177	-
7th	259	167	-	-
8th	287	187	-	-
9th	296	216	-	-
10th	322	223	-	-

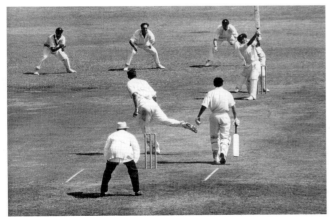

Gary Bartlett, the non-striking batsman, admires Zin Harris' lofted drive during their partnership of 73 in the first test.

Graham Dowling scored 74 and 58 on debut. It augured well for his future as a successful test opener.

MILESTONES

- Graham Dowling (93) made his test debut.

- Godfrey Lawrence's 8-53 was the best analysis by a South African fast bowler in 73 years of test cricket.

55   SOUTH AFRICA v NEW ZEALAND *(Third Test)*

at Newlands, Cape Town on 1, 2, 3, 4 January, 1962
Toss : New Zealand. Umpires : D. Collins and J.E. Warner
New Zealand won by 72 runs

Noel McGregor took advantage of splendid batting conditions to score 68 of New Zealand's 116-3 shortly after lunch on the first day. John Reid and Zin Harris added 93 runs in even time, scoring with the ease against an attack rendered toothless by the excellent batting wicket.

When Reid was caught at backward point on 92 he had accumulated 1001 runs for the South African tour. New Zealand did not squander this promising start with Murray Chapple, the number six batsman, providing splendid support for Harris and the pair were still at the wicket when stumps were drawn; 337-4, Harris 92 and Chapple 58.

Next day Harris struggled for almost an hour to advance through the nineties, finally securing his maiden test century before being stumped. The last six New Zealand wickets fell for only 48 runs, but the total of 385 was the best achieved by either side so far in the series. Bowling for South Africa, Syd Burke toiled through a marathon 54 overs for his six wickets.

The expectant crowd of 11,000 were shocked as the New Zealand openers were again at the batting crease by the end of the day's play. Fine bowling by Frank Cameron (5- 48) and Jack Alabaster (4-61) had seen South Africa bundled out in less than four hours for 190 runs. Excellent fielding was highlighted by eight catches being held.

Reid decided not to enforce the follow-on. His bowlers were no longer fresh and the wicket had a reputation for breaking up and he preferred to see his opponents bat fourth. However, his reasoning seemed shaky when half of his batsmen were dismissed for 106.

Timely contributions from Artie Dick, Chapple and Gary Bartlett improved the odds. Dick's unbeaten 50 was full of forthright strokes and his last wicket stand of 58 with Cameron, carried the total over 200 before Reid declared.

Burke was again the best of the South African bowlers with five wickets. Curiously, despite his 11 wickets in this match on his test debut, he would not appear in the remaining two tests. Chasing 408 runs in 475 minutes, South Africa was 54-2 at the end of the third day.

With the score at 100-3 Jackie McGlew and Roy McLean began a partnership that grew to worrying proportions for New Zealand. The pair added 101 in better than even time before McGlew (63) snicked Bartlett into the gloves of Dick.

McLean continued to hook and cut in grand style, supplementing these powerful shots with scampered singles.

After completing his fifth test century and reaching 113 he also fell to Bartlett, who was able to extract more bounce from the wicket than any other bowler. Alabaster and his right-arm leg-spinners was the linchpin of the attack, bowling 50 overs and taking his second four wicket bag for the match.

Unfortunately, radio listeners in New Zealand were denied the chance to hear New Zealand's first victory in 31 tests played overseas, and only the second in its test history. The link from South Africa failed in the early hours of the morning, when South Africa needed 80 runs and had three wickets in hand.

NEW ZEALAND

S.N.McGregor	b Burke	68	run out		20
G.T.Dowling	lbw b Lawrence	0	c Barlow b Burke		12
J.T.Sparling	c Elgie b Burke	19	c Waite b Burke		9
J.R.Reid*	c Bromfield b McKinnon	92	c Bromfield b Burke		14
P.G.Z.Harris	st Waite b Bromfield	101	c Bland b Burke		30
M.E.Chapple	c Waite b Burke	69	b Burke		33
A.E.Dick†	c Waite b Burke	4	(8) not out		50
G.A.Bartlett	c Waite b Burke	12	(7) st Waite b McKinnon		29
R.C.Motz	b Burke	0	c Barlow b Bromfield		0
J.C.Alabaster	c Farrer b Bromfield	1	st Waite b McKinnon		4
F.J.Cameron	not out	2	not out		10
Extras	(lb 8, nb 9)	17	(b 1)		1
TOTAL	(157.5 overs)	**385**	(88.1 overs) (9 wkts dec)		**212**

SOUTH AFRICA

D.J.McGlew*	c Bartlett b Motz	14	c Dick b Bartlett		63
E.J.Barlow	c Harris b Alabaster	51	c Reid b Alabaster		16
W.S.Farrer	c Dick b Alabaster	11	c Dowling b Alabaster		20
J.H.B.Waite†	c Chapple b Cameron	33	lbw b Alabaster		21
R.A.McLean	c Dick b Cameron	20	c Harris b Bartlett		113
K.C.Bland	b Alabaster	32	lbw b Reid		42
M.K.Elgie	c Chapple b Alabaster	6	c Harris b Cameron		12
S.F.Burke	c Dick b Cameron	0	c Motz b Sparling		12
G.B.Lawrence	c Reid b Cameron	4	c Harris b Reid		0
A.H.McKinnon	not out	9	b Alabaster		4
H.D.Bromfield	lbw b Cameron	1	not out		0
Extras	(b 6, lb 2, nb 1)	9	(b 14, lb 13, w 4, nb 1)		32
TOTAL	(68.4 overs)	**190**	(142.2 overs)		**335**

Bowling	O	M	R	W	O	M	R	W
SOUTH AFRICA								
Burke	53.5	19	128	6	27.1	10	68	5
Lawrence	23	7	46	1				
McKinnon	19	6	42	1	17	7	32	2
Barlow	9	0	40	0	20	2	53	0
Bromfield	46	11	94	2	24	3	58	1
Elgie	7	2	18	0				
NEW ZEALAND								
Motz	11	2	30	1	24	9	69	0
Cameron	24.4	10	48	5	26	14	42	1
Alabaster	21	4	61	4	50	12	119	4
Bartlett	5	1	17	0	22	8	40	2
Sparling	6	1	22	0	6	3	12	1
Chapple	1	0	3	0				
Reid					14.2	8	21	2

Fall of Wickets

	NZ	SA	NZ	SA
	1st	*1st*	*2nd*	*2nd*
1st	15	36	28	27
2nd	59	67	40	54
3rd	116	85	44	100
4th	209	124	61	201
5th	357	157	106	273
6th	367	164	127	315
7th	369	165	158	317
8th	369	173	159	331
9th	370	185	163	335
10th	385	190	-	335

MILESTONES

- New Zealand's first test victory overseas.

- Artie Dick and Frank Cameron had a record tenth wicket partnership against South Africa of 49 unbeaten.

56 SOUTH AFRICA v NEW ZEALAND *(Fourth Test)*

at Wanderers Stadium, Johannesburg on 2, 3, 5 February, 1962
Toss : New Zealand. Umpires : H.C. Kidson and G. Parry
South Africa won by an innings and 51 runs

The extraordinary depth of fast bowling in South Africa was indicated by the selectors' ability to name six speedsters, not including Peter Pollock, in their squad for the fourth test. The now fit Neil Adcock would make his first appearance in the series, along with Peter Heine.

The tourists lost any chance of gaining a series lead when they were bundled out for 164 in 212 minutes on an easy wicket. Most of the New Zealanders were the authors of their own downfall, choosing the wrong shot in the circumstances.

Only John Reid batted with confidence. His innings of 60, made in 84 minutes, included a five and 10 fours and was ended by what he described as the best catch he had ever seen. With his dismissal the last six wickets fell for 34 runs, with "Goofy" Lawrence claiming five victims for 52. Jackie McGlew and Eddie Barlow batted through the remaining two and a half hours on the first day with the latter falling to a catch behind the wicket off the last ball of the day; 134-1.

Once again Roy McLean assisted his captain, McGlew, in an entertaining partnership of 112 in 84 minutes, of which McLean struck 15 boundaries in a whirlwind innings of 78. McGlew was the anchor of the innings, scoring his second hundred of the series. All the South African batsmen played aggressively and rampaged through to 464, a lead of 300.

Before stumps on the second day New Zealand's problems were compounded by the loss of three wickets for 51.

Reid resumed the next day on six and batted with great confidence despite his team's predicament and the continual loss of wickets. Nursing a shoulder dislocated the previous day, Paul Barton batted in dogged fashion scoring nine runs, while Reid dominated a partnership that added 54 runs.

Gary Bartlett joined his captain in a stand worth 84 before Reid was dismissed. In 259 minutes Reid had scored 142 runs out of 184. At this stage of the tour Reid's batting was being hailed as the finest ever seen in South Africa.

Lawrence captured four wickets in the second innings to give him his second bag of nine wickets in the series. The bouncier surface at the Wanderers Ground had enabled the home team to complete a convincing victory with a day to spare.

MILESTONES

- John Waite created a world test wicketkeeping record of 24 dismissals in a series.

- Neil Adcock became the second South African bowler to capture 100 wickets in test cricket.

Zin Harris, left, scored 101 and Frank Cameron took 5-58 in the third test. New Zealand went on to score their first test victory overseas. Table Mountain is in the background.

NEW ZEALAND

S.N.McGregor	c Waite b Lance	21	c McLean b Heine		0
G.T.Dowling	lbw b Lawrence	14	b Adcock		0
P.T.Barton	b Adcock	22	(7) c Waite b Lance		9
J.R.Reid*	c Bland b Lawrence	60	(5) c McGlew b Heine		142
P.G.Z.Harris	c Lawrence b Adcock	4	(3) b Adcock		46
M.E.Chapple	c Lawrence b Lance	11	(4) lbw b Lawrence		9
A.E.Dick†	b Lawrence	16	(6) c McLean b Lawrence		1
G.A.Bartlett	c Waite b Lawrence	0	c Waite b Lawrence		33
J.C.Alabaster	c Bromfield b Lance	2	c Waite b Lawrence		3
R.C.Motz	not out	10	lbw b Adcock		0
F.J.Cameron	lbw b Lawrence	2	not out		0
Extras	(lb 1, nb 1)	2	(lb 2, nb 4)		6
TOTAL	(53.1 overs)	**164**	(88.2 overs)		**249**

SOUTH AFRICA

D.J.McGlew*	run out	120
E.J.Barlow	c Dick b Reid	67
J.H.B.Waite†	c Dick b Alabaster	9
R.A.McLean	lbw b Motz	78
W.S.Farrer	c Bartlett b Alabaster	40
K.C.Bland	lbw b Reid	28
H.R.Lance	c Dick b Reid	7
G.B.Lawrence	c Harris b Motz	39
P.S.Heine	c Dick b Alabaster	31
N.A.T.Adcock	b Motz	17
H.D.Bromfield	not out	4
Extras	(b 1, lb 11, w 5, nb 7)	24
TOTAL	(124.2 overs)	**464**

Bowling	O	M	R	W	O	M	R	W		Fall of Wickets		
SOUTH AFRICA										NZ	SA	NZ
										1st	*1st*	*2nd*
Heine	12	2	45	0	24	5	78	2	1st	36	134	0
Adcock	10	4	23	2	24	12	40	3	2nd	40	170	23
Lawrence	16.1	3	52	5	22.2	10	57	4	3rd	76	282	38
Lance	13	6	30	3	13	0	50	1	4th	94	282	70
Bromfield	2	0	12	0	5	2	18	0	5th	130	351	84
NEW ZEALAND									6th	150	363	138
Motz	26.2	2	86	3					7th	150	367	222
Cameron	30	6	84	0					8th	150	422	244
Bartlett	18	1	57	0					9th	157	445	245
Alabaster	31	4	143	3					10th	164	464	249
Reid	16	3	55	3								
Chapple	3	0	15	0								

57 SOUTH AFRICA v NEW ZEALAND *(Fifth Test)*

at St George's Park, Port Elizabeth on 16, 17, 19, 20 February, 1962
Toss : New Zealand. Umpires : G.D. Gibbon and G. Parry
New Zealand won by 40 runs

South Africa went into the final test leading 2-1 and only needed a draw to win the series. Any advantage gained by John Reid winning his third successive toss seemed to have vanished when both openers were dismissed for 20 runs. Paul Barton, batting with a heavily strapped shoulder, was very cautious, while Reid was his effervescent best, hitting six boundaries in an innings of 26.

Noel McGregor and Zin Harris provided little support and half the team was out for 115. Artie Dick joined Barton and together they added a vital 65 runs before the brave and courageous innings of Barton ended at 109, scored in 276 minutes. Dick departed for a precious 46 and at the end of a slow day's play New Zealand were 242-7.

Gary Bartlett and Jack Alabaster carried the innings to a modest 275 all out. Diving to stop a ball, Jackie McGlew dislocated his shoulder in a replica of the accident that had happened to Barton in the fourth test. The South African captain dropped down the order to bat at eight and "Goofy" Lawrence was elevated to open with Eddie Barlow.

The tall fast bowler produced his best test score, 43, while more renowned batsmen struggled against tight bowling and excellent fielding. Graham Dowling, standing at short backward square-leg picked up three catches. All five New Zealand bowlers captured a wicket as the home team were dismissed for 190.

With their team trailing by 85 on the first innings the South African bowlers subjected the tourists' top order to a barrage of short-pitched deliveries. In his brief stay John Sparling was struck by Peter Pollock and suffered two broken ribs. Dowling and Harris survived a torrid 40 minutes and New Zealand was 36-1 at stumps on the second day.

Reid and Dowling shared a match-winning partnership of 125 runs for the fourth wicket as the home team seemed intent on playing for a draw. McGlew's field placing became very defensive and the over-rate slowed down to about 12 an hour. When the partnership was broken, the last five batsmen were swept away for 53 runs. New Zealand's innings of 228 left the home team an hour plus the whole of the fourth day in which to score 314 runs.

Both openers were dropped late on the third day, thus surviving to resume on the last morning at 38. South Africa reached 100-1 as the game swung their way. Barlow reached his third half-century of the series before Reid bowled him. A superb throw from McGregor, fielding some 60 metres from the bat at square leg, accounted for McGlew; 117-3.

This stranglehold was tightened as another three wickets fell with the total at 142. In the next 90 minutes the tourists seemed determined to let their opponents escape the noose.

Four catches were dropped before Colin Bland became the seventh wicket to fall at 193, with Lawrence following six runs later.

The game took another turn as Pollock and Neil Adcock defied the bowlers and, more alarmingly, began compiling runs at a brisk rate. In less than an hour the score advanced by 60 runs until it was terminated when Dick Motz bowled Adcock with the new ball.

Harry Bromfield defended stoutly for over half an hour before he popped a catch into the hands of McGregor at silly point. This gave the tourists victory by 40 runs and a squared series. It was appropriate that Reid should return the best bowling figures of the second innings – 4-44 off 45 overs.

Throughout the tour his sublime, attacking batting had overshadowed his skill with the ball. But always the man for the moment and a captain who led by example, Reid earned a just reward with this fine victory. In the tests Reid scored more runs than any two of his colleagues. The consistent bowling of Motz, Alabaster and Cameron, with the occasional fiery spell from Bartlett, and Reid's inspirational bursts, gave New Zealand its best all-round test attack to date.

The leadership of Reid, Chapple and manager Leggat developed the tourists' spirit, a quality most evident in their ability to overcome adversity in the vital test matches. They succeeded admirably.

THE LESSON SOUTH AFRICA CAN LEARN FROM THE KIWIS

Play cricket the "Reid" way

ALL those of you who read the News Magazine section of the SUN-DAY TIMES to share moments with Molly Reinhardt, and those crazy men of Calamity Gulch, most probably will have heard of John Reid, New Zealand's great cricket captain and batsman.

But you will also have heard of a six-foot South African named "Tiger" Lance, if you follow the fortunes of the Rangers Football Club, or have been listening to Test cricket commentaries.

"Tiger," the derivation of whose nickname remains a mystery to most cricketers, moves his giant frame only when it is absolutely necessary for him to move it, and then he is more like a languid leopard than a tiger.

He had been bowling to John Reid for some time on a January, 1962, morning at East London at considerable cost to his average.

He had delivered just about every kind of ball he was capable of delivering to Reid, and Reid had done just about everything to those deliveries except hit one of them into the ocean.

Long run

DESPAIRINGLY, "Tiger" trudged back to the beginning of his long loping run.

John Reid's batting was being hailed as the finest ever seen in South Africa.

NEW ZEALAND

G.T.Dowling	lbw b Adcock	2	lbw b Lawrence		78
J.T.Sparling	c Lance b Pollock	3	c Bromfield b Pollock		4
P.T.Barton	c Bromfield b Lance	109	(4) lbw b Pollock		2
J.R.Reid*	b Adcock	26	(5) c Bromfield b Lance		69
S.N.McGregor	b Pollock	10	(6) b Lawrence		24
P.G.Z.Harris	c McGlew b Bromfield	7	(3) c Bland b Adcock		13
A.E.Dick†	c Waite b Pollock	46	lbw b Lance		1
G.A.Bartlett	hit wicket b Adcock	29	c Barlow b Lawrence		18
J.C.Alabaster	lbw b Lawrence	24	c Adcock b Lawrence		7
R.C.Motz	c McLean b Lawrence	2	c Waite b Pollock		0
F.J.Cameron	not out	1	not out		0
Extras	(b 1, lb 7, nb 8)	16	(b 4, lb 6, nb 2)		12
TOTAL	**(111.2 overs)**	**275**	**(83.1 overs)**		**228**

SOUTH AFRICA

E.J.Barlow	c Dowling b Motz	20	b Reid		59
G.B.Lawrence	c Dick b Alabaster	43	(8) b Alabaster		17
J.H.B.Waite†	c Dowling b Cameron	0	(4) c Dowling b Reid		7
W.S.Farrer	c Dick b Motz	7	(2) lbw b Cameron		10
R.A.McLean	c McGregor b Bartlett	25	b Alabaster		10
K.C.Bland	lbw b Bartlett	12	lbw b Reid		32
H.R.Lance	st Dick b Reid	9	c Dick b Reid		9
D.J.McGlew*	not out	28	(3) run out		26
P.M.Pollock	lbw b Motz	8	not out		54
N.A.T.Adcock	c Dowling b Reid	5	b Motz		24
H.D.Bromfield	c Dick b Alabaster	21	c McGregor b Cameron		0
Extras	(lb 6, nb 6)	12	(b 6, lb 3, w 2, nb 14)		25
TOTAL	**(72.4 overs)**	**190**	**(144 overs)**		**273**

Bowling	O	M	R	W	O	M	R	W
SOUTH AFRICA								
Adcock	27	11	60	3	21	11	25	1
Pollock	28	9	63	3	24.1	5	70	3
Lawrence	26.2	7	71	2	28	5	85	4
Lance	14	4	50	1	8	0	36	2
Bromfield	16	7	15	1	2	2	0	0
NEW ZEALAND								
Cameron	11	2	46	1	18	6	48	2
Bartlett	8	4	10	2	9	3	26	0
Motz	14	7	33	3	20	11	34	1
Alabaster	25.4	7	63	2	52	23	96	2
Reid	14	6	26	2	45	27	44	4

Fall of Wickets	NZ 1st	SA 1st	NZ 2nd	SA 2nd
1st	4	34	4	57
2nd	20	39	37	101
3rd	82	65	50	117
4th	108	92	175	125
5th	115	112	185	133
6th	180	115	192	142
7th	225	125	216	193
8th	269	137	228	199
9th	272	143	228	259
10th	275	190	228	273

MILESTONES

• John Reid set a record aggregate for a season in South Africa with 1915 runs at an average of 68.37 with seven centuries. He headed off Denis Compton (1781), Neil Harvey (1526) and Jack Hobbs (1489).

All eyes are on the square-leg umpire as Artie Dick stumps Tiger Lance in the first innings of the fifth test. From left, Jack Alabaster, Jackie McGlew, Artie Dick, Tiger Lance and the bowler John Reid.

AVERAGES

New Zealand

BATTING	M	I	NO	Runs	HS	Ave
J.R. Reid	5	10	1	546	142	60.66
P.G.Z. Harris	5	10	1	284	101	31.55
M.E. Chapple	2	4	0	122	69	30.50
P.T. Barton	4	8	0	240	109	30.00
G.T. Dowling	4	8	0	238	78	29.75
S.N. McGregor	5	10	0	242	68	24.20
G.A. Bartlett	5	9	0	215	40	23.88
A.E. Dick	5	9	1	139	50*	17.37
F.J. Cameron	5	9	8	17	10*	17.00
J.T. Sparling	3	6	0	58	19	9.66
J.C. Alabaster	5	9	0	68	24	7.55
J.W. Guy	2	4	0	18	9	4.50
R.C. Motz	5	9	1	25	10*	3.12

BOWLING	O	M	R	W	Ave
J.R. Reid	109.2	47	217	11	19.72
F.J. Cameron	201.2	54	493	20	24.65
R.C. Motz	182.2	41	505	19	26.57
J.C. Alabaster	224.3	60	617	22	28.04
J.T. Sparling	13	5	34	1	34.00
G.A. Bartlett	114	26	326	8	40.75
M.E. Chapple	4	0	18	0	-

South Africa

BATTING	M	I	NO	Runs	HS	Ave
D.J. McGlew	5	9	2	426	127*	60.85
R.A. McLean	5	9	0	356	113	39.55
E.J. Barlow	5	9	0	330	67	36.66
P.S. Heine	1	1	0	31	31	31.00
J.H.B. Waite	5	9	0	263	101	29.22
P.M. Pollock	3	6	2	115	54*	28.75
K.C. Bland	5	9	0	205	42	22.77
G.B. Lawrence	5	8	0	141	43	17.62
W.S. Farrer	3	5	0	88	40	17.60
N.A.T. Adcock	2	3	0	46	24	15.33
A.H. McKinnon	1	2	1	13	9*	13.00
M.K. Elgie	3	6	0	75	56	12.50
S. O'Linn	2	4	1	36	17	12.00
H.D. Bromfield	5	8	4	37	21	9.25
H.R. Lance	2	3	0	25	9	8.33
S.F. Burke	1	2	0	12	12	6.00
K.A. Walter	2	3	0	11	10	3.66

BOWLING	O	M	R	W	Ave
N.A.T. Adcock	82	38	148	9	16.44
P.M. Pollock	128.4	35	299	17	17.58
S.F. Burke	81	29	196	11	17.81
G.B. Lawrence	222.2	62	512	28	18.28
H.R. Lance	48	10	166	7	23.71
A.H. McKinnon	36	13	74	3	24.66
K.A. Walter	82.3	20	197	6	32.83
H.D. Bromfield	151	40	321	8	40.12
P.S. Heine	36	7	123	2	61.50
M.K. Elgie	11	2	46	0	-
E.J. Barlow	43	7	130	0	-

1962/63 MCC in New Zealand

1962/63 was the beginning of change not only in society but also in cricket. The distinction between amateurs and professionals in England was abolished. Different ideas were being promoted. The front foot rule for no-balls was introduced. A Sunday one-day competition began in England and in July 1962 a communications satellite named "Telstar" was launched enabling the transmission of images around the world.

58 NEW ZEALAND v ENGLAND *(First Test)*

at Eden Park, Auckland on 23, 25, 26, 27 February, 1963
Toss : England. Umpires : J.M.A. Brown and R.W.R. Shortt
England won by an innings and 215 runs

The England openers were ill at ease on a damp wicket, and both fell to Frank Cameron before the score had reached 50. With his fifth ball at test level Bryan Yuile had Ted Dexter expertly caught by Paul Barton at slip; 74-3 at lunch.

New Zealand lost the initiative in the next session when Colin Cowdrey joined Ken Barrington in a brisk partnership that added 166 runs in even time. Barrington's century, his third in consecutive tests, arrived in 215 minutes. Peter Parfitt saw Barrington through to 126, when the latter became Cameron's fourth victim. His five-hour stay had produced a six and 15 fours. Barry Knight joined Parfitt to carry England to 328-5 at stumps.

Both batsmen completed centuries on the second day while establishing a new sixth wicket record for England of 240 runs in 215 minutes before Knight was bowled for 125. Parfitt was 131 not out when Dexter declared at 562-7.

Faced with a mammoth task to save the game New Zealand's top order submitted meekly to the pace of David Larter and three wickets were swept away in the first half-hour. Barry Sinclair and John Reid carried the score to 62 before Sinclair was caught. Shortly afterwards bad light sent players from the field an hour early with the score 66-4.

A defiant 59 by Reid was followed by an entertaining stand of 95 for the eighth wicket between Dick Motz and Yuile, but it was not enough to prevent New Zealand being asked to follow on after they were dismissed for 256. The home team's top order failed for the second time and at stumps New Zealand was 42-4 with Reid dropping down the order to bat at six.

In the first 16 minutes of the next morning Reid watched his team's hope of salvaging a draw vanish as Sinclair, Artie Dick and Yuile fell to Larter, while the score crept to 56. When New Zealand were dismissed for a meagre 89 Reid was 21 not out.

ENGLAND

D.S.Sheppard	c Dick b Cameron	12
R.Illingworth	c Reid b Cameron	20
K.F.Barrington	c Playle b Cameron	126
E.R.Dexter*	c Barton b Yuile	7
M.C.Cowdrey	c Barton b Cameron	86
P.H.Parfitt	not out	131
B.R.Knight	b Alabaster	125
F.J.Titmus	st Dick b Sparling	26
J.T.Murray†	not out	9
J.D.F.Larter		
L.J.Coldwell		
Extras	(b 18, lb 1, nb 1)	20
TOTAL	**(186 overs) (7 wkts dec)**	**562**

NEW ZEALAND

G.T.Dowling	b Coldwell	3	b Illingworth		14
W.R.Playle	c Dexter b Larter	0	c Dexter b Coldwell		4
P.T.Barton	c Sheppard b Larter	3	lbw b Titmus		16
J.R.Reid*	b Titmus	59	(6) not out		21
B.W.Sinclair	c Coldwell b Titmus	24	b Larter		2
J.T.Sparling	c Murray b Larter	3	(4) c Barrington b Illingworth		0
A.E.Dick†	run out	29	c Illingworth b Larter		0
B.W.Yuile	run out	64	lbw b Larter		1
R.C.Motz	c Murray b Knight	60	c & b Illingworth		20
J.C.Alabaster	b Knight	2	c Titmus b Illingworth		0
F.J.Cameron	not out	0	b Larter		1
Extras	(b 5, lb 3, w 1, nb 2)	11	(b 2, lb 8)		10
TOTAL	**(110.4 overs)**	**258**	**(53.1 overs)**		**89**

Bowling	O	M	R	W	O	M	R	W
NEW ZEALAND								
Motz	42	12	98	0				
Cameron	43	7	118	4				
Alabaster	40	6	130	1				
Yuile	21	4	77	1				
Reid	28	8	67	0				
Sparling	12	2	52	1				
ENGLAND								
Coldwell	27	9	66	1	5	2	4	1
Larter	26	12	51	3	14.1	3	26	4
Knight	10.4	2	23	2	10	2	13	0
Titmus	25	9	44	2	6	5	2	1
Barrington	12	4	38	0				
Dexter	9	4	20	0				
Illingworth	1	0	5	0	18	7	34	4

Fall of Wickets	E	NZ	NZ
	1st	1st	2nd
1st	24	0	15
2nd	45	7	42
3rd	63	7	42
4th	229	62	42
5th	258	71	46
6th	498	109	46
7th	535	161	56
8th	-	256	83
9th	-	258	83
10th	-	258	89

Playing in his first test, Bryan Yuile found himself coming in to bat in the unenviable position of New Zealand at 109-6 in reply to England's mammoth 562. He was initially very cautious but later, batting with Dick Motz, he became more adventuresome, particularly against the spinners.

MILESTONES

- Barry Sinclair (94) and Bryan Yuile (95) made their test debuts.

- Peter Parfitt and Barry Knight established a new sixth wicket record for England of 240.

- England's total of 562 for seven declared was the highest achieved by any team against New Zealand.

59 NEW ZEALAND v ENGLAND *(Second Test)*

at Basin Reserve, Wellington on 1, 2, 4 March, 1963
Toss : England. Umpires : D.P. Dumbleton and W.T. Martin
England won by an innings and 47 runs

After missing the first test because of injury, Fred Trueman dominated proceedings on the first morning with four wickets. He was aggressive, fast and moved the ball in the air as well as off the seam. He was simply too good for New Zealand.

When Mike Shrimpton was dismissed shortly after lunch for a valiant 28, seven New Zealand wickets had fallen for 96 runs. Bob Blair led the tail-end batsmen in three partnerships that doubled their team's total. With Bryan Yuile, 33 were added for the eighth wicket; with Bruce Morrison 21 for the ninth; and for the 10th wicket 44 runs with Frank Cameron.

Blair batted with carefree confidence and power against all the bowlers and remained unbeaten on 64 when the innings ended at 194. The crowd's applause for Blair, the batsman, had scarcely died away when he bowled David Sheppard with the second ball of England's innings. Nothing else untoward occurred as England reached 74-1.

On the second day Ken Barrington compiled 76, Ray Illingworth 46, and Ted Dexter, Barry Knight and Fred Titmus thirties while the New Zealand bowlers could feel satisfied in taking eight wickets for 276 by tea in cold and blustery conditions.

Colin Cowdrey, nursing a damaged hand, had come in at number eight and was joined by wicketkeeper Alan Smith when England's lead was 71. The pair batted through the last session to extend the advantage to 216, with Smith being twice dropped off Blair.

Cowdrey's unbeaten century was his first against New Zealand and completed his sequence of hundreds against all the test-playing countries. Dexter delayed his declaration for 20 minutes on the third day, allowing Cowdrey and Smith to set a new world test record of 163 for the ninth wicket.

Facing a deficit of 234 New Zealand were in dire straits, losing Reid's wicket, the third, with the score at 41 before Bill Playle and Barry Sinclair staged a recovery, adding 81 runs in 97 minutes. The wicket was now showing signs of turning and the right arm off-spinner, Titmus, and right arm leg-spinner, Barrington, bore the brunt of the attack.

Playle survived for 202 minutes for a gutsy 65. Following his demise the tailenders, who had performed heroically in the first innings, were unable to repeat the performance in the second. Only Artie Dick batted with assurance and hit five boundaries in his 38 not out. The game finished soon after tea on the third day.

NEW ZEALAND

Batsman	Dismissal (1st)	Score	Dismissal (2nd)	Score
G.T.Dowling	c Smith b Trueman	12	c Knight b Trueman	2
W.R.Playle	c Smith b Knight	23	c & b Illingworth	65
P.T.Barton	c Cowdrey b Trueman	0	c Barrington b Knight	3
J.R.Reid*	c Smith b Knight	0	c Barrington b Titmus	9
B.W.Sinclair	b Trueman	4	c & b Barrington	36
M.J.F.Shrimpton	lbw b Knight	28	c Parfitt b Barrington	10
A.E.Dick†	c Sheppard b Trueman	7	not out	38
B.W.Yuile	c Illingworth b Titmus	13	b Titmus	0
R.W.Blair	not out	64	c Larter b Titmus	5
B.D.Morrison	run out	10	c Larter b Titmus	0
F.J.Cameron	lbw b Barrington	12	lbw b Barrington	0
Extras	(b 13, lb 5, nb 3)	21	(b 13, lb 4, nb 2)	19
TOTAL	**(76.3 overs)**	**194**	**(98 overs)**	**187**

ENGLAND

Batsman	Dismissal	Score
D.S.Sheppard	b Blair	0
R.Illingworth	c Morrison b Blair	46
K.F.Barrington	c Dick b Reid	76
E.R.Dexter*	b Morrison	31
P.H.Parfitt	c Dick b Morrison	0
B.R.Knight	c Dick b Cameron	31
F.J.Titmus	run out	33
M.C.Cowdrey	not out	128
F.S.Trueman	b Cameron	3
A.C.Smith†	not out	69
J.D.F.Larter		
Extras	(b 3, lb 6, nb 2)	11
TOTAL	**(149 overs) (8 wkts dec)**	**428**

Bowling ENGLAND	O	M	R	W	O	M	R	W
Trueman	20	5	46	4	18	7	27	1
Larter	14	2	52	0	7	1	18	0
Knight	21	8	32	3	4	1	7	1
Titmus	18	3	40	1	31	15	50	4
Barrington	2.3	1	1	1	11	3	32	3
Dexter	1	0	2	0				
Illingworth					27	14	34	1

NEW ZEALAND	O	M	R	W
Blair	33	11	81	2
Morrison	31	5	129	2
Cameron	43	16	98	2
Reid	32	8	73	1
Yuile	10	1	36	0

Fall of Wickets	NZ 1st	E 1st	NZ 2nd
1st	32	0	15
2nd	32	77	18
3rd	35	125	41
4th	40	125	122
5th	61	173	126
6th	74	197	158
7th	96	258	159
8th	129	265	171
9th	150	-	179
10th	194	-	187

MILESTONES

- Bruce Morrison (96) and Michael Shrimpton (97) made their test debuts.

- Colin Cowdrey and Alan Smith set a new world test record of 163 runs for the ninth wicket.

60 NEW ZEALAND v ENGLAND *(Third Test)*

at Lancaster Park, Christchurch on 15, 16, 18, 19 March, 1963
Toss : New Zealand. Umpires : L.C. Johnston and W.T. Martin
England won by 7 wickets

After the halcyon days of the previous season, when John Reid's team had performed so well in South Africa, cricket supporters in New Zealand were plunged into a familiar sense of gloom. Live television coverage of the third test was perhaps regarded as a rather masochistic treat.

The early loss of Bill Playle was compensated by a partnership of 80 between Graham Dowling and Barry Sinclair but both fell before the total reached 80. John Reid had seldom batted well at Lancaster Park but he now delighted the crowd with an aggressive 74, his best effort at the ground in 14 years.

Mike Shrimpton began with extreme caution, gathering just eight runs in his first hour at the wicket. He was very much the junior partner when he and Reid added 67. When he was dismissed at 234 Trueman then captured three wickets in 11 balls to leave the innings in tatters.

On the second morning Trueman accounted for Dick Motz and Frank Cameron, increasing his tally to 7-75 off 31 overs as the innings ended at 266. The home team then rewarded the crowd of 19,000 with a grand performance in the field. Four England batsmen scored polished forties, but none completed a half-century. All the New Zealand bowlers dropped onto a tight length and commanded respect. England 244-8.

For the first time in the series the home team battled to a lead on the first innings but the slender advantage of 13 runs was completely dissipated when Playle and Paul Barton were dismissed with the second innings score at 17. Carrying on from where he had left off in the first innings, Reid displayed all the qualities of great batsmanship: footwork, wrists, economy of power, the great strokes of the game, and each one of them thoroughly under control.

In little more than four hours, he accumulated a precise century. Scoring 74 and 100, or 41 per cent of New Zealand's aggregate runs for the match, it was not surprising that he left to a standing ovation from the crowd and the visiting team. This might have been John Reid's finest game as a batsman in test cricket.

Regrettably, no other New Zealand player was able to stay with him and New Zealand were dismissed for 159. Three English batsmen were dismissed before the winning run was struck in the middle of the last afternoon.

In the last nine years New Zealand had played England, arguably the strongest bowling attack in test cricket in the world, 12 times and lost 10 games, seven of them by an innings and the other three by comfortable margins.

NEW ZEALAND

G.T.Dowling	c Dexter b Titmus	40	c Smith b Larter		22
W.R.Playle	c Barrington b Trueman	0	c Smith b Trueman		3
B.W.Sinclair	hit wicket b Trueman	44	lbw b Larter		0
J.R.Reid*	c Parfitt b Knight	74	b Titmus		100
P.T.Barton	c Smith b Knight	11	lbw b Knight		12
M.J.F.Shrimpton	c Knight b Trueman	31	b Titmus		8
A.E.Dick†	b Trueman	16	c Parfitt b Titmus		1
R.C.Motz	c Parfitt b Trueman	7	b Larter		3
R.W.Blair	c Parfitt b Trueman	0	b Titmus		0
J.C.Alabaster	not out	20	c Parfitt b Trueman		1
F.J.Cameron	c Smith b Trueman	1	not out		0
Extras	(b 1, lb 9, w 3, nb 9)	22	(lb 7, nb 2)		9
TOTAL	(118.2 overs)	**266**	(83.4 overs)		**159**

ENGLAND

D.S.Sheppard	b Cameron	42	b Alabaster		31
R.Illingworth	c Dick b Cameron	2			
K.F.Barrington	lbw b Motz	47	(2) c Reid b Blair		45
E.R.Dexter*	b Alabaster	46			
M.C.Cowdrey	c Motz b Blair	43	(3) not out		35
P.H.Parfitt	lbw b Reid	4	(4) c Shrimpton b Alabaster		31
B.R.Knight	b Blair	32	(5) not out		20
F.J.Titmus	c Dick b Motz	4			
F.S.Trueman	c Reid b Alabaster	11			
A.C.Smith†	not out	2			
J.D.F.Larter	b Motz	2			
Extras	(b 4, lb 6, w 5, nb 3)	18	(b 9, nb 2)		11
TOTAL	(95.5 overs)	**253**	(59.3 overs) (3 wkts)		**173**

Bowling	O	M	R	W	O	M	R	W		*Fall of Wickets*			
ENGLAND											NZ	E	NZ	E
Trueman	30.2	9	75	7	19.4	8	16	2			*1st*	*1st*	*2nd*	*2nd*
Larter	21	5	59	0	23	8	32	3		1st	3	11	16	70
Knight	23	5	39	2	10	3	38	1		2nd	83	87	17	96
Titmus	30	13	45	1	21	8	46	4		3rd	98	103	66	149
Dexter	9	3	8	0	10	2	18	0		4th	128	186	91	-
Barrington	5	0	18	0						5th	195	188	129	-
NEW ZEALAND										6th	234	210	133	-
Motz	19.5	3	68	3	20	6	33	0		7th	235	225	151	-
Cameron	24	6	47	2	12	3	38	0		8th	235	244	154	-
Blair	24	12	42	2	12	3	34	1		9th	251	250	159	-
Alabaster	20	6	47	2	15.3	5	57	2		10th	266	253	159	-
Reid	8	1	31	1										

MILESTONES

- Fred Trueman established a new world test record when he captured his 243rd wicket.

- New Zealand's score of 159 is the lowest all out total in tests to include an individual century.

AVERAGES

New Zealand

BATTING	M	I	NO	Runs	HS	Ave
J.R. Reid	3	6	1	263	100	52.60
R.W. Blair	2	4	1	69	64*	23.00
R.C. Motz	2	4	0	90	60	22.50
B.W. Yuile	2	4	0	78	64	19.50
M.J.F. Shrimpton	2	4	0	77	31	19.25
B.W. Sinclair	3	6	0	110	44	18.33
A.E. Dick	3	6	1	91	38*	18.20
W.R. Playle	3	6	0	95	65	15.83
G.T. Dowling	3	6	0	93	40	15.50
J.C. Alabaster	2	4	1	23	20*	7.66
P.T. Barton	3	6	0	45	16	7.50
B.D. Morrison	1	2	0	10	10	5.00
F.J. Cameron	3	6	2	14	12	3.50
J.T. Sparling	1	2	0	3	3	1.50

BOWLING	O	M	R	W	Ave
R.W. Blair	69	26	157	5	31.40
F.J. Cameron	122	32	301	8	37.62
J.C. Alabaster	75.3	17	234	5	46.80
J.T. Sparling	12	2	52	1	52.00
B.D. Morrison	31	5	129	2	64.50
R.C. Motz	81.5	21	199	3	66.33
J.R. Reid	68	17	171	2	85.50
B.W. Yuile	31	5	113	1	113.00

England

BATTING	M	I	NO	Runs	HS	Ave
M.C. Cowdrey	3	4	2	292	128*	146.00
K.F. Barrington	3	4	0	294	126	73.50
B.R. Knight	3	4	1	208	125	69.33
P.H. Parfitt	3	4	1	166	131*	55.33
E.R. Dexter	3	3	0	84	46	28.00
R. Illingworth	3	3	0	68	46	22.66
D.S. Sheppard	3	4	0	85	42	21.25
F.J. Titmus	3	3	0	63	33	21.00
F.S. Trueman	2	2	0	14	11	7.00
J.D.F. Larter	3	1	0	2	2	2.00
A.C. Smith	2	2	2	71	69*	-
J.T. Murray	1	1	1	9	9*	-
L.J. Coldwell	1	-	-	-	-	-

BOWLING	O	M	R	W	Ave
F.S. Trueman	88	29	164	14	11.71
R. Illingworth	46	21	73	5	14.60
B.R. Knight	78.4	21	152	9	16.88
F.J. Titmus	131	53	227	13	17.46
K.F. Barrington	30.3	8	89	4	22.25
J.D.F. Larter	105.1	31	238	10	23.80
L.J. Coldwell	32	11	70	2	35.00
E.R. Dexter	29	9	48	0	-

John Reid had seldom batted well at Lancaster Park. His aggressive 74 in the first innings was his best effort at the ground in 14 years. His 100 in the second innings was perhaps the greatest innings that he played in his life. The England team showed their appreciation by applauding him off the field.

The enigmatic Paul Barton looked stylish even when not scoring runs. Peter Parfitt is at slip.

1963/64 South Africa in New Zealand

South Africa arrived in New Zealand having squared a five test series with Australia. The enterprising batting of Eddie Barlow, who scored three hundreds in the series, the talented 19-year-old Graeme Pollock, who had made two hundreds, and the energetic fielding of Colin Bland were all eagerly looked forward to by the New Zealand public.

61 **NEW ZEALAND v SOUTH AFRICA** *(First Test)*

at Basin Reserve, Wellington on 21, 22, 24, 25 February, 1964
Toss : South Africa. Umpires : D.P. Dumbleton and W.T. Martin
Match drawn

The Basin Reserve was under periodic police surveillance to prevent the threat of action by anti-apartheid protesters. Batting first on an easy but slow wicket, the tourists found it difficult to score against a containing attack. The first seven batsmen bettered 20 but Bland's innings of 40 was the highest. Bad light ended the day 20 minutes early; 233-7.

A cold southerly swept the ground and a shivering crowd of 6000 saw only 186 runs scored on the second day. The South African bowlers bowled with precision rather than hostility and were supported by field placings designed to pin batsmen down and goad them into taking risks. With three down for 49 Barry Sinclair and Noel McGregor added 63 before Sinclair was dismissed, shortly before stumps, after batting 205 minutes; 117-4.

Solid batting in the middle order by McGregor, John Sparling and Murray Chapple occupied much of the third day. Chapple and Sparling added 86 runs for the fifth wicket. With a number of delicate cuts and glances, Chapple provided the most attractive batting of the innings and deserved the top score of 59. Once he left at 234 Peter Pollock captured the last four wickets in 23 deliveries to finish with 6-47.

The South African bowling attack had been exceptionally economical bowling 67 maidens during the innings. The game finally came to life in the last session of the day when Trevor Goddard and Barlow put on 79 runs in 96 minutes.

The opening partnership lasted another half-hour next morning and was worth 117 runs before Goddard was dismissed. Barlow hit 14 boundaries before he was caught behind eight runs short of a century. Buster Farrer and Bland continued at a merry pace, adding 75 in 47 minutes. The declaration was made at 218-2.

The pitch was too low and slow for New Zealand to confidently set about their run-chase, which required them to score 268 in four hours. There was sufficient time for test debutant Graham Gedye to complete a half-century.

MILESTONES

- Graham Gedye (98) and John Ward (99) made their test debuts.

SOUTH AFRICA				
T.L.Goddard*	b Cameron	24	b Reid	40
E.J.Barlow	b Cameron	22	c Ward b Cameron	92
A.J.Pithey	c Chapple b Motz	31		
W.S.Farrer	b Reid	30	(3) not out	38
K.C.Bland	c Ward b Blair	40	(4) not out	46
J.H.B.Waite†	b Blair	30		
D.T.Lindsay	b Cameron	27		
P.L.van der Merwe	b Motz	44		
D.B.Pithey	b Blair	7		
P.M.Pollock	c Dowling b Reid	24		
J.T.Partridge	not out	2		
Extras	(b 9, lb 3, nb 9)	21	(b 2)	2
TOTAL	(131.5 overs)	**302**	(66 overs) (2 wkts dec)	**218**

NEW ZEALAND				
G.T.Dowling	b Pollock	1	lbw b Bland	32
S.G.Gedye	lbw b Pollock	10	c van der Merwe b Pollock	52
B.W.Sinclair	lbw b Pithey D.B.	44	b Bland	0
J.R.Reid*	c Barlow b Partridge	16	b Goddard	12
S.N.McGregor	b Pithey D.B.	39	lbw b Van der Merwe	24
J.T.Sparling	lbw b Pollock	49	c van der Merwe b Pollock	1
M.E.Chapple	c Goddard b Partridge	59	not out	0
R.C.Motz	c Pithey D.B. b Pollock	2	not out	0
J.T.Ward†	b Pollock	5		
R.W.Blair	b Pollock	5		
F.J.Cameron	not out	1		
Extras	(b 10, lb 5, nb 7)	22	(b 6, lb 7, w 1, nb 3)	7
TOTAL	(152.5 overs)	**253**	(76 overs) (6 wkts)	**138**

Bowling	O	M	R	W	O	M	R	W		Fall of Wickets			
NEW ZEALAND										SA	NZ	SA	NZ
										1st	1st	2nd	2nd
Motz	25	3	68	2	15	2	53	0					
Cameron	30	13	58	3	19	6	60	1	1st	41	14	117	64
Blair	41	10	86	3	11	0	48	0	2nd	56	17	143	64
Reid	29.5	12	47	2	21	8	55	1	3rd	97	49	-	79
Sparling	6	1	22	0					4th	121	112	-	134
SOUTH AFRICA									5th	189	148	-	136
Pollock	31.5	9	47	6	16	4	31	2	6th	198	234	-	138
Partridge	45	24	50	2	14	8	10	0	7th	233	242	-	-
Goddard	38	21	42	0	16	10	11	1	8th	257	243	-	-
Barlow	11	0	38	0	2	1	13	0	9th	292	252	-	-
Pithey D.B.	24	11	53	2	14	3	34	0	10th	302	253	-	-
Bland	3	2	1	0	9	3	16	2					
van der Merwe					5	4	6	1					

Frank Cameron's first 13 overs yielded only 19 runs and saw him bowl both openers, including Trevor Goddard, who is backing up.

62 NEW ZEALAND v SOUTH AFRICA *(Second Test)*

at Carisbrook, Dunedin on 28, 29 February, 2, 3 March, 1964
Toss : New Zealand. Umpires : D.C. Burns and H.B. Cassie
Match drawn

No play was possible on the first day because of rain, which fell again on the afternoon of the second day, washing out the session after tea.

The home team could not score quickly on the heavy outfield. Wynne Bradburn scored a diligent 32 and Barry Sinclair played well but six wickets fell for 114. Sinclair had sensibly played himself in before beginning to attack short-pitched deliveries on his leg stump. His innings of 52 lasted almost three hours.

Murray Chapple's 37 in two hours, completed on the third morning, was the next best contribution to New Zealand's disappointing total of 149. After little more than two hours, when the visitors' opening partnership had realised 117 runs, John Reid had Trevor Goddard caught behind for 63.

By stumps, South Africa had lost nine batsmen for 209 and Reid's superb spell of 35 consecutive overs had resulted in six wickets for 60 runs. The New Zealand captain performed this Herculean task despite injuring a groin muscle early in the afternoon.

On the fourth morning, the South African innings concluded at 223, giving them a lead of 74, and a draw seemed inevitable. A solid opening by Graham Gedye and Bradburn took the score to 41 for one at lunch. After the break David Pithey floated up his right-arm off-spinners and had all the batsmen floundering hopelessly. Rain at three o'clock provided merciful relief for an hour.

When play resumed, New Zealand was in desperate straits at 79-8, just five runs in credit. Artie Dick, Bob Blair and Frank Cameron battled intelligently, mixing caution with aggression to take the score to 138, with Pithey capturing 6-58.

South Africa had 27 minutes in which to score 65 runs for victory. In the first four overs they made 25 but lost three wickets. When the task became 40 runs in the last 10 minutes, the game was terminated. The predictable draw eventuated but not before a struggle that was by turns grim and exciting.

MILESTONES

• Wynne Bradburn (100) made his test debut.

NEW ZEALAND

Batsman	Dismissal (1st)	Runs	Dismissal (2nd)	Runs
S.G.Gedye	c Waite b Partridge	6	b Pithey D.B.	25
W.P.Bradburn	b Pollock	32	lbw b Pithey D.B.	14
B.W.Sinclair	c Lindsay b Goddard	52	lbw b Goddard	11
J.R.Reid*	b Pollock	2	(7) c Bland b Pithey D.B.	2
S.N.McGregor	run out	3	(4) run out	11
J.T.Sparling	b Pollock	1	(5) b Pithey D.B.	1
M.E.Chapple	c Farrer b Pithey D.B.	37	(6) b Pithey D.B.	7
A.E.Dick†	c Pithey D.B. b Partridge	3	lbw b Pithey D.B.	22
R.C.Motz	c Pithey D.B. b Partridge	3	lbw b Pollock	0
R.W.Blair	b Partridge	0	not out	26
F.J.Cameron	not out	1	b Pollock	8
Extras	(b 3, lb 3, nb 3)	9	(lb 7, nb 4)	11
TOTAL	(94 overs)	**149**	(84.5 overs)	**138**

SOUTH AFRICA

Batsman	Dismissal (1st)	Runs	Dismissal (2nd)	Runs
T.L.Goddard*	c Dick b Reid	63		
E.J.Barlow	b Reid	49	hit wicket b Cameron	13
A.J.Pithey	run out	1		
W.S.Farrer	run out	39		
K.C.Bland	lbw b Reid	1	(1) not out	16
J.H.B.Waite†	c Sparling b Reid	4		
D.T.Lindsay	c Motz b Reid	20	(3) b Blair	1
P.L.van der Merwe	c Sinclair b Reid	8	(4) b Blair	0
D.B.Pithey	c Bradburn b Sparling	9	(5) not out	8
P.M.Pollock	b Cameron	6		
J.T.Partridge	not out	8		
Extras	(b 6, lb 4, nb 5)	15	(lb 4)	4
TOTAL	(105.2 overs)	**223**	(7 overs) (3 wkts)	**42**

Bowling	O	M	R	W	O	M	R	W
SOUTH AFRICA								
Pollock	27	13	53	3	10.5	2	25	2
Partridge	34	15	51	4	5	4	3	0
Bland	9	4	9	0				
Goddard	17	14	10	1	26	10	29	1
Barlow	3	0	11	0				
Pithey D.B.	4	1	6	1	35	11	58	6
van der Merwe					8	3	12	0
NEW ZEALAND								
Motz	6	1	23	0				
Cameron	17.3	3	40	1	4	0	22	1
Blair	13	3	35	0	3	0	16	2
Reid	35	15	60	6				
Chapple	27	14	41	0				
Sparling	7	2	9	1				

Fall of Wickets	NZ 1st	SA 1st	NZ 2nd	SA 2nd
1st	11	117	38	18
2nd	62	124	42	23
3rd	64	124	63	25
4th	98	130	64	-
5th	100	134	67	-
6th	100	158	72	-
7th	132	168	73	-
8th	142	185	79	-
9th	148	209	111	-
10th	149	223	138	-

New Zealand wicketkeeper Artie Dick, the only first-class cricketer to hail from Middlemarch in Otago.

63 NEW ZEALAND v SOUTH AFRICA *(Third Test)*

at Eden Park, Auckland on 13, 14, 16, 17 March, 1964
Toss : New Zealand. Umpires : J.M.A. Brown and E.C.A. MacKintosh
Match drawn

Torrential rain had fallen in Auckland just prior to this test and John Reid decided to give his bowlers first use of a green wicket. However, the pitch was revealed to be placid and Eddie Barlow and Trevor Goddard compiled their third century opening stand of the series. Fierce hitting by Colin Bland and busy partnerships with John Waite and Denis Lindsay carried South Africa to 327 for five at the end of the first day.

On the next morning, Bland was dismissed for 83 as the tourists tallied 371. The last five wickets fell for 32 runs with Blair returning the best figures of the innings, 4-85. By the end of a balmy day New Zealand had reached 185 for three after losing their third wicket at 76. Barry Sinclair, who was 104 not out, provided the heart of the home team's innings.

He was struck twice by deliveries from Peter Pollock but responded with some magnificent hook shots. Noel McGregor, his partner for much of the afternoon, was content to act as a foil and the pair added 109 runs in 160 minutes.

On the third morning Sinclair and McGregor carried their partnership through to 171 before the former was out for 138, the highest score made by a New Zealander in a home test. Without a further run being scored McGregor's back foot dislodged a bail as he hooked a ball to the boundary and he was out hit wicket for 62 in five hours.

The euphoria created by Saturday's fight back was replaced with utter despondency as the last seven batsmen lasted only an hour and a quarter for the addition of 16 runs; 263 all out. Once again, Goddard and Barlow gave their side an excellent start by adding 92 for the first wicket before Barlow, having completed his fourth half-century of the series, was bowled by Blair. South Africa finished the day 163 for two.

Chasing quick runs on the last morning, South Africa lost three more wickets before Goddard declared at 200-5. This gave the tourists 313 minutes in which to bowl New Zealand out while New Zealand needed 309 runs for victory.

Shortly after lunch, with the score at 49, Wynne Bradburn walked despite the umpire rejecting an appeal for a catch behind. Graham Gedye's contribution of 55 was to be the best of the innings. Goddard's nagging, parsimonious bowling prevented any attempt to seek quick runs and he chipped away four wickets for 18 off 17 overs. Artie Dick and Bob Cunis came together at 185 for eight and defied a cluster of close fieldsmen until an appeal against the light was upheld.

The outstanding player for New Zealand in the series was diminutive Barry Sinclair, who scored runs batting at number three in each of the three first innings, coming in with the first wicket falling at 14, 11 and 7. His scores of 44, 52 and 138 provided much-needed backbone to each innings.

Barry Sinclair scored the first century made by a New Zealander in a test at Eden Park. His innings of 138 was the highest score made by a New Zealander in a home test. Sinclair's form in the first innings of each game was exceptional with scores of 44, 52 and 138.

MILESTONES

- Bob Cunis (101) made his test debut.

- Barry Sinclair scored the first test century by a New Zealander at Eden Park. His 138 was the highest score made by a New Zealander in a home test.

- The partnership of 171 between Barry Sinclair and Noel McGregor was a new test record for the fourth wicket.

- After 19 tests, in which he captured 43 wickets, Bob Blair announced his retirement from test cricket.

- This was the last test that New Zealand played against South Africa until 1994.

SOUTH AFRICA

T.L.Goddard*	c Sinclair b Cameron	73	c McGregor b Blair		33
E.J.Barlow	c Shrimpton b Blair	61	b Blair		58
A.J.Pithey	c Bradburn b Blair	13			
R.G.Pollock	b Reid	30	c Sinclair b Cunis		23
K.C.Bland	lbw b Cameron	83	not out		21
J.H.B.Waite	c Dick b Cameron	28	(3) c Sinclair b Blair		41
D.T.Lindsay†	b Blair	37	(6) b Cunis		1
W.S.Farrer	lbw b Reid	21	(7) not out		5
D.B.Pithey	c Dick b Blair	1			
P.M.Pollock	c & b Reid	2			
J.T.Partridge	not out	0			
Extras	(b 2, lb 16, nb 4)	22	(lb 17, nb 1)		18
TOTAL	(125.5 overs)	**371**	(64.4 overs) (5 wkts dec)		**200**

NEW ZEALAND

S.G.Gedye	c Lindsay b Partridge	18	b Partridge		55
W.P.Bradburn	b Partridge	2	c Lindsay b Pithey D.B.		14
B.W.Sinclair	c Pithey A.J. b Barlow	138	c Partridge b Pithey D.B.		19
J.R.Reid*	c Lindsay b Partridge	19	b Goddard		37
S.N.McGregor	hit wicket b Pollock P.M.	62	c Barlow b Pithey D.B.		29
M.J.F.Shrimpton	lbw b Barlow	0	b Goddard		0
M.E.Chapple	b Partridge	4	lbw b Goddard		20
A.E.Dick†	b Pollock P.M.	1	not out		4
R.W.Blair	b Partridge	0	b Goddard		0
R.S.Cunis	lbw b Partridge	0	not out		4
F.J.Cameron	not out	0			
Extras	(b 4, lb 7, nb 8)	19	(b 3, lb 2, nb 4)		9
TOTAL	(131.3 overs)	**263**	(101 overs) (8 wkts)		**191**

Bowling	O	M	R	W	O	M	R	W
NEW ZEALAND								
Cunis	21	2	80	0	17.4	0	47	2
Cameron	39	8	107	3	13	1	39	0
Reid	29.5	12	77	3	13	2	39	0
Blair	36	8	85	4	21	2	57	3
SOUTH AFRICA								
Pollock P.M.	28.3	13	60	2	16	3	42	0
Partridge	40	10	86	6	24	8	47	1
Goddard	26	17	32	0	17	9	18	4
Pithey D.B.	12	3	33	0	25	13	40	3
Barlow	12	5	20	2	16	8	19	0
Bland	13	6	13	0				
Pollock R.G.					3	0	16	0

Fall of Wickets	SA 1st	NZ 1st	SA 2nd	NZ 2nd
1st	115	7	92	49
2nd	149	34	105	89
3rd	158	76	165	95
4th	202	247	187	145
5th	256	247	190	145
6th	339	260	-	180
7th	357	262	-	182
8th	362	263	-	185
9th	371	263	-	-
10th	371	263	-	-

AVERAGES

New Zealand

BATTING	M	I	NO	Runs	HS	Ave
B.W. Sinclair	3	6	0	264	138	44.00
S.N. McGregor	3	6	0	168	62	28.00
S.G. Gedye	3	6	0	166	55	27.66
M.E. Chapple	3	6	1	127	59	25.40
G.T. Dowling	1	2	0	33	32	16.50
W.P. Bradburn	2	4	0	62	32	15.50
J.R. Reid	3	6	0	88	37	14.66
J.T. Sparling	2	4	0	52	49	13.00
F.J. Cameron	3	4	3	10	8	10.00
A.E. Dick	2	4	1	30	22	10.00
R.W. Blair	3	5	1	31	26*	7.75
J.T. Ward	1	1	0	5	5	5.00
R.S. Cunis	1	2	1	4	4*	4.00
R.C. Motz	2	4	1	5	3	1.66
M.J.F. Shrimpton	1	2	0	0	0	0.00

BOWLING	O	M	R	W	Ave
J.R. Reid	128.4	49	278	12	23.16
R.W. Blair	125	23	327	12	27.25
J.T. Sparling	13	3	31	1	31.00
F.J. Cameron	122.2	31	326	9	36.22
R.S. Cunis	38.4	2	127	2	63.50
R.C. Motz	46	6	144	2	72.00
M.E. Chapple	27	14	41	0	-

South Africa

BATTING	M	I	NO	Runs	HS	Ave
K.C. Bland	3	6	3	207	83	69.00
E.J. Barlow	3	6	0	295	92	49.16
T.L. Goddard	3	5	0	233	73	46.60
W.S. Farrer	3	5	2	133	39	44.33
R.G. Pollock	1	2	0	53	30	26.50
J.H.B. Waite	3	4	0	103	41	25.75
P.L. van der Merwe	2	3	0	52	44	17.33
D.T. Lindsay	3	5	0	86	37	17.20
A.J. Pithey	3	3	0	45	31	15.00
P.M. Pollock	3	3	0	32	24	10.66
D.B. Pithey	3	4	1	25	9	8.33
J.T. Partridge	3	3	3	10	8*	-

BOWLING	O	M	R	W	Ave
P.M. Pollock	130.1	44	258	15	17.20
P.L. van der Merwe	13	7	18	1	18.00
D.B. Pithey	114	42	224	12	18.66
J.T. Partridge	162	69	247	13	19.00
K.C. Bland	34	15	39	2	19.50
T.L. Goddard	140	81	142	7	20.28
E.J. Barlow	44	14	101	2	50.50
R.G. Pollock	3	0	16	0	-

1964/65 Pakistan in New Zealand

Pakistan made its first visit to New Zealand, playing 12 matches, and went through undefeated. Led by the "Little Master", Hanif Mohammad, they struggled with the foreign conditions they encountered in New Zealand which helped the quicker bowlers.

64   NEW ZEALAND v PAKISTAN *(First Test)*

at Basin Reserve, Wellington on 22, 23, 25, 26 January, 1965
Toss : Pakistan. Umpires : D.E.A. Copps and W.T. Martin
Match drawn

A long spell of dry weather broke just before this match and the wicket surrounds and outfield were saturated when the players arrived at the ground. Less than two hours' play was possible when a start was eventually made in the afternoon. Hanif was rewarded for inserting New Zealand with an early wicket. Graham Dowling and Barry Sinclair survived until stumps with the score 54-1.

Dowling scored 29 in almost three hours before he was dismissed at 82. Sinclair, batting with confidence, was dismissed at 114-3. John Reid was immediately aggressive and hit 16 fours in his innings of 97 and with test debutant Bevan Congdon 109 runs were added for the fourth wicket.

As the wicket dried the Pakistan seamers obtained considerable movement off the pitch. Asif Iqbal sneaked a ball between Reid's bat and pad and bowled the New Zealand captain at 261. The next wicket fell at the same score and the last four at 266 in the space of five balls. Asif finished with 5-48 from his right-arm, gentle medium-pacers.

Pakistan began the third day on 26 without loss. However, to the delight of the crowd, three wickets fell in the first quarter of an hour with no addition to the score. Hanif was soon yorked by Richard Collinge and at 47 Saeed Ahmed became the fifth wicket to fall. Useful contributions by the late order, included a cautious 46 in 205 minutes by Abdul Kadir and pugnacious flourishes by Asif and Intikhab Alam helped Pakistan reach 187 all out.

New Zealand now needed quick runs to add to its lead of 79. In the 125 minutes remaining on the third day Dowling and Sinclair were dismissed and Graham Gedye managed to score only 17 runs in a total of 64. Once he departed, having taken 160 minutes to reach 26, the run-rate accelerated but wickets fell at regular intervals. Reid's declaration left the tourists a target of 259 in 188 minutes.

Pakistan was reeling at 19-5 in less than an hour as Collinge and Dick Motz exposed the visitors' dislike of fast bowling. Hanif's gamesmanship and time wasting agitated the crowd before Collinge bowled him for the second time in the game. Nasim-ul-Ghani, Asif and Intikhab defied a keen attack until stumps were drawn.

Asif completed a good double with six wickets and an unbeaten 52, which rescued Pakistan from an embarrassing predicament. New Zealand may well have won this test if the task of scoring runs in the second innings had been approached with more urgency.

NEW ZEALAND					
S.G.Gedye	b Asif	1	b Arif		26
G.T.Dowling	c Burki b Pervez	29	b Arif		19
B.W.Sinclair	c Nasim b Saeed	65	c Saeed b Pervez		17
B.E.Congdon	c Naushad b Asif	42	b Asif Iqbal		30
J.R.Reid*	b Arif	97	c Saeed b Pervez		14
S.N.McGregor	lbw b Asif	11	not out		37
B.W.Yuile	b Asif	4	(8) run out		7
A.E.Dick†	b Arif	1			
R.C.Motz	b Asif	0	(7) b Arif		13
R.O.Collinge	not out	0			
F.J.Cameron	lbw b Arif	0			
Extras	(b 2, lb 14)	16	(b 12, lb 3, nb 1)		16
TOTAL	(114.2 overs)	266	(80.4 overs) (7 wkts dec)		179

PAKISTAN					
Naushad Ali†	run out	11	c & b Motz		3
Mohammad Ilyas	b Collinge	13	c Reid b Motz		4
Saeed Ahmed	c Congdon b Motz	11	c Yuile b Collinge		4
Javed Burki	b Motz	0	c Dick b Collinge		0
Hanif Mohammad*	b Collinge	5	b Collinge		25
Abdul Kadir	c & b Motz	46	b Motz		0
Nasim-ul-Ghani	b Cameron	16	c Dowling b Reid		23
Asif Iqbal	c Sinclair b Yuile	30	not out		52
Intikhab Alam	b Motz	28	not out		13
Arif Butt	b Yuile	20			
Pervez Sajjad	not out	1			
Extras	(b 2, lb 4)	6	(b 8, lb 6, w 1, nb 1)		16
TOTAL	(95 overs)	187	(52 overs) (7 wkts)		140

Bowling PAKISTAN	O	M	R	W	O	M	R	W
Arif	22.2	10	46	3	29	10	62	3
Asif	25	11	48	5	20.4	6	33	1
Pervez	24	7	48	1	25	5	61	2
Intikhab	17	6	35	0	5	1	7	0
Saeed	16	7	40	1	1	1	0	0
Nasim	3	1	5	0				
Ilyas	7	1	28	0				
NEW ZEALAND								
Collinge	17	6	51	2	13	3	43	3
Cameron	19	11	33	1	8	5	10	0
Motz	20	9	45	4	15	6	34	3
Yuile	26	16	28	2	8	2	21	0
Reid	13	6	24	0	8	3	16	1

Fall of Wickets	NZ	P	NZ	P
	1st	1st	2nd	2nd
1st	1	26	35	3
2nd	82	26	62	8
3rd	114	26	83	10
4th	223	41	102	17
5th	261	47	140	19
6th	261	64	156	64
7th	266	114	179	104
8th	266	144	-	-
9th	266	179	-	-
10th	266	187	-	-

The old scoreboard and scorers' box, which also accommodated the local reporters, form the backdrop to Bevan Congdon's cut backward of point during his first test. He scored 42 and 30 and was watched by Pakistan's wicketkeeper Naushad Ali.

MILESTONES

- Richard Collinge (102) became New Zealand's third youngest test debutant, aged 18 years and 295 days.

- Bevan Congdon (103) also made his test debut.

65 NEW ZEALAND v PAKISTAN *(Second Test)*

at Eden Park, Auckland on 29, 30 Janaury, 1, 2 February, 1965
Toss : Pakistan. Umpires : E.C.A. MacKintosh and R.W.R. Shortt
Match drawn

On a docile wicket the tourists batted very conservatively through the first day. 71 of 131 overs were maidens and only 161 runs were scored, for the loss of eight wickets. Bryan Yuile captured the first wicket at 19 and took three more during the day off his 47 overs (34 maidens) which cost 33 runs. Javed Burki accumulated 63 runs in 225 minutes of dedicated batting.

Rain delayed a start on the second day for an hour and a half. A busy partnership between Intikhab Alam and Arif Butt added 52 for the ninth wicket before the innings ended at 226. Frank Cameron captured the last two wickets to finish with 4-36.

New Zealand began badly and had lost both openers with the score at 25. Ross Morgan and John Reid put on 76 in 94 minutes, with the New Zealand captain hitting a six and seven fours in his 52 before he was run out. Morgan completed his half-century by stumps, when the score was 122-4. Useful contributions by the tailenders carried the total to 214.

For the second time in as many tests Asif Iqbal captured five wickets in an innings. He was to have a long career in test cricket, playing 58 tests, and these were the only times he captured five wickets. His batting flourished and he scored 11 test centuries later in his career.

In the 200 minutes left on the afternoon of the third day the tourists reached 129-4. On the last morning Richard Collinge dismissed Hanif Mohammad for the fourth time in as many innings. Abdul Kadir almost batted through the innings, being last out for 58 after batting for more than five hours. Frank Cameron's five wickets gave him match figures of 9-70 off 49 overs and were his best at test level.

New Zealand had the reasonable task of scoring 220 in four hours and was given a bright start when Graham Dowling and Bevan Congdon added 68 in 73 minutes before the slow left-arm spinner Pervez Sajjad captured four wickets within 10 minutes with the score at 102. Dowling now adopted a defensive approach and was finally seventh out at 150 having stayed 290 minutes for his 62 runs. Yuile, 30 not out, and Artie Dick batted out time.

MILESTONES

- Ross Morgan (104) made his test debut.

PAKISTAN

Naushad Ali†	b Yuile	14	c Yuile b Reid		8
Abdul Kadir	c & b Yuile	12	b Collinge		58
Saeed Ahmed	c Dick b Yuile	17	c Dick b Cameron		16
Javed Burki	c sub (S.G.Gedye)b Cameron	63	c Congdon b Collinge		15
Nasim-ul-Ghani	c Dowling b Yuile	2	lbw b Cameron		14
Hanif Mohammad*	b Collinge	27	c Congdon b Collinge		27
Mohammad Ilyas	lbw b Cameron	10	lbw b Reid		36
Asif Iqbal	c Morgan b Collinge	3	b Cameron		0
Intikhab Alam	lbw b Cameron	45	c Morgan b Cameron		7
Arif Butt	b Cameron	20	c Dick b Cameron		0
Pervez Sajjad	not out	2	not out		0
Extras	(b 5, lb 4, nb 2)	11	(b 9, lb 8, nb 9)		26
TOTAL	(154 overs)	**226**	(100.1 overs)		**207**

NEW ZEALAND

G.T.Dowling	lbw b Asif	0	c Asif b Nasim		62
B.E.Congdon	b Asif	9	c Intikhab b Pervez		42
R.W.Morgan	b Pervez	66	b Asif		5
J.R.Reid*	run out	52	b Pervez		11
S.N.McGregor	c Hanif b Saeed	1	c Saeed b Pervez		0
P.G.Z.Harris	c Hanif b Asif	1	b Pervez		0
B.W.Yuile	b Asif	0	(8) not out		30
A.E.Dick†	b Saeed	19	(9) not out		3
R.C.Motz	c Naushad b Asif	31	(7) c Intikhab b Pervez		0
R.O.Collinge	b Arif	13			
F.J.Cameron	not out	5			
Extras	(b 7, lb 8, nb 2)	17	(b 6, lb 2, nb 5)		13
TOTAL	(98.4 overs)	**214**	(80 overs) (7 wkts)		**166**

Bowling	O	M	R	W	O	M	R	W
NEW ZEALAND								
Collinge	28	8	57	2	22.1	9	41	3
Motz	12	4	15	0	6	1	15	0
Cameron	26	11	36	4	23	11	34	5
Yuile	54	38	43	4	30	15	39	0
Reid	20	14	26	0	19	7	52	2
Harris	7	2	14	0				
Morgan	7	3	24	0				
PAKISTAN								
Arif	17.4	4	43	1	6	1	19	0
Asif	27	6	52	5	18	4	40	1
Intikhab	29	10	52	0	15	7	17	0
Pervez	15	4	35	1	25	7	42	5
Saeed	10	4	15	2	9	3	14	0
Ilyas					2	0	12	0
Nasim					5	2	9	1

Fall of Wickets	P	NZ	P	NZ
	1st	*1st*	*2nd*	*2nd*
1st	19	9	25	68
2nd	44	25	51	82
3rd	70	101	75	102
4th	99	113	95	102
5th	129	125	139	102
6th	151	127	197	102
7th	156	148	200	150
8th	159	195	207	-
9th	211	195	207	-
10th	226	214	207	-

This was the last time that the old scoreboard was used for recording a cricket test at Eden Park. Work began shortly afterwards on building terraces and positioning the scoreboard elsewhere.

66 NEW ZEALAND v PAKISTAN *(Third Test)*

at Lancaster Park, Christchurch on 12, 13, 15, 16 February, 1965
Toss : Pakistan. Umpires : F.R. Goodall and W.T. Martin
Match drawn

Although the tourists had a generous quota of 17 players in their party they called upon the services of the Otago coach Khalid (Billy) Ibadulla to play for them. Ibadulla had played test cricket for Pakistan previously, scoring 166 on debut against Australia in 1964. He eventually settled in Dunedin and became familiar to television viewers as an expert commentator on the game.

The previous two tests had provided intriguing, if not spectacular cricket, with three pedestrian days becoming charged with the excitement of a contest on the last day when the prospects of a result had suddenly loomed. It was unfortunate that the final test of the series was affected by rain on the first day.

Winning the toss for the third time, Hanif Mohammad elected to bat. All his batsmen struggled to come to terms with the New Zealand attack and when rain stopped play, 20 minutes before tea, the score was 109-7.

In cold weather, after a delayed start on the second morning, Mohammad Ilyas hit out to score 72 of 97 runs added to the overnight score. He was last out, just before lunch, stumped off Yuile for 88, which included a six and 10 fours, giving Pakistan a total of 206.

New Zealand soon lost both openers and Barry Sinclair retired hurt after losing sight of a ball from Mufasir-ul Haq that struck him in the face. He returned to the wicket with the home team in trouble at 112-6 and batted courageously until stumps; 130-7.

The swelling on Sinclair's face subsided during the rest day and he was joined in a 41 run partnership by Richard Collinge before he was ninth out, having made 46. Frank Cameron then provided support for Collinge who was the second-highest scorer, with 32, in a total of 202 all out.

The tourists produced their best batting of the series to reach 309-8 when Hanif declared having reached a century a few minutes before lunch on the last day. His vice-captain, Saeed Ahmed, who played an assortment of daring shots in compiling 87, had ably assisted him. Although Hanif had entertained the crowd with his cultured batting, he gave his bowlers little chance of dismissing New Zealand on a good batting wicket with only four hours remaining.

The highlight of New Zealand's attempt was the batting of Ross Morgan who progressed towards a century in only his second test appearance. Ten minutes from stumps he was caught and bowled by Mufasir with his score at 97, an innings that occupied 212 minutes and contained 13 boundaries. New Zealand was 223-5 when the match ended.

MILESTONES

- Peter Truscott (105) made his test debut.

- Richard Collinge dismissed Hanif Mohammad five times in the series. In the other innings Hanif was not out.

PAKISTAN

Khalid Ibadulla	c Ward b Cameron	28	b Collinge	9
Naushad Ali†	c Truscott b Motz	12	c Collinge b Yuile	20
Javed Burki	b Collinge	4	(4) b Collinge	12
Saeed Ahmed	c Ward b Cameron	1	(3) lbw b Reid	87
Hanif Mohammad*	c & b Collinge	10	not out	100
Mohammad Ilyas	st Ward b Yuile	88	b Yuile	13
Nasim-ul-Ghani	b Motz	5	b Collinge	12
Asif Iqbal	c Motz b Yuile	3	c Bartlett b Cameron	20
Intikhab Alam	c Sinclair b Yuile	27	c Reid b Yuile	15
Pervez Sajjad	b Motz	9	not out	0
Mufasir-ul-Haq	not out	8		
Extras	(lb 4, nb 7)	11	(b 9, lb 6, w 1, nb 5)	21
TOTAL	(83 overs)	**206**	(93.3 overs) (8 wkts dec)	**309**

NEW ZEALAND

B.E.Congdon	b Mufasir	21	c Hanif b Asif	8
P.B.Truscott	lbw b Asif	3	c & b Asif	26
B.W.Sinclair	c Naushad b Intikhab	46	(6) not out	7
R.W.Morgan	c Nasim b Mufasir	19	(3) c & b Mufasir	97
J.R.Reid*	b Asif	27	(4) c Ilyas b Intikhab	28
B.W.Yuile	c Hanif b Nasim	7	(5) c Ilyas b Pervez	42
G.A.Bartlett	b Pervez	1	not out	4
R.C.Motz	c Naushad b Pervez	21		
J.T.Ward†	c Naushad b Asif	2		
R.O.Collinge	c Hanif b Asif	32		
F.J.Cameron	not out	8		
Extras	(b 3, lb 3, w 1, nb 8)	15	(b 7, nb 4)	11
TOTAL	(98.5 overs)	**202**	(83 overs) (5 wkts)	**223**

Bowling NEW ZEALAND	O	M	R	W	O	M	R	W
Bartlett	18	6	47	0	14.3	2	46	0
Collinge	12	3	23	2	17	3	50	3
Cameron	24	15	29	2	14	2	61	1
Motz	18	4	48	3	17	7	43	0
Yuile	11	3	48	3	20	9	64	3
Reid					11	5	24	1
PAKISTAN								
Asif	25.5	9	46	4	16	6	29	2
Mufasir	29	11	50	2	8	1	34	1
Ibadulla	9	5	17	0	3	0	12	0
Pervez	21	6	53	2	21	8	33	1
Intikhab	7	1	17	1	21	6	60	1
Nasim	4	3	3	1	3	1	5	0
Saeed	3	2	1	0	8	1	25	0
Ilyas					3	0	14	0

Fall of Wickets

	P	NZ	P	NZ
	1st	1st	2nd	2nd
1st	36	7	27	18
2nd	41	34	58	41
3rd	42	76	97	98
4th	62	81	159	179
5th	66	83	199	219
6th	78	112	222	-
7th	81	129	254	-
8th	132	137	300	-
9th	160	178	-	-
10th	206	202	-	-

Richard Collinge, playing in his first test series, captured the prized wicket of Hanif Mohammad in five consecutive innings. Trevor Martin is the umpire.

AVERAGES

New Zealand

BATTING	M	I	NO	Runs	HS	Ave
R.W. Morgan	2	4	0	187	97	46.75
B.W. Sinclair	2	4	1	135	65	45.00
J.R. Reid	3	6	0	229	97	38.16
G.T. Dowling	2	4	0	110	62	27.50
B.E. Congdon	3	6	0	152	42	25.33
R.O. Collinge	3	3	1	45	32	22.50
B.W. Yuile	3	6	1	90	42	18.00
S.N. McGregor	2	4	1	49	37*	16.33
P.B. Truscott	1	2	0	29	26	14.50
S.G. Gedye	1	2	0	27	26	13.50
F.J. Cameron	3	3	2	13	8*	13.00
R.C. Motz	3	5	0	65	31	13.00
A.E. Dick	2	3	1	23	19	11.50
G.A. Bartlett	1	2	1	5	4*	5.00
J.T. Ward	1	1	0	2	2	2.00
P.G.Z. Harris	1	2	0	1	1	0.50

BOWLING	O	M	R	W	Ave
F.J. Cameron	114	55	203	13	15.61
R.O. Collinge	109.1	32	265	15	17.66
R.C. Motz	88	31	200	10	20.00
B.W. Yuile	149	83	243	12	20.25
J.R. Reid	71	35	142	4	35.50
P.G.Z. Harris	7	2	14	0	-
R.W. Morgan	7	3	24	0	-
G.A. Bartlett	32.3	8	93	0	-

Pakistan

BATTING	M	I	NO	Runs	HS	Ave
Hanif Mohammad	3	6	1	194	100*	38.80
Abdul Kadir	2	4	0	116	58	29.00
Mohammad Ilyas	3	6	0	164	88	27.33
Intikhab Alam	3	6	1	135	45	27.00
Saeed Ahmed	3	6	0	136	87	22.66
Asif Iqbal	3	6	1	108	52*	21.60
Khalid Ibadulla	1	2	0	37	28	18.50
Javed Burki	3	6	0	94	63	15.66
Arif Butt	2	3	0	40	20	13.33
Nasim-ul-Ghani	3	6	0	72	23	12.00
Pervez Sajjad	3	5	4	12	9	12.00
Naushad Ali	3	6	0	68	20	11.33
Mufasir-ul-Haq	1	1	1	8	8*	-

BOWLING	O	M	R	W	Ave
Nasim-ul-Ghani	15	7	22	2	11.00
Asif Iqbal	132.3	42	248	18	13.77
Pervez Sajjad	131	37	272	12	22.66
Arif Butt	75	25	170	7	24.28
Mufasir-ul-Haq	37	12	84	3	28.00
Saeed Ahmed	47	18	95	3	31.66
Intikhab Alam	94	31	188	2	94.00
Khalid Ibadulla	12	5	29	0	-
Mohammad Ilyas	12	1	54	0	-

1965 New Zealand in India, Pakistan and England

The team for this ambitious tour, which involved 10 tests and 16 other first-class matches, was announced after the third test against Pakistan. Eight of the players would be making their first overseas tour, five were under the age of 22 and three had appeared in half-a-dozen or fewer first-class matches.

The inclusion of Bert Sutcliffe, absent from test cricket for five years, but still the most capable of batsmen at the age of 41, was regarded as a wise addition to the generally youthful touring party. The naming of Walter Hadlee as manager, with his wealth of experience of English conditions, was also welcomed.

The first section of the tour, in India and Pakistan, was especially gruelling, with seven test matches to be played in succession and the majority of the team confronted for the first time with dusty, spinning wickets, extreme heat and dietary problems. Four days after leaving New Zealand the tourists took the field at Madras in the first of four tests against India. Pre-match practice plans had been frustrated by the team's luggage having been sent to Calcutta.

67 INDIA v NEW ZEALAND *(First Test)*

at Corporation Stadium, Madras on 27, 28 February, 1, 2 March, 1965
Toss : India. Umpires : Mohammad Yunus and S.K. Raghunatha Rao
Match drawn

The tourists' pace attack made no impression on the Indian openers and it was not until Vic Pollard was introduced to bowl his flat-trajectory off spinners that the slow but steady run rate was checked. Pollard captured three wickets in his first 21 overs for 19 runs. With Dick Motz claiming two wickets, India were struggling at 115-5. Chandu Borde and Salim Durani added 88 runs in even time to carry India to 225-6 at stumps.

Borde was caught off Motz at slip without improving his overnight score of 68. Wicketkeeper Farokh Engineer was immediately struck to the ground by a delivery from Motz. The next ball he swung to the square-leg-boundary, the first of 14 fours in a cavalier innings of 90, scored in less than two hours. His partner, Bapu Nadkarni, joined in the assault and 100 runs came up in 78 minutes, enabling India to reach 397 by the middle of the second afternoon.

The New Zealand opening pair, Graham Dowling and Terry Jarvis, were at ease against the medium-pace bowlers. Once the spinners, Durani and Venkataraghavan, appeared the run rate dried up. Barry Sinclair and John Reid took the tourists through to 93-2 by stumps. New Zealand struggled through the third day against an unrelenting spin attack.

Apart from an early flourish by Reid, who carried his overnight score of 16 to 42 (a six and seven fours) in the first quarter of an hour, the batting was cautious and less than 200 runs were scored, even though the Indian bowlers averaged 24 overs an hour. Seven of the tourists scored over 29 but Sutcliffe's 56 was the highest individual score.

John Ward and Richard Collinge continued and added 61 for the 10th wicket. With little chance of a result, India batted until Vijay Manjrekar completed his seventh test hundred. New Zealand enjoyed an hour's batting till stumps.

INDIA					
D.N.Sardesai	b Pollard	22	retired hurt		0
M.L.Jaisimha	c Morgan b Motz	51	c Collinge b Yuile		49
V.L.Manjrekar	c Dowling b Pollard	19	not out		102
C.G.Borde	c Reid b Motz	68	b Pollard		20
Nawab of Pataudi*	b Motz	9			
Hanumant Singh	c Ward b Pollard	0			
S.A.Durani	b Reid	34			
R.G.Nadkarni	c Collinge b Yuile	75			
F.M.Engineer†	c Pollard b Yuile	90			
R.F.Surti	not out	9	(5) not out		17
S.Venkataraghavan	b Collinge	4			
Extras	(b 10, lb 1, nb 5)	16	(b 3, lb 1, nb 7)		11
TOTAL	**(143.5 overs)**	**397**	**(58.1 overs) (2 wkts dec)**		**199**
NEW ZEALAND					
T.W.Jarvis	b Durani	9	not out		40
G.T.Dowling	b Venkataraghavan	29	not out		21
B.W.Sinclair	b Venkataraghavan	30			
J.R.Reid*	lbw b Nadkarni	42			
R.W.Morgan	lbw b Durani	39			
B.Sutcliffe	b Surti	56			
B.W.Yuile	c Nadkarni b Durani	0			
V.Pollard	c Venkataraghavan b Jaisimha	3			
R.C.Motz	b Nadkarni	11			
J.T.Ward†	not out	35			
R.O.Collinge	lbw b Borde	34	(nb 1)		1
Extras	(b 8, lb 10, w 3, nb 6)	27			
TOTAL	**(179 overs)**	**315**	**(21 overs) (0 wkts)**		**62**

Bowling	O	M	R	W	O	M	R	W	Fall of Wickets				
NEW ZEALAND										I	NZ	I	NZ
										1st	1st	2nd	2nd
Collinge	22.5	5	55	1	9	2	29	0					
Motz	30	6	87	3	19	1	57	0	1st	51	38	88	-
Reid	30	11	70	1					2nd	94	58	130	-
Yuile	20	7	62	2	11.1	0	53	1	3rd	94	119	-	-
Pollard	34	16	90	3	14	4	32	1	4th	107	139	-	-
Morgan	7	2	17	0	5	2	17	0	5th	114	200	-	-
INDIA									6th	202	200	-	-
Jaisimha	12	4	30	1	4	2	8	0	7th	232	227	-	-
Surti	33	12	55	1	1	0	10	0	8th	375	227	-	-
Durani	45	23	53	3	1	0	4	0	9th	378	254	-	-
Venkataraghavan	48	23	90	2					10th	397	315	-	-
Nadkarni	36	21	42	2									
Borde	5	2	18	1									
Pataudi					3	2	9	0					
Hanumant Singh					6	0	19	0					
Manjrekar					6	4	11	0					

MILESTONES

- Terry Jarvis (106) and Victor Pollard (107) made their test debuts.

- Farokh Engineer and Bapu Nadkarni created an Indian eighth wicket test partnership record of 143.

- John Ward and Richard Collinge created a New Zealand test record of 61 for the tenth wicket.

68 INDIA v NEW ZEALAND *(Second Test)*

at Eden Gardens, Calcutta on 5, 6, 7, 8 March, 1965
Toss : New Zealand. Umpires : S.K. Ganguli and A.R. Joshi
Match drawn

John Reid, in this 50th test match, entered the fray with his team uncomfortably placed at 37-2. He was immediately on the offensive and hit four sixes in 10 balls; two off "Tiny" Desai, who had been making the ball lift sharply, one off Salim Durani and one off M.L. Jaisimha. Graham Dowling played a watching brief while Reid scored 82 in 140 minutes.

With five wickets down for 152, the veteran Bert Sutcliffe was joined by Vic Pollard and 81 runs were added in even time. On Pollard's dismissal, at 233-6, Bruce Taylor somehow deflected a ball directed outside his leg-stump off the back of his bat, over his stumps and through the slips. By stumps on the first day New Zealand had reached 259-6; Taylor was on 13 and Sutcliffe 74.

The partnership continued the next morning. Before lunch Sutcliffe had passed beyond his 43rd first-class century and Taylor had achieved a hundred in his first test. When he was dismissed he had been at the wicket for 158 minutes and had hit three sixes and 14 fours. While Taylor provided much of the day's bravado, Sutcliffe was accumulating his runs with graceful strokes. Reid declared at 462, of which Sutcliffe had contributed an unbeaten 151 in 357 minutes.

Dick Motz and Taylor began bowling with great vigour and the Indian openers survived a number of edged shots. A remarkable day's test cricket ended with India 101-4 with Taylor having claimed two wickets.

The wicket and the humid atmosphere continued to assist the New Zealand bowlers on the third morning. Often the ball beat the bat or was snicked fortuitously. The Indian captain, the Nawab of Pataudi, survived a sharp chance off the first ball of the day and thereafter played a succession of classical shots all round the ground. He scored 153, including 29 boundaries, and shared a partnership worth 110 with Chandu Borde. The pick of the New Zealand bowlers were Taylor, who captured five wickets, and Bryan Yuile, who took three.

Holding a lead of 82 runs the tourists frittered away any chance of setting India a target as only four runs were scored in the half-hour left on the third day. By lunch on the fourth day New Zealand had slumped to a precarious 103 for seven before Graham Vivian and Pollard dispelled a suspicion that India might snatch a surprise win.

MILESTONES

- Bruce Taylor (108) and Graham Vivian (109) made their test debuts. It was also Vivian's debut in first-class cricket.

- Bruce Taylor created test history by becoming the first test debutant (and only the 12th player) to score a century and take five wickets in an innings in the same test.

- Bert Sutcliffe and Bruce Taylor shared a record seventh wicket stand of 163 runs.

- John Reid became the first New Zealand player to play in 50 tests.

- Four New Zealand players captured their first test wicket: Bruce Taylor, Bevan Congdon, Graham Vivian and Graham Dowling.

John Reid hooks to square-leg watched by Indian wicketkeeper Farokh Engineer during the course of his 42 runs in the first test.

Bruce Taylor walks off to the applause of his batting partner Bert Sutcliffe and the Indian team during the second test.

NEW ZEALAND

G.T.Dowling	lbw b Venkataraghavan	27	c Engineer b Gupte	23
B.E.Congdon	b Desai	9	c Borde b Desai	0
R.W.Morgan	c Engineer b Desai	20	(4) b Durani	33
J.R.Reid*	c Borde b Venkataraghavan	82	(5) lbw b Venkataraghavan	11
B.Sutcliffe	not out	151	(6) c Hanumant Singh b Venkataraghavan	6
B.W.Yuile	b Gupte	1	(3) lbw b Venkataraghavan	21
V.Pollard	c Jaisimha b Desai	31	b Jaisimha	43
B.R.Taylor	c Kunderan b Nadkarni	105	(10) not out	0
G.E.Vivian	b Desai	1	c Jaisimha b Nadkarni	43
R.C.Motz	lbw b Venkataraghavan	21	(8) c Nadkarni b Durani	0
J.T.Ward†	not out	1		
Extras	(b 10, lb 3)	13	(b 10, nb 1)	11
TOTAL	**(160 overs) (9 wkts dec)**	**462**	**(91.1 overs) (9 wkts dec)**	**191**

INDIA

M.L.Jaisimha	b Motz	22	c Morgan b Congdon	0
B.K.Kunderan	b Congdon	36	not out	12
F.M.Engineer†	c Pollard b Taylor	10	c Pollard b Dowling	45
C.G.Borde	c Pollard b Taylor	62		
R.G.Nadkarni	b Taylor	0		
Nawab of Pataudi*	c Ward b Taylor	153		
Hanumant Singh	c sub (T.W.Jarvis) b Yuile	31		
S.A.Durani	c sub (T.W.Jarvis) b Yuile	20	(4) b Vivian	23
R.B.Desai	c Ward b Yuile	0		
S.Venkataraghavan	b Taylor	7	(5) not out	0
B.P.Gupte	not out	3		
Extras	(b 23, lb 2, nb 11)	36	(b 11, lb 1)	12
TOTAL	**(105.5 overs)**	**380**	**(17 overs) (3 wkts)**	**92**

Bowling	O	M	R	W	O	M	R	W		Fall of Wickets				
INDIA											NZ	I	NZ	I
											1st	*1st*	*2nd*	*2nd*
Desai	33	6	128	4	12	6	32	1	1st		13	45	4	3
Jaisimha	20	6	73	0	15.1	12	21	1	2nd		37	61	37	52
Durani	15	3	49	0	18	10	34	2	3rd		138	100	61	92
Nadkarni	35	12	59	1	7	4	14	1	4th		139	101	83	-
Gupte	16	3	54	1	22	7	64	1	5th		152	211	97	-
Venkataraghavan	41	18	86	3	17	11	15	3	6th		233	301	103	-
NEW ZEALAND									7th		396	357	103	-
Motz	21	3	74	1					8th		407	357	184	-
Taylor	23.5	2	86	5					9th		450	371	191	-
Congdon	18	5	49	1	5	0	33	1	10th		-	380	-	-
Pollard	15	1	50	0										
Vivian	12	3	37	0	3	0	14	1						
Reid	2	1	5	0										
Yuile	14	3	43	3										
Dowling					6	2	19	1						
Sutcliffe					3	2	14	0						

69 INDIA v NEW ZEALAND *(Third Test)*

at Brabourne Stadium, Bombay on 12, 13, 14, 15 March, 1965
Toss : New Zealand. Umpires : M.V. Nagendra and S. Roy
Match drawn

After the early loss of Bevan Congdon and Barry Sinclair New Zealand's first innings was revived with a sound stand between Graham Dowling and Ross Morgan, which carried the score to 87-2 at lunch and eventually realised 134 runs in three hours. Dowling (109 not out) batted throughout the day to achieve his maiden test century. During the last session he had battled against cramp in his arms and was extremely weary when stumps were drawn at 227-5.

Dowling's fine innings ended at 129 (17 boundaries) after 278 minutes. John Reid, who was indisposed on the first day, batted at number seven and his 22 was the best score among the last four New Zealanders; 297 all out. The outstanding bowler for India was "Tiny' Desai. Standing only 5 foot 4 inches tall, he was the smallest fast-bowler to play test cricket. He generated his pace from a lengthy run-up.

India then suffered a dramatic collapse against the pace of Bruce Taylor and Dick Motz. Batsmen were hit repeatedly and John Ward picked up four catches behind the wicket from tentative shots. In his first five overs, Taylor took three wickets for 11. This fiery effort so exhausted him that he left

the field and collapsed in the dressing room.

He revived sufficiently to return after tea to take two more wickets and, with Motz and Congdon finishing with two apiece, India were dismissed for 88. Following on 209 runs in arrears, the home team lost Farokh Engineer before the end of the second day; 18-1.

Taylor took his second wicket of the innings early on the third morning but Dilip Sardesai and Jaisimha batted through until lunch; 99-2. Chandu Borde came to the crease at 107-3 and proceeded to play a stunning innings. In 152 minutes he scored 109 of 154 runs added with Sardesai. His aggression carried India well into credit before stumps. Sardesai had advanced sedately from six to 97, on the third day.

With Hanumant Singh 121 runs were added in the first session of the last day. Sardesai reached his century in 390 minutes and, suddenly revealing an array of full-blooded strokes, he brought up his double century in a further 160 minutes, enabling the Nawab of Pataudi to declare at 463-5.

The tourists made no attempt on the target of 254 in 2½ hours but so tired were they after two days in the field that wickets began to tumble. Graham Dowling and Barry Sinclair departed before a run was scored and with an hour remaining seven wickets were down for 46 as the Indian spinners created havoc. Taylor then produced the top score of the innings, a defiant 21, and Bryan Yuile and John Ward survived doggedly until stumps.

MILESTONES

- Dilip Sardesai and Hanumant Singh established a new Indian test record of 193 for the sixth wicket.

During the 185 minutes that he was at the crease, Ross Morgan used his feet intelligently when playing the Indian spinners. He and Graham Dowling added 134 for the third wicket.

NEW ZEALAND

G.T.Dowling	b Desai	129	c Engineer b Jaisimha		0
B.E.Congdon	c Engineer b Desai	3	c Hanumant Singh b Durani		14
B.W.Sinclair	b Desai	9	c Venkataraghavan b Desai		0
R.W.Morgan	b Chandrasekhar	71	b Chandrasekhar		11
B.Sutcliffe	run out	4	(6) c Durani b Chandrasekhar		1
V.Pollard	c Jaisimha b Desai	26	(7) c Borde b Durani		4
J.R.Reid*	lbw b Desai	22	(5) c Borde b Chandrasekhar		10
B.R.Taylor	c Hanumant Singh b Desai	8	b Venkataraghavan		21
B.W.Yuile	lbw b Durani	2	not out		8
R.C.Motz	not out	5			
J.T.Ward†	b Durani	0	(10) not out		4
Extras	(b 4, lb 13, nb 1)	18	(b 5, nb 2)		7
TOTAL	(129.2 overs)	**297**	(43 overs) (8 wkts)		**80**

INDIA

D.N.Sardesai	c Ward b Motz	4	not out		200
M.L.Jaisimha	c Ward b Taylor	4	(4) c Ward b Pollard		47
S.A.Durani	c Morgan b Taylor	4	c Ward b Taylor		6
C.G.Borde	c Ward b Taylor	25	(5) c Yuile b Taylor		109
Hanumant Singh	hit wicket b Taylor	0	(7) not out		75
Nawab of Pataudi*	c Ward b Congdon	9	b Motz		3
R.G.Nadkarni	lbw b Congdon	7			
F.M.Engineer†	run out	17	(2) c Reid b Taylor		6
R.B.Desai	c Reid b Motz	0			
S.Venkataraghavan	c Congdon b Taylor	7			
B.S.Chandrasekhar	not out	4			
Extras	(lb 4, nb 3)	7	(b 4, lb 5, w 1, nb 7)		17
TOTAL	(33.3 overs)	**88**	(154.4 overs) (5 wkts dec)		**463**

Bowling	O	M	R	W	O	M	R	W
INDIA								
Desai	25	9	56	6	9	5	18	1
Jaisimha	17	6	53	0	6	5	4	1
Chandrasekhar	23	6	76	1	14	7	25	3
Durani	20.2	10	26	2	7	2	16	2
Venkataraghavan	32	13	46	0	7	3	10	1
Nadkarni	12	7	22	0				
NEW ZEALAND								
Motz	15	4	30	2	29.4	11	63	1
Taylor	7.3	2	26	5	29	5	76	3
Congdon	9	5	21	2	17	6	44	0
Pollard	2	1	4	0	29	6	95	1
Yuile					25	8	76	0
Morgan					18	3	54	0
Reid					3	1	8	0
Sutcliffe					4	0	30	0

Fall of Wickets	NZ	I	I	NZ
	1st	*1st*	*2nd*	*2nd*
1st	13	4	8	0
2nd	31	8	18	0
3rd	165	13	107	18
4th	170	23	261	34
5th	227	38	270	37
6th	256	48	-	45
7th	276	71	-	46
8th	281	76	-	76
9th	297	77	-	-
10th	297	88	-	-

70 ## INDIA v NEW ZEALAND *(Fourth Test)*

at Feroz Shah Kotla, Delhi on 19, 20, 21, 22 March, 1965
Toss : New Zealand. Umpires : S.P. Pan and B. Satyaji Rao
India won by 7 wickets

The Indian captain, the Nawab of Pataudi, soon dispensed with his medium-pace attack and set an on-side field of five men for his spinners, who bowled a consistent line on the leg stump. By the end of the first day Venkataraghavan had bowled 44 overs and taken five wickets for 62 runs.

The best innings of the day was that of Ross Morgan whose dedicated approach defied the spinners. In the last half hour, with "Tiny" Desai bowling loosely with the new ball, Morgan hit 21 runs off two overs. This ferocious assault so damaged the ball that it was replaced. At stumps Morgan was 68 not out and New Zealand 235-7.

An eighth wicket stand between Morgan and John Ward ended at 256, Morgan (82) fell at 260 and two runs later the innings ended. The clever flight and pinpoint accuracy of Venkataraghavan had resulted in his taking eight wickets for 72 off 52 overs.

With the exception of Jaisimha the Indian top order had a feast against the New Zealand bowlers who toiled on a most unresponsive wicket. The tourists' resources were stretched

when John Ward damaged a thumb and Bevan Congdon replaced him as wicketkeeper. Vic Pollard, too, left the field with a pulled muscle.

India's first 50 came up in half an hour and the second-wicket partnership of 123 took 105 minutes. Dilip Sardesai completed his second consecutive century. In the last session Chandu Borde and Pataudi put on 100 runs to give the home team a commanding lead, having scored 340 runs in 280 minutes for the loss of only four wickets.

Pataudi carried on from 49 overnight to reach his second century of the series before Richard Collinge bowled him for 113. Collinge quickly took another two wickets (4-89) and India declared at 465-8.

Facing a deficit of 203 the tourists were soon in grave trouble when three wickets fell for 22 runs. Terry Jarvis showed great determination in countering the subtle Indian spinners, and when he was the sixth wicket to fall at 178 his innings of 77 had occupied 322 minutes. Collinge (54 not out with 10 boundaries) and Frank Cameron put on 51 runs for the ninth wicket in little more than half an hour. The four wickets taken in the second innings by Venkataraghavan gave him a bag of 12-152 for the match, in which he had bowled 112.3 overs.

NEW ZEALAND

G.T.Dowling	lbw b Venkataraghavan	7	lbw b Subramanya		0
T.W.Jarvis	b Venkataraghavan	34	b Venkataraghavan		77
R.W.Morgan	lbw b Venkataraghavan	82	c Venkataraghavan b Desai		4
B.E.Congdon	c Chandrasekhar b Venkataraghavan	48	b Chandrasekhar		7
J.R.Reid*	b Chandrasekhar	9	b Venkataraghavan		22
B.Sutcliffe	b Venkataraghavan	54	c Engineer b Chandrasekhar		54
B.R.Taylor	c Borde b Chandrasekhar	21	c Sardesai b Venkataraghavan		3
V.Pollard	b Venkataraghavan	27	c Engineer b Subramanya		6
J.T.Ward†	lbw b Venkataraghavan	11	(11) run out		0
R.O.Collinge	not out	4	(9) c Engineer b Venkataraghavan		54
F.J.Cameron	b Venkataraghavan	0	(10) not out		27
Extras	(b 8, lb 6, nb 3)	17	(b 15, lb 1, nb 2)		18
TOTAL	(125.1 overs)	**262**	(149.2 overs)		**272**

INDIA

D.N.Sardesai	c Jarvis b Morgan	106	not out		28
M.L.Jaisimha	c Dowling b Reid	10	(3) hit wicket b Cameron		1
Hanumant Singh	c Congdon b Collinge	82	(5) not out		7
C.G.Borde	c Jarvis b Cameron	87			
Nawab of Pataudi*	b Collinge	113	(4) b Reid		29
V.Subramanya	b Taylor	9			
F.M.Engineer†	b Collinge	5	(2) b Taylor		2
R.G.Nadkarni	not out	14			
R.B.Desai	b Collinge	7			
S.Venkataraghavan					
B.S.Chandrasekhar					
Extras	(b 23, lb 4, w 1, nb 4)	32	(lb 4, nb 2)		6
TOTAL	(113.4 overs) (8 wkts dec)	**465**	(9.1 overs) (3 wkts)		**73**

Bowling	O	M	R	W	O	M	R	W
INDIA								
Desai	9	2	36	0	18	3	35	1
Jaisimha	5	2	12	0	1	0	2	0
Subramanya	5	2	3	0	16	5	32	2
Venkataraghavan	51.1	26	72	8	61.2	30	80	4
Chandrasekhar	37	14	96	2	34	14	95	2
Nadkarni	16	8	21	0	19	13	10	0
Hanumant Singh	2	0	5	0				
NEW ZEALAND								
Taylor	18	4	57	1	4	0	31	1
Collinge	20.4	4	89	4				
Reid	24	4	89	1	1	0	3	1
Cameron	26	5	86	1	4	0	29	1
Morgan	15	1	68	1				
Pollard	10	1	44	0				
Sutcliffe					0.1	0	4	0

Fall of Wickets	NZ	I	NZ	I
	1st	*1st*	*2nd*	*2nd*
1st	27	56	1	9
2nd	54	179	10	13
3rd	108	240	22	65
4th	117	378	68	-
5th	130	414	172	-
6th	157	421	178	-
7th	194	457	179	-
8th	256	465	213	-
9th	260	-	264	-
10th	262	-	272	-

AVERAGES

New Zealand

BATTING	M	I	NO	Runs	HS	Ave
T.W. Jarvis	2	4	1	160	77	53.33
R.O. Collinge	2	3	1	92	54	46.00
B. Sutcliffe	4	7	1	274	151*	45.66
R.W. Morgan	4	7	0	260	82	37.14
G.T. Dowling	4	8	1	236	129	33.71
B.R. Taylor	3	6	1	158	105	31.60
J.R. Reid	4	7	0	198	82	28.28
F.J. Cameron	1	2	1	27	27*	27.00
G.E. Vivian	1	2	0	44	43	22.00
V. Pollard	4	7	0	140	43	20.00
J.T. Ward	4	6	3	51	35*	17.00
B.E. Congdon	3	6	0	81	48	13.50
B.W. Sinclair	2	3	0	39	30	13.00
R.C. Motz	3	4	1	37	21	12.33
B.W. Yuile	3	5	1	32	21	8.00

BOWLING	O	M	R	W	Ave
B.R. Taylor	82.2	13	276	15	18.40
G.T. Dowling	6	2	19	1	19.00
R.O. Collinge	52.3	11	173	5	34.60
B.E. Congdon	49	16	147	4	36.75
B.W. Yuile	70.1	18	234	6	39.00
R.C. Motz	114.4	25	311	7	44.42
G.E. Vivian	15	3	51	1	51.00
F.J. Cameron	30	5	115	2	57.50
J.R. Reid	60	17	175	3	58.33
V. Pollard	104	29	315	5	63.00
R.W. Morgan	45	8	156	1	156.00
B. Sutcliffe	7.1	2	48	0	-

India

BATTING	M	I	NO	Runs	HS	Ave
V.L. Manjrekar	1	2	1	121	102*	121.00
D.N. Sardesai	3	6	3	360	200*	120.00
C.G. Borde	4	6	0	371	109	61.83
Nawab of Pataudi	4	6	0	316	153	52.66
Hanumant Singh	4	6	2	195	82	48.75
B.K. Kunderan	1	2	1	48	36	48.00
R.G. Nadkarni	4	4	1	96	75	32.00
F.M. Engineer	4	7	0	175	90	25.00
M.L. Jaisimha	4	8	0	184	51	23.00
S.A. Durani	3	5	0	87	34	17.40
V. Subramanya	1	1	0	9	9	9.00
S. Venkataraghavan	4	4	1	18	7	6.00
R.B. Desai	3	3	0	7	7	2.33
R.F. Surti	1	2	2	26	17*	-
B.S. Chandrasekhar	2	1	1	4	4*	-
B.P. Gupte	1	1	1	3	3*	-

BOWLING	O	M	R	W	Ave
V. Subramanya	21	7	35	2	17.50
C.G. Borde	5	2	18	1	18.00
S. Venkataraghavan	257.3	124	399	21	19.00
S.A. Durani	106.2	48	182	9	20.22
R.B. Desai	106	31	305	13	23.46
B.S. Chandrasekhar	108	41	292	8	36.50
R.G. Nadkarni	125	65	168	4	42.00
B.P. Gupte	38	10	118	2	59.00
R.F. Surti	34	12	65	1	65.00
M.L. Jaisimha	80.1	37	203	3	67.66
Nawab of Pataudi	3	2	9	0	-
V.L. Manjrekar	6	4	11	0	-
Hanumant Singh	8	0	24	0	-

India required 70 runs to win with an hour remaining. The weather was deteriorating and drizzling rain added to the drama. The crowd of 12,000 was in a constant uproar and the players had difficulty in communicating with each other. The scorers, too, joined in the pandemonium and rarely did the scorebooks and the board tally. The winning runs were hit with 13 minutes to spare.

This was only India's 10th victory in 94 tests, 50 of which had been drawn, illustrating the implacable pitches that India played on at home. During the series 13 leg-before-wicket appeals had been decided in favour of the home team but only one Indian batsman had been given out in this manner.

Injury and sickness had seen all 15 members of the touring party play at least one test. The injury suffered by Ward was diagnosed as a chipped bone, which would require setting in plaster for three weeks. An urgent call was sent for Artie Dick to join the team for the rest of the tour.

Terry Jarvis battled intense heat, illness and spinners on a crumbling pitch, the likes of which he had never encountered before. His was a courageous vigil of 322 minutes in the fourth test.

71   PAKISTAN v NEW ZEALAND *(First Test)*

at Pindi Club Ground, Rawalpindi on 27, 28, 30 March, 1965
Toss : Pakistan. Umpires : Qamaruddin Butt and Shujauddin
Pakistan won by an innings and 64 runs

This was the first test to be played in Rawalpindi and Hanif Mohammad chose to give his bowlers first use of the clay wicket, which proved extraordinarily receptive to seam bowling and spin. In little more than an hour New Zealand had lost half its wickets for 39 runs, with Barry Sinclair the only batsman to reach double figures.

The wicket had lost some of its venom when Bert Sutcliffe was joined by Bruce Taylor who dominated the partnership of 52 runs in 45 minutes before Sutcliffe went for seven. Taylor's 76 in 88 minutes included a six and 13 fours. Bryan Yuile and Richard Collinge added 27 for the last wicket and New Zealand was all out for 175 in under four hours.

The left-arm finger-spin of Pervez Sajjad was virtually unplayable with the amount of abrupt turn that he extracted from the wicket. By the end of the first day Pakistan had reached 138 for three with Mohammad Ilyas and Saeed Ahmed both contributing half centuries in an 81-minute stand that realised 114 runs.

Despite another half-century by Asif Iqbal the visitors remained in contention by disposing of the next five batsmen for 82 runs. However, the last two wickets added 98 in even time with Mohammad Farooq, Pakistan's number 11, responsible for 47 rollicking runs; 318 all out.

By stumps on the second day New Zealand had accounted for only 59 of the 143-run deficit, but had lost six wickets. Sinclair and Terry Jarvis laboured through a second wicket stand of 39 but in the last 20 minutes four wickets fell for just two runs as the batsmen played like men blinded by the dust that puffed up as the ball landed and spun viciously.

Three more batsmen departed at the overnight total before Taylor and Collinge managed to scrape together 20 runs for the last wicket; 79 all out. Scarcely half an hour's play had been necessary on the third day before Pakistan achieved its first test victory in six years. At one stage New Zealand lost seven wickets while scoring two runs.

John Reid was forthright in his criticism of the wicket at Rawalpindi saying that it was the worst that he had ever played on in test cricket. He could not understand a wicket on which the ball turned so much on the first day being considered good enough for a test.

MILESTONES

- John Reid created a new world record by taking the field in his 53rd consecutive test, one more than Frank Woolley (1909 to 1926) and Peter May (1953 to 1959).

NEW ZEALAND

Batsman	First innings		Second innings	
G.T.Dowling	b Farooq	5	b Majid	0
T.W.Jarvis	c Naushad b Asif	4	c Majid b Salahuddin	17
B.W.Sinclair	b Farooq	22	c Salahuddin b Pervez	21
J.R.Reid*	b Salahuddin	4	(6) c Asif b Farooq	0
R.W.Morgan	c Farooq b Salahuddin	0	(4) b Pervez	6
B.Sutcliffe	b Pervez	7	(8) b Pervez	0
B.R.Taylor	b Pervez	76	(9) not out	7
A.E.Dick†	b Pervez	0	(7) b Farooq	0
V.Pollard	lbw b Pervez	15	(10) c Hanif b Pervez	0
B.W.Yuile	not out	11	(5) run out	1
R.O.Collinge	c Ilyas b Intikhab	15	c Asif b Farooq	8
Extras	(b 1, lb 7, nb 8)	16	(b 6, lb 10, nb 3)	19
TOTAL	(56.5 overs)	175	(47 overs)	79

PAKISTAN

Mohammad Ilyas	c Pollard b Reid	56
Naushad Ali†	b Reid	2
Saeed Ahmed	b Taylor	68
Javed Burki	b Collinge	6
Asif Iqbal	b Taylor	51
Hanif Mohammad*	b Pollard	16
Majid Khan	b Collinge	11
Salahuddin	not out	34
Intikhab Alam	c Yuile b Reid	1
Pervez Sajjad	c Dick b Taylor	18
Mohammad Farooq	c Dowling b Morgan	47
Extras	(b 5, lb 3)	8
TOTAL	(116.3 overs)	318

Bowling PAKISTAN	O	M	R	W	O	M	R	W
Asif	4	1	7	1	4	3	4	0
Majid	4	2	11	0	5	2	9	1
Farooq	16	3	57	2	12	3	25	3
Salahuddin	15	5	36	2	11	5	16	1
Pervez	16	5	42	4	12	8	5	4
Intikhab	1.5	0	6	1	3	2	1	0
NEW ZEALAND								
Collinge	21	9	36	2				
Taylor	15	3	38	3				
Pollard	22	6	80	1				
Reid	34	18	80	3				
Yuile	16	5	42	0				
Morgan	8.3	1	34	1				

Fall of Wickets	NZ	P	NZ
	1st	1st	2nd
1st	5	13	3
2nd	24	127	42
3rd	34	135	57
4th	39	148	58
5th	39	177	59
6th	91	215	59
7th	91	217	59
8th	143	220	59
9th	148	253	59
10th	175	318	79

The 1965 New Zealand team that toured India, Pakistan and England. Back row (from left): Barry Sinclair, Bryan Yuile, John Ward, Graham Vivian, Vic Pollard. Middle row: Ross Morgan, Dick Motz, Richard Collinge, Bruce Taylor, Terry Jarvis, Bevan Congdon. Front row: Bert Sutcliffe, John Reid (captain), Walter Hadlee (manager), Graham Dowling, Frank Cameron.

72 PAKISTAN v NEW ZEALAND *(Second Test)*

at Gaddafi Stadium, Lahore on 2, 3, 4, 6, 7 April, 1965
Toss : New Zealand. Umpires : Akhtar Hussain and Shujauddin
Match drawn

The chance for practice at Lahore before the second test was denied the tourists when torrential rain closed the airport and delayed their departure from Rawalpindi. Rain had also turned Gaddafi Stadium into a morass only a day before the test was due to begin.

On winning the toss John Reid sent the home team in on a damp pitch and was rewarded with three wickets before the total reached 50. By stumps Pakistan had lost another two wickets while progressing slowly to 176. The tourists had dropped five catches during the day and Richard Collinge had suffered an unhappy 19th birthday by putting down two chances, watching two more dropped off his bowling and being forced off the field before tea with a stomach complaint.

On a wicket that had now dried out, Hanif Mohammad and Majid Jehangir (later known as Majid Khan) added 217 runs for the sixth wicket in 277 minutes. Hanif declared the innings closed at 385-7 when he had reached 203. It was his 11th test century and his first at Lahore. It required 50 policemen to clear the wicket area of the hundreds of spectators who clambered over the fence to congratulate him.

The tireless Frank Cameron was the best of the New Zealand bowlers with 4-90 off 44 overs. Artie Dick was one of seven New Zealanders to be affected by illness over the first two days of this match. When he left the ground suffering from muscular influenza Reid took over the keeping gloves for the first time in seven years at test level.

Graham Dowling and Terry Jarvis batted for over four hours, accumulating 136 for the first wicket, before Jarvis was out for 55. Dowling and Barry Sinclair were subjected to a barrage of bouncers, as many as four in one over, as Hanif supported his bowlers with three men close in on the leg-side. Dowling (83 in five hours) was the only other wicket to fall before stumps when the score was 200-2.

After the rest day the visitors continued to bat steadily, losing only three wickets on the fourth day while adding 244 runs. Reid scored 88, including a six and 13 fours, and his partnership with Sinclair was worth 178. Sinclair batted in a most cultured manner and brought up his century after five hours. Despite the high humidity, the tourists had run between wickets with quick efficiency, a necessary tactic against Pakistan's defensive field settings and slow over rate. All the batsmen made a start and Reid was able to declare after an hour's play on the last day at 482-6, a lead of 97.

The New Zealand bowlers had captured four wickets by the time the home team edged ahead by two runs but, again, several relatively easy chances had been put down (one count suggested that the two teams dropped 17 catches in this match).

Reid relinquished the keeping duties to Bevan Congdon, a substitute fieldsman, who acted as New Zealand's third wicketkeeper in the game. He distinguished himself in effecting a stumping off the part-time bowling of Sinclair.

PAKISTAN

Mohammad Ilyas	c Dick b Cameron	17	c sub (R.C.Motz) b Taylor	4
Naushad Ali†	c Collinge b Cameron	9	b Cameron	29
Saeed Ahmed	b Pollard	23	(8) c & b Sutcliffe	4
Salahuddin	c Dick b Taylor	23	(3) b Cameron	25
Javed Burki	c Dick b Cameron	10	(4) c Reid b Sinclair	14
Hanif Mohammad*	not out	203		
Majid Khan	c Reid b Taylor	80	(5) c Reid b Sutcliffe	44
Asif Iqbal	lbw b Cameron	4	(6) c Sutcliffe b Pollard	43
Intikhab Alam	not out	10	(7) not out	5
Pervez Sajjad			(9) st sub (B.E.Congdon) b Sinclair	16
Mohammad Farooq			(10) not out	0
Extras	(b 2, lb 3, nb 1)	6	(b 6, lb 3, nb 1)	10
TOTAL	(167 overs) (7 wkts dec)	**385**	(77 overs) (8 wkts dec)	**194**

NEW ZEALAND

G.T.Dowling	c Naushad b Farooq	83
T.W.Jarvis	b Salahuddin	55
B.W.Sinclair	c Hanif b Intikhab	130
J.R.Reid*	lbw b Majid	88
R.W.Morgan	c Majid b Farooq	50
B.Sutcliffe	b Asif	23
B.R.Taylor	not out	25
V.Pollard	not out	8
A.E.Dick†		
F.J.Cameron		
R.O.Collinge		
Extras	(b 5, lb 8, nb 7)	20
TOTAL	(209 overs) (6 wkts dec)	**482**

Bowling	O	M	R	W	O	M	R	W	Fall of Wickets			
NEW ZEALAND										P	NZ	P
										1st	*1st*	*2nd*
Collinge	27	6	85	0	11	4	11	0	1st	14	136	5
Cameron	44	12	90	4	11	5	15	2	2nd	45	164	61
Reid	9	3	21	0					3rd	49	342	74
Pollard	42	20	76	1	19	6	41	1	4th	62	391	99
Morgan	17	8	46	0	8	1	32	0	5th	121	439	169
Taylor	28	9	61	2	7	3	15	1	6th	338	469	169
Sinclair					10	3	32	2	7th	362	-	173
Sutcliffe					11	4	38	2	8th	-	-	194
PAKISTAN									9th	-	-	-
Asif	33	12	85	1					10th	-	-	-
Majid	24	3	57	1								
Farooq	41	12	71	2								
Pervez	43	18	72	0								
Salahuddin	33	8	76	1								
Intikhab	33	5	92	1								
Saeed	1	0	1	0								
Ilyas	1	0	8	0								

Graham Dowling was batting fluently and was on 83 when he glanced Mohammad Farooq down the leg-side, where the ball was caught by Naushad Ali. Even though the ball was jarred out of the wicketkeeper's gloves the decision stood. Watching, from left, are Mohammad Ilyas, Barry Sinclair, Farooq and Hanif Mohammad.

MILESTONES

- Hanif Mohammad and Majid Jahangir established a Pakistan test record of 217 for the sixth wicket.

- Graham Dowling and Terry Jarvis created a New Zealand record of 136 for the first wicket against Pakistan.

- Barry Sinclair and John Reid created a New Zealand record for any wicket against Pakistan when they added 178 for the third wicket.

- Bevan Congdon became the second substitute to claim a stumping in a test. The first was England's Neville Tufnell at Durban 1909/10 when he took over from Bert Strudwick.

73 **PAKISTAN v NEW ZEALAND** *(Third Test)*

at National Stadium, Karachi on 9, 10, 11, 13, 14 April, 1965
Toss : New Zealand. Umpires : Daud Khan and Shujauddin
Pakistan won by 8 wickets

New Zealand was hard pressed to assemble a full team for the last match in Pakistan. Half the team were ill, while Graham Dowling had broken a bone in his right hand and John Ward's hand was still in plaster. It was their tenth test in 82 days and, coupled with a horrendous travelling schedule and the intense heat, their problems were not surprising.

The team greeted John Reid's decision to bat first on a concrete-like slab with considerable relief. Terry Jarvis and Artie Dick opened with a positive 50 in even time but the highlight on the first day was the masterful form shown by Reid who combined power with resolute defence. By stumps on the first day he was 101 not out in a total of 233-7.

Next day the New Zealand captain was the ninth out after he had reached 128 (three sixes and 15 fours) in 268 minutes. Asif Iqbal and Intikhab Alam each took three wickets.

The slow but sure batting of Saeed Ahmed then dominated proceedings. In 350 minutes he scored 172 runs while his team-mates contributed 97. Dick had great difficulty in keeping on a wicket that bounced erratically and he conceded 17 byes as extras comprised the second top score of 38. The New Zealanders fielded magnificently despite most of the players having to take turns off the field recovering from the debilitating effects of their illnesses.

New Zealand's second innings was a disappointing 223 and only Reid (76 in 195 minutes) and Bevan Congdon (57) curbed the tendency to play careless shots against an array of six bowlers, all of whom enjoyed success. On a tour in which there had been several significant 10th wicket stands, Frank Cameron and Congdon excelled in this innings, coming together at 160-9 and adding 63 in 108 minutes.

A maiden test century by Mohammad Ilyas ensured Pakistan of victory by tea on the final day. With Ilyas' opening partner content to play a minor role, the first wicket realised 121 runs, of which Naushad Ali scored 39.

Tired and weary, the New Zealanders were no match for Pakistan in spite of Reid's double of 128 and 76. From Karachi the team flew to Rome and journeyed overland for five days, visiting Venice, Interlaken, Lucerne, Frankfurt, Koblenz and Cologne before flying to London to begin a tour of England.

NEW ZEALAND

Batsman	Dismissal	Score	Dismissal 2	Score 2
T.W.Jarvis	lbw b Salahuddin	27	b Asif	0
A.E.Dick†	c Naushad b Asif	33	b Majid	2
B.W.Sinclair	c Majid b Farooq	24	lbw b Farooq	14
J.R.Reid*	b Asif	128	c Majid b Salahuddin	76
R.W.Morgan	lbw b Saeed	13	c Salahuddin b Pervez	25
B.E.Congdon	c sub (Masood-ul-Hasan) b Intikhab	17	(8) b Intikhab	57
B.R.Taylor	c Pervez b Intikhab	6	c Hanif b Intikhab	3
V.Pollard	b Farooq	1	(9) b Salahuddin	4
R.C.Motz	b Intikhab	0	(10) lbw b Intikhab	2
B.Sutcliffe	not out	13	(6) c Majid b Intikhab	18
F.J.Cameron	c Naushad b Asif	9	not out	10
Extras	(lb 2, nb 12)	14	(b 1, lb 3, nb 8)	12
TOTAL	(103 overs)	**285**	(99.4 overs)	**223**

PAKISTAN

Batsman	Dismissal	Score	Dismissal 2	Score 2
Mohammad Ilyas	lbw b Motz	20	st Dick b Reid	126
Naushad Ali†	c Taylor b Motz	9	c sub (G.E.Vivian) b Pollard	39
Saeed Ahmed	b Cameron	172	not out	19
Javed Burki	c Morgan b Pollard	29	not out	4
Hanif Mohammad*	b Reid	1		
Majid Khan	run out	12		
Salahuddin	not out	11		
Asif Iqbal	lbw b Cameron	4		
Intikhab Alam	c Dick b Congdon	3		
Pervez Sajjad	not out	8		
Mohammad Farooq				
Extras	(b 17, lb 12, nb 9)	38	(b 8, lb 2, w 1, nb 3)	14
TOTAL	(121 overs) (8 wkts dec)	**307**	(60 overs) (2 wkts)	**202**

Bowling PAKISTAN	O	M	R	W	O	M	R	W
Asif	11	3	35	3	14	7	29	1
Majid	20	1	63	0	8	0	30	1
Farooq	21	5	59	2	17	5	41	1
Salahuddin	6	4	3	1	26	5	56	2
Pervez	11	4	29	0	8	3	16	1
Intikhab	24	6	53	3	26.4	10	39	4
Saeed	10	3	29	1				
NEW ZEALAND								
Motz	22	11	35	2				
Cameron	28	7	70	2	11	3	29	0
Pollard	27	13	41	1	18	3	52	1
Taylor	15	2	54	0	14	3	43	0
Morgan	13	2	31	0	7	2	31	0
Reid	10	5	28	1	1	0	6	1
Congdon	6	3	10	1	9	2	27	0

Fall of Wickets	NZ 1st	P 1st	NZ 2nd	P 2nd
1st	50	21	0	121
2nd	76	84	10	198
3rd	123	198	45	-
4th	167	201	93	-
5th	206	248	129	-
6th	220	286	133	-
7th	226	290	151	-
8th	233	297	157	-
9th	268	-	160	-
10th	285	-	223	-

MILESTONES

- Bevan Congdon and Frank Cameron put on 63, a New Zealand last wicket record for all tests.

In his two innings of 128 and 76 John Reid scored over half his runs in boundaries.

AVERAGES

New Zealand

BATTING	M	I	NO	Runs	HS	Ave
J.R. Reid	3	5	0	296	128	59.20
B.W. Sinclair	3	5	0	211	130	42.20
B.R. Taylor	3	5	2	117	76	39.00
B.E. Congdon	1	2	0	74	57	37.00
G.T. Dowling	2	3	0	88	83	29.33
T.W. Jarvis	3	5	0	103	55	20.60
F.J. Cameron	2	2	1	19	10*	19.00
R.W. Morgan	3	5	0	94	50	18.80
B. Sutcliffe	3	5	1	61	23	15.25
B.W. Yuile	1	2	1	12	11*	12.00
R.O. Collinge	2	2	0	23	15	11.50
A.E. Dick	3	4	0	35	33	8.75
V. Pollard	3	5	1	28	15	7.00
R.C. Motz	1	2	0	2	2	1.00

BOWLING	O	M	R	W	Ave
B.W. Sinclair	10	3	32	2	16.00
R.C. Motz	22	11	35	2	17.50
B. Sutcliffe	11	4	38	2	19.00
F.J. Cameron	94	27	204	8	25.50
J.R. Reid	54	26	135	5	27.00
B.R. Taylor	79	20	211	6	35.16
B.E. Congdon	15	5	37	1	37.00
V. Pollard	128	48	290	5	58.00
R.O. Collinge	59	19	132	2	66.00
R.W. Morgan	53.3	14	174	1	174.00
B.W. Yuile	16	5	42	0	-

Pakistan

BATTING	M	I	NO	Runs	HS	Ave
Hanif Mohammad	3	3	1	220	203*	110.00
Saeed Ahmed	3	5	1	286	172	71.50
Mohammad Farooq	3	2	1	47	47	47.00
Salahuddin	3	4	2	93	34*	46.50
Mohammad Ilyas	3	5	0	223	126	44.60
Majid Khan	3	4	0	147	80	36.75
Asif Iqbal	3	4	0	102	51	25.50
Pervez Sajjad	3	3	1	42	18	21.00
Naushad Ali	3	5	0	88	39	17.60
Javed Burki	3	5	1	63	29	15.75
Intikhab Alam	3	4	2	19	10*	9.50

BOWLING	O	M	R	W	Ave
Pervez Sajjad	90	38	164	9	18.22
Intikhab Alam	88.3	23	191	9	21.22
Mohammad Farooq	107	28	253	10	25.30
Asif Iqbal	66	26	160	6	26.66
Salahuddin	91	27	187	7	26.71
Saeed Ahmed	11	3	30	1	30.00
Majid Khan	61	8	170	3	56.66
Mohammad Ilyas	1	0	8	0	-

74 ENGLAND v NEW ZEALAND (First Test)

at Edgbaston, Birmingham on 27, 28, 29, 31 May, 1 June, 1965
Toss : England. Umpires : C.S. Elliott and W.F.F. Price
England won by 9 wickets

In six first-class games in England New Zealand had struggled to find form, drawing four and having one win and one loss. In cold, dull weather a crowd of fewer than 4000 watched the home team compile 232 runs for the loss of three wickets on the first day. A shower had dampened the ground just before the start of play and the New Zealand bowlers had to contend with a wet ball that quickly lost its shine.

Both Ted Dexter and Ken Barrington, who had struggled for form in county matches, looked unsettled in the early stages of their innings. Dexter completed a half century and Barrington was 61 not out at stumps, having struck just two boundaries in a stay of more than three hours.

Barrington added only 24 runs during the second morning and was eventually the last English wicket to fall, having batted 437 minutes for his 137. The visitors had endured a very cold day in the field (coffee was provided at the drinks break) and the bowlers stuck to their task manfully with Dick Motz returning the best figures of 5-108. Richard Collinge maintained a good line and took 3-63 off 30 overs.

Graham Dowling and Bevan Congdon found few problems with the pace attack and it was not until Fred Titmus was introduced that the first wicket fell at 54. Titmus found the wicket provided considerable turn on the third morning and he took another three wickets to finish with 4-18 off 26 overs.

A bouncer from Fred Trueman struck Bert Sutcliffe on the right ear and he left the field. New Zealand collapsed dramatically to be all out for 116. Dick Brittenden described the innings as "amongst the worst in an undeniably dismal history of bad batting. It was nervous and inept batting, nearly every batsman losing his wicket to a bad shot."

Facing a huge deficit of 319 runs the New Zealanders produced a sterling performance in their follow-on innings with seven of the first eight batsmen scoring over 40. The highlight of the innings was the partnership between the veteran Sutcliffe and Vic Pollard who added 104 for the seventh wicket. This enabled New Zealand to reach its highest total against England (413) in 14 years. Pollard was left on 81 not out after playing with excellent judgement and correct technique for four hours. New Zealand's fine effort could not deny England an easy victory.

MILESTONES

• Fred Titmus captured his 100th test wicket for England.

• Bert Sutcliffe and Victor Pollard created a record seventh wicket stand against England of 104.

• This was England's seventh win in 11 tests at Edgbaston, where they had never lost.

ENGLAND

G.Boycott	c Dick b Motz	23	not out		44
R.W.Barber	b Motz	31	c sub (G.E.Vivian) b Morgan		51
E.R.Dexter	c Dick b Motz	57	not out		0
K.F.Barrington	c Dick b Collinge	137			
M.C.Cowdrey	b Collinge	85			
M.J.K.Smith*	lbw b Collinge	0			
J.M.Parks†	c Cameron b Reid	34			
F.J.Titmus	c Congdon b Motz	13			
T.W.Cartwright	b Motz	4			
F.S.Trueman	c Pollard b Cameron	3			
F.E.Rumsey	not out	21			
Extras	(b 10, lb 6, nb 11)	27	(nb 1)		1
TOTAL	(156.4 overs)	435	(30.5 overs) (1 wkt)		96

NEW ZEALAND

G.T.Dowling	b Titmus	32	b Barber		41
B.E.Congdon	c Smith b Titmus	24	b Titmus		47
B.W.Sinclair	b Titmus	14	st Parks b Barber		2
J.R.Reid*	b Trueman	2	c Barrington b Titmus		44
B.Sutcliffe	retired hurt	4	(7) c Titmus b Dexter		53
R.W.Morgan	c Parks b Barber	22	(5) lbw b Trueman		43
A.E.Dick†	c Titmus b Cartwright	0	(6) b Barber		42
V.Pollard	lbw b Titmus	4	not out		81
R.C.Motz	c Trueman b Cartwright	0	c & b Barber		21
R.O.Collinge	c Dexter b Barber	4	c Parks b Trueman		9
F.J.Cameron	not out	4	b Trueman		0
Extras	(b 1, lb 1, nb 4)	6	(b 17, lb 11, nb 2)		30
TOTAL	(63 overs)	116	(175.4 overs)		413

Bowling	O	M	R	W	O	M	R	W
NEW ZEALAND								
Collinge	29.4	8	63	3	5	1	14	0
Cameron	43	10	117	1	3	0	11	0
Motz	43	14	108	5	13	3	34	0
Pollard	18	4	60	0	1	0	5	0
Congdon	7	2	17	0	2	1	6	0
Reid	16	5	43	1	5	2	7	0
Morgan					1.5	0	18	1
ENGLAND								
Rumsey	9	2	22	0	17	5	32	0
Trueman	18	3	49	1	32.4	8	79	3
Titmus	26	17	18	4	59	30	85	2
Cartwright	7	3	14	2	12	6	12	0
Barber	3	2	7	2	45	15	132	4
Barrington					5	0	25	0
Dexter					5	1	18	1

Fall of Wickets				
	E	NZ	NZ	E
	1st	1st	2nd	2nd
1st	54	54	72	92
2nd	76	63	105	-
3rd	164	67	131	-
4th	300	86	145	-
5th	300	97	220	-
6th	335	104	249	-
7th	368	105	353	-
8th	391	108	386	-
9th	394	115	413	-
10th	435	-	413	-

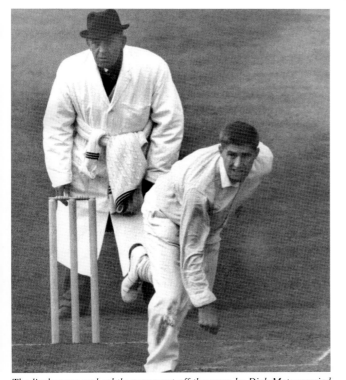

The lively pace and subtle movement off the seam by Dick Motz worried all the England batsmen.

75 ENGLAND v NEW ZEALAND *(Second Test)*

at Lord's on 17, 18, 19, 21, 22 June, 1965
Toss : New Zealand. Umpires : J.S. Buller and W.E. Phillipson
England won by 7 wickets

The England selectors created much controversy by dropping Ken Barrington for the test at Lord's. He was dropped because of the slow rate with which he had compiled his century in the first test.

New Zealand began badly when Bevan Congdon played back to the second ball of the match and was trapped in front by Fred Rumsey. In the left-armer's next over Barry Sinclair played back to a full-length ball and was bowled. Graham Dowling and Ross Morgan repeated this folly and after 67 minutes the tourists were four down for 28, with Rumsey having taken all four wickets for seven off as many overs. Lunch was taken with the score at 62-6.

A responsible partnership between Vic Pollard and Bruce Taylor carried the score to 154 before Fred Trueman bowled Taylor for 51 in stygian conditions. Pollard completed his second half-century of the series before New Zealand was dismissed for 175.

Dick Motz and Artie Dick combined to dismiss the England openers, Geoffrey Boycott and Bob Barber, cheaply before Ted Dexter began his innings with a flurry of six boundaries before stumps; 72-2.

Dexter continued to bat attractively when play eventually began on the second day but at 40 he was caught behind off Taylor for 62. Colin Cowdrey, who was affected by a back injury, now took up the dominant role and reached his 16th test century in four hours before the last six wickets fell for 36 runs, with Richard Collinge taking 4-17 in an explosive spell with the second new ball.

New Zealand overcame its first innings deficit of 132 for the loss of just one wicket, that of Congdon at 59. Dowling and Sinclair entertained a crowd of 23,000 with a sparkling partnership of 90 runs, 71 of which flowed in the hour after lunch. The *Times* correspondent later suggested: "When the tour is over this might be the hour the New Zealanders would like most of all to live again."

That promise faded when Peter Parfitt bowled Dowling on 66 and Sinclair miscued a sweep at a wide delivery from Barber to be caught for 72; 196-3. Ross Morgan and Pollard defended dourly and runs were accumulated at the rate of one an over. The scoring increased when the new ball was taken but just before stumps three wickets fell for seven; 261-7.

Play did not begin on the fourth day until after two. After an hour Collinge fell at 293 and 10 runs later Motz was caught having a mighty heave at Barber. Frank Cameron and Pollard added 44 for the 10th wicket before the patient Pollard was run out for 55, made in 258 minutes. England was 64-1 by stumps, leaving them 152 runs to score on the last day.

The advent of rain restricted the time available to little less than three hours. Despite fluctuating light conditions and the threat of rain Boycott and Dexter played most intelligently and a 126-run partnership saw England win with 15 minutes left.

NEW ZEALAND

B.E.Congdon	lbw b Rumsey	0	lbw b Titmus	26
G.T.Dowling	lbw b Rumsey	12	b Parfitt	66
B.W.Sinclair	b Rumsey	1	c Parks b Barber	72
J.R.Reid*	c Parks b Snow	21	b Titmus	22
R.W.Morgan	c Parfitt b Rumsey	0	lbw b Rumsey	35
V.Pollard	c & b Titmus	55	run out	55
A.E.Dick†	b Snow	7	c Parks b Snow	3
B.R.Taylor	b Trueman	51	c Smith b Snow	0
R.C.Motz	c Parks b Titmus	11	(10) c Snow b Barber	8
R.O.Collinge	b Trueman	7	(9) c Parks b Barber	21
F.J.Cameron	not out	3	not out	9
Extras	(b 3, lb 2, nb 2)	7	(b 8, lb 12, nb 10)	30
TOTAL	(74.5 overs)	**175**	(149 overs)	**347**

ENGLAND

G.Boycott	c Dick b Motz	14	lbw b Motz	76
R.W.Barber	c Dick b Motz	13	b Motz	34
E.R.Dexter	c Dick b Taylor	62	(4) not out	80
M.C.Cowdrey	c sub (T.W.Jarvis) b Collinge	119	(5) not out	4
P.H.Parfitt	c Dick b Cameron	11		
M.J.K.Smith*	c sub (T.W.Jarvis) b Taylor	44		
J.M.Parks†	b Collinge	2		
F.J.Titmus	run out	13	(3) c Dick b Motz	1
F.S.Trueman	b Collinge	3		
F.E.Rumsey	b Collinge	3		
J.A.Snow	not out	2		
Extras	(b 1, lb 7, w 1, nb 12)	21	(b 9, lb 5, nb 9)	23
TOTAL	(100.2 overs)	**307**	(60.5 overs) (3 wkts)	**218**

Bowling ENGLAND	O	M	R	W	O	M	R	W
Rumsey	13	4	25	4	26	10	42	1
Trueman	19.5	8	40	2	26	4	69	0
Dexter	8	2	27	0				
Snow	11	2	27	2	24	4	53	2
Titmus	15	7	25	2	39	12	71	2
Barber	8	2	24	0	28	10	57	3
Parfitt					6	2	25	1
NEW ZEALAND								
Collinge	28.2	4	85	4	15	1	43	0
Motz	20	1	62	2	19	5	45	3
Taylor	25	4	66	2	10	0	53	0
Cameron	19	6	40	1	13	0	39	0
Morgan	8	1	33	0	3	0	11	0
Reid					0.5	0	4	0

Fall of Wickets	NZ 1st	E 1st	NZ 2nd	E 2nd
1st	0	18	59	64
2nd	4	38	149	70
3rd	24	131	196	196
4th	28	166	206	-
5th	49	271	253	-
6th	62	285	258	-
7th	154	292	259	-
8th	160	300	293	-
9th	171	302	303	-
10th	175	307	347	-

MILESTONES

- The Sussex fast bowler John Snow made his debut for England. He was to play 49 tests from 1965 to 1976 and take 202 wickets.

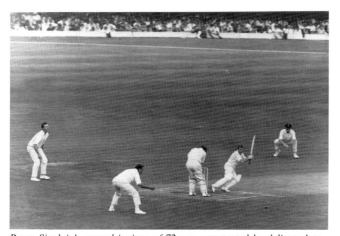

Barry Sinclair's second innings of 72 was punctuated by delicate late cuts off the slow bowlers. Jim Parks is the England wicketkeeper.

76   ENGLAND v NEW ZEALAND *(Third Test)*

at Headingley, Leeds on 8, 9, 10, 12, 13 July, 1965
Toss : England. Umpires : J.F. Crapp and C.S. Elliott
England won by an innings and 187 runs

The last ball of Bruce Taylor's third over took the edge of Bob Barber's bat and carried through to John Ward. That was New Zealand's only success on the first day as John Edrich and Ken Barrington prospered on an excellent batting wicket and their free strokes raced to the boundary across a lightning-fast outfield.

By the end of the day Edrich was 194 not out and Barrington 152 not out and England was happily situated at 366-1. In the previous three weeks Edrich had completed five centuries, two nineties and a fifty in eight innings. Barrington had replied in no uncertain terms to those, including the England selectors, who were critical of his slow batting in the first test.

The partnership was worth 369 when Barrington was caught behind off Dick Motz half an hour into the second day. His innings of 163 contained a seven and 26 fours. Edrich continued to dominate the bowling and became the eighth batsman to reach 300 in test cricket. After 522 minutes in the middle Edrich was unbeaten on 310, his five sixes and 52 fours being the most runs (238) scored in boundaries in any test innings.

John Reid said of the innings "There were magnificent lofted drives, some fine firm cover drives and periods in which he kept playing and missing repeatedly. How he failed to get a touch to some of those deliveries was incomprehensible."

Before the end of the day New Zealand had lost five wickets for 100, with Reid having contributed a bright 54, before being deceived by Ray Illingworth's faster ball, which trapped him in front.

Victor Pollard and Bryan Yuile put on 53 in the first hour on the third day until a calling mishap left Pollard helplessly stranded. The rest of the batting submitted to Illingworth and David Larter who both claimed four wickets. New Zealand's total of 193 was its best first-innings total of the series but it still left the tourists 353 runs behind. Rain swept across the ground preventing any further play before New Zealand began its second innings.

The fourth day also proceeded in a stop-start fashion according to the whims of the weather. Barry Sinclair and Graham Dowling shared a 63-run partnership for the second wicket and Pollard was on 50 (his fourth half-century of the series) when stumps were drawn at 161-9. Late in the day, when the tourists were 158 for five, Fred Titmus captured four wickets in one over without claiming a hat-trick. The match was concluded 15 minutes into the final day.

The 1965 New Zealand team had suffered defeat in the test series in India, Pakistan and England and had lost nine of their 26 first-class matches.

ENGLAND

R.W.Barber	c Ward b Taylor	13
J.H.Edrich	not out	310
K.F.Barrington	c Ward b Motz	163
M.C.Cowdrey	b Taylor	13
P.H.Parfitt	b Collinge	32
M.J.K.Smith*	not out	2
J.M.Parks†		
R.Illingworth		
F.J.Titmus		
F.E.Rumsey		
J.D.F.Larter		
Extras	(b 4, lb 8, nb 1)	13
TOTAL	(151 overs) (4 wkts dec)	**546**

NEW ZEALAND

G.T.Dowling	c Parks b Larter	5	b Rumsey	41
B.E.Congdon	c Parks b Rumsey	13	b Rumsey	1
B.W.Sinclair	c Smith b Larter	13	lbw b Larter	29
J.R.Reid*	lbw b Illingworth	54	c Barrington b Rumsey	5
R.W.Morgan	b Illingworth	1	(6) b Titmus	21
V.Pollard	run out	33	(5) c Cowdrey b Larter	53
B.W.Yuile	b Larter	46	c Cowdrey b Titmus	12
B.R.Taylor	c Parks b Illingworth	9	c & b Titmus	0
R.C.Motz	c Barber b Illingworth	3	c Barrington b Titmus	0
J.T.Ward†	not out	0	(11) not out	2
R.O.Collinge	b Larter	8	(10) b Titmus	0
Extras	(b 5, lb 1, w 2)	8	(nb 2)	2
TOTAL	(88.1 overs)	**193**	(84 overs)	**166**

Bowling	O	M	R	W	O	M	R	W
NEW ZEALAND								
Motz	41	8	140	1				
Taylor	40	8	140	2				
Collinge	32	7	87	1				
Yuile	17	5	80	0				
Morgan	6	0	28	0				
Pollard	11	2	46	0				
Congdon	4	0	12	0				
ENGLAND								
Rumsey	24	6	59	1	15	5	49	3
Larter	28.1	6	66	4	22	10	54	2
Illingworth	28	14	42	4	7	0	28	0
Titmus	6	2	16	0	26	17	19	5
Barber	2	0	2	0	14	7	14	0

Fall of Wickets				
	E	NZ	NZ	
	1st	1st	2nd	2nd
1st	13	15	4	
2nd	382	19	67	
3rd	407	53	75	
4th	516	61	86	
5th	-	100	111	
6th	-	153	158	
7th	-	165	158	
8th	-	173	158	
9th	-	181	158	
10th	-	193	166	

MILESTONES

- John Reid announced that this would be his last test match. He had played 58 tests in succession.

- John Edrich and Ken Barrington put on 369, the best for any wicket in England v New Zealand tests.

- Edrich became the seventh batsman in first-class cricket to score a fifty in nine consecutive innings. He became the ninth batsman to score a test match triple century, the fourth from England. The 238 runs in boundaries (52 fours and five sixes) was the most ever in a test innings.

Thirty-five years on, the tourists met for a reunion at the Basin Reserve. Back (from left): John Ward, Artie Dick, Bruce Taylor, Richard Collinge, Frank Cameron, Bryan Yuile. Front: Bevan Congdon, Bert Sutcliffe, John Reid, Barry Sinclair, Vic Pollard, Dr. Bill Treadwell.

AVERAGES

New Zealand

BATTING	M	I	NO	Runs	HS	Ave
B. Sutcliffe	1	2	1	57	53	57.00
V. Pollard	3	6	1	281	81*	56.20
G.T. Dowling	3	6	0	197	66	32.83
B.W. Yuile	1	2	0	58	46	29.00
J.R. Reid	3	6	0	148	54	24.66
B.W. Sinclair	3	6	0	131	72	21.83
R.W. Morgan	3	6	0	122	43	20.33
B.E. Congdon	3	6	0	111	47	18.50
F.J. Cameron	2	4	3	16	9*	16.00
B.R. Taylor	2	4	0	60	51	15.00
A.E. Dick	2	4	0	52	42	13.00
R.O. Collinge	3	6	0	49	21	8.16
R.C. Motz	3	6	0	43	21	7.16
J.T. Ward	1	2	2	2	2*	-

BOWLING	O	M	R	W	Ave
R.C. Motz	136	31	389	11	35.36
R.O. Collinge	110	21	292	8	36.50
J.R. Reid	21.5	7	54	1	54.00
B.R. Taylor	75	12	259	4	64.75
R.W. Morgan	18.5	1	90	1	90.00
F.J. Cameron	78	16	207	2	103.50
B.E. Congdon	13	3	35	0	-
B.W. Yuile	17	5	80	0	-
V. Pollard	30	6	111	0	-

England

BATTING	M	I	NO	Runs	HS	Ave
K.F. Barrington	2	2	0	300	163	150.00
E.R. Dexter	2	4	2	199	80*	99.50
M.C. Cowdrey	3	4	1	221	119	73.66
G. Boycott	2	4	1	157	76	52.33
R.W. Barber	3	5	0	142	51	28.40
F.E. Rumsey	3	2	1	24	21*	24.00
M.J.K. Smith	3	3	1	46	44	23.00
P.H. Parfitt	2	2	0	43	32	21.50
J.M. Parks	3	2	0	36	34	18.00
F.J. Titmus	3	3	0	27	13	9.00
T.W. Cartwright	1	1	0	4	4	4.00
F.S. Trueman	2	2	0	6	3	3.00
J.H. Edrich	1	1	1	310	310*	-
J.A. Snow	1	1	1	2	2*	-
R. Illingworth	1	-	-	-	-	-
J.D.F. Larter	1	-	-	-	-	-

BOWLING	O	M	R	W	Ave
T.W. Cartwright	19	9	26	2	13.00
F.J. Titmus	171	85	234	15	15.60
R. Illingworth	35	14	70	4	17.50
J.D.F. Larter	50.1	16	120	6	20.00
J.A. Snow	35	6	80	4	20.00
P.H. Parfitt	6	2	25	1	25.00
F.E. Rumsey	104	32	229	9	25.44
R.W. Barber	100	36	236	9	26.22
F.S. Trueman	96.3	23	237	6	39.50
E.R. Dexter	13	3	45	1	45.00
K.F. Barrington	5	0	25	0	-

1965/66 MCC in New Zealand

The England team, under Mike Smith, arrived after a tiring 23-match tour of Australia where they had drawn the series one-all. Although four members of the party did not travel to New Zealand, it was still a very experienced England side that played four matches on this small tour. Murray Chapple was a surprise selection as New Zealand captain. His abilities as a leader and tactician were not questioned but he had not batted with particular distinction for Central Districts.

77 NEW ZEALAND v ENGLAND *(First Test)*

at Lancaster Park, Christchurch on 25, 26, 28 February, 1 March, 1966
Toss : England. Umpires : F.R. Goodall and W.T. Martin
Match drawn

The wicket was soft after several days rain and Smith decided to bat first. Geoffrey Boycott and John Edrich soon fell to Dick Motz and, with the score at 47, Eric Russell was bowled, giving Motz his third wicket. As the wicket dried,

batting became easier and Smith and Peter Parfitt improved England's position with steady half-centuries.

England were 209-7 but were saved when the two Davids, Allen (88) and Brown (44), both made their highest test scores as they added 107 for the eighth wicket.

Chasing England's 342 Grahame Bilby and Mike Shrimpton opened with a bright partnership of 39 which was followed by a stand of 71 between Bevan Congdon and Barry Sinclair. Useful contributions by Vic Pollard and Chapple enabled Congdon to reach his maiden test century after 5½ hours' dedicated batting.

A vital partnership between Eric Petrie and Motz saw 118 runs added for the eighth wicket, with Petrie accumulating defensively and Motz hitting vigorously. New Zealand's innings ended an hour before stumps with a lead of five runs.

In the time remaining on the fourth day England suffered another shaky start and two wickets fell for 32 runs. At the beginning of the fifth day another two batsmen were dismissed cheaply before Smith and Parfitt put on 125 runs for the fifth wicket. Smith declared at 201-5, a lead of 195 runs with 140 minutes left for the chase.

Although New Zealand made no attempt on this target, Ken Higgs, a medium-fast bowler who obtained deceptive

Umpire Trevor Martin watches Gary Bartlett's front foot placement. The English media were more concerned about the legality of his action.

ENGLAND

G.Boycott	c Petrie b Motz	4	run out	4
W.E.Russell	b Motz	30	b Bartlett	25
J.H.Edrich	c Bartlett b Motz	2	lbw b Cunis	2
M.C.Cowdrey	c Bilby b Cunis	0	c Pollard b Motz	21
M.J.K.Smith*	c Puna b Pollard	54	c Bilby b Puna	87
P.H.Parfitt	c Congdon b Bartlett	54	not out	46
J.M.Parks†	c Petrie b Chapple	30	not out	4
D.A.Allen	c Chapple b Bartlett	88		
D.J.Brown	b Cunis	44		
K.Higgs	not out	8		
I.J.Jones	b Bartlett	0		
Extras	(b 6, lb 6, nb 16)	28	(b 4, lb 1, nb 7)	12
TOTAL	(127.2 overs)	342	(67 overs) (5 wkts dec)	201

NEW ZEALAND

G.P.Bilby	c Parks b Higgs	28	c Parks b Brown	3
M.J.F.Shrimpton	c Parks b Brown	11	c Smith b Allen	13
B.E.Congdon	c Smith b Jones	104	c Cowdrey b Higgs	4
B.W.Sinclair	c & b Higgs	23	c Parks b Higgs	0
V.Pollard	lbw b Higgs	23	not out	6
M.E.Chapple*	c Cowdrey b Jones	15	(7) c Parks b Higgs	0
G.A.Bartlett	c Parks b Brown	0	(8) c Brown b Parfitt	0
E.C.Petrie†	c Parks b Brown	55	(6) lbw b Higgs	1
R.C.Motz	c Parks b Jones	58	c Russell b Parfitt	2
R.S.Cunis	not out	8	not out	16
N.Puna	c Smith b Jones	1		
Extras	(b 7, lb 13, nb 1)	21	(b 2, lb 1)	3
TOTAL	(143.4 overs)	347	(48 overs) (8 wkts)	48

Bowling	O	M	R	W	O	M	R	W
NEW ZEALAND								
Motz	31	9	83	3	20	6	38	1
Bartlett	33.2	6	63	3	14	2	44	1
Cunis	31	9	63	2	19	3	58	1
Puna	18	6	54	0	14	6	49	1
Chapple	9	3	24	1				
Pollard	5	1	27	1				
ENGLAND								
Jones	28.4	9	71	4	7	3	13	0
Higgs	30	6	51	3	9	7	5	4
Allen	40	14	80	0	19	15	8	1
Boycott	12	6	30	0				
Parfitt	3	0	14	0	6	3	5	2
Parks					3	1	8	0

Fall of Wickets	E	NZ	E	NZ
	1st	*1st*	*2nd*	*2nd*
1st	19	39	18	5
2nd	28	41	32	19
3rd	47	112	48	21
4th	47	181	68	21
5th	160	202	193	22
6th	160	203	-	22
7th	209	237	-	22
8th	316	326	-	32
9th	342	344	-	-
10th	342	347	-	-

movement, soon undermined the defensive attitude of the top order. His nine overs cost only five runs, and he picked up four wickets. With more than an hour's play left the home team had lost seven wickets for 22 runs with Shrimpton (13) the only batsman to reach double figures.

Pollard batted resolutely for an hour and a half and together with Motz and Bob Cunis enabled New Zealand to salvage a draw. Despite the dreadful collapse on the last afternoon Chapple's men could reflect with some pride upon the fact that they had had a first-innings lead over England for only the fifth time in test matches between the two countries.

MILESTONES

- Murray Chapple was selected to captain New Zealand.

- Grahame Bilby (110) and Narotam (Tom) Puna (111) made their test debuts.

- Colin Cowdrey took his 100th catch in test cricket.

- Jim Parks equalled the England test record of five dismissals in an innings and eight in a match.

78 **NEW ZEALAND v ENGLAND** *(Second Test)*
at Carisbrook, Dunedin on 4, 5, 7, 8 March, 1966
Toss : New Zealand. Umpires : W.J.C. Gwynne and W.T. Martin
Match drawn

Murray Chapple was forced to withdraw from the team for the second test because of a pulled leg muscle. Barry Sinclair thus became New Zealand's third captain in as many tests.

Showers delayed the start of the first day's play until two o'clock. Sinclair decided to bat in cold, dismal weather and soon found himself at the wicket when both Grahame Bilby and Bevan Congdon were caught behind in the first 20 minutes. The England pace attack extracted appreciable lift and movement off the seam. Mike Shrimpton and Sinclair carried the score to 66 before the New Zealand captain was dismissed. Bad light stopped play with the home side 83-5.

Another two wickets were lost early on the second day before Eric Petrie and Dick Motz repeated their saving act from the previous game by adding 79 runs for the eighth wicket. In one over from David Allen, the England off-spinner, Motz hit three sixes and a four. All out for 192.

The New Zealand pace attack captured both England openers as well as John Edrich before the second day ended with England's score 103-3.

Mike Smith fell victim to the first ball of the next morning and Peter Parfitt followed soon after, at 119-5. A bout of influenza restricted Colin Cowdrey's batting and both he and John Murray were dropped before rain stopped play in the afternoon, with Cowdrey on 57 and Murray 38.

Resuming on the fourth day at 181-5 Murray, Barry

Knight and Allen all batted diligently before Smith declared at lunch with the score at 254-8. Cowdrey's unbeaten innings of 89 had occupied almost six hours.

Vic Pollard opened New Zealand's second innings, replacing Shrimpton who was suffering from flu. He was a victim of the capricious wicket, being bowled by a shooter from Ken Higgs which followed a ball pitched on a similar length that bounced over his head. New Zealand appeared to be safe when they reached tea having lost only three wickets. Immediately after the resumption Allen captured three wickets for four runs; 79-6.

Sinclair continued to play attacking shots until, with his score at 39 and the team total 100, he was splendidly caught at slip by Knight. England had a chance to win when the last batsman Tom Puna joined Petrie with 30 minutes remaining and the lead a meagre 54. Forthright batting saw the pair battle through until stumps thus earning New Zealand its second fortuitous draw.

When Dick Motz hit David Allen for 22 off one over (three sixes and a four) in the second test at Carisbrook he set a new test record for the most runs off a six-ball over.

NEW ZEALAND

G.P.Bilby	c Murray b Jones	3	c Parfitt b Higgs		21
M.J.F.Shrimpton	c Boycott b Higgs	38	(6) b Allen		0
B.E.Congdon	c Murray b Jones	0	b Parfitt		19
B.W.Sinclair*	b Knight	33	c Knight b Jones		39
V.Pollard	c Murray b Higgs	8	(2) b Higgs		2
R.W.Morgan	c Murray b Higgs	0	(5) c Smith b Allen		3
G.A.Bartlett	c Parfitt b Allen	6	c Knight b Allen		4
E.C.Petrie†	c Smith b Jones	28	not out		13
R.C.Motz	c Higgs b Knight	57	b Jones		1
R.S.Cunis	c Boycott b Allen	8	lbw b Allen		9
N.Puna	not out	3	not out		18
Extras	(b 4, lb 4)	8	(b 10, lb 6, nb 2)		18
TOTAL	(105.4 overs)	**192**	(82 overs) (9 wkts)		**147**

ENGLAND

G.Boycott	b Bartlett	5
W.E.Russell	b Motz	11
J.H.Edrich	c Bilby b Cunis	36
M.C.Cowdrey	not out	89
M.J.K.Smith*	c Pollard b Bartlett	20
P.H.Parfitt	c Pollard b Puna	4
J.T.Murray†	c Sinclair b Puna	50
B.R.Knight	c Bartlett b Motz	12
D.A.Allen	b Cunis	9
K.Higgs	not out	0
I.J.Jones		
Extras	(b 4, lb 6, nb 8)	18
TOTAL	(104 overs) (8 wkts dec)	**254**

Bowling ENGLAND	O	M	R	W	O	M	R	W
Jones	26	11	46	3	15	4	32	2
Higgs	20	6	29	3	13	7	12	2
Knight	32	14	41	2	3	1	3	0
Allen	27.4	9	68	2	33	17	46	4
Parfitt					17	6	30	1
Edrich					1	0	6	0
NEW ZEALAND								
Motz	32	7	76	2				
Bartlett	29	4	70	2				
Cunis	28	7	49	2				
Puna	14	2	40	2				
Pollard	1	0	1	0				

Fall of Wickets	NZ	E	NZ
	1st	1st	2nd
1st	4	9	8
2nd	6	32	27
3rd	66	72	66
4th	83	103	75
5th	83	119	75
6th	92	200	79
7th	100	213	100
8th	179	241	102
9th	181	-	112
10th	192	-	-

MILESTONES

• Barry Sinclair was selected to captain New Zealand.

• Dick Motz created a new test record by hitting 22 runs off a six-ball over, bowled to him by David Allen.

79 NEW ZEALAND v ENGLAND *(Third Test)*

at Eden Park, Auckland on 11, 12, 14, 15 March, 1966
Toss : New Zealand. Umpires : W.T. Martin and R.W.R. Shortt
Match drawn

Injuries to Gary Bartlett and Grahame Bilby provided the opportunity for Bruce Taylor, the 12th man in the previous tests, and Terry Jarvis to gain selection.

Barry Sinclair won the toss for the second time and then proceeded to dominate the rest of the day with his batting. The early loss of Mike Shrimpton was countered by a solid partnership of 77 between Jarvis and Bevan Congdon, with Congdon taking full advantage of being dropped on four and 11. Sinclair delighted the crowd with his free scoring while his team-mates came and went at the other end.

Just before stumps were drawn Sinclair hit David Allen through mid-wicket to complete his third test century after 178 minutes at the crease. During this time he had contributed 103 of the 136 runs scored off the bat.

Beginning the second day at 237-6 the home side added 59 runs before the last wicket fell. Sinclair's total of 114 included 11 boundaries and occupied 229 minutes. Allen, the off-spinner, took 5-123 in his 48 overs.

The England opener John Edrich was taken to hospital suffering from appendicitis and was unable to take any further part in the test. With his first ball in a test match in New Zealand Taylor bowled Peter Parfitt. Eric Russell and Colin Cowdrey both reached fifties as they compiled 118 for the second wicket. The match was nicely poised by the end of the second day with England having reached 181-4.

Once Taylor had disposed of Mike Smith early on the third morning, Vic Pollard wrapped up the England innings by claiming three wickets in five overs and giving his side the luxury of a lead of 74 on the first innings.

This advantage was soon squandered. Both of New Zealand's openers were dismissed without scoring. By the end of the day New Zealand had struggled through to 105-6 after 280 minutes. England had lost the services of their right-arm fast-medium bowler, David Brown, with a back injury that would hamper him if he were required to bat.

Soon after play resumed on the final day Pollard's stubborn stay of 155 minutes for 25 runs came to an end and the rest of the team capitulated leaving England 272 minutes in which to score 204 runs for victory. By now the wicket was playing low and slow and, against parsimonious bowling and defensive field settings, runs were very difficult to come by.

England lost the early wicket of Russell before Parfitt and Cowdrey came to terms with the wicket. The over rate slackened and Sinclair dropped men out of close catching positions. By tea, the tourists had lost two more wickets and now required 120 runs at one a minute. Sinclair was reluctant to bowl Puna, and Smith and Jim Parks found it impossible to maintain the required run-rate on an unresponsive wicket. The match dawdled to a draw.

The manager of the England side, S.C. (Billy) Griffith, said, "I think you let us off the hook. I would be more optimistic about New Zealand cricket, given the right approach, than you in New Zealand seem to be."

MILESTONES

• Barry Sinclair passed 1000 runs in test cricket in his 19th match.

• It was Sinclair's second century in successive tests at Eden Park. At that stage he was the only New Zealand batsman to have reached three figures in a test at Auckland whereas 12 visiting batsmen had done so.

NEW ZEALAND

T.W.Jarvis	c Parks b Jones	39	c Parks b Jones		0
M.J.F.Shrimpton	b Brown	6	lbw b Brown		0
B.E.Congdon	lbw b Higgs	64	run out		23
B.W.Sinclair*	c Russell b Jones	114	b Higgs		9
R.W.Morgan	c Smith b Allen	5	lbw b Knight		25
V.Pollard	c Knight b Allen	2	c Parks b Jones		25
E.C.Petrie†	c Smith b Higgs	12	(8) b Higgs		6
R.C.Motz	c Jones b Allen	16	(7) c Smith b Jones		14
B.R.Taylor	b Allen	18	b Higgs		6
R.S.Cunis	not out	6	c sub b Allen		8
N.Puna	c Russell b Allen	7	not out		2
Extras	(b 1, lb 4, nb 2)	7	(b 2, lb 7, nb 2)		11
TOTAL	(132.5 overs)	296	(102.4 overs)		129

ENGLAND

P.H.Parfitt	b Taylor	3	b Taylor		30
W.E.Russell	lbw b Motz	56	c Petrie b Taylor		1
M.C.Cowdrey	run out	59	lbw b Puna		27
M.J.K.Smith*	b Taylor	18	lbw b Cunis		30
J.M.Parks†	lbw b Taylor	38	not out		45
B.R.Knight	c Taylor b Pollard	25	not out		13
D.A.Allen	not out	7			
D.J.Brown	b Pollard	0			
K.Higgs	c Petrie b Pollard	0			
I.J.Jones	b Cunis	0			
J.H.Edrich	absent ill				
Extras	(b 11, lb 3, nb 2)	16	(b 4, lb 4, nb 5)		13
TOTAL	(88.5 overs)	222	(75 overs) (4 wkts)		159

Bowling	O	M	R	W	O	M	R	W
ENGLAND								
Brown	18	6	32	1	8.1	3	8	1
Jones	21	4	52	2	25	9	28	3
Higgs	28	13	33	2	28	11	27	3
Allen	47.5	12	123	5	23.3	7	34	1
Knight	16	7	40	0	18	9	21	1
Parfitt	2	0	9	0				
NEW ZEALAND								
Motz	15	4	42	1	16	1	32	0
Taylor	21	6	46	3	12	4	20	2
Cunis	25.5	8	45	1	18	5	33	1
Puna	22	2	70	0	12	4	27	1
Pollard	5	2	3	3	14	3	30	0
Shrimpton					2	1	1	0
Jarvis					1	0	3	0

Fall of Wickets				
	NZ	E	NZ	E
	1st	1st	2nd	2nd
1st	22	3	0	2
2nd	99	121	0	50
3rd	142	128	20	79
4th	153	175	48	112
5th	189	195	68	-
6th	237	215	88	-
7th	262	215	109	-
8th	264	219	118	-
9th	288	222	121	-
10th	296	-	129	-

AVERAGES

New Zealand

BATTING	M	I	NO	Runs	HS	Ave
B.W. Sinclair	3	6	0	218	114	36.33
B.E. Congdon	3	6	0	214	104	35.66
R.C. Motz	3	6	0	148	58	24.66
E.C. Petrie	3	6	1	115	55	23.00
T.W. Jarvis	1	2	0	39	39	19.50
R.S. Cunis	3	6	3	55	16*	18.33
N. Puna	3	5	3	31	18*	15.50
G.P. Bilby	2	4	0	55	28	13.75
V. Pollard	3	6	1	66	25	13.20
B.R. Taylor	1	2	0	24	18	12.00
M.J.F. Shrimpton	3	6	0	68	38	11.33
R.W. Morgan	2	4	0	33	25	8.25
M.E. Chapple	1	2	0	15	15	7.50
G.A. Bartlett	2	4	0	10	6	2.50

BOWLING	O	M	R	W	Ave
B.R. Taylor	33	10	66	5	13.20
V. Pollard	25	6	61	4	15.25
M.E. Chapple	9	3	24	1	24.00
G.A. Bartlett	76.2	12	177	6	29.50
R.S. Cunis	121.5	32	248	7	35.42
R.C. Motz	114	27	271	7	38.71
N. Puna	80	20	240	4	60.00
M.J.F. Shrimpton	2	1	1	0	-
T.W. Jarvis	1	0	3	0	-

England

BATTING	M	I	NO	Runs	HS	Ave
J.M. Parks	2	4	2	117	45*	58.50
D.A. Allen	3	3	1	104	88	52.00
J.T. Murray	1	1	0	50	50	50.00
M.C. Cowdrey	3	5	1	196	89*	49.00
M.J.K. Smith	3	5	0	209	87	41.80
P.H. Parfitt	3	5	1	137	54	34.25
B.R. Knight	2	3	1	50	25	25.00
W.E. Russell	3	5	0	123	56	24.60
D.J. Brown	2	2	0	44	44	22.00
J.H. Edrich	3	3	0	40	36	13.33
K. Higgs	3	3	2	8	8*	8.00
G. Boycott	2	3	0	13	5	4.33
I.J. Jones	3	2	0	0	0	0.00

BOWLING	O	M	R	W	Ave
K. Higgs	128	50	157	17	9.23
I.J. Jones	122.4	40	242	14	17.28
P.H. Parfitt	28	9	58	3	19.33
D.J. Brown	60.1	14	126	6	21.00
D.A. Allen	191	74	359	13	27.61
B.R. Knight	69	31	105	3	35.00
J.H. Edrich	1	0	6	0	-
J.M. Parks	3	1	8	0	-
G. Boycott	12	6	30	0	-

Barry Sinclair reached his century just prior to stumps on the first day at Eden Park. The England wicketkeeper is Jim Parks.

1967/68 India in New Zealand

The first Indian team to visit New Zealand arrived in February 1968 after a disappointing tour of Australia where they had lost all four tests. Their bowling attack, predominantly spin, found little assistance on Australian wickets and the Indian batsmen struggled against the Australian fast bowling.

80 NEW ZEALAND v INDIA *(First Test)*

at Carisbrook, Dunedin on 15, 16, 17, 19, 20 February, 1968
Toss : New Zealand. Umpires : D.E.A. Copps and W.T. Martin
India won by 5 wickets

Graham Dowling and Bruce Murray opened at a brisk rate with the latter the first man out at 45 after 42 minutes. The previously out-of-form Congdon batted cautiously while his partner paced his innings nicely, first taming and then mastering the Indian bowlers. In 247 minutes they added 155 before Congdon fell for 58. Dowling mixed solid defence with exciting attack until he was dismissed just prior to stumps for 143, which included two sixes and 16 fours. New Zealand finished at 248-5.

Bryan Yuile was run out at the start of the second day and two more wickets were lost in the first half-hour before Mark Burgess and Jack Alabaster added 69 for the ninth wicket, with Burgess scoring a half-century in his first test.

India appeared intent upon overhauling New Zealand's 350 before the end of the day. Farokh Engineer and Abid Ali chased every ball and were aided by short bowling from Dick Motz and Bruce Taylor which allowed them to indulge in hooks and pulls to the boundary. Ajit Wadekar and Rusi Surti also hurried along as India reached 202-3 at stumps.

All the Indian batsmen reached double figures as India took a lead of nine runs. Motz delivered a marathon 34 overs in capturing 5-86 runs. Alabaster's deceptive leg-spinners earned him three wickets. The Indian spinners found the wicket had developed a quirky nature much to their liking and New Zealand lost three wickets by stumps for 84.

The remaining New Zealand batsmen struggled with the off-spinner Erapalli Prasanna whose high flight and awkward bounce and turn enabled him to take six wickets and leave India a target of 200 runs with a day and a half remaining. The tourists began at a furious pace again and, once more, New Zealand fielding faltered under pressure. Three run outs were missed as the fieldsmen panicked into rushed returns.

Requiring 39 with seven wickets in hand India were delayed an hour because of rain. Wadekar enjoyed a splendid double of 80 and 71 to ensure India's victory by five wickets. Alabaster ensured his selection for the rest of the series with three wickets in each innings.

NEW ZEALAND

Batsman	Dismissal	Score	2nd Innings	Score
B.A.G.Murray	lbw b Desai	17	b Prasanna	54
G.T.Dowling	lbw b Abid Ali	143	c Borde b Nadkarni	10
B.E.Congdon	b Nadkarni	58	c Engineer b Prasanna	8
B.W.Sinclair*	c Wadekar b Bedi	0	run out	8
V.Pollard	b Abid Ali	20	(7) c Abid Ali b Bedi	15
M.G.Burgess	b Nadkarni	50	run out	39
B.W.Yuile	run out	4	(5) b Prasanna	2
B.R.Taylor	c Engineer b Abid Ali	7	(9) c Engineer b Prasanna	14
R.C.Motz	c Surti b Desai	10	(8) c sub (R.C.Saxena) b Prasanna	22
J.C.Alabaster	c Prasanna b Abid Ali	34	not out	13
R.I.Harford†	not out	0	lbw b Prasanna	6
Extras	(lb 5, nb 2)	7	(b 6, lb 6, nb 5)	17
TOTAL	**(157.3 overs)**	**350**	**(104 overs)**	**208**

INDIA

Batsman	Dismissal	Score	2nd Innings	Score
S.Abid Ali	c Sinclair b Taylor	21	run out	10
F.M.Engineer†	b Motz	63	c & b Alabaster	29
A.L.Wadekar	c Harford b Alabaster	80	c Murray b Alabaster	71
R.F.Surti	c Harford b Motz	28	b Alabaster	44
E.A.S.Prasanna	b Motz	23		
Nawab of Pataudi*	b Alabaster	24	(5) c & b Taylor	11
M.L.Jaisimha	c Yuile b Alabaster	17	(6) not out	11
C.G.Borde	c Pollard b Motz	21	(7) not out	15
R.G.Nadkarni	lbw b Taylor	12		
R.B.Desai	not out	32		
B.S.Bedi	c Yuile b Motz	22		
Extras	(b 2, lb 6, nb 8)	16	(b 1, lb 8)	9
TOTAL	**(124 overs)**	**359**	**(74.4 overs) (5 wkts)**	**200**

Bowling INDIA	O	M	R	W	O	M	R	W
Desai	21	3	61	2	7	1	15	0
Surti	11	1	51	0	4	1	3	0
Abid Ali	15	6	26	4	19	9	22	0
Bedi	37	10	90	1	22	11	44	1
Nadkarni	36.3	19	31	2	12	7	13	1
Prasanna	37	14	84	0	40	11	94	6
NEW ZEALAND								
Motz	34	7	86	5	11	2	39	0
Taylor	19	1	66	2	24	5	51	1
Alabaster	24	6	66	3	22	9	48	3
Pollard	19	5	55	0	10	1	30	0
Yuile	28	9	70	0	5	1	17	0
Congdon					1.4	1	6	0
Burgess					1	1	0	0

Fall of Wickets	NZ 1st	I 1st	NZ 2nd	I 2nd
1st	45	39	33	30
2nd	200	118	57	49
3rd	201	192	83	152
4th	243	215	91	163
5th	246	224	92	169
6th	252	258	120	-
7th	264	279	142	-
8th	281	300	187	-
9th	350	302	191	-
10th	350	359	208	-

Farokh Engineer breaks the wickets with both Bryan Yuile (left) and Mark Burgess (right) heading in the same direction. Yuile was the batsman run out. Seated in the front of the spectators are the three New Zealand selectors. From left, Ken Deas, Murray Chapple and Mac Anderson.

MILESTONES

- Mark Burgess (112), Roy Harford (113) and Bruce Murray (114) made their test debuts.

- Graham Dowling and Bevan Congdon established a new record second wicket partnership of 155.

- The partnership of 69 between Mark Burgess and Jack Alabaster equalled the New Zealand record for the ninth wicket.

81 NEW ZEALAND v INDIA *(Second Test)*

at Lancaster Park, Christchurch on 22, 23, 24, 26, 27 February, 1968
Toss : India. Umpires : F.R. Goodall and R.W.R. Shortt
New Zealand won by 6 wickets

The Lancaster Park wicket, mottled with bare patches of earth, encouraged Pataudi to put New Zealand in but his quicker bowlers could find no assistance. Graham Dowling and Bruce Murray put together an opening partnership of 126 before Murray was bowled for 74. Dowling, captaining New Zealand for the first time, scored his second century in as many tests, being 135 at stumps when the score was 273-3.

Successive century partnerships placed New Zealand in a strong position. Dowling and Mark Burgess added103 for the fourth wicket and Keith Thomson helped in a 119-run stand before Dowling was stumped. His innings of 239, in 556 minutes, contained five sixes, a five and 28 fours. It eclipsed Bert Sutcliffe's record of 230 against India in 1955/56.

New Zealand's total of 502 was only the second time that they had scored 500 in a test innings. Bishan Bedi was the best of the weary Indian bowlers, taking 6-126. Before bad light stopped play Dick Motz caught and bowled Abid Ali.

Accurate pace bowling, supported by splendid catching, never allowed the Indians a chance to get back into the contest. In spite of spirited resistance by Pataudi, Rusi Surti and Chandu Borde, who all scored half-centuries, Motz was not to be denied and his 6-63 ensured that India would follow on. Gary Bartlett's potency was diminished by no-ball problems. He was called 18 times in his 14 overs.

After the rest day India lost three wickets but rattled on 113 runs in the first session. Jack Alabaster achieved vital breakthroughs when he had Abid Ali and Ajit Wadekar caught behind the wicket in the space of three overs. Pataudi and Borde carried India's total into credit before Bartlett bowled both of them in the space of four balls. New Zealand's attack was weakened when Motz, who had been warned for running on the wicket, reoffended and was not allowed to bowl again in the innings.

India began the last day at 283-8. Seventeen runs were added before Bartlett wrapped up the tail, giving him six wickets for 38. New Zealand was left with a mere 88 runs for victory with most of the last day available. Bevan Congdon's

aggression ensured that they won handsomely. Alabaster now had the unique distinction of having participated in all four New Zealand test victories.

After the match the Indian manager, Ghulam Ahmed, said that Bartlett's bowling action was "a little suspect ... no bowler of his pace can get that extra bounce and speed from an occasional ball without some change in his action."

NEW ZEALAND

B.A.G.Murray	b Abid Ali	74	b Abid Ali	0
G.T.Dowling*	st Engineer b Prasanna	239	lbw b Bedi	5
B.E.Congdon	c Wadekar b Bedi	28	not out	61
V.Pollard	c Jaisimha b Bedi	1	c Jaisimha b Prasanna	9
M.G.Burgess	c Pataudi b Nadkarni	26	lbw b Bedi	1
K.Thomson	c Wadekar b Bedi	69	not out	0
G.A.Bartlett	c Wadekar b Bedi	22		
R.C.Motz	c sub (R.C.Saxena) b Bedi	1		
R.O.Collinge	c Pataudi. b Nadkarni	11		
J.C.Alabaster	c Wadekar b Bedi	1		
R.I.Harford†	not out	0		
Extras	(b 1, lb 13, w 1, nb 15)	30	(b 8, lb 1, nb 3)	12
TOTAL	(186.3 overs)	**502**	(40.4 overs) (4 wkts)	**88**

INDIA

S.Abid Ali	c & b Motz	7	c Harford b Alabaster	16
F.M.Engineer†	c Congdon b Motz	12	c Burgess b Bartlett	63
A.L.Wadekar	b Motz	15	c Murray b Alabaster	8
R.F.Surti	c Pollard b Motz	67	lbw b Pollard	45
Nawab of Pataudi*	c Murray b Pollard	52	b Bartlett	47
M.L.Jaisimha	c Murray b Collinge	1	(7) run out	15
C.G.Borde	lbw b Motz	57	(6) b Bartlett	33
R.G.Nadkarni	c Harford b Collinge	32	b Bartlett	29
E.A.S.Prasanna	c Dowling b Motz	7	c Pollard b Bartlett	7
B.S.Bedi	c Congdon b Collinge	3	c Murray b Bartlett	5
U.N.Kulkarni	not out	0	not out	1
Extras	(b 5, lb 8, nb 22)	35	(b 2, lb 11, nb 19)	32
TOTAL	(92.2 overs)	**288**	(98.5 overs)	**301**

Bowling	O	M	R	W	O	M	R	W		Fall of Wickets			
INDIA										NZ	I	I	NZ
										1st	1st	2nd	2nd
Kulkarni	13	3	38	0					1st	126	7	56	0
Surti	20	3	65	0	2.4	1	3	0	2nd	208	30	82	30
Abid Ali	18	4	40	1	3	0	13	1	3rd	214	50	107	70
Nadkarni	66	34	114	2	8	3	11	0	4th	317	153	186	79
Bedi	47.3	11	127	6	17	9	21	2	5th	436	154	230	-
Prasanna	19	2	83	1	8	1	18	1	6th	471	179	231	-
Jaisimha	3	1	5	0	2	0	10	0	7th	473	270	264	-
NEW ZEALAND									8th	498	281	278	-
Collinge	18.2	6	43	3	22	4	79	0	9th	502	287	300	-
Motz	21	6	63	6	14	5	37	0	10th	502	288	301	-
Bartlett	14	1	52	0	16.5	5	38	6					
Alabaster	15	7	36	0	31	13	63	2					
Pollard	24	7	59	1	15	2	52	1					

Graham Dowling scored 239 in his first test as New Zealand's captain.

MILESTONES

- Graham Dowling was selected to captain New Zealand.

- Keith Thomson (115) made his test debut.

- Graham Dowling's 239 was the highest individual score for New Zealand in a test. He joined Bert Sutcliffe, John Reid and Barry Sinclair as the only New Zealanders to score three or more test centuries.

- Gary Bartlett recorded the best bowling analysis for New Zealand in a test innings by taking 6-38.

- Bruce Murray equalled the New Zealand test record by taking four catches in the game.

82 NEW ZEALAND v INDIA *(Third Test)*

at Basin Reserve, Wellington on 29 February, 1, 2, 4 March, 1968
Toss : New Zealand. Umpires : D.E.A. Copps and W.T. Martin
India won by 8 wickets

On a day when showers and low cloud required the ground staff to emerge with the covers on five occasions, Graham Dowling may have regretted his decision to bat first. The weather conditions offered much assistance to what had previously looked a very ordinary Indian medium-pace attack.

The quicker bowlers were able to make the ball swing in the damp air and cut off a suspect wicket. Rusi Surti featured in the dismissal of New Zealand's first three batsmen for only 33 runs. Only Mark Burgess and Bevan Congdon looked assured as New Zealand ended the day at 147-4.

In 75 minutes on the second morning Erapalli Prasanna captured five wickets for 19 runs as he was able to extract varying turn from the bowler's footmarks. Several batsmen were guilty of attempting ill-judged sweep shots, a folly that would haunt the home team for the rest of the series. India ended the second day with a lead of 14 runs with five wickets in hand and Ajit Wadekar, impressing with wristy shots on the leg-side, on 78 not out.

On the third day Wadekar completed the only century in his test career. His contribution of 143, made in 371 minutes, helped India to a lead of 141 runs. With Gary Bartlett absent and Dick Motz and Bruce Taylor affected by stomach illness New Zealand's attack was restricted for much of the day. Roy Harford took five catches behind the wicket.

Before the home team batted again Dowling had the pitch rolled with the heavy roller. This ploy backfired with the Indian spinners able to make the ball leap and turn erratically. Only Burgess and Congdon, who added 86 runs in even time, displayed competent skills to counter the difficulties they faced. New Zealand collapsed to be all out for 199. Once more a sense of desperation seemed to provoke a suicidal urge in the batsman to attack recklessly. Bapu Nadkarni took 6-43 runs in his 30 overs. India now led the series 2–1.

NEW ZEALAND

G.T.Dowling*	c Wadekar b Surti	15	c Abid Ali b Nadkarni	14
B.A.G.Murray	run out	10	c Pataudi jnr. b Nadkarni	22
B.E.Congdon	c Wadekar b Surti	4	c Jaisimha b Bedi	51
M.G.Burgess	c Surti b Prasanna	66	(5) c Pataudi b Nadkarni	60
K.Thomson	b Surti	25	(6) c Wadekar b Nadkarni	0
V.Pollard	c Engineer b Nadkarni	24	(4) c Abid Ali b Nadkarni	1
B.R.Taylor	st Engineer b Prasanna	17	c Subramanya b Prasanna	28
R.C.Motz	c Surti b Prasanna	5	c Subramanya b Prasanna	9
R.O.Collinge	c Wadekar b Prasanna	5	c sub (R.C.Saxena) b Nadkarni	5
J.C.Alabaster	not out	3	not out	2
R.I.Harford†	c Engineer b Prasanna	1	c Subramanya b Prasanna	0
Extras	(b 2, nb 9)	11	(b 5, lb 2)	7
TOTAL	(89.2 overs)	**186**	(81.2 overs)	**199**

INDIA

S.Abid Ali	c Harford b Collinge	11	c Harford b Murray	36
F.M.Engineer†	run out	44	c Harford b Thomson	18
A.L.Wadekar	c Harford b Collinge	143	not out	5
R.F.Surti	c Congdon b Taylor	10	not out	0
Nawab of Pataudi*	c Harford b Taylor	30		
C.G.Borde	c Harford b Collinge	10		
M.L.Jaisimha	c Harford b Alabaster	20		
R.G.Nadkarni	c Murray b Alabaster	3		
V.Subramanya	not out	32		
E.A.S.Prasanna	b Taylor	1		
B.S.Bedi	run out	8		
Extras	(lb 8, nb 7)	15		0
TOTAL	(108.1 overs)	**327**	(13.3 overs) (2 wkts)	**59**

Bowling	O	M	R	W	O	M	R	W	Fall of Wickets	NZ	I	NZ	I
INDIA										1st	1st	2nd	2nd
Surti	22	6	44	3	8	1	31	0	1st	24	18	35	43
Abid Ali	8	0	31	0					2nd	30	78	42	57
Jaisimha	22	11	34	0	5	1	10	0	3rd	33	97	49	-
Bedi	2	0	12	0	16	5	42	1	4th	88	163	135	-
Nadkarni	17	8	22	1	30	12	43	6	5th	154	186	148	-
Prasanna	18.2	6	32	5	20.2	3	56	3	6th	155	256	179	-
Subramanya					2	1	10	0	7th	160	268	192	-
NEW ZEALAND									8th	169	295	193	-
Collinge	18	3	65	3	2	0	7	0	9th	182	296	199	-
Motz	20	5	62	0	3	0	21	0	10th	186	327	199	-
Taylor	27.1	9	59	3									
Alabaster	18	2	64	2	1	0	8	0					
Pollard	25	6	62	0	1	0	7	0					
Thomson					3.3	1	9	1					
Burgess					2	0	7	0					
Murray					1	1	0	1					

MILESTONES

- Roy Harford took five catches in India's first innings to create a new test record for New Zealand.

The New Zealand side which defeated India in the second test at Lancaster Park. Back row (from left): Allan Wright (manager), Mark Burgess, Richard Collinge, Bruce Murray, Gary Bartlett, Keith Thomson. Front row: Roy Harford, Dick Motz, Vic Pollard, Graham Dowling (captain), Jack Alabaster, Bryan Yuile (12th man), Bevan Congdon.

83 NEW ZEALAND v INDIA *(Fourth Test)*

at Eden Park, Auckland on 7, 8, 9, 11, 12 March, 1968
Toss : New Zealand. Umpires : D.E.A. Copps and W.T. Martin
India won by 272 runs

A long summer drought ended just as this test got under way. Graham Dowling sent India in to bat and in the second over caught Abid Ali off the bowling of Dick Motz. Rain fell after quarter of an hour and play could not resume until two o'clock. After Ajit Wadekar was dismissed, Farokh Engineer and Rusi Surti carried the score to 61-2 before the rain swept in again.

Water seeped under the covers overnight leaving a large damp patch at one end of the wicket. The Nawab of Pataudi and Chandu Borde proceeded cautiously on the second afternoon until bad light prevented a resumption after tea. India were 150-4. More than eight hours had now been lost to the weather and New Zealand's hopes of securing victory to square the series looked forlorn.

The last Indian wicket fell at 252 on the afternoon of the third day. Motz and Gary Bartlett were the leading wicket takers but Bartlett again no-balled frequently. New Zealand's response was dismal; all out for 140. The nagging accuracy of the Indian spinners frustrated the New Zealanders who adopted a "block or bash" approach. Although six batsmen reached double figures, the best effort in this sorry performance was Bevan Congdon's 27 runs.

Engineer gave India another positive start, collecting many of his 48 runs with aggressive hooks and cuts at short-pitched deliveries. Surti, who began the last day on 81, added 18 runs then offered three catching chances. The first two were put down but Mark Burgess made sure of the next opportunity to deprive this batsman of his maiden test century. Borde was not out on 65 when Pataudi declared at 261-5.

Although New Zealand had no prospect of scoring 374 runs to win, it seemed equally unlikely that the team would not survive the less than five hours remaining in the match. Dowling was safe and secure while the Indian spinners wrecked havoc with the other batsman. The occasional ball was scuttling through low on the wearing pitch.

Given this element of uncertainty, and the need for a defensive approach, it was extraordinary to see four batsmen caught on the boundary. New Zealand was routed for 101 in just three hours batting.

The Indian manager, Ghulam Ahmed said, "The main problem with New Zealand batsmen is that you have no practice against spinners, just as the Indian team has no practice against fast bowlers. Your wickets did not suit your fast bowlers but they favoured our spinners and that was the difference in the test series." He also observed that New Zealand cricket had definitely improved since the tour of India in 1965.

INDIA

Batsman	Dismissal	Runs	Dismissal	Runs
F.M.Engineer†	c Bartlett b Motz	44	c & b Alabaster	48
S.Abid Ali	c Dowling b Motz	1	c Murray b Taylor	22
A.L.Wadekar	c Ward b Bartlett	5	b Taylor	1
R.F.Surti	c Pollard b Bartlett	28	c Burgess b Bartlett	99
Nawab of Pataudi*	c Pollard b Motz	51	lbw b Pollard	6
C.G.Borde	c Alabaster b Pollard	41	not out	65
M.L.Jaisimha	c Pollard b Alabaster	19	not out	1
V.Subramanya	run out	3		
R.G.Nadkarni	c Burgess b Bartlett	21		
E.A.S.Prasanna	not out	3		
B.S.Bedi	c Murray b Motz	0		
Extras	(b 9, lb 3, w 2, nb 22)	36	(b 6, lb 4, nb 9)	19
TOTAL	(90.4 overs)	**252**	(96 overs) (5 wkts dec)	**261**

NEW ZEALAND

Batsman	Dismissal	Runs	Dismissal	Runs
G.T.Dowling*	c Engineer b Surti	8	b Bedi	37
B.A.G.Murray	c Engineer b Surti	17	c Jaisimha b Surti	3
B.E.Congdon	c Abid Ali b Nadkarni	27	c Surti b Nadkarni	3
M.G.Burgess	c Subramanya b Prasanna	11	c Bedi b Surti	18
B.W.Sinclair	b Bedi	20	b Prasanna	12
V.Pollard	run out	3	b Bedi	0
G.A.Bartlett	c Wadekar b Prasanna	0	(8) b Prasanna	11
B.R.Taylor	c Abid Ali b Bedi	7	(9) b Prasanna	0
R.C.Motz	c & b Prasanna	18	(10) c Engineer b Bedi	6
J.T.Ward†	not out	10	(7) b Prasanna	5
J.C.Alabaster	c Bedi b Prasanna	6	not out	0
Extras	(b 4, nb 9)	13	(b 3, lb 2, nb 1)	6
TOTAL	(77.1 overs)	**140**	(61.4 overs)	**101**

Bowling NEW ZEALAND	O	M	R	W	O	M	R	W
Motz	26.4	12	51	4	16	4	44	0
Bartlett	26	11	66	3	15	1	40	1
Taylor	17	4	49	0	22	4	60	2
Pollard	8	4	9	1	21	8	42	1
Alabaster	13	0	41	1	22	4	56	1
INDIA								
Surti	10	2	32	2	11	2	30	2
Jaisimha	7	3	14	0	3	1	5	0
Nadkarni	14	6	16	1	2	1	1	1
Prasanna	28.1	11	44	4	27	15	40	4
Bedi	17	8	21	2	17.4	11	14	3
Subramanya	1	1	0	0	1	0	5	0

Fall of Wickets	I	NZ	I	NZ
	1st	1st	2nd	2nd
1st	6	30	43	10
2nd	13	33	48	15
3rd	69	67	112	55
4th	132	74	127	74
5th	175	77	253	78
6th	215	88	-	78
7th	226	103	-	94
8th	244	106	-	95
9th	251	124	-	101
10th	252	140	-	101

MILESTONES

- Graham Dowling took his season's first-class aggregate to 968 runs in ten matches, a new record for the most runs in a season in New Zealand.

- New Zealand suffered its biggest defeat in terms of runs (272).

The electrifying pace of Gary Bartlett worried all the Indian batsmen in their first innings. Top scorer in the innings, the Indian captain, the Nawab of Pataudi views Bartlett from the safety of the non-striker's end.

AVERAGES

New Zealand

BATTING	M	I	NO	Runs	HS	Ave
G.T. Dowling	4	8	0	471	239	58.87
B.E. Congdon	4	8	1	240	61*	34.28
M.G. Burgess	4	8	0	271	66	33.87
K. Thomson	2	4	1	94	69	31.33
B.A.G. Murray	4	8	0	197	74	24.62
J.C. Alabaster	4	7	4	59	34	19.66
J.T. Ward	1	2	1	15	10*	15.00
B.R. Taylor	3	6	0	73	28	12.16
G.A. Bartlett	2	3	0	33	22	11.00
R.C. Motz	4	7	0	71	22	10.14
B.W. Sinclair	2	4	0	40	20	10.00
V. Pollard	4	8	0	73	24	9.12
R.O. Collinge	2	3	0	21	11	7.00
B.W. Yuile	1	2	0	6	4	3.00
R.I. Harford	3	5	2	7	6	2.33

BOWLING	O	M	R	W	Ave
B.A.G. Murray	1	1	0	1	0.00
K. Thomson	3.3	1	9	1	9.00
G.A. Bartlett	71.5	18	196	10	19.60
R.C. Motz	145.4	41	403	15	26.86
J.C. Alabaster	146	41	382	12	31.83
R.O. Collinge	60.2	13	194	6	32.33
B.R. Taylor	109.1	23	285	8	35.62
V. Pollard	123	33	316	4	79.00
B.E. Congdon	1.4	1	6	0	-
M.G. Burgess	3	1	7	0	-
B.W. Yuile	33	10	87	0	-

India

BATTING	M	I	NO	Runs	HS	Ave
C.G. Borde	4	7	2	242	65*	48.40
A.L. Wadekar	4	8	1	328	143	46.85
R.F. Surti	4	8	1	321	99	45.85
F.M. Engineer	4	8	0	321	63	40.12
V. Subramanya	2	2	1	35	32*	35.00
Nawab of Pataudi	4	7	0	221	52	31.57
R.G. Nadkarni	4	5	0	97	32	19.40
M.L. Jaisimha	4	7	2	84	20	16.80
S. Abid Ali	4	8	0	124	36	15.50
E.A.S. Prasanna	4	5	1	41	23	10.25
B.S. Bedi	4	5	0	38	22	7.60
R.B. Desai	1	1	1	32	32*	-
U.N. Kulkarni	1	2	2	1	1*	-

BOWLING	O	M	R	W	Ave
R.G. Nadkarni	185.3	90	251	14	17.92
E.A.S. Prasanna	197.5	63	451	24	18.79
S. Abid Ali	63	19	132	6	22.00
B.S. Bedi	176.1	65	371	16	23.18
R.F. Surti	88.4	17	259	7	37.00
R.B. Desai	28	4	76	2	38.00
V. Subramanya	4	2	15	0	-
U.N. Kulkarni	13	3	38	0	-
M.L. Jaisimha	42	17	78	0	-

1968/69 West Indies in New Zealand

After losing a test series in Australia, the West Indian team, which included a number of great players, some of who were in the twilight of their careers, arrived in New Zealand.

84 NEW ZEALAND v WEST INDIES (*First Test*)

at Eden Park, Auckland on 27, 28 February, 1, 3 March, 1969
Toss : West Indies. Umpires : E.C.A. MacKintosh and R.W.R. Shortt
West Indies won by 5 wickets

Glenn Turner made an inauspicious debut in the first of his 41 test appearances when he was caught off Wes Hall without scoring. This was the only occasion in 72 test innings in which Turner failed to score. Bevan Congdon dominated the first half of the day by scoring 85 in 150 minutes. His ability to cut the ball from in line with the leg stump to 30 cms wide of the off stump was never better exhibited.

However, the innings was in disarray at 152-6 when Bruce Taylor joined Bryan Yuile. Using a borrowed bat Taylor launched a furious assault upon the much-vaunted West Indian bowling. In 30 minutes he struck the fourth fastest half-century in test history and 56 minutes later he slammed Richard Edwards high over long-on to bring up his century with a six.

After 111 minutes his innings ended but by then he had made 124 with five sixes and 14 fours. This explosion of runs helped New Zealand reach 323 in 280 minutes. The tourists lost one wicket for 53 runs before stumps.

Joey Carew and Seymour Nurse saw the West Indies through to 197 before Nurse, who had survived a torrid time against Dick Motz early in his innings, was dismissed by Vic Pollard. Carew occupied the crease for 317 minutes in scoring 109, his only test century. From a position of great strength the tourists conspired to lose their last nine wickets for a meagre 79 runs.

Showers interrupted the third day's play four times but only 40 minutes were lost and the moisture made the wicket more docile. Dowling and Turner added 112 for the first wicket before Dowling was bowled for 71. Turner batted with the utmost dedication and occupied the crease for 222 minutes in his innings of 40.

Good contributions from Brian Hastings and Mark Burgess in the middle order and Motz and Bob Cunis at the tail allowed Dowling to declare at 297-8, with Pollard unbeaten on 51, early on the final morning. The West Indies were set a target of 345 to win in 315 minutes, with the requirement that 15 overs were to be bowled in the last hour.

An enthralling struggle developed through the afternoon. Roy Fredericks and Carew opened with a partnership of 50 made in 66 minutes. Nurse batted in sublime fashion, scoring 168 in 215 minutes. His timing was superb and his strokeplay elegant. There was not a shot invented that he didn't play.

With the help of Basil Butcher, 78 not out, 174 runs were added in 142 minutes, paving the way for a West Indian victory, achieved with three of the mandatory 15 overs remaining. Both sides displayed an adventurous spirit that saw 1244 runs scored for the loss of 33 wickets in four action-packed days.

NEW ZEALAND

Batsman	Dismissal	Runs	2nd Dismissal	Runs
G.T.Dowling*	c Hendriks b Edwards	18	b Edwards	71
G.M.Turner	c Sobers b Hall	0	b Edwards	40
B.E.Congdon	c Sobers b Gibbs	85	lbw b Edwards	7
B.F.Hastings	c Hendriks b Sobers	21	c Gibbs b Holford	31
M.G.Burgess	c Hendriks b Sobers	11	c Fredericks b Holford	30
V.Pollard	c & b Gibbs	4	(7) not out	51
B.W.Yuile	c Lloyd b Holford	20	(8) c Hendriks b Gibbs	1
B.R.Taylor	c Fredericks b Edwards	124	(6) c Gibbs b Holford	9
R.C.Motz	c Hall b Edwards	13	lbw b Sobers	23
R.S.Cunis	c Fredericks b Gibbs	13	not out	20
B.D.Milburn†	not out	4		
Extras	(b 5, lb 2, nb 3)	10	(b 3, lb 2, nb 9)	14
TOTAL	(73.4 overs)	323	(112.2 overs) (8 wkts dec)	297

WEST INDIES

Batsman	Dismissal	Runs	2nd Dismissal	Runs
R.C.Fredericks	b Motz	6	c Turner b Pollard	23
M.C.Carew	c Burgess b Yuile	109	c Hastings b Cunis	38
S.M.Nurse	c Turner b Pollard	95	c Yuile b Motz	168
C.H.Lloyd	lbw b Yuile	3	(5) run out	14
B.F.Butcher	c Hastings b Yuile	0	(4) not out	78
G.St A.Sobers*	c Milburn b Pollard	11	lbw b Taylor	0
D.A.J.Holford	c Burgess b Taylor	18	not out	4
J.L.Hendriks†	c Dowling b Taylor	15		
R.M.Edwards	c Milburn b Motz	2		
W.W.Hall	b Motz	1		
L.R.Gibbs	not out	0		
Extras	(b 2, lb 9, nb 5)	16	(b 12, lb 10, nb 1)	23
TOTAL	(79.7 overs)	276	(69 overs) (5 wkts)	348

Bowling	O	M	R	W	O	M	R	W
WEST INDIES								
Hall	8	1	34	1	8.2	4	8	0
Edwards	16	2	58	3	24	4	71	3
Gibbs	25.4	3	96	3	35	9	69	1
Sobers	19	1	87	2	30	7	79	1
Holford	5	1	38	1	15	1	56	3
NEW ZEALAND								
Motz	19	3	70	3	12	0	85	1
Taylor	16.7	2	48	2	11	1	54	1
Cunis	9	2	36	0	20	1	80	1
Yuile	15	2	64	3	14	2	58	0
Pollard	20	5	42	2	12	1	48	1

Fall of Wickets	NZ	WI	NZ	WI
	1st	1st	2nd	2nd
1st	8	25	112	50
2nd	28	197	122	122
3rd	92	212	131	296
4th	122	212	185	320
5th	135	225	200	320
6th	152	249	200	-
7th	232	269	201	-
8th	275	272	235	-
9th	315	274	-	-
10th	323	276	-	-

Bruce Taylor slams one of his five sixes, this one off David Holford. Wicketkeeper is Jackie Hendriks.

MILESTONES

- Brian Hastings (116), Barry Milburn (117) and Glenn Turner (118) made their test debuts.

- The eight-ball over was used at test and first class level and remained in force until 1979/80 when the NZCC reverted to six-ball overs.

- Bruce Taylor made the fifth fastest century in test cricket.

85 NEW ZEALAND v WEST INDIES *(Second Test)*

at Basin Reserve, Wellington on 7, 8, 10, 11 March, 1969
Toss : New Zealand. Umpires : E.C.A. MacKintosh and R.W.R. Shortt
New Zealand won by 6 wickets

Graham Dowling sent the visitors in to bat on a hard, lively, green wicket. Once Dick Motz found the right line, bowling at top speed he exploited the bounce and seam movement to dismiss three batsmen before lunch.

Clive Lloyd and Basil Butcher added a watchful 63 for the fourth wicket but once Bob Cunis had made the breakthrough wickets fell in a cluster; 181-7. While Motz was rested Jackie Hendricks and Charlie Griffith took advantage of some loose bowling to put on 60 runs in better than even time.

Motz returned and removed Griffith, his sixth wicket in the innings. Hendricks was joined by Richard Edwards, in a frustrating ninth wicket partnership of 46, and was left 54 not out when the innings ended at 297 just before stumps.

On a pitch that continued to assist the quick bowlers and with a strong, cold northerly sweeping down the ground the home team did well to reach 137 before losing its second wicket. Dowling departed at 41 and then Bevan Congdon and Glenn Turner added 96.

Turner batted resolutely until the middle of the afternoon, reaching 74 in 224 minutes, before he became the first of three victims taken by Edwards in three overs; 194-6. Useful contributions by Bryan Yuile, Bruce Taylor and Motz enabled New Zealand to tally 282 when the innings ended on the morning of the third day.

The West Indies began their second innings badly, being 38-4 at lunch. A sparkling partnership between Butcher, who made his second half-century of the game, and Gary Sobers threatened to wrench back the advantage from New Zealand's grasp until a superb ankle-high catch taken by Pollard, in the covers, sent Sobers back to the pavilion; 140-7.

Yuile and Motz bowled tightly to wrap up the innings at 148. Yuile finished with the best bowling figures of 3-25 but it had been Cunis (3-36) who had made the vital breakthroughs at the top and middle of the order.

The New Zealand bowlers had twice done their job and by the last session of the third day the responsibility of securing victory rested upon the shoulders of the batsmen who had 72 minutes, plus the last day, in which to score a modest 164.

The task was not made easy by the fast bowling duo of Edwards and Griffith. Prior to the home team beginning its second innings the West Indian side to visit England later in the year was announced. Neither bowler was included and both proceeded to vent their fury upon the New Zealanders.

WEST INDIES

R.C.Fredericks	c Milburn b Motz	15	c Hastings b Motz	2
M.C.Carew	c Taylor b Motz	17	run out	1
S.M.Nurse	b Motz	21	c Congdon b Cunis	16
B.F.Butcher	lbw b Motz	50	lbw b Yuile	59
C.H.Lloyd	c Milburn b Cunis	44	b Cunis	1
G.St A.Sobers*	c Morgan b Motz	20	c Pollard b Cunis	39
D.A.J.Holford	lbw b Cunis	1	b Yuile	12
J.L.Hendricks†	not out	54	b Motz	5
C.C.Griffith	c Congdon b Motz	31	b Yuile	4
R.M.Edwards	run out	22	run out	1
L.R.Gibbs	c Milburn b Yuile	2	not out	1
Extras	(b 3, lb 6, w 1, nb 10)	20	(nb 7)	7
TOTAL	**(65.4 overs)**	**297**	**(37.4 overs)**	**148**

NEW ZEALAND

G.T.Dowling*	c Gibbs b Griffith	21	c Hendriks b Griffith	23
G.M.Turner	c Sobers b Edwards	74	c Griffith b Edwards	1
B.E.Congdon	c Sobers b Carew	52	c Griffith b Edwards	4
B.F.Hastings	c Hendricks b Edwards	8	not out	62
V.Pollard	c Hendricks b Griffith	9		
R.W.Morgan	c Gibbs b Edwards	0	not out	16
B.W.Yuile	c Hendricks b Sobers	33	(5) lbw b Gibbs	37
B.R.Taylor	c Holford b Griffith	33		
R.C.Motz	c Gibbs b Edwards	18		
R.S.Cunis	lbw b Edwards	5		
B.D.Milburn†	not out	4		
Extras	(lb 7, nb 18)	25	(b 13, lb 4, w 1, nb 5)	23
TOTAL	**(83.7 overs)**	**282**	**(48.5 overs) (4 wkts)**	**166**

Bowling	O	M	R	W	O	M	R	W		Fall of Wickets			
NEW ZEALAND										WI	NZ	WI	NZ
										1st	*1st*	*2nd*	*2nd*
Motz	18	2	69	6	13	3	44	2	1st	27	41	2	20
Taylor	14	4	67	0	6	0	36	0	2nd	58	137	17	32
Cunis	18	4	76	2	12	2	36	3	3rd	67	152	36	39
Yuile	9.4	4	27	1	6.4	0	25	3	4th	130	169	38	113
Pollard	2	0	19	0					5th	174	169	92	-
Morgan	4	0	19	0					6th	177	194	116	-
WEST INDIES									7th	181	194	140	-
Griffith	26	2	92	4	15	6	29	1	8th	241	262	140	-
Edwards	24.7	5	84	5	11	2	42	2	9th	287	270	144	-
Sobers	9	2	22	1	8	2	22	0	10th	297	282	148	-
Gibbs	14	3	41	0	14.5	3	50	1					
Carew	10	3	18	1									

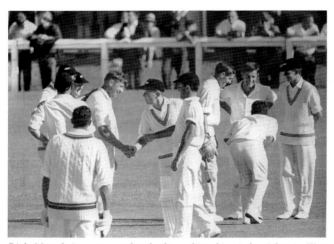

Dick Motz being congratulated after taking his sixth wicket in West Indies' first innings of the second test. From left, Bryan Yuile, Barry Milburn, Ross Morgan, Graham Dowling, Bevan Congdon and Glenn Turner.

Three batsmen fell for 39 runs as a bombardment of bouncers flew from the still lively wicket. Yuile came out as nightwatchman and the umpires asked Sobers to direct his bowlers not to aim the ball at the batsman's body.

Beginning the last day at 40 for three Brian Hastings and Yuile batted courageously before Yuile fell to the last ball before lunch. With rain falling on the hills surrounding the ground Hastings square cut a boundary to give New Zealand its fifth test victory.

MILESTONES

- Dick Motz captured his 86th wicket in test cricket, a record for a New Zealand bowler.

86 NEW ZEALAND v WEST INDIES *(Third Test)*

at Christchurch on 13, 14, 15, 17 March, 1969
Toss : West Indies. Umpires : E.C.A. MacKintosh and W.T. Martin
Match drawn

Before the match began Seymour Nurse announced that this would be his last test match. When Roy Fredericks was dismissed with the score at 16 Nurse embarked on a grandiose farewell gesture. With Joey Carew as his steadfast partner he batted with an easy exuberance that the New Zealand bowlers could do little to contain. Bad light stopped play half an hour after tea; 212-1, Nurse having completed a century in 3¼ hours.

When the partnership had added 231 Carew was well caught at slip by Glenn Turner for a patient 91. Nurse continued to display all the arts of a graceful batsman, augmenting his powerful drives off the back foot with delicate cuts and glides. His double century came up in 396 minutes.

Dick Motz struck a purple patch and in the space of 27 deliveries dismissed Basil Butcher, Clive Lloyd, Gary Sobers and David Holford. Nurse was the eighth batsman to fall at 413. His innings of 258 was scored in 476 minutes. Motz again demonstrated his supremacy among the New Zealand bowlers by taking 5-113 off 27 overs. Before stumps the home team lost Turner at 55 and Dowling at 63.

In warm, sunny conditions New Zealand struggled with the off-spin of Lance Gibbs and the leg-spin of Holford as they obtained sharp turn and variable bounce. Dismissed for 217, exactly 200 runs in arrears, New Zealand was asked to follow on. A sound opening by Dowling and Turner took the score to 115 without loss by the end of the third day.

The dismissal of Turner at the beginning of the fourth day, followed quickly by Dowling's demise, saw New Zealand lurching towards defeat. Brian Hastings found sound partners in Bevan Congdon and Vic Pollard and the danger was averted. Hastings's innings of 117 not out, made in 278 minutes, was his maiden test century and marked an excellent first series for the Canterbury batsman.

WEST INDIES		
R.C.Fredericks	c Turner b Motz	4
M.C.Carew	c Turner b Pollard	91
S.M.Nurse	st Milburn b Yuile	258
B.F.Butcher	lbw b Motz	29
C.H.Lloyd	c Yuile b Motz	3
G.St A.Sobers*	b Motz	0
D.A.J.Holford	b Motz	0
J.L.Hendriks†	c Milburn b Taylor	10
C.C.Griffith	c Pollard b Taylor	8
R.M.Edwards	st Milburn b Yuile	0
L.R.Gibbs	not out	0
Extras	(b 4, lb 9, nb 1)	14
TOTAL	**(101.4 overs)**	**417**

NEW ZEALAND				
G.T.Dowling*	lbw b Edwards	23	lbw b Sobers	76
G.M.Turner	b Gibbs	30	c Holford b Sobers	38
B.W.Yuile	lbw b Carew	17	(7) b Griffith	20
B.E.Congdon	b Gibbs	42	(3) b Sobers	43
B.F.Hastings	b Holford	0	(4) not out	117
M.G.Burgess	b Edwards	26	(5) c Sobers b Holford	2
V.Pollard	b Holford	21	(6) b Carew	44
B.R.Taylor	not out	43	not out	0
R.C.Motz	c Fredericks b Holford	6		
R.S.Cunis	c Carew b Holford	0		
B.D.Milburn†	c Holford b Gibbs	0		
Extras	(b 5, lb 3, w 1)	9	(b 10, lb 14, nb 3)	27
TOTAL	**(80.3 overs)**	**217**	**(118.4 overs) (6 wkts)**	**367**

Bowling	O	M	R	W	O	M	R	W		Fall of Wickets			
NEW ZEALAND											WI	NZ	NZ
Motz	27	3	113	5							1st	1st	2nd
Cunis	22	2	93	0						1st	16	55	115
Taylor	14.4	0	63	2						2nd	247	63	128
Pollard	18	6	64	1						3rd	326	95	203
Yuile	20	5	70	2						4th	340	117	210
WEST INDIES										5th	350	119	320
Sobers	8	3	21	0	31	8	70	3		6th	350	160	363
Griffith	5	2	15	0	13.4	1	55	1		7th	382	182	-
Edwards	15	4	30	2	21	6	67	0		8th	413	200	-
Gibbs	24.3	6	64	3	19	4	42	0		9th	417	216	-
Holford	20	5	66	4	25	5	82	1		10th	417	217	-
Carew	8	2	12	1	9	4	24	1					

Brian Hastings capped off a great first test series scoring 239 runs against a strong bowling attack. His 117 not out in New Zealand's second innings at Lancaster Park was well deserved.

AVERAGES

New Zealand BATTING	M	I	NO	Runs	HS	Ave	West Indies BATTING	M	I	NO	Runs	HS	Ave
B.R. Taylor	3	5	2	209	124	69.66	S.M. Nurse	3	5	0	558	258	111.60
B.F. Hastings	3	6	2	239	117*	59.75	B.F. Butcher	3	5	1	216	78*	54.00
B.E. Congdon	3	6	0	233	85	38.83	M.C. Carew	3	5	0	256	109	51.20
G.T. Dowling	3	6	0	232	76	38.66	J.L. Hendriks	3	4	1	84	54*	28.00
V. Pollard	3	5	1	129	51*	32.25	C.C. Griffith	2	3	0	43	31	14.33
G.M. Turner	3	6	0	183	74	30.50	G.St A. Sobers	3	5	0	70	39	14.00
B.W. Yuile	3	6	0	128	37	21.33	C.H. Lloyd	3	5	0	65	44	13.00
M.G. Burgess	2	4	0	69	30	17.25	R.C. Fredericks	3	5	0	50	23	10.00
R.W. Morgan	1	2	1	16	16*	16.00	D.A.J. Holford	3	5	1	35	18	8.75
R.C. Motz	3	4	0	60	23	15.00	R.M. Edwards	3	4	0	25	22	6.25
R.S. Cunis	3	4	1	38	20*	12.66	L.R. Gibbs	3	4	3	3	2	3.00
B.D. Milburn	3	3	2	8	4*	8.00	W.W. Hall	1	1	0	1	1	1.00

BOWLING	O	M	R	W	Ave	BOWLING	O	M	R	W	Ave
R.C. Motz	89	11	381	17	22.41	M.C. Carew	27	9	54	3	18.00
B.W. Yuile	65	13	244	9	27.11	R.M. Edwards	111.7	23	352	15	23.46
V. Pollard	52	12	173	4	43.25	D.A.J. Holford	66	12	242	9	26.88
R.S. Cunis	81	11	321	6	53.50	C.C. Griffith	59.4	11	191	5	38.20
B.R. Taylor	62.3	7	268	5	53.60	W.W. Hall	17	5	42	1	42.00
R.W. Morgan	4	0	19	0	-	G.St A. Sobers	105	23	301	7	43.00
						L.R. Gibbs	131.4	28	362	8	45.25

The New Zealand team of 1969 pictured at the start of their historic tour. Back row (from left): Barry Milburn, Brian Hastings, Ken Wadsworth, Hedley Howarth, Bruce Murray, Mark Burgess, Dayle Hadlee, Bob Cunis, Glenn Turner. Front: Bruce Taylor, Dick Motz, Vic Pollard, Graham Dowling (captain), Gordon Burgess (manager), Bevan Congdon, Bryan Yuile, Richard Collinge.

1969 New Zealand in England, India and Pakistan

Before the 1969 touring team was selected the Board of Control of the NZCC was required to consider the vexed question of Sunday play, which was becoming commonplace in England. The Presbyterian Church of New Zealand issued a statement saying that players omitted on these grounds would amount to "religious discrimination." Bruce Murray, Vic Pollard and Bryan Yuile were the players concerned, and all were chosen for the tour.

87 ENGLAND v NEW ZEALAND *(First Test)*

at Lord's on 24, 25, 26, 28 July, 1969
Toss : England. Umpires : J.S. Buller and A. Jepson
England won by 230 runs

None of the English newspapers gave New Zealand much chance of upsetting the home team and London's cricket followers seemed apathetic about the contest. Under a grey sky, the home team began batting on a curiously mottled pitch that had only a scant covering of grass. Dick Motz and Bruce Taylor created havoc among the England top order, aided by good catching.

Before lunch Dayle Hadlee, in his first test, dismissed Alan Knott with a spectacular catch off his own bowling. At lunch the England innings was in tatters at 68-5. Determined batting by Basil d'Oliveira, Ray Illingworth and Barry Knight carried England through to 190. The press launched a scathing attack upon the home team's batting while praising the visitors' excellent bowling and brilliant fielding.

By lunch on the second day Graham Dowling and Bevan Congdon had carried the score to 71-1 against some fiery bowling. After the break Illingworth exerted great pressure on the batsmen, marshalling his field with canny skill to support his own bowling and that of Derek Underwood.

Dayle Hadlee's first wicket in test cricket came from an unbelievable catch off his own bowling. The batsman was Alan Knott.

Between lunch and tea six batsmen fell for 75 runs and soon afterwards the last wicket fell at 169, with both spinners claiming four wickets.

Geoffrey Boycott and John Edrich were watchful in adding a vital 125 for the first wicket, which fell after lunch on the third day. Edrich and Phil Sharpe accelerated the scoring before Edrich was out for 115, which contained 20 boundaries. Wickets tumbled with 234-2 becoming 259-7 as the middle order batsmen attempted to force the pace against the accurate bowling of Hedley Howarth and Taylor. A solid innings by Knight, batting at eight, saw England through to 301-9 at stumps.

A last wicket of frolic by Knight and Alan Ward added 39 runs in even time at the start of the last day. England's total of 340 set New Zealand a target of 362. Underwood ensured that New Zealand would not challenge the target as he made the best use of the wicket's unpredictable bounce.

His subtle variation of flight and pace, aided by the treacherous wicket, claimed seven victims for 32 runs off 31 overs as the tourists collapsed to be all out for 131.

ENGLAND					
G.Boycott	c Congdon b Motz	0	c Turner b Pollard		47
J.H.Edrich	c Motz b Taylor	16	c Wadsworth b Hadlee		115
P.J.Sharpe	c Turner b Taylor	20	c Congdon b Howarth		46
K.W.R.Fletcher	b Motz	9	b Howarth		7
B.L.D'Oliveira	run out	37	c Wadsworth b Taylor		12
A.P.E.Knott†	c & b Hadlee	8	lbw b Howarth		10
R.Illingworth*	c Wadsworth b Howarth	53	c Wadsworth b Taylor		0
B.R.Knight	c Hadlee b Pollard	29	b Motz		49
D.J.Brown	not out	11	c Wadsworth b Taylor		7
D.L.Underwood	c Pollard b Howarth	1	b Motz		4
A.Ward	b Taylor	0	not out		19
Extras	(b 1, lb 3, w 1, nb 1)	6	(b 4, lb 15, nb 5)		24
TOTAL	(74.5 overs)	**190**	(140.4 overs)		**340**
NEW ZEALAND					
G.T.Dowling*	c Illingworth b Underwood	41	c Knott b Ward		4
G.M.Turner	c Knott b Ward	5	not out		43
B.E.Congdon	c Sharpe b Ward	41	c Fletcher b Underwood		17
B.F.Hastings	c Ward b Illingworth	23	c Knott b Underwood		0
V.Pollard	c Ward b Underwood	8	lbw b Underwood		0
M.G.Burgess	lbw b Illingworth	10	lbw b Underwood		6
K.J.Wadsworth†	lbw b Illingworth	14	(8) b Underwood		5
B.R.Taylor	c Brown b Illingworth	3	(7) b Underwood		0
R.C.Motz	b Underwood	15	c Knott b Underwood		23
D.R.Hadlee	c Illingworth b Underwood	1	c Sharpe b D'Oliveira		19
H.J.Howarth	not out	0	b Ward		4
Extras	(b 4, lb 4)	8	(b 5, lb 4, nb 1)		10
TOTAL	(87.3 overs)	**169**	(75.5 overs)		**131**

Bowling	O	M	R	W	O	M	R	W	Fall of Wickets				
NEW ZEALAND										E	NZ	E	NZ
Motz	19	5	46	2	39.4	17	78	2		*1st*	*1st*	*2nd*	*2nd*
Hadlee	14	2	48	1	16	5	43	1	1st	0	14	125	5
Taylor	13.5	4	35	3	25	4	62	3	2nd	27	76	199	27
Howarth	19	9	24	2	49	20	102	3	3rd	47	92	234	45
Pollard	9	1	31	1	8	2	20	1	4th	47	101	243	45
Burgess					3	0	11	0	5th	63	126	259	67
ENGLAND									6th	113	137	259	67
Brown	12	5	17	0	5	3	6	0	7th	158	146	259	73
Ward	14	2	49	2	10.5	0	48	2	8th	186	150	284	101
Underwood	29.3	16	38	4	31	18	32	7	9th	188	168	300	126
Knight	10	3	20	0	3	1	5	0	10th	190	169	340	131
Illingworth	22	8	37	4	18	9	24	0					
D'Oliveira					8	3	6	1					

The only batsman possessed with the resolute defensive technique required to survive in these circumstances was Glenn Turner, who was unbeaten on 43 after 253 minutes when the last wicket fell. Writing in the *Financial Times* Trevor Bailey said, "I feel the real villain is the pitch, which simply did not come up to the standards required for a test match."

MILESTONES

- Dayle Hadlee (119), Hedley Howarth (120) and Ken Wadsworth (121) made their test debuts.

- Glenn Turner became the first New Zealander, and the 16th player in all tests, to carry his bat through an innings.

88 ENGLAND v NEW ZEALAND *(Second Test)*

at Trent Bridge, Nottingham on 7, 8, 9, 11, 12 August, 1969
Toss : New Zealand. Umpires : C.S. Elliott and A.E.G. Rhodes
Match drawn

An injury to Glenn Turner meant that Bruce Murray opened the batting with Graham Dowling against a very quick attack on a lively wicket. Both openers were dismissed with the total at 53 but Bevan Congdon and Brian Hastings experienced little trouble and combined in a splendid third wicket stand worth 150 in 202 minutes.

After tea, with the new ball imminent, Congdon attempted to cut Ray Illingworth but the ball was too close to his body, took the edge of his bat and he was caught by Alan Knott; 203-3. Minutes later Hastings was dismissed for 83, which was to be the highest score by a New Zealander in the three-test series. Vic Pollard and Mark Burgess were also dismissed before stumps with the score at 231-6.

In 90 minutes on the second day New Zealand added 63 runs for the remaining four wickets. Dayle Hadlee's unbeaten 35 was the best contribution from the tailenders, who carried the total to a respectable 294. England lost Geoffrey Boycott in the last over before lunch, which was to be the tourists' only success for the rest of the day.

When stumps were drawn John Edrich and Phil Sharpe had both completed centuries and had added an unbroken 225 for the second wicket. Dick Brittenden described the bowling, which offered up a succession of full tosses and long hops, as "the worst I have seen from a New Zealand team."

The third day, a Saturday, was restricted to only 31 balls as a thunderstorm drenched the ground. In hot, steamy conditions after the rest day the New Zealand bowlers enjoyed favourable conditions. Sharpe was eventually dismissed for 111 while Edrich reached 155, made in 347 minutes.

Most of the other England batsmen were dismissed after making promising starts, and Illingworth declared at 451-8, a lead of 157. In gloomy conditions Dowling and Murray batted positively to score 37 before bad light stopped play after eight overs. Persistent rain on the final day saw the match abandoned.

NEW ZEALAND

G.T.Dowling*	b Ward	18	b Illingworth		22
B.A.G.Murray	c Knight b D'Oliveira	23	not out		40
B.E.Congdon	c Knott b Illingworth	66	not out		1
B.F.Hastings	c Sharpe b Illingworth	83			
V.Pollard	c Fletcher b Underwood	8			
M.G.Burgess	c Knight b Ward	2			
K.J.Wadsworth†	c D'Oliveira b Ward	21			
D.R.Hadlee	not out	35			
R.O.Collinge	c Knott b Knight	19			
R.C.Motz	b Ward	1			
H.J.Howarth	b Knight	3			
Extras	(b 1, lb 12, nb 2)	15	(lb 1, nb 2)		3
TOTAL	(127.5 overs)	294	(23 overs) (1 wkt)		66

ENGLAND

G.Boycott	b Motz	0
J.H.Edrich	b Hadlee	155
P.J.Sharpe	c & b Howarth	111
K.W.R.Fletcher	b Hadlee	31
B.L.D'Oliveira	c & b Hadlee	45
A.P.E.Knott†	c Burgess b Motz	15
R.Illingworth*	lbw b Collinge	33
B.R.Knight	not out	18
D.L.Underwood	c Collinge b Hadlee	16
J.A.Snow	not out	4
A.Ward		
Extras	(b 6, lb 12, w 1, nb 4)	23
TOTAL	(155 overs) (8 wkts dec)	451

Bowling	O	M	R	W	O	M	R	W		Fall of Wickets		
ENGLAND										NZ	E	NZ
										1st	1st	2nd
Snow	24	4	61	0	6	2	19	0				
Ward	23	3	61	4	3	0	14	0	1st	47	2	61
Knight	18.5	4	44	2	4	0	14	0	2nd	53	251	-
D'Oliveira	25	9	40	1	5	0	8	0	3rd	203	301	-
Underwood	22	8	44	1	3	1	5	0	4th	206	314	-
Illingworth	12	4	15	2	2	0	3	1	5th	212	344	-
Fletcher	3	1	14	0					6th	229	408	-
NEW ZEALAND									7th	244	408	-
Motz	36	5	97	2					8th	280	441	-
Collinge	29	6	88	1					9th	285	-	-
Hadlee	25	3	88	4					10th	294	-	-
Howarth	41	14	89	1								
Pollard	10	2	26	0								
Burgess	14	4	40	0								

MILESTONES

- This was the first time that New Zealand had played a test at Trent Bridge.

To the amazement of Phil Sharpe, at slip, and Alan Knott, the England wicketkeeper, Bevan Congdon gives himself room to hammer the ball through the off-side field.

89 ENGLAND v NEW ZEALAND *(Third Test)*

at The Oval on 21, 22, 23, 25, 26 August, 1969
Toss : New Zealand. Umpires : A.E. Fagg and T.W. Spencer
England won by 8 wickets

A delay of 15 minutes at the start of the first day was followed by interruptions in the morning and afternoon sessions because of rain and bad light. After John Snow bowled Bruce Murray in the first few minutes of the match, Glenn Turner and Bevan Congdon shared a 74-run partnership for the second wicket.

As at Lord's, Derek Underwood was able to make the ball bounce awkwardly and fizz away from the bat. Just before tea he had Congdon caught at slip and Turner was dismissed in the same manner immediately after the break. Four more wickets fell for 33 runs in the next hour to the combined spin of Underwood and Ray Illingworth; 123-7 at the end of the day's play.

Underwood (6-41 off 26 overs) completed the coup on the second morning when the last New Zealander was dismissed at 150. John Edrich and Geoffrey Boycott opened England's innings with a business-like 88 in 138 minutes, before the former drove at Bob Cunis and was bowled off his pads.

By tea the score had advanced to 131 for the loss of another three wickets thanks to the accuracy and penetration of Hedley Howarth and Cunis. Phil Sharpe and Alan Knott added 43 in even time before the latter was out and rain stopped play at 174-5. Howarth, with his high arm action and nagging accuracy, had bowled an impressive spell of 20 overs, capturing two wickets for 26 runs.

Dubious weather again affected the crowd numbers for a Saturday. In the hour's play before lunch Bruce Taylor delivered seven overs with the new ball, conceded seven runs and captured three wickets. When Phil Sharpe was dismissed leg-before-wicket early in the afternoon, Dick Motz became the first New Zealand bowler to capture 100 test wickets. The last two English batsmen, Alan Ward and Snow, ran riot in the last 22 minutes of England's innings, scoring 40 runs and extending the home team's total to 242.

The New Zealand openers survived the pace attack before Underwood was introduced with immediate success, capturing Murray and Glenn Turner before stumps were drawn at 71-2.

By lunch on the fourth day New Zealand had built up a credit of 30 runs thanks to diligent batting by Dowling and Brian Hastings. Hastings came in at number five and 219 minutes later was the last wicket to fall, having contributed 61 runs to the total of 229. Most of the other batsmen fell victim to Underwood, whose 6-60 gave him 12-101 in the match and 24-220 in the series.

With more than a day in which to score 138 England accounted for 32 of these runs in the 12 overs remaining on the fourth day and coasted to victory, in spite of rain on the fifth day.

The most disappointing feature of the series for New Zealand was the failure of its middle order batting to build on promising foundations. John Arlott, writing in the *Guardian* described the New Zealanders as "playing as keenly as ever but, by the standards of modern test cricket, they are unsophisticated."

NEW ZEALAND

B.A.G.Murray	b Snow	2	c & b Underwood		5
G.M.Turner	c Sharpe b Underwood	53	b Underwood		25
B.E.Congdon	c Sharpe b Underwood	24	c Knott b Ward		30
G.T.Dowling*	c Edrich b Illingworth	14	lbw b Snow		30
B.F.Hastings	b Illingworth	21	c Knott b Ward		61
V.Pollard	st Knott b Illingworth	13	c Denness b Underwood		9
B.R.Taylor	c Denness b Underwood	0	st Knott b Underwood		4
K.J.Wadsworth†	c Arnold b Underwood	2	c Knott b Snow		10
R.C.Motz	c Arnold b Underwood	16	c Denness b Underwood		11
R.S.Cunis	c Illingworth b Underwood	0	lbw b Underwood		7
H.J.Howarth	not out	0	not out		4
Extras	(nb 5)	5	(b 3, lb 11, nb 19)		33
TOTAL	**(82.3 overs)**	**150**	**(116.3 overs)**		**229**

ENGLAND

J.H.Edrich	b Howarth	68	c Wadsworth b Cunis	22
G.Boycott	b Cunis	46	b Cunis	8
M.H.Denness	c Wadsworth b Cunis	2	not out	55
P.J.Sharpe	lbw b Motz	48	not out	45
B.L.D'Oliveira	c Cunis b Howarth	1		
A.P.E.Knott†	c Murray b Taylor	21		
R.Illingworth*	c Wadsworth b Taylor	4		
G.G.Arnold	b Taylor	1		
D.L.Underwood	lbw b Taylor	3		
J.A.Snow	not out	21		
A.Ward	c Turner b Cunis	21		
Extras	(lb 5, nb 1)	6	(b 2, lb 4, nb 2)	8
TOTAL	**(98 overs)**	**242**	**(52.3 overs) (2 wkts)**	**138**

Bowling										
ENGLAND	O	M	R	W	O	M	R	W		
Arnold	8	2	13	0	10	3	17	0		
Snow	10	4	22	1	21	4	52	2		
Ward	5	0	10	0	18	10	28	2		
Illingworth	32.3	13	55	3	15	9	20	0		
Underwood	26	12	41	6	38.3	15	60	6		
D'Oliveira	1	0	4	0	14	9	19	0		
NEW ZEALAND										
Motz	19	6	54	1	9.3	1	35	0		
Taylor	21	9	47	4	4	0	11	0		
Cunis	19	3	49	3	11	3	36	2		
Howarth	34	14	66	2	23	10	32	0		
Pollard	5	1	20	0	5	1	16	0		

Fall of Wickets	NZ	E	NZ	E
	1st	1st	2nd	2nd
1st	3	88	22	19
2nd	77	118	39	56
3rd	90	118	88	-
4th	96	131	124	-
5th	118	174	153	-
6th	119	180	159	-
7th	123	188	200	-
8th	150	192	206	-
9th	150	202	224	-
10th	150	242	229	-

Phil Sharpe is lbw to Dick Motz as Motz became the first New Zealand bowler to capture 100 test wickets. Watching the proceedings from left are Bevan Congdon, Glenn Turner and wicketkeeper Ken Wadsworth. It was also Motz's last wicket in test cricket.

MILESTONES

- In his 32nd and last test match Dick Motz became the first New Zealand bowler to capture 100 test wickets.

AVERAGES

New Zealand

BATTING	M	I	NO	Runs	HS	Ave
G.M. Turner	2	4	1	126	53	42.00
B.F. Hastings	3	5	0	188	83	37.60
B.E. Congdon	3	6	1	179	66	35.80
D.R. Hadlee	2	3	1	55	35*	27.50
B.A.G. Murray	2	4	1	70	40*	23.33
G.T. Dowling	3	6	0	129	41	21.50
R.O. Collinge	1	1	0	19	19	19.00
R.C. Motz	3	5	0	66	23	13.20
K.J. Wadsworth	3	5	0	52	21	10.40
V. Pollard	3	5	0	38	13	7.60
M.G. Burgess	2	3	0	18	10	6.00
H.J. Howarth	3	5	3	11	4*	5.50
R.S. Cunis	1	2	0	7	7	3.50
B.R. Taylor	2	4	0	7	4	1.75

BOWLING	O	M	R	W	Ave
B.R. Taylor	63.5	17	155	10	15.50
R.S. Cunis	30	6	85	5	17.00
D.R. Hadlee	55	10	179	6	29.83
H.J. Howarth	166	67	313	8	39.12
R.C. Motz	123.1	34	310	7	44.28
V. Pollard	37	7	113	2	56.50
R.O. Collinge	29	6	88	1	88.00
M.G. Burgess	17	4	51	0	-

England

BATTING	M	I	NO	Runs	HS	Ave
J.H. Edrich	3	5	0	376	155	75.20
P.J. Sharpe	3	5	1	270	111	67.50
M.H. Denness	1	2	1	57	55*	57.00
B.R. Knight	2	3	1	96	49	48.00
B.L. D'Oliveira	3	4	0	95	45	23.75
R. Illingworth	3	4	0	90	53	22.50
G. Boycott	3	5	0	101	47	20.20
A. Ward	3	3	1	40	21	20.00
D.J. Brown	1	2	1	18	11*	18.00
K.W.R. Fletcher	2	3	0	47	31	15.66
A.P.E. Knott	3	4	0	54	21	13.50
D.L. Underwood	3	4	0	24	16	6.00
G.G. Arnold	1	1	0	1	1	1.00
J.A. Snow	2	2	2	25	21*	-

BOWLING	O	M	R	W	Ave
D.L. Underwood	150	70	220	24	9.16
R. Illingworth	101.3	43	154	10	15.40
A. Ward	73.5	15	210	10	21.00
B.L. D'Oliveira	53	21	77	2	38.50
B.R. Knight	35.5	8	83	2	41.50
J.A. Snow	61	14	154	3	51.33
K.W.R. Fletcher	3	1	14	0	-
D.J. Brown	17	8	23	0	-
G.G. Arnold	18	5	30	0	-

90 INDIA v NEW ZEALAND (*First Test*)

at Brabourne Stadium, Bombay on 25, 26, 27, 28, 30 September, 1969
Toss : India. Umpires : A.M. Mamsa and B. Satyaji Rao
India won by 60 runs

Political unrest was rife throughout India and rioting in Ahmedabad aroused fears for the players' safety. For this reason the first test was transferred to Bombay.

A crowd of 30,000 spectators, some of who grew restive at the slow over rate during the first day, watched the New Zealand bowlers exploit favourable conditions and bundle India out for 156. Ajit Wadekar was the only batsman not contained by the accurate attack, which found plenty of movement off a quickly prepared, well-grassed wicket. Bevan Congdon was the most successful of the bowlers, capturing three wickets. He also accounted for three catches in an excellent fielding performance.

New Zealand proceeded slowly to 70-1 at lunch on the second day. The spin bowling of Bishan Bedi and Erapalli Prasanna, with fieldsmen crowded close to the bat, continued to restrict the scoring throughout the day. Glenn Turner batted for 190 minutes for his 24 runs and Graham Dowling took over two hours for 32.

Congdon, however, used good footwork and an aggressive approach to unsettle the bowlers. By means of the sweep and cut shots he compiled 78 runs in 187 minutes. At the end of the second day the tourists had a lead of 48 runs with four wickets in hand.

Within an hour on the third day New Zealand was dismissed for 229, a hard-won lead of 73. A solid partnership between Wadekar and Chetan Chauhan took India's total past 100 for the loss of one wicket before a surprise bowling change saw Mark Burgess dismiss Chauhan for 34, made in 200 minutes. At the same score of 105 Wadekar was caught behind and Rusi Surti was bowled by Hadlee soon after.

Two quick successes on the fourth day, in front of a crowd of 47,000, saw India perilously placed. Together, the Nawab of Pataudi and Ashok Mankad produced the vital partnership of the game when they added 64 runs for the seventh wicket.

Hedley Howarth took a spectacular catch off his own bowling to dismiss Mankad. The Indian captain was eventually out for 67 after 282 minutes batting and India totalled 260. Dayle Hadlee captured three wickets in each innings.

With more than a day's play remaining, and India's lead a modest 187, the crowd urged on their favourites in the last hour. In order to dull the new ball of its shine, all returns to the bowlers were made by rolling the ball along the ground.

On the final morning Bedi and Prasanna were in complete command and the visitors' only response was to pop up catches to the close-in men. Both spinners ended up with eight wickets for the game. Dowling fought valiantly, being 36 not out after battling in vain for 156 minutes. It was a low scoring, slow scoring game.

INDIA

S.Abid Ali	c Congdon b Hadlee	3	run out	27
C.P.S.Chauhan	c Murray b Cunis	18	c Wadsworth b Burgess	34
A.L.Wadekar	c Congdon b Cunis	49	c Wadsworth b Taylor	40
R.F.Surti	c Hastings b Congdon	6	b Hadlee	1
Nawab of Pataudi*	c Congdon b Hadlee	18	c Howarth b Taylor	67
Hanumant Singh	c Wadsworth b Hadlee	1	c Wadsworth b Hadlee	13
A.V.Mankad	not out	19	(8) c & b Howarth	29
F.M.Engineer†	run out	20	(7) b Taylor	9
A.M.Pai	b Congdon	1	b Howarth	9
E.A.S.Prasanna	c Turner b Congdon	12	not out	17
B.S.Bedi	lbw b Taylor	4	c Wadsworth b Hadlee	4
Extras	(nb 5)	5	(lb 4, nb 6)	10
TOTAL	**(66.2 overs)**	**156**	**(136.2 overs)**	**260**

NEW ZEALAND

G.M.Turner	c Surti b Prasanna	24	c Surti b Prasanna	5
B.A.G.Murray	c Chauhan b Pai	17	c Surti b Prasanna	11
G.T.Dowling*	c Surti b Prasanna	32	(4) not out	36
B.E.Congdon	c Wadekar b Bedi	78	(5) c Surti b Bedi	4
B.F.Hastings	b Abid Ali	11	(6) c Wadekar b Bedi	7
M.G.Burgess	c Abid Ali b Pai	10	(7) c & b Bedi	0
K.J.Wadsworth†	c Wadekar b Bedi	14	(8) c Pataudi b Prasanna	13
H.J.Howarth	c Bedi b Prasanna	1	(11) c Engineer b Bedi	3
B.R.Taylor	c Mankad b Prasanna	21	c Abid Ali b Bedi	9
D.R.Hadlee	not out	0	c Pataudi b Prasanna	21
R.S.Cunis	run out	2	(3) c Wadekar b Bedi	12
Extras	(b 8, lb 5, nb 6)	19	(lb 1, nb 5)	6
TOTAL	**(117.3 overs)**	**229**	**(69.5 overs)**	**127**

Bowling	O	M	R	W	O	M	R	W
NEW ZEALAND								
Taylor	12.2	2	37	1	18	8	30	3
Hadlee	11	7	17	3	25.2	7	57	3
Cunis	14	5	31	2	22	6	50	0
Congdon	15	3	33	3	6	1	14	0
Howarth	14	5	33	0	45	21	69	2
Burgess					20	9	30	1
INDIA								
Pai	17	4	29	2	2	1	2	0
Abid Ali	11	1	23	1	2	1	1	0
Surti	6	2	10	0	2	1	2	0
Bedi	37	19	51	2	30.5	16	42	6
Prasanna	46.3	16	97	4	33	13	74	4

Fall of Wickets	I	NZ	I	NZ
	1st	1st	2nd	2nd
1st	4	27	44	10
2nd	34	78	105	31
3rd	45	97	105	31
4th	99	125	111	35
5th	99	165	165	49
6th	102	203	165	49
7th	131	204	229	76
8th	132	227	233	88
9th	151	227	243	115
10th	156	229	260	127

MILESTONES

- The crowd of 47,000 was the largest to watch a New Zealand team.

Bruce Murray rolls over at second slip after catching Chetan Chauhan off Bob Cunis in India's first innings. Observing the action from left are Ajit Wadekar, Ken Wadsworth, who was to take five catches in the match, and Glenn Turner.

91 INDIA v NEW ZEALAND *(Second Test)*

at Vidarbha C.A. Ground, Nagpur on 3, 4, 5, 7, 8 October, 1969
Toss : New Zealand. Umpires : S.P. Pan and V. Rajagopal
New Zealand won by 167 runs

This was the first test to be played in Nagpur. The tourists were surprised to see a pair of bullocks pulling the heavy roller over the wicket area prior to the match.

Graham Dowling chose to bat on a very hot day where the Indian medium-pacers were removed from the attack after six overs. Dowling and Bruce Murray refused to be tied down and were prepared to loft the ball over the in-field as they added 74 for the opening partnership.

When Murray departed Bevan Congdon continued his good form and New Zealand were well placed at tea at 185-2, with Dowling having made 69 in three hours. Mark Burgess and Congdon added 83 in 75 minutes before New Zealand stumbled in the last hour of play, losing three wickets to be 251-5 at stumps with Burgess 66 not out.

31 runs were added quickly at the start of the second day before three wickets fell in 10 minutes. A vigorous 26 by Dayle Hadlee enabled New Zealand to reach 319. New Zealand's attack seemed innocuous as India reached 139-2 at the start of the last over. Burgess then bowled Ajit Wadekar and had Venkataraghavan, the nightwatchman, caught at slip.

Burgess struck another significant blow early on the third day when he disposed of the Nawab of Pataudi. India slumped to a parlous 161-7 before Ambar Roy and Farokh Engineer gradually whittled away at the deficit putting on 73 for the seventh wicket. India was dismissed for 257, a deficit of 62.

The decisions that dismissed Murray (leg before) and Dowling (caught behind) were controversial and, with Congdon and Burgess also out before stumps, 81-4, the game was evenly poised at the end of the third day.

Glenn Turner and Vic Pollard made worthwhile contributions before the Indian spinners regained control. A most useful tail-end stand by Hadlee and Hedley Howarth added 43 and left India a day and a half in which to score 277. Venkataraghavan celebrated his return to test cricket by troubling all the batsmen and claiming six wickets.

India was making satisfactory progress when they went to tea with the score at 44-1. In the next session Howarth and Pollard swept away six wickets. The fielding was as exceptional as Howarth's bowling.

Resuming on the last day at 86-7 the spinners were not to be denied as New Zealand recorded its first overseas test win in seven years. Howarth, who took five wickets for 34 and nine for 100 in the match, was the obvious hero. He took three exceptional caught-and-bowleds.

NEW ZEALAND

G.T.Dowling*	lbw b Venkataraghavan	69	c Engineer b Venkataraghavan	18
B.A.G.Murray	c Abid Ali b Prasanna	30	lbw b Abid Ali	2
B.E.Congdon	c Engineer b Bedi	64	(4) c Abid Ali b Bedi	7
M.G.Burgess	lbw b Prasanna	89	(5) c Chauhan b Venkataraghavan	12
G.M.Turner	c Surti b Bedi	2	(3) c Chauhan b Venkataraghavan	57
V.Pollard	c Wadekar b Abid Ali	10	c Wadekar b Prasanna	29
B.W.Yuile	b Bedi	9	b Prasanna	10
K.J.Wadsworth†	c & b Bedi	1	lbw b Venkataraghavan	5
D.R.Hadlee	c Chauhan b Venkataraghavan	26	c & b Venkataraghavan	32
R.S.Cunis	lbw b Venkataraghavan	7	c Chauhan b Venkataraghavan	2
H.J.Howarth	not out	0	not out	17
Extras	(b 4, lb 6, nb 2)	12	(b 12, lb 8, nb 3)	23
TOTAL	(130 overs)	**319**	(105.1 overs)	**214**

INDIA

S.Abid Ali	c Dowling b Pollard	63	c Congdon b Cunis	0
C.P.S.Chauhan	c Turner b Yuile	14	c Congdon b Howarth	19
A.L.Wadekar	b Burgess	32	c & b Howarth	23
R.F.Surti	b Howarth	26	c Murray b Howarth	0
S.Venkataraghavan	c Turner b Burgess	0	(8) lbw b Burgess	4
Nawab of Pataudi*	c Wadsworth b Burgess	7	(5) lbw b Howarth	28
A.V.Mankad	c & b Howarth	10	(6) c Congdon b Pollard	7
A.Roy	b Pollard	48	(7) c & b Howarth	2
F.M.Engineer†	b Howarth	40	st Wadsworth b Pollard	19
E.A.S.Prasanna	lbw b Howarth	3	b Pollard	0
B.S.Bedi	not out	0	not out	5
Extras	(b 4, lb 7, nb 3)	14	(b 2)	2
TOTAL	(99.2 overs)	**257**	(55.5 overs)	**109**

Bowling	O	M	R	W	O	M	R	W		Fall of Wickets			
INDIA										NZ	I	NZ	I
										1st	*1st*	*2nd*	*2nd*
Surti	9	3	27	0	3	0	3	0					
Abid Ali	12	2	31	1	9	4	7	1	1st	74	55	5	1
Venkataraghavan	31	9	59	3	30.1	8	74	6	2nd	123	95	41	44
Bedi	45	18	98	4	32	13	46	1	3rd	206	139	59	44
Prasanna	33	10	92	2	31	10	61	2	4th	208	143	79	49
NEW ZEALAND									5th	244	145	144	60
Hadlee	12	2	32	0	5	2	14	0	6th	284	150	146	79
Cunis	15	6	45	0	4	2	8	1	7th	286	161	152	84
Pollard	19.2	6	36	2	11.5	4	21	3	8th	288	234	168	102
Howarth	30	5	66	4	23	11	34	5	9th	316	243	171	104
Yuile	15	6	41	1	3	1	8	0	10th	319	257	214	109
Burgess	8	4	23	3	6	0	18	1					
Congdon					3	1	4	0					

MILESTONES

- This was New Zealand's sixth test victory.

Instrumental in New Zealand's sixth test victory, Hedley Howarth leads the team from the field, acknowledged by his captain Graham Dowling, wearing a garland of flowers. From left are Ken Wadsworth, Mark Burgess, Glenn Turner, Vic Pollard, Bruce Murray, Bevan Congdon and Bryan Yuile.

92 INDIA v NEW ZEALAND *(Third Test)*

at Lal Bahadur Shastri Stadium, Hyderabad on 15, 16, 18, 19, 20 October, 1969
Toss : New Zealand. Umpires : S. Bhattacharya and M.V. Nagendra
Match drawn

Graham Dowling and Bruce Murray gave the tourists the best of starts for the deciding test of the series, with a 106-run partnership. Dowling was run out for 42 but his partner continued to bat fluently on his way to 80. Once Murray departed, with the score at 128, the Indian spinners encountered no opposition and in 73 minutes seven wickets tumbled for 38 runs; 181-9 at stumps.

The second day was washed out by persistent rain from a cyclone. There was a misunderstanding between the match officials, the groundsman, and the New Zealand management about the cutting of the pitch. Dowling's opinion was upheld which meant that play began on the third day 75 minutes late and New Zealand's innings was immediately terminated.

On a slightly damp pitch, from which tufts of grass protruded, Dayle Hadlee and Bob Cunis were almost unplayable. Assisted by keen catching, a procession of batsmen trudged back from the middle as India lost their ninth wicket with the score at 49. A plucky partnership between Venkataraghavan and Bishan Bedi carried the home team to 89 all out. Hadlee, with four for 30, and Cunis, three for 12, had exceptional bowling analyses.

The crowd's dismay at the end of the Indian innings was aggravated by an unfortunate incident. A young man ran onto the field to congratulate the last pair of Indian batsmen. A member of the army, wielding a long bamboo cane, struck him forcefully across the face.

His blood-soaked shirt was waved to the crowd who began to riot. Some swarmed onto the playing area. Fires were lit in the stands and an attempt was made to set the scoreboard alight. Windows were smashed in the rooms where the players were sheltering.

The fourth day saw an engrossing battle of tactics. The tourists wanted quick runs to extend their lead but the home team tried to delay this moment of reckoning by restricting New Zealand's ability to score rapidly. Defensive fields were set and the over-rate dropped from 18 an hour to 15.

Dowling played a sheet-anchor role, occupying the crease for 253 minutes. New Zealand slumped to 144-7 before Glenn Turner and Bruce Taylor added 31 runs in 43 minutes to enable Dowling to declare at stumps at 175-8.

Requiring 267 runs for victory India once again struggled with the bowling of Hadlee and Cunis and was 76-7 when fate delivered a cruel blow. A heavy shower fell in the middle of the afternoon and, although the sun soon reappeared, the umpires were reluctant to remove the covers and admonished the New Zealanders' endeavours to assist the groundsmen in their somewhat perfunctory attempts to mop up the wicket.

When the decision was made to abandon play another riot threatened as disgruntled spectators hurled chairs and bricks onto the field, fires were lit and army squads with teargas equipment took up positions on the perimeter. Thus a test that had already witnessed bizarre interruptions ended in confused and tense circumstances as the New Zealand team were denied the chance to win their first test series.

NEW ZEALAND

G.T.Dowling*	run out	42	lbw b Abid Ali		60
B.A.G.Murray	c Jaisimha b Prasanna	80	lbw b Prasanna		26
G.M.Turner	c Indrajitsinhji b Bedi	2	(9) not out		15
B.E.Congdon	c Pataudi b Prasanna	3	(3) c Prasanna b Venkataraghavan		18
B.F.Hastings	c Venkataraghavan b Prasanna	2	(4) c Venkataraghavan b Prasanna		21
M.G.Burgess	lbw b Bedi	2	(5) b Abid Ali		3
B.R.Taylor	c Gandotra b Prasanna	16	b Venkataraghavan		18
D.R.Hadlee	c Pataudi b Prasanna	1	b Abid Ali		0
K.J.Wadsworth†	run out	14	(6) lbw b Prasanna		5
R.S.Cunis	c Solkar b Abid Ali	7	not out		0
H.J.Howarth	not out	5			
Extras	(lb 7)	7	(b 6, lb 3)		9
TOTAL	(99.1 overs)	**181**	(82 overs) (8 wkts dec)		**175**

INDIA

S.Abid Ali	b Taylor	4	c Howarth b Taylor		5
K.S.Indrajitsinhji†	lbw b Cunis	7	c Dowling b Cunis		12
A.L.Wadekar	c Congdon b Hadlee	9	c Wadsworth b Hadlee		14
M.L.Jaisimha	c Hastings b Cunis	0	c Taylor b Hadlee		0
Nawab of Pataudi*	c Murray b Hadlee	0	lbw b Cunis		9
A.Roy	c Wadsworth b Hadlee	0	c Wadsworth b Hadlee		4
A.Gandotra	c Wadsworth b Howarth	18	b Cunis		15
E.D.Solkar	c Murray b Cunis	0	not out		13
S.Venkataraghavan	not out	25	not out		2
E.A.S.Prasanna	b Hadlee	2			
B.S.Bedi	c Dowling b Congdon	20			
Extras	(b 1, lb 3)	4	(lb 2)		2
TOTAL	(54.2 overs)	**89**	(46.4 overs) (7 wkts)		**76**

Bowling	O	M	R	W	O	M	R	W
INDIA								
Jaisimha	4	0	13	0	4	2	2	0
Abid Ali	12.1	5	17	1	27	7	47	3
Venkataraghavan	17	5	33	0	16	3	40	2
Bedi	34	14	52	2	9	2	19	0
Solkar	3	1	8	0				
Prasanna	29	13	51	5	26	7	58	3
NEW ZEALAND								
Hadlee	17	5	30	4	10.4	2	31	3
Taylor	10	2	20	1	8	2	18	1
Cunis	14	7	12	3	12	5	12	3
Congdon	3.2	1	7	1	5	3	4	0
Howarth	9	2	12	1	5	2	4	0
Burgess	1	0	4	0	6	3	5	0

Fall of Wickets

	NZ 1st	I 1st	NZ 2nd	I 2nd
1st	106	5	45	10
2nd	122	21	86	20
3rd	128	21	127	21
4th	132	21	133	34
5th	133	21	141	44
6th	135	27	141	50
7th	136	28	144	66
8th	158	46	175	-
9th	166	49	-	-
10th	181	89	-	-

MILESTONES

- Graham Dowling became the third New Zealander to pass 2000 runs in test cricket.

Perhaps the most unusual photograph of a New Zealand touring team. From left: Ken Wadsworth, Mark Burgess, Bruce Taylor, Bryan Yuile, Gordon Burgess (manager), Glenn Turner, Hedley Howarth, Graham Dowling (captain), Richard Collinge, Bob Cunis, Vic Pollard, Brian Hastings, Bruce Murray, Barry Milburn, Dick Brittenden (NZPA) and Dayle Hadlee.

AVERAGES

New Zealand

BATTING	M	I	NO	Runs	HS	Ave
G.T. Dowling	3	6	1	257	69	51.40
B.E. Congdon	3	6	0	174	78	29.00
B.A.G. Murray	3	6	0	166	80	27.66
G.M. Turner	3	6	1	105	57	21.00
V. Pollard	1	2	0	39	29	19.50
M.G. Burgess	3	6	0	116	89	19.33
D.R. Hadlee	3	6	1	80	32	16.00
B.R. Taylor	2	4	0	64	21	16.00
H.J. Howarth	3	5	3	26	17*	13.00
B.F. Hastings	2	4	0	41	21	10.25
B.W. Yuile	1	2	0	19	10	9.50
K.J. Wadsworth	3	6	0	52	14	8.66
R.S. Cunis	3	6	1	30	12	6.00

BOWLING	O	M	R	W	Ave
V. Pollard	31.1	10	57	5	11.40
D.R. Hadlee	81	25	181	13	13.92
B.E. Congdon	32.2	9	62	4	15.50
M.G. Burgess	41	16	80	5	16.00
B.R. Taylor	48.2	14	105	6	17.50
R.S. Cunis	81	31	158	9	17.55
H.J. Howarth	126	46	218	12	18.16
B.W. Yuile	18	7	49	1	49.00

India

BATTING	M	I	NO	Runs	HS	Ave
A.L. Wadekar	3	6	0	167	49	27.83
F.M. Engineer	2	4	0	88	40	22.00
A.V. Mankad	2	4	1	65	29	21.66
Nawab of Pataudi	3	6	0	129	67	21.50
C.P.S. Chauhan	2	4	0	85	34	21.25
S. Abid Ali	3	6	0	102	63	17.00
A. Gandotra	1	2	0	33	18	16.50
S. Venkataraghavan	2	4	2	31	25*	15.50
A. Roy	2	4	0	54	48	13.50
E.D. Solkar	1	2	1	13	13*	13.00
B.S. Bedi	3	5	2	33	20	11.00
K.S. Indrajitsinhji	1	2	0	19	12	9.50
E.A.S. Prasanna	3	5	1	34	17*	8.50
R.F. Surti	2	4	0	33	26	8.25
Hanumant Singh	1	2	0	14	13	7.00
A.M. Pai	1	2	0	10	9	5.00
M.L. Jaisimha	1	2	0	0	0	0.00

BOWLING	O	M	R	W	Ave
A.M. Pai	19	5	31	2	15.50
S. Abid Ali	73.1	20	126	7	18.00
S. Venkataraghavan	94.1	25	206	11	18.72
B.S. Bedi	187.5	82	308	15	20.53
E.A.S. Prasanna	198.3	69	433	20	21.65
E.D. Solkar	3	1	8	0	-
M.L. Jaisimha	8	2	15	0	-
R.F. Surti	20	6	42	0	-

93 PAKISTAN v NEW ZEALAND *(First Test)*
at National Stadium, Karachi on 24, 25, 26, 27 October, 1969
Toss : Pakistan. Umpires : Idrees Baig and Munawar Hussain
Match drawn

The reputation of the wicket at Karachi prompted the New Zealand selectors to include all three of their specialist spinners and only two medium-pacers. Glenn Turner was a notable omission from the batting order.

Hanif and Sadiq Mohammad began cautiously in a 55-run opening stand that lasted 140 minutes. After lunch the New Zealand spinners suddenly obtained sharp turn and bounce and nine wickets fell for 199 before stumps.

Sadiq battled on and top scored with 69 before falling to Hedley Howarth, who made the most of the wicket's vagaries and captured five for 66. He was well supported by Bryan Yuile and Dayle Hadlee, both of whom took two wickets.

A spirited last wicket partnership between Mohammad Nazir and Asif Masood carried the score through to 220. Graham Dowling and Bruce Murray began New Zealand's innings with a blitz of 30 runs off the first six overs.

The introduction of Intikhab Alam with his right-arm leg-breaks and Nazir's right-arm off-spinners restricted the scoring before Nazir began capturing wickets.

A century partnership between Yuile and Hadlee kept the fieldsmen busy and came up in 90 minutes. This positive approach helped New Zealand to a total of 274.

Nazir enjoyed a marvellous test debut capturing seven wickets to go with his 29 not out in the first innings. He was to play another 13 test matches for Pakistan and these two efforts remained his best.

With Pakistan 83 for three the New Zealanders began to wilt in the heat. Their usual agility in the field was no longer apparent and three catches were dropped. That batting was not easy on this wicket is indicated by the fact that Mushtaq, regarded as a dashing stroke-maker in English county cricket, took two hours to score 19 runs. Bryan Yuile had an impressive spell in the last session, bowling 16 overs and taking two wickets for 23 runs.

After lunch on the third day a sense of urgency seized Intikhab and he declared once he was dismissed for 47. Set a target of 230 runs in 195 minutes the tourists were immediately on the back foot, stumbling to 11-3, with the left-arm slow bowler Pervez Sajjad capturing all three.

Brian Hastings defended dourly while Mark Burgess continued to attack. When Pollard came to the crease he was also aggressive. Although the gesture could not possibly win the game for New Zealand it did at least prevent a timid submission.

Hedley Howarth bowls Sadiq Mohammad for 69 in Pakistan's first innings at Karachi. Howarth is wearing a sun hat while the umpire's head is enclosed in a towel to protect him from the searing sun.

PAKISTAN

Batsman	Dismissal	R	2nd innings	R
Hanif Mohammad	c Yuile b Howarth	22	lbw b Yuile	35
Sadiq Mohammad	b Howarth	69	run out	37
Younis Ahmed	c Dowling b Howarth	8	(5) c Dowling b Cunis	62
Mushtaq Mohammad	b Yuile	14	c Murray b Howarth	19
Zaheer Abbas	c Murray b Yuile	12	(6) c Burgess b Hadlee	27
Asif Iqbal	st Wadsworth b Howarth	22	(3) c Hastings b Yuile	0
Intikhab Alam*	c Congdon b Howarth	0	(8) c Yuile b Cunis	47
Wasim Bari†	c Murray b Hadlee	15	(7) c Congdon b Howarth	19
Mohammad Nazir	not out	29	not out	17
Pervez Sajjad	b Hadlee	0		
Asif Masood	c Howarth b Hadlee	17		
Extras	(b 2, lb 10)	12	(b 13, lb 7)	20
TOTAL	(97.2 overs)	**220**	(134.4 overs) (8 wkts dec)	**283**

NEW ZEALAND

Batsman	Dismissal	R	2nd innings	R
G.T.Dowling*	b Nazir	40	lbw b Pervez	3
B.A.G.Murray	c Hanif b Nazir	50	c Asif Iqbal b Pervez	6
B.E.Congdon	c Sadiq b Pervez	20	c Sadiq b Pervez	2
B.F.Hastings	b Nazir	22	b Pervez	9
M.G.Burgess	b Nazir	21	c Asif Iqbal b Pervez	45
V.Pollard	b Nazir	2	not out	28
B.W.Yuile	not out	47	not out	5
K.J.Wadsworth†	st Bari b Pervez	0		
D.R.Hadlee	lbw b Mushtaq	56		
R.S.Cunis	b Nazir	5		
H.J.Howarth	b Nazir	0		
Extras	(b 6, lb 3, nb 2)	11	(b 12, lb 2)	14
TOTAL	(85.1 overs)	**274**	(63 overs) (5 wkts)	**112**

Bowling NEW ZEALAND	O	M	R	W	O	M	R	W
Hadlee	17.2	5	27	3	16	5	31	1
Cunis	11	5	18	0	15.4	4	38	2
Congdon	8	5	14	0				
Howarth	33	10	80	5	31	13	60	2
Pollard	15	5	34	0	31	11	50	0
Yuile	13	3	35	2	35	13	70	2
Burgess					6	1	14	0
PAKISTAN								
Masood	3	0	18	0	2	1	7	0
Asif Iqbal	3	0	12	0	2	0	2	0
Intikhab	13	3	51	0	5	1	18	0
Nazir	30.1	3	99	7	14	5	15	0
Pervez	31	7	71	2	24	12	33	5
Mushtaq	5	0	12	1	12	5	20	0
Sadiq					2	0	2	0
Hanif					2	1	1	0

Fall of Wickets	P 1st	NZ 1st	P 2nd	NZ 2nd
1st	55	92	75	9
2nd	78	99	75	10
3rd	111	125	83	11
4th	121	139	133	44
5th	135	144	183	92
6th	142	163	195	-
7th	153	164	244	-
8th	191	264	283	-
9th	191	273	-	-
10th	220	274	-	-

MILESTONES

- The three Mohammad brothers, Mushtaq, Sadiq and Hanif all played in the first test. Another brother, Wazir, was one of the selectors who chose the team. Only once before had three brothers appeared in the same test eleven (the three Graces, E.M., G.F. and W.G. played for England against Australia in 1880).

- It was Hanif Mohammad's final test match. In 55 tests he had scored 12 centuries with a highest score of 337. His aggregate was 3915 runs at an average of 43.98.

94 PAKISTAN v NEW ZEALAND *(Second Test)*

at Gaddafi Stadium, Lahore on 30, 31 October, 1, 2 November, 1969
Toss : Pakistan. Umpires : Akhtar Hussain and Umar Khan
New Zealand won by 5 wickets

Dayle Hadlee and Bruce Taylor had immediate success when Pakistan chose to bat, capturing a wicket apiece while 13 runs were scored in 50 minutes. Bevan Congdon claimed two wickets and the home team was struggling at lunch at 43-4.

Hedley Howarth and Vic Pollard bowled unchanged throughout the next session. Mushtaq Mohammad (25) and Asif Iqbal (20) put on 31 for the fifth wicket, the biggest partnership and the best individual scores in the innings. Once the stand was broken the batting lurched from crisis to crisis. Both spinners picked up three wickets with the last falling just before tea at 114.

New Zealand ended the day losing the wicket of Graham Dowling. Gordon Burgess, the touring manager, lodged an official complaint about the state of the wicket to the Pakistan authorities after the first day's play.

A match-winning century partnership in 130 minutes between Bruce Murray and Brian Hastings compensated for the loss of Congdon early on the second day. Murray made his highest test score of 90 in five hours. Although Hastings continued to bat with assurance, Pervez Sajjad spun his way through the rest of the New Zealand order claiming 7-74. Hastings was unbeaten on 80 in a disappointing total of 241.

The Pakistan openers began the third day chipping away at the deficit of 127. Once the breakthrough was made at 30, wickets fell regularly and, at 85 for five, Pakistan was facing a humiliating drubbing. Shafqat Rana refused to surrender and by stumps was on 91, having carried the home team past the threat of an innings defeat and leading Pakistan to 202-8.

Pakistan's remaining two wickets fell quickly at the start of the fourth day. For the second consecutive innings five bowlers shared the spoils. New Zealand's progress towards a target of 82 was faltering, with the loss of three early wickets, before Mark Burgess and Hastings adopted aggressive tactics to ensure New Zealand's victory, their first over Pakistan.

There was considerable local criticism of Pakistan's slow batting in the first two tests. The home team had averaged 31.7 runs an hour compared to New Zealand's 41. Mushtaq's efforts were regarded with particular dismay. In four innings he had occupied the crease for over six hours for the miserable return of 59 runs.

PAKISTAN

Batsman	Dismissal	R	Dismissal	R
Sadiq Mohammad	b Congdon	16	c & b Howarth	17
Salahuddin	c Wadsworth b Taylor	2	b Taylor	11
Younis Ahmed	b Hadlee	0	(5) c Murray b Pollard	19
Mushtaq Mohammad	c Wadsworth b Pollard	25	c Yuile b Howarth	1
Shafqat Rana	c Murray b Congdon	4	(6) c Hastings b Hadlee	95
Asif Iqbal	c Murray b Pollard	20	(3) c Congdon b Yuile	22
Intikhab Alam*	c Dowling b Howarth	6	b Pollard	11
Wasim Bari†	c Burgess b Pollard	7	c Murray b Hadlee	11
Salim Altaf	c Hastings b Howarth	1	lbw b Hadlee	0
Mohammad Nazir	c Wadsworth b Howarth	12	not out	4
Pervez Sajjad	not out	6	lbw b Taylor	2
Extras	(b 9, lb 6)	15	(b 4, lb 9, nb 2)	15
TOTAL	(67.4 overs)	**114**	(105.5 overs)	**208**

NEW ZEALAND

Batsman	Dismissal	R	Dismissal	R
G.T.Dowling*	b Salim	10	c Salahuddin b Pervez	9
B.A.G.Murray	c Shafqat b Pervez	90	c Asif b Pervez	8
B.E.Congdon	lbw b Pervez	22	c Shafqat b Nazir	5
B.F.Hastings	not out	80	c Mushtaq b Nazir	16
M.G.Burgess	c Mushtaq b Pervez	0	not out	29
V.Pollard	c Bari b Pervez	11	st Bari b Nazir	0
B.W.Yuile	c Asif b Pervez	2	not out	4
D.R.Hadlee	c & b Pervez	0		
B.R.Taylor	b Pervez	0		
K.J.Wadsworth†	b Salim	13		
H.J.Howarth	b Salim	4		
Extras	(b 1, lb 6, nb 2)	9	(b 4, lb 5, nb 2)	11
TOTAL	(115 overs)	**241**	(32.3 overs) (5 wkts)	**82**

Bowling NEW ZEALAND	O	M	R	W	O	M	R	W		Fall of Wickets			
										P	NZ	P	NZ
										1st	1st	2nd	2nd
Hadlee	7	3	10	1	17	4	27	3					
Taylor	9	3	12	1	19.5	7	27	2	1st	8	20	30	19
Congdon	10	4	15	2	8	4	17	0	2nd	13	61	48	28
Howarth	21.4	13	35	3	26	7	63	2	3rd	33	162	56	29
Pollard	20	7	27	3	20	7	32	2	4th	39	162	66	66
Yuile					14	6	16	1	5th	70	184	85	78
Burgess					1	0	11	0	6th	83	186	117	-
PAKISTAN									7th	87	188	194	-
Salim	17	3	33	3	4	0	12	0	8th	90	188	194	-
Asif	4	0	6	0	2	1	2	0	9th	100	230	205	-
Pervez	40	15	74	7	14	6	38	2	10th	114	241	208	-
Nazir	36	15	54	0	12.3	4	19	3					
Mushtaq	8	1	34	0									
Intikhab	10	2	31	0									

MILESTONES

- The victory was New Zealand's seventh in test cricket and its first over Pakistan.

Bryan Yuile (in cap) and Mark Burgess leave the field at Lahore with New Zealand having won their first test in Pakistan by five wickets.

95   PAKISTAN v NEW ZEALAND (*Third Test*)

at Dacca Stadium on 8, 9, 10, 11 November 1969
Toss : New Zealand. Umpires : Daud Khan and Shujauddin
Match drawn

When the New Zealand team arrived in Dacca a curfew had been in force for several days after outbreaks of disorder. A close inspection of the wicket revealed that it consisted of rolled and baked mud without a blade of grass. Pakistan did not want to lose a test series and New Zealand only needed a draw to win the series. A war of attrition was created before a ball had been bowled.

Play began at the unusually early hour of 9.30 am. Batting first, the visitors were dismayed to find the ball kept very low, even when pitched short of a length. Batsmen were committed to playing from the front foot and found it difficult to propel strokes with any power.

From the 112 overs bowled on the first day only 154 of New Zealand's 172 runs came from the bat. Glenn Turner displayed exemplary concentration throughout the day. When stumps were drawn at 172-4 he was one run away from a century, after six hours of grinding labour.

Turner's Herculean effort continued for 85 minutes on the second day before he was dismissed for 110. His maiden test century contained only seven boundaries. Mark Burgess, who shared in the best partnership of the innings, 79 runs for the fifth wicket, hit nine fours in his 59, scored in a relatively hasty 160 minutes.

The grand offerings of Turner and Burgess were deflated when the last six New Zealand wickets fell for 47 runs. The total of 273 runs had taken 535 minutes. By stumps, after 47 overs, three wickets had fallen for 92 runs.

The tempo of the match increased on the third morning, with aggressive batting from Shafqat Rana and Aftab Baloch carrying the score to 150 before Vic Pollard broke through. New Zealand's total was in sight when Shafqat and Asif Iqbal rattled on 51 runs in even time.

Asif continued to plunder the New Zealand spinners. He hooked, pulled and drove his way to 92, scoring 13 boundaries before he was dismissed.

The Pakistan captain, Intikhab Alam, then declared at 290-7. To the delight of the crowd of 25,000 the first four New Zealand wickets fell for 25 before the first innings heroes, Turner and Burgess, battled their way through to stumps; 55-4.

The left-arm spin of Pervez Sajjad and the right-arm leg breaks of Intikhab excited the fervent spectators as the two bowlers ran through New Zealand's batting. With 4½ hours' play remaining the tourists had a precarious lead of 118 runs, with two wickets in hand, when Bob Cunis joined Burgess at the crease.

Cunis' average on the tour so far was a meagre 7.4 so expectations were not great in the New Zealand camp. For

109 minutes this pair defied an increasingly frustrated series of bowling changes. Cunis defended stubbornly as Burgess produced the innings of his career, scoring his maiden test century as they added 96.

With Pakistan requiring 184 in 150 minutes Cunis carried on his dream day by dismissing four batsmen in seven overs before crowd disturbances and, finally, rain ended the game.

NEW ZEALAND

B.A.G.Murray	b Asif	7	c Asif b Intikhab		2
G.M.Turner	c Shafqat b Pervez	110	c Intikhab b Pervez		26
G.T.Dowling*	c Asif b Intikhab	15	c Bari b Intikhab		2
B.E.Congdon	c Pervez b Intikhab	6	b Pervez		0
B.F.Hastings	b Intikhab	22	b Pervez		3
M.G.Burgess	c Bari b Pervez	59	not out		119
V.Pollard	c Shafqat b Intikhab	2	b Intikhab		11
D.R.Hadlee	c Burki b Intikhab	16	lbw b Intikhab		0
K.J.Wadsworth†	c Bari b Salim	7	c Gul b Pervez		0
R.S.Cunis	lbw b Salim	0	b Shafqat		23
H.J.Howarth	not out	0	c Wasim b Intikhab		2
Extras	(b 14, lb 11, nb 4)	29	(b 2, lb 8, nb 2)		12
TOTAL	(166.3 overs)	**273**	(101.4 overs)		**200**

PAKISTAN

Aftab Gul	c & b Howarth	30	b Cunis		5
Sadiq Mohammad	c Turner b Pollard	21	b Cunis		3
Javed Burki	c Turner b Howarth	22	not out		17
Shafqat Rana	run out	65	(5) c Dowling b Cunis		3
Aftab Baloch	lbw b Pollard	25			
Asif Iqbal	c Wadsworth b Howarth	92	(4) b Cunis		16
Intikhab Alam*	b Howarth	20	(6) not out		3
Wasim Bari†	not out	6			
Salim Altaf					
Mohammad Nazir					
Pervez Sajjad					
Extras	(b 6, lb 3)	9	(b 1, lb 3)		4
TOTAL	(101.1 overs) (7 wkts dec)	**290**	(15 overs) (4 wkts)		**51**

Bowling	O	M	R	W	O	M	R	W
PAKISTAN								
Salim	19.3	6	27	2	11	4	18	0
Asif	13	4	22	1	7	2	8	0
Pervez	48	20	66	2	34	11	60	4
Intikhab	56	26	91	5	39.4	13	91	5
Nazir	30	15	38	0	3	1	3	0
Sadiq					2	1	4	0
Baloch					2	0	2	0
Shafqat					3	1	2	1
NEW ZEALAND								
Hadlee	17	2	41	0	7	0	17	0
Cunis	23	5	65	0	7	0	21	4
Congdon	14	2	41	0				
Howarth	33.1	8	85	4				
Pollard	14	2	49	2	1	0	9	0

Fall of Wickets

	NZ	P	NZ	P
	1st	1st	2nd	2nd
1st	13	53	12	7
2nd	67	55	14	12
3rd	99	81	17	40
4th	147	150	25	46
5th	226	201	70	-
6th	241	277	92	-
7th	251	290	92	-
8th	271	-	101	-
9th	272	-	197	-
10th	273	-	200	-

MILESTONES

• This was New Zealand's first test series win.

• Mark Burgess and Bob Cunis created a New Zealand test record for the ninth wicket with their partnership of 96.

• This was the last test match played by Pakistan in Dacca. In 1971 civil war broke out in East Pakistan, which eventually resulted in the creation of Bangladesh.

• It was estimated that 432,000 people attended the five tests in India and 250,000 watched the four tests in Pakistan.

AVERAGES

New Zealand

BATTING	M	I	NO	Runs	HS	Ave
M.G. Burgess	3	6	2	273	119*	68.25
G.M. Turner	1	2	0	136	110	68.00
B.W. Yuile	2	4	3	58	47*	58.00
B.F. Hastings	3	6	1	152	80*	30.40
B.A.G. Murray	3	6	0	163	90	27.16
D.R. Hadlee	3	4	0	72	56	18.00
G.T. Dowling	3	6	0	79	40	13.16
V. Pollard	3	6	1	54	28*	10.80
R.S. Cunis	2	3	0	28	23	9.33
B.E. Congdon	3	6	0	55	22	9.16
K.J. Wadsworth	3	4	0	20	13	5.00
H.J. Howarth	3	4	1	6	4	2.00
B.R. Taylor	1	1	0	0	0	0.00

BOWLING	O	M	R	W	Ave
B.R. Taylor	28.5	10	39	3	13.00
D.R. Hadlee	81.2	19	153	8	19.12
H.J. Howarth	144.5	51	323	16	20.18
R.S. Cunis	56.4	14	142	6	23.66
B.W. Yuile	62	22	121	5	24.20
V. Pollard	101	32	201	7	28.71
B.E. Congdon	40	15	87	2	43.50
M.G. Burgess	7	1	25	0	-

Pakistan

BATTING	M	I	NO	Runs	HS	Ave
Mohammad Nazir	3	4	3	62	29*	62.00
Shafqat Rana	2	4	0	167	95	41.75
Javed Burki	1	2	1	39	22	39.00
Asif Iqbal	3	6	0	172	92	28.66
Hanif Mohammad	1	2	0	57	35	28.50
Sadiq Mohammad	3	6	0	163	69	27.16
Aftab Baloch	1	1	0	25	25	25.00
Younis Ahmed	2	4	0	89	62	22.25
Zaheer Abbas	1	2	0	39	27	19.50
Aftab Gul	1	2	0	35	30	17.50
Intikhab Alam	3	6	1	87	47	17.40
Asif Masood	1	1	0	17	17	17.00
Mushtaq Mohammad	2	4	0	59	25	14.75
Wasim Bari	3	5	1	58	19	14.50
Salahuddin	1	2	0	13	11	6.50
Pervez Sajjad	3	3	1	8	6*	4.00
Salim Altaf	2	2	0	1	1	0.50

BOWLING	O	M	R	W	Ave
Shafqat Rana	3	1	2	1	2.00
Pervez Sajjad	191	71	342	22	15.54
Salim Altaf	51.3	13	90	5	18.00
Mohammad Nazir	125.4	43	228	10	22.80
Intikhab Alam	123.4	45	282	10	28.20
Asif Iqbal	31	7	52	1	52.00
Mushtaq Mohammad	25	6	66	1	66.00
Hanif Mohammad	2	1	1	0	-
Aftab Baloch	2	0	2	0	-
Sadiq Mohammad	4	1	6	0	-
Asif Masood	5	1	25	0	-

Graham Dowling and manager Gordon Burgess can see themselves in the polished pitch at Dacca which was devoid of any grass.

1970/71 MCC in New Zealand

A strong MCC side had won the Ashes against Australia in 1970/71 by two tests to nil in a controversial series. They arrived in New Zealand without their two main players, John Snow and Geoffrey Boycott, but they were still a powerful combination.

96 NEW ZEALAND v ENGLAND *(First Test)*

at Lancaster Park, Christchurch on 25, 26, 27 February, 1 March, 1971
Toss : New Zealand. Umpires : C.S. Elliott and W.T. Martin
England won by 8 wickets

The pitch at Lancaster Park looked suspect from the outset. It was rumoured that a well-known official had interfered with the preparation. A series of careless shots saw Bruce Murray, Bevan Congdon and Ross Morgan dismissed in Ken Shuttleworth's first eight overs; 19-3.

The introduction of Derek Underwood saw the ball begin to turn and bounce erratically and the New Zealand batsmen slipped back into the nightmare days of 1969. In less than three hours New Zealand were dismissed for 65 with Underwood taking 6-12. With the playing surface suspect, he was virtually unplayable.

When stumps were drawn a few minutes early because of bad light England had not fared much better on this difficult pitch. They had lost their first three batsmen before John Hampshire and Basil d'Oliveira saw the day out at 56-3.

Overnight rain made the bowlers' run-ups slippery. Hampshire (40) fell to Hedley Howarth at 95 but Ray Illingworth joined d'Oliveira to bring up England's 100, and this pair added another 88 runs before Mike Shrimpton bowled Illingworth. D'Oliveira completed a stunning century in 216 minutes before being bowled by a clever wrong'un from Shrimpton. Howarth took four wickets but the surprise was the leg-spin and wrong'uns bowled by Shrimpton in taking 3-33.

Batting a second time New Zealand lost both Murray and Dowling for a run apiece. Glenn Turner was elevated from six to four in the batting order and he and Congdon carried the score to 54-2 before bad light stopped play.

Rain prevented play until after lunch and the third wicket remained intact while another 29 runs were added before Underwood bowled Congdon. Turner continued to bat with the utmost concentration. Vic Pollard helped add 52 and later Bob Cunis provided another of his stubborn tailend innings as 57 runs were added before Turner was dismissed. His 76 occupied 309 minutes.

A flurry of runs saw New Zealand end at 254. For the second time in the game Underwood captured six wickets. England required little more than two hours to score the 89 runs required for victory.

NEW ZEALAND

G.T.Dowling*	c Edrich b Underwood	13	c Luckhurst b Lever	1
B.A.G.Murray	c Taylor b Shuttleworth	1	b Shuttleworth	1
B.E.Congdon	c Taylor b Shuttleworth	1	b Underwood	55
R.W.Morgan	c Luckhurst b Shuttleworth	6	(5) b Underwood	0
M.J.F.Shrimpton	c Fletcher b Underwood	0	(6) c Illingworth b Underwood	8
G.M.Turner	b Underwood	11	(4) b Underwood	76
V.Pollard	b Wilson	18	lbw b Underwood	34
K.J.Wadsworth†	c Fletcher b Underwood	0	c Fletcher b Wilson	1
R.S.Cunis	b Underwood	0	b Shuttleworth	35
H.J.Howarth	st Taylor b Underwood	0	c Illingworth b Underwood	25
R.O.Collinge	not out	3	not out	7
Extras	(b 9, lb 1, w 1, nb 1)	12	(b 6, lb 3, w 1, nb 1)	11
TOTAL	(37.6 overs)	65	(97.3 overs)	254

ENGLAND

B.W.Luckhurst	c Wadsworth b Collinge	10	not out	29
J.H.Edrich	lbw b Cunis	12	c Wadsworth b Collinge	2
K.W.R.Fletcher	b Collinge	4	c Howarth b Collinge	2
J.H.Hampshire	c Turner b Howarth	40	not out	51
B.L.D'Oliveira	b Shrimpton	100		
R.Illingworth*	b Shrimpton	36		
R.W.Taylor†	st Wadsworth b Howarth	4		
D.Wilson	c Murray b Howarth	5		
P.Lever	b Howarth	4		
K.Shuttleworth	b Shrimpton	5		
D.L.Underwood	not out	0		
Extras	(b 1, lb 9, nb 1)	11	(b 1, lb 4)	5
TOTAL	(67.5 overs)	231	(25 overs) (2 wkts)	89

Bowling ENGLAND	O	M	R	W	O	M	R	W
Lever	5	4	1	0	15	3	30	1
Shuttleworth	8	1	14	3	12	1	27	2
D'Oliveira	3	1	2	0				
Underwood	11.6	7	12	6	32.3	7	85	6
Illingworth	6	3	12	0	17	5	45	0
Wilson	4	2	12	1	21	6	56	1
NEW ZEALAND								
Collinge	12	2	39	2	7	2	20	2
Cunis	13	2	44	1	8	0	17	0
Howarth	19	7	46	4	4	0	17	0
Pollard	9	3	45	0	3	1	9	0
Shrimpton	11.5	0	35	3	3	0	21	0
Congdon	3	0	11	0				

Fall of Wickets

	E 1st	NZ 1st	E 2nd	NZ 2nd
1st	4	20	1	3
2nd	7	26	6	11
3rd	19	31	83	-
4th	28	95	83	-
5th	33	188	99	-
6th	54	213	151	-
7th	54	220	152	-
8th	62	224	209	-
9th	62	231	231	-
10th	65	231	254	-

MILESTONES

- One of the umpires to stand in the test was Charlie Elliott, a well-known English umpire, who was in New Zealand on a Churchill Fellowship.

- Derek Underwood captured his 1000th first-class wicket in New Zealand's second innings.

Graham Dowling caught by John Edrich off Derek Underwood. Other players are, from left, John Hampshire, Alan Knott, Basil d'Oliveira and Ray Illingworth.

97 NEW ZEALAND v ENGLAND *(Second Test)*

at Eden Park, Auckland on 5, 6, 7, 8 March, 1971
Toss : New Zealand. Umpires : E.C.A. MacKintosh and R.W.R. Shortt
Match drawn

Graham Dowling took a chance by sending England in to bat on a hard, green-looking wicket but by claiming three wickets before lunch it proved to be a successful gamble. Bob Cunis found the wicket conducive to his lively off-cutters and immaculate length.

England was in deep strife when its fifth wicket fell at 111 and even deeper in the mire when the sixth wicket fell at 145. Alan Knott and Peter Lever offered chances early in their partnership, which was to add 149 runs, before Knott was bowled for 101. Cunis was just as demanding at the end of the day as at the start and ended with 6-76, the best bowling of his career.

Glenn Turner and Dowling gave New Zealand its best start in a test for several years, combining for three hours in a 91-run stand. When Turner's 264-minute vigil ended with his score at 65 New Zealand were 142-4, with Derek Underwood claiming three wickets, all caught and bowled. Mark Burgess and Mike Shrimpton defied the possibility of an abject collapse and batted safely through until stumps.

A crowd of 15,000 attended the first Sunday's play in test cricket in New Zealand. They had the satisfaction of watching Burgess (along with Cunis, a home-town favourite) advance from 50 to 104. His partnership with Shrimpton (46) had almost doubled New Zealand's tally from 142 to 283. Dowling made a bold decision to declare at 313-7, eight runs behind England's total. By stumps, England was 78 for four and the game was delicately poised for the fourth day.

Colin Cowdrey, with the aid of a runner, stayed with Knott until almost lunchtime when two wickets fell quickly. Over lunch some of the home team might have entertained hopes of victory with the score at 166-6. Knott, who had a special penchant for frustrating New Zealand bowlers, had other ideas. When Cunis finally bowled him, four runs short of his second century in the match, he had made the game safe for England.

MILESTONES

• Murray Webb (122) made his test debut.

• It was the first time that a test had been played on a Sunday in New Zealand.

• Alan Knott and Peter Lever added 149 runs, a record for England's seventh wicket against New Zealand.

ENGLAND

J.H.Edrich	c Morgan b Webb	1	c Burgess b Collinge		24
B.W.Luckhurst	c Dowling b Cunis	14	c Wadsworth b Webb		15
M.C.Cowdrey	c Congdon b Cunis	54	(6) b Collinge		45
J.H.Hampshire	c Turner b Cunis	9	(3) c Wadsworth b Cunis		0
B.L.D'Oliveira	c Morgan b Congdon	58	(9) b Collinge		5
R.Illingworth*	c Wadsworth b Cunis	0	(4) c Turner b Collinge		22
A.P.E.Knott†	b Collinge	101	b Cunis		96
P.Lever	c Wadsworth b Cunis	64	(7) lbw b Howarth		0
K.Shuttleworth	c Wadsworth b Cunis	0	(8) c Wadsworth b Morgan		11
R.G.D.Willis	c Burgess b Collinge	7	lbw b Cunis		3
D.L.Underwood	not out	1	not out		8
Extras	(b 1, lb 4, nb 7)	12	(b 5, lb 3)		8
TOTAL	(72.6 overs)	**321**	(84.7 overs)		**237**

NEW ZEALAND

G.M.Turner	c & b Underwood	65	not out		8
G.T.Dowling*	c & b Underwood	53	not out		31
B.E.Congdon	b Underwood	0			
R.W.Morgan	c & b Underwood	8			
M.G.Burgess	c Edrich b Willis	104			
M.J.F.Shrimpton	lbw b Underwood	46			
K.J.Wadsworth†	c Hampshire b Willis	16			
R.S.Cunis	not out	5			
H.J.Howarth	not out	2			
R.O.Collinge					
M.G.Webb					
Extras	(b 7, lb 4, nb 3)	14	(lb 1)		1
TOTAL	(106 overs) (7 wkts dec)	**313**	(16 overs) (0 wkts)		**40**

Bowling	O	M	R	W	O	M	R	W
NEW ZEALAND								
Webb	18	0	94	1	11	0	50	1
Collinge	18.6	5	51	2	19	6	41	4
Cunis	24	4	76	6	21.7	5	52	3
Howarth	7	0	41	0	21	8	37	1
Congdon	2	0	18	1				
Shrimpton	3	0	29	0	6	0	33	0
Morgan					6	0	16	1
ENGLAND								
Lever	19	3	43	0	2	0	6	0
Shuttleworth	17	3	49	0	4	0	12	0
Willis	14	2	54	2	6	1	15	0
Underwood	38	12	108	5	2	2	0	0
Illingworth	18	4	45	0				
Luckhurst					2	0	6	0

Fall of Wickets	E	NZ	E	NZ
	1st	1st	2nd	2nd
1st	8	91	26	-
2nd	38	91	27	-
3rd	59	121	62	-
4th	111	142	67	-
5th	111	283	143	-
6th	145	302	152	-
7th	294	307	177	-
8th	297	-	199	-
9th	317	-	218	-
10th	321	-	237	-

Bob Cunis maintained an immaculate length during this test and finished with his best test analysis of 6-76 and 3-52.

1971/72 New Zealand in West Indies

New Zealand broke new ground when they toured the West Indies. A surprise awaited the tourists. The West Indies, the home of fast bowlers Learie Constantine, Wes Hall and Charlie Griffith, produced mainly lifeless tracks lacking bounce. Murray Webb was surprisingly chosen to partner Bob Cunis instead of Bruce Taylor for the first test.

98 WEST INDIES v NEW ZEALAND *(First Test)*

at Sabina Park, Kingston on 16, 17, 18, 19, 21 February, 1972
Toss : West Indies. Umpires : J.R. Gayle and D. Sang Hue
Match drawn

The home side took full advantage of batting on a perfect wicket. New Zealand toiled all day for just one wicket, that of Joey Carew at 78. Roy Fredericks, who was dropped at 46 and 84 and completed his first test century, and Lawrence Rowe, a stylish left-hand batsman, who was an aggressive hooker of fast bowling and an exponent of the late-cut, dominated the rest of the day. By the end of the day Rowe was six runs short of a century on debut and the total was 273-1.

To the delight of the Jamaican crowd, their favourite player, Rowe, reached his century. Fredericks' innings of 163 was made in 408 minutes and the partnership was worth 269. Rowe, playing for Jamaica against New Zealand 10 days earlier, had scored 227, so when he reached his double-century the crowd was ecstatic. When he was finally dismissed for 214 the spectators surged on to the field, hoisted him shoulder high and carried him off in a tumult of arms and bobbing heads.

The declaration at 508-4 was a blessed relief for the weary visitors who, not surprisingly, batted in a desultory manner and lost three wickets for 49 by stumps.

At lunch Glenn Turner was 64 and New Zealand was struggling at 128-5. The next two sessions produced 152 runs without the loss of a wicket. Turner had progressed to 164 by the end of the day and his partner Ken Wadsworth was on 50. The score was 280-5 and the pair had restored New Zealand's honour.

The follow-on target of 309 was exceeded before Wadsworth departed for 78, made in 284 minutes. The partnership had realised 220. When the last New Zealand wicket fell at 386 Turner was left unbeaten on 223, having carried his bat throughout the innings lasting 572 minutes.

Enjoying a lead of 122 runs on the first innings the home team was keen to score quickly enough to enable a tempting declaration. They ended the day at 168-3.

After fielding for 153 overs in intense heat in West Indies' first innings, Glenn Turner batted throughout New Zealand's reply which lasted 572 minutes. Michael Findlay is the West Indian wicketkeeper.

WEST INDIES

R.C.Fredericks	c & b Howarth	163	b Congdon		33
M.C.Carew	lbw b Congdon	43	b Congdon		22
L.G.Rowe	c Dowling b Howarth	214	not out		100
C.A.Davis	c Turner b Cunis	31	b Howarth		41
M.L.C.Foster	not out	28	not out		13
G.St A.Sobers*	not out	13			
D.A.J.Holford					
T.M.Findlay†					
L.R.Gibbs					
G.C.Shillingford					
U.G.Dowe					
Extras	(b 1, lb 11, nb 4)	16	(b 9)		9
TOTAL	(153 overs) (4 wkts dec)	**508**	(53.4 overs) (3 wkts dec)		**218**

NEW ZEALAND

G.T.Dowling*	lbw b Dowe	4	b Holford		23
G.M.Turner	not out	223	b Holford		21
T.W.Jarvis	b Shillingford	7	(6) lbw b Holford		0
M.G.Burgess	b Dowe	15	c & b Dowe		101
B.E.Congdon	c & b Holford	11	(3) run out		16
B.F.Hastings	c Sobers b Gibbs	16	(5) b Holford		13
K.J.Wadsworth†	c Fredericks b Dowe	78	not out		36
R.S.Cunis	c Findlay b Shillingford	0	not out		13
H.J.Howarth	lbw b Holford	16			
J.C.Alabaster	c Dowe b Gibbs	2			
M.G.Webb	lbw b Shillingford	0			
Extras	(b 9, lb 1, nb 4)	14	(b 5, lb 6, nb 2)		13
TOTAL	(187.5 overs)	**386**	(108 overs) (6 wkts)		**236**

Bowling									Fall of Wickets				
NEW ZEALAND	O	M	R	W	O	M	R	W		WI	NZ	WI	NZ
										1st	1st	2nd	2nd
Webb	25	4	86	0	5	1	34	0					
Cunis	34	3	118	1	20.4	2	87	0	1st	78	4	44	50
Congdon	23	2	55	1	11	2	45	2	2nd	347	25	57	51
Alabaster	25	4	110	0					3rd	428	48	155	96
Howarth	44	6	108	2	17	6	43	1	4th	488	75	-	131
Burgess	2	0	15	0					5th	-	108	-	135
WEST INDIES									6th	-	328	-	214
Dowe	29	5	75	3	13	3	46	1	7th	-	329	-	-
Shillingford	26.5	8	63	3	11	2	32	0	8th	-	361	-	-
Sobers	11	3	20	0	13	5	16	0	9th	-	364	-	-
Holford	44	18	64	2	33	12	55	4	10th	-	386	-	-
Gibbs	45	9	94	2	21	8	42	0					
Foster	14	8	20	0	9	5	12	0					
Fredericks	4	1	5	0	4	0	14	0					
Carew	9	0	29	0	4	1	6	0					
Davis	5	3	2	0									

Gary Sobers postponed his declaration until Rowe reached precisely 100. His combination of a century and a double century in a test debut is unique. New Zealand's target was 341 in little more than five hours. With two hours remaining, and five wickets down for 135, Mark Burgess was joined by Wadsworth.

The situation did not deter Burgess' aggressive intent as he reached his hundred in 183 minutes, his third century in his last three tests. On his dismissal Wadsworth and Bob Cunis took New Zealand through to safety at 236-6.

MILESTONES

- Lawrence Rowe became the first player to score a double century and century in his first test.

- Glenn Turner became the fourth player to bat through a test innings for a second time. The other three were Bill Woodfull (Australia), Len Hutton (England) and Bill Lawry (Australia).

- Mark Burgess scored his third test century in consecutive tests after making 119 not out against Pakistan in 1969/70 and 104 against England in 1970/71.

99 **WEST INDIES v NEW ZEALAND** *(Second Test)*

at Queen's Park Oval, Port of Spain on 9, 10, 11, 12, 14 March, 1972
Toss : West Indies. Umpires : R.G. Gosein and D. Sang Hue
Match drawn

Although Graham Dowling had an injured back he decided to play. The opposing captain, Gary Sobers, believing that the patchy pitch might have a little early life, sent New Zealand in to bat. His decision seemed to be vindicated when New Zealand lost their fifth wicket with the score at 78.

Bevan Congdon, in one session, enjoyed more luck than a batsman might expect in a season. He was missed three times before he had reached 34 and, shortly afterwards, should have been stumped. Bruce Taylor's first three scoring shots produced two, four and six. In the next 90 minutes he hit 46 of 69 runs while Congdon crept past his half-century in almost four hours. By stumps Congdon was 85 and his new partner, Bob Cunis, was on 20 as the visitors struggled through to 211-7.

The partnership was terminated after the pair had added 136 and Cunis had completed the only half-century of his test career. Congdon continued throughout the innings to finish with 166 not out. He persevered for 527 minutes, with great determination, to see his team accumulate 348. New Zealand contained the West Indian batsmen to have them 68-2 at stumps.

Taylor, Hedley Howarth and Congdon succeeded in capturing another six wickets during the third day while only 220 runs were added as all the batsmen made a start but only

Roy Fredericks (69) and Charlie Davis (90) made substantial scores.

Inshan Ali and Vanburn Holder frustrated the New Zealanders for over an hour at the start of the fourth day. Taylor, with the new ball, claimed both players to finish with four wickets. By now the wicket was very placid and, with the exception of Graham Dowling, all the top-order batsmen were able to accumulate runs at a rate of two runs per over.

A declaration was made on the fifth day, leaving West Indies a target of 296 runs in 200 minutes. They began by scoring at a run a minute for the first hour before the bowlers tightened their line and more defensive fields were set. Four sharp catches were taken and the West Indies defended dourly for the last 20 overs.

After the game Dowling had his back put in a brace at the hospital. It showed no improvement so he returned to New Zealand and retired from test cricket.

NEW ZEALAND

G.T.Dowling*	c Carew b Sobers	8	c Holder b Gibbs	10
G.M.Turner	c Carew b Sobers	2	b Sobers	95
B.E.Congdon	not out	166	c Holford b Inshan Ali	82
M.G.Burgess	c Findlay b Holder	32	not out	62
B.F.Hastings	c Rowe b Inshan Ali	3	not out	29
G.E.Vivian	lbw b Holder	0		
K.J.Wadsworth†	c & b Holford	7		
B.R.Taylor	b Foster	46		
R.S.Cunis	c & b Holder	51		
H.J.Howarth	lbw b Holder	0		
J.C.Alabaster	c Carew b Inshan Ali	18		
Extras	(b 6, nb 9)	15	(b 3, nb 7)	10
TOTAL	**(175.5 overs)**	**348**	**(140 overs) (3 wkts dec)**	**288**

WEST INDIES

R.C.Fredericks	c Wadsworth b Howarth	69	c Hastings b Taylor	31
M.C.Carew	lbw b Taylor	4	c Vivian b Taylor	28
L.G.Rowe	b Congdon	22	c & b Howarth	1
C.A.Davis	c Turner b Howarth	90	not out	29
M.L.C.Foster	b Howarth	23	c Burgess b Taylor	3
G.St A.Sobers*	c Wadsworth b Congdon	19	b Alabaster	9
D.A.J.Holford	lbw b Congdon	14	not out	9
T.M.Findlay†	b Taylor	16		
Inshan Ali	c Burgess b Taylor	25		
V.A.Holder	b Taylor	30		
L.R.Gibbs	not out	3		
Extras	(b 12, lb 9, w 1, nb 4)	26	(b 8, w 1, nb 2)	11
TOTAL	**(155.1 overs)**	**341**	**(46 overs) (5 wkts)**	**121**

Bowling	O	M	R	W	O	M	R	W					
WEST INDIES									**Fall of Wickets**				
										NZ	WI	NZ	WI
Holder	32	13	60	4	15	5	17	0		*1st*	*1st*	*2nd*	*2nd*
Sobers	26	7	40	2	20	3	54	1	1st	5	18	35	59
Gibbs	29	6	64	0	35	14	67	1	2nd	16	65	174	66
Inshan Ali	46.5	10	92	2	33	8	60	1	3rd	66	143	218	68
Holford	22	6	45	1	17	2	50	0	4th	77	200	-	73
Davis	3	1	9	0	4	2	5	0	5th	78	239	-	95
Foster	9	5	12	1	7	2	9	0	6th	99	245	-	-
Carew	3	0	8	0	5	0	10	0	7th	168	270	-	-
Fredericks	5	3	3	0	4	2	6	0	8th	304	281	-	-
NEW ZEALAND									9th	307	327	-	-
Cunis	22	5	67	0	5	0	33	0	10th	348	341	-	-
Taylor	20.1	9	41	4	12	2	26	3					
Howarth	53	17	102	3	20	8	36	1					
Congdon	39	19	56	3	1	1	0	0					
Alabaster	21	7	49	0	4	2	5	1					
Vivian					4	2	10	0					

MILESTONES

- Glenn Turner and Mark Burgess passed 1000 runs in test cricket.

- Graham Dowling retired, having played 39 tests, 19 as captain, with four test victories. He scored 2306 runs at an average of 31.16, with three centuries.

Bevan Congdon batted for 527 minutes to take his side from the perilous position of 99-5 to 348. He then bowled 39 overs and conceded only 56 runs while claiming three wickets. It was no wonder he was named the Man of the Match.

100 WEST INDIES v NEW ZEALAND (*Third Test*)

at Kensington Oval, Bridgetown on 23, 24, 25, 26, 28 March, 1972
Toss : West Indies. Umpires : H.B. de C. Jordan and F.C.P. Kippins
Match drawn

The enforced retirement of Graham Dowling opened the way for Bevan Congdon to become the captain. Bruce Taylor achieved lively bounce and, by cutting the ball away, soon had the West Indies in trouble. Within the first hour Taylor had three wickets and Bob Cunis one and the score was 12-4.

By lunch it had advanced to 44-5. The carnage continued throughout the afternoon session until the home side had been dismissed for 133. Taylor became the first New Zealand bowler to capture seven wickets in a test innings. It was an exceptional performance. By stumps Glenn Turner and Terry Jarvis had taken the score to 31, but not without some difficulty.

The wicket performed more sedately the next day but New Zealand still lost three wickets in scoring 112. With the game in the balance Brian Hastings joined Congdon and they began a partnership which was to take their team to the brink of victory. At first they were cautious, then they began running with zest and playing shots all round the wicket.

Congdon reached his second consecutive century before he was dismissed after 258 minutes for 126. The partnership had been worth 175. The tourists were in a commanding position at stumps; 297-5.

Soon after play commenced on the third day Hastings completed his century. Useful contributions by Graham Vivian, Ken Wadsworth and Cunis saw New Zealand reach 422, a lead of 289 on the first innings. Ninety-eight runs of the deficit had been accounted for by the end of the third day with a loss of two wickets.

The first ball after lunch on the fourth day saw West Indies 171-5. This brought Gary Sobers to the crease, batting at number seven, to partner Charlie Davis. When bad light stopped play half an hour early, they had completed a century partnership and established a slight lead without further loss of wickets.

Soon after the start of play on the last morning Sobers, on 87, sparred at Taylor. The ball carried to Jarvis at first slip and spilled to the ground. Turner put down a chance off Davis and these errors put paid to any chance the tourists had of winning the test. Sobers, cricket's greatest all-round player, reached his 25th century (his first against New Zealand) and the partnership was worth 254 when he was dismissed.

With three hours remaining there was a remote chance of a New Zealand victory if the tail could be swept away quickly. Davis, supported by David Holford, soon quashed that pleasant speculation and the match ended in a draw. Don Cameron, the NZPA journalist with the team, described this "chastening experience" as " the catch and the match that got away."

WEST INDIES

R.C.Fredericks	c Hastings b Cunis	5	lbw b Cunis		28
M.C.Carew	c Morgan b Taylor	1	c Turner b Howarth		45
L.G.Rowe	c Wadsworth b Taylor	0	lbw b Congdon		51
C.A.Davis	c Jarvis b Taylor	1	(5) run out		183
G.St A.Sobers*	c Wadsworth b Congdon	35	(7) c Vivian b Taylor		142
M.L.C.Foster	c Wadsworth b Taylor	22	lbw b Taylor		4
D.A.J.Holford	c Wadsworth b Taylor	3	(8) c Wadsworth b Congdon		50
T.M.Findlay†	not out	44	(4) c Morgan b Howarth		9
Inshan Ali	b Taylor	3	not out		12
V.A.Holder	b Congdon	3	not out		16
G.C.Shillingford	c Morgan b Taylor	15			
Extras	(nb 1)	1	(b 6, lb 9, w 1, nb 8)		24
TOTAL	(49.3 overs)	133	(214 overs) (8 wkts)		564

NEW ZEALAND

G.M.Turner	c Holford b Holder	21
T.W.Jarvis	lbw b Shillingford	26
B.E.Congdon*	lbw b Holder	126
M.G.Burgess	c Fredericks b Sobers	19
B.F.Hastings	lbw b Sobers	105
R.W.Morgan	c Fredericks b Inshan Ali	2
G.E.Vivian	b Sobers	38
K.J.Wadsworth†	not out	15
B.R.Taylor	lbw b Sobers	0
R.S.Cunis	c Findlay b Holder	27
H.J.Howarth	b Shillingford	8
Extras	(lb 13, nb 22)	35
TOTAL	(163.2 overs)	422

Bowling										Fall of Wickets			
NEW ZEALAND	O	M	R	W	O	M	R	W			WI	NZ	WI
											1st	1st	2nd
Cunis	10	3	26	1	38	8	130	1					
Taylor	20.3	6	74	7	33	3	108	2		1st	6	54	48
Congdon	16	3	26	2	31	7	66	2		2nd	6	68	91
Howarth	3	1	6	0	74	24	138	2		3rd	6	112	105
Morgan					30	8	78	0		4th	12	287	163
Vivian					8	2	20	0		5th	44	293	171
WEST INDIES										6th	52	356	425
Holder	40	13	91	3						7th	83	369	518
Sobers	29	6	64	4						8th	99	369	544
Shillingford	24.2	7	65	2						9th	102	412	-
Davis	10	3	19	0						10th	133	422	-
Inshan Ali	35	11	81	1									
Holford	9	0	20	0									
Foster	14	2	40	0									
Fredericks	2	0	7	0									

MILESTONES

- Bruce Taylor's 7-74 were the best bowling figures for New Zealand in a test.

- Bevan Congdon became the 12th captain of New Zealand.

- The partnership of 175 between Bevan Congdon and Brian Hastings was a New Zealand record for the fourth wicket.

- Gary Sobers exceeded Colin Cowdrey's record aggregate of 7459 test runs.

- West Indies' second innings total of 564 was the highest against New Zealand.

One of Bruce Taylor's seven first innings wickets was David Holford caught by wicketkeeper Ken Wadsworth. Taylor's final analysis of 7-74 was the best for New Zealand. From left, Mark Burgess, Terry Jarvis Graham Vivian, Glenn Turner, Wadsworth, Holford and Taylor.

101 WEST INDIES v NEW ZEALAND *(Fourth Test)*

at Bourda, Georgetown on 6, 7, 8, 9, 11 April, 1972
Toss : West Indies. Umpires : H.B. de C. Jordan and F.C.P. Kippins
Match drawn

In New Zealand's game the previous week, against Guyana, 1183 runs had been scored, six centuries made, including 259 by Glenn Turner, and only 19 wickets captured. Gary Sobers had no hesitation in batting when he won the toss on a pitch resembling a motorway, with a very fast outfield and small boundaries.

The first three batsmen were untroubled by the bowlers. Clive Lloyd, who had made a century in each innings for Guyana against New Zealand, was in superb form and had his home crowd in buoyant mood before he was run out in a misunderstanding with Charlie Davis.

The crowd booed and jeered and, moment's later, Bruce Taylor was showered with bottles on the boundary. Bevan Congdon attempted to placate the chanting crowd but the fracas continued.

The players, who had gathered in the middle, now left the field. Lloyd appealed for calm from the broadcasting box. Play was resumed after a break of 20 minutes. For the remaining 40 minutes Davis' every move excited a chorus of abuse and he was given a police escort to the team's hotel at the end of the day; 201-4.

Showers restricted play on the second day to 2½ hours and the total advanced to 310-7. Sobers delayed his declaration on the third day until Alvin Kallicharran reached his century on his home ground, in his maiden test; 365-7. Glenn Turner and Terry Jarvis relished the opportunity to bat on such a genial pitch and both were unbeaten with half-centuries to their names when play ended at 163 without loss.

Jarvis was caught off a sliced drive for 182 after 540 minutes of intense concentration and the partnership was worth 387. Congdon joined Turner who ended the day at 210 in a total of 410-1.

Refreshed after the rest day Turner advanced his score to better Graham Dowling's New Zealand individual total of 239. His stoic powers of concentration failed him just before lunch when he was adjudged leg-before-wicket for 259.

Mark Burgess, who had awaited his summons for two full days, was quickly bowled and Brian Hastings and Congdon might well have batted the rest of the day but the New Zealand captain decided to declare to give his men a chance to stretch their legs.

MILESTONES

- Glenn Turner's 259 was the highest score by a New Zealander in a test.

- Bruce Taylor captured his 300th first-class wicket.

- Alvin Kallicharran made a century on test debut.

- New Zealand's 543 for three was its highest test score.

Terry Jarvis drives fluently through the on side watched by Lawrence Rowe and Michael Findlay. In reply to West Indies 365, Jarvis and Glenn Turner began with a New Zealand first-class record opening partnership of 387.

WEST INDIES

R.C.Fredericks	c Turner b Cunis	41	not out	42
G.A.Greenidge	c Wadsworth b Taylor	50	not out	35
L.G.Rowe	b Congdon	31		
C.H.Lloyd	run out	43		
C.A.Davis	c Wadsworth b Taylor	28		
A.I.Kallicharran	not out	100		
G.St A.Sobers*	c Burgess b Taylor	5		
D.A.J.Holford	lbw b Congdon	28		
T.M.Findlay†	not out	15		
V.A.Holder				
A.B.Howard				
Extras	(b 10, lb 5, w 1, nb 8)	24	(b 4, lb 2, w 1, nb 2)	9
TOTAL	**(135 overs) (7 wkts dec)**	**365**	**(40 overs) (0 wkts)**	**86**

NEW ZEALAND

G.M.Turner	lbw b Howard	259
T.W.Jarvis	c Greenidge b Holford	182
B.E.Congdon*	not out	61
M.G.Burgess	b Howard	8
B.F.Hastings	not out	18
R.W.Morgan		
G.E.Vivian		
K.J.Wadsworth†		
B.R.Taylor		
R.S.Cunis		
H.J.Howarth		
Extras	(lb 11, nb 4)	15
TOTAL	**(268 overs) (3 wkts dec)**	**543**

Bowling	O	M	R	W	O	M	R	W		Fall of Wickets		
NEW ZEALAND										WI	NZ	WI
										1st	1st	2nd
Cunis	24	5	61	1	5	2	13	0	1st	79	387	-
Taylor	37	7	105	3	6	3	9	0	2nd	103	482	-
Congdon	33	7	86	2					3rd	160	496	-
Howarth	38	10	79	0	9	3	12	0	4th	178	-	-
Vivian	3	0	10	0	3	0	16	0	5th	237	-	-
Morgan					9	3	10	0	6th	244	-	-
Burgess					5	3	12	0	7th	305	-	-
Turner					2	1	5	0	8th	-	-	-
Jarvis					1	1	0	0	9th	-	-	-
WEST INDIES									10th	-	-	-
Holder	24	8	39	0								
Sobers	42	15	76	0								
Lloyd	36	11	74	0								
Howard	62	16	140	2								
Holford	54	24	78	1								
Greenidge	14	4	34	0								
Davis	25	8	42	0								
Kallicharran	6	1	17	0								
Rowe	5	0	28	0								

102 WEST INDIES v NEW ZEALAND *(Fifth Test)*

at Queen's Park Oval, Port of Spain on 20, 21, 22, 23, 25, 26 April, 1972
Toss : West Indies. Umpires : R.G. Gosein and D. Sang Hue
Match drawn

In an endeavour to break the series stalemate it was decided that this test would be played over six days. Regrettably, rain interrupted play on part of the second, third and fifth days.

Gary Sobers won the toss for the fifth time in the series and decided to bat. Geoff Greenidge and Roy Fredericks were untroubled in putting on 86 runs before lunch. By the time the score reached 107 they were both out. Charlie Davis began uneasily but Alvin Kallicharran was quickly into his stride, slamming 14 off one over from Hedley Howarth.

The partnership added 101 in even time before Davis was dismissed. In less than three hours Kallicharran completed his second consecutive test century, which included a six and 13 fours, before he was out; 278-5 at stumps.

The last five wickets added 90 in between stoppages for rain. David Holford, who had made 46 before he limped off after pulling a hamstring, scored the bulk of these runs. The tourists made a disastrous start in their first innings. Glenn

Turner and Bevan Congdon, the men most likely to aid New Zealand's cause, were both bundled out cheaply.

The diminutive left-arm, back-of-the-hand spinner, Inshan Ali, proved difficult to read and created havoc with his deceptive flight. Terry Jarvis and Brian Hastings survived the last over; 53-4.

New Zealand lost both overnight batsmen while adding 70 runs on a much-abbreviated day. When play resumed on the fourth morning 46 runs were required to avoid the follow on. When the last wicket fell at 162 New Zealand were seven short of the target. Curiously, Sobers did not enforce the follow-on despite the fact that in Inshan Ali, with figures of 5-59, he appeared to hold a trump card.

The match looked to have swung New Zealand's way when West Indies lost their eighth wicket at 123. Bruce Taylor again dominated the batsmen, taking five wickets, ably supported by Howarth with three. The hobbling Holford, with a runner, and Vanburn Holder then added 56 for the ninth wicket before Holford was run out; 192-9 at stumps.

After the rest day the innings ended at 194. A fine rally by the tailenders had given the West Indies a lead of 400 with almost two full days left. Turner and Jarvis had put on 51 runs before rain washed out the remainder of the day's play.

When play resumed on the sixth morning New Zealand's only hope of saving the series was to bat through the day for a draw. With 105 minutes remaining seven wickets were down for 188 with only Turner (50) and Congdon (58) having offered much resistance. Taylor joined Ken Wadsworth and immediately offered a bat-pad chance that spilled out of the grasp of Frederick's hand.

For the rest of the day the pair batted stubbornly to save the game. Their partnership defined the tour. By grit, determination and a great resolve to fight to the utmost of their ability they held their own against superior opposition.

One of the heroes of New Zealand's tour of West Indies was Ken Wadsworth. The wicketkeeper's energetic approach, encouragement of the fieldsmen and his batting, which came to the fore in moments of crisis, were invaluable.

MILESTONES

- Bruce Taylor's 27 wickets in the series was a record for New Zealand.

- Glenn Turner's 672 runs was the highest aggregate in a series for New Zealand.

WEST INDIES

R.C.Fredericks	run out	60	c Turner b Taylor		15
G.A.Greenidge	c Hastings b Howarth	38	c Wadsworth b Taylor		21
A.I.Kallicharran	c Wadsworth b Cunis	101	c Vivian b Taylor		18
C.A.Davis	c Hastings b Morgan	40	c Taylor b Howarth		23
C.H.Lloyd	c Howarth b Taylor	18	c Congdon b Howarth		5
T.M.Findlay†	b Congdon	9	(7) lbw b Howarth		6
D.A.J.Holford	retired hurt	46	(9) run out		25
G.St A.Sobers*	c Hastings b Howarth	28	(6) b Taylor		2
Inshan Ali	c Wadsworth b Taylor	0	(8) lbw b Taylor		16
V.A.Holder	c & b Taylor	12	b Cunis		42
R.R.Jumadeen	not out	3	not out		2
Extras	(b 2, lb 6, nb 5)	13	(b 5, lb 12, nb 2)		19
TOTAL	**(128.4 overs)**	**368**	**(74.2 overs)**		**194**

NEW ZEALAND

G.M.Turner	b Holder	1	c Findlay b Holder		50
T.W.Jarvis	c Sobers b Inshan Ali	40	lbw b Inshan Ali		22
B.E.Congdon*	c Findlay b Lloyd	11	b Sobers		58
M.G.Burgess	b Inshan Ali	5	c Greenidge b Inshan Ali		6
R.S.Cunis	c Findlay b Inshan Ali	2			
B.F.Hastings	c Findlay b Jumadeen	27	(5) c Lloyd b Holder		11
G.E.Vivian	b Sobers	24	(6) lbw b Holder		4
B.R.Taylor	b Sobers	26	(9) not out		42
R.W.Morgan	c Holder b Inshan Ali	4	(8) b Holder		2
K.J.Wadsworth†	st Findlay b Inshan Ali	1	(7) not out		40
H.J.Howarth	not out	0			
Extras	(b 3, lb 6, nb 12)	21	(b 2, lb 1, w 1, nb 14)		18
TOTAL	**(75.4 overs)**	**162**	**(155 overs) (7 wkts)**		**253**

Bowling NEW ZEALAND	O	M	R	W	O	M	R	W
Cunis	20	5	61	1	4.2	0	21	1
Taylor	19.4	1	74	3	24	8	41	5
Congdon	31	6	73	1	15	2	39	0
Howarth	51	17	109	2	29	8	70	3
Morgan	7	0	38	1	2	1	4	0
WEST INDIES								
Holder	16	1	37	1	26	12	41	4
Sobers	11	5	17	2	29	12	45	1
Lloyd	3	0	10	1				
Inshan Ali	26.4	8	59	5	51	16	99	2
Jumadeen	19	9	18	1	45	22	46	0
Greenidge					1	0	2	0
Fredericks					2	1	2	0
Kallicharran					1	1	0	0

Fall of Wickets		WI 1st	NZ 1st	WI 2nd	NZ 2nd
1st		92	18	35	62
2nd		107	39	48	105
3rd		208	51	66	122
4th		265	53	73	157
5th		265	86	90	157
6th		312	106	90	181
7th		348	142	97	188
8th		360	150	123	-
9th		368	162	179	-
10th		-	162	194	-

AVERAGES

New Zealand

BATTING	M	I	NO	Runs	HS	Ave
G.M. Turner	5	8	1	672	259	96.00
B.E. Congdon	5	8	2	531	166*	88.50
K.J. Wadsworth	5	6	3	177	78	59.00
T.W. Jarvis	4	6	0	277	182	46.16
B.R. Taylor	4	4	1	114	46	38.00
B.F. Hastings	5	8	2	222	105	37.00
M.G. Burgess	5	8	1	248	101	35.42
R.S. Cunis	5	5	1	93	51	23.25
G.E. Vivian	4	4	0	66	38	16.50
G.T. Dowling	2	4	0	45	23	11.25
J.C. Alabaster	2	2	0	20	18	10.00
H.J. Howarth	5	4	1	24	16	8.00
R.W. Morgan	3	3	0	8	4	2.66
M.G. Webb	1	1	0	0	0	0.00

BOWLING	O	M	R	W	Ave
B.R. Taylor	172.2	39	478	27	17.70
B.E. Congdon	200	49	446	13	34.30
H.J. Howarth	338	100	703	14	50.21
R.S. Cunis	183	33	617	6	102.83
R.W. Morgan	48	12	130	1	130.00
J.C. Alabaster	50	13	164	1	164.00
T.W. Jarvis	1	1	0	0	-
G.M. Turner	2	1	5	0	-
M.G. Burgess	7	3	27	0	-
G.E. Vivian	18	4	56	0	-
M.G. Webb	30	5	120	0	-

West Indies

BATTING	M	I	NO	Runs	HS	Ave
A.I. Kallicharran	2	3	1	219	101	109.50
L.G. Rowe	4	7	1	419	214	69.83
C.A. Davis	5	9	1	466	183	58.25
R.C. Fredericks	5	10	1	487	163	54.11
G.A. Greenidge	2	4	1	144	50	48.00
G.St A. Sobers	5	8	1	253	142	36.14
D.A.J. Holford	5	7	2	175	50	35.00
V.A. Holder	4	5	1	103	42	25.75
T.M. Findlay	5	6	2	99	44*	24.75
M.C. Carew	3	6	0	143	45	23.83
M.L.C. Foster	3	6	2	93	28*	23.25
C.H. Lloyd	2	3	0	66	43	22.00
G.C. Shillingford	2	1	0	15	15	15.00
Inshan Ali	3	5	1	56	25	14.00
R.R. Jumadeen	1	2	2	5	3*	-
L.R. Gibbs	2	1	1	3	3*	-
U.G. Dowe	1	-	-	-	-	-
A.B. Howard	1	-	-	-	-	-

BOWLING	O	M	R	W	Ave
V.A. Holder	153	52	285	12	23.75
U.G. Dowe	42	8	121	4	30.25
G.C. Shillingford	62.1	17	160	5	32.00
G.St A. Sobers	181	56	332	10	33.20
Inshan Ali	192.3	53	391	11	35.54
D.A.J. Holford	179	62	312	8	39.00
R.R. Jumadeen	64	31	64	1	64.00
A.B. Howard	62	16	140	2	70.00
C.H. Lloyd	39	11	84	1	84.00
L.R. Gibbs	130	37	267	3	89.00
M.L.C. Foster	53	22	93	1	93.00
A.I. Kallicharran	7	2	17	0	-
L.G. Rowe	5	0	28	0	-
G.A. Greenidge	15	4	36	0	-
R.C. Fredericks	21	7	37	0	-
M.C. Carew	21	1	53	0	-
C.A. Davis	47	17	77	0	-

1972/73 Pakistan in New Zealand

Of the 17 Pakistan players who arrived in this country after an eventful tour of Australia, four were veterans of the 1964/65 visit to New Zealand. Most of the senior members of the team were full-time professionals engaged by various English county clubs.

103 NEW ZEALAND v PAKISTAN *(First Test)*

at Basin Reserve, Wellington on 2, 3, 4, 5 February, 1973
Toss : Pakistan. Umpires : E.C.A. MacKintosh and W.T. Martin
Match drawn

Light rain delayed the start of play, handicapping the New Zealand bowlers who had to use a damp ball in strong, blustery winds. Sadiq Mohammad and Majid Khan both recovered from an uncomfortable start to their innings, and began to take toll of short deliveries. The left-handed Sadiq executed violent square-cuts and vicious pulls off his hips and reached his century in 227 minutes. Majid was more graceful and orthodox. They were together at stumps with the score at 196-2.

Majid was caught off Taylor for 79 in the first over of the second day when the partnership had added 171. By lunch Pakistan had reached a formidable 307-4. The next six wickets tumbled for an additional 50 runs. There were 19 boundaries in Sadiq's innings of 166. John Parker, who would have opened New Zealand's batting, had suffered a broken thumb while fielding on the first day and took no further part in the game.

The Pakistan pace attack seemed to find more in the wicket than had their opposition. New Zealand was struggling at 77-2 when bad light halted proceedings.

It was left to Brian Hastings and Mark Burgess to weather the fiery Sarfraz Nawaz after Glenn Turner had been dismissed at the beginning of the third day. Together they added 128 runs in 140 minutes before Intikhab Alam deceived Burgess with his flight and accepted a simple catch. Hastings' cautious innings contained only four boundaries in 72 runs.

With a flurry of slashes through and over the slip field Richard Hadlee enjoyed a rollicking debut with the bat, contributing 46 of New Zealand's last 64 runs. Pakistan ended the day at 64-2.

Sadiq completed an excellent double with 68 and for the second time in the match Majid scored 79. The remaining batsmen chased quick runs before a token declaration was made at 290-6. Requiring 322 in two hours there was a brittle response from the New Zealand top order that caused some anxiety. Salim Altaf dispatched Terry Jarvis and Bevan Congdon in his first over and Hastings in his third. All three batsmen failed to score.

MILESTONES

- Richard Hadlee (123) and John Parker (124) made their test debuts.

Richard Hadlee provided a taste of things to come in his first innings at test level. His cavalier innings included many unorthodox shots and contributed 46 of the last 64 runs in New Zealand's total of 325.

PAKISTAN

Sadiq Mohammad	c sub (D.R.O'Sullivan) b Hadlee	166	c Congdon b Howarth		68
Talat Ali	c Turner b Collinge	6	lbw b Taylor		2
Zaheer Abbas	c Hadlee b Taylor	2	c Wadsworth b Collinge		8
Majid Khan	c Congdon b Taylor	79	c Burgess b Howarth		79
Asif Iqbal	c & b Hadlee	39	c Hastings b Howarth		23
Wasim Raja	c Congdon b Taylor	10	c sub (D.R.O'Sullivan) b Howarth		41
Intikhab Alam*	run out	16	not out		53
Wasim Bari†	retired hurt	13			
Salim Altaf	c Howarth b Taylor	14	(8) not out		6
Sarfraz Nawaz	c Wadsworth b Collinge	0			
Pervez Sajjad	not out	1			
Extras	(b 1, lb 5, nb 5)	11	(b 4, lb 2, nb 4)		10
TOTAL	(90.4 overs)	**357**	(71 overs) (6 wkts dec)		**290**

NEW ZEALAND

G.M.Turner	c Intikhab b Sarfraz	43	not out		49
T.W.Jarvis	c Majid b Sarfraz	0	c Majid b Salim		0
B.E.Congdon*	run out	19	c & b Salim		0
B.F.Hastings	c Majid b Sarfraz	72	c Bari b Salim		0
M.G.Burgess	c & b Intikhab	79	not out		21
B.R.Taylor	c Zaheer b Majid	5			
K.J.Wadsworth†	c Asif b Sarfraz	28			
R.J.Hadlee	c Asif b Salim	46			
H.J.Howarth	not out	3			
R.O.Collinge	b Salim	0			
J.M.Parker	absent hurt				
Extras	(b 9, lb 9, nb 12)	30	(lb 1, w 1, nb 6)		8
TOTAL	(74.4 overs)	**325**	(26 overs) (3 wkts)		**78**

Bowling	O	M	R	W	O	M	R	W	Fall of Wickets				
NEW ZEALAND										P	NZ	P	NZ
										1st	*1st*	*2nd*	*2nd*
Hadlee	18	0	84	2	7	0	28	0					
Collinge	20	1	63	2	13	1	50	1	1st	20	4	20	1
Taylor	24.4	1	110	4	11	2	63	1	2nd	26	55	35	1
Howarth	25	6	73	0	31	7	99	4	3rd	197	88	129	11
Congdon	3	0	16	0	9	0	40	0	4th	271	216	177	-
PAKISTAN									5th	308	221	202	-
Salim	16.4	3	70	2	6	1	15	3	6th	308	261	255	-
Sarfraz	29	5	126	4	5	1	15	0	7th	334	302	-	-
Asif	2	1	6	0					8th	342	325	-	-
Intikhab	13	1	55	1	3	0	11	0	9th	357	325	-	-
Pervez	5	0	19	0	4	1	5	0	10th	-	-	-	-
Majid	9	2	19	1									
Raja					4	0	10	0					
Sadiq					3	0	13	0					
Talat					1	0	1	0					

104 **NEW ZEALAND v PAKISTAN** *(Second Test)*

at Carisbrook, Dunedin on 7, 8, 9, 10 February, 1973
Toss : Pakistan. Umpires : D.E.A. Copps and R.W.R. Shortt
Pakistan won by an innings and 166 runs

A sudden drop in temperature, from 32 °C to 16 °C, just before the test began saw the New Zealanders take the field bundled up in sweaters bemoaning the fact that they had lost the toss for the seventh consecutive test. The score was 107-2 at lunch but rain came and ended the day's play.

Early on the second day Dayle Hadlee obtained the prized wicket of Sadiq Mohammad. This brought together the last of the recognised Pakistan batsmen, Mushtaq Mohammad and Asif Iqbal. They played cautiously until lunch but then launched an audacious assault on the New Zealand bowling. The next session produced 139 runs, with both players completing their centuries. In the last 75 minutes of their 4½ hour partnership runs flowed at the rate of two a minute.

The fourth wicket had realised 350 runs when Asif was dismissed for 175, his highest test innings. After 383 minutes Mushtaq brought up his first test double century. The New Zealand bowlers had been mauled by a display of sublime stroke-making. The two New Zealand spinners, Vic Pollard,

playing his first test in two years, and David O'Sullivan, had been blasted out of the attack. Their 31 fruitless overs had cost 145 runs and 400 runs were scored in the day.

Following the early loss of Terry Jarvis, Glenn Turner and Bevan Congdon added 58 in a style that revived memories of their batting in the West Indies. The pitch was beginning to show signs of wear and after Intikhab Alam dismissed Turner off a miscued sweep shot he then captured his next five wickets for 16 runs off nine overs. Ken Wadsworth attacked, almost recklessly, in making 45 and New Zealand were dismissed for 156 with Intikhab taking 7-52.

Facing a deficit of 351 Turner and Jarvis looked comfortable against the quick bowlers. When the shine had been taken off the ball Intikhab and Mushtaq Mohammed returned to the attack. The right-arm wrist-spinners found increasing turn and erratic bounce with their leg-breaks.

Their top-spinners and wrong-uns came through at deceptive heights that caused further havoc. Pollard and Wadsworth rallied the innings to reach 123-5 at the end of a day that had seen New Zealand lose 15 wickets for 279.

It required only an hour for the visiting leg-spinners to capture the final five wickets. Pollard continued to bluster along defiantly until, on 61, he became Intikhab's 11th victim in the game. It was the first time in four years of captaining Pakistan that Intikhab had led them to victory.

PAKISTAN

Sadiq Mohammad	b Hadlee	61			
Zaheer Abbas	c Wadsworth b Hadlee	15			
Majid Khan	c & b Taylor	26			
Mushtaq Mohammad	c Wadsworth b Congdon	201			
Asif Iqbal	c Hastings b Taylor	175			
Wasim Raja	not out	8			
Intikhab Alam*	c Pollard b Howarth	3			
Wasim Bari†	not out	2			
Salim Altaf					
Sarfraz Nawaz					
Pervez Sajjad					
Extras	(lb 13, nb 3)	16			
TOTAL	(123 overs) (6 wkts dec)	**507**			

NEW ZEALAND

G.M.Turner	c Mushtaq b Intikhab	37	c Mushtaq b Intikhab		24
T.W.Jarvis	c Mushtaq b Sarfraz	7	c Bari b Mushtaq		39
B.E.Congdon*	c Bari b Intikhab	35	c Majid b Mushtaq		7
B.F.Hastings	c Sarfraz b Intikhab	4	b Mushtaq		9
M.G.Burgess	b Intikhab Alam	10	c Pervez b Intikhab		4
V.Pollard	c Sarfraz b Intikhab	3	b Intikhab		61
B.R.Taylor	c Sarfraz b Intikhab	0	(8) run out		3
K.J.Wadsworth†	b Mushtaq	45	(7) c Majid b Intikhab		17
D.R.Hadlee	st Bari b Intikhab	1	c Majid b Mushtaq		0
D.R.O'Sullivan	c Raja b Mushtaq	4	b Mushtaq		1
H.J.Howarth	not out	4	not out		7
Extras	(b 1, lb 2, nb 3)	6	(b 5, lb 7, nb 1)		13
TOTAL	(51.5 overs)	**156**	(49.4 overs)		**185**

Bowling	O	M	R	W	O	M	R	W	Fall of Wickets			
NEW ZEALAND										P	NZ	NZ
										1st	*1st*	*2nd*
Hadlee	24	3	100	2					1st	23	15	48
Taylor	22	3	91	2					2nd	81	73	57
Congdon	17	1	72	1					3rd	126	84	78
Howarth	29	6	83	1					4th	476	87	87
Pollard	13	2	64	0					5th	504	99	91
O'Sullivan	18	2	81	0					6th	504	99	127
PAKISTAN									7th	-	104	150
Salim Altaf	5	0	23	0	4	2	11	0	8th	-	116	159
Sarfraz Nawaz	5	0	20	1	4	0	16	0	9th	-	139	169
Intikhab Alam	21	3	52	7	18.4	2	78	4	10th	-	156	185
Pervez Sajjad	17	5	40	0	3	0	10	0				
Mushtaq	3.5	1	15	2	18	2	49	5				
Wasim Raja					2	0	8	0				

MILESTONES

- David O'Sullivan (125) made his test debut.

- The fourth wicket partnership of 350 between Mushtaq Mohammad and Asif Iqbal was a Pakistan test record for any wicket.

- Mushtaq Mohammad joined West Indies' Denis Atkinson as the only players to score a double century and take five wickets in an innings of the same test.

- The day after the test, the teams played a 40-over one-day game in Christchurch. It was New Zealand's first one-day international. They won by 22 runs.

Dayle Hadlee is delighted to claim the first Pakistan wicket to fall, having Zaheer Abbas caught by Ken Wadsworth with the score at 23. From left, Wadsworth, Sadiq Mohammad, Zaheer, Glenn Turner, umpire Dick Shortt, Hadlee and Terry Jarvis.

105 NEW ZEALAND v PAKISTAN *(Third Test)*

at Eden Park, Auckland on 16, 17, 18, 19 February, 1973
Toss : Pakistan. Umpires : E.C.A. MacKintosh and W.T. Martin
Match drawn

Because the Auckland test involved Sunday play Vic Pollard was not available and Rodney Redmond took his place.

Batting on a hard wicket that afforded some bounce in the first session Pakistan lost both openers with the score at 43. Majid Khan, Mushtaq Mohammad and Asif Iqbal all batted fluently and took advantage of loose bowling to take the score quickly through to 238.

Majid, after scoring a stylish 110, became one of Ken Wadsworth's four catches taken that day. Wasim Raja, and Intikhab Alam were also caught by Wadsworth after bright cameo innings. Bruce Taylor captured his 100th test wicket when he dismissed Intikhab.

Several useful contributions by the lower-order batsmen, including a stand of 48 for the last wicket between Salim

Altaf and Pervez Sajjad, enabled Pakistan to bat on beyond lunch on the second day taking the score from 300-7 to 402 all out.

The wicket was docile when Redmond and Glenn Turner came out to open. Redmond was given an uncomfortable introduction to test cricket by Salim and Sarfraz Nawaz. With the introduction of spin he launched an all-out attack, taking 12 off Intikhab's first over.

Turner was content to give Redmond as much of the strike as possible. Their partnership reached 100 in 90 minutes. In one of Majid's overs Redmond struck the first five balls to the boundary. The crowd was intoxicated by his audacity.

When Redmond reached 99 several hundred spectators, whose enthusiasm was greater than their mathematical ability, surged onto the field and mobbed him. After being freed, Redmond hit the next ball through the covers, and the scene was re-enacted. When he was dismissed shortly afterwards the partnership was worth 159. Turner's supporting role ended in the last over of the day with his score on 58.

On the third morning New Zealand stumbled from 180-2 to 251-9. Intikhab captured five wickets in the morning for 12 runs off 13 overs. With Brian Hastings 31 not out and Richard Collinge yet to score New Zealand lunched uneasily, as they still required two runs to avoid the follow-on.

This achieved, Hastings grew in confidence and began to play freely, while his partner stretched a long front leg down the wicket to smother the spin. The run rate accelerated as Hastings reached his century and Collinge his half-century.

When Hastings was bowled for 110 the pair had added a world record 151 for the tenth wicket and Collinge was 68 not out. The team total exactly matched Pakistan's 402. The visitors reached 73-3 when play ended.

Pakistan was intent on retaining its one-nil lead in the series and was aided by the New Zealand fielding effort that included four dropped catches. By the time all ten wickets were captured New Zealand faced a target of 272 for victory in less than two hours.

In this time Redmond completed a fine double, making 56 to go with his 107 in the first innings. The test and the series dawdled through to a quiet conclusion.

MILESTONES

- Rodney Redmond (126) made his test debut. He became the third New Zealander to make a century in his first test.

- Ken Wadsworth equalled Roy Harford's record of five wicketkeeping dismissals in an innings.

- Bruce Taylor captured his 100th test wicket and went past Dick Motz's previous record.

- Brian Hastings and Richard Collinge set a new world record of 151 for the tenth wicket.

- Richard Collinge's 68 not out was the highest test score by a number eleven batsman.

- Brian Hastings became the eighth New Zealander to score 1000 runs in test cricket.

PAKISTAN

Sadiq Mohammad	c Wadsworth b Collinge	33	c Hadlee b Taylor		38
Zaheer Abbas	c Turner b Taylor	10	c Turner b Taylor		0
Majid Khan	c Wadsworth b Taylor	110	c Wadsworth b Howarth		33
Mushtaq Mohammad	c Hastings b Congdon	61	b Howarth		52
Asif Iqbal	b Taylor	34	(6) lbw b Congdon		39
Wasim Raja	c Wadsworth b Collinge	1	(7) b Collinge		49
Intikhab Alam*	c Wadsworth b Taylor	34	(8) b Howarth		2
Wasim Bari†	c & b Howarth	30	(9) lbw b Hadlee		27
Salim Altaf	not out	53	(5) lbw b Congdon		11
Sarfraz Nawaz	c Wadsworth b Howarth	2	c Taylor b Collinge		4
Pervez Sajjad	lbw b Congdon	24	not out		8
Extras	(b 1, lb 3, nb 6)	10	(b 3, lb 3, nb 2)		8
TOTAL	(117.5 overs)	402	(78.7 overs)		271

NEW ZEALAND

R.E.Redmond	c Mushtaq b Pervez	107	c Intikhab b Raja		56
G.M.Turner	c Sarfraz b Intikhab	58	b Raja		24
B.E.Congdon*	b Intikhab	24	not out		6
B.F.Hastings	b Wasim	110	(5) not out		4
M.G.Burgess	b Intikhab	2	(4) c Mushtaq b Raja		1
T.W.Jarvis	lbw b Intikhab	0			
K.J.Wadsworth†	c Sadiq b Intikhab	6			
B.R.Taylor	c Majid b Pervez	2			
D.R.Hadlee	b Intikhab	0			
H.J.Howarth	c Majid b Mushtaq	8			
R.O.Collinge	not out	68			
Extras	(b 8, lb 6, nb 3)	17	(b 1)		1
TOTAL	(90.6 overs)	402	(24 overs) (3 wkts)		92

Bowling	O	M	R	W	O	M	R	W		Fall of Wickets			
NEW ZEALAND											P	NZ	P	NZ
											1st	1st	2nd	2nd
Collinge	24	2	72	2	7	2	19	2	1st	43	159	4	80
Hadlee	18	3	100	0	5.7	0	35	1	2nd	43	180	61	81
Taylor	32	9	86	4	19	5	66	2	3rd	147	203	99	87
Howarth	32	5	86	2	31	11	99	3	4th	233	205	116	-
Congdon	11.5	0	48	2	16	3	44	2	5th	238	205	159	-
PAKISTAN									6th	267	225	203	-
Salim	20	1	58	0	4	0	17	0	7th	295	235	206	-
Sarfraz	16	1	85	0	4	0	13	0	8th	342	236	238	-
Intikhab	30	4	127	6					9th	354	251	242	-
Majid	3	0	30	0	3	0	11	0	10th	402	402	271	-
Pervez	15	3	50	2									
Mushtaq	5	0	26	1									
Raja	1.6	0	9	1	8	2	32	3					
Sadiq					5	1	18	0					

AVERAGES

New Zealand

BATTING	M	I	NO	Runs	HS	Ave
R.E. Redmond	1	2	0	163	107	81.50
R.O. Collinge	2	2	1	68	68*	68.00
G.M. Turner	3	6	1	235	58	47.00
R.J. Hadlee	1	1	0	46	46	46.00
B.F. Hastings	3	6	1	199	110	39.80
V. Pollard	1	2	0	64	61	32.00
K.J. Wadsworth	3	4	0	96	45	24.00
M.G. Burgess	3	6	1	117	79	23.40
H.J. Howarth	3	4	3	22	8	22.00
B.E. Congdon	3	6	1	91	35	18.20
T.W. Jarvis	3	5	0	46	39	9.20
D.R. O'Sullivan	1	2	0	5	4	2.50
B.R. Taylor	3	4	0	10	5	2.50
D.R. Hadlee	2	3	0	1	1	0.33
J.M. Parker	1	-	-	-	-	-

BOWLING	O	M	R	W	Ave
R.O. Collinge	64	6	204	7	29.14
B.R. Taylor	108	20	416	13	32.00
H.J. Howarth	148	35	440	10	44.00
B.E. Congdon	56.5	4	220	5	44.00
R.J. Hadlee	25	0	112	2	56.00
D.R. Hadlee	46.7	6	235	3	78.33
V. Pollard	13	2	64	0	-
D.R. O'Sullivan	18	2	81	0	-

Pakistan

BATTING	M	I	NO	Runs	HS	Ave
Mushtaq Mohammad	2	3	0	314	201	104.66
Sadiq Mohammad	3	5	0	366	166	73.20
Majid Khan	3	5	0	327	110	65.40
Asif Iqbal	3	5	0	310	175	62.00
Salim Altaf	3	4	2	84	53*	42.00
Wasim Bari	3	4	2	72	30	36.00
Pervez Sajjad	3	3	2	33	24	33.00
Wasim Raja	3	5	1	109	49	27.25
Intikhab Alam	3	5	1	108	53*	27.00
Zaheer Abbas	3	5	0	35	15	7.00
Talat Ali	1	2	0	8	6	4.00
Sarfraz Nawaz	3	3	0	6	4	2.00

BOWLING	O	M	R	W	Ave	
Mushtaq Mohammad	26.5	3	90	8	11.25	
Wasim Raja	15.6	2	59	4	14.75	
Intikhab Alam	85.4	10	323	18	17.94	
Salim Altaf	55.4	7	194	5	38.80	
Sarfraz Nawaz	63	7	275	5	55.00	
Majid Khan	15	2	60	1	60.00	
Pervez Sajjad	44	9	124	2	62.00	
Talat Ali	1	0	1	0	-	-
Asif Iqbal	2	1	6	0	-	-
Sadiq Mohammad	8	1	31	0	-	-

A scintillating display by Rodney Redmond saw him become the third New Zealander to make a century on debut. The other two, Jack Mills and Bruce Taylor, were also left-hand batsmen. It was to be his only test.

1973 New Zealand in England

The first two-thirds of the tour, comprising 12 first-class games, was dominated by rain and the quest of Glenn Turner to score 1000 runs before the end of May, which he succeeded in doing. With Hedley Howarth unfit, Bevan Congdon went into the match relying on a four-man pace attack.

106   ENGLAND v NEW ZEALAND *(First Test)*

at Trent Bridge, Nottingham on 7, 8, 9, 11, 12 June, 1973
Toss : England. Umpires : D.J. Constant and A.E.G. Rhodes
England won by 38 runs

Geoffrey Boycott and Dennis Amiss were painfully slow as England laboured to score 69 in the first session. Lively bowling by Bruce Taylor and Dayle Hadlee saw England struggle through to stumps with the score at 216-9 with both bowlers taking four wickets.

Alan Knott and Norman Gifford carried their partnership through to 59 and England's total to 250. The England bowlers, John Snow, Geoff Arnold and Tony Greig, were able to find more in the Trent Bridge pitch than had the New Zealanders.

Once Glenn Turner became the second wicket to fall, with the total at 31, the innings fell into disarray and New Zealand was all out for 97 with extras the top score. It was little consolation that in the last two hours four England wickets were claimed for 72, of which Amiss and Greig had added an unbroken 48.

The pair added a further 117 in the morning session. Greig, the more belligerent aggressor, made 139 before he was lbw to Richard Collinge, the pick of the visiting bowlers. The partnership had added 210. Amiss lost two more partners, both to Vic Pollard, before he acknowledged his hundred after batting for 315 minutes. He was 138 not out when the innings was declared closed at 325-8.

Needing the huge total of 479 to win New Zealand lost Turner and John Parker before stumps for 16. Congdon had been hit in the face by a ball from Snow and there was doubt whether he would be able to continue.

On the fourth morning Congdon took his place at the wicket and played the major role in one of cricket's great fightbacks. When four batsmen were dismissed the total was 130 and Vic Pollard joined Congdon in a resolute stand. It was to last until 13 minutes before stumps when Congdon played a tired shot to Arnold and was bowled for 176. His innings was technically faultless and was characterised by doggedness and determination.

New Zealand began the last day at 315-5 with Pollard 74 and 162 runs needed. The score advanced to 400 before Ken Wadsworth was caught at second slip off Arnold. Pollard defied the opposition bowlers for 437 minutes before he was out for 116. New Zealand's gallant effort ended at 440.

In pursuit of 479 to win, Bevan Congdon played a heroic hand after being struck in the face by a bouncer from John Snow and went on to make 176. At leg-gully is Dennis Amiss, with Snow on the boundary.

ENGLAND

G.Boycott	lbw b Taylor	51	run out	1
D.L.Amiss	c Wadsworth b Taylor	42	not out	138
G.R.J.Roope	lbw b Hadlee D.R.	28	c Wadsworth b Collinge	2
A.R.Lewis	c Wadsworth b Taylor	2	c Wadsworth b Taylor	2
K.W.R.Fletcher	lbw b Hadlee D.R.	17	b Hadlee D.R.	8
A.W.Greig	c Parker b Collinge	2	lbw b Collinge	139
R.Illingworth*	b Hadlee D.R.	8	c Parker b Pollard	3
A.P.E.Knott†	b Congdon	49	c Hastings b Pollard	2
J.A.Snow	b Hadlee D.R.	8	b Hadlee R.J.	7
G.G.Arnold	c Wadsworth b Taylor	1	not out	10
N.Gifford	not out	25		
Extras	(lb 10, nb 7)	17	(b 4, lb 6, nb 3)	13
TOTAL	(107.4 overs)	**250**	(97 overs) (8 wkts dec)	**325**

NEW ZEALAND

G.M.Turner	c Roope b Greig	11	c Roope b Arnold	9
J.M.Parker	c Knott b Greig	2	c Illingworth b Snow	6
B.E.Congdon*	run out	9	b Arnold	176
B.F.Hastings	c Roope b Arnold	3	lbw b Arnold	11
M.G.Burgess	c Knott b Arnold	0	c Knott b Arnold	26
V.Pollard	not out	16	lbw b Greig	116
K.J.Wadsworth†	c Knott b Greig	0	c Roope b Arnold	46
B.R.Taylor	c Knott b Snow	19	lbw b Snow	11
D.R.Hadlee	b Snow	0	hit wicket b Greig	14
R.J.Hadlee	b Snow	0	not out	4
R.O.Collinge	b Greig	17	b Greig	0
Extras	(b 8, lb 6, nb 6)	20	(lb 13, w 1, nb 7)	21
TOTAL	(41.4 overs)	**97**	(188.1 overs)	**440**

Bowling	O	M	R	W	O	M	R	W	Fall of Wickets				
NEW ZEALAND										E	NZ	E	NZ
										1st	1st	2nd	2nd
Collinge	27	6	62	1	24	7	43	2	1st	92	24	2	16
Hadlee R.J.	26	5	64	0	19	3	79	1	2nd	106	31	8	16
Taylor	29	7	53	4	23	3	87	1	3rd	108	34	11	68
Hadlee D.R.	19	6	42	4	13	2	51	1	4th	140	34	24	130
Congdon	6.4	1	12	1	9	1	28	0	5th	147	45	234	307
Pollard					9	3	24	2	6th	161	45	241	402
ENGLAND									7th	162	71	263	414
Snow	13	5	21	3	43	10	104	2	8th	184	72	311	414
Arnold	18	8	23	2	53	15	131	5	9th	191	72	-	440
Greig	10.4	0	33	4	45.1	10	101	3	10th	250	97	-	440
Roope					9	2	17	0					
Gifford					17	7	35	0					
Illingworth					21	7	31	0					

John Arlott wrote in the *Guardian* that England was grateful rather than proud to have won. "Never before in test cricket have one of the lesser sides forced their way up from humiliation to so close a sight of a win against a major country."

MILESTONES

- Alan Knott and Norman Gifford had a record tenth-wicket stand of 59 for England against New Zealand.

- New Zealand's total of 440 was the second highest achieved in the fourth innings of a test.

107 ENGLAND v NEW ZEALAND *(Second Test)*

at Lord's on 21, 22, 23, 25, 26 June, 1973
Toss : New Zealand. Umpires : A.E. Fagg and T.W. Spencer
Match drawn

North London was hazy and humid when Congdon sent England in after he won his first toss in eight tests. The initial attack from Bruce Taylor and Richard Collinge was sharp and later Hedley Howarth was able to turn and flight the ball.

Geoffrey Boycott looked ominous until he indulged in an uncharacteristic piece of miscalculated aggression and hooked Collinge straight to John Parker at square leg. At 148-2 Graham Roope and Keith Fletcher were looking well set. Within 19 minutes Howarth inflicted deep wounds in the English side. Roope was out for 56, Hastings caught Fletcher and Dayle Hadlee removed Ray Illingworth.

Tony Greig lived a charmed life, picking up runs with mis-hits and deflections. He survived while wickets fell regularly at the other end. The day ended with England on 240-9 and Collinge, Hadlee and Howarth each taking three wickets.

England was dismissed for 253 and New Zealand lost Glenn Turner and Parker with only 10 on the board. The England bowlers, sensing another victory, bowled with venom and vigour as Bevan Congdon and Brian Hastings battled valiantly.

After lunch the pair flourished with decisive running between the wickets. The tourists had struggled through 38 overs to reach their first 50 runs while the second 50 was reached in 18 overs. Hastings was dismissed for a determined 86 after the pair had added 190. At stumps Congdon was 100 not out and Howarth yet to score.

The nightwatchman, Howarth, stayed for 92 minutes while 49 runs were added. In glorious conditions the batsmen entertained the Lord's crowd with sublime batsmanship. Congdon's second century in two innings lasted 515 minutes before he was out for 175.

Mark Burgess drove fluently when he took over from Congdon and assisted Vic Pollard to add 117 before he was bowled for 105. During the day 293 runs were added for the loss of three wickets, with Pollard being 77 not out.

Pollard became the third century-maker in the innings, being 105 not out when the innings ended at 551. Dennis Amiss and Boycott gave England a strong start, putting on 112 before Amiss was out. Howarth caught and bowled Boycott when he was 92. England were 272-2 at stumps, still 74 behind.

Roope and Greig went within half an hour, which boosted the morale of the visitors, but Illingworth stayed with Fletcher for an invaluable two hours. Hope was again rekindled when Pollard and Howarth captured four wickets for 33. England was 368-8 with a lead of 70 and 92 minutes remaining.

Fletcher was playing the test innings of his career when Arnold, who was dropped by Ken Wadsworth on nought, joined him. Fletcher then launched a vicious assault on the weary bowlers and when he departed for 178 he had saved England from defeat.

ENGLAND					
G.Boycott	c Parker b Collinge	61	c & b Howarth		92
D.L.Amiss	c Howarth b Hadlee	9	c & b Howarth		53
G.R.J.Roope	lbw b Howarth	56	c Parker b Taylor		51
K.W.R.Fletcher	c Hastings b Howarth	25	c Taylor b Collinge		178
A.W.Greig	c Howarth b Collinge	63	c Wadsworth b Hadlee		12
R.Illingworth*	c Collinge b Hadlee	3	c Turner b Howarth		22
A.P.E.Knott†	b Hadlee	0	c Congdon b Howarth		0
C.M.Old	b Howarth	7	c Congdon b Pollard		7
J.A.Snow	b Taylor	2	c Hastings b Pollard		0
G.G.Arnold	not out	8	not out		23
N.Gifford	c Wadsworth b Collinge	8	not out		2
Extras	(lb 1, w 1, nb 9)	11	(b 8, lb 3, nb 12)		23
TOTAL	(106 overs)	253	(196 overs) (9 wkts)		463

NEW ZEALAND		
G.M.Turner	c Greig b Arnold	4
J.M.Parker	c Knott b Snow	3
B.E.Congdon*	c Knott b Old	175
B.F.Hastings	lbw b Snow	86
H.J.Howarth	hit wicket b Old	17
M.G.Burgess	b Snow	105
V.Pollard	not out	105
K.J.Wadsworth†	c Knott b Old	27
B.R.Taylor	b Old	11
D.R.Hadlee	c Fletcher b Old	6
R.O.Collinge		
Extras	(lb 5, nb 7)	12
TOTAL	(204.5 overs) (9 wkts dec)	551

Bowling	O	M	R	W	O	M	R	W	Fall of Wickets			
NEW ZEALAND										E	NZ	E
										1st	1st	2nd
Collinge	31	8	69	3	19	4	41	1	1st	24	5	112
Taylor	19	1	54	1	34	10	90	1	2nd	116	10	185
Hadlee	26	4	70	3	25	2	79	1	3rd	148	200	250
Congdon	5	2	7	0	8	3	22	0	4th	165	249	274
Howarth	25	6	42	3	70	24	144	4	5th	171	330	335
Pollard					39	11	61	2	6th	175	447	339
Hastings					1	0	3	0	7th	195	523	352
ENGLAND									8th	217	535	368
Snow	38	4	109	3					9th	237	551	460
Arnold	41	6	108	1					10th	253	-	-
Old	41.5	7	113	5								
Roope	6	1	15	0								
Gifford	39	6	107	0								
Illingworth	39	12	87	0								

MILESTONES

- It was the first time that New Zealand had three century-makers in one test innings.

- New Zealand's total of 551 was their highest in tests.

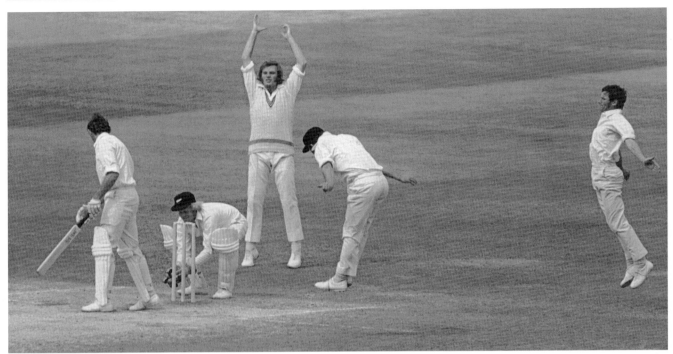

The moment when the probability of a test victory became a disappointing draw. Hedley Howarth, Brian Hastings and Bevan Congdon display different faces of abject disappointment as Ken Wadsworth fails to catch Geoff Arnold off the second ball he received. Arnold and Keith Fletcher went on to add 92 for the ninth wicket.

108 ENGLAND v NEW ZEALAND *(Third Test)*

at Headingley, Leeds on 5, 6, 7, 9, 10 July, 1973
Toss : New Zealand. Umpires : H.D. Bird and C.S. Elliott
England won by an innings and 1 run

The conditions were ideally suited for the England bowlers John Snow, Chris Old and Graham Arnold and when New Zealand had reached 24 they dealt a body blow. In the space of four balls John Parker, Bevan Congdon and then Glenn Turner were out, leaving Mark Burgess and Brian Hastings contemplating a major salvage operation.

They grimly set about the task, scoring 38 in 53 minutes to lunch and progressing more serenely afterwards. Hastings went at 78 and Vic Pollard joined Burgess to continue the battle. They were quick to seize on half-volleys from Old and dispatched both Ray Illingworth and Derek Underwood when they were trying to play a containing role.

Together they added 106 before Pollard went out for 62, followed 30 minutes later when the resolute Burgess was caught in the slips off Old for 87. Dayle Hadlee hit boldly at the end of the day for the visitors to reach 262-9.

Fourteen runs were added next morning. England then reached 70 for the loss of one wicket with Geoffrey Boycott dominating proceedings with 45. Heavy rain prevented any further play after the lunch break.

When play began on the third day the New Zealand bowlers did not use the conditions, which were totally in their favour. Graham Roope was an early victim but the other England batsmen welcomed the bowlers' policy of thudding the ball into the spongy wicket instead of keeping it pitched up. Playing in front of his home crowd, Boycott went on to score his first century against New Zealand in 203 minutes.

Keith Fletcher and, to a lesser extent, Ray Illingworth provided the substance with Boycott, scoring 81 and 65 respectively, of England's 337-6.

The left-arm fast bowling of Richard Collinge richly deserved five wickets when England was dismissed for 419 prior to lunch on the fourth day. Apart from Turner, New Zealand's second innings was a disappointing affair as they struggled to counter the trio of Snow, Old and particularly Arnold (better known as "Horse" because of his initials, G.G.) who captured 5-27 off 22 overs.

Turner could be counted unfortunate when he was adjudged lbw to Snow early on the last day, as he was on the verge of batting through a test innings for the third time.

MILESTONES

• Geoffrey Boycott joined a select group who had scored hundreds against each of the test-playing countries.

NEW ZEALAND

Batsman	1st innings		2nd innings	
G.Boycott	c Parker b Collinge	61	c & b Howarth	92
G.M.Turner	lbw b Old	11	lbw b Snow	81
J.M.Parker	c Knott b Arnold	8	c Knott b Arnold	4
B.E.Congdon*	c Knott b Arnold	0	c Knott b Arnold	2
B.F.Hastings	lbw b Arnold	18	b Old	10
M.G.Burgess	c Roope b Old	87	lbw b Old	18
V.Pollard	c Boycott b Old	62	c Roope b Arnold	3
K.J.Wadsworth†	b Old	8	b Arnold	5
B.R.Taylor	c Fletcher b Greig	20	c Roope b Snow	1
D.R.Hadlee	b Snow	34	lbw b Snow	0
R.O.Collinge	b Snow	5	b Arnold	0
H.J.Howarth	not out	8	not out	15
Extras	(b 5, lb 7, w 1, nb 2)	15	(b 1, lb 2)	3
TOTAL	(98.4 overs)	**276**	(70.3 overs)	**142**

ENGLAND

G.Boycott	c Parker b Congdon	115
D.L.Amiss	lbw b Collinge	8
G.R.J.Roope	c Turner b Collinge	18
K.W.R.Fletcher	c Howarth b Collinge	81
A.W.Greig	c Howarth b Congdon	0
R.Illingworth*	lbw b Taylor	65
A.P.E.Knott†	c Wadsworth b Taylor	21
C.M.Old	lbw b Collinge	34
J.A.Snow	c Howarth b Collinge	6
G.G.Arnold	c Wadsworth b Hadlee	26
D.L.Underwood	not out	20
Extras	(b 5, lb 16, w 1, nb 3)	25
TOTAL	(145.1 overs)	**419**

Bowling

ENGLAND	O	M	R	W	O	M	R	W
Snow	21.4	4	52	2	19.3	4	34	3
Arnold	27	8	62	3	22	11	27	5
Old	20	4	71	4	14	1	41	2
Underwood	11	4	27	0	7	2	14	0
Greig	13	4	29	1	6	1	22	0
Illingworth	6	0	20	0	2	1	1	0

NEW ZEALAND	O	M	R	W
Collinge	34	7	74	5
Taylor	31	3	111	2
Hadlee	23.1	2	98	1
Congdon	32	10	54	2
Howarth	18	6	44	0
Pollard	7	4	13	0

Fall of Wickets

	NZ 1st	E 1st	NZ 2nd
1st	24	23	16
2nd	24	71	20
3rd	24	190	39
4th	78	190	85
5th	184	280	88
6th	202	300	94
7th	215	339	95
8th	227	346	97
9th	233	365	106
10th	276	419	142

AVERAGES

New Zealand

BATTING	M	I	NO	Runs	HS	Ave
V. Pollard	3	5	2	302	116	100.66
B.E. Congdon	3	5	0	362	176	72.40
M.G. Burgess	3	5	0	236	105	47.20
H.J. Howarth	2	3	2	40	17	40.00
B.F. Hastings	3	5	0	128	86	25.60
G.M. Turner	3	5	0	116	81	23.20
K.J. Wadsworth	3	5	0	86	46	17.20
B.R. Taylor	3	5	0	62	20	12.40
D.R. Hadlee	3	5	0	54	34	10.80
R.O. Collinge	3	4	0	22	17	5.50
J.M. Parker	3	5	0	23	8	4.60
R.J. Hadlee	1	2	1	4	4*	4.00

BOWLING	O	M	R	W	Ave
R.O. Collinge	135	32	289	12	24.08
V. Pollard	55	18	98	4	24.50
H.J. Howarth	113	36	230	7	32.85
D.R. Hadlee	106.1	16	340	10	34.00
B.E. Congdon	60.4	17	123	3	41.00
B.R. Taylor	136	24	395	9	43.88
R.J. Hadlee	45	8	143	1	143.00
B.F. Hastings	1	0	3	0	–

England

BATTING	M	I	NO	Runs	HS	Ave
G. Boycott	3	5	0	320	115	64.00
D.L. Amiss	3	5	1	250	138*	62.50
K.W.R. Fletcher	3	5	0	309	178	61.80
A.W. Greig	3	5	0	216	139	43.20
N. Gifford	2	3	2	35	25*	35.00
G.G. Arnold	3	5	3	68	26	34.00
G.R.J. Roope	3	5	0	155	56	31.00
R. Illingworth	3	5	0	101	65	20.20
C.M. Old	2	3	0	48	34	16.00
A.P.E. Knott	3	5	0	72	49	14.40
J.A. Snow	3	5	0	23	8	4.60
A.R. Lewis	1	2	0	4	2	2.00
D.L. Underwood	1	1	1	20	20*	–

BOWLING	O	M	R	W	Ave
C.M. Old	75.5	12	225	11	20.45
G.G. Arnold	161	48	351	16	21.93
A.W. Greig	74.5	15	185	8	23.12
J.A. Snow	135.1	27	320	13	24.61
G.R.J. Roope	15	3	32	0	–
D.L. Underwood	18	6	41	0	–
R. Illingworth	68	20	139	0	–
N. Gifford	56	13	142	0	–

The individual highlight of the tour of England was Glenn Turner scoring 1000 runs before the end of May. Mark Burgess and Northamptonshire wicketkeeper George Sharp offer congratulations.

1973/74 New Zealand in Australia

Over the years, the Australian authorities regarded their nearest cricketing neighbours with either indifference or disdain, sending second-string selections on occasional visits to New Zealand and pitting New Zealand sides touring Australia only against state sides.

It was a breakthrough for New Zealand cricket officials when they arranged for a "twin tour" with Australia for the 1973/74 season. Six of the team that had toured England were unavailable – Bruce Taylor, Richard Collinge, Hedley Howarth, Mark Burgess, Vic Pollard and Rodney Redmond.

109 AUSTRALIA v NEW ZEALAND (*First Test*)

at Melbourne Cricket Ground on 29, 30 December 1973, 1, 2 Jan, 1974
Toss : Australia. Umpires : T.F. Brooks and J.R. Collins
Australia won by an innings and 25 runs

New Zealand could have gained an immediate advantage in Richard Hadlee's first over. Keith Stackpole, an overly aggressive opener, slashed three of the first five balls for runs. The sixth ball was short and again Stackpole swung but got an edge. Mike Shrimpton and Brian Hastings collided in their haste to grab the catch and the moment was lost.

Stackpole and Paul Sheahan compiled 75 for the first wicket. Stackpole went on to score his first test hundred on his home ground and with the Australian captain, Ian Chappell, added 128 for the second wicket, with Chappell scoring 54.

Greg Chappell and Doug Walters shared a stand of 92 for the fourth wicket in 81 minutes. By stumps Australia had reached 335-4 and the visitors could only look back on a day of missed catches and ordinary fielding.

Dayle Hadlee removed Walters, Ian Davis and Rod Marsh next day but any thoughts of a quick wrap-up were thwarted by Gary Gilmour, who slammed a maiden test half-century, and Kerry O'Keeffe, who scored 40, to take Australia through to 462, where they declared with eight wickets down.

Batting with a damaged hand Glenn Turner was struck a blow on it and he battled intense pain and squally conditions before he was caught for 7, made in 72 minutes. When rain prevented further play New Zealand were 51-3.

Two wickets fell early the next day before John Morrison and Ken Wadsworth put on 89, each in his own way. Morrison was watchful and defiant whereas Wadsworth rose to the challenge by attacking at every opportunity. Wadsworth's 80 was the highest score in his 33-test career.

Still 26 in arrears, New Zealand began its second innings with Morrison taking Turner's place as opener. The visitors ended the day 85-3.

Wadsworth and Dayle Hadlee tried some big hitting the next morning but it was only a matter of time before Australia inflicted an innings defeat on New Zealand.

MILESTONES

• Bryan Andrews (127) and John Morrison (128) made their test debuts.

Rival wicketkeepers Ken Wadsworth and Australian Rodney Marsh both enjoyed excellent series with the bat, as well as with the gloves. Both were fiercely competitive but still found time for enjoyment, even in the heat of battle.

AUSTRALIA

K.R.Stackpole	c Parker b Shrimpton	122
A.P.Sheahan	c Wadsworth b Hadlee D.R.	28
I.M.Chappell*	c Hadlee R.J. b Shrimpton	54
G.S.Chappell	c Wadsworth b Congdon	60
K.D.Walters	c Wadsworth b Hadlee D.R.	79
I.C.Davis	c Wadsworth b Hadlee D.R.	15
R.W.Marsh†	c Parker b Hadlee D.R.	6
K.J.O'Keeffe	not out	40
G.J.Gilmour	b Congdon	52
A.A.Mallett		
A.R.Dell		
Extras	(lb 4, w 1, nb 1)	6
TOTAL	(101.5 overs) (8 wkts dec)	**462**

NEW ZEALAND

G.M.Turner	c Gilmour b Dell	6	absent hurt		
J.M.Parker	c Chappell I.M. b O'Keeffe	27	(1) c Chappell I.M. b Walters	23
M.J.F.Shrimpton	c Marsh b Gilmour	16	b Walters	22
B.F.Hastings	b O'Keeffe	1	c Marsh b Mallett	22
B.E.Congdon*	st Marsh b Mallett	31	c Marsh b Mallett	14
J.F.M.Morrison	c Marsh b Gilmour	44	(2) c Marsh b Walters	16
K.J.Wadsworth†	c Chappell G.S. b Gilmour	80	(6) c Stackpole b Mallett	30
R.J.Hadlee	c Marsh b Gilmour	9	(7) c Chappell I.M. b O'Keeffe	6
D.R.Hadlee	run out	2	(8) c & b O'Keeffe	37
D.R.O'Sullivan	c Davis b Mallett	6	(9) c & b Mallett	8
B.Andrews	not out	0	(10) not out	5
Extras	(b 8, lb 5, nb 2)	15	(b 8, lb 9)	17
TOTAL	(79.7 overs)	**237**	(81.6 overs)	**200**

Bowling	O	M	R	W	O	M	R	W		Fall of Wickets			
NEW ZEALAND											A	NZ	NZ
											1st	1st	2nd
Hadlee R.J.	25	4	104	0						1st	75	19	37
Andrews	19	2	100	0						2nd	203	47	54
Hadlee D.R.	20	2	102	4						3rd	212	51	83
O'Sullivan	22	3	80	0						4th	304	56	109
Shrimpton	7	0	39	2						5th	345	100	113
Congdon	8.5	1	31	2						6th	363	189	134
AUSTRALIA										7th	381	215	150
Dell	22	7	54	1	5	0	9	0		8th	462	230	188
Gilmour	22	4	75	4	3	0	16	0		9th	-	237	200
Chappell G.S.	4	2	4	0	7	3	18	0		10th	-	237	-
Mallett	16.7	2	46	2	24	4	63	4					
O'Keeffe	14	4	40	2	29.6	12	51	2					
Chappell I.M.	1	0	3	0									
Walters					13	4	26	3					

110 AUSTRALIA v NEW ZEALAND *(Second Test)*

at Sydney Cricket Ground on 5, 6, 7, 9, 10 January, 1974
Toss : Australia. Umpires : P.R. Enright and M.G. O'Connell
Match drawn

Ian Chappell sent New Zealand in to bat but the immediate success belonged to the openers John Parker and John Morrison who stayed together for more than an hour and a half before Chappell was forced to call on his "shock bowler", Doug Walters, who had Morrison caught in his first over and took all three wickets that fell before lunch.

Jeremy Coney, playing in his first test, aided Parker in putting New Zealand back on a steady road with a partnership of 80 in 110 minutes. Parker's maiden test hundred occupied 258 minutes and included ten fours. Ken Wadsworth again took charge, racing to 54 before Chappell brought Walters back and the part-time bowler had immediate success, capturing Wadsworth to finish with four wickets in the day.

New Zealand was 273-7 overnight and after an hour's delay the next morning, the tailenders added 39 for a final tally of 312. The cloudy, humid conditions were ideal for Richard Hadlee and Bryan Andrews and they reduced the home side to 21-3 before Ian Chappell and Walters batted resolutely to add 77 for the fourth wicket.

When Coney took his third catch there was no further respite and the Australians tumbled to 162 all out. Richard Hadlee had taken four wickets, brother Dayle three and Andrews two.

Rain ruled out any play on the third day, which was followed by the rest day. The New Zealanders played themselves into a commanding position led by Morrison in only his second test. His 117 was achieved in 261 minutes and was the shining beacon in the side's total of 305.

Brian Hastings (83) was the ideal complement to his younger team-mate and together they added 124 in 97 minutes. Congdon's declaration left Australia to score 456 in 54 minutes and a full day. Keith Stackpole and Ian Chappell were both out before stumps but Sydney's rain returned and there was no play on the fifth day.

The game lifted the morale of the New Zealanders and showed the Australian public that they were not "a bunch of mugs".

NEW ZEALAND

J.M.Parker	c Marsh b Walker	108	c Marsh b Chappell G.S.	11
J.F.M.Morrison	c Chappell G.S. b Walters	28	c Davis b Chappell I.M.	117
M.J.F.Shrimpton	b Walters	0	c & b Walters	28
B.E.Congdon*	c Marsh b Walters	4	b Gilmour	17
B.F.Hastings	c Marsh b Walker	16	b Chappell G.S.	83
J.V.Coney	c Stackpole b O'Keeffe	45	(7) c Davis b Chappell G.S.	11
K.J.Wadsworth†	c Marsh b Walters	54	(6) c Chappell G.S. b Gilmour	2
D.R.Hadlee	c & b Chappell G.S.	14	(9) not out	18
R.J.Hadlee	c Chappell I.M. b Chappell G.S.	17	(8) run out	1
D.R.O'Sullivan	not out	3	lbw b Gilmour	1
B.Andrews	c Marsh b Gilmour	17		
Extras	(lb 2, nb 4)	6	(b 4, lb 11, w 1)	16
TOTAL	(86.6 overs)	**312**	(75.2 overs) (9 wkts dec)	**305**

AUSTRALIA

A.P.Sheahan	c Coney b Andrews	7	not out	14
K.R.Stackpole	c Morrison b Hadlee R.J.	8	lbw b Hadlee R.J.	2
I.M.Chappell*	c Hastings b Hadlee D.R.	45	lbw b Hadlee R.J.	6
G.S.Chappell	c Coney b Andrews	0	not out	8
K.D.Walters	c Coney b Hadlee D.R.	41		
I.C.Davis	c Andrews b Hadlee R.J.	29		
R.W.Marsh†	c Wadsworth b Hadlee D.R.	10		
K.J.O'Keeffe	c Wadsworth b Hadlee R.J.	9		
G.J.Gilmour	c Wadsworth b Congdon	3		
A.A.Mallett	lbw b Hadlee R.J.	0		
M.H.N.Walker	not out	2		
Extras	(lb 5, nb 3)	8		0
TOTAL	(44.4 overs)	**162**	(8.3 overs) (2 wkts)	**30**

Bowling	O	M	R	W	O	M	R	W		Fall of Wickets			
AUSTRALIA											NZ	A	NZ	A
											1st	1st	2nd	2nd
Gilmour	18.6	3	70	1	21.2	1	70	3		1st	78	20	23	10
Walker	22	2	71	2						2nd	78	20	94	22
Chappell G.S.	19	2	76	2	16	3	54	3		3rd	90	21	120	-
Walters	11	0	39	4	11	0	54	1		4th	113	98	244	-
Mallett	8	0	30	0	14	1	65	0		5th	193	115	255	-
O'Keeffe	8	2	20	1	10	0	40	0		6th	221	133	276	-
Chappell I.M.					3	0	6	1		7th	268	150	282	-
NEW ZEALAND										8th	292	157	292	-
Hadlee R.J.	9.4	2	33	4	4.3	0	16	2		9th	293	160	305	-
Andrews	9	1	40	2	4	0	14	0		10th	312	162	-	-
Hadlee D.R.	13	3	52	3										
Congdon	13	2	29	1										

MILESTONES

• Jeremy Coney (129) made his test debut.

Following New Zealand's listless batting in the first test, the two New Zealand openers, John Parker and John Morrison, made centuries in the second test at the Sydney Cricket Ground. Morrison, left, and Parker toast each other's success.

111 AUSTRALIA v NEW ZEALAND *(Third Test)*

at Adelaide Oval on 26, 27, 28, 30, 31 January, 1974
Toss : Australia. Umpires : J.R. Collins and P.R. Enright
Australia won by an innings and 57 runs

On a day made for batting, on a hard pitch and with the weather enervating for the bowlers and fieldsmen, it was surprising that the two Hadlees and Lance Cairns won the first session, claiming three wickets for 73 runs.

Greg Chappell and Doug Walters regained some control with a stand of 100 before Congdon bowled Chappell to make the score 173-4. Walters then reached his half-century in 95 minutes and raced to 94 in 133 minutes before falling to David O'Sullivan.

Australia's tail had been exposed but Rod Marsh and Kerry O'Keeffe saw the side through to stumps at 332-6, thanks to the generosity of dropped catches.

By the time they were separated they had added 168 for the seventh wicket and the belligerent Marsh was the last man out for 133 out of a total of 477.

Geoff Dymock made a dream start to test cricket having John Parker caught by Marsh with his second ball and New Zealand never really recovered from being one for one. Glenn Turner, John Morrison and Bevan Congdon occupied the middle without scoring significantly and it was left to the lower-order big hitters, Ken Wadsworth and the two Hadlees, to clothe the innings in some sort of respectability.

Trailing by 259 runs Ian Chappell enforced the follow on and, although Turner and Parker provided a start of 56, the second innings was no better than the first as left-arm, fast-medium bowler Dymock, cut his way through the feeble batting, Congdon excepted. The day ended with New Zealand 98-4. Adelaide's humidity turned to rain and the fourth day was washed out, raising hopes of salvation for the tourists.

Four more wickets fell for 65 runs on the last morning before rain reappeared. Congdon, playing a typically defiant innings, protested in vain when the umpires required play to continue in light rain. More than an hour and a half was lost with four stoppages, and Congdon and Cairns returned to the field on three separate occasions before Cairns was dismissed during the last hour of play.

AUSTRALIA

K.R.Stackpole	c Parker b Hadlee D.R.	15
A.J.Woodcock	c Coney b Cairns	27
I.M.Chappell*	c Hadlee R.J. b Cairns	22
G.S.Chappell	b Congdon	42
K.D.Walters	b O'Sullivan	94
I.C.Davis	c Congdon b O'Sullivan	15
R.W.Marsh†	st Wadsworth b O'Sullivan	132
K.J.O'Keeffe	lbw b Hadlee R.J.	85
A.A.Mallett	c Wadsworth b O'Sullivan	11
A.G.Hurst	c Hastings b O'Sullivan	16
G.Dymock	not out	0
Extras	(b 3, lb 6, nb 9)	18
TOTAL	**(120.5 overs)**	**477**

NEW ZEALAND

J.M.Parker	c Marsh b Dymock	0	c Chappell I.M. b Dymock	22
G.M.Turner	lbw b Hurst	20	c O'Keeffe b Dymock	34
J.F.M.Morrison	c Chappell I.M. b O'Keeffe	40	c Chappell I.M. b O'Keeffe	4
B.F.Hastings	c Woodcock b O'Keeffe	23	c Stackpole b Dymock	7
B.E.Congdon*	run out	13	not out	71
J.V.Coney	c Marsh b Dymock	8	b Dymock	17
K.J.Wadsworth†	lbw b Chappell I.M.	48	c Marsh b O'Keeffe	16
D.R.Hadlee	c Chappell G.S. b Mallett	29	c Chappell G.S. b Mallett	0
R.J.Hadlee	c Chappell I.M. b Mallett	20	c Marsh b O'Keeffe	15
D.R.O'Sullivan	b O'Keeffe	2	c Chappell I.M. b Dymock	4
B.L.Cairns	not out	4	c Chappell I.M. b Mallett	0
Extras	(b 4, lb 4, nb 3)	11	(b 2, lb 8, nb 2)	12
TOTAL	**(87.3 overs)**	**218**	**(89.5 overs)**	**202**

Bowling	O	M	R	W	O	M	R	W	Fall of Wickets			
NEW ZEALAND										A	NZ	NZ
										1st	1st	2nd
Hadlee R.J.	28	3	102	1								
Hadlee D.R.	21	2	76	1					1st	21	1	56
Cairns	21	4	73	2					2nd	67	35	65
O'Sullivan	35.5	4	148	5					3rd	73	84	65
Congdon	15	1	60	1					4th	173	89	73
AUSTRALIA									5th	221	105	105
Hurst	19	3	56	1	10	2	17	0	6th	232	110	130
Dymock	19	5	44	2	27	7	58	5	7th	400	176	143
Walters	1	0	2	0	3	0	17	0	8th	452	209	170
Mallett	23	6	46	2	21.5	9	47	2	9th	472	214	197
O'Keeffe	24.3	9	55	3	28	12	51	3	10th	477	218	202
Chappell I.M.	1	0	4	1								

MILESTONES

• Lance Cairns (130) made his test debut.

• Rod Marsh and Kerry O'Keeffe created a new Australian record of 168 for the seventh wicket.

AVERAGES

New Zealand

BATTING	M	I	NO	Runs	HS	Ave
J.F.M. Morrison	3	6	0	249	117	41.50
K.J. Wadsworth	3	6	0	230	80	38.33
J.M. Parker	3	6	0	191	108	31.83
B.E. Congdon	3	6	1	150	71*	30.00
B.F. Hastings	3	6	0	152	83	25.33
B. Andrews	2	3	2	22	17	22.00
J.V. Coney	2	4	0	81	45	20.25
D.R. Hadlee	3	6	1	100	37	20.00
G.M. Turner	2	3	0	60	34	20.00
M.J.F. Shrimpton	2	4	0	66	28	16.50
R.J. Hadlee	3	6	0	68	20	11.33
D.R. O'Sullivan	3	6	1	24	8	4.80
B.L. Cairns	1	2	1	4	4*	4.00

BOWLING	O	M	R	W	Ave
M.J.F. Shrimpton	7	0	39	2	19.50
D.R. Hadlee	54	7	230	8	28.75
B.E. Congdon	36.5	4	120	4	30.00
R.J. Hadlee	66.7	9	255	7	36.42
B.L. Cairns	21	4	73	2	36.50
D.R. O'Sullivan	57.5	7	228	5	45.60
B. Andrews	32	3	154	2	77.00

Australia

BATTING	M	I	NO	Runs	HS	Ave
K.D. Walters	3	3	0	214	94	71.33
K.J. O'Keeffe	3	3	1	134	85	67.00
R.W. Marsh	3	3	0	148	132	49.33
K.R. Stackpole	3	4	0	147	122	36.75
G.S. Chappell	3	4	1	110	60	36.66
I.M. Chappell	3	4	0	127	54	31.75
G.J. Gilmour	2	2	0	55	52	27.50
A.J. Woodcock	1	1	0	27	27	27.00
A.P. Sheahan	2	3	1	49	28	24.50
I.C. Davis	3	3	0	59	29	19.66
A.G. Hurst	1	1	0	16	16	16.00
A.A. Mallett	3	2	0	11	11	5.50
M.H.N. Walker	1	1	1	2	2*	-
G. Dymock	1	1	1	0	0*	-
A.R. Dell	1	-	-	-	-	-

BOWLING	O	M	R	W	Ave
I.M. Chappell	5	0	13	2	6.50
G. Dymock	46	12	102	7	14.57
K.D. Walters	39	4	138	8	17.25
K.J. O'Keeffe	114.1	39	257	11	23.36
G.J. Gilmour	65	8	231	8	28.87
A.A. Mallett	107.4	22	297	10	29.70
G.S. Chappell	46	10	152	5	30.40
M.H.N. Walker	22	2	71	2	35.50
A.R. Dell	27	7	63	1	63.00
A.G. Hurst	29	5	73	1	73.00

Left-arm spinner David O'Sullivan was the pick of the New Zealand bowlers in the third test at Adelaide, claiming 5-148 in Australia's first innings.

1973/74 Australia in New Zealand

112 NEW ZEALAND v AUSTRALIA *(First Test)*

at Basin Reserve, Wellington on 1, 2, 3, 5, 6 March, 1974
Toss : Australia. Umpires : D.E.A. Copps and F.R. Goodall
Match drawn

Within a fortnight of the three-test series in Australia a strong Australian side arrived in New Zealand for three more tests. The first day's play saw the players wrapped up against a cold southerly. The early advantage lay with the home side when both Australian openers were out at 55, however that was the end of New Zealand's success for the day.

The Chappell brothers took control and the only time that they were not scoring runs was during the lunch and tea intervals. Their contrasting styles were never more evident than during their record 264-run partnership: Ian, the aggressive battler with improvised shots; Greg, the master of the classics, almost arrogant in the exhibition of his skills. Ian's contribution was 145 in 283 minutes. At the end of the day Australia were 372-4, Greg Chappell 162 not out.

The declaration was made shortly after lunch on the second day at 511-6, with Greg Chappell undefeated on 247 made in 410 minutes. The early loss of John Parker was compensated by a forthright partnership between Glenn Turner and John Morrison which ended after 108 runs had been added when Turner was caught at cover for 79; 161-2 at stumps.

Rain delayed play for 90 minutes at the start of the third day and Morrison soon left for 66. Bevan Congdon and Brian Hastings showed that the wicket was batsman-friendly as they took New Zealand beyond the follow-on target of 312 and both scored centuries in their partnership of 229.

During the fourth day New Zealand's momentum foundered when six wickets fell while only 39 runs were added. Hedley Howarth and Murray Webb contributed an entertaining 47 before the innings closed at 484.

Australia's second innings was a repetition of the first, as Ian Chappell preferred batting to declaring. Ian Redpath fell seven runs short of a century. The two Chappells then continued to bat in the same masterly style as in the first innings with the same results, centuries to both of them. Statisticians had a field day throughout the match.

MILESTONES

- The match aggregate of 1455 was the highest for a test in New Zealand.

- Greg Chappell's aggregate of 380 was a record for one batsman in a test.

- It was the first time that brothers had scored a hundred in both innings of a test.

- The Chappells' first innings partnership of 264 was the highest for any wicket for Australia against New Zealand.

- The partnership of 229 between Bevan Congdon and Brian Hastings, for the fourth wicket, was New Zealand's highest against Australia.

- New Zealand made their highest total against Australia.

AUSTRALIA

Batsman	Dismissal (1st)	Runs	Dismissal (2nd)	Runs
K.R.Stackpole	b Webb	10	b Collinge	27
I.R.Redpath	c Coney b Hadlee	19	c Howarth b Congdon	93
I.M.Chappell*	c Wadsworth b Webb	145	c Hadlee b Howarth	121
G.S.Chappell	not out	247	c Wadsworth b Collinge	133
I.C.Davis	c Wadsworth b Hadlee	16	c Wadsworth b Howarth	8
K.D.Walters	c Howarth b Collinge	32	c Morrison b Hadlee	8
R.W.Marsh†	lbw b Congdon	22	c Collinge b Congdon	17
K.J.O'Keeffe			c Howarth b Congdon	2
M.H.N.Walker			not out	22
A.A.Mallett			not out	4
G.Dymock				
Extras	(b 1, lb 4, nb 15)	20	(b 4, lb 4, w 1, nb 16)	25
TOTAL	(105.5 overs) (6 wkts dec)	**511**	(101 overs) (8 wkts)	**460**

NEW ZEALAND

Batsman	Dismissal	Runs
G.M.Turner	c Redpath b O'Keeffe	79
J.M.Parker	lbw b Walker	10
J.F.M.Morrison	b Walker	66
B.E.Congdon*	c Davis b Mallett	132
B.F.Hastings	c Chappell I.M. b Dymock	101
J.V.Coney	c Chappell G.S. b Walker	13
K.J.Wadsworth†	b Dymock	5
D.R.Hadlee	c Davis b O'Keeffe	9
R.O.Collinge	run out	2
H.J.Howarth	not out	29
M.G.Webb	c O'Keeffe b Dymock	12
Extras	(b 10, lb 5, nb 11)	26
TOTAL	(169 overs)	**484**

Bowling NEW ZEALAND	O	M	R	W	O	M	R	W
Webb	21	1	114	2	19	0	93	0
Collinge	24	3	103	1	19	3	60	2
Hadlee	27	7	107	2	21	2	106	1
Howarth	21	0	113	0	25	3	97	2
Congdon	12.5	0	54	1	13	1	60	3
Coney					2	0	13	0
Hastings					2	0	6	0
AUSTRALIA								
Walker	41	11	107	3				
Dymock	35	7	77	3				
Walters	8	1	39	0				
Mallett	41	8	117	1				
O'Keeffe	33	9	83	2				
Chappell G.S.	7	0	27	0				
Chappell I.M.	4	0	8	0				

Fall of Wickets	A 1st	NZ 1st	A 2nd
1st	13	28	67
2nd	55	136	208
3rd	319	169	294
4th	359	398	318
5th	431	409	359
6th	511	423	414
7th	-	423	433
8th	-	430	433
9th	-	437	-
10th	-	484	-

John Morrison plays a ball off his pads during his second wicket partnership of 108 with Glenn Turner. Keith Stackpole and Rodney Marsh are the Australian fieldsmen.

113 NEW ZEALAND v AUSTRALIA *(Second Test)*

at Lancaster Park, Christchurch on 8, 9, 10, 12, 13 March, 1974
Toss : New Zealand. Umpires : J.B.R. Hastie and R.L. Monteith
New Zealand won by 5 wickets

Drizzle delayed the start by more than two hours and, when the toss was made, Bevan Congdon, who won the toss for only the third time in 14 tests, sent Australia in. Keith Stackpole lasted only four runs before Richard Collinge bowled him, and the New Zealand bowlers remained in the ascendancy for the rest of the day.

The ball was moving in the air and off the pitch, and only the experienced Ian Redpath showed sufficient application and determination. He was 55 not out when Australia ended the day at 128-5.

Rod Marsh, with a bright 38, helped Redpath add 53 the next morning, but the New Zealand bowlers were not to be denied and Australia lost its last four wickets for the addition of 42. Redpath was out for 71. Richard Hadlee, Collinge and Congdon each took three wickets and they were supported by fielding and catching that was world-class.

New Zealand scored 59 in 88 minutes before the first wicket fell, that of John Parker lbw to Geoff Dymock for 18, but thereafter the side's chances seemed to rest squarely on Glenn Turner's shoulders. He was 99 not out and New Zealand 194-5 at stumps.

It took Turner almost half an hour to reach his century the next morning, his first test hundred in New Zealand, but he was out in the following over. The rest of the New Zealand batting contributed little and the side finished with 255, a lead of 32.

Australia began their second innings disastrously, losing Stackpole and the two Chappells with their lead just one run. Redpath again steadied the cause and, with Ian Davis, added 106 before he was out for 58. Davis, who went on to 50, and Doug Walters fought a rearguard action but when Walters was leg-before to Dayle Hadlee on the fourth morning, Australia had no answer left.

The Hadlees had taken four wickets each and Australia was all out for 259, leaving New Zealand 228 to get for an historic first victory and all but two days in which to do it.

A decisive partnership of 115 between Turner and Brian Hastings restored New Zealand's fortunes after they lost their first three wickets with the score at 62. The dismissal of Hastings in the last over added tension to the fifth day's prospects as Turner was 85 not out and New Zealand 177-4.

In due course Turner reached his second hundred of the game and New Zealand achieved their momentous victory. It had been an engrossing match. For once, New Zealand had bowled precisely as the conditions required and caught every snick, there were 12 in the two innings, and Turner had shown exceptional skill to lead the batting.

AUSTRALIA

K.R.Stackpole	b Collinge	4	c Wadsworth b Collinge	9
I.R.Redpath	c & b Collinge	71	c Howarth b Hadlee R.J.	58
I.M.Chappell*	b Hadlee R.J.	20	b Collinge	1
G.S.Chappell	c Howarth b Congdon	25	c Coney b Hadlee R.J.	6
I.C.Davis	lbw b Hadlee R.J.	5	c Congdon b Hadlee R.J.	50
K.D.Walters	b Hadlee R.J.	6	lbw b Hadlee D.R.	65
R.W.Marsh†	b Congdon	38	c & b Hadlee D.R.	4
K.J.O'Keeffe	c Wadsworth b Congdon	3	not out	23
M.H.N.Walker	not out	18	c Howarth b Hadlee D.R.	4
A.A.Mallett	b Collinge	1	(11) c Wadsworth b Hadlee R.J.	11
G.Dymock	c Congdon b Hadlee D.R.	13	(10) c Wadsworth b Hadlee D.R.	0
Extras	(b 1, lb 6, nb 12)	19	(b 16, lb 4, nb 8)	28
TOTAL	(58.2 overs)	223	(67.4 overs)	259

NEW ZEALAND

G.M.Turner	c Stackpole b Chappell G.S.	101	not out	110
J.M.Parker	lbw b Dymock	18	c Marsh b Walker	26
J.F.M.Morrison	c Marsh b Chappell G.S.	12	lbw b Walker	0
B.E.Congdon*	c Chappell I.M. b Walker	8	run out	2
B.F.Hastings	c Marsh b Walker	19	b Mallett	46
J.V.Coney	c Marsh b Dymock	15	c Marsh b Chappell G.S.	14
K.J.Wadsworth†	c Marsh b Mallett	24	not out	9
D.R.Hadlee	c Marsh b Dymock	11		
R.J.Hadlee	lbw b Walker	23		
H.J.Howarth	c Chappell I.M. b Walker	0		
R.O.Collinge	not out	1		
Extras	(b 4, lb 8, nb 11)	23	(b 4, lb 14, nb 5)	23
TOTAL	(73.6 overs)	255	(83.6 overs) (5 wkts)	230

Bowling	O	M	R	W	O	M	R	W
NEW ZEALAND								
Hadlee R.J.	14	2	59	3	18.4	3	71	4
Collinge	21	4	70	3	9	0	37	2
Hadlee D.R.	12.2	2	42	1	20	2	75	4
Congdon	11	2	33	3	9	3	26	0
Howarth					11	2	22	0
AUSTRALIA								
Walker	19.6	5	60	4	28	10	50	2
Dymock	24	6	59	3	25	5	84	0
Walters	7	1	34	0				
Chappell G.S.	20	2	76	2	17.6	5	38	1
Mallett	3	1	3	1	13	4	35	1

Fall of Wickets	A	NZ	A	NZ
	1st	1st	2nd	2nd
1st	8	59	12	51
2nd	45	90	26	55
3rd	101	104	33	62
4th	120	136	139	177
5th	128	171	142	206
6th	181	213	160	-
7th	190	220	232	-
8th	194	241	238	-
9th	196	242	239	-
10th	223	255	259	-

MILESTONES

- Glenn Turner became the first New Zealand batsman to score a century in each innings of a test.

- It was New Zealand's eighth test victory and their first over Australia.

Glenn Turner became the first New Zealand batsman to score a century in each innings of a test.

114 NEW ZEALAND v AUSTRALIA *(Third Test)*

at Eden Park, Auckland on 22, 23, 24 March, 1974
Toss : New Zealand. Umpires : D.E.A. Copps and W.R.C. Gardiner
Australia won by 297 runs

The Eden Park pitch had been unresponsive for bowlers in first-class matches during the season and an effort to inject some life by transplanting grass did not help — when Bevan Congdon pressed his thumb on to it, a clear imprint remained. The toss became crucial and when Congdon won it he immediately inserted his opponents.

Before a ball hit the pitch, however, Richard Hadlee dismissed Keith Stackpole, caught off a full toss with the first ball. Three more wickets fell to the rampant Richard Collinge by the time 37 was on the board and when Ian Chappell went, Australia were 64-5. Doug Walters and Rod Marsh combined in a blend of survival and aggression, adding 86 in 74 minutes, before Collinge dismissed Marsh for his fifth wicket of the day.

Walters' century in such adverse conditions was beyond belief as the ball exploded from a good length, a condition that Congdon's slower paced deliveries exploited to maximum effect in claiming four wickets.

New Zealand's reply, Glenn Turner apart, was identical to Australia's as batsmen struggled to come to terms with the cantankerous pitch. By stumps New Zealand had lost eight batsmen for 85 runs; 18 wickets had fallen for 306 runs on a pitch that Ian Chappell tersely labelled as "bloody awful".

The New Zealand innings finished at 112, a deficit of 109 runs, early on the second day. Stackpole completed a pair for the match but Redpath and Ian Chappell ensured that their side would not capitulate so quickly with a careful partnership of 67 for the second wicket.

Greg Chappell replaced his brother and he dominated the next 49 runs, scoring 38 of them. Thus emerged the pattern of the innings, with Redpath remaining steadfast at one end while a succession of partners came and went. Redpath's century was achieved in 225 minutes and he was 150 not out at stumps with Australia 330-9.

Within 23 minutes Collinge terminated Australia's second innings, claiming his fourth wicket, and his ninth for the match, while Redpath remained unbeaten. With the playing time of the match not having reached the halfway stage New Zealand needed 456 runs for victory.

New Zealand made a valiant start with 77 by lunch and another 30 before the first wicket fell, John Parker for 34. John Morrison went in the same over and in the next 43 minutes another four wickets fell for 20 runs as Max Walker and Gary Gilmour ripped the heart out of the local side.

When Turner was caught by Ian Chappell off Walker the game was as good as over. For the fourth consecutive innings Turner scored the bulk of New Zealand's runs.

MILESTONES

- Ian Redpath became the seventh Australian to bat through a test innings and the first player to do so in New Zealand.

AUSTRALIA

K.R.Stackpole	c Parker b Hadlee R.J.	0	c Congdon b Collinge	0
I.R.Redpath	c Wadsworth b Collinge	13	not out	159
I.M.Chappell*	c Turner b Collinge	37	lbw b Collinge	35
G.S.Chappell	c Howarth b Collinge	0	c Wadsworth b Howarth	38
I.C.Davis	c Hastings b Collinge	0	c Parker b Howarth	5
K.D.Walters	not out	104	c Parker b Congdon	5
R.W.Marsh†	c Hastings b Collinge	45	c Hadlee R.J. b Howarth	47
K.J.O'Keeffe	c Morrison b Congdon	0	c Burgess b Collinge	32
G.J.Gilmour	c Morrison b Congdon	1	b Hadlee R.J.	4
M.H.N.Walker	c Burgess b Congdon	7	b Hadlee R.J.	0
A.A.Mallett	c Turner b Congdon	7	c Parker b Collinge	6
Extras	(b 4, lb 1, nb 2)	7	(b 4, lb 4, w 1, nb 6)	15
TOTAL	(46.2 overs)	**221**	(79.4 overs)	**346**

NEW ZEALAND

G.M.Turner	c Chappell G.S. b Mallett	41	c Chappell I.M. b Walker	72
J.M.Parker	lbw b Gilmour	11	c Marsh b Gilmour	34
J.F.M.Morrison	c Marsh b Walker	9	c Marsh b Gilmour	0
B.E.Congdon*	lbw b Gilmour	4	c Marsh b Walker	4
B.F.Hastings	b Gilmour	0	lbw b Walker	1
M.G.Burgess	c Marsh b Gilmour	7	c Stackpole b Walker	6
K.J.Wadsworth†	c Marsh b Gilmour	0	c Chappell G.S. b Mallett	21
H.J.Howarth	c Gilmour b Mallett	0	(10) not out	3
D.R.Hadlee	b Mallett	4	(8) c Walters b Mallett	4
R.J.Hadlee	c Chappell I.M. b Mallett	13	(9) b Hadlee R.J.	1
R.O.Collinge	not out	8	c Chappell I.M. b O'Keeffe	4
Extras	(b 4, lb 4, nb 10)	15	(b 3, lb 2, nb 3)	8
TOTAL	(30.2 overs)	**112**	(53 overs)	**158**

Bowling	O	M	R	W	O	M	R	W
NEW ZEALAND								
Hadlee R.J.	9	1	45	1	9	1	50	2
Collinge	18	4	82	5	16.4	0	84	4
Hadlee D.R.	9	0	41	0	7	0	48	0
Congdon	10.2	0	46	4	19	1	66	1
Howarth					28	5	83	3
AUSTRALIA								
Walker	10	4	11	1	19	8	39	4
Gilmour	15	3	64	5	16	0	52	2
Mallett	5.2	0	22	4	13	6	51	2
O'Keeffe					5	1	8	2

Fall of Wickets

	A 1st	NZ 1st	A 2nd	NZ 2nd
1st	0	16	2	107
2nd	32	28	69	107
3rd	37	34	118	112
4th	37	40	132	115
5th	64	62	143	116
6th	150	62	230	127
7th	154	63	315	145
8th	162	72	330	147
9th	191	102	330	147
10th	221	112	346	158

By the time Australia had reached 64 in their first innings five wickets had fallen, four to the strong left-arm fast bowling of Richard Collinge. At the end of the test he had his best match analysis of 9-166.

AVERAGES

New Zealand

BATTING	M	I	NO	Runs	HS	Ave
G.M. Turner	3	5	1	403	110*	100.75
B.F. Hastings	3	5	0	167	101	33.40
B.E. Congdon	3	5	0	150	132	30.00
J.M. Parker	3	5	0	99	34	19.80
J.F.M. Morrison	3	5	0	87	66	17.40
H.J. Howarth	3	4	2	32	29*	16.00
K.J. Wadsworth	3	5	1	59	24	14.75
J.V. Coney	2	3	0	42	15	14.00
R.J. Hadlee	2	3	0	37	23	12.33
M.G. Webb	1	1	0	12	12	12.00
R.O. Collinge	3	4	2	15	8*	7.50
D.R. Hadlee	3	4	0	28	11	7.00
M.G. Burgess	1	2	0	13	7	6.50

BOWLING	O	M	R	W	Ave
R.J. Hadlee	50.4	7	225	10	22.50
B.E. Congdon	74.6	7	285	12	23.75
R.O. Collinge	107.4	14	436	17	25.64
D.R. Hadlee	106.2	13	419	8	52.37
H.J. Howarth	85	10	315	5	63.00
M.G. Webb	40	1	207	2	103.50
B.F. Hastings	2	0	6	0	-
J.V. Coney	2	0	13	0	-

Australia

BATTING	M	I	NO	Runs	HS	Ave
G.S. Chappell	3	6	1	449	247*	89.80
I.R. Redpath	3	6	1	413	159*	82.60
I.M. Chappell	3	6	0	359	145	59.83
K.D. Walters	3	6	1	220	104*	44.00
R.W. Marsh	3	6	0	173	47	28.83
M.H.N. Walker	3	5	2	51	22*	17.00
K.J. O'Keeffe	3	5	1	60	32	15.00
I.C. Davis	3	6	0	84	50	14.00
K.R. Stackpole	3	6	0	50	27	8.33
A.A. Mallett	3	5	1	29	11	7.25
G. Dymock	2	2	0	13	13	6.50
G.J. Gilmour	1	2	0	5	4	2.50

BOWLING	O	M	R	W	Ave
G.J. Gilmour	31	3	116	7	16.57
M.H.N. Walker	117.6	38	267	14	19.07
K.J. O'Keeffe	38	10	91	4	22.75
A.A. Mallett	75.2	19	228	9	25.33
G. Dymock	84	18	220	6	36.66
G.S. Chappell	48.6	7	141	3	47.00
I.M. Chappell	4	0	8	0	-
K.D. Walters	15	2	73	0	-

New Zealand enjoyed their first test victory over Australia at Lancaster Park. Back row (left to right): Hedley Howarth, Richard Hadlee, Jeremy Coney, Richard Collinge, Barry Hadlee (12th man), John Morrison, John Parker. Front row: Ken Deas (manager), Ken Wadsworth, Bevan Congdon (captain), Glenn Turner, Dayle Hadlee, Brian Hastings.

1974/75 MCC in New Zealand

England had been subjected to some fearsome fast bowling by Dennis Lillee and Jeff Thomson on their tour of Australia and had lost the Ashes 4-1. With improved air transport, questions were being raised as to the value of tours to New Zealand being just an adjunct of tours to Australia.

115 NEW ZEALAND v ENGLAND (First Test)

at Eden Park, Auckland on 20, 21, 22, 23, 25 February, 1975
Toss : England. Umpires : D.E.A. Copps and W.R.C. Gardiner
England won by an innings and 83 runs

The pitch looked ideal for batting but it was Dayle Hadlee who made his presence felt when he had both openers back in the dressing room for 36. Only one further wicket was to fall that day when Hedley Howarth dismissed John Edrich for 64 when the score was 153.

Ewen Chatfield's first three overs in test cricket conceded 29 runs and the England captain, Mike Denness, used these quick runs as a platform on which to build a substantial innings and reach his hundred in 217 minutes. His partner at stumps was Keith Fletcher and the score was 319-3.

The partnership added a further 100 runs on the second day before Denness was out for 181, with the pair adding 266. Fletcher continued to flourish, adding 78 with Tony Greig and 81 with Alan Knott, before he was out for 214 made in 443 minutes. Denness declared at 593-6. Glenn Turner was out in Geoff Arnold's first over but New Zealand survived until stumps without further loss.

John Morrison and John Parker advanced their partnership to 116 until after lunch on the third day when Greig captured the first of his ten wickets in the match by dismissing Morrison. Three more wickets fell cheaply before Ken Wadsworth joined Parker in arresting the decline. After six hours of honest endeavour Parker reached his century as they took the score from 173-5 to 285 at stumps.

Parker was dismissed to the third ball next day and when Wadsworth followed soon after, the rest of the innings collapsed and New Zealand, with 326, had to follow on. For the second time in the game Morrison shored up one end as batsmen came and went.

After Morrison scored his second 58 of the match the only other resistance came from Geoff Howarth who was still in at stumps, with New Zealand 161-9. Greig had taken another five wickets with his mixture of fast-medium pacers and off-spinners.

Howarth and Chatfield added another 23 in 47 minutes, with Howarth reaching 51. The game came to a sickening and sudden end as Chatfield played a bouncer from Peter Lever onto his head and was knocked unconscious. Chatfield's heart stopped beating for several seconds but quick action by the MCC physiotherapist, Bernard Thomas, and a St. John

Ambulance brigade officer averted tragedy.

Comment on the outcome of the test concentrated almost exclusively on the manner in which it finished rather than any examination of New Zealand's failures.

ENGLAND		
D.L.Amiss	c Wadsworth b Hadlee	19
B.Wood	c Parker b Hadlee	0
J.H.Edrich	c Congdon b Howarth H.J.	64
M.H.Denness*	c Parker b Congdon	181
K.W.R.Fletcher	c Hadlee b Congdon	216
A.W.Greig	b Howarth G.P.	51
A.P.E.Knott†	not out	29
C.M.Old	not out	9
D.L.Underwood		
G.G.Arnold		
P.Lever		
Extras	(b 2, lb 14, nb 8)	24
TOTAL	(153 overs) (6 wkts dec)	**593**

NEW ZEALAND					
J.F.M.Morrison	c Amiss b Greig	58	c Fletcher b Greig	58
G.M.Turner	c Amiss b Arnold	8	c Knott b Lever	2
J.M.Parker	c Knott b Underwood	121	(5) c Edrich b Greig	13
B.E.Congdon*	c Old b Greig	2	(3) b Underwood	18
B.F.Hastings	c Knott b Old	13	(4) c Amiss b Lever	0
G.P.Howarth	c Wood b Greig	6	not out	51
K.J.Wadsworth†	lbw b Underwood	58	c Fletcher b Underwood	6
D.R.Hadlee	c sub (B.W.Luckhurst) b Underwood	22	c Edrich b Greig	1
H.J.Howarth	c Fletcher b Greig	9	b Greig	4
R.O.Collinge	not out	0	c Fletcher b Greig	0
E.J.Chatfield	c Fletcher b Greig	0	retired hurt	13
Extras	(b 5, lb 4, nb 20)	29	(lb 6, nb 12)	18
TOTAL	(89 overs)	**326**	(57.5 overs)	**184**

Bowling	O	M	R	W	O	M	R	W
NEW ZEALAND								
Collinge	24	6	75	0				
Hadlee	20	2	102	2				
Chatfield	19	2	95	0				
Congdon	30	3	115	2				
Howarth H.J.	46	9	135	1				
Howarth G.P.	14	1	47	1				
ENGLAND								
Arnold	20	4	69	1	6	1	31	0
Lever	20	4	75	0	11.5	0	37	2
Greig	26	4	98	5	15	3	51	5
Underwood	16	6	38	3	25	9	47	2
Old	7	3	17	1				

Fall of Wickets	E 1st	NZ 1st	NZ 2nd
1st	4	9	3
2nd	36	125	42
3rd	153	131	46
4th	419	166	99
5th	497	173	102
6th	578	285	131
7th	-	315	134
8th	-	326	140
9th	-	326	140
10th	-	326	-

The test ended in dramatic fashion when Ewen Chatfield deflected a bouncer from England pace bowler Peter Lever onto his head. Chatfield's heart stopped beating and it was only the quick intervention of England's physiotherapist, Bernard Thomas, that averted tragedy. Recognisable, from left, are Dennis Amiss, umpire Ralph Gardiner and Barry Wood. Tony Greig gesticulates for medical assistance.

MILESTONES

- Ewen Chatfield (131) and Geoff Howarth (132) made their test debuts.

- Mike Denness and Keith Fletcher established a record partnership of 266 for the fourth wicket for England against New Zealand.

- England's total of 593 was the highest made against New Zealand.

116 NEW ZEALAND v ENGLAND *(Second Test)*

at Lancaster Park, Christchurch on 28 February, 1, 2, 3, 4, 5 March, 1975
Toss : England. Umpires : D.E.A. Copps amd W.R.C. Gardiner
Match drawn

Heavy rain prevented any play on the first two scheduled days and the New Zealand and England authorities agreed to eliminate the rest day and play the test over four days.

The toss became of vital importance and Mike Denness did not have to think twice when he won it. Geoff Arnold, bowling in conditions ideally suited to him, removed Morrison first ball, and Glenn Turner and Bevan Congdon were required to muster a desperate defence. The quick loss of Brian Hastings, after Congdon was caught in the gully, brought John Parker to the wicket before bad light brought an early end to play.

Turner and Parker continued through to 181 the next day in better conditions, although the England bowlers maintained an agonisingly slow over-rate of about 10 overs an hour. Shortly after lunch Turner's vigil ended when he was out leg-before to Arnold for 98. The spectators did not appreciate Arnold's extravagant genuflections of thanks to the umpire when the decision went his way. Ken Wadsworth, Dayle Hadlee and Lance Cairns all contributed before the innings closed at 342.

Dennis Amiss and Barry Wood made 57 before stumps and another 23 the next morning before Wood fell to Hadlee. The rest of the day belonged to Amiss as he went to lunch at 80 and tea at 148, his century having arrived in 247 minutes. Bad light stopped play more than an hour early and a return of rain ruled out any further play in the match.

NEW ZEALAND

J.F.M.Morrison	c Hendrick b Arnold	0
G.M.Turner	lbw b Arnold	98
B.E.Congdon*	c Wood b Hendrick	38
B.F.Hastings	c Wood b Lever	0
J.M.Parker	c Edrich b Greig	41
G.P.Howarth	b Underwood	11
K.J.Wadsworth†	c Lever b Greig	58
D.R.Hadlee	c Greig b Arnold	22
B.L.Cairns	c & b Hendrick	39
H.J.Howarth	lbw b Underwood	9
R.O.Collinge	not out	0
Extras	(b 3, lb 9, w 1, nb 13)	26
TOTAL	**(89.5 overs)**	**342**

ENGLAND

D.L.Amiss	not out	164
B.Wood	c Wadsworth b Hadlee	33
J.H.Edrich	c Hadlee b Howarth H.J.	11
M.H.Denness*	not out	59
K.W.R.Fletcher		
A.W.Greig		
A.P.E.Knott†		
D.L.Underwood		
G.G.Arnold		
P.Lever		
M.Hendrick		
Extras	(lb 3, nb 2)	5
TOTAL	**(83 overs) (2 wkts)**	**272**

Bowling	O	M	R	W	O	M	R	W
ENGLAND								
Arnold	25	5	80	3				
Lever	18	2	66	1				
Hendrick	20	2	89	2				
Underwood	13.5	3	35	2				
Greig	9	1	27	2				
Wood	4	0	19	0				
NEW ZEALAND								
Collinge	19	3	63	0				
Hadlee	19	2	61	1				
Cairns	13	5	44	0				
Congdon	7	2	27	0				
Howarth H.J.	18	5	53	1				
Howarth G.P.	7	0	19	0				

Fall of Wickets

	NZ	E
	1st	*1st*
1st	0	80
2nd	64	121
3rd	66	-
4th	181	-
5th	208	-
6th	212	-
7th	267	-
8th	318	-
9th	338	-
10th	342	-

John Parker shared a fourth wicket partnership of 115 with Glenn Turner. The England captain, Mike Denness, is the fieldsman.

1975/76 India in New Zealand

The Indian team, led by Bishan Bedi, arrived in New Zealand in January for three tests before heading to the West Indies for four more. Unseasonal rain swept the country and played havoc with all cricket. Glenn Turner was appointed to lead the New Zealand side although Bevan Congdon would continue to play.

117 NEW ZEALAND v INDIA *(First Test)*

at Eden Park, Auckland on 24, 25, 26, 28 January, 1976
Toss : New Zealand. Umpires : D.E.A. Copps and R.L. Monteith
India won by 8 wickets

On a pitch described as "rolled-out porridge" the Indian opening bowlers had nine overs and did not bowl again in the innings. Sunil Gavaskar, standing in for Bedi who had injured a calf muscle, kept the pressure on John Morrison and Congdon by continually switching his spinners around and setting tight, attacking fields. Congdon's patience snapped and he was caught at long-on for 54.

The innings then went into decline and 110-1 became 155-5 before Mark Burgess, Ken Wadsworth and Dayle Hadlee had mini-partnerships which carried the score to 263. Bhagwat Chandrasekhar, bowling his right-arm leg-spinners, hit a purple patch and took three wickets as the last four fell for three runs.

New Zealand had an early breakthrough on the second day but, thereafter, most of the day went India's way and the few chances New Zealand had were not accepted. Gavaskar was dropped three times and Surinder Amarnath twice. To add to New Zealand's mortification, two promising run-out chances went begging. Not surprisingly, Gavaskar and Amarnath both made hundreds as they added 204, with Amarnath's being on his test debut.

The momentum stayed with India on the third day as Mohinder Amarnath and Madan Lal were untroubled to add 93 for the seventh wicket. The tailenders all contributed to take their team's score to 414. Congdon again showed his liking for Eden Park by taking all four wickets to fall that day, to end with 5-65, his best test return.

The subtle flowing off-spin of Erapalli Prasanna had accounted for both openers by the time the score had reached 39. Congdon and John Parker showed sensible application, adding 122 by stumps when the score was 161-2.

Parker was dismissed in the first over of the fourth day and his dismissal was effectively the end of New Zealand's fight. The remaining batsmen seemed totally flummoxed by Prasanna's flight and guile and Gavaskar's attacking fields. The last eight wickets tumbled for 54 runs with Prasanna returning 8-76. India was untroubled to score the 68 they needed for victory.

NEW ZEALAND

J.F.M.Morrison	c & b Chandrasekhar	46	c Viswanath b Prasanna		23
G.M.Turner*	c Gavaskar b Chandrasekhar	23	c Madan Lal b Prasanna		13
B.E.Congdon	c Madan Lal b Prasanna	54	c Gavaskar b Prasanna		54
J.M.Parker	b Chandrasekhar	17	c Vengsarkar b Prasanna		70
B.F.Hastings	lbw b Prasanna	8	b Prasanna		1
M.G.Burgess	c Prasanna b Venkataraghavan	31	lbw b Chandrasekhar		6
K.J.Wadsworth†	c Gavaskar b Prasanna	41	b Chandrasekhar		19
D.R.Hadlee	b Chandrasekhar	24	c Vengsarkar b Prasanna		0
D.R.O'Sullivan	c Amarnath S. b Chandrasekhar	0	c Amarnath S. b Prasanna		1
H.J.Howarth	c & b Chandrasekhar	0	(11) not out		1
R.O.Collinge	not out	3	(10) c Amarnath S. b Prasanna		13
Extras	(b 5, lb 12, nb 2)	19	(b 4, lb 8, nb 2)		14
TOTAL	(87 overs)	**266**	(70.2 overs)		**215**

INDIA

S.M.Gavaskar*	c Turner b Howarth	116	not out	35
D.B.Vengsarkar	lbw b Collinge	7	c Turner b Howarth	6
S.Amarnath	c sub (G.N.Edwards)) b Hadlee	124	lbw b Howarth	9
G.R.Viswanath	c Wadsworth b Hadlee	0	not out	11
B.P.Patel	c Morrison b Congdon	10		
S.Venkataraghavan	c Congdon b Howarth	1		
M.Amarnath	b Congdon	64		
Madan Lal	c Turner b Congdon	27		
S.M.H.Kirmani†	b Congdon	14		
E.A.S.Prasanna	not out	25		
B.S.Chandrasekhar	b Congdon	0		
Extras	(b 13, lb 9, nb 4)	26	(b 7, nb 3)	10
TOTAL	(121.7 overs)	**414**	(14.2 overs) (2 wkts)	**71**

Bowling	O	M	R	W	O	M	R	W
INDIA								
Madan Lal	5	0	14	0	4	4	0	0
Amarnath M.	4	1	16	0	2	0	8	0
Chandrasekhar	30	6	94	6	22.2	2	85	2
Venkataraghavan	24	4	59	1	19	8	32	0
Prasanna	24	5	64	3	23	5	76	8
NEW ZEALAND								
Collinge	19	3	61	1	2	0	14	0
Hadlee	18	3	71	2	3	0	15	0
Congdon	26.7	3	65	5				
Howarth	29	6	97	2	5.2	3	15	2
O'Sullivan	29	4	94	0	4	1	17	0

Fall of Wickets	NZ	I	NZ	I
	1st	1st	2nd	2nd
1st	38	16	32	38
2nd	110	220	39	56
3rd	144	220	161	-
4th	145	270	169	-
5th	155	270	180	-
6th	211	275	180	-
7th	263	368	180	-
8th	263	369	182	-
9th	263	414	214	-
10th	266	414	215	-

After a disastrous morning session, where catches were dropped with gay abandon, Bevan Congdon caught Venkataraghavan in the gully. From left, umpire Bob Monteith, Hedley Howarth, the bowler, Surinder Amarnath, John Parker, Congdon, Richard Collinge, Venkataraghavan, Glenn Turner, Ken Wadsworth and John Morrison.

MILESTONES

- Glenn Turner was appointed the New Zealand captain.

- Surinder Amarnath scored a test century on debut, a feat his father, Lala, had also accomplished, against England, in 1933/34.

- Sunil Gavaskar and Surinder Amarnath established a new second wicket record partnership of 204 for India against New Zealand.

- Bevan Congdon became the second New Zealander to score over 3000 runs in test cricket.

- Erapalli Prasanna's 8-76 were the best bowling figures in a test at Eden Park.

118 NEW ZEALAND v INDIA *(Second Test)*

at Lancaster Park, Christchurch on 5, 6, 7, 8, 9, 10 February, 1976
Toss : India. Umpires : D.E.A. Copps and W.R.C. Gardiner
Match drawn

Richard Collinge bowled with fire and enthusiasm in the opening overs but the Indian openers, Sunil Gavaskar and the 20-year-old Dilip Vengsakar, responded in like mind and appeared unwilling to ease their way cautiously into the match. Collinge used his height to extract steepling lift and, when he found the correct line, he found the edge of the bat and had all four wickets to fall by lunch, with India on 98.

The diminutive right-handed batsman Gundappa Viswanath and Mohinder Amarnath restored order to the Indian batting. Viswanath was severe on Richard Hadlee's short length, with powerful cuts, forward and backward of point. Dayle Hadlee broke the partnership when it had doubled the score, and he claimed another two wickets as India tottered at 206-8.

Bishan Bedi and Syed Kirmani, both displaying inventive and improvised batting techniques, added a rollicking 52. Their enterprise allowed India to reach 270. Collinge ended the innings with his best test figures of 6-63.

Glenn Turner and John Morrison batted with extreme caution and diligence, putting on 56 before Morrison was dismissed. Bevan Congdon and Turner continued to solidify the home team's position, adding 114 for the second wicket. Turner completed his third test century in four test innings at Lancaster Park (the fourth had yielded 98 against England).

Rain ended the day 36 minutes early and washed out any play on the Saturday. Agreement was reached to use the rest day as a playing day. Play began on the Sunday and there were frequent stops for more sawdust to absorb the worst of the surface water. New Zealand added another 144 runs.

Rain continued to interrupt the fifth day, during which Richard Hadlee and Hedley Howarth added 42 for the last wicket while Kirmani ended with six dismissals in the New

Zealand innings of 403, a lead of 133.

It was apparent that an early breakthrough was needed for New Zealand to win. Gavaskar and, later, his brother-in-law, Viswanath, proved to be efficacious spoilers with 71 and 79 respectively. Rain had the final say when India was 255-6, and the match was drawn.

INDIA					
S.M.Gavaskar	c Burgess b Collinge	22	c Howarth b Hadlee D.R.		71
D.B.Vengsarkar	c Wadsworth b Collinge	16	c Wadsworth b Hadlee R.J.		30
S.Amarnath	b Collinge	11	c Wadsworth b Collinge		21
G.R.Viswanath	c Turner b Hadlee D.R.	83	c Wadsworth b Roberts		79
B.P.Patel	c Burgess b Collinge	8	c Morrison b Parker		7
M.Amarnath	lbw b Congdon	45	c Wadsworth b Howarth		30
Madan Lal	c Wadsworth b Hadlee D.R.	5	not out		4
S.M.H.Kirmani†	lbw b Collinge	27	not out		1
E.A.S.Prasanna	c Roberts b Hadlee D.R.	1			
B.S.Bedi*	c Howarth b Collinge	30			
B.S.Chandrasekhar	not out	2			
Extras	(b 6, lb 4, nb 10)	20	(b 2, lb 3, w 1, nb 6)		12
TOTAL	(60.6 overs)	270	(79 overs) (6 wkts)		255

NEW ZEALAND		
J.F.M.Morrison	lbw b Madan Lal	31
G.M.Turner*	c Kirmani b Amarnath M.	117
B.E.Congdon	st Kirmani b Bedi	58
J.M.Parker	c Bedi b Amarnath M.	44
M.G.Burgess	c & b Madan Lal	31
A.D.G.Roberts	lbw b Madan Lal	17
K.J.Wadsworth†	c Kirmani b Madan Lal	29
D.R.Hadlee	c Kirmani b Madan Lal	10
R.J.Hadlee	c Kirmani b Amarnath M.	33
R.O.Collinge	c Kirmani b Amarnath M.	0
H.J.Howarth	not out	8
Extras	(b 8, lb 14, nb 3)	25
TOTAL	(132.1 overs)	403

Bowling	O	M	R	W	O	M	R	W	Fall of Wickets			
NEW ZEALAND										I	NZ	I
										1st	1st	2nd
Collinge	16.6	0	63	6	14	1	36	1	1st	32	56	60
Hadlee R.J.	12	1	75	0	14	2	64	1	2nd	41	170	97
Hadlee D.R.	16	0	76	3	12	1	52	1	3rd	52	254	138
Congdon	16	3	36	1	5	2	5	0	4th	98	260	175
Howarth					22	7	48	1	5th	196	293	250
Parker					5	2	24	1	6th	204	325	250
Roberts					5	1	12	1	7th	204	347	-
Burgess					2	1	2	0	8th	206	360	-
INDIA									9th	258	361	-
Madan Lal	43	9	134	5					10th	270	403	-
Amarnath M.	25.1	5	63	4								
Chandrasekhar	15	2	60	0								
Bedi	33	7	59	1								
Prasanna	16	1	62	0								

With the second test destined for a draw, Glenn Turner provided a touch of humour by threatening to trample on one of the Indian batsmen who had dived to make his ground. Mark Burgess and Ken Wadsworth are amused bystanders.

MILESTONES

- Andy Roberts (133) made his test debut.

- Syed Kirmani equalled the world test record of six dismissals in an innings. He joined Wally Grout (Australia), John Murray (England) and Denis Lindsay (South Africa).

119 NEW ZEALAND v INDIA *(Third Test)*

at Wellington on 13, 14, 15, 17 February, 1976
Toss : India. Umpires : W.R.C. Gardiner and R.L. Monteith
New Zealand won by an innings and 33 runs

Richard Hadlee who had bowled indifferently throughout the season was surprisingly preferred to Hedley Howarth and, with Lance Cairns also included, New Zealand went into the deciding test with an all-seam attack. As there were weather interruptions for each of the first three days India had to be wondering if the sun ever shone in New Zealand.

Sunil Gavaskar and Dilip Vengsakar were untroubled to take the score through to 40 when a double bowling change saw fortunes also change, radically. In the space of 10 runs the Hadlee brothers picked up four wickets. After lunch a fifth wicket fell with the total at 92 and India was heading for disaster.

Brijesh Patel began his innings by playing and missing and Syed Kirmani looked decidedly uncomfortable against the quick attack. Kirmani seemed to take heart from a dropped catch when he was three, and he and Patel, now playing with rare panache in very cold conditions, went on to add 116 runs. When Patel was out for 81 India's fight was over. They lost their last four wickets for three runs; 220 all out.

A cold southerly wind had all the players wearing numerous jerseys as Glenn Turner and John Morrison played cautiously, adding 55 against their opponent's mixed use of pace and spin. When Bevan Congdon replaced Morrison he was more enterprising and reached another half-century, his fourth in four innings, only to lose his wicket two runs later.

Turner, who had been in control without being dominant for his 64, was enticed out of his ground and was stumped. With John Parker and Andy Roberts out cheaply New Zealand ended the shortened day at 170-5.

Mark Burgess and Lance Cairns were complete opposites together on the third day; Burgess the gifted and elegant stroke-maker; Cairns the journeyman who used the bat like a club. Both were effective as they added a vital 90 in two hours.

India had three captains in the space of one hour as Bishan Bedi was hospitalised with tonsillitis and he was soon joined by his replacement, Gavaskar, with a broken cheekbone when he was struck by a ball from Cairns' bat. Erapalli Prasanna took over the leadership for the rest of an innings that saw Burgess end with 95 and New Zealand enjoy a comfortable lead of 114.

In glorious conditions India had a slow uphill battle early in its second innings and, later, a rapid downhill slide. Richard Hadlee began the decline with the last ball before lunch when he had Viswanath brilliantly caught at gully by Congdon.

With Gavaskar unable to bat, the resulting debacle saw six wickets fall for 19 runs in 46 minutes, giving New Zealand victory by 33 runs and squaring the series. Richard Hadlee captured 7-23 and marked his arrival as an exceptional test player.

INDIA

S.M.Gavaskar	c Wadsworth b Hadlee R.J.	22	absent hurt		
D.B.Vengsarkar	c Wadsworth b Hadlee R.J.	20	(1) c Turner b Collinge		4
S.Amarnath	c Roberts b Hadlee R.J.	2	(2) c Burgess b Hadlee R.J.		27
G.R.Viswanath	c Turner b Hadlee D.R.	4	(3) c Congdon b Hadlee R.J.		20
B.P.Patel	c Congdon b Cairns	81	(4) c Wadsworth b Hadlee R.J.		3
M.Amarnath	lbw b Collinge	26	(5) c Roberts b Hadlee D.R.		13
Madan Lal	b Hadlee D.R.	3	not out		2
S.M.H.Kirmani†	c Wadsworth b Hadlee R.J.	49	(6) c Burgess b Hadlee R.J.		1
E.A.S.Prasanna	not out	0	(8) b Hadlee R.J.		0
B.S.Bedi*	run out	2	(9) b Hadlee R.J.		2
B.S.Chandrasekhar	b Cairns	0	(10) b Hadlee R.J.		0
Extras	(lb 8, nb 3)	11	(b 5, lb 2, nb 2)		9
TOTAL	**(73.7 overs)**	**220**	**(26.3 overs)**		**81**

NEW ZEALAND

G.M.Turner*	st Kirmani b Bedi	64
J.F.M.Morrison	c Kirmani b Madan Lal	12
B.E.Congdon	c Viswanath b Chandrasekhar	52
J.M.Parker	c Gavaskar b Bedi	5
M.G.Burgess	lbw b Madan Lal	95
A.D.G.Roberts	c Kirmani b Chandrasekhar	0
K.J.Wadsworth†	c Gavaskar b Bedi	10
B.L.Cairns	c sub (E.D.Solkar) b Amarnath M.	47
R.J.Hadlee	c Prasanna b Madan Lal	12
D.R.Hadlee	c Kirmani b Chandrasekhar	13
R.O.Collinge	not out	5
Extras	(lb 15, nb 4)	19
TOTAL	**(113.7 overs)**	**334**

Bowling	O	M	R	W	O	M	R	W		Fall of Wickets			
NEW ZEALAND											I	NZ	I
Collinge	12	1	33	1	5	0	21	1			1st	1st	2nd
Cairns	20.7	2	57	2	4	1	9	0		1st	40	55	10
Hadlee D.R.	18	1	51	2	9	2	19	1		2nd	46	103	46
Hadlee R.J.	14	1	35	4	8.3	0	23	7		3rd	47	117	62
Congdon	9	1	33	0						4th	50	155	75
INDIA										5th	92	155	77
Amarnath M.	18.2	2	60	1						6th	101	180	77
Madan Lal	38	4	116	3						7th	217	270	77
Bedi	27	6	63	3						8th	218	301	79
Chandrasekhar	22.5	2	55	3						9th	220	324	81
Prasanna	8	2	21	0						10th	220	334	-

MILESTONES

- It was New Zealand's ninth test win and the first by an innings.

- Richard Hadlee's figures of 7-23 in the second innings and his match analysis of 11-58 were both New Zealand test records.

AVERAGES

New Zealand

BATTING	M	I	NO	Runs	HS	Ave
B.E. Congdon	3	4	0	218	58	54.50
G.M. Turner	3	4	0	217	117	54.25
B.L. Cairns	1	1	0	47	47	47.00
M.G. Burgess	3	4	0	163	95	40.75
J.M. Parker	3	4	0	136	70	34.00
J.F.M. Morrison	3	4	0	112	46	28.00
K.J. Wadsworth	3	4	0	99	41	24.75
R.J. Hadlee	2	2	0	45	33	22.50
D.R. Hadlee	3	4	0	47	24	11.75
R.O. Collinge	3	4	2	21	13	10.50
H.J. Howarth	2	3	2	9	8*	9.00
A.D.G. Roberts	2	2	0	17	17	8.50
B.F. Hastings	1	2	0	9	8	4.50
D.R. O'Sullivan	1	2	0	1	1	0.50

BOWLING	O	M	R	W	Ave
A.D.G. Roberts	5	1	12	1	12.00
R.J. Hadlee	48.3	4	197	12	16.41
R.O. Collinge	68.6	5	228	10	22.80
B.E. Congdon	56	9	139	6	23.16
J.M. Parker	5	2	24	1	24.00
D.R. Hadlee	76	7	284	9	31.55
H.J. Howarth	56.3	16	160	5	32.00
B.L. Cairns	24.7	3	66	2	33.00
M.G. Burgess	2	1	2	0	-
D.R. O'Sullivan	33	5	111	0	-

India

BATTING	M	I	NO	Runs	HS	Ave
S.M. Gavaskar	3	5	1	266	116	66.50
G.R. Viswanath	3	6	1	197	83	39.40
M. Amarnath	3	5	0	178	64	35.60
S. Amarnath	3	6	0	194	124	32.33
S.M.H. Kirmani	3	5	1	92	49	23.00
B.P. Patel	3	5	0	109	81	21.80
D.B. Vengsarkar	3	6	0	83	30	13.83
Madan Lal	3	5	2	41	27	13.66
E.A.S. Prasanna	3	4	2	26	25*	13.00
B.S. Bedi	2	3	0	34	30	11.33
S. Venkataraghavan	1	1	0	1	1	1.00
B.S. Chandrasekhar	3	4	1	2	2*	0.66

BOWLING	O	M	R	W	Ave
E.A.S. Prasanna	71	13	223	11	20.27
B.S. Chandrasekhar	89.7	12	294	11	26.72
M. Amarnath	49.3	8	147	5	29.40
B.S. Bedi	60	13	122	4	30.50
Madan Lal	90	17	264	8	33.00
S. Venkataraghavan	43	12	91	1	91.00

Richard Hadlee had a New Zealand record match analysis of 11-58 in the third test. He leads the team off. From left, Mark Burgess, Bhagwat Chandrasekhar, John Parker, Andy Roberts, Richard Hadlee, Dayle Hadlee, Bevan Congdon, Richard Collinge, Ken Wadsworth, Glenn Turner (captain) and John Morrison.

1976/77 New Zealand in Pakistan and India

Bevan Congdon, Hedley Howarth and Dayle Hadlee were unavailable to tour and Brian Hastings announced his retirement from international cricket. Tragedy forced a change from the original selection when Ken Wadsworth withdrew in June because of ill health and the cricket world was saddened by his death in August at the age of 29.

The president of the Pakistan board of control, Abdul Kardar, who had captained Pakistan in their first 23 tests ordered a change to the team selected and Intikhab Alam and Wasim Raja were drafted in.

120 PAKISTAN v NEW ZEALAND *(First Test)*

at Gaddafi Stadium, Lahore on 9, 10, 11, 13 October, 1976
Toss : Pakistan. Umpires : Amanullah Khan and Shujauddin
Pakistan won by 6 wickets

On a dry, brown pitch Richard Hadlee had remarkable success in the first session as his fast pace and accuracy proved too much for three of Pakistan's most vaunted batsmen, Majid Khan, Sadiq Mohammad and Mushtaq Mohammad. Part-time off-spinner Mark Burgess bowled Zaheer Abbas to have the home team 68-4 at lunch.

Hadlee took ill during lunch and, after the break, Javed Miandad and Asif Iqbal plundered the bowling. In two hours to tea they added 161, their century partnership taking only 85 minutes. Their partnership ended after 281 was added when Miandad was caught off Peter Petherick for 163.

Raja hit the next ball hard but low and back to Petherick who held the catch. Intikhab, surrounded by eight fieldsmen, played forward to the next ball which hit his glove and Geoff Howarth dived to his left to hold an excellent catch and complete the first hat-trick by a New Zealander in a test match. The day ended with Pakistan 349-7.

A further 68 runs were added on the second day as Asif stroked his way to 166 before he was bowled by Hadlee who captured five wickets in the innings. Chasing 417 New Zealand's top order struggled with the bounce of Sarfraz Nawaz and the pace of Imran Khan and were badly positioned when they lost their fourth wicket at 72.

In spite of a tenacious innings of 38 from Howarth and a breezy 27 from Hadlee the last six wickets succumbed to the leg-spin guile of Intikhab and Mushtaq, and New Zealand were required to follow on.

They began disastrously when John Morrison, Glenn Turner and Howarth were out with the score at one. John Parker and Mark Burgess began the resuscitation with a 61-run partnership in 88 minutes.

Robert Anderson, playing in his first test, looked totally at ease and, with a combination of sharp running and sensible batting, he and Burgess added 183 before Anderson was out to Mushtaq only eight short of a century.

Burgess was out next ball, bowled by Intikhab for 111, his fifth test century. Stout efforts by Warren Lees, Hadlee and David O'Sullivan enabled New Zealand to reach a total of 360, meritorious considering the early disasters.

Pakistan was untroubled in reaching the target to win the game by six wickets. Four players playing in their first test, Anderson, Petherick, Lees and Miandad all outshone the established stars.

PAKISTAN

Batsman		Runs		Runs
Majid Khan	c Lees b Hadlee	23	c Turner b Collinge	21
Sadiq Mohammad	c Burgess b Hadlee	5	c Parker b Howarth	38
Zaheer Abbas	b Burgess	15	c Morrison b Petherick	15
Mushtaq Mohammad*	b Hadlee	4	(5) c Morrison b Petherick	5
Javed Miandad	c Hadlee b Petherick	163	(4) not out	25
Asif Iqbal	b Hadlee	166	not out	1
Wasim Raja	c & b Petherick	0		
Intikhab Alam	c Howarth b Petherick	0		
Imran Khan	c Burgess b Hadlee	29		
Sarfraz Nawaz	lbw b O'Sullivan	4		
Wasim Bari†	not out	2		
Extras	(b 1, lb 2, nb 3)	6		0
TOTAL	(80.5 overs)	**417**	(18.7 overs) (4 wkts)	**105**

NEW ZEALAND

Batsman		Runs		Runs
J.F.M.Morrison	c Bari b Sarfraz	3	c Zaheer b Sarfraz	0
G.M.Turner*	c Raja b Sarfraz	8	b Imran Khan	1
G.P.Howarth	c & b Intikhab	38	c Sadiq b Sarfraz	0
J.M.Parker	c Bari b Imran	9	lbw b Imran	22
M.G.Burgess	b Imran Khan	17	b Intikhab	111
R.W.Anderson	c Mushtaq b Intikhab	14	c Majid b Mushtaq	92
W.K.Lees†	st Bari b Intikhab	8	c Mushtaq b Imran	42
R.J.Hadlee	c Raja b Mushtaq	27	c Majid b Miandad	42
D.R.O'Sullivan	c Miandad b Mushtaq	8	(11) not out	23
R.O.Collinge	c Bari b Intikhab	8	(9) b Imran Khan	0
P.J.Petherick	not out	1	(10) c Mushtaq b Sarfraz	1
Extras	(b 1, lb 4, nb 11)	16	(b 4, lb 11, nb 11)	26
TOTAL	(49.4 overs)	**157**	(92.4 overs)	**360**

Bowling	O	M	R	W	O	M	R	W
NEW ZEALAND								
Collinge	14	0	81	0	6	0	30	1
Hadlee	19	0	121	5	5	0	36	0
Burgess	4	1	20	1				
O'Sullivan	25.5	3	86	1				
Petherick	18	1	103	3	4.7	2	26	2
Howarth					3	0	13	1
PAKISTAN								
Sarfraz	13	5	33	2	18	1	69	3
Imran	15	1	57	2	21	4	59	4
Asif	2	0	10	0				
Intikhab	16.4	6	35	4	26	4	85	1
Mushtaq	3	0	6	2	13	2	56	1
Raja					7	0	31	0
Miandad					7.4	1	34	1

Fall of Wickets

	P 1st	NZ 1st	NZ 2nd	P 2nd
1st	23	9	1	49
2nd	33	26	1	74
3rd	44	64	1	74
4th	55	72	62	96
5th	336	99	245	—
6th	336	105	245	—
7th	336	106	306	—
8th	408	146	306	—
9th	413	149	315	—
10th	417	157	360	—

MILESTONES

- Robert Anderson (134), Warren Lees (135) and Peter Petherick (136) all made their test debuts.

- Peter Petherick took New Zealand's first test hat-trick. He was the second from any country to do so on debut.

- Mark Burgess and Robert Anderson combined for a record fifth wicket stand of 183 against all countries.

- Javed Miandad became the second Pakistan batsman to score a century on test debut. At 19 years and 119 days he was the third youngest from any country to score a test century.

Geoff Howarth dives to catch Intikhab Alam, and Peter Petherick has New Zealand's first test hat-trick. Players from left are: John Morrison, Robert Anderson, Richard Collinge, Warren Lees, Intikhab, Glenn Turner, Asif Iqbal, Howarth, Petherick and John Parker.

121 PAKISTAN v NEW ZEALAND *(Second Test)*

at Niaz Stadium, Hyderabad on 23, 24, 25, 27 October, 1976
Toss : Pakistan. Umpires : Amanullah Khan and Shakoor Rana
Pakistan won by 10 wickets

The look of the dry, grassless pitch meant that the winning of the toss would be crucial. "We lost the toss and we lost heart," was how Lance Cairns later described it.

Neither Richard Hadlee nor Cairns could make effective use of the conditions and although Peter Petherick and David O'Sullivan were brought on within an hour, Sadiq Mohammad and Majid Khan merrily went on their way. They had 100 on the board in less than two hours. The first relief that the visitors had was when Sadiq retired with cramp when he was 56 and the second was when part-time bowler Andy Roberts had Zaheer Abbas out for 12.

The third occurred when O'Sullivan enticed Majid out of his ground to become Warren Lees' first test stumping. Mushtaq Mohammad dominated the rest of the day with an innings of controlled power. New Zealand had trouble throughout the afternoon with various players having to leave the field because of illness. Play ended at 289-3.

Mushtaq and Asif Iqbal produced 164 for the fourth wicket, with Mushtaq reaching his eighth test century. Sadiq replaced him when he was out and rapidly built on the innings that he had started the previous day. He reached 103 in the final over before tea and his brother declared. New Zealand did not fare well, losing three wickets for 75, but ended the day with Glenn Turner and Mark Burgess both not out.

Early on the third day Turner was struck a blow on his left elbow which made holding the bat almost impossible. He was soon caught behind off Imran Khan and Burgess also fell to the same combination. There were several minor contributions from the remaining batsmen but as nothing was higher than 30, New Zealand were forced to follow on for the second test in a row. Turner lasted momentarily but Geoff Howarth and John Parker raised hopes with a confident stand of 65.

The pitch was now badly scuffed up and in these difficult circumstances Parker and Roberts showed admirable discipline and determination. It was Pakistan's third right-arm leg-spinner, Javed Miandad, who captured both their wickets, as well as that of Lees, to end with match figures of 5-94.

Intikhab claimed four wickets in succession leaving Pakistan requiring one run for victory. The match ended with more than a day to spare and the pitch bore more resemblance to a beach strip than a test strip.

PAKISTAN

Sadiq Mohammad	not out	103		
Majid Khan	st Lees b O'Sullivan	98		
Zaheer Abbas	lbw b Roberts	11		
Javed Miandad	c sub (N.M.Parker) b Cairns	25		
Mushtaq Mohammad*	run out	101		
Asif Iqbal	st Lees b Petherick	73		
Imran Khan	c Turner b O'Sullivan	13		
Intikhab Alam	lbw b Hadlee	4		
Sarfraz Nawaz	c Turner b Petherick	10	(1) not out	4
Wasim Bari†	not out	13	(2) not out	0
Farrukh Zaman				
Extras	(b 17, lb 3, nb 2)	22		0
TOTAL	(128 overs) (8 wkts dec)	**473**	(0.5 overs) (0 wkts)	**4**

NEW ZEALAND

G.M.Turner*	c Bari b Imran	49	b Sarfraz	2
G.P.Howarth	b Sarfraz	0	c Miandad b Mushtaq	23
J.M.Parker	c Miandad b Imran	7	c Mushtaq b Miandad	82
A.D.G.Roberts	c Bari b Sarfraz	8	b Miandad	33
M.G.Burgess	c Bari b Imran	33	c sub (Wasim Raja) b Intikhab	21
R.W.Anderson	b Intikhab	30	c Zaheer Abbas b Intikhab	4
W.K.Lees†	lbw b Intikhab	15	c sub (Mohsin Khan) b Miandad	29
B.L.Cairns	c Majid b Miandad	18	lbw b Intikhab	3
R.J.Hadlee	not out	28	c Bari b Intikhab	0
D.R.O'Sullivan	b Miandad	4	b Sarfraz	23
P.J.Petherick	b Sarfraz	0	not out	12
Extras	(b 13, lb 8, nb 6)	27	(b 15, lb 2, nb 5)	22
TOTAL	(73.6 overs)	**219**	(80.4 overs)	**254**

Bowling	O	M	R	W	O	M	R	W		Fall of Wickets			
NEW ZEALAND											P	NZ	NZ	P
											1st	1st	2nd	2nd
Hadlee	19	1	77	1						1st	164	5	5	-
Cairns	26	7	101	1						2nd	176	27	70	-
Roberts	8	1	23	1						3rd	220	38	147	-
Petherick	36	5	158	2						4th	384	101	158	-
O'Sullivan	39	10	92	2						5th	387	111	172	-
Lees					0.5	0	4	0		6th	410	161	190	-
PAKISTAN										7th	415	178	193	-
Sarfraz	17.6	4	53	3	10.4	1	45	2		8th	427	200	193	-
Imran	15	4	41	3	16	1	53	0		9th	-	208	226	-
Intikhab	20	7	51	2	20	7	44	4		10th	-	219	254	-
Farrukh	6	1	8	0	4	1	7	0						
Miandad	8	1	20	2	19	2	74	3						
Mushtaq	7	2	19	0	9	4	9	1						
Majid					2	2	0	0						

The New Zealand team that toured Pakistan and India in 1976/77. Back: David O'Sullivan, Geoff Howarth, Murray Parker, Andy Roberts, Gary Troup, Lance Cairns, Robert Anderson, Peter Petherick, Warren Lees. Front: Richard Hadlee, John Morrison, Glenn Turner (captain), Murray Chapple (manager), John Parker, Mark Burgess, Richard Collinge.

122 PAKISTAN v NEW ZEALAND (Third Test)

at National Stadium, Karachi on 30, 31 October, 1, 3, 4 November, 1976
Toss : Pakistan. Umpires : Shakoor Rana and Shujauddin
Match drawn

It was almost a pleasure for the touring side to see the pitch prepared at Karachi as it was well grassed and more like they were used to. Glenn Turner's injured elbow prevented him from playing and John Parker took over the captaincy.

For the third time in the series Pakistan won the toss and Mushtaq's decision to bat virtually ensured the side would not lose the test. Richard Hadlee beat Majid Khan three times in his first two overs but thereafter Majid gave a superlative batting exhibition as, with grace and elegance, he stroked the ball to all corners of the ground. By lunch he had scored 108 of the undefeated partnership of 141 with Sadiq Mohammad.

In the first hour after lunch New Zealand fought back, claiming three wickets for 27 runs, and Mushtaq was dropped in the slips off Hadlee at the beginning of his innings. From 161-3 the total became 338-3 at stumps as Javed Miandad scored his second century of the series.

Miandad and Mushtaq continued in a similar attacking vein until Warren Lees caught Mushtaq off Hadlee for 107. Their partnership had added 252 in 295 minutes. Imran Khan kept the tempo up while watching the prodigious Miandad showcase his talent by scoring 206, which included two sixes and 29 fours.

After ten hours fielding in intense heat it was not surprising that both openers were out with only 10 on the board. John Parker and Andy Roberts overcame the crisis to reach 67 by stumps.

Imran captured three wickets in the first hour: Parker, Roberts and Robert Anderson. With a blend of caution and aggression Mark Burgess and Lees added 91. Hadlee replaced Burgess, and Lees continued to shine against the spin bowling. Runs poured in as Lees scored his maiden test and first-class hundred in 198 minutes.

Not to be out-done, Hadlee effortlessly hit four sixes in his 87 as the pair added 186. By stumps New Zealand were 399-7 and 295 had been accrued in the last five hours for the loss of only two wickets.

The valiant batting of Lees came to an end after 338 minutes when he had scored 152 and Lance Cairns, despite a stomach complaint, smashed the bowling for 52. New Zealand was all out for 468.

The run scoring orgy continued for the rest of the fourth day as Pakistan chased quick runs against a depleted attack. Mushtaq's declaration left New Zealand to score 388 in six hours. John Morrison, Murray Parker and Roberts made bold efforts but, at 94-4, survival became paramount.

Anderson and Lees both added worthwhile contributions and Hadlee and Cairns resisted all Pakistan's efforts in the final 15 overs.

MILESTONES

- John Parker became New Zealand's fourteenth test captain.

- Murray Parker (137) made his test debut.

- Majid Khan became the fourth player to score a century before lunch on the first day of a test. The others were Australians Victor Trumper, Charlie Macartney and Don Bradman.

- The 186-run stand between Warren Lees and Richard Hadlee was a New Zealand record for the seventh wicket.

PAKISTAN

Sadiq Mohammad	not out	103		
Sadiq Mohammad	c Burgess b Hadlee	34	c Lees b Collinge	31
Majid Khan	c Burgess b Collinge	112	run out	50
Zaheer Abbas	b O'Sullivan	3	c Lees b O'Sullivan	16
Javed Miandad	c Hadlee b Collinge	206	(5) st Lees b O'Sullivan	85
Mushtaq Mohammad*	c Lees b Hadlee	107	(6) not out	67
Asif Iqbal	c Lees b Hadlee	12	(4) st Lees b Roberts	30
Imran Khan	c O'Sullivan b Hadlee	59	not out	4
Intikhab Alam	lbw b O'Sullivan	0		
Sarfraz Nawaz	lbw b Cairns	15		
Shahid Israr†	not out	7		
Sikander Bakht				
Extras	(b 3, lb 5, nb 2)	10	(lb 4, nb 3)	7
TOTAL	(105.2 overs) (9 wkts dec)	**565**	(47.4 overs) (5 wkts dec)	**290**

NEW ZEALAND

N.M.Parker	c Israr b Sarfraz	2	c Imran b Intikhab	40
J.F.M.Morrison	b Sarfraz	4	c Mushtaq b Sikander	31
J.M.Parker*	c Majid b Imran	24	c Sadiq b Miandad	16
A.D.G.Roberts	b Imran	39	b Sikander	45
M.G.Burgess	c Miandad b Sarfraz	44	c Majid b Miandad	1
R.W.Anderson	lbw b Imran	8	lbw b Imran	30
W.K.Lees†	b Sikander	152	c Asif b Imran	46
R.J.Hadlee	c Israr b Intikhab	87	not out	30
B.L.Cairns	not out	52	not out	9
D.R.O'Sullivan	c Mushtaq b Intikhab	1		
R.O.Collinge	b Intikhab	3		
Extras	(b 12, lb 7, nb 33)	52	(b 4, lb 5, nb 5)	14
TOTAL	(103.5 overs)	**468**	(79.6 overs) (7 wkts)	**262**

Bowling	O	M	R	W	O	M	R	W
NEW ZEALAND								
Collinge	21	1	141	2	12	0	88	1
Hadlee	20.2	1	138	4	12	0	75	0
Cairns	28	2	142	1				
O'Sullivan	35	6	131	2	17	0	96	2
Morrison	1	0	3	0	2	0	6	0
Roberts					4.4	2	18	1
PAKISTAN								
Sarfraz	20	1	84	3				
Imran	24.6	4	107	3	21.6	1	104	2
Sikander	16	3	68	1	8	2	38	2
Intikhab	20.7	5	76	3	17	5	42	1
Mushtaq	6	2	30	0	6	2	9	0
Miandad	10	3	34	0	17	4	45	2
Majid	5	2	17	0	9	4	6	0
Sadiq	1	1	0	0	1	0	4	0

Fall of Wickets

	P 1st	NZ 1st	NZ 2nd	P 2nd
1st	147	5	76	43
2nd	151	10	88	90
3rd	161	93	137	91
4th	413	93	137	93
5th	427	104	275	140
6th	524	195	-	200
7th	525	381	-	241
8th	548	433	-	-
9th	565	434	-	-
10th	-	468	-	-

Warren Lees walks from the middle after having played a ball from Sikander Bakht on to his leg stump. His innings of 152 saved New Zealand from following on. The other batsman is Lance Cairns.

AVERAGES

New Zealand

BATTING	M	I	NO	Runs	HS	Ave
R.J. Hadlee	3	6	2	214	87	53.50
W.K. Lees	3	6	0	292	152	48.66
B.L. Cairns	2	4	2	82	52*	41.00
M.G. Burgess	3	6	0	227	111	37.83
A.D.G. Roberts	2	4	0	125	45	31.25
R.W. Anderson	3	6	0	178	92	29.66
J.M. Parker	3	6	0	160	82	26.66
N.M. Parker	1	2	0	42	40	21.00
G.P. Howarth	2	4	0	61	38	15.25
G.M. Turner	2	4	0	60	49	15.00
D.R. O'Sullivan	3	5	1	59	23*	14.75
J.F.M. Morrison	2	4	0	38	31	9.50
P.J. Petherick	2	4	2	14	12*	7.00
R.O. Collinge	2	3	0	11	8	3.66

BOWLING	O	M	R	W	Ave
G.P. Howarth	3	0	13	1	13.00
M.G. Burgess	4	1	20	1	20.00
A.D.G. Roberts	12.4	3	41	2	20.50
P.J. Petherick	58.7	8	287	7	41.00
R.J. Hadlee	75.2	2	447	10	44.70
D.R. O'Sullivan	116	19	405	7	57.85
R.O. Collinge	53	1	340	4	85.00
B.L. Cairns	54	9	243	2	121.50
W.K. Lees	0.5	0	4	0	-
J.F.M. Morrison	3	0	9	0	-

Pakistan

BATTING	M	I	NO	Runs	HS	Ave
Javed Miandad	3	5	1	504	206	126.00
Mushtaq Mohammad	3	5	1	284	107	71.00
Asif Iqbal	3	5	1	282	166	70.50
Majid Khan	3	5	0	304	112	60.80
Sadiq Mohammad	3	5	1	211	103*	52.75
Imran Khan	3	4	1	105	59	35.00
Zaheer Abbas	3	5	0	60	16	12.00
Sarfraz Nawaz	3	4	1	33	15	11.00
Intikhab Alam	3	3	0	4	4	1.33
Wasim Raja	1	1	0	0	0	0.00
Wasim Bari	2	3	3	15	13*	-
Shahid Israr	1	1	1	7	7*	-
Farrukh Zaman	1	-	-	-	-	-
Sikander Bakht	1	-	-	-	-	-

BOWLING	O	M	R	W	Ave
Sarfraz Nawaz	79.2	12	284	13	21.84
Intikhab Alam	120.4	34	333	15	22.20
Javed Miandad	61.4	11	207	8	25.87
Imran Khan	113.4	15	421	14	30.07
Mushtaq Mohammad	44	12	129	4	32.25
Sikander Bakht	24	5	106	3	35.33
Sadiq Mohammad	2	1	4	0	-
Asif Iqbal	2	0	10	0	-
Farrukh Zaman	10	2	15	0	-
Majid Khan	16	8	23	0	-
Wasim Raja	7	0	31	0	-

123 INDIA v NEW ZEALAND *(First Test)*

at Wankhede Stadium, Bombay on 10, 11, 13, 14, 15 November
Toss : India. Umpires : J. Reuben and B. Satyaji Rao
India won by 162 runs

There was no respite for the New Zealand touring team of 1976 when they began their series against India six days after playing Pakistan. For the fourth test running New Zealand were resigned to a long, hot first day in the field and, with wayward bowling from the three pace men, Sunil Gavaskar and Aunshuman Gaekwad cruised to an opening partnership of 120.

When David O'Sullivan dismissed Gaekwad his replacement, Mohinder Amarnath, was also untroubled. Gavaskar made his first test century in India but then lost concentration and was caught by a diving Lance Cairns at long-on for 119. The sweltering day ended with India 228-4.

The next morning Richard Hadlee was a revitalised bowler and, with the new ball, he ripped out three batsmen before Syed Kirmani found an imaginative partner in the form of Bishan Bedi. Together they delayed the visitors' celebrations as they plundered 105 for the ninth wicket, and India totalled 399. New Zealand survived the last 105 minutes with great difficulty losing only one wicket; 48-1.

The third day provided an absorbing struggle as Glenn Turner and John Parker battled tenaciously against India's skilful spinners. They brought all their Worcestershire expertise to bear by defending stoutly, placing their shots neatly and running swiftly between the wickets as they added 106.

Turner's 65 was likened to a three-figure performance. Parker reached his third test century in 280 minutes but was immediately run out in a mix-up with Mark Burgess. New Zealand lost three wickets in the day for 186 runs.

On the fourth morning New Zealand's determined resistance ceased. For once, the middle order batting failed dismally and the last six wickets produced only 64 runs. There were no answers to the spin of Bedi, "Venkat" and "Chandra". India sought victory by scoring runs quickly. An electrifying innings by Brijesh Patel, who scored 45 from the first 21 balls he faced had the crowd in a frenzy, as he compiled 82 and India scored 178-4.

A further 24 runs in 30 minutes before the declaration was made left New Zealand 209 minutes in which to score 304. Turner's early dismissal by Madan Lal was the only wicket taken in the game by India's opening attack. The amount of turn extracted by the three spinning wizards soon had the Kiwis concentrating on survival rather than victory.

Their efforts, though, proved unavailing as they slumped to 67-7. A gritty effort by Lees and Collinge led to a bright rearguard action that gained them 65 before Lees was bowled. Bedi's left-arm spinning fingers gave him a match winning 5-27 from 33 overs.

INDIA

S.M.Gavaskar	c Cairns b Petherick	119	c Burgess b Hadlee		14
A.D.Gaekwad	lbw b O'Sullivan	42			
M.Amarnath	c O'Sullivan b Hadlee	45	(2) c Roberts b Collinge		30
G.R.Viswanath	b Petherick	10	(3) st Lees b Petherick		39
B.P.Patel	b Cairns	4	(4) c sub (R.W.Anderson)		
			b Collinge		82
A.V.Mankad	c & b Hadlee	16	(5) not out		27
Madan Lal	c Parker N.M. b Hadlee	8	(6) not out		8
S.M.H.Kirmani†	c Parker J.M. b Petherick	88			
S.Venkataraghavan	c Turner b Hadlee	3			
B.S.Bedi*	c Parker J.M. b Cairns	36			
B.S.Chandrasekhar	not out	20			
Extras	(b 2, lb 1, nb 5)	8	(lb 1, nb 1)		2
TOTAL	(142.5 overs)	**399**	(58 overs) (4 wkts dec)		**202**

NEW ZEALAND

G.M.Turner*	c Amarnath b Venkataraghavan	65	c Gavaskar b Madan Lal		6
N.M.Parker	c Kirmani b Chandrasekhar	9	c Amarnath b Chandrasekhar		14
J.M.Parker	run out	104	b Bedi		7
M.G.Burgess	c sub (K.D.Ghavri) b Bedi	42	c Gavaskar b Bedi		0
A.D.G.Roberts	lbw b Chandrasekhar	2	c Mankad b Bedi		16
W.K.Lees†	c Kirmani b Chandrasekhar	7	b Venkataraghavan		42
R.J.Hadlee	c Kirmani b Venkataraghavan	17	c Patel b Bedi		7
B.L.Cairns	b Chandrasekhar	12	st Kirmani b Venkataraghavan		1
D.R.O'Sullivan	c Venkataraghavan b Bedi	3	(10) not out		7
R.O.Collinge	c Kirmani b Venkataraghavan	26	(9) c Madan Lal b Bedi		36
P.J.Petherick	not out	0	c Amarnath b Chandrasekhar		1
Extras	(b 1, lb 6, nb 4)	11	(b 4)		4
TOTAL	(153.3 overs)	**298**	(80.2 overs)		**141**

Bowling	O	M	R	W	O	M	R	W
NEW ZEALAND								
Collinge	15	5	41	0	12	2	45	2
Hadlee	29	5	95	4	16	0	76	1
Cairns	34	8	76	2				
Roberts	6	0	27	0	6	1	13	0
O'Sullivan	27	9	62	1	10	6	21	0
Petherick	31.5	6	90	3	14	4	45	1
INDIA								
Madan Lal	9	2	27	0	6	0	13	1
Amarnath	13	3	33	0	3	0	9	0
Bedi	50.3	22	71	2	33	18	27	5
Chandrasekhar	44	13	77	4	19.2	5	59	2
Venkataraghavan	37	11	79	3	19	9	29	2

Fall of Wickets				
	I	NZ	I	NZ
	1st	1st	2nd	2nd
1st	120	37	24	6
2nd	188	143	63	25
3rd	218	220	118	27
4th	218	228	175	27
5th	239	238	-	50
6th	241	239	-	64
7th	247	267	-	67
8th	252	267	-	132
9th	357	298	-	136
10th	399	298	-	141

David O'Sullivan demands, and gets, a leg-before decision against Aunshuman Gaekwad. Joining in the appeal are Mark Burgess, Glenn Turner and Warren Lees.

124 INDIA v NEW ZEALAND *(Second Test)*

at Modi Stadium, Kanpur on 18, 19, 20, 21, 23 November, 1976
Toss : India. Umpires : M.V. Nagendra and M.S. Sivasankariah
Match drawn

The pitch prepared for the test in Kanpur had all the grass shaved off and was hard and presented a shiny surface. In front of a partisan crowd, the home side took full use of a pitch made for batting.

It was heartbreaking toil for the bowlers and Peter Petherick and David O'Sullivan shouldered the bulk of the work as the Indian batsmen went smoothly about accumulating runs, each one greeted by a deafening roar. The total clicked over regularly, 116-1 at lunch, 231-4 at tea and 304-4 at stumps.

The stately progress continued the next day through to an hour before stumps when Bishan Bedi, having reached his half-century, the sixth batsman in the innings to do so, declared at 524-9. Geoff Howarth was dropped before he scored but he and Glenn Turner saw New Zealand safely through to stumps at 54-0.

Turner dominated the tourists' reply, scoring his seventh and last test century before he was third out at 224. With Howarth he added 54 for the first wicket; with John Parker 64 for the second and 114 with Mark Burgess for the third. As the day came to a close New Zealand lost five wickets for 26 and were perilously poised to follow on at 265-7.

The fourth day began with Andy Roberts playing an intelligent innings as he and the last three batsmen added 85. Roberts played his shots with assurance and finished 84 not out, his best score in tests.

For the rest of the day India sought quick runs and the stylish Aunshuman Gaekwad and the hard-hitting Gundappa Viswanath were delighted to oblige, adding 163, with Viswanath reaching his century two balls before stumps.

New Zealand faced the daunting task of scoring 383 for victory when Turner and Parker began the innings. Turner again batted with surety but was given out, caught at short

Glenn Turner created a New Zealand test record by scoring his seventh test century; it was also his last in test cricket. He lofts the ball over mid-wicket watched by Sunil Gavaskar and Syed Kirmani.

gully, when it appeared that the ball had gone from his boot.

The game appeared lost at the tea break with New Zealand seven wickets down. Warren Lees again demonstrated his ability in a crisis, this time with keen assistance from O'Sullivan. They defied all that the Indian spinners could conjure in the last two hours, finishing 49 and 23 not out.

INDIA

S.M.Gavaskar	b O'Sullivan	66	b Hadlee		15
A.D.Gaekwad	c Lees b Hadlee	43	not out		77
M.Amarnath	b O'Sullivan	70	c Parker N.M. b Hadlee		8
G.R.Viswanath	lbw b Roberts	68	not out		103
B.P.Patel	b Petherick	13			
A.V.Mankad	lbw b Troup	50			
S.M.H.Kirmani†	c Turner b O'Sullivan	64			
K.D.Ghavri	c Troup b Petherick	37			
S.Venkataraghavan	c & b Petherick	27			
B.S.Bedi*	not out	50			
B.S.Chandrasekhar	not out	10			
Extras	(b 17, lb 4, w 1, nb 4)	26	(lb 4, nb 1)		5
TOTAL	(168 overs) (9 wkts dec)	**524**	(52 overs) (2 wkts dec)		**208**

NEW ZEALAND

G.M.Turner*	c Viswanath b Bedi	113	(2) c Venkataraghavan b Bedi	35
G.P.Howarth	c Kirmani b Ghavri	19	(6) c Mankad b Venkataraghavan	4
J.M.Parker	c Ghavri b Bedi	34	lbw b Bedi	17
M.G.Burgess	c Ghavri b Bedi	54	lbw b Venkataraghavan	24
A.D.G.Roberts	not out	84	c Mankad b Chandrasekhar	9
N.M.Parker	lbw b Venkataraghavan	6	(1) lbw b Chandrasekhar	18
W.K.Lees†	b Chandrasekhar	3	not out	49
R.J.Hadlee	b Chandrasekhar	0	c Venkataraghavan b Bedi	10
D.R.O'Sullivan	c Chandrasekhar b Venkataraghavan	15	not out	23
G.B.Troup	c Amarnath b Venkataraghavan	0		
P.J.Petherick	c Kirmani b Chandrasekhar	13		
Extras	(lb 9)	9	(lb 4)	4
TOTAL	(142.5 overs)	**350**	(117 overs) (7 wkts)	**193**

Bowling	O	M	R	W	O	M	R	W		Fall of Wickets			
NEW ZEALAND											I	NZ	I	NZ
Hadlee	29	2	121	1	15	1	56	2			1st	1st	2nd	2nd
Troup	20	3	69	1	10	0	47	0	1st	79	54	23	43
Roberts	19	5	53	1					2nd	193	118	45	59
O'Sullivan	50	14	125	3	16	1	49	0	3rd	196	224	-	86
Petherick	45	12	109	3	11	0	51	0	4th	217	225	-	97
Howarth	5	0	21	0					5th	312	241	-	110
INDIA									6th	341	250	-	114
Ghavri	12	3	16	1	6	2	35	0	7th	413	250	-	134
Amarnath	5	0	23	0	4	2	5	0	8th	450	291	-	-
Bedi	41	12	80	3	40	23	42	3	9th	493	298	-	-
Chandrasekhar	36.5	6	102	3	33	15	61	2	10th	-	350	-	-
Venkataraghavan	48	9	120	3	34	20	46	2					

MILESTONES

- Gary Troup (138) made his test debut.

- India's total of 524-9d was the highest innings in test cricket without an individual hundred.

- India's innings was only the eighth instance where all eleven batsmen reached double figures.

- Glenn Turner's seventh test century was a New Zealand record.

125 INDIA v NEW ZEALAND *(Third Test)*

at M.A. Chidambaram Stadium, Madras on 26, 27, 28, 30, November, 1, 2 December, 1976
Toss : India. Umpires : Mohammad Ghouse and K.B. Ramaswami
India won by 216 runs

With the series still undecided the test was extended to six days. Unfortunately, Madras was in the middle of its worst monsoon period since 1902. The rain prevented one umpire from getting to Madras and the other became ill, so two local umpires, without test experience, were appointed.

It was to become a regrettable decision. Glenn Turner's diabolical luck at the toss persisted and he lost for the sixth successive time in the six tests played in Asia.

There was no play on the first day and play finally began just prior to lunch on the second day with Lance Cairns dismissing both openers in his first two overs. New Zealand's bad luck continued when Richard Hadlee had to leave the field after three overs and Gundappa Viswanath exploited the lack of a fast bowler on a conducive pitch to lead India to 162-4 at stumps.

Hadlee returned the next day and with Cairns reduced India to 181-7. Venkataraghavan added 17 with Syed Kirmani before the New Zealanders became incensed by an umpiring decision to give Kirmani not out. The pair added a further invaluable 57 to rub salt into the wounds.

The umpires later cautioned Hadlee about intimidatory bowling to Bishan Bedi. Cairns fully deserved his best test return of 5-55. He shouldered the brunt of the bowling in intense humidity and never wilted.

Only two hours' play was possible on the fourth day, during which New Zealand reached 84 for two. The pitch did not inspire confidence as it was crumbling in parts as well as still having some damp spots. The outfield, not cut during the match, was dreadfully slow. On the fifth day Bedi and Chandrasekhar removed the remaining eight wickets for only 56 runs as they made the ball leap and turn prodigiously.

As on the previous days the pitch was livelier during the first session. India's second innings began in sensational fashion. Aunshuman Gaekwad, trying to avoid a lifting ball from Hadlee, knocked his leg bail off.

The square leg umpire said that a breeze had blown off the bail and that the batsman was not out. Two appeals for catches at the wicket off Mohinder Amarnath were rejected, and then Sunil Gavaskar was adjudged stumped when Warren Lees had dropped the ball.

Bedi's declaration set New Zealand 360 for victory on the sixth day but their fate was sealed by lunch when they had lost four wickets. The Indian spinners were not to be denied as they again exploited the conditions favourable to their skills. Bedi ended the game with nine wickets as New Zealand lost by 216 runs. During the series the Indian spin-bowling trio captured 50 wickets in three tests.

INDIA

Batsman	Dismissal	Runs	2nd innings	Runs
S.M.Gavaskar	b Cairns	2	st Lees b O'Sullivan	43
A.D.Gaekwad	c Parker b Cairns	0	b Hadlee	11
M.Amarnath	c Petherick b Cairns	21	c Morrison b Hadlee	55
G.R.Viswanath	c Lees b Hadlee	87	st Lees b O'Sullivan	17
B.P.Patel	run out	33	not out	40
A.V.Mankad	b Cairns	14	c Burgess b Petherick	21
S.M.H.Kirmani†	lbw b Petherick	44		
K.D.Ghavri	c Petherick b Hadlee	8		
S.Venkataraghavan	c sub (R.O.Collinge) b Cairns	64		
B.S.Bedi*	c Cairns b Hadlee	5		
B.S.Chandrasekhar	not out	1		
Extras	(b 7, lb 8, w 1, nb 3)	19	(b 11, lb 2, nb 1)	14
TOTAL	(133.1 overs)	**298**	(61.5 overs) (5 wkts dec)	**201**

NEW ZEALAND

Batsman	Dismissal	Runs	2nd innings	Runs
G.M.Turner*	c Kirmani b Chandrasekhar	37	c Amarnath b Chandrasekhar	5
J.F.M.Morrison	c Kirmani b Ghavri	7	c Chandrasekhar b Ghavri	1
J.M.Parker	c Patel b Ghavri	9	c Kirmani b Chandrasekhar	38
M.G.Burgess	b Bedi	40	run out	15
A.D.G.Roberts	c Venkataraghavan b Chandrasekhar	1	c Gavaskar b Bedi	0
G.P.Howarth	c Venkataraghavan b Bedi	3	c Chandrasekhar b Bedi	18
W.K.Lees†	c Venkataraghavan b Bedi	9	c sub (Madan Lal) b Bedi	21
R.J.Hadlee	c Gaekwad b Bedi	21	c Amarnath b Bedi	5
B.L.Cairns	c Mankad b Bedi	5	not out	8
D.R.O'Sullivan	c Venkataraghavan b Chandrasekhar	0	c Patel b Chandrasekhar	21
P.J.Petherick	not out	0	lbw b Venkataraghavan	1
Extras	(b 1, lb 2, nb 5)	8	(b 7, lb 1, nb 2)	10
TOTAL	(55.4 overs)	**140**	(67 overs)	**143**

Bowling NEW ZEALAND	O	M	R	W	O	M	R	W
Hadlee	21	7	37	3	17	3	52	2
Cairns	33.1	11	55	5	16	2	49	0
Roberts	17	5	32	0	2	0	4	0
O'Sullivan	34	9	69	0	20	3	70	2
Petherick	25	5	77	1	6.5	0	12	1
Howarth	3	1	9	0				
INDIA								
Ghavri	13	3	32	2	8	4	14	1
Amarnath	8	3	17	0	3	1	6	0
Bedi	16.4	4	48	5	22	12	22	4
Chandrasekhar	16	5	28	3	20	3	64	3
Venkataraghavan	2	0	7	0	14	8	27	1

Fall of Wickets	I 1st	NZ 1st	I 2nd	NZ 2nd
1st	0	17	33	2
2nd	3	37	86	21
3rd	60	91	118	50
4th	137	99	142	53
5th	167	101	201	79
6th	167	103	-	85
7th	181	133	-	103
8th	255	133	-	114
9th	276	136	-	142
10th	298	140	-	143

Lance Cairns shouldered the brunt of the bowling. He toiled in intense heat for 33 overs and thoroughly deserved his best test figures of 5-55.

AVERAGES

New Zealand

BATTING	M	I	NO	Runs	HS	Ave
G.M. Turner	3	6	0	261	113	43.50
J.M. Parker	3	6	0	209	104	34.83
R.O. Collinge	1	2	0	62	36	31.00
M.G. Burgess	3	6	0	175	54	29.16
W.K. Lees	3	6	1	131	49*	26.20
A.D.G. Roberts	3	6	1	112	84*	22.40
D.R. O'Sullivan	3	6	2	69	23*	17.25
N.M. Parker	2	4	0	47	18	11.75
G.P. Howarth	2	4	0	44	19	11.00
R.J. Hadlee	3	6	0	60	21	10.00
B.L. Cairns	2	4	1	26	12	8.66
P.J. Petherick	3	5	2	15	13	5.00
J.F.M. Morrison	1	2	0	8	7	4.00
G.B. Troup	1	1	0	0	0	0.00

BOWLING	O	M	R	W	Ave
B.L. Cairns	83.1	21	180	7	25.71
R.J. Hadlee	127	18	437	13	33.61
P.J. Petherick	133.4	27	384	9	42.66
R.O. Collinge	27	7	86	2	43.00
D.R. O'Sullivan	157	42	396	6	66.00
G.B. Troup	30	3	116	1	116.00
A.D.G. Roberts	50	11	129	1	129.00
G.P. Howarth	8	1	30	0	-

India

BATTING	M	I	NO	Runs	HS	Ave
S.M.H. Kirmani	3	3	0	196	88	65.33
G.R. Viswanath	3	6	1	324	103*	64.80
B.S. Bedi	3	3	1	91	50*	45.50
A.D. Gaekwad	3	5	1	173	77*	43.25
S.M. Gavaskar	3	6	0	259	119	43.16
B.P. Patel	3	5	1	172	82	43.00
M. Amarnath	3	6	0	229	70	38.16
A.V. Mankad	3	5	1	128	50	32.00
S. Venkataraghavan	3	3	0	94	64	31.33
K.D. Ghavri	2	2	0	45	37	22.50
Madan Lal	1	2	1	16	8*	16.00
B.S. Chandrasekhar	3	3	3	31	20*	-

BOWLING	O	M	R	W	Ave
B.S. Bedi	203.1	91	290	22	13.18
B.S. Chandrasekhar	169.1	47	391	17	23.00
K.D. Ghavri	39	12	97	4	24.25
S. Venkataraghavan	154	57	308	11	28.00
Madan Lal	15	2	40	1	40.00
M. Amarnath	36	9	93	0	-

1976/77 Australia in New Zealand

126 NEW ZEALAND v AUSTRALIA *(First Test)*

at Lancaster Park, Christchurch on 18, 19, 20, 22, 23 February, 1977
Toss : New Zealand. Umpires : D.E.A. Copps and F.R. Goodall
Match drawn

Glenn Turner's decision to put Australia in seemed justified at the tea interval when they were 208-6 but Gary Gilmour joined Doug Walters and the pair decimated the attack in the final session, adding 137. Walters was 129 at stumps, his century having taken 163 minutes.

In the first hour the next morning they added another 80 runs, with Gilmour completing his only test century. Walters was the last man out for the highest of his 15 test centuries, 250, compiled in 394 minutes. He had begun in an uncertain manner but soon flourished with magnificent driving and deft placement.

His giant score emphasised the seriousness of three let-offs by wicketkeeper Warren Lees, two catches and one stumping. The second day ended with New Zealand 106-3 and the follow on figure of 353, let alone the target of 552, seemed far away.

Mark Burgess took the attack to Dennis Lillee when play began after lunch on the third day. Lillee's first five overs conceded 40, mainly to Burgess. When the eighth wicket fell at 265 the Australians were thwarted by a stubborn partnership between Hedley Howarth and Dayle Hadlee that was to stretch into the fourth day. The pair added 73 and Hedley Howarth made his only test half-century.

There were still 15 runs required to avoid the follow on when Ewen Chatfield came to the crease. Tension rose as the runs were acquired, forcing Australia to bat a second time. Intermittent rain shortened the playing time and Australia were contained by shrewd, defensive field placements and accurate bowling, so that Greg Chappell's declaration left New Zealand 350 to get in 390 minutes.

Bevan Congdon built on a solid opening of 70 with an aggressive partnership with Burgess that took their team score at tea to 203 for three. The pressure of scoring 147 was too great and wickets were whittled away before Dayle Hadlee again defied the Australians and Congdon was undefeated for 107 when the game was drawn.

MILESTONES

- Graham "Jock" Edwards (139) made his test debut.

- Doug Walters and Gary Gilmour added 217, an Australian record for the seventh wicket.

- Bevan Congdon equalled Glenn Turner's record of seven test hundreds.

AUSTRALIA				
A.Turner	b Chatfield	3	lbw b Hadlee D.R.	20
I.C.Davis	c Howarth G.P. b Hadlee R.J.	34	c Lees b Hadlee R.J.	22
R.B.McCosker	c Parker b Hadlee D.R.	37	not out	77
G.S.Chappell*	c Turner b Hadlee R.J.	44	c Parker b Howarth H.J.	0
G.J.Cosier	b Hadlee R.J.	23	run out	2
K.D.Walters	c Howarth H.J. b Hadlee D.R.	250	not out	20
R.W.Marsh†	c Parker b Howarth H.J.	2		
G.J.Gilmour	b Chatfield	101		
K.J.O'Keeffe	run out	8		
D.K.Lillee	c Hadlee R.J. b Chatfield	19		
M.H.N.Walker	not out	10		
Extras	(b 7, lb 10, nb 4)	21	(lb 10, nb 3)	13
TOTAL	**(110.5 overs)**	**552**	**(43 overs) (4 wkts dec)**	**154**

NEW ZEALAND				
G.M.Turner*	c Turner b O'Keeffe	15	c & b O'Keeffe	36
G.P.Howarth	c Marsh b O'Keeffe	42	c Marsh b Gilmour	28
B.E.Congdon	c Gilmour b Walker	23	not out	107
J.M.Parker	c Marsh b O'Keeffe	34	c McCosker b Walker	21
M.G.Burgess	c Marsh b Walker	66	c McCosker b Walker	39
G.N.Edwards	c Gilmour b O'Keeffe	34	c Marsh b Walker	15
W.K.Lees†	c Marsh b Lillee	14	c Marsh b Lillee	3
R.J.Hadlee	c Marsh b O'Keeffe	3	(9) c Cosier b Walker	15
H.J.Howarth	b Walker	61	(8) b Lillee	0
D.R.Hadlee	not out	37	not out	8
E.J.Chatfield	b Lillee	5		
Extras	(lb 9, w 2, nb 12)	23	(lb 12, w 1, nb 8)	21
TOTAL	**(95.2 overs)**	**357**	**(84 overs) (8 wkts)**	**293**

Bowling	O	M	R	W	O	M	R	W	Fall of Wickets				
NEW ZEALAND										A	NZ	A	NZ
										1st	1st	2nd	2nd
Hadlee R.J.	29	1	155	3	13	4	41	1	1st	9	60	37	70
Chatfield	31	4	125	3	11	1	34	0	2nd	76	65	67	70
Hadlee D.R.	24.5	1	130	2	8	0	28	1	3rd	78	91	68	128
Congdon	7	0	27	0	1	0	1	0	4th	112	189	82	218
Howarth H.J.	19	2	94	1	10	4	37	1	5th	205	193	-	238
AUSTRALIA									6th	208	220	-	245
Lillee	31.2	6	119	2	18	1	70	2	7th	425	223	-	245
Gilmour	10	0	48	0	10	0	48	1	8th	454	265	-	260
Walker	26	7	66	3	25	4	65	4	9th	504	338	-	-
O'Keeffe	28	5	101	5	20	4	56	1	10th	552	357	-	-
Chappell					11	0	33	0					

Hedley Howarth compiled his best test score of 61. His innings helped New Zealand to avoid the follow on. Batting with him is Richard Hadlee.

127 NEW ZEALAND v AUSTRALIA *(Second Test)*

at Eden Park, Auckland on 25, 26, 27 February, 1 March, 1977
Toss : Australia. Umpires : D.E.A.Copps and W.R.C. Gardiner
Australia won by 10 wickets

Unusually for Eden Park a hard, well-grassed surface was prepared for the test and Dennis Lillee and Max Walker attacked the batsmen mercilessly with pace, bounce, swing and seam that only Geoff Howarth looked at ease against. For the second time in two tests he was dismissed when he looked in total control.

With the score at 121-5 New Zealand was saved from a shuddering collapse by stocky Jock Edwards who counter-attacked with stunning clean hit boundaries. In three overs he hit Gary Gilmour for 12, nine and 11 and had the crowd on their feet cheering. The sheer pace and direction of Lillee was rewarded with 5-51 and showed why he was regarded as one of the greatest fast bowlers to have ever played.

A large crowd, in excess of 19,000, watched enthralled as Australia struggled to come to terms with the vagaries of the pitch as Greg Chappell and Rick McCosker played cautiously. At tea the score was 171-3 and with the fall of another three wickets the noise from the terraces reached crescendo pitch and the main recipient was Richard Hadlee.

The effect was that he bowled too fast for three overs and virtually burnt himself out. He ended the day with one wicket for 105, but he could count himself most unlucky, having at least four chances missed off his bowling. Gary Gilmour and Kerry O'Keeffe weathered the storm and began a partnership that was to be spread over two days and took Australia from a tricky position to a dominant one. They added 93 and gave their side a first innings lead of 148.

Lillee began New Zealand's second innings in devastating form, demolishing the top order to take 4-19. Hadlee came to the crease in the ninth over at 31-5 and immediately took the attack to Lillee. A six hit into the terraces rejuvenated their voice and excitement mounted as Hadlee hit Lillee for 28 off three overs.

With Mark Burgess he added 105 runs before his colourful defiance concluded for 81 and emphasised how much he had matured in the previous year. Lillee ran through the tail to claim 6-72 and finish with match figures of 11-124.

Writing later, Richard Hadlee said: "It was the first time in my experience that a crowd reaction had been so startling, so vociferous, so demanding, so appreciative. It was a most moving emotional experience to hear that roar."

NEW ZEALAND

Batsman	Dismissal 1st	Runs	Dismissal 2nd	Runs
G.M.Turner*	c Marsh b Walker	4	c Walters b Lillee	23
G.P.Howarth	c McCosker b Lillee	59	c Turner b Lillee	2
B.E.Congdon	c Marsh b Lillee	25	c McCosker b Lillee	1
J.M.Parker	c Cosier b Lillee	20	c Turner b Walker	5
M.G.Burgess	c Marsh b Walters	1	b Walker	38
G.N.Edwards†	c Lillee b Gilmour	51	c Marsh b Lillee	0
R.J.Hadlee	c McCosker b Lillee	44	b Chappell	81
B.L.Cairns	b Chappell	2	c Lillee b Walker	7
H.J.Howarth	b Walker	5	lbw b Lillee	6
P.J.Petherick	c Marsh b Lillee	4	b Lillee	1
E.J.Chatfield	not out	0	not out	4
Extras	(lb 7, nb 7)	14	(b 4, lb 2, nb 1)	7
TOTAL	(66.3 overs)	**229**	(42.7 overs)	**175**

AUSTRALIA

Batsman	Dismissal 1st	Runs	Dismissal 2nd	Runs
I.C.Davis	b Chatfield	13	not out	6
A.Turner	c Edwards b Cairns	30	not out	20
R.B.McCosker	c Edwards b Cairns	84		
G.S.Chappell*	run out	58		
G.J.Cosier	c & b Cairns	21		
K.D.Walters	c Hadlee b Chatfield	16		
R.W.Marsh†	lbw b Hadlee	4		
G.J.Gilmour	b Chatfield	64		
K.J.O'Keeffe	c Congdon b Hadlee	32		
D.K.Lillee	not out	23		
M.H.N.Walker	c Turner b Chatfield	9		
Extras	(b 9, lb 9, nb 5)	23	(lb 1, nb 1)	2
TOTAL	(97.1 overs)	**377**	(3.5 overs) (0 wkts)	**28**

Bowling	O	M	R	W	O	M	R	W
AUSTRALIA								
Lillee	17.3	4	51	5	15.7	2	72	6
Walker	24	6	60	2	17	4	70	3
Gilmour	7	0	56	1	1	0	11	0
Chappell	13	4	28	1	9	4	15	1
Walters	4	1	20	1				
O'Keeffe	1	1	0	0				
NEW ZEALAND								
Hadlee	28	2	147	2	2	0	11	0
Chatfield	27.1	3	100	4	1.5	0	15	0
Cairns	28	9	69	3				
Congdon	5	1	8	0				
Howarth H.J.	5	1	16	0				
Petherick	4	2	14	0				

Fall of Wickets

	NZ 1st	A 1st	NZ 2nd	A 2nd
1st	6	31	10	-
2nd	63	56	12	-
3rd	112	171	23	-
4th	113	202	31	-
5th	121	217	31	-
6th	177	221	136	-
7th	202	245	162	-
8th	211	338	163	-
9th	228	364	169	-
10th	229	377	175	-

Watched by a crowd of 19,000 Ewen Chatfield bowled with his consistent metronomic accuracy and deserved his four wickets. The umpire is Dennis Copps.

1977/78 England in New Zealand

After three first-class games in New Zealand, England entered the first test with a question mark firmly against their batting. In the three games to date their batting lacked purpose, dedication and the skills that one normally associated with an England touring side. As Glenn Turner was staying in England making arrangements for his benefit year, New Zealand entered this game with a new captain in Mike Burgess.

128 NEW ZEALAND v ENGLAND *(First Test)*
at Basin Reserve, Wellington on 10, 11, 12, 14, 15 February, 1978
Toss : England. Umpires : W.R.C. Gardiner and R.L. Monteith
New Zealand won by 72 runs

Geoffrey Boycott, captaining England for only the second time, won the toss and asked New Zealand to bat first. Grey skies and a howling, blustering northerly made conditions most unpleasant for both batsmen and fieldsmen. A very confident appeal for caught behind to John Wright off the first ball was rejected, much to the disgust of the behind-the-wicket England fieldsmen. It took him 52 minutes to get off the mark.

Robert Anderson and extras scored the bulk of the opening partnership of 42 as Wright struggled for survival. Wright made one of the slowest half-centuries in test cricket taking 272 minutes to reach the mark. The England bowlers bowled at a rate of 10 overs per hour. When the umpires stopped play for bad light New Zealand was 152-3, Wright having batted 340 minutes for 55.

The gale that blew from the northern end changed direction and gusted equally strongly from the southern end on the second day. Wright's vigil ended without addition to his score and, under sustained hostility from Chris Old, New Zealand lost their last six wickets for 37 runs. Old deserved his best test figures of 6-54, which were a just reward for his tenacity and strength bowling into strong winds.

England's reply was similar to New Zealand's and Boycott revealed all his skill in fending off dangerous deliveries from Richard Collinge and Richard Hadlee on the cantankerous pitch. The highlight of the afternoon was Collinge capturing his 100th test victim.

Beginning the third day at 89-2 England maintained the slow tempo of the game as Boycott set out to bat through the innings. Graham Roope's 37 was the only bright feature of the innings. His dismissal, just prior to tea, cleared the way for the floodgates to open and the last six wickets fell for just 32 runs.

The decisive moment in New Zealand's first victory over England – Richard Collinge bowls England's master batsman Geoffrey Boycott at the start of the second innings. The fact has yet to register with Warren Lees and John Parker.

Hadlee bowled with great fire in his middle spell and Collinge was persistently on the line of the off stump. Bevan Congdon at one stage bowled 11 overs for two runs while Boycott's innings occupied 442 minutes of correct batting.

At lunch on the fourth day New Zealand were comfortably placed at 75-1. Bob Willis then produced a devastating spell of bowling, extracting awkward lift from the deteriorating pitch and exposing the New Zealanders' defensive weaknesses. From 82-2 the home side slid ignominiously to be 123 all out.

England came out after tea needing only 137 for victory. A yorker from Collinge bowled Boycott and lifted the hopes of the New Zealand team and the despondency of the crowd. It was Collinge's 500th first-class wicket and probably the one that has given him the most satisfaction. Collinge had the first three wickets with the score at 18 before Hadlee caught his enthusiasm and wickets tumbled to him.

Some balls exploded from the pitch, while others scuttled along the ground. Batting was impossible. At stumps England were 53-8. In the four hours from lunch 17 wickets had fallen for 101 runs.

Misty drizzle delayed play for 41 minutes on the last day. New Zealand made cricket history by dismissing England for 64, with Hadlee capturing 6-26 to give him match figures of 10-100.

MILESTONES

- Mark Burgess became the 14th captain of New Zealand.

- Stephen Boock (140) and John Wright (141) made their test debuts.

- New Zealand won their first test against England after 48 years and 48 matches.

- Richard Collinge captured his 100th test wicket and his 500th first-class wicket.

129 NEW ZEALAND v ENGLAND *(Second Test)*

at Lancaster Park, Christchurch on 24, 25, 26, 28 Feb, 1 March, 1978
Toss : England. Umpires : F.R. Goodall and R.L. Monteith
England won by 174 runs

On a well grassed, hard Lancaster Park pitch the New Zealand attack of Richard Collinge and Richard Hadlee carried on where they finished at the Basin Reserve with the first three England wickets falling for only 26 runs.

Graham Roope led a charmed life, being dropped twice, but he survived for 225 minutes and sapped the New Zealand seam bowlers of their effectiveness. Geoff Miller was batting well, before he was hit on the head and had to retire hurt.

With half the England side out, and Miller in hospital, the England innings was tottering at 128-5 when Bob Taylor joined Ian Botham. By stumps the score was 172-5.

Twenty-two-year-old Botham, playing in his fourth test, steered England into a winning position by scoring 103. In

NEW ZEALAND					
J.G.Wright	lbw b Botham	55	c Roope b Willis	19
R.W.Anderson	c Taylor b Old	28	lbw b Old	26
G.P.Howarth	c Botham b Old	13	c Edmonds b Willis	21
M.G.Burgess*	b Willis	9	c Boycott b Botham	6
B.E.Congdon	c Taylor b Old	44	c Roope b Willis	0
J.M.Parker	c Rose b Willis	16	c Edmonds b Willis	4
W.K.Lees†	c Taylor b Old	1	lbw b Hendrick	11
R.J.Hadlee	not out	27	c Boycott b Willis	2
D.R.Hadlee	c Taylor b Old	1	c Roope b Botham	2
R.O.Collinge	b Old	1	c Edmonds b Hendrick	6
S.L.Boock	b Botham	4	not out	0
Extras	(b 12, lb 3, w 1, nb 13)	29	(b 2, lb 9, w 2, nb 13)	26
TOTAL	(87.6 overs)	**228**	(44.3 overs)	**123**

ENGLAND					
B.C.Rose	c Lees b Collinge	21	not out	5
G.Boycott*	c Congdon b Collinge	77	b Collinge	1
G.Miller	b Boock	24	c Anderson b Collinge	4
R.W.Taylor†	c & b Collinge	8	(7) run out	0
D.W.Randall	c Burgess b Hadlee R.J.	4	(4) lbw b Collinge	9
G.R.J.Roope	c Lees b Hadlee R.J.	37	(5) c Lees b Hadlee R.J.	0
I.T.Botham	c Burgess b Hadlee R.J.	7	(6) c Boock b Hadlee R.J.	19
C.M.Old	b Hadlee R.J.	10	lbw b Hadlee R.J.	9
P.H.Edmonds	lbw b Congdon	4	c Parker b Hadlee R.J.	11
M.Hendrick	lbw b Congdon	0	c Parker b Hadlee R.J.	0
R.G.D.Willis	not out	6	c Howarth b Hadlee R.J.	3
Extras	(lb 4, nb 13)	17	(nb 3)	3
TOTAL	(94.4 overs)	**215**	(27.3 overs)	**64**

Bowling	O	M	R	W	O	M	R	W
ENGLAND								
Willis	25	7	65	2	15	2	32	5
Hendrick	17	2	46	0	10	2	16	2
Old	30	11	54	6	9	2	32	1
Edmonds	3	1	7	0	1	0	4	0
Botham	12.6	2	27	2	9.3	3	13	2
NEW ZEALAND								
Hadlee R.J.	28	5	74	4	13.3	4	26	6
Collinge	18	5	42	3	13	5	35	3
Hadlee D.R.	21	5	47	0	1	1	0	0
Boock	10	5	21	1				
Congdon	17.4	11	14	2				

Fall of Wickets	NZ	E	NZ	E
	1st	*1st*	*2nd*	*2nd*
1st	42	39	54	2
2nd	96	89	82	8
3rd	114	108	93	18
4th	152	126	93	18
5th	191	183	98	38
6th	193	188	99	38
7th	194	203	104	53
8th	196	205	116	53
9th	208	206	123	63
10th	228	215	123	64

Warren Lees follows the direction of a ball struck through the covers by Ian Botham . It was to be Botham's first test century.

conjunction with Taylor he added 160 runs and turned the tables irreversibly. Returning from his sickbed, Miller joined Phil Edmonds in a rollicking stand of 70. Strangely enough, Hadlee was used as a stock bowler.

Miller continued and added a further 23 runs off 21 balls. His had been a gutsy innings in the best tradition of cricket. Robert Anderson batted aggressively as New Zealand chased 418. He hit the medium-pace bowlers hard in the arc between extra cover and third man before he was bowled by a ball from Edmonds that spun out of the bowlers' footmarks. When the umpires stopped play because of fading light, New Zealand was precariously positioned at 122-4.

In perfect conditions New Zealand were struggling against the swing and pace of Botham and the left-arm spin of Edmonds. Had John Parker been caught when on 10, New Zealand may not have avoided the follow on. Botham added five wickets to his century for a memorable test double.

Seeking quick runs England's batsmen went for their strokes. Ewen Chatfield controversially ran out Derek Randall at the bowlers end, without a prior warning. This action precipitated an outburst, for and against, by the media.

Chasing 280 in six hours New Zealand were bowled out of any chance of victory by a magnificent spell of ferocious pace bowling by Bob Willis, who captured four wickets in seven overs. England fielded well and took some splendid sharp catches. The ball seemed to follow Botham around the field for three catches while he captured a further three wickets to give him an all-rounder's dream match.

MILESTONES

- Ian Botham joined the group of test players who had scored a century and taken five wickets in an innings in the same test. He was to repeat the feat another four times in his career of 102 tests.

130 NEW ZEALAND v ENGLAND *(Third Test)*
at Eden Park, Auckland on 4, 5, 6, 8, 9, 10 March, 1978
Toss : New Zealand. Umpires : W.R.C. Gardiner and J.B.R. Hastie
Match drawn

With the series level, the third and deciding test was played over six days. From the outset the wicket was placid and the teams played like marathon runners at the start of a race, aware that there was a long time for the match to be played.

New Zealand lost both openers with the score at 32. Geoff Howarth had been out of touch for most of the season and he initially struggled for survival. The only time he looked authoritative was when he was allowed to drive on the front foot. He reached his half-century in 253 minutes.

Jock Edwards brought some light to the game during the second day with a flamboyant innings of 55, helping to add 96 for the sixth wicket with Howarth. For 515 minutes Howarth continued to bat like a man determined not to get out and he had 122 to his name when he departed. New Zealand lost their last five wickets for only 37 runs. Botham was again England's star, capturing 5-109.

The war of attrition continued on the third day, during which only 59 overs were bowled and England added 142 runs. Boycott looked totally untroubled and it came as a great surprise when he was dismissed by Collinge after 233 minutes of dedicated service. The out-of-form Clive Radley began uncertainly but survived until stumps with England 172-2.

England made the game safe for themselves, as well as opening up possibilities for victory, mainly through the straight bat of Radley. At stumps on the fourth day England was 390-5. Radley had batted 616 minutes for his 154 not out. It was an innings built on singles and caution.

Roope and Botham added colour with their half-centuries but England squandered their position of strength when they lost their last five wickets for 39 runs. Stephen Boock captured his first five-wicket bag in test cricket as England's lead was restricted to 114 runs.

With 10 hours still remaining, there was no sign of wear on the pitch. If anything, it was even more docile. Robert Anderson and John Wright had 50 on the board in 12 overs. The day ended with New Zealand 112-2.

The sixth and final day meandered along with every New Zealand batsman reaching double figures, while Howarth reached the record books by scoring his second century in the game, this time batting for only 323 minutes.

ENGLAND

B.C.Rose	c Howarth b Chatfield	11	c Lees b Collinge	7
G.Boycott*	lbw b Collinge	8	run out	26
D.W.Randall	c Burgess b Hadlee	0	run out	13
G.R.J.Roope	c Burgess b Hadlee	50	(6) not out	9
G.Miller	c Congdon b Collinge	89		
C.T.Radley	c Lees b Hadlee	15		
I.T.Botham	c Lees b Boock	103	(4) not out	30
R.W.Taylor†	run out	45		
C.M.Old	b Hadlee	8	(5) b Collinge	1
P.H.Edmonds	c Lees b Collinge	50		
R.G.D.Willis	not out	6		
Extras	(b 14, lb 9, nb 10)	33	(b 4, lb 3, nb 3)	10
TOTAL	**(145.5 overs)**	**418**	**(22 overs) (4 wkts dec)**	**96**

NEW ZEALAND

J.G.Wright	c & b Edmonds	4	c Roope b Willis	0
R.W.Anderson	b Edmonds	62	b Willis	15
G.P.Howarth	c Edmonds b Willis	5	c Edmonds b Old	1
M.G.Burgess*	c Roope b Botham	29	not out	6
B.E.Congdon	lbw b Botham	20	c Botham b Willis	0
J.M.Parker	not out	53	c Botham b Edmonds	16
W.K.Lees†	c Miller b Botham	0	b Willis	0
R.J.Hadlee	b Edmonds	1	c Botham b Edmonds	39
R.O.Collinge	c Edmonds b Botham	32	c Miller b Botham	0
S.L.Boock	c Taylor b Edmonds	2	c Taylor b Botham	0
E.J.Chatfield	c Edmonds b Botham	3	lbw b Botham	6
Extras	(b 4, lb 1, nb 19)	24	(lb 6, nb 16)	22
TOTAL	**(92.7 overs)**	**235**	**(27 overs)**	**105**

Bowling	O	M	R	W	O	M	R	W		Fall of Wickets				
NEW ZEALAND											E	NZ	E	NZ
											1st	*1st*	*2nd*	*2nd*
Hadlee	43	10	147	4	6	1	17	0						
Collinge	26.5	6	89	3	9	2	29	2		1st	15	37	25	2
Chatfield	37	8	94	1	5	0	22	0		2nd	18	52	48	14
Congdon	18	11	14	0	2	0	18	0		3rd	26	82	67	19
Boock	21	11	41	1						4th	127	119	74	25
ENGLAND										5th	128	148	-	25
Willis	20	5	45	1	7	2	14	4		6th	288	151	-	59
Old	14	4	55	0	7	2	14	1		7th	294	153	-	81
Botham	24.7	6	73	5	7	1	38	3		8th	305	211	-	90
Edmonds	34	11	38	4	6	2	22	2		9th	375	216	-	95
										10th	418	235	-	105

Geoff Howarth came of age as a test batsman when he scored a century in each innings of the test at Eden Park.

NEW ZEALAND

J.G.Wright	c Taylor b Lever	4	c Taylor b Edmonds		25
R.W.Anderson	c Gatting b Botham	17	c Botham b Miller		55
G.P.Howarth	c Roope b Willis	122	b Miller		102
M.G.Burgess*	c Randall b Botham	50	c Taylor b Edmonds		17
B.E.Congdon	c Miller b Botham	5	c Roope b Lever		20
J.M.Parker	lbw b Botham	14	(7) not out		47
G.N.Edwards†	lbw b Lever	55	(6) c Randall b Lever		54
R.J.Hadlee	c Roope b Botham	1	b Miller		10
B.L.Cairns	b Lever	11	lbw b Edmonds		20
R.O.Collinge	not out	5	not out		12
S.L.Boock	c Edmonds b Willis	1			
Extras	(b 5, lb 10, nb 15)	30	(b 6, lb 4, nb 10)		20
TOTAL	**(105.6 overs)**	**315**	**(118 overs) (8 wkts)**		**382**

ENGLAND

G.Boycott*	c Burgess b Collinge	54
D.W.Randall	lbw b Hadlee	30
C.T.Radley	c Wright b Collinge	158
G.R.J.Roope	c Burgess b Boock	68
M.W.Gatting	b Boock	0
I.T.Botham	c Edwards b Collinge	53
R.W.Taylor†	b Boock	16
G.Miller	lbw b Collinge	15
P.H.Edmonds	b Boock	8
J.K.Lever	c & b Boock	1
R.G.D.Willis	not out	0
Extras	(b 6, lb 6, w 4, nb 10)	26
TOTAL	**(156.3 overs)**	**429**

Bowling	O	M	R	W	O	M	R	W		Fall of Wickets			
ENGLAND											NZ	E	NZ
Willis	26.6	8	57	2	10	3	42	0			1st	1st	2nd
Lever	34	5	96	3	17	4	59	2	1st		12	52	69
Botham	34	4	109	5	13	1	51	0	2nd		32	115	98
Edmonds	10	2	23	0	45	15	107	3	3rd		113	254	125
Miller	1	1	0	0	30	10	99	3	4th		129	258	185
Gatting					1	0	1	0	5th		182	355	272
Roope					1	0	2	0	6th		278	396	287
Randall					1	0	1	0	7th		285	418	305
NEW ZEALAND									8th		302	427	350
Hadlee	31	6	107	1					9th		314	428	-
Collinge	38	9	98	4					10th		315	429	-
Cairns	33	9	63	0									
Congdon	26	8	68	0									
Boock	28.3	4	67	5									

MILESTONES

- Geoff Howarth became the second New Zealand batsman, after Glenn Turner, to score a century in each innings of a test match.

- Richard Collinge captured his 112th test wicket to become New Zealand's leading wicket-taker.

AVERAGES

New Zealand

BATTING	M	I	NO	Runs	HS	Ave
G.N. Edwards	1	2	0	109	55	54.50
G.P. Howarth	3	6	0	264	122	44.00
J.M. Parker	3	6	2	150	53*	37.50
R.W. Anderson	3	6	0	203	62	33.83
M.G. Burgess	3	6	1	117	50	23.40
J.G. Wright	3	6	0	107	55	17.83
R.J. Hadlee	3	6	1	80	39	16.00
B.L. Cairns	1	2	0	31	20	15.50
B.E. Congdon	3	6	0	89	44	14.83
R.O. Collinge	3	6	2	56	32	14.00
E.J. Chatfield	1	2	0	9	6	4.50
W.K. Lees	2	4	0	12	11	3.00
S.L. Boock	3	5	1	7	4	1.75
D.R. Hadlee	1	2	0	3	2	1.50

BOWLING	O	M	R	W	Ave
S.L. Boock	59.3	20	129	7	18.42
R.O. Collinge	104.5	27	293	15	19.53
R.J. Hadlee	121.3	26	371	15	24.73
B.E. Congdon	63.4	30	114	2	57.00
E.J. Chatfield	42	8	116	1	116.00
D.R. Hadlee	22	6	47	0	-
B.L. Cairns	33	9	63	0	-

England

BATTING	M	I	NO	Runs	HS	Ave
C.T. Radley	2	2	0	173	158	86.50
I.T. Botham	3	5	1	212	103	53.00
G.R.J. Roope	3	5	1	164	68	41.00
G. Boycott	3	5	0	166	77	33.20
G. Miller	3	4	0	132	89	33.00
P.H. Edmonds	3	4	0	73	50	18.25
R.W. Taylor	3	4	0	69	45	17.25
R.G.D. Willis	3	4	3	15	6*	15.00
B.C. Rose	2	4	1	44	21	14.66
D.W. Randall	3	5	0	56	30	11.20
C.M. Old	2	4	0	28	10	7.00
J.K. Lever	1	1	0	1	1	1.00
M.W. Gatting	1	1	0	0	0	0.00
M. Hendrick	1	2	0	0	0	0.00

BOWLING	O	M	R	W	Ave
R.G.D. Willis	103.6	27	255	14	18.21
I.T. Botham	101	17	311	17	18.29
C.M. Old	60	21	150	8	18.75
P.H. Edmonds	99	31	201	9	22.33
J.K. Lever	51	9	155	5	31.00
M. Hendrick	27	4	62	2	31.00
G. Miller	31	11	99	3	33.00
M.W. Gatting	1	0	1	0	-
D.W. Randall	1	0	1	0	-
G.R.J. Roope	1	0	2	0	-

1978 New Zealand in England

131 **ENGLAND v NEW ZEALAND** *(First Test)*

at The Oval on 27, 28, 29, 31 July, 1 August, 1978
Toss : New Zealand. Umpires : D.J. Constant and B.J. Meyer
England won by 7 wickets

The England bowlers were able to obtain swing while the ball was new. After the loss of Robert Anderson, John Wright and Geoff Howarth were able to negate this advantage and had the largest partnership for New Zealand (123) of the test series. Mark Burgess and Howarth added 60 with attractive but sensible batting.

Following his success of twin hundreds at Eden Park, Howarth failed by only six runs to score his third test hundred on the trot. Ironically he was dismissed off perhaps the worst long-hop bowled in the game.

The last hour of the day cost New Zealand their main chance of victory as they lost four wickets for 33 runs and gave England an advantage that they never relinquished. It was a "should have been" day.

The pace of Bob Willis, with the new ball, quickly terminated New Zealand's innings as he captured three wickets in three overs to finish with five for the innings. There was a sensational start to the England innings when Brendon Bracewell, at the age of 18, captured a wicket off his third ball and another seven balls later to have England 7-2.

Clive Radley and David Gower rather fortuitously survived dropped catches and stemmed the tide, adding 116. Anderson was involved in the run out of both players but not before Gower had made a century of charm and grace. England was 225-7 in reply to New Zealand's 234.

England's last three batsmen added 52 even though conditions favoured the bowlers as the ball swung in the humid atmosphere. Before the scores were level New Zealand lost three wickets to attacking shots. Bruce Edgar and Bevan Congdon fought doggedly against the vast swing of Botham and the considerable spin of Edmonds. New Zealand ended a disastrous day only 78 runs in front and with only three wickets remaining. Rain washed out the fourth day.

Lance Cairns and Congdon took their partnership to 69 face-saving runs before Cairns departed at 182-8 and the last two wickets fell at the same score. There was never much prospect of England not being able to score the 138 runs needed for victory, particularly as Graham Gooch attacked boldly and scored 91 of the runs needed.

MILESTONES

- Brendon Bracewell (142) and Bruce Edgar (143) made their test debuts.

- Bevan Congdon set a new record for New Zealand with his 59th test appearance.

A dramatic photograph of Brendon Bracewell who captured two wickets in his first two overs at test level. At 18 years 316 days he was the fourth youngest New Zealander to play test cricket. David Gower is the England batsman backing up.

NEW ZEALAND

J.G.Wright	c Radley b Willis	62	lbw b Botham	25
R.W.Anderson	b Old	4	c Taylor b Botham	2
G.P.Howarth	c Edmonds b Botham	94	b Willis	0
B.A.Edgar	c & b Miller	0	b Edmonds	38
M.G.Burgess*	lbw b Willis	34	lbw b Botham	7
B.E.Congdon	run out	2	b Edmonds	36
G.N.Edwards†	b Miller	6	c Brearley b Edmonds	11
R.J.Hadlee	c Brearley b Willis	5	b Edmonds	7
B.L.Cairns	lbw b Willis	5	b Miller	27
B.P.Bracewell	c Taylor b Willis	0	b Miller	0
S.L.Boock	not out	3	not out	0
Extras	(b 1, lb 7, nb 11)	19	(b 8, lb 10, nb 11)	29
TOTAL	(104.2 overs)	**234**	(105.1 overs)	**182**

ENGLAND

J.M.Brearley*	c Edwards b Bracewell	2	lbw b Boock	11
G.A.Gooch	lbw b Bracewell	0	not out	91
C.T.Radley	run out	49	lbw b Bracewell	2
D.I.Gower	run out	111	c Howarth b Cairns	11
G.R.J.Roope	b Boock	14	not out	10
G.Miller	lbw b Cairns	0		
I.T.Botham	c Bracewell b Boock	22		
R.W.Taylor†	c Edwards b Hadlee	8		
P.H.Edmonds	lbw b Hadlee	28		
C.M.Old	c Edwards b Cairns	16		
R.G.D.Willis	not out	3		
Extras	(b 15, lb 8, nb 3)	26	(b 2, lb 3, nb 8)	13
TOTAL	(134.5 overs)	**279**	(52.3 overs) (3 wkts)	**138**

Bowling	O	M	R	W	O	M	R	W
ENGLAND								
Willis	20.2	9	42	5	13	2	39	1
Old	20	7	43	1	5	2	13	0
Botham	22	7	58	1	19	2	46	3
Miller	25	10	31	2	34	19	35	2
Edmonds	17	2	41	0	34.1	23	20	4
NEW ZEALAND								
Hadlee	21.5	6	43	2	11.3	3	18	0
Bracewell	17	8	46	2	13	3	26	1
Cairns	40	16	65	2	7	0	21	1
Boock	35	18	61	2	20	6	55	1
Congdon	21	6	38	0	1	0	5	0

Fall of Wickets	NZ	E	NZ	E
	1st	1st	2nd	2nd
1st	7	1	15	26
2nd	130	7	19	51
3rd	131	123	30	82
4th	191	165	70	–
5th	197	166	86	–
6th	207	208	105	–
7th	224	212	113	–
8th	230	232	182	–
9th	230	257	182	–
10th	234	279	182	–

132 ENGLAND v NEW ZEALAND *(Second Test)*

at Trent Bridge, Nottingham on 10, 11, 12, 14 August, 1978
Toss : England. Umpires : D.J. Constant and T.W. Spencer
England won by an innings and 119 runs

The first stanza of the game between Richard Hadlee and Geoffrey Boycott was intriguing. Twice in the opening overs Boycott looked dangerously near to being out lbw to balls that seamed back. Then, when on two, he was dropped at third slip.

The batsmen gradually gained the ascendancy, though they were kept under tight rein. Graham Gooch and Boycott added 111 then Clive Radley helped Boycott with a further 129. The importance of the early morning let-off for Boycott was emphasised when he made his 16th test century in 320 minutes. England was 252-2.

When England passed 300 for the loss of only two wickets it appeared as though it would amass a gigantic total. Even though David Gower and Mike Brearley added sufficient runs, the New Zealand bowlers, spearheaded by Hadlee, refused to let up and, unlike the opening day, the bowlers had the full support of the fieldsmen. England all out 419.

Two wickets to Ian Botham, as well as a bouncer that hit Geoff Howarth on the head and forced him to retire, illustrated the skills of Botham in delivering telling blows to New Zealand, which finished the day 35-3.

The third day began in Stygian gloom and, after two balls had been bowled, the umpires came off for bad light. When play began three hours later there was sufficient time for New Zealand to be dismissed and commence their second innings. Botham continued from where he left off the previous evening, bowling at a brisk pace with a barrage of bouncers as well as moving the ball considerably in the air.

When Hadlee was smartly caught by Gooch, Botham had taken his test tally of wickets to 50 in only his 10th game, an amazing feat. The England wicketkeeper Bob Taylor held five catches, once more emphasising his excellence in this specialist position.

With two days of the game remaining New Zealand contributed greatly to their self-destruction on the fourth day. Robert Anderson, desperate to get off the mark, ran himself out. Bruce Edgar and Howarth comfortably added 50 in even time before Howarth was caught at second slip. For over two hours John Parker and Edgar flourished until a light shower forced a 15-minute delay.

Upon resumption Parker slipped on the damp surface and was cruelly run out. For four hours Edgar soldiered on, displaying impeccable concentration to both spin and pace alike. Once he was dismissed, Phil Edmonds and Botham polished off the last seven wickets for only 42 runs. England's fielding and catching gave them an edge over New Zealand that they exploited to the full.

ENGLAND

G.Boycott	c & b Hadlee	131
G.A.Gooch	c Burgess b Bracewell	55
C.T.Radley	lbw b Hadlee	59
D.I.Gower	c Cairns b Boock	46
J.M.Brearley*	c Parker b Bracewell	50
P.H.Edmonds	b Cairns	6
G.Miller	c Howarth b Boock	4
I.T.Botham	c Hadlee b Boock	8
R.W.Taylor†	b Hadlee	22
R.G.D.Willis	not out	1
M.Hendrick	c Edwards b Bracewell	7
Extras	(b 16, lb 12, w 1, nb 11)	40
TOTAL	(180.5 overs)	**429**

NEW ZEALAND

B.A.Edgar	c Taylor b Botham	6	c Botham b Edmonds	60
R.W.Anderson	lbw b Botham	19	run out	0
G.P.Howarth	not out	31	c Botham b Hendrick	34
S.L.Boock	c Taylor b Willis	8	(10) lbw b Edmonds	2
J.M.Parker	c Taylor b Hendrick	0	(4) run out	38
M.G.Burgess*	c Taylor b Botham	5	(5) c Brearley b Edmonds	7
B.E.Congdon	c Hendrick b Botham	27	(6) c Brearley b Botham	4
G.N.Edwards†	c Taylor b Botham	0	(7) c & b Edmonds	18
B.L.Cairns	b Edmonds	9	(8) lbw b Botham	0
R.J.Hadlee	c Gooch b Botham	4	(9) c Taylor b Botham	11
B.P.Bracewell	b Edmonds	0	not out	0
Extras	(lb 1, w 1, nb 9)	11	(lb 6, w 1, nb 9)	16
TOTAL	(69.4 overs)	**120**	(92.1 overs)	**190**

Bowling	O	M	R	W	O	M	R	W
NEW ZEALAND								
Hadlee	42	11	94	4				
Bracewell	33.5	2	110	3				
Cairns	38	7	85	1				
Congdon	39	15	71	0				
Boock	28	18	29	2				
ENGLAND								
Willis	12	5	22	1	9	0	31	0
Hendrick	15	9	18	1	20	7	30	1
Botham	21	9	34	6	24	7	59	3
Edmonds	15.4	5	21	2	33.1	15	44	4
Miller	6	1	14	0	6	3	10	0

Fall of Wickets	E	NZ	NZ
	1st	1st	2nd
1st	111	22	5
2nd	240	27	63
3rd	301	30	127
4th	342	47	148
5th	350	49	152
6th	364	99	164
7th	374	99	168
8th	419	110	180
9th	427	115	190
10th	429	120	190

MILESTONES

- Bevan Congdon established a new record aggregate for runs for New Zealand, passing John Reid's 3428.

Bruce Edgar stolidly resisted for four hours and was 60 in New Zealand's second innings when he was caught by Ian Botham, fielding in a helmet at short leg. Mark Burgess, the non-striker, surveys the scene. From left, Mike Hendrick, Bob Taylor, umpire Tom Spencer, Edgar, Phil Edmonds, Mike Brearley and Clive Radley.

133 ENGLAND v NEW ZEALAND *(Third Test)*

at Lord's on 24, 25, 26, 28 August, 1978
Toss : New Zealand. Umpires : H.D. Bird and B.J. Meyer
England won by 7 wickets

New Zealand went about restoring its tarnished cricket image after Burgess had won the toss. From the outset there was variable bounce in the pitch and a good deal of movement through the air and off the turf. This required batting of the soundest calibre to weather the initial onslaught.

John Wright and Bruce Edgar, in the first of what was to become many test opening partnerships for New Zealand, added 65. At 117-3 New Zealand were struggling but a scintillating partnership of 130 runs, between Geoff Howarth and Mark Burgess, swung the game back to the batting side. It was an excellent return to form by Burgess. New Zealand 280-5, with Howarth on 105.

It was vital for the tourists that Robert Anderson and Richard Hadlee stayed to support Howarth but Ian Botham again proved to be New Zealand's nemesis by capturing six wickets. Howarth's innings of 123 occupied 361 minutes. It was his third century against England in seven innings and took his aggregate to 506. Both England openers were out with the score at 66, before David Gower and Clive Radley, both heavy scorers in early encounters, added 109 runs before stumps.

The third day was a day of shocks for ardent New Zealand followers as the New Zealand team firstly surprised to capture the last seven England wickets for 78 runs and thus earned a first innings lead of 50. The second surprise was

nowhere near as pleasant when they lost their first seven wickets for only 37 runs in their second innings.

The day began with Gower and Radley adding a further 67 runs. After lunch, with the new ball, Richard Collinge and Hadlee completely dominated the England batting with Hadlee taking three wickets for eight runs and Collinge providing adequate support in taking two. Batsmen on both sides had doubt about the height that the ball would bounce, while the inconsistency was becoming more erratic.

The combination of Bob Willis, with violent bounce from not too short of a length, and the swing and aggression of Botham proved too much for New Zealand. In the 110 minutes between tea and stumps they lost seven for 37. New Zealand's tactic of using both Stephen Boock and Brendon Bracewell as nightwatchmen was highly questionable and they were both destroyed within minutes of reaching the crease.

The visitors added a further 30 runs the next morning with Botham taking five for 39, giving him 11 for the match and 24 for the series. Requiring only 118, for victory Hadlee had alarm bells ringing in the England camp when he bowled Boycott in his third over and with the next ball bowled Radley, equally as comprehensively.

NEW ZEALAND

J.G.Wright	c Edmonds b Botham	17	b Botham		12
B.A.Edgar†	c Edmonds b Embury	39	b Botham		4
G.P.Howarth	c Taylor b Botham	123	(9) not out		14
J.M.Parker	lbw b Hendrick	14	c Taylor b Botham		3
M.G.Burgess*	lbw b Botham	68	c Hendrick b Botham		14
B.E.Congdon	c Emburey b Botham	2	c Taylor b Willis		3
R.W.Anderson	b Botham	16	(3) c Taylor b Willis		1
R.J.Hadlee	c Brearley b Botham	0	(10) run out		5
R.O.Collinge	c Emburey b Willis	19	(11) b Botham		0
S.L.Boock	not out	4	(7) c Radley b Willis		0
B.P.Bracewell	st Taylor b Emburey	4	(8) c Hendrick b Willis		0
Extras	(b 4, lb 18, w 4, nb 7)	33	(lb 3, nb 8)		11
TOTAL	(143.1 overs)	339	(37.1 overs)		67

ENGLAND

G.A.Gooch	c Boock b Hadlee	2	not out		42
G.Boycott	c Hadlee b Bracewell	24	b Hadlee		4
C.T.Radley	c Congdon b Hadlee	77	b Hadlee		0
D.I.Gower	c Wright b Boock	71	c Congdon b Bracewell		46
J.M.Brearley*	c Edgar b Hadlee	33	not out		8
I.T.Botham	c Edgar b Collinge	21			
R.W.Taylor†	lbw b Hadlee	1			
P.H.Edmonds	c Edgar b Hadlee	5			
J.E.Emburey	b Collinge	2			
M.Hendrick	b Bracewell	12			
R.G.D.Willis	not out	7			
Extras	(b 7, lb 5, nb 22)	34	(lb 3, w 4, nb 11)		18
TOTAL	(112.3 overs)	289	(30.5 overs) (3 wkts)		118

Bowling

ENGLAND	O	M	R	W	O	M	R	W
Willis	29	9	79	1	16	8	16	4
Hendrick	28	14	39	1				
Botham	38	13	101	6	18.1	4	39	5
Edmonds	12	3	19	0				
Emburey	26.1	12	39	2	3	2	1	0
Gooch	10	0	29	0				
NEW ZEALAND								
Hadlee	32	9	84	5	13.5	2	31	2
Collinge	30	9	58	2	6	1	26	0
Bracewell	19.3	1	68	2	6	0	32	1
Boock	25	10	33	1	5	1	11	0
Congdon	6	1	12	0				

Fall of Wickets

	NZ	E	NZ	E
	1st	*1st*	*2nd*	*2nd*
1st	65	2	10	14
2nd	70	66	14	14
3rd	117	180	20	84
4th	247	211	29	-
5th	253	249	33	-
6th	290	255	37	-
7th	290	258	37	-
8th	321	263	43	-
9th	333	274	57	-
10th	339	289	67	-

MILESTONES

- Bevan Congdon played his 61st and last test match for New Zealand.

AVERAGES

New Zealand

BATTING	M	I	NO	Runs	HS	Ave
G.P. Howarth	3	6	2	296	123	74.00
J.G. Wright	2	4	0	116	62	29.00
B.A. Edgar	3	6	0	147	60	24.50
M.G. Burgess	3	6	0	135	68	22.50
J.M. Parker	2	4	0	55	38	13.75
B.E. Congdon	3	6	0	74	36	12.33
B.L. Cairns	2	4	0	41	27	10.25
R.O. Collinge	1	2	0	19	19	9.50
G.N. Edwards	2	4	0	35	18	8.75
R.W. Anderson	3	6	0	42	19	7.00
S.L. Boock	3	6	3	17	8	5.66
R.J. Hadlee	3	6	0	32	11	5.33
B.P. Bracewell	3	6	1	4	4	0.80

BOWLING	O	M	R	W	Ave
R.J. Hadlee	121.1	31	270	13	20.76
B.P. Bracewell	89.2	14	282	9	31.33
S.L. Boock	113	53	189	6	31.50
R.O. Collinge	36	10	84	2	42.00
B.L. Cairns	85	23	171	4	42.75
B.E. Congdon	67	22	126	0	-

England

BATTING	M	I	NO	Runs	HS	Ave
G.A. Gooch	3	5	2	190	91*	63.33
D.I. Gower	3	5	0	285	111	57.00
G. Boycott	2	3	0	159	131	53.00
C.T. Radley	3	5	0	187	77	37.40
J.M. Brearley	3	5	1	104	50	26.00
G.R.J. Roope	1	2	1	24	14	24.00
I.T. Botham	3	3	0	51	22	17.00
C.M. Old	1	1	0	16	16	16.00
P.H. Edmonds	3	3	0	39	28	13.00
R.W. Taylor	3	3	0	31	22	10.33
M. Hendrick	2	2	0	19	12	9.50
J.E. Emburey	1	1	0	2	2	2.00
G. Miller	2	2	0	4	4	2.00
R.G.D. Willis	3	3	3	11	7*	-

BOWLING	O	M	R	W	Ave
I.T. Botham	142.1	42	337	24	14.04
P.H. Edmonds	112	48	145	10	14.50
R.G.D. Willis	99.2	33	229	12	19.08
J.E. Emburey	29.1	14	40	2	20.00
G. Miller	71	33	90	4	22.50
M. Hendrick	63	30	87	3	29.00
C.M. Old	25	9	56	1	56.00
G.A. Gooch	10	0	29	0	-

The helmeted Clive Radley takes evasive action as Geoff Howarth strikes another majestic boundary in his 123. This was Howarth's third century in six tests against England in which he had aggregated 560 runs.

1978/79 Pakistan in New Zealand

Pakistan were weakened by the demands of World Series Cricket that saw Imran Khan, Zaheer Abbas and Asif Iqbal committed to play in Australia during the first test. Dropped catches at crucial times during the first day denied New Zealand a complete breakthrough after they had won the toss and asked Pakistan to bat first.

134 NEW ZEALAND v PAKISTAN *(First Test)*

at Lancaster Park, Christchurch on 2, 3, 4, 6, 7 February, 1979
Toss : New Zealand. Umpires : J.B.R. Hastie and R.L. Monteith
Pakistan won by 128 runs

Javed Miandad was dropped off a simple catch to mid-on when he was on nought. This error proved vital in the whole context of this game. When he was bowled by Hadlee, with the second new ball, he had batted 235 minutes and had scored 81 runs. It was a mixed bag of an innings, with many streaky edges complementing shots of a class player. Easy chances were also dropped off Mushtaq Mohammad and Sarfraz Nawaz. At stumps Pakistan was 220-6.

Sarfraz continued to haunt the New Zealand team, taking his side through to 271. Richard Hadlee captured five wickets. Bruce Edgar anchored the home team's reply, finishing the day 70 not out as New Zaland ended in a strong position of 142-2. Players and critics alike praised the wicket as being one of the best seen in New Zealand for many years.

Edgar, resolute and determined, achieved his first test century next morning, but watched with dismay as four wickets fell at the other end in the session before lunch. When he was eventually caught behind he had batted 414 minutes for his 129. Apart from some flourishes by Hadlee, the remainder of the New Zealand batting was disappointing and their lead of only 19 was inexcusable.

Mudassar Nazar had to retire hurt with a badly bruised finger and if Jeremy Coney had not dropped Miandad when he was on six, Pakistan would have been in great strife. Instead, they ended the day 99-1.

The batting genius of Miandad dominated the fourth day. Once any chances of an early breakthrough had been eliminated, Pakistan went onto the attack. Miandad revealed superb reflexes and an amazing ability to run quickly between the wickets for a very sustained period of time. All told, he batted 411 minutes and hit 17 fours and one six. Mushtaq's declaration left New Zealand 390 minutes to score 305.

On a pitch still playing perfectly, New Zealand's second innings was destroyed by the leg-spin and googly bowling of Mushtaq, who captured five wickets, and Wasim Raja, four. Few of the New Zealanders had the technique to counter this form of attack. Many people were surprised by Pakistan's easy win by 128 runs, considering that they were without four of their better players.

PAKISTAN

Batsman	Dismissal	Runs	Dismissal	Runs
Mudassar Nazar	c Edgar b Bracewell	7	retired hurt	4
Talat Ali	c Wright b Hadlee	40	c Coney b Hadlee	61
Mohsin Khan	lbw b Hadlee	12	lbw b Coney	7
Javed Miandad	b Hadlee	81	not out	160
Haroon Rashid	c Howarth b Hadlee	40	b Cairns	35
Wasim Raja	c Boock b Cairns	12	c Hadlee b Coney	17
Mushtaq Mohammad*	lbw b Hadlee	10	c Burgess b Hadlee	12
Sarfraz Nawaz	not out	31	b Hadlee	4
Wasim Bari†	b Cairns	9		
Anwar Khan	c Lees b Boock	12	(9) not out	3
Sikander Bakht	c Edgar b Boock	0		
Extras	(b 5, lb 8, nb 4)	17	(b 1, lb 19)	20
TOTAL	(92.6 overs)	271	(93 overs) (6 wkts dec)	323

NEW ZEALAND

Batsman	Dismissal	Runs	Dismissal	Runs
B.A.Edgar	c Bari b Sikander	129	c Sarfraz b Sikander	16
J.G.Wright	c Bari b Sikander	27	b Mushtaq	21
G.P.Howarth	c Raja b Mushtaq	19	(4) b Mushtaq	0
M.G.Burgess*	c Miandad b Sikander	16	(5) c Sarfraz b Raja	6
J.M.Parker	c Bari b Sarfraz	2	(6) lbw b Mushtaq	33
J.V.Coney	c Miandad b Mushtaq	6	(3) c Mohsin b Raja	36
W.K.Lees†	c & b Mushtaq	8	c Bari b Raja	19
R.J.Hadlee	c Bari b Raja	42	c Sikander b Raja	4
B.L.Cairns	lbw b Mushtaq	11	not out	23
S.L.Boock	b Raja	1	(11) c Mohsin b Mushtaq	0
B.P.Bracewell	not out	0	(10) st Bari b Mushtaq	5
Extras	(b 8, lb 9, nb 12)	29	(b 4, lb 6, nb 3)	13
TOTAL	(88.4 overs)	290	(56 overs)	176

Bowling	O	M	R	W	O	M	R	W
NEW ZEALAND								
Hadlee	25	2	62	5	26	4	83	3
Bracewell	12	1	50	1	7	0	53	0
Coney	7	3	10	0	12	1	33	2
Cairns	31	5	96	2	23	7	46	1
Boock	14.6	5	22	2	19	4	70	0
Howarth	3	1	14	0	6	0	18	0
PAKISTAN								
Sarfraz	24	7	67	1	8	3	22	0
Sikander	21	4	88	3	6	0	14	1
Mushtaq	25	4	60	4	22	5	59	5
Anwar	4	0	12	0				
Raja	10.4	5	18	2	20	3	68	4
Mudassar	4	1	16	0				

Fall of Wickets	P	NZ	P	NZ
	1st	1st	2nd	2nd
1st	19	63	24	33
2nd	48	96	128	62
3rd	75	147	209	62
4th	135	151	273	77
5th	183	176	298	98
6th	198	200	316	136
7th	242	254	-	142
8th	255	288	-	152
9th	271	289	-	176
10th	271	290	-	176

A resolute and determined Bruce Edgar made 129 in the first test.

135 NEW ZEALAND v PAKISTAN (*Second Test*)

at McLean Park, Napier on 16, 17, 18, 19, 20, 21 February, 1979
Toss : Pakistan. Umpires : F.R. Goodall and S.J. Woodward
Match drawn

Because of alteration works at the Basin Reserve, Napier became the first official test match venue in New Zealand outside the main metropolitan centres. Pakistan was able to play the players contacted to World Series Cricket.

Mushtaq Mohammad may have regretted his decision to bat first in the early stages, when his side were 33-3, but a partnership of 85 by Javed Miandad and Asif Iqbal slowly began to turn things to Pakistan's advantage. Slowly but surely the graceful Asif assumed control and he soon passed the milestone of 3000 runs in test cricket. After 227 minutes he had his 10th century in test cricket. It was a completely professional innings that showed his years of experience. Pakistan was 207-5 at stumps.

The depth of the Pakistan batting was most aptly illustrated when one considers that the first five wickets made 181 and the last five wickets a further 179 to give Pakistan a solid score of 360. Wasim Raja was the main contributor to the lower half of the batting and Sarfraz Nawaz gave him admirable support.

Raja flowed into his drives and cuts and looked for boundaries off all the bowlers. Before rain washed out play, Bruce Edgar was caught on the leg-side from a ball that stood up on him after a series of deliveries had tended to keep low.

Rain fell on Saturday evening and Sunday's weather was atrocious. Play was abandoned and this became the rest day. Following 30 hours of continuous rain it was little short of a miracle that McLean Park was fit for play on Monday morning.

John Wright and Geoff Howarth rewrote the record book with a partnership of 195 runs in 255 minutes. Howarth's 114 was his fourth test century within 12 months and was, perhaps, artistically his best. From the moment he came in he struck the ball sweetly.

Wright's role was less flamboyant than Howarth's but it was his highest score in test cricket. He was hit several times by Imran Khan yet did not flinch and throughout his 307 minutes stay, always got into line. Mark Burgess played an aggressive cameo to have New Zealand 298-5 at stumps.

Weather-induced interruptions dotted the fourth day, which saw New Zealand reach 402, a lead of 42, and Jeremy Coney scored his first 50 in test cricket. A draw was now inevitable and interest on the final day centred on whether Majid Khan would score a century. He was unbeaten on 119 when the match ended.

Right: In 1978 Australia's Graham Yallop became the first batsman to wear a helmet in a test match. By 1979 they had become accepted for batsmen and close-in fieldsmen. John Wright made his best score of 88 and Javed Miandad wore the new grill protection for the face.

PAKISTAN

Majid Khan	c Lees b Cairns	29	not out		119
Talat Ali	b Hadlee	4	b Hadlee		13
Zaheer Abbas	c Parker b Cairns	2	c & b Boock		40
Javed Miandad	run out	26			
Asif Iqbal	b Cairns	104			
Mushtaq Mohammad*	c Lees b Hadlee	24	(4) c Cairns b Boock		28
Wasim Raja	lbw b Hadlee	74			
Imran Khan	c Lees b Hadlee	3	(5) not out		27
Sarfraz Nawaz	c Edgar b Coney	31			
Wasim Bari†	not out	37			
Sikander Bakht	lbw b Troup	19			
Extras	(b 2, lb 3, nb 2)	7	(b 2, lb 1, w 4)		7
TOTAL	(104.5 overs)	**360**	(86 overs) (3 wkts dec)		**234**

NEW ZEALAND

B.A.Edgar	c Mushtaq b Imran	3
J.G.Wright	c Miandad b Sikander	88
G.P.Howarth	b Sikander	114
J.M.Parker	lbw b Sikander	3
M.G.Burgess*	c Miandad b Imran	40
J.V.Coney	lbw b Sikander	69
S.L.Boock	b Imran	4
W.K.Lees†	b Imran	8
R.J.Hadlee	c Sikander b Imran	11
B.L.Cairns	c Zaheer b Mushtaq	13
G.B.Troup	not out	3
Extras	(b 10, lb 14, nb 22)	46
TOTAL	(101.3 overs)	**402**

Bowling	O	M	R	W	O	M	R	W
NEW ZEALAND								
Hadlee	25	3	101	4	14	1	56	1
Cairns	19	1	86	3	11	2	23	0
Troup	22.5	2	86	1	16	3	25	0
Boock	12	3	41	0	30	6	77	2
Coney	25	9	38	1	10	2	21	0
Howarth	1	0	1	0	5	1	25	0
PAKISTAN								
Imran	33	6	106	5				
Sarfraz	26	5	90	0				
Sikander	17	2	67	4				
Mushtaq	17.3	0	70	1				
Raja	3	1	10	0				
Majid	5	1	13	0				

Fall of Wickets	P	NZ	P
	1st	1st	2nd
1st	19	24	27
2nd	23	219	110
3rd	42	230	188
4th	128	241	-
5th	180	292	-
6th	221	301	-
7th	228	318	-
8th	283	351	-
9th	313	388	-
10th	360	402	-

MILESTONES

- McLean Park became the 50th test match venue.

- John Wright and Geoff Howarth established a New Zealand record second wicket partnership of 195.

- Richard Hadlee became the fourth New Zealand bowler to capture 100 test wickets.

136 NEW ZEALAND v PAKISTAN *(Third Test)*

at Eden Park, Auckland on 23, 24, 25, 27, 28 February, 1979
Toss : Pakistan. Umpires : F.R. Goodall and J.B.R. Hastie
Match drawn

By lunch on the first day New Zealand was struggling to stay in the game, being five wickets down for 68 runs. A combination of good bowling, poor batting and the glue-like gloves of Wasim Bari all contributed to New Zealand's dire situation. Three of the players were caught playing at balls at least a foot wide of the off stump.

After lunch Jeremy Coney was involved in three vital partnerships. The first, with Warren Lees, was worth 49, then he added 57 with Lance Cairns. Another 43, in combination with Richard Hadlee, helped pull New Zealand through to an adequate total of 229-9 at stumps.

The highlight of the day was Bari becoming the first wicketkeeper to take seven catches in one test innings. Many of the catches were straightforward but the one offered by John Wright was a superb effort taken wide of leg slip. The helmeted Hadlee continued to attack the Pakistan bowlers with his own inventive brand of batting and, together with Gary Troup, added 42 runs.

Hadlee dismissed Talat Ali and was unlucky when, next ball, Zaheer Abbas, an outstanding batsman by world standards who had 12 test innings against New Zealand for an aggregate of only 137 runs, edged the delivery safely between Lees and Bruce Edgar. He was to make the most of this and two other let-offs by scoring a competent 135 in 388 minutes.

Thanks to Zaheer's century and fine supporting roles played by Mushtaq, Miandad, Asif and Imran, who all reached the 30s, Pakistan reached 321-6. Hadlee, off the field for a large part of the day with a damaged ankle, a strained groin and a heavily bruised right bicep, returned and, in a purple patch, captured the last four wickets for only 12 runs to finish with 5-104. The pick of the New Zealand bowlers was Lance Cairns who laboured assiduously and without luck for most of the innings.

The highlights of New Zealand's second innings were a dogged innings of 71 by Mark Burgess and, for the fourth time in as many innings, Coney proving a stumbling block for the Pakistan bowlers. A combination of bad light, bad weather and bad catching allowed New Zealand to escape from this game with a draw after rain spoiled most of the last day.

MILESTONES

- John Reid (144) made his test debut.

- Wasim Bari created a test wicketkeeping record by taking seven catches in an innings.

To combat the bounce of Imran Khan, Jeremy Coney devised his own method of defence by leaping high into the line of the ball. Unorthodox though it appeared, it was effective as he scored 82 and 49.

PAKISTAN

J.G.Wright	c Bari b Sikander	32	b Sarfraz	10
B.A.Edgar	c Bari b Imran	1	b Imran	0
G.P.Howarth	c Bari b Sarfraz	5	c Raja b Sikander	38
J.F.Reid	c Bari b Imran	0	(5) c Majid b Mushtaq	19
M.G.Burgess*	c Sarfraz b Sikander	3	(4) c Asif b Sarfraz	71
J.V.Coney	c Bari b Sarfraz	82	c Mushtaq b Imran	49
W.K.Lees†	c Bari b Sarfraz	25	not out	45
B.L.Cairns	c Bari b Asif	17	b Sarfraz	4
R.J.Hadlee	not out	53	c Talat b Sarfraz	5
G.B.Troup	c Mushtaq b Sikander	7		
S.L.Boock	c Miandad b Imran	0		
Extras	(b 5, lb 3, w 1, nb 20)	29	(b 8, lb 13, w 1, nb 18)	40
TOTAL	(55.7 overs)	**254**	(91.2 overs)(8 wkts dec)	**281**

NEW ZEALAND

Majid Khan	b Cairns	10		
Talat Ali	c Lees b Hadlee	1	(1) not out	8
Zaheer Abbas	c Lees b Troup	135		
Javed Miandad	lbw b Cairns	30		
Asif Iqbal	c Coney b Cairns	35		
Mushtaq Mohammad*	lbw b Hadlee	48		
Wasim Raja	c Coney b Troup	19		
Imran Khan	c Lees b Hadlee	33		
Sarfraz Nawaz	c Howarth b Hadlee	5	(2) not out	0
Wasim Bari†	not out	25		
Sikander Bakht	c Cairns b Hadlee	6		
Extras	(b 4, lb 7, nb 1)	12		0
TOTAL	(103 overs)	**359**	(0.6 overs) (0 wkts)	**8**

Bowling	O	M	R	W	O	M	R	W
NEW ZEALAND								
Imran	17.7	2	77	3	32	9	72	2
Sarfraz	15	3	56	3	28.2	9	61	4
Asif	7	1	24	1	2	0	5	0
Sikander	16	4	68	3	18	2	64	1
Mushtaq					11	2	39	1
NEW ZEALAND								
Hadlee	27	3	104	5	0.6	0	8	0
Troup	22	2	70	2				
Cairns	28	5	94	3				
Coney	19	4	51	0				
Boock	6	0	28	0				
Howarth	1	1	0	0				

Fall of Wickets	P	NZ	P	NZ
	1st	1st	2nd	2nd
1st	11	5	1	-
2nd	31	22	52	-
3rd	32	118	85	-
4th	50	195	121	-
5th	60	231	205	-
6th	109	273	261	-
7th	166	321	275	-
8th	209	322	281	-
9th	251	345	-	-
10th	254	359	-	-

AVERAGES

New Zealand

BATTING	M	I	NO	Runs	HS	Ave
J.V. Coney	3	5	0	242	82	48.40
J.G. Wright	3	5	0	178	88	35.60
G.P. Howarth	3	5	0	176	114	35.20
B.A. Edgar	3	5	0	149	129	29.80
R.J. Hadlee	3	5	1	115	53*	28.75
M.G. Burgess	3	5	0	136	71	27.20
W.K. Lees	3	5	1	105	45*	26.25
B.L. Cairns	3	5	1	68	23*	17.00
J.M. Parker	2	3	0	38	33	12.66
G.B. Troup	2	2	1	10	7	10.00
J.F. Reid	1	2	0	19	19	9.50
B.P. Bracewell	1	2	1	5	5	5.00
S.L. Boock	3	4	0	5	4	1.25

BOWLING	O	M	R	W	Ave
R.J. Hadlee	117.6	13	414	18	23.00
B.L. Cairns	112	20	345	9	38.33
J.V. Coney	73	19	153	3	51.00
S.L. Boock	82.6	18	238	4	59.50
G.B. Troup	61.5	7	181	3	60.33
B.P. Bracewell	19	1	103	1	103.00
G.P. Howarth	16	3	58	0	-

Pakistan

BATTING	M	I	NO	Runs	HS	Ave
Javed Miandad	3	5	2	297	160*	99.00
Majid Khan	2	3	1	158	119*	79.00
Wasim Bari	3	3	2	71	37*	71.00
Asif Iqbal	2	2	0	139	104	69.50
Zaheer Abbas	2	3	0	177	135	59.00
Haroon Rashid	1	2	0	75	40	37.50
Imran Khan	2	3	1	63	33	31.50
Wasim Raja	3	4	0	122	74	30.50
Talat Ali	3	6	1	127	61	25.40
Mushtaq Mohammad	3	5	0	122	48	24.40
Sarfraz Nawaz	3	4	1	71	31*	23.66
Anwar Khan	1	2	1	15	12	15.00
Mudassar Nazar	1	2	1	11	7	11.00
Mohsin Khan	1	2	0	19	12	9.50
Sikander Bakht	3	3	0	25	19	8.33

BOWLING	O	M	R	W	Ave
Wasim Raja	33.4	9	96	6	16.00
Mushtaq Mohammad	75.3	11	228	11	20.72
Sikander Bakht	78	12	301	12	25.08
Imran Khan	82.7	17	255	10	25.50
Asif Iqbal	9	1	29	1	29.00
Sarfraz Nawaz	101.2	27	296	8	37.00
Anwar Khan	4	0	12	0	-
Majid Khan	5	1	13	0	-
Mudassar Nazar	4	1	16	0	-

1979/80 West Indies in New Zealand

West Indies came to New Zealand after humiliating Australia, winning the second and third tests by 10 wickets and 408 runs respectively. As Mark Burgess was unfit, Geoff Howarth was appointed New Zealand's 15th test captain. New Zealand was celebrating 50 years of test cricket and this was the seventh test to be played at Carisbrook.

137 **NEW ZEALAND v WEST INDIES** *(First Test)*

at Carisbrook, Dunedin on 8, 9, 10, 12, 13 February, 1980
Toss : West Indies. Umpires : F.R. Goodall and J.B.R. Hastie
New Zealand won by 1 wicket

Conjecture about Richard Hadlee's fitness for a test, after not having played a first-class match since 1 January, faded in the first 30 minutes when he took three wickets. Coming from faster wickets in Australia, West Indies could attribute their poor score of 140 to playing across the line too often.

The surface of the wicket was hard and devoid of grass but there was a great deal of moisture under the surface, which meant the ball bounced inconsistently, sometimes keeping very low. The last man out was Desmond Haynes who batted doggedly and suppressed his natural inclination to attack the

bowling. Bruce Edgar and John Wright survived a nasty spell of 70 minutes to leave New Zealand 30-0 at stumps.

The two openers and Geoff Howarth contended with the pace of the West Indies and the peculiarities of the pitch to fight their way through to 109 for the loss of only one wicket. The cornerstone of New Zealand's batting was Edgar's dedicated 300-minute occupation of the crease. The dismissal of Howarth saw the New Zealand innings nosedive as six wickets fell for only 59 runs.

With the innings in tatters Lance Cairns and Hadlee embarked on a spectacular 35-minute partnership that yielded 54 runs. Colin Croft was the most dangerous of the bowlers and his angled deliveries always caused concern.

Rain restricted play to 75 minutes on the third day but in that time Richard Hadlee reached his half-century off 62 balls. West Indies' top order batsmen failed to learn from their first innings and continued to play across the line of the ball and were 29-4 before Collis King joined Haynes, who continued to be watchful and selected his shots carefully.

Their partnership added 87 and when Deryck Murray added a further 64 runs with Haynes the West Indies had

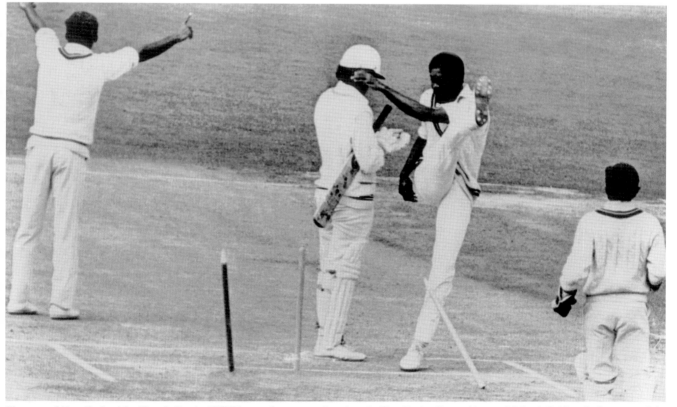

The tour of New Zealand by West Indies in 1979/80 was the most acrimonious in New Zealand's test history. Michael Holding had an appeal for caught behind off John Parker rejected. In anger he kicked over the stumps while a composed Parker adjusted his gloves.

played up to their ability for the first time in four days. The introduction of the second new ball at 180-5 saw Hadlee and Gary Troup swing the game back in New Zealand's direction, with four wickets falling for 29 runs.

Haynes accrued his runs like an experienced batsman accustomed to compiling test centuries rather than scoring his first. At stumps West Indies were 210-9.

When Haynes finally went for 105, after 435 minutes, New Zealand were left the task of scoring a paltry 104 for victory in 235 minutes. The visitors were stung into action and bowled like the champions they were. Their line was more accurate, their length was fuller and their pace increased.

Care, caution and ultra-defence were the watchwords of the batsmen. In an atmosphere of great tension and animosity New Zealand collapsed to 54-7, with all the recognised batsmen out. Hadlee, hit the first boundary of the innings but when Joel Garner bowled him with the score at 73 New Zealand's chances were written off.

Cairns and Troup somehow survived until tea with New Zealand requiring nine runs with two wickets remaining. With the score at 100 Cairns was caught and Stephen Boock, whose highest score was eight, came in with four runs wanted. Amid high tension the pair ran a quick leg-bye, there was almost a run out but the match was won by one wicket.

The match precipitated much truculent behaviour from the West Indies team and management for the rest of their tour.

MILESTONES

- Geoff Howarth became New Zealand's 15th test captain.

- Peter Webb (145) made his test debut.

- It was New Zealand's 11th test win.

- Richard Hadlee broke Richard Collinge's record for most test wickets for New Zealand.

- Richard Hadlee's four lbw decisions in the first innings equalled the record for tests. His seven lbws in the match and the total of 12 in the game were new records.

138 NEW ZEALAND v WEST INDIES *(Second Test)*

at Lancaster Park, Christchurch on 22, 23, 24, 26, 27 February, 1980
Toss : New Zealand. Umpires : F.R. Goodall and S.J. Woodward
Match drawn

After the controversial test in Dunedin the West Indies then had an unsatisfactory game against Wellington, which they lost on a dubious pitch at Lower Hutt. The visitors became noted for their rudeness, arrogance, petulance and lack of leadership. In return, the West Indies complained about the quality of the New Zealand pitches and umpiring.

Geoff Howarth invited the visitors to bat first on a hard wicket with a reasonable coverage of grass. For the third time in three innings, the top three wickets were taken with the score at 28. Gordon Greenidge and Alvin Kallicharran, however, were untroubled by the bowling and when the score was 166-3 it was a godsend for the New Zealand attack when the umpires took the players from the field because of rain.

The visitors failed to build on a great start and lost their last seven wickets for only 38 runs. Two wickets fell on the same score three times in the innings as Lance Cairns returned his best test figures of 6-85. For the third time in as many innings the New Zealand side did not drop a catch. Rain again stopped play with New Zealand 15-0 in reply to 228.

The visiting pace bowlers turned on a ferocious display on the third day and New Zealand struggled. Geoff Howarth and John Parker batted with courage and took many blows to the body. An appeal for caught behind when Howarth was 68 was rejected, adding to the West Indies frustration. When tea was taken Howarth was 99 not out but only the two umpires and two batsmen emerged 20 minutes later.

For the next 12 minutes the West Indies staged a sit-down strike in an attempt to have umpire Fred Goodall removed. When they belatedly returned to the playing arena the West Indies were jeered by 12,000 spectators and drifted through the next two hours hardly seeming to care about cricket.

At the end of the day they emptied their dressing room and told New Zealand Cricket that six players were going home. The day ended with New Zealand 248-4, Howarth having

WEST INDIES

C.G.Greenidge	c Cairns b Hadlee	2	lbw b Hadlee		3
D.L.Haynes	c & b Cairns	55	c Webb b Troup		105
L.G.Rowe	lbw b Hadlee	1	lbw b Hadlee		12
A.I.Kallicharran	lbw b Hadlee	0	c Cairns b Troup		0
C.H.Lloyd*	lbw b Hadlee	24	c Lees b Hadlee		5
C.L.King	c Coney b Troup	14	c Boock b Cairns		41
D.L.Murray†	c Edgar b Troup	6	lbw b Hadlee		30
D.R.Parry	b Boock	17	c & b Hadlee		1
J.Garner	c Howarth b Cairns	0	b Hadlee		2
M.A.Holding	lbw b Hadlee	4	c Cairns b Troup		3
C.E.H.Croft	not out	0	not out		1
Extras	(lb 8, nb 9)	17	(lb 4, nb 5)		9
TOTAL	**(69.5 overs)**	**140**	**(108.4 overs)**		**212**

NEW ZEALAND

J.G.Wright	b Holding	21	b Holding		11
B.A.Edgar	lbw b Parry	65	c Greenidge b Holding		6
G.P.Howarth*	c Murray b Croft	33	c Greenidge b Croft		11
J.M.Parker	b Croft	0	c Murray b Garner		5
P.N.Webb	lbw b Parry	5	(6) lbw b Garner		5
J.V.Coney	b Holding	8	(5) lbw b Croft		2
W.K.Lees†	run out	18	lbw b Garner		0
R.J.Hadlee	c Lloyd b Garner	51	b Garner		17
B.L.Cairns	b Croft	30	c Murray b Holding		19
G.B.Troup	c Greenidge b Croft	0	not out		7
S.L.Boock	not out	0	not out		2
Extras	(b 5, lb 2, nb 11)	18	(b 7, lb 5, nb 7)		19
TOTAL	**(95.5 overs)**	**249**	**(50 overs) (9 wkts)**		**104**

Bowling	O	M	R	W	O	M	R	W
NEW ZEALAND								
Hadlee	20	9	34	5	36	13	68	6
Troup	17	6	26	2	36.4	13	57	3
Cairns	19.5	4	32	2	25	10	63	1
Boock	13	4	31	1	11	4	15	0
WEST INDIES								
Holding	22	5	50	2	16	7	24	3
Croft	25	3	64	4	11	2	25	2
Garner	25.5	8	51	1	23	6	36	4
King	1	0	3	0				
Parry	22	6	63	2				

Fall of Wickets	WI 1st	NZ 1st	WI 2nd	NZ 2nd
1st	3	42	4	15
2nd	4	109	21	28
3rd	4	110	24	40
4th	72	133	29	44
5th	91	145	117	44
6th	105	159	180	44
7th	124	168	186	54
8th	135	232	188	73
9th	136	236	209	100
10th	140	249	212	-

reached his fifth century in nine tests, bruised but undefeated.

The next day was a rest day for the players but a busy and tense one for New Zealand administrators. For the first time in modern cricket, players were on the verge of breaking their contractual obligations. The implications for the future of international cricket were enormous. At the end of the day the West Indies manager, Willie Rodriguez, held a press conference stating that the tour would continue.

In Colin Croft's first over on the fourth day an appeal for a leg-side wicketkeeping catch was declined. Croft told umpire Goodall, standing in his 50th first-class game, "Why don't you stick to teaching? You're no **** use in this game!" The two umpires walked 30 metres to speak to Clive Lloyd in the slips.

In his next over, Croft had a confrontation with the batsman, Richard Hadlee. Then, Goodall no-balled Croft and, on his way back to his mark, Croft swept off the bails at the non-striker's end. During his next delivery Croft ran in strongly then veered towards the umpire so that his right elbow struck Goodall.

It was an act of unbridled dissent. Lloyd, arms folded in the slips, again did nothing and awaited the deputation. Lloyd said he would speak to Croft at the end of the over.

Regrettably, the unseemly behaviour of the rest of the visitors, with the exception of Desmond Haynes, was equally unprofessional. Howarth made 147 in 348 minutes and Jeremy Coney and Hadlee took full advantage of slovenly fielding and dropped catches to add 99 runs for the seventh wicket. Hadlee reached his first test century off only 88 balls.

Facing a deficit of 232 on the first innings Haynes and Gordon Greenidge thrashed some tired looking bowling on a gentle strip, adding 157 for the first wicket from 40 overs.

The final day saw 290 runs scored for the loss of only five wickets. There were three centuries and one near century. Unfortunately, the antics on the field will be recalled in the history books long after the good features are forgotten.

John Parker fought bravely with Geoff Howarth to add 122 in 135 minutes, taking New Zealand's fragile batting to unexpected riches and eventually a lead of 232 on the first innings in the second test.

WEST INDIES

Batsman	Dismissal 1	Runs	Dismissal 2	Runs
C.G.Greenidge	c Boock b Troup	91	c Lees b Troup	97
D.L.Haynes	c Parker b Hadlee	0	c Cairns b Coney	122
L.G.Rowe	lbw b Cairns	11	c Boock b Howarth	100
C.L.King	b Cairns	0	(6) not out	100
A.I.Kallicharran	c Wright b Cairns	75	(4) c Lees b Troup	0
C.H.Lloyd*	c Howarth b Cairns	14	(5) b Boock	7
D.L.Murray†	c Webb b Cairns	6	not out	1
J.Garner	c sub (P.E.McEwan) b Cairns	0		
C.E.H.Croft	b Hadlee	0		
A.M.E.Roberts	not out	17		
M.A.Holding	lbw b Hadlee	0		
Extras	(b 1, lb 9, nb 4)	14	(b 5, lb 8, w 1, nb 6)	20
TOTAL	**(89.3 overs)**	**228**	**(119 overs) (5 wkts dec)**	**447**

NEW ZEALAND

Batsman	Dismissal	Runs
J.G.Wright	b Croft	5
B.A.Edgar	c Murray b Holding	21
P.N.Webb	b Roberts	1
G.P.Howarth*	b Holding	147
J.M.Parker	b Garner	42
J.V.Coney	c King b Roberts	80
W.K.Lees†	c Rowe b Garner	3
R.J.Hadlee	b Kallicharran	103
B.L.Cairns	run out	1
G.B.Troup	not out	13
S.L.Boock	c & b Kallicharran	6
Extras	(b 18, lb 6, nb 14)	38
TOTAL	**(130.4 overs)**	**460**

Bowling	O	M	R	W	O	M	R	W
NEW ZEALAND								
Hadlee	23.3	5	58	3	22	7	64	0
Troup	21	7	38	1	27	7	84	2
Cairns	32	8	85	6	28	8	107	0
Coney	13	2	33	0	19	2	71	1
Boock					18	3	69	1
Howarth					5	0	32	1
WEST INDIES								
Roberts	29	6	82	2				
Holding	29	5	97	2				
Garner	28	4	75	2				
Croft	24	3	78	1				
King	9	0	70	0				
Kallicharran	6.4	1	16	2				
Rowe	5	2	4	0				

Fall of Wickets

	WI 1st	NZ 1st	WI 2nd
1st	1	15	225
2nd	28	18	233
3rd	28	53	234
4th	190	175	268
5th	190	267	436
6th	210	292	-
7th	210	391	-
8th	214	404	-
9th	224	448	-
10th	228	460	-

MILESTONES

- Gordon Greenidge and Alvin Kallicharran equalled the record fourth wicket partnership of 162 for West Indies against New Zealand.

- Geoff Howarth and Jeremy Coney set a new seventh wicket record partnership of 99 for New Zealand against West Indies.

- Richard Hadlee became the first New Zealand test player to take 100 wickets and score over 1000 runs.

- Desmond Haynes and Gordon Greenidge set a first wicket record of 225 for West Indies against New Zealand.

139 NEW ZEALAND v WEST INDIES *(Third Test)*
at Eden Park, Auckland on 29 February, 1, 2, 3, 4, 5 March, 1980
Toss : New Zealand. Umpires : W.R.C. Gardiner and J.B.R. Hastie
Match drawn

For the first time in 50 years of test cricket New Zealand arrived at the final test in a home series in the position where they could not lose the series.

In murky conditions, with the pitch looking unusually green, West Indies were sent in to bat and lost both openers by the time 36 runs had been scored. Lawrence Rowe and Alvin Kallicharran were batting well, before a senseless run out, followed by a poor hook shot, saw both of them out with the total at 116. Drizzle drove the players from the ground but not before Collis King was caught. The day ended at 145-5.

Drizzle persisted throughout the second day and West Indies lost their last five wickets for an addition of 74 runs. Gary Troup and Richard Hadlee both claimed four wickets. John Wright and Bruce Edgar compiled 43 by stumps.

Rain prevented play on the scheduled third day, which became the rest day, and on Monday Wright and Edgar gave New Zealand its best start of the series, 75 in 140 minutes. Geoff Howarth and Edgar then garnered a further 96.

The dismissal of Howarth saw Paul McEwan and John Parker come and go. Then Edgar entered into a torturous 60-minute period where he advanced his score through the 90s to his century which arrived after 376 minutes. Jeremy Coney proved an admirable ally over the latter stages of the day, which ended with New Zealand 239-4.

New Zealand lost its last six wickets for only 66 runs as Joel Garner, taking full advantage of his excessive height, proved almost unplayable with a series of well-directed yorkers. His 6-56 was his best reward in a test match.

Few people thought, when play began on the fifth day with West Indies 121-2, that there was any chance of a decision. An excellent spell of left-arm fast-medium bowling by Troup was rewarded with six wickets. A declaration left New Zealand 180 to win in 154 minutes.

Because of illness, there was a shuffling around in the New Zealand batting order but the weather had the final say. It was a series dogged by ill will, accusations of cheating and terrible sportsmanship.

Warren Lees tosses the ball high. Gary Troup spreadeagles himself in joy and Lawrence Rowe looks downcast on learning that he is caught behind for five in West Indies' second innings.

MILESTONES

- Paul McEwan (146) made his test debut.

- New Zealand won its first test series at home after 50 years of trying.

- Gary Troup became the third New Zealander to take 10 wickets in a test after Jack Cowie and Richard Hadlee.

- Richard Hadlee equalled Jack Cowie's record of 19 wickets for a three-match series.

WEST INDIES

C.G.Greenidge	c McEwan b Hadlee	7	c Lees b Cairns		74
D.L.Haynes	c Edgar b Cairns	9	b Troup		48
L.G.Rowe	run out	50	c Lees b Troup		5
A.I.Kallicharran	c Cairns b Troup	46	lbw b Troup		25
C.H.Lloyd*	c Wright b Troup	11	(6) c Lees b Troup		42
C.L.King	c Troup b Hadlee	23	(5) c Howarth b Troup		9
D.L.Murray†	c Lees b Hadlee	16	lbw b Cairns		7
A.M.E.Roberts	not out	35	c McEwan b Troup		26
J.Garner	b Troup	3	b Hadlee		7
M.A.Holding	lbw b Hadlee	5	not out		16
C.E.H.Croft	b Troup	6			
Extras	(b 1, lb 7, nb 1)	9	(b 1, lb 2, nb 2)		5
TOTAL	**(84.2 overs)**	**220**	**(94.1 overs) (9 wkts dec)**		**264**

NEW ZEALAND

J.G.Wright	c Greenidge b Croft	23	c Haynes b Kallicharran		23
B.A.Edgar	b Roberts	127	(5) not out		22
G.P.Howarth*	c Haynes b Croft	47	(2) run out		1
P.E.McEwan	c Murray b Croft	5	(3) b Garner		21
J.M.Parker	lbw b Garner	0	(4) run out		1
J.V.Coney	not out	49	not out		1
W.K.Lees†	b Garner	23			
R.J.Hadlee	c Murray b Garner	7			
B.L.Cairns	c Murray b Garner	1			
G.B.Troup	b Garner	0			
S.L.Boock	lbw b Garner	0			
Extras	(b 4, lb 11, nb 8)	23	(lb 3, nb 1)		4
TOTAL	**(138.2 overs)**	**305**	**(36 overs) (4 wkts)**		**73**

Bowling									Fall of Wickets				
NEW ZEALAND	O	M	R	W	O	M	R	W		WI	NZ	WI	NZ
										1st	1st	2nd	2nd
Hadlee	31	8	75	4	29	8	62	1	1st	10	75	86	4
Troup	31.2	11	71	4	29.1	5	95	6	2nd	36	171	92	30
Cairns	20	9	56	1	30	7	76	2	3rd	116	185	137	32
Boock	2	0	9	0	6	1	26	0	4th	116	186	147	71
WEST INDIES									5th	146	241	169	-
Roberts	34	6	90	1	9	2	24	0	6th	167	277	193	-
Holding	33	3	54	0	4	1	11	0	7th	169	299	228	-
Croft	33	6	81	3	10	4	17	0	8th	178	303	239	-
Garner	36.2	15	56	6	9	1	17	1	9th	197	303	264	-
King	2	1	1	0					10th	220	305	-	-
Kallicharran					4	4	0	1					

AVERAGES

New Zealand

BATTING	M	I	NO	Runs	HS	Ave
B.A. Edgar	3	5	1	241	127	60.25
G.P. Howarth	3	5	0	239	147	47.80
J.V. Coney	3	5	2	140	80	46.66
R.J. Hadlee	3	4	0	178	103	44.50
J.G. Wright	3	5	0	83	23	16.60
P.E. McEwan	1	2	0	26	21	13.00
B.L. Cairns	3	4	0	51	30	12.75
W.K. Lees	3	4	0	44	23	11.00
G.B. Troup	3	4	2	20	13*	10.00
J.M. Parker	3	5	0	48	42	9.60
S.L. Boock	3	4	2	8	6	4.00
P.N. Webb	2	3	0	11	5	3.66

BOWLING	O	M	R	W	Ave
R.J. Hadlee	161.3	50	361	19	19.00
G.B. Troup	162.1	49	371	18	20.61
G.P. Howarth	5	0	32	1	32.00
B.L. Cairns	154.5	46	419	12	34.91
S.L. Boock	50	12	150	2	75.00
J.V. Coney	32	4	104	1	104.00

West Indies

BATTING	M	I	NO	Runs	HS	Ave
A.M.E. Roberts	2	3	2	78	35*	78.00
D.L. Haynes	3	6	0	339	122	56.50
C.G. Greenidge	3	6	0	274	97	45.66
C.L. King	3	6	1	187	100*	37.40
L.G. Rowe	3	6	0	179	100	29.83
A.I. Kallicharran	3	6	0	146	75	24.33
C.H. Lloyd	3	6	0	103	42	17.16
D.L. Murray	3	6	1	66	30	13.20
D.R. Parry	1	2	0	18	17	9.00
M.A. Holding	3	5	1	28	16*	7.00
C.E.H. Croft	3	4	2	7	6	3.50
J. Garner	3	5	0	12	7	2.40

BOWLING	O	M	R	W	Ave
A.I. Kallicharran	10.4	5	16	3	5.33
J. Garner	122.1	34	235	14	16.78
C.E.H. Croft	103	18	265	10	26.50
D.R. Parry	22	6	63	2	31.50
M.A. Holding	104	21	236	7	33.71
A.M.E. Roberts	72	14	196	3	65.33
L.G. Rowe	5	2	4	0	-
C.L. King	12	1	74	0	-

What became a celebratory habit – Richard Hadlee puffs on a cheroot while opening a bottle of champagne watched by his teammates. From left, Warren Lees, Lance Cairns, Bruce Edgar, Jeremy Coney and John Wright. It was to become a familiar sight during the 1980s.

1980/81 New Zealand in Australia

The three-month tour of Australia, encompassing three tests and the novelty of the recently inaugurated three-way one-day series, took place over a period of 106 days. In this time New Zealand was scheduled to play 27 matches and a further five if they qualified for the final round of the ODI series. It was one of the most arduous tours undertaken by any New Zealand sports team.

140 AUSTRALIA v NEW ZEALAND (First Test)

at Brisbane Cricket Ground on 28, 29, 30 November, 1981
Toss : Australia. Umpires : R.C. Bailhache and M.W. Johnson
Australia won by 10 wickets

In the five days prior to this test match New Zealand played Australia in two one-day games. On winning the toss Greg Chappell asked New Zealand to bat first on a green, hard wicket. The two New Zealand left-hand opening batsmen, John Wright and Bruce Edgar, were untroubled to add 64 for the first wicket. Three loose shots saw both openers and Paul McEwan out with the score at 76.

Geoff Howarth and John Parker, in spite of the high temperatures, added 117 in 132 minutes, both batsmen playing their shots with ease and fluidity. In the first 69 minutes after the tea break, New Zealand was to lose seven wickets for a paltry 32 runs.

The speed of Len Pascoe triggered the collapse but the chief destroyer was the right-arm leg-spin bowler Jim Higgs who, in the course of 14 balls, captured four wickets for only nine runs.

Resuming at 14-0 John Dyson, and Graeme Wood were the essence of caution. Slowly they accrued runs and didn't appear to be in any trouble. A slower ball from Lance Cairns deceived Dyson. Chappell and Allan Border also batted with assurance in assisting Wood to build a large Australian score. Wood's 111 was scored in 318 minutes.

A superb piece of fielding by Mark Burgess ran out Border and then, with the new ball, Richard Hadlee and Cairns made deep inroads into the Australian batting in a collapse reminiscent of New Zealand's the previous night. Australia were 278-7 at stumps.

New Zealand did well to restrict Australia to a first innings lead of 80. The man responsible for this was Cairns, who varied his pace cleverly, and none of the Australians really mastered his moving deliveries. Wickets then fell at six, nine and 14 before lunch, all to the pace of Dennis Lillee.

New Zealand slipped to an embarrassing 61-7 before left-handers Edgar and Hadlee showed resolution and courage and got into line with the ball. In spite of the wickets toppling all around him Edgar remained unflustered and worked the ball diligently wherever he could.

In partnership with Hadlee he added a little character to the New Zealand innings. Lillee's 6-56 was the sixteenth time in 43 tests that he had taken five or more wickets in an innings. His change of pace, hostility and superb control were too much for the touring side. Dyson and Wood quickly hit off the required runs.

For the first part of the tour to Australia, Bruce Edgar grew a beard. In New Zealand's second innings he and Richard Hadlee were equal top scorers with 51. The next best score was eight, made by the last batsman, Brendon Bracewell.

NEW ZEALAND

Batsman		1st		2nd
J.G.Wright	c Marsh b Pascoe	29	c Walters b Lillee	1
B.A.Edgar	c Marsh b Lawson	20	c Hughes b Lillee	51
P.E.McEwan	c Border b Lillee	6	c Hughes b Lillee	0
G.P.Howarth*	c & b Higgs	65	c Wood b Lillee	4
J.M.Parker	b Pascoe	52	c Dyson b Lawson	4
M.G.Burgess	c Chappell b Pascoe	0	c Wood b Lillee	2
I.D.S.Smith†	c Hughes b Lillee	7	c Hughes b Pascoe	7
R.J.Hadlee	c Marsh b Higgs	10	(9) not out	51
B.L.Cairns	c Border b Higgs	0	(10) c Border b Lillee	0
J.G.Bracewell	not out	6	(8) c Border b Lawson	0
B.P.Bracewell	b Higgs	0	b Pascoe	8
Extras	(lb 18, w 5, nb 7)	30	(b 4, lb 4, w 1, nb 5)	14
TOTAL	(70.1 overs)	**225**	(41.1 overs)	**142**

AUSTRALIA

Batsman		1st		2nd
G.M.Wood	c Parker b Bracewell J.G.	111	not out	32
J.Dyson	lbw b Cairns	30	not out	24
G.S.Chappell*	c McEwan b Cairns	35		
K.J.Hughes	c Wright b Hadlee	9		
A.R.Border	run out	36		
K.D.Walters	b Cairns	17		
R.W.Marsh†	b Hadlee	8		
D.K.Lillee	c Parker b Cairns	24		
G.F.Lawson	c sub (S.L.Boock) b Hadlee	16		
L.S.Pascoe	b Cairns	5		
J.D.Higgs	not out	1		
Extras	(b 1, lb 7, nb 5)	13	(b 2, lb 2, nb 3)	7
TOTAL	(115.5 overs)	**305**	(21.3 overs) (0 wkts)	**63**

Bowling	O	M	R	W	O	M	R	W
AUSTRALIA								
Lillee	18	7	36	2	15	1	53	6
Pascoe	19	4	41	3	13.1	2	30	2
Lawson	12	2	39	1	8	0	26	2
Chappell	4	1	18	0				
Higgs	16.1	3	59	4	5	1	19	0
Walters	1	0	2	0				
NEW ZEALAND								
Hadlee	37	8	83	3	6	0	28	0
Bracewell B.P.	22	8	71	0	3	3	0	0
Cairns	38.5	11	87	5	7.3	3	16	0
Bracewell J.G.	18	5	51	1	5	0	12	0

Fall of Wickets	NZ	A	NZ	A
	1st	1st	2nd	2nd
1st	64	80	6	-
2nd	71	145	9	-
3rd	76	160	14	-
4th	193	225	30	-
5th	193	235	34	-
6th	209	250	58	-
7th	209	258	61	-
8th	210	299	114	-
9th	221	299	114	-
10th	225	305	142	-

MILESTONES

- John Bracewell (147) and Ian Smith (148) made their test debuts

141 AUSTRALIA v NEW ZEALAND (Second Test)

at W.A.C.A. Ground, Perth on 12, 13, 14 December, 1980
Toss : Australia. Umpires : A.R. Crafter and D.G. Weser
Australia won by 8 wickets

The sustained hostility of Dennis Lillee, Rodney Hogg and Len Pascoe, coupled with some indiscreet shots, saw New Zealand virtually lose this test in the first 80 minutes of the game when they tumbled to be 28-4.

A resolute partnership between Jeremy Coney and Mark Burgess, of 88 runs for the fifth wicket in 152 minutes, was the only effective answer New Zealand could mount. Once the partnership was broken there was very little resistance from the remaining batsman and the last six wickets fell for only 80 runs. Even though the tourists had been in Australia for six weeks the batting had that early-season look about it.

There was some consolation for New Zealand before the end of the first day when they dismissed Graeme Wood. They could have had an even greater prize off the last delivery of the day from Richard Hadlee when Greg Chappell appeared most fortunate to survive an appeal for lbw.

With some scathing criticism in the morning papers as to the quality of New Zealand's batting still fresh in their minds the team had cause for a wry smile when they had Australia 68-5. Two of the old warhorses of Australian cricket, Doug Walters and Rodney Marsh, began the revival. The evergreen Walters scored eight blazing boundaries in an entertaining innings of 55. When he reached 24 he became the sixth Australian to reach 5000 runs in test cricket, joining Don Bradman, Neil Harvey, Bill Lawry and Ian and Greg Chappell.

When Australia's eighth wicket fell they still trailed New Zealand's mediocre score by nine runs. After a shaky start Marsh went on the offensive and found a useful ally in Pascoe and they added 57 vital runs. Marsh was finally caught by Coney off Hadlee for a breezy 91.

It was an excellent performance by the New Zealand pace attack, with Gary Troup again performing well but without tangible success. Trailing by 69 runs New Zealand slipped further behind when Bruce Edgar was out for his second duck of the match.

The visitors battled valiantly against the Australian pace on the third morning, none more so than the night watchman John Bracewell who unflinchingly took a barrage of fast balls on his body. But application as well as courage was needed and where the pace attack failed Jim Higgs' leg-spin succeeded.

After 236 minutes New Zealand was all out for 121 and Australia needed only 53 runs to win. After some anxious moments the target was achieved.

Mark Burgess, captaining New Zealand in place of the injured Geoff Howarth, said that it was one of the best batting wickets that he had played on. There was much criticism of playing tests interspersed with one-day internationals and transcontinental travel, as the batting on both sides was ordinary.

One of Richard Hadlee's five wickets in Australia's first innings was Dennis Lillee. He was brilliantly caught and bowled by the New Zealand pace man.

NEW ZEALAND

J.G.Wright	b Pascoe	10	c Marsh b Hogg	3
B.A.Edgar	c Border b Lillee	0	c Hughes b Pascoe	0
J.M.Parker	c Chappell b Hogg	3	(4) c Hughes b Hogg	18
P.E.McEwan	c Marsh b Lillee	8	(5) c Marsh b Lillee	16
J.V.Coney	b Hogg	71	(6) c Marsh b Higgs	0
M.G.Burgess*	c Hughes b Lillee	43	(7) lbw b Higgs	18
W.K.Lees†	c Marsh b Pascoe	5	(8) not out	25
R.J.Hadlee	c Hughes b Pascoe	23	(9) c Chappell b Higgs	0
J.G.Bracewell	lbw b Lillee	6	(3) run out	16
B.L.Cairns	c Pascoe b Lillee	13	c Border b Higgs	6
G.B.Troup	not out	0	c Marsh b Lillee	0
Extras	(lb 3, w 2, nb 9)	14	(lb 12, w 2, nb 5)	19
TOTAL	**(73.5 overs)**	**196**	**(48.1 overs)**	**121**

AUSTRALIA

G.M.Wood	c Bracewell b Hadlee	0	c Lees b Hadlee	0
J.Dyson	c Bracewell b Cairns	28	not out	25
G.S.Chappell*	c Cairns b Troup	12	c Lees b Hadlee	13
K.J.Hughes	c Lees b Hadlee	3	not out	16
A.R.Border	b Cairns	10		
K.D.Walters	c Coney b Hadlee	55		
R.W.Marsh†	c Coney b Hadlee	91		
D.K.Lillee	c & b Hadlee	8		
R.M.Hogg	b Cairns	3		
L.S.Pascoe	not out	30		
J.D.Higgs	c Coney b Cairns	7		
Extras	(b 3, lb 4, w 1, nb 10)	18	(lb 1)	1
TOTAL	**(81.1 overs)**	**265**	**(22.1 overs) (2 wkts)**	**55**

Bowling	O	M	R	W	O	M	R	W		Fall of Wickets			
AUSTRALIA										NZ	A	NZ	A
										1st	1st	2nd	2nd
Lillee	23.5	5	63	5	15.1	7	14	2					
Hogg	16	5	29	2	10	2	25	2	1st	6	0	0	3
Pascoe	20	3	61	3	10	1	30	1	2nd	13	22	27	31
Chappell	7	3	5	0	3	1	7	0	3rd	24	25	38	-
Higgs	5	1	13	0	8	2	25	4	4th	28	50	63	-
Walters	2	0	11	0	2	1	1	0	5th	116	68	64	-
NEW ZEALAND									6th	133	156	73	-
Hadlee	27	8	87	5	11.1	4	20	2	7th	171	176	115	-
Troup	22	5	57	1	1	0	1	0	8th	177	187	115	-
Cairns	28.1	7	88	4	5	2	17	0	9th	196	244	121	-
Bracewell	4	1	15	0	5	0	16	0	10th	196	265	121	-

142 AUSTRALIA v NEW ZEALAND *(Third Test)*

at Melbourne Cricket Ground on 26, 27, 28, 29, 30 December, 1980
Toss : New Zealand. Umpires : R.C. Bailhache and A.R. Crafter
Match drawn

In front of an enthusiastic crowd of 28,671 for the Boxing Day test Geoff Howarth sent Australia in to bat on a much-criticised pitch that had been described as resembling a strip of black iron sand with a thin line of grass down the middle.

Batting was never easy with the ball keeping very low and only the superior skills of Greg Chappell, Kim Hughes, Allan Border and Doug Walters were able to cope with Richard Hadlee and Lance Cairns. Jeremy Coney provided a surprise bonus capturing the wickets of Border and Rodney Marsh in one over prior to stumps, when the score was 222-6.

Walters and Dennis Lillee took their partnership through to 69 before Cairns began his 25th over of the game. Lillee was yorked with the first ball. Rodney Hogg was run out off the fifth ball and the next ball bowled Pascoe. Three wickets in one over revived New Zealand's hopes. When the Australian score was 279-9, with Walters 77 and Higgs 1, Cairns bowled a languid long-hop to Higgs.

The tailender ducked awkwardly, the ball glanced off his gloves which were above his head, and flew into the hands of Lees. To the shock of the crowd the umpire, Robin Bailhache, called the Cairns' delivery a no-ball under the intimidatory rule. Howarth remonstrated with Bailhache for some minutes but the ruling stood and Higgs continued batting. Great Australian cricketers such as Richie Benaud, Ray Lindwall and Ian Chappell regarded the decision as ludicrous.

The extra 42 runs in 65 minutes that this partnership added was ultimately the difference between the winning and drawing of the game. Walters reached his 15th test century.

New Zealand's innings was quickly thrown into disarray by the guile of Higgs who had both openers in quick succession to leave New Zealand 32-2 at tea. Howarth and John Parker provided New Zealand's best batting performance of the series, bringing up a century partnership in 115 minutes.

Both overnight batsmen were out early with the score at 163. Mark Burgess and Coney added 84 for the fifth wicket. A spectacular storm swept across the ground and flooded it, ending play for the day at 3 pm with New Zealand 251-6.

Play began 80 minutes late on the fourth day because of the damp outfield. Coney occupied the crease for 219 minutes to remain unbeaten on 55 at the end of New Zealand's innings. The Australians were intent on scoring quick runs but the frequency of balls skidding precluded this. Astute bowling by Hadlee and Cairns had Australia dismissed for 188.

The task of scoring 193 in 54 overs was made monumental by the pitch. Wright, Edgar and Howarth tried to make a race of it but, when four wickets fell for six runs and the score became 101-5, the visitors closed the game up.

AUSTRALIA

G.M.Wood	c Lees b Hadlee	0	c Lees b Hadlee	21
J.Dyson	b Troup	13	lbw b Cairns	16
G.S.Chappell*	c Coney b Hadlee	42	b Hadlee	78
K.J.Hughes	c Parker b Hadlee	51	b Hadlee	30
A.R.Border	c Cairns b Coney	45	c Lees b Hadlee	9
K.D.Walters	b Coney	107	run out	2
R.W.Marsh†	c Parker b Coney	1	lbw b Cairns	0
D.K.Lillee	b Cairns	27	c Coney b Bracewell	8
R.M.Hogg	run out	0	b Hadlee	12
L.S.Pascoe	b Cairns	0	not out	0
J.D.Higgs	not out	6	b Hadlee	0
Extras	(b 7, lb 13, w 3, nb 6)	29	(b 6, lb 4, nb 2)	12
TOTAL	**(121.3 overs)**	**321**	**(87.2 overs)**	**188**

NEW ZEALAND

J.G.Wright	c Chappell b Higgs	4	c Wood b Hogg	44
B.A.Edgar	lbw b Higgs	21	run out	25
G.P.Howarth*	b Hogg	65	lbw b Chappell	20
J.M.Parker	c Marsh b Pascoe	56	lbw b Chappell	1
M.G.Burgess	lbw b Pascoe	49	(6) not out	10
J.V.Coney	not out	55	(5) lbw b Hogg	3
J.G.Bracewell	c Chappell b Pascoe	0		
W.K.Lees†	lbw b Hogg	4	(7) b Lillee	7
R.J.Hadlee	c Border b Hogg	9	(8) not out	5
B.L.Cairns	lbw b Higgs	18		
G.B.Troup	c Hughes b Hogg	1		
Extras	(b 13, lb 12, nb 10)	35	(b 2, lb 8, w 1, nb 2)	13
TOTAL	**(108.2 overs)**	**317**	**(54 overs) (6 wkts)**	**128**

Bowling	O	M	R	W	O	M	R	W		Fall of Wickets			
NEW ZEALAND										A	NZ	A	NZ
										1st	1st	2nd	2nd
Hadlee	39	8	89	3	27.2	7	57	6					
Troup	26	5	54	1	11	1	31	0	1st	0	27	25	50
Cairns	35	6	83	2	33	13	65	2	2nd	32	32	64	95
Bracewell	9	0	38	0	15	5	22	1	3rd	75	157	111	97
Coney	12.3	6	28	3	1	0	1	0	4th	159	163	131	101
AUSTRALIA									5th	190	247	131	101
Lillee	21	4	49	0	13	3	30	1	6th	192	247	131	121
Hogg	26.2	9	60	4	8	1	14	2	7th	261	264	149	-
Higgs	29	6	87	3	12	4	24	0	8th	261	280	185	-
Pascoe	26	6	75	3	11	1	35	0	9th	261	316	188	-
Border	4	1	6	0	2	1	5	0	10th	321	317	188	-
Chappell	2	0	5	0	7	4	7	2					
Hughes					1	1	0	0					

MILESTONES

- Richard Hadlee was named Man of the Series.

- Doug Walters and Jimmy Higgs created a tenth wicket partnership record of 60 for tests between Australia and New Zealand.

There was a controversial decision made by umpire Robin Bailhache when Australia was 279-9. Lance Cairns bowled a long-hop to Jimmy Higgs who gloved it to Warren Lees. Under the intimidatory rule, Bailhache called the delivery a no-ball and Higgs was given not out. From left, Higgs looks unconcerned, Lees turns away in disbelief, Lance Cairns and Mark Burgess listen while Bailhache makes a point to Geoff Howarth. Doug Walters, back to the camera, made the most of the reprieve to continue on to his 15th test century.

AVERAGES

New Zealand

BATTING	M	I	NO	Runs	HS	Ave
J.V. Coney	2	4	1	129	71	43.00
G.P. Howarth	2	4	0	154	65	38.50
R.J. Hadlee	3	6	2	98	51*	24.50
M.G. Burgess	3	6	1	122	49	24.40
J.M. Parker	3	6	0	134	56	22.33
B.A. Edgar	3	6	0	117	51	19.50
J.G. Wright	3	6	0	91	44	15.16
W.K. Lees	2	4	1	41	25*	13.66
P.E. McEwan	2	4	0	30	16	7.50
B.L. Cairns	3	5	0	37	18	7.40
I.D.S. Smith	1	2	0	14	7	7.00
J.G. Bracewell	3	5	1	28	16	7.00
B.P. Bracewell	1	2	0	8	8	4.00
G.B. Troup	2	3	1	1	1	0.50

BOWLING	O	M	R	W	Ave
J.V. Coney	13.3	6	29	3	9.66
R.J. Hadlee	147.3	35	364	19	19.15
B.L. Cairns	147.3	42	356	13	27.38
G.B. Troup	60	11	143	2	71.50
J.G. Bracewell	56	11	154	2	77.00
B.P. Bracewell	25	11	71	0	-

Australia

BATTING	M	I	NO	Runs	HS	Ave
K.D. Walters	3	4	0	181	107	45.25
G.S. Chappell	3	5	0	180	78	36.00
J. Dyson	3	6	2	136	30	34.00
G.M. Wood	3	6	1	164	111	32.80
K.J. Hughes	3	5	1	109	51	27.25
A.R. Border	3	4	0	100	45	25.00
R.W. Marsh	3	4	0	100	91	25.00
L.S. Pascoe	3	4	2	35	30*	17.50
D.K. Lillee	3	4	0	67	27	16.75
G.F. Lawson	1	1	0	16	16	16.00
J.D. Higgs	3	4	2	14	7	7.00
R.M. Hogg	2	3	0	15	12	5.00

BOWLING	O	M	R	W	Ave
R.M. Hogg	60.2	17	128	10	12.80
D.K. Lillee	106	27	245	16	15.31
J.D. Higgs	75.1	17	227	11	20.63
G.S. Chappell	23	9	42	2	21.00
G.F. Lawson	20	2	65	3	21.66
L.S. Pascoe	99.1	17	272	12	22.66
K.J. Hughes	1	1	0	0	-
A.R. Border	6	2	11	0	-
K.D. Walters	5	1	14	0	-

1980/81 India in New Zealand

This was the first test to be played at the Basin Reserve since 1978. Major renovations had taken place which transformed the rectangular shape into an oval with grassy banks on the eastern side. Other changes included the new R.A. Vance Stand, named after the chairman of NZCC's Board of Control.

143 NEW ZEALAND v INDIA *(First Test)*

at Basin Reserve, Wellington on 21, 22, 23, 25 February, 1981
Toss : India. Umpires : F.R. Goodall and S.J. Woodward
New Zealand won by 62 runs

Asked to bat first in front of 12,500 spectators New Zealand had reached 200 when they lost their third wicket, thanks to solid contributions from their top order. Ravi Shastri, aged 18 and playing within 24 hours of arriving in New Zealand as a replacement, caught and bowled Jeremy Coney for his first test wicket.

New Zealand's batting on the second day centred on Geoff Howarth. He was undefeated on 137 when the innings closed for 375. He drove imperially, wide of the covers and, by opening the face of his bat when he was driving, he managed to work the ball past point.

India were progressing comfortably at 70-1, when Lance Cairns swung the ball in deceptively from outside the off to bowl Sunil Gavaskar and three balls later, accounted for Gavaskar's brother-in-law, Gundappa Viswanath, in identical fashion. At stumps India was 133-4.

Sandip Patil lived up to his reputation as an exhilarating right-hand batsman by taking 13 runs off one of Richard Hadlee's first overs on the third morning. In the hour to lunch India's resistance collapsed and they lost five wickets for 37 runs, giving Cairns 5-33.

New Zealand's smiles were to be short-lived as Kapil Dev tore into their top order. John Wright and John Reid were beaten with sharp, moving deliveries while Bruce Edgar, Jock Edwards and Coney all succeeded in hooking the ball high to fine leg, where they were caught. Shastri concluded the innings by capturing three wickets in four balls, all catches taken by Dilip Vengsarkar fielding close to the bat. New Zealand's total of 100 was their lowest score against India. It was a dismal batting performance.

With the weather holding fine India had two full days at their disposal to score 253 runs for victory on a pitch that was still in first-class condition. The outcome of the match was decided in the first session of the fourth day when India lost four wickets for only 75 runs, with their three main batsmen dismissed.

Hadlee was the Hadlee of old. His length was better than the first innings and all the batsmen had difficulties facing him. New Zealand fielded superbly, throwing themselves for the ball even though the outfield was as hard as concrete. They were well supported by Ian Smith, the wicketkeeper, who took seven catches in the game.

There had been no cricket at the Basin Reserve since 1978. The ground had been transformed from a large rectangle into a circular cricket oval. The new R.A.Vance Grandstand was a welcome addition for both players and spectators.

NEW ZEALAND

Batsman	1st innings	Runs	2nd innings	Runs
J.G.Wright	c Binny b Yograj	32	c Viswanath b Kapil Dev	8
B.A.Edgar	c Kirmani b Patil	39	c Patil b Binny	28
J.F.Reid	c Kirmani b Patil	46	lbw b Kapil Dev	7
G.P.Howarth*	not out	137	c Kirmani b Patil	7
J.V.Coney	c & b Shastri	4	c sub (T.E.Srinivasan) b Kapil Dev	8
G.N.Edwards	c Kirmani b Kapil Dev	23	c sub (T.E.Srinivasan) b Kapil Dev	6
I.D.S.Smith†	c Vengsarkar b Kapil Dev	20	not out	15
R.J.Hadlee	c Kirmani b Binny	20	c Kirmani b Binny	7
B.L.Cairns	c Gavaskar b Kapil Dev	13	c Vengsarkar b Shastri	0
M.C.Snedden	b Shastri	2	c Vengsarkar b Shastri	0
G.B.Troup	c Gavaskar b Shastri	0	c Vengsarkar b Shastri	0
Extras	(b 4, lb 17, w 1, nb 17)	39	(lb 10, w 2, nb 2)	14
TOTAL	(119 overs)	375	(49 overs)	100

INDIA

Batsman	1st innings	Runs	2nd innings	Runs
S.M.Gavaskar*	b Cairns	23	b Snedden	12
C.P.S.Chauhan	c Coney b Troup	17	b Hadlee	1
D.B.Vengsarkar	lbw b Cairns	39	c Smith b Hadlee	26
G.R.Viswanath	b Cairns	0	b Troup	9
S.M.Patil	c Smith b Troup	64	c Smith b Cairns	42
K.B.J.Azad	b Cairns	20	b Hadlee	16
Kapil Dev	c Smith b Troup	0	(8) c Hadlee b Troup	9
S.M.H.Kirmani†	run out	13	(7) b Cairns	11
R.M.H.Binny	b Snedden	11	not out	26
R.J.Shastri	not out	3	c Smith b Snedden	19
Yograj Singh	c Smith b Cairns	4	c Smith b Hadlee	6
Extras	(b 10, lb 13, nb 6)	29	(b 2, lb 5, nb 6)	13
TOTAL	(72.4 overs)	223	(75.3 overs)	190

Bowling	O	M	R	W	O	M	R	W
INDIA								
Kapil Dev	38	9	112	3	16	4	34	4
Yograj	15	3	63	1				
Binny	22	4	67	1	12	4	26	2
Shastri	28	9	54	3	3	0	9	3
Patil	16	4	40	2	17	10	12	1
Azad					1	0	5	0
NEW ZEALAND								
Hadlee	16	4	62	0	22.3	7	65	4
Cairns	19.4	8	33	5	19	8	30	2
Snedden	20	7	56	1	17	5	39	2
Troup	17	5	43	3	13	4	34	2
Coney					4	1	9	0

Fall of Wickets	NZ	I	NZ	I
	1st	1st	2nd	2nd
1st	60	32	17	10
2nd	101	70	35	30
3rd	200	70	35	30
4th	215	116	58	75
5th	245	183	73	111
6th	292	183	78	117
7th	331	198	99	136
8th	364	213	100	136
9th	375	218	100	170
10th	375	223	100	190

MILESTONES

- Martin Snedden (149) made his test debut.

- It was New Zealand's 12th test victory and third in succession at Wellington.

- Geoff Howarth's 137 not out was the highest innings for New Zealand at the Basin Reserve.

- Ian Smith took seven catches in the match, equalling the test record for dismissals by a New Zealander shared by Artie Dick and Roy Harford.

144 **NEW ZEALAND v INDIA** *(Second Test)*

at Lancaster Park, Christchurch on 6, 7, 8, 9, 10, 11 March, 1981
Toss : India. Umpires : J.B.R. Hastie and D.A. Kinsella
Match drawn

India chose to play both left-arm spinners, Ravi Shastri and Dilip Doshi, so it was imperative that Sunil Gavaskar bat first when he won the toss.

The lunchtime score of 86-0 was a complete travesty of justice. Geoff Howarth kept an attacking field for the entire session and at least half of the runs that were scored were accumulated at third man. At no stage did the batsmen get on top and yet at lunch they had established a good start.

Both were dismissed in the same manner "c Smith b Hadlee"; Gavaskar for 53 and Chetan Chauhan for 78. No sooner had Chauhan been dismissed than the players came off the field because of bad light. At stumps India was 168-2.

Over the next three days 13 hours were lost through bad light and rain, which meant there was very little prospect of a result. Taking the second new ball, Richard Hadlee demolished the Indian batting and for the 11th time in his test career captured five wickets in the innings. Martin Snedden and Jeremy Coney ably supported him in dismissing India for 255. The last nine wickets had fallen for 87 runs.

John Wright began the New Zealand innings as if it were a one-day match. After his dismissal the two left-handers, Bruce Edgar and John Reid, batted through the rest of the day adding 66 runs in 114 minutes; 93-1.

With a draw evident the final day was played in the best conditions of the match and proved to be batting practice for the New Zealand team, especially for Reid. He quietly worked his runs, picking gaps on the on-side and occasionally unleashing a correct off drive wide of the covers. Together with Edgar 125 runs were added in 222 minutes.

India's wicketkeeper Syed Kirmani was injured during the game and Yashpal Sharma replaced him. He had a good view of John Reid scoring his first test century, 123 not out.

After facing 350 deliveries in 356 minutes Reid struck the first ball after tea to square-leg for his ninth four of the innings and brought up his first test century. He continued to show his forthright character by batting throughout the day to remain 123 not out.

The two Indian spinners, Shastri and Doshi, both bowled with pinpoint accuracy and were able to make the ball turn slowly. They bowled 44 maiden overs in their combined total of 91 overs and only conceded 132 runs.

INDIA

S.M.Gavaskar*	c Smith b Hadlee	53
C.P.S.Chauhan	c Smith b Hadlee	78
D.B.Vengsarkar	b Snedden	61
G.R.Viswanath	b Hadlee	7
S.M.Patil	c Reid b Hadlee	4
Yashpal Sharma	c Howarth b Hadlee	0
Kapil Dev	c & b Snedden	0
S.M.H.Kirmani†	retired hurt	9
K.D.Ghavri	c Reid b Coney	17
R.J.Shastri	not out	12
D.R.Doshi	b Coney	0
Extras	(b 4, lb 5, nb 5)	14
TOTAL	(127 overs)	**255**

NEW ZEALAND

J.G.Wright	c Vengsarkar b Ghavri	18
B.A.Edgar	lbw b Shastri	49
J.F.Reid	not out	123
G.P.Howarth*	c sub (T.E.Srinivasan) b Doshi	26
J.V.Coney	c Chauhan b Patil	15
G.N.Edwards	b Shastri	23
I.D.S.Smith†	not out	11
R.J.Hadlee		
B.L.Cairns		
G.B.Troup		
M.C.Snedden		
Extras	(b 6, lb 8, nb 7)	21
TOTAL	(145 overs) (5 wkts)	**286**

Bowling	O	M	R	W
NEW ZEALAND				
Hadlee	33	12	47	5
Troup	26	5	60	0
Cairns	33	16	57	0
Snedden	23	8	63	2
Coney	9	4	12	2
Howarth	3	2	2	0
INDIA				
Kapil Dev	22	2	60	0
Ghavri	10	4	33	1
Patil	12	4	14	1
Doshi	49	23	67	1
Shastri	42	21	65	2
Chauhan	5	1	12	0
Gavaskar	3	1	11	0
Vengsarkar	2	1	3	0

Fall of Wickets

	I	NZ
	1st	1st
1st	114	27
2nd	168	152
3rd	200	201
4th	210	235
5th	210	265
6th	224	-
7th	224	-
8th	255	-
9th	255	-
10th	-	-

MILESTONES

* Chetan Chauhan achieved the unusual distinction of being the only player to score 2000 runs in test cricket without having scored a century. He and Sunil Gavaskar shared 10 century opening partnerships, a record for India.

145 NEW ZEALAND v INDIA *(Third Test)*

at Eden Park, Auckland on 13, 14, 15, 17, 18 March, 1981
Toss : India. Umpires : F.R. Goodall and S.J. Woodward
Match drawn

India were desperate to win and square the series and one would have thought that the groundsman had been imported from India to assist them in this venture. The texture of the soil appeared loose and likely to break up and the grass was fresh and new. India did not hesitate to play off-spinner Shivlal Yadav, thus going into the test with three spinners.

Martin Snedden, playing in his first test match on his home ground, made a spectacular beginning to the game. He had Gavaskar caught behind and Dilip Vengsarkar caught at fourth slip with the score only 10. Wickets continued to tumble until India was in a precarious position at 124-8.

John Bracewell turned his off-spinners prodigiously and occasionally extracted difficult bounce even before lunch on the first day. The final session belonged to Syed Kirmani and Yadav who added 64 runs with sensible batting, assisted by three dropped catches. At stumps India was 184-8.

Bracewell claimed the last two wickets to finish with 4-61, but not before the partnership had added 105. The loss of Bruce Edgar to the second ball he faced was overcome by determined batting from John Wright and John Reid. Their concentration did not waver as a cluster of fieldsmen surrounded them. They were together at stumps with Reid 66, Wright 55 and the score 127-1.

Reid was out for 74 and Geoff Howarth went immediately. The threat of the Indian spinners was negated by Jeremy Coney's long reach and Wright's dogged determination. After 414 minutes Wright reached his first century in 30 test innings with a six. Later in the day Jock Edwards and Lance Cairns both batted aggressively in valuable partnerships with Coney, who reached 50 for the sixth time in 25 tests.

With a lead of 128 New Zealand appeared to be safe when India lost their first three wickets for only 93 runs. Dilip Vengsarkar and Gundappa Viswanath battled valiantly and India went into the last day with a lead of 69 runs with Gavaskar saying that the wicket was "spinning like a top."

Sandip Patil began the fifth day with a brilliant onslaught. His innings of 57 included seven fours and one six and 50 runs were scored in the first hour. His dismissal opened the floodgates and in the next hour India lost five wickets for only 37 runs. The star for New Zealand was Bracewell with 5-75, giving him nine wickets for the match. He was ably supported by Cairns whose 33 overs was a superb piece of containing bowling.

Needing 157 to win in two full sessions New Zealand adopted an aggressive policy with changes to the batting order but when four wickets fell for 12 runs Howarth settled for a one-nil series win, much to the dislike of some of the spectators.

MILESTONES

- It was the second time New Zealand had won a home test series.

- Syed Kirmani and Shivlal Yadav equalled India's record against New Zealand of 105 for the eighth wicket.

INDIA

S.M.Gavaskar*	c Smith b Snedden	5	c Wright b Bracewell		33
C.P.S.Chauhan	c Cairns b Bracewell	36	c Cairns b Bracewell		7
D.B.Vengsarkar	c Howarth b Snedden	0	(5) not out		52
S.M.Patil	c Smith b Cairns	19	(6) b Bracewell		57
G.R.Viswanath	lbw b Hadlee	2	(4) run out		46
T.E.Srinivasan	c Smith b Bracewell	29	(3) c Wright b Cairns		19
R.J.Shastri	c & b Cairns	5	(9) run out		9
S.M.H.Kirmani†	b Bracewell	78	b Bracewell		1
Kapil Dev	b Cairns	4	(7) c Edgar b Cairns		14
N.S.Yadav	c Hadlee b Bracewell	43	c Smith b Bracewell		1
D.R.Doshi	not out	3	b Cairns		2
Extras	(b 5, lb 3, nb 6)	14	(b 23, lb 7, nb 13)		43
TOTAL	(130.3 overs)	**238**	(120.5 overs)		**284**

NEW ZEALAND

J.G.Wright	c Kirmani b Chauhan	110	not out		33
B.A.Edgar	c Shastri b Patil	0	c Kirmani b Kapil Dev		1
J.F.Reid	c Viswanath b Shastri	74	(6) lbw b Doshi		0
G.P.Howarth*	c sub (R.M.H.Binny) b Shastri	0	(5) c Chauhan b Doshi		2
J.V.Coney	c & b Doshi	65	(7) not out		0
G.N.Edwards	c & b Doshi	34	(3) c & b Shastri		47
R.J.Hadlee	c Chauhan b Yadav	0	(4) b Shastri		2
B.L.Cairns	c Gavaskar b Shastri	41			
I.D.S.Smith†	b Shastri	10			
J.G.Bracewell	lbw b Shastri	1			
M.C.Snedden	not out	0			
Extras	(b 14, lb 10, nb 7)	31	(b 3, lb 4, nb 3)		10
TOTAL	(186 overs)	**366**	(62 overs) (5 wkts)		**95**

Bowling	O	M	R	W	O	M	R	W
NEW ZEALAND								
Hadlee	27	11	49	1	21	3	65	0
Snedden	22	7	52	2	13	4	40	0
Cairns	27	13	37	3	35.5	16	47	3
Coney	9	1	14	0	4	1	3	0
Bracewell	42.3	17	61	4	41	19	75	5
Howarth	3	0	11	0	6	3	11	0
INDIA								
Kapil Dev	20	6	34	0	10	6	15	1
Patil	6	4	2	1	4	0	8	0
Yadav	33	8	91	1	11	4	20	0
Doshi	69	34	79	2	19	9	18	2
Shastri	56	13	125	5	18	8	24	2
Chauhan	2	0	4	1				

Fall of Wickets

	P	NZ	P	NZ
	1st	*1st*	*2nd*	*2nd*
1st	9	0	43	1
2nd	10	148	50	83
3rd	43	152	93	87
4th	50	241	143	94
5th	97	301	236	95
6th	100	302	260	-
7th	114	332	261	-
8th	124	354	277	-
9th	229	365	279	-
10th	238	366	284	-

Jock Edwards played a short but aggressive innings of 34, much to the delight of his followers in Auckland.

AVERAGES

New Zealand

BATTING	M	I	NO	Runs	HS	Ave
J.F. Reid	3	5	1	250	123*	62.50
J.G. Wright	3	5	1	201	110	50.25
G.P. Howarth	3	5	1	172	137*	43.00
I.D.S. Smith	3	4	2	56	20	28.00
G.N. Edwards	3	5	0	133	47	26.60
B.A. Edgar	3	5	0	117	49	23.40
J.V. Coney	3	5	1	92	65	23.00
B.L. Cairns	3	3	0	54	41	18.00
R.J. Hadlee	3	4	0	29	20	7.25
J.G. Bracewell	1	1	0	1	1	1.00
M.C. Snedden	3	3	1	2	2	1.00
G.B. Troup	2	2	0	0	0	0.00

BOWLING	O	M	R	W	Ave
J.G. Bracewell	83.3	36	136	9	15.11
B.L. Cairns	134.3	61	204	13	15.69
J.V. Coney	26	7	38	2	19.00
G.B. Troup	56	14	137	5	27.40
R.J. Hadlee	119.3	37	288	10	28.80
M.C. Snedden	95	31	250	7	35.71
G.P. Howarth	12	5	24	0	-

India

BATTING	M	I	NO	Runs	HS	Ave
D.B. Vengsarkar	3	5	1	178	61	44.50
S.M. Patil	3	5	0	186	64	37.20
R.M.H. Binny	1	2	1	37	26*	37.00
S.M.H. Kirmani	3	5	1	112	78	28.00
C.P.S. Chauhan	3	5	0	139	78	27.80
S.M. Gavaskar	3	5	0	126	53	25.20
T.E. Srinivasan	1	2	0	48	29	24.00
N.S. Yadav	1	2	0	44	43	22.00
K.B.J. Azad	1	2	0	36	20	18.00
K.D. Ghavri	1	1	0	17	17	17.00
R.J. Shastri	3	5	2	48	19	16.00
G.R. Viswanath	3	5	0	64	46	12.80
Kapil Dev	3	5	0	27	14	5.40
Yograj Singh	1	2	0	10	6	5.00
D.R. Doshi	2	3	1	5	3*	2.50
Yashpal Sharma	1	1	0	0	0	0.00

BOWLING	O	M	R	W	Ave
S.M. Patil	55	22	76	5	15.20
C.P.S. Chauhan	7	1	16	1	16.00
R.J. Shastri	147	51	277	15	18.46
R.M.H. Binny	34	8	93	3	31.00
Kapil Dev	106	27	255	8	31.87
D.R. Doshi	137	66	164	5	32.80
K.D. Ghavri	10	4	33	1	33.00
Yograj Singh	15	3	63	1	63.00
N.S. Yadav	44	12	111	1	111.00
D.B. Vengsarkar	2	1	3	0	-
K.B.J. Azad	1	0	5	0	-
S.M. Gavaskar	3	1	11	0	-

1981/82 Australia in New Zealand

146 **NEW ZEALAND v AUSTRALIA** *(First Test)*
at Basin Reserve, Wellington on 26, 27, 28 February, 1, 2 March, 1982
Toss : Australia. Umpires : F.R. Goodall and S.J. Woodward
Match drawn

The 56 days prior to the Australians coming to Wellington were the third driest on record according to the Meteorological Office. Following heavy rain over the previous three days the first day's play was officially abandoned before 9 am. It was ironic that this day's loss of play was the first day of cricket cancelled at the Basin Reserve in the two years since the opening of the Vance Stand.

John Wright and Bruce Edgar were very circumspect in their approach when play did begin and they could not be tempted into making strokes outside the line of the stumps. There was life on the pitch but the Australian pace attack was erratic and only 18 runs were scored in the first hour. New Zealand was 107-1 at stumps on the shortened day.

There was only time for 51 minutes of play the next day but in this time Jeff Thomson bowled four of the best and fastest overs seen at the ground. A southerly gale swept through Cook Strait and ensured that there would be no cricket on the fourth day.

For the first time in five days the weather was suitable for cricket and Edgar's long stay of 336 minutes, spread over four days, was terminated when he was lbw to Terry Alderman. The game meandered to a draw.

MILESTONES

• Martin Crowe (150) made his test debut.

During the 66 minutes that it took John Wright to get off the mark, some comments from Dennis Lillee brought a smile to both their faces.

NEW ZEALAND		
B.A.Edgar	lbw b Alderman	55
J.G.Wright	c Chappell b Yardley	38
J.F.M.Morrison	b Thomson	15
G.P.Howarth*	not out	58
J.V.Coney	lbw b Yardley	1
M.D.Crowe	run out	9
R.J.Hadlee	b Thomson	21
I.D.S.Smith†	c Chappell b Yardley	11
B.L.Cairns	not out	19
M.C.Snedden		
E.J.Chatfield		
Extras	(b 5, lb 19, w 4, nb 11)	39
TOTAL	(116 overs) (7 wkts dec)	**266**
AUSTRALIA		
G.M.Wood	b Cairns	41
B.M.Laird	not out	27
J.Dyson	not out	12
G.S.Chappell*		
K.J.Hughes		
A.R.Border		
R.W.Marsh†		
D.K.Lillee		
B.Yardley		
T.M.Alderman		
J.R.Thomson		
Extras	(lb 2, nb 3)	5
TOTAL	(38 overs) (1 wkt)	**85**

Bowling	O	M	R	W
AUSTRALIA				
Thomson	26	13	35	2
Alderman	44	20	93	1
Lillee	15	5	32	0
Chappell	8	2	18	0
Yardley	23	10	49	3
NEW ZEALAND				
Hadlee	7	2	15	0
Snedden	8	1	24	0
Cairns	11	4	20	1
Chatfield	8	5	7	0
Crowe	4	1	14	0

Fall of Wickets		
	A	NZ
	1st	1st
1st	86	65
2nd	120	-
3rd	149	-
4th	162	-
5th	186	-
6th	212	-
7th	246	-
8th	-	-
9th	-	-
10th	-	-

147 NEW ZEALAND v AUSTRALIA *(Second Test)*

at Auckland on 12, 13, 14, 15, 16 March, 1982
Toss : New Zealand. Umpires : B.A. Bricknell and S.J. Woodward
New Zealand won by 5 wickets

The normal assistance given the faster bowlers on the first morning at Eden Park was missing as the pitch played very placidly and all in favour of the batsmen. It was thus surprising that Australia had lost three wickets for 76 runs at lunch.

The signs appeared most ominous when Greg Chappell raced through 30 runs in the first 30 minutes after lunch. The turning point in the match occurred when John Dyson steered a ball off his pads to backward square-leg which was brilliantly fielded and returned in one movement by Lance Cairns to run Chappell out.

There was a similar mix-up off the next ball that resulted in Allan Border also being run out. In two balls the Australian innings had gone from bad to mad (120-5) and in a short time the Australian bottom order was wafted away. The visitors were all out for 210. New Zealand was 35-2 by stumps.

Rarely in New Zealand test cricket have New Zealand batsmen so totally dominated a day's play. New Zealand scored 206 for the loss of only Geoff Howarth's wicket. The lynchpin of the performance was Bruce Edgar. He ensured that no wickets fell at one end while Howarth, who was in quite majestic form, scored freely at the other as they added 87 in 129 minutes.

Jeremy Coney once again rose to the atmosphere of test cricket. He played straight and watchfully at the start and, as his innings developed, so his assurance of shots on the leg-side and aggressive cover drives came into play. After taking 197 minutes to get to his fifty, Edgar reached his century in 278 minutes. Bad light stopped play with 88 minutes remaining and New Zealand 241-3.

As in the previous day's play, the hero was Edgar who continued to play each ball on its merits. His was a chanceless, marathon innings that lasted 516 minutes. Before Bruce Yardley bowled Coney for 73, he and Edgar had added 154 in 217 minutes and New Zealand had an overall lead of 177.

On the fourth day the pitch was slow enough to reduce even the quicker bowlers to gentle medium pace. Bruce Laird and Graeme Wood went a long way to wiping off the deficit with a century opening partnership. Wood again excelled at taking balls on the line of the leg stump and working them effortlessly to the leg-side boundaries, and he reached his seventh test century in 259 minutes.

When he was dismissed at 167-2 the game looked to be heading for a draw. During the afternoon, John Morrison, who had only bowled two overs in first-class cricket in the season, was introduced into the attack with his left-arm slows. He bowled 32 overs and completely closed down one end while Cairns snuck two yorkers through Dyson and Kim Hughes.

The last day began with Australia 241-4 and Chappell hit the first ball to Edgar in the covers. Richard Hadlee, in an inspired spell of 50 balls, captured four wickets for 14 runs, leaving New Zealand with 4½ hours to score 104 runs for victory. Justice was done when Morrison captured the last two wickets, giving him his only wickets in test cricket.

John Wright and Morrison went cheaply but Edgar again played a valuable stayer's innings while Howarth added the style of a rapier and Cairns the firepower of a blunderbuss from the other end. When play began at 10.30 am no one in the ground would have anticipated that by 2.32 pm New Zealand would have achieved a memorable victory over Australia by five wickets.

AUSTRALIA					
B.M.Laird	c Smith b Troup	38	lbw b Hadlee		39
G.M.Wood	c Smith b Cairns	9	c Snedden b Cairns		100
J.Dyson	b Snedden	33	b Cairns		33
K.J.Hughes	c Smith b Troup	0	b Cairns		17
G.S.Chappell*	run out	32	c Edgar b Hadlee		24
A.R.Border	run out	0	c Howarth b Morrison		38
R.W.Marsh†	b Troup	33	c Crowe b Hadlee		3
B.Yardley	b Hadlee	25	c Coney b Hadlee		0
J.R.Thomson	lbw b Hadlee	13	lbw b Hadlee		4
D.K.Lillee	c Crowe b Troup	9	c Smith b Morrison		5
T.M.Alderman	not out	0	not out		0
Extras	(lb 2, nb 16)	18	(b 4, lb 5, nb 8)		17
TOTAL	(68.3 overs)	**210**	(138 overs)		**280**

NEW ZEALAND					
B.A.Edgar	c & b Yardley	161	c Lillee b Yardley		29
J.G.Wright	c Yardley b Lillee	4	c Laird b Alderman		4
J.F.M.Morrison	b Lillee	11	c Marsh b Lillee		8
G.P.Howarth*	run out	56	c Chappell b Yardley		19
J.V.Coney	b Yardley	73	(6) not out		5
M.D.Crowe	c Wood b Lillee	2			
R.J.Hadlee	c Chappell b Yardley	25	not out		6
I.D.S.Smith†	lbw b Yardley	5			
B.L.Cairns	c Lillee b Alderman	14	(5) b Border		34
M.C.Snedden	not out	18			
G.B.Troup	c Border b Alderman	4			
Extras	(b 4, lb 7, w 1, nb 2)	14	(lb 4)		4
TOTAL	(150.3 overs)	**387**	(29.4 overs) (5 wkts)		**109**

Bowling NEW ZEALAND	O	M	R	W	O	M	R	W
Hadlee	20	7	38	2	28	9	63	5
Troup	18.3	3	82	4	15	4	31	0
Cairns	17	7	38	1	44	10	85	3
Snedden	12	5	26	1	8	2	22	0
Howarth	1	0	8	0	4	2	4	0
Coney					4	1	6	0
Morrison					35	16	52	2
AUSTRALIA								
Thomson	23	8	52	0				
Alderman	24.3	5	59	2	7	0	30	1
Lillee	39	7	106	3	13	5	32	1
Yardley	56	22	142	4	7.4	2	40	2
Border	3	2	11	0	2	1	3	1
Chappell	5	2	3	0				

Fall of Wickets	A	NZ	A	NZ
	1st	1st	2nd	2nd
1st	19	15	106	4
2nd	75	35	167	17
3rd	76	122	196	44
4th	120	276	202	97
5th	120	291	241	103
6th	131	326	254	-
7th	173	345	254	-
8th	187	352	260	-
9th	203	366	277	-
10th	210	387	280	-

MILESTONES

- It was New Zealand's second test victory at Eden Park.

- Bruce Edgar's 161 was the highest score by a New Zealand batsman in a test against Australia. It was also the highest score by a New Zealand player in a test at Eden Park.

Jeremy Coney again responded to the dramatic atmosphere of test cricket with an innings of charm, sharing a partnership of 154 with Bruce Edgar in the second test. Bruce Laird hovers in close on the leg-side.

148 **NEW ZEALAND v AUSTRALIA** *(Third Test)*

at Lancaster Park, Christchurch on 19, 20, 21, 22 March, 1982
Toss : New Zealand. Umpires : F.R. Goodall and D.A. Kinsella
Australia won by 8 wickets

For the third time in the series, the captain winning the toss asked the other side to bat first. Graham Wood began as he finished in Auckland, completely untroubled by the bowlers and stroking the ball with supreme ease. In 105 minutes at the crease he had nine boundaries and 64 runs.

Until misty drizzle drove the player from the field, 71 minutes before time, Greg Chappell held the innings together and was 76 not out at stumps, when the score was 202-5.

Richard Hadlee's first ball of the second over was square driven for four and one of the great master classes for batsmen began. In Gary Troup's second over Chappell plundered four boundaries and two twos to take his total from 83 to 103. It was his 20th century in 76 tests. He scored 100 runs in 107 minutes in the morning's play before he was dismissed. Those who saw this innings will never forget it.

Bruce Edgar was dismissed after one hour's batting with the score at 33, just as the formidable pair of Dennis Lillee and Jeff Thomson hit top gear. Their pace and ferocity scythed through the New Zealand batting, leaving them 98-8 at stumps in reply to Australia's 353.

Martin Snedden and Hadlee fought a brave rearguard action in a bid to avoid the follow-on with a partnership of 62 but, with only five runs needed, both players were dismissed. Even though Lillee was off the field with a damaged right knee, Chappell asked New Zealand to follow on.

Edgar and Morrison were soon dismissed but John Wright and Geoff Howarth formed a useful partnership and added 93 runs that restored New Zealand's sagging batting performance. With his bowlers tiring Chappell was forced to use Allan Border, who succeeded in dismissing Howarth in his first over. During the next 19 overs four wickets succumbed for 37 runs.

Amidst all this misery Wright threw off the shackles of dour play that had occasionally marked his test career and began to play some truly outstanding shots. In a dismal day's batting his innings of 91 not out was a shining beacon.

Of the 51 runs that Wright added on the fifth day, 40 of them were from boundaries. He not only drove Thomson with great power straight but also swayed back towards square leg and cut viciously past point. Cairns and Snedden both provided adequate support to ensure that Australia would have to bat again. The Australians lost two wickets in scoring the 69 required for victory which enabled them to square the series.

AUSTRALIA						
B.M.Laird	c Smith b Troup	12	c Edgar b Snedden			31
G.M.Wood	c Crowe b Hadlee	64	c Coney b Hadlee			15
J.Dyson	c Hadlee b Snedden	1	not out			14
G.S.Chappell*	c Smith b Coney	176	not out			3
K.J.Hughes	b Hadlee	12				
A.R.Border	b Snedden	6				
R.W.Marsh†	c Cairns b Hadlee	23				
B.Yardley	c Cairns b Hadlee	8				
J.R.Thomson	b Hadlee	25				
D.K.Lillee	c & b Hadlee	7				
T.M.Alderman	not out	1				
Extras	(b 2, lb 8, nb 8)	18	(b 2, lb 2, nb 2)			6
TOTAL	(89.5 overs)	**353**	(25.3 overs) (2 wkts)			**69**
NEW ZEALAND						
B.A.Edgar	c Dyson b Alderman	22	c Marsh b Alderman			11
J.G.Wright	c Marsh b Lillee	13	b Alderman			141
J.F.M.Morrison	lbw b Thomson	8	lbw b Chappell			4
G.P.Howarth*	c Alderman b Thomson	9	c Wood b Border			41
J.V.Coney	b Lillee	0	b Border			0
M.D.Crowe	c Marsh b Lillee	0	b Yardley			9
R.J.Hadlee	c Marsh b Thomson	40	c Alderman b Yardley			0
I.D.S.Smith†	b Thomson	0	c Wood b Yardley			0
B.L.Cairns	run out	3	lbw b Yardley			16
M.C.Snedden	b Alderman	32	b Border			20
G.B.Troup	not out	0	not out			8
Extras	(b 8, lb 2, w 1, nb 11)	22	(b 4, lb 7, w 2, nb 9)			22
TOTAL	(52.2 overs)	**149**	(97.3 overs)			**272**

Bowling	O	M	R	W	O	M	R	W
NEW ZEALAND								
Hadlee	28.5	5	100	6	8	2	10	1
Troup	11	1	53	1				
Snedden	18	2	89	2	4	0	15	1
Cairns	21	3	74	0	9	1	28	0
Coney	8	2	15	1	1	0	2	0
Morrison	3	0	4	0	2	1	6	0
Wright					1	0	2	0
Crowe					0.3	0	0	0
AUSTRALIA								
Thomson	21	5	51	4	19	5	54	0
Alderman	19.2	3	63	2	23	5	66	2
Lillee	12	6	13	3				
Chappell					18	5	30	1
Yardley					27	7	80	4
Border					10.3	4	20	3

Fall of Wickets	A	NZ	NZ	A
	1st	1st	2nd	2nd
1st	50	33	21	24
2nd	57	57	36	60
3rd	82	57	129	-
4th	128	57	133	-
5th	145	67	162	-
6th	237	82	166	-
7th	256	82	166	-
8th	340	87	215	-
9th	352	149	249	-
10th	353	149	272	-

MILESTONES

- Greg Chappell became the second-highest run scorer for Australia, exceeding Neil Harvey's 6149 runs.

- When Rodney Marsh caught Martin Crowe in the first innings he became the first wicketkeeper to make 300 dismissals in test cricket.

- Paid attendances on the tour exceeded $200,000, making this the best attended and most profitable tour of New Zealand.

John Wright proved his ability to play shots in test cricket. He scored over half of New Zealand's dismal second innings total of 272. Boundaries accounted for 74 per cent of his runs.

AVERAGES

New Zealand

BATTING	M	I	NO	Runs	HS	Ave
B.A. Edgar	3	5	0	278	161	55.60
G.P. Howarth	3	5	1	183	58*	45.75
J.G. Wright	3	5	0	200	141	40.00
M.C. Snedden	3	3	1	70	32	35.00
R.J. Hadlee	3	5	1	92	40	23.00
B.L. Cairns	3	5	1	86	34	21.50
J.V. Coney	3	5	1	79	73	19.75
G.B. Troup	2	3	2	12	8*	12.00
J.F.M. Morrison	3	5	0	46	15	9.20
M.D. Crowe	3	4	0	20	9	5.00
I.D.S. Smith	3	4	0	16	11	4.00
E.J. Chatfield	1	-	-	-	-	-

BOWLING	O	M	R	W	Ave
R.J. Hadlee	91.5	25	226	14	16.14
J.V. Coney	13	3	23	1	23.00
J.F.M. Morrison	40	17	62	2	31.00
G.B. Troup	44.3	8	166	5	33.20
M.C. Snedden	50	10	176	4	44.00
B.L. Cairns	102	25	245	5	49.00
J.G. Wright	1	0	2	0	-
E.J. Chatfield	8	5	7	0	-
G.P. Howarth	5	2	12	0	-
M.D. Crowe	4.3	1	14	0	-

Australia

BATTING	M	I	NO	Runs	HS	Ave
G.S. Chappell	3	4	1	235	176	78.33
G.M. Wood	3	5	0	229	100	45.80
B.M. Laird	3	5	1	147	39	36.75
J. Dyson	3	5	2	93	33	31.00
R.W. Marsh	3	3	0	59	33	19.66
A.R. Border	3	3	0	44	38	14.66
J.R. Thomson	3	3	0	42	25	14.00
B. Yardley	3	3	0	33	25	11.00
K.J. Hughes	3	3	0	29	17	9.66
D.K. Lillee	3	3	0	21	9	7.00
T.M. Alderman	3	3	3	1	1*	-

BOWLING	O	M	R	W	Ave
A.R. Border	15.3	7	34	4	8.50
B. Yardley	113.4	41	311	13	23.92
D.K. Lillee	79	23	183	7	26.14
J.R. Thomson	89	31	192	6	32.00
T.M. Alderman	117.5	33	311	8	38.87
G.S. Chappell	31	9	51	1	51.00

1982/83 Sri Lanka in New Zealand

The Sri Lankan cricket team arrived in New Zealand a year after achieving full membership of the ICC. It had the misfortune to lose its captain, Duleep Mendis, and vice captain, Roy Dias, with hand injuries prior to the first test. In their absence Somachandra de Silva was appointed captain for the tests. Leading bowler Ashantha de Mel was also missing through injury.

New Zealand's players had spent the previous two months playing in a one-day series and the test was their first first-class match in eight weeks. Certain members of the team did not look attuned to the demands of test cricket. Glenn Turner was playing his first test after a six-year absence.

149   NEW ZEALAND v SRI LANKA *(First Test)*

at Lancaster Park, Christchurch on 4, 5, 6 March, 1983
Toss : Sri Lanka. Umpires : F.R. Goodall and D.A. Kinsella
New Zealand won by an innings and 25 runs

Both Bruce Edgar and Turner played strokes of an attacking nature having 50 on the board at the end of 10 overs. Turner played with refreshing freedom and had six fours before he was out with the score at 59. Edgar and John Wright consolidated matters but, when the score reached 93, they were both dismissed as was Geoff Howarth, without scoring.

Jeff Crowe, playing in his first test, helped Jeremy Coney add 44 for the fourth wicket and the only danger that the batsmen looked to be in was with their running between the wickets. It came as no surprise when Crowe's innings ended with a run out. Coney was never in any great trouble, playing straight and offering no chances. He was 69 not out and Warren Lees was on 20 when the day ended at 217-7.

Coney was run out for 84, attempting to run a quick single on the second day. New Zealand's lower order revival continued with brisk partnerships of 42 between Lees and Martin Snedden and 52 between Lees and Ewen Chatfield. Lees, who began his innings looking diffident and unsure, flourished as his confidence grew and his stroke making became more fluent. New Zealand's last three wickets doubled the score made by the first seven and they ended with 344.

Sri Lanka's innings was dominated by the correct, defensive batting of Sidath Wettimuny who displayed a cast-iron defence and proved most adept at judging which balls to leave. Mixing his in-swingers with leg-breaks and leg-cutters Lance Cairns made the initial breakthrough, which was later backed up by Richard Hadlee's pace.

When the last two wickets fell at the start of the third day Sidath Wettimuny remained unbeaten on 63 and the follow-on was enforced. Sri Lanka struggled from the outset as the pitch appeared to have freshened up and, in humid, warm conditions, the ball swung prodigiously, and the game concluded on the third day.

NEW ZEALAND		
G.M.Turner	c de Alwis b John	32
B.A.Edgar	c Wettimuny M.de S.	
	b Ratnayeke	39
J.G.Wright	b Ratnayake	13
G.P.Howarth*	c Goonasekera b Ratnayeke	0
J.J.Crowe	run out	12
J.V.Coney	run out	84
R.J.Hadlee	b John	12
B.L.Cairns	c Wettimuny M.de S.	
	b Ratnayeke	3
W.K.Lees†	b de Silva	89
M.C.Snedden	c sub (S.A.R.Silva)	
	b Ratnayeke	22
E.J.Chatfield	not out	10
Extras	(lb 14, w 2, nb 12)	28
TOTAL	**(101.5 overs)**	**344**

SRI LANKA				
S.Wettimuny	not out	63	lbw b Cairns	7
M.de S.Wettimuny	c Lees b Cairns	17	c Lees b Snedden	5
E.R.N.S.Fernando	b Cairns	0	b Cairns	46
Y.Goonasekera	c Lees b Cairns	4	c Turner b Cairns	8
R.S.Madugalle	run out	34	c Lees b Snedden	23
D.S.de Silva*	c Lees b Hadlee	7	b Chatfield	52
J.R.Ratnayeke	run out	0	lbw b Cairns	7
R.G.de Alwis†	c Turner b Hadlee	0	c Hadlee b Snedden	3
S.Jeganathan	lbw b Cairns	6	b Chatfield	8
R.J.Ratnayake	c Coney b Hadlee	1	c Howarth b Chatfield	0
V.B.John	lbw b Hadlee	0	not out	3
Extras	(b 2, lb 7, nb 3)	12	(b 1, lb 6, w 1, nb 5)	13
TOTAL	**(53.3 overs)**	**144**	**(81.5 overs)**	**175**

Bowling SRI LANKA	O	M	R	W	O	M	R	W
Ratnayake	31	8	125	2				
John	12	2	45	2				
Ratnayeke	31	9	93	3				
de Silva	22.5	10	41	1				
Jeganathan	5	2	12	0				
NEW ZEALAND								
Hadlee	13.3	1	33	4	22	12	27	0
Snedden	10	1	30	0	23	6	48	3
Cairns	15	6	49	4	20	7	47	4
Chatfield	15	4	20	0	16.5	3	40	3

Fall of Wickets	NZ 1st	SL 1st	SL 2nd
1st	59	49	14
2nd	93	49	26
3rd	93	56	46
4th	93	104	95
5th	137	121	108
6th	159	129	124
7th	171	133	133
8th	250	141	168
9th	292	144	170
10th	344	144	175

Warren Lees top scored for New Zealand with 89.

MILESTONES

- Jeff Crowe (151) made his test debut.

- It was New Zealand's first test against Sri Lanka.

- It was New Zealand's 14th win in test cricket.

- Sidath Wettimuny became the 24th batsman to carry his bat through a test innings.

- Sidath and Mithra Wettimuny were the third set of brothers to open in a test.

150 NEW ZEALAND v SRI LANKA *(Second Test)*

at Basin Reserve, Wellington on 11, 12, 13, 14, 15 March, 1983
Toss : New Zealand. Umpires : I.C. Higginson and S.J. Woodward
New Zealand won by 6 wickets

Play did not begin until 4.45 pm and in the hour's play possible, which saw both Wettimuny brothers dismissed, the batsmen were confronted with a forest of slip fieldsmen.

A commendable partnership of 130 between Ranjan Madugalle and Somachandra de Silva brought Sri Lanka riches that appeared beyond them. Madugalle played beautifully. The secret of the power with which he hit his 12 boundary shots came from almost perfect timing.

He moved into position behind the ball and anything wide of the wicket was dispatched with certainty. De Silva played and missed more times than a batsman would in one season but he managed to survive 227 minutes for an invaluable 61.

The run-out of Madugalle saw the last six wickets fall for 62 runs — Ravi Ratnayeke scoring the bulk of them with 29 not out. Ewen Chatfield was rewarded with 4-66.

Sri Lanka's bowlers dominated most of the third day. The portly Vinothen John and enthusiastic 19-year-old Rumesh Ratnayake extracted more spiteful bounce than their New Zealand counterparts had. When John Wright had his nose broken by Rumesh Ratnayake, the bowler was almost as distressed as the batsman and had to be consoled by his teammates and the umpires before he could continue to bowl.

A partnership of 71 between an out-of-form Geoff Howarth and a circumspect Jeff Crowe temporarily halted Sri Lanka. Yohan Goonasekera took four catches but the rest of the Sri Lankan catching was mediocre. Richard Hadlee and Lance Cairns were both dropped on nought and, had the catches been taken, New Zealand would have been in dire straits.

Both players went for their shots and rode their luck and batted profitably in a belligerent manner. New Zealand conceded a lead of 39 but Martin Snedden and Hadlee were stung into action and captured three wickets before stumps.

The fourth day was shortened by two hours because of misty drizzle and indifferent light. The batsmen were besotted with the cut shot and only succeeded in nicking through to the safe gloves of Warren Lees. Needing 133 for victory, New Zealand won by six wickets.

MILESTONES

- It was New Zealand's 15th test win and the first time they had won consecutive tests.

- John Wright passed 1000 test runs.

- Warren Lees made eight dismissals in the game to set a New Zealand record and his five in the second innings equalled the New Zealand record.

SRI LANKA

S.Wettimuny	c Cairns b Hadlee	8	c Coney b Hadlee	9
M.de S.Wettimuny	c Coney b Snedden	6	c Cairns b Snedden	0
E.R.N.S.Fernando	c Wright b Hadlee	12	c Lees b Snedden	12
Y.Goonasekera	c Lees b Cairns	13	(5) c Lees b Chatfield	23
R.S.Madugalle	run out	79	(6) c Lees b Hadlee	13
D.S.de Silva*	lbw b Chatfield	61	(7) c Lees b Snedden	0
S.A.R.Silva†	c Lees b Chatfield	8	(4) c Crowe b Hadlee	0
J.R.Ratnayeke	not out	29	b Hadlee	12
S.Jeganathan	c Lees b Chatfield	5	c Lees b Chatfield	0
R.J.Ratnayake	b Snedden	12	c sub (M.D.Crowe) b Chatfield	1
V.B.John	c Wright b Chatfield	0	not out	8
Extras	(b 1, lb 5, nb 1)	7	(b 5, lb 10)	15
TOTAL	(100.5 overs)	**240**	(53 overs)	**93**

NEW ZEALAND

G.M.Turner	c Goonasekera b John	10	b Ratnayeke	29
B.A.Edgar	c John b Ratnayake	10	not out	47
J.G.Wright	c de Silva b Ratnayake	14		
G.P.Howarth*	c Wettimuny S. b de Silva	36	(3) c Silva b John	1
J.J.Crowe	c Silva b Ratnayake	36	(4) b Ratnayake	11
J.V.Coney	c Goonasekera b John	2	(5) c Goonasekera b de Silva	17
R.J.Hadlee	c Goonasekera b John	30	(6) not out	17
W.K.Lees†	c Goonasekera b John	0		
B.L.Cairns	c de Silva b John	45		
M.C.Snedden	lbw b Ratnayake	5		
E.J.Chatfield	not out	2		
Extras	(b 4, lb 3, w 3, nb 1)	11	(lb 11, nb 1)	12
TOTAL	(72.2 overs)	**201**	(37.1 overs) (4 wkts)	**134**

Bowling	O	M	R	W	O	M	R	W
NEW ZEALAND								
Hadlee	25	9	47	2	17	5	34	4
Snedden	24	5	56	2	17	7	21	3
Chatfield	26.5	7	66	4	12	5	15	3
Cairns	20	5	53	1	7	2	8	0
Coney	5	2	11	0				
SRI LANKA								
Ratnayake	24	5	81	4	15	0	46	1
John	25.2	9	60	5	8	2	38	1
Ratnayeke	14	3	36	0	8.1	4	20	1
de Silva	9	5	13	1	6	1	18	1

Fall of Wickets

	SL	NZ	SL	NZ
	1st	1st	2nd	2nd
1st	14	12	0	59
2nd	14	33	12	62
3rd	34	104	12	81
4th	48	107	57	116
5th	178	141	61	-
6th	191	141	61	-
7th	194	145	78	-
8th	220	163	81	-
9th	239	169	83	-
10th	240	201	93	-

Ewen Chatfield had a match analysis of 38.5 overs, 12 maidens, seven wickets for 81 runs.

1983 New Zealand in England

New Zealand's non-stop diet of one-day cricket meant the team was ill-prepared for test cricket and were weakened with Glenn Turner's unavailability for the tests that followed the World Cup played in England in 1983.

151 ENGLAND v NEW ZEALAND *(First Test)*

at The Oval on 14, 15, 16, 17, 18 July, 1983
Toss : England. Umpires : H.D. Bird and D.G.L. Evans
England won by 189 runs

Richard Hadlee gave New Zealand an ideal start, taking two early wickets. England were soon 116-5 and opening batsman Chris Tavare had his mouth stitched after receiving a blow from Hadlee's bowling. Derek Randall began with his usual nervousness but then asserted himself to successfully combat the bowlers. Sloppy batting saw the rest of the England innings deteriorate, with Hadlee capturing 6-53.

New Zealand's joy at dismissing England for 209 quickly turned to despair as they lost three of their top-order batsmen for 17 runs. At 41-5 Jeremy Coney and Hadlee both played straight and looked remarkably composed. Hadlee took his courage into his hands and, off 78 balls, he scored the best 84 runs that he had made so far in test cricket.

Coney's was an innings of character and dedication, which ended when he was run out going for a short single. As Bob Willis had knocked over the top order, Ian Botham knocked over the tail. Tavare and Graeme Fowler played cautiously and both were undefeated at stumps; 146-0.

New Zealand bowled sensibly and fielded brilliantly to restrict England to 194 runs for the day. Tavare and Fowler made centuries and shared in a record opening stand worth 223. No praise can be too high for John Bracewell and Coney who restricted England to only 58 runs in a two-hour session and claimed three wickets in doing so. England 340-6.

Allan Lamb became the third batsman to score a century in the innings but his was a laboured affair. New Zealand, set 460 to win, were reeling at 26-2 with both John Wright and Geoff Howarth looking far from confident. They battled through 46 overs, adding 104 runs, leaving New Zealand to score 330 for victory on the last day.

New Zealand contributed greatly to their own demise on the final day with two needless run outs. Following the partnership between Wright and Howarth, which added 120 runs, Howarth found an able ally in Martin Crowe and together they added 51 runs.

After lunch the left-arm spin of Phil Edmonds and right-arm off-spin of Vic Marks ran through the middle order, with three wickets each as the visitors lost six wickets for 31 runs. There were two run outs in each of the visitors' innings. New Zealand could rightfully feel disappointed, having failed to capitalise on their first day's effort.

ENGLAND					
G.Fowler	lbw b Hadlee	1	run out		105
C.J.Tavare	run out	45	c Howarth b Bracewell		109
D.I.Gower	b Hadlee	11	c Howarth b Hadlee		25
A.J.Lamb	b Cairns	24	not out		102
I.T.Botham	b Hadlee	15	run out		26
D.W.Randall	not out	75	c Coney b Hadlee		3
V.J.Marks	c Lees b Hadlee	4	c Crowe M.D. b Bracewell		2
P.H.Edmonds	c & b Bracewell	12	not out		43
R.W.Taylor†	lbw b Hadlee	0			
R.G.D.Willis*	c Crowe J.J. b Bracewell	4			
N.G.Cowans	b Hadlee	3			
Extras	(b 6, lb 6, nb 3)	15	(b 8, lb 23)		31
TOTAL	(70.4 overs)	**209**	(189.2 overs) (6 wkts dec)		**446**

NEW ZEALAND					
J.G.Wright	c Gower b Willis	0	run out		88
B.A.Edgar	c Taylor b Willis	12	c Taylor b Willis		3
J.J.Crowe	c Randall b Willis	0	c Lamb b Willis		9
G.P.Howarth*	b Cowans	4	c Taylor b Edmonds		67
M.D.Crowe	b Willis	0	c Taylor b Edmonds		33
J.V.Coney	run out	44	lbw b Marks		2
R.J.Hadlee	c & b Botham	84	c Taylor b Marks		11
J.G.Bracewell	c & b Botham	7	(9) c Gower b Marks		0
W.K.Lees†	not out	31	(8) run out		8
B.L.Cairns	c Lamb b Botham	2	c Willis b Edmonds		32
E.J.Chatfield	c Willis b Botham	0	not out		10
Extras	(lb 6, nb 6)	12	(b 3, lb 1, nb 3)		7
TOTAL	(57 overs)	**196**	(110.1 overs)		**270**

Bowling	O	M	R	W	O	M	R	W
NEW ZEALAND								
Hadlee	23.4	6	53	6	37.2	7	99	2
Chatfield	17	3	48	0	35	9	85	0
Cairns	17	3	63	1	30	7	67	0
Bracewell	8	4	16	2	54	13	115	2
Crowe M.D.	5	0	14	0	3	0	9	0
Coney					27	11	39	0
Howarth					3	2	1	0
ENGLAND								
Willis	20	8	43	4	12	3	26	2
Cowans	19	3	60	1	11	2	41	0
Botham	16	2	62	4	4	0	17	0
Edmonds	2	0	19	0	40.1	16	101	3
Marks					43	20	78	3

Fall of Wickets	E	NZ	E	NZ
	1st	1st	2nd	2nd
1st	2	0	223	10
2nd	18	1	225	26
3rd	67	10	269	146
4th	104	17	322	197
5th	116	41	329	202
6th	154	125	336	210
7th	184	149	-	228
8th	191	182	-	228
9th	202	188	-	228
10th	209	196	-	270

The all-round skills of Richard Hadlee dominated the first two days of the test.

MILESTONES

- Jeff Crowe joined brother Martin to become the fifth pair of brothers to play for New Zealand in a test.

- Richard Hadlee's 6-53 was the best analysis by a New Zealand bowler in a test in England.

- Chris Tavare and Graham Fowler added 223 for the first wicket, a record for England against New Zealand.

152 ENGLAND v NEW ZEALAND *(Second Test)*

at Headingley, Leeds on 28, 29, 30 July, 1 August, 1983
Toss : New Zealand. Umpires : D.J. Constant and B.J. Meyer
New Zealand won by 5 wickets

For the seventh time, on winning the toss, Geoff Howarth inserted the opposition and the decision appeared to have backfired when England reached 135-2, with Allan Lamb in full flow and Chris Tavare, rock solid, adding 100.

Ian Botham appeared about to annihilate the New Zealand attack, taking 18 off one Ewen Chatfield over but Lance Cairns replied with a brilliant spell in mid-afternoon. His line, length, swing, cut and enthusiasm dumbfounded the England batsmen as he captured seven wickets.

Bruce Edgar had to leave the field after he was hit on the hipbone and the blow induced temporary paralysis. John Wright and Martin Crowe slowly but surely built a substantial total to go to tea at 166-1. In 20 dismal minutes the score was reduced to 169-4.

Jeremy Coney and Richard Hadlee stemmed the flow, adding 49, before Edgar returned to stay with Hadlee until stumps, with New Zealand 252-5. Hadlee had reached his half-century off 89 balls.

Edgar's brave innings, lasting 282 minutes, was the linchpin of the remaining New Zealand innings. Useful partnerships with Hadlee, John Bracewell and Lance Cairns took New Zealand to a satisfactory first innings lead of 152.

The Headingley pitch, which had been damp on the first day, was now cracked with uneven bounce. Chatfield exploited these conditions, claiming both openers. David Gower and Lamb looked comfortable before Coney bowled Lamb.

Attempting a sweep shot, Botham deflected the ball high over his head to be caught; again, Coney was the bowler. Throughout a mini-collapse Gower played a most responsible innings as England ended the day at 154-6.

The last four wickets added a further 98 as Gower dominated the batting proceedings with a splendid unbeaten 112. Initially, the attack of Hadlee and Cairns was unsuccessful, and it was Chatfield who broke a stubborn stand, aided by Ian Smith, to give him his first five-wicket haul in test cricket and Smith his seventh catch in the match. Cairns claimed the remaining three wickets to give him 10 for the match.

Victory, jubilation, champagne and smiles. After 52 years and 28 tests New Zealand finally won a test in England. It was a triumph for Lance Cairns who took 10-144 and was rightfully made the Man of the Match. Back row (from left): John Bracewell, Martin Crowe, Ewen Chatfield, Jeff Crowe, Ian Smith, Trevor Franklin. Front row: Sir Allan Wright (manager), John Wright, Geoff Howarth, Lance Cairns, Richard Hadlee, Jeremy Coney, Bruce Edgar, Martin Snedden.

Bob Willis was inspired to capture five wickets with the score at 83 and cause some trepidation in the hearts of New Zealanders but they were not to be denied and achieved their first test victory over England in England. It was ironic that New Zealand's victory should have been achieved with Hadlee remaining wicketless for the game.

Writing in the *Daily Mirror*, Richie Benaud wrote, "Howarth, more than anyone else is responsible for New Zealand's victory. He has shown himself an outstanding leader, calm under pressure and as an ambassador for the game and his team."

ENGLAND

Batsman	Dismissal	Runs	Dismissal	Runs
G.Fowler	c Smith b Chatfield	9	c Smith b Chatfield	19
C.J.Tavare	c Smith b Coney	69	b Chatfield	23
D.I.Gower	c Coney b Cairns	9	not out	112
A.J.Lamb	c Crowe M.D. b Cairns	58	b Coney	28
I.T.Botham	c Howarth b Cairns	38	c Howarth b Coney	4
D.W.Randall	c Coney b Cairns	4	c Smith b Chatfield	16
P.H.Edmonds	c Smith b Cairns	8	c Smith b Chatfield	0
G.R.Dilley	b Cairns	0	c Smith b Chatfield	15
R.W.Taylor†	not out	10	b Cairns	9
R.G.D.Willis*	c Crowe J.J. b Coney	9	c Coney b Cairns	4
N.G.Cowans	c Bracewell b Cairns	0	c Crowe M.D. b Cairns	10
Extras	(b 4, lb 7)	11	(b 8, lb 3, w 1)	12
TOTAL	(89.2 overs)	**225**	(87 overs)	**252**

NEW ZEALAND

Batsman	Dismissal	Runs	Dismissal	Runs
J.G.Wright	c Willis b Cowans	93	c Randall b Willis	26
B.A.Edgar	b Willis	84	c Edmonds b Willis	2
G.P.Howarth*	run out	13	c Randall b Willis	20
M.D.Crowe	lbw b Cowans	37	c Lamb b Willis	1
J.J.Crowe	run out	0	b Willis	13
J.V.Coney	c Gower b Willis	19	not out	10
R.J.Hadlee	b Cowans	75	not out	6
J.G.Bracewell	c Dilley b Edmonds	16		
I.D.S.Smith†	c Tavare b Willis	2		
B.L.Cairns	not out	24		
E.J.Chatfield	lbw b Willis	0		
Extras	(b 1, lb 4, w 1, nb 8)	14	(b 8, lb 7, nb 10)	25
TOTAL	(139.3 overs)	**377**	(27.1 overs) (5 wkts)	**103**

Bowling	O	M	R	W	O	M	R	W	Fall of Wickets				
NEW ZEALAND										E	NZ	E	NZ
										1st	*1st*	*2nd*	*2nd*
Hadlee	21	9	44	0	26	9	45	0	1st	18	52	39	11
Chatfield	22	8	67	1	29	5	95	5	2nd	35	168	44	42
Cairns	33.2	14	74	7	24	2	70	3	3rd	135	169	116	60
Coney	12	3	21	2	8	1	30	2	4th	175	169	126	61
Bracewell	1	0	8	0					5th	185	218	142	83
ENGLAND									6th	205	304	142	-
Willis	23.3	6	57	4	14	5	35	5	7th	205	348	190	-
Dilley	17	4	36	0	8	2	16	0	8th	209	351	217	-
Botham	26	9	81	0	0.1	0	4	0	9th	225	377	221	-
Cowans	28	8	88	3	5	0	23	0	10th	225	377	252	-
Edmonds	45	14	101	1									

MILESTONES

- It was New Zealand's 16th test victory and their first in England.

- Lance Cairns' 7-74 was the best analysis by a New Zealand bowler in a test innings in England.

- Bob Willis claimed his 300th test wicket, the fourth bowler to do so.

153 **ENGLAND v NEW ZEALAND (*Third Test*)**
at Lord's on 11, 12, 13, 15 August, 1983
Toss : New Zealand. Umpires : D.J. Constant and D.G.L. Evans
England won by 127 runs

From the start there was unpredictable bounce in a pitch that dominated proceedings throughout the match. An eroded and pitted ridge just short of a length at one end, from which the ball lifted almost vertically, was the main source of concern.

David Gower was 21 when he was dropped by Lance Cairns in Martin Crowe's first over and this let-off was crucial to the result of the game. Chris Tavare reached another crucial half-century as Gower completed his second successive century.

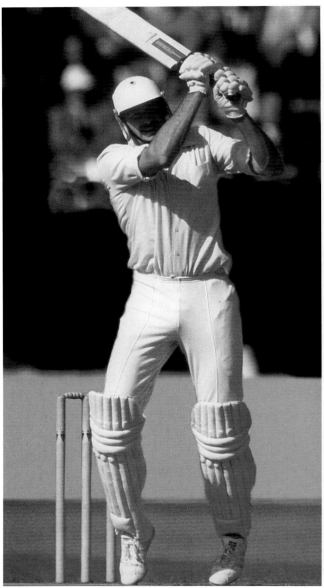

Jeremy Coney played an innings of character and determination.

At this stage Crowe was exhibiting raw aggression and was forcing the batsmen into hurrying their shots, something that the top line bowlers had not done all day. New Zealand appeared to have got back into the game when England were 218-5 but a stubborn partnership saw Mike Gatting and Bob Taylor add 61 runs before stumps; England 279-5.

There was renewed pace and hostility in Richard Hadlee's attack on the second day and the last five wickets fell for 47, with Hadlee claiming five wickets for the 15th time in 43 tests. Bruce Edgar and Martin Crowe added 98 for the third wicket but both batsmen had to play to their limits. For 32 overs they defied England and in the period after tea scored 69 off 14 overs to put New Zealand into a dominant position.

In the final hour the game swung back dramatically to England. In his first test, left-arm spinner Nick Cook spun a web of destruction to leave New Zealand 176-6 at stumps.

New Zealand's fall became a sharp decline as the last four wickets fell for 15 runs. From the time Crowe went out, New Zealand lost eight wickets for 44 runs. Ian Botham was the destroyer in the morning, thumping the ball short of a length up into the New Zealand batsmen and Lamb, at short gully, held three catches. England's commanding first-innings lead of 135 gave them a strong grip on the game.

Bowling at the same end as Cook, Evan Gray gave New Zealand heart by capturing the important wickets of Gower, Lamb and Gatting in his first spell of test match bowling.

His line was excellent, and he exploited the inconsistencies of the pitch very well. Botham enjoyed good fortune, scoring his first fifty in almost a year. For the second time in the game Bob Taylor played an unnoticed innings that was a great assistance to his team.

New Zealand was left to score 347 for victory when the last three England wickets fell in 21 deliveries. The pitch was still erratic, with some balls exploding and others scuttling through low. Batting was very much a lottery. Coney took his courage in his hands and played the hook shot to great effect but his was a lone effort. England went two-one up in the series, winning by 127 runs.

MILESTONES

- Evan Gray (152) made his test debut.

- It was the 75th test match played at Lord's.

- Bob Taylor made his 150th dismissal in test cricket.

154 ENGLAND v NEW ZEALAND *(Fourth Test)*

at Trent Bridge, Nottingham on 25, 26, 27, 28, 29 August, 1983
Toss : England. Umpires : H.D. Bird and B.J. Meyer
England won by 165 runs

Injuries to John Wright, with a broken toe, and Ian Smith, a broken finger, forced changes in the New Zealand side for the deciding fourth test. The England selectors decided to increase their batting strength to ensure that their 2-1 lead in the series would not be lost through inept batting.

For the third time David Gower was in sublime form and was looking dangerous when Lance Cairns squeezed the ball under his bat and bowled him. John Bracewell had three of the first five England wickets to fall. From 169-5 Ian Botham and Derek Randall turned the game on its head with an explosive partnership worth 186 runs in 135 minutes.

Botham hit a whirlwind match-winning century and Randall was by no means overshadowed in the batting carnage. By stumps they were both out but the damage had been done; England 362-7.

England's last three wickets added another 58 valuable runs. Bruce Edgar and Geoff Howarth batted impressively, adding 76 for the second wicket. Because Martin Crowe had dislocated a finger, the batting order was rearranged and Jeremy Coney came in at number four. At 124-2 Nick Cook, the innocent-looking left-arm spinner who had been successful at Lord's, struck again in the last hour, taking four wickets and leaving New Zealand 135-7.

Spirited batting by Crowe, Martin Snedden and Cairns saw the last three wickets contribute 72, which gave England a lead of 213. Bob Willis decided not to enforce the follow-on.

ENGLAND

C.J.Tavare	b Crowe	51	c Crowe b Hadlee	16
C.L.Smith	lbw b Hadlee	0	c Coney b Hadlee	43
D.I.Gower	lbw b Crowe	108	c Crowe b Gray	34
A.J.Lamb	c sub (J.J.Crowe) b Chatfield	17	c Hadlee b Gray	4
M.W.Gatting	c Wright b Hadlee	81	b Gray	15
I.T.Botham	lbw b Cairns	8	c Coney b Chatfield	61
R.W.Taylor†	b Hadlee	16	c & b Coney	7
N.A.Foster	c Smith b Hadlee	10	c Wright b Hadlee	3
N.G.B.Cook	b Chatfield	16	c Bracewell b Chatfield	5
R.G.D.Willis*	c Smith b Hadlee	7	not out	2
N.G.Cowans	not out	1	c Smith b Chatfield	1
Extras	(b 3, lb 3, w 2, nb 3)	11	(b 5, lb 6, nb 9)	20
TOTAL	(120.3 overs)	326	(89.3 overs)	211

NEW ZEALAND

J.G.Wright	c Lamb b Willis	11	c Taylor b Botham	12
B.A.Edgar	c Willis b Cook	70	c Lamb b Cowans	27
G.P.Howarth*	b Cook	25	c Taylor b Willis	0
M.D.Crowe	b Botham	46	c Foster b Cowans	12
J.V.Coney	b Cook	7	c Gatting b Foster	68
E.J.Gray	c Lamb b Botham	11	c Lamb b Cook	17
J.G.Bracewell	c Gower b Cook	0	(8) lbw b Willis	4
R.J.Hadlee	c Botham b Cook	0	(7) b Willis	30
B.L.Cairns	c Lamb b Botham	5	b Cook	16
I.D.S.Smith†	c Lamb b Botham	3	not out	17
E.J.Chatfield	not out	5	c & b Cook	2
Extras	(lb 5, nb 3)	8	(b 3, lb 4, nb 7)	14
TOTAL	(84.4 overs)	191	(69.2 overs)	219

Bowling	O	M	R	W	O	M	R	W	Fall of Wickets			
NEW ZEALAND										E	NZ	E	NZ
Hadlee	40	15	93	5	26	7	42	3		1st	1st	2nd	2nd
Cairns	23	8	65	1	3	0	9	0	1st	3	18	26	15
Chatfield	36.3	8	116	2	13.3	4	29	3	2nd	152	49	79	17
Crowe	13	1	35	2					3rd	175	147	87	57
Coney	8	7	6	0	6	4	9	1	4th	191	159	119	61
Bracewell					11	4	29	0	5th	218	176	147	108
Gray					30	8	73	3	6th	288	176	154	154
ENGLAND									7th	290	176	199	158
Willis	13	6	28	1	12	5	24	3	8th	303	183	208	190
Foster	16	5	40	0	12	0	35	1	9th	318	184	210	206
Cowans	9	1	30	0	11	1	36	2	10th	326	191	211	219
Botham	20.4	6	50	4	7	2	20	1					
Cook	26	11	35	5	27.2	9	90	3					

England's batsmen began with a sequence of dashing shots and expensive mistakes and it was only the determination of Allan Lamb that saw them to a modest total by the end of the day.

England was tottering at 188-7 but, for the third consecutive day, the last session belonged totally to England as Lamb and Cook added a vital partnership of 64 during which Lamb went through to his second century of the series. By claiming the last two batsmen Hadlee ended with 200 test wickets.

New Zealand required 511 for victory. At 31-3 they were struggling but Edgar and Coney commandeered the crease for the next two and a half hours as they fought gallantly to come to terms with England's bowling. Edgar passed 50 for the fourth time in the series and it was a jubilant England side that saw him caught at silly-point towards the end of the day.

There was character in New Zealand's chase of a forlorn cause as their last five wickets added a further 178 on the fifth day. Coney continued to bat with dedicated concentration and his innings lasted 280 minutes. Hadlee drove with both controlled and improvised power from the outset and had 13 boundaries in his unbeaten 92. England won by 165 runs and took the series three games to one.

MILESTONES

- Trevor Franklin (153) made his test debut.

- Richard Hadlee established a new series record of 21 wickets and captured his 200th test wicket. He was named Man of the Series, having also scored 301 runs.

In something of a surprise for the first day of a test match, the right-arm off-spinner John Bracewell captured three of the first five wickets to fall with the score at 169.

ENGLAND

C.J.Tavare	c Cairns b Snedden	4	c sub (J.J.Crowe) b Bracewell		13
C.L.Smith	c Howarth b Bracewell	31	c Howarth b Snedden		4
D.I.Gower	b Cairns	72	c Cairns b Bracewell		33
A.J.Lamb	c Howarth b Bracewell	22	not out		137
M.W.Gatting	lbw b Bracewell	14	c Lees b Cairns		11
I.T.Botham	lbw b Snedden	103	c Edgar b Gray		27
D.W.Randall	c Edgar b Hadlee	83	b Hadlee		13
R.W.Taylor†	b Bracewell	21	b Hadlee		0
N.G.B.Cook	c Lees b Snedden	4	c Lees b Cairns		26
R.G.D.Willis*	not out	25	b Hadlee		16
N.G.Cowans	c Bracewell b Cairns	7	b Hadlee		0
Extras	(b 11, lb 14, nb 9)	34	(b 6, lb 10, w 1)		17
TOTAL	(124.4 overs)	**420**	(92 overs)		**297**

NEW ZEALAND

T.J.Franklin	c Smith b Botham	2	b Willis		7
B.A.Edgar	c Gatting b Cook	62	c Gower b Cook		76
G.P.Howarth*	c & b Cook	36	c Tavare b Cowans		24
J.V.Coney	c Gatting b Cook	20	(5) c Taylor b Cook		68
E.J.Gray	run out	7	(6) c Gatting b Smith		3
R.J.Hadlee	c Smith b Cowans	3	(8) not out		92
W.K.Lees†	lbw b Cook	1	c Lamb b Cowans		7
M.D.Crowe	c & b Cook	34	(4) c Taylor b Cowans		0
M.C.Snedden	b Cowans	9	c Taylor b Cook		12
B.L.Cairns	c Gower b Cowans	26	b Cook		11
J.G.Bracewell	not out	1	c Taylor b Smith		28
Extras	(lb 5, nb 1)	6	(b 2, w 1, nb 14)		17
TOTAL	(82 overs)	**207**	(129 overs)		**345**

Bowling	O	M	R	W	O	M	R	W	Fall of Wickets				
NEW ZEALAND										E	NZ	E	NZ
										1st	*1st*	*2nd*	*2nd*
Hadlee	30	7	98	1	28	5	85	4					
Snedden	28	7	69	3	8	1	40	1	1st	5	4	5	18
Cairns	33.4	9	77	2	20	9	36	2	2nd	94	80	58	67
Bracewell	28	5	108	4	21	2	88	2	3rd	136	124	61	71
Coney	2	0	10	0					4th	156	127	92	156
Gray	3	0	24	0	15	4	31	1	5th	169	131	149	161
ENGLAND									6th	355	135	188	184
Botham	14	4	33	1	25	4	73	0	7th	356	135	188	228
Willis	10	2	23	0	19	3	37	1	8th	379	157	252	264
Cowans	21	8	74	3	21	2	95	3	9th	407	201	297	290
Cook	32	14	63	5	50	22	87	4	10th	420	207	297	345
Gatting	5	2	8	0	2	1	5	0					
Smith					12	2	31	2					

AVERAGES

New Zealand

BATTING	M	I	NO	Runs	HS	Ave
R.J. Hadlee	4	8	2	301	92*	50.16
B.A. Edgar	4	8	0	336	84	42.00
J.G. Wright	3	6	0	230	93	38.33
J.V. Coney	4	8	1	238	68	34.00
G.P. Howarth	4	8	0	189	67	23.62
M.D. Crowe	4	8	0	163	46	20.37
B.L. Cairns	4	7	1	116	32	19.33
W.K. Lees	2	4	1	47	31*	15.66
I.D.S. Smith	2	3	1	22	17*	11.00
M.C. Snedden	1	2	0	21	12	10.50
E.J. Gray	2	4	0	38	17	9.50
J.G. Bracewell	4	7	1	56	28	9.33
E.J. Chatfield	3	5	2	17	10*	5.66
J.J. Crowe	2	4	0	22	13	5.50
T.J. Franklin	1	2	0	9	7	4.50

BOWLING	O	M	R	W	Ave
J.V. Coney	63	26	115	5	23.00
R.J. Hadlee	232	65	559	21	26.61
M.C. Snedden	36	8	109	4	27.25
B.L. Cairns	184	52	461	16	28.81
M.D. Crowe	21	1	58	2	29.00
E.J. Gray	48	12	128	4	32.00
J.G. Bracewell	123	28	364	10	36.40
E.J. Chatfield	153	37	440	11	40.00
G.P. Howarth	3	2	1	0	-

England

BATTING	M	I	NO	Runs	HS	Ave
A.J. Lamb	4	8	2	392	137*	65.33
D.I. Gower	4	8	1	404	112*	57.71
C.J. Tavare	4	8	0	330	109	41.25
D.W. Randall	3	6	1	194	83	38.80
I.T. Botham	4	8	0	282	103	35.25
G. Fowler	2	4	0	134	105	33.50
M.W. Gatting	2	4	0	121	81	30.25
P.H. Edmonds	2	4	1	63	43*	21.00
C.L. Smith	2	4	0	78	43	19.50
R.G.D. Willis	4	7	2	67	25*	13.40
N.G.B. Cook	2	4	0	51	26	12.75
R.W. Taylor	4	7	1	63	21	10.50
G.R. Dilley	1	2	0	15	15	7.50
N.A. Foster	1	2	0	13	10	6.50
N.G. Cowans	4	7	1	22	10	3.66
V.J. Marks	1	2	0	6	4	3.00

BOWLING	O	M	R	W	Ave
R.G.D. Willis	123.3	38	273	20	13.65
C.L. Smith	12	2	31	2	15.50
N.G.B. Cook	135.2	56	275	17	16.17
V.J. Marks	43	20	78	3	26.00
I.T. Botham	112.5	27	340	10	34.00
N.G. Cowans	125	25	447	12	37.25
P.H. Edmonds	87.1	30	221	4	55.25
N.A. Foster	28	5	75	1	75.00
M.W. Gatting	7	3	13	0	-
G.R. Dilley	25	6	52	0	-

The 1983 New Zealand team in England. Back row (from left): Peter Borrie (doctor), Ian Smith, Jeff Crowe, John Bracewell, Trevor Franklin, Evan Gray, Jeremy Coney, Martin Snedden, Sean Tracy, Martin Crowe, John O'Sullivan (scorer), Front: Warren Lees, Ewen Chatfield, Richard Hadlee, Geoff Howarth (captain), Sir Allan Wright (manager), John Wright, Lance Cairns, Bruce Edgar.

1983/84 England in New Zealand

Within four months of England beating New Zealand in the fourth test at Trent Bridge, Bob Willis' side were on a full tour of New Zealand. Exceptionally heavy rain raised fears that the wicket at would be substandard for the first test.

155   NEW ZEALAND v ENGLAND *(First Test)*

at Basin Reserve, Wellington on 20, 21, 22, 23, 24 January, 1984
Toss : New Zealand. Umpires : F.R. Goodall and S.J. Woodward
Match drawn

For the ninth time in 18 test matches Geoff Howarth won the toss and for the first time decided to bat first. In good batting conditions the New Zealand display was dismal, with the exception of Jeff Crowe, who made his first test fifty. New Zealand ended the day at 212-9.

New Zealand was back in the game when Lance Cairns captured the first five wickets with the score at 115. He defeated his victims with deliveries that dipped in late. However, the hero became the villain when he dropped a straightforward catch off Botham before the batsman had scored.

Derek Randall joined Botham in extricating their side from its precarious position with aggressive batting. Two more dropped catches allowed Botham to reach his 13th test century. The partnership was worth 178 when stumps were drawn, with England 293-5.

The third day began with both batsmen in such an exuberant mood that 54 runs were added in the first hour. The epic partnership was broken after they had added 232. There was a touch of drama about Randall reaching his century as he remained scoreless on 99 for 50 minutes.

On completing his century he took the attack to the New Zealand bowlers and was finally dismissed for 164. In the circumstances, the bowling figures of Cairns were exceptional. England's lead of 244, with half the playing time still left and the weather set fair, saw New Zealand in a hopeless position, with defeat almost a certainty. John Wright and Bruce Edgar found runs easy to come by batting a second time but both were out before stumps when the score had reached 92-2.

Howarth looked authoritative before he was run out at the bowler's end. Martin Crowe survived a salvo of bouncers peppered at him by the England quicks. He showed great maturity in playing very straight and resisted the temptation to essay hooks at Botham, becoming New Zealand's third youngest test centurion after batting 276 minutes. He and Jeremy Coney added 114 runs for the fourth wicket. Coney was unbeaten on 76, with New Zealand 335-7.

A perfect day greeted New Zealand's tenuous position of a lead of 91 runs with only three wickets standing. Coney maintained complete control for the day and scored his first

test century after 327 minutes of hard graft. For 131 minutes he encouraged Cairns to play in a most disciplined way as they added 119 and made the game safe for their side. Coney's defiance lasted for 488 minutes.

NEW ZEALAND

J.G.Wright	c Cook b Botham	17	c Foster b Cook		35
B.A.Edgar	c Taylor b Botham	9	c Taylor b Willis		30
G.P.Howarth*	c Gower b Botham	15	run out		34
M.D.Crowe	b Willis	13	c Botham b Gatting		100
J.J.Crowe	c Taylor b Foster	52	lbw b Botham		3
J.V.Coney	c Gower b Cook	27	not out		174
R.J.Hadlee	c Gatting b Botham	24	c Lamb b Foster		18
M.C.Snedden	c Taylor b Willis	11	c Taylor b Foster		16
I.D.S.Smith†	lbw b Botham	24	b Cook		29
B.L.Cairns	c Gatting b Willis	3	c sub (G.Fowler) b Willis		64
E.J.Chatfield	not out	4	b Cook		0
Extras	(b 4, lb 9, nb 7)	20	(b 4, lb 14, w 2, nb 14)		34
TOTAL	**(93.4 overs)**	**219**	**(187.3 overs)**		**537**

ENGLAND

C.J.Tavare	b Cairns	9	not out		36
C.L.Smith	c Hadlee b Cairns	27	not out		30
D.I.Gower	c Hadlee b Cairns	33			
A.J.Lamb	c Crowe M.D. b Cairns	13			
M.W.Gatting	lbw b Cairns	19			
I.T.Botham	c Crowe J.J. b Cairns	138			
D.W.Randall	c Crowe M.D. b Hadlee	164			
R.W.Taylor†	run out	14			
N.G.B.Cook	c Smith b Cairns	7			
N.A.Foster	c Howarth b Hadlee	10			
R.G.D.Willis*	not out	5			
Extras	(lb 8, nb 16)	24	(nb 3)		3
TOTAL	**(132.5 overs)**	**463**	**(22 overs) (0 wkts)**		**69**

Bowling	O	M	R	W	O	M	R	W		Fall of Wickets			
ENGLAND										NZ	E	NZ	E
										1st	1st	2nd	2nd
Willis	19	7	37	3	37	8	102	2	1st	34	41	62	-
Botham	27.4	8	59	5	36	6	137	1	2nd	39	51	79	-
Foster	24	9	60	1	37	12	91	2	3rd	56	84	153	-
Cook	23	11	43	1	66.3	26	153	3	4th	71	92	165	-
Gatting					8	4	14	1	5th	114	115	279	-
Smith					3	1	6	0	6th	160	347	302	-
NEW ZEALAND									7th	174	372	334	-
Hadlee	31.5	6	97	2					8th	200	386	402	-
Snedden	21	3	101	0	7	2	28	0	9th	208	426	520	-
Cairns	45	10	143	7					10th	219	463	537	-
Chatfield	28	6	68	0	5	0	24	0					
Crowe M.D.	3	0	20	0	6	1	11	0					
Coney	4	1	10	0									
Edgar					3	1	3	0					
Crowe J.J.					1	1	0	0					

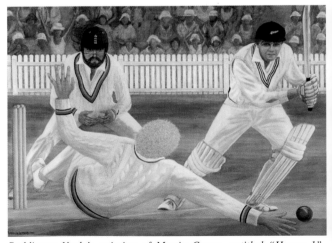

Paddianne Neely's painting of Martin Crowe, entitled "Hogan 1". Crowe became the third-youngest New Zealand test centurion, making his first test century in his eighth test. The helmeted Mike Gatting and David Gower crowded him at the start of his innings.

The scoreboard at the end of the match, showing New Zealand's record total of 537 for a home test. It also records the first test centuries for Martin Crowe and Jeremy Coney.

MILESTONES

- Lance Cairns became the fifth New Zealand bowler to take 100 test wickets. Bob Willis became England's leading wicket-taker in tests with 308 victims.

- Ian Botham scored a century and took five wickets in an innings for the fifth time in his test career. Jeremy Coney and Lance Cairns created a New Zealand ninth wicket record with their partnership of 118.

- New Zealand's second innings total of 537 was a record for New Zealand in a home test and the best total achieved by any team in a test at the Basin Reserve.

156 NEW ZEALAND v ENGLAND *(Second Test)*

at Lancaster Park, Christchurch on 3, 4, 5 February, 1984
Toss : New Zealand. Umpires : F.R. Goodall and S.J. Woodward
New Zealand won by an innings and 132 runs

Fears about the unpredictability of the pitch were confirmed in the opening overs when Bob Willis got a ball to rear wildly over John Wright's head and fly for four byes. The New Zealand batsmen were most circumspect in batting on a pitch where some balls were holding and not coming on to the bat and where others were taking off and flying at a nasty height.

Throughout the day the England bowlers were guilty of bowling inaccurately and too short. Jeff Crowe and Jeremy Coney batted proficiently, adding 50. Coney's dismissal brought Richard Hadlee to the crease and it is hard to imagine a more exhilarating innings than that which he played.

He took advantage of the barrage of short bowling, working it with neat deflections off his hip, cutting savagely and smashing pull shots to backward square-leg. He augmented these strokes with daringly lofted drives. Hadlee reached his fifty off only 47 balls and was out for 99 off 81 deliveries.

Runs came at a staggering pace. Hadlee and Ian Smith added 78 in 46 minutes. The England over rate was terrible and that New Zealand were able to average 4.25 runs an over on such a suspect pitch reflected clearly how badly England bowled. The day ended with New Zealand 307 all out and England 7-1.

A fine, misty drizzle prevented play beginning until 4.30 pm. Few in the sparse crowd would have, in their wildest dreams, imagined the dramatic cricket they were about to witness. Hadlee, with his high action, thrived in the conditions, committing the visitors to play at every delivery and he had three of them out in seven balls.

The batsmen became tentative and nervous, being unsure of the height of the bounce and unable to fathom the movement in the air. The New Zealand pace attack exploited the conditions and were supported by splendid catching. In 90 minutes England lost six wickets for only 46 runs, ending the day at 53-7.

There was a yell of triumph from the New Zealanders with the dismissal of Norman Cowans as, for the first time in 59 tests between the two countries, England had been forced to follow on. Ten minutes after lunch the game reverted to the crazy pattern of the previous day and in one hour six wickets fell. This time, left-arm spinner Stephen Boock was the destroyer.

With Ewen Chatfield keeping the batsmen to a meagre ration of one an over, Boock was able to float the ball up to the batsmen and create havoc. When England's sixth wicket fell they were only 33. For the next hour New Zealand experienced a strange sensation – they did not get any wickets as Bob Taylor and Derek Randall played sensibly.

Once Taylor was run out the remaining three wickets fell quickly and New Zealand were victorious by an innings and 132. Of the 20 wickets captured, 13 were taken by the cluster of fieldsmen around the batsman, some of them with exceptional catches.

MILESTONES

- It was New Zealand's 17th test win, its largest winning margin and quickest in terms of time played at 12 hours and one minute.

- It was the first time in the 20th century that England had failed to reach three figures in either innings.

NEW ZEALAND

J.G.Wright	c Taylor b Cowans	25
B.A.Edgar	c Randall b Pigott	1
G.P.Howarth*	b Cowans	9
M.D.Crowe	c Tavare b Botham	19
J.J.Crowe	lbw b Cowans	47
J.V.Coney	c Botham b Pigott	41
R.J.Hadlee	c Taylor b Willis	99
I.D.S.Smith†	not out	32
B.L.Cairns	c Taylor b Willis	2
S.L.Boock	c Taylor b Willis	5
E.J.Chatfield	lbw b Willis	0
Extras	(b 8, lb 11, w 2, nb 6)	27
TOTAL	(72.1 overs)	**307**

ENGLAND

G.Fowler	b Boock	4	c Howarth b Boock	10
C.J.Tavare	c Crowe J.J. b Hadlee	3	c Smith b Hadlee	6
D.I.Gower	lbw b Hadlee	2	c Cairns b Hadlee	8
A.J.Lamb	c Smith b Chatfield	11	c Coney b Chatfield	9
D.W.Randall	c Coney b Hadlee	0	(7) c Cairns b Hadlee	25
I.T.Botham	c Chatfield b Cairns	18	c Crowe M.D. b Boock	0
M.W.Gatting	not out	19	(5) c Hadlee b Boock	0
R.W.Taylor†	c Crowe J.J. b Cairns	2	run out	15
A.C.S.Pigott	lbw b Cairns	4	not out	8
R.G.D.Willis*	b Chatfield	6	c Howarth b Hadlee	0
N.G.Cowans	c Coney b Chatfield	4	c Smith b Hadlee	7
Extras	(lb 6, nb 3)	9	(lb 2, nb 3)	5
TOTAL	(50.2 overs)	**82**	(51 overs)	**93**

Bowling	O	M	R	W	O	M	R	W
ENGLAND								
Willis	22.1	5	51	4				
Botham	17	1	88	1				
Pigott	17	7	75	2				
Cowans	14	2	52	3				
Gatting	2	0	14	0				
NEW ZEALAND								
Hadlee	17	9	16	3	18	6	28	5
Cairns	19	5	35	3	9	3	21	0
Boock	6	3	12	1	13	3	25	3
Chatfield	8.2	3	10	3	11	1	14	1

Fall of Wickets

	E 1st	NZ 1st	E 2nd
1st	30	7	15
2nd	42	9	23
3rd	53	10	25
4th	87	10	31
5th	137	41	31
6th	203	41	33
7th	281	47	72
8th	291	58	76
9th	301	72	80
10th	307	82	93

A combination of aggression in the field and some excellent catching gave New Zealand an overwhelming victory at Lancaster Park. That spirit is captured as Martin Crowe dives in an attempt to catch Mike Gatting off Richard Hadlee. From left, Stephen Boock, John Wright, Lance Cairns, Jeremy Coney, Jeff Crowe, Geoff Howarth, Ian Smith, Hadlee, umpire Steve Woodward and Martin Crowe.

157 NEW ZEALAND v ENGLAND (*Third Test*)

at Eden Park, Auckland on 10, 11, 12, 14, 15 February, 1984
Toss : New Zealand. Umpires : F.R. Goodall and S.J. Woodward
Match drawn

New Zealand were determined to win the series against England and to do so they had to take full advantage of batting first.

After the early setback of losing Bruce Edgar, John Wright and Geoff Howarth batted studiously and accumulated runs carefully. At 111-3 New Zealand were badly placed on such a placid pitch. Jeff Crowe replaced his brother and, initially, struggled against Bob Willis but survived. When bad light and rain stopped play New Zealand were 140-4.

When play started at midday both Wright and Crowe began with indifferent shots but continued to bat until after lunch when their partnership was broken after adding 154 runs in 199 minutes. Wright's vigil lasted 387 minutes and virtually assured New Zealand would not lose the game.

After an injury-ridden season Wright enjoyed his moment of glory and his third test century, in spite of batting for a long period with a sore back. From his hesitant start Jeff Crowe blossomed, scoring his first test century, being severe with balls on his legs and at the same time stroking the ball through the covers with grace.

Ian Smith, for the fourth time in as many innings, played an invaluable knock. With six wickets down for 302 it was important, in the context of the series, that New Zealand lost no more wickets – they didn't. Smith was 26 not out, Jeff Crowe 115 and New Zealand 354-6 at the end of the day.

Blustery winds, grey skies, frequent rain showers and interruptions marred the third day. Jeff Crowe's maiden test century had reached 128 and occupied 384 minutes when his partnership with Smith was ended. Throughout the day Smith was very convincing, particularly when playing the ball short of a length outside the line of his off stump.

He approached his century with adrenaline pumping. Smith still needed 15 when Ewen Chatfield came in and drama was added to the occasion as rain showers swept across the ground, driving the players from the field. Finally, Smith celebrated his century by lofting two giant sixes off Vic Marks before the declaration was made at 496-9.

England was in an invidious position of batting to save the game for the last two days. There was no chance at all of their squaring the series and the only objective was to make as many runs as possible. They applied themselves professionally and, though they faced 107 overs, lost only two wickets for 184 runs on the fourth day. Chris Smith laboured hard for 459 minutes to score 91.

The final day saw Derek Randall score his second century of the season and Ian Botham bat flamboyantly for 70. The New Zealand bowlers bowled 96 maiden overs in England's total of 439. The draw gave New Zealand the series win.

New Zealand's three century-makers in the third test. From left: Ian Smith, John Wright and Jeff Crowe.

NEW ZEALAND

J.G.Wright	b Willis	130	not out	11
B.A.Edgar	lbw b Willis	0	not out	0
G.P.Howarth*	c Randall b Cowans	35		
M.D.Crowe	c Botham b Willis	16		
J.J.Crowe	b Marks	128		
J.V.Coney	b Cowans	9		
R.J.Hadlee	b Marks	3		
I.D.S.Smith†	not out	113		
B.L.Cairns	c Cowans b Foster	28		
S.L.Boock	lbw b Marks	2		
E.J.Chatfield	not out	6		
Extras	(lb 19, nb 7)	26	(lb 1, nb 4)	5
TOTAL	(169.2 overs) (9 wkts dec)	**496**	(5 overs) (0 wkts)	**16**

ENGLAND

G.Fowler	c Smith b Hadlee	0
C.L.Smith	c Smith b Cairns	91
D.I.Gower	b Boock	26
A.J.Lamb	lbw b Cairns	49
D.W.Randall	c Wright b Chatfield	104
R.W.Taylor†	st Smith b Boock	23
I.T.Botham	run out	70
V.J.Marks	c Smith b Chatfield	6
N.A.Foster	not out	18
R.G.D.Willis*	c Smith b Hadlee	3
N.G.Cowans	c Cairns b Boock	21
Extras	(b 7, lb 13, nb 8)	28
TOTAL	(227.3 overs)	**439**

Bowling	O	M	R	W	O	M	R	W
ENGLAND								
Willis	34	7	109	3	3	1	7	0
Botham	29	10	70	0				
Cowans	36	11	98	2	2	1	4	0
Foster	30	8	78	1				
Marks	40.2	9	115	3				
NEW ZEALAND								
Hadlee	43	12	91	2				
Cairns	40	19	52	2				
Boock	61.3	28	103	3				
Chatfield	46	23	72	2				
Crowe M.D.	17	5	62	0				
Coney	13	8	13	0				
Howarth	7	1	18	0				

Fall of Wickets	NZ	E	NZ
	1st	*1st*	*2nd*
1st	3	0	-
2nd	74	48	-
3rd	111	143	-
4th	265	234	-
5th	293	284	-
6th	302	371	-
7th	385	387	-
8th	451	391	-
9th	461	396	-
10th	-	439	-

MILESTONES

- It was New Zealand's first test series win over England.

- The fourth wicket partnership of 154 between John Wright and Jeff Crowe was a New Zealand record in tests against England.

- It was the first time that three New Zealand players had scored centuries in the same innings in a test at home.

AVERAGES

New Zealand

BATTING	M	I	NO	Runs	HS	Ave
I.D.S. Smith	3	4	2	198	113*	99.00
J.V. Coney	3	4	1	251	174*	83.66
J.J. Crowe	3	4	0	230	128	57.50
J.G. Wright	3	5	1	218	130	54.50
M.D. Crowe	3	4	0	148	100	37.00
R.J. Hadlee	3	4	0	144	99	36.00
B.L. Cairns	3	4	0	97	64	24.25
G.P. Howarth	3	4	0	93	35	23.25
M.C. Snedden	1	2	0	27	16	13.50
B.A. Edgar	3	5	1	40	30	10.00
E.J. Chatfield	3	4	2	10	6*	5.00
S.L. Boock	2	2	0	7	5	3.50

BOWLING	O	M	R	W	Ave
R.J. Hadlee	109.5	33	232	12	19.33
S.L. Boock	80.3	34	140	7	20.00
B.L. Cairns	113	37	251	12	20.91
E.J. Chatfield	98.2	33	188	6	31.33
J.J. Crowe	1	1	0	0	-
B.A. Edgar	3	1	3	0	-
G.P. Howarth	7	1	18	0	-
J.V. Coney	17	9	23	0	-
M.D. Crowe	26	6	93	0	-
M.C. Snedden	28	5	129	0	-

England

BATTING	M	I	NO	Runs	HS	Ave
C.L. Smith	2	3	1	148	91	74.00
D.W. Randall	3	4	0	293	164	73.25
I.T. Botham	3	4	0	226	138	56.50
N.A. Foster	2	2	1	28	18*	28.00
A.J. Lamb	3	4	0	82	49	20.50
M.W. Gatting	2	3	1	38	19*	19.00
C.J. Tavare	2	4	1	54	36*	18.00
D.I. Gower	3	4	0	69	33	17.25
R.W. Taylor	3	4	0	54	23	13.50
A.C.S. Pigott	1	2	1	12	8*	12.00
N.G. Cowans	2	3	0	32	21	10.66
N.G.B. Cook	1	1	0	7	7	7.00
V.J. Marks	1	1	0	6	6	6.00
G. Fowler	2	3	0	14	10	4.66
R.G.D. Willis	3	4	1	14	6	4.66

BOWLING	O	M	R	W	Ave
R.G.D. Willis	115.1	28	306	12	25.50
M.W. Gatting	10	4	28	1	28.00
N.G. Cowans	52	14	154	5	30.80
A.C.S. Pigott	17	7	75	2	37.50
V.J. Marks	40.2	9	115	3	38.33
N.G.B. Cook	89.3	37	196	4	49.00
I.T. Botham	109.4	25	354	7	50.57
N.A. Foster	91	29	229	4	57.25
C.L. Smith	3	1	6	0	-

1983/84 New Zealand in Sri Lanka

Within four days of their final one-day international against England, New Zealand embarked on a pioneering tour of Sri Lanka. Unseasonal weather allowed little play in three warm-up games prior to the first test. When the team arrived in Kandy there were talks of shifting the game to Colombo. Following the cancellation of the first day's play there were hostile scenes from the crowd, which had been seated in humid conditions for more than three hours.

158 SRI LANKA v NEW ZEALAND (*First Test*)

at Asgiriya Stadium, Kandy on 9, 10, 11, 13, 14 March, 1984
Toss : New Zealand. Umpires : H.C. Felsinger and P.W. Vidanagamage
New Zealand won by 165 runs

Geoff Howarth seemed to relish his return to the role of opener and completely dominated the partnership with John Wright. They added 97 for the first wicket. It was the first time that Howarth had passed 50 in his last 10 test innings. When rain and bad light stopped play New Zealand were 120-1.

New Zealand could be partially excused their disappointing batting when the first eight batsmen all scored over 20 but only Howarth exceeded 50. After 12 days they had yet to have net practice, none being available, and they were still acclimatising to the intense heat and humidity.

The day was a triumph for Vinothen John who was able to cut the ball into the right-hand batsmen and thoroughly deserved his 5-86. New Zealand 276; Sri Lanka 50-2.

On the rest day New Zealand had their first formal practice session. At the start of the fourth day they claimed three wickets for the addition of 11 runs and when the ninth wicket fell at 155 it appeared they would have a considerable first innings lead. John and Amerasinghe hit the ball hard against the fast-tiring attack and added 61 for the last wicket. With Sri Lanka dismissed for 215 New Zealand sought quick runs and was 77-2.

The fifth day was an intriguing battle of tactics, with New Zealand rearranging their batting order in the search for quick runs but being frustrated as the Sri Lankans meandered slowly through their overs, averaging less than 12 an hour. Howarth made his second half-century of the game and New Zealand declared, leaving Sri Lanka 263 to score in 130 minutes plus 20 overs.

In a dramatic six-over spell Richard Hadlee reaped four wickets at the cost of only eight runs and, with Stephen Boock claiming two wickets, Sri Lanka were reeling at 18-6. Hadlee's display was outstanding. He unsettled the batsmen with his faster delivery when he forced them to play six balls in every over.

The New Zealand touring team in Sri Lanka in 1984. From left, Steve McMorran (NZPA correspondent), Geoff Howarth (captain), Bas McBurney (manager), Ron Brierley (supporter), Jeff Crowe, John Wright, Jeremy Coney, Richard Hadlee, Ian Smith, Derek Stirling, Lance Cairns, Bruce Edgar, John Reid, John Bracewell, Ewen Chatfield, Martin Crowe, Richard Edmunds (doctor) and Stephen Boock.

With nothing to lose, Arjuna Ranatunga and Guy de Alwis both chanced their arms, with Ranatunga being particularly severe on John Bracewell, who conceded 51 runs in five overs. Bracewell was to have his revenge, catching his aggressor off his own bowling. Boock finished with his best test return of 5-28 and Sri Lanka was dismissed in 27.3 overs.

During the course of the day 16 wickets had fallen for 221 runs in just over four hours. At the end of the game a large crowd gathered in front of the pavilion. Orderly at first, they exploded in frustration and annoyance at their team's dismal performance and the riot police were called to disburse them.

at a somnolent pace throughout the day, with drinks breaks taken every 45 minutes. Only 145 runs were scored in the day from 78 overs. In addition to the heat and the unhurried batting New Zealand dropped five catches and Martin Crowe dislocated a finger.

Within an hour New Zealand captured the last four wickets for the addition of 29 runs with Cairns, moving the ball prodigiously, claiming three. Jeff Crowe and Jeremy Coney provided stubborn resistance with a partnership worth 61 after the third wicket fell at 66. At stumps New Zealand were 164-5; Sri Lanka 174.

The promise of a substantial first innings lead was quickly eliminated when four wickets fell for the addition of only 12 runs as Ravi Ratnayeke bowled with fire finished with 5-42. Sri Lanka lost their first two wickets before they had passed New Zealand's lead of 24.

With the side tottering, Sidath Wettimuny and Roy Dias established the first substantial partnership of the tour against New Zealand. At stumps they were both undefeated, having added 120. Dias was the aggressor, Wettimuny the defender. Together they were in perfect harmony. A further three catches were dropped by the visitors.

Although the pitch was showing signs of wear and the bounce was becoming slightly unpredictable, the partnership was only broken after 257 minutes when Wettimuny was struck in the groin by a delivery from Richard Hadlee and had to retire hurt.

NEW ZEALAND

G.P.Howarth*	c de Alwis b John	62	lbw b John		60
J.G.Wright	lbw b John	45	c de Alwis b John		4
J.F.Reid	c Kaluperuma b Amerasinghe	26	c Ranatunga b de Silva		30
M.D.Crowe	c Ratnayake b de Silva	26	(5) st de Alwis b de Silva		8
J.J.Crowe	c sub (S.H.U.Karnain) b John	20	(8) c Amerasinghe b Kaluperuma		9
J.V.Coney	lbw b Ratnayake	25	(10) not out		3
R.J.Hadlee	c Ranatunga b John	29	(6) c sub (S.H.U.Karnain) b Kaluperuma		27
I.D.S.Smith†	b Ranatunga	30	(9) not out		31
B.L.Cairns	c de Alwis b Ranatunga	0	(7) c Wettimuny b de Silva		2
J.G.Bracewell	c de Silva b John	2	(4) c Amerasinghe b John		21
S.L.Boock	not out	4			
Extras	(b 1, lb 1, w 5)	7	(b 3, w 3)		6
TOTAL	(100.1 overs)	276	(54.5 overs) (8 wkts dec)		201

SRI LANKA

S.Wettimuny	c Coney b Hadlee	0	c Smith b Hadlee		5
E.R.N.S.Fernando	c Hadlee b Boock	29	lbw b Hadlee		2
S.M.S.Kaluperuma	c Howarth b Bracewell	18	c Crowe J.J. b Boock		5
R.J.Ratnayake	c Smith b Hadlee	6	(9) lbw b Boock		12
L.R.D.Mendis*	c Bracewell b Hadlee	5	(4) b Hadlee		0
R.S.Madugalle	c Crowe M.D. b Hadlee	33	(5) c Bracewell b Hadlee		2
A.Ranatunga	c Bracewell b Cairns	20	(6) c & b Bracewell		51
D.S.de Silva	b Bracewell	11	(7) c Coney b Boock		0
R.G.de Alwis†	lbw b Boock	26	(8) c Howarth b Boock		19
V.B.John	not out	27	c Wright b Boock		0
A.M.J.G.Amerasinghe	run out	34	not out		0
Extras	(lb 2, nb 4)	6	(nb 1)		1
TOTAL	(79.5 overs)	215	(27.3 overs)		97

Bowling	O	M	R	W	O	M	R	W
SRI LANKA								
John	29.1	7	86	5	17.5	1	73	3
Ratnayake	15	4	45	1				
Ranatunga	9	3	17	2	4	0	14	0
de Silva	29	6	69	1	21	2	59	3
Amerasinghe	12	3	45	1	8	2	32	0
Kaluperuma	6	3	7	0	4	0	17	2
NEW ZEALAND								
Hadlee	20.5	7	35	4	7	4	8	4
Cairns	18	3	71	1	4	1	6	0
Crowe M.D.	3	1	4	0				
Boock	23	7	63	2	9.3	4	28	5
Bracewell	15	4	36	2	7	1	54	1

Fall of Wickets	NZ	SL	NZ	SL
	1st	1st	2nd	2nd
1st	97	0	14	3
2nd	124	38	75	12
3rd	165	55	111	12
4th	169	55	126	14
5th	210	61	133	18
6th	236	89	137	18
7th	266	120	167	55
8th	266	132	167	97
9th	272	155	-	97
10th	276	215	-	97

MILESTONES

- It was New Zealand's 18th win in test cricket. This was the first full test tour by any country to Sri Lanka

159 SRI LANKA v NEW ZEALAND *(Second Test)*

at Sinhalese Sports Club Ground, Colombo on 16, 17, 18, 20, 21 March, 1984
Toss : New Zealand. Umpires : D.P. Buultjens and H.C. Felsinger
Match drawn

Following the riots in Kandy 250 policemen and four riot squads were stationed at the ground to ensure that nothing untoward occurred in the second test.

Sent in by Geoff Howarth the Sri Lankan batsmen played

Even though the drinks were taken every 45 minutes, the suffocating heat sapped the energy from the players. Jeff Crowe toiled hard to reach 50 on the hottest day of the test.

Dias hit 17 boundaries in his innings of 108 that dominated Sri Lanka's total of 289. Duleep Mendis made a sporting declaration that left New Zealand 260 runs to make in 350 minutes. By stumps New Zealand had scored six of the required total.

The early loss of Howarth and John Reid, to the bowling of Vinothen John, ruled out any chance of New Zealand going for victory. Precariously placed, they looked to an out-of-form John Wright to consolidate the innings. At 48-3, Martin Crowe, still suffering from a dislocated finger and with stomach pains and influenza, joined Wright.

Both batsmen concentrated on occupying the crease to the extent that in the two-hour session between lunch and tea only 26 runs were scored. They batted together for 35 overs before Wright made an indiscretion and was out for 48, made in 275 minutes. It was a bizarre innings from Crowe, normally a brilliant strokemaker. After 95 minutes he had scored three. He and Coney saw off the second new ball and saved the game.

SRI LANKA

S.Wettimuny	c Coney b Chatfield	26	c Hadlee b Chatfield	65
E.R.N.S.Fernando	b Crowe M.D.	8	c Crowe J.J. b Hadlee	0
S.M.S.Kaluperuma	b Boock	23	c Cairns b Hadlee	2
R.L.Dias	run out	16	b Cairns	108
L.R.D.Mendis*	b Hadlee	1	(6) b Chatfield	36
R.S.Madugalle	not out	44	(7) c Crowe J.J. b Chatfield	36
A.Ranatunga	c Smith b Cairns	6	(8) run out	7
J.R.Ratnayeke	lbw b Hadlee	22	(5) c & b Hadlee	12
D.S.de Silva	c Coney b Cairns	0	not out	13
R.G.de Alwist	c Smith b Cairns	2	b Chatfield	2
V.B.John	c Smith b Cairns	0	not out	3
Extras	(b 5, lb 7, w 8, nb 6)	26	(, lb 4, nb 1)	5
TOTAL	(90.5 overs)	**174**	(127 overs) (9 wkts dec)	**289**

NEW ZEALAND

G.P.Howarth*	b John	24	c Kaluperuma b John	10
J.G.Wright	c Dias b John	20	c de Silva b Ranatunga	48
J.F.Reid	c de Alwis b John	7	lbw b John	0
J.J.Crowe	b Ratnayeke	50	c de Alwis b Ranatunga	16
J.V.Coney	c John b de Silva	30	(6) not out	20
R.J.Hadlee	b Ratnayeke	19		
S.L.Boock	c Madugalle b Ratnayeke	4		
M.D.Crowe	c Kaluperuma b Ratnayeke	0	(5) not out	19
I.D.S.Smith†	c Kaluperuma b Ratnayeke	7		
B.L.Cairns	lbw b de Silva	14		
E.J.Chatfield	not out	9		
Extras	(b 4, lb 6, w 1, nb 3)	14	(b 4, lb 4, nb 2)	10
TOTAL	(64.3 overs)	**198**	(86 overs) (4 wkts)	**123**

Bowling	O	M	R	W	O	M	R	W
NEW ZEALAND								
Hadlee	22	12	27	2	30	14	58	3
Cairns	24.5	6	47	4	22	3	79	1
Chatfield	20	7	35	1	29	9	78	4
Crowe M.D.	13	5	21	1				
Boock	11	2	18	1	42	16	65	0
Coney					4	3	4	0
SRI LANKA								
John	24	1	89	3	21	11	26	2
Ratnayeke	21	8	42	5	21	11	17	0
Kaluperuma	1	0	3	0	6	3	10	0
Ranatunga	4	1	11	0	18	7	29	2
de Silva	14.3	6	39	2	19	10	31	0
Madugalle					1	1	0	0

Fall of Wickets

	SL	NZ	SL	NZ
	1st	1st	2nd	2nd
1st	25	38	3	10
2nd	66	53	13	10
3rd	68	66	176	48
4th	69	127	209	89
5th	99	151	234	-
6th	111	166	244	-
7th	152	166	245	-
8th	153	171	278	-
9th	165	178	282	-
10th	174	198	-	-

MILESTONES

• Roy Dias became the first Sri Lankan to score a test century against New Zealand.

• Martin Crowe took 210 minutes to reach 10. It was the longest time taken by anyone to reach double figures in a test innings.

160 SRI LANKA v NEW ZEALAND *(Third Test)*

at Colombo Cricket Club Ground on 24, 25, 26, 28, 29 March, 1984
Toss : Sri Lanka. Umpires : K.T. Francis and P.W. Vidanagamage
New Zealand won by an innings and 61 runs

Richard Hadlee began his 50th test match by bowling Sidath Wettimuny with the last ball of his first over and then dismissed Ravi Ratnayeke in his second.

By lunch the position looked hopeless for Sri Lanka, who were 63-5, but once again some quality batting from Ranjan Madugalle, ably assisted by Arjuna Ranatunga, swung the game back onto an equal footing. They added 105 before Madugalle had to retire hurt after compiling 87. The day ended with Sri Lanka 230-8.

Ewen Chatfield captured the remaining two wickets and he and Hadlee each finished with five in the innings. John Reid and Martin Crowe shared a third wicket partnership of 100 after New Zealand had lost their first two wickets for 32. Reid ended the day unbeaten on 56, with New Zealand 153-3.

Having come in as nightwatchman Stephen Boock surprised everyone by still being unbeaten when lunch was taken. He delighted in playing a hook shot and a cover drive off both quick bowlers as he passed double figures for the first time in 17 test innings. He added 83 runs with Reid.

Jeff Crowe and Jeremy Coney played support roles as Reid continued his marathon innings throughout the third day for an additional 100 personal runs. He displayed remarkable powers of concentration and endurance in the oppressive heat.

During the day 187 runs were added, and only two wickets lost. It was not uncommon for the drinks break to take eight minutes as bowlers changed their boots and batsmen kept changing their gloves.

Following the rest day Reid and Coney made their partnership worth 133 before Reid was dismissed for 180, made in 685 minutes off 445 balls. Coney soon reached his 11th half-century in 31 tests and continued to increase the run tempo, with a valuable contribution also coming from Ian Smith. New Zealand's lead of 203 was substantial and at stumps Sri Lanka were 69-3 and their fate seemed set.

As in the first innings Madugalle and Ranatunga were the only batsmen to make a fight of it. Hadlee, for the second time in the game, took five wickets, and was assisted by the guileful bowling of Boock, who thoroughly deserved his return of 3-32 off 16 overs. New Zealand won by an innings and 61 runs.

MILESTONES

• It was New Zealand's 19th test victory and its first by an innings overseas.

• In his 50th test match Richard Hadlee captured 10 wickets in a match for the fourth time. He ended the series with 23 wickets, a New Zealand record in a three-game series.

SRI LANKA

Batsman	Dismissal	Score	Dismissal (2nd)	Score
S.Wettimuny	b Hadlee	4	c Coney b Hadlee	2
S.M.S.Kaluperuma	b Hadlee	16	c Coney b Hadlee	18
J.R.Ratnayeke	lbw b Hadlee	0	(7) b Boock	2
R.L.Dias	c Smith b Chatfield	10	absent hurt	
L.R.D.Mendis*	c Crowe J.J. b Chatfield	19	(6) b Boock	10
R.S.Madugalle	not out	89	(3) c Wright b Bracewell	38
A.Ranatunga	c sub (B.A.Edgar) b Chatfield	37	(4) c Wright b Boock	50
D.S.de Silva	c Smith b Hadlee	17	(5) c Smith b Hadlee	1
R.G.de Alwis†	c Boock b Hadlee	28	(8) c Bracewell b Hadlee	10
A.M.J.G.Amerasinghe	c Wright b Chatfield	15	(9) b Hadlee	5
V.B.John	c & b Chatfield	12	(10) not out	0
Extras	(lb 4, nb 5)	9	(w 1, nb 5)	6
TOTAL	**(82 overs)**	**256**	**(57 overs)**	**142**

NEW ZEALAND

Batsman	Dismissal	Score
G.P.Howarth*	lbw b Ratnayeke	7
J.G.Wright	c de Alwis b Ratnayeke	18
J.F.Reid	c & b Amerasinghe	180
M.D.Crowe	c de Alwis b Ratnayeke	45
S.L.Boock	b John	35
J.J.Crowe	lbw b John	18
J.V.Coney	c de Alwis b Amerasinghe	92
R.J.Hadlee	c Kaluperuma b de Silva	0
I.D.S.Smith†	b John	42
J.G.Bracewell	c Kaluperuma b de Silva	0
E.J.Chatfield	not out	1
Extras	(b 5, lb 8, w 2, nb 6)	21
TOTAL	**(175 overs)**	**459**

Bowling	O	M	R	W	O	M	R	W
NEW ZEALAND								
Hadlee	22	4	73	5	16	7	29	5
Chatfield	22	5	63	5	9	2	27	0
Crowe M.D.	6	2	22	0	5	2	13	0
Boock	20	9	51	0	16	2	32	3
Bracewell	9	2	31	0	11	4	35	1
Coney	3	0	7	0				
SRI LANKA								
John	37	8	99	3				
Ratnayeke	40	9	128	3				
Ranatunga	16	5	18	0				
de Silva	42	4	95	2				
Amerasinghe	30	4	73	2				
Kaluperuma	10	2	25	0				

Fall of Wickets	SL 1st	NZ 1st	SL 2nd
1st	4	13	6
2nd	4	32	63
3rd	22	132	63
4th	32	214	79
5th	63	253	101
6th	182	386	105
7th	222	391	136
8th	227	429	138
9th	249	436	142
10th	256	459	-

John Reid, watched by wicketkeeper Guy de Alwis, strokes another boundary. His 180 was a marathon of concentration lasting 11½ hours.

AVERAGES

New Zealand

BATTING	M	I	NO	Runs	HS	Ave
J.V. Coney	3	5	2	170	92	56.66
J.F. Reid	3	5	0	243	180	48.60
I.D.S. Smith	3	4	1	110	42	36.66
G.P. Howarth	3	5	0	163	62	32.60
J.G. Wright	3	5	0	135	48	27.00
M.D. Crowe	3	5	1	98	45	24.50
J.J. Crowe	3	5	0	113	50	22.60
S.L. Boock	3	3	1	43	35	21.50
R.J. Hadlee	3	4	0	75	29	18.75
J.G. Bracewell	2	3	0	23	21	7.66
B.L. Cairns	2	3	0	16	14	5.33
E.J. Chatfield	2	2	2	10	9*	-

BOWLING	O	M	R	W	Ave
R.J. Hadlee	117.5	48	230	23	10.00
E.J. Chatfield	80	23	203	10	20.30
S.L. Boock	121.3	40	257	11	23.36
B.L. Cairns	68.5	13	203	6	33.83
J.G. Bracewell	42	11	156	4	39.00
M.D. Crowe	27	10	60	1	60.00
J.V. Coney	7	3	11	0	-

Sri Lanka

BATTING	M	I	NO	Runs	HS	Ave
R.S. Madugalle	3	6	2	242	89*	60.50
R.L. Dias	2	3	0	134	108	44.66
A. Ranatunga	3	6	0	171	51	28.50
A.M.J.G. Amerasinghe	2	4	1	54	34	18.00
S. Wettimuny	3	6	0	102	65	17.00
R.G. de Alwis	3	6	0	87	28	14.50
V.B. John	3	6	3	42	27*	14.00
S.M.S. Kaluperuma	3	6	0	82	23	13.66
L.R.D. Mendis	3	6	0	71	36	11.83
E.R.N.S. Fernando	2	4	0	39	29	9.75
J.R. Ratnayeke	2	4	0	36	22	9.00
R.J. Ratnayake	1	2	0	18	12	9.00
D.S. de Silva	3	6	1	42	17	8.40

BOWLING	O	M	R	W	Ave
A. Ranatunga	51	16	89	4	22.25
V.B. John	129	28	373	16	23.31
J.R. Ratnayeke	82	28	187	8	23.37
S.M.S. Kaluperuma	27	8	62	2	31.00
D.S. de Silva	125.3	28	293	8	36.62
R.J. Ratnayake	15	4	45	1	45.00
A.M.J.G. Amerasinghe	50	9	150	3	50.00
R.S. Madugalle	1	1	0	0	-

1984/85 New Zealand in Pakistan

Within seven months of one tour in Asia, New Zealand cricket was gearing itself for another to Pakistan. Geoff Howarth was unavailable for the tour and Jeremy Coney led the side. During the 1984 English County Cricket Championship Richard Hadlee completed the double of 1000 runs and 100 wickets, the first player to do so since 1967. It was a great blow when he declined to tour Pakistan.

161 PAKISTAN v NEW ZEALAND (First Test)

at Gaddafi Stadium, Lahore on 16, 17, 18, 19, 20 November, 1984
Toss : New Zealand. Umpires : Mahboob Shah and Shakeel Khan
Pakistan won by 6 wickets

There was a dreadful lack of concentration among the top batsmen when New Zealand stumbled to an indigestible lunch at 57-5. The ploy of opening the batting with Jeff Crowe and Bruce Edgar and batting John Wright at four failed dismally. Martin Crowe and Ian Smith were the only two batsmen to display true form. Too many players were

dismissed with indiscreet shots, particularly to the left-arm spinner Iqbal Qasim. A score of 157 by New Zealand was a losing total.

Pakistan ended the second day at 189-7 as New Zealand bowled themselves back into the match, supported by solid fielding. The star was John Reid, who took three spectacular catches in the gully area.

Ewen Chatfield claimed all three wickets next morning to restrict Pakistan's lead to 64. Wright and Edgar, restored to the opening position, both played lovely attacking shots and by lunch had eliminated the deficit. None of the Pakistan bowlers seemed to pose particular problems for them, with the exception of Abdul Qadir, whose right-arm leg-spinners and wrong'uns needed careful watching.

With the score at 123-1 New Zealand stumbled, losing three wickets in the space of 11 runs to a great piece of fielding, a fine delivery and a bad umpiring decision. It was a period of disquiet for New Zealand but Jeff Crowe and Coney looked to have put things right with a partnership of 68 before Coney was dismissed minutes before stumps. Stephen Boock, the nightwatchman, immediately departed, leaving New Zealand 216-6.

The Pakistan spinning duo quickly wrapped up the New Zealand innings, leaving the home side only 178 to go one-

Jeremy Coney appears to be asking for divine guidance as he studies the Pakistan book of rules.

NEW ZEALAND

J.J.Crowe	c Dalpat b Mudassar	0	(5) b Iqbal		43
B.A.Edgar	b Mudassar	3	lbw b Hafeez		26
M.D.Crowe	c Omar b Qadir	55	c sub (Ramiz Raja) b Iqbal		33
J.G.Wright	c Anil Dalpat b Azeem Hafeez	1	(1) run out		65
J.F.Reid	lbw b Mudassar Nazar	2	(4) b Qadir		6
J.V.Coney*	c Mohsin Khan b Iqbal	7	c Dalpat b Hafeez		26
E.J.Gray	c sub (Ramiz Raja) b Iqbal	12	(8) c Mudassar b Qadir		6
I.D.S.Smith†	c Iqbal b Hafeez	41	(9) not out		11
D.A.Stirling	b Iqbal	16	(10) c Dalpat b Iqbal		10
S.L.Boock	c Miandad b Iqbal	13	(7) c Miandad b Qadir		0
E.J.Chatfield	not out	6	c Omar b Iqbal		0
Extras	(b 1)	1	(b 8, lb 2, w 1, nb 4)		15
TOTAL	**(74.4 overs)**	**157**	**(83 overs)**		**241**

PAKISTAN

Mudassar Nazar	c Reid b Stirling	26	b Boock		16
Mohsin Khan	c Reid b Gray	58	c & b Gray		38
Qasim Omar	c Crowe J.J. b Boock	13	lbw b Stirling		20
Javed Miandad	c Reid b Gray	11	not out		48
Zaheer Abbas*	c Crowe M.D. b Boock	43	c Smith b Gray		31
Salim Malik	lbw b Stirling	10	not out		24
Abdul Qadir	c Coney b Chatfield	14			
Anil Dalpat†	b Crowe M.D.	11			
Iqbal Qasim	c Coney b Chatfield	22			
Azeem Hafeez	c Boock b Chatfield	11			
Tauseef Ahmed	not out	0			
Extras	(nb 2)	2	(lb 4)		4
TOTAL	**(93.2 overs)**	**221**	**(65.1 overs) (4 wkts)**		**181**

Bowling

PAKISTAN	O	M	R	W	O	M	R	W
Mudassar	11	5	8	3	10	1	30	0
Hafeez	18	9	40	2	13	5	37	2
Qadir	21	6	58	1	26	4	82	3
Iqbal	22.4	10	41	4	30	10	65	4
Tauseef	2	0	9	0	4	0	17	0

NEW ZEALAND	O	M	R	W	O	M	R	W
Stirling	27	7	71	2	15.1	2	60	1
Crowe M.D.	7	1	21	1				
Gray	8	1	19	2	18	0	45	2
Chatfield	27.2	7	57	3	13	7	12	0
Boock	24	7	53	2	17	2	56	1
Coney					2	1	4	0

Fall of Wickets

	NZ	P	NZ	P
	1st	1st	2nd	2nd
1st	0	54	66	33
2nd	11	84	123	77
3rd	28	103	138	77
4th	31	114	140	138
5th	50	144	208	-
6th	76	165	210	-
7th	120	188	220	-
8th	124	189	220	-
9th	146	212	235	-
10th	157	221	241	-

up in the series. Some typically tight-fisted bowling from Chatfield, who conceded only 12 runs from 13 overs, and accurate spin bowling from the left-arm pair of Evan Gray and Boock caused Pakistan some anxious moments before confident batting by Javed Miandad and Zaheer Abbas decided the game.

Throughout the match umpiring decisions had been crucial and there was disappointment in both camps at the number of faulty findings.

MILESTONES

- Jeremy Coney became the 17th captain of New Zealand.

- Derek Stirling (154) made his test debut.

- Zaheer Abbas became the 20th batsman to score 5000 runs in test cricket.

162 PAKISTAN v NEW ZEALAND (*Second Test*)

at Niaz Stadium, Hyderabad on 25, 26, 27, 29, 30 November, 1984
Toss : New Zealand. Umpires : Khizer Hayat and Mian Mohammad Aslam
Pakistan won by 7 wickets

A week before the game the ground had been a foot under water and there had been liberal loads of sand spread on the ground to help it dry.

John Wright and Bruce Edgar were both out at 30, the former to a questionable umpiring decision. John Reid arrived at the crease and was still there at the end of the day's play, having reached his third test century in 251 minutes. Reid's was a calm, purposeful, confident and capable innings that held New Zealand together.

He shared a fifth wicket stand of 62 with Jeff Crowe and later with Evan Gray a further 74 for the seventh wicket. Of the seven wickets that New Zealand lost for 239 runs during the day, four decisions given by umpire Khizer Hayat were suspect. The previous season the Indian captain, Sunil Gavaskar, also complained of his incompetence.

Dismissing New Zealand for 267 Pakistan made inroads into the total with a partnership of 103 for the third wicket between Javed Miandad and Qasim Omar. Miandad was full of business but he lost three partners in quick succession at the end of the second day, which ended with Pakistan 159-5.

In spite of the fact that Miandad scored his 12th century, in his 100th test innings, New Zealand ended with a first-innings lead of 37 thanks to an inspired spell of bowling by Stephen Boock. His line and length were impeccable, his flight tantalising, and he was able to turn the occasional ball sharply. John Bracewell gave him support and it was the first test triumph for New Zealand's spinners for some time.

If the New Zealand spinners prospered, so did Pakistan's. Through a combination of good bowling, careless shots and more peculiarities in umpiring New Zealand lost eight wickets

for 159 on the third day. During his innings Martin Crowe had an on-field conference with his captain Jeremy Coney and team manager Ian Taylor, after he had been told by the umpires to change his shoes. His shoes were not changed.

For the second time in the game Jeff Crowe batted purposefully, firm in his idea, strong of stroke, and he had with him an equally resolute Ian Smith to share in a brisk stand of 45.

An additional 30 runs for the last two wickets had Pakistan requiring 227 for victory. New Zealand's prospects of victory were very real when Martin Crowe, in his role of opening bowler, had the first two wickets with the score at 13 and Miandad facing to prevent the hat-trick.

For the rest of the match the batting of Miandad and Mudassar Nazar, both of whom scored centuries, was exceptional. Both were impregnable in defence and had a glittering array of handsome shots. They added 212 to give Pakistan victory by seven wickets and a series win as well.

After the game Jeremy Coney read a prepared statement by the manager, Ian Taylor, which stated that his players were disillusioned by the standards of the umpiring.

That the complaints were not taken as the grizzle of losers was shown by the appointment of a committee of inquiry comprising Hanif Mohammed and former test umpire Shuja-ud-din. It would later report that four of the decisions against New Zealand and two against Pakistan were "confusing".

NEW ZEALAND

Batsman	Dismissal	Score	Dismissal	Score
J.G.Wright	c Dalpat b Iqbal	18	c Dalpat b Iqbal	22
B.A.Edgar	c Malik b Qadir	11	lbw b Mudassar	1
M.D.Crowe	b Qadir	19	(4) st Dalpat b Iqbal	21
J.F.Reid	lbw b Hafeez	106	(3) lbw b Qadir	21
J.V.Coney*	c Manzoor b Qadir	6	b Iqbal	5
J.J.Crowe	c Malik b Zaheer	39	lbw b Iqbal	57
I.D.S.Smith†	c Iqbal b Zaheer	6	c Mudassar b Hafeez	34
E.J.Gray	lbw b Mudassar	25	c Omar b Iqbal	5
J.G.Bracewell	c Mudassar b Qadir	0	c & b Qadir	0
D.A.Stirling	not out	11	b Qadir	11
S.L.Boock	lbw b Qadir	12	not out	4
Extras	(b 13, nb 1)	14	(b 1, lb 4, nb 3)	8
TOTAL	**(108.3 overs)**	**267**	**(56.1 overs)**	**189**

PAKISTAN

Batsman	Dismissal	Score	Dismissal	Score
Mudassar Nazar	c Crowe M.D. b Bracewell	28	c Coney b Boock	106
Mohsin Khan	c Gray b Boock	9	b Crowe M.D.	2
Qasim Omar	c Coney b Boock	45	lbw b Crowe M.D.	0
Javed Miandad	c Crowe J.J. b Boock	104	not out	103
Anil Dalpat†	b Bracewell	1		
Zaheer Abbas*	st Smith b Boock	2		
Salim Malik	b Boock	1		
Manzoor Elahi	c Crowe J.J. b Boock	19	(5) not out	4
Abdul Qadir	lbw b Boock	11		
Iqbal Qasim	c Crowe J.J. b Bracewell	8		
Azeem Hafeez	not out	0		
Extras	(lb 2)	2	(b 5, lb 7, nb 3)	15
TOTAL	**(91.1 overs)**	**230**	**(64.4 overs) (3 wkts)**	**230**

Bowling	O	M	R	W	O	M	R	W
PAKISTAN								
Mudassar	7	4	14	1	5	2	8	1
Hafeez	18	4	29	1	8	2	34	1
Iqbal	33	6	80	1	24.1	7	78	5
Qadir	40.3	11	108	5	18	3	59	3
Manzoor	2	1	2	0				
Zaheer	8	1	21	2	1	0	5	0
NEW ZEALAND								
Stirling	3	0	11	0	4	0	26	0
Crowe M.D.	3	0	8	0	8	1	29	2
Coney	10	4	8	0	4	1	9	0
Boock	37	12	87	7	23.4	4	69	1
Bracewell	16.1	3	44	3	14	3	36	0
Gray	22	4	70	0	11	0	49	0

Fall of Wickets	NZ	P	NZ	P
	1st	1st	2nd	2nd
1st	30	26	2	14
2nd	30	50	34	14
3rd	74	153	58	226
4th	88	154	71	-
5th	150	159	80	-
6th	164	169	125	-
7th	238	191	149	-
8th	239	215	149	-
9th	243	230	167	-
10th	267	230	189	-

MILESTONES

- The test was the 1000th played since the first match between England and Australia in Melbourne in 1876/77.

- Stephen Boock's bowling figures of 7-87 were the best by a New Zealand slow bowler in test cricket.

- Javed Miandad became the second Pakistan player to score a century in each innings of a match.

163 **PAKISTAN v NEW ZEALAND** *(Third Test)*
at National Stadium, Karachi on 10, 11, 12, 14, 15 December, 1984
Toss : Pakistan. Umpires : Javed Akhtar and Shakoor Rana
Match drawn

New Zealand's opening attack of Derek Stirling and Martin Crowe, with Paul McEwan as first change, looked a fill-in affair but it proved to be effective and difficult to score off. At 124-5 New Zealand were halted by resolute batting from two younger members of the Pakistan side, Salim Malik and Wasim Raja, who added 79 to have Pakistan 203-5 at stumps.

Despite a determined bowling effort by Stirling and continued success for Stephen Boock, who each took four wickets, Pakistan ended with 328 thanks to a stand of 89 between Anil Dalpat and Iqbal Qasim. By the end of the day New Zealand was 99-1, due almost entirely to a display of batting pyrotechnics by John Wright who was 81 not out as the strokes flowed, clean and powerful.

Wright could not sustain his brilliant form the next day. Whereas his 81 had taken two hours it took him a further 90 minutes to reach his century. John Reid, again showing enormous powers of concentration, fell three runs short of what would have been his second century of the series. With all the batsmen finding true form New Zealand ended the day at 316-4.

A ninth wicket stand between McEwan and John Bracewell enabled New Zealand to stretch its lead to 98. When Pakistan lost their second wicket at 33 there was a faint hope for the visitors. Shakoor Rana rejected an appeal for a catch at the wicket from Javed Miandad off Bracewell with the score at 77. The refusal outraged the tourists.

Jeremy Coney had a few words to the umpire, who then made a memorable statement, "I swear to God I am not a cheat." He then invited everyone to leave the field, and look at the television replays of the incident. Coney was about to lead his team from the field when the other umpire, Javed Akhatar, called everyone back to their senses.

Pakistan was still in danger of defeat when they lost their fifth wicket at 130. Malik and Raja weathered the storm once again and their unbroken partnership of 178 kept intact Pakistan's unbeaten record at Karachi. Malik scored the fastest century of the series in 173 minutes.

MILESTONES

- Anil Dalpat and Iqbal Qasim created an eighth wicket record for Pakistan against New Zealand with their partnership of 89.

In Pakistan's first innings left-arm spinner Stephen Boock returned the best bowling figures for a New Zealand slow bowler, claiming 7-87.

PAKISTAN

Batsman	Dismissal	Runs	Dismissal (2nd)	Runs
Mudassar Nazar	c Smith b Stirling	5	c McEwan b Stirling	0
Shoaib Mohammad	c Smith b Stirling	31	c McEwan b Boock	34
Qasim Omar	lbw b Boock	45	c & b Crowe M.D.	17
Javed Miandad	c Smith b Crowe M.D.	13	c Crowe J.J. b Boock	58
Zaheer Abbas*	c Smith b Stirling	14	c Smith b Bracewell	3
Salim Malik	c & b Crowe M.D.	50	not out	119
Wasim Raja	lbw b Stirling	51	not out	60
Abdul Qadir	c Wright b Boock	7		
Anil Dalpat†	b Boock	52		
Iqbal Qasim	not out	45		
Azeem Hafeez	lbw b Boock	0		
Extras	(b 5, lb 6, w 1, nb 3)	15	(b 2, lb 8, nb 7)	17
TOTAL	(120 overs)	328	(94 overs) (5 wkts)	308

NEW ZEALAND

Batsman	Dismissal	Runs
J.G.Wright	c Dalpat b Iqbal	107
B.A.Edgar	run out	15
J.F.Reid	c Iqbal b Hafeez	97
M.D.Crowe	lbw b Raja	45
J.J.Crowe	c Miandad b Hafeez	62
J.V.Coney*	c & b Iqbal	16
P.E.McEwan	not out	40
I.D.S.Smith†	c Malik b Iqbal	0
D.A.Stirling	c Omar b Iqbal	7
J.G.Bracewell	c Dalpat b Hafeez	30
S.L.Boock	c Dalpat b Hafeez	0
Extras	(b 1, lb 5, nb 1)	7
TOTAL	(157.4 overs)	426

Bowling	O	M	R	W	O	M	R	W
NEW ZEALAND								
Stirling	29	5	88	4	14	1	82	1
Crowe M.D.	21	4	81	2	10	3	26	1
McEwan	4	1	6	0	2	0	7	0
Boock	41	19	83	4	30	10	83	2
Coney	5	3	5	0				
Bracewell	20	5	54	0	33	11	83	1
Crowe J.J.					2	0	9	0
Wright					1	0	1	0
Reid					2	0	7	0
PAKISTAN								
Mudassar	15.4	2	45	0				
Hafeez	46.4	9	132	4				
Iqbal	57	13	133	4				
Raja	33	8	97	1				
Zaheer	5.2	1	13	0				

Fall of Wickets	P 1st	NZ 1st	P 2nd
1st	14	83	5
2nd	80	163	37
3rd	92	258	119
4th	102	292	126
5th	124	338	130
6th	204	352	-
7th	226	353	-
8th	315	361	-
9th	319	426	-
10th	328	426	-

AVERAGES

New Zealand

BATTING	M	I	NO	Runs	HS	Ave
J.F. Reid	3	5	0	232	106	46.40
J.G. Wright	3	5	0	213	107	42.60
J.J. Crowe	3	5	0	201	62	40.20
M.D. Crowe	3	5	0	173	55	34.60
I.D.S. Smith	3	5	1	92	41	23.00
D.A. Stirling	3	5	1	55	16	13.75
J.V. Coney	3	5	0	60	26	12.00
E.J. Gray	2	4	0	48	25	12.00
B.A. Edgar	3	5	0	56	26	11.20
J.G. Bracewell	2	3	0	30	30	10.00
S.L. Boock	3	5	1	29	13	7.25
E.J. Chatfield	1	2	1	6	6*	6.00
P.E. McEwan	1	1	1	40	40*	-

BOWLING	O	M	R	W	Ave
E.J. Chatfield	40.2	14	69	3	23.00
S.L. Boock	172.4	54	431	17	25.35
M.D. Crowe	49	9	165	6	27.50
D.A. Stirling	92.1	15	338	8	42.25
E.J. Gray	59	5	183	4	45.75
J.G. Bracewell	83.1	22	217	4	54.25
J.G. Wright	1	0	1	0	-
J.F. Reid	2	0	7	0	-
J.J. Crowe	2	0	9	0	-
P.E. McEwan	6	1	13	0	-
J.V. Coney	21	9	26	0	-

Pakistan

BATTING	M	I	NO	Runs	HS	Ave
Wasim Raja	1	2	1	111	60*	111.00
Javed Miandad	3	6	2	337	104	84.25
Salim Malik	3	5	2	204	119*	68.00
Iqbal Qasim	3	3	1	75	45*	37.50
Shoaib Mohammad	1	2	0	65	34	32.50
Mudassar Nazar	3	6	0	181	106	30.16
Mohsin Khan	2	4	0	107	58	26.75
Qasim Omar	3	6	0	140	45	23.33
Manzoor Elahi	1	2	1	23	19	23.00
Anil Dalpat	3	3	0	64	52	21.33
Zaheer Abbas	3	5	0	93	43	18.60
Abdul Qadir	3	3	0	32	14	10.66
Azeem Hafeez	3	3	1	11	11	5.50
Tauseef Ahmed	1	1	1	0	0*	-

BOWLING	O	M	R	W	Ave
Zaheer Abbas	14.2	2	39	2	19.50
Mudassar Nazar	48.4	14	105	5	21.00
Iqbal Qasim	166.5	46	397	18	22.05
Abdul Qadir	105.3	24	307	12	25.58
Azeem Hafeez	103.4	29	272	10	27.20
Wasim Raja	33	8	97	1	97.00
Manzoor Elahi	2	1	2	0	-
Tauseef Ahmed	6	0	26	0	-

Martin Crowe works a ball backward of point while Pakistan wicketkeeper Anil Dalpat lifts his gloves with a flourish.

1984/85 Pakistan in New Zealand

Less than a month after the series in Pakistan had ended Javed Miandad brought Pakistan for a nine-match tour of New Zealand. Geoff Howarth was again named New Zealand captain and also chosen to open the innings with John Wright. Before the match, critics expressed doubt about the pitch, predicting that it would assist the Pakistan spinners.

164 **NEW ZEALAND v PAKISTAN** *(First Test)*
at Basin Reserve, Wellington on 18, 19, 20, 21, 22 January, 1985
Toss : New Zealand. Umpires : G.C. Morris and S.J. Woodward
Match drawn

Howarth appeared to be growing in confidence at the beginning of New Zealand's innings and, before he was run out for 33, he had displayed some of his former batting charm. John Reid was the cornerstone of New Zealand's innings with his easy footwork and his handsome, if occasional, attacking strokes.

He and Martin Crowe nullified the threat of Abdul Qadir's whippy right-arm leg-spinners and the pinpoint accuracy of his left-arm colleague, Iqbal Qasim. There was turn but it was too slow. Reid ended the day 86 not out and New Zealand was 220-4.

With Coney's dismissal, early on the second day, the two left-handers, Reid and Richard Hadlee, cemented New Zealand's position with a partnership of 145. Hadlee, the aggressor, made 89. Reid's innings ended after he had faced 427 balls in making 148. He had shared stands of 37 with

Howarth, 65 with Martin Crowe, 92 with Coney, 145 with Hadlee and 39 with Ian Smith. Lance Cairns and Smith rammed home New Zealand's advantage by taking the score to 485-7.

After 173 overs had been bowled with the original ball, Miandad took the new ball at the start of the third day and New Zealand's innings finished at 492. The New Zealand pace attack failed to worry the batsmen and it was Stephen Boock who sowed the seeds of doubt and was the key figure as Pakistan lost ground steadily.

When the sixth wicket had fallen at 187, one had been run out and Boock had the other five. He bowled a tantalising length and was not afraid to keep the ball pitched up. Salim Malik played shots all round the ground until he was caught off a full toss from Hadlee. It was Hadlee's 1000th dismissal in first-class cricket.

Starting the fourth day at 236-7 Pakistan was in grave danger of having to follow on. However, there was no question of meek submission from Qadir and Anil Dalpat. They batted in a forthright manner and, when Qadir was dismissed, Iqbal was equally resolute.

Starting its second innings with a lead of 170 New Zealand hoped for authoritative batting to yield quick runs.

Jeremy Coney, who scored 48, sweeps a ball past Shoaib Mohammad. The other Pakistan fieldsmen are Anil Dalpat and Iqbal Qasim.

NEW ZEALAND

G.P.Howarth*	run out	33	c Dalpat b Hafeez		17
J.G.Wright	c Shoaib b Hafeez	11	lbw b Mudassar		11
J.F.Reid	b Hafeez	148	c Qadir b Iqbal		3
M.D.Crowe	c Dalpat b Iqbal	37	c Qadir b Iqbal		33
J.J.Crowe	c Shoaib b Iqbal	4	not out		19
J.V.Coney	b Qadir	48	not out		18
R.J.Hadlee	c Miandad b Hafeez	89			
I.D.S.Smith†	c & b Mudassar	65			
B.L.Cairns	b Hafeez	36			
S.L.Boock	c Dalpat b Hafeez	0			
E.J.Chatfield	not out	3			
Extras	(b 5, lb 12, nb 1)	18	(lb 2)		2
TOTAL	(175 overs)	**492**	(45 overs) (4 wkts)		**103**

PAKISTAN

Mudassar Nazar	c & b Boock	38
Mohsin Khan	c Wright b Boock	40
Shoaib Mohammad	run out	7
Qasim Omar	b Boock	8
Javed Miandad*	c Smith b Boock	30
Salim Malik	c Cairns b Hadlee	66
Wasim Raja	c Crowe M.D. b Boock	14
Abdul Qadir	c Smith b Hadlee	54
Anil Dalpat†	c Smith b Chatfield	15
Iqbal Qasim	not out	27
Azeem Hafeez	c Boock b Cairns	3
Extras	(b 9, lb 9, nb 2)	20
TOTAL	(129.4 overs)	**322**

Bowling	O	M	R	W	O	M	R	W		Fall of Wickets		
PAKISTAN										NZ	P	NZ
Mudassar	29	5	80	1	6	3	13	1		*1st*	*1st*	*2nd*
Hafeez	48	12	127	5	15	3	51	1	1st	24	62	24
Qadir	51	13	142	1	8	1	18	0	2nd	61	85	30
Iqbal	41	5	105	2	16	8	19	2	3rd	126	95	42
Raja	2	0	10	0					4th	138	102	73
Shoaib	1	0	4	0					5th	230	161	-
Miandad	3	1	7	0					6th	375	187	-
NEW ZEALAND									7th	414	223	-
Hadlee	32	11	70	2					8th	488	288	-
Cairns	27.4	5	65	1					9th	488	309	-
Chatfield	25	10	52	1					10th	492	322	-
Boock	45	18	117	5								

The first two overs yielded 19 runs but it took New Zealand a further 19 overs to reach 50, with Iqbal proving most difficult to score off.

By day's end New Zealand was 103-4, 273 runs ahead, with the chance of some quick runs on the last morning and the prospect of winning the game, but a storm overnight saw the game abandoned.

MILESTONES

- New Zealand's total of 492 was their highest against Pakistan.

- John Reid and Richard Hadlee established a new record sixth wicket partnership against Pakistan of 145.

- Richard Hadlee became the second New Zealand cricketer to capture 1000 first-class wickets, the first being Clarrie Grimmett, who played most of his cricket in Australia.

165 NEW ZEALAND v PAKISTAN *(Second Test)*

at Eden Park, Auckland on 25, 26, 27, 28 January, 1985
Toss : New Zealand. Umpires : F.R. Goodall and S.J. Woodward
New Zealand won by an innings and 99 runs

Eden Park was unusually green and play was late starting owing to overnight rain. Pakistan was sent in to bat in a damp and heavy atmosphere with the humidity high – an ideal situation for swing and seam bowlers.

Pakistan negotiated the first stanza of the game, losing only two wickets in scoring 93. Excellent catches by Jeremy Coney and Martin Crowe altered the situation but it was the ball from Ewen Chatfield, bowled to Javed Miandad, which flew from near a length, touched his glove and carried to Ian Smith that was crucial. With their top batsman and leader gone the remaining Pakistan batsmen showed a deep distrust of almost everything they saw.

Salim Malik was the exception. He still managed to play silky shots in unfriendly conditions. The accuracy of Chatfield, the swing and seam of Lance Cairns and the general hostility of Richard Hadlee reduced Pakistan to 169, their lowest score in a test against New Zealand.

By the end of the second day New Zealand was firmly in control, thanks to a positive outlook by the batsman. John Wright set the pace, personally scoring 26 off the first three overs, before settling into a more normal run rate. With the score at 108 he was dismissed for 66 but that was the last glimmer of hope for Pakistan as John Reid and Martin Crowe settled into a stand that realised 137.

It was highly skilful and entertaining batting as Crowe went to his fifty from only 70 balls and Reid showed much more freedom than he had been allowed at Wellington. Close of play saw New Zealand 248-3, 79 ahead, with Reid on 73.

Reid continued on the third day, giving the bowlers no

glimmer of hope, as he drove and cut beautifully, hooked occasionally and soon reached another test century as well as his 1000th run in test cricket.

Light showers interrupted play and, after one break, a delivery from Azeem Hafeez deflected off Reid's bat and then onto his chin requiring him to retire and have five stitches inserted. Reid returned and was still batting at the end of the day, on 158, with New Zealand 451-9.

When New Zealand declared overnight, leading by 282, Pakistan had to bat for two days to save the match. The erratic bounce on the previous afternoon may have dented their batting confidence or maybe it was another murky morning.

With the exception of Mudassar Nazar Pakistan adopted a cavalier approach, which was never a viable proposition against the disciplined bowling and the vagaries of the pitch. Mudassar was the last man dismissed as, once again, Hadlee, Cairns and Chatfield captured nine wickets between them.

PAKISTAN

Batsman	First innings		Second innings	
Mudassar Nazar	lbw b Hadlee	12	b Cairns	89
Mohsin Khan	c Coney b Cairns	26	c Coney b Hadlee	1
Qasim Omar	c Crowe M.D. b Cairns	33	c Cairns b Chatfield	22
Javed Miandad*	c Smith b Chatfield	26	(5) c Smith b Chatfield	1
Zaheer Abbas	c Crowe J.J. b Cairns	6	(6) c sub (B.P.Bracewell) b Hadlee	12
Salim Malik	not out	41	(4) c Cairns b Chatfield	0
Wasim Raja	c Smith b Chatfield	4	c Wright b Boock	11
Abdul Qadir	run out	0	lbw b Cairns	10
Anil Dalpat†	c Crowe J.J. b Hadlee	7	lbw b Cairns	6
Wasim Akram	c Crowe M.D. b Hadlee	0	(11) not out	0
Azeem Hafeez	c Boock b Hadlee	6	(10) lbw b Cairns	17
Extras	(lb 5, nb 3)	8	(lb 11, nb 3)	14
TOTAL	**(66.5 overs)**	**169**	**(59.4 overs)**	**183**

NEW ZEALAND

G.P.Howarth*	c Miandad b Mudassar	13
J.G.Wright	c Malik b Akram	66
J.F.Reid	not out	158
M.D.Crowe	c sub (Shoaib Mohammad) b Qadir	84
S.L.Boock	c Raja b Hafeez	10
J.J.Crowe	run out	30
J.V.Coney	c Dalpat b Mudassar	25
R.J.Hadlee	c Mohsin b Hafeez	13
I.D.S.Smith†	c Miandad b Akram	7
B.L.Cairns	b Hafeez	23
E.J.Chatfield	not out	1
Extras	(b 6, lb 9, nb 6)	21
TOTAL	**(147 overs) (9 wkts dec)**	**451**

Bowling NEW ZEALAND	O	M	R	W	O	M	R	W
Hadlee	19.5	3	60	4	17	1	66	2
Cairns	29	10	73	3	19.4	8	49	4
Chatfield	14	5	24	2	19	5	47	3
Coney	4	1	7	0				
Boock					4	2	10	1
PAKISTAN								
Hafeez	47	10	157	3				
Akram	34.4	4	105	2				
Mudassar	34	5	85	2				
Qadir	22	5	52	1				
Raja	1	0	3	0				
Malik	8.2	2	34	0				

Fall of Wickets	P	NZ	P
	1st	1st	2nd
1st	33	60	13
2nd	58	108	54
3rd	93	245	54
4th	105	278	57
5th	111	359	79
6th	115	366	122
7th	123	387	140
8th	147	411	152
9th	151	447	178
10th	169	-	183

MILESTONES

- It was New Zealand's 20th test win and its first at home against Pakistan. New Zealand had now beaten all current test-playing countries at home.

- John Reid scored his 1000th run in his 12th test and 20th innings. Bert Sutcliffe and Glenn Turner had each reached four figures in their 13th test, Sutcliffe in his 22nd innings and Turner in his 26th.

John Reid pulls one of the 15 boundaries that highlighted his innings of 148. Javed Miandad is in the background,

166 NEW ZEALAND v PAKISTAN *(Third Test)*

at Carisbrook, Dunedin on 9, 10,11, 13, 14 February, 1985
Toss : New Zealand. Umpires : F.R. Goodall and G.C. Morris
New Zealand won by 2 wickets

In a first-class match between Otago and Auckland prior to the test fast bowlers had dominated proceedings to such an extent that neither team chose a spinner for the test match.

The wicket was hard and grassy when Pakistan was sent in to bat. They appeared to have weathered the storm when they went to lunch at 76-1. Qasim Omar and Javed Miandad gave a delightful display by adding 141 for the third wicket.

The game's fortunes swung dramatically when Omar was caught off Coney for 96 and in the last half-hour of the day four further wickets fell. From a position of strength at 241-2, Pakistan had fallen to 251-7 and Richard Hadlee had his 19th five wicket bag.

Pakistan was dismissed for 274 early on the second day, which turned out to be frustrating for New Zealand. All the batsmen, except Jeff Crowe, established themselves only to get out unexpectedly, mainly from rash strokes. Martin Crowe and Jeremy Coney fought hard against the fast left-arm bowler Wasim Akram, aged 18, and playing in his second test match.

The third day began with New Zealand 201-6 but the last four wickets added only 19. Qasim Omar batted excellently once again. Short and athletically built he radiated enthusiasm as he timed the ball through the covers. By now the occasional ball was skidding through making the pitch decidedly two-paced. Pakistan's total of 109-5 gave them a lead of 163 in the evenly balanced contest.

After the rest day Omar was more subdued and, eventually, was dismissed for 89. A vital last-wicket partnership between Rashid Khan and Akram added an energetic 42 in an hour, leaving New Zealand 278 for victory.

The run-chase began inauspiciously with three of the first four wickets falling to the precocious Akram with the total at 23. Martin Crowe and Coney again stopped the rot and batted through the final session, leaving New Zealand 164 runs to get on the last day and Pakistan needing six wickets for a face-saving victory.

Crowe and Coney carried on from where they left off, defending dourly most of the time, attacking strongly on occasions. It was an absorbing struggle. When Crowe was dismissed for 84, the partnership had been worth 157. By lunch the score had advanced to 192. New Zealand needed 86 more runs, and Pakistan five wickets.

Not for the first time in the game there was a dramatic collapse as Hadlee and Smith were dismissed. Cairns, not wearing a helmet, was felled by a bouncer from Akram and had to be assisted from the field, almost certainly unable to resume.

New Zealand's prospects looked gloomy when Ewen Chatfield joined Coney with 50 runs remaining to be scored. Akram mounted a short-pitched attack against Chatfield and was warned by the umpires, adding to the tension. Coney continued to take singles at almost every opportunity, and eventually reached his century in 337 minutes.

Chatfield presented a broad defence for most of the time and, occasionally, was hit on the body as well as the helmet. He faced 84 of the last 132 balls bowled as the pair added 50 to give their team victory. It was a great escape.

MILESTONES

- It was New Zealand's 21st test victory.

- Wasim Akram, aged 18, became the youngest player in test history to take 10 wickets in a test.

- Richard Hadlee captured his 250th test wicket.

- Javed Miandad became the youngest player to score 5000 test runs.

PAKISTAN

Batsman	Dismissal	Runs	Dismissal	Runs
Mudassar Nazar	c Crowe J.J. b Hadlee	18	c Coney b Bracewell	5
Mohsin Khan	run out	39	c Crowe M.D. b Hadlee	27
Qasim Omar	c Crowe J.J. b Coney	96	c Smith b Chatfield	89
Javed Miandad*	c Smith b Hadlee	79	c Reid b Hadlee	2
Zaheer Abbas	c Reid b Hadlee	6	lbw b Cairns	0
Rashid Khan	c Crowe M.D. b Hadlee	0	(9) b Bracewell	37
Anil Dalpat†	b Bracewell	16	b Chatfield	21
Salim Malik	lbw b Hadlee	0	(6) b Cairns	9
Tahir Naqqash	c Wright b Hadlee	0	(8) run out	1
Azeem Hafeez	c Smith b Bracewell	4	b Chatfield	7
Wasim Akram	not out	1	not out	8
Extras	(b 1, lb 2, nb 12)	15	(b 1, lb 9, nb 7)	17
TOTAL	(94.2 overs)	274	(88.4 overs)	223

NEW ZEALAND

Batsman	Dismissal	Runs	Dismissal	Runs
G.P. Howarth*	b Akram	23	c Mohsin b Akram	17
J.G. Wright	c Qasim b Hafeez	32	c Mohsin b Hafeez	1
J.F. Reid	b Akram	24	c Dalpat b Akram	0
M.D. Crowe	c Miandad b Akram	57	c Mudassar b Tahir	84
J.J. Crowe	lbw b Wasim Akram	6	lbw b Akram	0
J.V. Coney	c Dalpat b Rashid	24	not out	111
R.J. Hadlee	c Dalpat b Rashid	18	b Hafeez	11
I.D.S. Smith†	lbw b Tahir	12	c Miandad b Akram	6
B.L. Cairns	c Dalpat b Akram	6	retired hurt	0
B.P. Bracewell	c Rashid b Tahir	3	c Tahir b Akram	4
E.J. Chatfield	not out	2	not out	21
Extras	(b 7, lb 5, nb 1)	13	(b 5, lb 6, w 1, nb 11)	23
TOTAL	(85.4 overs)	220	(99.4 overs) (8 wkts)	278

Bowling

NEW ZEALAND

	O	M	R	W	O	M	R	W
Hadlee	24	5	51	6	26	9	59	2
Bracewell	18.2	1	81	2	14.4	2	48	2
Cairns	22	0	77	0	22	5	41	2
Chatfield	24	6	46	0	26	5	65	3
Coney	6	1	16	1				

PAKISTAN

	O	M	R	W	O	M	R	W
Rashid	23	7	64	2	9	2	33	0
Hafeez	20	6	65	1	32	9	84	2
Akram	26	7	56	5	33	10	72	5
Tahir	16.4	4	23	2	16.4	1	58	1
Mudassar					9	2	20	0

Fall of Wickets

	P 1st	NZ 1st	P 2nd	NZ 2nd
1st	25	41	5	4
2nd	100	81	72	5
3rd	241	84	75	23
4th	243	92	76	23
5th	245	149	103	180
6th	251	185	157	208
7th	251	203	166	217
8th	255	205	169	228
9th	273	216	181	-
10th	274	220	223	-

AVERAGES

New Zealand

BATTING	M	I	NO	Runs	HS	Ave
J.F. Reid	3	5	1	333	158*	83.25
J.V. Coney	3	5	2	226	111*	75.33
M.D. Crowe	3	5	0	295	84	59.00
R.J. Hadlee	3	4	0	131	89	32.75
J.G. Wright	3	5	0	121	66	24.20
I.D.S. Smith	3	4	0	90	65	22.50
B.L. Cairns	3	4	1	65	36	21.66
G.P. Howarth	3	5	0	103	33	20.60
J.J. Crowe	3	5	1	59	30	14.75
S.L. Boock	2	2	0	10	10	5.00
B.P. Bracewell	1	2	0	7	4	3.50
E.J. Chatfield	3	4	4	27	21*	-

BOWLING	O	M	R	W	Ave
R.J. Hadlee	118.5	29	306	16	19.12
S.L. Boock	49	20	127	6	21.16
J.V. Coney	10	2	23	1	23.00
E.J. Chatfield	108	31	234	9	26.00
B.L. Cairns	120.2	28	305	10	30.50
B.P. Bracewell	33	3	129	4	32.25

Pakistan

BATTING	M	I	NO	Runs	HS	Ave
Qasim Omar	3	5	0	248	96	49.60
Mudassar Nazar	3	5	0	162	89	32.40
Salim Malik	3	5	1	116	66	29.00
Javed Miandad	3	5	0	138	79	27.60
Mohsin Khan	3	5	0	133	40	26.60
Abdul Qadir	2	3	0	64	54	21.33
Rashid Khan	1	2	0	37	37	18.50
Anil Dalpat	3	5	0	65	21	13.00
Wasim Raja	2	3	0	29	14	9.66
Wasim Akram	2	4	3	9	8*	9.00
Azeem Hafeez	3	5	0	37	17	7.40
Shoaib Mohammad	1	1	0	7	7	7.00
Zaheer Abbas	2	4	0	24	12	6.00
Tahir Naqqash	1	2	0	1	1	0.50
Iqbal Qasim	1	1	1	27	27*	-

BOWLING	O	M	R	W	Ave
Wasim Akram	93.4	21	233	12	19.41
Tahir Naqqash	33.2	5	81	3	27.00
Iqbal Qasim	57	13	124	4	31.00
Azeem Hafeez	162	40	484	12	40.33
Rashid Khan	32	9	97	2	48.50
Mudassar Nazar	78	15	198	4	49.50
Abdul Qadir	81	19	212	2	106.00
Shoaib Mohammad	1	0	4	0	-
Javed Miandad	3	1	7	0	-
Wasim Raja	3	0	13	0	-
Salim Malik	8.2	2	34	0	-

Richard Hadlee captured his 250th test wicket while taking 6-51 in Pakistan's first innings.

1984/85 New Zealand in West Indies

By 1985 West Indies were regarded as the most accomplished team in the world. Their fast bowling strength was unlike anything previously seen in test cricket and their batsmen were colourful, technically correct and highly innovative. Memories were still fresh in West Indies of their tour of New Zealand in 1980 where they thought that they had been ambushed by the patriotism of the home-town umpires.

167 **WEST INDIES v NEW ZEALAND** (*First Test*)

at Queen's Park Oval, Port of Spain on 29, 30, 31 March, 2, 3 April, 1985
Toss : West Indies. Umpires : D.M. Archer and C.E. Cumberbatch
Match drawn

Vivian Richards, the captain of the West Indies, spent time consulting his team before deciding to bat when he won the toss on a wicket that was damp in the middle and described as decidedly unstable at one end.

Richard Hadlee struck twice before the score reached ten but Gordon Greenidge and Richie Richardson produced a partnership of calibre, weathering the malice of Hadlee and the accuracy of Chatfield, adding 185 for the third wicket. Both were dismissed within two runs of each other at 196 after Greenidge had completed an even century.

Ewen Chatfield, who had toiled hard in the sun the previous day, was rewarded with four wickets in the space of 23 balls as the home team lost their last five wickets for 30 runs. The early loss of Ken Rutherford saw John Wright and Jeff Crowe bat sensibly against the awesome pace attack.

Wright was all concentration and determination, while Crowe was in sparkling form, with straight drives being a feature of his innings, as they added 109. Geoff Howarth and Jeremy Coney were unbeaten at stumps; 166-4.

There was only sufficient time for 54 runs to be added on the fourth day for the loss of Coney's wicket. So far on the tour Howarth's batting appeared like a faded memory but this day he was a resolute leader, inspiring by example, as he spent 3½ hours compiling 45. The searing pace of Michael Holding tore through the tail, capturing three of the five wickets that fell for 39 runs, as New Zealand totalled 262.

As Greenidge was injured West Indies' second innings was opened by Richardson and he was one of two batsmen removed with the score at 58. Desmond Haynes and Richards sought quick runs and added 114 in breezy style. Both were out before stumps, with West Indies 226-4.

Nine overs were bowled on the last day before the declaration was made. Chatfield finished with six wickets for the innings, giving him ten in the match.

New Zealand's target was an unlikely 307. They lost their fifth wicket at 83 with two hours still to play and West Indies, sensing victory, put fierce pressure on Coney and Hadlee. Their stand was of heroic proportions and ensured a draw.

WEST INDIES				
C.G.Greenidge	b Boock	100		
D.L.Haynes	c Rutherford b Hadlee	0	(1) c Crowe M.D. b Chatfield	78
H.A.Gomes	c Smith b Hadlee	0	c & b Chatfield	25
R.B.Richardson	c Hadlee b Coney	78	(2) c Smith b Chatfield	3
I.V.A.Richards*	b Hadlee	57	(4) b Cairns	78
A.L.Logie	b Chatfield	24	(5) b Cairns	42
P.J.L.Dujon†	b Chatfield	15	(6) b Chatfield	5
M.D.Marshall	c sub (J.G.Bracewell) b Chatfield	0	(7) c Coney b Chatfield	1
R.A.Harper	c Howarth b Chatfield	0	(8) not out	11
M.A.Holding	lbw b Hadlee	12	(9) c Crowe J.J. b Chatfield	8
J.Garner	not out	0		
Extras	(b 1, lb 16, nb 4)	21	(lb 3, nb 7)	10
TOTAL	(106.3 overs)	**307**	(72 overs) (8 wkts dec)	**261**

NEW ZEALAND				
J.G.Wright	c Richardson b Harper	40	lbw b Holding	19
K.R.Rutherford	c Haynes b Marshall	0	run out	0
J.J.Crowe	c & b Harper	64	c Garner b Marshall	27
M.D.Crowe	lbw b Holding	3	c Haynes b Marshall	2
G.P.Howarth*	c sub (P.V.Simmons) b Holding	45	b Marshall	14
J.V.Coney	lbw b Marshall	25	c Dujon b Marshall	44
R.J.Hadlee	c Garner b Holding	18	not out	39
I.D.S.Smith†	c Logie b Holding	10	not out	11
B.L.Cairns	c Harper b Garner	8		
S.L.Boock	c sub (P.V.Simmons) b Garner	3		
E.J.Chatfield	not out	4		
Extras	(b 12, lb 11, nb 19)	42	(b 17, lb 6, nb 8)	31
TOTAL	(100.3 overs)	**262**	(81 overs) (6 wkts)	**187**

Bowling	O	M	R	W	O	M	R	W
NEW ZEALAND								
Hadlee	24.3	6	82	4	17	2	58	0
Chatfield	28	11	51	4	22	4	73	6
Cairns	26	3	93	0	19	2	70	2
Boock	19	5	47	1	14	4	57	0
Coney	9	3	17	1				
WEST INDIES								
Marshall	25	3	78	2	26	4	65	4
Garner	21.3	8	41	2	18	2	41	0
Holding	29	8	79	4	17	6	36	1
Harper	22	11	33	2	14	7	19	0
Richards	2	0	7	0	2	1	1	0
Gomes	1	0	1	0	2	1	2	0
Richardson					1	1	0	0
Logie					1	1	0	0

Fall of Wickets	WI	NZ	WI	NZ
	1st	1st	2nd	2nd
1st	5	1	10	0
2nd	9	110	58	40
3rd	194	113	172	59
4th	196	132	226	76
5th	236	182	239	83
6th	267	223	240	158
7th	267	225	241	-
8th	269	248	261	-
9th	302	250	-	-
10th	307	262	-	-

Viv Richards awaits developments from this delivery by Ewen Chatfield who finished with his best test analysis of 10-124, becoming the fifth New Zealander to take 10 wickets in a match.

MILESTONES

- Ken Rutherford (155) made his test debut.

- Richard Hadlee, when he scored 31, had attained 2000 runs and 250 wickets in test cricket. Ian Botham (England) and Kapil Dev (India) were the only other test cricketers to achieve this feat.

- Ewen Chatfield became the fifth New Zealand bowler to take 10 wickets in a match.

168 WEST INDIES v NEW ZEALAND *(Second Test)*

at Bourda, Georgetown on 6, 7, 8, 10, 11 April, 1985
Toss : West Indies. Umpires : L.H. Barker and D.J. Narine
Match drawn

The docile nature of the pitch and the short boundaries had always loaded the dice in favour of batsmen on the Bourda Oval and so it was for the second test. There was some movement at the start of the first day but the pitch quickly reinforced its reputation for heartlessness.

After Ewen Chatfield bowled Gordon Greenidge it was to be a further 215 minutes before the second wicket fell. Desmond Haynes was bowled for 90 after he, and the accomplished Richie Richardson, had added 190 without risk or complication. The West Indies ended the day at 291-2.

Larry Gomes, who scored 54, was the only wicket to fall before lunch on the second day as Richardson continued untroubled. Richardson's marathon stay ended when he was run out for 185 — an innings that lasted 465 minutes and contained 25 boundaries.

Even at 407-5 the only respite for the visiting bowlers were periodic showers as Gus Logie and Jeffrey Dujon scored fifties and, for the third time in the innings, there was a century partnership.

Viv Richards declared at the overnight score of 511-6 and New Zealand began its quest of scoring 312 to avoid the follow-on. The fall of the fourth wicket at 98 made New Zealand's chances look doubtful. Jeremy Coney found a partner of similar steely resolve in Martin Crowe and, when play ended 34 minutes early through rain, they were still together with the total at 230-4, Crowe 72 and Coney 65.

Coney was out when the partnership had realised 142. It had given the side a much-needed boost in confidence. Crowe continued his conscientious innings. Joined by Ian Smith the follow-on was avoided as the keeper settled in to play an invaluable hand.

Crowe, aged 22, continued to bat like an old master and his marathon innings concluded after 571 minutes with his score at 188. It was the largest score made against West Indies, in West Indies, for a decade, and it enabled New Zealand to reach 440 to ensure that the only result would be a draw. The partnership with Smith was worth 143 runs.

WEST INDIES

C.G.Greenidge	b Chatfield	10	c & b Coney		69
D.L.Haynes	b Hadlee	90	c Smith b Hadlee		9
R.B.Richardson	run out	185	(4) c Crowe J.J. b Cairns		60
H.A.Gomes	lbw b Cairns	53	(5) c sub (J.G.Bracewell)		
			b Rutherford		35
I.V.A.Richards*	st Smith b Coney	40	(8) not out		7
A.L.Logie	c Howarth b Hadlee	52	not out		41
P.J.L.Dujon†	not out	60	b Cairns		3
C.G.Butts			(3) c Smith b Hadlee		9
M.D.Marshall					
M.A.Holding					
J.Garner					
Extras	(b 1, lb 16, w 1, nb 3)	21	(b 7, lb 25, w 1, nb 2)		35
TOTAL	(152.5 overs) (6 wkts dec)	**511**	(95 overs) (6 wkts dec)		**268**

NEW ZEALAND

J.G.Wright	run out	27
K.R.Rutherford	c Dujon b Garner	4
J.J.Crowe	b Marshall	22
M.D.Crowe	lbw b Garner	188
G.P.Howarth*	c Haynes b Marshall	4
J.V.Coney	c Richards b Holding	73
R.J.Hadlee	c Dujon b Marshall	16
I.D.S.Smith†	lbw b Marshall	53
B.L.Cairns	b Holding	3
S.L.Boock	b Holding	0
E.J.Chatfield	not out	3
Extras	(b 12, lb 2, w 6, nb 27)	47
TOTAL	(151.5 overs)	**440**

Bowling	O	M	R	W	O	M	R	W
NEW ZEALAND								
Hadlee	25.5	5	83	2	16	3	32	2
Chatfield	30	3	122	1	16	3	43	0
Cairns	32	5	105	1	18	4	47	2
Boock	43	11	107	0	18	3	52	0
Coney	18	2	62	1	10	3	20	1
Howarth	4	1	15	0	5	4	2	0
Rutherford					9	1	38	1
Wright					3	1	2	0
WEST INDIES								
Marshall	33	3	110	4				
Garner	27.5	5	72	2				
Holding	28	6	89	3				
Butts	47	12	113	0				
Richards	8	1	22	0				
Gomes	8	2	20	0				

Fall of Wickets

	WI	NZ	WI
	1st	1st	2nd
1st	30	8	22
2nd	221	45	46
3rd	327	81	150
4th	394	98	191
5th	407	240	207
6th	511	261	225
7th	-	404	-
8th	-	415	-
9th	-	415	-
10th	-	440	-

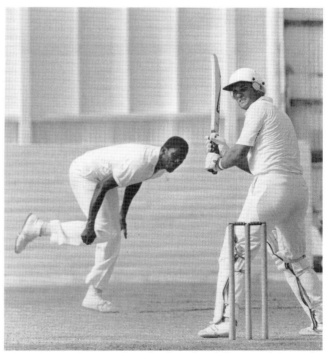

Martin Crowe takes a single to fine-leg off Joel Garner to bring up his century. His 188 was the sixth highest score made by a New Zealander in a test.

MILESTONES

- John Wright passed 2000 runs in his 39th test.

- Martin Crowe passed 1000 runs in his 21st test.

- Martin Crowe and Ian Smith added 143 runs for the seventh wicket, a New Zealand record against West Indies.

169 WEST INDIES v NEW ZEALAND *(Third Test)*

at Kensington Oval, Bridgetown on 26, 27, 28, 30 April, 1 May, 1985
Toss : West Indies. Umpires : D.M. Archer and L.H. Barker
West Indies won by 10 wickets

On two tours of the West Indies, New Zealand had now played seven drawn tests and they were the only visiting side the West Indies had not defeated at home. Kensington Oval had the reputation of being the fastest and liveliest pitch in the region, so a fourth fast bowler was included in the home side.

Rain restricted play to only 92 minutes on the first day and the pitch played as predicted – spitefully. Geoff Howarth, John Wright and Ken Rutherford were dismissed with the score at one. Batting was life-threatening against the electrifying pace and bounce of Joel Garner, Malcolm Marshall and Michael Holding. Jeff Crowe defended for 75 minutes for one run before rain mercifully brought an early end to the day with New Zealand 19-4.

There was rather more resistance on the second day but New Zealand was all out 40 minutes before tea for 94, their lowest score in the West Indies. The fieldsmen behind the

wicket supported their bowlers by holding seven catches. Jeff Crowe's innings of 21 was an innings of raw courage.

Trailing by only three runs, with only one wicket down, West Indies were in an extremely strong position before Martin Crowe was given a bowl for the first time in six tests. Within two overs he had two wickets and Richard Hadlee captured one to make the scoreboard 95-4. The third day began well enough for New Zealand with the bowlers sniping away at West Indies batting.

When seven wickets were down the home team's lead was only 80 but Viv Richards was still batting. Discarding his often flamboyant approach he applied himself to building up the innings significantly. Helping in the restoration was Marshall who, after taking four wickets in New Zealand's first innings, showed that he was a more than capable batsman. They added 83 in 97 minutes as Richards went on to his 19th test century in 192 minutes.

Joel Garner and Marshall capitalised on a tiring attack by adding 70 for the ninth wicket in better than even time to give West Indies a lead of 242. Jeff Crowe distinguished himself by taking four catches in the slips and Ian Smith, the wicketkeeper, took three.

Batting a second time, all the New Zealand batsmen struggled against Marshall's bowling. With the run-up of a sprinter, and one of the fastest arms in the history of test

Jeremy Coney was given a torrid time as he accumulated 83 in 222 minutes. He is seen lofting Malcolm Marshall for four.

NEW ZEALAND

G.P.Howarth*	c Greenidge b Garner	1	c Haynes b Marshall		5
J.G.Wright	c Dujon b Marshall	0	c Richardson b Davis		64
K.R.Rutherford	c Richards b Marshall	0	c Holding b Marshall		2
M.D.Crowe	hit wicket b Holding	14	c Dujon b Marshall		2
J.J.Crowe	c Dujon b Davis	21	b Davis		4
J.V.Coney	c Richardson b Marshall	12	c Logie b Marshall		83
I.D.S.Smith†	c Greenidge b Marshall	2	c & b Marshall		26
R.J.Hadlee	c Logie b Davis	29	c Greenidge b Davis		3
D.A.Stirling	c Logie b Davis	6	b Marshall		3
S.L.Boock	c Dujon b Garner	1	c Haynes b Marshall		22
E.J.Chatfield	not out	0	not out		4
Extras	(nb 8)	8	(b 8, lb 1, w 2, nb 19)		30
TOTAL	(47.4 overs)	**94**	(80.3 overs)		**248**

WEST INDIES

C.G.Greenidge	c Crowe J.J. b Hadlee	2	not out	4
D.L.Haynes	c Smith b Hadlee	62	not out	5
R.B.Richardson	lbw b Crowe M.D.	22		
H.A.Gomes	c Crowe J.J. b Crowe M.D.	0		
W.W.Davis	c Smith b Stirling	16		
I.V.A.Richards*	c Crowe M.D. b Boock	105		
A.L.Logie	c Crowe J.J. b Chatfield	7		
P.J.L.Dujon†	b Hadlee	3		
M.D.Marshall	c Crowe J.J. b Chatfield	63		
J.Garner	not out	37		
M.A.Holding	c Smith b Stirling	1		
Extras	(b 2, lb 8, w 6, nb 2)	18	(w 1)	1
TOTAL	(93.1 overs)	**336**	(1.4 overs) (0 wkts)	**10**

Bowling	O	M	R	W	O	M	R	W
WEST INDIES								
Marshall	15	3	40	4	25.3	6	80	7
Garner	15	9	14	2	19	5	56	0
Holding	7	4	12	1	1	0	2	0
Davis	10.4	5	28	3	18	0	66	3
Richards					13	3	25	0
Gomes					4	0	10	0
NEW ZEALAND								
Hadlee	26	5	86	3				
Chatfield	28	10	57	2				
Stirling	14.1	0	82	2				
Crowe M.D.	10	2	25	2				
Boock	15	1	76	1	1	1	0	0
Rutherford					0.4	0	10	0

Fall of Wickets

	NZ 1st	WI 1st	NZ 2nd	WI 2nd
1st	1	12	26	-
2nd	1	91	35	-
3rd	1	91	45	-
4th	18	95	60	-
5th	37	142	108	-
6th	44	161	141	-
7th	80	174	149	-
8th	87	257	226	-
9th	90	327	235	-
10th	94	336	248	

cricket, his pace was electric and his bouncer horrific. John Wright played an innings of character for 64 and was never afraid to play attacking shots when he was able to.

At 60-4 Jeremy Coney, who had been bedridden with an acute viral infection for the previous three days, joined him. For the third time in the series Coney displayed exceptional batting skills which saw him bat for the remaining 222 minutes of the day and be on 81 when it concluded at 228-8.

Stephen Boock matched Coney in nerve and determination as they added 77 for the eighth wicket and took the game into the final day, when Marshall finished the innings with seven wickets to give him 11 for the match.

MILESTONES

- Jeff Crowe set a New Zealand record by taking four catches in an innings.

170 WEST INDIES v NEW ZEALAND (*Fourth Test*)

at Sabina Park, Kingston on 4, 5, 6, 8 May, 1985
Toss : New Zealand. Umpires : D.M. Archer and J.R. Gayle
West Indies won by 10 wickets

Geoff Howarth won the toss for the first time and sent West Indies in on a wicket that seemed to hold no mystery for the batsmen. It was thought that New Zealand preferred to face the West Indies blitz after the sting had gone from a new pitch.

The best pair of opening batsmen in world cricket, Gordon Greenidge and Desmond Haynes, were untroubled adding 82 before Martin Crowe again became a partnership-breaker. When Richard Hadlee claimed two wickets off successive balls, Viv Richards and Gus Logie, Howarth's gamble appeared to have paid off at 207-5. Larry Gomes and Jeff Dujon denied New Zealand further success until Gomes was caught at square leg in the last over; West Indies 273-6.

Dujon steered the lower order to add 90 further runs. Hadlee captured four wickets, from an economical 28.4 overs, and Martin Crowe took four catches. As to be expected, New Zealand ran into trouble early in its innings, losing three wickets for 37 runs.

The rain that began to fall during the tea break freshened the pitch and encouraged the West Indies bowlers to launch their fiercest onslaught of the tour. Watchfulness and courage were the passwords for John Wright and Jeremy Coney as they had to survive a continual barrage of bouncers aimed to hit the body and not the stumps.

Joel Garner made one lift savagely which broke Coney's left forearm and ended his participation in the match. Play ended with New Zealand 65-4. At the end of the day's play a former test player, Rohan Kanhai, said that it was not the way the game should be played.

When New Zealand's innings terminated for 138, on the third morning, they were asked to follow on, facing a deficit of 225. The early loss of Wright brought Jeff Crowe to join Howarth to begin one of the great partnerships in the history of New Zealand cricket.

For the first time on the tour Howarth rediscovered his timing of old and handsome drives and elegant cuts crossed the boundaries. Jeff Crowe's was a classic affair, reaching his second test century in 192 minutes off 163 deliveries. The bowlers who had dominated proceedings earlier in the day were now totally dominated by the pair as New Zealand reached 211-1 off 58 overs. It was a remarkable recovery for a beleaguered and bruised team.

The rest day had rejuvenated the fearsome attack when play began on the fourth day. The partnership reached 210 before Crowe was out and Howarth followed four balls later. There was some resistance from Hadlee and John Bracewell but West Indies could not be denied their series win by two tests to nil.

WEST INDIES

C.G.Greenidge	c Crowe J.J. b Crowe M.D.	46	not out	33
D.L.Haynes	c Crowe J.J. b Coney	76	not out	24
R.B.Richardson	c Richardson b Coney	30		
H.A.Gomes	c Wright b Hadlee	45		
I.V.A.Richards*	lbw b Hadlee	23		
A.L.Logie	c Crowe M.D. b Hadlee	0		
P.J.L.Dujon†	c Bracewell b Troup	70		
M.D.Marshall	lbw b Bracewell	26		
W.W.Davis	c Crowe M.D. b Troup	0		
J.Garner	c Crowe M.D. b Hadlee	12		
C.A.Walsh	not out	12		
Extras	(b 7, lb 9, w 1, nb 6)	23	(b 1, lb 1)	2
TOTAL	(116.4 overs)	**363**	(17 overs) (0 wkts)	**59**

NEW ZEALAND

G.P.Howarth*	c Gomes b Marshall	5	c Garner b Walsh	84
J.G.Wright	b Davis	53	c Dujon b Garner	10
J.J.Crowe	c Richardson b Garner	2	c Marshall b Richards	112
M.D.Crowe	c Davis b Walsh	6	c Dujon b Walsh	1
J.V.Coney	retired hurt	4	absent hurt	
K.R.Rutherford	c Dujon b Marshall	1	(5) lbw b Marshall	5
I.D.S.Smith†	b Garner	0	(6) b Marshall	9
R.J.Hadlee	c Dujon b Davis	18	(7) c Walsh b Marshall	14
J.G.Bracewell	not out	25	(8) c Gomes b Marshall	27
G.B.Troup	c Marshall b Davis	0	(9) c Richardson b Garner	2
E.J.Chatfield	b Davis	2	(10) not out	0
Extras	(b 4, lb 1, w 2, nb 15)	22	(b 7, lb 4, nb 8)	19
TOTAL	(55.5 overs)	**138**	(102.4 overs)	**283**

Bowling	O	M	R	W	O	M	R	W
NEW ZEALAND								
Hadlee	28.4	11	53	4	5	1	15	0
Troup	17	1	87	2	3	0	13	0
Chatfield	26	5	85	0	2	0	10	0
Crowe M.D.	10	2	30	1				
Bracewell	21	5	54	1	4	0	14	0
Coney	14	3	38	2				
Smith					3	1	5	0
WEST INDIES								
Marshall	17	3	47	2	28.4	8	66	4
Garner	16	0	37	2	19	8	41	2
Davis	13.5	5	19	4	21	1	75	0
Walsh	9	1	30	1	16	4	45	2
Richards					14	2	34	1
Gomes					3	0	11	0
Richardson					1	1	0	0

Fall of Wickets	WI	NZ	NZ	WI
	1st	*1st*	*2nd*	*2nd*
1st	82	11	13	-
2nd	144	15	223	-
3rd	164	37	223	-
4th	207	65	228	-
5th	207	68	238	-
6th	273	106	242	-
7th	311	113	259	-
8th	311	122	281	-
9th	339	138	283	-
10th	363	-	-	-

MILESTONES

- Geoff Howarth and Jeff Crowe shared a partnership of 210 for the second wicket, a record for New Zealand against all opponents.

- Martin Crowe equalled brother Jeffrey's record of four catches in an innings, established in the previous test.

AVERAGES

New Zealand

BATTING	M	I	NO	Runs	HS	Ave
J.G. Bracewell	1	2	1	52	27	52.00
J.V. Coney	4	6	1	241	83	48.20
J.J. Crowe	4	7	0	252	112	36.00
M.D. Crowe	4	7	0	216	188	30.85
J.G. Wright	4	7	0	213	64	30.42
R.J. Hadlee	4	7	1	137	39*	22.83
G.P. Howarth	4	7	0	158	84	22.57
I.D.S. Smith	4	7	1	111	53	18.50
E.J. Chatfield	4	6	5	13	4*	13.00
S.L. Boock	3	4	0	26	22	6.50
B.L. Cairns	2	2	0	11	8	5.50
D.A. Stirling	1	2	0	9	6	4.50
K.R. Rutherford	4	7	0	12	5	1.71
G.B. Troup	1	2	0	2	2	1.00

BOWLING	O	M	R	W	Ave
M.D. Crowe	20	4	55	3	18.33
R.J. Hadlee	143	33	409	15	27.26
J.V. Coney	51	11	137	5	27.40
E.J. Chatfield	152	36	441	13	33.92
D.A. Stirling	14.1	0	82	2	41.00
K.R. Rutherford	9.4	1	48	1	48.00
G.B. Troup	20	1	100	2	50.00
B.L. Cairns	95	14	315	5	63.00
J.G. Bracewell	25	5	68	1	68.00
S.L. Boock	110	25	339	2	169.50
J.G. Wright	3	1	2	0	-
I.D.S. Smith	3	1	5	0	-
G.P. Howarth	9	5	17	0	-

West Indies

BATTING	M	I	NO	Runs	HS	Ave
R.B. Richardson	4	6	0	378	185	63.00
I.V.A. Richards	4	6	1	310	105	62.00
D.L. Haynes	4	8	2	344	90	57.33
C.G. Greenidge	4	7	2	264	100	52.80
J. Garner	4	3	2	49	37*	49.00
A.L. Logie	4	6	1	166	52	33.20
P.J.L. Dujon	4	6	1	156	70	31.20
H.A. Gomes	4	6	0	158	53	26.33
M.D. Marshall	4	4	0	90	63	22.50
R.A. Harper	1	2	1	11	11*	11.00
C.G. Butts	1	1	0	9	9	9.00
W.W. Davis	2	2	0	16	16	8.00
M.A. Holding	3	3	0	21	12	7.00
C.A. Walsh	1	1	1	12	12*	-

BOWLING	O	M	R	W	Ave
M.D. Marshall	170.1	30	486	27	18.00
W.W. Davis	63.3	11	188	10	18.80
M.A. Holding	82	24	218	9	24.22
C.A. Walsh	25	5	75	3	25.00
R.A. Harper	36	18	52	2	26.00
J. Garner	136.2	37	302	10	30.20
I.V.A. Richards	39	7	89	1	89.00
R.B. Richardson	2	2	0	0	-
A.L. Logie	1	1	0	0	-
H.A. Gomes	18	3	44	0	-
C.G. Butts	47	12	113	0	-

Jeremy Coney clutches his left arm, which was broken by a delivery from Joel Garner during the first innings of the fourth test. None of the West Indies players show any concern.

1985/86 New Zealand in Australia

The announcement of New Zealand's tour of Australia brought the end of Geoff Howarth's reign as captain. Jeremy Coney, who had led the team to Pakistan when Howarth was unavailable, took over. A rebel Australian team, led by former captain Kim Hughes, was touring South Africa thus weakening the powerful, usually all-conquering Australian test team. Glenn Turner was appointed as assistant manager for New Zealand. His primary role was to coach and advise.

171 AUSTRALIA v NEW ZEALAND *(First Test)*

at Brisbane Cricket Ground on 8, 9, 10, 11, 12 November, 1985
Toss : New Zealand. Umpires : A.R. Crafter and R.A. French
New Zealand won by an innings and 41 runs

On a humid day, with thick cloud cover, conditions could not have been more perfect for Richard Hadlee to begin one of the great masterclasses of bowling in the history of test cricket. When bad light stopped play after tea Australia was 146-4 and Hadlee had all four wickets.

In similar conditions the next day Hadlee continued his demolition of Australia. He ended with nine wickets as the last six wickets fell for 31 runs. Pace, accuracy, swing, seam and cut had all been exhibited in a great bowling display that was the fourth best return in test cricket.

In reply to 179, New Zealand were 103-2 at tea and John Reid and Martin Crowe were embarking on a memorable partnership that added 106 in the last session. Reid's bat was broad and his determination and dedication were unquestioned. Crowe took half an hour to make his first run but, thereafter, was utterly masterful as punishing drives, savage cuts and powerful hooks along the ground sped to the boundary. It was controlled, calculating cricket that had New Zealand 209-2 at stumps.

The partnership proceeded mercilessly the next day. The new ball only increased the flow of boundaries. Crowe went from 87 to 102 in five strokes from seven balls. Reid was a victim of cramps on both days and spent more than an hour in the 90s. When Allan Border brilliantly caught Reid for 108 the partnership had been worth 224.

The remaining four partnerships of the innings built upon this wonderful platform adding 53, 65, 44 and 78. Martin Crowe's innings ended after 472 minutes during which he hit 26 fours and equalled his own highest test score of 188. In semi-darkness Vaughan Brown and Hadlee rubbed salt into the wounds, adding 78 in 63 minutes, taking New Zealand's total to 553-7 and its highest first-innings advantage of 374.

It appeared as if it would be a humiliating defeat for Australia when their fifth wicket fell at 67. Border had never reached a half-century in a test against New Zealand but the soundness of his defence was matched by the quality of his occasional attacking strokes as, with Greg Matthews, he went about restoring the reputation of Australian batsmen.

For the best part of four hours they battled tenaciously until Hadlee, with the new ball, disposed of Matthews for 115 after the pair had added 197 for the sixth wicket, leaving Australia 266-6 at the end of the fourth day.

Hadlee captured three of the remaining four wickets to end with six for the innings and 15 for the game. Border was undefeated on 152.

AUSTRALIA						
K.C.Wessels	lbw b Hadlee	70	c Brown b Chatfield			3
A.M.J.Hilditch	c Chatfield b Hadlee	0	c Chatfield b Hadlee			12
D.C.Boon	c Coney b Hadlee	31	c Smith b Chatfield			1
A.R.Border*	c Edgar b Hadlee	1	not out			152
G.M.Ritchie	c Crowe M.D. b Hadlee	8	c Coney b Snedden			20
W.B.Phillips†	b Hadlee	34	b Hadlee			2
G.R.J.Matthews	b Hadlee	2	c Coney b Hadlee			115
G.F.Lawson	c Hadlee b Brown	8	(9) c Brown b Chatfield			7
C.J.McDermott	c Coney b Hadlee	9	(8) c & b Hadlee			5
D.R.Gilbert	not out	0	c Chatfield b Hadlee			10
R.G.Holland	c Brown b Hadlee	0	b Hadlee			0
Extras	(b 9, lb 5, nb 2)	16	(lb 3, nb 3)			6
TOTAL	(76.4 overs)	**179**	(116.5 overs)			**333**

NEW ZEALAND		
B.A.Edgar	c Phillips b Gilbert	17
J.G.Wright	lbw b Matthews	46
J.F.Reid	c Border b Gilbert	108
M.D.Crowe	b Matthews	188
J.V.Coney*	c Phillips b Lawson	22
J.J.Crowe	c Holland b Matthews	35
V.R.Brown	not out	36
R.J.Hadlee	c Phillips b McDermott	54
I.D.S.Smith†	not out	2
M.C.Snedden		
E.J.Chatfield		
Extras	(b 2, lb 11, nb 32)	45
TOTAL	(161 overs) (7 wkts dec)	**553**

Bowling	O	M	R	W	O	M	R	W		Fall of Wickets		
NEW ZEALAND										A	NZ	A
										1st	*1st*	*2nd*
Hadlee	23.4	4	52	9	28.5	9	71	6	1st	1	36	14
Chatfield	18	6	29	0	32	9	75	3	2nd	70	85	16
Snedden	11	1	45	0	19	3	66	1	3rd	72	309	16
Crowe M.D.	5	0	14	0	9	2	19	0	4th	82	362	47
Brown	12	5	17	1	25	9	96	0	5th	148	427	67
Coney	7	5	8	0	3	1	3	0	6th	150	471	264
AUSTRALIA									7th	159	549	272
Lawson	36.5	8	96	1					8th	175	-	291
McDermott	31	3	119	1					9th	179	-	333
Gilbert	39	9	102	2					10th	179	-	333
Matthews	31	5	110	3								
Holland	22	3	106	0								
Border	0.1	0	0	0								
Wessels	1	0	7	0								

MILESTONES

- Vaughan Brown (156) made his test debut. It was New Zealand's 22nd test win, the first win in Australia and the first by an innings against Australia.

- New Zealand's total of 553-7d was its highest in a test.

- Richard Hadlee's 9-52 was the best bowling by a New Zealander in a test innings and the fourth best ever. His match figures of 15-123 were the best by a New Zealander and the eighth best in all test cricket.

- The partnership of 224 for the third wicket between John Reid and Martin Crowe was a New Zealand record against all countries.

New Zealand completed an outstanding performance in beating Australia by an innings and 41 runs. From left, John Reid, Ian Smith, Allan Border, Richard Hadlee, Martin Snedden, John Wright, Bruce Edgar, Jeremy Coney (captain), Ewen Chatfield, Martin Crowe, Vaughan Brown, Jeff Crowe.

172 AUSTRALIA v NEW ZEALAND (Second Test)

at Sydney Cricket Ground on 22, 23, 24, 25, 26 November, 1985
Toss : Australia. Umpires : M.W. Johnson and B.E. Martin
Australia won by 4 wickets

Sydney's notorious reputation for assisting spin bowlers saw New Zealand discard Ewen Chatfield and bring over John Bracewell to partner Stephen Boock.

Bruce Edgar and John Wright got New Zealand off to a solid start before Wright departed after lunch with the score at 79. Edgar followed soon after reaching his half-century in 240 minutes. Bowling right-arm leg-spinners Bob Holland spun his way through the middle order. New Zealand was 169-9 when Bracewell and Boock played the most attractive cricket of the day and by stumps had added 48, unbroken.

Common sense and an ability to hit boundaries off bad balls saw them become only the 11th pair in test history to score a hundred for the last wicket. They both made their highest test scores in adding 124 for the 10th wicket.

Australia were struggling in reply to 293 when the fifth wicket fell at 71. Greg Ritchie and Greg Matthews then defied the accurate bowling as they made their stand worth 100 in two hours. Australia ended the day at 175-5.

Australia lost their last four wickets in the space of 25 minutes, giving New Zealand a lead of 66. Richard Hadlee had another five-wicket bag and was well supported by Bracewell and Boock.

The game appeared to have swung completely New Zealand's way when Edgar and Wright had their first, and only, century opening partnership. Disaster struck when both openers and Martin Crowe were dismissed in the space of seven runs.

Coney was bowled by Holland with the third ball the following day, at the overnight score of 119, and John Reid followed soon after as the innings collapsed before the Australian spinners, with Holland claiming 10 wickets for

the match. After an excellent start New Zealand had lost 10 wickets for 93 runs. Bad light and rain shortened the day, with Australia 36-1 requiring a further 224 for victory.

A second wicket stand of 105 between Wayne Phillips and David Boon saw Australia halfway to their target. The slow outfield and accurate, but not dangerous, bowling saw Australia requiring 90 in the last hour with six wickets in hand. David Hookes and Matthews went for their shots in the gathering gloom and their stand reached 50 in 31 minutes to give their side a deserved win.

NEW ZEALAND

J.G.Wright	c O'Donnell b Bright	38	c & b Matthews	43
B.A.Edgar	c Border b Holland	50	c & b Holland	52
J.F.Reid	c Kerr b Holland	7	b Matthews	19
M.D.Crowe	run out	8	b Holland	0
J.V.Coney*	c Border b Holland	8	b Holland	7
J.J.Crowe	b Holland	13	c & b Holland	6
V.R.Brown	lbw b Holland	0	b Bright	15
I.D.S.Smith†	c Hookes b Bright	28	c & b Bright	12
R.J.Hadlee	lbw b Holland	5	lbw b Gilbert	26
J.G.Bracewell	not out	83	not out	2
S.L.Boock	lbw b Gilbert	37	c Boon b Bright	3
Extras	(b 6, lb 8, nb 2)	16	(b 1, lb 4, nb 3)	8
TOTAL	**(124.3 overs)**	**293**	**(102.5 overs)**	**193**

AUSTRALIA

W.B.Phillips†	b Bracewell	31	c Bracewell b Boock	63
R.B.Kerr	lbw b Hadlee	7	c Wright b Bracewell	7
D.C.Boon	lbw b Hadlee	0	c Reid b Bracewell	81
A.R.Border*	b Bracewell	20	st Smith b Bracewell	11
G.M.Ritchie	c Crowe J.J. b Hadlee	89	c Crowe M.D. b Hadlee	13
D.W.Hookes	run out	0	not out	38
G.R.J.Matthews	c Smith b Hadlee	50	lbw b Hadlee	32
S.P.O'Donnell	not out	20	not out	2
R.J.Bright	lbw b Boock	1		
D.R.Gilbert	c Smith b Hadlee	0		
R.G.Holland	st Smith b Boock	0		
Extras	(b 5, lb 2, nb 2)	9	(b 3, lb 9, nb 1)	13
TOTAL	**(97.5 overs)**	**227**	**(97.1 overs) (6 wkts)**	**260**

Bowling	O	M	R	W	O	M	R	W	Fall of Wickets				
AUSTRALIA										NZ	A	NZ	A
Gilbert	20.3	6	41	1	9	2	22	1		*1st*	*1st*	*2nd*	*2nd*
O'Donnell	6	2	13	0	5	4	4	0	1st	79	19	100	27
Bright	34	12	87	2	17.5	3	39	3	2nd	92	22	106	132
Matthews	17	3	32	0	30	11	55	2	3rd	109	48	119	144
Holland	47	19	106	6	41	16	68	4	4th	112	71	119	163
NEW ZEALAND									5th	128	71	131	192
Hadlee	24	2	65	5	27.1	10	58	2	6th	128	186	137	258
Crowe M.D.	5	2	15	0	2	1	7	0	7th	161	224	162	-
Bracewell	25	9	51	2	30	7	91	3	8th	166	225	163	-
Boock	29.5	14	53	2	22	4	49	1	9th	169	226	190	-
Brown	13	3	35	0	7	0	28	0	10th	293	227	193	-
Coney	1	0	1	0	9	1	15	0					

John Bracewell, watched by David Boon, put on 124 for the last wicket with Stephen Boock.

MILESTONES

- The partnership of 124 between John Bracewell and Stephen Boock was a record for the 10th wicket between New Zealand and Australia.

173 AUSTRALIA v NEW ZEALAND *(Third Test)*

at W.A.C.A. Ground, Perth on 30 November, 1, 2, 3, 4 December, 1985
Toss : New Zealand. Umpires : R.C. Isherwood and P.J. McConnell
New Zealand won by 6 wickets

The WACA ground had undergone the first stages of a renovation plan. The whole cricket arena had been relaid and the spongy turf was dangerous for fieldsmen and almost impenetrable by batsmen. The pitch had variable bounce. On the last day some balls lifted alarmingly, whereas others sometimes skidded low. Over the entire game, 29 hours and 34 minutes, only 39 fours and two sixes were struck.

Richard Hadlee continued his absolute mastery over the Australian batsmen with another five-wicket haul. Ewen Chatfield was at his parsimonious best in claiming both opening batsmen before retiring with a groin strain caused by the spongy run-up. He returned in mid-afternoon strapped up but handicapped and bowled from a shorter run.

A deflection by Bruce Edgar in the day's first over brought him a boundary; he was able to add only one other while batting throughout the day. Australia's bowling, led by Geoff Lawson, was wonderfully accurate and the outfield extremely slow. Edgar's determination and dedication never wavered throughout a long and trying day and he reached his third consecutive half-century in the series in 289 minutes.

Martin Crowe knuckled down admirably to a situation that did not suit his attacking talents. The pair did their job so efficiently that they added 129 and by day's end New Zealand still had eight wickets intact and were just 19 short of Australia's total.

The third day was dominated by Australia as they fought their way back into the game. The overnight pair of Edgar and Crowe scored only a single between them and the rest of the New Zealand batsmen struggled as the last eight wickets were mopped up for 115 runs.

The lead of 96 was not nearly as large as had looked likely but it was distinctly useful and made to look better by the capture of two Australian wickets for 38, from 28 overs, by the close of play.

Ninety-five overs for 201 runs and five wickets was New Zealand's return for the fourth day. All batsmen were uncomfortable with the bounce which was becoming more unpredictable. The Australian captain, Allan Border, found resolute allies in David Boon and Greg Ritchie and shared in two 80-run partnerships before New Zealand fought back after tea. A slow, but dramatic, day ended with Australia on 239-7, a lead of 143, and the series in the balance.

Within half an hour the innings was over with Hadlee claiming another six wickets. New Zealand's target of 164 looked distant considering the shooters, the lift from a length and the dreadfully slow outfield but a series of moderate partnerships saw New Zealand reach its target.

Australian journalist Mike Coward wrote: "It was a magnificent achievement by a homely, unpretentious and highly professional cricket team and just reward for controlling 13 of the 15 days."

AUSTRALIA				
W.B.Phillips†	c Smith b Chatfield	37	c Smith b Chatfield	10
R.B.Kerr	c Smith b Chatfield	17	b Hadlee	0
D.C.Boon	c Bracewell b Hadlee	12	b Hadlee	50
A.R.Border*	c Smith b Hadlee	12	b Hadlee	83
G.M.Ritchie	lbw b Coney	6	c Crowe M.D. b Coney	44
D.W.Hookes	c Bracewell b Coney	14	b Bracewell	7
G.R.J.Matthews	b Hadlee	34	lbw b Hadlee	14
G.F.Lawson	c Crowe J.J. b Hadlee	11	c Crowe J.J. b Hadlee	21
C.J.McDermott	b Chatfield	36	lbw b Bracewell	11
D.R.Gilbert	not out	12	b Hadlee	3
R.G.Holland	c Crowe M.D. b Hadlee	4	not out	0
Extras	(lb 6, nb 2)	8	(b 2, lb 5, nb 9)	16
TOTAL	(83.5 overs)	203	(131.5 overs)	259

NEW ZEALAND				
J.G.Wright	c Phillips b Lawson	20	b Gilbert	35
B.A.Edgar	c Hookes b McDermott	74	c Border b Matthews	16
J.F.Reid	b Gilbert	7	c Phillips b Gilbert	28
M.D.Crowe	lbw b McDermott	71	not out	42
J.V.Coney*	c Phillips b Lawson	19	b Gilbert	16
J.J.Crowe	lbw b Holland	17	not out	2
R.J.Hadlee	c Hookes b Holland	26		
I.D.S.Smith†	c Matthews b Lawson	12		
J.G.Bracewell	not out	28		
B.L.Cairns	c Ritchie b Holland	0		
E.J.Chatfield	c Phillips b Lawson	3		
Extras	(b 1, lb 7, nb 14)	22	(b 7, lb 7, nb 11)	25
TOTAL	(157 overs)	299	(74 overs) (4 wkts)	164

Bowling	O	M	R	W	O	M	R	W	Fall of Wickets				
NEW ZEALAND										A	NZ	A	NZ
										1st	1st	2nd	2nd
Hadlee	26.5	6	65	5	39	11	90	6	1st	38	43	3	47
Cairns	14	1	50	0	26	6	59	0	2nd	63	55	28	77
Chatfield	16	6	33	3	30	9	47	1	3rd	78	184	109	121
Coney	21	11	43	2	8	5	9	1	4th	85	191	195	149
Bracewell	6	3	6	0	28.5	8	47	2	5th	85	215	207	-
AUSTRALIA									6th	114	253	214	-
Lawson	47	12	79	4	21	7	35	0	7th	131	256	234	-
McDermott	33	9	66	2	13	1	27	0	8th	159	273	251	-
Gilbert	31	9	75	1	23	5	48	3	9th	190	276	255	-
Holland	40	12	63	3	8	1	27	0	10th	203	299	259	-
Matthews	5	3	6	0	9	3	13	1					
Hookes	1	0	2	0									

MILESTONES

- It was New Zealand's first series win against Australia.

- In three tests in Australia Richard Hadlee captured 33 wickets. Only George Lohmann, who took 35 for England against South Africa in 1895/96, had captured more in a three-match series.

Under almost impossible conditions, Martin Crowe played an innings of grit, determination and character. His scores of 71 and 42 not out won plaudits from the Australian media and ensured that New Zealand won the series 2-1.

AVERAGES

New Zealand

BATTING	M	I	NO	Runs	HS	Ave
M.D. Crowe	3	5	1	309	188	77.25
B.A. Edgar	3	5	0	209	74	41.80
J.G. Wright	3	5	0	182	46	36.40
J.F. Reid	3	5	0	169	108	33.80
R.J. Hadlee	3	4	0	111	54	27.75
V.R. Brown	2	3	1	51	36*	25.50
S.L. Boock	1	2	0	40	37	20.00
J.J. Crowe	3	5	1	73	35	18.25
I.D.S. Smith	3	4	1	54	28	18.00
J.V. Coney	3	5	0	72	22	14.40
E.J. Chatfield	2	1	0	3	3	3.00
B.L. Cairns	1	1	0	0	0	0.00
J.G. Bracewell	2	3	3	113	83*	-
M.C. Snedden	1	-	-	-	-	-

BOWLING	O	M	R	W	Ave
R.J. Hadlee	169.3	42	401	33	12.15
E.J. Chatfield	96	30	184	7	26.28
J.V. Coney	49	23	79	3	26.33
J.G. Bracewell	89.5	27	195	7	27.85
S.L. Boock	51.5	18	102	3	34.00
M.C. Snedden	30	4	111	1	111.00
V.R. Brown	57	13	176	1	176.00
M.D. Crowe	21	5	55	0	-
B.L. Cairns	40	7	109	0	-

Australia

BATTING	M	I	NO	Runs	HS	Ave
A.R. Border	3	6	1	279	152*	55.80
G.R.J. Matthews	3	6	0	247	115	41.16
K.C. Wessels	1	2	0	73	70	36.50
G.M. Ritchie	3	6	0	180	89	30.00
W.B. Phillips	3	6	0	177	63	29.50
D.C. Boon	3	6	0	175	81	29.16
D.W. Hookes	2	4	1	59	38*	19.66
C.J. McDermott	2	4	0	61	36	15.25
G.F. Lawson	2	4	0	47	21	11.75
D.R. Gilbert	3	5	2	25	12*	8.33
R.B. Kerr	2	4	0	31	17	7.75
A.M.J. Hilditch	1	2	0	12	12	6.00
R.G. Holland	3	5	1	4	4	1.00
R.J. Bright	1	1	0	1	1	1.00
S.P. O'Donnell	1	2	2	22	20*	-

BOWLING	O	M	R	W	Ave
R.J. Bright	51.5	15	126	5	25.20
R.G. Holland	158	51	370	13	28.46
G.R.J. Matthews	92	25	216	6	36.00
D.R. Gilbert	122.3	31	288	8	36.00
G.F. Lawson	104.5	27	210	5	42.00
C.J. McDermott	77	13	212	3	70.66
A.R. Border	0.1	0	0	0	-
D.W. Hookes	1	0	2	0	-
K.C. Wessels	1	0	7	0	-
S.P. O'Donnell	11	6	17	0	-

1985/86 Australia in New Zealand

Interest was greater than normal for the first day of a test with Richard Hadlee one short of 300 test wickets. The news that Australia was batting soon had Wellingtonians queuing to get into the ground but they had a long time to wait for Hadlee's milestone to arrive.

174 NEW ZEALAND v AUSTRALIA *(First Test)*

at Basin Reserve, Wellington on 21, 22, 23, 24, 25 February, 1986
Toss : New Zealand. Umpires : F.R. Goodall and S.J. Woodward
Match drawn

David Boon and Geoff Marsh provided an excellent platform for the Australian innings as they scored 104 in 151 minutes, with their running between the wickets exploiting slow fieldsmen. The moment the crowd had been waiting for occurred when Allan Border was adjudged lbw to Hadlee with the score at 166-4.

Greg Ritchie and Greg Matthews were diligent and their aggressive running between the wickets saw the New Zealand fielding disintegrate. Both players were 55 not out and their partnership had added 119 in almost even time when play ended at 285-4.

Matthews and Ritchie began the second day as they had finished the first, utterly on top of the bowling. Classic fall-faced drives from Ritchie and powerful shots on the leg-side from Matthews, plus more audacious singles, saw the partnership reach 213 and place Australia in an almost impregnable position.

When Matthews was dismissed for 130 it was his second test hundred against New Zealand in four tests. His dismissal saw the last five Australian wickets fall for a paltry 21 runs. Stu Gillespie made his test debut as a nightwatchman even though he had bowled 27 tiring overs into a blustery northerly wind as New Zealand finished the day at 70-2.

To the surprise of his team-mates Gillespie soldiered on and stayed for 114 minutes. Martin Crowe was the fifth New Zealand wicket to fall with the score at 138. Ken Rutherford,

An historic moment was a long time coming for Richard Hadlee on the first day of this test. Requiring one wicket to reach his 300th, the Australian score had advanced to 166-3 before an appeal for lbw against Allan Border was dramatically upheld.

after his nightmare experience in West Indies, showed no sign of nerves, stroking the ball sweetly from the outset.

Jeremy Coney was more conservative and restrained. Both batsmen were troubled by the tall left-armer Bruce Reid who ended Rutherford's first test half-century after the partnership had been worth 109. In 67 minutes before stumps Coney and Hadlee attacked the second new ball, adding 64.

Only 77 minutes of play was possible on the fourth day owing to swirling blankets of mist and rain but in that time New Zealand went from 311-6 to 379 without further loss of wickets. A minute before rain washed out play for the day Coney reached his third test century, made in 288 minutes. From the outset Hadlee was in his most belligerent mood and scored 72 of the partnership worth 132.

The ground was awash and there was no chance of play on the fifth day.

AUSTRALIA

D.C.Boon	c Smith b Troup	70
G.R.Marsh	c Coney b Chatfield	43
W.B.Phillips	b Gillespie	32
A.R.Border*	lbw b Hadlee	13
G.M.Ritchie	b Troup	92
G.R.J.Matthews	c Rutherford b Coney	130
S.R.Waugh	c Smith b Coney	11
T.J.Zoehrer†	c sub (J.G.Bracewell) b Coney	18
C.J.McDermott	b Hadlee	2
B.A.Reid	not out	0
S.P.Davis	c & b Hadlee	0
Extras	(b 2, lb 9, w 4, nb 9)	24
TOTAL	(146.1 overs)	**435**

NEW ZEALAND

T.J.Franklin	c Border b McDermott	0
B.A.Edgar	c Waugh b Matthews	38
J.F.Reid	c Phillips b Reid	32
S.R.Gillespie	c Border b Reid	28
M.D.Crowe	b Matthews	19
K.R.Rutherford	c sub (R.J.Bright) b Reid	65
J.V.Coney*	not out	101
R.J.Hadlee	not out	72
I.D.S.Smith†		
G.B.Troup		
E.J.Chatfield		
Extras	(b 2, lb 6, w 1, nb 15)	24
TOTAL	(126.3 overs) (6 wkts)	**379**

Bowling	O	M	R	W
NEW ZEALAND				
Hadlee	37.1	5	116	3
Chatfield	36	10	96	1
Troup	28	6	86	2
Gillespie	27	2	79	1
Coney	18	7	47	3
AUSTRALIA				
McDermott	25.3	5	80	1
Davis	25	4	70	0
Reid	31	6	104	3
Matthews	37	10	107	2
Border	4	3	1	0
Waugh	4	1	9	0

Fall of Wickets

	A	NZ
	1st	1st
1st	104	0
2nd	143	57
3rd	166	94
4th	166	115
5th	379	138
6th	414	247
7th	418	-
8th	435	-
9th	435	-
10th	435	-

MILESTONES

- Stu Gillespie (157) made his test debut.

- Richard Hadlee became the sixth player to capture 300 test wickets.

- Jeremy Coney and Ken Rutherford created a new sixth wicket record of 109 for New Zealand against Australia.

- Jeremy Coney and Richard Hadlee created a new seventh wicket record of 132 for New Zealand against Australia.

at Lancaster Park, Christchurch on 28 February, 1, 2, 3, 4 March, 1986
Toss : New Zealand. Umpires : B.L. Aldridge and F.R. Goodall
Match drawn

When Jeremy Coney won the toss he had no hesitation in asking Australia to bat on a cold day that threatened rain. Australia plummeted from a position of strength shortly before lunch, at 57 without loss, to lose their fifth wicket with the score at 74.

Allan Border, who had never exceeded 38 in a test innings in New Zealand, was kept scoreless for 25 minutes before finding his confidence. He was joined by 20-year-old Steve Waugh and together they kept New Zealand at bay for the rest of the day. During the afternoon, when his score reached 78, Border became the fourth Australian after Sir Donald Bradman, Greg Chappell and Neil Harvey to score 6000 runs in test cricket. Waugh scored his first test half-century as the pair added 150 runs in 192 minutes. Australia 224-5.

Border reached his 17th test century in 287 minutes and was eventually out for 140 enabling Australia's last five wickets to add 290. Richard Hadlee had a marathon workload of 44.4 overs in capturing seven wickets. New Zealand struggled to 48 for three in the hour and a half to stumps.

Before a run was scored on the third day Ken Rutherford was dismissed. This brought Jeremy Coney to join Martin Crowe and the pair were in delightful touch, with Crowe reaching 51 in 130 minutes before he was felled by a Bruce Reid bouncer and required six stitches in his chin. Coney's feet were moving and straight drives and imperial strokes through the off side off the back foot flowed from his cultivated bat.

Ian Smith aided Coney in adding 66 in 79 minutes and when he was dismissed Martin Crowe returned to the crease, this time wearing a helmet. At the tea interval Coney was 95 and Crowe 76 but such was Crowe's confidence that he reached his century before Coney, with a succession of outstanding boundary shots.

John Bracewell demands, and gets, a decision from umpire Brian Aldridge. Ray Bright caught by Ian Smith.

Two balls after Crowe had reached his century, in 156 balls, Coney was out, caught at deep backward square leg for an excellent 98. Crowe was the last player dismissed for a spine-tingling 137. It was one of the bravest and most emotional innings seen in test cricket in New Zealand. New Zealand finished the day a mere 25 runs behind Australia, having batted 155 minutes and 45.1 overs fewer.

Any chance of a decision being reached was virtually washed away when there was only time for 94 minutes of play on the fourth day, but on the fifth Australia was in trouble when the sixth wicket fell and the score was only 130. The only thing between Australia and defeat was the wide bat of Border who, for the second time in the game, scored a century.

John Bracewell had his most inspired spell of bowling in test cricket, claiming four wickets with his tantalising off-spinners that demanded respect from all those who faced them.

176 NEW ZEALAND v AUSTRALIA *(Third Test)*

at Eden Park, Auckland on 13, 14, 15, 16, 17 March, 1986
Toss : Australia. Umpires : R.L. McHarg and S.J. Woodward
New Zealand won by 8 wickets

After fifteen successive tests between Australia and New Zealand in which the captain winning the toss had fielded first Allan Border broke the sequence by deciding to bat.

Geoff Marsh played comfortably from the front foot. Wayne Phillips, whose form in New Zealand had been spasmodic, survived for 246 minutes without ever looking at ease. They added 168 for the second wicket and a huge score looked inevitable at 191-1 but in the last half-hour Marsh, after scoring his first test century, and Border were dismissed to leave the honours even for the day. Australia; 227-4.

Greg Ritchie dominated the morning session of the second day and effortlessly reached his half-century in 106 minutes. The pick of the New Zealand bowlers was John Bracewell, who captured four wickets The last five Australian wickets fell for 21 runs. John Wright and Bruce Edgar had their best start of the series, reaching 73, before 12 deliveries from Greg Matthews snared three wickets without any addition to the score. New Zealand were 75-3 in reply to Australia's 314.

New Zealand was in strife when the fifth wicket fell at 107, with Wright reaching his fifty in 139 minutes. For the third time in as many games Coney proved to be in excellent form. He countered the spin and bounce of Matthews and Ray Bright with nimble footwork and powerful drives. In three consecutive innings Coney had scores of 101 not out, 98 and 93. In each case he arrived at a moment of crisis and played his team into safer waters with positive stroke making.

The fourth day was dominated by an outstanding performance of the off-spinners' art from Bracewell. When he bowled Border, his confidence soared. He was able to make the ball spin sharply from the pitch and the variable

AUSTRALIA

G.R.Marsh	b Hadlee	28	lbw b Bracewell		15
D.C.Boon	c Coney b Hadlee	26	c Coney b Troup		6
W.B.Phillips	c Smith b Chatfield	1	b Hadlee		25
A.R.Border*	b Chatfield	140	not out		114
G.M.Ritchie	lbw b Hadlee	4	c Smith b Bracewell		11
G.R.J.Matthews	c Smith b Hadlee	6	c sub (J.J.Crowe) b Hadlee		3
S.R.Waugh	lbw b Hadlee	74	c Smith b Bracewell		1
T.J.Zoehrer†	c Coney b Hadlee	30	c Rutherford b Bracewell		13
R.J.Bright	c Smith b Bracewell	21	not out		21
D.R.Gilbert	b Hadlee	15			
B.A.Reid	not out	1			
Extras	(b 1, lb 9, nb 8)	18	(lb 6, w 1, nb 3)		10
TOTAL	(152.4 overs)	**364**	(94 overs) (7 wkts dec)		**219**

NEW ZEALAND

B.A.Edgar	lbw b Reid	8	c & b Matthews		9
J.G.Wright	c Zoehrer b Gilbert	10	not out		4
J.F.Reid	c Zoehrer b Waugh	2	not out		0
M.D.Crowe	c Waugh b Reid	137			
K.R.Rutherford	lbw b Gilbert	0			
J.V.Coney*	c Reid b Waugh	98			
R.J.Hadlee	c Zoehrer b Reid	0			
I.D.S.Smith†	b Waugh	22			
J.G.Bracewell	c Marsh b Reid	20			
G.B.Troup	lbw b Waugh	10			
E.J.Chatfield	not out	2			
Extras	(b 6, lb 8, nb 16)	30	(nb 3)		3
TOTAL	(107.3 overs)	**339**	(14 overs) (1 wkt)		**16**

Bowling	O	M	R	W	O	M	R	W	Fall of Wickets				
NEW ZEALAND										A	NZ	A	NZ
										1st	1st	2nd	2nd
Hadlee	44.4	8	116	7	25	4	47	2	1st	57	17	15	13
Troup	34	4	104	0	15	0	50	1	2nd	58	29	32	-
Chatfield	36	13	56	2	17	6	29	0	3rd	58	29	76	-
Coney	9	0	28	0	3	1	10	0	4th	64	48	120	-
Bracewell	27	9	46	1	33	12	77	4	5th	74	124	129	-
Crowe	2	1	4	0					6th	251	190	130	-
Reid					1	1	0	0	7th	319	263	166	-
AUSTRALIA									8th	334	311	-	-
Reid	34.3	8	90	4	4	0	7	0	9th	358	331	-	-
Gilbert	26	4	106	2	7	4	9	0	10th	364	339	-	-
Waugh	23	6	56	4									
Bright	18	6	51	0									
Matthews	6	1	22	0	3	3	0	1					

MILESTONES

- Allan Border joined the group of players who had twice scored a century in each innings of a test – West Indians George Headley and Clyde Walcott, Herbert Sutcliffe of England, Sunil Gavaskar of India and Greg Chappell of Australia.

On a parched pitch, John Bracewell ripped his off-spinners to destroy the Australian batsmen in their second innings, claiming 6-32. He became the first New Zealand slow bowler to take 10 wickets in a match.

bounce from the pitch was another problem for the batsmen to solve.

David Boon, who batted throughout the innings, was the only player to play him with any certainty. Ewen Chatfield, who allowed only 19 runs off his 18 overs while capturing three wickets, ably supported Bracewell. Australia's dismissal for 103 left New Zealand five sessions in which to score the 160 runs necessary for victory. New Zealand went to stumps at 85-1 with Wright 46 not out and Ken Rutherford 22.

Seven thousand spectators were at Eden Park to witness New Zealand's victory by eight wickets, with Wright scoring his second fifty of the game and Rutherford battling 285 minutes for his half-century.

MILESTONES

- Gary Robertson (158) made his test debut.

- It was New Zealand's first home series win over Australia.

- John Bracewell became the first New Zealand slow bowler to take 10 wickets in a test. His 6-32 was the best return by a New Zealand slow bowler in a test in New Zealand and the best figures by a New Zealander in a test at Eden Park.

- David Boon became the seventh Australian to carry his bat through an innings.

- Tim Zoehrer became the first player in test cricket to act as nightwatchman in both innings of a test.

AUSTRALIA

D.C.Boon	c Coney b Hadlee	16	not out	58
G.R.Marsh	c Coney b Hadlee	118	lbw b Hadlee	0
W.B.Phillips	c Smith b Bracewell	62	c Bracewell b Chatfield	15
A.R.Border*	c Smith b Chatfield	17	(5) b Bracewell	6
T.J.Zoehrer†	c Coney b Robertson	9	(4) lbw b Chatfield	1
G.M.Ritchie	c Smith b Chatfield	56	lbw b Chatfield	1
G.R.J.Matthews	b Bracewell	5	st Smith b Bracewell	4
S.R.Waugh	c Reid b Bracewell	1	b Bracewell	0
R.J.Bright	c Smith b Hadlee	5	b Bracewell	0
C.J.McDermott	lbw b Bracewell	9	b Bracewell	6
B.A.Reid	not out	0	c Hadlee b Bracewell	8
Extras	(b 2, lb 11, nb 3)	16	(lb 4)	4
TOTAL	(135.3 overs)	**314**	(60 overs)	**103**

NEW ZEALAND

J.G.Wright	c Zoehrer b McDermott	56	c Boon b Matthews	59
B.A.Edgar	lbw b Matthews	24	b Reid	1
K.R.Rutherford	b Matthews	0	not out	50
M.D.Crowe	lbw b Matthews	0	not out	23
J.F.Reid	c Phillips b Bright	16		
J.V.Coney*	c Border b McDermott	93		
R.J.Hadlee	b Reid	33		
I.D.S.Smith†	b Waugh	3		
J.G.Bracewell	c Boon b Bright	4		
G.K.Robertson	st Zoehrer b Matthews	12		
E.J.Chatfield	not out	1		
Extras	(b 7, lb 8, nb 1)	16	(b 18, lb 4, nb 5)	27
TOTAL	(97 overs)	**258**	(84.4 overs) (2 wkts)	**160**

Bowling NEW ZEALAND	O	M	R	W	O	M	R	W
Hadlee	31	12	60	3	20	7	48	1
Robertson	24	6	91	1				
Chatfield	29	10	54	2	18	9	19	3
Crowe	3	2	4	0				
Bracewell	43.3	19	74	4	22	8	32	6
Coney	5	0	18	0				
AUSTRALIA								
McDermott	17	2	47	2	14	3	29	0
Reid	19	2	63	1	12.4	2	30	1
Matthews	34	15	61	4	31	18	46	1
Bright	22	4	58	2	23	12	29	0
Waugh	5	1	14	1	4	1	4	0

Fall of Wickets	A 1st	NZ 1st	A 2nd	NZ 2nd
1st	25	73	0	6
2nd	193	73	28	106
3rd	225	73	35	-
4th	225	103	59	-
5th	278	107	62	-
6th	293	170	71	-
7th	294	184	71	-
8th	301	203	71	-
9th	309	250	85	-
10th	314	258	103	-

AVERAGES

New Zealand

BATTING	M	I	NO	Runs	HS	Ave
J.V. Coney	3	3	1	292	101*	146.00
M.D. Crowe	3	4	1	179	137	59.66
R.J. Hadlee	3	3	1	105	72*	52.50
J.G. Wright	2	4	1	129	59	43.00
K.R. Rutherford	3	4	1	115	65	38.33
S.R. Gillespie	1	1	0	28	28	28.00
J.F. Reid	3	4	1	50	32	16.66
B.A. Edgar	3	5	0	80	38	16.00
I.D.S. Smith	3	2	0	25	22	12.50
J.G. Bracewell	2	2	0	24	20	12.00
G.K. Robertson	1	1	0	12	12	12.00
G.B. Troup	2	1	0	10	10	10.00
T.J. Franklin	1	1	0	0	0	0.00
E.J. Chatfield	3	2	2	3	2*	-

BOWLING	O	M	R	W	Ave
J.G. Bracewell	125.3	48	229	15	15.26
R.J. Hadlee	157.5	36	387	16	24.18
E.J. Chatfield	136	48	254	8	31.75
J.V. Coney	35	8	103	3	34.33
S.R. Gillespie	27	2	79	1	79.00
G.B. Troup	77	10	240	3	80.00
G.K. Robertson	24	6	91	1	91.00
J.F. Reid	1	1	0	0	-
M.D. Crowe	5	3	8	0	-

Australia

BATTING	M	I	NO	Runs	HS	Ave
A.R. Border	3	5	1	290	140	72.50
D.C. Boon	3	5	1	176	70	44.00
G.R. Marsh	3	5	0	204	118	40.80
G.M. Ritchie	3	5	0	164	92	32.80
G.R.J. Matthews	3	5	0	148	130	29.60
W.B. Phillips	3	5	0	135	62	27.00
S.R. Waugh	3	5	0	87	74	17.40
R.J. Bright	2	4	1	47	21*	15.66
D.R. Gilbert	1	1	0	15	15	15.00
T.J. Zoehrer	3	5	0	71	30	14.20
B.A. Reid	3	4	3	9	8	9.00
C.J. McDermott	2	3	0	17	9	5.66
S.P. Davis	1	1	0	0	0	0.00

BOWLING	O	M	R	W	Ave
S.R. Waugh	36	9	83	5	16.60
G.R.J. Matthews	111	47	236	8	29.50
B.A. Reid	101.1	18	294	9	32.66
C.J. McDermott	56.3	10	156	3	52.00
D.R. Gilbert	33	8	115	2	57.50
R.J. Bright	63	22	138	2	69.00
A.R. Border	4	3	1	0	-
S.P. Davis	25	4	70	0	-

1986 New Zealand in England

New Zealand journeyed to England with the unenviable record of having won only one test and lost 19 of the 31 played. John Reid announced his retirement from international cricket and Richard Hadlee, who was having his benefit season with Nottinghamshire, was available only for the three tests and the two one-day internationals.

New Zealand crowned their most successful cricket year with an historic series victory over England in England and completed a tour of 15 first-class matches unbeaten.

177 ENGLAND v NEW ZEALAND (First Test)

at Lord's on 24, 25, 26, 28, 29 July, 1986
Toss : England. Umpires : H.D. Bird and A.G.T. Whitehead
Match drawn

England looked to have the makings of a considerable score at 196-2 but Hadlee returned towards the end of the day and, from the pavilion end, captured three wickets for 15 runs as England finished at 248-5.

Short stoppages for bad light enabled Hadlee and Willie Watson to operate unchanged for the rest of England's innings, which saw the last five wickets fall for 59 runs. For the seventh time in 10 consecutive innings Hadlee had taken five or more wickets. Bruce French, who also played at Nottingham with Hadlee, was hit on the back of the head by the New Zealand pace bowler and was unable to take his place behind the stumps for the rest of the game.

Bill Athey began the keeper's role before being replaced by Bob Taylor, aged 45, who last played for England in 1984. After the loss of two early wickets Bruce Edgar and Martin Crowe steadied the innings and both were 52 not out when the day ended with New Zealand 127-2.

The game of musical chairs with England's wicketkeeper took on another phase when the Hampshire wicketkeeper Bobby Parks, whose grandfather and father had both played for England, took the gloves on the third day. Edgar and Crowe were not separated until after lunch, by which time the partnership had been worth 210 runs.

Edgar was gritty and sensibly cautious for the 358 minutes that he was at the crease and Crowe dominated the bowlers — his driving, particularly on the on-side was exceptional. His fifth test century came in 299 minutes. The remainder of the innings was kept under control by tight bowling, from Graham Dilley and Phil Edmonds, and excellent catching.

New Zealand lost their last wicket with the first ball of the fourth day to end with a lead of 35. Unfortunately, rain and bad light allowed only 47 overs to be bowled, in which time England lost three wickets for 110.

For New Zealand to have a chance of victory it was imperative that they cleaned up the rest of the innings before lunch on the final day. Maintaining an admirable mixture of concentration, restraint and well-timed strokes, Gooch completed his seventh test century and his third at Lord's and finished with 183 to ensure a draw.

ENGLAND

G.A.Gooch	c Smith b Hadlee	18	c Watson b Bracewell	183
M.D.Moxon	lbw b Hadlee	74	lbw b Hadlee	5
C.W.J.Athey	c Crowe J.J. b Hadlee	44	b Gray	16
D.I.Gower	c Crowe M.D. b Bracewell	62	b Gray	3
M.W.Gatting*	b Hadlee	2	c Crowe M.D. b Gray	26
P.Willey	lbw b Watson	44	b Bracewell	42
P.H.Edmonds	c Crowe M.D. b Hadlee	6	not out	9
B.N.French†	retired hurt	0		
G.R.Dilley	c Smith b Hadlee	17		
N.A.Foster	b Watson	8		
N.V.Radford	not out	12		
Extras	(b 6, lb 7, nb 7)	20	(lb 6, w 1, nb 4)	11
TOTAL	(118.5 overs)	**307**	(120.4 overs) (6 wkts dec)	**295**

NEW ZEALAND

J.G.Wright	b Dilley	0	c Gower b Dilley	0
B.A.Edgar	c Gatting b Gooch	83	c Gower b Foster	0
K.R.Rutherford	c Gooch b Dilley	0	not out	24
M.D.Crowe	c & b Edmonds	106	not out	11
J.J.Crowe	c Gatting b Edmonds	18		
J.V.Coney*	c Gooch b Radford	51		
E.J.Gray	c Gower b Edmonds	11		
R.J.Hadlee	b Edmonds	19		
I.D.S.Smith†	c Edmonds b Dilley	18		
J.G.Bracewell	not out	1		
W.Watson	lbw b Dilley	1		
Extras	(b 4, lb 9, w 6, nb 15)	34	(lb 4, nb 2)	6
TOTAL	(140.1 overs)	**342**	(15 overs) (2 wkts)	**41**

Bowling	O	M	R	W	O	M	R	W		Fall of Wickets			
NEW ZEALAND										E	NZ	E	NZ
										1st	1st	2nd	2nd
Hadlee	37.5	11	80	6	27	3	78	1					
Watson	30	7	70	2	17	2	50	0	1st	27	2	9	0
Crowe M.D.	8	1	38	0	4	0	13	0	2nd	102	5	68	8
Coney	4	0	12	0					3rd	196	215	72	-
Bracewell	26	8	65	1	23.4	7	57	2	4th	198	218	136	-
Gray	13	9	29	0	46	14	83	3	5th	237	274	262	-
Rutherford					3	0	8	0	6th	258	292	295	-
ENGLAND									7th	271	310	-	-
Dilley	35.1	9	82	4	6	3	5	1	8th	285	340	-	-
Foster	25	6	56	0	3	1	13	1	9th	307	340	-	-
Radford	25	4	71	1					10th	-	342	-	-
Edmonds	42	10	97	4	5	0	18	0					
Gooch	13	6	23	1									
Gower					1	0	1	0					

Martin Crowe showed his affinity for batting at his finest at Lord's. He dominated the bowlers, driving impeccably on the on-side to register his fifth test century.

MILESTONES

- Willie Watson (159) made his test debut.

- The second wicket partnership of 210 between Bruce Edgar and Martin Crowe was a record for New Zealand against England.

- Phil Edmonds became the 26th bowler to take one hundred test wickets for England.

- Jeremy Coney became the fourth New Zealand player to score four consecutive test fifties.

178 ENGLAND v NEW ZEALAND *(Second Test)*

at Trent Bridge, Nottingham on 7, 8, 9, 11, 12 August, 1986
Toss : New Zealand. Umpires : D.J. Constant and K.E. Palmer
New Zealand won by 8 wickets

Jeremy Coney's bold gamble of asking England to bat paid dividends when both openers were out with the score at 43. David Gower and Bill Athey both looked comfortable and untroubled by the attack and went on to their half centuries.

Gower was out for a delightfully compiled 71, lbw to Evan Gray, to a ball that spun sharply out of the bowler's footmarks and kept low. This exposed England's lengthy tail to Richard Hadlee and, for the 27th time, he captured five or more wickets in a test innings and England ended 240-9.

In reply to England's 256 John Wright batted with refreshing freedom and was second out for 58 when the score was 85. New Zealand was in the delicate position of 144 with the loss of their five top batsmen but for the rest of the day Hadlee played in his own rousing style and received loyal assistance from Gray, who defended dourly for two hours, to ensure that New Zealand did not lose further wickets. New Zealand was 211-5 at stumps.

The partnership had added an invaluable 95 when Hadlee was dismissed for 68. John Bracewell was quick to attack any loose deliveries and swept the English spinners to good effect in reaching 50 off 85 balls. Gray's concentration remained unruffled and, when he was finally caught bat-pad off Phil Edmonds, he had been at the crease 299 minutes and seen his team's score improve by 176 runs. It was arguably the vital innings of the series.

Derek Stirling, using his reach, strength and batting ability added a further 65 runs. An impudent pull shot to square leg gave Bracewell his first test century in 257 minutes. As well as Bracewell, Gray, Stirling and Watson all bettered their previous best test scores as the last five wickets added 269 runs to give New Zealand a lead of 157.

The vital wicket of Graham Gooch was captured by Bracewell to leave England in a perilous situation with two days remaining. Rain restricted play to only 43 minutes on the fourth day but not before two wickets were taken.

Overcast conditions prevailed for the fifth day and the spinners, Gray and Bracewell, both extracted turn and occasionally made the ball bounce higher than the batsmen expected. John Emburey and Derek Pringle took England's score from 104-6 to 178 before Pringle was dismissed with the deficit wiped off. More importantly for the tourists it had occupied 95 minutes.

The new ball in Hadlee's hands signalled the end of England's resistance. Martin Crowe and Coney took New Zealand to victory by eight wickets with nine overs to spare.

ENGLAND

G.A.Gooch	lbw b Hadlee	18	c Coney b Bracewell		17
M.D.Moxon	b Hadlee	9	c Smith b Hadlee		23
C.W.J.Athey	lbw b Watson	55	(4) c Smith b Bracewell		6
D.I.Gower	lbw b Gray	71	(5) c Crowe J.J. b Bracewell		26
M.W.Gatting*	b Hadlee	17	(6) c Smith b Gray		4
D.R.Pringle	c Watson b Stirling	21	(7) c Gray b Stirling		9
J.E.Emburey	c Smith b Hadlee	8	(8) c Crowe M.D. b Hadlee		75
P.H.Edmonds	c Smith b Hadlee	0	(3) lbw b Hadlee		20
J.G.Thomas	b Hadlee	28	c Gray b Stirling		10
B.N.French†	c Coney b Watson	21	not out		12
G.C.Small	not out	2	lbw b Hadlee		12
Extras	(b 1, lb 3, nb 2)	6	(b 4, lb 9, w 1, nb 2)		16
TOTAL	(89.5 overs)	**256**	(95.1 overs)		**230**

NEW ZEALAND

J.G.Wright	c Athey b Small	58	b Emburey	7
B.A.Edgar	lbw b Thomas	8		
J.J.Crowe	c French b Small	23	(2) lbw b Small	2
M.D.Crowe	c Edmonds b Emburey	28	(3) not out	48
J.V.Coney*	run out	24	(4) not out	20
E.J.Gray	c Athey b Edmonds	50		
R.J.Hadlee	c Gooch b Thomas	68		
J.G.Bracewell	c Moxon b Emburey	110		
I.D.S.Smith†	lbw b Edmonds	2		
D.A.Stirling	b Small	26		
W.Watson	not out	8		
Extras	(lb 4, w 2, nb 2)	8		0
TOTAL	(169.5 overs)	**413**	(24 overs) (2 wkts)	**77**

Bowling	O	M	R	W	O	M	R	W		Fall of Wickets				
NEW ZEALAND											E	NZ	E	NZ
Hadlee	32	7	80	6	33.1	15	60	4			1st	1st	2nd	2nd
Stirling	17	3	62	1	18	5	48	2		1st	18	39	23	5
Gray	13	4	30	1	24	9	55	1		2nd	43	85	47	19
Watson	16.5	6	51	2	9	3	25	0		3rd	126	92	63	-
Coney	7	1	18	0						4th	170	142	87	-
Bracewell	4	1	11	0	11	5	29	3		5th	176	144	98	-
ENGLAND										6th	191	239	104	-
Small	38	12	88	3	8	3	10	1		7th	191	318	178	-
Thomas	39	5	124	2	4	0	16	0		8th	205	326	203	-
Pringle	20	1	58	0	2	0	16	0		9th	240	391	203	-
Edmonds	28	11	52	2	4	1	16	0		10th	256	413	230	-
Emburey	42.5	17	87	2	6	1	15	1						
Gooch	2	2	0	0										
Gower					0.0	0	4	0						

Evan Gray's contribution was a major factor in New Zealand winning the test.

MILESTONES

- It was New Zealand's 24th test victory.

- Richard Hadlee set a test record by taking five wickets in an innings for the 27th time. He also equalled the record of 10 wickets in a match seven times.

- Ian Smith established a new record of 97 dismissals by a New Zealand wicketkeeper.

179 ENGLAND v NEW ZEALAND *(Third Test)*

at The Oval on 21, 22, 23, 25, 26 August, 1986
Toss : England. Umpires : H.D. Bird and D.R. Shepherd
Match drawn

Ian Botham returned from a two-month ban from international and first-class cricket after he had admitted that he had smoked cannabis. Needing a victory to square the series Mike Gatting asked New Zealand to bat first.

Play was 35 minutes late in starting and the ball swung in the damp air and moved off the seam. Botham's storybook comeback began with the first ball he bowled, which dismissed Bruce Edgar. Thirteen balls later Jeff Crowe was trapped in front of his leg stump and Botham became the holder of the record for the most test wickets — 356.

John Wright battled courageously in the difficult conditions and reached a well-earned fifty for the 17th time in his test career. When play was curtailed early because of rain New Zealand were 142-4, with Wright not out 63.

For the second day, before a full house, rain and bad light allowed only 59 overs to be bowled. Because of heavy overnight rain the outfield was much slower and runs were harder to come by. The overnight stand between Wright and Evan Gray was extended to 69 before three wickets fell in quick succession.

Soldiering on valiantly at one end had been Wright who realised a long-held ambition, after playing county cricket for ten seasons, of scoring a test century against England in England. He found another worthy partner in Tony Blain who, playing in his first test, showed the characteristic determination that had distinguished the touring party from its opponents. Their partnership of 54 was terminated when Wright was bowled after facing 344 balls. At stumps New Zealand was 257-8.

Blain, Derek Stirling and Ewen Chatfield helped New Zealand's cause admirably by occupying the crease for another 50 minutes while adding another 30 valuable runs.

Stirling's good work with the bat was undone when his opening bowling spell was neither fast nor accurate and provided ample opportunity for the England batsmen to score boundaries. David Gower and Mike Gatting salvaged England's fortunes from 62-3 with the best England batting

of the season, adding 219 in 223 minutes.

Richie Benaud commented that he'd never seen Gower bat with such sustained brilliance as he completed his 13th test century. Gatting had begun scratchily but, as his innings developed, so his footwork improved and his shot production rivalled Gower's.

Hurricane Charlie affected all of the British Isles and only 66 minutes of play was possible. Chatfield quickly disposed of Gower but Gatting, who was belligerent from the outset, scored at a run a ball to reach his sixth test century in his last 18 tests. Botham continued to display his prodigious all-round ability by hitting 24 runs off one Stirling over before rain came and continued to fall for the next two days.

Only 14 hours 20 minutes of the scheduled 30 hours playing time had been possible.

MILESTONES

- Tony Blain (160) made his test debut.

- New Zealand won its first test series in England.

- John Wright became the first New Zealander to score a test century at the Oval.

- Ian Botham became the holder of the record for the most test wickets, overtaking Dennis Lillee's record of 355.

NEW ZEALAND

J.G.Wright	b Edmonds	119	not out	7
B.A.Edgar	c Gooch b Botham	1	not out	0
J.J.Crowe	lbw b Botham	8		
M.D.Crowe	lbw b Dilley	13		
J.V.Coney*	c Gooch b Botham	38		
E.J.Gray	b Dilley	30		
R.J.Hadlee	c French b Edmonds	6		
J.G.Bracewell	c Athey b Emburey	3		
T.E.Blain†	c Gooch b Dilley	37		
D.A.Stirling	not out	18		
E.J.Chatfield	c French b Dilley	5		
Extras	(b 1, w 1, nb 7)	9		0
TOTAL	(128.2 overs)	**287**	(1 overs) (0 wkts)	**7**

ENGLAND

G.A.Gooch	c Stirling b Hadlee	32
C.W.J.Athey	lbw b Hadlee	17
D.I.Gower	b Chatfield	131
A.J.Lamb	b Chatfield	0
M.W.Gatting*	b Chatfield	121
I.T.Botham	not out	59
J.E.Emburey	not out	9
B.N.French†		
P.H.Edmonds		
G.R.Dilley		
G.C.Small		
Extras	(lb 9, w 5, nb 5)	19
TOTAL	(90.5 overs) (5 wkts dec)	**388**

Bowling	O	M	R	W	O	M	R	W
ENGLAND								
Dilley	28.2	4	92	4				
Small	18	5	36	0				
Botham	25	4	75	3	1	0	7	0
Emburey	31	15	39	1				
Edmonds	22	10	29	2				
Gooch	4	1	15	0				
NEW ZEALAND								
Hadlee	23.5	6	92	2				
Stirling	9	0	71	0				
Chatfield	21	7	73	3				
Gray	21	4	74	0				
Bracewell	11	1	51	0				
Coney	5	0	18	0				

Fall of Wickets	NZ	E	NZ
	1st	1st	2nd
1st	17	38	-
2nd	31	62	-
3rd	59	62	-
4th	106	285	-
5th	175	326	-
6th	192	-	-
7th	197	-	-
8th	251	-	-
9th	280	-	-
10th	287	-	-

AVERAGES

New Zealand

BATTING	M	I	NO	Runs	HS	Ave
M.D. Crowe	3	5	2	206	106	68.66
J.G. Bracewell	3	3	1	114	110	57.00
J.V. Coney	3	4	1	133	51	44.33
D.A. Stirling	2	2	1	44	26	44.00
J.G. Wright	3	6	1	191	119	38.20
T.E. Blain	1	1	0	37	37	37.00
R.J. Hadlee	3	3	0	93	68	31.00
E.J. Gray	3	3	0	91	50	30.33
K.R. Rutherford	1	2	1	24	24*	24.00
B.A. Edgar	3	5	1	92	83	23.00
J.J. Crowe	3	4	0	51	23	12.75
I.D.S. Smith	2	2	0	20	18	10.00
W. Watson	2	2	1	9	8*	9.00
E.J. Chatfield	1	1	0	5	5	5.00

BOWLING	O	M	R	W	Ave
R.J. Hadlee	153.5	42	390	19	20.52
E.J. Chatfield	21	7	73	3	24.33
J.G. Bracewell	75.4	22	213	6	35.50
W. Watson	72.5	18	196	4	49.00
E.J. Gray	117	40	271	5	54.20
D.A. Stirling	44	8	181	3	60.33
K.R. Rutherford	3	0	8	0	-
J.V. Coney	16	1	48	0	-
M.D. Crowe	12	1	51	0	-

England

BATTING	M	I	NO	Runs	HS	Ave
D.I. Gower	3	5	0	293	131	58.60
G.A. Gooch	3	5	0	268	183	53.60
J.E. Emburey	2	3	1	92	75	46.00
P. Willey	1	2	0	86	44	43.00
M.W. Gatting	3	5	0	170	121	34.00
B.N. French	3	3	2	33	21	33.00
M.D. Moxon	2	4	0	111	74	27.75
C.W.J. Athey	3	5	0	138	55	27.60
J.G. Thomas	1	2	0	38	28	19.00
G.R. Dilley	2	1	0	17	17	17.00
D.R. Pringle	1	2	0	30	21	15.00
G.C. Small	2	2	1	14	12	14.00
P.H. Edmonds	3	4	1	35	20	11.66
N.A. Foster	1	1	0	8	8	8.00
A.J. Lamb	1	1	0	0	0	0.00
I.T. Botham	1	1	1	59	59*	-
N.V. Radford	1	1	1	12	12*	-

BOWLING	O	M	R	W	Ave
G.R. Dilley	69.3	16	179	9	19.88
P.H. Edmonds	101	32	212	8	26.50
I.T. Botham	26	4	82	3	27.33
G.C. Small	64	20	134	4	33.50
J.E. Emburey	79.5	33	141	4	35.25
G.A. Gooch	19	9	38	1	38.00
N.A. Foster	28	7	69	1	69.00
J.G. Thomas	43	5	140	2	70.00
N.V. Radford	25	4	71	1	71.00
D.I. Gower	1	0	5	0	-
D.R. Pringle	22	1	74	0	-

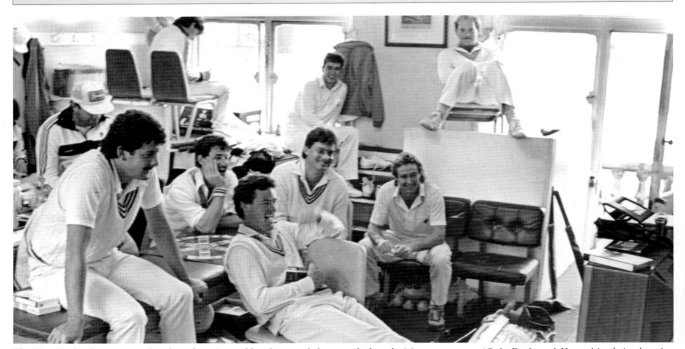

The New Zealand team are relaxed as the rain tumbles down and they watch the television programme 'Only Fools and Horses' in their changing room. From left, Derek Stirling, Richard Hadlee, John Bracewell, Evan Gray, Willie Watson, Tony Blain and Jeff Crowe.

1986/87 West Indies in New Zealand

West Indies arrived in New Zealand with seven of their players past the age of 30, which meant it was an enormously experienced side. They had won six of their last seven tests.

180 NEW ZEALAND v WEST INDIES *(First Test)*

at Basin Reserve, Wellington on 20, 21, 22, 23, 24 February, 1987
Toss : West Indies. Umpires : B.L. Aldridge and S.J. Woodward
Match drawn

Viv Richards won the toss and asked New Zealand to bat first on a brown, rather than green, strip. The experiment of playing Jeremy Coney at number three failed and New Zealand were 19-2. John Wright and Jeff Crowe were the only New Zealand batsmen to show real defiance with Wright being severe on the leg-side.

He displayed discipline and coolness in the face of many short-pitched deliveries during an innings that lasted 245 minutes. Joel Garner's height made him extremely difficult to play. At stumps New Zealand were badly placed at 205-8.

Replying to New Zealand's total of 228 Gordon Greenidge and Desmond Haynes, opening the innings for the 90th time in test cricket, shared their 10th century partnership, adding 150 for the first wicket. Haynes overcame the pain of a badly bruised and swollen jaw with two painkillers and reached his ninth test century in 236 minutes. The visitors ended the day 10 runs behind with eight wickets in hand.

A forthright bowling effort from all the bowlers saw New Zealand claw their way back from the brink of defeat as the last eight wickets were captured for the addition of 127 runs. It was significant that the wicket was taking spin and the batsmen dismissed during the day were less comfortable against the spinning ball than the quicker deliveries.

With a deficit of 117 New Zealand began the second innings in almost identical fashion to the first with Ken Rutherford and Coney both out with only 20 on the board. Wright and Martin Crowe survived the last session to finish 91-2.

A fierce northerly wind throughout the fourth day created a huge problem for the visitors as none of their pace attack were comfortable bowling into the gale and so Richards, bowling off a miniscule run up, accepted the role. Wright and Crowe consolidated their rescue attempt with extraordinary discipline by batting together until after tea. Crowe was dismissed after 385 minutes for 119, with the partnership adding 241 runs. It was the only wicket to fall during the day.

A beautiful day greeted the players for the final day. After 177 overs Richards took the new ball, but to no effect, as Wright continued his marathon and those batsmen who did get to bat were untroubled. Wright's 138 was both mentally and physically a monumental effort. During the course of the game he had occupied the crease for 828 minutes.

NEW ZEALAND

Batsman	1st innings		2nd innings	
J.G.Wright	c Garner b Richards	75	c & b Gomes	138
K.R.Rutherford	c Logie b Garner	6	lbw b Garner	6
J.V.Coney*	c Logie b Marshall	3	c Richards b Garner	4
M.D.Crowe	lbw b Walsh	3	c Holding b Richards	119
D.N.Patel	c Garner b Walsh	18	b Walsh	20
J.J.Crowe	c Logie b Garner	37	not out	27
J.G.Bracewell	lbw b Garner	17	not out	28
R.J.Hadlee	not out	35		
I.D.S.Smith†	lbw b Garner	0		
S.L.Boock	c Garner b Marshall	3		
E.J.Chatfield	lbw b Garner	0		
Extras	(lb 7, nb 24)	31	(b 10, lb 10, nb 24)	44
TOTAL	(89 overs)	228	(177 overs) (5 wkts dec)	386

WEST INDIES

Batsman	1st innings		2nd innings	
C.G.Greenidge	c Rutherford b Chatfield	78	c Rutherford b Boock	25
D.L.Haynes	b Bracewell	121	c Hadlee b Boock	13
H.A.Gomes	c Smith b Hadlee	18	not out	8
R.B.Richardson	b Boock	37	not out	0
I.V.A.Richards*	c Smith b Chatfield	24		
A.L.Logie	c Coney b Hadlee	3		
P.J.L.Dujon†	c Smith b Chatfield	22		
M.D.Marshall	c & b Boock	30		
M.A.Holding	c sub (T.D.Ritchie) b Chatfield	0		
J.Garner	not out	0		
C.A.Walsh	c Hadlee b Boock	1		
Extras	(b 1, lb 8, w 1, nb 1)	11	(b 3, lb 1)	4
TOTAL	(128 overs)	345	(22 overs) (2 wkts)	50

Bowling	O	M	R	W	O	M	R	W
WEST INDIES								
Marshall	22	3	57	2	20	6	43	0
Garner	27	5	51	5	30	9	72	2
Walsh	12	1	46	2	34	13	59	1
Holding	16	4	34	0	21	4	65	0
Richards	11	3	32	1	47	13	86	1
Gomes	1	0	1	0	21	6	37	1
Richardson					4	1	4	0
NEW ZEALAND								
Hadlee	31	9	77	2	4	0	12	0
Chatfield	39	14	102	4	4	0	13	0
Coney	3	0	8	0				
Bracewell	14	5	47	1	7	2	13	0
Boock	35	14	76	3	7	4	8	2
Crowe M.D.	3	1	13	0				
Patel	3	0	13	0				

Fall of Wickets	NZ 1st	WI 1st	NZ 2nd	WI 2nd
1st	10	150	13	33
2nd	19	208	20	46
3rd	46	232	261	-
4th	107	278	301	-
5th	153	287	331	-
6th	181	289	-	-
7th	192	339	-	-
8th	192	343	-	-
9th	226	344	-	-
10th	228	345	-	-

John Wright, left, and Martin Crowe both scored hundreds to save the game for New Zealand. Their partnership of 241 runs was a record for the third wicket for New Zealand against all countries.

MILESTONES

- Dipak Patel (161) made his test debut.

- John Wright and Jeremy Coney were both playing in their 50th test match.

- Ian Smith became the first New Zealand wicketkeeper to make one hundred dismissals in test cricket.

- John Wright and Martin Crowe added 241 for the third wicket, a New Zealand record against all countries.

- Martin Crowe became the first New Zealander to score a century in five consecutive series.

- John Wright's second innings, lasting 582 minutes, was the longest test innings for New Zealand at home.

- Joel Garner became the second West Indies bowler to capture 250 test wickets.

181 NEW ZEALAND v WEST INDIES (*Second Test*)

at Eden Park, Auckland on 27, 28 February, 1, 2, 3 March, 1987
Toss : West Indies. Umpires : F.R. Goodall and G.C. Morris
West Indies won by 10 wickets

Following the test in Wellington, Michael Holding, for the third time, announced his retirement from test cricket and returned home with his total of test wickets at 249.

Although the pitch had been covered 12 days prior to the test it was the dampest pitch prepared at Eden Park in 13 years and the visitors lost two early wickets. Gordon Greenidge and Richie Richardson were watchful, particularly Richardson, when Stephen Boock was brought into the attack before lunch.

After the lunch break Greenidge took to Boock's bowling and plundered 48 from six overs. Showers continually interrupted play but not before Greenidge had reached his 13th test century and had partnered Gus Logie in adding 80, unbeaten, before stumps were drawn with the West Indies 211-4.

More showers also interrupted the second day's play and Martin Crowe took his second exceptional catch in the gully off Richard Hadlee. On joining Greenidge, Jeff Dujon displayed his excellent batting prowess, the pair adding 165 for the sixth wicket. Greenidge prospered by being dropped on 135, 148 and 187, all easy catches. He completed his third double century and batted 534 minutes, hitting seven sixes and 20 fours.

West Indies declared at their overnight total of 418-9. The pace attack of Malcolm Marshall, Tony Gray and Courtney Walsh was able to make the ball seam sharply and caused all the batsmen trouble. Altogether, nine catches were taken, some brilliantly, as the batting was blasted away. Ian Smith displayed his best form for some time in a test and his was the

only resistance in a generally substandard batting display. Bad light shortened the day for the home team who followed on 261 runs behind.

Only two and a half hours play was possible on the fourth day but it was sufficient time for both openers to depart, leaving New Zealand's hopes of saving the match in the hands of the brothers Crowe or the weather.

There were only two brief interruptions by the weather on the fifth day, making 14 interruptions during the game. It seemed as if West Indies would win with time to spare when the fifth wicket fell at 126. Martin Crowe was courageously defying all the bowlers. The gritty John Bracewell joined him and together they embarked on an heroic stand of 107.

Crowe completed his seventh test century before Walsh, with the new ball, scythed through the tail to finish with five wickets in the innings for the first time in his test career. It was New Zealand's first loss at home in five years.

WEST INDIES

D.L.Haynes	c Crowe M.D. b Hadlee	1	not out	6
C.G.Greenidge	b Hadlee	213	not out	10
H.A.Gomes	c Smith b Chatfield	5		
R.B.Richardson	c Smith b Hadlee	41		
I.V.A.Richards*	b Hadlee	14		
A.L.Logie	c Crowe M.D. b Hadlee	34		
P.J.L.Dujon†	b Boock	77		
M.D.Marshall	c Crowe J.J. b Boock	6		
C.G.Butts	not out	8		
A.H.Gray	lbw b Hadlee	8		
C.A.Walsh				
Extras	(b 4, lb 3, nb 4)	11		0
TOTAL	(142.4 overs) (9 wkts dec)	**418**	(1.3 overs) (0 wkts)	**16**

NEW ZEALAND

J.G.Wright	c Richardson b Marshall	11	c Logie b Walsh	7
K.R.Rutherford	b Marshall	12	c Richardson b Marshall	5
J.J.Crowe	c Dujon b Walsh	1	c Gray b Walsh	21
M.D.Crowe	c Dujon b Marshall	10	c Logie b Gray	104
D.N.Patel	c Greenidge b Butts	21	lbw b Marshall	5
J.V.Coney*	c Logie b Gray	15	c Dujon b Gray	17
J.G.Bracewell	c Richardson b Gray	7	lbw b Gomes	43
R.J.Hadlee	c Dujon b Butts	0	c Richardson b Walsh	14
I.D.S.Smith†	not out	40	c Richards b Walsh	10
S.L.Boock	c Dujon b Gray	0	c Dujon b Walsh	4
E.J.Chatfield	c Logie b Marshall	4	not out	0
Extras	(b 12, lb 2, nb 22)	36	(b 7, lb 8, nb 28)	43
TOTAL	(53 overs)	**157**	(111.2 overs)	**273**

Bowling	O	M	R	W	O	M	R	W		Fall of Wickets				
NEW ZEALAND											WI	NZ	NZ	WI
											1st	1st	2nd	2nd
Hadlee	41.4	7	105	6	1	0	9	0	1st		7	30	10	-
Chatfield	37	14	88	1	0.3	0	7	0	2nd		14	38	14	-
Boock	25	6	96	2					3rd		109	39	83	-
Bracewell	17	2	53	0					4th		131	69	91	-
Coney	11	2	22	0					5th		219	81	126	-
Crowe M.D.	5	1	9	0					6th		384	95	233	-
Patel	6	0	38	0					7th		400	101	250	-
WEST INDIES									8th		402	109	260	-
Marshall	17	3	43	4	33	7	71	2	9th		418	109	269	-
Walsh	14	5	34	1	30.2	6	73	5	10th		-	157	273	-
Butts	12	4	21	2	26	6	61	0						
Gray	10	1	45	3	18	4	44	2						
Gomes					4	1	9	1						

MILESTONES

- Richard Hadlee created a new world record by taking five or more wickets in a test innings for the 28th time.

- Martin Crowe equalled the record held by Glenn Turner and Bevan Congdon when he completed his seventh test century. Aged 24 he was the youngest New Zealander to pass 2000 runs in test cricket.

Top scorer in New Zealand's mediocre first innings of 157 was Ian Smith. He indulged in his favourite cut shot to good effect in his 40 not out. Smith had taken his 100th catch in test cricket in the previous game.

182 NEW ZEALAND v WEST INDIES *(Third Test)*

at Lancaster Park, Christchurch on 12, 13, 14, 15 March, 1987
Toss : New Zealand. Umpires : G.C. Morris and S.J. Woodward
New Zealand won by 5 wickets

After the emphatic loss at Auckland, New Zealand faced a daunting prospect to save the series. Not only would they have to win the test but the long-range forecast suggested that bad weather would interfere with the game.

The first day dawned in depressing fashion with rain falling and play was abandoned. On winning the toss, Jeremy Coney invited West Indies to bat.

Hardly had the match begun when the drama started. With his seventh ball Richard Hadlee bowled Desmond Haynes and in the next over Ewen Chatfield sent Gordon Greenidge's

middle stump cartwheeling.

Hadlee was strangely wayward in his opening spell and came off after only four overs, where he had bowled five no-balls, a most un-Hadlee like occurrence. Chatfield, however, was giving an object lesson in the seamer's art and captured three of the first four wickets to fall with the score at 56.

Coney held three successive catches at second slip off Hadlee as West Indies were dismissed in 36.3 overs for 100, their fifth lowest total in test cricket.

New Zealand made an unpromising start, with both Phil Horne and John Wright caught by Viv Richards at first slip before the Crowe brothers consolidated New Zealand's position, taking the score to 117 at stumps.

Both brothers reached their half-centuries before Martin played a premeditated hook at Malcolm Marshall and was bowled for 83, the partnership adding 156. This signalled a mini-collapse with Dipak Patel and Jeff Crowe following in quick succession to see New Zealand tenuously placed at 181-5.

Coney and John Bracewell set about restoring the innings during the middle session. Although they scored only 60 runs, no wickets fell as the batsmen fought to protect their wickets, as well as their bodies, from the four-pronged pace attack. After tea the New Zealanders surprised West Indies with an all-out assault on the bowling.

Bracewell hit both Courtney Walsh and Joel Garner for huge sixes. He and Coney added an invaluable 89, with the badly bruised Bracewell scoring a punishing 66. New Zealand declared at 332-9 and still had 30 minutes bowling at the West Indies openers. It was the first time in 57 tests that West Indies had trailed an opponent by more than 200 runs on the first innings.

The visitors made another disastrous start to the day's play when both Haynes and Greenidge were dismissed for the addition of two runs. It was a strange West Indian innings, with the first nine batsmen all scoring double figures but Marshall's 45 being the highest in the total of 264. Bowling with pinpoint accuracy and moving the ball either way off the seam, Martin Snedden captured his first five-wicket haul in a test match.

There was great tension as New Zealand lost five wickets in scoring the necessary 33 runs needed for victory against the unbridled pace and venom of the bowlers. All 35 wickets that fell in the game went to pace bowlers and it was just West Indies fifth loss in 62 test matches since 1980.

Against the odds, New Zealand had defended its recent proud record of not losing a test series at home since 1978/79.

MILESTONES

- Phil Horne (162) made his test debut.

- Jeremy Coney retired after playing his 52nd test.

WEST INDIES

C.G.Greenidge	b Chatfield	2	c Smith b Hadlee	16
D.L.Haynes	b Hadlee	0	c Horne b Chatfield	19
R.B.Richardson	c Crowe M.D. b Hadlee	37	c Crowe M.D. b Hadlee	19
H.A.Gomes	c Crowe J.J. b Chatfield	8	c Coney b Crowe M.D.	33
I.V.A.Richards*	c Smith b Chatfield	1	c Smith b Snedden	38
A.L.Logie	c Coney b Hadlee	6	c Crowe J.J. b Snedden	19
P.J.L.Dujon†	c Coney b Hadlee	6	c Crowe M.D. b Snedden	39
M.D.Marshall	c Snedden b Chatfield	2	b Hadlee	45
J.Garner	c Coney b Hadlee	0	c Wright b Snedden	11
A.H.Gray	not out	10	c Crowe M.D. b Snedden	3
C.A.Walsh	b Hadlee	14	not out	8
Extras	(lb 6, nb 8)	14	(b 2, lb 4, nb 8)	14
TOTAL	(36.3 overs)	**100**	(70.3 overs)	**264**

NEW ZEALAND

J.G.Wright	c Richards b Walsh	6	c Richards b Gray	2
P.A.Horne	c Richards b Garner	9	c Gray b Walsh	0
J.J.Crowe	c Dujon b Gray	55	c Gray b Walsh	2
M.D.Crowe	b Marshall	83	not out	9
D.N.Patel	c Dujon b Gray	0	c Richardson b Walsh	9
J.V.Coney*	run out	36	c Gray b Garner	2
J.G.Bracewell	c Haynes b Garner	66	not out	2
R.J.Hadlee	not out	25		
I.D.S.Smith	c Dujon b Garner	7		
M.C.Snedden	c Logie b Garner	7		
E.J.Chatfield	not out	1		
Extras	(b 6, lb 2, w 1, nb 28)	37	(nb 7)	7
TOTAL	(100.5 overs) (9 wkts dec)	**332**	(10.1 overs) (5 wkts)	**33**

Bowling	O	M	R	W	O	M	R	W
NEW ZEALAND								
Hadlee	12.3	2	50	6	23	2	101	3
Chatfield	18	8	30	4	16	3	42	1
Snedden	6	1	14	0	18.3	2	68	5
Bracewell					7	0	34	0
Crowe M.D.					6	0	13	1
WEST INDIES								
Marshall	27	2	75	1				
Garner	19	2	79	4	1	0	3	1
Walsh	24.5	3	78	1	5.1	0	16	3
Gray	17	4	47	2	4	1	14	1
Richards	9	3	29	0				
Gomes	4	1	16	0				

Fall of Wickets

	WI 1st	NZ 1st	WI 2nd	NZ 2nd
1st	2	12	37	1
2nd	6	23	37	3
3rd	44	179	80	13
4th	56	180	129	27
5th	56	181	133	30
6th	64	270	160	-
7th	67	294	237	-
8th	70	307	241	-
9th	75	330	255	-
10th	100	-	264	-

Martin Snedden claimed five wickets in a test innings for the first time. It was a testimony to the consistency of his line that all five dismissals went to catches behind the wicket, ranging from wicketkeeper to gully.

AVERAGES

New Zealand

BATTING	M	I	NO	Runs	HS	Ave
M.D. Crowe	3	6	1	328	119	65.60
J.G. Bracewell	3	6	2	163	66	40.75
J.G. Wright	3	6	0	239	138	39.83
R.J. Hadlee	3	4	2	74	35*	37.00
J.J. Crowe	3	6	1	143	55	28.60
I.D.S. Smith	3	4	1	57	40*	19.00
J.V. Coney	3	6	0	77	36	12.83
D.N. Patel	3	6	0	73	21	12.16
K.R. Rutherford	2	4	0	29	12	7.25
M.C. Snedden	1	1	0	7	7	7.00
P.A. Horne	1	2	0	9	9	4.50
E.J. Chatfield	3	4	2	5	4	2.50
S.L. Boock	2	3	0	7	4	2.33

BOWLING	O	M	R	W	Ave
M.C. Snedden	24.3	3	82	5	16.40
R.J. Hadlee	113.1	20	354	17	20.82
S.L. Boock	67	24	180	7	25.71
E.J. Chatfield	114.3	39	282	10	28.20
M.D. Crowe	14	2	35	1	35.00
J.G. Bracewell	45	9	147	1	147.00
J.V. Coney	14	2	30	0	-
D.N. Patel	9	0	51	0	-

West Indies

BATTING	M	I	NO	Runs	HS	Ave
C.G. Greenidge	3	6	1	344	213	68.80
P.J.L. Dujon	3	4	0	144	77	36.00
R.B. Richardson	3	5	1	134	41	33.50
D.L. Haynes	3	6	1	160	121	32.00
C.A. Walsh	3	3	2	23	14	23.00
M.D. Marshall	3	4	0	83	45	20.75
I.V.A. Richards	3	4	0	77	38	19.25
H.A. Gomes	3	5	1	72	33	18.00
A.L. Logie	3	4	0	62	34	15.50
A.H. Gray	2	3	1	21	10*	10.50
J. Garner	2	3	0	11	11	3.66
M.A. Holding	1	1	0	0	0	0.00
C.G. Butts	1	1	1	8	8*	-

BOWLING	O	M	R	W	Ave
J. Garner	77	16	205	12	17.08
A.H. Gray	49	10	150	8	18.75
C.A. Walsh	120.2	28	306	13	23.53
H.A. Gomes	30	8	63	2	31.50
M.D. Marshall	119	21	289	9	32.11
C.G. Butts	38	10	82	2	41.00
I.V.A. Richards	67	19	147	2	73.50
R.B. Richardson	4	1	4	0	-
M.A. Holding	37	8	99	0	-

1986/87 New Zealand in Sri Lanka

A late invitation to tour Sri Lanka in April and May was seen as an excellent opportunity to prepare a new wave of international players, as Bruce Edgar and Jeremy Coney had announced their retirements. John Wright was excused from going to Sri Lanka, so that he could organise his benefit at Derbyshire, and Stephen Boock was unavailable for business reasons. Jeff Crowe was appointed the 18th captain of New Zealand.

183 SRI LANKA v NEW ZEALAND (*First Test*)

at Colombo Cricket Club Ground on 16, 18, 19, 20, 21 April, 1987
Toss : New Zealand. Umpires : P.W. Vidanagamage and
W.A.U. Wickremasinghe
Match drawn

Unfortunately, the first test at Colombo was as exciting as watching men sleep. On a lifeless pitch 803 runs were scored in five days for the loss of only 15 wickets. The game became one for various milestones and records.

It was a game that saw the bat totally dominate the ball and both sides play in an ultra-defensive fashion.

MILESTONES

- Jeff Crowe became the 18th captain of New Zealand.

- Andrew Jones (163) made his test debut.

- Brendon Kuruppu became the first Sri Lankan to score a century on his test debut and only the third from any country to score a double century on test debut.

- Ewen Chatfield became the sixth New Zealand bowler to take 100 test wickets.

- Jeff Crowe and Evan Gray set a new fifth wicket partnership of 61 for New Zealand versus Sri Lanka.

- Jeff Crowe and Richard Hadlee set a New Zealand record for the sixth wicket against all countries with their unbroken partnership of 246.

- Jeff Crowe's century, scored in 516 minutes, was the third slowest in test cricket.

- Richard Hadlee scored the 100th test century for New Zealand.

Political events took their toll and caused the abandonment of New Zealand's second tour of Sri Lanka. Shortly after the completion of the test a bomb exploded at a bus depot in Colombo, one kilometre from the team's hotel, killing 150.

While the team had been in Sri Lanka there had been daily occurrences of terrorist activity. Previously it had been sporadic but it seemed that violence was spiralling as government troops fought the Tamil separatists.

The players expressed a wish to return home from the strife-ridden country and the tour was terminated with two tests and four one-day games unplayed.

SRI LANKA		
R.S.Mahanama	c Smith b Chatfield	16
D.S.B.P.Kuruppu†	not out	201
A.P.Gurusinha	lbw b Hadlee	22
R.L.Dias	c Bracewell b Hadlee	25
A.Ranatunga	c Smith b Bracewell	15
L.R.D.Mendis*	c Bracewell b Hadlee	12
R.S.Madugalle	c Hadlee b Gray	60
J.R.Ratnayeke	c Crowe M.D. b Bracewell	12
R.J.Ratnayeke	c Bracewell b Hadlee	17
S.D.Anurasiri	c Smith b Chatfield	1
A.K.Kuruppuarachchi	not out	0
Extras	(lb 4, w 1, nb 11)	16
TOTAL	**(173.5 overs) (9 wkts dec)**	**397**

NEW ZEALAND		
K.R.Rutherford	c Madugalle b Ratnayake	11
P.A.Horne	c Kuruppu b Anurasiri	16
A.H.Jones	lbw b Ratnayeke	38
M.D.Crowe	c Mendis b Ratnayeke	27
J.J.Crowe*	not out	120
E.J.Gray	c Ranatunga b Kuruppuarachchi	31
R.J.Hadlee	not out	151
J.G.Bracewell		
I.D.S.Smith†		
M.C.Snedden		
E.J.Chatfield		
Extras	(lb 2, w 4, nb 6)	12
TOTAL	**(163 overs) (5 wkts)**	**406**

Bowling	O	M	R	W
NEW ZEALAND				
Hadlee	38.5	10	102	4
Chatfield	38	11	104	2
Crowe M.D.	7	4	13	0
Snedden	16	4	41	0
Bracewell	47	14	98	2
Gray	27	12	35	1
SRI LANKA				
Ratnayake	32	7	79	1
Kuruppuarachchi	20	3	64	1
Ranatunga	23	10	43	0
Ratnayeke	37	6	111	2
Anurasiri	36	13	67	1
Gurusinha	9	1	17	0
Madugalle	2	0	6	0
Dias	4	0	17	0

Fall of Wickets		
	SL	NZ
	1st	1st
1st	29	20
2nd	70	51
3rd	129	90
4th	166	99
5th	210	160
6th	319	-
7th	342	-
8th	382	-
9th	383	-
10th	-	-

Jeff Crowe scored a century in his first test as captain. On a lifeless pitch he battled for 516 minutes to score the third-slowest test century.

1987/88 New Zealand in Australia

One month after Australia had won the World Cup in India the majority of those players were selected for the first test. A storm over the ground, three nights prior to the test, created major problems for the groundsman and the pitch was still damp when Allan Border won the toss and invited the visitors to bat under a heavy cloud cover.

184   AUSTRALIA v NEW ZEALAND *(First Test)*

at Brisbane Cricket Ground on 4, 5, 6, 7 December, 1987
Toss : Australia. Umpires : A.R. Crafter and M.W. Johnson
Australia won by 9 wickets

There was considerable movement and disconcerting bounce for the bowlers. New Zealand was fortunate that the bowlers were all wayward with their direction, otherwise their total of 181-9 at stumps would have been considerably less.

John Wright stuck to the grim task of survival for 172 minutes, while Martin Crowe accumulated his runs with style. His dismissal opened the floodgates for a disastrous last session in which six wickets fell for the addition of only 48 runs.

Danny Morrison showed the nervousness that one would expect in a young fast bowler playing in his first test match and his first three overs cost 15 runs. Conditions still favoured the bowlers and the Australian openers, Geoff Marsh and David Boon, did well in compiling 65 for the first wicket. Four wickets were down at 131 before Steve Waugh joined Boon to add 88 and give Australia a healthy advantage.

The value of Boon's innings could not be overrated as he alone looked capable of coping with the New Zealand attack and he reached his century in 249 minutes. Morrison, coming back with the old ball, bowled impressively to restrict Australia's lead to only 33 and have them six wickets down.

A tenacious innings, lasting 151 minutes, by Peter Sleep saw Australia work their way through to a lead of 119 runs. A close look at the scoreboard shows how much Australia were indebted to Boon's wonderful innings. Even the most cynical Australian critics waxed eloquently about Morrison's test debut of four wickets.

Batting a second time New Zealand wickets tumbled regularly but Andrew Jones struggled with grim determination to survive. Survive he did, scoring 45 runs in 141 minutes against a much-improved bowling attack. At stumps, with their score at 131-5 and two days remaining, it appeared as though the only thing that could save New Zealand was a tropical storm.

Three wickets fell quickly at the beginning of the fourth day and, when Morrison came to the crease, Dipak Patel decided to go for his shots . Silky cuts, authoritative drives and exciting hook shots raced to the boundary in the next hour as 52 runs were added for the ninth wicket.

Australia had one day and two sessions in which to score the necessary 94 needed for victory. This was achieved for the loss of Boon's wicket and Australia coasted to victory by nine wickets.

NEW ZEALAND

K.R.Rutherford	c Veletta b Reid	0	c Dyer b McDermott		2
J.G.Wright	c Dyer b Hughes	38	lbw b Reid		15
A.H.Jones	b McDermott	4	c Border b Reid		45
M.D.Crowe	c Waugh b Hughes	67	c Jones b Hughes		23
J.J.Crowe*	lbw b Waugh	16	lbw b Reid		12
D.N.Patel	c Dyer b McDermott	17	c Dyer b Hughes		62
R.J.Hadlee	c Boon b Hughes	8	c Marsh b McDermott		24
J.G.Bracewell	c Veletta b McDermott	11	c Dyer b McDermott		0
I.D.S.Smith†	lbw b Reid	2	c Veletta b Reid		9
D.K.Morrison	c Waugh b McDermott	0	c Dyer b Waugh		2
E.J.Chatfield	not out	0	not out		1
Extras	(b 1, lb 7, w 4, nb 11)	23	(b 6, lb 1, w 1, nb 9)		17
TOTAL	(93.2 overs)	**186**	(79 overs)		**212**

AUSTRALIA

G.R.Marsh	c Bracewell b Hadlee	25	not out	31
D.C.Boon	run out	143	lbw b Bracewell	24
D.M.Jones	b Hadlee	2	not out	38
A.R.Border*	lbw b Morrison	9		
M.R.J.Veletta	c Rutherford b Bracewell	4		
S.R.Waugh	c Jones b Morrison	21		
P.R.Sleep	c & b Bracewell	39		
G.C.Dyer†	lbw b Hadlee	8		
C.J.McDermott	c Wright b Morrison	22		
M.G.Hughes	c Smith b Morrison	5		
B.A.Reid	not out	8		
Extras	(b 3, lb 5, w 2, nb 9)	19	(lb 1, w 1, nb 2)	4
TOTAL	(117.5 overs)	**305**	(32.1 overs) (1 wkt)	**97**

Bowling AUSTRALIA	O	M	R	W	O	M	R	W
Reid	25	10	40	2	25	6	53	4
McDermott	22.2	6	43	4	21	2	79	3
Hughes	18	5	40	3	17	7	57	2
Waugh	22	9	35	1	2	1	2	1
Sleep	6	1	20	0	14	5	14	0
NEW ZEALAND								
Hadlee	31	5	95	3	8	3	14	0
Morrison	28	7	86	4	8	0	32	0
Chatfield	34	11	58	0				
Bracewell	24.5	3	58	2	13	3	32	1
Patel					3.1	0	18	0

Fall of Wickets	NZ 1st	A 1st	NZ 2nd	A 2nd
1st	0	65	18	37
2nd	28	72	20	-
3rd	80	110	66	-
4th	133	131	103	-
5th	143	219	104	-
6th	153	219	142	-
7th	175	250	142	-
8th	180	286	152	-
9th	181	291	204	-
10th	186	305	212	-

MILESTONES

• Danny Morrison (164) made his test debut.

Dipak Patel arrived at the crease at 103-4 with New Zealand facing certain defeat. He unleashed a succession of flowing shots as he made 62. This begged the question as to why his best score in his previous six test innings was only 21.

185 AUSTRALIA v NEW ZEALAND *(Second Test)*

at Adelaide Oval on 11, 12, 13, 14, 15 December, 1987
Toss : New Zealand. Umpires : R.C. Bailhache and S.G. Randell
Match drawn

The day began badly for New Zealand when Jeff Crowe, promoting himself to the role of opener, was dismissed third ball. For the next 198 minutes a grim John Wright and an effervescent Andrew Jones defied the Australian attack. Australia's main strike bowler, Bruce Reid, damaged a muscle in his lower back and, after visiting Adelaide Hospital for X-rays, was destined not to play again for the season.

Wright was lifting the tempo, cutting and pulling Tim May's right-arm off-spinners to the boundary before he was dismissed when the partnership had added 128. Martin Crowe arrived at the crease determined to dominate the Australian slow bowlers and in next to no time had hit three fours and one gigantic six.

There was a touch of nervousness as Jones got close to his century and he could easily have been run out when on 98. A rousing pull shot through mid-wicket, off Craig McDermott, gave him his first test century in his third test. At stumps Jones was 128 and Crowe 88 in the total of 268-2.

Runs came at a fast pace as Crowe, recording his eighth test hundred, and Jones continued as they had left off the previous day. They were both out within five runs after their partnership had added 213.

At 346-4 the innings became becalmed. In the remaining 243 minutes only a further 145 were added even though the temperatures were in the mid-30s and the Australian attack was limited by the absence of Reid. Strangely enough, after each partnership was broken two wickets fell very quickly.

Allan Border was the cornerstone of Australia's reply though he was fortunate to survive a stumping chance off Evan Gray on 57 when a ball spun sharply out of the footmarks and beat Ian Smith. Nine runs later Jeff Crowe took what appeared to be an outstanding catch off Border but asked him to continue batting as the ball had hit the ground. Indeed a noble act of sportsmanship.

At day's end Border had reached his 22nd test hundred and Australia were still 60 runs short of avoiding the follow-on with six wickets remaining.

The fourth day belonged to the strong-willed Border as he went on relentlessly to his first test double-century in 596 minutes. Assisted by Peter Sleep and Greg Dyer, who both scored half-centuries, Australia gained a lead of nine runs. John Bracewell and Gray both bowled with great accuracy and Richard Hadlee was his inimitable excellent self.

They were splendidly supported by the fieldsmen, who made Australia struggle for every run in temperatures averaging over 40°C. The final day was occupied by New Zealand batting, with neither side having a chance to push for victory.

NEW ZEALAND

J.J.Crowe*	c Veletta b Reid	0	c Boon b May		19
J.G.Wright	c Waugh b May	45	b McDermott		8
A.H.Jones	run out	150	c Border b Sleep		64
M.D.Crowe	c sub (M.G.Hughes) b Sleep	137	c Border b Sleep		8
D.N.Patel	c Marsh b McDermott	35	c Boon b May		40
E.J.Gray	c Boon b McDermott	23	c Border b May		14
R.J.Hadlee	c & b Jones	36	(9) not out		3
J.G.Bracewell	c Sleep b McDermott	32			
I.D.S.Smith†	not out	8	(8) c Dyer b Sleep		5
M.C.Snedden	c Veletta b McDermott	0	(7) not out		8
D.K.Morrison					
Extras	(b 3, lb 7, w 1, nb 8)	19	(b 2, lb 4, nb 7)		13
TOTAL	(174.5 overs) (9 wkts dec)	485	(85 overs) (7 wkts)		182

AUSTRALIA

G.R.Marsh	c Gray b Hadlee	30
D.C.Boon	b Hadlee	6
D.M.Jones	c Smith b Hadlee	0
A.R.Border*	st Smith b Bracewell	205
S.R.Waugh	lbw b Snedden	61
P.R.Sleep	c Smith b Morrison	62
M.R.J.Veletta	c sub (K.R.Rutherford) b Bracewell	10
G.C.Dyer†	run out	60
C.J.McDermott	lbw b Hadlee	18
T.B.A.May	not out	14
B.A.Reid	c Smith b Hadlee	5
Extras	(b 2, lb 13, w 1, nb 9)	25
TOTAL	(195 overs)	496

Bowling AUSTRALIA	O	M	R	W	O	M	R	W
Reid	7	0	21	1				
McDermott	45.5	10	135	4	10	3	29	1
Waugh	31	11	71	0	10	4	17	0
May	54	13	134	1	30	10	68	3
Sleep	34	5	109	1	32	14	61	3
Jones	3	1	5	1	3	2	1	0
NEW ZEALAND								
Hadlee	42	16	68	5				
Morrison	22	0	89	1				
Bracewell	48	8	122	2				
Snedden	32	6	89	1				
Gray	44	10	102	0				
Patel	7	3	11	0				

Fall of Wickets

	NZ	A	NZ
	1st	1st	2nd
1st	0	29	16
2nd	128	29	57
3rd	341	85	77
4th	346	201	139
5th	398	355	153
6th	405	380	170
7th	473	417	179
8th	481	451	-
9th	485	489	-
10th	-	496	-

Andrew Jones took great delight in scoring 150 at Adelaide after the Australian media had been harshly critical of his batting ability in the previous test. He let the reporters know what he thought of their judgement when he walked off the field at the end of the first day.

MILESTONES

- Martin Crowe scored his eighth test century, a New Zealand record.

- John Wright and Andrew Jones created a record second wicket partnership of 128 for New Zealand against Australia.

- Allan Border became Australia's greatest run-scorer in test cricket, passing Greg Chappell's 7110.

- Andrew Jones became the ninth New Zealander to score a century and a fifty in a test match.

186 AUSTRALIA v NEW ZEALAND *(Third Test)*

at Melbourne Cricket Ground on 26, 27, 28, 29, 30 December, 1987
Toss : Australia.   Umpires : A.R. Crafter and R.A. French
Match drawn

A massive crowd of 51,087 assured a lively Boxing Day in Melbourne. Many in the crowd amused themselves with things other than cricket.

John Wright and Andrew Jones had added 87 before Jones was given out, having made 40, in most controversial circumstances when he turned Craig McDermott fine on the leg side and Greg Dyer dived far to his left to catch the ball, rolled twice and sat on the ground with the ball now in his right hand.

The decision to give him out created a brouhaha and became media headlines for the remainder of the test. Wright was dismissed for 99 after 310 minutes of diligent batting. Martin Crowe played in an imperial manner to be 76 not out with his side 242-5.

The early dismissal of Crowe and the failure of the remaining batsmen, with the exception of Ian Smith who batted gaily in scoring 44, saw New Zealand dismissed for 317. Australia had lost half its wickets for 170 at stumps.

Steve Waugh, overnight not out on 55, was dismissed second ball of the third day to raise New Zealand's hopes. Peter Sleep, who in the previous two tests had featured in vital partnerships, became the mainstay of the innings, forming a series of vital partnerships with the lower-order batsmen as he compiled 90. Tony Dodemaide's fifty was a fine debut innings and ensured that Australia led by 40.

New Zealand sought quick runs throughout the fourth day and the first seven batsmen scored in excess of 20. With the score at 272-5 the innings disintegrated before the medium pace bowling of Dodemaide and the last four wickets fell in the final 40 minutes for 13 runs. The Australian media thought that a lead of 245, with nine wickets down, was insufficient to stop Australia winning easily.

Dodemaide claimed his sixth wicket at the beginning of the fifth day. At tea, Australia needed 100 runs with seven wickets in hand and 40 overs left. The immediate loss of Border and a splendid spell from John Bracewell, which saw him tie down the Australian batsmen, gave the visitors hope.

The final hour, and 20 overs, began with Australia requiring just 41 runs for victory and New Zealand needing five wickets. The crowd of 24,000, which brought the aggregate

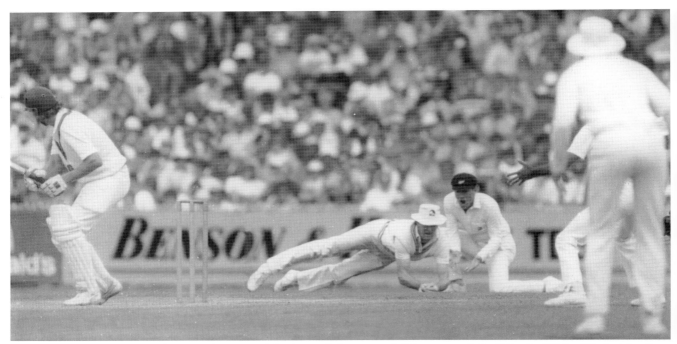

Australia lose their first wicket in their second innings as John Bracewell dives across Jeff Crowe to catch Geoff Marsh off Richard Hadlee's bowling.

crowd to over 127,000 for the five days, was totally involved in the dramatic events that took place.

Three wickets, Sleep, Dyer and Dodemaide fell to Richard Hadlee, and Bracewell captured Mike Veletta. With 30 balls remaining and the last pair, Craig McDermott and Mike Whitney, at the crease, the Australians were intent on saving the game.

Each ball was bowled in deathly silence and the crowd cheered the result. Danny Morrison twice had lbw decisions against McDermott rejected. The draw gave Australia its first series win since 1984, and the first in Border's time as captain.

NEW ZEALAND

P.A.Horne	c Dyer b Dodemaide	7	c Boon b Dodemaide	27
J.G.Wright	c Dyer b McDermott	99	b Sleep	43
A.H.Jones	c Dyer b McDermott	40	run out	20
M.D.Crowe	c Veletta b McDermott	82	c Border b Dodemaide	79
J.J.Crowe*	lbw b McDermott	6	c Boon b Sleep	25
D.N.Patel	b McDermott	0	c Dyer b Dodemaide	38
J.G.Bracewell	c Dyer b Whitney	9	(8) c Veletta b Dodemaide	1
R.J.Hadlee	c Dodemaide b Whitney	11	(7) lbw b Sleep	29
I.D.S.Smith†	c Jones b Whitney	44	c Dyer b Dodemaide	12
D.K.Morrison	c Border b Whitney	0	b Dodemaide	0
E.J.Chatfield	not out	6	not out	1
Extras	(b 1, lb 4, nb 8)	13	(b 2, lb 8, nb 1)	11
TOTAL	(110.3 overs)	**317**	(92.3 overs)	**286**

AUSTRALIA

D.C.Boon	lbw b Hadlee	10	c Crowe M.D. b Morrison	54
G.R.Marsh	c sub (K.R.Rutherford) b Hadlee	13	c Bracewell b Hadlee	23
D.M.Jones	c Smith b Hadlee	4	c Crowe M.D. b Chatfield	8
A.R.Border*	c Crowe J.J. b Bracewell	31	lbw b Hadlee	43
M.R.J.Veletta	lbw b Hadlee	31	c Patel b Bracewell	39
S.R.Waugh	c Jones b Bracewell	55	c Patel b Chatfield	10
P.R.Sleep	lbw b Hadlee	90	lbw b Hadlee	20
G.C.Dyer†	run out	21	c Smith b Hadlee	4
A.I.C.Dodemaide	c Smith b Morrison	50	lbw b Hadlee	3
C.J.McDermott	b Morrison	33	not out	10
M.R.Whitney	not out	0	not out	2
Extras	(lb 8, nb 11)	19	(b 1, lb 9, nb 4)	14
TOTAL	(145.4 overs)	**357**	(92 overs) (9 wkts)	**230**

Bowling	O	M	R	W	O	M	R	W					
AUSTRALIA									**Fall of Wickets**				
										NZ	A	NZ	A
										1st	*1st*	*2nd*	*2nd*
McDermott	35	8	97	5	10	1	43	0	1st	32	24	73	45
Whitney	33.3	6	92	4	20	5	45	0	2nd	119	30	76	59
Dodemaide	20	4	48	1	28.3	10	58	6	3rd	187	31	158	103
Waugh	10	1	44	0					4th	221	78	178	147
Sleep	12	1	31	0	26	5	107	3	5th	223	121	220	176
Jones					8	3	23	0	6th	254	170	272	209
NEW ZEALAND									7th	254	213	272	209
Hadlee	44	11	109	5	31	9	67	5	8th	280	293	281	216
Morrison	27.4	5	93	2	16	2	54	1	9th	294	354	285	227
Chatfield	30	10	55	0	21	6	41	2	10th	317	357	286	-
Bracewell	32	8	69	2	24	5	58	1					
Patel	12	6	23	0									

MILESTONES

- John Wright became the third New Zealand batsman to pass 3000 runs in test cricket.

- Martin Crowe became the seventh batsman to score 4000 first-class runs in a calendar year.

- Allan Border took his 100th test catch.

- Richard Hadlee became the first bowler to take 10 wickets in a test eight times.

- Tony Dodemaide became the first Australian in 93 years to take five wickets and score a half-century on test debut.

AVERAGES

New Zealand

BATTING	M	I	NO	Runs	HS	Ave
M.D. Crowe	3	6	0	396	137	66.00
A.H. Jones	3	6	0	323	150	53.83
J.G. Wright	3	6	0	248	99	41.33
D.N. Patel	3	6	0	192	62	32.00
R.J. Hadlee	3	6	1	111	36	22.20
E.J. Gray	1	2	0	37	23	18.50
P.A. Horne	1	2	0	34	27	17.00
I.D.S. Smith	3	6	1	80	44	16.00
J.J. Crowe	3	6	0	78	25	13.00
J.G. Bracewell	3	5	0	53	32	10.60
M.C. Snedden	1	2	1	8	8*	8.00
K.R. Rutherford	1	2	0	2	2	1.00
D.K. Morrison	3	4	0	2	2	0.50
E.J. Chatfield	2	4	4	8	6*	-

BOWLING	O	M	R	W	Ave
R.J. Hadlee	156	44	353	18	19.61
J.G. Bracewell	141.5	27	339	8	42.37
D.K. Morrison	101.4	14	354	8	44.25
E.J. Chatfield	85	27	154	2	77.00
M.C. Snedden	32	6	89	1	89.00
D.N. Patel	22.1	9	52	0	-
E.J. Gray	44	10	102	0	-

Australia

BATTING	M	I	NO	Runs	HS	Ave
A.R. Border	3	4	0	288	205	72.00
P.R. Sleep	3	4	0	211	90	52.75
D.C. Boon	3	5	0	237	143	47.40
S.R. Waugh	3	4	0	147	61	36.75
G.R. Marsh	3	5	1	122	31*	30.50
C.J. McDermott	3	4	1	83	33	27.66
A.I.C. Dodemaide	1	2	0	53	50	26.50
G.C. Dyer	3	4	0	93	60	23.25
M.R.J. Veletta	3	4	0	84	39	21.00
D.M. Jones	3	5	1	52	38*	13.00
B.A. Reid	2	2	1	13	8*	13.00
M.G. Hughes	1	1	0	5	5	5.00
T.B.A. May	1	1	1	14	14*	-
M.R. Whitney	1	2	2	2	2*	-

BOWLING	O	M	R	W	Ave
A.I.C. Dodemaide	48.3	14	106	7	15.14
B.A. Reid	57	16	114	7	16.28
M.G. Hughes	35	12	97	5	19.40
C.J. McDermott	144.1	30	426	17	25.05
D.M. Jones	14	6	29	1	29.00
M.R. Whitney	53.3	11	137	4	34.25
P.R. Sleep	124	31	342	7	48.85
T.B.A. May	84	23	202	4	50.50
S.R. Waugh	75	26	169	2	84.50

1987/88 England in New Zealand

After two games in New Zealand, England travelled to Australia for two bicentenary games before returning for the tests in New Zealand. Spectator interest was not as high as in past tours and this could be attributed to the weather and the slow cricket played in the tests.

187 NEW ZEALAND v ENGLAND *(First Test)*

at Lancaster Park, Christchurch on 12, 13, 14, 16, 17 February, 1988
Toss : New Zealand. Umpires : B.L. Aldridge and S.J. Woodward
Match drawn

Jeff Crowe had no hesitation in sending England in to bat after he won the toss. Richard Hadlee was on the verge of becoming the world's leading wicket-taker in test cricket and the conditions appeared to be tailor-made for him. It was ironic that two team mates at Nottingham, Chris Broad and Tim Robinson, played England into a solid position after the early loss of a wicket.

Prior to the tea interval Hadlee pulled a calf muscle that prevented him from bowling again for the rest of the season. Broad reached his fourth test century in 283 minutes and, together with Robinson, who made 70, they added 168 for the second wicket as England ended the first day at 235-4.

With the exception of some distinctive batting from John Emburey England capitulated to fine seam bowling by Ewen Chatfield and Danny Morrison, who restricted England to 319. Graham Dilley found conditions favourable and generated pace and made the ball lift disconcertingly to take the first four New Zealand wickets with the score at 40.

New Zealand began the third day at 83-4 with the objective of getting past the follow-on figure of 120. Hadlee, who had Martin Crowe as his runner, assisted Jeff Crowe in achieving this goal and was the last player to be dismissed, for 37, as the tailenders put up little resistance. Dilley finished with the impressive figures of 6-38 off 24.5 overs.

England made a slow start to its second innings. Once again, bad light cut play short when England had reached 55-2. Throughout the day runs had been at a premium as the pitch continued to make strokeplay difficult. With two days left to play England had a lead of 206 and, with eight wickets in hand, were in a strong position.

Inclement weather prevented any play before 4 pm and, before the score reached 100, England had lost four more wickets to the excellent bowling of Chatfield and Martin Snedden.

Chatfield had to leave the field with a leg strain, having bowled 72 overs in the match, conceding only 123 runs and capturing eight wickets. Snedden also claimed wickets and England's second innings finished at 152.

Weather again prevented play starting on time on a pitch that was becoming more cantankerous and soon New Zealand lost its fourth wicket at 78. Andrew Jones showed that his success in Australia had been no fluke as he and John Bracewell batted with considerable character to salvage a draw. After the game it was discovered that Jones had batted with a broken bone in his wrist.

ENGLAND					
B.C.Broad	c Smith b Snedden	114	c sub (M.J.Greatbatch) b Chatfield	20
M.D.Moxon	c Jones b Morrison	1	c Jones b Chatfield	27
R.T.Robinson	c Smith b Morrison	70	c Wright b Chatfield	2
M.W.Gatting*	c sub (M.J.Greatbatch) b Morrison	8	b Snedden	23
C.W.J.Athey	c sub (M.J.Greatbatch) b Morrison	22	c Smith b Snedden	19
D.J.Capel	c Bracewell b Chatfield	11	c Crowe M.D. b Chatfield	0
J.E.Emburey	c Jones b Morrison	42	run out	19
B.N.French†	c Smith b Chatfield	7	c Crowe J.J. b Snedden	3
P.A.J.DeFreitas	c Morrison b Chatfield	4	lbw b Snedden	16
P.W.Jarvis	c Smith b Chatfield	14	not out	10
G.R.Dilley	not out	7	c Jones b Morrison	2
Extras	(lb 11, w 1, nb 7)	19	(lb 7, nb 4)	11
TOTAL	(120.1 overs)	319	(74.1 overs)	152

NEW ZEALAND					
J.G.Wright	c Moxon b Dilley	10	lbw b Dilley	23
T.J.Franklin	c Athey b Dilley	10	lbw b Dilley	12
A.H.Jones	c French b Dilley	8	not out	54
M.D.Crowe	c Moxon b Dilley	5	c French b Jarvis	6
J.J.Crowe*	c French b DeFreitas	28	lbw b DeFreitas	0
J.G.Bracewell	c French b Dilley	31	not out	20
R.J.Hadlee	c French b Dilley	37		
I.D.S.Smith†	c Capel b Jarvis	13		
M.C.Snedden	lbw b DeFreitas	0		
D.K.Morrison	b Jarvis	0		
E.J.Chatfield	not out	0		
Extras	(b 2, lb 12, nb 12)	26	(b 6, lb 4, nb 5)	15
TOTAL	(81.5 overs)	168	(77 overs) (4 wkts)	130

Bowling NEW ZEALAND	O	M	R	W	O	M	R	W
Hadlee	18	3	50	0				
Morrison	21.1	3	69	5	21.1	4	64	1
Chatfield	42	13	87	4	30	13	36	4
Snedden	33	9	86	1	23	8	45	4
Bracewell	6	1	16	0				
ENGLAND								
DeFreitas	22	6	39	2	19	6	26	1
Dilley	24.5	10	38	6	18	5	32	2
Capel	10	2	32	0	13	5	16	0
Jarvis	21	8	43	2	17	7	30	1
Emburey	4	3	2	0	10	4	16	0

Fall of Wickets	E	NZ	E	NZ
	1st	1st	2nd	2nd
1st	7	20	32	37
2nd	175	25	38	43
3rd	186	32	55	61
4th	219	40	95	78
5th	237	96	96	-
6th	241	131	99	-
7th	248	151	118	-
8th	260	155	125	-
9th	285	156	147	-
10th	319	168	152	-

The New Zealand team that played England in Christchurch. Back row (from left): Dave Elder (manager), Martin Snedden, Andrew Jones, Trevor Franklin, Mark Greatbatch (12th man), Danny Morrison. Front row: Ian Smith, Martin Crowe, John Wright, Jeff Crowe (captain), Richard Hadlee, Ewen Chatfield, John Bracewell.

MILESTONES

- Andrew Jones equalled the New Zealand record of four catches in a match.

- Mark Greatbatch took three catches as a substitute fieldsman.

188 NEW ZEALAND v ENGLAND *(Second Test)*

at Eden Park, Auckland on 25, 26, 27, 28, 29 February, 1988
Toss : England. Umpires : F.R. Goodall and R. L. McHarg
Match drawn

Auckland's capricious weather seemed to point in the direction of assistance for anyone capable of swinging the ball and so it proved no surprise when Mike Gatting invited the home team to bat.

Off the first ball of the match, John Wright bisected wicketkeeper and first slip at catchable height and at 12 he was dropped at third slip. Together with Trevor Franklin 77 was scored before Franklin was dismissed. During the afternoon Wright became more dominant, quick to seize on the short ball, either through mid-wicket or backward of point.

In two hours batting with Martin Crowe 71 were added for the third wicket. Wright's seventh test century was reached in 326 minutes as New Zealand progressed to 186-3, on a day dotted with frustrating stoppages for showers.

Wright's resolute innings was terminated off the first ball of the second day and triggered a disappointing slump as New Zealand lost 5-77 in the morning session. The tail wagged sufficiently to take New Zealand to 301, with Graham Dilley finishing with five wickets for the fifth time in his last six tests. England, led by Martyn Moxon, was untroubled to reach 97 for the loss of one.

England pressed on with Moxon and Tim Robinson producing a second wicket stand of 108. The arrival of Gatting at the crease heralded the most aggressive batting of the test so far and 76 runs were added in 110 minutes. Moxon became bogged down in the nervous nineties, when the new ball was introduced, and was eventually caught by Jeff Crowe off Ewen Chatfield for 99.

The New Zealand pace attack used the new ball to great effect, claiming five further wickets before stumps for the addition of 91 runs. Only John Emburey prevented England from collapsing for less than 300. With a lead of one run and with only two wickets in hand England had once again let New Zealand off the hook. Chatfield claimed the remaining two wickets at the start of the fourth day to finish with the astonishing figures of four for 37 off 31.1 overs.

There was an encouraging start to New Zealand's second innings as Franklin began in a positive frame of mind and, together with Wright, added 117 for the opening stand. When

Franklin was dismissed for 62 there was a worrying collapse as New Zealand lost five wickets for 37 runs and were teetering on the edge of defeat.

Mark Greatbatch, playing in his first test, and Martin Snedden, the night watchman, were both prepared to sell their wickets dearly. They were still together at lunch and the England team were becoming most frustrated. By batting 162 minutes Snedden had performed his task admirably, as did John Bracewell and Ian Smith, who followed him. Greatbatch scored a match-saving century.

With New Zealand teetering on the edge of defeat at 153-5, Mark Greatbatch was assisted by Martin Snedden, John Bracewell and Ian Smith to almost double the score and save the game. Greatbatch became the fourth New Zealander to score a century on debut. All four were left-handed batsmen.

MILESTONES

- Mark Greatbatch (165) made his test debut and became the fourth New Zealander to score a hundred on debut.

- Ian Smith became the first New Zealand wicketkeeper to pass 1000 runs in test cricket and make 100 dismissals.

NEW ZEALAND

Batsman	Dismissal (1st)	Score	Dismissal (2nd)	Score
J.G.Wright	c French b Dilley	103	c French b Radford	49
T.J.Franklin	b Jarvis	27	b Dilley	62
J.J.Crowe*	c Capel b Dilley	11	lbw b Dilley	1
M.D.Crowe	c Capel b Emburey	36	lbw b Jarvis	26
M.J.Greatbatch	c French b Dilley	11	not out	107
K.R.Rutherford	b Capel	29	b Emburey	2
J.G.Bracewell	c Moxon b Dilley	9	(8) lbw b Gatting	38
I.D.S.Smith†	c French b Jarvis	23	(9) not out	23
M.C.Snedden	c Moxon b Dilley	14	(7) c French b Capel	20
D.K.Morrison	not out	14		
E.J.Chatfield	c French b Capel	10		
Extras	(b 1, lb 2, w 2, nb 9)	14	(b 8, lb 8, nb 6)	22
TOTAL	(134.2 overs)	**301**	(169 overs) (7 wkts dec)	**350**

ENGLAND

Batsman	Dismissal	Score
B.C.Broad	c Crowe M.D. b Bracewell	9
M.D.Moxon	c Crowe J.J. b Chatfield	99
R.T.Robinson	c Morrison b Bracewell	54
M.W.Gatting*	c Smith b Morrison	42
N.H.Fairbrother	c Smith b Chatfield	1
D.J.Capel	c Bracewell b Morrison	5
J.E.Emburey	c Smith b Chatfield	45
B.N.French†	c Franklin b Bracewell	13
P.W.Jarvis	c Smith b Snedden	10
N.V.Radford	b Chatfield	8
G.R.Dilley	not out	8
Extras	(b 12, lb 12, nb 5)	29
TOTAL	(141.1 overs)	**323**

Bowling	O	M	R	W	O	M	R	W		Fall of Wickets		
ENGLAND										NZ	E	NZ
										1st	1st	2nd
Dilley	28	9	60	5	23	9	44	2				
Jarvis	33	9	74	2	27	8	54	1	1st	77	27	117
Radford	30	4	79	0	20	3	53	1	2nd	98	135	119
Capel	26.2	4	57	2	21	5	40	1	3rd	169	211	119
Emburey	17	7	28	1	57	23	91	1	4th	191	220	150
Gatting					17	4	40	1	5th	207	222	153
Fairbrother					2	0	9	0	6th	219	234	232
Moxon					2	0	3	0	7th	254	267	296
NEW ZEALAND									8th	262	282	-
Morrison	32	7	95	2					9th	279	308	-
Chatfield	31.1	15	37	4					10th	301	323	-
Bracewell	39	8	88	3								
Snedden	34	14	71	1								
Rutherford	5	1	8	0								

189 NEW ZEALAND v ENGLAND *(Third Test)*

at Basin Reserve, Wellington on 3, 4, 5, 6, 7 March 1988
Toss : New Zealand. Umpires : B.L. Aldridge and S.J. Woodward
Match drawn

At the completion of the second test it was announced that John Wright would replace Jeff Crowe as captain. Throughout the long summer in Australia and New Zealand Crowe had struggled to justify his position as a batsman. In five tests he had scored only 118 runs in 10 completed innings.

During the season the Basin Reserve had lacked pace and bounce and it was deemed necessary to play two slow bowlers. With six specialist batsmen and four specialist bowlers New Zealand was delighted when John Wright won his first toss as test captain and decided to bat.

From the outset the scoring rate was pedestrian and the innings had been in progress 189 minutes before Wright was out for 36 and the total was 79. Robert Vance and Martin Crowe combated the accurate Phil DeFreitas and the spin of Eddie Hemmings and John Emburey before Vance was run out, failing to respond to a call for a third run.

Graham Dilley struggled throughout the day with niggly injuries, leaving the field for long spells. The hero of the second test, Mark Greatbatch, joined Crowe and they added 60 before stumps. New Zealand 192-3.

Crowe and Greatbatch were untroubled on the docile pitch

as they added 155 for the fourth wicket. Coming as it did, on top of a debut century at Eden Park, Greatbatch confirmed his easy adjustment to the extra demands of test match play. Crowe completed his ninth test century off 254 balls before Mike Gatting captured his wicket on the stroke of afternoon tea for 143.

Ken Rutherford and John Bracewell began their partnership cautiously but in the last session 110 were added as New Zealand batted England out of any chance of victory. Gatting was overheard to say to his team as they took the field on the third day, "I wonder if they intend batting for five days?"

The partnership between Rutherford and Bracewell continued at a steady pace, with Bracewell making 54 and Rutherford completing his first test century in 228 minutes. Knowing that a declaration was intended Ian Smith literally smashed 33 runs off 19 balls. New Zealand declared at 512 -6 at lunch on the third day.

Chris Broad and Martyn Moxon batted effortlessly for three hours until Stephen Boock induced a false stroke from Broad to bowl him for 61. Gatting joined Moxon after Ewen

Dwarfed by the scoreboard that records the joyous tale, Ken Rutherford returns undefeated with his first test century "up in lights".

Chatfield quickly disposed of Tim Robinson. Together they added 51 before stumps were drawn, leaving England 183-2.

After three days of splendid conditions and reasonable crowds the weather went sour as Cyclone Bola caused extensive flooding and wiped out the final two days of play.

NEW ZEALAND

J.G.Wright*	c Fairbrother b Capel	36
T.J.Franklin	lbw b DeFreitas	14
R.H.Vance	run out	47
M.D.Crowe	lbw b Gatting	143
M.J.Greatbatch	c DeFreitas b Emburey	68
K.R.Rutherford	not out	107
J.G.Bracewell	c Fairbrother b Capel	54
I.D.S.Smith†	not out	33
D.K.Morrison		
S.L.Boock		
E.J.Chatfield		
Extras	(lb 10)	10
TOTAL	**(197 overs) (6 wkts dec)**	**512**

ENGLAND

B.C.Broad	b Boock	61
M.D.Moxon	not out	81
R.T.Robinson	c Smith b Chatfield	0
M.W.Gatting*	not out	33
N.H.Fairbrother		
D.J.Capel		
J.E.Emburey		
B.N.French†		
P.A.J.DeFreitas		
E.E.Hemmings		
G.R.Dilley		
Extras	(lb 6, nb 2)	8
TOTAL	**(79 overs) (2 wkts)**	**183**

Bowling	O	M	R	W
ENGLAND				
Dilley	11	1	36	0
DeFreitas	50.1	21	110	1
Capel	39	7	129	2
Emburey	45.5	10	99	1
Hemmings	45	15	107	0
Gatting	6	1	21	1
NEW ZEALAND				
Morrison	6	0	41	0
Chatfield	23	10	38	1
Bracewell	23	9	44	0
Boock	26	9	53	1
Rutherford	1	0	1	0

Fall of Wickets	NZ 1st	E 1st
1st	33	129
2nd	70	132
3rd	132	-
4th	287	-
5th	336	-
6th	470	-
7th	-	-
8th	-	-
9th	-	-
10th	-	-

MILESTONES

- John Wright became New Zealand's 19th test captain.

- Robert Vance (166) made his test debut.

- Martin Crowe and Mark Greatbatch established a new fourth wicket record of 155 runs for New Zealand against England.

- Ken Rutherford and John Bracewell established a new sixth wicket record of 134 for New Zealand against England.

- John Wright passed 20,000 runs in first-class cricket.

AVERAGES

New Zealand

BATTING	M	I	NO	Runs	HS	Ave
M.J. Greatbatch	2	3	1	186	107*	93.00
K.R. Rutherford	2	3	1	138	107*	69.00
A.H. Jones	1	2	1	62	54*	62.00
R.H. Vance	1	1	0	47	47	47.00
I.D.S. Smith	3	4	2	92	33*	46.00
J.G. Wright	3	5	0	221	103	44.20
M.D. Crowe	3	5	0	216	143	43.20
J.G. Bracewell	3	5	1	152	54	38.00
R.J. Hadlee	1	1	0	37	37	37.00
T.J. Franklin	3	5	0	125	62	25.00
D.K. Morrison	3	2	1	14	14*	14.00
M.C. Snedden	2	3	0	34	20	11.33
J.J. Crowe	2	4	0	40	28	10.00
E.J. Chatfield	3	2	1	10	10	10.00
S.L. Boock	1	-	-	-	-	-

BOWLING	O	M	R	W	Ave
E.J. Chatfield	126.1	51	198	13	15.23
D.K. Morrison	80.2	14	269	8	33.62
M.C. Snedden	90	31	202	6	33.66
J.G. Bracewell	68	18	148	3	49.33
S.L. Boock	26	9	53	1	53.00
K.R. Rutherford	6	1	9	0	-
R.J. Hadlee	18	3	50	0	-

England

BATTING	M	I	NO	Runs	HS	Ave
M.D. Moxon	3	4	1	208	99	69.33
B.C. Broad	3	4	0	204	114	51.00
M.W. Gatting	3	4	1	106	42	35.33
J.E. Emburey	3	3	0	106	45	35.33
R.T. Robinson	3	4	0	126	70	31.50
C.W.J. Athey	1	2	0	41	22	20.50
G.R. Dilley	3	3	2	17	8*	17.00
P.W. Jarvis	2	3	1	34	14	17.00
P.A.J. DeFreitas	2	2	0	20	16	10.00
N.V. Radford	1	1	0	8	8	8.00
B.N. French	3	3	0	23	13	7.66
D.J. Capel	3	3	0	16	11	5.33
N.H. Fairbrother	2	1	0	1	1	1.00
E.E. Hemmings	1	-	-	-	-	-

BOWLING	O	M	R	W	Ave
G.R. Dilley	104.5	34	210	15	14.00
M.W. Gatting	23	5	61	2	30.50
P.W. Jarvis	98	32	201	6	33.50
P.A.J. DeFreitas	91.1	33	175	4	43.75
D.J. Capel	109.2	23	274	5	54.80
J.E. Emburey	133.5	47	236	3	78.66
N.V. Radford	50	7	132	1	132.00
M.D. Moxon	2	0	3	0	-
N.H. Fairbrother	2	0	9	0	-
E.E. Hemmings	45	15	107	0	-

1988/89 New Zealand in India

190 INDIA v NEW ZEALAND *(First Test)*
at M. Chinnaswamy Stadium, Bangalore on 12, 13, 14, 16, 17 November, 1988
Toss : India. Umpires : S.K. Ghosh and P.D. Reporter
India won by 172 runs

The Indian opener Arun Lal edged Richard Hadlee's 13th delivery to Chris Kuggeleijn and Hadlee had created a new world record of 374 test wickets. Navjot Sidhu, returning to test cricket after five seasons, began uncertainly but he and Dilip Vengsarkar flourished as they took the score to 184-2, when Vengsarkar retired on 73 because of cramp in his left-hand. Sidhu was the third player dismissed, for 116, and India ended at 243-3.

In the space of 84 deliveries Hadlee broke the back of India's batting, taking three wickets, and India's score tumbled to 294-7. The situation was retrieved by Ravi Shastri and Kiran More as a further 84 runs were added, allowing India to declare at 384-9. John Wright and Trevor Franklin were given a glimpse of things to come when India opened the bowling with right-arm off-spinner Ashad Ayub.

Wright and Franklin faced four different spin bowlers with a cluster of fieldsmen surrounding them as they fought to come to terms with this different attack. Survival was the priority, runs were secondary and all the batsmen grafted industriously. The last 18 overs of the day were to be fatal for New Zealand as four wickets fell for 22. During the day India bowled 104 overs and New Zealand added just 136 runs.

On the rest day a viral fever, with malaria-type symptoms, swept through the New Zealand team, leaving 12 of the touring party of 15 incapacitated. When play began on the fourth day Hadlee, one of the overnight batsmen, was still in bed at the hotel. Ian Smith, batting in place of Hadlee, was daring and within three overs had scattered the cluster of fieldsmen to the boundaries.

When he was cruelly adjudged lbw two runs were still required to save the follow-on. A desperately ill Kuggeleijn was bowled first ball and was replaced by an ashen-looking Hadlee, who denied Kapil Dev a hat-trick, then slashed the ball to the boundary to save the follow-on.

India was successful in seeking quick runs, declaring at 141-1. Fielding for New Zealand were five substitutes including Jeremy Coney, now a radio broadcaster, and Ken Nicholson, a former Otago player doing television commentary. The openers, Wright and Franklin, adopted a more aggressive approach and by stumps had reached 73 without loss. searching for the target of 337 to win.

Richard Hadlee created a world record of 374 test wickets when he had Arun Lal caught by Chris Kuggeleijn at third slip off his 13th delivery of the test. From left: John Bracewell, Mark Greatbatch and Ian Smith follow the flight of the ball.

New Zealand's courageous struggle evaporated in 43.4 overs as they lost all 10 wickets for 81 runs. On a pitch that was now turning as much as 80 cms and bouncing inconsistently, Ayub and Hirwani were unplayable.

INDIA

K.Srikkanth	b Hadlee	1	not out	58
Arun Lal	c Kuggeleijn b Hadlee	6	c & b Gray	33
N.S.Sidhu	c Jones b Gray	116	not out	43
D.B.Vengsarkar*	b Hadlee	75		
M.Azharuddin	c Smith b Hadlee	42		
W.V.Raman	b Hadlee	3		
R.J.Shastri	c Rutherford b Gray	54		
Kapil Dev	c Jones b Chatfield	24		
K.S.More†	lbw b Kuggeleijn	46		
Arshad Ayub	not out	2		
N.D.Hirwani	not out	0		
Extras	(b 4, lb 4, nb 7)	15	(b 5, lb 2)	7
TOTAL	(142 overs) (9 wkts dec)	**384**	(28 overs) (1 wkt dec)	**141**

NEW ZEALAND

T.J.Franklin	c Azharuddin b Arshad Ayub	28	b Hirwani	16
J.G.Wright*	c Arun Lal b Arshad Ayub	22	lbw b Hirwani	58
A.H.Jones	c Srikkanth b Arshad Ayub	45	lbw b Hirwani	17
M.J.Greatbatch	c Srikkanth b Raman	14	c Kapil Dev b Arshad Ayub	10
K.R.Rutherford	c Arun Lal b Hirwani	14	(6) lbw b Hirwani	0
E.J.Gray	lbw b Hirwani	1	(5) c Srikkanth b Hirwani	2
R.J.Hadlee	b Kapil Dev	5	(8) not out	13
J.G.Bracewell	c More b Arshad Ayub	3	(10) c Arun Lal b Arshad Ayub	11
I.D.S.Smith†	lbw b Kapil Dev	30	lbw b Hirwani	25
E.J.Chatfield	not out	4	(11) c Vengsarkar b Arshad Ayub	0
C.M.Kuggeleijn	lbw b Kapil Dev	0	(7) c More b Arshad Ayub	0
Extras	(b 6, lb 8, nb 9)	23	(b 10, nb 2)	12
TOTAL	(122.3 overs)	**189**	(78.4 overs)	**164**

Bowling	O	M	R	W	O	M	R	W
NEW ZEALAND								
Hadlee	30	10	65	5				
Chatfield	30	12	53	1	14	0	61	0
Kuggeleijn	13	2	50	1				
Gray	45	8	128	2	6	0	39	1
Bracewell	24	1	80	0	8	0	34	0
INDIA								
Kapil Dev	9.3	4	24	3	4	0	16	0
Arshad Ayub	48	21	51	4	35.4	12	53	4
Hirwani	31	12	62	2	30	10	59	6
Shastri	14	8	11	0	7	1	21	0
Raman	17	8	26	1	2	0	5	0
Srikkanth	3	2	1	0				

Fall of Wickets	I	NZ	I	NZ
	1st	1st	2nd	2nd
1st	9	58	64	77
2nd	10	62	-	92
3rd	236	118	-	107
4th	244	128	-	113
5th	254	135	-	113
6th	258	140	-	113
7th	294	149	-	113
8th	378	183	-	143
9th	384	183	-	164
10th	-	189	-	164

MILESTONES

- Richard Hadlee became the greatest wicket-taker in test history. He also overtook Clarrie Grimmett's record of 1424 first-class wickets, the most by a New Zealander.

- Chris Kuggeleijn (167) made his test debut.

- Five substitute fieldsmen on the field at one time was unprecedented in test cricket.

191 **INDIA v NEW ZEALAND** *(Second Test)*

at Wankhede Stadium, Bombay on 24, 25, 26, 27, 29 November, 1988
Toss : New Zealand. Umpires : R.B. Gupta and V.K. Ramaswamy
New Zealand won by 136 runs

A damp pitch assisted the Indian spinners to make the ball turn appreciably but as the heat of the day wore on the turn became slower. John Wright and Mark Greatbatch were the dominant batsmen at the top of the order.

New Zealand could have lost the test match when five wickets went for 75 in the session between lunch and tea as the batsmen were undone by penetrative spin bowling.

However, from 158-8 John Bracewell and Danny Morrison saved the day, batting through to stumps when the score was 231-8. Bracewell had made his fourth fifty in test cricket.

Kris Srikkanth was entertainingly aggressive, striking three sixes during a partnership worth 100 in 119 minutes with his captain Dilip Vengsarkar. New Zealand bounced back in the final session, capturing six wickets for 91 runs, and leaving India four runs short of New Zealand's 236 with nine wickets down.

Richard Hadlee bowled five deliveries at the start of the third day before claiming his fifth wicket. Despite the fact that Kapil Dev made the ball swing disconcertingly in the steamy atmosphere, Wright and Andrew Jones batted positively, taking the score to 73 before Wright was controversially given out.

Greatbatch and Jones attacked judiciously, taking the score to 149-3 before disaster struck in the form of leg-spinner Narendra Hirwani and off-spinner Arshad Ayub, and six wickets fell for 49 runs. New Zealand ended the day with a tenuous lead of only 184 with two days remaining and Ian Smith and Bracewell defending doggedly.

By playing their natural attacking games Smith and Bracewell plundered 69 runs, with Smith scoring 54 before he was given out contentiously caught off the middle of his pad. Ewen Chatfield, not for the first time in his test career, made an invaluable contribution, batting for one hour while another vital 29 runs were added with Bracewell.

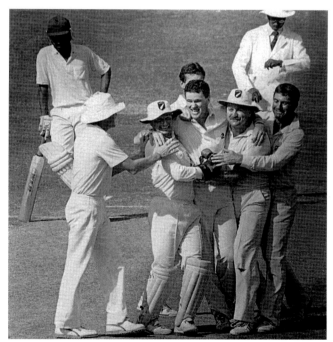

India's reputation of being masters of spin bowling was severely dented when John Bracewell captured six wickets in their second innings at Bombay. Excited team mates Ian Smith, Mark Greatbatch and John Wright converge upon him after another success.

With India needing 282 runs for victory, Srikkanth's dismissal ·with the first ball of the second innings by Hadlee gave New Zealand the psychological boost that they so desperately needed.

India's innings was disintegrating at 89-5, with Bracewell causing problems as his close cluster of fieldsmen pressurised the Indian batsmen. For a short time Kapil Dev played audaciously but an injudicious shot led to his downfall. Stumps were drawn with India 137-7 and requiring 145 to win.

New Zealand took only 21 minutes on the fifth day to wrap up the test victory and square the series. Many thought that it was a just reward for the character and tenacity of the team after their experiences in the first test. Bracewell had an outstanding double of 52 and 32 and took 2-81 and 5-51.

NEW ZEALAND

T.J.Franklin	st More b Arshad Ayub	18	c More b Kapil Dev		2
J.G.Wright*	c More b Hirwani	33	lbw b Hirwani		36
A.H.Jones	lbw b Kapil Dev	3	lbw b Arshad Ayub		78
M.J.Greatbatch	lbw b Shastri	46	b Hirwani		31
K.R.Rutherford	c Srikkanth b Hirwani	6	c Arun Lal b Arshad Ayub		17
T.E.Blain	c Kapil Dev b Shastri	16	lbw b Arshad Ayub		5
R.J.Hadlee	c Patel b Hirwani	10	c Vengsarkar b Hirwani		1
I.D.S.Smith†	b Shastri	13	c Vengsarkar b Arshad Ayub		54
J.G.Bracewell	c More b Shastri	52	(10) c & b Arshad Ayub		32
D.K.Morrison	not out	27	(9) c More b Hirwani		0
E.J.Chatfield	b Kapil Dev	0	not out		2
Extras	(lb 5, nb 7)	12	(b 4, lb 8, w 1, nb 8)		21
TOTAL	**(93.3 overs)**	**236**	**(115 overs)**		**279**

INDIA

K.Srikkanth	c Franklin b Hadlee	94	lbw b Hadlee		0
Arun Lal	lbw b Hadlee	9	c Greatbatch b Hadlee		47
N.S.Sidhu	lbw b Chatfield	6	b Bracewell		14
D.B.Vengsarkar*	c Blain b Bracewell	25	b Bracewell		0
M.Azharuddin	c Greatbatch b Bracewell	9	c Rutherford b Bracewell		21
R.J.Shastri	b Chatfield	32	c Smith b Hadlee		6
Kapil Dev	b Hadlee	7	c Wright b Bracewell		36
K.S.More†	b Hadlee	28	b Bracewell		2
Arshad Ayub	c Bracewell b Hadlee	10	not out		4
R.G.M.Patel	c Rutherford b Hadlee	0	c Smith b Hadlee		0
N.D.Hirwani	not out	2	c Chatfield b Bracewell		3
Extras	(lb 5, nb 7)	12	(b 5, lb 4, nb 3)		12
TOTAL	**(75.5 overs)**	**234**	**(49.4 overs)**		**145**

Bowling	O	M	R	W	O	M	R	W
INDIA								
Kapil Dev	15.3	4	48	2	24	5	52	1
Patel	4	0	14	0	10	0	37	0
Arshad Ayub	25	10	42	1	33	11	50	5
Hirwani	31	6	82	3	38	7	93	4
Shastri	18	1	45	4	10	1	35	0
NEW ZEALAND								
Hadlee	20.5	5	49	6	16	3	39	4
Morrison	16	1	58	0	6	1	27	0
Chatfield	18	6	41	2	10	1	19	0
Bracewell	21	6	81	2	17.4	3	51	6

Fall of Wickets

	NZ	I	NZ	I
	1st	1st	2nd	2nd
1st	36	26	2	0
2nd	43	34	73	48
3rd	67	134	149	54
4th	83	150	163	89
5th	110	150	169	89
6th	121	172	176	134
7th	141	209	176	134
8th	158	224	181	141
9th	234	229	250	142
10th	236	234	279	145

MILESTONES

- It was New Zealand's 27th test victory.

- John Wright became New Zealand's greatest test run-scorer, overtaking Bevan Congdon's 3448 runs.

- John Bracewell and Danny Morrison set a ninth wicket record of 76 for New Zealand against India.

- Dilip Vengsarkar became the seventh player to appear in 100 tests.

- Richard Hadlee captured 10 wickets in a test for the ninth time.

192 INDIA v NEW ZEALAND (*Third Test*)

at Lal Bahadur Shastri Stadium, Hyderabad on 2, 3, 4, 6 December, 1988
Toss : New Zealand. Umpires : S.K. Ghosh and R.B. Gupta
India won by 10 wickets

There was a general air of excitement in Hyderabad for the crucial third test. Two results in two tests and the dramatic way in which both games had pivoted from session to session had made for more absorbing cricket and crowd appeal.

New Zealand's elation at winning the toss soon turned to disappointment as six wickets fell for 91 runs midway through the first day. Once again, the tantalising off-spinners of Arshad Ayub created havoc as he bowled a long and accurate spell and, aided by a helpful pitch, his sharp spin made him most difficult to play.

It was only an unbeaten stand of 137 between Mark Greatbatch and Ian Smith that put New Zealand in a relatively sound position of 228-6 at the end of the first day's play. Greatbatch was solidity itself while Smith was effervescent, cutting, pulling and sweeping to great effect. Even though Greatbatch had been at the crease two hours longer, Smith actually drew level with Greatbatch when he reached 57.

India wrapped up New Zealand's innings early on the second day as four wickets fell for 26 runs. Bowling with the second new ball, test debutant Sanjeev Sharma claimed three wickets in his last four overs. Greatbatch remained undefeated on 90. It was an innings of great character.

Kris Srikkanth batted in his adventurous manner and when he was fourth out for 69, India were 150. The mercurial Mohammad Azharuddin and resolute Ravi Shastri took India to 215-4 at stumps.

The early loss of Shastri was offset by an exhilarating partnership of 62 in 65 minutes between Kapil Dev and Azharuddin. It was the third of the last four partnerships to pass 60 and threatened to take the game completely away from New Zealand. Martin Snedden, playing in his first test of the series, was the pick of the bowlers, capturing four wickets. He appeared to gain momentum off the pitch from his co-ordinated action.

Requiring 105 to make India bat a second time, Trevor Franklin and John Wright began in grand style and both looked solid, even with the introduction of the spin twins Ayub and right-arm leg-spinner Narendra Hirwani. With the score at 49 New Zealand's day soured as three wickets fell in the last eight overs, much to the delight of the crowd of 25,000. New Zealand ended at 65-3.

Apart from a rapid-fire innings by Richard Hadlee and an unyielding innings by Wright, the rest of the batting was simply swept away, firstly by the spinners and, towards the finish, by Kapil Dev. John Wright was the last wicket to fall after 231 minutes of valiant batting. Throughout the tour he was consistency itself.

New Zealand's last seven wickets had fallen for only 59

runs and eight batsmen could muster only a paltry 10 runs between them. It was a galling loss. In spite of the fact that all the wickets suited spin bowling Hadlee still managed to capture 18 wickets in three games. Of 60 New Zealand wickets that fell in the series the Indian spinners took 47, with Ayub taking 21 and Hirwani 20.

NEW ZEALAND

T.J.Franklin	c Arun Lal b Arshad Ayub	7	c Kapil Dev b Hirwani	15
J.G.Wright*	c & b Arshad Ayub	17	c & b Shastri	62
A.H.Jones	c Kapil Dev b Arshad Ayub	8	c Vengsarkar b Arshad Ayub	5
M.J.Greatbatch	not out	90	(5) lbw b Hirwani	5
T.E.Blain	b Hirwani	15	(6) c Arun Lal b Hirwani	0
C.M.Kuggeleijn	c Vengsarkar b Hirwani	7	(7) c Sharma b Arshad Ayub	0
R.J.Hadlee	c Azharuddin b Arshad Ayub	1	(8) c More b Kapil Dev	31
I.D.S.Smith†	c Srikkanth b Kapil Dev	79	(9) b Kapil Dev	0
J.G.Bracewell	c Vengsarkar b Sharma	3	(10) lbw b Kapil Dev	0
M.C.Snedden	lbw b Sharma	0	(4) lbw b Arshad Ayub	0
E.J.Chatfield	c Srikkanth b Sharma	0	not out	0
Extras	(b 8, lb 11, w 1, nb 7)	27	(lb 1, w 5)	6
TOTAL	(95 overs)	**254**	(65.3 overs)	**124**

INDIA

K.Srikkanth	c Bracewell b Snedden	69	not out	18
Arun Lal	c Greatbatch b Hadlee	8	not out	0
N.S.Sidhu	c Franklin b Snedden	19		
D.B.Vengsarkar*	c Hadlee b Chatfield	32		
R.J.Shastri	c Franklin b Chatfield	42		
M.Azharuddin	c Smith b Chatfield	81		
Kapil Dev	c Wright b Hadlee	40		
K.S.More†	c Bracewell b Snedden	0		
Arshad Ayub	c Smith b Hadlee	19		
S.K.Sharma	not out	18		
N.D.Hirwani	c & b Snedden	17		
Extras	(lb 9, nb 4)	13	(nb 4)	4
TOTAL	(106.3 overs)	**358**	(2.1 overs) (0 wkts)	**22**

Bowling	O	M	R	W	O	M	R	W
INDIA								
Kapil Dev	26	6	71	1	10	3	21	3
Sharma	17	4	37	3	4	0	13	0
Arshad Ayub	30	9	55	4	25	12	36	3
Shastri	6	2	15	0	3.3	1	10	1
Hirwani	15	2	51	2	23	10	43	3
Srikkanth	1	0	6	0				
NEW ZEALAND								
Hadlee	34	7	99	3				
Chatfield	33	6	82	3	1	0	5	0
Snedden	18.3	3	69	4	1	0	13	0
Bracewell	18	1	86	0				
Kuggeleijn	3	0	13	0	0.1	0	4	0

Fall of Wickets

	I	NZ	NZ	I
	1st	1st	2nd	2nd
1st	25	17	49	-
2nd	33	48	58	-
3rd	38	116	60	-
4th	82	150	71	-
5th	90	217	75	-
6th	91	279	80	-
7th	230	281	118	-
8th	246	310	118	-
9th	248	322	124	-
10th	254	358	124	-

Ian Smith reached his second fifty in successive innings off 76 balls. He played many audacious shots during his partnership with Mark Greatbatch which was worth 139.

AVERAGES

New Zealand

BATTING	M	I	NO	Runs	HS	Ave
M.J. Greatbatch	3	6	1	196	90*	39.20
J.G. Wright	3	6	0	228	62	38.00
I.D.S. Smith	3	6	0	201	79	33.50
D.K. Morrison	1	2	1	27	27*	27.00
A.H. Jones	3	6	0	156	78	26.00
J.G. Bracewell	3	6	0	101	52	16.83
T.J. Franklin	3	6	0	86	28	14.33
R.J. Hadlee	3	6	1	61	31	12.20
K.R. Rutherford	2	4	0	37	17	9.25
T.E. Blain	2	4	0	36	16	9.00
E.J. Chatfield	3	6	3	6	4*	2.00
C.M. Kuggeleijn	2	4	0	7	7	1.75
E.J. Gray	1	2	0	3	2	1.50
M.C. Snedden	1	2	0	0	0	0.00

BOWLING	O	M	R	W	Ave
R.J. Hadlee	100.5	25	252	18	14.00
M.C. Snedden	19.3	3	82	4	20.50
J.G. Bracewell	88.4	11	332	8	41.50
E.J. Chatfield	106	25	261	6	43.50
E.J. Gray	51	8	167	3	55.66
C.M. Kuggeleijn	16.1	2	67	1	67.00
D.K. Morrison	22	2	85	0	-

India

BATTING	M	I	NO	Runs	HS	Ave
K. Srikkanth	3	6	2	240	94	60.00
N.S. Sidhu	3	5	1	198	116	49.50
M. Azharuddin	3	4	0	153	81	38.25
R.J. Shastri	3	4	0	134	54	33.50
D.B. Vengsarkar	3	4	0	132	75	33.00
Kapil Dev	3	4	0	107	40	26.75
Arun Lal	3	6	1	103	47	20.60
K.S. More	3	4	0	76	46	19.00
Arshad Ayub	3	4	2	35	19	17.50
N.D. Hirwani	3	4	2	22	17	11.00
W.V. Raman	1	1	0	3	3	3.00
R.G.M. Patel	1	2	0	0	0	0.00
S.K. Sharma	1	1	1	18	18*	-

BOWLING	O	M	R	W	Ave
Arshad Ayub	196.4	75	287	21	13.66
S.K. Sharma	21	4	50	3	16.66
N.D. Hirwani	168	47	390	20	19.50
Kapil Dev	89	22	232	10	23.20
R.J. Shastri	58.3	14	137	5	27.40
W.V. Raman	19	8	31	1	31.00
K. Srikkanth	4	2	7	0	-
R.G.M. Patel	14	0	51	0	-

1988/89 Pakistan in New Zealand

On his arrival in New Zealand the captain of Pakistan, Imran Khan, stated that his target was to become the first team to win a series in New Zealand in the 1980s.

■ NEW ZEALAND v PAKISTAN *(First Test)*

at Carisbrook, Dunedin on 3, 4, 5, 6, 7 February, 1989
Toss : Not made. Umpires : R.S Dunne and S.J. Woodward
Abandoned without a ball being bowled

Rain washed out play on the first three days and the authorities abandoned the game and substituted a one-day international. The match was the fourth test to be abandoned without a ball bowled. The others (all England against Australia) were in 1890 and 1938 at Manchester and 1971 at Melbourne.

193 NEW ZEALAND v PAKISTAN *(Second Test)*

at Basin Reserve, Wellington on 10, 11, 12, 13, 14 February, 1989
Toss : Pakistan. Umpires : R.S. Dunne and S.J. Woodward
Match drawn

Imran won the toss and, to the surprise of everyone, put New Zealand in. It was soon apparent that the pitch was very slow and of no assistance to the bowlers. Two loose shots off the medium-paced Mudassar Nazar provided the opportunity for Andrew Jones and Martin Crowe to rebuild the innings.

Jones assaulted the Pakistan bowling and lived dangerously and inventively, and provided the highlight of the day's play, scoring 86 of the partnership worth 149. Martin Crowe was more circumspect than usual and was 89 not out at stumps with New Zealand 229-4.

The partnership between the Crowe brothers was worth 114, with Jeff quietly restoring his test career while Martin Crowe scored his 10th test hundred in 346 minutes. Until he was dismissed for 174, mistiming a hook off Salim Jaffer, Martin Crowe was indomitable. Ian Smith continued his fine batting form of the season with a bright, assertive 40 not out, adding 48 for the last wicket with Ewen Chatfield.

Chasing New Zealand's 447 Pakistan ended the third day at 205-2 as Javed Miandad and Shoaib Mohammad were forthright in their occupancy of the crease. Miandad, normally dashing and full of shots, put his head down and Shoaib, son of the great Hanif, showed that he had inherited his father's patience. Miandad 87 and Shoaib 89 were both not out at stumps.

The fourth day saw a meagre return of only 196 runs for the loss of a further two wickets, with Shoaib scoring only 70 of them. Miandad was dismissed after scoring his 20th test century and Salim Malik and Imran Khan were the major contributors to partnerships that ensured a drawn test. After 12 hours of occupation Shoaib finally left the batting arena for 167. Imran declared ten runs behind New Zealand.

After John Wright went, Robert Vance and Jones availed themselves of excellent conditions, taking the score to 107-1. Salim Jaffer, bowling into a gentle southerly, produced prodigious swing and wickets began to tumble. Suddenly, the nature of the wicket was of no importance as the ball moved alarmingly in the air. New Zealand slumped to 186-7, conceding a major psychological victory to the tourists.

NEW ZEALAND					
R.H.Vance	c Yousuf b Mudassar	5	lbw b Imran		44
J.G.Wright*	c Yousuf b Mudassar	7	c Miandad b Imran		19
A.H.Jones	c Shoaib b Jaffer	86	c sub (Ramiz Raja) b Jaffer		39
M.D.Crowe	c Miandad b Jaffer	174	lbw b Salim Jaffer		0
D.N.Patel	lbw b Imran	0	c Yousuf b Jaffer		2
J.J.Crowe	b Qadir	39	b Jaffer		23
J.G.Bracewell	b Imran	15	lbw b Jaffer		0
R.J.Hadlee	c Rizwan b Jaffer	32	c sub (Ramiz Raja) b Imran		7
I.D.S.Smith†	not out	40	not out		29
D.K.Morrison	lbw b Khan	0	not out		1
E.J.Chatfield	run out	14			
Extras	(b 10, lb 14, nb 11)	35	(b 10, lb 6, nb 6)		22
TOTAL	**(169.4 overs)**	**447**	**(61 overs) (8 wkts)**		**186**

PAKISTAN		
Mudassar Nazar	c & b Morrison	6
Rizwan-uz-Zaman	lbw b Hadlee	18
Shoaib Mohammad	b Hadlee	163
Javed Miandad	lbw b Hadlee	118
Salim Malik	c Smith b Bracewell	38
Imran Khan*	b Chatfield	71
Aamer Malik	not out	8
Salim Yousuf†	c Jones b Hadlee	4
Abdul Qadir	not out	0
Salim Jaffer		
Aaqib Javed		
Extras	(b 1, lb 8, nb 3)	12
TOTAL	**(195 overs) (7 wkts dec)**	**438**

Bowling	O	M	R	W	O	M	R	W	Fall of Wickets			
PAKISTAN										NZ	P	NZ
										1st	1st	2nd
Imran	46.4	18	75	3	17	8	34	3				
Jaffer	34	5	94	3	17	4	40	5	1st	13	14	36
Mudassar	22	5	59	2					2nd	18	54	107
Aaqib	34	5	103	0	13	1	57	0	3rd	167	274	108
Qadir	29	4	83	1	14	3	39	0	4th	168	325	117
Aamer	4	1	9	0					5th	282	422	128
NEW ZEALAND									6th	321	430	132
Hadlee	54	14	101	4					7th	389	437	140
Morrison	36	10	96	1					8th	398	-	180
Chatfield	53	21	82	1					9th	399	-	-
Patel	12	3	27	0					10th	447	-	-
Bracewell	40	8	123	1								

Once Martin Crowe reached his 10th test century, he unveiled a succession of shots that were beautifully executed.

MILESTONES

- Aaqib Javed became the second-youngest player to play test cricket at the age of 16 years and 189 days.

- Martin Crowe became the first New Zealand batsman to score 10 test hundreds. His 174 equalled the highest score by a New Zealander at the Basin Reserve.

- Javed Miandad and Shoaib Mohammad put on 220 for the third wicket, a Pakistan record against New Zealand.

- Shoaib Mohammad's innings of 720 minutes was the longest played in New Zealand.

194 NEW ZEALAND v PAKISTAN *(Third Test)*

at Eden Park, Auckland on 24, 25, 26, 27, 28 February, 1989
Toss : Pakistan. Umpires : B.L. Aldridge and S.J. Woodward
Match drawn

On a pitch that would not have been out of place in Pakistan, Imran Khan, having won the toss, decided to bat. The day belonged to Shoaib Mohammad and Javed Miandad and they both completed centuries before stumps; 289-2.

Shoaib looked more assertive than during his mammoth effort in Wellington. Miandad had an indiscreet slog at the second ball he received from Stephen Boock but for the rest of his innings he was a great player toying with an attack.

Shoaib was run out but the home side had to wait a further 147 runs for another wicket and were reduced to three bowlers as Richard Hadlee left the field with a leg injury. At 480 Miandad was superbly caught by Ian Smith off Ewen Chatfield for 271, his seventh hundred against New Zealand.

Salim Malik and Imran Khan batted freely on the third morning on a pitch showing no signs of wear. Their partnership was worth 136 when the declaration was made at 616-5.

Robert Vance played with refreshing freedom in scoring his only test half-century. Wicketkeeper is Salim Yousuf.

Wright was out at 13 and Robert Vance and Andrew Jones began an arduous repair operation. Just when it seemed the day would be safely negotiated both of them were dismissed as well as the nightwatchman Martin Snedden, leaving New Zealand precariously positioned at 133-4.

As the partnership between Martin Crowe and Mark Greatbatch grew so did a constant chorus of concerted appeals, subjecting the umpires to tremendous pressure. When the partnership was worth 154, both batsmen and John Bracewell were removed and Jeff Crowe had to survive a hat-trick with the first ball after tea. He and Ian Smith survived until stumps, with New Zealand 360-7.

Next day New Zealand was dismissed for 403 and asked to follow on but there was never any chance of a result.

PAKISTAN

Mudassar Nazar	lbw b Hadlee	5			
Rizwan-uz-Zaman	c Crowe J.J. b Boock	15			
Shoaib Mohammad	run out	112			
Javed Miandad	c Smith b Chatfield	271			
Aamer Malik	c Crowe J.J. b Bracewell	56			
Salim Malik	not out	80			
Imran Khan*	not out	69			
Salim Yousuf†					
Abdul Qadir					
Tauseef Ahmed					
Salim Jaffer					
Extras	(lb 7, nb 1)	8			
TOTAL	(203 overs) (for 5 wkts dec)	**616**			

NEW ZEALAND

R.H.Vance	c Shoaib b Qadir	68	c Yousuf b Mudassar		31
J.G.Wright*	c Rizwan b Tauseef	2	c Yousuf b Qadir		36
A.H.Jones	run out	47	c Yousuf b Mudassar		0
M.D.Crowe	c Yousuf b Jaffer	78	not out		9
S.L.Boock	c Mudassar b Qadir	8			
M.J.Greatbatch	b Qadir	76	(5) not out		13
J.J.Crowe	c Miandad b Qadir	33			
J.G.Bracewell	b Qadir	0			
I.D.S.Smith†	c Mudassar b Imran	58			
R.J.Hadlee	not out	14			
E.J.Chatfield	c Aamer b Qadir	0			
Extras	(b 7, lb 2, nb 10)	19	(nb 10)		10
TOTAL	(184.1 overs)	**403**	(50.4 overs) (3 wkts)		**99**

Bowling NEW ZEALAND	O	M	R	W	O	M	R	W
Hadlee	28	7	68	1				
Chatfield	65	14	158	1				
Boock	70	10	229	1				
Bracewell	37	4	138	1				
Jones	3	0	16	0				
PAKISTAN								
Jaffer	18	6	44	1	8	4	18	0
Imran	34	9	76	1	5.4	1	13	0
Tauseef	69	28	106	1	12	4	23	0
Qadir	58.1	18	160	6	16	7	27	1
Shoaib	2	1	1	0	1	0	5	0
Mudassar	3	1	7	0	8	2	13	2

Fall of Wickets	P	NZ	NZ
	1st	1st	2nd
1st	10	13	68
2nd	44	122	71
3rd	292	123	76
4th	439	132	-
5th	480	286	-
6th	-	294	-
7th	-	294	-
8th	-	388	-
9th	-	388	-
10th	-	403	-

MILESTONES

- Pakistan's 616-5 was the highest score against New Zealand.

- Javed Miandad's 271 was the second-highest test score in New Zealand and his 21st test hundred.

- Shoaib Mohammad and Javed Miandad put on 248, a new third wicket record for Pakistan against New Zealand.

- Martin Crowe became the third New Zealander to score 3000 test runs.

- Imran Khan became the third player to score 3000 test runs and take 300 test wickets.

1989/90 New Zealand in Australia

195 **AUSTRALIA v NEW ZEALAND** *(Only Test)*
at W.A.C.A. Ground, Perth on 24, 25, 26, 27, 28 November, 1989
Toss : New Zealand. Umpires : R.J. Evans and P.J. McConnell
Match drawn

David Boon relished batting against the New Zealand bowlers and he attacked relentlessly. He punished anything loose and made capital with many boundaries hit well over the slips and gully cordons. He added 145 with Tom Moody for the second wicket and at stumps he was 169, Allan Border 45 and Australia 296-2.

Boon went for 200, after 451 minutes, but Dean Jones was a problem for New Zealand until he was lbw for 99. Australia declared at 521-9 and New Zealand was 25-0 at stumps.

In Wright, Mark Greatbatch and Martin Crowe New Zealand had batsmen capable of counter-attacking Australia's fast, short-pitched bowling, playing shots square on both sides of the wicket. On the rare occasion that the ball was pitched up both Crowe and Greatbatch revealed sumptuous

drives. Lion-hearted Merv Hughes displayed great stamina to claim four of the six wickets that fell in the last session as the visitors limped to 218-8 at stumps.

New Zealand had to follow on and both openers were soon out. Greatbatch took 39 minutes to score but, by the time he reached 50, New Zealand were 107-4 and facing defeat. Jeff Crowe assisted Greatbatch and at the end of the fourth day they were on 42 and 69 in a total of 168-4.

On the last day Chris Cairns had to avoid a hat-trick and for 93 minutes received a bombardment of short-pitched bowling. Meanwhile, Greatbatch was engineering one of the great rearguard actions in test cricket.

Martin Snedden then stayed 202 minutes until play ended. Thanks to Greatbatch, New Zealand had salvaged a respectable draw out of what should have been a disaster.

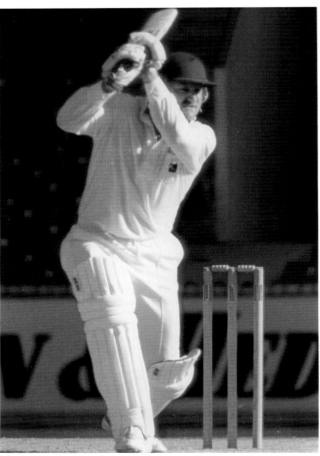

Mark Greatbatch's 146 not out was one of the greatest match-saving innings in test cricket history.

AUSTRALIA

M.A.Taylor	c Wright b Morrison	9	
D.C.Boon	c Wright b Snedden	200	
T.M.Moody	c Smith b Snedden	61	
A.R.Border*	b Morrison	50	
D.M.Jones	lbw b Morrison	99	
S.R.Waugh	c Greatbatch b Snedden	17	
I.A.Healy†	c Crowe J.J. b Patel	28	
M.G.Hughes	c Wright b Snedden	16	
G.F.Lawson	b Morrison	1	
C.G.Rackemann	not out	15	
T.M.Alderman			
Extras	(b 1, lb 9, w 2, nb 13)	25	
TOTAL	(158.1 overs) (9 wkts dec)	**521**	

NEW ZEALAND

J.G.Wright*	b Rackemann	34	c Border b Lawson		3
R.H.Vance	b Alderman	4	c Alderman b Rackemann		8
M.J.Greatbatch	c Healy b Hughes	76	not out		146
M.D.Crowe	lbw b Alderman	62	c Taylor b Moody		30
D.N.Patel	c Boon b Hughes	0	lbw b Alderman		7
J.J.Crowe	c Healy b Rackemann	7	lbw b Hughes		49
I.D.S.Smith†	c Lawson b Hughes	11	c Border b Hughes		0
C.L.Cairns	c Healy b Hughes	1	lbw b Hughes		28
M.C.Snedden	not out	13	not out		33
D.K.Morrison	c Border b Lawson	3			
W.Watson	lbw b Alderman	4			
Extras	(b 1, lb 6, w 4, nb 5)	16	(lb 14, nb 4)		18
TOTAL	(92.4 overs)	**231**	(162 overs) (7 wkts)		**322**

Bowling	O	M	R	W	O	M	R	W
NEW ZEALAND								
Morrison	39.1	8	145	4				
Cairns	12	2	60	0				
Snedden	42	10	108	4				
Watson	37	7	118	0				
Patel	28	5	80	1				
AUSTRALIA								
Alderman	25.4	7	73	3	32	14	59	1
Lawson	22	5	54	1	38	12	88	1
Rackemann	20	4	39	2	31	21	23	1
Hughes	20	7	51	4	36	8	92	3
Moody	4	1	6	0	17	6	23	1
Border	1	0	1	0	5	2	17	0
Jones					3	2	6	0

Fall of Wickets	A	NZ	NZ
	1st	1st	2nd
1st	28	28	11
2nd	177	84	11
3rd	316	173	79
4th	361	178	107
5th	395	191	189
6th	449	204	189
7th	489	206	234
8th	490	212	-
9th	521	226	-
10th	-	231	-

MILESTONES

* Chris Cairns (168) made his test debut. He and Lance Cairns became New Zealand's fourth father and son combination to play test cricket.

* Mark Greatbatch's hundred in 462 minutes was the slowest century made in test cricket in Australia.

* David Boon's 200 was the highest test score at Perth.

1989/90 India in New Zealand

Willie Watson broke his thumb at practice and was replaced by Richard Hadlee, who had recuperated from an operation on his achilles tendon performed in early December.

196 NEW ZEALAND v INDIA *(First Test)*

at Lancaster Park, Christchurch on 2, 3, 4, 5 February, 1990
Toss : New Zealand. Umpires : R.S. Dunne and S.J. Woodward
New Zealand won by 10 wickets

John Wright struggled with the swing bowling of Manoj Prabhakar at first but the arrival of Andrew Jones seemed to provide an attacking spark for Wright and the pair picked up the scoring momentum, with Wright growing in confidence as he began cutting the ball savagely. A six hit over the long-on boundary brought Jones his fifty off 82 balls.

Mark Greatbatch joined Wright and by stumps they had added 73, with Wright on 127; 255-3. The two added a further 52 next day before Greatbatch left. Ken Rutherford had scored 226 for Otago against India prior to the test, yet he was most unconvincing in the early stages of this innings.

The loss of Wright for 185, his highest test score, caused a mini-collapse as John Bracewell and Ian Smith departed in quick succession. Responsibility brought the best out in Rutherford, and he and Hadlee captivated the crowd with the excellence of their strokeplay as they added 64 in quick time.

India lost a wicket in Hadlee's first over and again by the time 27 runs had been scored. Wayward bowling by Danny Morrison saw Mohammad Azharuddin and Navjot Sidhu plunder the attack in a display that electrified the crowd. Azharuddin had 31 from only 21 balls before Hadlee struck again in the penultimate over, leaving India 97-3. Hadlee, on his home ground, ended the day on 399 test wickets.

Morrison's opening spell was again erratic and only notable for the fact that he broke a knuckle on the forefinger of Sidhu's right-hand. Changing ends, Morrison became inspired as India lost their last seven wickets for 18 runs. Morrison took 5-75, his second five-wicket bag. Martin Snedden, who claimed two wickets, ably assisted him.

Following on 295 behind, India enjoyed its best opening partnership for 20 tests, with Prabhakar and Woorkeri Raman adding 80 before Snedden bowled Prabhakar. An emotional scene followed when Hadlee bowled Sanjay Manjrekar to become the first player to capture 400 test wickets.

He was presented with 400 roses as the crowd stood and cheered for five minutes. At the end of the day Raman was 85 and India 210-5. Steady bowling and sound fielding saw India out for 296 to give New Zealand a win by 10 wickets.

Danny Morrison destroyed India's first innings when he took five wickets in six overs as the visitors tumbled from 146-3 to 164 all out. Sachin Tendulkar was out first ball.

NEW ZEALAND

T.J.Franklin	c Prabhakar b Kapil Dev	20			
J.G.Wright*	b Raju	185			
A.H.Jones	c Raju b Hirwani	52			
M.D.Crowe	lbw b Raju	24			
M.J.Greatbatch	b Wassan	46			
K.R.Rutherford	b Kapil Dev	69			
J.G.Bracewell	b Hirwani	0			
I.D.S.Smith†	lbw b Raju	9			
R.J.Hadlee	c Hirwani b Prabhakar	28			
M.C.Snedden	lbw b Kapil Dev	3	(1) not out	1
D.K.Morrison	not out	1	(2) not out	1
Extras	(b 3, lb 12, nb 7)	22		0
TOTAL	**(155.3 overs)**	**459**	**(0.5 overs) (0 wkts)**	**2**

INDIA

W.V.Raman	lbw b Hadlee	0	c Jones b Morrison	96
N.S.Sidhu	lbw b Morrison	51	absent hurt	
S.V.Manjrekar	c Jones b Hadlee	5	b Hadlee	4
M.Azharuddin*	lbw b Hadlee	48	b Bracewell	30
S.L.V.Raju	c Crowe b Snedden	31	(8) c Smith b Snedden	21
S.R.Tendulkar	c Smith b Morrison	0	c Smith b Bracewell	24
M.Prabhakar	c Smith b Snedden	1	(2) b Snedden	40
Kapil Dev	c Snedden b Morrison	4	(7) lbw b Hadlee	25
K.S.More†	c Smith b Morrison	1	(5) b Hadlee	11
A.Wassan	c Smith b Morrison	2	(9) not out	24
N.D.Hirwani	not out	1	(10) c Bracewell b Hadlee	0
Extras	(b 5, lb 5, nb 10)	20	(b 6, lb 2, nb 13)	21
TOTAL	**(45.5 overs)**	**164**	**(91.5 overs)**	**296**

Bowling	O	M	R	W	O	M	R	W		Fall of Wickets			
INDIA										NZ	I	I	NZ
										1st	1st	2nd	2nd
Kapil Dev	28.3	4	89	3					1st	26	0	80	-
Prabhakar	38	8	114	1	0.5	0	2	0	2nd	131	27	85	-
Wassan	25	3	95	1					3rd	182	88	135	-
Raju	35	12	86	3					4th	307	146	160	-
Hirwani	29	9	60	2					5th	374	146	206	-
NEW ZEALAND									6th	375	148	242	-
Hadlee	14	1	45	3	22.5	3	69	4	7th	394	153	254	-
Morrison	16	2	75	5	19	0	94	1	8th	448	158	289	-
Snedden	12.5	4	20	2	25	5	59	2	9th	454	161	296	-
Bracewell	3	0	14	0	20	3	45	2	10th	459	164	-	-
Rutherford					5	0	21	0					

MILESTONES

- It was New Zealand's 28th test victory.

- Richard Hadlee became the first bowler to take 400 test wickets.

- John Wright and Mark Greatbatch created a fourth wicket record of 125 against India.

- John Wright made his eighth test hundred and his highest score in test cricket.

197 NEW ZEALAND v INDIA *(Second Test)*

at McLean Park, Napier on 9, 10, 11, 12, 13 February, 1990
Toss : India. Umpires : B.L. Aldridge and S.J. Woodward
Match drawn

The first test to be scheduled at Napier since 1978/79 was ruined by rain. The Napier area, which had been having semi-drought conditions, was deluged with rain in the two days before the game and no play was possible until 11.30 am on the second day.

Play began dramatically with Richard Hadlee getting Woorkeri Raman lbw to the first ball of the game. The breakthrough set in action a slow rebuilding exercise that saw only 55 runs scored by lunch. Manoj Prabhakar persevered for 204 minutes before notching up his fifty as black clouds turned into a thunderstorm when India was 126-2.

Danny Morrison created a stir when he had two Indian captains out with successive deliveries. He bowled the current captain, Mohammad Azharuddin, and had his predecessor, Dilip Vengsarkar, caught by Ian Smith. Meanwhile, Prabhakar had been continuing in a determined fashion.

His new partner, Sachin Tendulkar, displayed the best batting technique of all the team and, when Prabhakar was dismissed for 95, he assumed the role of senior batsman, although only 16 years 294 days old. He and the diminutive wicketkeeper, Kiran More, proved worthy adversaries by going for their shots. They added 128 in 187 minutes, with More striking 11 boundaries in his score of 73; India 348-7.

Tendulkar began the fourth day 80 not out and all interest centred on whether he would become the youngest person to score a century in a test. Two fours off Morrison suggested that he would but, in his youthful excitement to score with an off drive, he tried once too often against Morrison and the result was a lofted chance to Wright, who held the catch.

Three balls later Morrison bowled Atul Wassan to claim his second five-wicket bag of the series and India declared at 358-9. John Wright and Trevor Franklin were untroubled by the Indian attack on the slow wicket and when Franklin was dismissed for 50 their partnership had been worth 149. Wright had recorded his ninth test century off 189 balls. Bad light ended play and rain caused the fifth day to be abandoned.

INDIA		
W.V.Raman	lbw b Hadlee	0
M.Prabhakar	c Smith b Hadlee	95
S.V.Manjrekar	c Smith b Morrison	42
M.Azharuddin*	b Morrison	33
D.B.Vengsarkar	c Smith b Morrison	0
S.R.Tendulkar	c Wright b Morrison	88
Kapil Dev	lbw b Hadlee	4
K.S.More†	c Franklin b Snedden	73
S.L.V.Raju	not out	3
A.Wassan	b Morrison	0
N.D.Hirwani	not out	1
Extras	(lb 5, nb 14)	19
TOTAL	(146 overs) (9 wkts dec)	**358**

NEW ZEALAND		
T.J.Franklin	c Kapil Dev b Wassan	50
J.G.Wright*	not out	113
A.H.Jones	not out	4
M.D.Crowe		
M.J.Greatbatch		
K.R.Rutherford		
J.G.Bracewell		
I.D.S.Smith†		
R.J.Hadlee		
M.C.Snedden		
D.K.Morrison		
Extras	(b 5, lb 3, w 1, nb 2)	11
TOTAL	(71 overs) (1 wkt)	**178**

Bowling	O	M	R	W
NEW ZEALAND				
Hadlee	35	11	73	3
Morrison	38	8	98	5
Snedden	42	10	104	1
Bracewell	22	2	50	0
Rutherford	9	0	28	0
INDIA				
Prabhakar	13	3	25	0
Kapil Dev	14	4	30	0
Wassan	15	2	48	1
Hirwani	18	7	40	0
Raju	11	4	27	0

Fall of Wickets

	I	NZ
	1st	1st
1st	0	149
2nd	92	-
3rd	150	-
4th	152	-
5th	210	-
6th	218	-
7th	346	-
8th	356	-
9th	356	-
10th	-	-

MILESTONES

- Sachin Tendulkar and Kiran More created an Indian record for the seventh wicket against New Zealand with their partnership of 128.

- The first-wicket stand of 149 between John Wright and Trevor Franklin was a New Zealand record against India.

- John Wright scored his ninth test century and became the eighth New Zealand player to score centuries in successive test innings.

For the second successive test, John Wright scored an enterprising century that contained obdurate sessions augmented with thrilling shots.

198 NEW ZEALAND v INDIA *(Third Test)*

at Eden Park, Auckland on 22, 23, 24, 25, 26 February, 1990
Toss : India. Umpires : B.L. Aldridge and R.S. Dunne
Match drawn

In conditions conducive to swing and seam bowling India had New Zealand reeling when they lost their sixth wicket at 85. Richard Hadlee's appearance signalled a change in the initiative as he immediately went on the attack, on-driving and flicking the ball backward of square and cutting savagely.

When Hadlee was joined by Ian Smith the momentum kept rolling and their hundred partnership came up in 97 minutes off 134 balls before Hadlee was bowled for 87. No sooner had he departed than Smith brought up his fifty off 56 balls. Now the senior partner, with the reliable Martin Snedden to prop up the other end, Smith bludgeoned the Indian bowlers unmercifully, scoring his second test century off 95 balls and reaching 150 just 23 balls later.

When Snedden departed for 22, 136 runs had been added off 90 balls. At stumps Smith was unbeaten on 169, made in 225 minutes of absolute mayhem. 387 runs had been scored in the day.

Smith went early and India, in spite of losing three early wickets, also played attractively. They were led by their captain, Mohammad Azharuddin, who scored his first test century outside India and Pakistan. He captivated the crowd with elegant drives and cajoled the ball across the boundary at square leg with strong wrists and superb timing.

Beginning the third day at 316-7, India began a most brutal assault on New Zealand's bowlers as Kiran More joined his skipper in flogging the attack, and 85 runs were added for the loss of More's wicket. New batsman Atul Wassan continued in similar vein, with 50 coming off the first five overs of the new ball. Azharuddin was last out for 192 sumptuous runs and India had a first innings lead of 91. Danny Morrison had taken his third five-wicket bag of the series.

At the halfway point of the match 873 runs had been scored at 4.66 per over and many in the crowd were talking about "the one-day test". Andrew Jones and John Wright were together at stumps with the score at 135-1.

Successive partnerships of 148, between Jones and Wright, and 179, between Jones and Martin Crowe had New Zealand at 334 when they lost their third wicket, Martin Crowe for

Ian Smith entered the record books with the highest score made in test cricket by a batsman batting at number nine. His 173 was the highest score made by a New Zealander in a test at Eden Park.

113. Jones had completed his second test century. The pitch was still perfect for batting when New Zealand declared at 482-5, with Jones 170 not out.

There was insufficient time for either side to forge a victory. The target left India 393 runs to make off 64 overs. It was never a serious challenge and India reached 149 without the loss of a wicket.

MILESTONES

- Shane Thomson (169) made his test debut.

- Richard Hadlee and Ian Smith created a new eighth wicket record of 103 for New Zealand against India.

- Ian Smith and Martin Snedden set a new ninth wicket record of 136 for New Zealand against all countries.

- Smith's 173 was the highest score by a number nine batsman in test cricket.

- Smith hit 24 runs off one over from Atul Wassan, equalling the test record for most runs off a six-ball over.

- Smith's 173 was the highest score by a New Zealander in a test at Eden Park and it was also the highest score by a New Zealand wicketkeeper in a test.

NEW ZEALAND

T.J.Franklin	c Tendulkar b Wassan	4	lbw b Prabhakar		2
J.G.Wright*	c Gursharan b Kapil Dev	3	c Wassan b Hirwani		74
A.H.Jones	c More b Prabhakar	19	not out		170
M.D.Crowe	c More b Wassan	24	lbw b Hirwani		113
M.J.Greatbatch	b Wassan	4	c Gursharan b Wassan		43
K.R.Rutherford	c Prabhakar b Wassan	20	c More b Hirwani		8
S.A.Thomson	c More b Kapil Dev	22	not out		43
R.J.Hadlee	b Hirwani	87			
I.D.S.Smith†	lbw b Prabhakar	173			
M.C.Snedden	c More b Prabhakar	22			
D.K.Morrison	not out	0			
Extras	(lb 9, nb 4)	13	(b 4, lb 14, nb 12)		30
TOTAL	(92.2 overs)	**391**	(159 overs) (5 wkts dec)		**483**

INDIA

W.V.Raman	c Franklin b Hadlee	8	not out		72
M.Prabhakar	lbw b Snedden	36	not out		63
S.V.Manjrekar	b Morrison	16			
D.B.Vengsarkar	c Smith b Morrison	47			
M.Azharuddin*	c Rutherford b Thomson	192			
S.R.Tendulkar	c Smith b Morrison	5			
Gursharan Singh	c & b Thomson	18			
Kapil Dev	c Jones b Hadlee	22			
K.S.More†	lbw b Morrison	50			
A.Wassan	b Morrison	53			
N.D.Hirwani	not out	0			
Extras	(b 1, lb 11, w 1, nb 22)	35	(lb 9, nb 5)		14
TOTAL	(104.3 overs)	**482**	(45 overs) (0 wkts)		**149**

Bowling	O	M	R	W	O	M	R	W
INDIA								
Kapil Dev	29.2	6	85	2	31	4	101	0
Prabhakar	29.2	3	123	3	38	6	118	1
Wassan	16.4	1	108	4	25	5	80	1
Hirwani	17	1	66	1	46	11	143	3
Raman					19	10	23	0
NEW ZEALAND								
Hadlee	30	8	123	2	4	1	9	0
Morrison	30	3	145	5	7	1	34	0
Snedden	26	4	110	1	12	1	29	0
Thomson	18.3	3	92	2	9	1	30	0
Jones					9	1	28	0
Rutherford					3	0	10	0
Greatbatch					1	1	0	0

Fall of Wickets

	NZ 1st	I 1st	NZ 2nd	I 2nd
1st	8	15	7	-
2nd	29	65	155	-
3rd	29	71	334	-
4th	51	215	396	-
5th	64	223	406	-
6th	85	263	-	-
7th	131	308	-	-
8th	234	396	-	-
9th	370	482	-	-
10th	391	482	-	-

AVERAGES

New Zealand

BATTING	M	I	NO	Runs	HS	Ave
J.G. Wright	3	4	1	375	185	125.00
A.H. Jones	3	4	2	245	170*	122.50
I.D.S. Smith	3	2	0	182	173	91.00
S.A. Thomson	1	2	1	65	43*	65.00
R.J. Hadlee	3	2	0	115	87	57.50
M.D. Crowe	3	3	0	161	113	53.66
K.R. Rutherford	3	3	0	97	69	32.33
M.J. Greatbatch	3	3	0	93	46	31.00
T.J. Franklin	3	4	0	76	50	19.00
M.C. Snedden	3	3	1	26	22	13.00
J.G. Bracewell	2	1	0	0	0	0.00
D.K. Morrison	3	3	3	2	1*	-

BOWLING	O	M	R	W	Ave
R.J. Hadlee	105.5	24	319	12	26.58
D.K. Morrison	110	14	446	16	27.87
M.C. Snedden	117.5	24	322	6	53.66
J.G. Bracewell	45	5	109	2	54.50
S.A. Thomson	27.3	4	122	2	61.00
M.J. Greatbatch	1	1	0	0	-
A.H. Jones	9	1	28	0	-
K.R. Rutherford	17	0	59	0	-

India

BATTING	M	I	NO	Runs	HS	Ave
M. Azharuddin	3	4	0	303	192	75.75
M. Prabhakar	3	5	1	235	95	58.75
N.S. Sidhu	1	1	0	51	51	51.00
W.V. Raman	3	5	1	176	96	44.00
K.S. More	3	4	0	135	73	33.75
S.R. Tendulkar	3	4	0	117	88	29.25
S.L.V. Raju	2	3	1	55	31	27.50
A. Wassan	3	4	1	79	53	26.33
D.B. Vengsarkar	2	2	0	47	47	23.50
Gursharan Singh	1	1	0	18	18	18.00
S.V. Manjrekar	3	4	0	67	42	16.75
Kapil Dev	3	4	0	55	25	13.75
N.D. Hirwani	3	4	3	2	1*	2.00

BOWLING	O	M	R	W	Ave
S.L.V. Raju	46	16	113	3	37.66
A. Wassan	81.4	11	331	7	47.28
N.D. Hirwani	110	28	309	6	51.50
Kapil Dev	102.5	18	305	5	61.00
M. Prabhakar	119.1	20	382	5	76.40
W.V. Raman	19	10	23	0	-

1989/90 Australia in New Zealand

After months of fine weather the immediate pre-test preparations could not have been worse as a storm submerged almost two-thirds of the Basin Reserve three days before the game. Prior to the match Richard Hadlee informed a media conference that it would be his last test in New Zealand.

199 NEW ZEALAND v AUSTRALIA (Only Test)
at Basin Reserve, Wellington on 15, 16, 17, 18, 19 March, 1990
Toss : Australia. Umpires : R.S. Dunne and S.J. Woodward
New Zealand won by 9 wickets

Play began at 2 pm on the first day and Border decided to bat upon winning the toss. The pitch was damp and slow and the outfield decidedly soft. To the surprise of all, the Australian innings terminated after 198 minutes, all out for 110.

Danny Morrison, Martin Snedden and Hadlee exploited conditions brilliantly and were assisted by sharp catching. Openers John Wright and Trevor Franklin saw their way through 14 overs to be unbeaten at stumps; 18-0.

Misty rain enveloped Wellington and play began at 2.30 pm after which New Zealand lost three wickets advancing their score to 93. Wright and Franklin added 48 for the first wicket and Andrew Jones assisted Wright to add 41 for the second. As stumps approached, both were dismissed and Snedden, the nightwatchman, joined Mark Greatbatch.

At 123-5 Snedden was intent on avoiding a New Zealand collapse. His batting ground to a halt as he spent 94 minutes scoreless, a world record for test cricket. Snedden's vigil, lasting 171 minutes, ended with him scoring 23. Hadlee, John Bracewell and Morrison all reached double figures but there was nothing substantial in the innings of 202.

When Bracewell began bowling in Australia's second innings he immediately found bite in the wicket and quickly dismissed David Boon. Peter Taylor, who had top scored with 29, batting at eight, in the first innings, came in as nightwatchman with Australia 57-2.

Taylor recorded the first half-century of the test and, in collaboration with Border, the pair took Australia on the road to recovery as they added 103. The second new ball suited Bracewell better, as it gripped and turned more, and he ran through the lower order, claiming the last four wickets in the space of eight runs to end with six for the innings.

The fifth day was a triumph for John Wright who, in four home tests, had scored three hundreds, two against India and one against Australia. Aided by Franklin and Jones, he saw New Zealand through to their target.

AUSTRALIA				
M.A.Taylor	lbw b Morrison	4	(2) lbw b Hadlee	5
G.R.Marsh	b Morrison	4	(1) c Rutherford b Bracewell	41
D.C.Boon	lbw b Hadlee	0	c Smith b Bracewell	12
A.R.Border*	lbw b Morrison	1	(5) not out	78
D.M.Jones	c Wright b Snedden	20	(6) lbw b Morrison	0
S.R.Waugh	b Hadlee	25	(7) c Greatbatch b Hadlee	25
I.A.Healy†	b Snedden	0	(8) c Rutherford b Bracewell	10
P.L.Taylor	c Wright b Hadlee	29	(4) c Smith b Morrison	87
G.D.Campbell	lbw b Hadlee	4	b Bracewell	0
C.G.Rackemann	not out	6	b Bracewell	1
T.M.Alderman	b Hadlee	4	st Smith b Bracewell	1
Extras	(lb 6, nb 7)	13	(lb 6, nb 3)	9
TOTAL	(45.2 overs)	110	(109.2 overs)	269

NEW ZEALAND				
T.J.Franklin	c Marsh b Taylor P.L.	28	c Healy b Campbell	18
J.G.Wright*	c Healy b Alderman	36	not out	117
A.H.Jones	c & b Border	18	not out	33
M.C.Snedden	b Alderman	23		
M.J.Greatbatch	c Healy b Taylor P.L.	16		
K.R.Rutherford	c Healy b Taylor P.L.	12		
J.J.Crowe	lbw b Alderman	9		
R.J.Hadlee	lbw b Campbell	18		
I.D.S.Smith†	c Taylor M.A. b Campbell	1		
J.G.Bracewell	not out	19		
D.K.Morrison	c Taylor M.A. b Alderman	12		
Extras	(b 2, lb 5, nb 3)	10	(b 2, lb 10, nb 1)	13
TOTAL	(121 overs)	202	(63.4 overs) (1 wkt)	181

Bowling NEW ZEALAND	O	M	R	W	O	M	R	W
Hadlee	16.2	5	39	5	25	3	70	2
Morrison	10	4	22	3	24	8	58	2
Snedden	15	2	33	2	25	5	46	0
Rutherford	2	0	8	0				
Bracewell	2	1	2	0	34.2	11	85	6
Jones					1	0	4	0
AUSTRALIA								
Alderman	29	9	46	4	14	8	27	0
Rackemann	32	17	42	0	15	4	39	0
Taylor P.L.	33	19	44	3	11	3	39	0
Campbell	21	3	51	2	7	2	23	1
Border	6	3	12	1	10.4	5	27	0
Jones					6	3	14	0

Fall of Wickets	A 1st	NZ 1st	A 2nd	NZ 2nd
1st	4	48	27	53
2nd	9	89	54	-
3rd	9	89	91	-
4th	12	111	194	-
5th	38	123	194	-
6th	44	150	232	-
7th	70	151	261	-
8th	87	152	261	-
9th	103	171	267	-
10th	110	202	269	-

MILESTONES

* Richard Hadlee took his 100th five-wicket bag in first-class cricket and his 35th in tests. He became the fourth player in tests to score 3000 runs and take 300 wickets.

* Andrew Jones scored his 1000th run in test cricket.

* Martin Snedden set a test record for the longest time without adding to his score, staying on six for 94 minutes.

* John Bracewell established a record for a New Zealand spin bowler in tests when he took his 87th test wicket.

* John Wright scored his 10th test century.

* It was New Zealand's sixth test victory against Australia.

John Bracewell, John Wright, Martin Crowe, Mark Greatbatch, Ken Rutherford, Richard Hadlee, Jeff Crowe and Ian Smith.

1990 New Zealand in England

Throughout the month of May England had been bathed in sunshine but, regrettably, continual interruptions for rain ruined the first test. Not one session was uninterrupted during the five days.

200 **ENGLAND v NEW ZEALAND** *(First Test)*
at Trent Bridge, Nottingham on 7, 8, 9, 11, 12 June, 1990
Toss : New Zealand. Umpires : H.D. Bird and J.H. Hampshire
Match drawn

Conditions were excellent when play began. New Zealand made a cautious start, scoring 16 runs in the first 16 overs, before the first interruption occurred. Upon returning, John Wright went and this set the pattern for a day that ended with New Zealand 171-5. Martin Crowe, who scored his 12th test half-century, was the only batsman to look comfortable.

Play was restricted to five overs on the second day and only 53 minutes on the third as New Zealand were dismissed for 208 with right-arm medium-quick bowler Phillip DeFreitas being rewarded for an industrious spell, taking five wickets. Martin Snedden was involved in an unusual piece of trivia. He batted on each of the first three days for a total of 42 minutes, facing 29 balls, without scoring.

The fourth day saw Michael Atherton's temperament as an opening batsman illustrated at this level of cricket. He accrued 78 not out of England's stumps total of 187-5.

On the fifth day Atherton completed his first test century although John Bracewell and Snedden kept England's run-rate under control, conceding only 129 runs from their combined 71 overs. It was an inconclusive draw in a test which marked the end of England's spell of golden weather.

MILESTONES

- Mark Priest (170) made his test debut.

- Ian Smith, became the 10th wicketkeeper in test cricket to make 150 dismissals.

- This was New Zealand's 200th test. It had taken 42 years and two months to record the first 100 tests but only 18 years and two months for the second hundred. After 200 tests New Zealand's record was won 29, lost 79, drawn 92.

- The announcement that Richard Hadlee had been created a Knight in the Queen's Birthday Honours occurred between the first and the second test. He became the sixth cricketer to be knighted but the first to be so honoured while still playing.

In the four county games leading up to the first test Andrew Jones had scored 301 runs in six innings with a lowest score of 41. He continued his consistent streak even though the conditions were difficult and there were numerous stoppages for rain.

NEW ZEALAND

T.J.Franklin	b Malcolm	33	not out	22
J.G.Wright*	c Stewart b Small	8	c Russell b Small	1
A.H.Jones	c Stewart b Malcolm	39	c Russell b DeFreitas	13
M.D.Crowe	b DeFreitas	59		
M.J.Greatbatch	b Hemmings	1		
M.W.Priest	c Russell b DeFreitas	26		
M.C.Snedden	c Gooch b DeFreitas	0		
J.G.Bracewell	c Gooch b Small	28		
R.J.Hadlee	b DeFreitas	0		
I.D.S.Smith†	not out	2		
D.K.Morrison	lbw b DeFreitas	0	(4) not out	0
Extras	(b 1, lb 10, w 1)	12		0
TOTAL	**(89 overs)**	**208**	**(17 overs) (2 wkts)**	**36**

ENGLAND

G.A.Gooch*	lbw b Hadlee	0
M.A.Atherton	c Snedden b Priest	151
A.J.Stewart	c Smith b Hadlee	27
A.J.Lamb	b Hadlee	0
R.A.Smith	c Smith b Bracewell	55
N.H.Fairbrother	c Franklin b Snedden	19
R.C.Russell†	c Snedden b Morrison	28
P.A.J.DeFreitas	lbw b Bracewell	14
G.C.Small	c Crowe b Hadlee	26
E.E.Hemmings	not out	13
Extras	(b 2, lb 3, nb 3)	8
TOTAL	**(138 overs) (9 wkts dec)**	**345**

Bowling	O	M	R	W	O	M	R	W
ENGLAND								
Small	29	9	49	2	6	2	14	1
Malcolm	19	7	48	2	7	2	22	0
Hemmings	19	6	47	1	2	2	0	0
DeFreitas	22	6	53	5	2	2	0	1
NEW ZEALAND								
Hadlee	33	6	89	4				
Morrison	22	3	96	1				
Snedden	36	17	54	1				
Bracewell	35	8	75	2				
Priest	12	4	26	1				

Fall of Wickets			
	NZ	E	NZ
	1st	*1st*	*2nd*
1st	16	0	8
2nd	75	43	36
3rd	110	45	-
4th	121	141	-
5th	170	168	-
6th	174	260	-
7th	191	302	-
8th	191	306	-
9th	203	340	-
10th	208	-	-

201 ENGLAND v NEW ZEALAND *(Second Test)*

at Lord's on 21, 22, 23, 25, 26 June, 1990
Toss : New Zealand. Umpires : M.J. Kitchen and D.R. Shepherd
Match drawn

It was appropriate that Sir Richard Hadlee's first game after his knighthood was the test at Lord's. When he led the team out on the first day he was accorded a standing ovation from the packed ground. Unfortunately, after 51 minutes rain swept over the ground and ended the day's play.

Hadlee and Danny Morrison began the second day with some menacing bowling that went unrewarded as Graham Gooch and Alec Stewart struggled for survival. The pair were dominating before Gooch fell victim to a caught-and-bowled chance to John Bracewell when he was 85 and the score was 151. Stewart later reached his maiden test half-century.

Both Allan Lamb and Robin Smith appreciated the excellent batting conditions and runs came at a faster clip before Morrison and Hadlee made inroads into England's batting towards the close, when England's score was 329-8.

John Wright and Trevor Franklin became the first New Zealand opening pair to share a century stand at Lord's, in spite of the numerous interruptions caused by inclement weather. At stumps, Wright was 84, while Franklin was 60 and New Zealand were 156-0.

Wright failed by two to record a century at the most famous of grounds and Franklin spent an agonising 45 minutes on 98 before reaching his. It was also his first test century and came in 435 minutes.

With New Zealand appearing to be in a powerful position at 278-1 England speedster Devon Malcolm shattered whatever complacency may have existed by claiming three of the next four wickets that fell for the addition of only seven runs. Mark Greatbatch was joined by Hadlee who immediately went on the attack, racing to 50 off 42 balls. He was particularly severe on the fast-medium bowlers.

The crowd were delighted as 123 runs were added in 106 minutes of picket-thumping batting before Hadlee was dismissed by his Nottingham team mate, Eddie Hemmings, for 86.

New Zealand extended their first innings lead to 128 when they were finally dismissed for 462 early on the fifth day. Any hope for New Zealand to surprise England hinged on an early breakthrough. As the wicket was playing truly there was little chance of an unlikely success being achieved. Rather, it became an exhibition of batting practice with the final test in mind. Five of the six batsmen who reached the crease stayed for more than an hour.

MILESTONES

- Trevor Franklin's century was the 500th test century scored in England.

ENGLAND

G.A.Gooch*	c & b Bracewell	85	b Hadlee	37
M.A.Atherton	b Morrison	0	c Bracewell b Jones	54
A.J.Stewart	lbw b Hadlee	54	c sub (M.W.Priest) b Bracewell	42
A.J.Lamb	lbw b Snedden	39	not out	84
R.A.Smith	c Bracewell b Morrison	64	hit wicket b Bracewell	0
N.H.Fairbrother	c Morrison b Bracewell	2	not out	33
R.C.Russell†	b Hadlee	13		
P.A.J.DeFreitas	c Franklin b Morrison	38		
G.C.Small	b Morrison	3		
E.E.Hemmings	b Hadlee	0		
D.E.Malcolm	not out	0		
Extras	(lb 13, w 1, nb 22)	36	(b 8, lb 8, nb 6)	22
TOTAL	(89.4 overs)	334	(78 overs) (4 wkts dec)	272

NEW ZEALAND

T.J.Franklin	c Russell b Malcolm	101
J.G.Wright*	c Stewart b Small	98
A.H.Jones	c Stewart b Malcolm	49
M.D.Crowe	c Russell b Hemmings	1
M.J.Greatbatch	b Malcolm	47
K.R.Rutherford	c Fairbrother b Malcolm	0
R.J.Hadlee	b Hemmings	86
J.G.Bracewell	run out	4
I.D.S.Smith†	c Small b Malcolm	27
M.C.Snedden	not out	13
D.K.Morrison	not out	2
Extras	(b 12, lb 15, w 2, nb 5)	34
TOTAL	(157.4 overs) (9 wkts dec)	462

Bowling	O	M	R	W	O	M	R	W
NEW ZEALAND								
Hadlee	29	5	113	3	13	2	32	1
Morrison	18.4	4	64	4	16	0	81	0
Snedden	21	4	72	1				
Bracewell	21	3	72	2	34	13	85	2
Jones					12	3	40	1
Rutherford					3	0	18	0
ENGLAND								
Malcolm	43	14	94	5				
Small	35	4	127	1				
DeFreitas	35.4	1	122	0				
Hemmings	30	13	67	2				
Gooch	13	7	25	0				
Atherton	1	1	0	0				

Fall of Wickets	E	NZ	E
	1st	1st	2nd
1st	3	185	68
2nd	151	278	135
3rd	178	281	171
4th	216	284	175
5th	226	285	-
6th	255	408	-
7th	319	415	-
8th	322	425	-
9th	332	448	-
10th	334	-	-

Trevor Franklin languished for 45 minutes on 98 before scoring his maiden test century at Lord's, the home of cricket, thus accomplishing every schoolboy's dream.

202 ENGLAND v NEW ZEALAND (*Third Test*)

at Edgbaston, Birmingham on 5, 6, 7, 9, 10 July, 1990
Toss : New Zealand. Umpires : J.W. Holder and B.J. Meyer
England won by 114 runs

Apart from being the final test for Sir Richard Hadlee it was also the last test for Martin Snedden and John Bracewell, and possibly John Wright's last as captain. With the first two rain-affected tests being drawn it meant that the whole tour would probably be judged on the result of the third test.

After being sent in to bat, England posted its fifty at limited-overs pace in the 13th over. Michael Atherton maintained the heartening consistency, from an England viewpoint, by reaching his third fifty of the series. He and Graham Gooch added 174 for the first wicket, with Gooch being 95 not out at stumps.

The middle order contributed little and, when Gooch was out for 154, England was 316-6. All the lower order made worthwhile contributions and England was finally dismissed for 435.

New Zealand was struggling on the third day when it lost its third wicket at 90. Trevor Franklin, for the third time in the first innings of each test, occupied the crease in excess of three hours, so highly did he value his wicket. His partnership of 71 with Mark Greatbatch was the only substantial batting of the innings, which ended at 249. Off-spinner Eddie Hemmings, at the age of 41, returned his best test figures of 6-58.

England was proceeding well at 129-3, with Atherton again directing their batting fortunes. Operating in unison, Hadlee and Bracewell bowled New Zealand into a strong position, claiming the last seven wickets for 29 runs. In his last eight overs in test cricket Hadlee took 5-17, with a wicket off his last ball.

In search of 345, on a pitch noticeably more variable in bounce, Andrew Jones and Wright got New Zealand off to a good start and the fourth day ended with New Zealand 101-2.

New Zealand's hope for success rested on being able to hold out the menacing fast bowling of Devon Malcolm. They were unable to do so as wickets tumbled at regular intervals until they were all out for 230. It was a test that marked the end of an era for New Zealand.

ENGLAND

G.A.Gooch*	c Hadlee b Morrison	154	b Snedden	30
M.A.Atherton	lbw b Snedden	82	c Rutherford b Bracewell	70
A.J.Stewart	c Parore b Morrison	9	lbw b Bracewell	15
A.J.Lamb	c Parore b Hadlee	2	st Parore b Bracewell	4
R.A.Smith	c Jones b Bracewell	19	c & b Hadlee	14
N.H.Fairbrother	lbw b Snedden	2	lbw b Bracewell	3
R.C.Russell†	b Snedden	43	c sub (J.J.Crowe) b Hadlee	0
C.C.Lewis	c Rutherford b Bracewell	32	c Parore b Hadlee	1
G.C.Small	not out	44	not out	11
E.E.Hemmings	c Parore b Hadlee	20	b Hadlee	0
D.E.Malcolm	b Hadlee	0	b Hadlee	0
Extras	(b 4, lb 15, nb 9)	28	(lb 6, nb 4)	10
TOTAL	**(141.5 overs)**	**435**	**(49 overs)**	**158**

NEW ZEALAND

T.J.Franklin	c Smith b Hemmings	66	lbw b Malcolm	5
J.G.Wright*	c Russell b Malcolm	24	c Smith b Lewis	46
A.H.Jones	c Russell b Malcolm	2	c Gooch b Small	40
M.D.Crowe	lbw b Lewis	11	lbw b Malcolm	25
M.J.Greatbatch	b Malcolm	45	c Atherton b Hemmings	22
K.R.Rutherford	c Stewart b Hemmings	29	c Lamb b Lewis	18
R.J.Hadlee	c Atherton b Hemmings	8	b Malcolm	13
J.G.Bracewell	b Hemmings	25	(9) c Atherton b Malcolm	0
A.C.Parore†	not out	12	(8) c Lamb b Lewis	20
M.C.Snedden	lbw b Hemmings	2	not out	21
D.K.Morrison	b Hemmings	1	b Malcolm	6
Extras	(b 9, lb 11, w 2, nb 2)	24	(lb 9, w 1, nb 4)	14
TOTAL	**(98.3 overs)**	**249**	**(91.4 overs)**	**230**

Bowling	O	M	R	W	O	M	R	W
NEW ZEALAND								
Hadlee	37.5	8	97	3	21	3	53	5
Morrison	26	7	81	2	3	1	29	0
Snedden	35	9	106	3	9	0	32	1
Bracewell	42	12	130	2	16	5	38	4
Jones	1	0	2	0				
ENGLAND								
Small	18	7	44	0	16	5	56	1
Malcolm	25	7	59	3	24.4	8	46	5
Lewis	19	5	51	1	22	3	76	3
Hemmings	27.3	10	58	6	29	13	43	1
Atherton	9	5	17	0				

Fall of Wickets

	E	NZ	E	NZ
	1st	1st	2nd	2nd
1st	170	45	50	25
2nd	193	67	87	85
3rd	198	90	99	111
4th	245	161	129	125
5th	254	163	136	155
6th	316	185	141	163
7th	351	223	146	180
8th	381	230	157	180
9th	435	243	158	203
10th	435	249	158	230

Martin Snedden was one of three players to bow out of test cricket after this match. The other two were newly knighted Sir Richard Hadlee and John Bracewell.

MILESTONES

- Adam Parore (171) made his test debut.

- John Bracewell became the second player to complete the double of 1000 runs and 100 wickets in the same test, the other being Kapil Dev. He was the second New Zealand cricketer to achieve the double.

- Sir Richard Hadlee captured his 36th five-wicket bag.

- England's total of 158 was its lowest score in a home test against New Zealand.

- Graham Gooch became the 11th England player to score 5000 test runs.

AVERAGES

New Zealand

BATTING	M	I	NO	Runs	HS	Ave
T.J. Franklin	3	5	1	227	101	56.75
J.G. Wright	3	5	0	177	98	35.40
A.C. Parore	1	2	1	32	20	32.00
I.D.S. Smith	2	2	1	29	27	29.00
M.J. Greatbatch	3	4	0	115	47	28.75
A.H. Jones	3	5	0	143	49	28.60
R.J. Hadlee	3	4	0	107	86	26.75
M.W. Priest	1	1	0	26	26	26.00
M.D. Crowe	3	4	0	96	59	24.00
M.C. Snedden	3	4	2	36	21*	18.00
K.R. Rutherford	2	3	0	47	29	15.66
J.G. Bracewell	3	4	0	57	28	14.25
D.K. Morrison	3	5	2	9	6	3.00

BOWLING	O	M	R	W	Ave
R.J. Hadlee	133.5	24	384	16	24.00
M.W. Priest	12	4	26	1	26.00
J.G. Bracewell	148	41	400	12	33.33
A.H. Jones	13	3	42	1	42.00
M.C. Snedden	101	30	264	6	44.00
D.K. Morrison	85.4	15	351	7	50.14
K.R. Rutherford	3	0	18	0	-

England

BATTING	M	I	NO	Runs	HS	Ave
M.A. Atherton	3	5	0	357	151	71.40
G.A. Gooch	3	5	0	306	154	61.20
G.C. Small	3	4	2	84	44*	42.00
A.J. Lamb	3	5	1	129	84*	32.25
R.A. Smith	3	5	0	152	64	30.40
A.J. Stewart	3	5	0	147	54	29.40
P.A.J. DeFreitas	2	2	0	52	38	26.00
R.C. Russell	3	4	0	84	43	21.00
C.C. Lewis	1	2	0	33	32	16.50
N.H. Fairbrother	3	5	1	59	33*	14.75
E.E. Hemmings	3	4	1	33	20	11.00
D.E. Malcolm	3	4	2	4	4*	2.00

BOWLING	O	M	R	W	Ave
D.E. Malcolm	118.4	38	269	15	17.93
E.E. Hemmings	107.3	44	215	10	21.50
P.A.J. DeFreitas	59.4	9	175	6	29.16
C.C. Lewis	41	8	127	4	31.75
G.C. Small	104	27	290	5	58.00
M.A. Atherton	10	6	17	0	-
G.A. Gooch	13	7	25	0	-

The New Zealand team in England 1990. Back row (from left): Adam Parore, Danny Morrison, Ken Rutherford, Mark Priest. Second row: Bob Cunis (coach), Trevor Franklin, Shane Thomson, Andrew Jones, Mark Greatbatch, Jonathan Millmow, Pat Culpan (scorer), Mark Plummer (physiotherapist). Front: Jeff Crowe, Martin Snedden, John Bracewell, Ian Taylor (manager), John Wright (captain), Martin Crowe, Richard Hadlee, Ian Smith.

1990/91 New Zealand in Pakistan

With the retirement of Sir Richard Hadlee, John Bracewell and Martin Snedden, and with the unavailability of former skipper John Wright, Jeff Crowe and Andrew Jones, New Zealand faced the toughest tour of its recent history.

203 PAKISTAN v NEW ZEALAND *(First Test)*

at National Stadium, Karachi on 10, 11, 12, 14, 15 October, 1990
Toss : Pakistan. Umpires : Feroz Butt and Mahboob Shah
Pakistan won by an innings and 43 runs

Javed Miandad returned to captain Pakistan for the fifth time. As the temperatures hovered around the century mark it was agreed to bowl a minimum of 72 overs each day. Sent in to bat, New Zealand soon found itself facing the vaunted Pakistan opening bowlers Wasim Akram and Waqar Younis. Their prodigious swing bowling was a new phenomenon for the New Zealanders.

At 51-3 they were in trouble but Mark Greatbatch found a welcome ally in Ken Rutherford and the pair took the sting from the Pakistan attack, managing to turn the pressure back on the home bowlers as they added 116. On the stroke of stumps both were dismissed, leaving New Zealand 175-5.

New Zealand's hope that the tail could wag were not realised as, in 55 minutes, the last five wickets were captured, meaning that the last seven wickets had fallen for 29 runs. The poor start to the day was not helped by the ease with which the Pakistan opening batsmen, Ramiz Raja and Shoaib Mohammad, went about their duties for the rest of the day. By stumps the pair had added 159. The New Zealanders fielded brilliantly to assist the beleaguered bowlers.

The third day was a continuation of the hard slog of the second day and Shoaib replicated the batting occupation of the crease that he had displayed in the previous series in New Zealand. When he reached his century it was his first on his home ground, as his previous two innings there had seen him dismissed in the 90s.

After 655 minutes of disciplined batting Shoaib achieved his double-century. Twenty-five years earlier his father, Hanif Mohammed, had made 203 not out against John Reid's team in Lahore, the identical score made by his son.

Staring at a deficit of 237 New Zealand were soon in strife as well pitched-up, vicious, in-swinging yorkers kept hitting the pads or the stumps. The only batsman with the ability to counter the exceptionally skilled bowlers, Wasim and Waqar, was Martin Crowe. When he finally ran out of partners at the start of the fifth morning he had made 68 out of New Zealand's total of 194.

With five lbw decisions in the second innings, to bring the visitors total to nine for the game, the perennial question of neutral umpires was again raised, with some justification.

NEW ZEALAND

Batsman	1st innings		2nd innings	
T.J.Franklin	c Yousuf b Waqar	16	b Akram	0
D.J.White	c Yousuf b Akram	9	b Akram	18
M.J.Greatbatch	c & b Ijaz	43	lbw b Aaqib	21
M.D.Crowe*	c Ramiz b Waqar	7	not out	68
K.R.Rutherford	b Aaqib	79	lbw b Aaqib	0
D.N.Patel	lbw b Waqar	2	lbw b Akram	19
D.K.Morrison	lbw b Akram	4	(9) b Akram	0
G.E.Bradburn	not out	11	(7) c Salim b Waqar	2
I.D.S.Smith†	lbw b Akram	4	(8) b Waqar	14
C.Pringle	b Waqar	0	lbw b Qadir	20
W.Watson	lbw b Akram	0	lbw b Waqar	11
Extras	(b 5, lb 11, w 2, nb 3)	21	(b 7, lb 9, nb 5)	21
TOTAL	**(84.5 overs)**	**196**	**(62.4 overs)**	**194**

PAKISTAN

Batsman		Runs
Ramiz Raja	c Crowe b Bradburn	78
Shoaib Mohammad	not out	203
Salim Malik	c Rutherford b Pringle	43
Javed Miandad*	lbw b Morrison	27
Wasim Akram	run out	28
Ijaz Ahmed	b Watson	9
Salim Yousuf†	c Crowe b Morrison	13
Abdul Qadir	not out	6
Tauseef Ahmed		
Aaqib Javed		
Waqar Younis		
Extras	(b 3, lb 11, w 1, nb 11)	26
TOTAL	**(140.3 overs) (6 wkts dec)**	**433**

Bowling	O	M	R	W	O	M	R	W		Fall of Wickets			
PAKISTAN											NZ	P	NZ
Akram	29.5	12	44	4	24	5	60	4			1st	1st	2nd
Waqar	22	7	40	4	15.4	4	39	3		1st	28	172	4
Aaqib	16	4	37	1	12	1	45	2		2nd	37	239	23
Qadir	7	1	32	0	10	2	32	1		3rd	51	288	56
Tauseef	5	0	18	0	1	0	2	0		4th	167	360	57
Ijaz	5	0	9	1						5th	174	384	96
NEW ZEALAND										6th	181	413	103
Morrison	28.3	5	86	2						7th	181	-	119
Pringle	25	3	68	1						8th	194	-	120
Watson	40	8	125	1						9th	195	-	173
Bradburn	17	3	56	1						10th	196	-	194
Patel	24	6	62	0									
Crowe	6	1	22	0									

Ken Rutherford played a wonderful assortment of strokes against an exceptional bowling attack.

MILESTONES

- Martin Crowe became New Zealand's 20th test captain.

- Grant Bradburn (172), Chris Pringle (173) and David White (174) made their test debuts.

- Shoaib Mohammad and Ramiz Raja set a Pakistan record against New Zealand of 172 for the first wicket.

- Martin Crowe became New Zealand's second-highest run-scorer in tests.

204 PAKISTAN v NEW ZEALAND *(Second Test)*

at Gaddafi Stadium, Lahore on 18, 19, 20, 22, 23 October, 1990
Toss : New Zealand. Umpires : Athar Zaidi and Salim Badar
Pakistan won by 9 wickets

Martin Crowe's decision to bat first on a grassy pitch seemed incongruous as Pakistan had added a further quick bowler to their side at the expense of a spinner.

The Pakistan bowlers worked cohesively together and it was only a belligerent innings of 33 by Ian Smith, from 41 deliveries, that boosted the total to 160. Adding to New Zealand's misery was the fact that, in the 48 minutes before stumps, Pakistan's openers managed to score 43, with Ramiz Raja playing some powerful on-side shots.

The assault continued at the start of the second day before Ramiz was dismissed for 48. Pakistan's total of 98 had been made in 87 minutes and the visitors' attack was in shreds. It was to the bowlers' great credit that they found their length and direction and closed the flood of runs to a mere trickle.

Once again the seemingly immovable Shoaib Mohammad, most of whose body was hidden by oversized protective gear, was moving his way towards yet another century. By stumps Pakistan had reached the security of 252-4 but Shoaib had been dismissed for 105.

On the third day Ijaz Ahmed was respectful of the New Zealand bowlers in gathering 86 runs and was mainly responsible for Pakistan's lunchtime score of 337-5. In a superb spell after lunch Willie Watson swept all before him to record his best figures in a test match, 6-78 off 36 overs, before Pakistan declared at 373-9.

The New Zealand openers struggled again and, when Danny Morrison came out as nightwatchman to join Crowe, New Zealand had lost their third wicket for 57. Morrison survived a further half an hour at the start of the fourth day before Waqar Younis bowled him.

Crowe had been most patient and, when Ken Rutherford joined him, the pair defied the rampaging fast bowlers for 209 minutes as they added 132 runs and built up hopes of New Zealand being able to salvage a draw. By stumps the tenacious Crowe had achieved his century after 463 minutes. It was his 12th and most courageous test century.

Crowe was the silent partner on the last day as the last four wickets fell for 34 runs and he remained unbeaten on 108 made in 552 minutes. Playing in only his seventh test, Waqar Younis returned his best test figures of 7-86 and captured 10 wickets for the match to proclaim to the cricketing world his undoubted brilliance.

Requiring only 75 runs, Pakistan lost one wicket before they had their victory.

NEW ZEALAND

T.J.Franklin	c Akram b Jaffer	11	c Yousuf b Jaffer	25
D.J.White	c Yousuf b Akram	3	b Waqar	1
M.J.Greatbatch	b Waqar	11	b Waqar	6
M.D.Crowe*	c Malik b Aaqib	20	not out	108
K.R.Rutherford	lbw b Akram	23	(6) lbw b Waqar	60
D.N.Patel	b Waqar	4	(7) c Yousuf b Jaffer	7
G.E.Bradburn	lbw b Jaffer	8	(8) c sub (Aamer Sohail) b Waqar	14
I.D.S.Smith†	c Yousuf b Qadir	33	(9) c Jaffer b Qadir	8
C.Pringle	c Ramiz b Waqar	9	(10) b Waqar	7
D.K.Morrison	c Yousuf b Qadir	0	(5) b Waqar	7
W.Watson	not out	0	lbw b Waqar	0
Extras	(b 5, lb 13, w 5, nb 15)	38	(b 17, lb 10, nb 17)	44
TOTAL	(59 overs)	**160**	(115.5 overs)	**287**

PAKISTAN

Ramiz Raja	c Greatbatch b Watson	48	c Crowe b Morrison	11
Shoaib Mohammad	b Morrison	105	not out	42
Salim Malik	lbw b Watson	6	not out	19
Javed Miandad*	c Smith b Bradburn	43		
Ijaz Ahmed	c Greatbatch b Watson	86		
Salim Yousuf†	c Rutherford b Pringle	33		
Wasim Akram	c Bradburn b Watson	1		
Waqar Younis	b Watson	17		
Salim Jaffer	not out	10		
Aaqib Javed	c Crowe b Watson	7		
Abdul Qadir				
Extras	(b 4, lb 1, nb 12)	17	(lb 1, w 1, nb 3)	5
TOTAL	(125 overs) (9 wkts dec)	**373**	(20.3 overs) (1 wkt)	**77**

Bowling	O	M	R	W	O	M	R	W	Fall of Wickets				
PAKISTAN										NZ	P	NZ	P
										1st	1st	2nd	2nd
Akram	16	3	43	2	9	4	15	0					
Waqar	15	6	20	3	37.5	11	86	7	1st	7	98	10	27
Jaffer	12	2	37	2	25	8	62	2	2nd	30	117	18	-
Aaqib	13	2	37	1	21	9	40	0	3rd	39	192	57	-
Qadir	3	1	5	2	19	4	43	1	4th	79	246	74	-
Shoaib					2	0	8	0	5th	99	317	206	-
Ijaz					2	0	6	0	6th	103	337	228	-
NEW ZEALAND									7th	143	342	264	-
Morrison	29	9	103	1	8	2	36	1	8th	147	363	277	-
Pringle	31	6	112	1	7	4	10	0	9th	154	373	287	-
Watson	36	10	78	6	2	0	12	0	10th	160	-	287	-
Patel	16	5	43	0	3	0	13	0					
Bradburn	13	4	32	1									
White					0.3	0	5	0					

In extreme heat Willie Watson was tireless, bowling his right-arm medium-pacers. Playing in his fifth test, he returned the figures of 6-78 off 36 overs. They were to be the best of his 15-test career.

MILESTONES

- Salim Yousuf became the second Pakistan wicketkeeper to score 1000 runs in test cricket without scoring a century. The other was Wasim Bari.

- Martin Crowe's century, made in 463 minutes, was the slowest test hundred made against Pakistan.

205 PAKISTAN v NEW ZEALAND *(Third Test)*

at Iqbal Stadium, Faisalabad on 26, 28, 29, 30, 31 October, 1990
Toss : New Zealand. Umpires : Athar Zaidi and Salim Badar
Pakistan won by 65 runs

Martin Crowe won the toss at Faisalabad and put Pakistan in to bat on a green, fast track. Pakistan scored 35 before the drinks break with most of their runs coming off Chris Pringle. Given one more over, he had Shoaib Mohammad slash at a wide delivery to be caught in gully. From then on Pringle was lethal; every ball, a potential wicket-taker.

He kept a strict line on off stump and with the assistance of four catches to Ian Smith he moved the ball about to capture 7-52 as Pakistan plunged to be all out for 102. In reply, the visitors reached 36 before Waqar Younis captured four wickets for the cost of one run, and they ended the day at 40-4.

Danny Morrison, who had come in as nightwatchman, did his job so well that he batted for 242 minutes. During this time he assisted Crowe to add 52 for the fifth wicket and helped Smith with 77 for the sixth.

Smith reached his half-century off 34 balls and hit 11 fours from the 49 balls he faced before he was out for 61. Useful contributions from Grant Bradburn and Pringle gave New Zealand a lead of 115. Younis was again New Zealand's bogeyman, claiming another seven wickets.

Two century stands involving Shoaib, 131 with Salim Malik, and 111 with Javed Miandad, not only placed Pakistan in a dominant position but also allowed Shoaib to score his third century of the series. After lunch on the fourth day Pringle dismissed both Shoaib and Miandad within five runs of each other and Danny Morrison found some final reward when he swept through the lower order, capturing four wickets in 27 balls as Pakistan lost its last seven wickets for 48 runs.

New Zealand's task of scoring 243 runs for victory was always going to be difficult and, once again, some dubious umpiring decisions that were criticised by the local correspondents, were made at crucial times. In spite of encouraging batting by Dipak Patel and Bradburn, who together added 84, Younis claimed another five wickets to enable his side to win by 65 runs.

Disclosures after the tour revealed that the New Zealanders had observed the Pakistanis doctoring the ball either with fingernails or bottle tops and that Pringle had experimented with such tactics in the third test to great effect.

PAKISTAN

Ramiz Raja	c Smith b Pringle	20	lbw b Watson		16
Shoaib Mohammad	c Crowe b Pringle	15	c sub (A.C.Parore) b Pringle		142
Salim Malik	c Smith b Pringle	4	(4) c & b Crowe		71
Javed Miandad*	c Smith b Pringle	25	(5) c Bradburn b Pringle		55
Ijaz Ahmed	c Horne b Watson	5	(6) c Horne b Pringle		6
Salim Yousuf†	c Morrison b Watson	14	(3) c Crowe b Pringle		13
Naved Anjum	c Smith b Pringle	10	b Morrison		22
Tauseef Ahmed	c Rutherford b Pringle	1	not out		12
Waqar Younis	b Pringle	0	c Rutherford b Morrison		0
Salim Jaffer	lbw b Watson	0	b Morrison		2
Aaqib Javed	not out	0	c sub (A.C.Parore) b Morrison		4
Extras	(b 3, nb 5)	8	(b 1, lb 8, nb 5)		14
TOTAL	(40.3 overs)	**102**	(139.5 overs)		**357**

NEW ZEALAND

T.J.Franklin	b Waqar	25	c Ijaz b Aaqib		12
P.A.Horne	c Ramiz b Jaffer	0	lbw b Waqar		12
M.J.Greatbatch	c Yousuf b Waqar	8	(4) b Aaqib		0
M.D.Crowe*	c Tauseef b Jaffer	31	(5) c Yousuf b Waqar		10
K.R.Rutherford	b Waqar	0	(6) c Yousuf b Jaffer		25
D.N.Patel	lbw b Waqar	0	(7) c Yousuf b Jaffer		45
D.K.Morrison	c Shoaib b Waqar	25	(3) c Yousuf b Aaqib		0
I.D.S.Smith†	c Malik b Tauseef	61	(9) c & b Waqar		21
G.E.Bradburn	c Yousuf b Waqar	18	(8) not out		30
C.Pringle	not out	24	c Yousuf b Waqar		0
W.Watson	lbw b Waqar	2	lbw b Waqar		2
Extras	(b 12, lb 8, nb 3)	23	(b 10, lb 5, w 1, nb 4)		20
TOTAL	(76.2 overs)	**217**	(58.5 overs)		**177**

Bowling	O	M	R	W	O	M	R	W
NEW ZEALAND								
Morrison	9	3	18	0	29.5	3	105	4
Pringle	16	5	52	7	43	12	100	4
Watson	15.3	5	29	3	44	23	77	1
Patel					6	0	21	0
Crowe					11	5	22	1
Bradburn					6	1	23	0
PAKISTAN								
Waqar	30.2	13	76	7	23.5	9	54	5
Aaqib	10	5	24	0	17	1	57	3
Naved	6	4	13	0				
Jaffer	20	5	47	2	18	4	51	2
Tauseef	10	2	37	1				

Fall of Wickets	P	NZ	NZ	P
	1st	1st	2nd	2nd
1st	35	36	33	23
2nd	37	37	61	25
3rd	42	37	192	28
4th	65	37	300	31
5th	82	89	314	45
6th	92	166	321	64
7th	98	171	349	148
8th	102	178	349	171
9th	102	207	353	171
10th	102	217	357	177

MILESTONES

- Javed Miandad became the fifth batsman to score 8000 runs in test cricket.

- Chris Pringle's 7-52 were the third-best figures by a New Zealand bowler in test cricket. He became the second New Zealand bowler to take 11 wickets in a match.

- Ian Smith scored the fastest half-century (34 balls) by a New Zealand batsman in tests.

- Shoaib Mohammad had now scored five hundreds in five consecutive tests against New Zealand.

- Mark Greatbatch completed 1000 runs in his 17th test.

- Waqar Younis, aged 19, took 29 wickets in the three tests.

Chris Pringle playing in only his third test recorded the third-best bowling figures in an innings for a New Zealander; 7-52. He became the second New Zealand bowler to capture 11 wickets in a test. Pringle admitted afterwards to "doctoring" one side of the ball.

AVERAGES

New Zealand

BATTING	M	I	NO	Runs	HS	Ave
M.D. Crowe	3	6	2	244	108*	61.00
K.R. Rutherford	3	6	0	187	79	31.16
I.D.S. Smith	3	6	0	141	61	23.50
G.E. Bradburn	3	6	2	83	30*	20.75
T.J. Franklin	3	6	0	89	25	14.83
M.J. Greatbatch	3	6	0	89	43	14.83
D.N. Patel	3	6	0	77	45	12.83
C. Pringle	3	6	1	60	24*	12.00
D.J. White	2	4	0	31	18	7.75
P.A. Horne	1	2	0	12	12	6.00
D.K. Morrison	3	6	0	36	25	6.00
W. Watson	3	6	1	15	11	3.00

BOWLING	O	M	R	W	Ave
C. Pringle	122	30	342	13	26.30
W. Watson	137.3	46	321	11	29.18
D.K. Morrison	104.2	22	348	8	43.50
M.D. Crowe	17	6	44	1	44.00
G.E. Bradburn	36	8	111	2	55.50
D.J. White	0.3	0	5	0	-
D.N. Patel	49	11	139	0	-

Pakistan

BATTING	M	I	NO	Runs	HS	Ave
Shoaib Mohammad	3	5	2	507	203*	169.00
Javed Miandad	3	4	0	150	55	37.50
Salim Malik	3	5	1	143	71	35.75
Ramiz Raja	3	5	0	173	78	34.60
Ijaz Ahmed	3	4	0	106	86	26.50
Salim Yousuf	3	4	0	73	33	18.25
Naved Anjum	1	2	0	32	22	16.00
Wasim Akram	2	2	0	29	28	14.50
Tauseef Ahmed	2	2	1	13	12*	13.00
Salim Jaffer	2	3	1	12	10*	6.00
Waqar Younis	3	3	0	17	17	5.66
Aaqib Javed	3	3	1	11	7	5.50
Abdul Qadir	2	1	1	6	6*	-

BOWLING	O	M	R	W	Ave
Waqar Younis	144.4	50	315	29	10.86
Ijaz Ahmed	7	0	15	1	15.00
Wasim Akram	78.5	24	162	10	16.20
Salim Jaffer	75	19	197	8	24.62
Abdul Qadir	39	8	112	4	28.00
Aaqib Javed	89	22	240	7	34.28
Tauseef Ahmed	16	2	57	1	57.00
Shoaib Mohammad	2	0	8	0	-
Naved Anjum	6	4	13	0	-

1990/91 Sri Lanka in New Zealand

206 **NEW ZEALAND v SRI LANKA** *(First Test)*
at Basin Reserve, Wellington on 31 January, 1, 2, 3, 4 February, 1991
Toss : Sri Lanka. Umpires : B.L. Aldridge and S.J. Woodward
Match drawn

Sri Lanka's decision to insert New Zealand on a pitch that was greener than for many seasons was quickly rewarded when three wickets fell for 33 runs. A gale-force wind saw the umpires dispose with the bails for over an hour, which highlighted the performance of Graeme Labrooy who bowled 23 overs into the wind and claimed four wickets. New Zealand's total of 174 was disappointing.

The New Zealand bowlers were unable to come to terms with the gale on the second day as Aravinda de Silva, with Asanka Gurusinha and Arjuna Ranatunga, flayed the bowling unmercifully. Sri Lanka passed New Zealand's total for the loss of two wickets as de Silva and Gurusinha added 143.

Gurusinha was correct and methodical making 70 but it was de Silva's dazzling footwork and hitting the ball square to both sides of the wicket that was exceptional. His century came in 171 minutes and his double-century in 352 minutes.

Ranatunga fed him most of the bowling as the pair went on to make the highest partnership for any wicket against New Zealand. Sri Lanka lost only one wicket on day two in scoring 348 runs with de Silva 203 not out and Ranatunga 52.

Prior to lunch on the third day de Silva set a new ground record in tests, beating South African Jackie McGlew's 255 made in 1952-53. Following de Silva's dismissal for 267, Danny Morrison came into his own, taking three wickets in quick succession, and the innings terminated at 497. Facing a massive deficit of 323 John Wright and Trevor Franklin had reduced that margin by 91 runs at stumps.

The openers had achieved their fourth century opening partnership before Franklin went at 134 and Wright at 148. Andrew Jones and Martin Crowe began their partnership still 175 runs in arrears.

Crowe took 27 minutes to get off the mark but went on to reach his century in 250 minutes while Jones resolutely went about the task in hand. By stumps New Zealand had reached 369-2 and a lead of 46, with Crowe 126 and Jones 82.

The final day became a day of rewriting world and New Zealand test cricket statistics as Jones and Crowe went on to establish a new world test record partnership.

NEW ZEALAND

T.J.Franklin	c sub (S.T.Jayasuriya) b Labrooy	3	lbw b Ramanayake	39
J.G.Wright	c Gurusinha b Labrooy	15	c Tillakaratne b Ramanayake	88
A.H.Jones	c Tillakaratne b Ratnayake	5	c sub (M.A.W.R.Madurasinghe)	
			b Ramanayake	186
M.D.Crowe*	c Tillakaratne b Ramanayake	30	c Tillakaratne b Ranatunga	299
M.J.Greatbatch	c Gurusinha b Labrooy	13	not out	14
K.R.Rutherford	c Tillakaratne b Ratnayake	25		
G.E.Bradburn	c Tillakaratne b Ramanayake	14		
I.D.S.Smith†	c Senanayake b Ratnayake	28		
C.Pringle	lbw b Labrooy	0		
D.K.Morrison	b Ratnayake	13		
W.Watson	not out	10		
Extras	(b 1, lb 7, w 1, nb 9)	18	(lb 9, w 1, nb 35)	45
TOTAL	(58.2 overs)	**174**	(220.3 overs) (4 wkts)	**671**

SRI LANKA

C.P.Senanayake	c Smith b Watson	0
H.P.Tillakaratne†	c Greatbatch b Morrison	21
A.P.Gurusinha	c Crowe b Watson	70
P.A.de Silva	c Bradburn b Morrison	267
A.Ranatunga*	hit wicket b Morrison	55
E.A.R.de Silva	c Smith b Morrison	26
G.F.Labrooy	c Wright b Morrison	0
R.J.Ratnayake	b Watson	26
C.P.H.Ramanayake	not out	14
K.P.J.Warnaweera	b Watson	3
R.S.Mahanama	absent hurt	
Extras	(lb 7, nb 8)	15
TOTAL	(151.1 overs)	**497**

Bowling	O	M	R	W	O	M	R	W
SRI LANKA								
Ratnayake	18.2	6	45	4	30	1	101	0
Labrooy	23	5	68	4	26	1	88	0
Ramanayake	11	3	39	2	40	5	122	2
Warnaweera	6	1	14	0	34	8	75	0
Ranatunga					19.3	4	60	2
de Silva E.A.R.					56	14	141	0
de Silva P.A.					8	0	59	0
Gurusinha					7	0	16	0
NEW ZEALAND								
Morrison	44	6	153	5				
Watson	46.1	10	121	4				
Pringle	31	4	116	0				
Bradburn	26	5	83	0				
Rutherford	2	0	11	0				
Jones	2	0	6	0				

Fall of Wickets	NZ	SL	NZ
	1st	1st	2nd
1st	5	8	134
2nd	18	41	148
3rd	33	184	615
4th	75	362	671
5th	78	449	-
6th	108	449	-
7th	124	454	-
8th	131	487	-
9th	150	497	-
10th	174	-	-

The elegance of Martin Crowe driving straight during his record-breaking innings of 299.

MILESTONES

- Martin Crowe's 299 remains the New Zealand test record.
- Crowe's partnership of 467 with Andrew Jones was the highest for any wicket in test cricket
- Umpire Steve Woodward, standing in his 24th test, equalled the New Zealand record.
- Aravinda de Silva and Arjuna Ranatunga created a fourth wicket record of 178 for Sri Lanka against New Zealand.
- John Wright and Trevor Franklin put on 134, a New Zealand record opening stand against Sri Lanka.

207 NEW ZEALAND v SRI LANKA (*Second Test*)

at Trust Bank Park, Hamilton on 22, 23, 24, 25, 26 February, 1991
Toss : New Zealand. Umpires : B.L. Aldridge and R.S. Dunne
Match drawn

Hamilton became the 64th test cricket venue and the sixth in New Zealand after renovations, including extending the pavilion and re-laying the wicket, had been completed.

For the second successive test Arjuna Ranatunga asked New Zealand to bat first when he won the toss and again his gamble paid off as both openers were out before lunch, with the score at 40. Martin Crowe and Andrew Jones looked as if they were taking off from their record-breaking efforts of the first test when they added 50 run in 63 minutes.

Ian Smith joined Wasim Bari of Pakistan and Bob Taylor of England as the only test wicketkeepers to take seven dismissals in one innings.

The loss of two quick wickets saw Shane Thomson join Jones and they batted for the remainder of the day, resurrecting New Zealand's fortunes. Jones joined the ranks of New Zealand test players to have scored centuries in successive innings, while Thomson was impressive, playing some fine drives. The day ended with New Zealand 221-4.

After the pair had added 113 Rumesh Ratnayake found a new lease of life and began to move the ball either way. He was instrumental in the final six wickets falling for 57 runs and New Zealand finishing with 296.

When Aravinda de Silva was the third batsman dismissed at 41 New Zealand was in a strong position. Throughout all the fuss Asanka Gurusinha was unmoved and accumulated his runs without risk. During the afternoon Crowe went over on his ankle and took no further part in the series. The home side could only ruminate on a series of dropped catches during the innings.

When play began on the third day, with Sri Lanka 180-5, Gurusinha was 81 not out. He reached his century in 312 minutes. Ian Smith ended the innings with seven catches as Sri Lanka were dismissed for 253. John Wright and Trevor Franklin provided a much more solid start and, once Wright found the measure of the pitch, he quickly launched into his favoured drives and raced to his century in 183 minutes, setting up the game for a declaration.

New Zealand sought quick runs from the outset of the fourth day when, for the second time in the game, Jones and Thompson shared a century partnership. Jones reached his second century of the game off the last ball before tea and the declaration was made, leaving Sri Lanka to score 418 to win.

Charith Senanayake and Chandika Hathurusingha attacked all the bowling, adding 95 in 116 minutes and leaving Sri Lanka to score 309 on the last day with nine wickets standing.

After Hathurusingha had set the platform with an excellent 81, de Silva fell quickly, dashing Sri Lanka's hopes. Gurusinha dominated the rest of the innings, scoring his second century of the match.

MILESTONES

- Ian Smith equalled the test record of seven catches in an innings.

- Andrew Jones became the third New Zealander to score a century in each innings of a test, the others being Glenn Turner and Geoff Howarth. He became the first New Zealand player to score three centuries in successive test innings.

- Asanka Gurusinha scored a century in each innings.

- It was only the second instance of players on opposing sides scoring two hundreds each. The other occasion was in 1946/47 at Adelaide when Arthur Morris (Australia) and Dennis Compton (England) achieved the same feat.

- John Wright and Trevor Franklin beat their own first wicket record for New Zealand against Sri Lanka, set in Wellington, by adding 161 for the first wicket.

- Sanath Jayasuriya made his test debut for Sri Lanka.

NEW ZEALAND

T.J.Franklin	c de Silva P.A. b Gurusinha	15	b Ratnayake		69
J.G.Wright	c Hathurusingha b Labrooy	21	c Tillakaratne b Ramanayake		101
A.H.Jones	c Tillakaratne b Ratnayake	122	(4) not out		100
M.D.Crowe*	c Tillakaratne b Ranatunga	36			
K.R.Rutherford	c Tillakaratne b Ramanayake	0	b de Silva E.A.R.		6
S.A.Thomson	b Ramanayake	36	c Tillakaratne b de Silva E.A.R.		55
D.N.Patel	not out	26	b Labrooy		9
I.D.S.Smith†	c Senanayake b Ratnayake	7	not out		6
D.K.Morrison	c Tillakaratne b Ratnayake	0	(3) c Jayasuriya b Ramanayake		0
C.Pringle	b Ratnayake	9			
W.Watson	c Tillakaratne b Ratnayake	4			
Extras	(lb 16, nb 4)	20	(b 3, lb 9, w 2, nb 14)		28
TOTAL	(120.4 overs)	**296**	(105 overs) (6 wkts dec)		**374**

SRI LANKA

C.P.Senanayake	c Smith b Pringle	5	c Jones b Watson		64
U.C.Hathurusingha	c Smith b Morrison	23	c sub (M.J.Greatbatch) b Thomson		81
A.P.Gurusinha	c Thomson b Morrison	119	(4) c Smith b Morrison		102
P.A.de Silva	c Smith b Watson	1	(5) c & b Patel		6
H.P.Tillakaratne†	c Smith b Pringle	12	(6) c sub (G.E.Bradburn) b Patel		26
S.T.Jayasuriya	lbw b Patel	35			
C.P.H.Ramanayake	run out	13	(3) c sub (M.J.Greatbatch) b Watson		11
A.Ranatunga*	c Smith b Morrison	21	(7) not out		20
E.A.R.de Silva	c Smith b Watson	0	(8) not out		11
G.F.Labrooy	c Smith b Watson	6			
R.J.Ratnayake	not out	1			
Extras	(lb 4, nb 13)	17	(b 4, lb 11, nb 8)		23
TOTAL	(93.4 overs)	**253**	(125 overs) (6 wkts)		**344**

Bowling SRI LANKA	O	M	R	W	O	M	R	W
Ratnayake	29.4	10	77	5	27	4	70	1
Labrooy	22	6	46	1	20	2	65	1
Ramanayake	27	9	52	2	26	5	97	2
Gurusinha	14.2	3	36	1	4	1	12	0
de Silva E.A.R.	14	2	35	0	24	6	89	2
Ranatunga	13.4	1	34	1				
Hathurusingha					2	0	15	0
de Silva P.A.					2	0	14	0
NEW ZEALAND								
Morrison	26	6	77	3	25	4	85	1
Pringle	20	5	64	2	12	2	46	0
Watson	26.4	8	65	3	37	8	75	2
Patel	15	4	33	1	39	13	90	2
Thomson	6	1	10	0	8	3	18	1
Jones					4	1	15	0

Fall of Wickets	NZ 1st	SL 1st	NZ 2nd	SL 2nd
1st	40	8	161	95
2nd	40	38	162	121
3rd	125	41	209	238
4th	126	83	222	245
5th	239	163	327	300
6th	239	185	359	320
7th	258	240	-	-
8th	270	246	-	-
9th	288	246	-	-
10th	296	253	-	-

208   **NEW ZEALAND v SRI LANKA** *(Third Test)*

at Eden Park, Auckland on 1, 2, 3, 4, 5 March, 1991
Toss : New Zealand. Umpires : B.L. Aldridge and R.L. McHarg
Match drawn

Ian Smith, captaining the side for the injured Martin Crowe, sent Sri Lanka in to bat on winning the toss. Chris Cairns, playing in his first test in New Zealand, captured his first test wickets and announced his arrival as a test player by worrying Asanka Gurusinha and Aravinda de Silva.

Runs came at a good rate as de Silva was in audacious form and it was only an impetuous hook shot that brought about his downfall on 96. At the end of the day there was a pyrotechnic display from Graeme Labrooy who hit two sixes and one four off the first three balls he faced.

When Sri Lanka's innings terminated before lunch on the second day Labrooy was 70 not out and the total was 380. John Wright again dominated the early batting and when he

was dismissed for 84 the total was 140-3. However, the middle order batting was disappointing and five wickets were down at stumps for 194.

Rain showers interrupted the third day which saw New Zealand stage a minor recovery. Mark Greatbatch, who had not scored a test half-century in his last 16 innings, led the way, batting 266 minutes for a diligent 65. Sri Lanka enjoyed a 63 run first-innings lead before bad light stopped play. They had lost two wickets, extending the lead to 129.

The morning session saw another display of imperial batting by de Silva. Successive short balls were deposited into the square-leg grandstand and Shane Thomson was driven into the grandstand behind cover. Chandika Hathurusingha was no silent partner as the pair added 145. His 74 was an elegant affair.

Aravinda de Silva achieved his second century of the series but his dismissal saw Thomson and Cairns share five wickets for 12 runs, one of the few times that bowlers had prospered in the series. To win the test New Zealand needed to score 383 runs.

At the beginning of the fifth day New Zealand required a run rate of 3.72 per over, by lunch it had risen to 4.87 and they had lost both openers. The early loss of Greatbatch and Ken Rutherford following lunch virtually put paid to the chase, but not before Andrew Jones brought up his now traditional half-century.

SRI LANKA

C.P.Senanayake	c Smith b Cairns	20	c Greatbatch b Cairns		8
U.C.Hathurusingha	b Watson	13	c Smith b Cairns		74
A.P.Gurusinha	lbw b Cairns	50	c & b Cairns		29
P.A.de Silva	c Smith b Cairns	96	c Morrison b Thomson		123
A.Ranatunga*	c Smith b Cairns	34	c Thomson b Cairns		30
H.P.Tillakaratne†	lbw b Morrison	31	c Cairns b Thomson		3
S.T.Jayasuriya	c Smith b Watson	18	not out		12
E.A.R.de Silva	c Jones b Patel	2	(9) c Greatbatch b Thomson		0
G.F.Labrooy	not out	70	(8) c Morrison b Cairns		1
R.J.Ratnayake	c Greatbatch b Watson	18	c Greatbatch b Morrison		20
C.P.H.Ramanayake	c Smith b Morrison	1	b Morrison		0
Extras	(b 2, lb 15, w 1, nb 9)	27	(b 1, lb 5, nb 13)		19
TOTAL	(105 overs)	**380**	(98 overs)		**319**

NEW ZEALAND

T.J.Franklin	lbw b Ratnayake	13	c Tillakaratne b Labrooy		31
J.G.Wright	c Ranatunga b Ramanayake	84	c Tillakaratne b Ramanayake		20
A.H.Jones	c Ratnayake b de Silva E.A.R.	27	lbw b Labrooy		73
M.J.Greatbatch	lbw b Labrooy	65	b Labrooy		7
K.R.Rutherford	c Gurusinha b de Silva E.A.R.	15	b Labrooy		6
S.A.Thomson	lbw b Ratnayake	1	not out		80
D.N.Patel	c Labrooy b Ramanayake	41	not out		16
I.D.S.Smith*†	b Ratnayake	3			
C.L.Cairns	c de Silva P.A. b Labrooy	17			
D.K.Morrison	lbw b Labrooy	7			
W.Watson	not out	5			
Extras	(b 1, lb 7, nb 31)	39	(b 1, lb 9, nb 18)		28
TOTAL	(125.3 overs)	**317**	(99 overs) (5 wkts)		**261**

Bowling NEW ZEALAND	O	M	R	W	O	M	R	W
Morrison	21	5	87	2	20	3	74	2
Cairns	32	5	136	4	27	6	75	5
Watson	31.5	11	81	3	9	1	23	0
Thomson	12.1	6	22	0	19	5	63	3
Patel	8	2	37	1	23	6	78	0
SRI LANKA								
Labrooy	21.3	6	48	3	19	6	42	4
Ramanayake	26	7	96	2	19	4	62	1
Ratnayake	33	3	83	3	21	3	44	0
de Silva E.A.R.	39	8	67	2	25	4	61	0
Gurusinha	6	2	15	0	2	1	1	0
Ranatunga					7	1	23	0
Jayasuriya					6	1	18	0

Fall of Wickets	SL 1st	NZ 1st	SL 2nd	NZ 2nd
1st	34	63	9	39
2nd	61	139	56	80
3rd	132	140	201	95
4th	223	170	276	117
5th	234	172	282	217
6th	255	247	282	-
7th	273	257	285	-
8th	325	299	288	-
9th	356	304	319	-
10th	380	317	319	-

Jones and Thomson shared their third century partnership of the series. Thomson's 80 not out was his test best to date, as were his bowling figures of 3-63.

MILESTONES

- Ian Smith became the 21st test captain of New Zealand and the first wicketkeeper to lead his side. He also made his 400th first-class dismissal.

- Graeme Labrooy created a world test record by reaching 50 with only 13 scoring shots. It was also the first test half-century made without a single.

- Andrew Jones set a New Zealand record for a home three-test series by scoring 513 runs.

- Chris Cairns captured his first five-wicket bag in first-class cricket.

Chris Cairns made his test debut 13 tests earlier. Because of injuries this was only his second test. Cairns ended the test with his first five-wicket bag and nine for the game. It was not only a great boost for the young man but also for cricket and New Zealand.

AVERAGES

New Zealand

BATTING	M	I	NO	Runs	HS	Ave
M.D. Crowe	2	3	0	365	299	121.66
A.H. Jones	3	6	1	513	186	102.60
S.A. Thomson	2	4	1	172	80*	57.33
J.G. Wright	3	6	0	329	101	54.83
D.N. Patel	2	4	2	92	41	46.00
M.J. Greatbatch	2	4	1	99	65	33.00
T.J. Franklin	3	6	0	170	69	28.33
W. Watson	3	3	2	19	10*	19.00
C.L. Cairns	1	1	0	17	17	17.00
I.D.S. Smith	3	4	1	44	28	14.66
G.E. Bradburn	1	1	0	14	14	14.00
K.R. Rutherford	3	5	0	52	25	10.40
D.K. Morrison	3	4	0	20	13	5.00
C. Pringle	2	2	0	9	9	4.50

BOWLING	O	M	R	W	Ave
C.L. Cairns	59	11	211	9	23.44
S.A. Thomson	45.1	15	113	4	28.25
W. Watson	150.4	38	365	12	30.41
D.K. Morrison	136	24	476	13	36.61
D.N. Patel	85	25	238	4	59.50
C. Pringle	63	11	226	2	113.00
K.R. Rutherford	2	0	11	0	-
A.H. Jones	6	1	21	0	-
G.E. Bradburn	26	5	83	0	-

Sri Lanka

BATTING	M	I	NO	Runs	HS	Ave
P.A. de Silva	3	5	0	493	267	98.60
A.P. Gurusinha	3	5	0	370	119	74.00
U.C. Hathurusingha	2	4	0	191	81	47.75
A. Ranatunga	3	5	1	160	55	40.00
S.T. Jayasuriya	2	3	1	65	35	32.50
G.F. Labrooy	3	4	1	77	70*	25.66
R.J. Ratnayake	3	4	1	65	26	21.66
C.P. Senanayake	3	5	0	97	64	19.40
H.P. Tillakaratne	3	5	0	93	31	18.60
E.A.R. de Silva	3	5	1	39	26	9.75
C.P.H. Ramanayake	3	5	1	39	14*	9.75
K.P.J. Warnaweera	1	1	0	3	3	3.00
R.S. Mahanama	1	-	-	-	-	-

BOWLING	O	M	R	W	Ave
G.F. Labrooy	131.3	26	357	13	27.46
R.J. Ratnayake	159	27	420	13	32.30
A. Ranatunga	40.1	6	117	3	39.00
C.P.H. Ramanayake	149	33	468	11	42.54
A.P. Gurusinha	33.2	7	80	1	80.00
E.A.R. de Silva	158	34	393	4	98.25
U.C. Hathurusingha	2	0	15	0	-
S.T. Jayasuriya	6	1	18	0	-
P.A. de Silva	10	0	73	0	-
K.P.J. Warnaweera	40	9	89	0	-

1991/92 England in New Zealand

209 **NEW ZEALAND v ENGLAND** *(First Test)*

at Lancaster Park, Christchurch on 18, 19, 20, 21, 22 January, 1992
Toss : New Zealand. Umpires : B.L. Aldridge and R.S. Dunne
England won by an innings and 4 runs

Martin Crowe's decision to ask England to bat first misfired when his bowlers failed to exploit any early life in the pitch. After the first hour it was a batsman's paradise and the first eight English batsmen, with the exception of Graham Gooch, took full advantage of it.

Alec Stewart and Robin Smith set the tone for the day by adding 179 in just 50 overs and maiden overs were as rare as wickets taken. Stewart compiled his highest test score of 148 and England ended the first day at 310-4.

England continued on the second day with three partnerships exceeding 75. Allan Lamb became the second batsman in the innings, after Robin Smith, to be dismissed in the 90s. A bonus for England was the uninhibited hitting of Chris Lewis who unfurled drives and cuts of genuine quality in scoring 70 off 73 balls. England declared at 580-9.

Rain delayed play and only 70 overs were possible on the third day. John Wright and Blair Hartland began confidently,

adding 51 for the first wicket, before the left-arm spinner Phil Tufnell relegated the home side's top order to the pavilion, claiming four of the first five wickets to fall at 91.

The Kenyan-born all-rounder Dipak Patel, who had played county cricket for Worcestershire and was now a naturalised Kiwi, set about breaking up Tufnell's rhythm by using his feet and lofting the ball judiciously. He was 55 not out at stumps, New Zealand 169-6.

Patel and Chris Cairns added 50 in 48 minutes and the pair continued in a positive frame, adding 117 before Patel hesitated over taking a third run and was run out for 99, an inglorious end to a valiant innings. Cairns displayed maturity beyond his years in scoring his first test fifty but New Zealand's innings terminated at 312 and they were asked to follow on 268 behind.

Both Wright and Hartland were unfazed by the tired England attack and relished batting on a perfect surface. Only a debatable bat-pad decision against Hartland at the end of the day, with the score at 81, spoilt their enjoyment.

For 213 minutes on the fifth day Wright and Andrew Jones proved immovable as they easily countered the pace and whatever spin was used against them until Jones was dismissed on the stroke of tea at 182-3 ,with Wright 99 not

Dipak Patel had reached a majestic 97 when he pulled a short ball from Chris Lewis. It went wide of mid-on for an easy two but he was tempted to try for a third only to self destruct and run himself out for 99.

ENGLAND

G.A.Gooch*	c Smith b Morrison	2
A.J.Stewart	c Crowe b Morrison	148
G.A.Hick	lbw b Cairns	35
R.A.Smith	c Greatbatch b Pringle	96
A.J.Lamb	b Patel	93
R.C.Russell†	run out	36
D.A.Reeve	c Jones b Pringle	59
C.C.Lewis	b Pringle	70
D.R.Pringle	c Greatbatch b Patel	10
P.A.J.DeFreitas	not out	7
P.C.R.Tufnell		
Extras	(b 5, lb 10, w 1, nb 8)	24
TOTAL	(163 overs) (9 wkts dec)	**580**

NEW ZEALAND

B.R.Hartland	c Smith b Tufnell	22	c Smith b Tufnell	45
J.G.Wright	c Lamb b Tufnell	28	st Russell b Tufnell	99
A.H.Jones	lbw b Lewis	16	(4) c Russell b Pringle	39
M.J.Greatbatch	c Stewart b Tufnell	11	(6) c Smith b Tufnell	0
S.A.Thomson	b Tufnell	5	(7) lbw b Tufnell	0
D.N.Patel	run out	99	(8) c Pringle b Tufnell	6
M.D.Crowe*	c Stewart b Pringle	20	(5) c Pringle b Tufnell	48
C.L.Cairns	c Hick b Reeve	61	(9) c Smith b Tufnell	0
I.D.S.Smith†	lbw b DeFreitas	20	(10) c Russell b Lewis	1
D.K.Morrison	not out	8	(3) c Russell b Lewis	0
C.Pringle	c Hick b DeFreitas	6	not out	5
Extras	(b 1, lb 7, nb 8)	16	(b 1, lb 7, nb 13)	21
TOTAL	(127.4 overs)	**312**	(132.1 overs)	**264**

Bowling	O	M	R	W	O	M	R	W
NEW ZEALAND								
Morrison	33	5	133	2				
Cairns	30	3	118	1				
Pringle	36	4	127	3				
Thomson	15	3	47	0				
Patel	46	5	132	2				
Jones	3	0	8	0				
ENGLAND								
DeFreitas	32.4	16	54	2	23	6	54	0
Lewis	30	9	69	1	22	3	66	2
Pringle	15	2	54	1	21	5	64	1
Tufnell	39	10	100	4	46.1	25	47	7
Hick	3	0	11	0	14	8	11	0
Reeve	8	4	16	1	2	0	8	0
Smith					4	2	6	0

Fall of Wickets	E	NZ	NZ
	1st	1st	2nd
1st	6	51	81
2nd	95	52	81
3rd	274	73	182
4th	310	87	211
5th	390	91	222
6th	466	139	222
7th	544	256	236
8th	571	279	241
9th	580	306	250
10th	-	312	264

out. Wright was stranded on 99 for 25 minutes before he charged down the pitch at Tufnell and was stumped by a considerable margin.

With that, the floodgates opened and all, with the exception of Crowe, seemed mesmerised by Tufnell's flight. Last batsman Chris Pringle came out with 7.5 overs remaining and 18 runs needed to make England bat again. With time almost up Crowe gambled on hitting a four to save the game. The ball was caught at wide mid-off and the game was lost by an innings and four runs.

MILESTONES

- Blair Hartland (175) made his test debut.

- England's total of 580-9d was the highest test score made by any country at Lancaster Park.

- Martin Crowe passed 4000 test runs in his 57th test.

- Dipak Patel and Chris Cairns put on 117, a New Zealand record for the seventh wicket against England.

- John Wright became the third player in test history to be twice dismissed for 99. The others were Geoffrey Boycott and Mike Smith, both of England.

- It was the first time that four players were dismissed in the nineties in one test.

- Phil Tufnell's figures of 7-42 were the best by an overseas bowler in a test at Lancaster Park.

210 NEW ZEALAND v ENGLAND *(Second Test)*

at Eden Park, Auckland on 30, 31 January, 1, 2, 3 February, 1992
Toss : New Zealand. Umpires : B.L. Aldridge and R.S. Dunne
England won by 168 runs

The first day's play was restricted to 59 overs because of bad weather and, when Allan Lamb survived a hat-trick ball from Chris Cairns, the scoreboard showed England three wickets down for nine runs with the 21 year-old, stand-in wicketkeeper Adam Parore having taken three catches.

The wicket had a thick sole of grass and moisture in the pitch made batting a nightmare. Regrettably, the New Zealand slip cordon dropped three catches as New Zealand sought to claim total dominance. England struggled to be 146-7 at stumps.

Cairns captured three wickets on the second morning to give him 6-52 and, because of Derek Pringle's defiant 41, England reached 203. Parore ended with five catches.

Thanks to the first fifty partnership of the game, between Martin Crowe and Ken Rutherford, New Zealand reached 91 for the loss of two before the England bowlers, spearheaded by Chris Lewis, captured seven wickets and the home side slumped to 141-9.

With a lead of 61 gained early on the third day and the wicket still at its cantankerous worst, good fortune shone on England and Graham Gooch as he played and missed consistently after his team had lost two wickets cheaply. Aided by Robin Smith, he weathered the storm and provided the backbone of the innings.

Lamb replaced Smith, and immediately went on the attack, scoring 50 off 33 balls in 49 minutes; it was the impetus that England required. By comparison, Gooch's fifty had taken 181 minutes and his 16th test hundred duly arrived 73 minutes later. England was in a strong position at 272-6 when the third day ended.

On the fourth morning seven wickets, as many as had fallen on the previous day, went in a period of 42 minutes. The last four English wickets fell for two runs and the first three New Zealand wickets for seven runs. It befell Crowe and Rutherford to extricate New Zealand from its hopeless position. They battled the vagaries of the pitch diligently, adding 70 for the fourth wicket before they were parted.

After that, wickets fell at regular intervals and the brightest batting came from Murphy Su'a who hit 30 of his 36 not out in boundaries. The last two wickets fell at the beginning of the fifth day with England winning by an innings and 168 runs.

ENGLAND

G.A.Gooch*	c Parore b Morrison	4	run out		114
A.J.Stewart	c Parore b Cairns	4	c Parore b Su'a		8
G.A.Hick	lbw b Cairns	30	lbw b Su'a		4
R.A.Smith	c Parore b Cairns	0	b Morrison		35
A.J.Lamb	b Su'a	13	c Watson b Patel		60
D.A.Reeve	c Parore b Watson	22	lbw b Watson		25
C.C.Lewis	c Cairns b Watson	33	run out		23
R.C.Russell†	c Parore b Cairns	33	c Hartland b Cairns		24
D.R.Pringle	lbw b Cairns	41	lbw b Cairns		2
P.A.J.DeFreitas	c Crowe b Cairns	1	c Wright b Morrison		0
P.C.R.Tufnell	not out	6	not out		0
Extras	(lb 11, nb 5)	16	(b 8, lb 16, nb 2)		26
TOTAL	(83 overs)	**203**	(98.4 overs)		**321**

NEW ZEALAND

B.R.Hartland	lbw b Lewis	0	c Russell b DeFreitas		0
J.G.Wright	b Pringle	15	lbw b Lewis		0
A.H.Jones	c Smith b DeFreitas	14	lbw b DeFreitas		5
M.D.Crowe*	c Hick b Lewis	45	c Lamb b DeFreitas		56
K.R.Rutherford	c Russell b DeFreitas	26	c Stewart b Pringle		32
D.N.Patel	lbw b Lewis	24	c & b Tufnell		17
C.L.Cairns	c Hick b Tufnell	1	c Russell b Tufnell		24
A.C.Parore†	lbw b Pringle	0	lbw b Lewis		15
M.L.Su'a	not out	0	lbw b DeFreitas		36
D.K.Morrison	lbw b Lewis	0	run out		12
W.Watson	b Lewis	2	not out		5
Extras	(nb 15)	15	(lb 1, nb 11)		12
TOTAL	(63 overs)	**142**	(79 overs)		**214**

Bowling	O	M	R	W	O	M	R	W	Fall of Wickets				
NEW ZEALAND										E	NZ	E	NZ
										1st	1st	2nd	2nd
Morrison	17	2	55	1	21.4	6	66	2	1st	9	2	29	0
Cairns	21	4	52	6	19	6	86	2	2nd	9	35	33	0
Watson	24	13	41	2	26	10	59	1	3rd	9	91	93	7
Su'a	21	8	44	1	10	3	43	2	4th	31	102	182	77
Patel					22	7	43	1	5th	72	123	263	109
ENGLAND									6th	91	124	269	118
DeFreitas	16	2	53	2	27	11	62	4	7th	128	139	319	153
Lewis	21	5	31	5	27	4	83	2	8th	165	139	320	173
Pringle	15	7	21	2	7	2	23	1	9th	171	139	320	203
Reeve	7	1	21	0					10th	203	142	321	214
Tufnell	4	2	16	1	17	5	45	2					
Hick					1	1	0	0					

MILESTONES

- Murphy Su'a (176) made his test debut.

- England became the first side to win a series in New Zealand since Pakistan did so in 1978/79.

- Between 1978/79 and 1991/92 New Zealand had lost only two home tests – to Australia at Christchurch in 1981/82 and to West Indies at Auckland in 1986/87.

Adam Parore had taken three catches by the time the score had reached nine. Two of them were diving catches from chances which otherwise would have fallen short of first slip.

211 NEW ZEALAND v ENGLAND (*Third Test*)

at Basin Reserve, Wellington on 6, 7, 8, 9, 10 February, 1992
Toss : England. Umpires : B.L. Aldridge and R.S. Dunne
Match drawn

New Zealand's new ball attack was rendered completely ineffectual by abysmal catching with Graham Gooch being dropped at eight and nine. Four other catches were dropped on the first day.

The right-arm off-spin of Dipak Patel was introduced by the 32nd over and not only applied the brakes but captured the first four wickets. Alec Stewart, for the second time in the series, scored a century and was dismissed minutes before stumps for 107 with England 239-5.

Because the catches were taken on the second day and the England batsmen scored at a funereal pace New Zealand emerged with credit when they dismissed the visitors for 305 and ended the day at 104-1. John Wright and Andrew Jones displayed the skills that had made them both masters in the art of crease occupation and neither looked worried by the England attack.

The pair picked up the momentum, adding 77 in the morning session. Facing David Lawrence on 93, Wright sent a devastating pull shot for four and from the next ball repeated the shot to bring up his century in 352 minutes. Jones's century took seven minutes longer to compile.

When Wright was dismissed the partnership had added a record 241 and New Zealand passed England's total for the loss of only two wickets as Martin Crowe assisted Jones to add 64. The excellent work was undone by the great accuracy of the left-arm spinner Phil Tufnell and the right arm off-spinner Graeme Hick, who both toiled throughout the day and received their reward at the end of the day when four wickets fell for 31.

New Zealand began the fourth day at 340-6 and useful contributions by the tail enabled them to declare at 432-9, a lead of 127. England lost Gooch, Hick and Stewart before they were in credit and it was left to Robin Smith and Allan Lamb to ease England's fears going into the last day at 171-3.

At the beginning of the fifth day Lamb was adjudged caught at slip by Crowe off Chris Cairns. Ian Smith said that the ball did not carry, so Lamb stayed and added a further 69 runs with Robin Smith before going on to the highest score of his 14 test centuries, 142.

A mid-innings collapse, where three wickets fell in 32 balls, hinted at an outside chance of victory for New Zealand but Lamb found a determined ally in Jack Russell and a draw was assured.

When England fielded a second time right-arm fast bowler David Lawrence suffered a terrible injury when his left knee split apart after landing when he was bowling. His cries of pain were audible around a now-hushed ground and he had to be stretchered off the ground by his teammates.

ENGLAND

	1st innings		2nd innings	
G.A.Gooch*	b Patel	30	c Rutherford b Cairns	11
A.J.Stewart	b Morrison	107	c Smith b Patel	63
G.A.Hick	b Patel	43	c Smith b Su'a	22
R.A.Smith	c Rutherford b Patel	6	c & b Su'a	76
A.J.Lamb	c Smith b Patel	30	c Latham b Patel	142
D.A.Reeve	c Latham b Su'a	18	b Su'a	0
D.V.Lawrence	c Rutherford b Cairns	6		
I.T.Botham	c Cairns b Su'a	15	(7) lbw b Patel	1
R.C.Russell†	lbw b Morrison	18	(8) not out	24
P.A.J.DeFreitas	lbw b Morrison	3		
P.C.R.Tufnell	not out	2		
Extras	(b 4, lb 12, nb 11)	27	(lb 13, nb 7)	20
TOTAL	(118.1 overs)	**305**	(119.3 overs) (7 wkts dec)	**359**

NEW ZEALAND

	1st innings		2nd innings	
B.R.Hartland	c Botham b Lawrence	2	lbw b Botham	19
J.G.Wright	c Reeve b Tufnell	116	c Russell b Botham	0
A.H.Jones	b Hick	143	(4) lbw b Reeve	9
M.D.Crowe*	b Tufnell	30	(3) not out	13
K.R.Rutherford	run out	8	not out	2
R.T.Latham	b Hick	25		
D.N.Patel	lbw b Hick	9		
C.L.Cairns	c Russell b Botham	33		
I.D.S.Smith†	b Hick	21		
M.L.Su'a	not out	20		
D.K.Morrison	not out	0		
Extras	(b 1, lb 15, w 1, nb 8)	25		0
TOTAL	(192 overs) (9 wkts dec)	**432**	(24 overs) (3 wkts)	**43**

Bowling	O	M	R	W	O	M	R	W
NEW ZEALAND								
Morrison	22.1	6	44	3	23	5	63	0
Cairns	25	3	89	1	22	4	84	1
Su'a	36	10	62	2	33	10	87	3
Patel	34	10	87	4	41.3	12	112	3
Jones	1	0	7	0				
ENGLAND								
DeFreitas	8	4	12	0				
Lawrence	27	7	67	1	2.1	1	4	0
Tufnell	71	22	147	2	9	5	12	0
Hick	69	27	126	4				
Botham	14	4	53	1	8	1	23	2
Reeve	3	1	11	0	4.5	2	4	1

Fall of Wickets	E 1st	NZ 1st	E 2nd	NZ 2nd
1st	83	3	17	4
2nd	159	244	52	24
3rd	169	308	127	41
4th	215	312	249	-
5th	235	327	249	-
6th	248	340	254	-
7th	277	369	359	-
8th	286	404	-	-
9th	298	430	-	-
10th	305	-	-	-

MILESTONES

- Rod Latham (177) made his test debut.

- John Wright and Andrew Jones added 241 for the second wicket, a New Zealand test record against all countries.

- Ian Botham became the 13th player to appear in 100 test matches.

- Phil Tufnell bowled 71 overs in the first innings, a record for first-class cricket in New Zealand.

Andrew Jones began in a circumspect mood but as his innings developed so his shots became more regal. He hit 15 fours in his 143.

AVERAGES

New Zealand

BATTING	M	I	NO	Runs	HS	Ave
M.L. Su'a	2	3	2	56	36	56.00
J.G. Wright	3	6	0	258	116	43.00
M.D. Crowe	3	6	1	212	56	42.40
A.H. Jones	3	6	0	226	143	37.66
D.N. Patel	3	5	0	155	99	31.00
R.T. Latham	1	1	0	25	25	25.00
C.L. Cairns	3	5	0	119	61	23.80
K.R. Rutherford	2	4	1	68	32	22.66
B.R. Hartland	3	6	0	88	45	14.66
I.D.S. Smith	2	3	0	42	21	14.00
C. Pringle	1	2	1	11	6	11.00
A.C. Parore	1	2	0	15	15	7.50
W. Watson	1	2	1	7	5*	7.00
D.K. Morrison	3	5	2	20	12	6.66
M.J. Greatbatch	1	2	0	11	11	5.50
S.A. Thomson	1	2	0	5	5	2.50

BOWLING	O	M	R	W	Ave
M.L. Su'a	100	31	236	8	29.50
W. Watson	50	23	100	3	33.33
D.N. Patel	143.3	34	374	10	37.40
C.L. Cairns	117	20	429	11	39.00
C. Pringle	36	4	127	3	42.33
D.K. Morrison	116.5	24	361	8	45.12
A.H. Jones	4	0	15	0	-
S.A. Thomson	15	3	47	0	-

England

BATTING	M	I	NO	Runs	HS	Ave
A.J. Lamb	3	5	0	338	142	67.60
A.J. Stewart	3	5	0	330	148	66.00
R.A. Smith	3	5	0	213	96	42.60
C.C. Lewis	2	3	0	126	70	42.00
R.C. Russell	3	5	1	135	36	33.75
G.A. Gooch	3	5	0	161	114	32.20
G.A. Hick	3	5	0	134	43	26.80
D.A. Reeve	3	5	0	124	59	24.80
D.R. Pringle	2	3	0	53	41	17.66
I.T. Botham	1	2	0	16	15	8.00
D.V. Lawrence	1	1	0	6	6	6.00
P.A.J. DeFreitas	3	4	1	11	7*	3.66
P.C.R. Tufnell	3	3	3	8	6*	-

BOWLING	O	M	R	W	Ave
P.C.R. Tufnell	186.1	69	367	16	22.93
C.C. Lewis	100	21	249	10	24.90
I.T. Botham	22	5	76	3	25.33
P.A.J. DeFreitas	106.4	39	235	8	29.37
D.A. Reeve	24.5	8	60	2	30.00
D.R. Pringle	58	16	162	5	32.40
G.A. Hick	87	36	148	4	37.00
D.V. Lawrence	29.1	8	71	1	71.00
R.A. Smith	4	2	6	0	-

1992/93 New Zealand in Zimbabwe and Sri Lanka

After the ICC awarded Zimbabwe test status in mid-1992 New Zealand were confirmed as their second test opponents, India having played a test match two weeks earlier. The New Zealand tour, combined with the subsequent trip to Sri Lanka, offered an oustanding chance for the side to build on its World Cup performances.

212 **ZIMBABWE v NEW ZEALAND** *(First Test)*
at Bulawayo Athletic Club on 1, 2, 3, 4, 5 November, 1992
Toss : New Zealand. Umpires : H.D. Bird, K. Kanjee and I.D. Robinson
Match drawn

The first test was played in Bulawayo, situated in a drought-ridden part of southern Zimbabwe, but was shortened by 10 hours through heavy rain. Martin Crowe adopted a positive attitude by electing to bat and instructing his batsman to score their runs quickly. Mark Greatbatch, who had been outstanding in the World Cup with his belligerent batting, began at breakneck speed, registering his fifty off 39 balls.

Good fortune favoured his approach as he was dropped three times before he was dismissed for 87, dominating an opening stand of 116 with Rod Latham. Andrew Jones and Latham continued the onslaught to end the first day at 205-1.

Latham completed his first, and only, test century on the second morning before being run out for 119. Shortly after lunch, with the score at 325-3, heavy rain again fell and terminated the day's play. When the rain came, the local groundsman, a farmer, faced the dilemma of attending to the playing conditions or returning home to plant his vital crops.

Despite sunshine on day three play was unable to begin, as overnight rain had seeped under the covers. Zimbabwe were not keen to restart so Crowe declared New Zealand's innings closed, thus taking benefit of the ruling that allowed the fielding captain the final decision on whether play should proceed. In 41 overs Zimbabwe crawled to 54-1.

After 38 balls on the fourth morning Zimbabwe had slumped to 62-5 before David Houghton and Andy Flower shared a stand of 70 and removed the possibility of being asked to follow on. Dipak Patel, who had opened the bowling with his right arm off-spinners, ended with his career best test figures of 6-113.

Latham and Greatbatch again batted in one-day vein and, for the second time in the game, enjoyed a century opening partnership. In 35 overs New Zealand surged to 163-1, with Greatbatch 80 not out. On the last morning Greatbatch again fell just short of the century and Crowe's declaration left Zimbabwe an unlikely target of 329 to be made off approximately 73 overs. In perfect batting conditions Kevin

Arnott became Zimbabwe's second test centurion as the game petered out to a draw.

Rod Latham made 119 in the first test at Bulawayo.

MILESTONES

- Simon Doull (178) and Mark Haslam (179) made their test debuts.

- Bulawayo became the 69th test venue.

- Umpire Dickie Bird stood in a record 49th test.

- Mark Greatbatch and Rod Latham became the first New Zealand pair to share a century opening partnership in each innings of a test.

- Andrew Jones became the 12th New Zealander to score 2000 runs in test cricket.

NEW ZEALAND

Batsman	1st innings		2nd innings	
M.J.Greatbatch	c Campbell b Omarshah	88	c Houghton b Jarvis	48
R.T.Latham	run out	119	c Houghton b Flower G.W.	48
A.H.Jones	not out	67	retired hurt	39
M.D.Crowe*	c Jarvis b Traicos	42	(5) c Flower A. b Jarvis	6
K.R.Rutherford	not out	7	(7) not out	11
A.C.Parore†			(4) c Houghton b Jarvis	12
S.B.Doull			(6) b Traicos	2
D.N.Patel			not out	11
M.L.Su'a				
M.J.Haslam				
W.Watson				
Extras	(lb 3)	3	(b 1, lb 3, nb 1)	5
TOTAL	(96.1 overs) (3 wkts dec)	**325**	(48 overs) (5 wkts dec)	**222**

ZIMBABWE

Batsman	1st innings		2nd innings	
K.J.Arnott	c Crowe b Patel	30	not out	101
G.W.Flower	c Rutherford b Patel	29	c Latham b Patel	45
M.G.Burmester	c Haslam b Patel	0		
A.D.R.Campbell	run out	0	(3) not out	48
A.J.Pycroft	b Doull	2		
D.L.Houghton*	b Patel	36		
A.Flower†	c Haslam b Su'a	81		
A.H.Omarshah	c Parore b Su'a	28		
G.J.Crocker	b Patel	1		
A.J.Traicos	b Patel	4		
M.P.Jarvis	not out	2		
Extras	(lb 4, nb 2)	6	(lb 2, w 1)	3
TOTAL	(93.4 overs)	**219**	(71.1 overs) (1 wkt)	**197**

Bowling	O	M	R	W	O	M	R	W
ZIMBABWE								
Jarvis	26.1	4	87	0	11	0	38	3
Burmester	14	1	71	0				
Omarshah	14	6	46	1	7	0	36	0
Traicos	23.1	4	56	1	17	1	82	1
Crocker	14	1	57	0	5	0	30	0
Houghton	0.5	0	0	0				
Flower G.W.	4	2	5	0	8	0	32	1
NEW ZEALAND								
Su'a	9	3	18	2	6.1	2	9	0
Patel	40.4	12	113	6	28	7	60	1
Doull	15	6	29	1	4	1	8	0
Watson	7	3	10	0	7	2	21	0
Haslam	21	8	44	0	19	4	76	0
Jones	1	0	1	0				
Latham					3	2	6	0
Crowe					4	0	15	0

Fall of Wickets	NZ	Z	NZ	Z
	1st	1st	2nd	2nd
1st	116	54	102	92
2nd	243	56	181	-
3rd	314	59	193	-
4th	-	62	196	-
5th	-	64	204	-
6th	-	134	-	-
7th	-	194	-	-
8th	-	213	-	-
9th	-	213	-	-
10th	-	219	-	-

213 **ZIMBABWE v NEW ZEALAND** *(Second Test)*

at Harare Sports Club on 7, 9, 10, 11, 12 November, 1992
Toss : New Zealand. Umpires : H.D. Bird, K. Kanjee and I.D. Robinson
New Zealand won by 177 runs

New Zealand was given a positive start when Mark Greatbatch hit his third successive half-century. In the session after lunch Martin Crowe personally scored 96 of the 143 runs that were scored as he exhibited the full repertoire of classical stroke-making: silky drives, delicate cuts, savage pulls and effortless lofted drives over the boundary line. He reached his 14th test century in 134 minutes and he and Ken Rutherford added 168 in only 36 overs to leave New Zealand 314-6 at stumps.

When New Zealand were dismissed for 335 they had lost their last seven wickets for 36 runs. The New Zealand team, playing its 12th day out of 13, showed signs of tiredness and their effort in the field was substandard.

Zimbabwe began the third day at 173-3 and had advanced to 210 without further loss before Murphy Su'a induced a mini-collapse with the second new ball, capturing three wickets in seven balls. He also had Andy Flower dropped before he had scored. Shortly after lunch a thunderstorm

ended play for the day, with the home side 228-6.

High hopes of ending the Zimbabwe innings quickly foundered on more poor catching by the New Zealanders. Five chances were put down as the tailenders added 55 runs before a declaration was made at 283-9. Left-arm fast-medium bowler Su'a completed his first five-wicket haul in tests.

New Zealand made a hesitant start to their second innings, losing both openers with the score at 27. Crowe made a patient 61, despite a strained tendon in his right ankle and a hamstring twinge in his left thigh. It was left to Rutherford and Patel to provide the impetus that the innings required as they added 130 in even time.

Needing 315 to win Zimbabwe were quickly placed on the back foot by a rejuvenated bowling and fielding effort from the visitors. Patel led the bowlers, extracting turn and inconsistent bounce to confuse the batsmen, and finished with his second six-wicket bag of the series and his best test figures of 6-50. It was New Zealand's first test success in 14 matches.

NEW ZEALAND

Batsman	1st innings		2nd innings	
M.J.Greatbatch	c Flower A. b Brain	55	c Brandes b Brain	13
R.T.Latham	c Flower A. b Crocker	15	c Houghton b Brandes	10
A.H.Jones	c Pycroft b Brandes	8	st Flower A. b Traicos	28
M.D.Crowe*	c Burmester b Crocker	140	lbw b Patel	61
K.R.Rutherford	c Flower A. b Traicos	74	c Arnott b Brandes	89
D.N.Patel	c Campbell b Traicos	6	not out	58
A.C.Parore†	run out	2		
D.J.Nash	not out	11		
M.L.Su'a	c Arnott b Brandes	1		
W.Watson	b Brain	3		
M.J.Haslam	c Flower A. b Brain	3		
Extras	(lb 11, nb 6)	17	(lb 2, w 1)	3
TOTAL	(94 overs)	**335**	(82.4 overs) (5 wkts dec)	**262**

ZIMBABWE

Batsman	1st innings		2nd innings	
K.J.Arnott	b Watson	68	c Watson b Nash	10
G.W.Flower	lbw b Su'a	5	c Latham b Su'a	1
A.D.R.Campbell	c Su'a b Patel	52	c Greatbatch b Patel	35
A.J.Pycroft	b Su'a	60	c Latham b Watson	5
D.L.Houghton*	c Parore b Su'a	21	c Nash b Patel	2
A.Flower†	c Patel b Nash	14	c Parore b Patel	9
E.A.Brandes	c Parore b Su'a	0	c & b Patel	6
G.J.Crocker	b Su'a	12	c Greatbatch b Haslam	33
D.H.Brain	c Su'a b Patel	11	c Su'a b Patel	17
M.G.Burmester	not out	30	not out	17
A.J.Traicos	not out	1	lbw b Patel	0
Extras	(lb 7, nb 2)	9	(lb 2)	2
TOTAL	(123 overs) (9 wkts dec)	**283**	(50.3 overs)	**137**

Bowling	O	M	R	W	O	M	R	W
NEW ZEALAND								
Brandes	22	6	49	2	19.4	3	59	2
Brain	18	5	49	3	16	2	52	1
Crocker	15	1	65	2	7	0	24	0
Burmester	10	2	34	0	9	1	44	0
Traicos	23	1	82	2	27	8	70	2
Flower G.W.	6	0	45	0	4	0	11	0
NEW ZEALAND								
Su'a	37	8	85	5	12	3	30	1
Nash	28	10	59	1	8	3	19	1
Watson	25	6	51	1	3	2	3	1
Patel	33	7	81	2	17.3	5	50	6
Haslam					10	2	33	1

Fall of Wickets	NZ	Z	NZ	Z
	1st	1st	2nd	2nd
1st	44	7	21	3
2nd	73	114	27	15
3rd	131	136	77	28
4th	299	210	132	34
5th	306	211	262	56
6th	313	211	-	62
7th	321	239	-	71
8th	327	239	-	91
9th	330	275	-	137
10th	335	-	-	137

MILESTONES

• Dion Nash (180) made his test debut.

• It was Zimbabwe's first defeat in test cricket.

• Ken Rutherford reached 1000 test runs in his 32nd test.

New Zealand became the first country to beat Zimbabwe in a test match, primarily because Dipak Patel was able to extract turn and find erratic bounce from a worn pitch as he claimed 6-50. This was to be his best bowling performance in a test career lasting 37 tests.

214 **SRI LANKA v NEW ZEALAND** *(First Test)*

at Tyronne Fernando Stadium, Moratuwa on 27, 28, 29 November, 1, 2 December, 1992
Toss : Sri Lanka. Umpires : K.T. Francis and T.M. Samarasinghe
Match drawn

Before a ball was bowled in the second leg of the tour in Sri Lanka a bomb-carrying motorcyclist rammed a car carrying a vice-admiral and three of his staff outside the New Zealanders' hotel. The explosion saw body parts strewn for over 100 metres and the team requested to come home. The chairman of New Zealand Cricket, Peter McDermott, immediately flew to Sri Lanka to save the tour.

Six of the tourists, Mark Greatbatch, Rod Latham, Dipak Patel, Gavin Larsen, Willie Watson and coach Warren Lees opted to return to New Zealand and were replaced by John Wright, Grant Bradburn, Michael Owens and Justin Vaughan. The original three-test itinerary was changed and the second

test to be staged at Moratuwa became the first of a two-match series.

A wet outfield delayed the start of play and New Zealand was struggling when the fourth wicket fell with the score at 87. A tenacious partnership between Ken Rutherford and Chris Harris saw no further wickets fall, and bad light stopped play at 139-4.

The pair extended their stand to 151, as Rutherford recorded his second test century, while the obstinate Harris batted 312 minutes to make 56 in his first test innings. The last six wickets fell for the addition of only 50 runs.

Two successive century partnerships involving Roshan Mahanama, firstly 138 with Asanka Gurusinha and then 133 with Aravinda de Silva, saw New Zealand's total of 288 overtaken for the loss of two wickets. Mahanama's hopes of continuing on from his maiden test century to a double century were ended emphatically when he was run out by Harris for 153.

Rain frustrated Sri Lanka in their attempt to seek victory. It prevented play beginning on time and ended play early. Two wickets fell quickly when play did begin and Sri Lanka declared at 327-6.

Blair Hartland and Wright were intent on occupying the crease and required 26 overs to wipe out the deficit of 39 runs. The day ended with Hartland having scored his first test half-century and Wright being 38 not out and their unbroken partnership worth 104.

In spite of the fact that there was a flurry of early wickets, which saw New Zealand stumble to 136-3, the rest of the last day was mainly academic. It was enlivened by an attractive innings of 53 by Ken Rutherford, his fourth successive test half-century. New Zealand's second innings of 195 occupied 103 overs as they played for a draw.

Ken Rutherford top-scored with 105 in the first test.

NEW ZEALAND

J.G.Wright	c Gurusinha b Ramanayake	11	(2) st Wickremasinghe b Anurasiri	42
B.R.Hartland	c de Silva b Liyanage	3	(1) lbw b Ramanayake	52
A.H.Jones	c Mahanama b Liyanage	35	c Wickremasinghe b Ramanayake	14
M.D.Crowe*	c Ranatunga b Warnaweera	19	c Tillakaratne b Anurasiri	11
K.R.Rutherford	c Wickremasinghe b Hathurusingha	105	lbw b Warnaweera	53
C.Z.Harris	b Warnaweera	56	(7) not out	0
J.T.C.Vaughan	b Liyanage	17	(6) not out	0
A.C.Parore†	c Wickremasinghe b Anurasiri	3		
D.J.Nash	c Wickremasinghe b Liyanage	4		
M.L.Su'a	b Anurasiri	0		
M.B.Owens	not out	0		
Extras	(b 5, lb 12, w 2, nb 16)	35	(lb 8, w 1, nb 14)	23
TOTAL	**(133.5 overs)**	**288**	**(103 overs) (5 wkts)**	**195**

SRI LANKA

R.S.Mahanama	run out	153
U.C.Hathurusingha	c Jones b Nash	10
A.P.Gurusinha	c Vaughan b Su'a	43
P.A.de Silva	c Nash b Su'a	62
H.P.Tillakaratne	b Owens	1
A.Ranatunga*	c Parore b Owens	3
A.G.D.Wickremasinghe†	not out	13
C.P.H.Ramanayake	not out	10
D.K.Liyanage		
S.D.Anurasiri		
K.P.J.Warnaweera		
Extras	(lb 7, w 9, nb 16)	32
TOTAL	**(92 overs) (6 wkts dec)**	**327**

Bowling	O	M	R	W	O	M	R	W
SRI LANKA								
Ramanayake	23	2	57	1	17	6	27	2
Liyanage	26.5	6	82	4	17	4	48	0
Hathurusingha	8	4	12	1	10	6	22	0
Anurasiri	34	11	55	2	26	11	32	2
Warnaweera	34	15	46	2	25	15	31	1
de Silva	4	2	8	0				
Gurusinha	1	0	6	0				
Ranatunga	3	2	5	0	7	2	26	0
Tillakaratne					1	0	1	0
NEW ZEALAND								
Su'a	25	6	62	2				
Owens	17	3	63	2				
Nash	18	2	62	1				
Vaughan	14	0	56	0				
Harris	15	5	64	0				
Jones	1	0	3	0				
Crowe	2	0	10	0				

Fall of Wickets	NZ	SL	NZ
	1st	1st	2nd
1st	6	27	110
2nd	44	164	122
3rd	77	297	136
4th	87	299	160
5th	238	300	194
6th	265	309	-
7th	273	-	-
8th	283	-	-
9th	286	-	-
10th	288	-	-

MILESTONES

- Chris Harris (181), Michael Owens (182) and Justin Vaughan (183) made their test debuts.

- Ken Rutherford and Chris Harris put on 151, a record for the fifth wicket for New Zealand against Sri Lanka.

- Roshan Mahanama and Asanka Gurusinha put on 137, a second wicket record for Sri Lanka against New Zealand.

- Chris Harris scored the third-slowest fifty for New Zealand in a test.

- John Wright became the first New Zealander to score 5000 test runs.

215 SRI LANKA v NEW ZEALAND *(Second Test)*

at Sinhalese Sports Club Ground, Colombo on 6, 7, 8, 9 December 1992
Toss : Sri Lanka. Umpires : I. Anandappa and T.M. Samarasinghe
Sri Lanka won by 9 wickets

Sri Lanka's imposing first innings total of 394 owed much to Roshan Mahanama's second consecutive century. Such was his command that of the first 66 runs scored in the morning, Chandika Hathurusingha only made 13. The pair added 102

for the first wicket, with the stylish Mahanama reaching his hundred off 128 balls.

The bowling, which had been wayward prior to lunch, struggled manfully in the searing heat to restrict the batsmen but Arjuna Ranatunga and Hashan Tillakaratane added 92 with a delightful array of strokes. Sri Lanka; 303-6.

After 328 minutes Tillakaratane's innings of 93 came to an end after he and Don Anurasiri had frustrated New Zealand further by adding 69 for the eighth wicket. Michael Owens displayed great stamina and improved accuracy in claiming four wickets.

Following their century partnership of the previous test John Wright and Blair Hartland were untroubled, reaching 57 before the two unorthodox right-arm off-spinners, Jayananda Warnaweera and Muttiah Muralitharan, struck in tandem with devastating results.

By stumps New Zealand had lost seven wickets for the addition of 43 runs and none of the batsmen were able to fathom the mysteries posed to them. The last three wickets

Michael Owens, a replacement in the team, was quick to seize his chance at test level, claiming four wickets in Sri Lanka's first innings.

were swept away for the addition of two more runs off 19 balls. New Zealand's total of 102 was one of its most lamentable batting efforts of the last decade.

It was left to New Zealand's most experienced pair of Wright and Martin Crowe to bolster New Zealand's follow-on effort after two wickets had fallen for 30 runs. It was a partnership of contrasts, with Wright unyielding in defence and Crowe conducting a masterclass in stroke production as they added 159 for the third wicket. Crowe departed first for 107, which included four sixes and 10 fours, and Wright's vigil ended after 231 minutes for 50.

The fourth day began with New Zealand 277-6. The Sri Lankan attack was again based on the two off-spinners and the left-arm slow bowling of Anurasiri. Surrounded by a hoard of pickpocket fieldsmen Adam Parore displayed good technique and excellent temperament in batting for over three hours as he engineered the last two wickets to add 75. It was his first test half-century.

Muralitharan had match figures of 7-156. In the years to come he was to better this analysis, many, many times. Sri Lanka achieved its target of 70 runs for the loss of Mahanama's wicket, thus securing a comfortable victory with a day to spare.

MILESTONES

- It was Sri Lanka's first test win in 11 tests against New Zealand and their first series win against New Zealand.

- Hashan Tillakaratane took seven catches, equalling the test record by a fielder.

- Hashan Tillakaratane and Don Anurasiri had an eighth wicket stand of 69, a Sri Lankan record against New Zealand.

SRI LANKA

R.S.Mahanama	c Bradburn b Owens	109	c Parore b Owens	29
U.C.Hathurusingha	c Harris b Owens	27	not out	26
A.P.Gurusinha	st Parore b Bradburn	22	not out	14
P.A.de Silva	c Parore b Pringle	3		
A.Ranatunga*	c Parore b Su'a	76		
H.P.Tillakaratne	c Parore b Bradburn	93		
A.G.D.Wickremasinghe†	c Rutherford b Owens	2		
D.K.Liyanage	c Parore b Su'a	16		
S.D.Anurasiri	c Su'a b Owens	24		
M.Muralitharan	not out	4		
K.P.J.Warnaweera	c Crowe b Bradburn	5		
Extras	(b 3, lb 4, w 3, nb 3)	13	(lb 2, nb 2)	4
TOTAL	(128.4 overs)	394	(14.4 overs) (1 wkt)	73

NEW ZEALAND

B.R.Hartland	c Gurusinha b Warnaweera	21	c Muralitharan b Gurusinha	21
J.G.Wright	c Wickremasinghe b Warnaweera	30	c Mahanama b Muralitharan	50
A.H.Jones	c Tillakaratne b Warnaweera	20	c Tillakaratne b Warnaweera	5
M.D.Crowe*	b Muralitharan	0	c Tillakaratne b Muralitharan	107
K.R.Rutherford	c Tillakaratne b Warnaweera	0	c sub (S.T.Jayasuriya) b Warnaweera	38
C.Z.Harris	run out	9	lbw b Anurasiri	19
A.C.Parore†	lbw b Muralitharan	5	c Tillakaratne b Muralitharan	60
G.E.Bradburn	c Tillakaratne b Liyanage	1	c Wickremasinghe b Anurasiri	7
M.L.Su'a	not out	2	b Muralitharan	0
C.Pringle	b Liyanage	0	c Tillakaratne b Liyanage	23
M.B.Owens	c Anurasiri b Muralitharan	0	not out	8
Extras	(lb 4, w 1, nb 9)	14	(b 2, lb 8, nb 13)	23
TOTAL	(52.1 overs)	102	(119 overs)	361

Bowling

NEW ZEALAND	O	M	R	W	O	M	R	W
Su'a	26	7	50	2	2	0	14	0
Owens	30	7	101	4	6	1	36	1
Pringle	32	7	85	1	2	1	5	0
Bradburn	37.4	4	134	3	3	1	8	0
Harris	3	0	17	0				
Jones					1.4	1	8	0
SRI LANKA								
Liyanage	9	3	9	2	12	3	35	1
Gurusinha	4	1	15	0	8	1	19	1
Anurasiri	6	1	13	0	22	4	54	2
Hathurusingha	7	3	14	0	3	2	2	0
Warnaweera	14	3	25	4	34	4	107	2
Muralitharan	12.1	3	22	3	40	5	134	4

Fall of Wickets

	SL 1st	NZ 1st	NZ 2nd	SL 2nd
1st	102	58	23	36
2nd	160	61	30	-
3rd	167	64	189	-
4th	182	65	240	-
5th	274	89	240	-
6th	287	98	261	-
7th	316	100	285	-
8th	385	101	286	-
9th	385	101	317	-
10th	394	102	361	-

The New Zealand team in Sri Lanka. Back row (from left): Adam Parore, Justin Vaughan, Murphy Su'a, Blair Hartland, Chris Harris, Chris Pringle, Michael Owens, Dion Nash, Grant Bradburn, Mark Haslam. Front: Mark Plummer (physiotherapist), John Wright, Leif Dearsley (manager), Martin Crowe (captain), Andrew Jones, Ken Rutherford.

1992/93 Pakistan in New Zealand

Pakistan, engaged in a series in Australia, asked for a test and three one-day internationals when they had a fortnight's lull. Finger injuries meant that John Wright and Martin Crowe were unavailable and Ken Rutherford became the test captain.

216 NEW ZEALAND v PAKISTAN *(Only Test)*

at Trust Bank Park, Hamilton on 2, 3, 4, 5 January 1993
Toss : New Zealand. Umpires : B.L. Aldridge and R.S. Dunne
Pakistan won by 33 runs

Danny Morrison and Murphy Su'a had Pakistan struggling at 12-3 before Javed Miandad exhibited the true art of batting on a seamer-friendly pitch, compiling his 65th score of 50 or more in tests. His 92 steered his team to 216, while Su'a returned his best test figures of 5-73.

Pakistan's poor catching enabled Mark Greatbatch and Blair Hartland to survive against the ferocity of Wasim Akram and Waqar Younis with as many as three balls each over threatening the batsmen's heads. Courageously, they brought up their 100 partnership in 180 minutes but not before Hartland had his helmet hit twice and broken.

Once Hartland was dismissed, wickets fell at regular intervals and Greatbatch's monumental effort concluded 10 minutes from stumps when he was lbw to Waqar for 133, made in 427 minutes.

New Zealand's innings ended at 264 the next day with Adam Parore being the sixth batsman in the innings dismissed lbw. New Zealand appeared to have the game won when Pakistan were 39-5, still nine runs in arrears.

Left-arm seamer Murphy Su'a has his exuberant appeal against Javed Miandad answered in the affirmative.

Morrison captured four of the first five wickets but Inzamam-ul-Haq and Rashid Latif added 80 vital runs and gave their bowlers something of a target. When Pakistan was dismissed for 174 New Zealand required just 127 for victory.

A fiery opening spell by Akram saw him capture three wickets before stumps and leave New Zealand requiring 88 runs on the final day with seven wickets remaining.

Andrew Jones and Parore survived a further 40 minutes before a freakish reflex catch by Asif Mujtaba saw Jones depart with the total at 65. Fast bowling of the highest calibre tore through the remaining six wickets for 28 with Younis and Akram each claiming five wickets as Pakistan seized an improbable victory by 33 runs.

PAKISTAN

Ramiz Raja	c Rutherford b Su'a	4	(2) c Parore b Morrison	8
Aamer Sohail	c Owens b Morrison	0	(1) b Morrison	0
Asif Mujtaba	c Owens b Su'a	0	lbw b Morrison	11
Javed Miandad*	b Su'a	92	lbw b Su'a	12
Salim Malik	c Parore b Morrison	14	c Su'a b Morrison	0
Inzamam-ul-Haq	c Morrison b Su'a	23	lbw b Owens	75
Wasim Akram	c Greatbatch b Patel	27	(8) b Patel	15
Rashid Latif†	not out	32	(7) c Rutherford b Su'a	33
Waqar Younis	run out	13	not out	4
Mushtaq Ahmed	lbw b Su'a	2	c Rutherford b Morrison	10
Aaqib Javed	c Greatbatch b Morrison	1	c Hartland b Patel	2
Extras	(w 4, nb 4)	8	(lb 2, nb 2)	4
TOTAL	(69.3 overs)	**216**	(55.1 overs)	**174**

NEW ZEALAND

M.J.Greatbatch	lbw b Waqar	133	(2) c Sohail b Akram	8
B.R.Hartland	st Latif b Mushtaq	43	(1) b Wasim Akram	9
A.H.Jones	lbw b Akram	2	c Mujtaba b Waqar	19
R.T.Latham	lbw b Akram	2	(6) b Waqar	0
K.R.Rutherford*	c Latif b Mushtaq	14	(7) c Sohail b Akram	9
C.Z.Harris	lbw b Waqar	6	(8) b Waqar	9
D.N.Patel	lbw b Mushtaq	12	(9) b Waqar	4
A.C.Parore†	lbw b Akram	16	(5) c Latif b Akram	13
M.L.Su'a	c Latif b Waqar	0	(10) lbw b Akram	0
D.K.Morrison	not out	3	(4) lbw b Akram	0
M.B.Owens	b Waqar	0	not out	0
Extras	(b 1, lb 15, w 1, nb 16)	33	(b 1, lb 11, nb 10)	22
TOTAL	(109 overs)	**264**	(43.3 overs)	**93**

Bowling NEW ZEALAND	O	M	R	W	O	M	R	W
Morrison	19.4	3	42	3	15	2	41	5
Su'a	24	2	73	5	13	1	47	2
Owens	12	3	48	0	7	0	19	1
Patel	14	2	53	1	20.1	5	65	2
PAKISTAN								
Akram	31	9	66	3	22	4	45	5
Waqar	28	11	59	4	13.3	4	22	5
Mushtaq	38	10	87	3				
Aaqib	7	2	24	0	8	2	14	0
Sohail	5	2	12	0				

Fall of Wickets	P 1st	NZ 1st	P 2nd	NZ 2nd
1st	4	108	4	19
2nd	4	111	20	31
3rd	12	117	25	32
4th	45	147	25	65
5th	87	164	39	67
6th	158	193	119	71
7th	176	254	158	88
8th	202	256	158	88
9th	208	257	171	88
10th	216	264	174	93

MILESTONES

- Ken Rutherford became New Zealand's 22nd test captain.
- Waqar Younis took his 100th test wicket in his 20th test.
- Wasim Akram completed the test double of 1000 runs and 100 wickets.
- Javed Miandad ended the match with 8569 runs, the third highest on the all-time test list.
- Six lbws in New Zealand's first innings equalled the record for test cricket.

1992/93 Australia in New Zealand

▮217▮ NEW ZEALAND v AUSTRALIA *(First Test)*
at Lancaster Park, Christchurch on 25, 26, 27, 28 February, 1993
Toss : New Zealand. Umpires : B.L. Aldridge and C.E. King
Australia won by an innings and 60 runs

Heavy rain in the week before the match meant that preparation of the pitch was minimal. The dark green appearance convinced Martin Crowe to ask the visitors to bat first.

Thanks to wayward bowling the Australians were able to build a solid base with Mark Taylor typifying this grafting approach as he batted 140 minutes before scoring his first boundary. His 82 was the first time in 17 test innings that he had scored a half-century. Justin Langer played in a similar manner to be 63 not out at stumps; Australia 217-3.

Allan Border, intent on playing a long innings, came to the crease when Langer was dismissed in the first over of the second day. Initially the pace and movement of Danny Morrison worried him and it took him 90 minutes before his trademark pulls, cover drives and cuts were played with confidence.

After 160 minutes he drove Dipak Patel to the mid-wicket boundary to bring up his fifty and, more importantly, he became test cricket's greatest run-scorer, passing Sunil Gavaskar's record of 10,122 runs. Steve Waugh, Ian Healy and Merv Hughes all batted aggressively as Australia totalled 485. In dull conditions Craig McDermott dismissed both Mark Greatbatch and Andrew Jones before stumps, leaving New Zealand 30-2.

John Wright anchored one end for 270 minutes, scoring 39 off only 20 scoring shots, before he was sixth out with the score at 138. The Australians did not intimidate Ken Rutherford and one back-foot drive from McDermott went for six over the extra cover boundary.

Prior to this game Shane Warne had taken 14 wickets in eight tests. His first seven overs were maidens, and his confidence and competence grew immeasurably as he captured three wickets for 23 off 22 overs. All out for 182, 303 behind, New Zealand was immediately in trouble when it followed on. At the close of play New Zealand was 37-3.

New Zealand's position was perilous when the fifth wicket fell at 92 before Rutherford produced his finest test innings in New Zealand, reaching his third test century with shots to every corner of the ground. After his dismissal, for 102, Murphy Su'a made a lively 44 and, with Hughes and Warne both claiming four wickets, Australia completed their first test victory in New Zealand since 1981/82.

AUSTRALIA

D.C.Boon	c Parore b Owens	15
M.A.Taylor	c Crowe b Morrison	82
J.L.Langer	lbw b Morrison	63
M.E.Waugh	c Parore b Patel	13
S.R.Waugh	lbw b Owens	62
A.R.Border*	c Parore b Morrison	88
I.A.Healy†	c Morrison b Owens	54
M.G.Hughes	c Cairns b Patel	45
P.R.Reiffel	c Greatbatch b Su'a	18
S.K.Warne	not out	22
C.J.McDermott	c Jones b Cairns	4
Extras	(b 2, lb 6, w 5, nb 6)	19
TOTAL	**(157.3 overs)**	**485**

NEW ZEALAND

M.J.Greatbatch	c Healy b McDermott	4	c Reiffel b Hughes	0
J.G.Wright	lbw b Warne	39	b McDermott	14
A.H.Jones	lbw b McDermott	8	c Border b McDermott	10
M.D.Crowe*	c Taylor b Hughes	15	lbw b Hughes	14
K.R.Rutherford	b Warne	57	c Healy b Warne	102
C.L.Cairns	c Boon b McDermott	0	c Taylor b Warne	21
A.C.Parore†	c Boon b Reiffel	6	c Boon b Warne	5
D.N.Patel	c McDermott b Hughes	35	b Warne	8
M.L.Su'a	c Healy b Reiffel	0	b Hughes	44
D.K.Morrison	not out	4	c Healy b Hughes	19
M.B.Owens	lbw b Warne	0	not out	0
Extras	(b 2, lb 4, w 4, nb 4)	14	(lb 2, nb 4)	6
TOTAL	**(86 overs)**	**182**	**(94.5 overs)**	**243**

Bowling

NEW ZEALAND	O	M	R	W	O	M	R	W
Morrison	36	11	81	3				
Su'a	33	5	106	1				
Cairns	31.3	9	87	1				
Owens	26	9	58	3				
Patel	31	3	145	2				
AUSTRALIA								
McDermott	21	4	73	3	19	6	45	2
Hughes	21	10	44	2	24.5	6	62	4
Reiffel	18	8	27	2	18	3	59	0
Waugh S.R.	4	2	9	0	2	2	0	0
Warne	22	12	23	3	26	7	63	4
Waugh M.E.					5	1	12	0

Fall of Wickets

	A	NZ	NZ
	1st	1st	2nd
1st	33	4	0
2nd	149	18	19
3rd	170	53	24
4th	217	124	51
5th	264	128	92
6th	363	138	110
7th	435	150	144
8th	441	152	190
9th	480	181	242
10th	485	182	243

The New Zealand team that played against Australia. Back row (from left): Mark Plummer (physiotherapist), Murphy Su'a, Chris Harris, Willie Watson, Michael Owens, Dipak Patel, Tony Blain, Warren Lees (coach). Front row: Leif Dearsley (manager), Andrew Jones, John Wright, Martin Crowe (captain), Ken Rutherford, Mark Greatbatch, Danny Morrison.

MILESTONES

- Allan Border became the leading run-scorer in test cricket, overtaking Sunil Gavaskar's record of 10,122 runs.

- It was the second time in the season that Ken Rutherford had scored a century and a fifty in the same test match.

- Merv Hughes claimed his 500th first-class wicket.

- It was the first time in test cricket that Shane Warne was named Man of the Match.

218 NEW ZEALAND v AUSTRALIA *(Second Test)*

at Basin Reserve, Wellington on 4, 5, 6, 7, 8 March, 1993
Toss : Australia. Umpires : B.L. Aldridge and R.S. Dunne
Match drawn

Indifferent weather saw only 12.1 overs bowled on the first day after New Zealand was sent in on a pitch conducive to seam. Steve Waugh dropped John Wright in the slips when he was on nought and this had a major effect on the game.

Mark Greatbatch dominated the early scoring and when his partnership with Wright reached 100 it was the fourth time in five tests that he had been involved in a century stand. Wright made the Australians rue the dropped catch by occupying the crease for 361 minutes for his indomitable 72. His partner in the latter stages of the day, Martin Crowe, was in imperial form, taking boundaries off all the bowlers as he attempted to lift the run-rate.

The third day began with New Zealand 237-3 and Ken Rutherford and Crowe began positively, adding a further 50 in even time. When Rutherford was dismissed at 287 the Australian fast bowlers exploited the strong southerly wind and gloomy conditions to capture the last seven wickets for 42. Craig McDermott captured three wickets in 15 balls, including Crowe, who misjudged the line and was bowled for 98. The loss of David Boon and Mark Taylor, after they had been untroubled compiling 92 for the first wicket, left the game evenly poised at 107-2.

When Danny Morrison took the second new ball Australia was well placed at 229-4 with Allan Border and Steve Waugh batting in accomplished style. In the space of 43 balls Morrison captured the remaining six wickets with some formidably fast bowling to finish with 7-89, a New Zealand test record against Australia at the Basin Reserve. During this carnage Wright hurt his ankle and Andrew Jones opened New Zealand's second innings, which began badly with Australia claiming three for 40 by stumps.

The overnight pair of Jones and Tony Blain (who had replaced the injured Adam Parore the day before the game) added 71 sensible runs as New Zealand attempted to bat out the day. Blain used his feet to counter the leg-spin of Shane Warne and scored his first test fifty. Wright hobbled his way to the wicket using Mark Greatbatch as a runner and defied the opposition for 217 minutes, thus enabling New Zealand to draw the game and keep the series alive.

Danny Morrison found good rhythm, accuracy, pace and movement to return his best test analysis of 7-89. As the senior member of the bowling attack he led by example.

NEW ZEALAND

M.J.Greatbatch	c Taylor b Reiffel	61	b McDermott	0
J.G.Wright	c Healy b Hughes	72	(6) not out	46
A.H.Jones	b Reiffel	4	(2) lbw b Warne	42
M.D.Crowe*	b McDermott	98	(3) lbw b McDermott	3
K.R.Rutherford	c Healy b Hughes	32	(4) c Healy b Reiffel	11
T.E.Blain†	b Hughes	1	(5) c Healy b Warne	51
C.L.Cairns	c Border b McDermott	13	lbw b McDermott	14
D.N.Patel	not out	13	c Healy b Waugh M.E.	25
D.K.Morrison	c Warne b McDermott	2	not out	0
W.Watson	c Taylor b Warne	3		
M.B.Owens	b Warne	0		
Extras	(b 7, lb 11, w 2, nb 10)	30	(b 8, lb 8, w 1, nb 1)	18
TOTAL	(135 overs)	**329**	(115 overs) (7 wkts)	**210**

AUSTRALIA

M.A.Taylor	run out	50
D.C.Boon	c & b Morrison	37
J.L.Langer	c Blain b Watson	24
M.E.Waugh	c & b Owens	12
S.R.Waugh	c Blain b Morrison	75
A.R.Border*	lbw b Morrison	30
I.A.Healy†	c Rutherford b Morrison	8
M.G.Hughes	c Wright b Morrison	8
P.R.Reiffel	lbw b Morrison	7
S.K.Warne	c Greatbatch b Morrison	22
C.J.McDermott	not out	7
Extras	(lb 14, nb 4)	18
TOTAL	(101.4 overs)	**298**

Bowling	O	M	R	W	O	M	R	W
AUSTRALIA								
McDermott	31	8	66	3	23	9	54	3
Hughes	35	9	100	3	11	5	22	0
Reiffel	23	8	55	2	16	7	27	1
Waugh S.R.	15	7	28	0				
Warne	29	9	59	2	40	25	49	2
Waugh M.E.	2	1	3	0	8	3	12	1
Border					12	5	15	0
Taylor					4	2	15	0
Boon					1	1	0	0
NEW ZEALAND								
Morrison	26.4	5	89	7				
Cairns	24	3	77	0				
Watson	29	12	60	1				
Owens	21	3	54	1				
Patel	1	0	4	0				

Fall of Wickets	NZ	A	NZ
	1st	1st	2nd
1st	111	92	4
2nd	120	105	9
3rd	191	128	30
4th	287	153	101
5th	289	229	131
6th	307	237	154
7th	308	251	202
8th	314	258	-
9th	329	271	-
10th	329	298	-

MILESTONES

- Danny Morrison's figures of 7-89 were the best for New Zealand against Australia in New Zealand and the second best in New Zealand by a New Zealander.

- John Wright and Mark Greatbatch put on 111, a first wicket record for New Zealand against Australia.

- John Wright became the second New Zealander, after Glenn Turner, to score 25,000 first-class runs.

- John Wright batted a total of 581 minutes for his scores of 72 and 46 not out.

219 NEW ZEALAND v AUSTRALIA *(Third Test)*

at Eden Park, Auckland on 12, 13, 14, 15, 16 March, 1993
Toss : Australia. Umpires : B.L. Aldridge and C.E. King
New Zealand won by 5 wickets

Allan Border's decision to bat first looked reasonable at 38-0 but, when clouds swept over the ground, Danny Morrison and Willie Watson became almost unplayable as they swung the ball away and cut it back in at pace, with precise accuracy.

Six wickets fell for the addition of 10 runs before Steve Waugh found an unlikely ally in Merv Hughes and together they added 53 for the seventh wicket. Just before tea the players left the field because of bad light and drizzle with Australia 139-9.

Without addition to the score Morrison claimed his sixth wicket in what had been an inspiring performance. The first seven New Zealand batsmen all reached double figures, with Ken Rutherford's 43 the highest, as they cautiously went about building a substantial lead. They were aided by Border who did not bowl Shane Warne, except for a solitary over before lunch, until the 68th over by which time New Zealand had scored 178-4. At stumps the leg-spinner had taken 3-5 off 10 overs and New Zealand were 206-8.

New Zealand extended their lead to 85 and Martin Crowe's gamble of opening the bowling with Dipak Patel paid immense dividends when Mark Taylor was stumped in the first over and Justin Langer was lbw in the second. Damien Martyn batted with style and panache and David Boon defended stubbornly as the pair combined in the only partnership of the game to exceed 100, adding 107 in 113 minutes.

The battling instincts of Border were never more clearly exhibited as he reached his 60th test half century. He was assisted by Ian Healy to add 65 for the sixth wicket. Prior to stumps Healy became Patel's fifth wicket of the day; Australia 226-6.

For the second time in the game Hughes contributed vital runs, 31 not out, as Australia were dismissed for 285, leaving New Zealand 201 for victory, which would square the series at one-all. Mark Greatbatch, obviously impressed with the one-day ploy of opening the bowling with Patel, adopted his one-day approach at the beginning of New Zealand's second innings, flamboyantly attacking McDermott and Hughes.

His 29 off 30 balls broke the ice and New Zealand continued to bat positively. It was entrusted to Rutherford and Tony Blain to add 67, unbeaten, for the sixth wicket to give New Zealand victory by five wickets and their third successive victory over Australia at Eden Park.

MILESTONES

- John Wright retired from test cricket after 82 matches. He had scored 5334 runs.

- Danny Morrison, playing in his 29th test, became the eighth New Zealand bowler to capture 100 test wickets.

- Ian Healy made his 150th dismissal in his 47th test.

- It was New Zealand's seventh win in 29 tests against Australia.

- Shane Warne established an Australian record for a series in New Zealand by claiming 17 wickets.

The new electronic scoreboard provided replays as well as the score and was a wonderful facility for the spectators at Eden Park.

AUSTRALIA

D.C.Boon	lbw b Watson	20	lbw b Su'a	53
M.A.Taylor	lbw b Morrison	13	st Blain b Patel	3
J.L.Langer	c Blain b Morrison	0	lbw b Patel	0
D.R.Martyn	c Blain b Watson	1	c Greatbatch b Patel	74
S.R.Waugh	c Jones b Watson	41	lbw b Patel	0
A.R.Border*	c Blain b Morrison	0	c Harris b Watson	71
I.A.Healy†	c Jones b Morrison	0	c Blain b Patel	24
M.G.Hughes	c Morrison b Patel	33	not out	31
P.R.Reiffel	c Blain b Morrison	9	b Watson	1
S.K.Warne	not out	3	c Jones b Morrison	2
C.J.McDermott	b Morrison	6	c Wright b Watson	10
Extras	(lb 7, nb 6)	13	(b 1, lb 7, nb 8)	16
TOTAL	(55.4 overs)	139	(106 overs)	285

NEW ZEALAND

J.G.Wright	c Taylor b McDermott	33	run out	33
M.J.Greatbatch	c Border b Hughes	32	b Hughes	29
A.H.Jones	c Healy b Hughes	20	b Warne	26
M.D.Crowe*	c Taylor b Waugh	31	c Langer b Warne	25
K.R.Rutherford	st Healy b Warne	43	not out	53
C.Z.Harris	c Taylor b Warne	13	lbw b Waugh	0
T.E.Blain†	c Healy b McDermott	15	not out	24
D.N.Patel	c Healy b Warne	2		
M.L.Su'a	c Waugh b Warne	3		
D.K.Morrison	not out	10		
W.Watson	lbw b Hughes	0		
Extras	(b 7, lb 10, nb 5)	22	(lb 10, nb 1)	11
TOTAL	(95.5 overs)	224	(72.4 overs) (5 wkts)	201

Bowling	O	M	R	W	O	M	R	W
NEW ZEALAND								
Morrison	18.4	5	37	6	33	8	81	1
Su'a	14	3	27	0	18	4	56	1
Watson	19	9	47	3	19	5	43	3
Patel	4	0	21	1	34	10	93	5
Harris					2	1	4	0
AUSTRALIA								
McDermott	19	6	50	2	12	3	38	0
Hughes	24.5	6	67	3	15.4	2	54	1
Reiffel	22	6	63	0	6	1	19	0
Warne	15	12	8	4	27	8	54	2
Waugh	14	6	19	1	6	1	15	1
Martyn	1	1	0	0				
Border					6	2	11	0

Fall of Wickets

	A	NZ	A	NZ
	1st	1st	2nd	2nd
1st	38	60	5	44
2nd	38	91	8	65
3rd	39	97	115	109
4th	39	144	119	129
5th	43	178	160	134
6th	48	200	226	-
7th	101	205	261	-
8th	121	206	271	-
9th	133	224	274	-
10th	139	224	285	-

AVERAGES

New Zealand

BATTING	M	I	NO	Runs	HS	Ave
K.R. Rutherford	3	6	1	298	102	59.60
J.G. Wright	3	6	1	237	72	47.40
M.D. Crowe	3	6	0	186	98	31.00
T.E. Blain	2	4	1	91	51	30.33
M.J. Greatbatch	3	6	0	126	61	21.00
D.N. Patel	3	5	1	83	35	20.75
A.H. Jones	3	6	0	110	42	18.33
D.K. Morrison	3	5	3	35	19	17.50
M.L. Su'a	2	3	0	47	44	15.66
C.L. Cairns	2	4	0	48	21	12.00
C.Z. Harris	1	2	0	13	13	6.50
A.C. Parore	1	2	0	11	6	5.50
W. Watson	2	2	0	3	3	1.50
M.B. Owens	2	3	1	0	0*	0.00

BOWLING	O	M	R	W	Ave
D.K. Morrison	114.2	29	288	17	16.94
W. Watson	67	26	150	7	21.42
M.B. Owens	47	12	112	4	28.00
D.N. Patel	70	13	263	8	32.87
M.L. Su'a	65	12	189	2	94.50
C.L. Cairns	55.3	12	164	1	164.00
C.Z. Harris	2	1	4	0	-

Australia

BATTING	M	I	NO	Runs	HS	Ave
A.R. Border	3	4	0	189	88	47.25
S.R. Waugh	3	4	0	178	75	44.50
M.G. Hughes	3	4	1	117	45	39.00
D.R. Martyn	1	2	0	75	74	37.50
M.A. Taylor	3	4	0	148	82	37.00
D.C. Boon	3	4	0	125	53	31.25
S.K. Warne	3	4	2	49	22*	24.50
J.L. Langer	3	4	0	87	63	21.75
I.A. Healy	3	4	0	86	54	21.50
M.E. Waugh	2	2	0	25	13	12.50
C.J. McDermott	3	4	1	27	10	9.00
P.R. Reiffel	3	4	0	35	18	8.75

BOWLING	O	M	R	W	Ave
S.K. Warne	159	73	256	17	15.05
C.J. McDermott	125	36	326	13	25.07
M.G. Hughes	132.2	38	349	13	26.84
M.E. Waugh	15	5	27	1	27.00
S.R. Waugh	41	18	71	2	35.50
P.R. Reiffel	103	33	250	5	50.00
D.C. Boon	1	1	0	0	-
D.R. Martyn	1	1	0	0	-
M.A. Taylor	4	2	15	0	-
A.R. Border	18	7	26	0	-

Martin Crowe's tactic of opening the bowling with Dipak Patel in Australia's second innings proved to be inspirational as Tony Blain stumped Mark Taylor and Justin Langer was lbw – both to Patel.

1993/94 New Zealand in Australia

Before the first test New Zealand had lost to West Australia but had an excellent victory over a strong New South Wales side. Throughout the tour the team was dogged by a variety of injuries that required replacement players to be flown in.

220 AUSTRALIA v NEW ZEALAND (*First Test*)

at W.A.C.A. Ground, Perth on 12, 13, 14, 15, 16 November, 1993
Toss : New Zealand. Umpires : D.B. Hair and A.J. McQuillan
Match drawn

Because of rain, play was delayed until after lunch, which meant two long sessions of 140 and 180 minutes for New Zealand to field after they sent Australia in to bat. Chris Cairns dismissed Michael Slater and David Boon, off consecutive deliveries, with the score at 37.

Mark Taylor was the linchpin for the first four hours of Australia's batting, playing with great discipline in scoring 64. For the seventh time in test cricket Danny Morrison dismissed Allan Border. The visitors had done well to have Australia 229-6, with Ian Healy 30 not out.

The last four Australian wickets added 200 runs, mainly through a partnership between Healy and Paul Reiffel. They added 93 in almost even time. Reiffel scored his first test fifty and Healy his second test century. A belligerent innings by Craig McDermott took Australia to 398 and the visitors were left to rue some disappointing catching.

Debutant Glenn McGrath captured his first test wicket, that of Mark Greatbatch, caught behind when the score was 25. Andrew Jones and Blair Pocock defied the Australian bowlers until just before stumps when Pocock was caught at short-leg. New Zealand was 123-2, with Jones 62 not out.

Jones passed 50 for the first time in 16 test innings and went on to record his seventh test century, finishing with 143 in 351 minutes. Cairns and Tony Blain put on 102 and took New Zealand to within four of Australia's total when Blain departed for a gutsy 36 early on the fourth day. Cairns' 78 was his highest score in test cricket. When Willie Watson, responding to a quick single, tore his hamstring, Crowe declared the innings closed at 419, a lead of 21.

Cairns bowled one over at the start of Australia's second innings before he left the field with bruised heels. This left only three bowlers, Morrison, Su'a and Patel, to contain the Australians, and Taylor, Slater and Boon exploited this weakness to the full. They were blessed with several controversial umpiring decisions in the batsmen's favour.

Border was able to declare at 323-1, leaving New Zealand 65 overs to score an unlikely victory target of 303. By tea New Zealand were 105 for three. Crowe, batting with a damaged right-knee, which later necessitated him flying back to New Zealand for an operation, Rutherford and Patel all played diligently to save the game.

AUSTRALIA

M.A.Taylor	b Cairns	64	(2) not out	142
M.J.Slater	c Patel b Cairns	10	(1) c Blain b Patel	99
D.C.Boon	c Rutherford b Cairns	0	not out	67
M.E.Waugh	lbw b Morrison	36		
A.R.Border*	c Rutherford b Morrison	16		
S.R.Waugh	c Blain b Patel	44		
I.A.Healy†	not out	113		
P.R.Reiffel	c Jones b Watson	51		
S.K.Warne	c Patel b Cairns	11		
C.J.McDermott	b Su'a	35		
G.D.McGrath	lbw b Su'a	0	(lb 6, nb 9)	15
Extras	(b 4, lb 7, nb 7)	18		
TOTAL	**(114.5 overs)**	**398**	**(87 overs) (1 wkt dec)**	**323**

NEW ZEALAND

M.J.Greatbatch	c Healy b McGrath	18	c Healy b McDermott	0
B.A.Pocock	c Boon b McDermott	34	c Healy b McGrath	28
A.H.Jones	c Healy b Waugh M.E.	143	lbw b Waugh M.E.	45
M.D.Crowe*	c Taylor b Reiffel	42	not out	31
K.R.Rutherford	c Healy b McDermott	17	lbw b Waugh S.R.	39
D.N.Patel	c Waugh S.R. b Reiffel	20	not out	18
C.L.Cairns	b Warne	78		
T.E.Blain†	lbw b McDermott	36		
M.L.Su'a	not out	14		
D.K.Morrison	lbw b McGrath	0		
W.Watson	not out	0		
Extras	(b 1, lb 6, nb 10)	17	(lb 1, nb 4)	5
TOTAL	**(159.1 overs) (9 wkts dec)**	**419**	**(62 overs) (4 wkts)**	**166**

Bowling

NEW ZEALAND	O	M	R	W	O	M	R	W
Morrison	35	4	113	2	25	5	80	0
Cairns	28	4	113	4	1	0	12	0
Watson	24	11	52	1				
Su'a	19.5	2	72	2	20	0	71	0
Patel	8	0	37	1	39	4	144	1
Pocock					2	0	10	0
AUSTRALIA								
McDermott	40	10	127	3	13	3	40	1
McGrath	39	12	92	2	16	6	50	1
Reiffel	24	2	75	2	7	2	25	0
Warne	37.1	6	90	1	13	6	23	0
Waugh M.E.	13	5	18	1	6	4	17	1
Waugh S.R.	4	0	10	0	7	2	10	1
Border	2	2	0	0				

Fall of Wickets

	A	NZ	A	NZ
	1st	1st	2nd	2nd
1st	37	25	198	0
2nd	37	100	-	66
3rd	100	199	-	85
4th	129	239	-	145
5th	164	275	-	-
6th	198	292	-	-
7th	291	394	-	-
8th	329	413	-	-
9th	398	418	-	-
10th	398	-	-	-

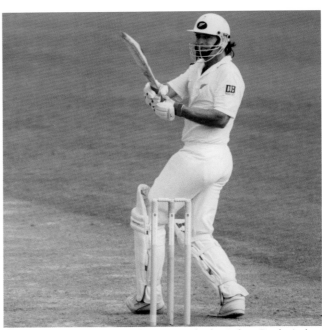

For nine minutes short of six hours, on a lively pitch at Perth, Andrew Jones fought the belligerence of the pace attack with solid defence but was prepared to hook when the opportunity presented itself.

MILESTONES

- Blair Pocock (184) made his test debut.

- Glenn McGrath, who was to play 110 tests for Australia, made his test debut.

- Craig McDermott, in his 50th test, became the eighth Australian bowler to claim 200 test wickets.

- Mark Taylor and Michael Slater established a new first wicket record of 198 for Australia against New Zealand.

- Mark Taylor became the first player to score centuries on all six of Australia's current test grounds.

221 **AUSTRALIA v NEW ZEALAND** *(Second Test)*

at Bellerive Oval, Hobart on 26, 27, 28, 29 November, 1993
Toss : Australia. Umpires : D.B. Hair and W.P. Sheahan
Australia won by an innings and 222 runs

With Martin Crowe undergoing arthroscopic surgery on his right knee in Auckland, Ken Rutherford became captain. The scourge of dropped catches continued to plague the visitors and both Michael Slater and Mark Taylor were dropped within the first hour as 65 runs were scored before Taylor departed.

David Boon and Slater took toll of the inexperienced attack, adding 235 in quick time for the second wicket. Bad balls were methodically put away to the boundary and short singles were stolen off better balls. Slater's 168 was not only his highest score in test cricket but also his highest in first-class cricket. Boon was 105 not out at stumps, his 18th test century; Australia 329-2.

The bad habits continued on the second day when the success of dismissing Boon was followed by the disappointment of Allan Border being dropped when three. This opened the way for the stylish Mark Waugh to become the third centurymaker of the innings and share a partnership of 150 in even time with Border. When Australia declared at 544-6 New Zealand had squandered seven missed chances, Danny Morrison suffering most with four off his bowling.

In the session before stumps New Zealand was fortunate to be only two wickets down for 81 as both not out batsmen, Andrew Jones 34 and Ken Rutherford 15, had been dropped.

The third day was a total disaster for New Zealand as they lost 13 wickets scoring 207 runs. The damage in the first innings was done by the accurate off-spin bowling of Tim May, whose arm-ball proved difficult for the visitors to detect as he took his third five-wicket bag in tests. New Zealand lost their last eight wickets for 56 runs.

Craig McDermott again captured the first wicket before the spinners took control. During the English summer Shane

Warne had taken 34 wickets in six tests and had been acclaimed by world critics as a great leg-spin bowler. He now reinforced his growing reputation, capturing six wickets for 31.

His length was impeccable, his spin occasionally prodigious and his use of top-spinners and flippers created total confusion for the New Zealand batsmen, with the exception of Rutherford and, in both innings, Tony Blain. Warne and May shared 16 wickets in the game as New Zealand made the same score in both innings – 161.

AUSTRALIA

M.A.Taylor	c Jones b Su'a	27
M.J.Slater	c Morrison b Patel	168
D.C.Boon	c Jones b Doull	106
M.E.Waugh	c Doull b de Groen	111
A.R.Border*	c & b Morrison	60
S.R.Waugh	not out	25
I.A.Healy†	c Doull b de Groen	1
P.R.Reiffel	not out	23
S.K.Warne		
T.B.A.May		
C.J.McDermott		
Extras	(b 7, lb 2, nb 14)	23
TOTAL	(139 overs) (6 wkts dec)	**544**

NEW ZEALAND

M.J.Greatbatch	c May b McDermott	12	c Waugh M.E. b McDermott	0
B.A.Pocock	lbw b Waugh M.E.	9	st Healy b Warne	15
A.H.Jones	c Healy b May	47	c Border b Waugh M.E.	18
K.R.Rutherford*	c Taylor b May	17	b Warne	55
D.N.Patel	c Taylor b Warne	18	lbw b May	16
C.Z.Harris	c Waugh M.E. b May	0	b May	4
T.E.Blain†	c Warne b May	40	c & b Warne	29
M.L.Su'a	c Taylor b Warne	6	b Warne	5
D.K.Morrison	c Waugh M.E. b May	0	b Warne	0
S.B.Doull	lbw b Warne	0	c May b Warne	1
R.P.de Groen	not out	0	not out	3
Extras	(b 2, lb 1, nb 9)	12	(b 2, lb 5, nb 8)	15
TOTAL	(82.3 overs)	**161**	(77.5 overs)	**161**

Bowling	O	M	R	W	O	M	R	W
NEW ZEALAND								
Morrison	33	4	125	1				
Su'a	24	3	102	1				
Doull	21	0	99	1				
de Groen	36	9	113	2				
Patel	23	3	78	1				
Harris	2	0	18	0				
AUSTRALIA								
McDermott	15	3	29	1	17	8	42	1
Reiffel	5	1	13	0	12	1	28	0
Waugh S.R.	4	1	8	0				
Waugh M.E.	9	4	7	1	4	0	8	1
May	31.3	10	65	5	25	13	45	2
Warne	18	5	36	3	19.5	9	31	6

Fall of Wickets

	A	NZ	NZ
	1st	*1st*	*2nd*
1st	65	15	1
2nd	300	47	29
3rd	335	84	84
4th	485	105	103
5th	501	107	111
6th	502	117	133
7th	-	137	149
8th	-	138	149
9th	-	139	158
10th	-	161	161

MILESTONES

- Richard de Groen (185) made his test debut.

- Michael Slater and David Boon created a new Australian record of 235 for the second wicket against New Zealand.

- Australia's total of 544-6d was its highest total against New Zealand in Australia.

- It was New Zealand's heaviest test defeat and Australia's fourth most emphatic.

- David Boon became the fifth Australian to pass 6000 runs in test cricket.

- It was the first time that Australia had fielded a team with 500 test caps.

Tony Blain extended well forward to counter the spin of Shane Warne and Tim May in both innings. Mark Taylor and wicketkeeper Ian Healy watch him.

222 AUSTRALIA v NEW ZEALAND *(Third Test)*

at Brisbane Cricket Ground on 3, 4, 5, 6, 7 December, 1993
Toss : New Zealand. Umpires : P.D. Parker and S.G. Randell
Australia won by an innings and 96 runs

In spite of Blair Pocock going for a duck, Bryan Young and Andrew Jones batted with renewed determination and shared the largest partnership of the innings, worth 94, before they were both out within two runs of one another. Another partnership developed between Ken Rutherford and Mark Greatbatch but when it was broken after 69 runs had been scored, five wickets fell for the addition of a meagre 11 runs, with Danny Morrison, as he had in his three preceding innings, left scoreless.

Throughout the series Tony Blain had been a model of consistency and determination. He was still there at stumps on 20 not out with New Zealand, failing to capitalise on an excellent batting wicket, 208-9.

New Zealand's innings ended at 233 on the second morning after the last-wicket partnership between Blain and Richard de Groen had added 40. Australia's reply was spread over three days, with six batsmen scoring over 50, and Allan Border and Steve Waugh reaching three figures. For the third successive test New Zealand's catching was mediocre and all five demoralised bowlers used by New Zealand conceded over 100 runs.

The highlights of the run-fest were two partnerships, the first between Border and Steve Waugh that added 155 after New Zealand's first-innings total had been eclipsed. After Border's dismissal Ian Healy became Australia's first video-replay victim when he was given run out. The second partnership between Shane Warne and Steve Waugh was unbroken with 142 runs in 133 minutes spread over the third and fourth days, interrupted by bad light and rain.

A poised Young, for the second time in his debut test, battled the Australians with admirable tenacity before Warne bowled him around his legs for 53. Jones and Greatbatch were snuffed out within four runs and New Zealand was once again on the back foot. For 201 minutes Ken Rutherford played a courageous, but lone, hand as wickets tumbled around him.

Glenn McGrath took three wickets and Warne captured four for the second time in the game. Australia won by an innings and 96 runs and claimed the Trans-Tasman Trophy.

MILESTONES

- Bryan Young (186) made his test debut.

- Allan Border, playing in his 150th test match on his adopted home ground, scored his 27th and last test century. He also took his 150th catch in the field, a record for test cricket.

- Australia's total of 607-6d was their highest score against New Zealand.

- Ian Healy moved into second place, behind Rodney Marsh, for dismissals by an Australian test wicketkeeper, overtaking Wally Grout's 187.

- It was the second time in test cricket history that a side had five bowlers conceding 100, the other being West Indies against Australia in 1954/55.

- Shane Warne's 72 wickets in a calendar year was the most by a slow bowler.

NEW ZEALAND

B.A.Pocock	c Healy b McDermott	0	c Healy b McDermott	11
B.A.Young	c Healy b Waugh M.E.	38	b Warne	53
A.H.Jones	b Warne	56	c Border b Warne	15
K.R.Rutherford*	c Boon b McDermott	36	c Warne b McGrath	86
M.J.Greatbatch	c Healy b McDermott	35	lbw b McDermott	2
C.L.Cairns	c & b Warne	5	c Healy b McGrath	16
D.N.Patel	c Boon b May	1	(8) b Warne	3
T.E.Blain†	not out	42	(7) b McGrath	18
D.K.Morrison	c Healy b Warne	0	not out	20
S.B.Doull	c Healy b McDermott	10	c Taylor b Warne	24
R.P.de Groen	c Border b Warne	3	b May	6
Extras	(b 2, lb 3, nb 2)	7	(b 7, lb 12, nb 5)	24
TOTAL	(105.3 overs)	**233**	(103 overs)	**278**

AUSTRALIA

M.J.Slater	c Blain b Patel	28
M.A.Taylor	c Pocock b Doull	53
D.C.Boon	c Blain b Doull	89
M.E.Waugh	c Greatbatch b Cairns	68
A.R.Border*	c Patel b de Groen	105
S.R.Waugh	not out	147
I.A.Healy†	run out	15
S.K.Warne	not out	74
T.B.A.May		
C.J.McDermott		
G.D.McGrath		
Extras	(b 6, lb 13, nb 9)	28
TOTAL	(183 overs) (6 wkts dec)	**607**

Bowling AUSTRALIA	O	M	R	W	O	M	R	W		Fall of Wickets			
											NZ	A	NZ
											1st	1st	2nd
McDermott	23	11	39	4	25	4	63	2	1st		2	80	34
McGrath	20	7	45	0	21	1	66	3	2nd		96	82	80
Waugh S.R.	3	0	13	0					3rd		98	227	81
Waugh M.E.	10	4	14	1	6	1	30	0	4th		167	277	84
May	21	7	51	1	16	3	41	1	5th		170	436	138
Warne	28.3	12	66	4	35	11	59	4	6th		174	465	187
NEW ZEALAND									7th		174	-	218
Morrison	33	3	104	0					8th		178	-	230
Cairns	36	7	128	1					9th		193	-	265
Doull	33	5	105	2					10th		233	-	278
de Groen	46	14	120	1									
Patel	33	4	125	1									
Jones	2	0	6	0									

AVERAGES

New Zealand

BATTING	M	I	NO	Runs	HS	Ave
M.D. Crowe	1	2	1	73	42	73.00
A.H. Jones	3	6	0	324	143	54.00
B.A. Young	1	2	0	91	53	45.50
K.R. Rutherford	3	6	0	250	86	41.66
T.E. Blain	3	5	1	165	42*	41.25
C.L. Cairns	2	3	0	99	78	33.00
B.A. Pocock	3	6	0	97	34	16.16
D.N. Patel	3	6	1	76	20	15.20
M.L. Su'a	2	3	1	25	14*	12.50
M.J. Greatbatch	3	6	0	67	35	11.16
S.B. Doull	2	4	0	35	24	8.75
R.P. de Groen	2	4	2	12	6	6.00
D.K. Morrison	3	5	1	20	20*	5.00
C.Z. Harris	1	2	0	4	4	2.00
W. Watson	1	1	1	0	0*	-

BOWLING	O	M	R	W	Ave
C.L. Cairns	65	11	253	5	50.60
W. Watson	24	11	52	1	52.00
S.B. Doull	54	5	204	3	68.00
R.P. de Groen	82	23	233	3	77.66
M.L. Su'a	63.5	5	245	3	81.66
D.N. Patel	103	11	384	4	96.00
D.K. Morrison	126	16	422	3	140.66
A.H. Jones	2	0	6	0	-
B.A. Pocock	2	0	10	0	-
C.Z. Harris	2	0	18	0	-

Australia

BATTING	M	I	NO	Runs	HS	Ave
S.R. Waugh	3	3	2	216	147*	216.00
M.A. Taylor	3	4	1	286	142*	95.33
D.C. Boon	3	4	1	262	106	87.33
S.K. Warne	3	2	1	85	74*	85.00
M.J. Slater	3	4	0	305	168	76.25
P.R. Reiffel	2	2	1	74	51	74.00
M.E. Waugh	3	3	0	215	111	71.66
I.A. Healy	3	3	1	129	113*	64.50
A.R. Border	3	3	0	181	105	60.33
C.J. McDermott	3	1	0	35	35	35.00
G.D. McGrath	2	1	0	0	0	0.00
T.B.A. May	2	-	-	-	-	-

BOWLING	O	M	R	W	Ave
S.K. Warne	151.3	49	305	18	16.94
M.E. Waugh	48	18	94	5	18.80
T.B.A. May	93.3	33	202	9	22.44
C.J. McDermott	133	39	340	12	28.33
S.R. Waugh	18	3	41	1	41.00
G.D. McGrath	96	26	253	6	42.16
P.R. Reiffel	48	6	141	2	70.50
A.R. Border	2	2	0	0	-

Bryan Young underwent a career change after several seasons of playing for Northern Districts as their wicketkeeper and lower order batsman. He fashioned himself into an opening batsman. Playing in his first test he enjoyed an excellent double of 38 and 53 against the Australian attack.

1993/94 Pakistan in New Zealand

The only controversy of Pakistan's tour occurred before the team left their homeland when the appointed vice-captain of the team, Waqar Younis, said that he and nine other players would not tour if the original captain, Wasim Akram, led the side. Consequently Salim Malik was made captain and Asif Mujtaba became vice-captain.

223 NEW ZEALAND v PAKISTAN (First Test)

at Eden Park, Auckland on 10, 11, 12 February, 1994
Toss : Pakistan. Umpires : H.D. Bird and R.S. Dunne
Pakistan won by 5 wickets

The pitch prepared for this game was substandard, aiding the quicker bowlers on both sides with inconsistent bounce that was occasionally excessive from off a length. Hence the batting of both teams looked below test standard.

New Zealand went to lunch, after being sent in to bat, at 67 for one. Bryan Young became the second of Rashid Latif's nine catches in the game when he was dismissed with the first ball after lunch for 29. The mainstay of New Zealand's innings was another courageous batting effort from Andrew Jones, who defied the bowlers for 212 minutes, scoring 66.

He shared a partnership with Mark Greatbatch that added 75 in 47 minutes. Greatbatch hit eight fours and one six as he attacked the right-arm leg-spinner Mushtaq Ahmed unmercifully. Mushtaq had the last say, claiming the wickets of Greatbatch, Jones and Chris Cairns. This tore the heart out of New Zealand's middle order and opened the way for Akram and Younis to demolish the lower order and have New Zealand out for 242. The game swung back in New Zealand's favour when the first four Pakistan batsmen were dismissed by stumps for 61.

The last five Pakistan wickets added 128 runs as they struggled against the bustling inswingers of Simon Doull and the bounce that Richard de Groen extracted from the pitch, and New Zealand dismissed Pakistan for 215. With New Zealand's lead a slender 27, the pace and sublime skill of Akram reduced New Zealand to 44-6 before Chris Cairns and Doull attacked courageously, adding 36 in 33 minutes.

New Zealand were all out for 110, made off 32.1 overs. Akram's analysis of 6-43 was his best in test cricket. Thirty wickets had fallen in the first two days and Pakistan was left requiring 138 for victory.

Aamer Sohail played a match-winning innings of 78, showing fine judgement with his defence and his ability to find the boundary, which he did eleven times during his innings. Young took three catches in each innings. Pakistan won by five wickets with over half the playing time of the game remaining.

NEW ZEALAND

Batsman	Dismissal	Runs	Dismissal (2nd)	Runs (2nd)
B.A.Young	c Latif b Waqar	29	c Latif b Akram	0
B.A.Pocock	c Latif b Akram	0	c Mujtaba b Akram	10
A.H.Jones	c Latif b Mushtaq	66	c Latif b Akram	6
K.R.Rutherford*	b Waqar	14	b Waqar	18
M.J.Greatbatch	c Malik b Mushtaq	48	c Inzamam b Akram	0
S.A.Thomson	c Latif b Waqar	29	c Latif b Waqar	0
C.L.Cairns	c Malik b Mushtaq	6	c Mujtaba b Rehman	31
T.E.Blain†	c Mushtaq b Akram	26	c Latif b Rehman	4
S.B.Doull	c & b Waqar	0	c Malik b Akram	29
R.P.de Groen	c Mushtaq b Akram	2	not out	0
M.B.Owens	not out	2	c Latif b Akram	0
Extras	(b 4, lb 8, w 1, nb 7)	20	(b 4, lb 5, nb 3)	12
TOTAL	(68.3 overs)	242	(32.1 overs)	110

PAKISTAN

Batsman	Dismissal	Runs	Dismissal (2nd)	Runs (2nd)
Saeed Anwar	c Blain b Cairns	16	c Young b de Groen	7
Aamer Sohail	c Jones b de Groen	16	c Young b Thomson	78
Asif Mujtaba	c Blain b Doull	8	c & b Doull	0
Mushtaq Ahmed	c Young b Doull	0		
Salim Malik*	c Young b Doull	18	(4) c Young b de Groen	11
Basit Ali	c Blain b Cairns	25	(5) c & b Doull	7
Inzamam-ul-Haq	c Young b de Groen	43	(6) not out	20
Rashid Latif†	lbw b Doull	30	(7) not out	13
Wasim Akram	c Blain b de Groen	35		
Waqar Younis	c Cairns b Doull	11		
Ata-ur-Rehman	not out	2		
Extras	(lb 6, nb 5)	11	(lb 3, nb 2)	5
TOTAL	(57.4 overs)	215	(41 overs) (5 wkts)	141

Bowling	O	M	R	W	O	M	R	W
PAKISTAN								
Akram	22.3	9	50	3	16.1	4	43	6
Waqar	15	2	46	4	10	3	35	2
Rehman	14	3	55	0	6	1	23	2
Mushtaq	17	1	79	3				
NEW ZEALAND								
Cairns	18	2	75	2	6	1	15	0
Owens	7	1	28	0	2	0	10	0
Doull	15	2	66	5	16	0	48	2
de Groen	17.4	5	40	3	13	3	48	2
Thomson					4	1	17	1

Fall of Wickets

	NZ 1st	P 1st	NZ 2nd	P 2nd
1st	3	17	0	21
2nd	67	36	8	25
3rd	95	48	31	56
4th	170	50	35	73
5th	175	87	40	119
6th	185	93	44	-
7th	228	141	67	-
8th	228	176	103	-
9th	233	207	110	-
10th	242	215	110	-

MILESTONES

• Wasim Akram became the third Pakistan bowler to capture 200 test wickets. It was his 51st test.

• Waqar Younis took his 150th wicket in his 26th test.

• Pakistan wicketkeeper Rashid Latif took a record nine catches in the match.

• Bryan Young became the first New Zealand fieldsman to take six catches in a test.

Richard de Groen's bustling, fast-medium deliveries were accorded due respect by the batsmen. His match analysis of 5-88 was well deserved.

224 NEW ZEALAND v PAKISTAN *(Second Test)*

at Basin Reserve, Wellington on 17, 18, 19, 20 February, 1994
Toss : New Zealand. Umpires : B.L. Aldridge and H.D. Bird
Pakistan won by an innings and 12 runs

Ken Rutherford decided to bat on a hard and fast pitch but one of the openers was again dismissed in the first over of the game. When New Zealand lost their fourth wicket at 100, 19 year-old right-arm fast-medium bowler Ata-ur-Rehman had taken three of the wickets, overshadowing his illustrious companions. Wasim Akram and Waqar Younis shared the remaining spoils as New Zealand was dismissed for a disappointing 175.

After losing Aamer Sohail and nightwatchman Akram Raza at 36 the remaining Pakistan batsmen provided a scintillating batting display. They were led by the graceful left-hand batsman Saeed Anwar, who was to score the first of his 11 test centuries.

He shared a partnership of 197 with Basit Ali at almost a run a ball to set the tone for the remainder of the innings. During the second day Pakistan added 363 for the loss of three wickets, with Salim Malik on 62 and Inzamam-ul-Haq on 63 both well set for the following day.

Both batsmen completed their centuries and carried their fifth wicket partnership to 258 before Malik was caught and bowled by Matthew Hart. Malik declared with a lead of 373. For the fourth innings of the series New Zealand began badly with both openers out and the score at six.

As had been the case in the previous three years Andrew Jones was given the role of steadying the ship and, again, the dire nature of the situation brought his highly competitive spirit to the fore. For 224 minutes he got in behind the ball, taking several on the body, as he defied his tormentors while scoring 76. Rutherford was a more aggressive lieutenant as he partnered Jones, adding 114 for the third wicket.

On the fourth day the pitch was more benign and Akram had to persevere with control and subtle change of pace, and was made to work hard for his wickets. An unlikely ninth-wicket stand between Tony Blain and Danny Morrison added 74 with both players recording their highest test scores. It was finally broken when Akram had Blain caught. For the second test running Akram had recorded his best innings analysis. This time, he took 7-119 off 37 overs and secured his second Man of the Match award.

MILESTONES

- Matthew Hart (187) made his test debut.
- Pakistan's total of 548-5d was the highest test score by an overseas side at the Basin Reserve.
- It was New Zealand's fourth successive test defeat and the third by an innings.
- For the previous 22 years the curator at the Basin Reserve was Wes Armstrong. During his time he had prepared 18 test pitches. New Zealand had won five, drawn 12 and this was the only loss.

Mark Greatbatch adopted an aggressive counter-attack method against the fearsome Pakistan attack, top-scoring with 45 in New Zealand's first innings.

NEW ZEALAND

B.A.Young	lbw b Akram	0	(2) b Akram		4
B.A.Pocock	b Rehman	16	(1) b Waqar		0
A.H.Jones	lbw b Rehman	43	b Akram		76
K.R.Rutherford*	c Raza b Rehman	7	c Raza b Rehman		63
M.J.Greatbatch	c Latif b Waqar	45	c Latif b Akram		10
S.A.Thomson	b Akram	7	c Rehman b Akram		47
T.E.Blain†	c Anwar b Waqar	8	c Basit b Akram		78
M.N.Hart	not out	12	b Akram		7
D.K.Morrison	c Rashid Latif b Akram	5	(10) lbw b Waqar		42
S.B.Doull	c Basit b Waqar	17	(9) c Malik b Akram		15
R.P.de Groen	b Akram	4	not out		1
Extras	(lb 7, nb 4)	11	(b 1, lb 5, nb 12)		18
TOTAL	(67 overs)	**175**	(95.2 overs)		**361**

PAKISTAN

Saeed Anwar	run out	169
Aamer Sohail	lbw b Morrison	2
Akram Raza	c Blain b Morrison	0
Basit Ali	b Thomson	85
Salim Malik*	c & b Hart	140
Inzamam-ul-Haq	not out	135
Asif Mujtaba		
Rashid Latif†		
Wasim Akram		
Waqar Younis		
Ata-ur-Rehman		
Extras	(b 5, lb 6, nb 6)	17
TOTAL	(137.2 overs) (5 wkts dec)	**548**

Bowling	O	M	R	W	O	M	R	W	Fall of Wickets	NZ 1st	P 1st	NZ 2nd
PAKISTAN												
Wasim Akram	24	10	60	4	37	7	119	7	1st	0	34	3
Waqar Younis	22	5	51	3	25.2	4	111	2	2nd	40	36	6
Ata-ur-Rehman	15	4	50	3	18	1	86	1	3rd	49	233	120
Akram Raza	6	4	7	0	12	4	25	0	4th	100	290	143
Aamer Sohail					1	0	1	0	5th	126	548	209
Salim Malik					2	0	13	0	6th	128	-	216
NEW ZEALAND									7th	140	-	244
Morrison	31	4	139	2					8th	149	-	276
de Groen	31	8	104	0					9th	170	-	350
Doull	27	6	112	0					10th	175	-	361
Hart	31.2	9	102	1								
Thomson	17	3	80	1								

225 NEW ZEALAND v PAKISTAN (*Third Test*)

at Lancaster Park, Christchurch on 24, 25, 26, 27, 28 February, 1994
Toss : New Zealand. Umpires : R.S. Dunne and K.T. Francis
New Zealand won by 5 wickets

New Zealand's old nemesis, poor catching, revisited the team on the first-day of the third test when they dropped six catches after sending Pakistan in to bat first. Saeed Anwar was dropped off Danny Morrison's first and second overs. After these two lucky let-offs he and Aamer Sohail enjoyed the first century opening stand of the series.

The New Zealand bowlers, led by Morrison, fought back admirably in the afternoon session, claiming five wickets. The stocky, right-hand batsman Basit Ali dominated the latter part of the visitors' innings, scoring 103 of the 180 runs added while he was at the wicket.

Chasing 344 New Zealand inevitably lost an early wicket, before Bryan Young and Andrew Jones adopted a positive approach to the awesome Pakistan pace bowlers. Jones raced to his fastest fifty in 39 tests, made off 46 balls but, when the wickets began to tumble after Young departed at 109, Jones took a further 83 balls to advance his score to 81 before he ran himself out.

He had exercised strict discipline yet attacked judiciously and audaciously, which he did at the outset of his innings at Waqar Younis' expense. Younis blitzed through the New Zealand middle order with a spell of 5-19, to give him an analysis of 6-78 for the innings. With New Zealand trailing by 144, Morrison and Doull, the pick of the New Zealand bowlers in the first innings, each had an opening batsman out when the second day ended with Pakistan 8-2.

Morrison and Matthew Hart worked their way through the visitors' batting, which would have been piteous if Basit Ali had not again batted flamboyantly, to see Pakistan dismissed prior to stumps for 179. With two days remaining New Zealand needed 324 for a face-saving victory.

Jones was run out for the second time in the game with New Zealand at 76-2. By the time the experienced Rutherford and Greatbatch were out, with the score at 133-4, the game appeared safe for Pakistan. However, Northern Districts team-mates Young and Shane Thomson, with only nine test appearances between them, turned the game by batting for the rest of the day, with Young, reaching his century in 376 minutes and Thomson being 93 not out.

The last rites were administered early on the fifth day with Thomson ending 120 not out and New Zealand the victors by five wickets.

PAKISTAN

Saeed Anwar	c Young b Doull	69	c Blain b Morrison	0
Aamer Sohail	c Hartland b Doull	60	c Young b Doull	3
Atif Rauf	c Greatbatch b Morrison	16	c Young b Doull	9
Salim Malik*	b Hart	18	(5) c Pringle b Morrison	23
Basit Ali	c Hartland b Pringle	103	(6) run out	67
Inzamam-ul-Haq	c Greatbatch b Doull	5	(7) c sub b Morrison	20
Rashid Latif†	c Hartland b Thomson	27	(8) c & b Hart	3
Wasim Akram	c Greatbatch b Morrison	5	(9) b Hart	17
Akram Raza	not out	29	(4) st Blain b Hart	26
Waqar Younis	c Doull b Morrison	2	c Blain b Morrison	10
Aamer Nazir	b Morrison	0	not out	0
Extras	(lb 6, w 1, nb 3)	10	(nb 1)	1
TOTAL	(97 overs)	**344**	(65.3 overs)	**179**

NEW ZEALAND

B.R.Hartland	c Basit b Waqar	3	(2) c Inzamam b Akram	10
B.A.Young	lbw b Nazir	38	(1) b Akram	120
A.H.Jones	run out	81	run out	26
K.R.Rutherford*	c Inzamam b Waqar	7	lbw b Akram	13
M.J.Greatbatch	lbw b Akram	1	c Inzamam b Waqar	1
S.A.Thomson	c Latif b Waqar	3	not out	120
T.E.Blain†	lbw b Waqar	0	not out	11
M.N.Hart	b Akram	6		
S.B.Doull	lbw b Waqar	17		
D.K.Morrison	not out	6		
C.Pringle	b Waqar	0		
Extras	(b 5, lb 9, nb 24)	38	(lb 5, nb 18)	23
TOTAL	(56 overs)	**200**	(107 overs) (5 wkts)	**324**

Bowling	O	M	R	W	O	M	R	W
NEW ZEALAND								
Morrison	24	3	105	4	21.3	5	66	4
Doull	25	3	93	3	5	0	13	2
Pringle	33	6	83	1	17	3	41	0
Hart	9	2	37	1	18	5	47	3
Thomson	6	0	20	1	4	0	12	0
PAKISTAN								
Akram	22	5	54	2	38	6	105	3
Waqar	19	1	78	6	27	6	84	1
Nazir	15	2	54	1	16	0	59	0
Raza					19	5	49	0
Sohail					2	1	5	0
Malik					4	1	13	0
Anwar					1	0	4	0

Fall of Wickets

	P	NZ	P	NZ
	1st	*1st*	*2nd*	*2nd*
1st	125	12	0	22
2nd	147	109	4	76
3rd	169	124	26	119
4th	195	139	53	133
5th	206	147	77	287
6th	254	147	133	-
7th	261	147	152	-
8th	339	186	154	-
9th	344	198	171	-
10th	344	200	179	-

MILESTONES

- It was New Zealand's 32nd test victory.

- New Zealand's 324 was their highest fourth innings total to win a test.

- Wasim Akram's 25 wickets was a record for a three-test series in New Zealand.

- Basit Ali, Bryan Young and Shane Thomson made their maiden test centuries.

Following two successive defeats by Pakistan, no critic considered New Zealand capable of extending the visitors during their tour. Conceding a lead of 144 after each side had batted once, defeat was a foregone conclusion. Bryan Young, left, and Shane Thomson both scored maiden test centuries to give New Zealand their 32nd test victory.

AVERAGES

New Zealand

BATTING	M	I	NO	Runs	HS	Ave
A.H. Jones	3	6	0	298	81	49.66
S.A. Thomson	3	6	1	206	120*	41.20
B.A. Young	3	6	0	191	120	31.83
D.K. Morrison	2	3	1	53	42	26.50
T.E. Blain	3	6	1	127	78	25.40
K.R. Rutherford	3	6	0	122	63	20.33
C.L. Cairns	1	2	0	37	31	18.50
M.J. Greatbatch	3	6	0	105	48	17.50
S.B. Doull	3	5	0	78	29	15.60
M.N. Hart	2	3	1	25	12*	12.50
B.R. Hartland	1	2	0	13	10	6.50
B.A. Pocock	2	4	0	26	16	6.50
R.P. de Groen	2	4	2	7	4	3.50
M.B. Owens	1	2	1	2	2*	2.00
C. Pringle	1	1	0	0	0	0.00

BOWLING	O	M	R	W	Ave
S.B. Doull	88	11	332	12	27.66
D.K. Morrison	76.3	12	310	10	31.00
M.N. Hart	58.2	16	186	5	37.20
R.P. de Groen	61.4	16	192	5	38.40
S.A. Thomson	31	4	129	3	43.00
C.L. Cairns	24	3	90	2	45.00
C. Pringle	50	9	124	1	124.00
M.B. Owens	9	1	38	0	-

Pakistan

BATTING	M	I	NO	Runs	HS	Ave
Inzamam-ul-Haq	3	5	2	223	135*	74.33
Basit Ali	3	5	0	287	103	57.40
Saeed Anwar	3	5	0	261	169	52.20
Salim Malik	3	5	0	210	140	42.00
Aamer Sohail	3	5	0	159	78	31.80
Akram Raza	2	3	1	55	29*	27.50
Rashid Latif	3	4	1	73	30	24.33
Wasim Akram	3	3	0	57	35	19.00
Atif Rauf	1	2	0	25	16	12.50
Waqar Younis	3	3	0	23	11	7.66
Asif Mujtaba	2	2	0	8	8	4.00
Mushtaq Ahmed	1	1	0	0	0	0.00
Aamir Nazir	1	2	1	0	0*	0.00
Ata-ur-Rehman	2	1	1	2	2*	-

BOWLING	O	M	R	W	Ave
Wasim Akram	159.4	41	431	25	17.24
Waqar Younis	118.2	21	405	18	22.50
Mushtaq Ahmed	17	1	79	3	26.33
Ata-ur-Rehman	53	9	214	6	35.66
Aamir Nazir	31	2	113	1	113.00
Saeed Anwar	1	0	4	0	-
Aamer Sohail	3	1	6	0	-
Salim Malik	6	1	26	0	-
Akram Raza	37	13	81	0	-

1993/94 India in New Zealand

The seventh and last test of the 1993/94 season was memorable for the debut of Stephen Fleming but rain and dismal light eliminated so much time that only a draw was possible.

226 NEW ZEALAND v INDIA *(Only Test)*

at Trust Bank Park, Hamilton on 19, 20, 21, 22, 23 March, 1994
Toss : New Zealand. Umpires : B.L. Aldridge and Khizer Hayat
Match drawn

The first day was restricted to 38.5 overs, during which time Ken Rutherford scored 43 not out of New Zealand's 81-3. All the home team struggled with the pace and bounce of the tall right-arm fast-medium bowler Javagal Srinath.

Eight New Zealand batsmen reached double figures but only Rutherford, with 63, scored over 20. The Indian spinning trio of Anil Kumble, right-arm leg-spin, Rajesh Chauhan, right-arm off-spin and Venkatapathy Raju, left-arm spin, were rightfully accorded respect as they all exerted pressure on the batsmen, the last seven of whom fell for 87 runs.

Makeshift opener Nayan Mongia, the Indian wicketkeeper, played cautiously and shared an enthralling third wicket partnership with Sachin Tendulkar of 51. Tendulkar played a stunning cameo, scoring 43 off 47 balls, which included seven boundaries.

On the third day Mongia's vigil concluded after 227 minutes when he was run out for 45. It was left to the Indian captain Mohammad Azharuddin to play defensively as he was uncertain of the uneven bounce of the pitch. Once he was bowled, sweeping at Shane Thomson who was now bowling right-arm off-spin, the remaining five Indian wickets fell for 63 runs, giving them a lead of 59.

Stephen Fleming made his debut batting at number five. He displayed maturity above his age by scoring an elegant 92 in his second innings.

Blair Hartland and Bryan Young gave New Zealand their best opening stand in their last 14 test innings, being unbeaten at stumps at 39-0. The partnership advanced to 57 before Hartland was dismissed early on the fourth day. The pitch had evened out and Young and Rutherford were untroubled in adding 116 for the second wicket, with both scoring half centuries. Rutherford made his second fifty of the game.

Both fell in quick succession to Chauhan which allowed debutant Fleming to display his wares, including fluent drives to both sides of the wicket off both front and back foot. He reached stumps on 67, with New Zealand 306-5.

Regrettably, the expectation of the final day failed to materialise when Fleming was dismissed for 92. Rutherford's declaration left India the difficult task of scoring 310 off 66 overs. In spite of Navjot Sidhu and Mongia combining to score 102 in 124 minutes the game petered out to a draw, with Sidhu scoring an interesting 98.

NEW ZEALAND

Batsman	1st innings	Runs	2nd innings	Runs
B.R.Hartland	c Chauhan b Kapil Dev	0	(2) c Mongia b Srinath	25
B.A.Young	c Kumble b Srinath	13	(1) c Mongia b Chauhan	85
K.R.Rutherford*	b Kumble	63	b Chauhan	59
M.J.Greatbatch	c Azharuddin b Srinath	12	c Manjrekar b Kumble	27
S.P.Fleming	c Kambli b Srinath	16	c Kapil Dev b Chauhan	92
S.A.Thomson	c Manjrekar b Raju	12	b Raju	26
A.C.Parore†	c & b Chauhan	9	c Mongia b Kapil Dev	17
M.N.Hart	b Chauhan	17	not out	20
D.J.Nash	not out	10	not out	9
D.K.Morrison	lbw b Srinath	3		
C.Pringle	b Raju	18		
Extras	(lb 9, nb 5)	14	(b 2, lb 1, nb 5)	8
TOTAL	(97.2 overs)	187	(129 overs) (7 wkts dec)	368

INDIA

Batsman	1st innings	Runs	2nd innings	Runs
N.R.Mongia†	run out	45	b Hart	38
N.S.Sidhu	b Morrison	10	c Parore b Hart	98
V.G.Kambli	c Young b Pringle	9	b Pringle	19
S.R.Tendulkar	c Nash b Thomson	43	not out	11
M.Azharuddin*	b Thomson	63		
S.V.Manjrekar	c Young b Morrison	29	(5) not out	8
Kapil Dev	c Fleming b Nash	18		
A.R.Kumble	c Fleming b Morrison	7		
R.K.Chauhan	not out	12		
S.L.V.Raju	c Young b Morrison	2		
J.Srinath	c Parore b Pringle	1		
Extras	(lb 6, w 1)	7	(lb 3)	3
TOTAL	(102.3 overs)	246	(59 overs) (3 wkts)	177

Bowling	O	M	R	W	O	M	R	W
INDIA								
Srinath	31	8	60	4	33	4	104	1
Kapil Dev	9	2	29	1	16	2	43	1
Kumble	23	8	34	1	27	6	68	1
Raju	13.2	5	14	2	24	6	53	1
Chauhan	21	6	41	2	29	5	97	3
NEW ZEALAND								
Morrison	30	9	52	4	8	1	15	0
Nash	20	5	57	1	13	6	25	0
Pringle	22.3	8	52	2	12	2	29	1
Hart	19	5	33	0	15	2	66	2
Thomson	11	1	46	2	11	1	39	0

Fall of Wickets

	NZ 1st	I 1st	NZ 2nd	I 2nd
1st	1	25	56	102
2nd	21	38	172	140
3rd	49	89	176	167
4th	100	138	220	-
5th	122	183	265	-
6th	124	216	317	-
7th	154	226	355	-
8th	155	227	-	-
9th	158	237	-	-
10th	187	246	-	-

MILESTONES

- Stephen Fleming (188) made his test debut.

- Ken Rutherford passed 2000 runs in his 45th test.

- Sachin Tendulkar passed 2000 runs in his 32nd test.

- Mohammed Azharuddin passed 4000 runs in his 62nd test.

1994 New Zealand in England

New Zealand's record in England going into the first test was appalling, as was their ill-luck, with injuries to Danny Morrison, Chris Pringle and Michael Owens. The five bowlers used in this test had 14 test appearances and only 22 wickets between them. New Zealand had rarely had such an inexperienced group of bowlers. Though it was the middle of summer in England, all five days were played under stygian skies and were accompanied by strong cold winds. Amazingly, only ten overs were lost to rain and bad light.

227 **ENGLAND v NEW ZEALAND** *(First Test)*

at Trent Bridge, Nottingham on 2, 3, 4, 5, 6 June, 1994
Toss : New Zealand. Umpires : H.D. Bird and S.A. Bucknor
England won by an innings and 90 runs

Phil DeFreitas was recalled to the England side for the 14th time and had his away-swingers working effectively as he captured four of the top five batsmen. Stephen Fleming was poised and reached his fifty off 98 balls, and Adam Parore, Dion Nash and Matthew Hart all battled valiantly at the end of the innings.

By the end of the second day England had overtaken New Zealand's total of 254 thanks to an accomplished partnership between Graham Gooch and Michael Atherton that had produced 261. Gooch, who had been unavailable for England's tour of the West Indies, was approaching his 40th birthday and batted in a regal manner, thundering shots to all corners of the ground and was 152 not out at the end of the day's play. On the stroke of time Atherton bought up his sixth test century.

The loss of Atherton, without adding to his score, was the first of six wickets that fell during the third day as England sedately added a further 239. Gooch, who had scored his 20th test hundred, continued to bat like the master batsman he was against the visiting novices. He raised his second test double-century in 388 minutes. Robin Smith led the other batsmen as they accumulated the substantial total of 516-6 by the end of the third day.

DeFreitas bludgeoned his second test fifty in his 50th test innings before Atherton declared at 567-8 with England enjoying a massive lead of 316. New Zealand's second innings was a replica of their first, with Young being the only player to score over 50.

Following a mini-collapse, when four wickets were lost while 25 runs were added, Adam Parore and Hart provided sturdy resistance, adding 51 in 128 minutes and taking play into the fifth day. DeFreitas ended with five wickets, giving him nine for the game, when he concluded Parore's 3½ hour effort. The game ended with England winning by an innings and 90 runs.

NEW ZEALAND

Batsman	Dismissal	Runs	2nd innings	Runs
B.A.Young	c Hick b DeFreitas	15	(2) c Rhodes b Fraser	53
B.R.Hartland	c Hick b DeFreitas	6	(1) lbw b DeFreitas	22
K.R.Rutherford*	lbw b DeFreitas	25	c Atherton b Such	14
M.D.Crowe	c Rhodes b White	16	lbw b DeFreitas	28
S.P.Fleming	c White b DeFreitas	54	c White b Hick	11
S.A.Thomson	c Hick b Fraser	14	c White b Such	6
A.C.Parore†	c Rhodes b Malcolm	38	c Rhodes b DeFreitas	42
G.R.Larsen	c Fraser b Such	8	c Stewart b DeFreitas	2
M.N.Hart	c Hick b Fraser	36	lbw b Fraser	22
D.J.Nash	c Rhodes b Malcolm	19	c Rhodes b DeFreitas	5
H.T.Davis	not out	0	not out	0
Extras	(lb 6, nb 14)	20	(lb 1, nb 20)	21
TOTAL	(93.4 overs)	251	(106.3 overs)	226

ENGLAND

Batsman	Dismissal	Runs
M.A.Atherton*	c Parore b Larsen	101
A.J.Stewart	c Larsen b Davis	8
G.A.Gooch	c Crowe b Thomson	210
G.A.Hick	b Nash	18
R.A.Smith	run out	78
C.White	c Larsen b Hart	19
S.J.Rhodes†	c Thomson b Nash	49
P.A.J.DeFreitas	not out	51
A.R.C.Fraser	c Fleming b Larsen	8
P.M.Such		
D.E.Malcolm		
Extras	(lb 9, w 6, nb 10)	25
TOTAL	(174.4 overs) (8 wkts dec)	567

Bowling ENGLAND	O	M	R	W	O	M	R	W
Malcolm	17.4	5	45	2	10	2	39	0
Fraser	21	10	40	2	23	8	53	2
DeFreitas	23	4	94	4	22.3	4	71	5
Such	19	7	28	1	34	12	50	2
White	13	3	38	1	3	3	0	0
Hick					14	6	12	1
NEW ZEALAND								
Davis	21	0	93	1				
Nash	36	5	153	2				
Larsen	44.4	11	116	2				
Hart	35	7	123	1				
Thomson	38	6	73	1				

Fall of Wickets	NZ	E	NZ
	1st	*1st*	*2nd*
1st	13	16	59
2nd	37	279	95
3rd	66	314	95
4th	78	375	141
5th	108	414	141
6th	168	482	141
7th	188	528	147
8th	194	567	201
9th	249	-	224
10th	251	-	226

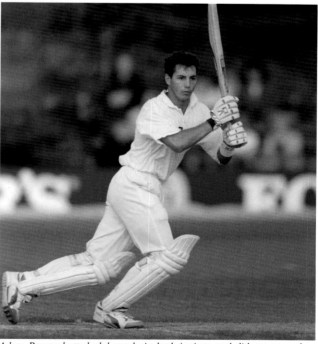

Adam Parore batted obdurately in both innings and did not concede a bye in 173.4 overs.

MILESTONES

- Heath Davis (189) and Gavin Larsen (190) made their test debuts.

- Phillip DeFreitas became the 100th bowler to capture 100 test wickets.

- Michael Atherton and Graham Gooch shared their fourth double-century partnership to go with five other century partnerships.

- England's total of 567-8d was its highest in 38 tests against New Zealand in England.

- West Indies' Steve Bucknor became the first overseas umpire to stand in a test in England.

228 ENGLAND v NEW ZEALAND *(Second Test)*

at Lord's on 16, 17, 18, 19, 20 June, 1994
Toss : New Zealand. Umpires : S.A. Bucknor and N.T. Plews
Match drawn

Bryan Young became the first of the 11 lbw decisions given during the game when Angus Fraser dismissed him in this manner in the first over of the match. When Ken Rutherford was out for 37, New Zealand were uncomfortably placed at 67-3.

Martin Crowe, restricted in movement when batting because of a brace on his right knee, then made the centre of Lord's, a ground that had always been dear to him, the stage from which he exhibited all the wonderful shots in his repertoire as he completed his 16th test century off 157 balls. For much of the day his partner was Shane Thomson and, so well did he play, that at no stage was he in the shadow of Crowe as they added 178 at better than a run a minute.

With both Thomson and Crowe dismissed at 360 the last four wickets added a valiant 116, mainly thanks to Adam Parore, who for the third successive time played a substantial innings, and Dion Nash, who made his first test fifty off 92 balls.

New Zealand's total of 476 looked catchable when Alec Stewart tore into the visitors attack, hitting nine boundaries before he was out within the first hour of England's reply. Michael Atherton and Graham Gooch were more sedate, taking England through to 94-1 at stumps.

Three wickets fell for six runs at the start of Saturday's play before a packed Lord's as Nash swung the ball away from the right-handers at a brisk pace. Matthew Hart was metronomically accurate, keeping Graeme Hick and Craig White very circumspect as they added 92, before a return from Nash ran out White for 51.

When Nash took an athletic return catch from Fraser and then had Paul Taylor caught by Parore it gave him his first five-wicket bag in test cricket and left England on the verge of having to follow on. The last pair overcame the hurdle and with two days remaining New Zealand had a lead of 195.

There was a frenzied start to the beginning of the fourth day, as Phil DeFreitas captured three wickets in his first four overs. Young, who scored an enterprising 94, stemmed the collapse and combined with Stephen Fleming to add 115 for the fourth wicket. This enabled New Zealand to declare after tea and leave England 407, the highest victory target ever attained to win a test. Atherton and Stewart were untroubled to add 56 before stumps.

Two early wickets to Nash, coupled with several overs where he did everything but dismiss Stewart, meant England abandoned their opportunity for a dramatic victory and settled for the conservative option of surviving the day. They achieved the latter, with Stewart scoring 119 and bad light threatening to shorten the day.

Nash completed an exceptional all-round game with another five wickets. The silent bowling hero was Hart, who bowled 85 overs during the game, with 44 maidens, and conceded only 105 runs.

Dion Nash had figures of 11-169 and also scored a half-century.

NEW ZEALAND

B.A.Young	lbw b Fraser	0	(2) c Hick b Such	94
B.A.Pocock	c Smith b Such	10	(1) lbw b DeFreitas	2
K.R.Rutherford*	c Stewart b DeFreitas	37	lbw b DeFreitas	0
M.D.Crowe	c Smith b DeFreitas	142	b DeFreitas	9
S.P.Fleming	lbw b Fraser	41	lbw b Taylor	39
S.A.Thomson	run out	69	not out	38
A.C.Parore†	c Rhodes b Taylor	40	not out	15
M.N.Hart	b Such	25		
D.J.Nash	b White	56		
C.Pringle	c Hick b DeFreitas	14		
M.B.Owens	not out	2		
Extras	(b 3, lb 15, w 1, nb 21)	40	(lb 4, nb 10)	14
TOTAL	(149.1 overs)	476	(68 overs) (5 wkts dec)	211

ENGLAND

M.A.Atherton*	lbw b Hart	28	c Young b Nash	33
A.J.Stewart	c Parore b Nash	45	c Crowe b Nash	119
G.A.Gooch	lbw b Nash	13	lbw b Nash	0
R.A.Smith	c & b Nash	6	c Parore b Nash	23
G.A.Hick	c Young b Pringle	58	lbw b Pringle	37
C.White	run out	51	c Thomson b Nash	9
S.J.Rhodes†	not out	32	not out	24
P.A.J.DeFreitas	c Parore b Thomson	11	lbw b Owens	3
A.R.C.Fraser	c & b Nash	10	lbw b Hart	2
J.P.Taylor	c Parore b Nash	0	not out	0
P.M.Such	c Parore b Nash	4		
Extras	(b 4, lb 12, nb 7)	23	(b 2, lb 1, nb 1)	4
TOTAL	(121 overs)	281	(108 overs) (8 wkts)	254

Bowling	O	M	R	W	O	M	R	W
ENGLAND								
Fraser	36	9	102	2	15	0	50	0
DeFreitas	35	8	102	3	16	0	63	3
Taylor	20	4	64	1	6	2	18	1
Such	30	8	84	2	25	5	55	1
White	21.1	4	84	1	4	1	21	0
Gooch	5	1	13	0				
Hick	2	0	9	0	2	2	0	0
NEW ZEALAND								
Owens	7	0	34	0	10	3	35	1
Nash	25	6	76	6	29	8	93	5
Pringle	23	5	65	1	16	5	41	1
Hart	44	21	50	1	41	23	55	1
Thomson	22	8	40	1	12	4	27	0

Fall of Wickets	NZ	E	NZ	E
	1st	1st	2nd	2nd
1st	0	65	9	60
2nd	39	95	9	60
3rd	67	95	29	136
4th	138	101	144	210
5th	318	193	170	217
6th	350	225	-	240
7th	391	241	-	244
8th	397	265	-	250
9th	434	271	-	-
10th	476	281	-	-

MILESTONES

- During Martin Crowe's 16th century he joined John Wright as the only other New Zealander to pass 5000 test runs.

- Martin Crowe and Shane Thomson put on 180, a fifth wicket record for New Zealand against England.

- Dion Nash became the first player to take 10 wickets and score a half-century in 91 tests played at Lord's.

229 ENGLAND v NEW ZEALAND *(Third Test)*

at Old Trafford, Manchester on 30 June, 1, 2, 4, 5 July, 1994
Toss : England. Umpires : S.B. Lambson and D.R. Shepherd
Match drawn

Fresh from his triumph at Lord's, Dion Nash had tongues wagging when he dismissed Alec Stewart and Graham Gooch off successive balls with England's score at 37. It was the third time that Nash had dismissed Gooch in the last seven balls that he had bowled to him.

Lacking genuine pace, all the visiting bowlers concentrated their attack on and outside the off stump and succeeded in frustrating the England batsmen, inducing impatient shots that led to their downfall. These tactics suited Michael Atherton and he provided the sheet-anchor innings to steer England to 199-4 at stumps.

Poised on 96 overnight Atherton soon reached his seventh test hundred and his third against New Zealand before becoming Nash's third wicket. England's fortunes were revived when Phil DeFreitas and Darren Gough, playing in his first test, both played their natural attacking way as they added 130 for the eighth wicket and delighted the spectators but thwarted the fieldsmen.

Gough, who was to have another 85 test innings in his colourful career, never scored more than the 65 that he scored this day. England's total of 382 was considerably more than thought possible when they were 235-7.

New Zealand was off to a bad start when the extra pace and power of Gough eliminated Mark Greatbatch with a sharp lifter that deflected off his gloves to Graham Hick off the fifth ball of the innings. There was more variety in England's attack with the introduction of the pace of Gough, the swing of DeFreitas, the change of pace of Chris White and the accuracy of Angus Fraser, and they had New Zealand 84-4 at stumps.

Martin Crowe, who scored an enterprising 70, provided the only resistance for New Zealand in their lowly total of 151. During the England innings Crowe had left the field feeling the side effects from medication taken for flu prior to the game. The England management rightfully objected to his being substituted as he had entered the match unwell.

Crowe attacked whenever possible and reached his 50 off as many balls and 46 of his 70 runs came from boundaries. Forced to follow on New Zealand again stumbled, losing five wickets for 132 before Crowe and the consistent Adam Parore added 63 in gloomy conditions and stumps were drawn two hours early.

Sunday had been announced as a rest day, so as not to compete against the men's singles final at Wimbledon, which was won by Pete Sampras against Goran Ivanisevic. Ironically, with New Zealand on the verge of defeat this was the sunniest day of the test. The following day was restricted to 18 overs, during which time no wickets fell as New Zealand increased their score by 48.

On the final day rain interrupted the first session twice, before Parore's resolute innings of 71 ended after 213 minutes and he and Crowe had added 141. Crowe's defiant 114, plus further stoppages for rain, saw New Zealand emerge with a draw, thanks to Wimbledon.

MILESTONES

- Darren Gough made his test debut for England.

- Graham Gooch took his 100th test catch.

- Martin Crowe and Adam Parore put on 131, a New Zealand sixth wicket record against England.

- It was England's first home test series win since 1990.

ENGLAND

M.A.Atherton*	lbw b Nash	111
A.J.Stewart	c Pringle b Nash	24
G.A.Gooch	c Young b Nash	0
R.A.Smith	b Owens	13
G.A.Hick	c Nash b Owens	20
C.White	c Hart b Owens	42
S.J.Rhodes†	c Parore b Nash	12
P.A.J.DeFreitas	b Owens	69
D.Gough	c sub b Pringle	65
A.R.C.Fraser	c Thomson b Hart	10
P.M.Such	not out	5
Extras	(lb 8, w 1, nb 2)	11
TOTAL	**(146.3 overs)**	**382**

NEW ZEALAND

B.A.Young	c Rhodes b DeFreitas	25	lbw b DeFreitas	8
M.J.Greatbatch	c Hick b Gough	0	c DeFreitas b White	21
K.R.Rutherford*	c Gooch b DeFreitas	7	c Rhodes b Gough	13
S.P.Fleming	c Rhodes b Gough	14	c Hick b Fraser	11
M.D.Crowe	c Gooch b White	70	c Hick b DeFreitas	115
M.N.Hart	c Atherton b Gough	0	(8) not out	16
S.A.Thomson	c Rhodes b DeFreitas	9	(6) c Smith b Gough	21
A.C.Parore†	c Rhodes b White	7	(7) c Gooch b DeFreitas	71
D.J.Nash	not out	8	not out	6
C.Pringle	b White	0		
M.B.Owens	c Stewart b Gough	4		
Extras	(nb 7)	7	(b 8, lb 13, nb 5)	26
TOTAL	**(57.3 overs)**	**151**	**(106.2 overs) (7 wkts)**	**308**

Bowling	O	M	R	W	O	M	R	W
NEW ZEALAND								
Nash	39	9	107	4				
Owens	34	12	99	4				
Pringle	39	12	95	1				
Hart	27.3	9	50	1				
Thomson	7	1	23	0				
ENGLAND								
Fraser	12	3	17	0	19	7	34	1
Gough	16.3	2	47	4	31.2	5	105	2
DeFreitas	17	2	61	3	30	6	60	3
Such	5	2	8	0	10	2	39	0
White	7	1	18	3	14	3	36	1
Gooch					2	0	13	0

Fall of Wickets	E	NZ	NZ
	1st	1st	2nd
1st	37	2	8
2nd	37	12	34
3rd	68	47	48
4th	104	82	73
5th	203	93	132
6th	224	113	273
7th	235	125	287
8th	365	140	-
9th	372	140	-
10th	382	151	-

AVERAGES

New Zealand

BATTING	M	I	NO	Runs	HS	Ave
M.D. Crowe	3	6	0	380	142	63.33
A.C. Parore	3	6	1	213	71	42.60
B.A. Young	3	6	0	195	94	32.50
S.A. Thomson	3	6	1	157	69	31.40
D.J. Nash	3	5	2	94	56	31.33
S.P. Fleming	3	6	0	170	54	28.33
M.N. Hart	3	5	1	99	36	24.75
K.R. Rutherford	3	6	0	96	37	16.00
B.R. Hartland	1	2	0	28	22	14.00
M.J. Greatbatch	1	2	0	21	21	10.50
C. Pringle	2	2	0	14	14	7.00
M.B. Owens	2	2	1	6	4	6.00
B.A. Pocock	1	2	0	12	10	6.00
G.R. Larsen	1	2	0	10	8	5.00
H.T. Davis	1	2	2	0	0*	-

BOWLING	O	M	R	W	Ave
D.J. Nash	129	28	429	17	25.23
M.B. Owens	51	15	168	5	33.60
G.R. Larsen	44.4	11	116	2	58.00
C. Pringle	78	22	201	3	67.00
M.N. Hart	147.3	60	278	4	69.50
S.A. Thomson	79	19	163	2	81.50
H.T. Davis	21	0	93	1	93.00

England

BATTING	M	I	NO	Runs	HS	Ave
M.A. Atherton	3	4	0	273	111	68.25
D. Gough	1	1	0	65	65	65.00
S.J. Rhodes	3	4	2	117	49	58.50
G.A. Gooch	3	4	0	223	210	55.75
A.J. Stewart	3	4	0	196	119	49.00
P.A.J. DeFreitas	3	4	1	134	69	44.66
G.A. Hick	3	4	0	133	58	33.25
C. White	3	4	0	121	51	30.25
R.A. Smith	3	4	0	120	78	30.00
P.M. Such	3	2	1	9	5*	9.00
A.R.C. Fraser	3	4	0	30	10	7.50
J.P. Taylor	1	2	1	0	0*	0.00
D.E. Malcolm	1	-	-	-	-	-

BOWLING	O	M	R	W	Ave
G.A. Hick	18	8	21	1	21.00
P.A.J. DeFreitas	143.3	24	451	21	21.47
D. Gough	47.5	7	152	6	25.33
C. White	62.1	15	197	6	32.83
J.P. Taylor	26	6	82	2	41.00
D.E. Malcolm	27.4	7	84	2	42.00
A.R.C. Fraser	126	37	296	7	42.28
P.M. Such	123	36	264	6	44.00
G.A. Gooch	7	1	26	0	-

After making 142 and 39 in the previous test, Martin Crowe continued his stunning form, scoring 70 and 115. Watched by Steve Rhodes, he caresses one of the 15 boundaries in his 115 to backward point.

1994/95 New Zealand in South Africa

This was New Zealand's third tour of South Africa and their first test against South Africa since they had been readmitted to international cricket in 1991. Winning the toss was vital, as both sides were suspicious of the pitch that had visible cracks from the outset.

230 **SOUTH AFRICA v NEW ZEALAND** *(First Test)*
at Wanderers Stadium, Johannesburg on 25, 26, 27, 28, 29 November, 1994
Toss : New Zealand. Umpires : K.E. Liebenberg and I.D. Robinson
New Zealand won by 137 runs

The loss of an early wicket was off-set by an audacious innings by Stephen Fleming, who hit 10 fours in his innings of 48. Martin Crowe and Ken Rutherford combined in a stand of 126, made in 42 overs, which ended when Rutherford was bowled for 68. Crowe was more sedate and at the end of the day was 81 not out, with the total at 242-4.

Crowe was out at the start of the second day and it was left to Shane Thomson, who scored an elegant 84 of the 136 accumulated while he was at the crease, to take New Zealand to 354-8. A crucial last wicket stand of 57 between Simon Doull and Richard de Groen, made in 38 frenetic minutes, swelled New Zealand's total to 411. Within an hour South Africa was 38-3. It was determined batting by Daryll Cullinan that led a recovery to 109-4 by stumps.

The recovery continued on the third day led by wicketkeeper and strong-minded batsman Dave Richardson, who batted with a guard to project his recently broken right thumb. With his side facing the follow-on he dominated a stand worth 57 for the ninth wicket with Clive Eksteen, who contributed nine. Richardson was the last man out for a test-best score of 93.

Resuming with a lead of 132 New Zealand lost a wicket to the first ball bowled by Fanie de Villiers. It was the 14th time in the last 22 New Zealand test openings that the first wicket had fallen in single figures. De Villiers changed ends and in the space of nine balls removed Bryan Young, Crowe and Rutherford to have the visitors 34-5.

On the fourth day the match was delicately poised at 81-5 as Thomson and Adam Parore continued their partnership, which had begun on the third day, extending it to 69. Useful contributions by the lower order, for the second time in the game, saw New Zealand finish with 194. Hard-working, right-arm medium-fast bowler Craig Matthews claimed a five-wicket bag. With the target 327 runs on a wearing pitch, Brian McMillan and Hansie Cronje advanced South Africa to 128-2 by stumps.

The cracks had widened considerably after four days of sun and general wear and tear, and batting became most difficult on the fifth day. A match-winning spell of three for 17 by Doull proved decisive at the start of play. Matthew

Hart bowled his left-arm spinners accurately into the rough and claimed five wickets as the last seven South Africans were dismissed for 37 and New Zealand had won a test that had had as many twists as a maze.

Matthew Hart ran through the tail of South Africa's batting in both innings to bowl New Zealand to only their third test win against South Africa.

NEW ZEALAND

B.A.Young	c McMillan b Snell	7	(2) c Richardson b de Villiers	18
D.J.Murray	c Richardson b de Villiers	25	(1) lbw b de Villiers	0
S.P.Fleming	b de Villiers	48	c Richardson b Matthews	15
M.D.Crowe	lbw b Snell	83	b de Villiers	0
K.R.Rutherford*	c Cronje b Eksteen	68	c McMillan b de Villiers	0
S.A.Thomson	b Matthews	84	b Snell	29
A.C.Parore†	c McMillan b Matthews	13	c Richardson b Matthews	49
M.N.Hart	c Richardson b Matthews	0	b Matthews	34
D.J.Nash	c Hudson b Eksteen	18	c Richardson b Matthews	20
S.B.Doull	not out	31	not out	14
R.P.de Groen	b Snell	26	b Matthews	0
Extras	(lb 5, w 2, nb 1)	8	(b 9, lb 4, w 1, nb 1)	15
TOTAL	(145.5 overs)	411	(75 overs)	194

SOUTH AFRICA

A.C.Hudson	c Parore b Nash	10	lbw b Doull	2
G.Kirsten	c Crowe b de Groen	9	lbw b Hart	33
B.M.McMillan	c Murray b Nash	5	lbw b Doull	42
W.J.Cronje*	lbw b de Groen	20	c Parore b de Groen	62
D.J.Cullinan	c Parore b Doull	58	c Crowe b Doull	12
J.N.Rhodes	lbw b Doull	37	lbw b Doull	0
D.J.Richardson†	lbw b Nash	93	c & b Hart	6
R.P.Snell	c Crowe b Hart	16	c Doull b Hart	1
C.R.Matthews	c Crowe b Hart	4	b Hart	6
C.E.Eksteen	c Fleming b Hart	9	b Hart	0
P.S.de Villiers	not out	6	not out	1
Extras	(b 6, lb 6)	12	(b 17, lb 6, w 1)	24
TOTAL	(92 overs)	279	(78.4 overs)	189

Bowling	O	M	R	W	O	M	R	W
SOUTH AFRICA								
de Villiers	34	8	78	2	23	9	52	4
Snell	33.5	9	112	3	16	5	54	1
Matthews	28	3	98	3	19	9	42	5
McMillan	24	8	56	0	2	1	1	0
Eksteen	23	10	49	2	14	5	32	0
Cronje	3	0	13	0	1	1	0	0
NEW ZEALAND								
Nash	24	6	81	3	8	2	17	0
Doull	21	6	70	2	15	5	33	4
de Groen	21	2	59	2	12	3	21	1
Hart	26	7	57	3	32.4	7	77	5
Thomson					11	6	18	0

Fall of Wickets	NZ 1st	SA 1st	NZ 2nd	SA 2nd
1st	7	20	0	9
2nd	79	28	32	70
3rd	92	38	33	130
4th	218	73	33	150
5th	249	147	34	150
6th	280	148	103	167
7th	280	173	130	175
8th	354	197	168	180
9th	354	254	190	184
10th	411	279	194	189

MILESTONES

- Darrin Murray (191) made his test debut.

- It was New Zealand's 33rd test win and third in 15 tests against South Africa.

- Martin Crowe surpassed Jeremy Coney's New Zealand record of 64 test catches.

- Martin Crowe became the first test player to be in a winning side against eight different countries.

- Simon Doull and Richard de Groen set a 10th wicket record of 57 for New Zealand against South Africa.

231 SOUTH AFRICA v NEW ZEALAND (Second Test)

at Kingsmead, Durban on 26, 27, 28, 29, 30 December, 1994
Toss : New Zealand. Umpires : Khizer Hayat and C.J. Mitchley
South Africa won by 8 wickets

There was a four-week gap between the first and second tests when New Zealand, South Africa, Sri Lanka and Pakistan competed in a one-day tournament for the Mandela Trophy. New Zealand played badly, losing five of their six games, with the other being abandoned.

Their first-class game against Boland at Paarl, prior to the second test, was called off after one over on the second day when the umpires decreed that the pitch constituted a danger to the batsmen. Boland had made 83 and were 31-3 after New Zealand had been dismissed for 86 when the decision to abandon the match was made.

It was at Paarl that the infamous cannabis-smoking incident occurred that saw Stephen Fleming, Matthew Hart and Dion Nash fined by the tour management and 24 days later suspended from playing against the West Indies in three one-day internationals after they had initially been selected.

Irresolute batting plagued New Zealand in both innings as top order batsmen flirted, fatally, with hook and pull shots that led to their downfall. Shane Thomson came to the crease at 65-4 and counter-attacked, being particularly severe on anything short, and his first seven scoring shots included five fours and one six.

Fanie de Villiers and right-arm fast bowler Stephen Jack shared the first five wickets to fall before Brian McMillan claimed three wickets in 19 balls to have New Zealand 114-8. Fortunately for New Zealand bad light prevented any play after tea with their score at 130-8, with Thomson reaching his fifty from 54 balls.

Danny Morrison and Thomson continued their partnership of the previous day, adding 66 before Gary Kirsten brilliantly caught Thomson on 82, off another mis-hit hook shot. Morrison's defiant innings of 24 occupied 140 minutes and was an object lesson to his team's leading batsmen.

South Africa also made a poor start and it was left to 29-year-old John Commins, playing in his first test, to share two successive stands, of 48 with Kirsten and 49 with Daryll Cullinan, that steered South Africa to 110-2 before Morrison captured three quick wickets to have them 122-5. Bad light again shortened the day.

A vital last wicket partnership of 44 between Dave Richardson and de Villiers gave their team a lead of 41 with Simon Doull and Morrison bowling well in tandem to claim five and four wickets respectively. New Zealand's second innings was built around an obdurate, history-making innings by Brian Young. He had been batting for two hours to be 18 not out of New Zealand's 48-3, when bad light terminated the third day.

The following day he went on to record the third-slowest fifty in test cricket, made in 333 minutes off 229 balls. For the second time in the game New Zealand was dismissed for less than 200. Led by Kirsten and Commins, who added 97 for the second wicket, South Africa were untroubled to reach the 152 required for victory and thus square the series.

MILESTONES

- Martin Crowe became New Zealand's leading test run scorer when he overtook John Wright's 5334.

- Bryan Young scored the third-slowest fifty in test cricket in 333 minutes. Only England's Trevor Bailey, 357 minutes, and Chris Tavare, 350 minutes, were slower.

NEW ZEALAND

Batsman	1st innings			2nd innings	
B.A.Young	b Jack		2	(2) c Cullinan b McMillan	51
D.J.Murray	c Richardson b de Villiers		38	(1) lbw b de Villiers	0
S.P.Fleming	c Jack b de Villiers		4	(5) c Richardson b Jack	31
M.D.Crowe	c de Villiers b Jack		18	c Richardson b McMillan	10
K.R.Rutherford*	c Commins b de Villiers		0	(3) c Commins b McMillan	6
S.A.Thomson	c Kirsten b de Villiers		82	b Cronje	35
A.C.Parore†	c Kirsten b McMillan		5	run out	1
M.N.Hart	c Cronje b McMillan		5	c Richardson b Kirsten	6
S.B.Doull	c Richardson b McMillan		0	c Richardson b de Villiers	19
D.K.Morrison	not out		24	c McMillan b de Villiers	12
C.Pringle	c Kirsten b de Villiers		0	not out	6
Extras	(lb 4, nb 3)		7	(lb 11, nb 4)	15
TOTAL	(82 overs)		185	(100.2 overs)	192

SOUTH AFRICA

Batsman	1st innings			2nd innings	
A.C.Hudson	c Young b Morrison		8	c Parore b Doull	6
G.Kirsten	c Parore b Doull		29	not out	66
J.B.Commins	c Hart b Doull		30	c Young b Hart	45
D.J.Cullinan	lbw b Doull		34	not out	25
W.J.Cronje*	c Thomson b Morrison		19		
J.N.Rhodes	c Fleming b Hart		1		
B.M.McMillan	b Doull		17		
D.J.Richardson†	not out		39		
C.R.Matthews	c Parore b Morrison		7		
S.D.Jack	c Crowe b Morrison		0		
P.S.de Villiers	c Fleming b Doull		28		
Extras	(lb 6, nb 8)		14	(lb 9, nb 2)	11
TOTAL	(86.5 overs)		226	(45.4 overs) (2 wkts)	153

Bowling	O	M	R	W	O	M	R	W
SOUTH AFRICA								
de Villiers	24	7	64	5	31.2	10	56	3
Jack	16	7	32	2	15	3	45	1
Matthews	19	11	37	0	12	3	17	0
McMillan	19	8	40	3	30	8	53	3
Cronje	4	1	8	0	10	6	10	1
Kirsten					2	2	0	1
NEW ZEALAND								
Morrison	25	4	70	4	15	1	56	0
Doull	29.5	9	73	5	15	5	26	1
Pringle	15	5	23	0				
Hart	17	2	54	1	13.4	2	52	1
Thomson					2	1	10	0

Fall of Wickets	NZ 1st	SA 1st	NZ 2nd	SA 2nd
1st	9	13	2	20
2nd	19	61	11	117
3rd	62	110	28	-
4th	65	111	81	-
5th	66	122	144	-
6th	102	141	144	-
7th	114	168	153	-
8th	114	182	153	-
9th	180	182	179	-
10th	185	226	192	-

The New Zealand team to South Africa in 1994/95 photographed at the Wanderers, Johannesburg. Back row (from left): Lee Germon, Dion Nash, Stephen Fleming, Richard de Groen, Simon Doull, Murphy Su'a, Blair Hartland, Matthew Hart, Darrin Murray, Mark Plummer (physiotherapist). Front row: Geoff Howarth (coach), Chris Pringle, Adam Parore, Bryan Young, Ken Rutherford (captain), Martin Crowe, Chris Harris, Shane Thomson, Mike Sandilands (manager).

232 SOUTH AFRICA v NEW ZEALAND (Third Test)

at Newlands, Cape Town on 2, 3, 4, 5, 6 January, 1995
Toss : New Zealand. Umpires : K.T. Francis and S.B. Lambson
South Africa won by 7 wickets

An aggressive approach was evident from the first overs bowled by South Africa on a hard, fast pitch where all their fiery bowlers threatened the visitors' upper bodies. Brian McMillan, playing on his home ground, delighted the 17,000 spectators on the first day by taking three of the first five wickets to fall for 96.

Ken Rutherford led a fight-back, adding 83 with Stephen Fleming, who had been swapped in the batting order with Adam Parore. It was disappointing when Rutherford, for the fourth time in the series, self-destructed, pulling recklessly to mid-wicket when he had made 56.

On the second day Fleming and Matthew Hart extended their partnership to 66 before the refined Fleming, when he had scored 79, became the first of three wickets that Stephen Jack took in 11 balls to reduce New Zealand to 254-9. Chris Pringle scored a flamboyant 30 , contributing all the runs off the bat in a last-wicket stand of 33, with Danny Morrison being in nought not out after 52 minutes at the crease.

Gary Kirsten and Rudi Styne put on 106 before the innocuous off-spin of Shane Thomson dismissed both of them and Daryll Cullinan before stumps, with South Africa 152-3.

South Africa took a stranglehold of the test by dominating the third day's play, scoring a further 229 runs while only losing another four wickets. The South African captain, Hansie Cronje, scored a patient 112 but was on 59 when Hart dropped him at mid-wicket off the tireless Simon Doull.

For the third time in the first innings of South Africa's reply, Dave Richardson thwarted the visitors. Batting at number eight he went on to scored his maiden test century. It was most appropriate that Richardson was later named the Man of the Match and the Series. Because of his efforts, South Africa reached 440 and a lead of 152.

By stumps, where New Zealand were 121-4, the match and the series were very much in South Africa's favour. Bryan Young, for the second time in the game, held the innings together with his 42 not out taking over four hours to compile on a still benign pitch.

When Young succumbed to a failed hook shot it was left to Fleming to prolong the resistance until de Villiers mopped up the last three wickets to give him another five wicket haul and 20 wickets for the series. South Africa scored the 87 runs required for an historic victory and it was fitting that Cronje struck the winning boundary to give his side victory and the series 2-1.

MILESTONES

- Not since Dr W.G. Grace captained England against Australia in 1888 had a team come back from behind to win a three-test series. It was one of test cricket's longest standing records.

- Hansie Cronje passed 1000 test runs. It was his fourth test century, all of them leading to a victory for his side.

NEW ZEALAND

Batsman	Dismissal	Runs	Dismissal	Runs
B.A.Young	lbw b McMillan	45	c Kirsten b McMillan	51
D.J.Murray	c Kirsten b McMillan	5	lbw b de Villiers	3
A.C.Parore†	run out	2	c Eksteen b de Villiers	34
M.D.Crowe	c Richardson b Jack	18	c Richardson b McMillan	5
K.R.Rutherford*	c Kirsten b McMillan	56	lbw b McMillan	26
S.A.Thomson	b McMillan	0	run out	16
S.P.Fleming	b Jack	79	c Richardson b de Villiers	53
M.N.Hart	c Richardson b Jack	24	c de Villiers b Jack	7
S.B.Doull	c Cronje b Jack	6	c Rhodes b de Villiers	25
D.K.Morrison	not out	0	lbw b de Villiers	1
C.Pringle	b de Villiers	30	not out	0
Extras	(lb 13, nb 10)	23	(b 5, lb 6, w 1, nb 6)	18
TOTAL	(114.5 overs)	288	(111.1 overs)	239

SOUTH AFRICA

Batsman	Dismissal	Runs	Dismissal	Runs
G.Kirsten	b Thomson	64	lbw b Hart	25
P.J.R.Steyn	lbw b Thomson	38	c Doull b Thomson	12
J.B.Commins	c Rutherford b Hart	27	not out	10
D.J.Cullinan	c Young b Thomson	5	hit wicket b Hart	28
W.J.Cronje*	c Pringle b Hart	112	not out	14
J.N.Rhodes	b Doull	18		
B.M.McMillan	lbw b Pringle	18		
D.J.Richardson†	c Crowe b Doull	109		
C.E.Eksteen	b Hart	22		
S.D.Jack	c Murray b Morrison	7		
P.S.de Villiers	not out	1		
Extras	(b 7, lb 3, w 1, nb 8)	19		0
TOTAL	(181.2 overs)	440	(31.2 overs) (3 wkts)	89

Bowling SOUTH AFRICA	O	M	R	W	O	M	R	W
de Villiers	28.5	7	90	1	28.1	9	61	5
Jack	27	7	69	4	19	7	50	1
McMillan	26	5	65	4	25	9	52	3
Cronje	5	3	8	0	7	3	15	0
Eksteen	26	10	36	0	31	16	46	0
Kirsten	2	0	7	0	1	0	4	0
NEW ZEALAND								
Morrison	34	7	100	1	4	1	5	0
Doull	34.2	12	55	2				
Pringle	28	5	69	1				
Hart	54	8	141	3	15.2	2	51	2
Thomson	31	7	65	3	12	3	33	1

Fall of Wickets

	NZ 1st	SA 1st	NZ 2nd	SA 2nd
1st	17	106	19	37
2nd	19	119	63	37
3rd	61	125	73	69
4th	95	161	115	-
5th	96	225	131	-
6th	179	271	154	-
7th	245	325	173	-
8th	255	410	224	-
9th	255	429	230	-
10th	288	440	239	-

AVERAGES

New Zealand

BATTING	M	I	NO	Runs	HS	Ave
S.A. Thomson	3	6	0	246	84	41.00
S.P. Fleming	3	6	0	230	79	38.33
B.A. Young	3	6	0	174	51	29.00
K.R. Rutherford	3	6	0	156	68	26.00
S.B. Doull	3	6	2	95	31*	23.75
M.D. Crowe	3	6	0	134	83	22.33
D.J. Nash	1	2	0	38	20	19.00
D.K. Morrison	2	4	2	37	24*	18.50
C. Pringle	2	4	2	36	30	18.00
A.C. Parore	3	6	0	104	49	17.33
R.P. de Groen	1	2	0	26	26	13.00
M.N. Hart	3	6	0	76	34	12.66
D.J. Murray	3	6	0	71	38	11.83

BOWLING	O	M	R	W	Ave
S.B. Doull	115.1	37	257	14	18.35
R.P. de Groen	33	5	80	3	26.66
M.N. Hart	158.4	28	432	15	28.80
S.A. Thomson	56	17	126	4	31.50
D.J. Nash	32	8	98	3	32.66
D.K. Morrison	78	13	231	5	46.20
C. Pringle	43	10	92	1	92.00

South Africa

BATTING	M	I	NO	Runs	HS	Ave
D.J. Richardson	3	4	1	247	109	82.33
W.J. Cronje	3	5	1	227	112	56.75
G. Kirsten	3	6	1	226	66*	45.20
J.B. Commins	2	4	1	112	45	37.33
P.S. de Villiers	3	4	3	36	28	36.00
D.J. Cullinan	3	6	1	162	58	32.40
P.J.R. Steyn	1	2	0	50	38	25.00
B.M. McMillan	3	4	0	82	42	20.50
J.N. Rhodes	3	4	0	56	37	14.00
C.E. Eksteen	2	3	0	31	22	10.33
R.P. Snell	1	2	0	17	16	8.50
A.C. Hudson	2	4	0	26	10	6.50
C.R. Matthews	2	3	0	17	7	5.66
S.D. Jack	2	2	0	7	7	3.50

BOWLING	O	M	R	W	Ave
G. Kirsten	5	2	11	1	11.00
P.S. de Villiers	169.2	50	401	20	20.05
B.M. McMillan	126	39	267	13	20.53
C.R. Matthews	78	26	194	8	24.25
S.D. Jack	77	24	196	8	24.50
R.P. Snell	49.5	14	166	4	41.50
W.J. Cronje	30	14	54	1	54.00
C.E. Eksteen	94	41	163	2	81.50

Shane Thomson was the most improved batsman in the three tests in South Africa, aggregating 246 runs at an average of 41.00.

1994/95 West Indies in New Zealand

The 1994/95 season marked the Centenary of New Zealand Cricket and included a tour by West Indies, a quadrangular one-day tournament with India, Australia and South Africa, followed by a centenary test against South Africa. At the end of the season New Zealand hosted a tour by Sri Lanka.

From the time the team returned from South Africa until the last one-day international was played against Sri Lanka, New Zealand cricket was embroiled in unsavoury publicity.

Coach and manager on the South African tour, Geoff Howarth and Mike Sandilands, resigned, as did Graham Dowling, the Executive Director of New Zealand Cricket. The entire administrative structure of New Zealand Cricket was subsequently changed.

233 NEW ZEALAND v WEST INDIES *(First Test)*

at Lancaster Park, Christchurch on 3, 4, 5, 6, 7 February, 1995
Toss : West Indies. Umpires : B.L. Aldridge and N.T. Plews
Match drawn

Rain before and during the first three days meant that a result would be impossible to achieve when New Zealand, being sent in to bat, were still batting well into the fourth day. There was only time for 11.4 overs on the first day and New Zealand advanced their score to 221-6 by stumps on the second day, when 76 overs were bowled.

Darrin Murray played a brave innings for three hours for his highest test score of 43. The youthful duo of Stephen Fleming and Adam Parore both batted sensibly and used fast footwork to evade dangerous deliveries as well as playing stylish shots.

No play was possible on the third day and it was late starting on the fourth when Parore and Matthew Hart advanced their partnership from 11 to 118 in 163 minutes. Both players made their highest test score. Hart made 45 and Parore 100 not out, at which time Rutherford declared at 341-8.

Over the previous year Parore had been as technically good as any of his team-mates and his attitude towards playing at the highest level always hinted that his batting would be a on a par with his keeping as top-class.

For a short time there was a glimmer of hope of victory when an inspired spell of accurate, probing fast bowling from Danny Morrison had the West Indies reeling at 98-5, with Morrison having four. The only dampener on New Zealand's first session of fielding was that Dion Nash broke a finger.

The final day saw Shivnarine Chanderpaul play watchfully and later, when the pressure had lifted, he watched partner Kenny Benjamin bat rumbustiously striking 85 off 87 balls to enable the last five wickets to add 214. Morrison captured the last two wickets to give him six for the innings.

NEW ZEALAND

B.A.Young	c Murray b Walsh	19	c Murray b Benjamin K.C.G.	21
D.J.Murray	c Campbell b Ambrose	43	c Murray b Walsh	8
A.H.Jones	c Williams b Benjamin K.C.G.	12	not out	10
K.R.Rutherford*	c Murray b Ambrose	11	not out	16
S.P.Fleming	c Lara b Walsh	56		
S.A.Thomson	c Benjamin W.K.M. b Benjamin K.C.G.	20		
A.C.Parore†	not out	100		
M.N.Hart	c & b Benjamin W.K.M.	45		
D.J.Nash	c Campbell b Ambrose	3		
S.B.Doull				
D.K.Morrison				
Extras	(b 12, lb 5, nb 15)	32	(lb 1, nb 5)	6
TOTAL	(124.1 overs) (8 wkts dec)	**341**	(32 overs) (2 wkts)	**61**

WEST INDIES

S.C.Williams	c Parore b Morrison	10
S.L.Campbell	lbw b Morrison	51
B.C.Lara	b Morrison	2
J.C.Adams	c Doull b Morrison	13
K.L.T.Arthurton	run out	1
S.Chanderpaul	b Thomson	69
J.R.Murray†	c Murray b Thomson	28
W.K.M.Benjamin	b Doull	85
C.E.L.Ambrose	b Morrison	33
C.A.Walsh*	not out	0
K.C.G.Benjamin	c Parore b Morrison	5
Extras	(lb 11, nb 4)	15
TOTAL	(96.2 overs)	**312**

Bowling

WEST INDIES	O	M	R	W	O	M	R	W
Ambrose	31.1	12	57	3	3	0	7	0
Walsh	30	5	69	2	4	1	8	1
Benjamin W.K.M.	33	4	94	1	5	1	12	0
Benjamin K.C.G.	25	7	91	2	6	0	12	1
Chanderpaul	3	1	10	0	2	2	0	0
Arthurton	2	0	3	0	5	1	9	0
Adams					3	1	4	0
Lara					4	0	8	0

NEW ZEALAND	O	M	R	W
Morrison	26.2	9	69	6
Nash	5	2	11	0
Doull	22	5	85	1
Hart	25	2	75	0
Thomson	18	3	61	2

Fall of Wickets

	NZ 1st	WI 1st	NZ 2nd
1st	32	10	33
2nd	63	21	33
3rd	92	49	-
4th	97	54	-
5th	128	98	-
6th	210	155	-
7th	328	232	-
8th	341	299	-
9th	-	307	-
10th	-	312	-

MILESTONES

- Danny Morrison overtook Lance Cairns' tally of 130 wickets to be New Zealand's second-highest wicket-taker behind Richard Hadlee. It was his ninth five-wicket haul.

Danny Morrison became New Zealand's second-highest test wicket-taker when his 6-69 took him past Lance Cairns' total of 130. It was the ninth time that he had taken five or more wickets in an innings.

234 NEW ZEALAND v WEST INDIES *(Second Test)*

at Basin Reserve, Wellington on 10, 11, 12, 13 February, 1995
Toss : West Indies. Umpires : R.S. Dunne and V.K. Ramaswamy
West Indies won by an innings and 322 runs

Twenty-four hours before the test began Shane Thomson fell over an advertising hoarding and needed eight stitches below his knee. He was pronounced fit to play the following day but he fielded in the unaccustomed position of first slip and didn't bowl a ball during the West Indies mammoth innings.

At the end of the first day's play, when the visitors had reached 356-3, Jimmy Adams, who was 87 not out, rated the pitch at "nine point plenty" out of 10 for batting. Sherwin Campbell, who had made 51 on his debut in the previous test, batted with refreshing freedom on the first morning and if he had not slowed down when he damaged a hamstring he might have reached a century.

After Campbell was caught at long-leg for 88, Brian Lara and Adams toyed with the despairing attack as they added 221. Lara's 147, his fourth test century, included 24 fours and showed why he was acknowledged as the greatest modern batsman now playing.

The carnage continued unabated on the second day as Adams went on to complete his fourth test century. Keith Arthurton, Shivnarine Chanderpaul and Junior Murray all delighted the spectators with thrilling, inventive strokeplay, none more so than the West Indian wicketkeeper Murray who made the only test century of his career from 88 balls. The total of 660-5 declared was the highest ever made in a test against New Zealand.

With the pitch still in excellent condition New Zealand's first innings reply of 216 was disappointing as Bryan Young, Darrin Murray, Ken Rutherford, Stephen Fleming and Adam Parore all made good starts but only Murray had the tenacity to bat for over three hours.

Courtney Walsh, denied steepling bounce, his normal ally, concentrated on the basics of his trade, line and length, and gave each batsman no respite from his nagging examination, which extended over the third and fourth days. He captured 7-37 and 6-18, both times beating his previous best test return of 6-62.

MILESTONES

- New Zealand lost by an innings and 322 runs, its heaviest test loss. It was the fourth-biggest margin in test history.

- Courtney Walsh's match figures of 13-55 were the best in a test in New Zealand, beating Derek Underwood's 12-97 for England at Lancaster Park in 1970/71. Walsh's figures of 7-37 were the best in an innings at the Basin Reserve, beating Frank Woolley's 7-76 in 1929/30.

- Courtney Walsh captured his 250th test wicket in his 70th test. He was the fourth West Indies bowler to reach the milestone.

- Brian Lara and Jimmy Adams added 221, a third wicket record for West Indies against New Zealand.

- Matthew Hart and Murphy Su'a conceded the most runs by any New Zealand bowler going wicketless in a first-class innings.

WEST INDIES

S.C.Williams	c Parore b Doull	26
S.L.Campbell	c Su'a b Morrison	88
B.C.Lara	lbw b Morrison	147
J.C.Adams	c Su'a b Doull	151
K.L.T.Arthurton	run out	70
S.Chanderpaul	not out	61
J.R.Murray†	not out	101
C.E.L.Ambrose		
C.A.Walsh*		
K.C.G.Benjamin		
R.Dhanraj		
Extras	(lb 6, nb 10)	16
TOTAL	(169.2 overs) (5 wkts dec)	**660**

NEW ZEALAND

B.A.Young	lbw b Walsh	29	b Walsh		0
D.J.Murray	lbw b Ambrose	52	b Walsh		43
A.H.Jones	c Murray b Walsh	0	lbw b Benjamin		2
K.R.Rutherford*	lbw b Dhanraj	22	lbw b Ambrose		5
S.P.Fleming	c Lara b Walsh	47	b Walsh		30
S.A.Thomson	b Walsh	6	b Dhanraj		8
A.C.Parore†	c Adams b Walsh	32	not out		5
M.N.Hart	c Lara b Dhanraj	0	c Ambrose b Dhanraj		1
M.L.Su'a	c Murray b Walsh	6	c Arthurton b Walsh		8
S.B.Doull	b Walsh	0	lbw b Walsh		0
D.K.Morrison	not out	0	c Murray b Walsh		14
Extras	(b 1, lb 14, nb 7)	22	(lb 2, nb 4)		6
TOTAL	(84.4 overs)	**216**	(40.2 overs)		**122**

Bowling	O	M	R	W	O	M	R	W	Fall of Wickets			
NEW ZEALAND										WI	NZ	NZ
										1st	1st	2nd
Morrison	29	5	82	2					1st	85	50	0
Su'a	44	4	179	0					2nd	134	52	3
Doull	37.2	5	162	2					3rd	355	108	15
Hart	46	4	181	0					4th	449	135	70
Jones	13	2	50	0					5th	521	160	93
WEST INDIES									6th	-	196	93
Ambrose	19	9	32	1	5	1	17	1	7th	-	197	97
Walsh	20.4	7	37	7	15.2	8	18	6	8th	-	207	106
Dhanraj	33	6	97	2	12	2	49	2	9th	-	211	106
Benjamin	12	1	35	0	8	0	36	1	10th	-	216	122

A beautiful day at the Basin Reserve. The major buildings from left are the Brierley Pavilion, the old grandstand, overshadowed by the Carillon, and the R.A.Vance Grandstand.

1994/95 South Africa in New Zealand

235 **NEW ZEALAND v SOUTH AFRICA** *(Only Test)*

at Eden Park, Auckland on 4, 5, 6, 7, 8 March, 1995
Toss : South Africa. Umpires : R.S. Dunne and D.B. Hair
South Africa won by 93 runs

The one-off Centenary test was played on an excellent pitch at Eden Park one month after New Zealand's humiliating thrashing by the West Indies. The first session was lost to rain and the South Africans were indebted to Daryll Cullinan who was 82 not out, compiled on his 28th birthday, out of a total 153-3. Between periods of extreme caution Cullinan displayed a full repertoire of shots and 58 of his eventual total of 96 came from boundaries.

Sent in as a nightwatchman Clive Eksteen remained scoreless for 64 minutes before getting off the mark. South Africa was kept at 2.8 runs per over primarily by the accuracy of Danny Morrison, Dion Nash and Gavin Larsen. New Zealand ended the day at 94-1, with Brian Young and Darrin Murray accumulating 86 for the first wicket, their best return as an opening pair.

Though the first nine New Zealand batsmen all reached double figures there was only a series of moderate partnerships. Continuing to grow in confidence, Adam Parore cut, hooked and drove on both sides of the wicket off the front foot, with flair and polish. For the second innings of the game all the wickets fell to the pace bowlers.

New Zealand's slim lead of 34 was quickly wiped off as Gary Kirsten and the recalled Andrew Hudson methodically took the score to 123 before Kirsten became one of Parore's six catches in the game. Hansie Cronje was venturesome

towards the end of the fourth day, hitting Dipak Patel twice over mid-wicket for six and Matthew Hart once over long-off for six, reaching his fifty off 67 balls and leaving South Africa with a lead of 198 with six wickets in hand and the last day to play.

Cronje continued to play positively and, in spite of tight bowling, reached his fifth century before making an enterprising declaration that left New Zealand requiring 275 to win off 64 overs. A run-a-ball alliance between Ken Rutherford and Stephen Fleming worth 64 had the game well balanced at the tea break with New Zealand 114-3.

Fleming went third ball after the interval, followed at 145 by Rutherford for a valiant 56. Fanie de Villiers, Allan Donald and Craig Matthews bundled out the last six wickets for 36, giving South Africa victory by 93 runs with seven overs remaining.

SOUTH AFRICA					
G.Kirsten	b Larsen	16	c Parore b Nash		76
P.J.R.Steyn	c Patel b Morrison	46	c Rutherford b Patel		13
A.C.Hudson	c Parore b Nash	1	c Young b Patel		64
D.J.Cullinan	c Murray b Morrison	96	c Parore b Hart		12
C.E.Eksteen	c Fleming b Nash	21			
W.J.Cronje*	c Crowe b Morrison	41	(5) c Hart b Larsen		101
J.N.Rhodes	c Parore b Nash	0	(6) b Larsen		28
D.J.Richardson†	c Parore b Nash	18	(7) not out		8
C.R.Matthews	c Parore b Larsen	26	(8) not out		4
P.S.de Villiers	c Hart b Larsen	12			
A.A.Donald	not out	4			
Extras	(lb 13)	13	(lb 1, nb 1)		2
TOTAL	**(105.3 overs)**	**294**	**(105 overs) (6 wkts dec)**		**308**
NEW ZEALAND					
B.A.Young	c Richardson b Donald	74	c Cullinan b de Villiers		4
D.J.Murray	c Kirsten b Cronje	25	c Matthews b de Villiers		24
M.D.Crowe	c Hudson b de Villiers	16	c Cullinan b Matthews		14
S.P.Fleming	b Matthews	17	c Richardson b Matthews		27
K.R.Rutherford*	c Richardson b Cronje	28	c Hudson b de Villiers		56
A.C.Parore†	c Richardson b Donald	89	c Cullinan b Eksteen		24
M.N.Hart	lbw b Matthews	28	(8) c Richardson b de Villiers		6
G.R.Larsen	not out	26	(9) c Richardson b Donald		1
D.N.Patel	c Richardson b Donald	15	(7) run out		12
D.J.Nash	lbw b de Villiers	1	lbw b Matthews		6
D.K.Morrison	c Cullinan b Donald	0	not out		0
Extras	(lb 5, w 1, nb 3)	9	(b 1, lb 4, nb 2)		7
TOTAL	**(140.4 overs)**	**328**	**(55.5 overs)**		**181**

Bowling	O	M	R	W	O	M	R	W	Fall of Wickets				
NEW ZEALAND										SA	NZ	SA	NZ
										1st	1st	2nd	2nd
Morrison	26	9	53	3	23	6	78	0	1st	41	86	41	11
Nash	27	13	72	4	22	3	67	1	2nd	42	108	123	42
Larsen	24.3	7	57	3	18	6	31	2	3rd	145	137	135	50
Hart	11	3	45	0	12	3	50	1	4th	168	144	218	114
Patel	17	2	54	0	30	6	81	2	5th	230	226	277	145
SOUTH AFRICA									6th	230	268	300	167
Donald	32.4	11	88	4	8	2	44	1	7th	230	303	-	174
de Villiers	36	13	78	2	18	6	42	4	8th	276	321	-	174
Matthews	32	11	66	2	12.5	3	47	3	9th	276	322	-	179
Cronje	17	3	48	2	3	1	18	0	10th	294	328	-	181
Eksteen	23	9	43	0	14	5	25	1					

The accuracy of the busy Gavin Larsen was a notable feature of the Centenary test match against South Africa. His match analysis of five wickets for 88 runs off 42.3 overs, of which 13 were maidens, was a fine performance.

MILESTONES

- It was South Africa's first test win in New Zealand in 42 years.

- Hansie Cronje scored his fifth test century in his 21st test match. Each match in which he had scored a century ended in victory for South Africa.

- David Richardson took seven catches in the game.

1994/95 Sri Lanka in New Zealand

236 NEW ZEALAND v SRI LANKA *(First Test)*

at McLean Park, Napier on 11, 12, 13, 14, 15 March, 1995
Toss : New Zealand. Umpires : D.B. Cowie and S.G. Randell
Sri Lanka won by 241 runs

Drought conditions were again broken when a test match was scheduled at McLean Park. The players were confronted by a hard pitch with a dense covering of grass that saw 13 wickets fall on the first day after Ken Rutherford had won the toss and sent Sri Lanka in to bat.

Making his debut for New Zealand Kerry Walmsley, 203 cm tall, had his first test wicket with the seventh ball that he bowled. The other members of the quartet of pace bowlers, Danny Morrison, Dion Nash and Gavin Larsen, thrived on the helpful conditions and had Sri Lanka at 88-6.

Arjuna Ranatunga and 21-year-old Chaminda Vaas halted the triumphant procession by taking runs off the erratic Walmsley and adding 49 for the seventh wicket. This enabled Sri Lanka to recover and be all out for 183.

Any thoughts that the pitch was flattening out were dispelled when Sri Lanka captured three wickets in the first 20 balls, leaving New Zealand 33-3 at stumps, with Stephen Fleming and Rutherford being the overnight batsmen.

On the second day a misty morning enabled the quicker Sri Lankan bowlers to gain sharp movement off the pitch and through the air to expose the frailties of the New Zealand batsmen who crumbled to be all out for 109, giving Sri Lanka a lead of 74. Vaas claimed his best test figures of 5-47.

Larsen had two lbw appeals answered in the affirmative as Sri Lanka laboured at 22-3 before Aravinda de Silva showed exceptional skill, scoring fifty off 71 balls and, with Hashan Tillakaratne defending dourly, taking Sri Lanka through until bad light ended the day at 92-3.

Tillakaratne, 74 in 301 minutes, and debutant keeper Chamara Dunusinghe, 91 in 323 minutes, helped Sri Lanka to 352 all out just before lunch on the fourth day. New Zealand needed 427 to win in five sessions.

They were well placed at 108-1, with Darrin Murray and Mark Greatbatch well-established, but Muttiah Muralitharan began to extract considerable turn and had both of them, and Fleming, out before stumps, leaving New Zealand 139-4.

The youthful pair of Vaas and Muralitharan ripped out the remaining batsmen before lunch on the last day, each taking five wickets, to give Sri Lanka their first overseas test win.

SRI LANKA

A.P.Gurusinha	b Walmsley	2	lbw b Larsen	8
D.P.Samaraweera	c Young b Walmsley	33	run out	6
S.Ranatunga	c Larsen b Nash	12	lbw b Larsen	7
P.A.de Silva	c Parore b Nash	0	c Parore b Morrison	62
H.P.Tillakaratne	lbw b Morrison	9	c Young b Nash	74
A.Ranatunga*	c Young b Walmsley	55	b Morrison	28
C.I.Dunusinghe†	c Rutherford b Larsen	11	b Morrison	91
W.P.U.J.C.Vaas	not out	33	b Walmsley	36
G.P.Wickramasinghe	c Fleming b Morrison	13	c sub (M.N.Hart) b Larsen	16
M.Muralitharan	c Nash b Larsen	8	not out	10
K.R.Pushpakumara	c Larsen b Morrison	1	c Parore b Morrison	0
Extras	(lb 6)	6	(b 2, lb 7, nb 5)	14
TOTAL	(69 overs)	**183**	(144.3 overs)	**352**

NEW ZEALAND

B.A.Young	c Dunusinghe b Wickramasinghe	2	c Samaraweera b Muralitharan	14
D.J.Murray	b Vaas	1	c Dunusinghe b Vaas	36
M.J.Greatbatch	lbw b Wickramasinghe	1	c Tillakaratne b Muralitharan	46
S.P.Fleming	c Ranatunga S. b Vaas	35	c Tillakaratne b Muralitharan	0
K.R.Rutherford*	c Tillakaratne b Pushpakumara	32	c Dunusinghe b Vaas	20
S.A.Thomson	c Muralitharan b Vaas	8	c Gurusinha b Muralitharan	4
A.C.Parore†	c Dunusinghe b Wickramasinghe	7	c Tillakaratne b Muralitharan	17
G.R.Larsen	c Dunusinghe b Vaas	0	not out	21
D.J.Nash	lbw b Pushpakumara	0	c Dunusinghe b Vaas	0
D.K.Morrison	not out	7	c Gurusinha b Vaas	0
K.P.Walmsley	b Vaas	4	c Dunusinghe b Vaas	4
Extras	(b 5, lb 1, w 1, nb 5)	12	(b 6, lb 11, nb 6)	23
TOTAL	(42.5 overs)	**109**	(84.4 overs)	**185**

Bowling	O	M	R	W	O	M	R	W
NEW ZEALAND								
Morrison	19	5	40	3	25.3	5	61	4
Walmsley	17	3	70	3	38	7	112	1
Nash	16	4	28	2	36	12	87	1
Larsen	17	6	39	2	39	13	73	3
Thomson					6	3	10	0
SRI LANKA								
Wickramasinghe	19	7	33	3	13	2	42	0
Vaas	18.5	3	47	5	26.4	10	43	5
Pushpakumara	5	1	23	2	9	2	19	0
Muralitharan					36	15	64	5

Fall of Wickets

	SL	NZ	SL	NZ
	1st	1st	2nd	2nd
1st	15	2	14	37
2nd	40	4	21	108
3rd	40	6	22	108
4th	54	53	121	112
5th	64	65	165	141
6th	88	78	205	141
7th	137	79	294	166
8th	166	94	323	181
9th	178	104	352	181
10th	183	109	352	185

Mark Greatbatch accumulates more runs backward of square-leg in his second innings of 46.

MILESTONES

- Kerry Walmsley (192) made his test debut.

- Chaminda Vaas took his first five-wicket bag and became the first Sri Lankan bowler to take 10 wickets in a match.

- Muttiah Muralitharan had his best test analysis of 5-64.

- Arjuna Ranatunga became the first Sri Lankan to score 3000 test runs.

237 NEW ZEALAND v SRI LANKA *(Second Test)*

at Carisbrok, Dunedin on 18, 19, 20, 21, 22 March, 1995
Toss : New Zealand. Umpires : D.M. Quested and V.K. Ramaswamy
Match drawn

Over the 1994/95 season New Zealand played eight tests and it was rare that the same medium-fast bowling attack played consecutive tests because of injuries decimating the personnel from test to test. The eighth and last test was no different as Danny Morrison and Dion Nash were both injured and were replaced by Murphy Su'a and Chris Pringle to partner Kerry Walmsley from the previous test. New Zealand had to win this test to square the series.

Sri Lanka was sent in to bat and was out moments before stumps for 233. The first wicket added 42 and the last 39 and the rest of the innings contained useful partnerships but nothing substantial. Pringle and right-arm off-spinner Dipak Patel shared the wickets with three each.

Attempting to take a catch, Ken Rutherford split the webbing between two fingers and took no further part in the game. Gavin Larsen was entrusted with the captaincy and, when he was off the field, Mark Greatbatch took over.

Rain shortened the second day but not before Darrin Murray and Greatbatch had both been dismissed for ducks by Chaminda Vaas, and the home team finished at 95-2 with Bryan Young 44 not out and Stephen Fleming 39 not out.

The alliance of Young and Fleming accomplished a rare occurrence among the New Zealand batsmen – a century partnership – that was terminated when Fleming was run out for 66. Young batted for 381 minutes for 84. Patel became the third player in the innings to reach fifty and the total of 307 enabled New Zealand to lead by 74 with two days to play on what was now a most benign pitch.

When New Zealand captured the first three visitors Sri Lanka's lead was only seven but two left-hand batsmen, Asanka Gurusinha and Hashan Tillakaratane, were strong-willed in their team's quest for their first series win overseas. They slowly and safely accumulated runs and carried their partnership through the last two sessions of the fourth day and the morning session of the fifth day, adding 192 before Tillakaratane was dismissed for 108. Gurusinha's indomitable effort of 127 occupied 516 minutes.

By the time that Arjuna Ranatunga, the Sri Lankan captain, came to the crease, his team was on the brink of their historic accomplishment and he delighted in scoring 90 before being the last man dismissed.

MILESTONES

- Sri Lanka won their first test series overseas.
- Chaminda Vaas had his best analysis of 6-87 as well as his highest test score of 51.

SRI LANKA					
A.P.Gurusinha	c Patel b Pringle	28	b Su'a		127
D.P.Samaraweera	b Su'a	33	lbw b Su'a		5
S.Ranatunga	c Young b Pringle	22	c Parore b Patel		23
P.A.de Silva	c Patel b Walmsley	18	c Murray b Patel		13
A.Ranatunga*	c Young b Larsen	0	(6) c Parore b Larsen		90
H.P.Tillakaratne	c Young b Patel	36	(5) c Murray b Patel		108
C.I.Dunusinghe†	lbw b Pringle	0	c Fleming b Patel		11
W.P.U.J.C.Vaas	c Fleming b Su'a	51	c Parore b Walmsley		3
G.P.Wickramasinghe	c Fleming b Patel	10	c Parore b Walmsley		9
M.Muralitharan	c Larsen b Patel	8	run out		7
K.R.Pushpakumara	not out	17	not out		1
Extras	(lb 6, nb 4)	10	(b 6, lb 5, nb 3)		14
TOTAL	(87.5 overs)	233	(168.4 overs)		411

NEW ZEALAND					
B.A.Young	c Gurusinha b Vaas	84	not out		0
D.J.Murray	c Dunusinghe b Vaas	0	not out		0
M.J.Greatbatch	lbw b Vaas	0			
S.P.Fleming	run out	66			
A.C.Parore†	c de Silva b Vaas	19			
D.N.Patel	b Muralitharan	52			
G.R.Larsen	c Gurusinha b Muralitharan	16			
M.L.Su'a	not out	20			
C.Pringle	c Ranatunga S. b Vaas	4			
K.P.Walmsley	b Vaas	0			
K.R.Rutherford*	absent hurt				
Extras	(b 3, lb 28, nb 15)	46			0
TOTAL	(139 overs)	307	(0.1 overs) (0 wkts)		0

Bowling	O	M	R	W	O	M	R	W
NEW ZEALAND								
Su'a	20.5	5	43	2	26	3	97	2
Walmsley	18	4	41	1	38	8	121	2
Pringle	15	1	51	3	22	8	55	0
Patel	21	3	62	3	57	20	96	4
Larsen	13	2	30	1	25.4	14	31	1
SRI LANKA								
Wickramasinghe	26	6	49	0				
Vaas	40	9	87	6	0.1	0	0	0
Muralitharan	50	20	77	2				
Pushpakumara	16	3	42	0				
de Silva	1	0	11	0				
Gurusinha	6	2	10	0				

Fall of Wickets	SL	NZ	SL	NZ
	1st	1st	2nd	2nd
1st	42	26	11	-
2nd	67	26	63	-
3rd	94	140	81	-
4th	97	196	273	-
5th	122	197	295	-
6th	122	244	344	-
7th	157	291	355	-
8th	178	303	377	-
9th	194	307	405	-
10th	233	-	411	-

Dipak Patel had an excellent all-round game. He took two catches, seven wickets for 158 runs and also made 52.

1995/96 New Zealand in India

The fallout from the dismal performance by New Zealand in its centenary season continued when Ken Rutherford opted to play his cricket for the South African province Transvaal. Glenn Turner was appointed not only the convener of the national selectors but also coach of the team. Lee Germon, who had played 76 first-class games for Canterbury, was chosen as captain without having played test cricket.

The tour to India over October and November saw the test series played during the monsoon months. The three test venues all lay in the path of the monsoon and, with the exception of Bangalore, the other two tests were washed out.

238 INDIA v NEW ZEALAND *(First Test)*

at M. Chinnaswamy Stadium, Bangalore on 18, 19, 20 October, 1995
Toss : New Zealand. Umpires : S.K. Bansal and M.J. Kitchen
India won by 8 wickets

Germon's first act as his country's captain was successful when he won the toss and elected to bat. The new skills learned in English county cricket by Javagal Srinath at Gloucestershire were evident when he captured three of the first six wickets to fall with the score at a paltry 71.

At this stage Germon came in to bat and, by exhibiting fast footwork and good technique, he was the only batsman to take the battle to the tormenting Indian trio of spinners, the pick of whom was Anil Kumble the right-arm leg-spinner who was playing in front of his home crowd. With his googly working effectively Kumble ended with four for 39.

Lee Germon became the first New Zealander to captain the test team on debut since Tom Lowry in the country's first test in 1929/30. As the 23rd captain of New Zealand he led by example, top scoring in both innings.

New Zealand's 145 was disappointing but Dion Nash and Danny Morrison bowled in a lively fashion to have India struggling at 54-3. Ajay Jadeja, a dangerous opening batsman ideally suited to one-day cricket, partnered Mohammad Azharuddin in a stand that determined the game.

They added 95, with Jadeja compiling his maiden test fifty. Azharuddin went on to 87 before he was bowled by Chris Cairns, one of four wickets Cairns captured in a stunning spell of 22 balls after lunch on the second day. India's last six wickets toppled for 17 runs and they led by 83.

New Zealand lost five wickets in wiping off the arrears and it was left to Stephen Fleming and Cairns to survive until stumps with New Zealand 125-5, a lead of 42, and only five wickets remaining with three days left to play.

Fleming and Cairns were dismissed early on the third day but Germon again resisted Kumble and Venkatapathy Raju. Nash and Matthew Hart assisted the captain to add 99 for the last three wickets, but the spectators in Bangalore were delighted when Kumble ended with another five wickets.

India's target was 151. Jadeja took the attack to the bowlers before he was brilliantly caught by Adam Parore, in the covers, for 73 made off 93 balls. Jadeja and Manoj Prabhakar added 101 for the first wicket and the winning runs were made, giving India victory by eight wickets after three days play. The following day, the monsoon struck.

NEW ZEALAND

Batsman	Dismissal	Runs	Dismissal (2nd)	Runs
B.A.Young	c Tendulkar b Raju	14	(2) lbw b Prabhakar	8
M.J.Greatbatch	b Srinath	10	(1) b Prabhakar	16
A.C.Parore	lbw b Srinath	2	lbw b Srinath	3
M.D.Crowe	c Tendulkar b Kumble	11	lbw b Kumble	24
S.P.Fleming	c Mongia b Srinath	16	c & b Kumble	41
S.A.Thomson	c Mongia b Chauhan	17	c Mongia b Kumble	6
C.L.Cairns	c Manjrekar b Raju	15	b Srinath	23
L.K.Germon*†	c Tendulkar b Kumble	48	lbw b Kumble	41
D.J.Nash	lbw b Kumble	0	c Kumble b Raju	17
M.N.Hart	c Prabhakar b Kumble	1	not out	27
D.K.Morrison	not out	1	c Azharuddin b Kumble	9
Extras	(b 4, lb 5, nb 1)	10	(b 8, lb 10)	18
TOTAL	(65 overs)	**145**	(73.2 overs)	**233**

INDIA

Batsman	Dismissal	Runs	Dismissal (2nd)	Runs
M.Prabhakar	c Germon b Morrison	4	c Greatbatch b Hart	43
A.Jadeja	c Young b Morrison	59	c Parore b Hart	73
S.V.Manjrekar	lbw b Nash	15	not out	29
S.R.Tendulkar	c Young b Nash	4	not out	0
M.Azharuddin*	b Cairns	87		
V.G.Kambli	c Parore b Nash	27		
N.R.Mongia†	lbw b Cairns	1		
A.R.Kumble	not out	6		
J.Srinath	b Cairns	0		
R.K.Chauhan	c Young b Morrison	1		
S.L.V.Raju	c Hart b Cairns	0		
Extras	(lb 8, w 4, nb 12)	24	(lb 3, nb 3)	6
TOTAL	(70.4 overs)	**228**	(40.5 overs) (2 wkts)	**151**

Bowling	O	M	R	W	O	M	R	W	Fall of Wickets				
INDIA										NZ	I	NZ	I
										1st	1st	2nd	2nd
Prabhakar	6	0	15	0	8	3	23	2					
Srinath	14	5	24	3	15	6	41	2	1st	14	11	19	101
Raju	16	6	47	2	14	2	43	1	2nd	22	45	32	145
Kumble	18	5	39	4	27.2	4	81	5	3rd	30	54	36	-
Chauhan	11	7	11	1	9	1	27	0	4th	44	149	58	-
NEW ZEALAND									5th	71	211	80	-
Morrison	18	5	61	3	7	1	34	0	6th	71	214	130	-
Cairns	17.4	5	44	4	6	1	13	0	7th	114	220	134	-
Nash	16	3	50	3	7	1	26	0	8th	114	220	173	-
Hart	7	1	28	0	9.5	3	34	2	9th	144	227	210	-
Thomson	12	3	37	0	11	1	41	0	10th	145	228	233	-

MILESTONES

- Lee Germon (193) made his test debut.

- Germon became the 23rd test captain of New Zealand.

- Bryan Young scored his 1000th test run.

- Anil Kumble captured his 100th test wicket, on his home ground, in his 21st test. He was the 12th Indian bowler to reach the mark, ten of them being spin bowlers.

- New Zealand had lost six of their last eight tests.

239 INDIA v NEW ZEALAND *(Second Test)*

at M.A. Chidambaram Stadium, Madras on 25, 26, 27, 28, 29 October, 1995
Toss : India. Umpires : K.T. Francis and S. Venkataraghavan
Match drawn

The second test began two days after a total eclipse of the sun which had captivated all the people of India. Unfortunately, monsoon rain washed out three complete days and interfered with the other two, so that little more than five hours' play was possible. Another villain was the relaid outfield that did not allow the water to run away into the drains.

When play began at 2.30 pm on the first day there was only time for 35.3 overs and India's score had reached 54-1. Chris Cairns had the bowling figures of 11-5-8-0.

The next two days were washed out and there was only time for a further two hours' play on the fourth day, where the highlight was Sachin Tendulkar scoring a quick fifty off 67 balls.

Not out 41 at the completion of the match was Manoj Prabhakar, who had batted for the entire course of the game, 304 minutes, one of the slowest innings in the history of test cricket. Rain and damp ground conditions saw no play possible on the fifth day.

MILESTONES

- Roger Twose (194) made his test debut.

- Only 71.1 overs were bowled, making it the shortest test, in terms of balls bowled, in Indian test cricket.

The New Zealand team in India in 1995/96. Back row (from left): Mark Plummer (physiotherapist), Roger Twose, Simon Doull, Mark Haslam, Aaron Gale. Middle row: Bryan Young, Dion Nash, Chris Cairns, Stephen Fleming, Matthew Hart, Shane Thomson. Front row: Gren Alabaster (manager), Danny Morrison, Mark Greatbatch, Lee Germon (captain), Martin Crowe, Adam Parore, Glenn Turner (coach).

INDIA

M.Prabhakar	not out	41
A.Jadeja	b Nash	3
N.S.Sidhu	c Twose b Cairns	33
S.R.Tendulkar	not out	52
M.Azharuddin*		
V.G.Kambli		
N.R.Mongia†		
A.R.Kumble		
J.Srinath		
R.K.Chauhan		
S.L.V.Raju		
Extras	(lb 1, w 1, nb 13)	15
TOTAL	(71.1 overs) (2 wkts)	**144**

NEW ZEALAND

M.J.Greatbatch
R.G.Twose
A.C.Parore
M.D.Crowe
S.P.Fleming
S.A.Thomson
C.L.Cairns
L.K.Germon*†
D.J.Nash
M.J.Haslam
D.K.Morrison

Bowling NEW ZEALAND	O	M	R	W		Fall of Wickets *I*
						1st
Morrison	14	3	34	0		
Cairns	16	7	18	1	1st	18
Nash	15	3	22	1	2nd	73
Haslam	17.1	4	50	0	3rd	-
Thomson	9	0	19	0	4th	-
					5th	-
					6th	-
					7th	-
					8th	-
					9th	-
					10th	-

240 **INDIA v NEW ZEALAND** *(Third Test)*
at Barabati Stadium, Cuttack on 8, 9, 10, 11, 12 November, 1995
Toss : India. Umpires : V.K. Ramaswamy and I.D. Robinson
Match drawn

The monsoon swept in off the Bay of Bengal and ruined this test, with no play being possible on the second and third days. Regrettably, human error prevented play on the third day, when it was found that the pitch had been saturated by water seeping through holes in the multi-layered covers.

Play began on time on the first day and India had reached 120-3 when rain interfered. Both Chris Cairns and Dion Nash caused all the batsmen problems with the amount of movement they got off the seam.

When play began on the second day the movement was still there and the pair reduced India to 188-6 before wicketkeeper Nayan Mongia and right-arm off-spinner Aashish Kapoor both scored over 40 to highlight that batting was not utterly impossible. India declared their innings closed at the completion of the fourth day's play at 296-8.

Having made his test debut 19 days earlier Roger Twose finally went to the crease at the start of the fifth day and batted for three and a half hours, adding 86 for the first wicket with Mark Greatbatch, who made a welcome return to form.

Playing his first test for five years Narendra Hirwani bamboozled the majority of the leaden-footed visitors with his orthodox right-arm leg-spinners mixed liberally with googlies as he captured six wickets. Stephen Fleming did not bat owing to a stomach upset. The draw gave India a 1-0 series win.

MILESTONES

- India had not been beaten in a home series in nine years.

- After playing in the first five one-day internationals Martin Crowe flew home saying that his knee, which had hampered him in the past few years, would take no more and he was retiring from cricket. This was his 77th test match. He had the most test runs for New Zealand (5444), most test centuries (17) and most catches by a fieldsman (71).

Monsoon rains ruined New Zealand's tour of India. Dion Nash captured one wicket on the first day of the third test and three more on the fourth day to end with 4-62 as rain ensured the game would end in a draw.

INDIA

M.Prabhakar	c Crowe b Nash	22
A.Jadeja	c Hart b Cairns	45
N.S.Sidhu	c Fleming b Nash	41
S.R.Tendulkar	b Cairns	2
M.Azharuddin*	lbw b Cairns	35
V.G.Kambli	c Germon b Nash	28
N.R.Mongia†	not out	45
A.R.Kapoor	st Germon b Haslam	42
A.R.Kumble	c Greatbatch b Nash	2
J.Srinath	not out	21
N.D.Hirwani		
Extras	(lb 10, nb 3)	13
TOTAL	**(89.5 overs) (8 wkts dec)**	**296**

NEW ZEALAND

M.J.Greatbatch	c Jadeja b Hirwani	50
R.G.Twose	lbw b Hirwani	36
A.C.Parore	c Mongia b Hirwani	12
M.D.Crowe	c Kambli b Hirwani	15
C.L.Cairns	c Jadeja b Hirwani	13
L.K.Germon*†	run out	2
M.N.Hart	c Srinath b Hirwani	8
D.J.Nash	not out	10
D.K.Morrison	lbw b Kumble	0
M.J.Haslam	not out	1
S.P.Fleming		
Extras	(b 7, lb 19, nb 2)	28
TOTAL	**(88 overs) (8 wkts)**	**175**

Bowling	O	M	R	W
NEW ZEALAND				
Morrison	13	0	52	0
Cairns	26.5	4	95	3
Nash	29	4	62	4
Twose	1	0	5	0
Haslam	15	1	42	1
Hart	5	0	30	0
INDIA				
Prabhakar	5	2	10	0
Srinath	8	3	16	0
Kapoor	17	3	32	0
Kumble	27	12	32	1
Hirwani	31	10	59	6

Fall of Wickets

	I	NZ
	1st	1st
1st	69	85
2nd	75	109
3rd	77	130
4th	143	139
5th	172	151
6th	188	155
7th	254	166
8th	267	166
9th	-	-
10th	-	-

AVERAGES

New Zealand

BATTING	M	I	NO	Runs	HS	Ave
R.G. Twose	2	1	0	36	36	36.00
L.K. Germon	3	3	0	91	48	30.33
S.P. Fleming	3	2	0	57	41	28.50
M.J. Greatbatch	3	3	0	76	50	25.33
M.N. Hart	2	3	1	36	27*	18.00
C.L. Cairns	3	3	0	51	23	17.00
M.D. Crowe	3	3	0	50	24	16.66
D.J. Nash	3	3	1	27	17	13.50
S.A. Thomson	2	2	0	23	17	11.50
B.A. Young	1	2	0	22	14	11.00
A.C. Parore	3	3	0	17	12	5.66
D.K. Morrison	3	3	1	10	9	5.00
M.J. Haslam	2	1	1	1	1*	-

BOWLING	O	M	R	W	Ave
D.J. Nash	67	11	160	8	20.00
C.L. Cairns	66.3	17	170	8	21.25
M.N. Hart	21.5	4	92	2	46.00
D.K. Morrison	52	9	181	3	60.33
M.J. Haslam	32.1	5	92	1	92.00
R.G. Twose	1	0	5	0	-
S.A. Thomson	32	4	97	0	-

India

BATTING	M	I	NO	Runs	HS	Ave
M. Azharuddin	3	2	0	122	87	61.00
N.R. Mongia	3	2	1	46	45*	46.00
A. Jadeja	3	4	0	180	73	45.00
S.V. Manjrekar	1	2	1	44	29*	44.00
A.R. Kapoor	1	1	0	42	42	42.00
N.S. Sidhu	2	2	0	74	41	37.00
M. Prabhakar	3	4	1	110	43	36.66
S.R. Tendulkar	3	4	2	58	52*	29.00
V.G. Kambli	3	2	0	55	28	27.50
J. Srinath	3	2	1	21	21*	21.00
A.R. Kumble	3	2	1	8	6*	8.00
R.K. Chauhan	2	1	0	1	1	1.00
S.L.V. Raju	2	1	0	0	0	0.00
N.D. Hirwani	1	-	-	-	-	-

BOWLING	O	M	R	W	Ave
N.D. Hirwani	31	10	59	6	9.83
A.R. Kumble	72.2	21	152	10	15.20
J. Srinath	37	14	81	5	16.20
M. Prabhakar	19	5	48	2	24.00
S.L.V. Raju	30	8	90	3	30.00
R.K. Chauhan	20	8	38	1	38.00
A.R. Kapoor	17	3	32	0	-

1995/96 Pakistan in New Zealand

241 **NEW ZEALAND v PAKISTAN** *(Only Test)*
at Lancaster Park, Christchurch on 8, 9, 10, 11, 12 December, 1995
Toss : New Zealand. Umpires : B.C. Cooray and R.S. Dunne
Pakistan won by 161 runs

Erratic bowling by Danny Morrison and Chris Cairns was punished by Aamer Sohail and Ramiz Raja, who together hit 21 boundaries in adding 135 runs. Cairns broke the partnership and captured three wickets in 21 balls. In a dramatic collapse the last 10 wickets fell for 73 runs and Pakistan were dismissed for 208. Craig Spearman made a fluent 40 that enabled New Zealand to be 98-3 at stumps.

Roger Twose and Cairns added 102, with Twose defending dourly while Cairns was at his flamboyant best. They were both dismissed by Wasim Akram who captured five of the last six wickets to fall. Ijaz Ahmed and Inzamam-ul-Haq were unbeaten on 54 and 52 at stumps, with Pakistan 138-1.

This most cultured partnership, involving classic shots and flawless timing, continued the next day, as Ijaz continued on to his second test century in 11 days. The three sessions during the day saw Pakistan score 77, 75 and 79 as all the batsmen, with the exception of Basit Ali, applied themselves

diligently. The tourists had a commanding lead of 289 at the end of the third day, with three wickets remaining.

Pakistan's final total of 434 left New Zealand with 357 to win and a solid opening saw 50 on the board before the first wicket fell. In the space of the next hour the magic of Mushtaq Ahmed saw New Zealand lose five wickets and with it any chance of repeating their famous victory against the same opponents two years previously. Twose rallied the lower order batsmen, taking the game into its fifth day with New Zealand 158-7 at stumps. On the final day he reached his second half-century of the match and Mushtaq ended with the best test analysis of his 52-test career with 7-56.

MILESTONES

- Craig Spearman (195) made his test debut.

- Danny Morrison recorded his 23rd duck, thus equalling the record held by Bhagwat Chandrashekar of India.

- Ijaz Ahmed and Inzamam-ul-Haq put on 140, a Pakistan second wicket record against New Zealand.

- Waqar Younis captured his 200th test wicket in his 38th test, the youngest bowler (aged 24) to reach this landmark.

- Mushtaq Ahmed took 10 wickets in a test for the first time.

- It was the first test held in New Zealand in December.

Roger Twose scored two fifties in the match, batting for a total of 467 minutes.

PAKISTAN

Aamer Sohail	hit wicket b Cairns	88	b Patel		30
Ramiz Raja	lbw b Cairns	54	lbw b Morrison		62
Ijaz Ahmed	c Morrison b Larsen	30	c Germon b Nash		103
Inzamam-ul-Haq	lbw b Cairns	0	c Fleming b Nash		82
Salim Malik	c Germon b Nash	0	c Germon b Morrison		21
Basit Ali	c Germon b Larsen	5	lbw b Cairns		0
Rashid Latif†	c Spearman b Morrison	2	c Germon b Cairns		39
Wasim Akram*	c Young b Morrison	2	c Fleming b Cairns		19
Mushtaq Ahmed	lbw b Nash	5	c Germon b Larsen		24
Waqar Younis	not out	12	lbw b Larsen		34
Ata-ur-Rehman	c & b Cairns	5	not out		0
Extras	(lb 1, w 1, nb 3)	5	(b 5, lb 6, w 4, nb 5)		20
TOTAL	(54.1 overs)	**208**	(145 overs)		**434**

NEW ZEALAND

B.A.Young	c Latif b Rehman	16	c Latif b Mushtaq		18
C.M.Spearman	b Mushtaq	40	c Sohail b Mushtaq		33
A.C.Parore	c Latif b Rehman	9	lbw b Mushtaq		5
S.P.Fleming	st Latif b Mushtaq	25	lbw b Rehman		0
R.G.Twose	lbw b Akram	59	not out		51
C.L.Cairns	b Akram	76	c Malik b Mushtaq		8
L.K.Germon*†	c Latif b Akram	21	run out		12
D.N.Patel	c Sohail b Akram	3	b Mushtaq		15
G.R.Larsen	not out	5	c Sohail b Mushtaq		13
D.J.Nash	c Latif b Akram	11	b Waqar		22
D.K.Morrison	b Mushtaq	0	c Malik b Mushtaq		1
Extras	(lb 4, nb 17)	21	(b 3, lb 9, w 1, nb 4)		17
TOTAL	(91.4 overs)	**286**	(80.4 overs)		**195**

Bowling	O	M	R	W	O	M	R	W		Fall of Wickets				
NEW ZEALAND											P	NZ	P	NZ
Morrison	14	0	57	2	27	5	99	2			1st	1st	2nd	2nd
Cairns	11.1	2	51	4	35	6	114	3		1st	135	48	55	50
Larsen	15	2	44	2	29	10	58	2		2nd	146	65	195	57
Nash	11	3	43	2	30	6	91	2		3rd	148	73	224	60
Patel	3	1	12	0	24	8	61	1		4th	149	119	260	60
PAKISTAN										5th	177	221	265	75
Akram	24.5	4	53	5	11	3	31	0		6th	184	262	339	101
Waqar	16	2	60	0	26	6	73	1		7th	184	265	363	131
Rehman	17.1	4	47	2	9	1	23	1		8th	187	269	384	163
Mushtaq	30.4	4	115	3	34.4	13	56	7		9th	203	283	425	192
Sohail	3	0	7	0						10th	208	286	434	195

1995/96 Zimbabwe in New Zealand

Zimbabwe, who had played three matches in New Zealand during the 1992 World Cup, made their first test appearances in New Zealand.

242 NEW ZEALAND v ZIMBABWE *(First Test)*

at Trust Bank Park, Hamilton on 13, 14, 15, 16, 17 January, 1996
Toss : Zimbabwe. Umpires : L.H. Barker and D.M. Quested
Match drawn

Rain and inadequate drainage meant that the first test at Hamilton was always going to be a difficult situation from which to achieve victory, as only 110 overs were bowled in the first three days. New Zealand declared at lunch on the third day after 80 overs at 230-8, with Roger Twose having batted for 227 minutes for 42. Stephen Fleming was all class, stroking 49 in 83 minutes before he was run out.

Greg Loveridge, one of the four debutants for New Zealand, chosen for his right-arm leg-spin bowling, fractured his knuckle the ball after straight-driving Henry Olonga for four and took no further part in the only test of his career.

Chris Cairns soon had Zimbabwe reeling at 52-5. On the fourth day a resilient partnership between Guy Whittall and Paul Strang, worth 91 runs, ensured that Zimbabwe was only 34 behind New Zealand's first innings total.

Adam Parore's 84 not out off 177 balls enabled New Zealand to declare, for the second time in the test, at lunch on the fifth day at 222-5. Lee Germon was able to set a realistic target, challenging Zimbabwe to score 257 runs in two sessions and, with sensible, positive batting the visitors reached 143-3 before three dubious decisions left Zimbabwe no alternative but to bat out time.

Andy Flower, the Zimbabwean captain, observed the three decisions from the non-striker's end and was at his diplomatic best when he said after the game, "Those hiccups in the middle destroyed our momentum."

MILESTONES

- Geoff Allott (196), Nathan Astle (197), Robert Kennedy (198) and Greg Loveridge (199) made their test debuts.

- New Zealand's four debutants were the most in one test since 1961/62 (test 53).

- David Houghton reached his 1000th run in his 15th test.

- Lee Germon and Andy Flower were the first two wicketkeeper-captains to oppose each other in test history.

- Heath Streak became the first Zimbabwe bowler to capture 50 test wickets.

NEW ZEALAND

C.M.Spearman	c Flower A. b Streak	0	lbw b Streak	27
R.G.Twose	b Brandes	42	run out	8
S.P.Fleming	run out	49	c Flower A. b Strang P.A.	21
A.C.Parore	c Flower A. b Streak	16	not out	84
N.J.Astle	lbw b Streak	18	c Olonga b Strang B.C.	32
C.L.Cairns	c Flower A. b Streak	7	c Olonga b Brandes	7
L.K.Germon*†	c Carlisle b Olonga	24	not out	22
D.N.Patel	c Olonga b Strang P.A.	31		
G.R.Loveridge	retired hurt	4		
R.J.Kennedy	not out	2		
G.I.Allott	not out	0		
Extras	(b 4, lb 11, w 1, nb 21)	37	(b 4, lb 7, w 4, nb 6)	21
TOTAL	(80 overs) (8 wkts dec)	**230**	(75 overs) (5 wkts dec)	**222**

ZIMBABWE

G.W.Flower	b Cairns	5	c Germon b Cairns	59
S.V.Carlisle	c Germon b Cairns	4	c Fleming b Patel	19
A.D.R.Campbell	c Astle b Allott	5	(6) c Germon b Patel	3
D.L.Houghton	lbw b Cairns	31	lbw b Twose	31
A.Flower*†	c Spearman b Kennedy	6	not out	58
G.J.Whittall	c Germon b Kennedy	54	(3) c Kennedy b Twose	20
H.H.Streak	c Spearman b Cairns	24	lbw b Cairns	6
P.A.Strang	b Patel	49	not out	0
H.K.Olonga	c Germon b Kennedy	0		
E.A.Brandes	not out	3		
B.C.Strang	c Astle b Patel	4		
Extras	(lb 3, w 2, nb 6)	11	(lb 4, w 1, nb 7)	12
TOTAL	(74.5 overs)	**196**	(58 overs) (6 wkts)	**208**

Bowling										Fall of Wickets			
ZIMBABWE	O	M	R	W	O	M	R	W		NZ	Z	NZ	Z
										1st	*1st*	*2nd*	*2nd*
Streak	25	7	52	4	22	4	56	1					
Strang B.C.	24	11	51	0	5	1	19	1	1st	0	8	36	56
Olonga	14	2	65	1	3	1	20	0	2nd	67	13	63	99
Brandes	15	3	46	1	18	4	52	1	3rd	115	21	64	125
Strang P.A.	2	1	1	1	24	7	57	1	4th	143	41	121	143
Flower G.W.					3	1	7	0	5th	160	56	140	151
NEW ZEALAND									6th	164	98	-	177
Cairns	24	7	56	4	15	4	43	2	7th	216	189	-	-
Allott	17	5	51	1	7	0	49	0	8th	226	189	-	-
Kennedy	12	4	28	3	5	0	19	0	9th	-	191	-	-
Twose	5	1	14	0	10	4	36	2	10th	-	196	-	-
Patel	16.5	4	44	2	21	6	57	2					

Having been relieved of the wicketkeeper's duties by Lee Germon earlier in the season, Adam Parore made his first substantial score as a top order batsman scoring 84 not out in New Zealand's second innings.

243 NEW ZEALAND v ZIMBABWE *(Second Test)*

at Eden Park, Auckland on 20, 21, 22, 23, 24 January, 1996
Toss : New Zealand. Umpires : D.B. Cowie and Mahboob Shah
Match drawn

New Zealand won the toss and had the advantage of batting first on a benign pitch. After passing 200 for the loss of four wickets they would have been disappointed when they lost their last six wickets for 35 runs.

Craig Spearman played judiciously to give his side a comfortable beginning but it was left to the languid Stephen Fleming and the confident and powerful Chris Cairns to add 99 runs in good time. The two right-arm medium-pacers, Heath Streak and Bryan Strang, both ended with three wickets.

Each of New Zealand's first three bowlers had a wicket by the time Zimbabwe reached 50 but David Houghton and Andy Flower restored Zimbabwe's position, adding 88. When Houghton had reached 56 a full-pitched ball from Robert Kennedy hit his left foot on the full, breaking it.

Houghton continued to bat and, with the aid of a runner, ended the day 104 not out, a truly heroic innings in which he lingered on 99 for 19 anxious minutes before recording his fourth test century. Zimbabwe ended the day at 231-7. Houghton's foot was put in plaster overnight, ruling him out of the game. Eddo Brandes and Paul Strang had a boisterous partnership worth 79, which left Zimbabwe with a first-innings lead of 75.

For only the third time in 66 years of test cricket New Zealand's openers enjoyed a double-century opening partnership. At 214 Roger Twose was caught and bowled by Streak for 94 and Spearman followed eight minutes later for 112.

Fleming and Nathan Astle departed quickly but Adam Parore anchored the innings, allowing Cairns the freedom to display all the attacking shots in his considerable arsenal. He reached his maiden test century off 86 balls and, when he was dismissed, he had struck nine sixes and 10 fours and had added 166 with Parore off 171 balls. Requiring 367 for victory off 109 overs Zimbabwe ended the fourth day at 39-0.

On the final day the Zimbabwean openers, Grant Flower and Stuart Carlisle, were untroubled in adding 120 for the first wicket but Zimbabwe finally opted for a draw.

MILESTONES

• Stephen Fleming reached 1000 test runs in his 18th test.

• Andy Flower reached 1000 test runs in 16 tests.

• Chris Cairns captured his 50th test wicket in his 14th test.

• Chris Cairns hit nine sixes in his maiden test century, one short of Walter Hammond's record of 10 hit on the same ground in 1932/33 (test 12).

• Adam Parore reached 1000 test runs in his 26th test.

NEW ZEALAND

C.M.Spearman	c Flower G.W. b Strang B.C.	42	c Carlisle b Streak	112
R.G.Twose	c Flower A. b Brandes	18	c & b Streak	94
S.P.Fleming	c Carlisle b Whittall	84	c Wishart b Streak	3
A.C.Parore	c Flower A. b Strang B.C.	0	not out	76
N.J.Astle	c & b Brandes	14	c Flower A. b Brandes	13
C.L.Cairns	c & b Strang P.A.	57	b Streak	120
L.K.Germon*†	c Flower A. b Streak	25	not out	1
D.N.Patel	not out	7		
G.R.Larsen	lbw b Streak	0		
R.J.Kennedy	c Campbell b Streak	0		
G.I.Allott	c & b Strang B.C.	0		
Extras	(lb 3, nb 1)	4	(b 6, lb 15, nb 1)	22
TOTAL	(95.3 overs)	**251**	(133 overs) (5 wkts dec)	**441**

ZIMBABWE

G.W.Flower	lbw b Allott	5	c Kennedy b Patel	71
S.V.Carlisle	c Astle b Kennedy	12	c Fleming b Kennedy	58
G.J.Whittall	c Germon b Cairns	27	c Germon b Patel	10
D.L.Houghton	retired hurt	104		
A.Flower*†	lbw b Allott	35	(4) not out	45
A.D.R.Campbell	lbw b Allott	17	(5) c Germon b Twose	34
C.B.Wishart	b Larsen	7	(6) not out	12
H.H.Streak	b Cairns	2		
P.A.Strang	c Parore b Patel	44		
E.A.Brandes	c Astle b Patel	39		
B.C.Strang	not out	14		
Extras	(b 1, lb 11, w 2, nb 6)	20	(lb 6, w 2, nb 8)	16
TOTAL	(110 overs)	**326**	(100 overs) (4 wkts)	**246**

Bowling

ZIMBABWE	O	M	R	W	O	M	R	W
Streak	22	9	50	3	30	7	110	4
Brandes	18	3	69	2	13	3	41	1
Strang B.C.	31.3	8	64	3	27	8	64	0
Strang P.A.	12	2	29	1	43	7	142	0
Whittall	12	4	36	1	13	4	40	0
Campbell					2	0	3	0
Flower G.W.					5	0	20	0

NEW ZEALAND	O	M	R	W	O	M	R	W
Cairns	31	12	92	2	23	6	49	0
Allott	23	7	56	3	19	3	53	0
Kennedy	20	3	73	1	22	3	61	1
Larsen	21	8	30	1	5	3	8	0
Patel	12	0	60	2	27	7	60	2
Astle	3	1	3	0	1	0	4	0
Twose					3	1	5	1

Fall of Wickets

	NZ	Z	NZ	Z
	1st	*1st*	*2nd*	*2nd*
1st	50	5	214	120
2nd	78	38	217	144
3rd	86	50	221	145
4th	117	138	261	225
5th	216	196	427	-
6th	232	217	-	-
7th	244	222	-	-
8th	246	310	-	-
9th	246	326	-	-
10th	251	-	-	-

Chris Cairns lived up to his reputation as one of the world's most aggressive batsmen by blitzing 120 off 98 balls.

1995/96 New Zealand in West Indies

New Zealand made its third tour of the West Indies immediately following the 1996 World Cup played in India, Pakistan and Sri Lanka.

244 WEST INDIES v NEW ZEALAND *(First Test)*

at Kensington Oval, Bridgetown on 19, 20, 21, 23 April, 1996
Toss : West Indies. Umpires : S.A. Bucknor and P. Willey
West Indies won by 10 wickets

The game began disastrously for the tourists and they lost their first three wickets in the first half-hour for six runs. Adam Parore and Nathan Astle survived a torrid spell of fast bowling by Courtney Walsh and Curtly Ambrose on a fiery Kensington Oval pitch. Astle played in one-day mode and reached his first test fifty in 64 minutes with 10 boundaries.

At 154-4 part-time left-arm spinner Jimmy Adams was introduced. An innocuous slow delivery saw Parore dismissed by Adams' first ball. Adams then went on to capture five wickets in nine overs as New Zealand lost its last five wickets for 41 runs and was all out for 195. By stumps Sherwin Campbell and Brian Lara had accounted for half that total; 98-1.

The early loss of Lara slowed the West Indies progress before Campbell and Shivnarine Chanderpaul enjoyed a 155-run partnership for the fifth wicket. By the end of the second day both batsmen were undefeated, with each having made their highest test score. Campbell was on 149 and Chanderpaul 81 and West Indies was 334-4.

Campbell continued on the third day, bringing up his double-century in 648 minutes and, with further useful contributions from the lower order, the West Indies total of 472 gave them a lead of 277. New Zealand was again in trouble from the outset and lost their fourth wicket at 57. Another venturesome innings by Astle and another obdurate vigil by Vaughan took the game into the fourth day.

A feature of Nathan Astle's second innings of 125 was that he scored exactly 100 of his runs from boundaries, hitting two sixes and 22 fours.

Astle continued to attack and recorded his first test century in 169 minutes off 125 deliveries. His 125 included 22 fours and two sixes, precisely 100 runs from boundaries. He and Vaughan added 144, a record for the fifth wicket against the West Indies. Vaughan contributed 24. There was a surprising end to the New Zealand innings as Danny Morrison and Robert Kennedy added 45 for the last wicket in 34 minutes.

West Indies required 29 to win and in keeping with his Man of the Match award Campbell blithely scored them all. Parore suffered a groin injury while fielding and subsequently flew home early.

NEW ZEALAND					
C.M.Spearman	c Browne b Ambrose	0	c Lara b Thompson		20
R.G.Twose	c Samuels b Walsh	2	c Lara b Walsh		0
S.P.Fleming	c Chanderpaul b Walsh	1	c Samuels b Bishop		22
A.C.Parore	c Simmons b Adams	59	(7) c Campbell b Bishop		1
N.J.Astle	c Browne b Thompson	54	(4) c Campbell b Thompson		125
C.Z.Harris	c Lara b Thompson	0	(5) c Samuels b Bishop		0
J.T.C.Vaughan	c Bishop b Adams	44	(6) lbw b Bishop		24
L.K.Germon*†	c Chanderpaul b Adams	0	lbw b Walsh		23
G.R.Larsen	st Browne b Adams	12	lbw b Walsh		6
D.K.Morrison	not out	4	not out		26
R.J.Kennedy	c Browne b Adams	0	c Adams b Walsh		22
Extras	(lb 1, w 1, nb 17)	19	(lb 7, nb 29)		36
TOTAL	(62 overs)	**195**	(82 overs)		**305**

WEST INDIES					
S.L.Campbell	b Harris	208	not out		29
R.G.Samuels	lbw b Larsen	12	not out		0
B.C.Lara	c Spearman b Larsen	35			
P.V.Simmons	lbw b Larsen	22			
J.C.Adams	c Germon b Vaughan	21			
S.Chanderpaul	c Harris b Morrison	82			
C.O.Browne†	c Astle b Kennedy	20			
I.R.Bishop	c Germon b Harris	31			
C.E.L.Ambrose	c Germon b Vaughan	8			
C.A.Walsh*	not out	12			
P.I.C.Thompson	lbw b Morrison	1			
Extras	(lb 8, nb 12)	20			
TOTAL	(164.3 overs)	**472**	(4 overs) (0 wkts)		**29**

Bowling									
WEST INDIES	O	M	R	W	O	M	R	W
Ambrose	13	4	33	1	18	6	41	0
Walsh	17	6	30	2	22	3	72	4
Bishop	10	3	36	0	19	1	67	4
Thompson	8	0	58	2	14	1	77	2
Simmons	3	0	11	0				
Adams	9	4	17	5	6	1	32	0
Chanderpaul	2	0	9	0	3	1	9	0
NEW ZEALAND								
Morrison	29.3	4	120	2	2	0	8	0
Kennedy	22	3	89	1	2	0	21	0
Larsen	40	15	76	3				
Vaughan	34	10	81	2				
Harris	34	11	75	2				
Twose	4	0	20	0				
Astle	1	0	3	0				

Fall of Wickets				
	NZ	WI	NZ	WI
	1st	1st	2nd	2nd
1st	2	46	14	-
2nd	2	103	28	-
3rd	6	129	48	-
4th	86	182	57	-
5th	87	337	201	-
6th	154	386	215	-
7th	157	445	219	-
8th	186	458	254	-
9th	193	466	260	-
10th	195	472	305	-

MILESTONES

- Nathan Astle and Justin Vaughan put on 144, a fifth wicket record against West Indies.

- Danny Morrison and Robert Kennedy set a new 10th wicket record of 45 for New Zealand against West Indies.

- Sherwin Campbell became the eighth West Indies batsman to go on to 200 after having made his maiden test century. The others were Denis Atkinson, Gary Sobers, Rohan Kanhai, Seymour Nurse, Lawrence Rowe, Faoud Bacchus and Brian Lara.

Chris Cairns left the tour, claiming that a side strain meant that he was not fit to play. He did, however, play for his county, Nottinghamshire, while the second test was in progress. As a result of their "critical public comments" about Glenn Turner and the team management Cairns and Adam Parore were fined and severely censured by New Zealand Cricket. In July Steve Rixon, a former Australian wicketkeeper, replaced Turner as the New Zealand team coach. Turner blamed his removal as coach on the "major philosophical differences" between himself and New Zealand CEO Christopher Doig.

245 WEST INDIES v NEW ZEALAND *(Second Test)*

at Antigua Recreation Ground, St John's on 27, 28, 29 April, 1, 2 May, 1996
Toss : New Zealand. Umpires : L.H. Barker and C.J. Mitchley
Match drawn

Lee Germon asked West Indies to bat first and they ended the first day at 302-4. Left-handed batsman Robert Samuels, playing in his second test match, made an elegant 125. He was cast on 93 for 15 minutes before he struck Dipak Patel for four and six from consecutive balls to reach his century.

Jimmy Adams began the second day on 50 and went on to his first test century, converted into a double-century, with the last 100 being compiled off 112 balls. He shared a fifth wicket stand of 165 with the consistent Shivnarine Chanderpaul. New Zealand was 21-2 at stumps.

Craig Spearman and Stephen Fleming put on 89 which opened the way for Nathan Astle to continue a remarkable batting sequence. He made his test debut in February, in his first World Cup game he scored 101 against England, his first one-day international century and in the first test in West Indies, he scored his first test fifty and his first test century.

Batting in a slightly more subdued manner he scored his second successive test century and shared useful stands with Justin Vaughan and Chris Harris. A resolute partnership of 110 between Germon and Patel saw Patel make his highest score in test cricket for five years and enabled New Zealand to reach 437; a deficit of 111.

West Indies, led by some audacious shot production from Brian Lara, advanced to 89-1 before Danny Morrison and Vaughan engineered a collapse that gave the visitors a hint of victory as the home side tumbled to 147-7.

New Zealand were left with a victory target of 296 in 73 overs. For the fourth time in the series the opening partnership failed to reach 20 and when the third wicket fell at 39 New Zealand were left with no alternative but to play for a draw.

Stephen Fleming batted for over four hours for his 56 not out and for the fourth consecutive innings Vaughan batted for over 100 minutes, making 32.

MILESTONES

- Danny Morrison recorded his 24th duck, a test record.

- Dipak Patel passed 1000 runs in his 33rd test and became the fifth New Zealander to score 1000 runs and take 50 wickets.

- Nathan Astle became the 10th New Zealander to score test centuries in successive innings.

- Danny Morrison became the second New Zealand test bowler to capture five wickets in an innings on ten occasions.

WEST INDIES					
S.L.Campbell	run out	13	c Fleming b Vaughan	36
R.G.Samuels	b Harris	125	lbw b Morrison	4
B.C.Lara	c Germon b Patel	40	c Fleming b Morrison	74
P.V.Simmons	b Harris	59	c Vaughan b Harris	0
J.C.Adams	not out	208	c & b Vaughan	6
S.Chanderpaul	c Astle b Patel	41	b Morrison	8
C.O.Browne†	run out	18	lbw b Larsen	5
I.R.Bishop	c Fleming b Larsen	14	c Germon b Morrison	9
C.E.L.Ambrose	not out	21	lbw b Morrison	6
C.A.Walsh*			not out	17
R.Dhanraj			b Vaughan	9
Extras	(lb 3, nb 6)	9	(lb 2, nb 8)	10
TOTAL	**(166 overs) (7 wkts dec)**	**548**	**(61.3 overs)**	**184**

NEW ZEALAND					
C.M.Spearman	c Browne b Walsh	54	c Browne b Ambrose	24
R.G.Twose	b Ambrose	2	c Samuels b Ambrose	2
D.K.Morrison	lbw b Ambrose	0		
S.P.Fleming	c Browne b Bishop	39	(3) not out	56
N.J.Astle	c Simmons b Ambrose	103	(4) c Adams b Simmons	8
J.T.C.Vaughan	b Dhanraj	26	(5) lbw b Walsh	32
C.Z.Harris	c Adams b Ambrose	40	(6) c & b Dhanraj	4
L.K.Germon*†	c Browne b Ambrose	49	(7) not out	0
D.N.Patel	c Browne b Bishop	78		
G.R.Larsen	not out	17		
R.J.Kennedy	c Browne b Bishop	4		
Extras	(lb 7, nb 18)	25	(lb 1, w 2, nb 1)	4
TOTAL	**(138.3 overs)**	**437**	**(65 overs) (5 wkts)**	**130**

Bowling	O	M	R	W	O	M	R	W
NEW ZEALAND								
Morrison	26	6	124	0	20	2	61	5
Larsen	25	9	69	1	11	3	27	1
Vaughan	29	8	79	0	16.3	5	30	3
Patel	38	7	131	2				
Kennedy	13	2	59	0	10	2	30	0
Harris	35	11	83	2	4	0	34	1
WEST INDIES								
Ambrose	32	12	68	5	12	3	22	2
Walsh	27	5	70	1	16	5	32	1
Dhanraj	38	9	132	1	18	6	33	1
Bishop	26.3	6	90	3	7	1	25	0
Adams	13	1	60	0	2	1	5	0
Chanderpaul	2	0	10	0				
Simmons					10	6	12	1

Fall of Wickets	WI	NZ	WI	NZ
	1st	1st	2nd	2nd
1st	35	9	5	19
2nd	96	9	89	30
3rd	193	98	94	39
4th	280	108	119	96
5th	405	202	128	127
6th	448	276	133	-
7th	495	281	147	-
8th	-	391	155	-
9th	-	426	158	-
10th	-	437	184	-

Justin Vaughan proved difficult to dislodge. In four innings he batted a total of 548 minutes while scoring 126 runs.

1996/97 New Zealand in Pakistan

New Zealand journeyed to Sharjah and Pakistan during the Asian winter of November and December 1996. On the morning of the test the Pakistan captain Wasim Akram withdrew because of a damaged shoulder, leaving Pakistan with a depleted attack. Saeed Anwar took his place as captain. Justin Vaughan's consistency six months earlier in the West Indies saw him elevated to opener.

246 PAKISTAN v NEW ZEALAND *(First Test)*

at Gadaffi Stadium, Lahore on 21, 22, 23, 24 November, 1996
Toss : New Zealand. Umpires : Shakoor Rana and R.B. Tiffin
New Zealand won by 44 runs

Batting was always difficult as the ball came through low and with inconsistent bounce. It was not surprising that there were 15 lbw decisions in the match. Adam Parore and Dipak Patel, batting at number 10, were the only batsmen to score over 20 as the fast reverse-swinging yorkers of Waqar Younis and the leg-breaks and beautifully disguised googlies of Mushtaq Ahmed humbled New Zealand to be all out in 57.1 overs for 155.

An exceptional spell of right-arm swing and seam bowling by Simon Doull saw Pakistan perilously positioned at 52-5

at stumps. 15 wickets had fallen on day one for 207 runs.

Doull claimed his fifth wicket early on the second day before the ball was changed after it went out of shape. Moin Khan adopted an aggressive approach in scoring a feisty 59 but then became one of three consecutive lbw decisions to Vaughan's dipping medium pace. Bryan Young and Vaughan knocked off the deficit of 36 before the deceptive Mushtaq began to spin his web of destruction that left the game delicately poised with New Zealand 88-3.

The game was won and lost in the early stages of the third day when New Zealand lost their fifth wicket at 101 and Chris Cairns was dropped in the gully on seven. Boldness became his cry as he banished the ball to, and over, the boundary 15 times, scoring 93 off 89 balls while adding 141 with Stephen Fleming for the sixth wicket.

A vital last wicket stand between Fleming and Doull added 49 in 36 minutes, thus leaving Pakistan 276 to pursue in over two days. Fleming's strong-willed effort of 92 not out in 278 minutes was an innings of distinction.

Humiliation loomed for Pakistan when Doull repeated his magic of the first innings and reduced them to be five down at stumps for 46. The game took a further twist on the fourth day when debutant Mohammad Wasim, following a first innings duck, scored an unbeaten 109 and took his side to the brink of victory.

Simon Doull played a vital role with both bat and ball in New Zealand's 34th test victory.

NEW ZEALAND

Batsman	Dismissal 1	R	Dismissal 2	R
B.A.Young	lbw b Waqar	8	c Wasim b Mushtaq	36
J.T.C.Vaughan	lbw b Shahid	3	b Mushtaq	11
A.C.Parore	c Malik b Saqlain	37	lbw b Saqlain	15
S.P.Fleming	c Malik b Mushtaq	19	not out	92
N.J.Astle	lbw b Mushtaq	0	lbw b Mushtaq	3
M.J.Greatbatch	c Wasim b Waqar	18	b Waqar	1
C.L.Cairns	c Inzamam b Mushtaq	4	lbw b Mushtaq	93
C.Z.Harris	b Waqar	16	c Malik b Mushtaq	0
L.K.Germon*†	lbw b Waqar	0	lbw b Mushtaq	11
D.N.Patel	lbw b Mushtaq	26	lbw b Shahid	0
S.B.Doull	not out	15	st Moin b Saqlain	26
Extras	(b 4, lb 5)	9	(b 6, lb 16, nb 1)	23
TOTAL	(57.1 overs)	155	(85.2 overs)	311

PAKISTAN

Batsman	Dismissal 1	R	Dismissal 2	R
Saeed Anwar*	b Doull	8	lbw b Doull	0
Zahoor Elahi	c Fleming b Doull	22	c Young b Patel	6
Ijaz Ahmed	lbw b Cairns	3	b Doull	8
Inzamam-ul-Haq	c Astle b Doull	0	c Young b Cairns	14
Salim Malik	c Young b Doull	21	(6) c Germon b Doull	21
Mohammad Wasim	b Doull	0	(7) not out	109
Moin Khan†	lbw b Vaughan	59	(8) c Germon b Astle	38
Saqlain Mushtaq	lbw b Vaughan	23	(5) c Fleming b Vaughan	0
Waqar Younis	lbw b Vaughan	2	(10) b Patel	1
Mushtaq Ahmed	c Germon b Vaughan	25	(9) c Fleming b Patel	15
Shahid Nazir	not out	13	c Harris b Patel	1
Extras	(b 5, lb 7, nb 3)	15	(b 8, lb 8, nb 2)	18
TOTAL	(55.5 overs)	191	(71.1 overs)	231

Bowling	O	M	R	W	O	M	R	W
PAKISTAN								
Waqar	15	3	48	4	15	6	26	1
Shahid	8	3	15	1	16	1	84	1
Mushtaq	22.1	4	59	4	32	8	84	6
Saqlain	12	3	24	1	22.2	4	95	2
NEW ZEALAND								
Cairns	19	5	79	1	16	5	62	1
Doull	16	3	46	5	16	4	39	1
Harris	1	0	3	0	6	2	20	0
Vaughan	12.5	2	27	4	14	5	48	1
Patel	7	2	24	0	15.1	6	36	4
Astle					4	1	10	1

Fall of Wickets	NZ 1st	P 1st	NZ 2nd	P 2nd
1st	6	21	46	0
2nd	16	29	59	8
3rd	67	34	85	25
4th	70	37	88	26
5th	73	37	101	42
6th	83	85	242	60
7th	102	141	242	135
8th	102	143	262	211
9th	117	164	263	219
10th	155	191	311	231

MILESTONES

- It was New Zealand's second test win in Pakistan, their first since 1969/70.

- Mohammed Wasim made a century on test debut, the fourth Pakistan batsman to do so. The others were Khalid Ibadulla, Javed Miandad and Salim Malik.

247 PAKISTAN v NEW ZEALAND *(Second Test)*

at Rawalpindi Cricket Stadium on 28, 29, 30 November, 1 December, 1996
Toss : Pakistan. Umpires : L.H. Barker and Javed Akhtar
Pakistan won by an innings and 13 runs

On a lifeless pitch, devoid of grass, New Zealand was quickly placed on the back foot after being sent in to bat. Mohammad Zahid, aged 20, making his debut as a right-arm fast bowler did not have to wait long for his first two wickets in test cricket, courtesy of lbw decisions. Mushtaq Ahmed revelled in bowling to the New Zealand batsmen and the visitors were reduced to 111-7 by tea before Stephen Fleming and Lee Germon launched a recovery, enabling the tourists to reach 215-8 at stumps.

Germon reached his maiden test fifty and Mushtaq claimed his 16th wicket in three innings when New Zealand was dismissed for 249. Losing their first wicket at six did not deter Saeed Anwar and Ijaz Ahmed from toying with the visitors' attack and in the space of 65 overs they added 262 for the second wicket, each scoring boundary-filled centuries.

Anwar's dismissal for 149 saw the New Zealand bowlers, ably led by Chris Cairns, restrict and then demolish the last six wickets for 55 runs, with Cairns capturing his third five-wicket bag. With their team trailing by 181 the openers, Brian Young and Justin Vaughan, provided a solid reply, adding 69 without being dismissed by the end of the third day's play.

On the fourth day the partnership was broken at 82 when Zahid dismissed Vaughan and the floodgates burst open as the sheer, blistering pace of the youngster could only be countered by Young, whose innings of 61 occupied 171 minutes. New Zealand lost their last ten wickets for 86 runs in 30 overs, with Zahid writing himself into Pakistan and world cricket records, taking 11 wickets for the match. The series was drawn one game all.

During the two tests New Zealand lost 19 of their 40 wickets to lbw decisions – a remarkable statistic.

MILESTONES

- Mohammad Zahid became the first Pakistan bowler to take 10 wickets in his first test. He finished with 11-130, the seventh-best analysis by any test debutant. Unfortunately he suffered a severe back injury and his career was limited to five tests.

- Saeed Anwar and Ijaz Ahmed created a Pakistan record of 262 for the second wicket against New Zealand.

- Mushtaq Ahmed captured his 100th test wicket in his 26th test. In his last eight tests he had captured 63 wickets.

NEW ZEALAND

Batsman	Dismissal	Runs	Dismissal	Runs
B.A.Young	lbw b Mushtaq	39	c Zahoor b Zahid	61
J.T.C.Vaughan	lbw b Zahid	12	lbw b Zahid	27
A.C.Parore	lbw b Zahid	3	lbw b Zahid	6
S.P.Fleming	c Moin b Mushtaq	67	(7) c Moin b Shahid	4
N.J.Astle	c Moin b Mushtaq	11	lbw b Zahid	1
M.J.Greatbatch	c Anwar b Mushtaq	2	c Anwar b Mushtaq	19
C.L.Cairns	c Wasim b Mushtaq	9	(8) b Mushtaq	11
C.Z.Harris	lbw b Zahid	1	(9) lbw b Zahid	14
L.K.Germon*†	c Moin b Zahid	55	(4) b Zahid	0
D.N.Patel	c Ijaz b Mushtaq	21	lbw b Zahid	0
S.B.Doull	not out	1	not out	4
Extras	(b 4, lb 14, nb 10)	28	(lb 7, w 1, nb 13)	21
TOTAL	(74 overs)	249	(58 overs)	168

PAKISTAN

Batsman	Dismissal	Runs
Saeed Anwar*	c Doull b Cairns	149
Zahoor Elahi	c Fleming b Cairns	2
Ijaz Ahmed	lbw b Cairns	125
Mushtaq Ahmed	lbw b Harris	42
Inzamam-ul-Haq	c Vaughan b Harris	1
Salim Malik	b Cairns	78
Mohammad Wasim	c Cairns b Doull	5
Moin Khan†	lbw b Doull	2
Shahid Nazir	c & b Cairns	10
Mohammad Zahid	lbw b Astle	0
Mohammad Akram	not out	0
Extras	(lb 14, nb 2)	16
TOTAL	(126.4 overs)	430

Bowling PAKISTAN	O	M	R	W	O	M	R	W		Fall of Wickets			
											NZ	P	NZ
											1st	1st	2nd
Zahid	21	5	64	4	20	3	66	7		1st	33	6	82
Shahid	9	4	23	0	7	1	19	1	2nd		43	268	105
Akram	12	1	48	0	7	2	11	0	3rd		59	290	109
Mushtaq	30	3	87	6	22	7	52	2	4th		77	291	112
Malik	2	0	9	0	2	0	13	0	5th		87	376	119
NEW ZEALAND									6th		110	394	137
Doull	31	7	86	2					7th		111	398	137
Cairns	30.4	2	137	5					8th		192	419	163
Vaughan	17	1	72	0					9th		241	420	163
Astle	9	1	31	1					10th		249	430	168
Patel	15	4	33	0									
Harris	24	7	57	2									

The New Zealand team that toured Pakistan 1996/97. Back row (from left): Craig Spearman, Justin Vaughan, Robert Kennedy, Simon Doull, Glenn Jonas, Chris Cairns, Stephen Fleming, Matthew Hart, Nathan Astle. Front row: Chris Harris, Bryan Young, Adam Parore, Mark Greatbatch, Lee Germon (captain), Steve Rixon (coach), Dipak Patel, Tim Murdoch (manager), Mark Plummer (physiotherapist).

1996/97 England in New Zealand

248 **NEW ZEALAND v ENGLAND** *(First Test)*

at Eden Park, Auckland on 24, 25, 26, 27, 28 January, 1997
Toss : England. Umpires : S.A. Bucknor and R.S. Dunne
Match drawn

The England captain, Michael Atherton, was distraught to see his three pace bowlers bowl waywardly after he asked New Zealand to bat on a damp pitch. Blair Pocock, playing his first test since the New Zealand tour to England in 1994, appreciated the width and went on to score his first test fifty.

He put on 85 with Bryan Young while Alec Stewart, the England wicketkeeper, dived enthusiastically, gathering wide deliveries on both sides of the wicket. Stephen Fleming ended the first day on 58 and New Zealand were 233-5.

With the wicket improving by the hour Cairns, in particular, attacked the bowling, adding 118 with Fleming for the sixth wicket, of which his share was 67. Fleming's first test century came in 275 minutes and when he was last out for 129 New Zealand's total was 390. Atherton and Stewart were both in imperious form and were untroubled to take England through to 123-1 at the end of the second day.

After they had added 182 in four hours Atherton departed for 83 while Stewart went on, without difficulty, to score 179. With his dismissal there was a minor collapse and it was left to Graham Thorpe, so often the backbone of a crumbling England innings, to join with Dominic Cork and extract England from the mire, even if it was at a funereal pace.

On the fourth day England scored 155 off their last 61 overs, with Thorpe reaching his third test century and the partnership adding 114 in 177 minutes. Cork made his highest test score. New Zealand lost three wickets for 56 runs in the remaining time.

They started the fifth day 75 in arrears on a pitch that was perfect, if slow, for batting and each batsman knew that defence was the order of the day. By lunch the die had been cast as New Zealand lost five wickets before lunch in advancing their score to 105-8.

Adam Parore ran out Lee Germon and then charged Phil Tufnell and was stumped as panic set in. The afternoon session was only 37 minutes old, with New Zealand leading by 11, when Simon Doull was ninth out. Danny Morrison, holder of the record for the most test ducks, came to the wicket to join Nathan Astle who had been a silent observer of the earlier carnage.

For the remaining 165 minutes the pair stood firm – nothing could shift them. They both faced 133 balls and when time was mercifully called, Astle had scored his third century in seven tests and Morrison was undefeated on 14. They had effected one of New Zealand's great escapes.

Danny Morrison, left, and Nathan Astle saved the game for New Zealand with an unbroken last-wicket partnership of 106.

NEW ZEALAND

B.A.Young	lbw b Mullally	44	(2) c Hussain b Cork		3
B.A.Pocock	lbw b Gough	70	(1) lbw b Gough		20
A.C.Parore	c Stewart b Cork	6	st Stewart b Tufnell		33
S.P.Fleming	c & b Cork	129	c Crawley b Tufnell		9
N.J.Astle	c Stewart b White	10	(6) not out		102
J.T.C.Vaughan	lbw b Cork	3	(7) lbw b Tufnell		2
C.L.Cairns	c Stewart b White	67	(8) b Mullally		7
L.K.Germon*†	c Stewart b Gough	14	(5) run out		13
D.N.Patel	lbw b Gough	0	lbw b Mullally		0
S.B.Doull	c Knight b Gough	5	b Gough		26
D.K.Morrison	not out	6	not out		14
Extras	(b 5, lb 12, w 2, nb 17)	36	(lb 11, nb 8)		19
TOTAL	(131.5 overs)	**390**	(114 overs) (9 wkts)		**248**

ENGLAND

N.V.Knight	lbw b Doull	5
M.A.Atherton*	c & b Patel	83
A.J.Stewart†	c & b Doull	173
N.Hussain	c Fleming b Patel	8
G.P.Thorpe	hit wicket b Cairns	119
J.P.Crawley	run out	14
C.White	lbw b Vaughan	0
D.G.Cork	c Young b Morrison	59
D.Gough	c Germon b Morrison	2
A.D.Mullally	c Germon b Morrison	21
P.C.R.Tufnell	not out	19
Extras	(b 2, lb 12, w 2, nb 2)	18
TOTAL	(187.4 overs)	**521**

Bowling	O	M	R	W	O	M	R	W	*Fall of Wickets*			
ENGLAND										NZ	E	NZ
										1st	*1st*	*2nd*
Cork	32.5	8	96	3	16	3	45	1				
Mullally	27	11	55	1	26	11	47	2	1st	85	18	17
Gough	32	5	91	4	22	3	66	2	2nd	114	200	28
Tufnell	25	5	80	0	40	18	53	3	3rd	193	222	47
White	15	3	51	2	10	2	26	0	4th	210	304	88
NEW ZEALAND									5th	215	339	90
Morrison	24.4	4	104	3					6th	333	339	92
Doull	39	10	118	2					7th	362	453	101
Cairns	30	3	103	1					8th	362	471	105
Astle	14	3	33	0					9th	380	478	142
Vaughan	36	10	57	1					10th	390	521	-
Patel	44	10	92	2								

MILESTONES

- Stephen Fleming made his first test hundred in his 23rd test. He had reached 10 scores in excess of 50 in his preceding 22 tests.

- Alec Stewart's 173 was the highest score made by an England wicketkeeper in a test match.

- Nathan Astle and Danny Morrison put on 106 for the last-wicket, a record against England. It was the 10th highest last-wicket partnership in test cricket history.

249 NEW ZEALAND v ENGLAND (*Second Test*)

at Basin Reserve, Wellington on 6, 7, 8, 9, 10 February, 1997
Toss : New Zealand. Umpires : S.A. Bucknor and D.B. Cowie
England won by an innings and 68 runs

Having failed in their last two tests to seize victory when it was presented to them, England had the better of the second test when New Zealand erred in its decision to bat first in conditions conducive to swing and seam bowling.

In the two hours available for play on the first day New Zealand were reduced to 56-6 in 30 overs as New Zealand-born Andy Caddick and Darren Gough sliced through the flimsy defence, each capturing three cheap wickets.

In perfect conditions the following day Nathan Astle and Dipak Patel offered minor resistance before New Zealand were dismissed for 124. By stumps England had scored 204-3 and taken complete charge of the game, with Nasser Hussain and Graham Thorpe totally in control.

Daniel Vettori claimed his first test wicket, Hussain, who had also been has first first-class victim just 22 days previously, both times caught by Bryan Young at slip. It was a memorable debut for Vettori who had only played two first-class games prior to this test. For one so young his control was admirable and he appeared almost nerveless.

Thorpe scored his second successive century and shared century partnerships with Hussain, worth 107, and John Crowley, 118. At 331-4 Thorpe was stumped by Lee Germon off Patel and England's innings went into a steep decline. The last six wickets went for 53 runs, with Simon Doull's perseverance being rewarded by his fourth five-wicket bag. Blair Pocock and Young were unbeaten at the end of the third day, having added 48.

Rain prevented play until 3.15 pm on the fourth day. Young scored 56 of the opening partnership of 89 before he became the first of three batsmen to be dismissed by the England spinners Robert Croft and Phil Tufnell, and by stumps New Zealand were tottering at 124-4.

Pocock's resistance lasted for 336 minutes and was spread over three days before he succumbed to the second new ball and the match-winning combination of Gough and Caddick, who raced through the last six New Zealand wickets for only

30 runs. They claimed 15 wickets for 179 runs. England's win was their first victory in nine tests and their first win in an overseas test in two years.

NEW ZEALAND

B.A.Young	c Stewart b Gough	8	(2) c Stewart b Tufnell		56
B.A.Pocock	c Cork b Caddick	6	(1) c Knight b Gough		64
A.C.Parore	c Stewart b Gough	4	lbw b Croft		15
S.P.Fleming	c & b Caddick	1	c & b Croft		0
N.J.Astle	c Croft b Gough	36	(7) c Stewart b Gough		4
C.L.Cairns	c Hussain b Gough	3	(8) c Knight b Caddick		22
L.K.Germon*†	c Stewart b Caddick	10	(6) b Gough		11
D.N.Patel	c Cork b Caddick	45	(5) lbw b Croft		0
S.B.Doull	c Stewart b Gough	0	c Knight b Gough		0
G.I.Allott	c Knight b Cork	1	b Caddick		2
D.L.Vettori	not out	3	not out		2
Extras	(lb 5, nb 2)	7	(b 5, lb 4, nb 6)		15
TOTAL	(48.3 overs)	124	(103.2 overs)		191

ENGLAND

N.V.Knight	c Patel b Doull	8
M.A.Atherton*	lbw b Doull	30
A.J.Stewart†	c Fleming b Allott	52
N.Hussain	c Young b Vettori	64
G.P.Thorpe	st Germon b Patel	108
J.P.Crawley	c Germon b Doull	56
D.G.Cork	lbw b Astle	7
R.D.B.Croft	c Fleming b Doull	0
D.Gough	c Fleming b Doull	18
A.R.Caddick	c Allott b Vettori	20
P.C.R.Tufnell	not out	6
Extras	(b 3, lb 9, nb 2)	14
TOTAL	(137.3 overs)	**383**

Bowling	O	M	R	W	O	M	R	W		*Fall of Wickets*		
ENGLAND										NZ	E	NZ
										1st	1st	2nd
Cork	14	4	34	1	10	1	42	0		14	10	89
Caddick	18.3	5	45	4	27.2	11	40	2	1st	14	10	89
Gough	16	6	40	5	23	9	52	4	2nd	18	80	125
Croft					20	9	19	3	3rd	19	106	125
Tufnell					23	9	29	1	4th	19	213	125
NEW ZEALAND									5th	23	331	161
Doull	28	10	75	5					6th	48	331	164
Allott	31	6	91	1					7th	85	331	175
Vettori	34.3	10	98	2					8th	85	357	175
Cairns	4	2	8	0					9th	106	357	182
Astle	14	5	30	1					10th	124	383	191
Patel	24	6	59	1								
Pocock	2	0	10	0								

Blair Pocock was the sixth batsman dismissed in New Zealand's second innings, for 64. He had resisted the England bowlers for 336 minutes, spread over three days of intermittent rain.

MILESTONES

- Daniel Vettori (200) made his test debut. At 18 years and 10 days he became New Zealand's youngest test cricketer. He was 187 days younger than Doug Freeman who made his debut in 1932/33 (test 10).

- Blair Pocock scored the second-slowest test fifty, in terms of balls received, after Trevor Bailey of England against Australia in 1953.

- Simon Doull captured his 50th test wicket in his 15th test.

- Darren Gough returned the best match analysis of his 58-match test career.

250 NEW ZEALAND v ENGLAND (Third Test)

at Lancaster Park, Christchurch on 14, 15, 16, 17, 18 February, 1997
Toss : England. Umpires : R.S. Dunne and D.B. Hair
England won by 4 wickets

For the first time in 33 tests England fielded an unchanged side. Lee Germon injured his groin and was unable to play so Adam Parore returned as the wicketkeeper for the first time in 12 tests. Stephen Fleming was appointed captain.

New Zealand batted with greater consistency when they were asked to bat first on a well-grassed pitch. Playing in his first test Matt Horne showed true grit after Darren Gough had struck him on his left hand when he was 12. He added a further 30 and with Stephen Fleming took the score to 106 before he was dismissed. An X-ray revealed that he had a broken bone; New Zealand 229-4.

Parore relished his lower position in the batting order and, together with Chris Cairns, played many attractive drives and cuts as they both scored half-centuries. A combination of tight bowling and expansive attacking shots, particularly off the back foot, saw England nosedive to 104-5. Atherton's innings was exemplary, with his defence sound and his runs coming mainly from hooks and cuts.

Atherton became the seventh England player to bat through a test innings, being 94 not out. The innings terminated at 228, with all six New Zealand bowlers claiming a wicket. Geoff Allott returned his best test figures of four for 74. New Zealand enjoyed a first-innings lead of 118 but by losing six of their second innings wickets for 95 by the end of the third day's play they had squandered their position of strength.

A tenacious partnership between Cairns and Daniel Vettori added 71 for the eighth wicket leaving England a tantalising target of 305 for victory. By stumps Atherton had recorded his second fifty of the match, while Vettori's tantalising spin and flight had clearly highlighted who would be England's

danger man the following day.

England required a further 187 runs and New Zealand eight more wickets when play began on the fifth day. Atherton's marathon of concentration continued until he had completed his 11th test century. His dismissal, at 226-4 for 118, triggered a swing back to New Zealand as Vettori dismissed both Nasser Hussain and Graham Thorpe to have the visitors at 231-6, with Vettori having four wickets. John Crawley and Dominic Cork, however, held their nerve and added 76 to give England victory and the series, 2-0.

NEW ZEALAND

B.A.Young	b Cork	11	(2) c Knight b Tufnell	49
B.A.Pocock	c Atherton b Croft	22	(1) b Cork	0
M.J.Horne	c Thorpe b Gough	42	(8) c Stewart b Caddick	13
S.P.Fleming*	st Stewart b Croft	62	c Knight b Tufnell	11
N.J.Astle	c Hussain b Croft	15	c Hussain b Croft	5
A.C.Parore†	c Hussain b Croft	59	(3) c Stewart b Gough	8
C.L.Cairns	c Stewart b Caddick	57	(6) c Knight b Tufnell	52
S.B.Doull	run out	1	(7) c Knight b Croft	5
D.L.Vettori	run out	25	not out	29
H.T.Davis	c Hussain b Croft	8	b Gough	1
G.I.Allott	not out	8	c Stewart b Gough	1
Extras	(b 1, lb 16, nb 19)	36	(lb 8, nb 4)	12
TOTAL	(129.1 overs)	**346**	(88.3 overs)	**186**

ENGLAND

N.V.Knight	c Fleming b Allott	14	c Davis b Vettori	29
M.A.Atherton*	not out	94	c Parore b Astle	118
A.J.Stewart†	c sub (C.Z.Harris) b Allott	15	c Pocock b Vettori	17
N.Hussain	c Parore b Cairns	12	(5) c Fleming b Vettori	33
G.P.Thorpe	b Astle	18	(6) c & b Vettori	2
J.P.Crawley	c Parore b Allott	1	(7) not out	40
D.G.Cork	c Parore b Davis	16	(8) not out	39
R.D.B.Croft	c Davis b Astle	31		
D.Gough	b Vettori	0		
A.R.Caddick	c sub (C.Z.Harris) b Allott	4	(4) c Fleming b Doull	15
P.C.R.Tufnell	c Young b Doull	13		
Extras	(lb 4, w 1, nb 5)	10	(b 2, lb 8, w 1, nb 3)	14
TOTAL	(84.4 overs)	**228**	(146.4 overs) (6 wkts)	**307**

Bowling										Fall of Wickets			
ENGLAND	O	M	R	W	O	M	R	W		NZ	E	NZ	E
										1st	1st	2nd	2nd
Cork	20	3	78	1	6	2	5	1	1st	14	20	0	64
Caddick	32	8	64	1	10	1	25	1	2nd	78	40	42	116
Gough	21	3	70	1	13.3	5	42	3	3rd	106	70	61	146
Croft	39.1	5	95	5	31	13	48	2	4th	137	103	76	226
Tufnell	16	6	22	0	28	9	58	3	5th	201	104	80	226
Thorpe	1	1	0	0					6th	283	145	89	231
NEW ZEALAND									7th	288	198	107	-
Allott	18	3	74	4	12.4	2	32	0	8th	310	199	178	-
Doull	17.4	3	49	1	21	8	57	1	9th	337	210	184	-
Davis	18	2	50	1	18	6	43	0	10th	346	228	186	-
Vettori	12	4	13	1	57	18	97	4					
Cairns	8	5	12	1	10	1	23	0					
Astle	11	2	26	2	28	10	45	1					

MILESTONES

- Matthew Horne (201) made his test debut.

- Stephen Fleming, aged 23 years and 319 days, became New Zealand's 24th, and youngest, test captain.

- Michael Atherton became the seventh England player to carry his bat through a test innings.

- It was England's second-highest winning fourth innings total.

- Chris Cairns reached 1000 runs in his 21st test.

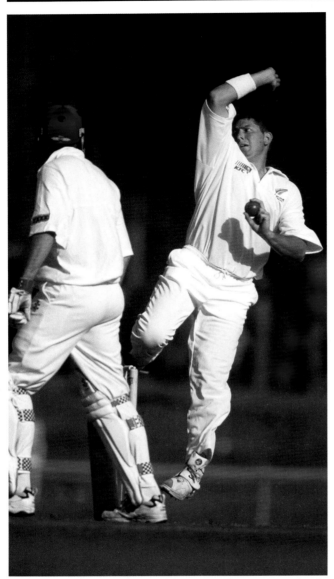

Geoff Allott had the best return of his ten-match test career when he claimed 4-74 in England's first innings.

AVERAGES

New Zealand

BATTING	M	I	NO	Runs	HS	Ave
D.L. Vettori	2	4	3	59	29*	59.00
S.P. Fleming	3	6	0	212	129	35.33
C.L. Cairns	3	6	0	208	67	34.66
N.J. Astle	3	6	1	172	102*	34.40
B.A. Pocock	3	6	0	182	70	30.33
B.A. Young	3	6	0	171	56	28.50
M.J. Horne	1	2	0	55	42	27.50
A.C. Parore	3	6	0	125	59	20.83
L.K. Germon	2	4	0	48	14	12.00
D.N. Patel	2	4	0	45	45	11.25
S.B. Doull	3	6	0	37	26	6.16
H.T. Davis	1	2	0	9	8	4.50
G.I. Allott	2	4	1	12	8*	4.00
J.T.C. Vaughan	1	2	0	5	3	2.50
D.K. Morrison	1	2	2	20	14*	-

BOWLING	O	M	R	W	Ave
D.L. Vettori	103.3	32	208	7	29.71
S.B. Doull	105.4	31	299	9	33.22
N.J. Astle	67	20	134	4	33.50
D.K. Morrison	24.4	4	104	3	34.66
G.I. Allott	61.4	11	197	5	39.40
D.N. Patel	68	16	151	3	50.33
J.T.C. Vaughan	36	10	57	1	57.00
C.L. Cairns	52	11	146	2	73.00
H.T. Davis	36	8	93	1	93.00
B.A. Pocock	2	0	10	0	-

England

BATTING	M	I	NO	Runs	HS	Ave
M.A. Atherton	3	4	1	325	118	108.33
A.J. Stewart	3	4	0	257	173	64.25
G.P. Thorpe	3	4	0	247	119	61.75
D.G. Cork	3	4	1	121	59	40.33
P.C.R. Tufnell	3	3	2	38	19*	38.00
J.P. Crawley	3	4	1	111	56	37.00
N. Hussain	3	4	0	117	64	29.25
A.D. Mullally	1	1	0	21	21	21.00
R.D.B. Croft	2	2	0	31	31	15.50
N.V. Knight	3	4	0	56	29	14.00
A.R. Caddick	2	3	0	39	20	13.00
D. Gough	3	3	0	20	18	6.66
C. White	1	1	0	0	0	0.00

BOWLING	O	M	R	W	Ave
R.D.B. Croft	90.1	27	162	10	16.20
D. Gough	127.3	31	361	19	19.00
A.R. Caddick	87.5	25	174	8	21.75
A.D. Mullally	53	22	102	3	34.00
P.C.R. Tufnell	132	47	242	7	34.57
C. White	25	5	77	2	38.50
D.G. Cork	98.5	21	300	7	42.85
G.P. Thorpe	1	1	0	0	-

1996/97 Sri Lanka in New Zealand

Lee Germon had missed New Zealand's last test against England through injury and was dropped when Sri Lanka began a two-test series. Fleming had demonstrated a refreshing attitude and inventiveness against England and was made captain for the season.

251 **NEW ZEALAND v SRI LANKA** *(First Test)*
at Carisbrook, Dunedin on 7, 8, 9, 10 March, 1997
Toss : Sri Lanka. Umpires : C.E. King and I.D. Robinson
New Zealand won by an innings and 36 runs

Arjuna Ranatunga invited New Zealand to bat first and his dejected team was kept in the field until tea the next day as New Zealand made its second-highest test score of 586-7. Bryan Young dominated the batting for 605 minutes, making 267 not out, the second-highest test score for New Zealand.

He shared century partnerships with Matt Horne (140) and Chris Cairns (123). He hit 37 fours and relished the excessively short-pitched bowling to score the majority of his runs off the back foot, square of the wicket on the off side. By good running he ensured that New Zealand maintained a run rate of four runs per over.

Simon Doull and Heath Davis reduced Sri Lanka to 78-4 by the end of the second day with Doull, in particular, swinging the ball both ways. Apart from a defiant 55 not out from Hashan Tillakaratane and some hitting by Romesh Kaluwitharana and Pramodya Wickramasinghe, there was little indication that the visitors were intent on battling to save the game.

Following on 364 runs behind the same dispirited approach saw Sri Lanka fall to 133-6. Kaluwitharana found a staunch ally in Chaminda Vaas and they indulged in attacking cricket, adding 137 for the seventh wicket in 109 minutes. Diminutive wicketkeeper and explosive batsman Kaluwitharana scored his third test century off 98 balls. Doull had the excellent match figures of 8-140 and New Zealand won by an innings and 36. It was their first home test win since February 1994.

MILESTONES

- Bryan Young's 267 not out was the second-highest innings for New Zealand in a test.

- It was the highest score by a New Zealand opener and the highest score by any player in a test at Dunedin.

- New Zealand's total was its second-highest total in tests.

- It was New Zealand's seventh test victory by an innings.

- Simon Doull had his fifth five-wicket bag in tests and his third of the season.

- Bryan Young and Matt Horne had a record second wicket partnership of 140 for New Zealand against Sri Lanka.

NEW ZEALAND

B.A.Young	not out	267
B.A.Pocock	c Mahanama b Vaas	18
M.J.Horne	c Mahanama b Ranatunga	66
S.P.Fleming*	c Zoysa b Wickramasinghe	51
N.J.Astle	b Vaas	27
D.L.Vettori	c Mahanama b Vaas	1
C.L.Cairns	c Mahanama b Zoysa	70
A.C.Parore†	c Wickramasinghe b Vaas	19
D.N.Patel	not out	30
S.B.Doull		
H.T.Davis		
Extras	(lb 14, w 2, nb 21)	37
TOTAL	(146 overs) (7 wkts dec)	**586**

SRI LANKA

S.T.Jayasuriya	b Doull	0	c Parore b Doull	50
R.S.Mahanama	lbw b Doull	26	b Doull	21
M.S.Atapattu	lbw b Doull	25	b Patel	22
P.A.de Silva	c Patel b Davis	3	lbw b Astle	0
A.Ranatunga*	c Young b Doull	14	c Horne b Vettori	13
H.P.Tillakaratne	not out	55	run out	8
R.S.Kaluwitharana†	c Fleming b Patel	43	c & b Vettori	103
W.P.U.J.C.Vaas	c Horne b Patel	2	c & b Davis	57
G.P.Wickramasinghe	c Parore b Davis	43	c Doull b Astle	0
D.N.T.Zoysa	c Young b Davis	0	not out	16
M.Muralitharan	c Cairns b Doull	0	c & b Doull	26
Extras	(lb 10, w 1)	11	(lb 9, nb 3)	12
TOTAL	(85.2 overs)	**222**	(86.3 overs)	**328**

Bowling	O	M	R	W	O	M	R	W
SRI LANKA								
Vaas	35	6	144	4				
Zoysa	40	6	112	1				
Wickramasinghe	25	4	117	1				
Muralitharan	33	6	136	0				
Ranatunga	5	0	29	1				
Jayasuriya	8	0	34	0				
NEW ZEALAND								
Doull	21.2	5	58	5	20.3	5	82	3
Davis	19	6	34	3	22	2	79	1
Horne	6	5	4	0	4	2	18	0
Astle	3	0	11	0	15	3	51	2
Patel	22	4	67	2	10	3	36	1
Vettori	14	5	38	0	15	3	53	2

Fall of Wickets	NZ	SL	SL
	1st	1st	2nd
1st	55	4	49
2nd	195	55	82
3rd	271	58	85
4th	337	58	99
5th	343	79	115
6th	466	135	133
7th	512	141	270
8th	-	214	271
9th	-	215	285
10th	-	222	328

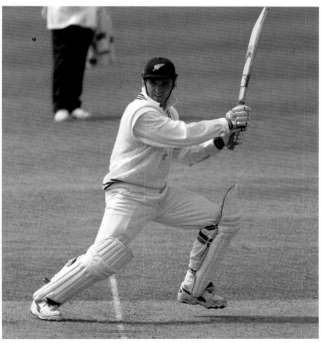

Bryan Young's 267 not out was the second-highest innings for New Zealand in test cricket after Martin Crowe's 299, also against Sri Lanka.

252 NEW ZEALAND v SRI LANKA *(Second Test)*

at Trust Bank Park, Hamilton on 14, 15, 16, 17 March, 1997
Toss : New Zealand. Umpires : D.B. Cowie and Mahboob Shah
New Zealand won by 120 runs

The pitch prepared for this fixture was mediocre for test cricket, being very slow with uneven bounce, which made batting extremely difficult. The saviour for New Zealand was Blair Pocock who made the highest score of his 15-match test career, scoring 85 off 288 balls. His was the perfect innings for the conditions, and 30 extras was the next highest contributor to New Zealand's total of 222.

Roshan Mahanama, who made 45, was the only Sri Lankan with the necessary technique and patience to offer lengthy resistance against the accuracy and control of Heath Davis, who went on to capture his first five-wicket bag. He was ably supported by the flight, guile and variations of pace of the outstandingly talented teenager Daniel Vettori. A further 53 extended New Zealand's lead to 105 by stumps.

New Zealand's lead was extended to 325 as Bryan Young, Stephen Fleming and Nathan Astle compiled workman-like

half-centuries and Simon Doull added a vital 25 at the end of the innings with his daring and innovative hitting. The 18-year-old Nuwan Zoysa captured another three wickets.

Mahanama once again provided the backbone of Sri Lanka's second innings, this time occupying the crease for 252 minutes while scoring 62. In a match where bowlers were dominant, the outstanding performance came from the youngest – Vettori – who captured five wickets in the second innings to lead New Zealand to victory by 120 runs.

Vettori's match analysis of 9-130 gave New Zealand their first series win since their visit to Zimbabwe in 1992/93. A fair comment on the pitch was that it was dug up and replaced a few weeks after the test concluded.

MILESTONES

- Daniel Vettori, at 18 years and 46 days, became the second-youngest player to capture five wickets in a test innings. The youngest was Nasim-ul-Ghani for Pakistan against West Indies at Georgetown in 1957/58.

- Muttiah Muralitharan became the first Sri Lankan bowler to capture 100 test wickets. It was his 27th test.

- It was the first time that New Zealand had achieved successive test wins since 1984/85 (tests 165 and 166).

- Sri Lanka fielded four left-arm bowlers, Chaminda Vaas, Nuwan Zoysa, Sajeewa de Silva and Sanath Jayasuriya.

Playing in his fourth test, Daniel Vettori became the second youngest player to take five wickets in an innings in a test match.

NEW ZEALAND

B.A.Pocock	c Tillakaratne b Muralitharan	85	c Mahanama b Zoysa		7
B.A.Young	run out	4	c Ranatunga b Dharmasena		62
M.J.Horne	b Zoysa	21	st Kaluwitharana b Muralitharan		16
S.P.Fleming*	c Mahanama b Zoysa	2	b Muralitharan		59
N.J.Astle	lbw b Zoysa	0	c Mahanama b Vaas		52
C.L.Cairns	c Ranatunga b Dharmasena	10	c sub U.D.U.Chandana) b Muralitharan		4
A.C.Parore†	run out	25	run out		2
D.N.Patel	c Dharmasena b Muralitharan	13	c de Silva P.A. b Dharmasena		4
D.L.Vettori	b Muralitharan	4	b Zoysa		6
S.B.Doull	c de Silva P.A. b Vaas	20	c Mahanama b Zoysa		25
H.T.Davis	not out	8	not out		2
Extras	(b 11, lb 9, nb 10)	30	(b 9, lb 11, w 7, nb 7)		34
TOTAL	(90.4 overs)	**222**	(97.4 overs)		**273**

SRI LANKA

S.T.Jayasuriya	c Astle b Davis	20	run out		3
R.S.Mahanama	lbw b Vettori	45	lbw b Doull		65
H.P.Tillakaratne	c Young b Doull	2	b Vettori		10
P.A.de Silva	c Parore b Vettori	1	(5) lbw b Doull		5
A.Ranatunga*	lbw b Davis	4	(6) c Doull b Vettori		33
R.S.Kaluwitharana†	c Parore b Davis	11	(7) lbw b Doull		13
H.D.P.K.Dharmasena	c Fleming b Davis	27	(8) not out		38
W.P.U.J.C.Vaas	c Pocock b Vettori	28	(4) c Patel b Vettori		8
D.N.T.Zoysa	c Doull b Vettori	14	c Parore b Vettori		13
K.S.C.de Silva	not out	0	c Young b Davis		0
M.Muralitharan	c Parore b Davis	5	c Cairns b Vettori		7
Extras	(lb 9, w 1, nb 3)	13	(b 4, lb 5, w 1)		10
TOTAL	(68.2 overs)	**170**	(76.2 overs)		**205**

Bowling	O	M	R	W	O	M	R	W
SRI LANKA								
Vaas	12.4	1	32	1	15	3	34	1
Zoysa	18	3	47	3	22.4	7	53	3
de Silva K.S.C.	15	4	36	0	10	2	29	0
Dharmasena	22	7	39	1	24	5	75	2
Muralitharan	22	4	43	3	26	7	62	3
Jayasuriya	1	0	5	0				
NEW ZEALAND								
Doull	13	4	19	1	15	4	34	3
Davis	20.2	3	63	5	17	4	35	1
Astle	3	1	8	0	3	1	9	0
Vettori	24	8	46	4	29.2	8	84	5
Patel	8	2	25	0	12	5	34	0

Fall of Wickets	NZ 1st	SL 1st	NZ 2nd	SL 2nd
1st	19	39	14	5
2nd	88	57	64	16
3rd	96	58	108	40
4th	100	76	183	50
5th	126	87	198	129
6th	172	93	201	147
7th	172	144	211	152
8th	178	154	239	185
9th	203	165	243	186
10th	222	170	273	205

1997/98 New Zealand in Zimbabwe

Zimbabwe was ranked eighth on the Wisden World Championship and New Zealand ninth. Some writers considered it a battle for test cricket's wooden spoon.

253 ZIMBABWE v NEW ZEALAND *(First Test)*

at Harare Sports Club on 18, 19, 20, 21, 22 September, 1997
Toss : New Zealand. Umpires : B.C. Cooray and I.D. Robinson
Match drawn

Zimbabwe were sent in to bat in humid conditions and Grant Flower made the most of his good fortune when he was caught at second slip, before scoring, off a no-ball, one of 24 bowled by Heath Davis in the game. After remaining scoreless for 40 minutes he broke free and at the end of a shortened day's play was 85 not out, out of Zimbabwe's 205-4.

The second day saw Grant Flower reach his third test century. His dismissal was one of Chris Cairns' five wickets in the innings, where he bowled within himself off a shortened run. Stephen Fleming held five catches to equal the test record for the most catches in an innings.

New Zealand's reply was a disappointing 207. Most of the batsmen got a start but only Stephen Fleming (52) and Adam Parore (42) batted over two hours. Zimbabwe had two right-arm leg-spinners in their attack, Paul Strang and Adam Huckle, and they captured two wickets each to spin their way past the last four wickets for 18 runs.

Grant Flower and Gavin Rennie strengthened Zimbabwe's hold on the game by adding 156 for the first wicket, a record partnership for any wicket against New Zealand. Grant Flower scored 151, his second century of the game. New Zealand slowed proceedings down by dropping their bowling rate below 10 overs per hour.

In a search of quick runs Zimbabwe lost their last eight wickets for 93 before declaring at 311-9. This left New Zealand the task of facing 128 overs to score 403 for victory.

The signs looked ominous for New Zealand at 122-5 but Cairns played an uncharacteristic, patient innings lasting 256 minutes while scoring 71. Parore scored a swashbuckling run-a-ball half-century, while Chris Harris and Daniel Vettori defended dourly. Emotions ran high in the latter stages of the game as New Zealand held on for the draw.

Stephen Fleming equalled two test records by taking five catches in one innings and seven catches in a match.

ZIMBABWE					
G.J.Rennie	c Fleming b Cairns	23	c Harris b O'Connor		57
G.W.Flower	c Parore b Cairns	104	c Fleming b O'Connor		151
A.Flower†	c Spearman b Cairns	8	c Parore b O'Connor		20
G.J.Whittall	c Fleming b O'Connor	33	run out		4
A.D.R.Campbell*	c Pocock b Astle	18	c Fleming b Davis		21
D.L.Houghton	lbw b Davis	23	c Davis b Astle		1
P.A.Strang	c Fleming b Davis	42	c Horne b Davis		17
H.H.Streak	c Fleming b Cairns	0	run out		0
J.A.Rennie	c Fleming b Davis	22	c. & b Astle		16
B.C.Strang	lbw b Cairns	1	not out		4
A.G.Huckle	not out	0			
Extras	(b 1, lb 5, w 4, nb 14)	24	(lb 12, nb 8)		20
TOTAL	(114.1 overs)	298	(91.5 overs) (9 wkts dec)		311

NEW ZEALAND					
C.M.Spearman	c Campbell b Strang B.C.	23	(2) c Flower A. b Huckle		33
B.A.Pocock	run out	21	(1) lbw b Streak		52
M.J.Horne	c Whittall b Streak	24	c Flower A. b Strang P.A.		0
S.P.Fleming*	c Flower A. b Strang B.C.	52	lbw b Strang B.C.		27
N.J.Astle	c Flower A. b Strang B.C.	7	c Flower G.W. b Strang B.C.		0
C.L.Cairns	run out	12	not out		71
A.C.Parore†	not out	42	lbw b Huckle		51
C.Z.Harris	lbw b Huckle	16	lbw b Streak		41
D.L.Vettori	c Rennie J.A. b Strang P.A.	2	c Rennie G.J. b Huckle		13
S.B.O'Connor	c Houghton b Strang P.A.	2	not out		1
H.T.Davis	c Rennie G.J. b Huckle	1			
Extras	(b 4, lb 1)	5	(b 6, lb 6, w 1, nb 2)		15
TOTAL	(84 overs)	207	(128 overs) (8 wkts)		304

Bowling	O	M	R	W	O	M	R	W
NEW ZEALAND								
O'Connor	26	1	104	1	26	3	73	3
Davis	20	1	57	3	13	2	45	2
Cairns	28.1	9	50	5	9	0	44	0
Astle	23	12	40	1	25.5	2	86	2
Vettori	4	0	14	0	13	2	40	0
Harris	13	5	27	0	5	3	11	0
ZIMBABWE								
Streak	23	2	63	1	21	3	52	2
Rennie J.A.	8	1	32	0	3	1	5	0
Strang B.C.	19	10	29	3	26	10	56	2
Strang P.A.	15	2	31	2	42	17	76	1
Whittall	5	0	15	0	5	1	19	0
Huckle	14	3	32	2	31	9	84	3

Fall of Wickets	Z	NZ	Z	NZ
	1st	1st	2nd	2nd
1st	47	44	156	63
2nd	57	44	218	64
3rd	117	89	231	116
4th	144	96	263	116
5th	214	135	264	122
6th	244	146	290	200
7th	244	189	290	266
8th	295	198	290	296
9th	298	204	311	-
10th	298	207	-	-

MILESTONES

- Shayne O'Connor (202) made his test debut.

- Zimbabwe fielded three sets of brothers in this test, Andy and Grant Flower, Gavin and John Rennie, Bryan and Paul Strang. This was unique in test cricket.

- Grant Flower became the first Zimbabwe batsman to score a century in each innings of a test.

- Flower and Gavin Rennie created a Zimbabwe record in tests against New Zealand by adding 156 for the first wicket.

- Stephen Fleming equalled two test records by taking five catches in an innings and seven in the match.

254 ZIMBABWE v NEW ZEALAND *(Second Test)*

at Queen's Sports Club, Bulawayo on 25, 26, 27, 28, 29 September, 1997
Toss : Zimbabwe. Umpires : S. Venkataraghavan and R.B. Tiffin
Match drawn

Grant Flower and John Rennie began with an opening stand of 144 and then Guy Whittall, professional occupation "big game hunter", hunted the New Zealand bowlers for almost eight hours as he scored 203, unbeaten, of Zimbabwe's 461.

New Zealand were 162-6 but Nathan Astle and Chris Harris added 97 for the seventh wicket. Both batsmen played the leg-spinners, Paul Strang and Adam Huckle, competently and rarely missed the opportunity to put away the bad ball. Astle was dismissed four short of a well-deserved century.

Vettori came to the crease with a highest first-class score of 29. He and Harris added 112, with Vettori favouring slashing cuts through the point area. He fell 10 runs short of becoming New Zealand's youngest test centurion. Huckle and Paul Strang captured nine wickets, while Harris made 71 of the 208 runs scored in the 278 minutes he was at the crease.

With a lead of 58 all the Zimbabwean top order batsmen contributed second-innings runs before Alistair Campbell was able to make a sporting declaration, a rarity in test cricket, leaving New Zealand a target of 286 off 68 overs.

The game was evenly poised at tea, with New Zealand 139-3. The run out of Stephen Fleming at 240-6 upset New Zealand's rhythm. When Vettori was run out in the final over, with four balls remaining and 11 runs required, Harris opted for defence. An enthralling game ended in a draw.

MILESTONES

- David Sewell (203) made his test debut.

- Nathan Astle and Chris Harris put on 97, a record seventh wicket partnership for New Zealand against Zimbabwe.

- Harris and Daniel Vettori added 112, a record eighth wicket partnership for New Zealand against Zimbabwe.

- Adam Huckle became the first Zimbabwe bowler to capture 10 wickets in a test.

ZIMBABWE

Batsman	Dismissal	R	Dismissal (2nd)	R
G.J.Rennie	c Harris b O'Connor	57	lbw b Astle	24
G.W.Flower	c Fleming b Vettori	83	run out	49
A.Flower†	c Harris b Vettori	39	c & b Harris	7
G.J.Whittall	not out	203	run out	45
A.D.R.Campbell*	c Astle b O'Connor	7	not out	59
D.L.Houghton	b Cairns	32	c Harris b Vettori	13
P.A.Strang	c Harris b Vettori	5	lbw b Vettori	2
H.H.Streak	lbw b Cairns	17	run out	1
B.C.Strang	c Fleming b Cairns	0	b Cairns	10
A.G.Huckle	c Parore b Vettori	0	not out	0
E.Z.Matambanadzo	c Fleming b O'Connor	4		
Extras	(lb 10, w 2, nb 2)	14	(b 2, lb 7, w 3, nb 5)	17
TOTAL	**(161 overs)**	**461**	**(64 overs) (8 wkts dec)**	**227**

NEW ZEALAND

Batsman	Dismissal	R	Dismissal (2nd)	R
C.M.Spearman	c Huckle b Strang P.A.	47	(2) c Campbell b Huckle	27
B.A.Pocock	lbw b Strang P.A.	27	(1) c Strang P.A. b Huckle	62
M.J.Horne	lbw b Strang P.A.	5	c Campbell b Huckle	29
S.P.Fleming*	c Strang P.A. b Huckle	27	run out	75
N.J.Astle	c sub (A.R.Whittall) b Huckle	96	c Flower G.W. b Strang P.A.	21
C.L.Cairns	c Rennie b Huckle	0	c Houghton b Huckle	8
A.C.Parore†	c Flower G.W. b Huckle	17	c Whittall b Huckle	23
C.Z.Harris	b Huckle	71	not out	12
D.L.Vettori	c Strang B.C. b Huckle	90	run out	7
S.B.O'Connor	run out	9	not out	0
D.G.Sewell	not out	1		
Extras	(b 1, lb 7, nb 5)	13	(b 5, lb 4, nb 2)	11
TOTAL	**(161.4 overs)**	**403**	**(68 overs) (8 wkts)**	**275**

Bowling

NEW ZEALAND

	O	M	R	W	O	M	R	W
Sewell	19	3	81	0	4	0	9	0
O'Connor	27	9	80	3	5	0	34	0
Cairns	36	11	97	3	11	1	49	1
Vettori	58	11	165	4	18	3	69	2
Harris	14	6	13	0	17	4	41	1
Astle	7	2	15	0	9	6	16	1

ZIMBABWE

	O	M	R	W	O	M	R	W
Streak	15	5	26	0				
Matambanadzo	15	4	52	0	2	0	14	0
Strang P.A.	47	19	110	3	23	1	81	1
Huckle	40.4	9	111	6	32	2	146	5
Strang B.C.	26	12	50	0	8	4	15	0
Whittall	6	1	14	0				
Flower G.W.	10	2	19	0	3	1	10	0
Campbell	2	0	13	0				

Fall of Wickets

	Z 1st	NZ 1st	Z 2nd	NZ 2nd
1st	144	60	75	41
2nd	148	76	80	89
3rd	218	92	91	138
4th	244	130	172	207
5th	322	130	202	221
6th	343	162	204	240
7th	416	259	205	260
8th	420	371	219	275
9th	421	389	-	-
10th	461	403	-	-

Chris Harris made the highest score in his 23-test career of 71.

1997/98 New Zealand in Australia

New Zealand entered the three-match test series low in confidence, having suffered innings defeats by both Queensland and New South Wales. Influenced by their ex-Australian wicketkeeper, Steve Rixon, now the New Zealand coach, New Zealand played Australia in a bold Australian-like fashion. Prior to the test Stephen Fleming insisted that they were not "a weak little under-age side but that his team had the ability to match their opponents, whether verbally or aggressively".

255 AUSTRALIA v NEW ZEALAND (First Test)

at Brisbane Cricket Ground on 7, 8, 9, 10, 11 November, 1997
Toss : New Zealand. Umpires : V.K. Ramaswamy and S.G. Randell
Australia won by 186 runs

Rain had kept the pitch covered for two days prior to the start and Fleming, on winning the toss, took advantage of the bowler-friendly conditions and asked Australia to bat. Wayward bowling by Simon Doull and Geoff Allott wasted the conditions but Chris Cairns, coming on as first change, relished them and removed four of the first five batsmen with the score at 53. Mark Taylor and Ian Healy staged a recovery, adding 117 for the sixth wicket, with Taylor, who had been in a batting slump, playing courageously to reach his 16th test hundred.

The new-found batting prowess of Paul Reiffel, who made his highest test score of 77, saw Australia fight their way to 373. The loss of Bryan Young in the second over brought the best out in Blair Pocock who, along with Fleming, defied the Australian attack for 175 minutes to add 98 before Pocock, on 57, became Shane Warne's first of seven victims for the game.

New Zealand batted for most of the third day, taking their overnight score of 134-3 through to 349, thanks to further scores in excess of fifty by Fleming (91), Cairns (64) and a most pleasing test debut by Craig McMillan, whose 54 included a memorable six over long-on off Warne.

From a position of parity New Zealand were on the verge of greater success when Australia lost their first four wickets for 105. The graceful Greg Blewett and the youthful Ricky Ponting hastened the scoring along with a series of scintillating shots that allowed Taylor to declare at 294-6, leaving New Zealand the last day to score 319 for victory.

The maturity and spirited attitude that New Zealand had displayed on the first four days disintegrated as they were all out for 132 in the face of sustained pressure from Glenn McGrath, who made the ball cut into the right-hand batsmen and away from the left. Warne wrapped up the tail, capturing three wickets, as New Zealand lost their last five wickets for 20 runs, thus giving Australia victory by 186 runs.

AUSTRALIA

M.A.Taylor*	c Young b Doull	112	(2) c Astle b Cairns	16
M.T.G.Elliott	c Young b Cairns	18	(1) c Fleming b Vettori	11
G.S.Blewett	c Vettori b Cairns	7	(4) c Fleming b Cairns	91
M.E.Waugh	c Vettori b Cairns	3	(5) c Fleming b Vettori	17
S.R.Waugh	lbw b Cairns	2	(6) c Parore b Cairns	23
R.T.Ponting	c Pocock b Doull	26	(7) not out	73
I.A.Healy†	b Doull	68	(3) c Fleming b Allott	25
P.R.Reiffel	c Parore b Allott	77	not out	28
S.K.Warne	c Fleming b Vettori	21		
M.S.Kasprowicz	not out	13		
G.D.McGrath	c Fleming b Doull	6		
Extras	(b 4, lb 9, w 1, nb 6)	20	(b 1, lb 4, nb 5)	10
TOTAL	(121 overs)	**373**	(100.5 overs) (6 wkts dec)	**294**

NEW ZEALAND

B.A.Young	c Taylor b Kasprowicz	1	(2) lbw b McGrath	45
B.A.Pocock	c Taylor b Warne	57	(1) c Taylor b Reiffel	3
N.J.Astle	run out	12	c Blewett b McGrath	14
S.P.Fleming*	lbw b Kasprowicz	91	c Healy b McGrath	0
D.L.Vettori	c Waugh S.R. b Blewett	14	(9) c Taylor b Warne	0
C.D.McMillan	lbw b Warne	54	(5) lbw b McGrath	0
C.L.Cairns	b McGrath	64	(6) b Reiffel	21
A.C.Parore†	c Taylor b Warne	12	(7) not out	39
C.Z.Harris	b Warne	13	(8) b Warne	0
S.B.Doull	not out	2	c Healy b McGrath	2
G.I.Allott	c Elliott b McGrath	4	lbw b Warne	0
Extras	(b 4, lb 4, nb 17)	25	(lb 2, nb 6)	8
TOTAL	(132.2 overs)	**349**	(62 overs)	**132**

Bowling NEW ZEALAND	O	M	R	W	O	M	R	W
Doull	30	6	70	4	19	5	44	0
Allott	31	3	117	1	19.5	4	60	1
Cairns	24	5	90	4	16	4	54	3
Vettori	21	5	46	1	36	13	87	2
Astle	11	2	20	0	1	0	14	0
Harris	4	1	17	0	9	0	30	0
AUSTRALIA								
McGrath	32.2	6	96	2	17	6	32	5
Kasprowicz	24	6	57	2	8	1	17	0
Warne	42	13	106	4	25	6	54	3
Reiffel	21	6	53	0	12	4	27	2
Waugh M.E.	7	2	18	0				
Blewett	6	2	11	1				

Fall of Wickets	A	NZ	A	NZ
	1st	1st	2nd	2nd
1st	27	2	24	4
2nd	46	36	36	55
3rd	50	134	72	68
4th	52	173	105	68
5th	108	210	163	69
6th	225	279	217	112
7th	294	317	-	115
8th	349	343	-	117
9th	359	343	-	126
10th	373	349	-	132

The Australian wicketkeeper Ian Healy joins in the applause for Craig McMillan reaching 50 in his first test innings.

MILESTONES

• Craig McMillan (204) made his test debut.

• Mark Taylor and Shane Warne became test cricket's most prolific fielder-bowler combination displacing Sobers-Gibbs, which accounted for 39 wickets. Daniel Vettori was the 40th batsman dismissed "c Taylor b Warne".

256 AUSTRALIA v NEW ZEALAND *(Second Test)*

at W.A.C.A. Ground, Perth on 20, 21, 22, 23 November, 1997
Toss : New Zealand. Umpires : G. Sharp and D.B. Hair
Australia won by an innings and 70 runs

There was an acrimonious atmosphere between the Australian Cricket Board and the Australian players throughout this test. The problem came near to a crisis point with talks of a players' strike gaining more headlines than the game. The Adelaide Oval curator, Les Burdett, prepared the pitch in Perth after the Perth groundsman resigned in protest at criticism of some of his pitches.

Batting first on a hard, fast pitch New Zealand were dismissed before the end of the first day for a paltry 217 as a result of a superb display of athletic catching that some critics at the ground rated as one of the most exciting fielding displays witnessed on Australian soil.

The best of the seven catches taken was by Mark Waugh off a Chris Cairns full-blooded blow. He leapt to his right at mid-wicket and floated gracefully before landing horizontal to the ground holding an exceptional one-handed catch.

Shayne O'Connor's left-arm deliveries caused the Australian top order batsmen concern.

Mark Waugh, whose position in the Australian test team was in jeopardy owing to a poor Ashes series in England and his double failure in the previous test, shared a 153-run partnership in 157 minutes with his twin brother Steve. This created a batting momentum that Ian Healy, Paul Reifel and Shane Warne carried through until Australia were dismissed just after tea on the third day for 461.

Little-known New South Wales right-arm fast bowler Simon Cook had replaced Glenn McGrath, who had suffered a groin injury in the previous test while taking 5-32. As Cook had been 12th man for New South Wales a few weeks earlier, it was indeed a surprise selection, but it paid off.

For the second time in the game Adam Parore looked a top-quality batsman, ideally suited to batting at number three. Cook finished the match with a flourish, capturing the last five wickets for 39 runs, giving himself match figures of 7-75 in his debut test. Midway through the fourth day Australia won by an innings and 70 runs.

NEW ZEALAND

B.A.Young	c Waugh S.R. b Kasprowicz	9	(2) run out	23
B.A.Pocock	c Healy b Cook	15	(1) c Blewett b Kasprowicz	1
A.C.Parore†	c Blewett b Reiffel	30	lbw b Kasprowicz	63
S.P.Fleming*	c Blewett b Warne	10	(5) c Blewett b Warne	4
N.J.Astle	c Healy b Reiffel	12	(6) lbw b Cook	19
C.D.McMillan	c Taylor b Kasprowicz	54	(7) lbw b Cook	23
C.L.Cairns	c Waugh M.E. b Warne	52	(8) b Cook	7
D.L.Vettori	not out	14	(4) c Taylor b Warne	1
S.B.Doull	c Taylor b Warne	8	c Waugh S.R. b Cook	17
S.B.O'Connor	c Waugh S.R. b Cook	7	c Taylor b Cook	7
G.I.Allott	b Warne	0	not out	2
Extras	(lb 3, nb 3)	6	(lb 2, nb 5)	7
TOTAL	**(74.4 overs)**	**217**	**(64.2 overs)**	**174**

AUSTRALIA

M.A.Taylor*	lbw b O'Connor	2
M.T.G.Elliott	c O'Connor b Cairns	42
G.S.Blewett	c Astle b O'Connor	14
M.E.Waugh	c Parore b Doull	86
S.R.Waugh	b O'Connor	96
I.A.Healy†	c Fleming b Cairns	85
R.T.Ponting	c Fleming b Cairns	16
P.R.Reiffel	c Fleming b Cairns	54
S.K.Warne	c O'Connor b Vettori	36
M.S.Kasprowicz	run out	9
S.H.Cook	not out	3
Extras	(b 6, lb 5, nb 7)	18
TOTAL	**(131.4 overs)**	**461**

Bowling	O	M	R	W	O	M	R	W
AUSTRALIA								
Kasprowicz	20	9	40	2	16	5	43	2
Reiffel	20	6	46	2	12	4	26	0
Cook	10	5	36	2	10.2	3	39	5
Warne	22.4	3	83	4	26	4	64	2
Blewett	2	1	9	0				
NEW ZEALAND								
Doull	21	3	78	1				
O'Connor	31.4	7	109	3				
Cairns	28	9	95	4				
Vettori	29	7	84	1				
Allott	22	3	84	0				

Fall of Wickets	NZ 1st	A 1st	NZ 2nd
1st	12	3	2
2nd	31	53	53
3rd	51	71	55
4th	72	224	84
5th	87	262	102
6th	161	287	137
7th	187	403	145
8th	197	449	160
9th	214	450	165
10th	217	461	174

MILESTONES

- Test history was made after tea on the first day when the floodlights were turned on because of poor light. It was the first time that a test was conducted under lights. ICC had approved the principle at a meeting five months earlier.

- Mark Waugh on-drove Daniel Vettori 130 metres onto the roof of the five-tiered Lillee-Marsh Stand. It was thought to be the biggest six hit at the ground.

- Steve Waugh became the seventh Australian to reach 6000 test runs.

- Ian Healy passed Rodney Marsh's 3663 runs to become Australia's highest-scoring test wicketkeeper.

- It was Mark Taylor's 20th win in 35 tests as Australian captain.

257 AUSTRALIA v NEW ZEALAND (*Third Test*)

at Bellerive Oval, Hobart on 27, 28, 29, 30 November, 1 December, 1997
Toss : Australia. Umpires : R.B. Tiffin and S.J. Davis
Match drawn

The test at Hobart was spoilt by fickle weather that saw most of the first day washed out and Australia's first innings occupying 554 minutes over 2½ days. Left-handed opening batsman Matthew Elliott, who had made two centuries in the Ashes tests in England, played patiently to bring up his third test century of the calendar year in 304 minutes.

He shared a second wicket partnership of 197 with Greg Blewett who was bowled by Simon Doull for 99 the over after Elliott (114) became Craig McMillan's first test wicket. Mark Waugh played, for him, an obdurate, but highly valuable innings, taking his team through to 400.

New Zealand enjoyed their best opening stand of the series, with Bryan Young and Matthew Horne adding 60. The continuing development of the batting talent of Adam Parore saw him and Horne add 132 to take New Zealand to 192-1 before the innings was torn asunder by Steve Waugh, the seventh bowler used by Australia. He dismissed Parore, Stephen Fleming and Nathan Astle in the space of six runs.

Towards the end of the fourth day, when the rain-affected match appeared doomed to be a dreary draw, Fleming's imaginative declaration, 149 runs behind Australia, challenged the home side to a game of cricket. It won the respect of both the Australian team and the cricketing public of both countries.

On the final day Mark Taylor scored a laborious 62 not out, while Blewett batted audaciously in scoring 56 off 65 balls. Taylor, in a somewhat defensive lunchtime declaration, left New Zealand to score 288 off 61 overs.

A pulsating offensive by Astle and Horne, who scored 72 off the first 52 balls bowled, gave New Zealand an excellent start. When the score had reached 93-1 New Zealand's expectations were dashed when three wickets fell for two runs as Shane Warne again showed his exceptional competitive edge. McMillan, Parore and Roger Twose kept their team close to the target but another collapse, when three

wickets fell for four runs, saw the last two batsmen, Simon Doull and Shayne O'Connor, hold on for the last 38 minutes to give the game a nail-biting finish.

At the end of the game Stephen Fleming said, "We came with the attitude of playing positive cricket and the fact that our performances in the middle haven't matched that hasn't changed the philosophy."

MILESTONES

- Matthew Horne, playing because of an injury to Blair Pocock, opened the innings for the third time in his first-class career and for the third time made a hundred. This was his maiden test century.

- Greg Blewett was bowled for 99 in a test for the second time in 1997.

- Shane Warne captured 19 wickets in the three tests, a record for Australia against New Zealand.

AUSTRALIA

M.T.G.Elliott	c Young b McMillan	114			
M.A.Taylor*	b O'Connor	18	(1) not out		66
G.S.Blewett	b Doull	99	b Vettori		56
M.E.Waugh	c Parore b O'Connor	81	(2) lbw b O'Connor		9
S.R.Waugh	c McMillan b Doull	7	(4) not out		2
R.T.Ponting	c Parore b Cairns	4			
I.A.Healy†	c Young b O'Connor	16			
P.R.Reiffel	c Young b Doull	19			
S.K.Warne	st Parore b Vettori	14			
M.S.Kasprowicz	c Doull b Cairns	20			
S.H.Cook	not out	0			
Extras	(lb 6, w 1, nb 1)	8	(b 4, lb 1)		5
TOTAL	(141.1 overs)	**400**	(38 overs) (2 wkts dec)		**138**

NEW ZEALAND

B.A.Young	b Reiffel	31	(6) c Ponting b Warne		10
M.J.Horne	c Elliott b Reiffel	133	(1) lbw b Reiffel		31
A.C.Parore†	lbw b Waugh S.R.	44	(7) c Elliott b Warne		41
S.P.Fleming*	c Healy b Waugh S.R.	0	st Healy b Warne		0
R.G.Twose	lbw b Warne	2	(8) run out		29
C.D.McMillan	lbw b Waugh S.R.	2	(5) c Taylor b Warne		41
N.J.Astle	not out	22	(2) c Ponting b Reiffel		40
C.L.Cairns	not out	10	(3) st Healy b Warne		18
D.L.Vettori			c Healy b Waugh S.R.		3
S.B.Doull			not out		1
S.B.O'Connor			not out		0
Extras	(b 1, lb 2, nb 4)	7	(b 2, lb 7)		9
TOTAL	(90 overs) (6 wkts dec)	**251**	(61 overs) (9 wkts)		**223**

Bowling	O	M	R	W	O	M	R	W		Fall of Wickets			
NEW ZEALAND										A	NZ	A	NZ
										1st	*1st*	*2nd*	*2nd*
Doull	33	11	87	3	8	1	28	0	1st	41	60	14	72
O'Connor	34	8	101	3	9	2	32	1	2nd	238	192	106	93
Cairns	35.1	13	86	2					3rd	238	192	-	93
Astle	12	5	32	0	7	0	25	0	4th	246	195	-	95
McMillan	15	4	43	1					5th	266	198	-	137
Vettori	12	1	45	1	14	1	48	1	6th	291	229	-	152
AUSTRALIA									7th	326	-	-	218
Kasprowicz	13	1	43	0	3	0	33	0	8th	353	-	-	221
Reiffel	14	8	27	2	14	2	47	2	9th	400	-	-	222
Warne	27	4	81	1	28	6	88	5	10th	400	-	-	-
Cook	13	2	50	0	4	0	17	0					
Waugh M.E.	8	2	17	0	6	1	19	0					
Blewett	5	1	10	0									
Waugh S.R.	9	2	20	3	6	4	10	0					
Elliott	1	1	0	0									

Playing in the unaccustomed position of opening batsman, because of an injury to Blair Pocock, Matt Horne made the most of the opportunity and scored his maiden test century.

AVERAGES

New Zealand

BATTING	M	I	NO	Runs	HS	Ave
M.J. Horne	1	2	0	164	133	82.00
A.C. Parore	3	6	1	229	63	45.80
C.L. Cairns	3	6	1	172	64	34.40
C.D. McMillan	3	6	0	174	54	29.00
N.J. Astle	3	6	1	119	40	23.80
B.A. Young	3	6	0	119	45	19.83
B.A. Pocock	2	4	0	76	57	19.00
S.P. Fleming	3	6	0	105	91	17.50
R.G. Twose	1	2	0	31	29	15.50
S.B. Doull	3	5	2	30	17	10.00
D.L. Vettori	3	5	1	32	14*	8.00
S.B. O'Connor	2	3	1	14	7	7.00
C.Z. Harris	1	2	0	13	13	6.50
G.I. Allott	2	4	1	6	4	2.00

BOWLING	O	M	R	W	Ave
C.L. Cairns	103.1	31	325	13	25.00
S.B. O'Connor	74.4	17	242	7	34.57
S.B. Doull	111	26	307	8	38.37
C.D. McMillan	15	4	43	1	43.00
D.L. Vettori	112	27	310	6	51.66
G.I. Allott	72.5	10	261	2	130.50
C.Z. Harris	13	1	47	0	-
N.J. Astle	31	7	91	0	-

Australia

BATTING	M	I	NO	Runs	HS	Ave
P.R. Reiffel	3	4	1	178	77	59.33
M.A. Taylor	3	5	1	214	112	53.50
G.S. Blewett	3	5	0	267	99	53.40
I.A. Healy	3	4	0	194	85	48.50
M.T.G. Elliott	3	4	0	185	114	46.25
R.T. Ponting	3	4	1	119	73*	39.66
M.E. Waugh	3	5	0	196	86	39.20
S.R. Waugh	3	5	1	130	96	32.50
S.K. Warne	3	3	0	71	36	23.66
M.S. Kasprowicz	3	3	1	42	20	21.00
G.D. McGrath	1	1	0	6	6	6.00
S.H. Cook	2	2	2	3	3*	-

BOWLING	O	M	R	W	Ave
S.R. Waugh	15	6	30	4	7.50
G.D. McGrath	49.2	12	128	7	18.28
S.H. Cook	37.2	10	142	7	20.28
S.K. Warne	170.4	36	476	19	25.05
P.R. Reiffel	93	30	226	8	28.25
G.S. Blewett	13	4	30	1	30.00
M.S. Kasprowicz	84	22	233	6	38.83
M.T.G. Elliott	1	1	0	0	-
M.E. Waugh	21	5	54	0	-

1997/98 Zimbabwe in New Zealand

258 NEW ZEALAND v ZIMBABWE *(First Test)*

at Basin Reserve, Wellington on 19, 20, 21, 22 February, 1998
Toss : Zimbabwe. Umpires : S.G. Randell and R.S. Dunne
New Zealand won by 10 wickets

Alistair Campbell, Zimbabwe's captain, included three spinners in his team for the Basin Reserve. Overnight rain shortened the first day's play but Campbell opted to bat first, thinking that the fourth innings would favour his slow men.

Unfortunately for the visitors the predominantly quick New Zealand attack thrived in the conditions and Zimbabwe never recovered from being 89-6. Campbell and Heath Streak fought tenaciously but Shayne O'Connor, who kept a full length, returned his best test figures of 4-52. Zimbabwe's 180 was never enough, even though Bryan Young was dismissed without a run on the board.

Six of the next seven batsmen all scored over 36 and all of them batted more than two hours. New Zealand ended the second day four runs behind Zimbabwe but with seven wickets in hand thanks to a cautious innings by Matthew Horne and a venturesome innings of 78 by Adam Parore.

The third day was dominated by a maiden test century from 21-year-old Craig McMillan. Having recently experienced the leg-spinner's art as performed by the master, Shane Warne, he found little difficulty in solving the problems posed by Zimbabwe's Adam Huckle and Paul Strang. He scored 92 of his 139 runs from boundary shots and showed scant regard to cricket's "nervous nineties" which he negotiated in five minutes.

There was a heightened sense of drama when, on 94, he lofted the ball to long-on where the strong wind took the ball over the boundary, where it was caught by Huckle. After an agonising delay the umpire ruled that it had cleared the ropes and was a six. Thus McMillan had his first test century. Zimbabwe began their second innings 231 runs in arrears and lost two wickets for 27 before stumps.

Murray Goodwin, who was born in Zimbabwe but spent his formative years in Western Australia, displayed genuine batting talent as he fought a rearguard action, scoring his third score in the 70s in his six test innings to date.

A stubborn stand between Campbell and Heath Streak threatened to take the game into the fifth day before Chris Cairns broke through, taking two of the last three wickets that fell for three runs. It was indeed timely that New Zealand claimed the extra half-hour and scored the 20 runs required for victory as rain swept through Wellington for the following two days.

Adam Parore keeps his eye on the ball as a return comes rifling in. He held four catches in Zimbabwe's first innings.

ZIMBABWE

Batsman	Dismissal	Runs	Dismissal (2nd)	Runs
G.J.Rennie	b Doull	13	lbw b Doull	15
G.W.Flower	b Nash	38	c & b Vettori	4
M.W.Goodwin	lbw b Vettori	8	(4) c Fleming b Cairns	72
G.J.Whittall	c Parore b O'Connor	6	(5) c Astle b Nash	22
A.Flower†	c Parore b O'Connor	2	(6) c O'Connor b Vettori	6
A.D.R.Campbell*	run out	37	(7) c Horne b Cairns	56
P.A.Strang	c Young b Doull	1	(8) b Cairns	0
H.H.Streak	lbw b O'Connor	39	(9) not out	43
A.R.Whittall	c Parore b Cairns	1	(3) run out	12
A.G.Huckle	c Parore b O'Connor	19	lbw b Vettori	0
M.Mbangwa	not out	0	lbw b Cairns	0
Extras	(lb 10, nb 6)	16	(b 6, lb 14)	20
TOTAL	(85.3 overs)	**180**	(106.3 overs)	**250**

NEW ZEALAND

Batsman	Dismissal	Runs	Dismissal (2nd)	Runs
B.A.Young	c Strang b Streak	0	(2) not out	10
M.J.Horne	c Flower A. b Mbangwa	44	(1) not out	9
A.C.Parore†	c Flower A. b Huckle	78		
S.P.Fleming*	c Campbell b Huckle	36		
N.J.Astle	c Flower A. b Streak	42		
C.D.McMillan	c Whittall A.R. b Huckle	139		
C.L.Cairns	run out	0		
D.J.Nash	b Strang	41		
D.L.Vettori	b Strang	16		
S.B.Doull	c Goodwin b Strang	8		
S.B.O'Connor	not out	2		
Extras	(b 1, lb 4)	5	(lb 1)	1
TOTAL	(145.1 overs)	**411**	(3.5 overs) (0 wkts)	**20**

Bowling	O	M	R	W	O	M	R	W
NEW ZEALAND								
Cairns	16	2	50	1	24.3	4	56	4
O'Connor	18.3	7	52	4	14	3	39	0
Doull	17	8	18	2	13	1	47	1
Nash	14	7	11	1	9	6	10	1
Vettori	20	10	39	1	41	18	73	3
McMillan					5	1	5	0
ZIMBABWE								
Streak	22	6	74	2	2	0	13	0
Mbangwa	17	4	42	1				
Strang	49.1	13	126	3				
Whittall G.J.	5	2	12	0				
Whittall A.R.	12	0	50	0				
Huckle	40	10	102	3	1.5	0	6	0

Fall of Wickets	Z 1st	NZ 1st	Z 2nd	NZ 2nd
1st	30	0	18	-
2nd	53	103	20	-
3rd	64	144	65	-
4th	70	179	110	-
5th	78	240	125	-
6th	89	254	155	-
7th	122	362	155	-
8th	131	388	249	-
9th	171	397	249	-
10th	180	411	250	-

MILESTONES

- It was New Zealand's 37th test victory.

- Steve Dunne equalled the New Zealand umpiring record, held by Brian Aldridge, by controlling his 26th test.

- Craig McMillan and Dion Nash added 108 for the seventh wicket, a record for New Zealand against Zimbabwe.

259 NEW ZEALAND v ZIMBABWE *(Second Test)*

at Eden Park, Auckland on 26, 27, 28 February, 1998
Toss : Zimbabwe. Umpires : S.G. Randell and D.B. Cowie
New Zealand won by an innings and 13 runs

The pitch looked as if it would assist spin from the outset so Shayne O'Connor was dropped and replaced by left-arm finger-spinner Mark Priest, who was selected for his second test eight years after his first. Zimbabwe followed suit and played their three spinners again.

Simon Doull had an inspired spell at the beginning of the match bowling 10 overs and taking 4-16. He was able to extract sharp bounce from a length and balls that were of a full length swung noticeably or seamed disconcertingly. From 98-6 Andy Flower and Paul Strang took the score to 157 before Chris Cairns disposed of the last three wickets to have Zimbabwe all out for 170.

The Zimbabwean right-arm fast-medium pair of Heath Streak and Pommie Mbangwa caused problems for New Zealand who were 69-3 before Matthew Horne, who had looked uncertain in the early stages of his innings, was joined by Nathan Astle. They added 243 at almost four runs an over.

Astle was dismissed for his fourth test century (112) and Horne fell 10 runs later to a tired shot after batting 394 minutes. There was no respite for Zimbabwe as Craig McMillan launched into a boisterous exhibition of shot making, reaching fifty off 38 balls. When he was out early on the third day New Zealand had a lead of 290.

Zimbabwe's second innings followed the same pattern as the first and they were soon 90-5. Andy Flower again showed he was the finest batsman produced by Zimbabwe, scoring 83 to go with his first innings score of 65, thus providing one third of the runs made by Zimbabwe in the game.

Paul Strang batted in his distinctive, somewhat unorthodox, way and by scoring 67 not out off 77 balls ended Zimbabwe's innings on a positive note, even though they made only 277. New Zealand thus won the series two-nil.

It was the first series that Cairns, Doull and Dion Nash had bowled in together as all three had suffered injuries throughout their careers. They captured 29 of the 40 wickets that New Zealand took in the two tests.

MILESTONES

- It was New Zealand's 38th test win and fourth consecutive home win – all achieved within four days.

- It was New Zealand's third test win inside three days and their seventh by an innings.

- Matthew Horne and Nathan Astle had a fourth wicket partnership of 243, a record against all countries and New Zealand's highest for any wicket against Zimbabwe.

- Nathan Astle reached his 1000th test run in his 18th test.

ZIMBABWE					
G.J.Rennie	c Parore b Doull	0	(2) c Fleming b Cairns	0
G.W.Flower	c Parore b Doull	13	(1) c Young b Nash	32
M.W.Goodwin	c Young b Doull	28	c McMillan b Nash	14
A.D.R.Campbell*	c Astle b Doull	11	c Horne b Vettori	22
A.Flower†	c McMillan b Nash	65	c Parore b Cairns	83
G.J.Whittall	c Young b Nash	1	lbw b Doull	10
H.H.Streak	c Fleming b Nash	12	lbw b Cairns	24
P.A.Strang	not out	30	not out	67
A.R.Whittall	lbw b Cairns	4	c Parore b Doull	3
A.G.Huckle	lbw b Cairns	0	b Doull	13
M.Mbangwa	b Cairns	0	c Fleming b Doull	0
Extras	(b 1, lb 3, nb 2)	6	(b 1, lb 6, nb 2)	9
TOTAL	(62.5 overs)	170	(94.4 overs)	277

NEW ZEALAND		
B.A.Young	b Streak	1
M.J.Horne	c Whittall G.J. b Mbangwa	157
A.C.Parore†	c Flower A. b Mbangwa	10
S.P.Fleming*	c Huckle b Mbangwa	19
N.J.Astle	c Flower G.W. b Streak	114
C.D.McMillan	c Flower A. b Strang	88
C.L.Cairns	c Strang b Streak	22
D.J.Nash	lbw b Strang	1
M.W.Priest	c Rennie b Strang	16
D.L.Vettori	c Campbell b Strang	0
S.B.Doull	not out	6
Extras	(b 8, lb 17, w 1)	26
TOTAL	(120.1 overs)	460

Bowling	O	M	R	W	O	M	R	W
NEW ZEALAND								
Doull	20	6	35	4	19.4	5	50	4
Cairns	16.5	5	56	3	29	9	81	3
Nash	18	4	41	3	10	5	13	2
Vettori	2	0	15	0	20	5	60	1
Astle	5	1	15	0				
Priest	1	0	4	0	14	0	51	0
McMillan					2	0	15	0
ZIMBABWE								
Streak	31	7	105	3				
Mbangwa	27	10	78	3				
Whittall G.J.	14	3	68	0				
Strang	18.1	0	54	4				
Whittall A.R.	11	1	37	0				
Huckle	13	1	66	0				
Goodwin	6	1	27	0				

Fall of Wickets	Z	NZ	Z
	1st	*1st*	*2nd*
1st	1	2	4
2nd	32	40	29
3rd	53	69	71
4th	54	312	71
5th	55	322	90
6th	98	382	156
7th	157	405	227
8th	168	431	234
9th	170	433	277
10th	170	460	277

Nathan Astle lofts a ball over the long-off boundary under the watchful gaze of Zimbabwean wicketkeeper Andy Flower.

1997/98 New Zealand in Sri Lanka

260 SRI LANKA v NEW ZEALAND *(First Test)*

at R. Premadasa Stadium on 27, 28, 29, 30, 31 May, 1998
Toss : New Zealand. Umpires : R.E. Koertzen and K.T. Francis
New Zealand won by 167 runs

The Sri Lankan policy of preparing their local pitches to suit the strength of their bowling attack – spin – came unstuck in the first test when Stephen Fleming won the toss and then played two substantial innings to provide his team with sufficient runs. The game concluded when the New Zealand spinners, Daniel Vettori and Paul Wiseman, exploited the conditions better to spin the visitors to victory.

Fleming and Adam Parore provided the backbone of New Zealand's first innings of 305, both scoring attractive half-centuries, while they batted against an attack that included six slow bowlers. Muttiah Muralitharan flighted his off-spinners to perfection, claiming five wickets.

Steady batting, after losing two early wickets to Chris Cairns, saw Sri Lanka fall 20 runs short of New Zealand's total. Mahela Jayawardene and Romesh Kaluwitharana accumulated runs against New Zealand's more varied attack.

The partnership between Fleming and Craig McMillan dominated the last session of the third day. They came together when New Zealand had lost their third wicket at 160 and, by dint of decisive footwork and positive stroke play, they combined to add 240 in 222 minutes to take New Zealand through to 400 after lunch on the fourth day.

Fleming played with total control to finish unbeaten on 176, his second test century. McMillan's second test hundred was more flamboyant as he scored 80 per cent of his runs in boundary shots, with six sixes and 13 fours.

Chasing 465 to win in 4½ sessions on a docile pitch where the ball was spinning but turning slowly, Sri Lanka ended the fourth day at 111-2, with the right-arm off-spinner Paul Wiseman having both wickets.

Jayawardene and Arivinda de Silva displayed their silky skills, taking Sri Lanka to lunch at 194-2. The first ball after lunch saw de Silva deceived by Vettori's arm ball and be adjudged lbw for 71 to begin a slide that saw the last eight wickets tumble for 103. Wiseman and Vettori bowled marathon spells and throughout the day were more aggressive than their more highly rated opponents.

NEW ZEALAND

Batsman	Dismissal 1	Runs	Dismissal 2	Runs
B.A.Young	c Kaluwitharana b Muralitharan	30	lbw b Bandaratilleke	11
M.J.Horne	b Bandaratilleke	15	c Ranatunga b Muralitharan	35
S.P.Fleming*	c Jayasuriya b Kalpage	78	not out	174
N.J.Astle	c Jayawardene b Kalpage	30	c Kaluwitharana b Jayasuriya	34
C.D.McMillan	lbw b Muralitharan	0	c Kalpage b Muralitharan	142
A.C.Parore†	c Jayasuriya b Wickramasinghe	67	c Kalpage b Muralitharan	1
C.L.Cairns	c Bandara b Muralitharan	20	c Jayasuriya b Muralitharan	6
C.Z.Harris	lbw b Wickramasinghe	19	not out	14
D.L.Vettori	c Kalpage b Muralitharan	20		
P.J.Wiseman	c Jayawardene b Muralitharan	6		
S.B.Doull	not out	1		
Extras	(lb 9, w 1, nb 9)	19	(b 5, lb 10, nb 12)	27
TOTAL	(105.2 overs)	**305**	(123 overs) (6 wkts dec)	**444**

SRI LANKA

Batsman	Dismissal 1	Runs	Dismissal 2	Runs
S.T.Jayasuriya	c Parore b Cairns	10	c Young b Wiseman	59
M.S.Atapattu	c Parore b Cairns	0	c Horne b Wiseman	16
D.P.M.D.Jayawardene	c Vettori b Wiseman	52	c Horne b Wiseman	54
P.A.de Silva	c Doull b McMillan	37	lbw b Vettori	71
A.Ranatunga	b Cairns	49	c & b Vettori	9
R.S.Kaluwitharana†	b Vettori	72	c Parore b McMillan	39
R.S.Kalpage	b Wiseman	6	c Young b Vettori	16
G.P.Wickramasinghe	lbw b Vettori	27	(9) c Young b Cairns	0
M.R.C.N.Bandaratilleke	run out	20	(8) c Horne b Wiseman	16
M.Muralitharan	b Vettori	0	not out	9
C.M.Bandara	not out	0	lbw b Wiseman	0
Extras	(lb 8, nb 4)	12	(b 1, lb 4, nb 3)	8
TOTAL	(90.2 overs)	**285**	(131.5 overs)	**297**

SRI LANKA

Bowler	O	M	R	W	O	M	R	W
Wickramasinghe	14	2	55	2	7	0	21	0
Jayawardene	3	0	10	0				
Bandaratilleke	22	6	51	1	39	8	105	1
Muralitharan	38.2	9	90	5	36	5	137	4
Bandara	13	3	41	0	8	0	38	0
Kalpage	15	2	49	2	15	4	51	0
de Silva					2	0	14	0
Jayasuriya					16	0	63	1

NEW ZEALAND

Bowler	O	M	R	W	O	M	R	W
Doull	12.2	2	43	0	3	0	15	0
Cairns	15	0	59	3	19	6	64	1
Harris	7	1	27	0	4	1	16	0
Vettori	24	8	56	3	51	23	101	3
Wiseman	20	4	61	0	46.5	17	82	5
McMillan	12	4	31	1	6	4	12	1
Astle					2	0	2	0

Fall of Wickets

	SL	NZ	SL	NZ
	1st	1st	2nd	2nd
1st	25	6	11	70
2nd	97	21	68	89
3rd	141	101	160	194
4th	141	105	400	216
5th	188	206	404	216
6th	229	221	416	239
7th	269	237	-	277
8th	282	284	-	279
9th	296	284	-	289
10th	305	285	-	297

Right-arm off-spinner Paul Wiseman became the fourth New Zealand bowler to capture five or more wickets on his debut.

MILESTONES

- It was New Zealand's 39th test win and the first time they had won three successive tests.

- Stephen Fleming passed 2000 runs in his 35th test.

- Stephen Fleming and Craig McMillan added 240 for the fourth wicket, a New Zealand record against Sri Lanka.

- Paul Wiseman became the fourth New Zealand bowler to capture five or more wickets in an innings on debut. The others were Fen Cresswell, Alec Moir and Bruce Taylor.

261 SRI LANKA v NEW ZEALAND *(Second Test)*

at Galle International Stadium on 3, 4, 5, 6, 7 June, 1998
Toss : New Zealand. Umpires : D.L. Orchard and B.C. Cooray
Sri Lanka won by an innings and 16 runs

An old Dutch fort provided a stunning backdrop for the 79th test cricket venue in the world at Galle. It also became the seventh test venue in Sri Lanka. A great deal of money had been spent on upgrading the surroundings but little had been spent on the pitch and the outfield, which were less than acceptable. Seven hours of play was lost on the first two days owing to poor drainage and leaking covers.

From the outset the ball spun and left-arm finger-spinner Niroshan Bandaratilleke claimed his first wicket when he had Matthew Horne out when the score was only five. At the end of the shortened first day he had taken three wickets for 10 runs off 15 overs. In the 55 minutes available on the second day he bowled Craig McMillan for his fourth wicket.

On the third day off-spin bowler Kumar Dharmasena, whose action was questioned by the ICC, captured the remaining five wickets with his zippy deliveries to dismiss

New Zealand for 193. By stumps Sri Lanka were four runs ahead with seven wickets remaining thanks to a scintillating innings from 21-year-old Mahela Jayawardene who countered the turn and erratic bounce to be 88 not out.

The canny Sri Lankan captain, Arjuna Ranatunga, nursed Jayawardene through some difficult moments during their invaluable partnership of 76 for the fourth wicket.

Jayawardene reached his first test century in his fourth test. The milestone was greeted with gusto by the crowd. A policeman set off rockets and a hot-dog vending machine exploded, sending clouds of smoke across the pavilion.

Jayawardene took advantage of the short-of-a-length bowling by the visiting spinners which allowed him to cut and hook with safety to reach 167. The final stanza of Sri Lanka's total of 323 was marked by Chris Harris initiating three run outs off his own bowling.

New Zealand's task was to survive for more than four sessions to save the match but for the second time in the game they collapsed to the highly promising Bandaratilleke who had three of the five wickets that fell for 94 before stumps.

Apart from Adam Parore, who defended stoutly, the remaining five wickets fell in 43 minutes for only 20 runs at the start of the fifth day. This gave Sri Lanka victory by an innings and 16, with Bandaratilleke finishing with a match analysis of 9-83 off 62 overs.

Chris Cairns appeals unsuccessfully during the test at Galle. In the following test in Colombo he became the third New Zealander to achieve the double of 1000 runs and 100 wickets in test cricket.

NEW ZEALAND

B.A.Young	c Jayasuriya b Bandaratilleke	46	c Tillakaratne b Bandaratilleke	11
M.J.Horne	c Kaluwitharana b Bandaratilleke	1	lbw b Bandaratilleke	3
S.P.Fleming*	lbw b Dharmasena	14	lbw b Muralitharan	10
N.J.Astle	c Tillakaratne b Dharmasena	53	b de Silva	13
D.L.Vettori	c Tillakaratne b Bandaratilleke	0	(9) run out	0
C.D.McMillan	b Bandaratilleke	13	(5) c Jayasuriya b Bandaratilleke	1
A.C.Parore†	c Jayasuriya b Dharmasena	30	(6) not out	32
C.L.Cairns	c Jayasuriya b Dharmasena	0	(7) c Tillakaratne b Bandaratilleke	16
C.Z.Harris	c Wickramasinghe b Dharmasena	4	(8) c Jayawardene b Muralitharan	9
P.J.Wiseman	st Kaluwitharana b Dharmasena	23	c Tillakaratne b Bandaratilleke	2
S.B.O'Connor	not out	0	c Jayasuriya b Muralitharan	0
Extras	(lb 7, nb 2)	9	(b 7, lb 7, w 1, nb 2)	17
TOTAL	**(101.1 overs)**	**193**	**(55 overs)**	**114**

SRI LANKA

S.T.Jayasuriya	c Harris b Vettori	21
M.S.Atapattu	c Vettori b Wiseman	35
D.P.M.D.Jayawardene	lbw b Harris	167
P.A.de Silva	lbw b Vettori	10
A.Ranatunga*	c O'Connor b Vettori	36
H.P.Tillakaratne	b Wiseman	10
R.S.Kaluwitharana†	run out	3
H.D.P.K.Dharmasena	run out	12
G.P.Wickramasinghe	c Harris b Vettori	12
M.R.C.N.Bandaratilleke	run out	4
M.Muralitharan	not out	2
Extras	(lb 9, nb 2)	11
TOTAL	**(106.4 overs)**	**323**

Bowling	O	M	R	W	O	M	R	W		NZ 1st	SL 1st	NZ 2nd
SRI LANKA												
Wickramasinghe	7	1	20	0	2	0	6	0	1st	5	44	18
Dharmasena	24.1	4	72	6	6	0	16	0	2nd	21	106	21
Bandaratilleke	38	13	47	4	24	9	36	5	3rd	90	135	40
Muralitharan	23	9	33	0	16	7	24	3	4th	90	211	41
Jayasuriya	4	1	8	0					5th	110	262	69
de Silva	5	2	6	0	7	1	18	1	6th	137	271	94
NEW ZEALAND									7th	137	301	103
O'Connor	4	0	13	0					8th	147	315	106
Cairns	5	0	20	0					9th	190	319	109
Wiseman	30	3	95	2					10th	193	323	114
Vettori	26	4	88	4								
Harris	25.4	6	56	1								
McMillan	11	3	30	0								
Astle	5	3	12	0								

MILESTONES

- Galle International Stadium became the 79th test venue in the world.

- Adam Parore and Paul Wiseman established a new record ninth wicket partnership against Sri Lanka of 43.

- Kumar Dharmasena took 6-72, the best bowling figures for Sri Lanka in a test against New Zealand.

262 SRI LANKA v NEW ZEALAND *(Third Test)*

at Sinhalese Sports Club Ground, Colombo on 10, 11, 12, 13 June, 1998
Toss : Sri Lanka. Umpires : V.K. Ramaswamy and P. Manuel
Sri Lanka won by 164 runs

New Zealand included three slow bowlers in the team so it was ironic that Chris Cairns captured five wickets in Sri Lanka's first innings of 206. Sri Lanka were in danger of recording a dismal total when they lost their fifth wicket at 102 but valiant efforts by Hashan Tillakaratane, Romesh Kaluwitharana and Pramodya Wickramasinghe doubled Sri Lanka's score.

The visiting batsmen, with the exception of Stephen Fleming, who fought valiantly for over five hours and was last out for 78, were bemused and bereft of strokes and the day ended with New Zealand all out for 183 and conceding a first innings lead of 13.

With three days remaining the game was evenly poised, although the pitch was showing signs of deteriorating. New Zealand's hopes were buoyed when Daniel Vettori, opening the bowling, had three of the first four wickets to fall for 36 before Arjuna Ranatunga and Tillakaratane combined to add 102 for the fifth wicket.

Bowling with great subtlety and control Vettori bowled New Zealand back into the game, capturing another three wickets to reduce Sri Lanka to 211-9. In 60 desperate and exciting minutes Kaluwitharana and Muralitharan blazed forth with a mixture of some brilliant strokes and some audacious slogs to add an invaluable 71 for the last wicket, a record for Sri Lanka against any country.

New Zealand required 296 to win and started the fourth day with ten on the board and all 10 wickets remaining. The total had reached 44 before the third umpire adjudged Bryan Young stumped off Muralitharan. The last wicket was captured one hour after lunch.

The remaining nine wickets fell for 87 runs as Muralitharan and Bandaratilleke proved to be unplayable. The test series that had began so well ended in utter humiliation as Sri Lanka won by 164 runs and won the series 2-1.

MILESTONES

- It was the first time since March 1988 (test 172) that New Zealand had fielded three slow bowlers.

- Chris Cairns became the ninth New Zealand bowler to capture 100 test wickets. It was his 33rd test and it was the first time that a father and son had each taken 100 wickets in tests. Lance Cairns reached the mark against England in 1983/84 (test 155).

- Chris Cairns became the third New Zealand player, after Sir Richard Hadlee and John Bracewell, to record the test double of 1000 runs and 100 wickets.

- Daniel Vettori, aged 19, reached 50 wickets in his 14th test. His 6-64 was his best first-class analyis as well as the best by a New Zealander in a test against Sri Lanka.

- It was only the fifth time in test history that a team winning the first test in a three-test series had lost the series.

SRI LANKA

Batsman	Dismissal (1st)	R	Dismissal (2nd)	R
S.T.Jayasuriya	c Young b Cairns	13	c Parore b Cairns	8
M.S.Atapattu	c Vettori b Wiseman	48	lbw b Vettori	5
D.P.M.D.Jayawardene	c Parore b Cairns	16	c Horne b Vettori	11
P.A.de Silva	c Spearman b Cairns	4	c Astle b Vettori	3
A.Ranatunga*	run out	4	c Cairns b Priest	64
H.P.Tillakaratne	c Young b McMillan	43	b Vettori	40
R.S.Kaluwitharana†	b McMillan	28	lbw b Priest	88
H.D.P.K.Dharmasena	c Parore b Cairns	11	b McMillan	11
G.P.Wickramasinghe	not out	24	c Fleming b Vettori	0
M.R.C.N.Bandaratilleke	lbw b Vettori	5	c Fleming b Vettori	7
M.Muralitharan	c Astle b Cairns	1	not out	26
Extras	(b 1, lb 8)	9	(b 8, lb 10, nb 1)	19
TOTAL	(88.4 overs)	206	(84.5 overs)	282

NEW ZEALAND

Batsman	Dismissal (1st)	R	Dismissal (2nd)	R
B.A.Young	c Atapattu b Bandaratilleke	2	st Kaluwitharana b Muralitharan	24
C.M.Spearman	c de Silva b Wickramasinghe	4	c & b Muralitharan	22
S.P.Fleming*	b Wickramasinghe	78	lbw b Muralitharan	3
N.J.Astle	c Atapattu b Dharmasena	16	c & b Muralitharan	16
M.J.Horne	c Tillakaratne b de Silva	35	c Kaluwitharana b Bandaratilleke	12
C.D.McMillan	st Kaluwitharana b de Silva	2	c Jayawardene b Muralitharan	1
A.C.Parore†	lbw b de Silva	19	b Bandaratilleke	2
C.L.Cairns	run out	6	b Bandaratilleke	26
M.W.Priest	c sub (A.S.A.Perera) b Muralitharan	12	b Bandaratilleke	2
D.L.Vettori	c Jayasuriya b Muralitharan	0	b Muralitharan	3
P.J.Wiseman	not out	1	not out	0
Extras	(b 11, lb 2, nb 5)	18	(b 6, lb 10, nb 4)	20
TOTAL	(86.3 overs)	193	(54.3 overs)	131

Bowling	O	M	R	W	O	M	R	W
NEW ZEALAND								
Cairns	17.4	1	62	5	17	0	75	1
Vettori	25	7	52	1	33	10	64	6
Priest	24	11	35	0	11.5	0	42	2
Wiseman	10	4	21	1	6	2	29	0
McMillan	12	5	27	2	14	2	46	1
Astle					3	0	8	0
SRI LANKA								
Wickramasinghe	6.3	3	7	2	6	2	5	0
Bandaratilleke	20	6	48	1	17	3	52	4
Dharmasena	18	4	35	1	10	2	14	1
de Silva	18.5	7	30	3	3	0	14	0
Muralitharan	23.1	3	60	2	18.3	8	30	5

Fall of Wickets	SL 1st	NZ 1st	SL 2nd	NZ 2nd
1st	24	5	12	44
2nd	52	7	16	57
3rd	56	30	24	63
4th	70	94	36	82
5th	102	98	138	93
6th	156	128	140	93
7th	163	143	188	105
8th	196	181	193	128
9th	201	183	211	131
10th	206	193	282	131

Daniel Vettori achieved his best first-class bowling analysis of 6-64 in Sri Lanka's second innings of the third test. He also passed 50 test wickets in his 14th test.

AVERAGES

New Zealand

BATTING	M	I	NO	Runs	HS	Ave
S.P. Fleming	3	6	1	357	174*	71.40
A.C. Parore	3	6	1	151	67	30.20
N.J. Astle	3	6	0	162	53	27.00
C.D. McMillan	3	6	0	159	142	26.50
B.A. Young	3	6	0	124	46	20.66
M.J. Horne	3	6	0	101	35	16.83
C.Z. Harris	2	4	1	46	19	15.33
C.M. Spearman	1	2	0	26	22	13.00
C.L. Cairns	3	6	0	74	26	12.33
P.J. Wiseman	3	5	2	32	23	10.66
M.W. Priest	1	2	0	14	12	7.00
D.L. Vettori	3	5	0	23	20	4.60
S.B. O'Connor	1	2	1	0	0*	0.00
S.B. Doull	1	1	1	1	1*	-

BOWLING	O	M	R	W	Ave
D.L. Vettori	159	52	361	17	21.23
C.L. Cairns	73.4	7	280	10	28.00
P.J. Wiseman	112.5	30	288	10	28.80
C.D. McMillan	55	18	146	5	29.20
M.W. Priest	35.5	11	77	2	38.50
C.Z. Harris	36.4	8	99	1	99.00
S.B. O'Connor	4	0	13	0	-
N.J. Astle	10	3	22	0	-
S.B. Doull	15.2	2	58	0	-

Sri Lanka

BATTING	M	I	NO	Runs	HS	Ave
D.P.M.D.Jayawardene	3	5	0	300	167	60.00
R.S.Kaluwitharana	3	5	0	230	88	46.00
A.Ranatunga	3	5	0	162	64	32.40
H.P.Tillakaratne	2	3	0	93	43	31.00
P.A.de Silva	3	5	0	125	71	25.00
S.T.Jayasuriya	3	5	0	111	59	22.20
M.S.Atapattu	3	5	0	104	48	20.80
M.Muralitharan	3	5	3	38	26*	19.00
G.P.Wickramasinghe	3	5	1	63	27	15.75
H.D.P.K.Dharmasena	2	3	0	34	12	11.33
R.S.Kalpage	1	2	0	22	16	11.00
M.R.C.N.Bandaratilleke	3	5	0	52	20	10.40
C.M.Bandara	1	2	1	0	0*	0.00

BOWLING	O	M	R	W	Ave
H.D.P.K.Dharmasena	58.1	10	137	8	17.12
M.Muralitharan	155	41	374	19	19.68
P.A.de Silva	35.5	10	82	4	20.50
M.R.C.N.Bandaratilleke	160	45	339	16	21.18
G.P.Wickramasinghe	42.3	8	114	4	28.50
R.S.Kalpage	30	6	100	2	50.00
S.T.Jayasuriya	20	1	71	1	71.00
D.P.M.D.Jayawardene	3	0	10	0	-
C.M.Bandara	21	3	79	0	-

1998/99 India in New Zealand

■ NEW ZEALAND v INDIA *(First Test)*

at Carisbrook, Dunedin on 18, 19, 20, 21, 22 December, 1998
Toss : India. Umpires : E.A. Nicholls and R.S. Dunne
Abandoned without a ball being bowled

Persistent rain saw the first test abandoned without a ball being bowled. It was the second time that Steve Dunne had been scheduled to umpire a test on his home ground and the second time that the game had been washed out. The previous occasion was in 1988/89 when Pakistan toured New Zealand.

263 NEW ZEALAND v INDIA *(Second Test)*

at Basin Reserve, Wellington on 26, 27, 28, 29, 30 December, 1998
Toss : India. Umpires : E.A. Nicholls and E.A. Watkin
New Zealand won by 4 wickets

The Basin Reserve was the venue for the second test, the first to be played in New Zealand on Boxing Day. It was called the Pohutukawa Boxing Day test as 38 of the 54 Pohutukawa trees encircling the ground were covered in scarlet flowers.

Simon Doull opened with one of the best spells in New Zealand test history and by the 11th over of the game he had captured four wickets and India were only 16. It required innings of the highest order from Mohammad Azharuddin and Sachin Tendulkar to take India to 99 before Doull struck again to claim another three wickets.

On the first day of the Pohutukawa Boxing Day test against India Simon Doull had one of the greatest opening spells of medium-fast, swing-seam bowling taking 7-65, including four wickets in his first six overs.

Azharuddin reached his 21st test century, making 103 of India's 208. Doull took 7-65, bowling a rigid line of wicket-to-wicket and swinging and seaming the ball both ways.

Steady batting by New Zealand's top order saw them reach 208 when Nathan Astle was the seventh wicket to fall. Determined batting by Dion Nash and Daniel Vettori added 137 in two minutes short of four hours and swung the game back in New Zealand's favour.

In India's second innings Tendulkar reached a hundred off 123 balls, as fine a century to have been scored in the 125-year history of first-class cricket at the ground.

Needing 212 New Zealand were 74-5 with Astle retired hurt with a broken bone in his left hand after being struck by a ball from Javagal Srinath. Craig McMillan and Chris Cairns added 137 in even time to bring a memorable, wildly fluctuating test to an end with victory for the home side.

INDIA

N.S.Sidhu	c Fleming b Doull	0	(2) lbw b Doull	34
A.Jadeja	lbw b Doull	10	(1) b Nash	22
R.S.Dravid	lbw b Doull	0	b Wiseman	28
S.C.Ganguly	c Parore b Doull	5	c Bell b Wiseman	48
S.R.Tendulkar	c Bell b Doull	47	c Fleming b Nash	113
M.Azharuddin*	not out	103	c Parore b Nash	48
N.R.Mongia†	c Astle b Doull	0	c Fleming b Doull	2
A.R.Kumble	c McMillan b Doull	11	c Nash b Vettori	23
J.Srinath	c Fleming b Nash	7	not out	27
B.K.V.Prasad	c Fleming b Vettori	15	c & b Astle	0
Harbhajan Singh	c Astle b McMillan	1	c Horne b McMillan	1
Extras	(lb 3, nb 6)	9	(b 3, lb 1, w 1, nb 5)	10
TOTAL	**(65.4 overs)**	**208**	**(115 overs)**	**356**

NEW ZEALAND

M.D.Bell	c Mongia b Prasad	4	c Dravid b Srinath	0
M.J.Horne	b Kumble	38	lbw b Kumble	31
S.P.Fleming*	run out	42	b Kumble	17
N.J.Astle	b Kumble	56	retired hurt	1
C.D.McMillan	c Dravid b Srinath	24	not out	74
A.C.Parore†	lbw b Kumble	2	run out	1
C.L.Cairns	c Tendulkar b Prasad	3	(8) c Jadeja b Srinath	61
D.J.Nash	not out	89	(9) not out	4
D.L.Vettori	b Tendulkar	57		
P.J.Wiseman	b Tendulkar	0	(7) lbw b Srinath	0
S.B.Doull	lbw b Kumble	0		
Extras	(b 13, lb 19, nb 5)	37	(b 9, lb 9, nb 8)	26
TOTAL	**(148.4 overs)**	**352**	**(60.3 overs) (6 wkts)**	**215**

Bowling	O	M	R	W	O	M	R	W
NEW ZEALAND								
Doull	24	7	65	7	25	10	49	2
Cairns	17	3	69	0	19	2	68	0
Nash	14	1	46	1	15	9	20	3
Vettori	7	0	20	1	20	6	92	1
Astle	2	0	5	0	7	3	7	1
McMillan	1.4	1	0	1	10	2	26	1
Wiseman					19	1	90	2
INDIA								
Srinath	36	6	89	1	19.3	1	82	3
Prasad	30	8	67	2	10	3	26	0
Kumble	45.4	17	83	4	23	6	70	2
Harbhajan Singh	25	6	61	0	5	1	11	0
Ganguly	6	0	13	0				
Tendulkar	6	2	7	2	3	0	8	0

Fall of Wickets	I	NZ	I	NZ
	1st	1st	2nd	2nd
1st	0	7	41	0
2nd	2	79	74	42
3rd	15	112	112	51
4th	16	162	200	67
5th	99	172	297	74
6th	99	179	304	211
7th	132	208	304	-
8th	149	345	346	-
9th	207	349	349	-
10th	208	352	356	-

MILESTONES

- Matthew Bell (206) made his test debut.

- It was New Zealand's 40th test win and their eighth at the Basin Reserve.

- Dion Nash and Daniel Vettori had an eighth wicket record stand of 137 for New Zealand against all countries.

264 NEW ZEALAND v INDIA *(Third Test)*

at WestpacTrust Park, Hamilton on 2, 3, 4, 5, 6 January, 1999
Toss : India. Umpires : R.E. Koertzen and D.B. Cowie
Match drawn

Mohammad Azharuddin's decision to field first was handsomely rewarded when Javagal Srinath captured two wickets in his first over. Roger Twose, who was dropped at third slip when on 7, then batted until the penultimate over, making 87. He shared two substantial partnerships, first 95 with Matthew Horne and then 160 with Craig McMillan. This led to New Zealand amassing a respectable total of 366 just after lunch on the second day.

The next day and a half were dominated by the flawless technique of Rahul Dravid. He was, initially, a keen observer in a partnership of 109 that was dominated by the superlative stroke play of Sachin Tendulkar, who again toyed with the bowlers in making 67, which included 46 runs in boundaries.

India was still trailing by 155 when Srinath joined Dravid early on the third day. Fortune favoured the boisterous Srinath who was dropped three times and missed being run out. He and the polished Dravid added 144, with both Dravid (190) and Srinath (76) making their best test scores to date and providing India with a first innings lead of 50.

India captured four quick wickets, two to the deceptive leg-spin of Tendulkar, with New Zealand's lead only 35. For the fourth successive innings McMillan's belligerence led a recovery. Together with Adam Parore a record-breaking 140

was added in even time. This eased the way for Chris Cairns, Dion Nash and Daniel Vettori to more than double the score of 225-6 for the next two wickets.

Cairns began cautiously before unleashing a series of massive front foot drives and thundering pulls as he scored his second test century. Nash and Vettori batted sensibly, as they had in every innings of the series, and provided Cairns with ideal partners who rotated the strike back to him.

Fleming delayed his declaration as three of his main bowlers, Nash, Vettori and Doull were incapacitated. With no chance of victory Dravid and Sourav Ganguly were untroubled and each was able to reach a century before stumps were drawn.

NEW ZEALAND				
M.D.Bell	c Mongia b Srinath	0	lbw b Tendulkar	25
M.J.Horne	b Srinath	63	c Mongia b Srinath	26
S.P.Fleming*	c Dravid b Srinath	0	b Prasad	18
R.G.Twose	c Mongia b Prasad	87	lbw b Tendulkar	4
C.D.McMillan	c Prasad b Kumble	92	c Mongia b Singh	84
A.C.Parore†	c sub b Prasad	21	c Singh b Kumble	50
P.J.Wiseman	c Ganguly b Singh	13		
C.L.Cairns	b Singh	2	(7) c Dravid b Kumble	126
D.J.Nash	not out	18	(8) run out	63
D.L.Vettori	b Srinath	24	(9) not out	43
S.B.Doull	c Kumble b Srinath	6		
Extras	(b 5, lb 19, w 2, nb 14)	40	(b 9, lb 7, w 1, nb 8)	25
TOTAL	**(121.2 overs)**	**366**	**(137.5 overs) (8 wkts dec)**	**464**

INDIA				
N.S.Sidhu	c Parore b Cairns	1	(2) b Cairns	13
A.Jadeja	c Nash b Doull	12	(1) c Parore b Cairns	21
R.S.Dravid	c McMillan b Cairns	190	not out	103
S.R.Tendulkar	lbw b Nash	67		
S.C.Ganguly	c Fleming b Doull	11	(4) not out	101
M.Azharuddin*	c Fleming b Cairns	4		
N.R.Mongia†	c Horne b Nash	7		
A.R.Kumble	c Parore b Doull	0		
J.Srinath	c Twose b Wiseman	76		
B.K.V.Prasad	not out	30		
R.Singh	c Fleming b Cairns	0		
Extras	(b 2, lb 4, w 8, nb 4)	18	(lb 9, nb 2)	11
TOTAL	**(128.3 overs)**	**416**	**(52.1 overs) (2 wkts)**	**249**

Bowling	O	M	R	W	O	M	R	W
INDIA								
Srinath	32.2	10	95	5	27	6	90	1
Prasad	33	10	61	2	33	8	75	1
Kumble	27	7	64	1	45.5	13	124	2
Singh	21	5	74	2	19	3	102	1
Ganguly	5	3	25	0	6	1	27	0
Tendulkar	3	0	23	0	7	0	30	2
NEW ZEALAND								
Doull	36	15	64	3	4	0	17	0
Cairns	22.3	3	107	4	9	1	30	2
Nash	37	11	98	2				
Vettori	16	3	71	0				
McMillan	4	0	24	0	17	4	59	0
Wiseman	13	2	46	1	12	0	80	0
Twose					9.1	0	50	0
Horne					1	0	4	0

Fall of Wickets	NZ	I	NZ	I
	1st	1st	2nd	2nd
1st	0	17	46	33
2nd	0	17	69	55
3rd	95	126	76	-
4th	255	164	85	-
5th	278	195	225	-
6th	311	204	225	-
7th	314	211	372	-
8th	315	355	464	-
9th	356	416	-	-
10th	366	416	-	-

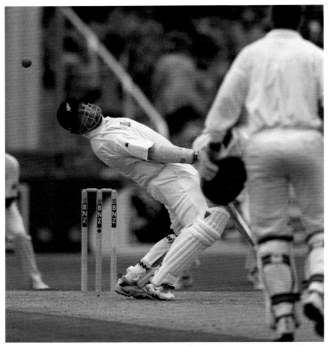

Roger Twose came to the crease at 0-2. He immediately avoided a bouncer from Javagal Srinath and continued to defy the Indian attack until the penultimate over of the day.

MILESTONES

- Roger Twose and Craig McMillan created a new fourth wicket record of 160 for New Zealand against India.

- Craig McMillan and Adam Parore created a new fifth wicket record of 140 for New Zealand against India.

- Rahul Dravid became the third Indian batsman to score a century in each innings of a test. The previous two were Sunil Gavaskar, who achieved the feat three times, and Vijay Hazare.

- It was New Zealand's third successive test series win.

1998/99 South Africa in New Zealand

Stephen Fleming suffered a groin injury in the first one-day international against India which ruled him out of playing in the three tests against South Africa. Dion Nash took his place as captain. A fungal disease ruined the cricket block at Eden Park so the ground staff dampened the strip and then rolled it with a heavy roller. A copious quantity of PVA glue was applied, with grass cuttings rolled into it, to give the appearance of a test pitch.

265 NEW ZEALAND v SOUTH AFRICA *(First Test)*

at Eden Park, Auckland on 27, 28 February, 1, 2, 3 March, 1999
Toss : New Zealand. Umpires : D.J. Harper and D.B. Cowie
Match drawn

No one had any idea of how the surface would play and Nash, on winning the toss, asked the visitors to bat. When they declared after 792 minutes, prior to lunch on the third day, South Africa had scored 621 and had lost only five wickets. The glue had reduced all the bowlers to the ranks of a gentle bowling machine and numerous batting records were created.

Gary Kirsten, a patient left-hand opener, was the first to appreciate the advantage that the batsmen had over their opponents, the bowlers. He finished the first day 109 not out.

Together with Daryll Cullinan, who was 89 not out, they had added 148.

They extended their partnership to 183 before Kirsten departed with the score 280-3. Cullinan, who five years earlier had shown his ability to bat long innings when he scored 337 not out for Transvaal against Northern Transvaal, continued to amass runs, though his scoring rate got slower as his innings progressed. He made 275 in two minutes short of 11 hours.

None of the New Zealand batsmen took full advantage of the batting-friendly pitch, which was best illustrated by the fact that New Zealand's last batsman, Geoff Allott, batted 101 minutes before he was dismissed for 0. New Zealand was untroubled to bat through the fifth day to draw the match with Twose, Horne and Astle each hitting half-centuries.

SOUTH AFRICA				
G.Kirsten	c Astle b Allott	128		
H.H.Gibbs	b Vettori	34		
J.H.Kallis	lbw b Doull	7		
D.J.Cullinan	not out	275		
W.J.Cronje*	c Allott b Harris	30		
J.N.Rhodes	c Twose b Harris	63		
S.M.Pollock	not out	69		
M.V.Boucher†				
L.Klusener				
A.A.Donald				
P.R.Adams				
Extras	(b 6, lb 7, nb 2)	15		
TOTAL	(200.1 overs) (5 wkts dec)	**621**		
NEW ZEALAND				
R.G.Twose	c Boucher b Donald	31	(3) c Cullinan b Klusener	65
M.J.Horne	b Adams	93	(1) b Adams	60
N.J.Astle	c Boucher b Donald	41	(4) not out	69
C.D.McMillan	c Boucher b Cronje	25	(5) not out	22
C.Z.Harris	not out	68		
A.C.Parore†	b Pollock	9		
M.D.Bell	b Klusener	6	(2) c Donald b Pollock	6
D.J.Nash*	c Boucher b Klusener	1		
D.L.Vettori	c Cronje b Adams	32		
S.B.Doull	c Gibbs b Adams	17		
G.I.Allott	c Pollock b Kallis	0		
Extras	(lb 21, w 2, nb 6)	29	(b 13, lb 2, w 2, nb 5)	22
TOTAL	(160.4 overs)	**352**	(84 overs) (3 wkts)	**244**

Bowling	O	M	R	W	O	M	R	W	Fall of Wickets				
NEW ZEALAND										SA	NZ	SA	NZ
										1st	1st	2nd	2nd
Doull	33	7	90	1					1st	76	80	15	-
Allott	38	5	153	1					2nd	97	170	104	-
Nash	28	2	97	0					3rd	280	210	193	-
Vettori	42	8	120	1					4th	354	210	-	-
Harris	45	10	94	2					5th	495	224	-	-
McMillan	5.1	0	24	0					6th	-	242	-	-
Astle	9	1	30	0					7th	-	251	-	-
SOUTH AFRICA									8th	-	294	-	-
Donald	27	16	40	2	9	2	20	0	9th	-	320	-	-
Pollock	28	11	51	1	13	5	21	1	10th	-	352	-	-
Klusener	27	8	60	2	13	6	26	1					
Adams	46	18	103	3	30	11	96	1					
Kallis	21.4	10	44	1	13	0	61	0					
Cullinan	2	1	8	0									
Cronje	9	2	25	1	6	4	5	0					

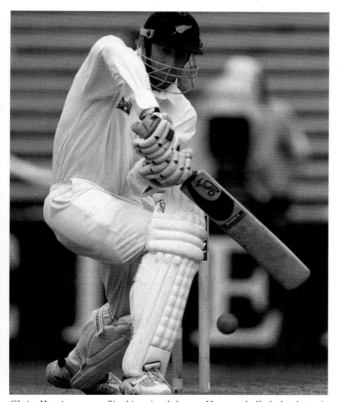

Chris Harris was unflinching in defence. He marshalled the last six wickets to deny the visiting bowlers for almost six hours.

MILESTONES

- Dion Nash became New Zealand's 25th captain.

- Daryl Cullinan's 275 not out was a South African test record score, beating Graeme Pollock's 274 against Australia at Durban in 1969/70.

- Gary Kirsten and Cullinan set a South African record of 183 for the third wicket against New Zealand.

- Cullinan and Jonty Rhodes set a South African record of 141 for the fifth wicket against New Zealand.

- Cullinan and Shaun Pollock set a South African record of 126 for the sixth wicket against New Zealand.

- Matthew Horne and Nathan Astle put on 90, a record for New Zealand's second wicket against South Africa.

- Geoff Allott broke John Wright's New Zealand record of 66 minutes without scoring, made in 1981/82 against Australia (test 146). He also broke Godfrey Evans' (England) world record of 97 minutes without scoring. Allott extended the record to 101 minutes.

266 NEW ZEALAND v SOUTH AFRICA (Second Test)

at Jade Stadium, Christchurch on 11, 12, 13, 14, 15 March, 1999
Toss : New Zealand. Umpires : K.T. Francis and D.M. Quested
Match drawn

The commercial reality of modern sport was highly visible as the venue that had been Lancaster Park for 117 years was now Jade Stadium. Lancaster Park had been the venue for 35 tests, of which New Zealand had won 7, lost 14 and drawn 14.

Dion Nash learnt from his lesson in the first test and opted to bat first on a good-looking natural pitch that had a tinge of green. Unfortunately, the New Zealand batsmen played in an exuberant manner and lost wickets more to batsmen's errors than to bowlers' skills.

From lunch, when they were 104 for three, they capitulated, losing their last seven wickets for 56. Allan Donald captured three wickets before leaving the field with a groin injury, while his bowling partner, Shaun Pollock, captured four.

New Zealand's total of 168 was disappointing, particularly as Gary Kirsten and Herschelle Gibbs were untroubled to take South Africa to 54 without loss at stumps.

Before this test Gibbs, a "coloured" player, had played 12 tests for a top score of 54. There was still a row in South Africa over "players of colour" being given a test position. Some critics opposed to Gibbs' selection argued that it reeked of tokenism. No doubt those in favour of Gibbs were delighted when he was 101 not out at stumps.

With Kirsten and Jacques Kallis scoring half-centuries South Africa were totally in charge at 229-1. Rain reduced the third day's play to just half an hour while the fourth day was also rain affected. When Hansie Cronje declared at the start of the fifth day Gibbs was 211 not out and Kallis 148. South Africa declared at 442 for the loss of one wicket. The unbroken partnership of 315 was the third-highest in all tests for South Africa.

There was time for only 54 overs on the final day and without Donald, and with the pitch playing perfectly, Bryan Young and Matthew Horne gave New Zealand their first century partnership for three years as they both batted comfortably.

Matt Horne (pictured) and Bryan Young shared an opening partnership of 107 in the second innings.

MILESTONES

- Gary Stead (207) made his test debut.

- Herschelle Gibbs and Jacques Kallis added 315 unbroken for the second wicket. It was a record for any wicket between New Zealand and South Africa and the third-highest for South Africa in all tests.

NEW ZEALAND

Batsman	Dismissal	Runs	2nd innings	Runs
M.J.Horne	c Kirsten b Kallis	36	(2) run out	56
B.A.Young	b Donald	5	(1) not out	55
R.G.Twose	c Cullinan b Pollock	0	not out	6
N.J.Astle	c Klusener b Donald	44		
G.R.Stead	c Boucher b Donald	27		
C.Z.Harris	c Adams b Pollock	0		
A.C.Parore†	c sub (D.M.Benkenstein) b Pollock	14		
D.J.Nash*	lbw b Adams	14		
D.L.Vettori	lbw b Adams	18		
S.B.Doull	c Boucher b Pollock	0		
G.I.Allott	not out	1		
Extras	(lb 4, nb 5)	9	(lb 5, nb 5)	10
TOTAL	(63.4 overs)	168	(54 overs) (1 wkt)	127

SOUTH AFRICA

Batsman	Dismissal	Runs
G.Kirsten	c Astle b Vettori	65
H.H.Gibbs	not out	211
J.H.Kallis	not out	148
D.J.Cullinan		
W.J.Cronje*		
J.N.Rhodes		
S.M.Pollock		
M.V.Boucher†		
L.Klusener		
P.R.Adams		
A.A.Donald		
Extras	(lb 12, nb 6)	18
TOTAL	(162 overs) (1 wkt dec)	442

Bowling	O	M	R	W	O	M	R	W	Fall of Wickets	NZ 1st	SA 1st	NZ 2nd
SOUTH AFRICA												
Donald	17.5	4	54	3								
Pollock	17	5	34	4	12	4	23	0	1st	13	127	107
Klusener	12	3	37	0	17	4	33	0	2nd	18	-	-
Kallis	5	1	21	1	6	2	13	0	3rd	60	-	-
Cronje	6.1	4	9	0	4	3	1	0	4th	112	-	-
Adams	5.4	2	9	2	15	0	52	0	5th	115	-	-
NEW ZEALAND									6th	115	-	-
Doull	25.5	9	48	0					7th	138	-	-
Allott	43	11	109	0					8th	157	-	-
Nash	22	5	46	0					9th	157	-	-
Astle	18.1	2	76	0					10th	168	-	-
Vettori	24	6	73	1								
Stead	1	0	1	0								
Harris	28	9	77	0								

267 NEW ZEALAND v SOUTH AFRICA *(Third Test)*

at Basin Reserve, Wellington on 18, 19, 20, 21, 22 March, 1999
Toss : New Zealand. Umpires : S. Venkataraghavan and R.S. Dunne
South Africa won by 8 wickets

For the only time in the three-match series the pitch was ideal for both batsmen and bowlers and the game was blessed with five sublime summer days. Dion Nash won the toss for the third time.

New Zealand recovered from losing four early wickets for 54 as Gary Stead and Chris Harris battled the constant fast-medium barrage. They survived their strenuous ordeal until almost stumps when Stephen Elworthy ended Stead's first test half-century and then disposed of the nightwatchman, Daniel Vettori, to take four wickets for the day. New Zealand were 211-6 at the close.

Shaun Pollock wiped out the remaining batsmen, claiming four wickets for four runs at the beginning of the second day and giving him five wickets on the ground where his father, Peter, had taken 6-47 in a test against New Zealand in 1963/64. New Zealand's last six wickets fell for 16 runs.

Gary Kirsten and Herschelle Gibbs had their worst start in the series, opening with 73. Gibbs played with more freedom in scoring his second successive century while Daryll Cullinan

continued to feast on the New Zealand bowlers. When he was caught and bowled by Nathan Astle on the third day, for 152, it was the first time that he had been dismissed while scoring 427 runs.

Hansie Cronje and Pollock reinforced South Africa's stranglehold on the game and provided bright interludes to extend South Africa's lead to 276. Vettori's stamina was again tested as he bowled 54 overs. His patience and excellent control were rewarded with four wickets.

Allan Donald's replacement, the tall, lean, right-arm medium-pacer Elworthy, aged 34, proved to be a more than adequate substitute as, for the second time in the game, he claimed four wickets. A quality of his bowling was reflected by the fact that seven of his wickets were top order batsmen. The pressure that he exerted by short-pitched, accurate bowling, allied with occasional sharp seam movement, in partnership with Pollock, unsettled the New Zealand batsmen.

Astle was dropped four times before he was 28 and only the defiance of Harris and Stead, for the second time in the game, as well as a rumbustious 38 from Simon Doull took play through to the fifth day.

The New Zealand public was amazed to witness the left-arm slow bowling of Paul Adams, who bowled Chinamen with an action that was aptly described as being "like a frog in a blender". Some of his deliveries completely bamboozled the lower order batting as he finished with 4-63.

NEW ZEALAND

Batsman	Dismissal	Runs	2nd innings	Runs
M.J.Horne	c Cullinan b Pollock	2	(2) lbw b Elworthy	27
B.A.Young	c Rhodes b Kallis	18	(1) c Boucher b Pollock	2
R.G.Twose	c Boucher b Elworthy	12	c Pollock b Elworthy	5
N.J.Astle	b Elworthy	20	b Elworthy	62
G.R.Stead	c Pollock b Elworthy	68	lbw b Elworthy	33
C.Z.Harris	c Rhodes b Pollock	68	b Adams	41
D.L.Vettori	c Kallis b Elworthy	4	(9) b Pollock	16
A.C.Parore†	c Cullinan b Pollock	5	(7) c Rhodes b Adams	19
D.J.Nash*	c Adams b Pollock	2	(8) c Boucher b Adams	27
S.B.Doull	c Boucher b Pollock	0	not out	38
S.B.O'Connor	not out	2	c Rhodes b Adams	2
Extras	(lb 18, nb 3)	21	(b 9, lb 7, nb 3)	19
TOTAL	(102.3 overs)	222	(105.3 overs)	291

SOUTH AFRICA

Batsman	Dismissal	Runs	2nd innings	Runs
G.Kirsten	b O'Connor	40	not out	12
H.H.Gibbs	c O'Connor b Vettori	120	run out	0
J.H.Kallis	c Horne b Nash	17	b Vettori	4
D.J.Cullinan	c & b Astle	152	not out	0
W.J.Cronje*	c Nash b Vettori	72		
J.N.Rhodes	c Young b Vettori	3		
S.M.Pollock	not out	43		
M.V.Boucher†	b Vettori	8		
L.Klusener	c Parore b Nash	19		
S.Elworthy	not out	3		
P.R.Adams				
Extras	(b 10, lb 6, nb 5)	21		0
TOTAL	(165 overs) (8 wkts dec)	498	(8.1 overs) (2 wkts)	16

Bowling	O	M	R	W	O	M	R	W	Fall of Wickets	NZ 1st	SA 1st	NZ 2nd	SA 2nd
SOUTH AFRICA													
Pollock	28.3	14	33	5	25	8	54	2	1st	7	73	8	6
Elworthy	27	10	66	4	28	5	93	4	2nd	32	105	35	14
Kallis	20	5	44	1	19	7	50	0	3rd	57	258	35	-
Klusener	15	7	33	0	11	7	15	0	4th	58	403	100	-
Adams	7	2	12	0	22.3	6	63	4	5th	203	415	152	-
Cronje	5	3	16	0					6th	207	420	196	-
NEW ZEALAND									7th	218	440	199	-
Doull	24	4	77	0					8th	219	489	233	-
O'Connor	24	4	89	1	4.1	0	9	0	9th	219	-	281	-
Nash	25	7	76	2					10th	222	-	291	-
Vettori	54	16	153	4	4	0	7	1					
Harris	22	0	66	0									
Astle	16	8	21	1									

MILESTONES

- Herschelle Gibbs and Daryll Cullinan put on 153, a South African third wicket record against New Zealand.

- Daryll Cullinan and Hansie Cronje put on 145, equalling the South African fourth wicket record against New Zealand.

A resolute 68 by Gary Stead against an aggressive South African attack was the dominant feature of the first day's play.

AVERAGES

New Zealand

BATTING	M	I	NO	Runs	HS	Ave
C.Z. Harris	3	4	1	177	68*	59.00
N.J. Astle	3	5	1	236	69*	59.00
C.D. McMillan	1	2	1	47	25	47.00
M.J. Horne	3	6	0	274	93	45.66
G.R. Stead	2	3	0	128	68	42.66
B.A. Young	2	4	1	80	55*	26.66
R.G. Twose	3	6	1	119	65	23.80
S.B. Doull	3	4	1	55	38*	18.33
D.L. Vettori	3	4	0	70	32	17.50
A.C. Parore	3	4	0	47	19	11.75
D.J. Nash	3	4	0	44	27	11.00
M.D. Bell	1	2	0	12	6	6.00
S.B. O'Connor	1	2	1	4	2*	4.00
G.I. Allott	2	2	1	1	1*	1.00

BOWLING	O	M	R	W	Ave
D.L. Vettori	124	30	353	7	50.42
S.B. O'Connor	28.1	4	98	1	98.00
D.J. Nash	75	14	219	2	109.50
C.Z. Harris	95	19	237	2	118.50
N.J. Astle	43.1	11	127	1	127.00
S.B. Doull	82.5	20	215	1	215.00
G.I. Allott	81	16	262	1	262.00
G.R. Stead	1	0	1	0	-
C.D. McMillan	5.1	0	24	0	-

South Africa

BATTING	M	I	NO	Runs	HS	Ave
D.J. Cullinan	3	3	2	427	275*	427.00
H.H. Gibbs	3	4	1	365	211*	121.66
G. Kirsten	3	4	1	245	128	81.66
J.H. Kallis	3	4	1	176	148*	58.66
W.J. Cronje	3	2	0	102	72	51.00
J.N. Rhodes	3	2	0	66	63	33.00
L. Klusener	3	1	0	19	19	19.00
M.V. Boucher	3	1	0	8	8	8.00
S.M. Pollock	3	2	2	112	69*	-
S. Elworthy	1	1	1	3	3*	-
A.A. Donald	2	-	-	-	-	-
P.R. Adams	3	-	-	-	-	-

BOWLING	O	M	R	W	Ave
S.M. Pollock	123.3	47	216	13	16.61
S. Elworthy	55	15	159	8	19.87
A.A. Donald	53.5	22	114	5	22.80
P.R. Adams	126.1	39	335	10	33.50
W.J. Cronje	30.1	16	56	1	56.00
L. Klusener	95	35	204	3	68.00
J.H. Kallis	84.4	25	233	3	77.66
D.J. Cullinan	2	1	8	0	-

1999 New Zealand in England

New Zealand reached the semi-final of the World Cup for the fourth time in the seventh tournament played in England over May and June 1999.

268 ENGLAND v NEW ZEALAND *(First Test)*

at Edgbaston, Birmingham on 1, 2, 3 July. 1999
Toss : New Zealand. Umpires : S.A. Bucknor and P. Willey
England won by 7 wickets

Dramatic reversals became a feature of this test, which was completed in 2½ days. Under grey skies there was a generous amount of lateral movement and with the batsmen intent on playing attacking shots that bordered on the reckless, New Zealand were dismissed for 226 at the end of the first day. Their plight would have been more severe had Adam Parore and Dion Nash not added 85 for the seventh wicket.

The second day was extremely sultry. After England lost Alec Stewart to the third ball of the day Mark Butcher and Nasser Hussain, England's two in-form batsmen, looked to have weathered the storm before Butcher was run out, which triggered a horrendous collapse that saw England 45-7 at lunch.

If Stephen Fleming had held a catch in the slips off Andy Caddick it would have been worse. Caddick and Alex Tudor attacked judiciously and between them had 13 boundaries to take England to 126, conceding New Zealand a lead of 100.

New Zealand-born Caddick, who had been out of the England test team for 15 months, had a point to prove, not only to the England selectors, but also to his old team-mates from Canterbury, New Zealand. Moving the ball prodigiously he personally accounted for five wickets as New Zealand out-collapsed England to be 52-8.

Fleming, having batted tenaciously through the carnage, now found a strong ally in Simon Doull and they doubled the total, mainly by Doull reaching his highest test score of 46. The third ball in England's quest for 208 again proved fatal to Stewart and England sent in Tudor as a night watchman on a day when 21 wickets had fallen for 236 runs.

The third day began in sunshine with a breeze and no hint of swing. England approached their task positively and from the first seven overs from Geoff Allott and Doull 45 runs were plundered. None of the New Zealand bowlers could find the correct line or length and, led by Tudor who was 99 not out at the end, England won by seven wickets.

Going from the perilous position of 45-7 in their first innings to winning the test by seven wickets was England's most spectacular recovery in 112 years. In 1886/87 England was dismissed by Australia in Sydney for 45. A second innings recovery set the Australians 110 to win, but England prevailed by 13 runs.

NEW ZEALAND

R.G.Twose	c Thorpe b Mullally	0	lbw b Caddick	0
M.J.Horne	lbw b Caddick	12	c Read b Mullally	1
S.P.Fleming*	c Thorpe b Tudor	27	c Read b Tufnell	25
N.J.Astle	c Read b Butcher	26	c Read b Mullally	9
C.D.McMillan	c Thorpe b Caddick	18	c Butcher b Mullally	15
C.L.Cairns	c & b Caddick	17	c Read b Caddick	3
A.C.Parore†	c Read b Mullally	73	c Stewart b Caddick	0
D.J.Nash	c Hussain b Tufnell	21	c Read b Caddick	0
D.L.Vettori	c Hussain b Tufnell	1	b Caddick	0
S.B.Doull	c Butcher b Tufnell	11	st Read b Tufnell	46
G.I.Allott	not out	7	not out	0
Extras	(b 1, lb 5, w 1, nb 6)	13	(b 1, lb 4, w 1, nb 2)	8
TOTAL	**(88.4 overs)**	**226**	**(37.1 overs)**	**107**

ENGLAND

M.A.Butcher	run out	11	c Parore b Nash	33
A.J.Stewart	lbw b Allott	1	b Allott	0
N.Hussain*	b Doull	10	(4) b Allott	44
G.P.Thorpe	c Astle b Allott	6	(5) not out	21
M.R.Ramprakash	c Parore b Cairns	0		
A.Habib	b Cairns	1		
C.M.W.Read†	c sub (C.Z.Harris) b Nash	1		
A.R.Caddick	c Parore b Nash	33		
A.J.Tudor	not out	32	(3) not out	99
A.D.Mullally	c Parore b Nash	0		
P.C.R.Tufnell	c Fleming b Cairns	6		
Extras	(b 8, lb 11, nb 6)	25	(b 7, lb 2, nb 5)	14
TOTAL	**(46.4 overs)**	**126**	**(43.4 overs) (3 wkts)**	**211**

Bowling	O	M	R	W	O	M	R	W
ENGLAND								
Mullally	26.4	5	72	2	16	3	48	3
Caddick	27	12	57	3	14	3	32	5
Tudor	11	2	44	1	5	2	15	0
Butcher	7	2	25	1				
Tufnell	17	9	22	3	2.1	0	7	2
NEW ZEALAND								
Allott	14	3	38	2	15	0	71	2
Doull	12	6	17	1	7	0	48	0
Cairns	9.4	3	35	3	4	0	18	0
Nash	11	6	17	3	7	0	29	1
Vettori					6	1	22	0
Astle					1	1	0	0
McMillan					3.4	0	14	0

Fall of Wickets	NZ	E	NZ	E
	1st	*1st*	*2nd*	*2nd*
1st	0	5	0	3
2nd	19	26	5	76
3rd	55	28	17	174
4th	73	33	39	-
5th	103	38	46	-
6th	104	40	46	-
7th	189	45	52	-
8th	191	115	52	-
9th	211	115	106	-
10th	226	126	107	-

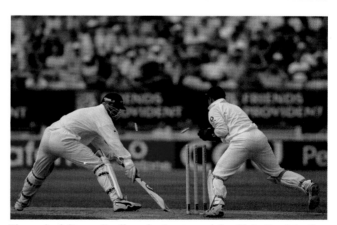

The end of Simon Doull as he is stumped by Chris Read in New Zealand's second innings.

MILESTONES

- It was Nasser Hussain's first test as England's captain.

- Chris Read, aged 20, became England's youngest wicketkeeper.

- England's first innings score of 126 was their lowest total at home against New Zealand.

- It was the first time that New Zealand had played a test where both teams completed their innings on the same day. It was the 16th time in all tests that this had occurred.

- Alex Tudor's 99 not out was the highest score by an England nightwatchman. The previous best was Harold Larwood's 98 in the first test of the bodyline series.

269 ENGLAND v NEW ZEALAND *(Second Test)*

at Lord's on 22, 23, 24, 25 July, 1999
Toss : England. Umpires : R.E. Koertzen and M.J. Kitchen
New Zealand won by 9 wickets

Simon Doull was ruled out of the tour with a knee problem. New Zealand replaced him with opening batsman Matthew Bell, thus placing more responsibility on to Chris Cairns and Dion Nash.

The two responded brilliantly by bowling incisively prior to and after lunch, when England went from 79-1 to 170-9. They were both able to swing the ball in the Stygian conditions that prevailed and only Alec Stewart and Nasser Hussain had the ability to survive for more than one hour. One of the features in Cairns' impressive bowling performance was his superb slower delivery, which caused great concern for the England batsmen.

New Zealand took full advantage of the fine conditions which nullified lateral movement of the ball and Matt Horne proved to be an immovable object for 307 minutes as he grafted diligently to his third test hundred. Nathan Astle and Roger Twose ably supported him to take New Zealand into the lead on the second day at 242-6.

The new-found defiant streak of self-belief in the New Zealanders was more evident on the third day as Daniel Vettori, the nightwatchman, counter-attacked with slashing cuts and drives through the off, and a further 116 was added for the last four wickets. This gave his side a comfortable lead of 172.

A well-struck square-cut by Adam Parore broke Hussain's right middle finger and prevented him from taking any further part in the game. As England had not appointed a vice-captain, Hussain appointed Graham Thorpe to captain the side in his absence.

Though most of England's batsmen got a start Stewart, Mark Butcher and Mark Ramprakash were guilty of poor shot selection, leading to their demise. The entire New Zealand attack bowled a consistent line on and outside the off-stump and all five tasted success.

The best resistance offered by England was a partnership of 78, England's highest in the game, between Chris Read and Andy Caddick for the seventh wicket. New Zealand were unhurried in pursuing the 60 runs required for victory, which they reached shortly after 5 pm on the fourth day.

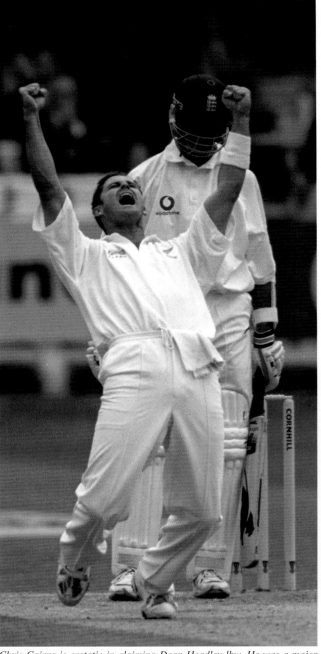

Chris Cairns is ecstatic in claiming Dean Headley lbw. He was a major contributor in New Zealand's first test win at Lord's in 13 attempts.

MILESTONES

- It was New Zealand's 41st test victory and their first test win at Lord's in 13 attempts.

- Chris Cairns took his sixth five-wicket bag in tests and captured his 500th first-class wicket.

- Alec Stewart became the ninth test player from England to make 6000 test runs.

ENGLAND

M.A.Butcher	c Parore b Cairns	8	c Astle b Vettori		20
A.J.Stewart	c Fleming b Nash	50	b Vettori		35
N.Hussain*	c Parore b Cairns	61	absent hurt		
G.P.Thorpe	c Astle b Cairns	7	b Cairns		7
M.R.Ramprakash	lbw b Nash	4	(3) c Parore b Astle		24
A.Habib	b Nash	6	(5) c Astle b Allott		19
C.M.W.Read†	b Cairns	0	lbw b Nash		37
A.R.Caddick	run out	18	c Fleming b Allott		45
D.W.Headley	lbw b Cairns	4	(6) c Fleming b Allott		12
A.D.Mullally	c Astle b Cairns	0	(9) c Twose b Cairns		10
P.C.R.Tufnell	not out	1	(10) not out		5
Extras	(b 5, lb 8, nb 14)	27	(b 5, lb 3, nb 7)		15
TOTAL	(61.1 overs)	**186**	(101.4 overs)		**229**

NEW ZEALAND

M.J.Horne	c Hussain b Headley	100	lbw b Caddick		26
M.D.Bell	lbw b Headley	15	not out		26
S.P.Fleming*	c Read b Mullally	1	not out		5
N.J.Astle	c Read b Mullally	43			
R.G.Twose	c Caddick b Headley	52			
C.D.McMillan	c Read b Caddick	3			
D.L.Vettori	c Thorpe b Tufnell	54			
A.C.Parore†	b Caddick	12			
C.L.Cairns	b Caddick	31			
D.J.Nash	c Mullally b Tufnell	6			
G.I.Allott	not out	1			
Extras	(b 1, lb 24, w 2, nb 13)	40	(b 2, nb 1)		3
TOTAL	(119.1 overs)	**358**	(23 overs) (1 wkt)		**60**

Bowling	O	M	R	W	O	M	R	W		Fall of Wickets			
NEW ZEALAND										E	NZ	E	NZ
										1st	*1st*	*2nd*	*2nd*
Allott	10	1	37	0	16.4	6	36	3	1st	35	43	55	37
Cairns	21.1	1	77	6	25	6	67	2	2nd	79	45	71	-
Nash	23	11	50	3	25	9	50	1	3rd	102	112	78	-
Astle	7	3	9	0	4	2	6	1	4th	112	232	97	-
Vettori					31	12	62	2	5th	123	239	123	-
ENGLAND									6th	125	242	127	-
Mullally	27	7	98	2	5	0	21	0	7th	150	275	205	-
Caddick	34	11	92	3	10	4	18	1	8th	165	345	216	-
Headley	27	7	74	3					9th	170	351	229	-
Tufnell	27.1	7	61	2	8	2	19	0	10th	186	358	-	-
Butcher	3	0	7	0									
Ramprakash	1	0	1	0									

270 ENGLAND v NEW ZEALAND *(Third Test)*

at Old Trafford, Manchester on 5, 6, 7, 8, 9 August, 1999
Toss : England. Umpires : D.R. Shepherd & R.B. Tiffin
Match drawn

Nasser Hussain's finger had not healed so Mark Butcher was appointed England captain. Following a busy season at Old Trafford the pitch prepared had been played on twice previously and had an unkempt look to it. The scribes agreed it would favour slow bowling in the latter stages of the game.

Rain reduced the first day by 29 overs. The pitch was slow and low and could not be trusted. The batsmen were determined to occupy the crease and Michael Atherton led by example with 11 in 135 minutes. Frequent interruptions allowed Chris Cairns and Dion Nash to remain fresh and threatening. The day ended at 108-5 and Michael Henderson of the *Telegraph* wrote, "Days do not come much duller than this."

Mark Ramprakash went on to make his highest test score, 69 not out, in 269 minutes, and England finished with 199. Peter Such batted 72 minutes for nought, for which he was accorded a rousing ovation as he left the field.

Matt Horne was dropped on nought, a chest-high catch at first slip by Graham Thorpe, off Andy Caddick, but then proceeded to play aggressively. Stephen Fleming maintained the impetus and Matthew Bell grew in confidence while the pitch was becoming more batting friendly.

New Zealand took charge, attacking from the outset of the third day. When Bell was finally dismissed for 83, his partnership with Nathan Astle was worth 153 and it was to be the only century partnership in the entire series. New Zealand had a lead of 64 with seven wickets remaining.

Astle led the attack on the spinners with three innovative shots clearing the ropes as he went to his fifth test century. Following the loss of three further wickets Craig McMillan and Cairns indulged in an even more explosive fashion for New Zealand to end the day at 399-6.

Before Fleming declared at 496, McMillan reached his third test century. New Zealand had a lead of 297 and England had to survive five sessions of play.

Sound batting by the experienced Atherton, Stewart and Thorpe, with 60 overs being lost to rain, saw England draw the game. After 12 days England and New Zealand were tied at 1-all even though New Zealand had won 11 of the 12 days.

ENGLAND

M.A.Butcher*	c Fleming b Cairns	5	lbw b Nash		9
M.A.Atherton	c Parore b Cairns	11	c Astle b Vettori		48
A.J.Stewart	c Parore b Nash	23	not out		83
G.P.Thorpe	c Bell b Vettori	27	not out		25
G.A.Hick	lbw b Nash	12			
M.R.Ramprakash	not out	69			
D.W.Headley	c Fleming b Harris	18			
C.M.W.Read†	b Harris	0			
A.R.Caddick	run out	12			
P.M.Such	c Bell b Vettori	0			
P.C.R.Tufnell	c Astle b Nash	1			
Extras	(b 6, lb 10, w 5)	21	(b 9, lb 7)		16
TOTAL	(109.1 overs)	**199**	(68 overs) (2 wkts)		**181**

NEW ZEALAND

M.J.Horne	b Caddick	39	
M.D.Bell	c Atherton b Headley	83	
S.P.Fleming*	lbw b Such	38	
N.J.Astle	c Such b Caddick	101	
R.G.Twose	lbw b Such	20	
C.D.McMillan	not out	107	
A.C.Parore†	c Butcher b Such	10	
C.L.Cairns	c Caddick b Tufnell	41	
D.J.Nash	c Caddick b Such	26	
C.Z.Harris	b Tufnell	3	
D.L.Vettori	not out	2	
Extras	(b 6, lb 17, nb 3)	26	
TOTAL	(160 overs) (9 wkts dec)	**496**	

Bowling	O	M	R	W	O	M	R	W		Fall of Wickets		
NEW ZEALAND										E	NZ	E
										1st	*1st*	*2nd*
Cairns	34	12	72	2	11	1	54	0	1st	13	46	19
Nash	31.1	15	46	3	10	3	26	1	2nd	54	110	118
Astle	11	5	14	0	3	1	7	0	3rd	60	263	-
Vettori	25	7	35	2	26	12	48	1	4th	83	280	-
Harris	8	4	16	2	18	6	30	0	5th	104	321	-
ENGLAND									6th	133	331	-
Caddick	39	11	112	2					7th	133	425	-
Headley	31	4	115	1					8th	152	476	-
Tufnell	46	12	111	2					9th	183	487	-
Such	41	11	114	4					10th	199	-	-
Hick	1	0	8	0								
Butcher	2	0	13	0								

MILESTONES

- When Daniel Vettori made his maiden first-class century against Leicestershire each member of the New Zealand team had made at least one first-class hundred.

- Craig McMillan passed 1000 runs in his 15th test.

- England conceded a first innings deficit of over 100 against New Zealand for the fourth test in a row.

Matthew Bell, watched by Chris Read, drives fluently through mid-off for one of the seven boundaries in his diligent innings of 83.

271 ENGLAND v NEW ZEALAND *(Fourth Test)*

at The Oval on 19, 20, 21, 22 August, 1999
Toss : England. Umpires : G. Sharp & S. Venkataraghavan
New Zealand won by 83 runs

In their previous first-class match New Zealand suffered a humiliating defeat to Essex by an innings and 40 runs. Geoff Allott had a strained back and Chris Cairns had developed leg troubles. It was hardly the ideal build-up for the decisive test at The Oval. In addition, heavy rain in London meant that the pitch had sweated for two days beneath the covers.

When Nasser Hussein sent New Zealand in to bat the bounce from the pitch was consistent but there was considerable lateral and seam movement which created doubt in the minds of most of the batsmen in both teams.

The two Matthews, Bell and Horne, tenaciously survived the first 26 overs; Andrew Caddick's first 12 overs conceding just four runs. At lunch New Zealand was 45-1 but was soon 104-7. Stephen Fleming defied the England attack for the remainder of the day, being 52 not out, New Zealand 170-7.

Daniel Vettori scored an invaluable 51 in a partnership with Fleming worth 78. Fleming's 66 not out was made in 331 minutes. England's reply was similar to the visitors' with the openers struggling for survival. After the fall of the first wicket, five others fell quickly for England to be 94-6.

Chris Cairns was adequately rewarded with 5-31, while Vettori spun the ball for 33 consecutive overs of top-quality spin to capture 3-36 to give New Zealand a lead of 83.

The lead was nullified when New Zealand were reduced to 37-6 before Cairns embarked on an heroic assault where he recovered the initiative by scoring 80 off 93 balls, during

which he straight-drove Phil Tufnell for four sixes. Dion Nash made three of their 50-run partnership.

England began their second innings requiring 246. They were aware that their last six test victories had been in games where they had conceded a first innings deficit.

The fourth day began with England 91-2 and Michael Atherton and Graham Thorpe well established. The partnership added 78 before Thorpe edged to slip to set off another collapse where eight wickets fell for 39 runs.

New Zealand's victory by 83 runs was a wonderful farewell to their coach for their last 26 tests, Steve Rixon. This series saw the establishment of Chris Cairns as a great world-class all-rounder, capable of winning a test with either bat or ball.

NEW ZEALAND

M.J.Horne	c Caddick b Irani	15	lbw b Giddins	10
M.D.Bell	c Stewart b Mullally	23	c Irani b Caddick	4
S.P.Fleming*	not out	66	c Thorpe b Caddick	4
N.J.Astle	c Stewart b Caddick	9	c Irani b Giddins	5
R.G.Twose	c Maddy b Giddins	1	c Stewart b Giddins	0
C.D.McMillan	b Tufnell	19	lbw b Mullally	26
A.C.Parore†	c Ramprakash b Tufnell	0	b Caddick	1
C.L.Cairns	b Mullally	11	c & b Mullally	80
D.J.Nash	c Ramprakash b Caddick	18	not out	10
D.L.Vettori	lbw b Tufnell	51	c Ramprakash b Tufnell	6
S.B.O'Connor	lbw b Caddick	1	b Tufnell	6
Extras	(b 9, lb 9, w 2, nb 2)	22	(lb 4, w 1, nb 5)	10
TOTAL	(102.1 overs)	**236**	(54 overs)	**162**

ENGLAND

M.A.Atherton	c Fleming b Nash	10	c Parore b Nash	64
D.L.Maddy	b Vettori	14	c Fleming b Nash	5
N.Hussain*	c Bell b Cairns	40	c Parore b O'Connor	9
G.P.Thorpe	c Fleming b Cairns	10	c Fleming b O'Connor	44
A.J.Stewart†	b Vettori	11	c Bell b Nash	12
M.R.Ramprakash	c Parore b Cairns	30	c Parore b Nash	0
R.C.Irani	lbw b Cairns	1	c Parore b Vettori	9
A.R.Caddick	b O'Connor	15	c Bell b Vettori	3
A.D.Mullally	c Bell b Vettori	5	c Twose b Cairns	3
P.C.R.Tufnell	not out	0	run out	1
E.S.H.Giddins	lbw b Cairns	0	not out	0
Extras	(b 1, lb 5, w 5, nb 6)	17	(b 2, lb 3, nb 7)	12
TOTAL	(80 overs)	**153**	(56.1 overs)	**162**

Bowling	O	M	R	W	O	M	R	W		Fall of Wickets				
ENGLAND											NZ	E	NZ	E
											1st	1st	2nd	2nd
Caddick	33.1	17	66	3	17	4	35	3						
Mullally	26	12	34	2	11	1	27	2		1st	39	25	15	23
Giddins	16	4	41	1	10	3	38	3		2nd	45	29	15	45
Tufnell	16	3	39	3	16	3	58	2		3rd	54	46	22	123
Irani	11	3	38	1						4th	62	87	22	143
NEW ZEALAND										5th	87	91	37	143
Cairns	19	8	31	5	15.1	3	50	1		6th	87	94	39	148
Nash	14	5	40	1	14	3	39	4		7th	104	141	79	157
O'Connor	13	3	30	1	11	3	32	2		8th	157	153	149	160
Vettori	33	12	46	3	16	6	36	2		9th	235	153	156	161
Astle	1	1	0	0						10th	236	153	162	162

MILESTONES

- It was New Zealand's 42nd test win, their first at The Oval.

- It was the first time New Zealand had won two tests in a series against England.

- Stephen Fleming overtook Martin Crowe's record of 71 catches in the field.

- For the first time in a home series of more than two tests England were unable to produce a century partnership.

- Michael Atherton reached 50 for the 50th time in tests.

- Chris Cairns hit four sixes. This took his test tally to 36, surpassing the New Zealand record of 33 shared by John Reid and Richard Hadlee.

AVERAGES

New Zealand

BATTING	M	I	NO	Runs	HS	Ave
M.D. Bell	3	5	1	151	83	37.75
C.D. McMillan	4	6	1	188	107*	37.60
S.P. Fleming	4	7	2	166	66*	33.20
N.J. Astle	4	6	0	193	101	32.16
C.L. Cairns	4	6	0	183	80	30.50
M.J. Horne	4	7	0	203	100	29.00
S.B. Doull	1	2	0	57	46	28.50
D.L. Vettori	4	6	1	114	54	22.80
D.J. Nash	4	6	1	81	26	16.20
A.C. Parore	4	6	0	96	73	16.00
R.G. Twose	4	6	0	73	52	12.16
S.B. O'Connor	1	2	0	7	6	3.50
C.Z. Harris	1	1	0	3	3	3.00
G.I. Allott	2	3	3	8	7*	-

BOWLING	O	M	R	W	Ave
D.J. Nash	135.1	52	297	17	17.47
S.B. O'Connor	24	6	62	3	20.66
C.L. Cairns	139	34	404	19	21.26
C.Z. Harris	26	10	46	2	23.00
D.L. Vettori	137	50	249	10	24.90
G.I. Allott	55.4	10	182	7	26.00
N.J. Astle	27	13	36	1	36.00
S.B. Doull	19	6	65	1	65.00
C.D. McMillan	3.4	0	14	0	-

England

BATTING	M	I	NO	Runs	HS	Ave
M.A. Atherton	2	4	0	133	64	33.25
N. Hussain	3	5	0	164	61	32.80
A.J. Stewart	4	8	1	215	83*	30.71
M.R. Ramprakash	4	6	1	127	69*	25.40
G.P. Thorpe	4	8	2	147	44	24.50
A.R. Caddick	4	6	0	126	45	21.00
M.A. Butcher	3	6	0	86	33	14.33
G.A. Hick	1	1	0	12	12	12.00
D.W. Headley	2	3	0	34	18	11.33
C.M.W. Read	3	4	0	38	37	9.50
D.L. Maddy	1	2	0	19	14	9.50
A. Habib	2	3	0	26	19	8.66
R.C. Irani	1	2	0	10	9	5.00
P.C.R. Tufnell	4	6	3	14	6	4.66
A.D. Mullally	3	5	0	18	10	3.60
P.M. Such	1	1	0	0	0	0.00
E.S.H. Giddins	1	2	1	0	0*	0.00
A.J. Tudor	1	2	2	131	99*	-

BOWLING	O	M	R	W	Ave
E.S.H. Giddins	26	7	79	4	19.75
A.R. Caddick	174.1	62	412	20	20.60
P.C.R. Tufnell	132.2	36	317	14	22.64
A.D. Mullally	111.4	28	300	11	27.27
P.M. Such	41	11	114	4	28.50
R.C. Irani	11	3	38	1	38.00
M.A. Butcher	12	2	45	1	45.00
D.W. Headley	58	11	189	4	47.25
A.J. Tudor	16	4	59	1	59.00
M.R. Ramprakash	1	0	1	0	-
G.A. Hick	1	0	8	0	-

New Zealand's win at The Oval clinched the series. Back (from left): Shayne O'Connor, Geoff Allott, Gilbert Enoka (player co-ordinator), Andrew Penn, John Graham (manager), Steve Rixon (coach), Roger Twose, Nathan Astle. Front: Adam Parore, Matthew Bell, Craig McMillan, Chris Cairns.

1999/00 New Zealand in India

272 **INDIA v NEW ZEALAND** *(First Test)*
at Punjab C.A. Stadium, Mohali on 10, 11, 12, 13, 14 October, 1999
Toss : New Zealand. Umpires : P.T. Manuel & S. Venkataraghavan
Match drawn

Few would have believed that after 4½ sessions where 20 wickets had fallen that the remaining 10½ sessions would only see another 10 wickets fall as the match meandered to a very tame draw.

New Zealand took full advantage of winning the toss and asked India to bat first. The pitch had retained some moisture and this enabled the ball to swing and seam. Dion Nash revelled in the conditions and his movement off the seam, combined with his pinpoint accuracy, left little margin for error. He richly deserved his best test analysis of 6-27 as India were bowled out for 83 in 27 overs.

By stumps New Zealand had a lead of 36 and still had seven wickets intact, thanks to a determined partnership of 91 between Craig Spearman and Stephen Fleming. They were watchful of the in-swingers from the tall Javagal Srinath and appeared untroubled by his bowling partners.

The pitch had dried by the second day and with it went all movement. It was deplorably slow and it got progressively lower and slower over the remainder of the match. New Zealand squandered the chance to build on the first day's effort when they lost their last seven wickets for 59. Srinath bowled with great determination and ended with 6-45.

The Indian openers Devang Gandhi and Sadagoppa Ramesh, who had both made ducks in the first innings, were more at home on the lifeless wicket and they wiped off the deficit of 132 with their partnership of 137.

Their cautious start laid the platform for Rahul Dravid and Sachin Tendulkar to add 229 for the third wicket. Tendulkar batted in a responsible manner, in keeping with his role as India's captain, and discarded his more flamboyant shots. Dravid was at his cultured and technical best in scoring 144. India's declaration left them time for 135 overs and New Zealand a target of 374. The pitch was so slow and low that neither side threatened to win the game.

India made their lowest score against New Zealand, mainly because of the excellent bowling of Dion Nash who captured a test best 6-27.

INDIA					
D.J.Gandhi	c Parore b Nash	0	lbw b Astle		75
S.Ramesh	b Nash	0	c & b Vettori		73
R.S.Dravid	c Astle b Cairns	1	b Vettori		144
S.R.Tendulkar*	b O'Connor	18	not out		126
S.C.Ganguly	b Nash	2	not out		64
V.R.Bharadwaj	c Parore b Cairns	0			
M.S.K.Prasad†	not out	16			
S.B.Joshi	c Spearman b O'Connor	0			
A.R.Kumble	c Spearman b Nash	7			
J.Srinath	c Astle b Nash	20			
B.K.V.Prasad	c Fleming b Nash	0			
Extras	(b 8, lb 5, nb 6)	19	(b 9, lb 7, nb 7)		23
TOTAL	(27 overs)	**83**	(183 overs) (3 wkts dec)		**505**

NEW ZEALAND					
M.J.Horne	c Ganguly b Srinath	6	c Ganguly b Joshi		33
M.D.Bell	b Srinath	0	lbw b Srinath		7
C.M.Spearman	c & b Kumble	51	c Ganguly b Joshi		35
S.P.Fleming*	lbw b Srinath	43	c Ganguly b Kumble		73
N.J.Astle	c Kumble b Srinath	45	c Prasad M.S.K. b Srinath		34
C.D.McMillan	lbw b Joshi	22	c Ramesh b Kumble		18
A.C.Parore†	not out	13	c Gandhi b Kumble		7
C.L.Cairns	b Prasad B.K.V.	7	not out		0
D.J.Nash	c Prasad M.S.K. b Srinath	2			
D.L.Vettori	b Srinath	0			
S.B.O'Connor	c Gandhi b Bharadwaj	2			
Extras	(b 5, lb 11, nb 8)	24	(b 24, lb 15, nb 5)		44
TOTAL	(91.1 overs)	**215**	(135 overs) (7 wkts)		**251**

Bowling	O	M	R	W	O	M	R	W		Fall of Wickets				
NEW ZEALAND											I	NZ	I	NZ
											1st	1st	2nd	2nd
Cairns	9	3	23	2	24	3	76	0		1st	2	7	137	24
Nash	11	3	27	6	37	16	79	0		2nd	3	8	181	95
O'Connor	7	1	20	2	18	3	73	0		3rd	7	99	410	108
Vettori					71	24	171	2		4th	10	156	-	186
Astle					31	8	82	1		5th	22	179	-	227
McMillan					2	0	8	0		6th	38	181	-	246
INDIA										7th	38	199	-	251
Srinath	22	9	45	6	31	9	63	2		8th	53	207	-	-
Prasad B.K.V.	19	6	56	1	16	7	24	0		9th	83	212	-	-
Ganguly	1	0	1	0						10th	83	215	-	-
Kumble	18	3	49	1	41	19	42	3						
Bharadwaj	14.1	4	26	1	13	3	34	0						
Joshi	17	8	22	1	28	12	38	2						
Tendulkar					6	2	11	0						

MILESTONES

- It was India's lowest score against New Zealand and their second-lowest score against all teams in India.

- Daniel Vettori's 71 overs in a test innings had only been exceeded once for New Zealand when Hedley Howarth sent down 74 overs in West Indies (test 100).

- India became the first team to be dismissed for under 100 in a test and score over 500 in their second innings.

273 INDIA v NEW ZEALAND *(Second Test)*

at Green Park, Kanpur on 22, 23, 24, 25 October, 1999
Toss : New Zealand. Umpires : D.J. Harper & A.V. Jayaprakash
India won by 8 wickets

The venue for the second test, Green Park, had an infamous history as the ground where Jusubhai Patel had taken 9-69 and 5-55 with his right-arm off-spinners in 1959 to give India their first victory against Australia. To this day members of that Australian team bemoan the fact that they were shafted.

This game began on a parched pitch, bereft of grass and guaranteed to crumble to dust from the opening over. New Zealand failed to take advantage of winning the toss as they lost four wickets before lunch. The middle order of Nathan Astle, Craig McMillan, Adam Parore, Chris Cairns and Dion Nash all fought valiantly, scoring between 34 and 53, but they were undone by the band of pickpocket fieldsmen who surrounded them when they were batting.

The slightest error was pounced upon and four batsmen were caught close in. New Zealand's total of 256 was only an adequate score. During the second day, on a pitch of uneven pace and bounce, none of the New Zealand attack bowled to their potential. Wide balls and half-volleys were punished unmercifully by Devang Ghandhi and Sadagoppa Ramesh who took India to 212-1 at the end of the second day by adding 162 for the first wicket.

From the start of the third day the ball was bringing up puffs of dust and the New Zealand bowlers were transformed into their best form. Leading them was Daniel Vettori, who had conceded 66 runs off 25 overs on the second day without capturing a wicket. In one golden spell he dispatched Sachin Tendulkar and Sourav Ganguly with successive balls and bowled Rahul Dravid four overs later.

Serious of thought and bowling with a curving, hovering flight he captured 6-61 during the day to have India out for 330 and restricted them to a lead of 74. There were two days left to play on a cantankerous strip of dirt.

Anil Kumble sealed New Zealand's fate when he claimed three wickets in 12 minutes prior to stumps on the third day. There were limited pockets of resistance from Adam Parore and Stephen Fleming but Kumble could not be denied as he snared six wickets.

In spite of India losing two early wickets Tendulkar and Gandhi were aggressive and India won by eight wickets with a day to spare. New Zealand not only lost the test but also lost McMillan with a broken finger.

As to be expected on a dry pitch bereft of grass and guaranteed to crumble, Daniel Vettori had a marathon performance, bowling 55 overs to claim six wickets.

MILESTONES

- Javagal Srinath captured his 150th test wicket.

- Anil Kumble captured his 250th test wicket. It was the third time that Kumble had taken 10 wickets in a match.

NEW ZEALAND

Batsman	First innings		Second innings	
M.J.Horne	c Prasad b Ganguly	5	lbw b Kumble	3
M.D.Bell	lbw b Srinath	15	lbw b Kumble	7
C.M.Spearman	c Ramesh b Kumble	12	(4) c Tendulkar b Harbhajan Singh	1
S.P.Fleming*	b Srinath	2	(5) c Dravid b Harbhajan Singh	31
N.J.Astle	lbw b Srinath	39	(6) c Bharadwaj b Kumble	0
C.D.McMillan	c Ramesh b Joshi	34	(8) lbw b Kumble	31
A.C.Parore†	c Dravid b Kumble	35	b Harbhajan Singh	48
C.L.Cairns	c Tendulkar b Kumble	53	(9) b Joshi	2
D.J.Nash	not out	41	(3) b Kumble	0
D.L.Vettori	c Bharadwaj b Harbhajan Singh	0	not out	8
P.J.Wiseman	c Bharadwaj b Kumble	0	lbw b Kumble	0
Extras	(b 7, nb 13)	20	(b 5, lb 9, nb 10)	24
TOTAL	(102.5 overs)	256	(66.5 overs)	155

INDIA

Batsman	First innings		Second innings	
D.J.Gandhi	c Fleming b Astle	88	not out	31
S.Ramesh	c Parore b Astle	83	b Cairns	5
R.S.Dravid	c Parore b Vettori	48	lbw b Nash	1
S.R.Tendulkar*	c Astle b Vettori	15	not out	44
S.C.Ganguly	c & b Vettori	0		
V.R.Bharadwaj	c Spearman b Wiseman	22		
M.S.K.Prasad†	c Fleming b Vettori	19		
S.B.Joshi	c Bell b Vettori	19		
A.R.Kumble	st Parore b Vettori	5		
J.Srinath	c Astle b Wiseman	0		
Harbhajan Singh	not out	1		
Extras	(b 14, lb 6, nb 10)	30	(lb 1, nb 1)	2
TOTAL	(148.1 overs)	330	(18.2 overs) (2 wkts)	83

Bowling	O	M	R	W	O	M	R	W
INDIA								
Srinath	22	9	62	3	9	5	12	0
Ganguly	4	0	15	1	1	0	2	0
Kumble	32.5	12	67	4	26.5	5	67	6
Harbhajan Singh	17	6	30	1	15	3	33	3
Joshi	25	7	63	1	15	6	27	1
Bharadwaj	2	0	12	0				
NEW ZEALAND								
Cairns	16	8	34	0	3	1	10	1
Nash	22	10	41	0	4	1	11	1
Vettori	55.1	11	127	6	6.2	2	22	0
Wiseman	29	10	81	2	5	0	39	0
Astle	26	12	27	2				

Fall of Wickets	NZ	I	NZ	I
	1st	1st	2nd	2nd
1st	7	162	16	5
2nd	33	214	16	7
3rd	40	243	17	-
4th	50	246	28	-
5th	112	255	33	-
6th	130	293	71	-
7th	172	311	128	-
8th	255	321	138	-
9th	255	326	150	-
10th	256	330	155	-

It was not until Stephen Fleming and Nathan Astle came together at 64-4 that the visitors offered strong resistance. Both Astle and Cairns played innings in direct contrast to their normal aggressive mode. They both made over 70 with Astle's effort occupying 323 minutes and Cairns 236. Anil Kumble's brisk, flat leg-spinners and googlies again proved an unfathomable puzzle.

Tendulkar did not enforce the follow-on. Instead he opted for further runs to allow his four main bowlers to have a rest. There was no chance that New Zealand could score 423 to win but India had a chance of victory as they had 101 overs to bowl New Zealand out. The slow pitch had the final say and the top four New Zealand batsmen were untroubled to see out time, giving India the series 1-0.

274 INDIA v NEW ZEALAND (*Third Test*)

at Sardar Patel Stadium, Ahmedabad on 29, 30, 31 October, 1, 2 November, 1999
Toss : India. Umpires : R.E. Koertzen & V.K. Ramaswamy
Match drawn

When India last played a test in Ahmedabad the pitch was described by a South African journalist as "poor" and South Africa were spun out within four days. The New Zealanders stayed behind in Kanpur and practised on the pitch that they had just been beaten on, expecting a repeat in Ahmedabad.

In appearance the pitch looked as if the dire predictions would come to pass but, in reality, it was the best pitch of the series as it failed to disintegrate, though it became very slow.

India's chance of losing the test was exhausted by the end of day one at 311-3. Left-hand opener Sadagoppa Ramesh took advantage of the slow nature of the pitch, which drew the teeth and the bounce of Chris Cairns and Dion Nash. When he was out at 182 he had shared partnerships of 82 with Rahul Dravid and 80 with Sachin Tendulkar.

Sourav Ganguly helped build on this excellent position. For the next five hours and 23 minutes he and Tendulkar rewrote the previous Indian record of 256 for the fourth wicket, made by the same pair against Sri Lanka two years earlier. Their partnership was worth 281 before Ganguly holed out. Tendulkar batted 494 minutes to complete his first test double-century and his highest first-class score of 217.

INDIA

Batsman	First innings		Second innings	
D.J.Gandhi	c Parore b Cairns	6	(1) c Parore b Nash	16
S.Ramesh	c Spearman b Harris	110	run out	12
R.S.Dravid	c Parore b Vettori	33	(2) b Cairns	15
S.R.Tendulkar*	c Nash b Vettori	217	(4) b Harris	53
S.C.Ganguly	c Nash b Astle	125		
A.Jadeja	b Vettori	13	(7) not out	12
M.S.K.Prasad†	b Vettori	2	(5) c Parore b Astle	17
A.R.Kumble	not out	27		
J.Srinath	not out	33	(6) not out	19
B.K.V.Prasad				
Harbhajan Singh				
Extras	(b 4, lb 7, nb 6)	17	(lb 4)	4
TOTAL	(167 overs) (7 wkts dec)	583	(32 overs) (5 wkts dec)	148

NEW ZEALAND

Batsman	First innings		Second innings	
G.R.Stead	c Ganguly b Kumble	17	(2) c Prasad M.S.K. b Harbhajan	78
M.J.Horne	c Dravid b Kumble	2	(1) c sub (V.R.Bharadwaj) b Kumble	41
D.L.Vettori	c sub (V.R.Bharadwaj) b Kumble	3		
C.M.Spearman	c Ramesh b Prasad B.K.V.	17	(3) not out	54
S.P.Fleming*	c Prasad M.S.K. b Srinath	48	(4) not out	64
N.J.Astle	c Ganguly b Prasad B.K.V.	74		
A.C.Parore†	lbw b Kumble	11		
C.L.Cairns	b Kumble	72		
C.Z.Harris	c Ramesh b Srinath	12		
D.J.Nash	not out	14		
P.J.Wiseman	lbw b Harbhajan Singh	3		
Extras	(b 8, lb 14, nb 13)	35	(b 1, lb 5, nb 9)	15
TOTAL	(141.4 overs)	308	(95 overs) (2 wkts)	252

Bowling	O	M	R	W	O	M	R	W
NEW ZEALAND								
Cairns	24	5	82	1	6	1	29	1
Nash	28	6	86	0	8	0	35	1
Vettori	57	5	200	4	2	0	23	0
Astle	17	2	55	1	5	0	13	1
Harris	17	3	64	1	11	0	44	1
Wiseman	24	2	85	0				
INDIA								
Srinath	35	11	72	2	15	3	59	0
Prasad B.K.V.	26	9	52	2	13	2	36	0
Kumble	48	21	82	5	31	16	57	1
Harbhajan Singh	30.4	8	78	1	26	7	55	1
Ganguly	2	1	2	0	4	0	20	0
Tendulkar					5	2	19	0
Dravid					1	1	0	0

Fall of Wickets	I	NZ	I	NZ
	1st	1st	2nd	2nd
1st	20	13	21	131
2nd	102	29	35	131
3rd	182	33	68	-
4th	463	65	114	-
5th	502	135	122	-
6th	518	166	-	-
7th	521	231	-	-
8th	-	284	-	-
9th	-	294	-	-
10th	-	308	-	-

MILESTONES

- It was Sachin Tendulkar's 21st century in 71 tests and his first test double-century.

- Sachin Tendulkar and Sourav Ganguly put on 281, an Indian fourth wicket record against all comers.

- India's 583-7d was its highest total against New Zealand.

- Daniel Vettori became the second New Zealand bowler after Stephen Boock to concede 200 runs in a test innings.

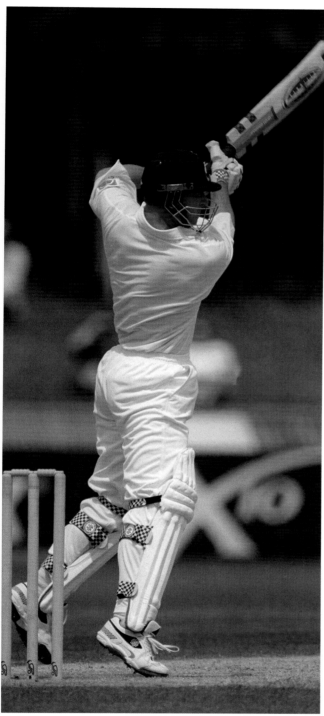

Craig Spearman was very watchful of the Indian spinners as his side batted to save the game. He had reached an unbeaten half-century when the game ended.

AVERAGES

New Zealand

BATTING	M	I	NO	Runs	HS	Ave
S.P. Fleming	3	6	1	261	73	52.20
G.R. Stead	1	2	0	95	78	47.50
N.J. Astle	3	5	0	192	74	38.40
C.M. Spearman	3	6	1	170	54*	34.00
C.L. Cairns	3	5	1	134	72	33.50
A.C. Parore	3	5	1	114	48	28.50
D.J. Nash	3	4	2	57	41*	28.50
C.D. McMillan	2	4	0	105	34	26.25
M.J. Horne	3	6	0	90	41	15.00
C.Z. Harris	1	1	0	12	12	12.00
M.D. Bell	2	4	0	29	15	7.25
D.L. Vettori	3	4	1	11	8*	3.66
S.B. O'Connor	1	1	0	2	2	2.00
P.J. Wiseman	2	3	0	3	3	1.00

BOWLING	O	M	R	W	Ave
D.J. Nash	110	36	279	8	34.87
N.J. Astle	79	22	177	5	35.40
D.L. Vettori	191.3	42	543	12	45.25
S.B. O'Connor	25	4	93	2	46.50
C.L. Cairns	82	21	254	5	50.80
C.Z. Harris	28	3	108	2	54.00
P.J. Wiseman	58	12	205	2	102.50
C.D. McMillan	2	0	8	0	-

India

BATTING	M	I	NO	Runs	HS	Ave
S.R. Tendulkar	3	6	2	435	217	108.75
S.C. Ganguly	3	5	1	244	125	61.00
D.J. Gandhi	3	5	1	200	88	50.00
S. Ramesh	3	6	0	287	110	47.83
R.S. Dravid	3	6	0	239	144	39.83
J. Srinath	3	4	2	72	33*	36.00
A. Jadeja	1	2	1	25	13	25.00
A.R. Kumble	3	3	1	39	27*	19.50
M.S.K. Prasad	3	4	1	54	19	18.00
V.R. Bharadwaj	2	2	0	22	22	11.00
S.B. Joshi	2	2	0	19	19	9.50
B.K.V. Prasad	2	1	0	0	0	0.00
Harbhajan Singh	2	1	1	1	1*	-

BOWLING	O	M	R	W	Ave
A.R. Kumble	197.4	76	364	20	18.20
J. Srinath	134	46	313	13	24.07
S.B. Joshi	85	33	150	5	30.00
Harbhajan Singh	88.4	24	196	6	32.66
S.C. Ganguly	12	1	40	1	40.00
B.K.V. Prasad	74	24	168	3	56.00
V.R. Bharadwaj	29.1	7	72	1	72.00
R.S. Dravid	1	1	0	0	-
S.R. Tendulkar	11	4	30	0	-

1999/00 West Indies in New Zealand

275 **NEW ZEALAND v WEST INDIES** *(First Test)*
at WestpacTrust Park, Hamilton on 16, 17, 18, 19, 20 December, 1999
Toss : West Indies. Umpires : D.B. Cowie & D.R. Shepherd
New Zealand won by 9 wickets

Fourteen minutes before stumps on the first day West Indies looked to be in an impregnable position at 276-0 with both openers, Sherwin Campbell and Adrian Griffith, having reached their centuries.

At 276 Campbell was caught by Adam Parore off Dion Nash. He had made 170 and hit 16 fours behind square, on the off-side, indicating his penchant for the cut shot and the inaccuracy of the bowlers. His partner Griffith had been more watchful and cautious and it was his first test century.

On a friendly pitch West Indies began the second day at 291-1. Chris Cairns and Daniel Vettori, who had both been wicketless at the end of the first day, worked well in tandem, claiming seven of the wickets to fall.

Cairns went around the wicket to the continual procession of six left-hand batsmen and claimed 3-14 off 11 overs while Vettori captured four wickets as the West Indies lost their last 10 wickets for 89 runs to be all out for 365. Solid

contributions from all the local top order enabled New Zealand to be 113-3 at the end of the second day.

Stephen Fleming was the linchpin of the innings, taking 226 minutes to make 66. Cairns came to the crease at 258-6 and was fortunate to be given the benefit of the doubt in a run out before he had scored. The side-on cameras were not available and the third umpire ruled that there was an element of doubt and therefore ruled in favour of the batsman.

Cairns accepted his good fortune by mounting a pulsating counter-attack and, with Craig McMillan, 116 runs were added in 123 minutes. New Zealand had a first innings lead of 28. The visitors began the fourth day in the worst possible way, losing three wickets for one run, and were saved by rain that wiped out the afternoon session with the score at 66-4.

In the first hundred minutes of the fifth day West Indies lost their remaining six wickets for 31 runs as Cairns tore through them to end with 7-27, the third-best bowling analysis for New Zealand.

He took 10 wickets in a match for the only time in his test career. When play ended on the first day he had 0-62 so he captured 10 wickets while conceding only 38 runs. Matthew Horne broke a finger as New Zealand reached their target of 70 for the loss of one wicket.

Chris Cairns was named Man of the Match after claiming 10 wickets and scoring 72 in the first test.

WEST INDIES					
A.F.G.Griffith	c Parore b Vettori	114	c Parore b Cairns		18
S.L.Campbell	c Parore b Nash	170	b Cairns		0
D.Ramnarine	c Parore b Cairns	8	(9) c & b Cairns		0
S.Chanderpaul	c Fleming b Astle	14	(3) c Parore b Cairns		0
B.C.Lara*	c Nash b Vettori	24	(4) c Parore b Nash		1
R.L.Powell	c Wiseman b Cairns	0	(5) c Spearman b Vettori		30
J.C.Adams	not out	17	(6) c sub (S.B.O'Connor) b Cairns		25
R.D.Jacobs†	c Spearman b Vettori	5	(7) run out		2
F.A.Rose	c Wiseman b Cairns	4	(8) lbw b Cairns		3
R.D.King	b Nash	1	lbw b Cairns		0
C.A.Walsh	b Vettori	0	not out		5
Extras	(lb 6, nb 2)	8	(b 7, lb 3, nb 3)		13
TOTAL	(135.1 overs)	**365**	(53.5 overs)		**97**

NEW ZEALAND					
G.R.Stead	b Walsh	22	b Walsh		16
M.J.Horne	c Rose b King	32	retired hurt		5
C.M.Spearman	b Ramnarine	27	not out		30
S.P.Fleming*	c Jacobs b Ramnarine	66			
D.L.Vettori	c Adams b King	29			
N.J.Astle	c Ramnarine b Walsh	48	(4) not out		7
C.D.McMillan	c Jacobs b King	51			
C.L.Cairns	c Campbell b Ramnarine	72			
A.C.Parore†	run out	8			
D.J.Nash	c Powell b King	6			
P.J.Wiseman	not out	0			
Extras	(b 4, lb 9, w 3, nb 16)	32	(b 4, lb 1, nb 7)		12
TOTAL	(130.2 overs)	**393**	(15 overs) (1 wkt)		**70**

Bowling	O	M	R	W	O	M	R	W		Fall of Wickets				
NEW ZEALAND											WI	NZ	WI	NZ
Cairns	31	11	73	3	22.5	10	27	7			1st	1st	2nd	2nd
Nash	28	12	63	2	7	1	37	1		1st	276	61	0	59
Vettori	34.1	9	83	4	22	12	20	1		2nd	289	67	0	-
Astle	16	2	67	1						3rd	311	107	1	-
Wiseman	22	10	51	0	2	0	3	0		4th	336	162	36	-
McMillan	4	1	22	0						5th	336	215	78	-
WEST INDIES										6th	336	258	85	-
Walsh	29	4	81	2	8	1	33	1		7th	345	374	90	-
Rose	27	4	103	0	6	0	28	0		8th	352	379	90	-
Ramnarine	36	10	82	3	1	0	4	0		9th	362	388	90	-
King	26.2	2	81	4						10th	365	393	97	-
Powell	5	2	13	0										
Adams	7	1	20	0										

MILESTONES

- It was New Zealand's 43rd test victory.

- Sherwin Campbell and Adrian Griffith put on 276, a West Indies record for any wicket against New Zealand.

- Chris Cairns reached 2000 test runs in his 43rd test.

- Chris Cairns joined father Lance in taking 10 wickets in a test. This was was the first time a father and son had both achieved the feat.

276 NEW ZEALAND v WEST INDIES *(Second Test)*

at Basin Reserve, Wellington on 26, 27, 28, 29 December, 1999
Toss : West Indies. Umpires : R.B. Tiffin & E.A. Watkin
New Zealand won by an innings and 105 runs

Brian Lara won the toss and sent New Zealand in to bat. Reon King claimed the first wicket and that brought the debutant Mathew Sinclair to the crease. He was still there at the end of the day, on 123, becoming the fifth New Zealander to score a century on debut. Supported by Stephen Fleming's 67, New Zealand were 263-3 at stumps.

Sinclair's innings of 214 concluded just prior to tea on the second day after he had batted for 534 minutes. He hit 18 of his 22 boundaries in the arc between third man and extra cover. He and Nathan Astle added 189 before Astle was run out going for a second run, trying to bring up Sinclair's 200.

Chris Cairns continued his remarkable all-round form when, for the fourth time in 10 tests in 1999, he captured a five-wicket bag. His variations of pace and controlled aggression sliced through the West Indies and only Adrian Griffith and Brian Lara had the skill to combat him.

When West Indies followed on 339 runs behind, Griffith, for the fourth time in four innings, batted defiantly for over two hours, finding a solid partner in Shivnarine Chanderpaul. Lara played some sumptuous shots in his three-hour stay before he had bad luck to be adjudged caught behind. Cairns was moving gingerly with a sore back so it was left to Dion Nash to wrap up the game and the series with a day to spare.

MILESTONES

- Mathew Sinclair (208) made his test debut.

- It was New Zealand's 44th test victory.

- Nathan Astle reached 2000 test runs in his 34th test.

- Mathew Sinclair became the fifth New Zealander to make a century on test debut.

- Sinclair and Nathan Astle created a new fourth wicket record of 189 for New Zealand against West Indies.

- New Zealand's total of 518-9d was their highest against West Indies.

NEW ZEALAND

C.M.Spearman	c Walsh b King	24
G.R.Stead	c Campbell b King	17
M.S.Sinclair	b King	214
S.P.Fleming*	c Adams b Chanderpaul	67
N.J.Astle	run out	93
C.D.McMillan	c Jacobs b King	31
C.L.Cairns	c Adams b Rose	31
A.C.Parore†	b Rose	5
D.J.Nash	not out	2
D.L.Vettori	c Campbell b Rose	2
S.B.O'Connor	not out	0
Extras	(b 5, lb 12, w 1, nb 14)	32
TOTAL	(173.3 overs) (9 wkts dec)	**518**

WEST INDIES

A.F.G.Griffith	c Fleming b Nash	67	run out		45
S.L.Campbell	lbw b Cairns	0	lbw b Cairns		3
N.O.Perry	c Parore b Cairns	3	(7) lbw b Astle		0
S.Chanderpaul	c Parore b Cairns	5	(3) c Parore b Nash		70
B.C.Lara*	b Vettori	67	(4) c Parore b Nash		75
J.C.Adams	c Stead b Vettori	8	(5) c Parore b Nash		4
R.D.Jacobs†	not out	19	(6) c Stead b Vettori		20
F.A.Rose	c Parore b Cairns	0	lbw b Cairns		10
R.D.King	run out	0	(10) not out		4
C.A.Walsh	b Cairns	0	(9) lbw b Nash		0
D.Ganga	absent hurt		absent hurt		
Extras	(b 4, lb 2, w 2, nb 2)	10	(b 1, lb 1, w 1)		3
TOTAL	(91 overs)	**179**	(83.1 overs)		**234**

Bowling	O	M	R	W	O	M	R	W
WEST INDIES								
Walsh	41	5	112	0				
King	36	11	96	4				
Rose	32.3	5	113	3				
Perry	32	5	120	0				
Adams	26	9	45	0				
Chanderpaul	6	1	15	1				
NEW ZEALAND								
Cairns	19	5	44	5	12.1	4	25	2
Nash	18	8	23	1	16	4	38	4
Vettori	31	10	69	2	32	8	86	1
O'Connor	19	8	25	0	16	3	50	0
Astle	4	1	12	0	7	0	33	1

Fall of Wickets	NZ	WI	WI
	1st	1st	2nd
1st	33	1	8
2nd	76	5	83
3rd	240	17	148
4th	429	129	154
5th	456	141	189
6th	507	174	204
7th	507	175	225
8th	514	176	225
9th	518	179	234
10th	-	-	

Mathew Sinclair became the fourth player to make a double-century on test debut.

1999/00 Australia in New Zealand

277 **NEW ZEALAND v AUSTRALIA** *(First Test)*
at Eden Park, Auckland on 11, 12, 13, 14, 15 March, 2000
Toss : Australia. Umpires : B.F. Bowden & S. Venkataraghavan
Australia won by 62 runs

Eden Park continued its history of preparing pitches that were different from traditional strips. There was a good grass cover but as there was also excess moisture below the surface it aided and abetted spin bowlers for the duration of what turned out to be an intriguing game.

Daniel Vettori was introduced into the New Zealand attack in the 10th over of the game and was greeted by Justin Langer hitting him for a four and a six. The spinning ball was gripping onto the surface and turning but was bouncing more like a tennis ball.

This upset the equilibrium of all the batsmen, with the exception of Mark Waugh, who nonchalantly compiled 74 not out, of Australia's 214. New Zealand struggled to reach 26-4 at stumps with the novice tearaway fast bowler Brett Lee claiming two wickets.

In a fascinating test match played on a wicket conducive to spin Daniel Vettori exploited the conditions expertly to have match figures of 12-149.

The second day saw a further 11 wickets fall for 251 runs. All the New Zealand middle order batted valiantly and it was Glenn McGrath who captured the last three wickets after lunch to have the figures of the innings of 4-33.

Wiseman opened the bowling for New Zealand when Australia batted a second time. An explosive cameo from Langer was the main contribution to Australia being 114-5 at stumps and in peril of defeat.

Sensible batting by Damien Martyn and Adam Gilchrist, aided by occasional stoppages for showers, assisted Australia's recovery, taking the score to 174 before Vettori bowled Martin for 36 to give him his 100th test wicket. Vettori claimed the stunning figures of 7-87 and match figures of 12-149.

Colin Miller, Australian right-arm medium-pace bowler, recently turned off-spinner at the age of 32, captured three of the first four New Zealand wickets to fall, for 43, in the quest for 281 runs. Nathan Astle and Craig McMillan stemmed the flow by adding 78 in 17 overs, with McMillan reaching fifty at a-run-a-ball. The third day ended with New Zealand 130 short of their target but with McMillan 57 not out and Cairns 20 not out and five wickets remaining. Hopes were high for a local victory.

Rain prevented play on the fourth day and delayed play on the fifth. When play began Cairns fell immediately to Miller and when Lee captured McMillan and Adam Parore in successive overs it was left to Shane Warne to capture the last wicket and keep Australia's winning sequence intact.

MILESTONES

- Daniel Vettori captured his 100th test wicket in his 29th test, aged 21 years 46 days. He was the second-youngest bowler to reach this milestone after India's Kapil Dev.

- Vettori took 10 wickets in a test for the first time. His match figures of 12-149 were the second-best for New Zealand behind Sir Richard Hadlee's 15-123 against Australia in 1985/86 (test 171).

- On the first afternoon floodlights were turned on during a test match in New Zealand for the first time.

- Stephen Fleming passed 3000 test runs in his 49th test.

- Shane Warne overtook Dennis Lillee's record of 355 test wickets for Australia when he claimed the last wicket of the game.

- Australia equalled their record of eight consecutive test wins established by Warwick Armstrong's Australian sides against England in 1920/21 and 1921.

AUSTRALIA

M.J.Slater	b Cairns	5	(2) c Horne b Cairns		6
G.S.Blewett	c Astle b Wiseman	17	(1) c Spearman b Vettori		8
J.L.Langer	st Parore b Wiseman	46	c Astle b Vettori		47
M.E.Waugh	not out	72	c Parore b Vettori		25
S.R.Waugh*	c Spearman b Vettori	17	c & b Wiseman		10
D.R.Martyn	c Astle b Vettori	17	b Vettori		36
A.C.Gilchrist†	lbw b Wiseman	7	c Fleming b Vettori		59
S.K.Warne	c Fleming b Vettori	7	c Wiseman b Vettori		12
B.Lee	c Parore b Vettori	6	not out		6
C.R.Miller	b Cairns	0	st Parore b Vettori		8
G.D.McGrath	c Spearman b Vettori	8	lbw b Wiseman		1
Extras	(b 7, lb 4, nb 1)	12	(b 7, lb 4)		11
TOTAL	(71 overs)	214	(77.5 overs)		229

NEW ZEALAND

M.J.Horne	c Blewett b McGrath	3	c Langer b Miller		11
C.M.Spearman	c Martyn b Lee	12	lbw b McGrath		4
M.S.Sinclair	lbw b Lee	8	lbw b Miller		6
P.J.Wiseman	b Lee	1	(11) c Gilchrist b Warne		9
S.P.Fleming*	st Gilchrist b Miller	21	(4) c Gilchrist b Miller		8
N.J.Astle	c Waugh M.E. b Warne	31	(5) b Warne		35
C.D.McMillan	b Warne	6	(6) c Warne b Lee		78
C.L.Cairns	c Gilchrist b McGrath	35	(7) c Waugh S.R. b Miller		20
A.C.Parore†	c Gilchrist b McGrath	11	(8) c Waugh S.R. b Lee		26
D.L.Vettori	not out	15	(9) c Warne b Miller		0
S.B.Doull	c Lee b McGrath	12	(10) not out		5
Extras	(b 4, lb 1, nb 3)	8	(b 7, lb 7, nb 2)		16
TOTAL	(62.1 overs)	163	(73.3 overs)		218

Bowling	O	M	R	W	O	M	R	W
NEW ZEALAND								
Cairns	18	0	71	2	4	1	13	1
Doull	14	6	21	0	5	1	8	0
Vettori	25	8	62	5	35	11	87	7
Wiseman	14	2	49	3	33.5	6	110	2
AUSTRALIA								
McGrath	11.1	2	33	4	23	8	33	1
Miller	22	8	38	1	18	5	55	5
Warne	22	4	68	3	20.3	5	80	2
Lee	7	4	19	2	12	4	36	2

Fall of Wickets	A 1st	NZ 1st	A 2nd	NZ 2nd
1st	10	5	7	15
2nd	77	25	46	25
3rd	78	25	67	25
4th	114	26	81	43
5th	138	80	107	121
6th	161	80	174	151
7th	184	102	202	195
8th	192	134	214	204
9th	193	143	226	204
10th	214	163	229	218

278 NEW ZEALAND v AUSTRALIA *(Second Test)*

at Basin Reserve, Wellington on 24, 25, 26, 27 March, 2000
Toss : New Zealand. Umpires : D.M. Quested & Riazuddin
Australia won by 6 wickets

For three days prior to the test in Wellington the pitch was covered. When it emerged on the morning of the test there was a yellowish tinge to the grass and most critics were surprised by Stephen Fleming's decision to bat first.

Brett Lee's extra speed accounted for Matthew Horne and Craig Spearman and set the tone for a disastrous morning that had New Zealand 69-5 at lunch. Nathan Astle and Chris Cairns staged a recovery and 135 runs were added in 32 overs before tea, with Adam Parore assisting after Astle's dismissal.

Cairns' third test century was studded with memorable strokes and enabled New Zealand to reach 298 in 80.5 overs. Australia lost Greg Blewett and the nightwatchman, Shane Warne, before stumps for 29.

Cairns the bowler dominated the first stanza of the second day as he accounted for Justin Langer and Mark Waugh. At 51-4 New Zealand had a long wait before they dismissed Michael Slater. With his captain, Steve Waugh, he added 199. The nimble-footed Slater entertained in grand style with shots all round the wicket off both the back and front foot as he scored his fourteenth test century. Daniel Vettori strained his back and could only be used in brief spells.

The partnership between Steve Waugh and Damien Martyn, which had made 68 the previous night, added a further 46 to extend Australia's lead. While Steve Waugh was at the crease making 151 not out the last five Australian wickets added 353 very substantial runs to give them a lead of 121.

In spite of Horne and Spearman beginning with 46 for the first wicket New Zealand was in dire straits at 88-5 and still 33 behind. Cairns, so often the catalyst for recovery over the last two years, took the attack to the visitors, hitting Warne into the R.A. Vance grandstand twice and Lee out of the ground at both fine-leg and over the sightscreen.

Fleming accumulated runs almost unnoticed and by stumps New Zealand was 189-5 with Fleming 53 not out and Cairns 61 not out. They both perished early on the fourth day and though Adam Parore played thoughtfully and Simon Doull rumbustiously, Australia required 174 to win the test and the series. They did so with a day to spare, losing only four wickets.

NEW ZEALAND

M.J.Horne	c Warne b Lee	4	b Lee		14
C.M.Spearman	c Gilchrist b Lee	4	c Langer b Miller		38
M.S.Sinclair	lbw b Miller	4	b Lee		0
S.P.Fleming*	c Miller b Warne	16	c Blewett b Miller		60
N.J.Astle	c Waugh M.E. b Warne	61	c Warne b Lee		14
C.D.McMillan	c Gilchrist b Lee	1	c Waugh M.E. b Warne		0
C.L.Cairns	c Blewett b Miller	109	lbw b McGrath		69
A.C.Parore†	c Gilchrist b Blewett	46	run out		33
D.L.Vettori	c Langer b Warne	27	c Waugh S.R. b Lee		8
S.B.Doull	c Slater b Warne	12	c Waugh S.R. b Warne		40
S.B.O'Connor	not out	2	not out		4
Extras	(b 1, lb 8, nb 3)	12	(b 3, lb 8, nb 3)		14
TOTAL	(80.5 overs)	298	(96.2 overs)		294

AUSTRALIA

M.J.Slater	c Parore b McMillan	143	(2) st Parore b Vettori		12
G.S.Blewett	c Astle b Doull	0	(1) b Cairns		25
S.K.Warne	lbw b Vettori	7			
J.L.Langer	c Parore b Cairns	12	(3) c Spearman b O'Connor		57
M.E.Waugh	c Sinclair b Cairns	3	(4) not out		44
S.R.Waugh*	not out	151	(5) c Fleming b O'Connor		15
D.R.Martyn	c Parore b McMillan	78	(6) not out		17
A.C.Gilchrist†	c Parore b O'Connor	3			
B.Lee	lbw b O'Connor	0			
C.R.Miller	c & b McMillan	4			
G.D.McGrath	c & b Cairns	14			
Extras	(lb 3, nb 3)	4	(b 2, lb 2, w 3)		7
TOTAL	(120.3 overs)	419	(54.1 overs) (4 wkts)		177

Bowling	O	M	R	W	O	M	R	W
AUSTRALIA								
McGrath	17	4	60	0	22.2	11	35	1
Lee	17	2	49	3	23	6	87	3
Miller	20	2	78	2	21	5	54	2
Warne	14.5	1	68	4	27	7	92	3
Blewett	8	1	24	1	3	0	15	0
Waugh S.R.	4	0	10	0				
NEW ZEALAND								
Cairns	26.3	2	110	3	13	2	45	1
Doull	19	2	78	1	10	2	35	0
Vettori	15	1	50	1	8	1	19	1
O'Connor	26	6	78	2	11	3	42	2
Astle	11	2	45	0	10.1	4	19	0
McMillan	23	10	57	3	2	0	13	0

Fall of Wickets	NZ 1st	A 1st	NZ 2nd	A 2nd
1st	4	8	46	22
2nd	9	29	46	83
3rd	18	47	69	110
4th	53	51	88	144
5th	66	250	88	-
6th	138	364	198	-
7th	247	375	205	-
8th	282	375	222	-
9th	287	382	276	-
10th	298	419	294	-

MILESTONES

- Stephen Fleming and Chris Cairns created a new sixth wicket record of 110 for New Zealand against Australia.

- Steve Waugh completed his 22nd test century. By scoring 151 not out he had now scored 150 plus against the eight other test-playing countries.

- It was an Australian record ninth successive test victory.

Adam Parore used his feet to good effect, striking two straight sixes in his first innings score of 46. Adam Gilchrist is the Australian wicketkeeper.

279 NEW ZEALAND v AUSTRALIA *(Third Test)*
at WestpacTrust Park, Hamilton on 31 March, 1, 2, 3 April, 2000
Toss : Australia. Umpires : R.S. Dunne & A.V. Jayaprakash
Australia won by 6 wickets

The remarkable accuracy of Glenn McGrath and the express speed of Brett Lee again caused New Zealand great concern. McGrath combined with Adam Gilchrist to dismiss both New Zealand openers and later the last two New Zealand batsmen to finish with four wickets. Lee claimed five successive wickets in the middle order with his blistering pace and it was only a gutsy and courageous 79 by Craig McMillan that saw New Zealand reached 232.

Early on the second day Australia was reeling when they lost their fifth wicket at 29. Shayne O'Connor, the tall left-arm medium-fast inswing bowler, was in the form of his life, capturing three wickets in five overs before Stephen Fleming made a tactical indiscretion and replaced him with Daryl Tuffey, the debutant.

Mark Waugh and Damien Martyn seized upon his bowling and 75 runs were added in just over an hour. Later Adam Gilchrist unleashed his own brand of aggression, reaching fifty in 53 minutes, as he and Martin added 119 in 91 minutes. O'Connor ended with five wickets by capturing the last two wickets, which left Martin stranded, undefeated on 89, his highest test score to date.

The constant loss of New Zealand's first four wickets for less than 89 in the six innings to date had them again on the back foot and the best partnership of the innings came between Chris Cairns and Paul Wiseman who added 55 for the eighth wicket.

Cairns completed the series by scoring another 71 to give him 341 runs at an average of 56.83. He had also struck 13 sixes as he fought class with belligerence. Gilchrist took five catches in each innings to create a new Australian test record of 10 dismissals in a match. Langer made 122 not out off 122 balls of the 210 required for victory and was described by his captain Steve Waugh as "the best batsman in the world at this moment". All spectators who saw this innings at the ground or on television could only concur, such was Langer's mastery.

The Australians had won all ten of their tests against Pakistan, India and New Zealand during the summer of 1999/00. They would extend their winning sequence to 16, a new world test record.

NEW ZEALAND

Batsman	Dismissal	Score	Dismissal (2nd)	Score
M.J.Horne	c Gilchrist b McGrath	12	run out	0
C.M.Spearman	c Gilchrist b McGrath	12	c Gilchrist b Lee	35
M.S.Sinclair	c Warne b Lee	19	lbw b Miller	24
S.P.Fleming*	lbw b Lee	30	c Gilchrist b Miller	2
N.J.Astle	lbw b Lee	0	c Gilchrist b Warne	26
C.D.McMillan	c Gilchrist b Lee	79	c Waugh M.E. b Warne	30
C.L.Cairns	c Martyn b Lee	37	b McGrath	71
A.C.Parore†	not out	12	c Gilchrist b McGrath	16
P.J.Wiseman	b Warne	1	c Gilchrist b Lee	16
D.R.Tuffey	c Gilchrist b McGrath	3	not out	1
S.B.O'Connor	c Gilchrist b McGrath	0	lbw b Lee	0
Extras	(b 5, lb 7, w 2, nb 13)	27	(lb 4, nb 4)	8
TOTAL	(82.5 overs)	**232**	(86.4 overs)	**229**

AUSTRALIA

Batsman	Dismissal	Score	Dismissal (2nd)	Score
M.L.Hayden	c Parore b O'Connor	2	(2) c Spearman b Wiseman	37
M.J.Slater	lbw b O'Connor	2	(1) lbw b O'Connor	9
S.K.Warne	lbw b O'Connor	10		
J.L.Langer	b Cairns	4	(3) not out	122
M.E.Waugh	c Sinclair b Wiseman	28	(4) c Sinclair b Wiseman	18
S.R.Waugh*	c Fleming b Cairns	3	(5) retired hurt	18
D.R.Martyn	not out	89	(6) lbw b O'Connor	4
A.C.Gilchrist†	c Horne b Wiseman	75	(7) not out	0
B.Lee	c McMillan b Cairns	8		
G.D.McGrath	b O'Connor	7		
C.R.Miller	c Tuffey b O'Connor	2		
Extras	(b 4, lb 6, nb 12)	22	(lb 1, nb 3)	4
TOTAL	(61.5 overs)	**252**	(41.3 overs) (4 wkts)	**212**

Bowling	O	M	R	W	O	M	R	W
AUSTRALIA								
McGrath	21.5	8	58	4	20	7	50	2
Lee	23	8	77	5	18.4	2	46	3
Warne	20	5	45	1	25	11	61	2
Miller	11	4	28	0	20	5	58	2
Martyn	7	4	12	0				
Waugh S.R.					3	0	10	0
NEW ZEALAND								
Cairns	22	7	80	3	10	1	60	0
O'Connor	15.5	5	51	5	11	1	53	2
Tuffey	9	0	75	0	11	1	52	0
Astle	4	3	5	0				
Wiseman	11	3	31	2	9	1	42	2
McMillan					0.3	0	4	0

Fall of Wickets

	NZ	A	NZ	A
	1st	*1st*	*2nd*	*2nd*
1st	22	3	3	13
2nd	42	16	49	96
3rd	53	17	71	190
4th	53	25	71	190
5th	131	29	111	-
6th	208	104	130	-
7th	212	223	165	-
8th	224	233	220	-
9th	227	248	228	-
10th	232	252	229	-

Shayne O'Connor, left, is congratulated by Daryl Tuffey, who was making his test debut. It was O'Connor's first and only five-wicket bag in his test career.

MILESTONES

- Daryl Tuffey (209) made his test debut.

- Shayne O'Connor, in his 12th test, captured the only five wicket bag of his career.

- Adam Gilchrist set a new Australian record with 10 dismissals in a test, beating Gil Langley, Rodney Marsh and Ian Healy with nine. Jack Russell (England) held the test record of 11 dismissals.

- Adam Gilchrist equalled the New Zealand first-class record of 10 dismissals in a match.

AVERAGES

New Zealand

BATTING	M	I	NO	Runs	HS	Ave
C.L. Cairns	3	6	0	341	109	56.83
C.D. McMillan	3	6	0	194	79	32.33
A.C. Parore	3	6	1	144	46	28.80
N.J. Astle	3	6	0	167	61	27.83
S.B. Doull	2	4	1	69	40	23.00
S.P. Fleming	3	6	0	137	60	22.83
C.M. Spearman	3	6	0	105	38	17.50
D.L. Vettori	2	4	1	50	27	16.66
M.S. Sinclair	3	6	0	61	24	10.16
M.J. Horne	3	6	0	44	14	7.33
P.J. Wiseman	2	4	0	27	16	6.75
D.R. Tuffey	1	2	1	4	3	4.00
S.B. O'Connor	2	4	2	6	4*	3.00

BOWLING	O	M	R	W	Ave
D.L. Vettori	83	21	218	14	15.57
S.B. O'Connor	63.5	15	224	11	20.36
C.D. McMillan	25.3	10	74	3	24.66
P.J. Wiseman	67.5	12	232	9	25.77
C.L. Cairns	93.3	13	379	10	37.90
S.B. Doull	48	11	142	1	142.00
N.J. Astle	25.1	9	69	0	-
D.R. Tuffey	20	1	127	0	-

Australia

BATTING	M	I	NO	Runs	HS	Ave
D.R. Martyn	3	6	2	241	89*	60.25
J.L. Langer	3	6	1	288	122*	57.60
S.R. Waugh	3	6	2	214	151*	53.50
M.E. Waugh	3	6	2	190	72*	47.50
A.C. Gilchrist	3	5	1	144	75	36.00
M.J. Slater	3	6	0	177	143	29.50
M.L. Hayden	1	2	0	39	37	19.50
G.S. Blewett	2	4	0	50	25	12.50
S.K. Warne	3	4	0	36	12	9.00
G.D. McGrath	3	4	0	30	14	7.50
B. Lee	3	4	1	20	8	6.66
C.R. Miller	3	4	0	14	8	3.50

BOWLING	O	M	R	W	Ave
B. Lee	100.4	26	314	18	17.44
G.D. McGrath	115.2	40	269	12	22.41
C.R. Miller	112	29	311	12	25.91
S.K. Warne	129.2	33	414	15	27.60
G.S. Blewett	11	1	39	1	39.00
D.R. Martyn	7	4	12	0	-
S.R. Waugh	7	0	20	0	-

2000/01 New Zealand in Zimbabwe

Before the game began, Guy Whittall withdrew from the Zimbabwe side in protest at the inclusion of David Mutendera, claiming that the selection was politically motivated against Craig Wishart. Wishart replaced Whittall.

280   ZIMBABWE v NEW ZEALAND (*First Test*)

at Queen's Sports Club, Bulawayo on 12, 13, 14, 15, 16 September, 2000
Toss : Zimbabwe. Umpires : D.B. Hair & R.B. Tiffin
New Zealand won by 7 wickets

On a placid pitch Zimbabwe meandered to tea at 105-2 against accurate but not threatening bowling. Although all the batsmen looked at ease, a total of 185-4 off 102 overs was a meagre return at the end of the first day's play.

Alistair Campbell completed his first test fifty in 17 tests, compiling 88. Paul Wiseman's off-breaks were rewarded with his second five-wicket bag. In the course of bowling 52 overs Daniel Vettori aggravated a back injury which was to keep him out of test cricket for another eight tests.

Horne reached his fourth test hundred on the third day and when he left for 110 New Zealand was in a delicate situation at 180-6. Throughout the day New Zealand failed to come to terms with the right-arm leg-spinner Paul Strang who had missed Zimbabwe's last 14 tests with a wrist injury. Conscientious batting by the lower order saw the last four wickets contribute 158 to take New Zealand to 338.

The most valiant innings played was by Vettori. He batted with a runner for 125 minutes, scoring 49. Paul Strang ended with eight wickets. At a stage when the game appeared destined to be drawn an invigorated New Zealand attack claimed five wickets for 100 runs.

On the last day Chris Cairns took four wickets off 29 balls leaving New Zealand requiring 132 for victory, which was achieved for the loss of three wickets. Darrell Hair, umpiring at square leg, no-balled left-arm spinner Grant Flower three times for throwing. It was the first time in almost 700 overs in international cricket that Grant Flower had been called.

ZIMBABWE

Batsman	Dismissal	Runs	Dismissal (2nd)	Runs
G.W.Flower	c Parore b Vettori	24	c Parore b O'Connor	3
G.J.Rennie	c McMillan b Wiseman	36	b Cairns	2
S.V.Carlisle	c Horne b Wiseman	38	b Wiseman	15
A.D.R.Campbell	lbw b Astle	88	lbw b Cairns	45
A.Flower†	c Astle b Cairns	29	lbw b Astle	22
C.B.Wishart	c Richardson b Wiseman	17	c Richardson b Wiseman	1
H.H.Streak*	c Parore b Wiseman	51	c McMillan b Wiseman	15
P.A.Strang	c Richardson b Wiseman	0	(9) not out	8
M.L.Nkala	not out	30	(8) c Sinclair b Cairns	0
B.C.Strang	c Parore b O'Connor	10	b Cairns	5
D.T.Mutendera	b Cairns	10	c Parore b Cairns	0
Extras	(b 5, lb 4, nb 8)	17	(lb 1, w 1, nb 1)	3
TOTAL	(175.2 overs)	**350**	(67.5 overs)	**119**

NEW ZEALAND

Batsman	Dismissal	Runs	Dismissal (2nd)	Runs
M.H.Richardson	c Carlisle b Streak	6	lbw b Rennie	13
M.J.Horne	lbw b Strang P.A.	110	(2) not out	43
M.S.Sinclair	lbw b Strang P.A.	12		
P.J.Wiseman	lbw b Strang P.A.	14		
S.P.Fleming*	c Rennie b Strang P.A.	11	(3) lbw b Strang P.A.	12
N.J.Astle	c Flower A. b Strang P.A.	0	(4) c Nkala b Strang P.A.	27
C.D.McMillan	c Flower A. b Strang P.A.	58	(5) not out	31
C.L.Cairns	b Streak	33		
A.C.Parore†	not out	32		
D.L.Vettori	c & b Strang P.A.	49		
S.B.O'Connor	c Campbell b Strang P.A.	4		
Extras	(lb 1, nb 8)	9	(lb 2, w 1, nb 3)	6
TOTAL	(153.5 overs)	**338**	(45.4 overs) (3 wkts)	**132**

Bowling

NEW ZEALAND	O	M	R	W	O	M	R	W
Cairns	28.2	9	77	2	14.5	5	31	5
O'Connor	30	7	63	1	9	5	8	1
McMillan	9	3	23	0				
Vettori	52	23	79	1				
Astle	11	6	9	1	18	10	24	1
Wiseman	45	16	90	5	25	8	54	3
Richardson					1	0	1	0
ZIMBABWE								
Streak	26	9	67	2	5	0	21	0
Nkala	21	7	43	0	2	1	2	0
Strang P.A.	51.5	12	109	8	20.4	3	49	2
Strang B.C.	25	7	63	0	2	0	10	0
Mutendera	14	4	29	0				
Flower G.W.	16	4	26	0	1.3	0	5	0
Rennie					13.3	0	40	1
Campbell					1	0	3	0

Fall of Wickets

	Z 1st	NZ 1st	Z 2nd	NZ 2nd
1st	40	15	6	27
2nd	91	52	23	43
3rd	120	109	23	93
4th	157	139	75	-
5th	206	139	86	-
6th	282	180	100	-
7th	291	252	100	-
8th	300	252	110	-
9th	323	330	119	-
10th	350	338	119	-

Paul Wiseman shouldered the spin duties when Daniel Vettori was unable to bowl in the second innings owing to a back injury.

MILESTONES

- Mark Richardson (210) made his test debut.

- It was New Zealand's 45th test victory.

- Adam Parore and Daniel Vettori added 78, a New Zealand record for the eighth wicket against Zimbabwe.

- Chris Cairns, in his 48th test, became New Zealand's second-highest wicket taker passing Danny Morrison's 160 victims, also from 48 tests.

- Paul Strang's figures of 8-109 were the best for Zimbabwe in tests.

Dion Nash (pictured) and Chris Cairns created an eighth wicket record against all countries of 144.

281 ZIMBABWE v NEW ZEALAND (Second Test)

at Harare Sports Club on 19, 20, 21, 22, 23 September, 2000
Toss : New Zealand. Umpires : I.D. Robinson & D.R. Shepherd
New Zealand won by 8 wickets

Eleven days prior to this match Mark Richardson had batted for 12 hours and 35 minutes in compiling 306 against Zimbabwe A at Kwekwe. Playing in his second test he was adjudged lbw for 99 in the last over of the day. He took full advantage of a docile pitch to limit himself to a minimum of strokes and display ironclad concentration. His partnership with Nathan Astle, worth 135, enabled New Zealand to reach 226-4 at the end of the first day.

An invigorating record stand of 144 between Chris Cairns and Dion Nash saw Cairns through to his fourth test century and took New Zealand through to their highest total against Zimbabwe, 465.

Zimbabwe, after losing an early wicket, progressed comfortably to 76-1 before accurate bowling from all five medium-pace bowlers saw them lose their last nine wickets for 90 runs. It was a woeful exhibition in conditions that were excellent for batting.

With Zimbabwe facing a deficit of 299 with two days remaining, all the signs indicated a comfortable victory for New Zealand, especially when Zimbabwe was 48-4. Guy Whittall, now reinstated, collaborated with Andy Flower to

add 133 for the fifth wicket to stem New Zealand's thrust to victory. Whittle advanced to his third test hundred, striking Astle for four, two and six off successive balls to end the fourth day 105 not out.

Whittle's defiant vigil lasted well into the final day and he remained unbeaten, scoring an epic 188. With Heath Streak, 151 were added, taking Zimbabwe to 330-5 before the third new ball saw Cairns and Shayne O'Connor claim four wickets in eight overs. Stubborn batting by Pommie Mbangwa teased New Zealand cruelly and when he was finally run out New Zealand had time for 18 overs to make 72, which they did with 16 balls to spare.

NEW ZEALAND

M.H.Richardson	lbw b Nkala	99		
C.M.Spearman	c Flower A. b Olonga	2	(1) c Rennie b Streak	2
M.S.Sinclair	c Carlisle b Olonga	44	not out	35
S.P.Fleming*	c Campbell b Mbangwa	9		
N.J.Astle	run out	86		
C.D.McMillan	lbw b Mbangwa	15		
C.L.Cairns	st Flower A. b Strang	124	(4) not out	19
A.C.Parore†	c Flower A. b Olonga	4	(2) c Carlisle b Streak	13
D.J.Nash	c Flower G.W. b Strang	62		
P.J.Wiseman	not out	1		
S.B.O'Connor	c Whittall b Flower G.W.	2		
Extras	(lb 3, w 2, nb 12)	17	(lb 2, w 1, nb 2)	5
TOTAL	**(160.3 overs)**	**465**	**(15.2 overs) (2 wkts)**	**74**

ZIMBABWE

G.W.Flower	c Parore b Astle	49	run out	10
G.J.Rennie	c Spearman b Cairns	4	c Spearman b O'Connor	1
S.V.Carlisle	c Sinclair b Cairns	31	c Fleming b Astle	20
A.D.R.Campbell	c Fleming b O'Connor	0	run out	10
A.Flower†	lbw b McMillan	48	c Sinclair b O'Connor	65
G.J.Whittall	c Parore b Astle	9	not out	188
H.H.Streak*	c Wiseman b O'Connor	8	lbw b Cairns	54
M.L.Nkala	c Parore b McMillan	0	lbw b O'Connor	0
P.A.Strang	c Parore b O'Connor	5	b Cairns	8
H.K.Olonga	c Parore b Nash	4	lbw b O'Connor	0
M.Mbangwa	not out	0	run out	5
Extras	(b 3, lb 3, w 1, nb 1)	8	(b 4, lb 4, nb 1)	9
TOTAL	**(92 overs)**	**166**	**(178.3 overs)**	**370**

Bowling	O	M	R	W	O	M	R	W		Fall of Wickets				
ZIMBABWE											NZ	Z	Z	NZ
											1st	1st	2nd	2nd
Olonga	27	5	115	3						1st	5	5	1	4
Streak	29	6	74	0	8	2	33	2		2nd	69	76	27	42
Nkala	15	0	60	1	3	0	17	0		3rd	91	77	39	-
Mbangwa	28	10	58	2	4.2	0	22	0		4th	226	118	48	-
Strang	38	11	80	2						5th	256	146	179	-
Flower G.W.	20.3	6	59	1						6th	302	151	330	-
Rennie	3	0	16	0						7th	318	151	335	-
NEW ZEALAND										8th	462	157	348	-
Cairns	17.1	7	33	2	33	7	80	2		9th	462	164	349	-
O'Connor	28	9	43	3	45	17	73	4		10th	465	166	370	-
Nash	17	11	25	1	17.3	8	28	0						
McMillan	12.5	2	29	2	20	4	53	0						
Astle	14	9	22	2	36	16	73	1						
Wiseman	3	0	8	0	27	11	55	0						

MILESTONES

- It was New Zealand's 46th test win.

- Stephen Fleming became New Zealand's most successful test captain, leading New Zealand to its 12th test victory in 29 tests. Geoff Howarth had 11 wins in 30 tests.

- Mark Richardson became the sixth New Zealander to be dismissed for 99 in a test.

- Chris Cairns and Dion Nash put on 144, an eighth wicket record for New Zealand against all countries.

- Andy Flower became the first Zimbabwe player to reach 3000 runs in test cricket.

2000/01 New Zealand in South Africa

New Zealand left Zimbabwe and headed to Kenya where they created a great surprise by beating India in the final of the first ICC Knockout in Nairobi with two balls to spare.

282 SOUTH AFRICA v NEW ZEALAND (*First Test*)

at Goodyear Park, Bloemfontein on 17, 18, 19, 20, 21 November, 2000
Toss : South Africa. Umpires : A.V. Jayaprakash & D.L. Orchard
South Africa won by 5 wickets

Injury decimated the New Zealand bowling attack, with Shayne O'Connor being the only pace bowler with any test wickets (44). Daryl Tuffey had none from his only test and Chris Martin was making his debut. Brooke Walker, the leg-spinner, was also making his test debut. Conversely, Allan Donald and Shaun Pollock had 483 wickets between them.

In spite of losing a wicket with the second ball of the game, South Africa built up a formidable total thanks to Jacques Kallis. He shared consecutive partnerships with Gary Kirsten, Daryll Cullinan and Neil McKenzie that

Stephen Fleming became the seventh New Zealand batsman to be dismissed for 99 in a test match.

produced 97, 66 and 115 respectively, while compiling his seventh test century and his biggest score to date, 160. With the exception of Lance Klusener, the South African lower order powered their way to an imposing 471 before they declared with nine wickets down.

The combined forces of Donald and Pollock ensured that New Zealand would not avoid the follow-on mark in spite of an obstinate innings from Stephen Fleming. There was great excitement when Donald dismissed O'Connor. It was his 300th test wicket and it was greeted with a three-gun salute from an armoured car parked near the boundary.

With the pitch playing slower and lower New Zealand wiped off the deficit of 242 for the loss of four, thanks to Mark Richardson's impregnable defence and excellent judgement of what to leave. He scored 77 in 256 minutes.

Fleming became the seventh New Zealander to be dismissed for 99 in a test, thereby failing to improve his fifty-to-century conversion rate, which stood at 26 to 2. Craig McMillan played an innings out of character, grafting 10 minutes longer than Richardson for 78.

After lunch on the fifth day Makhaya Ntini captured three wickets in three overs to take his first five-wicket bag. South Africa lost five wickets in scoring the 102 runs required for victory as Tuffey bowled with greater control and fire.

SOUTH AFRICA

Batsman	Dismissal	Runs	Dismissal (2nd)	Runs
H.H.Dippenaar	c Astle b O'Connor	0	c Parore b Tuffey	27
G.Kirsten	c Astle b Martin	31	lbw b O'Connor	1
J.H.Kallis	c Parore b O'Connor	160	lbw b Martin	13
D.J.Cullinan	b Walker	29	lbw b Tuffey	22
N.D.McKenzie	c Parore b Martin	55	not out	13
M.V.Boucher†	lbw b Walker	76	(7) not out	22
L.Klusener	b O'Connor	9	(6) c McMillan b Tuffey	4
N.Boje	c Tuffey b Astle	43		
S.M.Pollock*	c Sinclair b Martin	25		
A.A.Donald	not out	21		
M.Ntini				
Extras	(b 5, lb 7, nb 10)	22	(nb 1)	1
TOTAL	**(142.1 overs) (9 wkts dec)**	**471**	**(26.3 overs) (5 wkts)**	**103**

NEW ZEALAND

Batsman	Dismissal	Runs	Dismissal (2nd)	Runs
M.H.Richardson	b Donald	23	lbw b Donald	77
C.M.Spearman	c Klusener b Pollock	23	c McKenzie b Ntini	15
M.S.Sinclair	c Cullinan b Pollock	1	c Klusener b Donald	20
S.P.Fleming*	b Boje	57	c Kirsten b Donald	99
N.J.Astle	c Kallis b Ntini	37	b Ntini	8
C.D.McMillan	c Boucher b Donald	16	c Kirsten b Kallis	78
A.C.Parore†	lbw b Pollock	11	(8) c Kallis b Ntini	12
B.G.K.Walker	not out	27	(7) c Boucher b Ntini	10
D.R.Tuffey	b Pollock	0	b Ntini	6
S.B.O'Connor	lbw b Donald	15	b Ntini	0
C.S.Martin	c Boucher b Kallis	7	not out	0
Extras	(b 1, lb 7, w 2, nb 2)	12	(b 2, lb 10, w 1, nb 4)	17
TOTAL	**(89 overs)**	**229**	**(157.4 overs)**	**342**

Bowling	O	M	R	W	O	M	R	W
NEW ZEALAND								
O'Connor	30	4	87	3	7	0	28	1
Tuffey	26	6	96	0	8	1	38	3
Martin	22.1	4	89	3	5	3	18	1
Walker	27	4	92	2	6.3	2	19	0
Astle	24	5	57	1				
McMillan	13	2	38	0				
SOUTH AFRICA								
Donald	21	4	69	3	28	14	43	3
Pollock	22	10	37	4	25	11	47	0
Ntini	14	4	48	1	31.4	12	66	6
Kallis	13	5	30	1	23	4	88	1
Boje	16	4	35	1	40	14	61	0
Klusener	3	2	2	0	10	3	25	0

Fall of Wickets	SA 1st	NZ 1st	NZ 2nd	SA 2nd
1st	0	28	33	3
2nd	97	29	93	16
3rd	164	72	145	55
4th	279	151	175	69
5th	304	153	247	75
6th	330	176	285	-
7th	409	183	325	-
8th	429	185	340	-
9th	471	213	341	-
10th	-	229	342	-

MILESTONES

- Chris Martin (211) and Brooke Walker (212) made their test debuts.

- Allan Donald became the first South African bowler to claim 300 test wickets.

283 SOUTH AFRICA v NEW ZEALAND *(Second Test)*

at St George's Park, Port Elizabeth on 30 November, 1, 2, 3, 4 December, 2000
Toss : South Africa. Umpires : R.E. Koertzen & I.D. Robinson
South Africa won by 7 wickets

Sean Pollock misjudged the pitch when he asked New Zealand to bat first as it played truer than expected and it was only the sustained pressure exerted by the South African pace attack that continued to chip away at the New Zealand batsmen, breaking numerous emerging partnerships by dismissing whoever was batting with Mathew Sinclair. Thanks largely to Sinclair's watchfulness and patience, New Zealand ended the first day at 206-7, with Sinclair being 88 not out.

Sinclair and Shayne O'Connor, who was to compile the highest test score in his test career, provided the largest partnership of the innings of 73. Sinclair's was the last wicket to fall at 298 and his 150 was a testimony to his intense concentration and ability to work the ball off the back foot through the off field. Alan Donald and Shaun Pollock, with four wickets apiece, again proved the old cricket maxim that great fast bowlers come in pairs.

South Africa was struggling at 207-7 with Chris Martin's lively pace and ability to move the ball late into the right-hand batsmen demanding sound judgement and solid technique. Neil McKenzie, who had made his debut in a test series against Sri Lanka earlier in the year and scored only 54 runs in five innings, extended his test career with a fighting and stylish maiden century.

Nicky Boje batted at nine even though he had been South Africa's leading run-scorer in the one-day internationals, where he scored 355 runs, including two centuries. He and McKenzie established a new South African record partnership for the eighth wicket and gave their side a lead of 63. Nathan Astle bowled with remarkable stamina and economy. His 36 overs included 18 maidens and he conceded only 46 runs.

At the outset of New Zealand's second innings there was a request from the batting side to ask the St George's Park band to refrain from playing as it was disturbing the batsmen's concentration. With three of the top batsmen dismissed by the time New Zealand had wiped out the deficit, the band obviously had kept playing.

Mark Richardson's grit and determination in scoring 60 were again admirable. Stephen Fleming said after the game that "poor batsmanship and poor option-taking between lunch and tea on the fourth day cost us the game." In the period described his team lost five wickets for 69.

Lance Klusener claimed the last three wickets in 10 balls to dismiss the tourists for 148. South Africa was untroubled to win by seven wickets with a day to spare.

Playing in his second test, Chris Martin's lively pace and ability to move the ball late into right-hand batsmen was rewarded with four wickets in South Africa's first innings.

NEW ZEALAND

Batsman	Dismissal	Runs	Dismissal	Runs
M.H.Richardson	b Ntini	26	c Boucher b Pollock	60
C.M.Spearman	c Kirsten b Donald	16	lbw b Donald	0
M.S.Sinclair	c Kirsten b Donald	150	lbw b Boje	17
S.P.Fleming*	c & b Pollock	14	c Cullinan b Boje	8
N.J.Astle	lbw b Pollock	2	c Boucher b Ntini	18
C.D.McMillan	c Ntini b Pollock	39	lbw b Pollock	0
A.C.Parore†	c Boucher b Donald	2	c Kirsten b Ntini	5
B.G.K.Walker	c Cullinan b Pollock	3	lbw b Klusener	19
S.B.O'Connor	b Kallis	20	b Klusener	8
K.P.Walmsley	c Cullinan b Donald	5	lbw b Klusener	0
C.S.Martin	not out	5	not out	0
Extras	(b 4, lb 5, w 2, nb 5)	16	(b 6, lb 3, nb 4)	13
TOTAL	(126.3 overs)	298	(69.3 overs)	148

SOUTH AFRICA

Batsman	Dismissal	Runs	Dismissal	Runs
H.H.Dippenaar	lbw b Martin	35	lbw b O'Connor	0
G.Kirsten	c Parore b Walmsley	49	not out	47
J.H.Kallis	c Parore b Astle	12	c O'Connor b Martin	23
D.J.Cullinan	b Walker	33	b Walmsley	11
S.M.Pollock*	c Spearman b Martin	33		
N.D.McKenzie	c Spearman b McMillan	120	(5) not out	7
M.V.Boucher†	b O'Connor	0		
L.Klusener	c Parore b Martin	6		
N.Boje	c Parore b O'Connor	51		
A.A.Donald	lbw b Martin	9		
M.Ntini	not out	0		
Extras	(b 7, lb 4, w 2)	13	(lb 1)	1
TOTAL	(144.4 overs)	361	(34.1 overs) (3 wkts)	89

Bowling SOUTH AFRICA	O	M	R	W	O	M	R	W
Donald	26.3	2	69	4	7	1	16	1
Pollock	32	15	64	4	15	4	44	2
Kallis	21	8	44	1	7	2	17	0
Ntini	22	7	59	1	16	6	24	2
Klusener	6	2	8	0	9.3	5	8	3
Boje	19	5	45	0	15	2	30	2
NEW ZEALAND								
O'Connor	26.4	8	68	2	8	4	9	1
Martin	29	8	104	4	12	3	32	1
Walmsley	13	2	40	1	5	2	7	1
Walker	23	5	61	1	7.1	1	32	0
Astle	36	18	46	1	2	0	8	0
McMillan	17	6	31	1				

Fall of Wickets	NZ 1st	SA 1st	NZ 2nd	SA 2nd
1st	43	81	4	4
2nd	55	96	54	53
3rd	95	114	64	71
4th	101	151	111	-
5th	172	181	111	-
6th	194	184	115	-
7th	203	209	122	-
8th	276	345	147	-
9th	291	361	147	-
10th	298	361	148	-

MILESTONES

- Mathew Sinclair's 150 was the highest score by a New Zealand batsman against South Africa, beating John Reid's 142 at Johannesburg (test 56).

- Neil McKenzie and Nicky Boje added 136, a record eighth wicket partnership for South Africa against New Zealand.

284 SOUTH AFRICA v NEW ZEALAND *(Third Test)*

at Wanderers Stadium, Johannesburg on 8, 9, 10, 11, 12 December, 2000
Toss : South Africa. Umpires : D.L. Orchard & G. Sharp
Match drawn

Allan Donald was unable to play and Mfuneko Ngam replaced him. Ngam, who played in the Eastern Province, had modelled himself on Donald.

Play began on the second day after rain had prevented play on the first. Adam Parore was used as a makeshift opener and should have been Ngam's first wicket when he survived chances in his first and third overs. Ngam had to wait until after lunch, when the score had reached 83, before he had Mark Richardson caught by Mark Boucher for 46.

The fast-improving Makhaya Ntini dismissed Stephen Fleming and Nathan Astle in successive overs as five of the middle order were wiped out for 38. It took Hamish Marshall, in his debut test, one hour to get off the mark, during which time he was hit several times on the helmet. He displayed raw courage to remain unbeaten on 40 when New Zealand's innings ended at 200. Bad light stopped play when South Africa had lost Gary Kirsten caught at short leg by Richardson off Chris Martin for 10.

Rain continued to fall and prevented any play on the third and fourth days, leading to conjecture that the South African captain, Shaun Pollock, might be tempted to contrive a result on the fifth day similar to what had occurred at Centurion the previous year between Hansie Cronje and England's Michael Vaughan. On that occasion both teams had forfeited an innings, something which was unprecedented in test cricket. That test led to the eventual downfall of Cronje.

The fifth day continued as normal with Boeta Dippenaar taking advantage of a meaningless day in scoring his first test century. New Zealand's tour of Zimbabwe, Kenya and South Africa had been blighted by eight players having serious injuries that necessitated them returning to New Zealand.

NEW ZEALAND

Batsman	Dismissal	Runs
M.H.Richardson	c Boucher b Ngam	46
A.C.Parore†	c McKenzie b Ntini	10
M.S.Sinclair	c Klusener b Pollock	24
S.P.Fleming*	b Ntini	14
N.J.Astle	c Kallis b Ntini	12
C.D.McMillan	c Klusener b Kallis	4
H.J.H.Marshall	not out	40
B.G.K.Walker	lbw b Klusener	17
D.R.Tuffey	c Boucher b Ngam	8
S.B.O'Connor	c Kallis b Pollock	9
C.S.Martin	b Kallis	0
Extras	(b 2, lb 9, w 1, nb 4)	16
TOTAL	(93.5 overs)	200

SOUTH AFRICA

Batsman	Dismissal	Runs
H.H.Dippenaar	b O'Connor	100
G.Kirsten	c Richardson b Martin	10
N.Boje	c Sinclair b Martin	22
J.H.Kallis	not out	79
D.J.Cullinan	not out	31
N.D.McKenzie		
L.Klusener		
M.V.Boucher†		
S.M.Pollock*		
M.Ngam		
M.Ntini		
Extras	(lb 17, w 2)	19
TOTAL	(97 overs) 3 wkts dec	261

Bowling SOUTH AFRICA	O	M	R	W
Pollock	26	9	41	2
Ngam	19	8	34	2
Kallis	15.5	4	26	2
Ntini	18	9	29	3
Klusener	12	2	43	1
Boje	3	0	16	0
NEW ZEALAND				
O'Connor	15	5	52	1
Martin	15	4	43	2
Tuffey	19	4	60	0
Astle	26	15	31	0
McMillan	17	5	41	0
Marshall	1	0	4	0
Sinclair	4	0	13	0

Fall of Wickets	NZ 1st	SA 1st
1st	37	18
2nd	83	87
3rd	83	187
4th	112	-
5th	113	-
6th	117	-
7th	148	-
8th	174	-
9th	199	-
10th	200	-

MILESTONES

- Hamish Marshall (213) made his test debut.

- It was Shaun Pollock's first series win as captain.

Hamish Marshall took over one hour to get off the mark in his test debut. During this time he was hit several times on the helmet. He displayed courage of the highest order by still getting behind the ball and was undefeated on 40 when New Zealand was finally dismissed.

AVERAGES

New Zealand

BATTING	M	I	NO	Runs	HS	Ave
M.H. Richardson	3	5	0	232	77	46.40
M.S. Sinclair	3	5	0	212	150	42.40
S.P. Fleming	3	5	0	192	99	38.40
C.D. McMillan	3	5	0	137	78	27.40
B.G.K. Walker	3	5	1	76	27*	19.00
N.J. Astle	3	5	0	77	37	15.40
C.M. Spearman	2	4	0	54	23	13.50
S.B. O'Connor	3	5	0	52	20	10.40
A.C. Parore	3	5	0	40	12	8.00
C.S. Martin	3	5	3	12	7	6.00
D.R. Tuffey	2	3	0	14	8	4.66
K.P. Walmsley	1	2	0	5	5	2.50
H.J.H. Marshall	1	1	1	40	40*	-

BOWLING	O	M	R	W	Ave
K.P. Walmsley	18	4	47	2	23.50
C.S. Martin	83.1	22	286	11	26.00
S.B. O'Connor	86.4	21	244	8	30.50
D.R. Tuffey	53	11	194	3	64.66
B.G.K. Walker	63.4	12	204	3	68.00
N.J. Astle	88	38	142	2	71.00
C.D. McMillan	47	13	110	1	110.00
H.J.H. Marshall	1	0	4	0	-
M.S. Sinclair	4	0	13	0	-

South Africa

BATTING	M	I	NO	Runs	HS	Ave
N.D. McKenzie	3	4	2	195	120	97.50
J.H. Kallis	3	5	1	287	160	71.75
M.V. Boucher	3	3	1	98	76	49.00
N. Boje	3	3	0	116	51	38.66
G. Kirsten	3	5	1	138	49	34.50
H.H. Dippenaar	3	5	0	162	100	32.40
D.J. Cullinan	3	5	1	126	33	31.50
A.A. Donald	2	2	1	30	21*	30.00
S.M. Pollock	3	2	0	58	33	29.00
L. Klusener	3	3	0	19	9	6.33
M. Ntini	3	1	1	0	0*	-
M. Ngam	1	-	-	-	-	-

BOWLING	O	M	R	W	Ave
M. Ngam	19	8	34	2	17.00
M. Ntini	101.4	38	226	13	17.38
A.A. Donald	82.3	21	197	11	17.90
S.M. Pollock	120	49	233	12	19.41
L. Klusener	40.3	14	86	4	21.50
J.H. Kallis	79.5	23	205	5	41.00
N. Boje	93	25	187	3	62.33

2000/01 Zimbabwe in New Zealand

Zimbabwe played six matches in New Zealand with only one test being scheduled, the third Pohutukawa Boxing Day test at the Basin Reserve.

285 NEW ZEALAND v ZIMBABWE *(Only Test)*

at Basin Reserve, Wellington on 26, 27, 28, 29, 30 December, 2000
Toss : New Zealand. Umpires : B.C. Cooray & R.S. Dunne
Match drawn

The pitch was bare of grass and very dry and deceived the New Zealand team into thinking that it would assist slow bowlers when historical facts show that in the previous 36 tests played at the ground spinners had had little success.

Batting first in a fierce northerly gale New Zealand made heavy weather of the placid pitch, losing three wickets for 67. Mark Richardson continued his impressive record of consistency before he was run out at 145-4.

This brought together Nathan Astle and Craig McMillan, both of whom had been subjected to intense media speculation about their lack of form, attitude and performance in Africa. Both played to eliminate any risky shots, with the result they refrained from playing any. The three sessions on the first day yielded 63, 66 and 61 runs to have New Zealand 190-4.

Craig McMillan, right, congratulates Nathan Astle on reaching his century.

McMillan was the first dismissed when he was bowled by Brian Murphy's non-existent leg-spin for 142. The face-saving record partnership of 222 had occupied 311 minutes. Astle's marathon innings of 141 lasted 549 minutes.

New Zealand ended the second day at 475-6 and continued on the third day when only 29 overs were bowled owing to rain and bad light. Chris Martin seamed the ball disconcertingly in his opening spell to claim two wickets.

Gavin Rennie kept the New Zealand attack and their two spin bowlers at bay for 401 minutes, making 93. Andy Flower (79) and Trevor Madondo (74 not out) proved doughty fighters, untroubled by all the bowlers except Martin. In spite of token declarations on the last day the comatose nature of the pitch consigned this test to a boring draw.

NEW ZEALAND

M.H.Richardson	run out	75			
M.J.Horne	c Flower b Streak	1	(1) c Flower b Streak	0
M.S.Sinclair	lbw b Strang	9	(2) c Flower b Murphy	18
S.P.Fleming*	run out	22	(3) run out	55
N.J.Astle	c Carlisle b Strang	141	(4) not out	51
C.D.McMillan	b Murphy	142	(5) c Madondo b Strang	10
A.C.Parore†	not out	50	(6) not out	3
B.G.K.Walker	c Olonga b Strang	27		
P.J.Wiseman	not out	0		
S.B.O'Connor				
C.S.Martin				
Extras	(b 1, lb 8, w 5, nb 6)	20	(b 5, lb 5, nb 6)	16
TOTAL	**(181 overs) (7 wkts dec)**	**487**	**(40 overs) (4 wkts dec)**	**153**

ZIMBABWE

G.J.Whittall	b Martin	9	c Parore b O'Connor	6
G.J.Rennie	c Parore b McMillan	93	c Parore b Wiseman	37
S.V.Carlisle	c Horne b Martin	0	not out	16
A.D.R.Campbell	lbw b Martin	24	not out	0
A.Flower†	c Parore b Martin	79		
T.N.Madondo	not out	74		
D.A.Marillier	c Parore b Martin	28		
H.H.Streak*	not out	19		
B.A.Murphy				
B.C.Strang				
H.K.Olonga				
Extras	(b 3, lb 9, nb 2)	14	(lb 1)	1
TOTAL	**(138.5 overs) (6 wkts dec)**	**340**	**(30 overs) (2 wkts)**	**60**

Bowling	O	M	R	W	O	M	R	W		Fall of Wickets			
ZIMBABWE										NZ	Z	NZ	Z
										1st	1st	2nd	2nd
Streak	37	10	74	1	5	1	18	1					
Strang	46	16	116	3	11	2	25	1	1st	5	21	4	26
Olonga	30	2	105	0	2	0	12	0	2nd	22	23	44	57
Murphy	46	9	128	1	18	0	86	1	3rd	67	66	103	-
Whittall	22	6	55	0	4	3	2	0	4th	145	196	126	-
NEW ZEALAND									5th	367	237	-	-
Martin	32.5	11	71	5	5	2	6	0	6th	426	295	-	-
O'Connor	16	7	29	0	8	4	8	1	7th	487	-	-	-
Wiseman	54	13	131	0	6	2	15	1	8th	-	-	-	-
Walker	22	1	68	0	11	1	30	0	9th	-	-	-	-
McMillan	9	4	22	1					10th	-	-	-	-
Astle	5	2	7	0									

MILESTONES

- Nathan Astle and Craig McMillan put on 222, a record for the fifth wicket for New Zealand against Zimbabwe.

- Astle scored a century and a fifty in the same test for the second time in his career.

- Andy Flower scored his sixth consecutive test fifty, one short of Everton Weekes' record.

- Flower passed 1000 test runs for the calendar year.

2000/01 Pakistan in New Zealand

It is doubtful if any side that has toured New Zealand since Parr's All England XI in 1863/64 has attracted as much controversy as the side captained by Moin Khan and coached by Javed Miandad. On the team's return to Pakistan both were dismissed.

286 NEW ZEALAND v PAKISTAN (First Test)

at Eden Park, Auckland on 8, 9, 10, 11, 12 March, 2001
Toss : New Zealand. Umpires : D.B. Cowie & R.B. Tiffin
Pakistan won by 299 runs

It was the first time that a drop-in, or portable, pitch was used for a test match in New Zealand. Both captains expressed uncertainty over how it would perform and, not surprisingly, Stephen Fleming inserted the visitors when he won the toss.

None of the batsmen were troubled by the pitch and the first seven all batted for at least an hour. Yousuf Youhana delighted the spectators with his classic stroke-making. Younis Khan was more flamboyant and exciting and with 19-year-old Faisal Iqbal, Miandad's nephew, 132 was added to have Pakistan 270-4 by stumps at the end of the first day.

Daryl Tuffey is thrilled to get Younis Khan caught by Craig McMillan in the slips cordon.

New Zealand began the rain affected second day by getting both overnight batsmen out without adding to their scores. Chris Martin and Daryl Tuffey ended with four wickets each and Adam Parore took five catches. New Zealand was immediately on the back foot with both openers removed by the second over. A determined partnership between Stephen Fleming and Craig McMillan gave New Zealand some backbone but they still finished 94 runs in arrears.

The highlight of Pakistan's second innings was the second century partnership of the game between Younis and Faisal, this time worth an unbeaten 147, with Younis again displaying his prodigious talent and scoring the second century of what was to become an exceptional test career.

New Zealand began the task of scoring 431 to win in 138 overs in the best possible fashion when Mark Richardson and Matthew Bell put on 91 in 30 overs before Bell was run out shortly before stumps.

The air of self-confidence emanating from the New Zealand camp at the beginning of the last day at 105-1 was short-lived. With no addition to the score Richardson was caught off Saqlain Mushtaq, the only wicket of the eight that he was to capture in the match that wasn't bowled or lbw. The introduction of Mohammad Sami brought the game to a sensational conclusion.

PAKISTAN						
Imran Farhat	c Parore b Martin	23	c & b Wiseman			63
Salim Elahi	c Parore b Tuffey	24	c Wiseman b Tuffey			7
Misbah-ul-Haq	c Sinclair b McMillan	28	c Parore b Tuffey			10
Yousuf Youhana	c Parore b Martin	51	c Astle b Franklin			42
Younis Khan	c McMillan b Tuffey	91	(6) not out			149
Faisal Iqbal	c Fleming b Tuffey	42	(7) not out			52
Moin Khan*†	c Parore b Tuffey	47				
Saqlain Mushtaq	c Fleming b Martin	2	(5) c Parore b Tuffey			2
Waqar Younis	lbw b Martin	4				
Mushtaq Ahmed	c Parore b Franklin	19				
Mohammad Sami	not out	0				
Extras	(b 2, lb 7, nb 6)	15	(b 4, lb 6, nb 1)			11
TOTAL	(106 overs)	**346**	(103 overs) (5 wkts dec)			**336**

NEW ZEALAND						
M.H.Richardson	b Sami	1	c Farhat b Saqlain			59
M.D.Bell	c Moin b Waqar	0	run out			28
M.S.Sinclair	c Farhat b Sami	34	(4) c Youhana b Sami			10
S.P.Fleming*	b Saqlain	86	(5) lbw b Saqlain			5
N.J.Astle	b Mushtaq	0	(6) b Saqlain			1
C.D.McMillan	c Younis b Waqar	54	(7) c Saqlain b Sami			0
A.C.Parore†	not out	32	(8) not out			0
J.E.C.Franklin	lbw b Saqlain	0	(9) b Sami			0
P.J.Wiseman	lbw b Saqlain	9	(3) b Sami			8
D.R.Tuffey	b Saqlain	2	b Sami			0
C.S.Martin	b Sami	0	b Saqlain			0
Extras	(b 8, lb 20, nb 6)	34	(b 12, lb 7, nb 1)			20
TOTAL	(96.4 overs)	**252**	(59.4 overs)			**131**

Bowling	O	M	R	W	O	M	R	W	Fall of Wickets				
NEW ZEALAND										P	NZ	P	NZ
										1st	1st	2nd	2nd
Tuffey	34	13	96	4	17	3	43	3					
Martin	22	1	106	4	12	2	65	0	1st	46	1	21	91
Franklin	21	6	55	1	18	2	59	1	2nd	52	1	59	105
Wiseman	7	0	35	0	36	6	107	1	3rd	130	82	97	121
McMillan	14	5	34	1	7	0	27	0	4th	138	83	110	126
Astle	8	3	11	0	13	6	25	0	5th	270	194	189	127
PAKISTAN									6th	271	217	-	130
Waqar	22	8	44	2	11	2	31	0	7th	286	217	-	130
Sami	31.4	11	70	3	15	4	36	5	8th	294	237	-	130
Saqlain	20	3	48	4	25.4	12	24	4	9th	346	251	-	130
Mushtaq	23	8	62	1	8	2	21	0	10th	346	252	-	131

Running in like a sprinter his pace was electric and in seven overs he captured five wickets for six runs as the last eight wickets tumbled for 10 runs, leaving New Zealand humiliatingly beaten by 299 runs.

MILESTONES

- James Franklin (214) made his test debut.

- It was the first time that a portable pitch was used for a test match.

- It was Pakistan's ninth win over New Zealand in the last 11 tests between the nations.

- It was New Zealand's heaviest defeat by a runs margin, previously 297 by Australia at Eden Park in 1973/74 (test 114).

287 NEW ZEALAND v PAKISTAN *(Second Test)*

at Jade Stadium, Christchurch on 15, 16, 17, 18, 19 March, 2001
Toss : Pakistan. Umpires : D.J. Harper & D.M. Quested
Match drawn

The portable pitch used at Lancaster Park was so hard and so batsman-friendly that there was never any doubt about the outcome of the game – a boring draw. Three days after New Zealand were humiliated at Eden Park, losing eight wickets for 10 runs, the openers Mark Richardson and Matthew Bell restored the team's batting psyche with the first opening century partnership for New Zealand in 13 tests.

Mathew Sinclair dominated the rest of the innings. He remained unbeaten in scoring his second test double-century, being 204 not out, compiled in 520 minutes of intense concentration. When New Zealand ended its innings, Pakistan lost both its openers for 25, which suggested that better pickings were in store for the local bowlers.

The suggestion was only momentary as Inzamam-ul-Haq, with a cultured 130, and Faisal Iqbal added 132, which prepared the way for Yousuf Youhana to settle in to occupy the crease for 528 minutes in making 203.

Pakistan were content to defend their series lead by batting New Zealand out of the game. When their innings was tottering at 304-7 Saqlain Mushtaq provided a noble ally for Youhana. The slender right-hand batsman, who had 35 scores under 10 in 52 test innings, stayed 10 minutes longer than seven hours, scoring 101 not out. The partnership of 248 between Youhana and Saqlain was the highest of the five century partnerships made during the game. It took Pakistan to a first innings lead of 95 when they declared at 571-8.

With no chance of a decision, Richardson, Bell and Sinclair took full advantage of the friendly bowling on an almost unscarred cricket pitch that had seen 1243 runs scored for the loss of only 19 wickets.

NEW ZEALAND

M.H.Richardson	b Saqlain	46	not out	73
M.D.Bell	c Farhat b Saqlain	75	lbw b Younis	40
M.S.Sinclair	not out	204	not out	50
S.P.Fleming*	run out	32		
N.J.Astle	c Moin b Waqar	6		
G.E.Bradburn	c Farhat b Fazl	0		
C.D.McMillan	c Younis b Fazl	20		
A.C.Parore†	lbw b Saqlain	46		
D.R.Tuffey	b Fazl	13		
C.J.Drum	c Moin b Waqar	4		
C.S.Martin	b Waqar	0		
Extras	(b 2, lb 17, w 1, nb 10)	30	(b 15, lb 4, nb 14)	33
TOTAL	(156 overs)	**476**	(73 overs) (1 wkt dec)	**196**

PAKISTAN

Imran Farhat	c Drum b Martin	4
Ijaz Ahmed	hit wicket b Drum	11
Faisal Iqbal	c Fleming b McMillan	63
Inzamam-ul-Haq	c Fleming b Martin	130
Yousuf Youhana	c & b Richardson	203
Younis Khan	c Parore b Tuffey	0
Moin Khan*†	c Martin b Bradburn	28
Saqlain Mushtaq	not out	101
Waqar Younis	c Parore b Tuffey	12
Fazl-e-Akbar	not out	0
Mohammad Sami		
Extras	(b 5, lb 8, nb 6)	19
TOTAL	(210 overs) (8 wkts dec)	**571**

Bowling										Fall of Wickets			
PAKISTAN	O	M	R	W	O	M	R	W			NZ	P	NZ
											1st	1st	2nd
Waqar	34	6	114	3	8	1	18	0	1st		102	5	69
Sami	36	4	107	0	11	3	32	0	2nd		163	25	–
Fazl	32	6	87	3	7	0	26	0	3rd		248	157	–
Saqlain	48	11	134	3	24	5	44	0	4th		276	259	–
Younis	6	1	15	0	21	6	47	1	5th		282	260	–
Youhana					1	0	3	0	6th		327	304	–
Faisal					1	0	7	0	7th		428	552	–
NEW ZEALAND									8th		449	569	–
Tuffey	49	13	152	2					9th		468	–	–
Martin	41	9	153	2					10th		476	–	–
Drum	8	1	21	1									
Bradburn	42	10	124	1									
McMillan	31	13	47	1									
Astle	30	12	45	0									
Richardson	9	0	16	1									

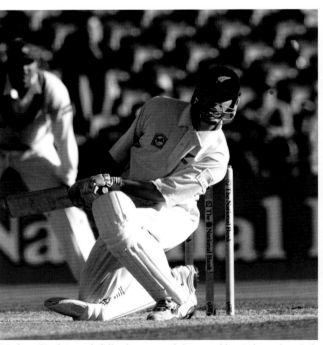

Mathew Sinclair took full advantage of the portable pitch used at Jade Stadium to score his second test double-century, being 204 not out when New Zealand's first innings ended at 476.

MILESTONES

- Chris Drum (215) made his test debut.

- Mathew Sinclair became the second New Zealander, after Glenn Turner, to score two test double-centuries.

- Sinclair's 204 was New Zealand's highest individual innings against Pakistan.

- Sinclair became the fifth player to have each of his first three test centuries pass 150.

- Yousuf Youhana passed 2000 runs in test cricket.

- Grant Bradburn returned to test cricket after a gap of eight years.

288 NEW ZEALAND v PAKISTAN (*Third Test*)

at WestpacTrust Park, Hamilton on 27, 28, 29, 30 March, 2001
Toss : New Zealand. Umpires : D.J. Harper & R.S. Dunne
New Zealand won by an innings and 185 runs

The third and final test of the series was played on a traditional, well-grassed pitch. In overcast conditions Stephen Fleming sent Pakistan in to bat and their openers attacked furiously, taking 28 off the first five overs. Irresponsible batting saw five wickets fall for a further 10 runs, with Chris Martin claiming the first four.

Daryl Tuffey demolished the remaining batsmen and the first innings was completed in the second over after lunch with Pakistan dismissed for 104. Both Martin and Tuffey made the ball seam and swing disconcertingly and each captured four wickets.

Mark Richardson and Matthew Bell, whose previous opening partnerships in the series were 1, 91, 102 and 69, outdid these efforts and by the end of the first day had added 160, with Bell 89 and Richardson 64, both undefeated, against dispirited bowling and fielding.

Rain prevented play on the second day and disrupted part of the third day but not before both openers completed their maiden test centuries.

Richardson was eventually dismissed with the third ball of the fourth day which then saw Craig McMillan bat in a highly creative fashion, with the reverse sweep being played to wondrous effect. In one over from Younis Khan he hit 444464 to create a new test record of 26 runs off a six-ball over. Together with Stephen Fleming 147 were added in 119 minutes.

McMillan perished in search of another six when he was caught on the third man boundary for 98 made off 97 balls. Fleming's declaration left New Zealand time to bowl 194 overs and Pakistan were required to score more than 303 runs to force New Zealand to bat for a second time.

Left-arm fast-medium James Franklin joined the bowling heroes of the first innings and within 50 overs they demolished

the visitors, with Franklin claiming his best test figures, while Adam Parore had seven catches for the game.

Pakistan had gone from winning by an innings and 299 runs in the first test to losing by an innings and 185 runs in the third test, 18 days later. This victory enabled New Zealand to square the series. It was not until after this test that the total disharmony within the Pakistan side emerged.

PAKISTAN

Imran Farhat	c Astle b Martin	24	c McMillan b Tuffey	1
Ijaz Ahmed	c Parore b Martin	5	c Parore b Franklin	17
Faisal Iqbal	c Bell b Martin	0	c Bradburn b Tuffey	5
Inzamam-ul-Haq*	lbw b Martin	5	c Tuffey b Franklin	20
Yousuf Youhana	c Parore b Tuffey	0	c Parore b Martin	16
Younis Khan	c Richardson b Tuffey	36	c Astle b Tuffey	4
Humayun Farhat†	c Parore b Tuffey	28	c Bradburn b Martin	26
Saqlain Mushtaq	run out	0	c Martin b Franklin	14
Waqar Younis	c Fleming b Franklin	0	c Parore b McMillan	4
Fazl-e-Akbar	c Parore b Tuffey	0	not out	0
Mohammad Akram	not out	1	c & b Franklin	4
Extras	(lb 3, nb 2)	5	(lb 2, nb 5)	7
TOTAL	(26.5 overs)	**104**	(49.5 overs)	**118**

NEW ZEALAND

M.H.Richardson	c Farhat b Fazl	106
M.D.Bell	lbw b Waqar	105
M.S.Sinclair	c Waqar b Fazl	27
C.D.McMillan	c Waqar b Fazl	98
S.P.Fleming*	not out	51
N.J.Astle		
G.E.Bradburn		
A.C.Parore†		
J.E.C.Franklin		
D.R.Tuffey		
C.S.Martin		
Extras	(lb 10, nb 10)	20
TOTAL	(112.2 overs) (4 wkts dec)	**407**

Bowling	O	M	R	W	O	M	R	W	Fall of Wickets			
NEW ZEALAND										P	NZ	P
										1st	1st	2nd
Tuffey	10.5	2	39	4	19	5	38	3	1st	28	181	10
Martin	10	3	52	4	15	2	48	2	2nd	28	239	20
Franklin	6	2	10	1	9.5	3	26	4	3rd	29	260	43
McMillan					5	3	2	1	4th	34	407	54
Astle					1	0	2	0	5th	38	-	69
PAKISTAN									6th	89	-	71
Waqar	31	2	98	1					7th	89	-	97
Fazl	27.2	6	85	3					8th	91	-	114
Akram	22	1	106	0					9th	103	-	114
Saqlain	31	6	82	0					10th	104	-	118
Younis	1	0	26	0								

MILESTONES

- It was New Zealand's 47th test victory and the win by an innings and 185 was New Zealand's largest in test cricket.

- Inzamam-ul-Haq captained Pakistan for the first time.

- Mark Richardson and Matthew Bell set a new first wicket record partnership of 181 for New Zealand against Pakistan.

- It was the third time that both New Zealand openers scored a century in the same test innings, Stewie Dempster and Jack Mills (test 2) and Glenn Turner and Terry Jarvis (test 101) having also achieved the feat.

- It was Pakistan's heaviest defeat in test cricket.

- Craig McMillan set a test record of 26 runs off a six-ball over. Five players had previously taken 24 off an over.

- McMillan and Stephen Fleming created a new fourth wicket partnership of 147 for New Zealand against Pakistan.

- Adam Parore, in his 70th match, surpassed Ian Smith's New Zealand record of 176 dismissals, made in 63 tests.

AVERAGES

New Zealand

BATTING	M	I	NO	Runs	HS	Ave
M.S. Sinclair	3	5	2	325	204*	108.33
A.C. Parore	3	3	2	78	46	78.00
M.H. Richardson	3	5	1	285	106	71.25
S.P. Fleming	3	4	1	174	86	58.00
M.D. Bell	3	5	0	248	105	49.60
C.D. McMillan	3	4	0	172	98	43.00
P.J. Wiseman	1	2	0	17	9	8.50
D.R. Tuffey	3	3	0	15	13	5.00
C.J. Drum	1	1	0	4	4	4.00
N.J. Astle	3	3	0	7	6	2.33
G.E. Bradburn	2	1	0	0	0	0.00
C.S. Martin	3	3	0	0	0	0.00
J.E.C. Franklin	2	2	0	0	0	0.00

BOWLING	O	M	R	W	Ave
M.H. Richardson	9	0	16	1	16.00
C.J. Drum	8	1	21	1	21.00
J.E.C. Franklin	54.5	13	150	7	21.42
D.R. Tuffey	129.5	36	368	16	23.00
C.S. Martin	100	17	424	12	35.33
C.D. McMillan	57	21	110	3	36.66
G.E. Bradburn	42	10	124	1	124.00
P.J. Wiseman	43	6	142	1	142.00
N.J. Astle	52	21	83	0	–

Pakistan

BATTING	M	I	NO	Runs	HS	Ave
Younis Khan	3	5	1	280	149*	70.00
Yousuf Youhana	3	5	0	312	203	62.40
Inzamam-ul-Haq	2	3	0	155	130	51.66
Faisal Iqbal	3	5	1	162	63	40.50
Moin Khan	2	2	0	75	47	37.50
Saqlain Mushtaq	3	5	1	119	101*	29.75
Humayun Farhat	1	2	0	54	28	27.00
Imran Farhat	3	5	0	115	63	23.00
Mushtaq Ahmed	1	1	0	19	19	19.00
Misbah-ul-Haq	1	2	0	38	28	19.00
Salim Elahi	1	2	0	31	24	15.50
Ijaz Ahmed	2	3	0	33	17	11.00
Waqar Younis	3	4	0	20	12	5.00
Mohammad Akram	1	2	1	5	4	5.00
Fazl-e-Akbar	2	3	2	0	0*	0.00
Mohammad Sami	2	1	1	0	0*	–

BOWLING	O	M	R	W	Ave
Saqlain Mushtaq	148.4	37	332	11	30.18
Mohammad Sami	93.4	22	245	8	30.62
Fazl-e-Akbar	66.2	12	198	6	33.00
Waqar Younis	106	19	305	6	50.83
Mushtaq Ahmed	31	10	83	1	83.00
Younis Khan	28	7	88	1	88.00
Yousuf Youhana	1	0	3	0	–
Faisal Iqbal	1	0	7	0	–
Mohammad Akram	22	1	106	0	–

The smiles tell the story. Mark Richardson, left, and Matthew Bell both scored centuries as they combined to add 181 for the first wicket. It was only the third time that both openers had scored a century in the same test innings for New Zealand.

2001/02 New Zealand in Australia

289 **AUSTRALIA** v **NEW ZEALAND** *(First Test)*
at Brisbane Cricket Ground on 8, 9, 10, 11, 12 November, 2001
Toss : New Zealand. Umpires : S.A. Bucknor & D.J. Harper
Match drawn

Justin Langer survived a raucous appeal in the first over after New Zealand sent Australia in to bat and for the next 251 minutes the two left-handed opening batsmen toyed with the visitors' bowling. Their contrasting strengths, Matthew Hayden powerful and bullying with Langer more technically precise and industrious, coupled with aggressive running between the wickets, saw them add 224.

New Zealand was back in the game at stumps when six wickets fell for 70 runs after Hayden was dismissed. New Zealand's saviour was Craig McMillan who took three cheap wickets after tea on the first day; Australia 294-6.

Continual breaks for rain over the next three days saw Australia declare at 486 after Gilchrist had reached his fourth test century. Brett Lee exhibited good batting skills in a partnership of 135.

Jason Gillespie's sharp pace and probing leg-cutters to right-hand batsmen had New Zealand 55-4 before the Canterbury trio of Nathan Astle, Chris Cairns and McMillan showed restrained resolution in the face of hostile fast bowling from Lee, who captured his first haul of five wickets for 12 months.

The fifth day was enthralling. Stephen Fleming declared as soon as New Zealand had avoided the follow-on and his counterpart Steve Waugh picked up the gauntlet after his side hit 82 off 14 overs before he declared, leaving New Zealand 284 to win in 57 overs on a good batting surface. The action of both captains had engineered a weather-doomed drawn test into a spine-tingling cricket match.

Mark Richardson departed from his normal defensive mode by playing more audaciously to reach 50 off 54 balls. The momentum was continued as Fleming and Astle added 100 off 19 overs. The tempo of the game was lifted a further notch as Cairns and McMillan hit four sixes between them, adding 51 in 39 balls.

A fine catch by Ricky Ponting off Cairns on the edge of the long-on boundary, when 20 was required off 10 balls, extinguished New Zealand's valiant chase and they ended the match a tantalising 10 runs short of the target. After the game both Dion Nash and Shayne O'Connor returned to New Zealand with injuries.

Apart from scoring 45 and 23 not out Craig McMillan distinguished himself by claiming three wickets with his energetic medium-pacers.

AUSTRALIA

J.L.Langer	c Vettori b McMillan	104	(4) not out		18
M.L.Hayden	c Richardson b Cairns	136	run out		13
R.T.Ponting	c Vettori b Cairns	5	not out		32
M.E.Waugh	lbw b Astle	0			
S.R.Waugh*	c Parore b McMillan	3			
D.R.Martyn	c Vettori b McMillan	4			
A.C.Gilchrist†	c sub (L.Vincent) b Cairns	118	(1) b Cairns		20
S.K.Warne	c Sinclair b Cairns	22			
B.Lee	c Parore b Cairns	61			
J.N.Gillespie	not out	20			
G.D.McGrath					
Extras	(lb 4, w 1, nb 8)	13	(nb 1)		1
TOTAL	(131 overs) (9 wkts dec)	**486**	(14 overs) (2 wkts dec)		**84**

NEW ZEALAND

M.H.Richardson	lbw b Gillespie	26	lbw b Warne		57
M.D.Bell	c Ponting b Gillespie	6	lbw b McGrath		5
M.S.Sinclair	c Ponting b Lee	3	st Gilchrist b Warne		23
S.P.Fleming*	c Gilchrist b Gillespie	0	run out		57
N.J.Astle	c Gilchrist b Lee	66	c Gillespie b Warne		49
C.D.McMillan	c Warne b Lee	45	(7) not out		23
C.L.Cairns	c Waugh S.R. b Lee	61	(6) c Ponting b Lee		43
A.C.Parore†	c Waugh S.R. b Lee	11	not out		3
D.J.Nash	not out	25			
D.L.Vettori	not out	3			
S.B.O'Connor					
Extras	(lb 15, nb 26)	41	(b 1, lb 9, w 1, nb 3)		14
TOTAL	(88.4 overs) (8 wkts dec)	**287**	(57 overs) (6 wkts)		**274**

Bowling										Fall of Wickets				
NEW ZEALAND	O	M	R	W	O	M	R	W			A	NZ	A	NZ
											1st	*1st*	*2nd*	*2nd*
Cairns	37	8	146	5	5	1	29	1						
Nash	30	6	93	0						1st	224	36	30	33
O'Connor	17.2	4	67	0						2nd	233	51	39	89
Vettori	13.4	0	65	0	2	0	8	0		3rd	235	51	-	90
Astle	19	7	46	1						4th	256	55	-	190
McMillan	14	1	65	3	7	0	47	0		5th	260	147	-	213
AUSTRALIA										6th	263	242	-	264
McGrath	26	6	80	0	20	4	66	1		7th	302	243	-	-
Gillespie	18.4	6	56	3	8	0	48	0		8th	437	271	-	-
Lee	23	6	67	5	10	0	53	1		9th	486	-	-	-
Warne	18	2	61	0	18	2	89	3		10th	-	-	-	-
Ponting	3	0	8	0										
Waugh M.E.					1	0	8	0						

MILESTONES

- Matthew Hayden became the first Queensland-born specialist batsman to score a test century at the "Gabba". Wicketkeeper Ian Healy had also scored a century there.

- Chris Cairns, playing in his 50th test, took his 11th five-wicket bag.

- Matthew Hayden and Justin Langer shared an opening stand of 224, a record for Australia against New Zealand.

- It was the highest opening partnership between two left-hand batsmen in test cricket.

- Adam Gilchrist and Brett Lee added 135, a new eighth wicket record for Australia against New Zealand.

- Steve Waugh took his 100th test catch.

290 AUSTRALIA v NEW ZEALAND *(Second Test)*

at Bellerive Oval, Hobart on 22, 23, 24, 25, 26 November, 2001
Toss : New Zealand. Umpires : S.A. Bucknor, S.J. Davis and J.H. Smeaton
Match drawn

Once again Stephen Fleming invited Australia to bat first and for the second time Matthew Hayden and Justin Langer plundered the bowling, this time to the tune of 223 for the first wicket. Langer again had luck on his side, being dropped at the start of the day before he became the major partner, being first out with his score at 123, his third consecutive test century.

With the exception of Ricky Ponting, the Australian middle order again squandered their opportunities, losing five wickets for 44. Damien Martyn, and Steve and Mark Waugh had contributed only 19 runs in six completed innings. Throughout the day Australia batted most purposefully and lifted their normal target of four runs per over to 4.5 to end the first day at 411-6.

Daniel Vettori had kept New Zealand in the game with an inspiring bowling performance, claiming four of the wickets. Ponting showed why some cricket critics classed him as the batting equal of Sachin Tendulkar when he finished the day 92 not out. The weather deteriorated and over the next four days only 140 of the possible 360 overs were bowled.

On the second day Ponting continued his masterclass of stroke-making with boundaries all round the ground. He was 157 not out when the declaration was made at 558-8, Australia's second-highest score against New Zealand. Bad light prevented the start of New Zealand's reply.

The third day was restricted to 35 overs, which New Zealand negotiated cautiously, losing Matthew Bell and Matthew Sinclair for 71 runs.

Craig McMillan and Fleming went about denying Australia a breakthrough during the 50 overs that could be played on the fourth day. They were subjected to a test of their technique and courage by the Australian three-pronged pace attack, as they added 97. Mercifully, the game was concluded when the skies opened prior to lunch on the fifth day with neither side completing an innings.

AUSTRALIA		
J.L.Langer	c Vettori b Cairns	123
M.L.Hayden	c Bond b Vettori	91
R.T.Ponting	not out	157
M.E.Waugh	b Vettori	12
S.R.Waugh*	lbw b Bond	0
D.R.Martyn	lbw b Vettori	0
A.C.Gilchrist†	b Vettori	39
S.K.Warne	b Astle	70
B.Lee	c McMillan b Vettori	41
J.N.Gillespie		
G.D.McGrath		
Extras	(b 3, lb 5, w 2, nb 15)	25
TOTAL	(124 overs) (8 wkts dec)	**558**

NEW ZEALAND		
M.H.Richardson	lbw b Gillespie	30
M.D.Bell	c Gilchrist b Warne	4
M.S.Sinclair	b Gillespie	23
S.P.Fleming*	lbw b McGrath	71
N.J.Astle	c Warne b Waugh M.E.	11
C.D.McMillan	b Gillespie	55
C.L.Cairns	c Gilchrist b McGrath	20
A.C.Parore†	not out	10
D.L.Vettori	not out	10
D.R.Tuffey		
S.E.Bond		
Extras	(lb 1, nb 8)	9
TOTAL	(105.2 overs) (7 wkts)	**243**

Bowling	O	M	R	W			Fall of Wickets		
NEW ZEALAND								A	NZ
								1st	1st
Cairns	28	3	122	1					
Tuffey	15	1	74	0			1st	223	11
Bond	28	0	135	1			2nd	238	53
Vettori	36	5	138	5			3rd	253	76
McMillan	8	0	51	0			4th	266	100
Astle	9	0	30	1			5th	267	197
AUSTRALIA							6th	336	219
McGrath	27	12	46	2			7th	481	223
Gillespie	28	14	45	3			8th	558	-
Warne	24.2	3	70	1			9th	-	-
Lee	19	5	51	0			10th	-	-
Waugh M.E.	7	1	30	1					

Not for the only time in this test was a New Zealand appeal rejected. Daniel Vettori, centre, looks flabbergasted at the rejection of a catch off Mark Waugh. Mathew Sinclair, left, and Adam Parore, right, continue appealing enthusiastically. Shortly afterwards Vettori bowled Waugh.

MILESTONES

- Shane Bond (216) made his test debut.

- Justin Langer became the first Australian since David Boon, in 1993, to score hundreds in three successive tests.

- Ricky Ponting scored his first test hundred in his native Tasmania. It was his ninth test century.

- It was the first time that Australia had scored over 400 runs in the first day's play since making 475 at the Oval in 1934.

- Stephen Fleming and Craig McMillan put on 97, a fifth wicket record against Australia.

291 AUSTRALIA v NEW ZEALAND *(Third Test)*

at W.A.C.A. Ground, Perth on 30 November, 1, 2, 3, 4 December, 2001
Toss : New Zealand. Umpires : D.B. Hair & I.D. Robinson
Match drawn

Lou Vincent's first half-hour in test cricket was notable for the fact that he looked as if he would not survive the next ball. He was fortunate that the bowler causing him the most concern, Glenn McGrath, had to leave the field after the ninth over and be treated for back spasms. From an inauspicious 19-2 Stephen Fleming and Vincent combined to tame their opponents, adding 193 runs in 244 minutes.

Vincent's innings went from struggling to spectacular, with one six and 15 fours showcasing his wide range of strokes as he became the sixth New Zealander to score a century on test debut. It was Fleming's first test century in 3½ years and his third in 63 tests. Brett Lee and Jason Gillespie brought Australia back into the game, using the second new ball effectively, to claim four wickets as New Zealand went from 264-4 to 281-7.

The overnight batsmen, Nathan Astle and Adam Parore, both advanced to their highest test scores of 156 not out and 110, as they added 253 for the eighth wicket in just over five hours. When the declaration was made at 534-9 the scoreboard had an unusual look, with four batsmen scoring centuries and none of the other six reaching double figures. Newcomers Shane Bond and Vincent were immediately into the action combining to dismiss Matthew Hayden for nought.

Australia was on the verge of following on when they lost their seventh wicket at 270 as a result of exceptional slow bowling by Daniel Vettori. He combined unfailing length and deceptive loop and outwitted six of the Australians. The last four wickets added 159 runs, mainly through the boisterous batting of Shane Warne, who made 99.

New Zealand began batting for a second time at the start of the fourth day with a lead of 183. Vincent, again revelling in the fast-paced pitch, punished the bowling in scoring a run-a-ball 54 to set the attacking tone for the New Zealand innings that enabled Fleming to declare after tea.

The Australians were set the uphill task of scoring a record 440 in a minimum of 107 overs. The task became more difficult when they lost Justin Langer and Ricky Ponting before stumps.

Successive partnerships of 51, 75, 65, 49 and 95 saw the test in a continual state of change as the Australians made a bold attempt to win. Umpire Ian Robinson turned down two appeals for caught behind but New Zealand derived much credit for holding Australia to three draws in the series, as Australia had won every test in their last two home series.

NEW ZEALAND					
M.H.Richardson	b Gillespie	9	run out		30
L.Vincent	c Waugh M.E. b Warne	104	c Waugh M.E. b Lee		54
M.S.Sinclair	lbw b McGrath	2	c Gilchrist b McGrath		29
S.P.Fleming*	lbw b Lee	105	(5) b Warne		4
N.J.Astle	not out	156	(6) c Langer b Gillespie		40
C.D.McMillan	lbw b Gillespie	4	(7) c Warne b Gillespie		19
D.L.Vettori	c Martyn b Gillespie	2	c Waugh S.R. b Lee		3
C.L.Cairns	c Gilchrist b Lee	8	(4) c Warne b Lee		42
A.C.Parore†	c McGrath b Lee	110	(8) not out		16
S.E.Bond	b Lee	0	b Lee		8
C.S.Martin					
Extras	(b 4, lb 15, w 2, nb 13)	34	(b 1, lb 6, nb 4)		11
TOTAL	**(162.5 overs) (9 wkts dec)**	**534**	**(71 overs) (9 wkts dec)**		**256**
AUSTRALIA					
J.L.Langer	c Parore b Cairns	75	c Vettori b Bond		0
M.L.Hayden	c Vincent b Bond	0	c Sinclair b Vettori		57
R.T.Ponting	c Parore b Martin	31	b Cairns		26
M.E.Waugh	c Bond b Vettori	42	b McMillan		86
S.R.Waugh*	c Parore b Vettori	8	run out		67
D.R.Martyn	c Fleming b Cairns	60	b Vettori		30
A.C.Gilchrist†	c Richardson b Vettori	0	not out		83
S.K.Warne	c Richardson b Vettori	99	run out		10
B.Lee	c McMillan b Vettori	17			
J.N.Gillespie	c Parore b Vettori	0	(9) not out		1
G.D.McGrath	not out	0			
Extras	(lb 2, w 1, nb 16)	19	(lb 3, w 2, nb 16)		21
TOTAL	**(103.4 overs)**	**351**	**(110 overs) (7 wkts)**		**381**

Bowling AUSTRALIA	O	M	R	W	O	M	R	W	Fall of Wickets	NZ 1st	A 1st	NZ 2nd	A 2nd
McGrath	27	11	72	1	17	4	63	1	1st	12	3	77	1
Gillespie	40	7	112	3	17	0	55	2	2nd	19	61	90	52
Lee	32.5	5	125	4	16	3	56	4	3rd	218	122	128	130
Warne	43	9	135	1	21	3	75	1	4th	264	137	151	195
Martyn	10	0	44	0					5th	269	191	199	244
Waugh M.E.	6	1	26	0					6th	272	192	208	339
Ponting	4	3	1	0					7th	281	270	241	355
NEW ZEALAND									8th	534	342	246	-
Cairns	23	5	86	2	15	2	72	1	9th	534	346	256	-
Bond	18	2	74	1	21	3	80	1	10th	-	351	-	-
Martin	23	4	88	1	12	0	51	0					
Vettori	34.4	7	87	6	45	11	142	2					
Astle	5	1	14	0	12	5	18	0					
McMillan					5	2	15	1					

MILESTONES

- Lou Vincent (217) made his test debut.

- Lou Vincent became the sixth New Zealander to score a century on debut after Jack Mills, Bruce Taylor, Rodney Redmond, Mark Greatbatch and Mathew Sinclair.

- Lou Vincent became the fourth touring player to score a century on debut in Australia, the last being the Nawab of Pataudi (England) in the first test of the bodyline series.

- Nathan Astle and Adam Parore added 253 for the eighth wicket. It was a record for New Zealand against all countries and the second-highest by any country.

- It was the first time since England did so in 1938 that four players had made centuries in one innings against Australia.

AVERAGES

New Zealand

BATTING	M	I	NO	Runs	HS	Ave
N.J. Astle	3	5	1	322	156*	80.50
L. Vincent	1	2	0	158	104	79.00
A.C. Parore	3	5	3	150	110	75.00
S.P. Fleming	3	5	0	237	105	47.40
C.D. McMillan	3	5	1	146	55	36.50
C.L. Cairns	3	5	0	174	61	34.80
M.H. Richardson	3	5	0	152	57	30.40
M.S. Sinclair	3	5	0	80	29	16.00
D.L. Vettori	3	4	2	18	10*	9.00
M.D. Bell	2	3	0	15	6	5.00
S.E. Bond	2	2	0	8	8	4.00
D.J. Nash	1	1	1	25	25*	-
S.B. O'Connor	1	-	-	-	-	-
D.R. Tuffey	1	-	-	-	-	-
C.S. Martin	1	-	-	-	-	-

BOWLING	O	M	R	W	Ave
D.L. Vettori	131.2	23	440	13	33.84
C.D. McMillan	34	3	178	4	44.50
C.L. Cairns	108	19	455	10	45.50
N.J. Astle	45	13	108	2	54.00
S.E. Bond	67	5	289	3	96.33
C.S. Martin	35	4	139	1	139.00
S.B. O'Connor	17.2	4	67	0	-
D.R. Tuffey	15	1	74	0	-
D.J. Nash	30	6	93	0	-

Australia

BATTING	M	I	NO	Runs	HS	Ave
R.T. Ponting	3	5	2	251	157*	83.66
J.L. Langer	3	5	1	320	123	80.00
A.C. Gilchrist	3	5	1	260	118	65.00
M.L. Hayden	3	5	0	297	136	59.40
S.K. Warne	3	4	0	201	99	50.25
B. Lee	3	3	0	119	61	39.66
M.E. Waugh	3	4	0	140	86	35.00
D.R. Martyn	3	4	0	94	60	23.50
J.N. Gillespie	3	3	2	21	20*	21.00
S.R. Waugh	3	4	0	78	67	19.50
G.D. McGrath	3	1	1	0	0*	-

BOWLING	O	M	R	W	Ave
B. Lee	100.5	19	352	14	25.14
J.N. Gillespie	111.4	27	316	11	28.72
M.E. Waugh	14	2	64	1	64.00
G.D. McGrath	117	37	327	5	65.40
S.K. Warne	124.2	19	430	6	71.66
R.T. Ponting	7	3	9	0	-
D.R. Martyn	10	0	44	0	-

It was the first time that four New Zealanders had scored a century in the same test innings. It was the first time since 1938 that four players had done this against Australia. From left: Nathan Astle, Adam Parore, Lou Vincent and Stephen Fleming.

2001/02 Bangladesh in New Zealand

Bangladesh arrived in New Zealand with very little experience of green, seaming wickets. It was their misfortune to arrive in New Zealand in December 2001 to find the country experiencing its wettest spring and early summer in living memory. The home side had been battle hardened after three difficult tests against Australia.

292 NEW ZEALAND v BANGLADESH *(First Test)*

at WestpacTrust Park, Hamilton on 18, 19, 20, 21, 22 December, 2001
Toss : Bangladesh. Umpires : A.L. Hill & D.L. Orchard
New Zealand won by an innings and 52 runs

Northern Districts was keen to show off WestpacTrust Park as over NZ$1 million had been spent refurbishing the ground. The only thing that happened on the first day was the toss, won by the Bangladesh captain Khaled Mashud, who decided to field first but, no sooner had he made that decision, than the rain came and washed out the first two days.

Mark Richardson scored 143, as New Zealand recorded their 48th test victory.

Play began on the third day and New Zealand were soon in trouble. By the 16th over they were 51-4. Mark Richardson played an innings of character and brought up his second test century in 261 minutes. Craig McMillan played according to the game situation, at first very cautiously and then, when the support bowlers were used, totally aggressively.

He and Richardson added 190 in 180 minutes as they accelerated the scoring rate, which had begun at 31 in the first hour, to 90 in the fourth. McMillan's fifth test century was scored off 136 balls. Play ended at 306-5 when rain again intervened with Richardson 140 and Chris Cairns 40.

New Zealand lost wickets quickly on the fourth morning as a further 59 runs were scored, enabling Fleming to declare at 365. Habibul Bashar, at this early stage in Bangladesh's test history their premier batsman, played positively, showing an almost instinctive desire to hook anything short.

The pace of Shane Bond, bowling on a grassy pitch, would have tested experienced test batsmen. For those whose cricket careers had been based on flat-rolled mud pitches, lacking pace, the leap was too much.

By the close of the day Bangladesh was 90-4, with Al Sahariar having made a courageous 53. The final day of the test saw the return to form of Chris Cairns as Bangladesh lost their last six wickets for 18 runs, with Cairns claiming five in 38 balls to end the innings with 7-53.

NEW ZEALAND

M.H.Richardson	c & b Sharif	143
L.Vincent	c & b Mortaza	0
M.S.Sinclair	c Mashud b Manjural	7
S.P.Fleming*	c Mashud b Mortaza	4
N.J.Astle	c Rokon b Manjural	5
C.D.McMillan	c Manjural b Mortaza	106
C.L.Cairns	b Sharif	48
A.C.Parore†	b Sharif	20
D.L.Vettori	lbw b Mahmud	0
S.E.Bond	not out	4
C.S.Martin		
Extras	(b 2, lb 18, w 5, nb 3)	28
TOTAL	(77.1 overs) (9 wkts dec)	**365**

BANGLADESH

Javed Omar	c Richardson b Cairns	9	lbw b Martin		15
Al Sahariar Rokon	c Sinclair b Bond	15	c Parore b Cairns		53
Habibul Bashar	c Martin b Vettori	61	c Parore b Cairns		1
Aminul Islam	c Parore b Bond	14	b Cairns		0
Mohammad Ashraful	c Sinclair b Vettori	1	c sub (C.J.Drum) b Bond		6
Sanuar Hossain	c Vincent b McMillan	45	b Bond		12
Khaled Mashud*†	c Bond b McMillan	6	c Fleming b Cairns		6
Khaled Mahmud	c Richardson b Bond	45	c Sinclair b Cairns		0
Mohammad Sharif	b Martin	0	not out		4
Mashrafe bin Mortaza	lbw b Bond	3	c Vincent b Cairns		2
Manjural Islam	not out	0	c Fleming b Cairns		1
Extras	(lb 1, nb 5)	6	(lb 4, nb 4)		8
TOTAL	(58.1 overs)	**205**	(46.2 overs)		**108**

Bowling	O	M	R	W	O	M	R	W
BANGLADESH								
Mortaza	27	3	100	3				
Manjural	18	5	66	2				
Sharif	20.1	2	114	3				
Mahmud	9	0	40	1				
Ashraful	3	0	25	0				
NEW ZEALAND								
Cairns	11	0	55	1	18.2	2	53	7
Bond	13.1	2	47	4	15	4	28	2
Martin	11	4	38	1	4	1	6	1
McMillan	8	1	39	2				
Vettori	15	4	25	2	9	4	17	0

Fall of Wickets

	NZ	B	B
	1st	1st	2nd
1st	1	24	39
2nd	19	32	42
3rd	29	92	42
4th	51	95	68
5th	241	121	90
6th	330	146	98
7th	357	155	98
8th	359	156	104
9th	365	204	107
10th	-	205	108

MILESTONES

- It was New Zealand's 48th test victory.

- It was the first test between New Zealand and Bangladesh.

- Because there was no play on the first two days the follow-on target was reduced to 150 runs.

- Chris Cairns' figures of 7-53 were the fifth-best by a New Zealand bowler in test cricket.

- Tony Hill made his debut as a test umpire.

293 NEW ZEALAND v BANGLADESH *(Second Test)*

at Basin Reserve, Wellington on 26, 27, 28, 29 December, 2001
Toss : New Zealand. Umpires : B.F. Bowden & D.J. Harper
New Zealand won by an innings and 74 runs

Intense rain a week out from the test saw the ground staff erect a tent to enable them to do their final preparation on the pitch, as the rain fell continuously. Not surprisingly, when Bangladesh were asked to bat the pitch was sluggish and lacking pace. Even so, Bangladesh got off to a horror start, losing two wickets in Chris Cairns' second over.

Under instructions from their coach, Australian Trevor Chapple, to occupy the crease, several of the top order were out to injudicious shots. Aminul Islam was the exception. He had achieved fame throughout his country when he scored a gritty 145 in Bangladesh's inaugural test against India in Dhaka in 2000.

He batted five minutes short of three hours for 42 as Bangladesh capitulated in 64 overs for 132. The New Zealand openers were untroubled to compile 72 before stumps with Mark Richardson being 38 and Matthew Horne 30.

No play was possible owing to rain on the second day, which also delayed the start of the third. The opening partnership of 104 was the ideal platform from which Stephen Fleming, Craig McMillan and Cairns could launch an all-out attack on the visitors. Each scored at a faster rate than the last enabling a declaration to be made at 341-6.

In the 20 overs available Shane Bond's pace was too much for the visitors as he captured three of the five wickets to fall for a paltry 67 runs at stumps. The innings lasted only one hour on the fourth day before Bangladesh were dismissed for 135, giving New Zealand victory by an innings and 74 and a 2-0 series win.

MILESTONES

- It was New Zealand's 49th test victory.

Umpire Brent (Billy) Bowden has an excellent view of Shane Bond, probably the fastest bowler to play for New Zealand in the last decade.

BANGLADESH

Javed Omar	c Vincent b Cairns	0	lbw b Bond		12
Al Sahariar Rokon	c Bond b Vettori	18	c Horne b Bond		0
Habibul Bashar	c Sinclair b Cairns	6	lbw b Drum		32
Aminul Islam	c Vincent b Bond	42	c Vettori b Bond		4
Mohammad Ashraful	c Fleming b Cairns	11	lbw b Vettori		10
Sanuar Hossain	run out	10	b Bond		7
Khaled Mahmud	c Parore b Drum	10	run out		4
Khaled Mashud*†	not out	10	not out		19
Hasibul Hussain	c Vincent b Drum	4	c Parore b Vettori		7
Manjural Islam	b Vettori	0	(11) c Sinclair b Cairns		0
Mashrafe bin Mortaza	run out	8	(10) b Cairns		29
Extras	(lb 4, w 1, nb 8)	13	(lb 7, w 1, nb 3)		11
TOTAL	(64 overs)	**132**	(41 overs)		**135**

NEW ZEALAND

M.H.Richardson	c Mortaza b Hasibul	83
M.J.Horne	c Mashud b Manjural	38
L.Vincent	c Mashud b Mortaza	23
S.P.Fleming*	c Mashud b Manjural	61
C.D.McMillan	run out	70
M.S.Sinclair	not out	19
C.L.Cairns	c Bashar b Manjural	36
A.C.Parore†		
D.L.Vettori		
S.E.Bond		
C.J.Drum		
Extras	(b 1, lb 6, w 1, nb 3)	11
TOTAL	(88 overs) (6 wkts dec)	**341**

Bowling	O	M	R	W	O	M	R	W	Fall of Wickets			
NEW ZEALAND										B	NZ	B
										1st	1st	2nd
Cairns	15	7	24	3	6	1	27	2	1st	0	104	5
Bond	13	4	21	1	15	5	54	4	2nd	6	148	28
Drum	11	1	26	2	3	0	9	1	3rd	49	153	41
Vettori	25	6	57	2	17	8	38	2	4th	81	283	62
BANGLADESH									5th	92	285	64
Mortaza	16	1	57	1					6th	108	341	75
Manjural	29	5	99	3					7th	114	-	79
Hasibul	21	3	88	1					8th	118	-	86
Islam	7	0	37	0					9th	119	-	135
Mahmud	12	2	42	0					10th	132	-	135
Ashraful	3	0	11	0								

2001/02 England in New Zealand

294 **NEW ZEALAND v ENGLAND** *(First Test)*

at Jade Stadium, Christchurch on 13, 14, 15, 16 March, 2002
Toss : New Zealand. Umpires : B.F. Bowden & E.A.R. de Silva
England won by 98 runs

Four days before this test the Super 12 rugby match between the Canterbury Crusaders and the Auckland Blues was played at Jade Stadium, meaning a drop-in pitch was used for the test. Experienced critics thought that whoever won the toss on a very juicy pitch would win the game and, after five balls of Chris Cairns' first over when England lost two wickets for no runs, they appeared to have judged correctly.

Michael Vaughan responded by hooking two sixes in an aggressive 27. A dropped catch when Nasser Hussain had reached 50 was capitalised on fully as Hussain was last out after making a courageous 106; England 228.

Matthew Hoggard exploited the bowler-friendly conditions, pitching the ball up and swinging it away from the right-hand batsmen, to capture the first five wickets to fall. Nightwatchman Daniel Vettori and Craig McMillan both scored 40 in a disappointing reply of 147, giving England a lead of 81 with the pitch drying out and becoming slightly easier to bat on.

From the overnight score of 63-2 England staggered to 106-5 as a result of encouraging bowling by test novices Chris Drum and Ian Butler. Regrettably for New Zealand Cairns had damaged his right knee and, apart from a token gesture at the end of the second day, was unable to bowl again for the rest of the season.

With England holding a lead of 187 Graham Thorpe, who was dropped on four by Nathan Astle, was joined by Andrew Flintoff who had managed only eight runs in his previous five test innings. Flintoff was confronted by a series of half volleys and hit five fours and a six from the first 14 balls he faced to ignite a partnership that was to add 281 runs against wilting bowlers.

Thorpe reached his 10th test hundred after 121 minutes and he began to emulate Flintoff's pulsating attack. He went on to be 200 not out, which at the time was the fourth-fastest double-hundred made, from 231 balls. Flintoff scored his first test hundred and England were able to declare leaving New Zealand to make 550 runs for victory or survive two days and 21 overs on a pitch that was now ideal for batting.

After tea on the final day New Zealand, in spite of valiant innings by Mark Richardson, Stephen Fleming and Astle, were heading for a predictable defeat at 333-9. A limping Cairns came to the crease, with Daniel Vettori as his runner, to join Astle who was 134 not out.

Andrew Caddick, who had played age-group cricket with the Canterbury members of the New Zealand side, was ecstatic when he captured his sixth wicket in the innings with the second new ball. In the next four overs from Hoggard and Caddick seven sixes and eight fours were struck.

Two balls from Caddick were hit straight over the grandstand and out of the ground. Astle let his intuition have free rein. His strokes were breathtakingly audacious and daring as he raced from 100 to 200 off 39 balls. He and Cairns added 118 in 55 minutes.

Three weeks earlier Adam Gilchrist had taken 212 balls to record the fastest double-hundred from balls received, beating Ian Botham's previous record of 220 balls. Astle's double-hundred required only 153 balls. He didn't break the record, he obliterated it. The game ended when he was caught behind for 222 and New Zealand had lost by 98 runs.

No one could argue with Lawrence Booth's statement in *Wisden* when he wrote, "It was perhaps the most glorious failure in the history of test cricket."

ENGLAND					
M.E.Trescothick	c Parore b Cairns	0	c Vettori b Butler		33
M.P.Vaughan	c Parore b Cairns	27	b Butler		0
M.A.Butcher	c Butler b Cairns	0	hit wicket b Butler		34
N.Hussain*	lbw b Drum	106	c Parore b Drum		11
G.P.Thorpe	c Fleming b Drum	17	not out		200
M.R.Ramprakash	c Parore b Astle	31	b Drum		11
A.Flintoff	lbw b Astle	0	c sub (M.N.McKenzie) b Astle		137
J.S.Foster†	lbw b Drum	19	not out		22
A.F.Giles	c Drum b Butler	8			
A.R.Caddick	lbw b Butler	0			
M.J.Hoggard	not out	0			
Extras	(b 1, lb 10, nb 9)	20	(b 6, lb 4, nb 10)		20
TOTAL	(81.2 overs)	**228**	(96.4 overs) (6 wkts dec)		**468**

NEW ZEALAND					
M.H.Richardson	lbw b Hoggard	2	c Foster b Caddick		76
M.J.Horne	c Thorpe b Hoggard	14	c Foster b Caddick		4
D.L.Vettori	c Foster b Hoggard	42	(8) c Flintoff b Giles		12
L.Vincent	b Hoggard	12	(3) c Butcher b Caddick		0
S.P.Fleming*	c Giles b Caddick	12	(4) c Foster b Flintoff		48
N.J.Astle	lbw b Hoggard	10	(5) c Foster b Hoggard		222
C.D.McMillan	c Vaughan b Hoggard	40	(6) c & b Caddick		24
C.L.Cairns	c Flintoff b Caddick	0	(11) not out		23
A.C.Parore†	lbw b Caddick	0	(7) b Caddick		1
C.J.Drum	not out	2	(9) lbw b Flintoff		0
I.G.Butler	c Hussain b Hoggard	0	(10) c Foster b Caddick		4
Extras	(lb 5, nb 8)	13	(b 9, lb 11, w 1, nb 16)		37
TOTAL	(51.2 overs)	**147**	(93.3 overs)		**451**

Bowling	O	M	R	W	O	M	R	W
NEW ZEALAND								
Cairns	15	4	58	3	4	0	8	0
Drum	20.2	8	36	3	32	6	130	2
Butler	16	2	59	2	23	2	137	3
Astle	18	10	32	2	5.4	0	20	1
Vettori	9	1	26	0	10	0	66	0
McMillan	3	1	6	0				
ENGLAND								
Caddick	18	8	50	3	25	8	122	6
Hoggard	21.2	7	63	7	24.3	5	142	1
Flintoff	12	2	29	0	16	1	94	2
Giles					28	6	73	1

Fall of Wickets	E	NZ	E	NZ
	1st	1st	2nd	2nd
1st	0	4	11	42
2nd	0	50	50	53
3rd	46	65	81	119
4th	83	79	85	189
5th	139	93	106	242
6th	151	117	387	252
7th	196	117	-	300
8th	214	117	-	301
9th	226	146	-	333
10th	228	147	-	451

MILESTONES

- Ian Butler (218) made his test debut.

- Matthew Hoggard's 7-63 was the best by an England pace bowler in New Zealand.

- Graham Thorpe and Andrew Flintoff put on 281, an England sixth wicket record against all countries.

- Nathan Astle's double-century, off 153 deliveries, was the fastest in test history in terms of balls received.

- Astle's 222 was the highest score by a New Zealand batsman against England.

- Astle hit 11 sixes in his innings, one short of the record of Wasim Akram for Pakistan against Zimbabwe in 1996/97.

- Astle and Chris Cairns put on 118, a 10th wicket record for New Zealand against England.

- New Zealand's 451 was the second-highest fourth innings score in a test. The highest was England's 654-5 against South Africa in the 1938/39 timeless test.

Nathan Astle played one of the most amazing innings in the 1594 tests played to date by scoring the fastest double-century off 153 balls.

295   NEW ZEALAND v ENGLAND *(Second Test)*

at Basin Reserve, Wellington on 21, 22, 23, 24, 25 March, 2002
Toss : New Zealand. Umpires : D.B. Hair & R.S. Dunne
Match drawn

A howling north-westerly wind brought with it heavy rain that wiped out the first day's play. Inadequate tarpaulin covers left the centre block boggy, which prevented play until 3.15 pm on the second day, in perfect summer conditions.

There was further embarrassment for the ground controllers of the Basin Reserve when the scoreboard was likened to a ransom note, as the players' names were constructed of letters of varying sizes. England was invited to bat and was 90-2 at stumps.

Nasser Hussain was 58 not out and England were four wickets down for 199 when the players came off the field for lunch to learn that Ben Hollioake, who had just recently played 16 one-day internationals for England had died in a car crash in Perth. Not surprisingly, England lost their last six wickets for 59 runs after lunch, with Ian Butler capturing four of them.

In reply to 280 Mark Richardson and Lou Vincent began a partnership that was blessed with good fortune as they added 119 for the second wicket. It was broken on the fourth day by Ashley Giles, who extracted turn with his left-arm finger spin and claimed four wickets, while Andrew Caddick, thumping the ball at pace into the pitch and having it threaten the upper body, swept to six wickets for the second time in the series. New Zealand's last nine wickets fell for 83, giving England a lead of 62.

This grew to 246 as Marcus Trescothick and Mark Butcher were untroubled by the inexperienced local fast-medium attack and were both unbeaten with England 184-1 at stumps, with Trescothick 77 and Butcher 57.

The final day began with England losing the two overnight batsmen within 29 runs. In their search for quick runs, Andrew Flintoff was promoted to number four and he unleashed his tremendous power to make 73 in 55 minutes, enabling England to declare. New Zealand's task was to bat out 86 overs or to score 356 runs.

Neither side came close to victory as Vincent scored his second fifty of the game and Stephen Fleming batted completely out of character for 11 runs in 142 minutes.

ENGLAND

M.E.Trescothick	c Vincent b Vettori	37	c Richardson b Vettori	88
M.P.Vaughan	c Fleming b Drum	7	c Drum b Vettori	34
M.A.Butcher	c Astle b Drum	47	c Martin b Drum	60
N.Hussain*	c Astle b Vettori	66	(5) not out	13
G.P.Thorpe	c Fleming b Martin	11	(6) not out	1
M.R.Ramprakash	b Butler	24		
A.Flintoff	c Drum b Butler	2	(4) c & b Vettori	75
J.S.Foster†	not out	25		
A.F.Giles	c McMillan b Butler	10		
A.R.Caddick	c Richardson b Martin	10		
M.J.Hoggard	c Parore b Butler	7		
Extras	(b 4, lb 2, w 6, nb 22)	34	(b 5, lb 13, nb 4)	22
TOTAL	(88.3 overs)	**280**	(65 overs) (4 wkts dec)	**293**

NEW ZEALAND

M.H.Richardson	c Giles b Caddick	60	c Thorpe b Giles	4
M.J.Horne	b Caddick	8	c Foster b Flintoff	38
L.Vincent	c Thorpe b Giles	57	lbw b Hoggard	71
S.P.Fleming*	c Thorpe b Caddick	3	b Hoggard	11
N.J.Astle	c Hussain b Giles	4	not out	11
C.D.McMillan	lbw b Caddick	41	not out	17
A.C.Parore†	c Ramprakash b Giles	0		
D.L.Vettori	c Thorpe b Caddick	11		
C.J.Drum	c Trescothick b Giles	2		
I.G.Butler	c Foster b Caddick	12		
C.S.Martin	not out	0		
Extras	(b 2, lb 9, nb 9)	20	(b 3, lb 1, nb 2)	6
TOTAL	(88.3 overs)	**218**	(84 overs) (4 wkts)	**158**

Bowling	O	M	R	W	O	M	R	W	Fall of Wickets				
NEW ZEALAND										E	NZ	E	NZ
										1st	1st	2nd	2nd
Butler	18.3	2	60	4	6	0	32	0					
Drum	24	6	85	2	16	2	78	1	1st	26	16	79	28
Martin	17	3	58	2	7	1	40	0	2nd	63	135	194	65
Vettori	25	3	62	2	24	1	90	3	3rd	133	138	209	128
Astle	1	0	1	0	9	4	18	0	4th	163	143	291	131
McMillan	3	0	8	0	3	0	17	0	5th	221	149	-	-
ENGLAND									6th	221	149	-	-
Caddick	28.3	8	63	6	17	6	31	0	7th	223	178	-	-
Hoggard	13	5	32	0	13	4	31	2	8th	238	201	-	-
Giles	37	3	103	4	33	11	53	1	9th	250	207	-	-
Flintoff	10	4	9	0	16	6	24	1	10th	280	218	-	-
Vaughan					5	1	15	0					

MILESTONES

- Mark Butcher reached 2000 test runs for England.

- Andrew Flintoff reached 50 off 33 balls. It was the equal sixth-fastest in test history.

- Stephen Fleming's 11 made in 142 minutes was one of the slowest innings in test cricket.

Lou Vincent continued to improve as an international top order batsman when he scored 57 and 71 against a good England attack.

296 NEW ZEALAND v ENGLAND *(Third Test)*

at Eden Park, Auckland on March 30, 31, April 1, 2, 3
Toss : New Zealand. Umpires : D.B. Cowie & S. Venkataraghavan
New Zealand won by 78 runs

For the second time in three tests a drop-in pitch was used at Eden Park and it proved something of a lottery. Early dampness meant the ball left pronounced pitch-marks that hardened up under the sun, creating conditions that Nasser Hussain referred to at the end of the match as "batting on corrugated iron".

For the third test running the New Zealand batsmen found Andrew Caddick's pace and bounce difficult to combat and he had three wickets when the score was 19-4. Chris Harris, batting at number four for the first time in a test, stymied and frustrated the England bowlers by lunging as far forward as possible to nullify the seam and lift. When rain and bad light stopped play New Zealand was 151-5.

There was no play on the second day and frequent showers and poor light restricted the third day to just 28 overs. In that time New Zealand were dismissed for 202, with Harris making his highest test score of 71.

England lost three wickets scoring 12, with Daryl Tuffey removing Marcus Trescothick and Mark Butcher in his first five balls. Only 28 overs of a possible 180 had been bowled in two days and many regarded the game as destined to be drawn.

Two new rules contributed to making the fourth day exceptional. The rule allowing lost time to be made up on the following days saw play begin at 10.00 am. After a brief flurry Tuffey and debutant André Adams demolished England, with Tuffey claiming six wickets and Adams three as England made 160, their lowest score in 22 tests.

The rule allowing lights at the ground to be switched on saw play continue to 6.50 pm, approximately 36 minutes after sunset, thus creating test cricket's long day's journey into night with the moon shining brightly. Nathan Astle and Chris Harris pursued quick runs and began an assault that saw 258 runs scored after tea off 41 overs.

Astle scored the second-fastest fifty for New Zealand off 38 balls. Craig McMillan drove with such fury that the England captain Hussain asked the umpires if the fielding side could appeal against the light as they were in danger of being hurt. He was refused as only the batsmen could appeal against the light.

England approached their chase for 311 runs off 105 overs on the fifth day positively.

Length and accuracy and the inconsistency of bounce from the pitch was always going to assist the bowlers and each of the New Zealand medium-fast attack captured three wickets to give New Zealand victory by 78 runs, levelling the series 1-1.

MILESTONES

- André Adams (219) made his test debut. He captured six wickets in what turned out to be his only test.

- It was New Zealand's 50th test victory.

- Andrew Caddick became the ninth England player to take 200 test wickets.

- Stephen Fleming became the first New Zealand player to take 100 catches in the field in tests.

- Adam Parore retired from test cricket. He had been the eighth wicketkeeper to complete 200 test dismissals. In 78 tests he scored 2865 runs at an average of 26.28, including two centuries.

- Chris Drum retired from test cricket after a brief career of five matches, including all three in the series against England.

NEW ZEALAND

M.H.Richardson	b Caddick	5	c sub b Butcher	25
L.Vincent	b Caddick	10	(9) c Giles b Hoggard	10
S.P.Fleming*	c Ramprakash b Hoggard	1	b Hoggard	1
C.Z.Harris	lbw b Flintoff	71	lbw b Butcher	43
N.J.Astle	c Thorpe b Caddick	2	c Butcher b Flintoff	65
C.D.McMillan	lbw b Caddick	41	not out	50
A.C.Parore†	c sub (U.Afzaal) b Flintoff	45	(2) c Thorpe b Hoggard	36
D.L.Vettori	lbw b Hoggard	3	c Foster b Flintoff	0
A.R.Adams	c Giles b Flintoff	7	(7) b Flintoff	11
D.R.Tuffey	c Butcher b Hoggard	0	b Hoggard	5
C.J.Drum	not out	2		
Extras	(lb 10, nb 5)	15	(b 3, lb 9, w 1, nb 10)	23
TOTAL	**(75.2 overs)**	**202**	**(63.1 overs) (9 wkts dec)**	**269**

ENGLAND

M.E.Trescothick	lbw b Tuffey	0	b Drum	14
M.P.Vaughan	c Parore b Adams	27	c Fleming b Drum	36
M.A.Butcher	c Richardson b Tuffey	0	c sub (B.G.K.Walker) b Astle	35
N.Hussain*	c Fleming b Drum	2	c & b Adams	82
G.P.Thorpe	b Tuffey	42	c Parore b Tuffey	3
M.R.Ramprakash	c Parore b Tuffey	9	b Tuffey	0
A.Flintoff	c Parore b Adams	29	b Tuffey	2
J.S.Foster†	not out	16	c Parore b Adams	23
A.F.Giles	lbw b Tuffey	0	not out	21
A.R.Caddick	b Tuffey	20	c Vettori b Drum	4
M.J.Hoggard	c Fleming b Adams	0	c Astle b Adams	2
Extras	(b 1, lb 11, nb 3)	15	(b 1, lb 8, nb 2)	11
TOTAL	**(45.4 overs)**	**160**	**(63 overs)**	**233**

Bowling	O	M	R	W	O	M	R	W		Fall of Wickets			
ENGLAND										NZ	E	NZ	E
										1st	1st	2nd	2nd
Caddick	25	5	70	4	11	3	41	0	1st	12	0	53	23
Hoggard	28.2	10	66	3	19.1	3	68	4	2nd	17	0	55	73
Flintoff	16	6	49	3	23	1	108	3	3rd	17	11	91	122
Butcher	5	3	6	0	9	2	34	2	4th	19	60	166	125
Giles	1	0	1	0	1	0	6	0	5th	86	75	217	125
NEW ZEALAND									6th	172	118	232	155
Tuffey	19	6	54	6	16	3	62	3	7th	191	122	235	204
Drum	10	3	45	1	10	0	52	3	8th	198	124	262	207
Adams	15.4	2	44	3	16	3	61	3	9th	200	159	269	230
McMillan	1	0	5	0					10th	202	160	-	233
Astle					19	6	44	1					
Vettori					2	0	5	0					

With the use of lights, play continued until 36 minutes after sunset and a clear moon was visible. Nasser Hussain, the England captain, appealed to the umpires to leave the field as the ferocious hitting of Nathan Astle and Craig McMillan was likely to injure his fieldsmen. The umpires rejected this appeal as only the batsmen had the right to appeal against the light.

AVERAGES

New Zealand

BATTING	M	I	NO	Runs	HS	Ave
N.J. Astle	3	6	1	314	222	62.80
C.Z. Harris	1	2	0	114	71	57.00
C.D. McMillan	3	6	2	213	50*	53.25
M.H. Richardson	3	6	0	172	76	28.66
L. Vincent	3	6	0	160	71	26.66
C.L. Cairns	1	2	1	23	23*	23.00
A.C. Parore	3	5	0	82	45	16.40
M.J. Horne	2	4	0	64	38	16.00
D.L. Vettori	3	5	0	68	42	13.60
S.P. Fleming	3	6	0	76	48	12.66
A.R. Adams	1	2	0	18	11	9.00
I.G. Butler	2	3	0	16	12	5.33
C.J. Drum	3	4	2	6	2*	3.00
D.R. Tuffey	1	2	0	5	5	2.50
C.S. Martin	1	1	1	0	0*	-

BOWLING	O	M	R	W	Ave
D.R. Tuffey	35	9	116	9	12.88
A.R. Adams	31.4	5	105	6	17.50
C.L. Cairns	19	4	66	3	22.00
N.J. Astle	52.4	20	115	4	28.75
I.G. Butler	63.3	6	288	9	32.00
C.J. Drum	112.2	25	426	12	35.50
C.S. Martin	24	4	98	2	49.00
D.L. Vettori	82	8	280	5	56.00
C.D. McMillan	20	1	102	0	-

England

BATTING	M	I	NO	Runs	HS	Ave
G.P. Thorpe	3	6	2	274	200*	68.50
N. Hussain	3	6	1	280	106	56.00
J.S. Foster	3	5	3	105	25*	52.50
A. Flintoff	3	6	0	245	137	40.83
M.A. Butcher	3	6	0	176	60	29.33
M.E. Trescothick	3	6	0	172	88	28.66
M.P. Vaughan	3	6	0	131	36	21.83
M.R. Ramprakash	3	5	0	75	31	15.00
A.F. Giles	3	4	1	39	21*	13.00
A.R. Caddick	3	4	0	34	20	8.50
M.J. Hoggard	3	4	1	9	7	3.00

BOWLING	O	M	R	W	Ave
A.R. Caddick	124.3	38	377	19	19.84
M.A. Butcher	14	5	40	2	20.00
M.J. Hoggard	119.2	34	402	17	23.64
A. Flintoff	93	20	313	9	34.77
A.F. Giles	100	20	236	6	39.33
M.P. Vaughan	5	1	15	0	-

2001/02 New Zealand in Pakistan

In September 2001 New Zealand cancelled a tour to Pakistan on the advice of the Government after terrorist activity in the major cities. It was rescheduled for April and May 2002.

▍297 PAKISTAN v NEW ZEALAND *(First Test)*

at Gadaffi Stadium, Lahore on 1, 2, 3 May, 2002
Toss : Pakistan. Umpires : S.A. Bucknor & R.E. Koertzen
Pakistan won by an innings and 324 runs

Within three balls of commencing his test career Robbie Hart had taken a catch off Northern District team mate Daryl Tuffey. There was little joy thereafter for New Zealand as they were completely outplayed in every department and registered their heaviest defeat in test cricket.

In searing temperatures all the New Zealand bowlers wilted as Inzamam-ul-Haq and Imran Nazir added 204 for the third wicket in less than four hours. Nazir reached his second test century before Mark Richardson took a splendid diving catch at mid-on. By stumps Pakistan were 354-4, with Inzamam 159 not out.

Shortly before lunch on the second day Inzamam reached 200. He began to suffer from cramp and was allowed to use Shahid Afridi as a runner for three overs. After lunch the privilege was denied. Reduced to walking singles, Inzamam set about hitting boundaries to and over the fence. Productive partnerships of 111 and 98 were shared with Saqlain Mushtaq and Shoaib Akhtar.

After hitting Brooke Walker for three sixes in one over Inzamam was caught at long-on attempting a fourth to be out for 329 made in 579 minutes. There was still time on the second day for New Zealand to capitulate to 58-6. Shoaib, using his yorker with extreme pace and accuracy, bowled the first four batsmen to fall, before he limped from the field with a sprained ankle.

Shoaib returned on the third day to claim a further two wickets to finish with six wickets for 11 runs. New Zealand

followed on 570 behind but knowing that Shoaib would not bowl again in the match. They were 186-3 before Danish Kaneria snaffled five wickets with his leg-breaks and well-disguised flipper. The game finished late in the day.

On the morning of the second test, to be played at the National Stadium in Karachi, a bomb exploded opposite the team's hotel, killing 14 people. The New Zealand team left the country the same evening.

PAKISTAN		
Imran Nazir	c Richardson b McMillan	127
Shahid Afridi	c Hart b Tuffey	0
Younis Khan	c Fleming b Vettori	27
Inzamam-ul-Haq	c Tuffey b Walker	329
Yousuf Youhana	c Fleming b Martin	29
Abdur Razzaq	lbw b Tuffey	25
Rashid Latif†	c & b Harris	7
Saqlain Mushtaq	b McMillan	30
Waqar Younis*	c & b McMillan	10
Shoaib Akhtar	st Hart b Walker	37
Danish Kaneria	not out	4
Extras	(b 1, lb 8, w 1, nb 8)	18
TOTAL	**(157.5 overs)**	**643**

NEW ZEALAND				
M.H.Richardson	b Shoaib	8	c Latif b Saqlain	32
M.J.Horne	b Shoaib	4	c Latif b Waqar	0
L.Vincent	c Latif b Danish	21	c Latif b Danish	57
S.P.Fleming*	b Shoaib	2	c sub (Mohammad Sami) b Danish	66
C.Z.Harris	b Shoaib	2	lbw b Razzaq	43
C.D.McMillan	c Afridi b Saqlain	15	lbw b Danish	2
R.G.Hart†	lbw b Waqar	4	b Danish	0
D.L.Vettori	c Waqar b Saqlain	7	c sub (Shoaib Malik) b Razzaq	5
B.G.K.Walker	lbw b Shoaib	0	not out	15
D.R.Tuffey	not out	6	c Younis b Danish	12
C.S.Martin	b Shoaib	0	c sub (Shoaib Malik) b Saqlain	0
Extras	(lb 1, nb 3)	4	(b 4, lb 6, nb 4)	14
TOTAL	**(30.2 overs)**	**73**	**(76.3 overs)**	**246**

Bowling	O	M	R	W	O	M	R	W		Fall of Wickets		
NEW ZEALAND										P	NZ	NZ
Tuffey	25	7	94	2						*1st*	*1st*	*2nd*
Martin	31	12	108	1					1st	1	12	3
Vettori	40	4	178	1					2nd	57	17	69
Walker	14.5	3	97	2					3rd	261	19	101
Harris	29	3	109	1					4th	355	21	186
McMillan	18	1	48	3					5th	384	53	193
PAKISTAN									6th	399	57	193
Waqar	10	6	21	1	9	1	38	1	7th	510	66	204
Shoaib	8.2	4	11	6					8th	534	67	227
Danish	6	1	19	1	32	3	110	5	9th	612	73	245
Saqlain	6	1	21	2	17.3	3	38	2	10th	643	73	246
Razzaq					14	2	47	2				
Afridi					4	1	3	0				

MILESTONES

- Robbie Hart (220) made his test debut.

- Inzamam-ul-Haq's 329 was the 10th-highest score in tests. He became the 16th batsman to make a triple-century.

- Inzamam scored 206 runs from boundaries, the second-highest amount in one test innings.

- Inzamam and Shoaib Akhtar added 98, a new ninth wicket record for Pakistan against New Zealand.

- Stephen Fleming reached 4000 test runs in his 69th test.

- It was Pakistan's biggest test victory.

- It was New Zealand's heaviest defeat.

- Steve Bucknor equalled Dickie Bird's record of umpiring 66 tests.

Chris Harris was one of only three of the visitors to bat for over 100 minutes in either innings.

2001/02 New Zealand in West Indies

298 **WEST INDIES v NEW ZEALAND** *(First Test)*
at Kensington Oval, Bridgetown, Barbados on 21, 22, 23, 24 June, 2002
Toss : West Indies. Umpires : R.E. Koertzen & S. Venkataraghavan
New Zealand won by 204 runs

West Indies had won the one-day series 3-1 and were confident of success in the tests. This confidence was borne out when New Zealand lost their fifth wicket at 117 following a middle order slump that saw four wickets fall for 29. However, Stephen Fleming played a captain's role and completed his fourth test hundred.

He was given admirable support by Robbie Hart who surpassed any expectations held for his batting by occupying the crease for 322 minutes as he added 108 with Fleming and then assisted the last four wickets to add a further 112. His total of 57 undefeated was the cornerstone of his team's 337, which demoralised the home team's self-belief.

West Indies batted recklessly after the pace of Bond undid Chris Gayle and Marlon Samuels in his third over. Only Shivnarine Chanderpaul showed any application and concentration against Vettori and Butler, who shared seven wickets, to reduce West Indies to their lowest test score at Kensington Oval in 67 years. Nine catches were taken by different players during the innings. Fleming chose not to enforce the follow-on.

At 88-5 early on the third afternoon, New Zealand appeared to be in danger of not playing the West Indies out of the game as Pedro Collins's left arm swinging deliveries caused concern to the batsmen. Nathan Astle counter-attacked taking 29 off three overs from Adam Sandford and, together with Fleming, who was batting at seven owing to a neck injury, put on 76.

For the second time in the game there were valuable contributions from the lower order batsmen that left West Indies the task of scoring 473 with over two days remaining.

It required just one day for the game to be over. In spite of Gayle and Brian Lara both scoring 73, Bond returned his best test figures when he captured the last three wickets, including Lara's, in 12 balls to finish with 5-78. It was an historic victory.

NEW ZEALAND					
M.H.Richardson	b Sanford	41	c Lara b Collins		0
L.Vincent	c Jacobs b Dillon	14	lbw b Collins		2
S.P.Fleming*	c Gayle b Hooper	130	(7) c Hinds b Sanford		34
C.Z.Harris	c Lara b Collins	0	lbw b Powell		19
N.J.Astle	c Lara b Dillon	2	c Lara b Collins		77
C.D.McMillan	lbw b Sanford	6	c Hooper b Collins		1
R.G.Hart†	not out	57	(8) c Hinds b Collins		24
D.L.Vettori	c Hinds b Collins	39	(9) b Sanford		11
D.R.Tuffey	lbw b Powell	28	(3) c Gayle b Hooper		31
S.E.Bond	b Powell	5	not out		6
I.G.Butler	run out	3	c Jacobs b Collins		26
Extras	(lb 8, nb 4)	12	(lb 8, w 1, nb 3)		12
TOTAL	(125.4 overs)	**337**	(90.4 overs)		**243**
WEST INDIES					
C.H.Gayle	c Vettori b Bond	3	lbw b Bond		73
W.W.Hinds	c McMillan b Tuffey	10	c Richardson b Vettori		37
R.R.Sarwan	c Butler b Bond	0	c Vettori b Bond		18
B.C.Lara	b Vettori	28	b Bond		73
C.L.Hooper*	c Tuffey b Butler	6	c Fleming b Tuffey		16
S.Chanderpaul	not out	35	c Fleming b Vettori		17
R.D.Jacobs†	c Astle b Vettori	4	c Astle b Vettori		6
P.T.Collins	c Vincent b Butler	8	(9) lbw b Bond		8
A.Sanford	c Hart b Butler	1	(10) not out		0
D.B.L.Powell	c Harris b Vettori	0	(8) c Astle b Butler		2
M.Dillon	c Fleming b Vettori	0	c Vincent b Bond		0
Extras	(lb 4, nb 8)	12	(b 5, lb 11, w 2, nb 1)		19
TOTAL	(42.1 overs)	**107**	(83 overs)		**269**

Bowling WEST INDIES	O	M	R	W	O	M	R	W	Fall of Wickets				
										NZ	WI	NZ	WI
										1st	1st	2nd	2nd
Dillon	28	6	73	2	6	3	11	0	1st	38	6	0	68
Collins	24	5	80	2	30.4	8	76	6	2nd	88	6	11	133
Powell	21	6	41	2	20	4	61	1	3rd	89	31	48	142
Sanford	28.4	7	101	2	17	5	68	2	4th	106	47	69	179
Hooper	13	5	21	1	17	8	19	1	5th	117	62	88	204
Gayle	10	3	12	0					6th	225	73	164	216
Sarwan	1	0	1	0					7th	278	90	181	222
NEW ZEALAND									8th	323	93	205	252
Bond	12	1	34	2	21	7	78	5	9th	333	103	213	269
Tuffey	7	3	16	1	15	5	43	1	10th	337	107	243	269
Butler	11	2	26	3	14	0	58	1					
Vettori	12.1	2	27	4	19	3	53	3					
Astle					5	4	4	0					
Harris					9	3	17	0					

The New Zealand team in the West Indies in 2002. Back row (from left): Zak Hitchcock (video analyst), Jeff Crowe (manager), Scott Styris, Chris Martin, Ian Butler, Daryl Tuffey, Shane Bond, Robbie Hart, Denis Aberhart (coach), Dayle Shackel (physiotherapist). Front row: Lou Vincent, Matt Horne, Nathan Astle, Stephen Fleming (captain), Craig McMillan, Daniel Vettori, Chris Harris, Mark Richardson.

MILESTONES

* It was New Zealand's 51st test victory.

* It was Stephen Fleming's 17th win as captain, exactly a third of all New Zealand's victories to date.

* It was New Zealand's first win in 12 tests in the Caribbean.

* It was only the fourth time that West Indies had lost in 39 tests played at Kensington Oval.

299 **WEST INDIES v NEW ZEALAND** *(Second Test)*

at Queen's Park, St George's on 28, 29, 30 June, 1, 2 July, 2002
Toss : West Indies. Umpires : R.E. Koertzen & S. Venkataraghavan
Match drawn

West Indies captain, Carl Hooper, was criticised when he won the toss for the sixth time in seven tests played in the Caribbean this season and sent New Zealand in. It was to be the fourth time that the opposition scored in excess of 300.

The pitch proved to be lifeless and Mark Richardson and Lou Vincent were untroubled adding 61 for the first wicket. The quick loss of Stephen Fleming and Chris Harris was countered by Nathan Astle assisting Richardson to add 123 for the fourth wicket. The introduction of the second new ball saw Richardson's balanced innings end for 95 as Pedro Collins claimed him and nightwatchman Daniel Vettori prior to stumps when New Zealand was 206-5.

The second day began with Collins dismissing Astle first ball, which brought Scott Styris to the crease. For the next 232 minutes Styris showed exceptional maturity for a player having his first innings in test cricket as he went on to make 107 and engineered the tailenders to add 165 for the last four wickets; New Zealand 373.

Chris Gayle played an innings that was to resurrect his career. His 204 featured shots of power and innovation and was the backbone of West Indies' reply of 470. Shane Bond captured five wickets for the second time in six days. Vincent was dropped twice off Collins, on two, before he and Richardson wiped off the home team's lead of 97, adding 117 for the first wicket.

Beginning the last day at 139-2, and poised to bat out the remainder of the day, the visitors lost three wickets for 18 runs. Craig McMillan had an injury that required three stitches in his hand so there was a chance that West Indies might play themselves into a position to square the series.

Styris and Robbie Hart initially calmed the nerves and then made the game safe by adding 99 runs. Rain limited the last two sessions to 23 overs, enabling New Zealand to draw and celebrate their first series win in the Caribbean.

NEW ZEALAND

M.H.Richardson	c Gayle b Collins	95	c Jacobs b Nagamootoo		71
L.Vincent	b Cuffy	24	b Sarwan		54
S.P.Fleming*	c Lara b Collins	6	c Lara b Hooper		5
C.Z.Harris	c Jacobs b Hooper	0	c Sarwan b Nagamootoo		17
N.J.Astle	lbw b Collins	69	c Hinds b Hooper		0
D.L.Vettori	c Jacobs b Collins	1			
C.D.McMillan	c Lara b Cuffy	14			
S.B.Styris	b Sanford	107	(6) not out		69
R.G.Hart†	c Hinds b Hooper	20	(7) not out		28
S.E.Bond	lbw b Chanderpaul	17			
I.G.Butler	not out	5			
Extras	(lb 6, w 2, nb 7)	15	(lb 7, nb 5)		12
TOTAL	(152.5 overs)	**373**	(131 overs) (5 wkts)		**256**

WEST INDIES

C.H.Gayle	c Hart b Bond	204
W.W.Hinds	b Bond	10
R.R.Sarwan	run out	39
B.C.Lara	c Hart b Styris	48
C.L.Hooper*	lbw b Bond	17
S.Chanderpaul	c Fleming b Bond	51
R.D.Jacobs†	c Styris b Butler	17
M.V.Nagamootoo	c Hart b Styris	32
P.T.Collins	lbw b Vettori	14
A.Sanford	c Butler b Bond	12
C.E.Cuffy	not out	0
Extras	(b 4, lb 2, w 5, nb 15)	26
TOTAL	(138.1 overs)	**470**

Bowling	O	M	R	W	O	M	R	W	Fall of Wickets			
WEST INDIES										NZ	WI	NZ
										1st	1st	2nd
Collins	30	9	68	4	17	7	28	0	1st	61	28	117
Cuffy	35	12	76	2	10	3	20	0	2nd	81	128	132
Sanford	22.5	4	74	1	14	3	27	0	3rd	82	204	148
Nagamootoo	33	9	88	0	42	16	75	2	4th	205	242	149
Hooper	25	3	44	2	34	10	66	2	5th	206	385	157
Gayle	3	1	5	0	6	2	7	0	6th	208	394	-
Chanderpaul	4	0	12	1	2	2	0	0	7th	256	441	-
Sarwan					6	0	26	1	8th	312	448	-
NEW ZEALAND									9th	361	470	-
Bond	30.1	7	104	5					10th	373	470	-
Butler	21	4	83	1								
Styris	25	3	88	2								
Vettori	41	9	134	1								
Astle	6	2	15	0								
Harris	15	4	40	0								

Batting at number eight, Scott Styris became the seventh New Zealand batsman to score a century on debut.

MILESTONES

- Scott Styris (221) made his test debut.

- Styris became the seventh New Zealand batsman to make a century on debut and the third, after Rodney Redmond (107 & 56) and Lou Vincent (104 & 54), to make a century and a fifty on debut.

- St George's, Grenada, became the 84th test venue.

2002/03 India in New Zealand

Ex-New Zealand captain John Wright was now the coach of India. The tour was blighted by rain, which favoured New Zealand's totally fast-medium attack. As a build-up to the World Cup seven one-day internationals were played after the two tests.

300   NEW ZEALAND v INDIA *(First Test)*

at Basin Reserve, Wellington on 12, 13, 14 December, 2002
Toss : New Zealand. Umpires : D.J. Harper & E.A.R. de Silva
New Zealand won by 10 wickets

That necessary component in every test victory, luck, blessed Stephen Fleming when he won the toss and asked India to bat first on a hard, green pitch whose spitefulness was fully exploited by the New Zealand attack, with Daryl Tuffey and Shane Bond knocking off the top order and Jacob Oram and Scott Styris taking care of the lower order.

Rahul Dravid displayed great technique and courage to score 76 in 247 minutes. In hindsight it was to be the longest innings and highest score by an Indian player in 39 further test innings to be played by the tourists.

New Zealand was placed in a winning position by a valiant innings from Mark Richardson that began during the last session on the first day and concluded early on the third day. He occupied the crease for 403 minutes, sharing vital partnerships of 63 with Fleming and 80 with Nathan Astle.

At 181-3 New Zealand appeared to be building up a substantial lead. However, they lost their last seven wickets for 76 as left-arm fast-medium Zaheer Khan claimed his first test haul of five wickets.

The match was decided in India's first 16 overs before lunch on the third day when Bond, bowling with a strong breeze behind him, captured three wickets off eight overs to have India 33-4. Only Sachin Tendulkar displayed the will to fight and when he was last out for 51 the innings had lasted just 38.1 overs. Bond took seven wickets in the game.

Richardson and Vincent scored the 36 runs required in 47 minutes. The game ended shortly after tea on the third day.

Jacob Oram's height enabled him to cause all the Indians concern over the amount of bounce that he was able to extract from the pitch.

INDIA

S.B.Bangar	c Styris b Tuffey	1	lbw b Oram	12
V.Sehwag	b Tuffey	2	lbw b Bond	12
R.S.Dravid	b Styris	76	b Bond	7
S.R.Tendulkar	lbw b Oram	8	b Bond	51
S.C.Ganguly*	c Vincent b Bond	17	c Hart b Bond	2
V.V.S.Laxman	c Hart b Bond	0	c Fleming b Oram	0
P.A.Patel†	c Vincent b Oram	8	c Fleming b Tuffey	10
A.B.Agarkar	c Astle b Styris	12	c McMillan b Tuffey	9
Harbhajan Singh	c McMillan b Styris	0	c Styris b Tuffey	1
Z.Khan	c Oram b Bond	19	c Styris b Oram	9
A.Nehra	not out	10	not out	0
Extras	(lb 1, w 1, nb 6)	8	(lb 1, nb 7)	8
TOTAL	**(58.4 overs)**	**161**	**(38.1 overs)**	**121**

NEW ZEALAND

M.H.Richardson	lbw b Khan	89	not out	14
L.Vincent	c Patel b Bangar	12	not out	21
S.P.Fleming*	b Khan	25		
C.D.McMillan	lbw b Bangar	9		
N.J.Astle	c Harbhajan Singh b Khan	41		
S.B.Styris	st Patel b Harbhajan Singh	0		
J.D.P.Oram	lbw b Harbhajan Singh	0		
R.G.Hart†	lbw b Khan	6		
D.L.Vettori	c Patel b Khan	21		
D.R.Tuffey	not out	9		
S.E.Bond	b Agarkar	2		
Extras	(b 6, lb 12, w 2, nb 8, pen 5)	33	(w 1)	1
TOTAL	**(91.1 overs)**	**247**	**(9.3 overs) (0 wkts)**	**36**

Bowling	O	M	R	W	O	M	R	W
NEW ZEALAND								
Bond	18.4	4	66	3	13.1	5	33	4
Tuffey	16	7	25	2	9	3	35	3
Oram	15	4	31	2	12	3	36	3
Styris	6	0	28	3	4	0	16	0
Astle	3	1	10	0				
INDIA								
Khan	25	8	53	5	3	0	13	0
Nehra	19	4	50	0	4.3	0	21	0
Agarkar	13.1	1	54	1				
Bangar	15	4	23	2				
Harbhajan Singh	17	4	33	2	2	1	2	0
Ganguly	2	0	11	0				

Fall of Wickets

	I 1st	NZ 1st	I 2nd	NZ 2nd
1st	2	30	23	-
2nd	9	96	31	-
3rd	29	111	31	-
4th	51	181	33	-
5th	55	182	36	-
6th	92	186	76	-
7th	118	201	88	-
8th	118	228	96	-
9th	147	237	121	-
10th	161	247	121	-

MILESTONES

- Jacob Oram (223) made his test debut.

- It was New Zealand's 52nd test victory.

- India had now lost their last four tests at the Basin Reserve.

- It was New Zealand's 11th test win at the Basin Reserve.

301 NEW ZEALAND v INDIA *(Second Test)*

at Westpac Park, Hamilton on 19, 20, 21, 22 December, 2002
Toss : New Zealand. Umpires : E.A.R de Silva & D.J. Harper
New Zealand won by 4 wickets

The city of Hamilton had its entire average December rainfall in the five days leading up to the test. Not surprisingly, there was no play on the first day and only 37 overs on the second.

Again the toss favoured New Zealand and when play began at 4.30 pm the excess of sideways movement achieved by Shane Bond and Daryl Tuffey totally confused the batsmen, with Tuffey being almost unplayable, as he captured four wickets in his first eight overs. V.V.S. Laxman top-scored with 23 and Harbhajan Singh (20) slogged effectively, hitting five boundaries in his nine-minute stay. India ended the truncated day 92-8.

Any thoughts that a night's rest would calm the vile nature of the pitch were shattered as the last two wickets fell in seven minutes to have India out for 99. Perhaps the heavy roller quietened the pitch temporarily as New Zealand progressed to 39-1, with Mark Richardson and Stephen Fleming playing and missing more often than not but surviving.

When Richardson did not play a shot at Zaheer Khan and was out lbw, New Zealand disintegrated and lost their last nine wickets for 55, to be out for 94 in 38.2 overs and giving India a first-innings lead of five. Zaheer Khan ended with his best test figures of 5-29.

Throughout his career Tuffey had shown a remarkable knack for claiming wickets at the beginning of an innings and he did so in India's second innings, dismissing both openers with the score at eight. Rahul Dravid and Sachin Tendulkar provided the most fluent batting of the game, adding 49. India totalled 154, with Jacob Oram and Tuffey having the identical figures of 4-41.

New Zealand ended an enthralling third day at 24-0, a day when 22 wickets fell, a number only matched three times in the last fifty years of test cricket.

Tension ebbed and flowed on the fourth and final day. New Zealand appeared comfortably placed at 89-2 before the talented left-arm medium-fast Ashish Nehra caused palpitations, capturing two quick wickets before Jacob Oram and Robbie Hart saw New Zealand home.

During the game 36 wickets fell in 179 overs, making the test gripping viewing with the average partnership worth 14 and a wicket falling every five overs.

MILESTONES

- It was New Zealand's 53rd test victory.

- It was the first time that New Zealand had beaten India twice in a series. India's first innings total of 99 was the lowest score to gain a first innings lead in a test.

- It was the first time in 1632 tests that both sides had been dismissed for under 100 in their first full innings.

- New Zealand's 94 was their lowest score against India.

- Rahul Dravid's score of 39 in India's second innings was the fourth-lowest top score in a completed test. The other instances were before 1890.

- Twenty-two wickets fell on the third day, matched only three times in the previous 50 years of tests.

- Daniel Vettori began the series with 139 test wickets. In comparison his fast-medium colleagues had an aggregate of 123 wickets. He did not bowl a ball in the series.

INDIA

S.B.Bangar	c Oram b Tuffey	1	c & b Tuffey		7
V.Sehwag	c Richardson b Bond	1	(7) c Tuffey b Bond		25
R.S.Dravid	c Hart b Tuffey	9	c sub (M.J.Mason) b Oram		39
S.R.Tendulkar	c Styris b Tuffey	9	b Tuffey		32
S.C.Ganguly*	c Fleming b Tuffey	5	c Hart b Oram		5
V.V.S.Laxman	b Bond	23	b Astle		4
P.A.Patel†	c Hart b Oram	8	(2) b Tuffey		0
Harbhajan Singh	b Bond	20	c Hart b Tuffey		18
Z.Khan	b Oram	0	c Astle b Oram		0
A.Nehra	c Fleming b Bond	7	c Hart b Oram		10
T.Yohannan	not out	0	not out		8
Extras	(lb 12, nb 4)	16	(lb 1, w 2, nb 3)		6
TOTAL	(38.2 overs)	**99**	(43.5 overs)		**154**

NEW ZEALAND

M.H.Richardson	lbw b Khan	13	c Patel b Nehra		28
L.Vincent	c Dravid b Khan	3	c Patel b Yohannan		9
S.P.Fleming*	c & b Khan	21	c Khan b Nehra		32
C.D.McMillan	c Dravid b Nehra	4	lbw b Nehra		18
N.J.Astle	c Harbhajan Singh b Nehra	0	c Patel b Khan		14
S.B.Styris	lbw b Harbhajan Singh	13	c Patel b Harbhajan Singh		17
J.D.P.Oram	c Tendulkar b Harbhajan Singh	3	not out		26
R.G.Hart†	lbw b Khan	3	not out		11
D.L.Vettori	c Laxman b Khan	6			
D.R.Tuffey	run out	13			
S.E.Bond	not out	0			
Extras	(b 1, lb 4, nb 10)	15	(lb 4, nb 1)		5
TOTAL	(38.2 overs)	**94**	(56.2 overs) (6 wkts)		**160**

Bowling	O	M	R	W	O	M	R	W
NEW ZEALAND								
Bond	14.2	7	39	4	10	0	58	1
Tuffey	9	6	12	4	16	3	41	4
Oram	10	1	22	2	12.5	2	41	4
Styris	2	0	10	0				
Astle	3	2	4	0	5	1	13	1
INDIA								
Khan	13.2	4	29	5	13	0	56	1
Yohannan	9	4	16	0	16	5	27	1
Nehra	8	3	20	2	16.2	4	34	3
Bangar	2	1	4	0				
Harbhajan Singh	6	0	20	2	11	0	39	1

Fall of Wickets

	I	NZ	I	NZ
	1st	*1st*	*2nd*	*2nd*
1st	1	7	2	30
2nd	11	39	8	52
3rd	26	47	57	89
4th	34	48	64	105
5th	40	60	85	136
6th	70	64	110	136
7th	91	69	130	-
8th	92	79	131	-
9th	93	94	136	-
10th	99	94	154	-

Daryl Tuffey took full advantage of the conditions and became an unerring destroyer, capturing four wickets for eight runs off eight overs.

2002/03 New Zealand in Sri Lanka

302 **SRI LANKA v NEW ZEALAND** *(First Test)*
at P. Saravanamuttu Stadium on 25, 26, 27, 28, 29 April, 2003
Toss : New Zealand. Umpires : D.J. Harper & S.J.A. Taufel
Match drawn

Following the loss of an early wicket, Mark Richardson and Stephen Fleming battled intense heat and accurate slow bowling with judicious use of their front pad. Their intense concentration was not broken until the first delivery of the second new ball from Chaminda Vaas, which bowled Richardson for 85 after the pair had added a record 172 for the second wicket, despite Richardson straining a hamstring and batting with a runner. At stumps New Zealand was 207-2 with Fleming 112 not out.

Fleming continued his heroic marathon throughout the second day until he declared at 515-7 after sharing profitable

partnerships of 157 with Scott Styris and 78 with Jacob Oram. For 665 minutes he defied the Sri Lankan bowlers in scoring 274 not out and won a psychological victory over Muralitharan. Sri Lanka's reply was cautiously measured as temporary captain Hashan Tillakaratane was determined to avoid defeat at all costs.

With the pitch playing placidly Sri Lanka reached 267-4 at the end of the third day thanks to half-centuries to four of their first six batsmen. Any chance of New Zealand pushing home an advantage, when Jayawardene was dismissed early on the fourth day, disappeared when the diminutive Kaluwitharana was audacious and thrilling, scoring 76 off 90 balls. Tillakaratane continued to play dourly and when a spectacular thunderstorm halted play he was 126 not out of Sri Lanka's 424-6.

He continued batting on the fifth day, which strangled what little life there was out of the game. When Daniel Vettori got three lbw decisions in five balls, Sri Lanka was left 32 runs in arrears. Batting a second time, Fleming stayed for one minute short of five hours, being 69 not out.

Stephen Fleming celebrated his 50th test as captain of New Zealand by making 274 not out, the highest score of his test career.

NEW ZEALAND

M.H.Richardson	b Vaas	85	(7) not out		6
M.J.Horne	c Dharmasena b Nissanka	4	(1) lbw b Lokuarachchi		42
S.P.Fleming*	not out	274	(2) not out		69
M.S.Sinclair	c Sangakkara b Dharmasena	17	(3) c sub (T.M.Dilshan) b Muralitharan		1
S.B.Styris	c Vaas b Dharmasena	63	(4) lbw b Lokuarachchi		16
J.D.P.Oram	c Lokuarachchi b Muralitharan	33	(5) c Kaluwitharana b Muralitharan		19
R.G.Hart†	c Jayawardene b Muralitharan	9	(6) c Sangakkara b Muralitharan		0
D.L.Vettori	lbw b Dharmasena	7			
P.J.Wiseman	not out	16			
D.R.Tuffey					
S.E.Bond					
Extras	(b 2, lb 3, w 1, nb 1)	7	(b 2, lb 5, nb 1)		8
TOTAL	(174.5 overs) (7 wkts dec)	**515**	(78 overs) (5 wkts dec)		**161**

SRI LANKA

M.S.Atapattu	lbw b Tuffey	0
S.T.Jayasuriya	b Bond	50
W.P.U.J.C.Vaas	c Fleming b Bond	4
K.C.Sangakkara	c Oram b Wiseman	67
D.P.M.D.Jayawardene	c Hart b Oram	58
H.P.Tillakaratne*	b Bond	144
R.S.Kaluwitharana†	c Sinclair b Wiseman	76
H.D.P.K.Dharmasena	lbw b Vettori	31
K.S.Lokuarachchi	not out	28
R.A.P.Nissanka	lbw b Vettori	0
M.Muralitharan	lbw b Vettori	0
Extras	(lb 21, w 1, nb 3)	25
TOTAL	(152 overs)	**483**

Bowling	O	M	R	W	O	M	R	W		Fall of Wickets		
SRI LANKA										NZ	SL	NZ
										1st	1st	2nd
Vaas	29	8	73	1	7	2	27	0				
Nissanka	23	9	53	1	6	1	18	0	1st	20	0	71
Dharmasena	40	7	132	3	16	7	21	0	2nd	192	11	76
Muralitharan	58.5	16	140	2	30	15	41	3	3rd	235	114	108
Lokuarachchi	18	2	83	0	19	2	47	2	4th	392	134	133
Jayasuriya	6	0	29	0					5th	471	267	133
NEW ZEALAND									6th	486	374	-
Tuffey	17	5	54	1					7th	499	444	-
Bond	28	6	97	3					8th	-	483	-
Oram	30	13	62	1					9th	-	483	-
Vettori	33	8	94	3					10th	-	483	-
Wiseman	41	13	127	2								
Styris	3	0	28	0								

MILESTONES

- It was Stephen Fleming's 50th test as captain. He became the eighth player to captain his country 50 times.

- Fleming aggregated 343 runs for the match. The previous highest by a New Zealander was Martin Crowe's 329 against Sri Lanka at Wellington in 1990/91 (test 206).

- Mark Richardson and Fleming created a new second wicket record of 172 for New Zealand against Sri Lanka.

303 SRI LANKA v NEW ZEALAND *(Second Test)*

at Asgiriya Stadium, Kandy on 3, 4, 5, 6, 7 May, 2003
Toss : New Zealand. Umpires : D.J. Harper & S.J.A. Taufel
Match drawn

The first five sessions were lost because of a saturated outfield that only became playable because of the mopping-up operation done by prisoners from a nearby jail.

After winning the toss New Zealand batted but were quickly in strife when they lost their first three wickets for 11 runs. The ever-reliable Mark Richardson halted the slide and was unbeaten on 32 at stumps with his side 75-4.

A first test fifty by Jacob Oram, and consistent batting throughout the line-up, saw New Zealand recover to 305, two

sessions into the third day. Daniel Vettori's innings ended when he was run out for 55. He collided head first with Marvan Atapattu which saw both players incapacitated for the remainder of the game. Vettori rolled his ankle and could not bowl and Atapattu, semi-concussed, was unable to bat.

Although Sri Lanka possessed several attacking batsmen Jayasuriya was the only one who appreciated that the pitch was slowly breaking up and accordingly played with his accustomed aggressiveness, making 92.

Hashan Tillakaratane was looking for his third successive test century but, after a stay of 336 minutes, missed his goal by seven runs. Paul Wiseman was rewarded with four wickets for a sustained, accurate spell.

In hindsight it was just as well for New Zealand that Sri Lanka had not batted with positive intent as Muralitharan spun the ball fiendishly on the fifth day, capturing five wickets, as New Zealand lost their last nine wickets for 74.

A gutsy stand, lasting 28.1 overs, by Robbie Hart and Wiseman saved the day for New Zealand who ended with a lead of 191 runs with only 38 overs left. Sri Lanka rejected the challenge, the series being left drawn nil-all.

Paul Wiseman helped Robbie Hart to occupy the crease for a vital 28.1 overs that extinguished any hope Sri Lanka had of winning the test.

NEW ZEALAND					
M.H.Richardson	c Sangakkara b Lokuarachchi	55	c Kaluwitharana b Nissanka	55	
M.J.Horne	c Kaluwitharana b Vaas	1	c Tillakaratne b Muralitharan	27	
S.P.Fleming*	lbw b Nissanka	0	c Kaluwitharana b Dharmasena	33	
M.S.Sinclair	lbw b Vaas	3	st Kaluwitharana b Muralitharan	0	
S.B.Styris	c Tillakaratne b Muralitharan	32	c Muralitharan b Vaas	1	
J.D.P.Oram	c Kaluwitharana b Lokuarachchi	74	lbw b Muralitharan	16	
R.G.Hart†	lbw b Muralitharan	31	c Kaluwitharana b Vaas	12	
D.L.Vettori	run out	55	b Muralitharan	0	
P.J.Wiseman	b Muralitharan	7	c Tillakaratne b Vaas	29	
D.R.Tuffey	c Jayawardene b Nissanka	15	c Jayasuriya b Muralitharan	1	
S.E.Bond	not out	10	not out	1	
Extras	(b 3, lb 7, w 5, nb 7)	22	(b 1, lb 6, nb 1)	8	
TOTAL	(111.5 overs)	**305**	(97.3 overs)	**183**	

SRI LANKA					
K.C.Sangakkara	c Hart b Tuffey	10	not out	27	
S.T.Jayasuriya	c Fleming b Wiseman	82	c Richardson b Bond	9	
D.P.M.D.Jayawardene	c Hart b Oram	15	not out	32	
H.P.Tillakaratne*	b Wiseman	93			
R.S.Kaluwitharana†	c Tuffey b Bond	20			
H.D.P.K.Dharmasena	c Fleming b Wiseman	5			
K.S.Lokuarachchi	c Tuffey b Oram	20			
W.P.U.J.C.Vaas	b Oram	22			
M.S.Atapattu	retired hurt	2			
R.A.P.Nissanka	b Wiseman	6			
M.Muralitharan	not out	2			
Extras	(b 6, lb 11, nb 4)	21	(lb 4)	4	
TOTAL	(97.3 overs)	**298**	(30 overs) (1 wkt)	**72**	

Bowling	O	M	R	W	O	M	R	W		Fall of Wickets			
SRI LANKA										NZ	SL	NZ	SL
										1st	*1st*	*2nd*	*2nd*
Vaas	22	8	48	2	15.3	6	31	3					
Nissanka	16.5	5	41	2	10	4	18	1	1st	6	30	65	14
Muralitharan	34	10	90	3	39	18	49	5	2nd	7	69	109	-
Jayasuriya	8	0	24	0	7	0	20	0	3rd	11	126	110	-
Dharmasena	15	5	40	0	12	2	32	1	4th	71	169	115	-
Lokuarachchi	16	5	52	2	14	3	26	0	5th	109	189	136	-
NEW ZEALAND									6th	189	234	139	-
Tuffey	20	6	45	1	9	3	18	0	7th	222	264	139	-
Bond	25	6	78	1	6	1	19	1	8th	237	285	179	-
Oram	20	2	54	3					9th	271	298	182	-
Wiseman	32.3	4	104	4	9	4	20	0	10th	305	-	183	-
Vettori					6	1	11	0					

MILESTONES

- Muttiah Muralitharan captured five wickets in an innings for the 37th time, overtaking Sir Richard Hadlee's record.

- Muralitharan claimed his 450th test wicket.

2003/04 New Zealand in India

Prior to the test the Indian media were unanimous that there had to be "payback" for the juicy, green conditions that led to India's downfall when they toured New Zealand eight months earlier. India's captain, Sourav Ganguly, believed that his two spinners, Anil Kumble and Harbhajan Singh, would be his key to winning the series. As it happened the pitch, made from imported red soil, held together for the duration of the test, providing excellent batting conditions.

304 INDIA v NEW ZEALAND (First Test)

at Sardar Patel Stadium, Ahmedabad on 8, 9, 10, 11, 12 October, 2003
Toss : India. Umpires : R.E. Koertzen & D.R. Shepherd
Match drawn

Rahul Dravid's elegant stroke play thrived, as it had done on previous occasions against New Zealand. He occupied the crease for almost 10 hours in scoring 222, his third test double century. When Ganguly declared, on reaching his personal hundred, India's total had reached 500-5. Zaheer Khan's left-arm pace immediately accounted for three New Zealand wickets. The day ended at 41-3.

Nathan Astle forged worthwhile partnerships of 91 with Scott Styris and a further 91 with Craig McMillan. Astle's 103 was his ninth test century. McMillan's 54 was meritorious, as he was recovering from knee surgery. New Zealand was 74 runs from avoiding the follow-on with three wickets left.

A gallant innings of 60 by Daniel Vettori, aided by his spinning colleague Paul Wiseman, saw them to the initial safety of 301 and on to 340. India, with a lead of 160, increased their batting tempo from the first innings but in the context of the game it was not fast enough in such good batting conditions. Their second declaration of the match set New Zealand a target of 370 for victory off 107 overs.

On the final day the temperature topped 40°C. At 86-4, with Kumble and Harbhajan looking threatening, Lou Vincent and McMillan led a spirited defiance. Neither of these batsmen had been selected for New Zealand's previous series against Sri Lanka and had something to prove. Along with Astle they saw the game safely to a draw.

INDIA

A.Chopra	c & b Vettori	42	c Styris b Vettori	31
V.Sehwag	lbw b Tuffey	29	c Hart b Oram	17
R.S.Dravid	c Hart b Oram	222	c Vincent b Wiseman	73
S.R.Tendulkar	c Astle b Styris	8	c Vettori b Wiseman	7
V.V.S.Laxman	c Wiseman b Vettori	64	c Vettori b Wiseman	44
S.C.Ganguly*	not out	100	b Wiseman	25
P.A.Patel†	not out	29	not out	29
Harbhajan Singh				
A.R.Kumble				
Z.Khan				
L.Balaji				
Extras	(b 2, lb 3, nb 1)	6	(b 4, lb 3)	7
TOTAL	**(159 overs) (5 wkts dec)**	**500**	**(44.5 overs) (6 wkts dec)**	**209**

NEW ZEALAND

M.H.Richardson	b Khan	6	c Chopra b Kumble	21
L.Vincent	c Patel b Khan	7	b Kumble	67
S.P.Fleming*	b Khan	1	(4) c Laxman b Harbhajan Singh	8
S.B.Styris	c Chopra b Harbhajan Singh	34	(5) lbw b Kumble	0
N.J.Astle	st Patel b Harbhajan Singh	103	(8) not out	51
C.D.McMillan	c Chopra b Sehwag	54	not out	83
J.D.P.Oram	c Dravid b Kumble	5	c Dravid b Harbhajan Singh	7
R.G.Hart†	lbw b Balaji	15		
D.L.Vettori	c Dravid b Kumble	60		
P.J.Wiseman	c Laxman b Khan	27		
D.R.Tuffey	not out	2	(3) b Kumble	8
Extras	(b 4, lb 18, nb 4)	26	(b 4, lb 11, nb 12)	27
TOTAL	**(131.1 overs)**	**340**	**(107 overs) (6 wkts)**	**272**

Bowling NEW ZEALAND	O	M	R	W	O	M	R	W
Tuffey	31	6	103	1	9	2	18	0
Oram	33	8	95	1	8	0	39	1
Styris	26	5	83	1				
Vettori	44	9	128	2	16	0	81	1
McMillan	4	1	6	0				
Wiseman	21	0	80	0	11.5	0	64	4
INDIA								
Khan	23	3	68	4	10	1	36	0
Balaji	26	7	84	1	11	4	21	0
Kumble	35.1	11	58	2	39	12	95	4
Harbhajan Singh	36	8	86	2	38	9	65	2
Sehwag	8	2	17	1	2	2	0	0
Tendulkar	3	2	5	0	7	0	40	0

Fall of Wickets	I	NZ	I	NZ
	1st	1st	2nd	2nd
1st	35	11	20	44
2nd	107	16	97	68
3rd	134	17	118	85
4th	264	108	166	86
5th	446	199	177	150
6th	-	223	209	169
7th	-	227	-	-
8th	-	265	-	-
9th	-	332	-	-
10th	-	340	-	-

New Zealand wicketkeeper Robbie Hart watches V.V.S. Laxman drive effortlessly through the offside.

MILESTONES

- Rahul Dravid and Sourav Ganguly put on 182, a record for the fifth wicket for India against New Zealand.

- Daniel Vettori became the fourth New Zealander to score 1000 runs and take 100 wickets in test cricket, the others being Richard Hadlee, John Bracewell and Chris Cairns.

- Nathan Astle scored a century and a fifty in a test for the third time.

- Astle's 103 was the first century scored by a New Zealander in a test in India since Glenn Turner in 1976/77 (test 124).

- Anil Kumble captured his 350th wicket in his 77th test.

305 INDIA v NEW ZEALAND *(Second Test)*

at Punjab C.A. Stadium, Mohali on 16, 17, 18, 19, 20 October, 2003
Toss : New Zealand. Umpires : R.E. Koertzen & D.R. Shepherd
Match drawn

Following the stalemate in Ahmedabad the second test was an even bigger batting bonanza with 10 batsmen spending over three hours at the crease, scoring six centuries and four fifties.

New Zealand batted for the first two and a half days in compiling their highest test score overseas before Stephen Fleming declared at 630-6. Mark Richardson and Lou Vincent were untroubled in compiling 231 for the first wicket and when Scott Styris replaced Vincent another 151 were added for the second wicket.

By the time of the declaration four batsmen had scored centuries, none faster than Craig McMillan who accelerated to his century off 130 balls, displaying shots of great power combined with cheeky improvisations. To show how one-sided the contest was in favour of batsmen India was 203-1 at the end of the third day with Virender Sehwag unbeaten on 128. Thus 833 runs had been plundered for the loss of seven wickets.

Laxman almost guided India past the follow-on figure of 430 by compiling a silky 104 not out. Daryl Tuffey forced India to follow on with a Herculean performance. At the start of the fifth day he effected a startling run out and then dismissed the last two batsmen in identical fashion, caught by wicketkeeper Robbie Hart.

India was instantly in danger when Tuffey dismissed Sehwag, Rahul Dravid and Sachin Tendulkar with the score at 18. When he was rested, Tuffey's amazing figures for the morning were 15 overs, three wickets for 25 runs. Aakash Chopra and Laxman again proved difficult to dislodge and the game, and the series, ended in a draw.

NEW ZEALAND

M.H.Richardson	c Kumble b Harbhajan Singh	145
L.Vincent	lbw b Kumble	106
S.B.Styris	lbw b Kumble	119
S.P.Fleming*	b Tendulkar	30
N.J.Astle	c Patel b Harbhajan Singh	18
C.D.McMillan	not out	100
R.G.Hart†	b Kumble	11
D.L.Vettori	not out	48
P.J.Wiseman		
D.R.Tuffey		
I.G.Butler		
Extras	(b 21, lb 28, w 1, nb 3)	53
TOTAL	**(198.3 overs) (6 wkts dec)**	**630**

INDIA

A.Chopra	c Astle b Tuffey	60	c Richardson b Wiseman	52
V.Sehwag	b Styris	130	c Fleming b Tuffey	1
R.S.Dravid*	c Hart b Butler	13	c Fleming b Tuffey	5
S.R.Tendulkar	c Richardson b Vettori	55	b Tuffey	1
V.V.S.Laxman	not out	104	not out	67
Yuvraj Singh	c Hart b Tuffey	20	not out	5
P.A.Patel†	c Richardson b Vettori	18		
A.R.Kumble	run out	5		
Harbhajan Singh	run out	8		
L.Balaji	c Hart b Tuffey	4		
Z.Khan	c Hart b Tuffey	0		
Extras	(b 2, lb 1, w 2, nb 2)	7	(lb 4, w 1)	5
TOTAL	**(172 overs)**	**424**	**(69 overs) (4 wkts)**	**136**

Bowling	O	M	R	W	O	M	R	W
INDIA								
Khan	26	8	95	0				
Balaji	30	10	78	0				
Tendulkar	22	3	55	1				
Kumble	66	18	181	3				
Harbhajan Singh	48	7	149	2				
Sehwag	5.3	1	22	0				
Yuvraj	1	0	1	0				
NEW ZEALAND								
Tuffey	29	5	80	4	14	4	30	3
Butler	35	7	116	1	5	1	12	0
Styris	19	7	40	1	4	2	4	0
Vettori	56	24	84	2	23	8	40	0
Wiseman	32	7	95	0	17	6	37	1
McMillan	1	0	6	0	6	3	9	0

Fall of Wickets			
	NZ	I	I
	1st	1st	2nd
1st	231	163	6
2nd	382	208	12
3rd	433	218	18
4th	447	330	128
5th	507	364	-
6th	540	388	-
7th	-	396	-
8th	-	408	-
9th	-	424	-
10th	-	424	-

The four centurions at Mohali, from left, Mark Richardson, Scott Styris, Lou Vincent and Craig McMillan.

MILESTONES

- Mark Richardson and Lou Vincent established a first wicket record of 231 for New Zealand against India.

- It was the first time in tests that the first three New Zealand batsmen had scored centuries in the same innings.

- It was the second time in tests that four New Zealanders had made a century in one innings, the first being against Australia in Perth in 2001/02 (test 291).

- New Zealand's score of 630-6d was its second-highest behind 671-4 against Sri Lanka at the Basin Reserve in 1990/91. It was New Zealand's highest test score overseas.

- This was the first New Zealand side not to have lost a series in India in five visits since 1969/70.

2003/04 Pakistan in New Zealand

306 **NEW ZEALAND v PAKISTAN** (*First Test*)

at Westpac Park, Hamilton on 19, 20, 21, 22, 23 December, 2003
Toss : New Zealand. Umpires : S.J. Davis & D.L. Orchard
Match drawn

It was probably the fact that when India played at Hamilton the previous year on a green pitch neither side scored 100 in their first innings, that influenced Inzamam-ul-Haq to ask New Zealand to bat first.

He was rewarded with the early wicket of Lou Vincent before Mark Richardson and Stephen Fleming combined for 101 for the second wicket until Richardson was run out for 44. The elegant Fleming reached his sixth hundred in 248 minutes. He lost four partners after tea and, when stumps were drawn at 296-5, Fleming was unbeaten on 125.

The early loss of Robbie Hart was followed by a record partnership of 125 for the eighth wicket between Fleming and Daniel Vettori. In his previous 48 tests Vettori had scored six half-centuries but in this innings he emerged from the shadows of "tailender" to "test centurion", reaching his first test hundred shortly after Fleming was out for 192.

Led by Vettori's 137 not out the last three New Zealand wickets added 249 at better than a run a minute. In reply to New Zealand's 563, a record score against Pakistan, the visitors' batsmen were consistent, with the first eight all scoring over 20.

Consistent rain limited play to 38.2 overs on the third day but not before Yasir Hameed, a right-hand batsman who earlier in the year became the second player to score a century in each innings on debut, exhibited graceful batting skills in scoring 80.

Daryl Tuffey captured five of the first six wickets to fall at 285 before wicketkeeper Moin Khan savaged the bowling and dominated the partnership with Mohammad Sami that added 152 for the seventh wicket. Moin's 137 was his fourth, and highest, test century in a career that began in 1990.

Rain delayed the start of the fifth day until after lunch, with New Zealand having a lead of 104. Sami sprinted in to bowl and found good rhythm and generated high speed, and wickets fell at an alarming rate before Jacob Oram and Vettori halted the slide. It was disappointing that a weak 48 overs had taken the gloss off New Zealand's performance of dominating the bulk of the game.

Daniel Vettori is congratulated by his Northern Districts and New Zealand team-mate Daryl Tuffey after scoring his first test hundred.

NEW ZEALAND

M.H.Richardson	run out	44	c Moin b Gul	15
L.Vincent	c Inzamam b Shabbir	8	c Farhat b Sami	4
S.P.Fleming*	lbw b Gul	192	c Moin b Sami	0
S.B.Styris	c Umar b Danish	33	c Umar b Sami	20
C.D.McMillan	c Umar b Danish	22	run out	2
C.L.Cairns	c Moin b Shabbir	11	b Gul	0
J.D.P.Oram	b Shabbir	6	not out	23
R.G.Hart†	c Youhana b Shabbir	10	b Sami	0
D.L.Vettori	not out	137	c Umar b Sami	20
D.R.Tuffey	b Gul	35	not out	1
I.G.Butler	c Farhat b Shabbir	7		
Extras	(b 4, lb 12, w 9, nb 33)	58	(lb 4, w 1, nb 6)	11
TOTAL	(151.2 overs)	563	(41.1 overs) (8 wkts)	96

PAKISTAN

Imran Farhat	c Hart b Oram	20
Taufeeq Umar	c Butler b Tuffey	27
Yasir Hameed	lbw b Tuffey	80
Yousuf Youhana	c Vincent b Tuffey	28
Inzamam-ul-Haq*	lbw b Tuffey	51
Abdur Razzaq	c Hart b Tuffey	48
Moin Khan†	lbw b Oram	137
Mohammad Sami	c Hart b Vettori	25
Shabbir Ahmed	c Hart b Butler	8
Umar Gul	c Vettori b Butler	3
Danish Kaneria	not out	0
Extras	(lb 4, w 11, nb 21)	36
TOTAL	(144.4 overs)	463

Bowling	O	M	R	W	O	M	R	W		*Fall of Wickets*		
PAKISTAN										NZ	P	NZ
Sami	27	2	126	0	16	4	44	5		*1st*	*1st*	*2nd*
Shabbir	43.2	9	117	5	10	7	10	0	1st	16	47	13
Gul	31	5	118	2	8.1	2	25	2	2nd	117	55	13
Razzaq	18	2	74	0	3	1	7	0	3rd	217	134	42
Danish	32	6	112	2	4	2	6	0	4th	249	209	42
NEW ZEALAND									5th	266	256	42
Tuffey	33	8	87	5					6th	274	285	47
Butler	23.4	6	113	2					7th	314	437	52
Oram	23	6	55	2					8th	439	453	95
Cairns	17	0	60	0					9th	538	462	-
Vettori	36	3	117	1					10th	563	463	-
Styris	12	4	27	0								

MILESTONES

- Stephen Fleming and Daniel Vettori created an eighth wicket record of 125 for New Zealand against Pakistan.

- Daniel Vettori and Daryl Tuffey created a ninth wicket record partnership of 99 for New Zealand against Pakistan.

- New Zealand's 563 was their highest total against Pakistan.

- Daniel Vettori's score of 137 not out was the fourth-highest made by a batsman batting at number nine. The highest was by Ian Smith who made 173 against India at Auckland in 1989/90 (test 198).

307 NEW ZEALAND v PAKISTAN *(Second Test)*

at Basin Reserve, Wellington on 26, 27, 28, 29, 30 December, 2003
Toss : New Zealand. Umpires : E.A.R. de Silva & D.L. Orchard
Pakistan won by 7 wickets

New Zealand had no qualms about batting first in Wellington under overcast conditions. Shoaib Akhtar castled Lou Vincent with his eighth ball and the players left the field because of bad light. After a lengthy delay Stephen Fleming was lbw four balls after play resumed.

With two wickets down for one run the situation was tailor-made for Mark Richardson to drop anchor and battle for survival, which he did for the rest of the truncated day, finishing on 53 of New Zealand's total of 151-5.

Richardson's obdurate innings lasted 438 minutes. When he departed for 82 Jacob Oram and ever-improving Daniel Vettori batted more aggressively and were associated in an 80-run stand. Oram's 97 was his highest test score and enabled New Zealand to finish on 366. Shoaib took 5-48.

Pakistan began the third day at 52-2 but New Zealand was initially thwarted by a cultured 60 from Yousuf Youhana. Taking the second new ball, with a strong northerly breeze behind him, Ian Butler wrecked Pakistan's innings taking five wickets in five overs to finish with his best test figures of 6-46.

It was a well-deserved success for the 22-year-old Butler, who bowled accurately and mixed his length from short to full with precision. Pakistan's last six wickets fell for 18 runs, a foretaste of worse to come. New Zealand's unexpected lead of 170 was extended to 245 by stumps, with Richardson 35 not out and nightwatchman Daryl Tuffey yet to score.

Pakistan were facing defeat with New Zealand leading by 265 runs and only three wickets down. Shoaib induced a wild slash from Richardson and his was the first of seven wickets to fall for eight runs. Pakistan now required 275 to win on a pitch playing well and the game not yet at the halfway mark.

Shoaib, the architect of the mayhem, took 11 wickets for 78 runs. It is debatable if any bowler in test history has had such a long run-up or sprinted in so fast. The end result of

which was rarely-equalled, extraordinary pace, allied with the ability to swing the ball both ways.

The visitors' batsmen then batted with great determination against a side that looked shell-shocked. Inzamam-ul-Haq and Youhana were untroubled in an unbroken partnership of 121 that gave Pakistan victory by six wickets.

Bowling with a strong wind behind him, Ian Butler removed five batsmen in five overs and ended with figures of 6-46.

NEW ZEALAND

M.H.Richardson	c Youhana b Shabbir	82	c Moin b Shoaib	41
L.Vincent	b Shoaib	0	lbw b Shoaib	4
S.P.Fleming*	lbw b Shoaib	0	lbw b Danish	24
R.A.Jones	b Razzaq	16	c Moin b Shoaib	7
S.B.Styris	c Moin b Shoaib	36	(6) b Shoaib	0
C.D.McMillan	lbw b Shabbir	26	(7) not out	3
R.G.Hart†	c Farhat b Shoaib	19	(10) b Shoaib	0
J.D.P.Oram	c Moin b Shabbir	97	lbw b Shabbir	3
D.L.Vettori	c Hameed b Sami	44	lbw b Shabbir	0
D.R.Tuffey	not out	9	(5) run out	13
I.G.Butler	c Moin b Shoaib	4	b Shoaib	0
Extras	(b 5, lb 14, w 3, nb 11)	33	(lb 4, w 1, nb 3)	8
TOTAL	(142.3 overs)	**366**	(53 overs)	**103**

PAKISTAN

Imran Farhat	c Hart b Oram	20	c Hart b Oram	14
Taufeeq Umar	c Oram b Tuffey	16	lbw b Vettori	34
Yasir Hameed	b Butler	3	c Hart b Butler	59
Yousuf Youhana	c Fleming b Vettori	60	not out	88
Inzamam-ul-Haq*	lbw b Oram	34	not out	72
Abdur Razzaq	b Butler	26		
Moin Khan†	c Vettori b Butler	19		
Mohammad Sami	c Hart b Butler	4		
Shoaib Akhtar	b Butler	0		
Shabbir Ahmed	not out	0		
Danish Kaneria	lbw b Butler	0		
Extras	(b 4, lb 3, w 1, nb 6)	14	(b 4, lb 2, nb 4)	10
TOTAL	(90 overs)	**196**	(74.5 overs) (3 wkts)	**277**

Bowling	O	M	R	W	O	M	R	W
PAKISTAN								
Shoaib	20.3	5	48	5	18	3	30	6
Sami	30	12	64	1	4	1	12	0
Shabbir	37	8	87	3	17	5	20	2
Danish	32	5	86	0	9	2	18	1
Razzaq	23	6	62	1	5	1	19	0
NEW ZEALAND								
Tuffey	24	9	46	1	14	5	41	0
Butler	20	6	46	6	18.5	1	100	1
Oram	22	5	49	2	9	1	34	1
Vettori	22	6	47	1	23	5	59	1
Styris	2	1	1	0	6	1	26	0
McMillan					4	0	11	0

Fall of Wickets

	NZ	P	NZ	P
	1st	1st	2nd	2nd
1st	1	27	8	37
2nd	1	30	43	75
3rd	41	60	73	156
4th	94	112	95	-
5th	145	168	95	-
6th	171	171	96	-
7th	247	194	101	-
8th	327	195	102	-
9th	361	196	103	-
10th	366	196	103	-

MILESTONES

- Richard Jones (223) made his test debut.

- Daniel Vettori took his 150th test wicket in his 46th test.

2003/04 South Africa in New Zealand

The portents for the tests were favourable for New Zealand when they won the one-day series 5-1. It was the first time that New Zealand had taken a series off South Africa in either form of cricket.

308 **NEW ZEALAND v SOUTH AFRICA** *(First Test)*
at Westpac Park, Hamilton on 10, 11, 12, 13, 14 March, 2004
Toss : South Africa. Umpires : S.J. Davis & R.B. Tiffin
Match drawn

A fungus killed the grass on the prepared pitch and a new one had to be developed at short notice. It was touch-and-go before New Zealand Cricket would allow the match to proceed. The new surface proved slow with low bounce and both South Africa's openers were dismissed forcing the pace. Jacques Kallis, having made centuries in the last four tests for South Africa against the West Indies before they came on tour, was dismissed for 92 and South Africa ended the day at 279-4.

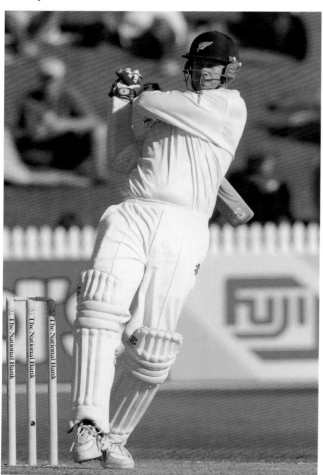

Jacob Oram scored 137 not out and saw New Zealand through to their highest total against South Africa.

Gary Kirsten dominated the second day's play, scoring his 21st and last test century and piloting South Africa through to 459. The last six wickets added 188, with Kirsten finishing on 137. Michael Papps, making his test debut, was 50 not out at stumps, with New Zealand 102-2. By now an abnormally large hole had developed at one end from the bowlers' follow-through. Optically it worried all the batsmen but in fact had little effect on the game.

The game appeared to be heading in the visitors' direction when New Zealand were reduced to 225-6 but, once again, the lower order came to the rescue and batted their side into a first innings lead of 50. Jacob Oram replicated Kirsten's innings only more profitably.

Oram made his first test hundred and with another debutant, Brendon McCullum, making 57, Vettori 53 and Paul Wiseman, his best test score of 36, the last four wickets added 294.

At the end of the fourth day's play South Africa were 84 ahead but had lost three wickets. The superior skills of Kallis, who scored 150 not out making it five successive tests where he had reached a century, were aided by Neil McKenzie and Kirsten, and ensured South Africa a draw.

SOUTH AFRICA

G.C.Smith*	c Oram b Vettori	25	c McCullum b Tuffey		5
H.H.Gibbs	c Styris b Vettori	40	c McCullum b Wiseman		47
J.A.Rudolph	c McCullum b Styris	72	b Cairns		0
J.H.Kallis	c Tuffey b Oram	92	not out		150
G.Kirsten	c Papps b Vettori	137	(6) not out		34
P.R.Adams	b Oram	7			
N.D.McKenzie	lbw b Vettori	10	(5) c Richardson b Wiseman		52
M.V.Boucher†	lbw b Styris	22			
S.M.Pollock	run out	10			
M.Ntini	run out	21			
A.Nel	not out	4			
Extras	(b 1, lb 5, w 1, nb 12)	19	(b 12, lb 5, nb 8)		25
TOTAL	(139.2 overs)	**459**	(116.1 overs) (4 wkts dec)		**313**

NEW ZEALAND

M.H.Richardson	lbw b Pollock	4			
M.H.W.Papps	lbw b Kallis	59	(1) c Boucher b Nel		12
S.P.Fleming*	lbw b Adams	27			
S.B.Styris	b Pollock	74	(3) not out		3
C.D.McMillan	lbw b Kallis	19			
C.L.Cairns	c Boucher b Ntini	28			
J.D.P.Oram	not out	119			
B.B.McCullum†	c Boucher b Kallis	57	(2) not out		19
D.L.Vettori	b Adams	53			
P.J.Wiseman	b Pollock	36			
D.R.Tuffey	c Boucher b Pollock	0			
Extras	(b 12, lb 11, nb 10)	33	(lb 1, w 1, nb 3)		5
TOTAL	(164.4 overs)	**509**	(16 overs) (1 wkt)		**39**

Bowling	O	M	R	W	O	M	R	W
NEW ZEALAND								
Tuffey	26	11	62	0	15	3	28	1
Oram	27	7	76	2	15	4	29	0
Cairns	18	2	52	0	15	3	48	1
Vettori	39.2	2	158	4	34	11	79	0
Wiseman	12	1	54	0	19	4	68	2
Styris	16	4	46	2	13	4	29	0
McMillan	1	0	5	0	5.1	0	15	0
SOUTH AFRICA								
Pollock	30.4	4	98	4	4	2	5	0
Ntini	29	9	74	1	4	0	15	0
Kallis	26	7	71	3				
Nel	27	8	91	0	4	0	15	1
Adams	45	11	118	2	3	1	2	0
Rudolph	5	0	20	0				
Smith	2	0	14	0				
McKenzie					1	0	1	0

Fall of Wickets

	SA	NZ	SA	NZ
	1st	1st	2nd	2nd
1st	51	20	15	34
2nd	79	75	16	-
3rd	211	127	108	-
4th	271	172	215	-
5th	281	223	-	-
6th	305	225	-	-
7th	364	309	-	-
8th	379	422	-	-
9th	415	509	-	-
10th	459	509	-	-

When the second new ball was taken, the umpires were concerned that the "crater" might be too dangerous for the left-handed Kirsten. The umpires asked the match referee, former West Indies captain Clive Lloyd, for his opinion as they were considering abandoning the game. The game continued but petered out to a draw.

MILESTONES

- Brendon McCullum (224) and Michael Papps (225) made their test debuts.

- Jacob Oram and Daniel Vettori put on 118, an eighth wicket record for New Zealand against South Africa.

- Oram and Paul Wiseman established a new ninth wicket record for New Zealand against South Africa of 87.

- 509 was New Zealand's highest total against South Africa, beating the previous best of 505 made in 1953/54 (test 29).

- Jacques Kallis became the second player, after Sir Donald Bradman, to score hundreds in five successive tests.

- Neil McKenzie passed 2000 test runs.

309 **NEW ZEALAND v SOUTH AFRICA** *(Second Test)*

at Eden Park, Auckland on 18, 19, 20, 21, 22 March, 2004
Toss : New Zealand. Umpires : Aleem Dar & E.A.R. de Silva
New Zealand won by 9 wickets

Stephen Fleming misread the drop-in pitch when he asked South Africa to bat first. At 177 without loss, after dedicated, polished batting by Graeme Smith and Herschelle Gibbs, things were drastic for New Zealand. Gibbs was dismissed with the last ball before tea for 80 and Smith with the first ball after tea for 88, to bring temporary relief.

Chris Martin, aged 29, was playing in his first test for two years and was a revelation. He was nine kg heavier than when he last played and generated more pace and had more control of his inswinging deliveries. Beginning the second day at 235-2, South Africa were reduced to 246-6 as Martin claimed three wickets and ended with his best test figures of 6-76. South Africa lost their last eight wickets for 61.

Despite New Zealand losing their first two wickets for 12, scintillating batting by Scott Styris, who counter-attacked to be 112 not out supported by the indomitable Mark Richardson and the vibrant Craig McMillan, saw New Zealand end the second day at 201-3.

Styris continued to bat in the manner of Greg Chappell, driving and pulling imperially on the on-side. His 170 was compiled off 224 balls. McMillan's 82 was dwarfed by a pulsating partnership between Chris Cairns and Jacob Oram and their alliance saw 225 runs plundered in less than three hours.

In a dominating display New Zealand scored 394 runs during the day, with the batsmen hitting 13 sixes. Cairns made 158, his highest score in first-class cricket, and Oram 90. For the second time in eight days New Zealand had scored in excess of 500 runs.

South Africa trailed by 299 and Martin bowled Smith with the first ball of the innings. For the second time in the game the visitors' top order batting was highly effective, taking their team past 230 before they lost their third wicket, thanks to Gibbs and the two Jacques, Rudolph and Kallis, sharing consecutive stands of 103 and 146.

Rudolph looked impregnable against all the bowlers and finished 154 not out as the last seven wickets were scythed away by Martin, whose final match analysis of 11-180 was the best by a New Zealander against South Africa. New Zealand's victory by nine wickets placed this performance as one of the most complete in its history of 309 tests.

SOUTH AFRICA					
G.C.Smith*	lbw b Martin	88	b Martin		0
H.H.Gibbs	b Cairns	80	lbw b Oram		61
J.A.Rudolph	c Papps b Martin	17	not out		154
J.H.Kallis	c McCullum b Martin	40	lbw b McMillan		71
G.Kirsten	b Oram	1	lbw b Martin		1
N.D.McKenzie	c Papps b Martin	27	c Papps b Martin		0
M.V.Boucher	c McMillan b Martin	4	c Fleming b Martin		10
S.M.Pollock†	b Tuffey	10	c Fleming b Martin		10
N.Boje	not out	12	c McCullum b Cairns		24
M.Ntini	c McCullum b Martin	0	c McMillan b Cairns		6
D.J.Terbrugge	lbw b Oram	0	c sub (J.A.H.Marshall) b Cairns		2
Extras	(lb 13, w 1, nb 3)	17	(b 6, lb 1, nb 3)		10
TOTAL	(123.3 overs)	296	(108.3 overs)		349

NEW ZEALAND					
M.H.Richardson	c Gibbs b Kallis	45	(2) c Boje b Ntini		10
M.H.W.Papps	c Boje b Pollock	0	(1) not out		8
S.P.Fleming*	c Kallis b Ntini	4	not out		31
S.B.Styris	c Pollock b Boje	170			
C.D.McMillan	b Pollock	82			
B.B.McCullum†	b Ntini	13			
C.L.Cairns	c Kallis b Smith	158			
J.D.P.Oram	b Ntini	90			
D.L.Vettori	not out	4			
D.R.Tuffey	b Pollock	13			
C.S.Martin	b Pollock	0			
Extras	(lb 10, nb 6)	16	(nb 4)		4
TOTAL	(148.5 overs)	595	(10.2 overs) (1 wkt)		53

Bowling	O	M	R	W	O	M	R	W
NEW ZEALAND								
Tuffey	24	7	41	1	4	1	13	0
Martin	31	7	76	6	23	5	104	5
Oram	28.3	6	60	2	27	13	47	1
Cairns	21	6	54	1	13.3	1	63	3
Styris	14	5	37	0	13	5	39	0
Vettori	5	1	15	0	24	4	73	0
McMillan					4	1	3	1
SOUTH AFRICA								
Pollock	32.5	6	113	4	5	1	16	0
Ntini	36	7	110	3	5	0	31	1
Terbrugge	22	4	93	0				
Kallis	23	1	108	1				
Boje	22	2	108	1	0.2	0	6	0
McKenzie	2	0	8	0				
Rudolph	6	0	26	0				
Smith	5	0	19	1				

Fall of Wickets	SA	NZ	SA	NZ
	1st	1st	2nd	2nd
1st	177	5	0	20
2nd	177	12	103	-
3rd	235	137	249	-
4th	236	285	250	-
5th	240	314	250	-
6th	246	349	272	-
7th	273	574	290	-
8th	289	578	327	-
9th	289	595	337	-
10th	296	595	349	-

MILESTONES

- It was New Zealand's 54th test win.

- It was the first time that New Zealand had beaten South Africa in a test at home in 13 attempts.

- Scott Styris' innings of 170 was the highest by a New Zealand batsman against South Africa.

- Chris Cairns and Jacob Oram created a record partnership of 225 for the seventh wicket for New Zealand against any country. It was also the highest partnership for any wicket for New Zealand against South Africa.

- Cairns' 158 was his highest score in all first-class cricket.

- New Zealand's 595 was its highest total against South Africa.

- Shaun Pollock overtook Allan Donald's South African test record of 330 wickets.

- Chris Martin entered the record books with his ninth successive scoreless innings in test cricket. His bowling analysis of 11-180 was the best for New Zealand against South Africa.

- Chris Cairns became the second New Zealand bowler to take 200 test wickets.

New Zealand defeated South Africa in a test at home for the first time. Back row (from left): Jacob Oram, Chris Cairns, Michael Papps, Mark Richardson, Scott Styris, Daniel Vettori, Craig McMillan and Daryl Tuffey. Front row: Chris Martin, Brendon McCullum, Stephen Fleming, Hamish Marshall.

310 **NEW ZEALAND v SOUTH AFRICA** *(Third Test)*

at Basin Reserve, Wellington on 26, 27, 28, 29, 30 March, 2004
Toss : South Africa. Umpires : Aleem Dar & E.A.R. de Silva
South Africa won by 6 wickets

A strong, blustery, northerly wind created problems for South Africa; who to bowl into it? It was only after Stephen Fleming and late replacement Mathew Sinclair had taken the score to 90-2 that the visitors found the answer, left-arm finger-spinner Nicky Boje. His trajectory was flat and his accuracy pinpoint, and for the duration of the test, whenever he trundled into the gale, he looked dangerous.

Solid contributions were forthcoming from Sinclair and Brendon McCullum, while Chris Cairns was his aggressive self. Looking a quality batsman, Jacob Oram ran out of batting partners as New Zealand finished at 297.

Graeme Smith and Herschelle Gibbs shared their seventh century opening partnership and Jacques Rudolph carried on from Auckland with another conscientious innings. South Africa ended the second day at 237-3.

Chris Martin produced a crucial spell with the second new ball when he captured three wickets in 16 deliveries. This triggered a now-expected South African collapse and their last seven wickets fell for 65, giving them a lead of only 19.

Before a third day crowd of 9020 New Zealand lost the verve that they had displayed the previous week and appeared to be overzealous in guarding their series lead.

From an overnight position of 128-5, Scott Styris and Cairns rekindled the aggressive intent by adding 70 off 15 overs but, when Cairns was caught at long-on and Styris was dismissed in the following over, Oram again found himself left with the tailenders as his batting colleagues.

South Africa required 234 for a face-saving win that would enable them to draw the series. New Zealand were indebted again to Martin who gave them a great start, claiming two of the first three wickets that fell by 36. Gary Kirsten, playing in his last test innings, revealed a great resolution to ensure that his last innings would be memorable, and it was.

He scored 76 and shared a partnership of 171 for the fourth wicket with Smith that saw South Africa comfortable winners by six wickets. Smith played a captain's innings to be 124 not out.

NEW ZEALAND					
M.H.Richardson	c Boucher b Kallis	14	(2) c Smith b Boje	37
M.H.W.Papps	lbw b Ntini	7	(1) lbw b Pollock	0
S.P.Fleming*	c Pollock b Boje	30	c Boucher b Nel	9
M.S.Sinclair	lbw b Boje	74	lbw b Pollock	21
S.B.Styris	b Boje	1	c & b Nel	73
B.B.McCullum†	lbw b Pollock	55	b Boje	3
C.L.Cairns	b Pollock	69	c van Jaarsveld b Boje	41
J.D.P.Oram	st Boucher b Boje	34	lbw b Boje	40
D.L.Vettori	c Boucher b Pollock	0	c van Jaarsveld b Ntini	9
M.J.Mason	c van Jaarsveld b Nel	3	run out	0
C.S.Martin	not out	1	not out	1
Extras	(b 2, lb 1, w 1, nb 5)	9	(b 1, lb 9, w 3, nb 5)	18
TOTAL	(104 overs)	**297**	(96.2 overs)	**252**

SOUTH AFRICA					
G.C.Smith*	b Cairns	47	not out	125
H.H.Gibbs	c sub (J.A.H.Marshall) b Martin	77	c Fleming b Martin	16
J.A.Rudolph	not out	93	b Martin	0
G.Kirsten	c McCullum b Martin	1	(5) lbw b Styris	76
M.van Jaarsveld	c Oram b Martin	59	(6) not out	13
J.H.Kallis	c McCullum b Martin	0	(4) lbw b Oram	1
M.V.Boucher†	c Papps b Martin	0		
S.M.Pollock	c Fleming b Oram	5		
N.Boje	b Cairns	25		
M.Ntini	c McCullum b Cairns	4		
A.Nel	c Oram b Cairns	0		
Extras	(lb 1, nb 4)	5	(lb 2, nb 1)	3
TOTAL	(99.5 overs)	**316**	(72.2 overs) (4 wkts)	**234**

Bowling SOUTH AFRICA	O	M	R	W	O	M	R	W	Fall of Wickets				
										NZ	SA	NZ	SA
										1st	1st	2nd	2nd
Pollock	29	2	85	3	22	10	65	2					
Ntini	21	6	63	1	20	6	50	1	1st	23	103	1	29
Kallis	7	5	4	1					2nd	23	130	42	31
Nel	27	9	77	1	21	5	58	2	3rd	90	136	73	36
Boje	20	2	65	4	33.2	7	69	4	4th	97	251	107	207
NEW ZEALAND									5th	163	265	111	-
Martin	20	6	55	5	18.2	2	65	2	6th	248	265	198	-
Mason	16	4	73	0	6	1	32	0	7th	257	270	201	-
Oram	11	3	21	1	11	3	23	1	8th	257	304	220	-
Vettori	26	6	76	0	18	2	53	0	9th	264	308	224	-
Cairns	16.5	2	60	4	10	2	19	0	10th	297	316	252	-
Styris	10	4	30	0	9	1	40	1					

Chris Martin was recalled to the New Zealand team at the age of 29 and took 18 wickets in the series at 16.66. It was an exceptional comeback.

MILESTONES

- Michael Mason (226) made his test debut.

- Stephen Fleming, playing in his 82nd test, became the third New Zealand player to score 5000 runs in test cricket after John Wright and Martin Crowe.

- Chris Martin became the third New Zealand bowler to take five wickets in three successive tests innings.

- Martin took 13 tests to capture 50 test wickets, a record for New Zealand.

- It was Gary Kirsten's 101st and last test. His 7289 runs and 21 centuries were South African records.

- Graeme Smith and Herschelle Gibbs shared their seventh century opening partnership, beating the South African record of six held by Eddie Barlow and Trevor Goddard.

AVERAGES

New Zealand

BATTING	M	I	NO	Runs	HS	Ave
J.D.P. Oram	3	4	1	283	119*	94.33
S.B. Styris	3	5	1	321	170	80.25
C.L. Cairns	3	4	0	296	158	74.00
C.D. McMillan	2	2	0	101	82	50.50
M.S. Sinclair	1	2	0	95	74	47.50
B.B. McCullum	3	5	1	147	57	36.75
P.J. Wiseman	1	1	0	36	36	36.00
S.P. Fleming	3	5	1	101	31*	25.25
D.L. Vettori	3	4	1	66	53	22.00
M.H. Richardson	3	5	0	110	45	22.00
M.H.W. Papps	3	6	1	86	59	17.20
D.R. Tuffey	2	2	0	13	13	6.50
C.S. Martin	2	3	2	2	1*	2.00
M.J. Mason	1	2	0	3	3	1.50

BOWLING	O	M	R	W	Ave
C.S. Martin	92.2	20	300	18	16.66
C.D. McMillan	10.1	1	23	1	23.00
C.L. Cairns	94.2	16	296	9	32.88
J.D.P. Oram	119.3	36	256	7	36.57
P.J. Wiseman	31	5	122	2	61.00
D.R. Tuffey	69	22	144	2	72.00
S.B. Styris	75	23	221	3	73.66
D.L. Vettori	146.2	26	454	4	113.50
M.J. Mason	22	5	105	0	-

South Africa

BATTING	M	I	NO	Runs	HS	Ave
J.A. Rudolph	3	6	2	336	154*	84.00
M. van Jaarsveld	1	2	1	72	59	72.00
J.H. Kallis	3	6	1	354	150*	70.80
G.C. Smith	3	6	1	290	125*	58.00
H.H. Gibbs	3	6	0	321	80	53.50
G. Kirsten	3	6	1	250	137	50.00
N. Boje	2	3	1	61	25	30.50
N.D. McKenzie	2	4	0	89	52	22.25
M.V. Boucher	3	4	0	36	22	9.00
S.M. Pollock	3	4	0	35	10	8.75
M. Ntini	3	4	0	31	21	7.75
P.R. Adams	1	1	0	7	7	7.00
A. Nel	2	2	1	4	4*	4.00
D.J. Terbrugge	1	2	0	2	2	1.00

BOWLING	O	M	R	W	Ave
N. Boje	75.4	11	248	9	27.55
S.M. Pollock	123.3	25	382	13	29.38
G.C. Smith	7	0	33	1	33.00
J.H. Kallis	56	13	183	5	36.60
M. Ntini	115	28	343	7	49.00
P.R. Adams	48	12	120	2	60.00
A. Nel	79	22	241	4	60.25
N.D. McKenzie	3	0	9	0	-
J.A. Rudolph	11	0	46	0	-
D.J. Terbrugge	22	4	93	0	-

2004 New Zealand in England

New Zealand was confident going to England, having lost only two of their last 13 tests. Three days before the match Michael Vaughan, the England captain, twisted his right knee and Marcus Trescothick was appointed captain. Andrew Strauss, a Middlesex player not chosen in the original squad, was selected to open and made a century on debut.

311 ENGLAND v NEW ZEALAND (*First Test*)

at Lord's on 20, 21, 22, 23, 24 May, 2004
Toss : England. Umpires : D.B. Hair & R.E. Koertzen
England won by 7 wickets

Minutes before the close of the first day Mark Richardson was denied a century by a controversial lbw decision. He described his obstinate 93, made in 378 minutes, as "dour, pokey and proddy" but it was the backbone of New Zealand's total of 284-5. Stephen Fleming, Nathan Astle and Jacob Oram all provided admirable support.

An explosive cameo of 82 by Chris Cairns, in 61 minutes, included six sixes. It was an unexpected adrenalin shot for the spectators, who were to witness 348 runs in the course of the day. Without the pace of Shane Bond, who in the county game prior to the test withdrew from the tour with a stress fracture of his back, New Zealand lacked true pace to unsettle the England top order.

Trescothick and Strauss began with a partnership of 190, made in 54 overs, before Trescothick departed for a fluent 86. The highlight for the North London crowd was when Strauss reached his test century on debut on his home ground.

Beginning the third day at 246-2 New Zealand seized the initiative by claiming four wickets for an additional 65 runs; 311-6. Andrew Flintoff and Geraint Jones counter-attacked efficiently by adding a vital 105 in 19 overs to give England an advantage of 55 runs. Brendon McCullum, playing in his fourth test, was promoted to number three when Astle was incapacitated with influenza. McCullum's tenacity and pulsating stroke production took him to within a heartbeat of his first test century.

He was out on the fourth day for 96 after he and Richardson had played New Zealand into a strong position of 180-2. Justice was done when Richardson scored 101 but, apart from Astle's 47 batting at number seven, New Zealand had frittered away their position of strength and England had the last day to score 278 for victory.

After Strauss was sacrificed for 86 in a run out with Nasser Hussain at 143-3, Hussain and Graham Thorpe thwarted the bowling with Hussain making fifty off 45 balls. He was 103 not out when England won by seven wickets. It had been an intriguing, wildly fluctuating test.

NEW ZEALAND

Batsman	1st innings		2nd innings	
M.H.Richardson	lbw b Harmison	93	c Jones G.O. b Harmison	101
S.P.Fleming*	c Strauss b Jones S.P.	34	c Hussain b Harmison	4
N.J.Astle	c Jones G.O. b Flintoff	64	(7) c Jones G.O. b Harmison	49
S.B.Styris	c Jones G.O. b Jones S.P.	0	c Hussain b Giles	4
C.D.McMillan	lbw b Hoggard	6	c Hussain b Giles	0
J.D.P.Oram	c Jones G.O. b Harmison	67	run out	4
D.R.Tuffey	b Harmison	8	(10) not out	14
C.L.Cairns	c Harmison b Flintoff	82	c Butcher b Giles	14
B.B.McCullum†	b Jones S.P.	5	(3) c Jones G.O. b Jones S.P.	96
D.L.Vettori	b Harmison	2	(9) c Jones G.O. b Harmison	5
C.S.Martin	not out	1	b Flintoff	7
Extras	(b 9, lb 6, w 2, nb 7)	24	(b 14, lb 16, nb 8)	38
TOTAL	(102.4 overs)	386	(121.1 overs)	336

ENGLAND

Batsman	1st innings		2nd innings	
M.E.Trescothick*	c McCullum b Oram	86	c & b Tuffey	2
A.J.Strauss	c Richardson b Vettori	112	run out	83
M.A.Butcher	c McCullum b Vettori	26	c Fleming b Martin	6
M.J.Hoggard	c McCullum b Oram	15		
N.Hussain	b Martin	34	(4) not out	103
G.P.Thorpe	b Cairns	3	(5) not out	51
A.Flintoff	c Richardson b Martin	63		
G.O.Jones†	c Oram b Styris	46		
A.F.Giles	c Oram b Styris	11		
S.P.Jones	b Martin	4		
S.J.Harmison	not out	0		
Extras	(b 4, lb 18, nb 19)	41	(b 7, lb 12, w 5, nb 13)	37
TOTAL	(124.3 overs)	441	(87 overs) (3 wkts)	282

Bowling ENGLAND	O	M	R	W	O	M	R	W
Hoggard	22	7	68	1	14	3	39	0
Harmison	31	7	126	4	29	8	76	4
Flintoff	21.4	7	63	2	16.1	5	40	1
Jones S.P.	23	8	82	3	23	5	64	1
Giles	5	0	32	0	39	8	87	3
NEW ZEALAND								
Tuffey	26	4	98	0	10	3	32	1
Martin	27	6	94	3	18	2	75	1
Oram	30	8	76	2	15	4	39	0
Cairns	16	2	71	1	6	0	27	0
Vettori	21	1	69	2	25	5	53	0
Styris	4.3	0	11	2	13	5	37	0

Fall of Wickets

	NZ 1st	E 1st	NZ 2nd	E 2nd
1st	58	190	7	18
2nd	161	239	180	35
3rd	162	254	187	143
4th	174	288	187	-
5th	280	297	203	-
6th	287	311	287	-
7th	324	416	290	-
8th	329	428	304	-
9th	338	441	310	-
10th	386	441	336	-

MILESTONES

• Andrew Strauss became the fourth player to make a century on debut at Lord's, the others being Harry Graham (Australia) 1893, John Hampshire (England) 1969 and Sourav Ganguly (India) 1996.

• Andrew Strauss became the 15th player to score a century on debut for England.

• Chris Cairns hit four sixes to take him past Viv Richard's test record of 84.

• England's 282 in the fourth innings was 64 runs more than their previous best to win a test at Lord's in 106 attempts.

• The two left-hand openers, Mark Richardson and Andrew Strauss, batted more than 22 hours and made 27% of the runs scored in the game.

• Two days after the test Nasser Hussain announced his retirement from test cricket. In 96 tests he made 5764 runs at 37.18 and scored 14 centuries. He captained England 45 times.

Mark Richardson batted for 378 minutes in the first innings and for 435 in the second, scoring 93 and 101.

From the beginning of England's innings Marcus Trescothick bristled with positive intent to score 132 and, together with Andrew Strauss, shared an opening partnership of 153. England ended the third day at 248-4.

In what was to become a feature of the series, England dominated the fourth day. New Zealand was smitten with injuries that saw Papps unable to field, Daniel Vettori pull a hamstring and Jacob Oram unable to bowl because of a side strain. During the day, five different players fielded as substitutes.

A rollicking batting performance by Andrew Flintoff and Geraint Jones saw 118 added at a rate of more than four runs per over. The diminutive Jones out-scored the stronger Flintoff, displaying beautifully timed shots to reach 100. With a deficit of 117, on a truculent pitch that was becoming more difficult, New Zealand ended the day at 105-5 with Papps and Vettori yet to bat. The test finished before lunch the next day with England winning comprehensively by nine wickets.

NEW ZEALAND

M.H.Richardson	b Saggers	13	c Jones b Hoggard		40
M.H.W.Papps	lbw b Flintoff	86	(9) c Vaughan b Harmison		0
S.P.Fleming*	c Vaughan b Harmison	97	(2) c Strauss b Flintoff		11
N.J.Astle	c Butcher b Saggers	2	lbw b Hoggard		8
S.B.Styris	c Jones b Harmison	21	c Jones b Hoggard		19
J.D.P.Oram	c Thorpe b Flintoff	39	(7) not out		36
C.L.Cairns	c Strauss b Harmison	41	(8) lbw b Hoggard		10
B.B.McCullum†	b Hoggard	54	(3) c Trescothick b Harmison		20
D.L.Vettori	b Harmison	35	absent hurt		
D.R.Tuffey	lbw b Hoggard	0	(6) c Jones b Harmison		7
C.S.Martin	not out	0	(10) run out		0
Extras	(b 5, lb 14, w 2)	21	(b 4, lb 4, nb 2)		10
TOTAL	(143.2 overs)	**409**	(42 overs)		**161**

ENGLAND

M.E.Trescothick	b Styris	132	not out		30
A.J.Strauss	c Tuffey b Vettori	62	c Astle b Tuffey		10
M.A.Butcher	lbw b Vettori	4	not out		5
M.P.Vaughan*	c Fleming b Styris	13			
G.P.Thorpe	b Martin	34			
A.Flintoff	c Martin b Styris	94			
G.O.Jones†	c Fleming b Cairns	100			
A.F.Giles	c Fleming b Martin	21			
M.J.Hoggard	c McCullum b Tuffey	4			
M.J.Saggers	c sub b Cairns	0			
S.J.Harmison	not out	0			
Extras	(b 25, lb 21, w 3, nb 13)	62			0
TOTAL	(133.1 overs)	**526**	(8 overs) (1 wkt)		**45**

Bowling	O	M	R	W	O	M	R	W		Fall of Wickets			
ENGLAND											NZ	E	NZ	E
											1st	1st	2nd	2nd
Hoggard	27	6	93	2	15	4	75	4		1st	33	153	39	18
Harmison	36.2	8	74	4	16	5	57	3		2nd	202	174	75	-
Flintoff	27	7	64	2	6	0	16	1		3rd	215	229	77	-
Saggers	30	6	86	2	5	3	5	0		4th	215	240	84	-
Trescothick	2	0	3	0						5th	263	339	91	-
Giles	19	1	67	0						6th	293	457	118	-
Vaughan	2	0	3	0						7th	355	491	144	-
NEW ZEALAND										8th	409	526	149	-
Tuffey	26.1	7	88	1	4	0	28	1		9th	409	526	161	-
Martin	30	9	127	2	4	1	17	0		10th	409	526	-	-
Styris	27	5	88	3										
Cairns	27	6	94	2										
Vettori	23	2	83	2										

312 ENGLAND v NEW ZEALAND *(Second Test)*

at Headingley, Leeds on 3, 4, 5, 6, 7 June, 2004
Toss : England. Umpires : S.A. Bucknor & S.J.A. Taufel
England won by 9 wickets

Rain restricted play to only 19 overs on the first day but in that time Mark Richardson had been bowled by Martin Saggers' first delivery in test cricket. The Headingley pitch was fast and Steve Harmison and Andrew Flintoff extracted unpredictable bounce and were a threat to the batsmen's bodies.

Michael Papps had a finger broken by Harmison and batted on courageously to record his highest test score of 86. He and Stephen Fleming, who was dismissed in the nineties for the fourth time in test cricket, added 169. Resilient batting saw New Zealand reach a useful 409, with Harmison taking four wickets for the third time in three outings.

MILESTONES

- Geraint Jones became the 10th England wicketkeeper to score a test century.

- There were 62 extras in England's first innings, the most New Zealand had ever conceded.

In spite of having a finger broken by a ball from Steve Harmison, Michael Papps batted courageously for over five hours, making 86. Wicketkeeper is Geraint Jones, born in New Guinea and raised in Queensland.

313 ENGLAND v NEW ZEALAND *(Third Test)*

at Trent Bridge, Nottingham on 10, 11, 12, 13 June, 2004
Toss : New Zealand. Umpires : D.J. Harper & S.J.A. Taufel
England won by 4 wickets

New Zealand took full advantage of batting first on a pitch without eccentric bounce to put themselves into a strong position, three days after their demoralising loss at Headingley.

Mark Richardson made, by his standards so far in the series, an express 73 before he was out, having added 163 in 52 overs with his captain Stephen Fleming. The latter was then joined by the out-of-luck Scott Styris who, after four innings, had totalled only 44 runs. The runs continued to flow as Fleming reached his seventh test century. Styris was 68 not out at stumps, with his team's score at 295-4.

Even though Styris reached his fourth test hundred off the identical number of balls as Fleming (161) the innings ended disappointingly on 384 with the last six wickets contributing only 76.

As Shane Bond and Daniel Vettori were injured the bowling stocks were decidedly weak. When Chris Martin (hamstring) and debutant Kyle Mills (side strain) retired, having only bowled 47 balls between them, it was decidedly

weaker. James Franklin, brought in for his third test from playing in Lancashire League Cricket for Rishton, acquitted himself well, claiming four wickets. Chris Cairns, who was playing in his farewell test and opening the bowling for the first time in 19 tests, captured five wickets in an innings for the 13th time in his career.

The visitors failed to build on their lead of 65 even though Richardson, Fleming and Styris all batted with aplomb. New Zealand had a lead of 159 when the first wicket fell but the remaining nine wickets added only 114 as the pace of Harmison and Flintoff and the left-arm spin of Ashley Giles caused poor shot selection and brought about their downfall.

For the third time in the series New Zealand had squandered a position of power within a session. Mark Richardson was the linchpin of the series, batting for 21 hours and 53 minutes and scoring the most runs for either side, 369. He had faced a monumental 971 deliveries, of which 799 were dot balls.

In the history of test cricket no side had ever scored 284 runs in the fourth innings to win a test match at Trent Bridge. Mature batting by Graham Thorpe, 104 not out, aided initially by Mark Butcher, 59, and at the finish by Giles, 36 not out, saw England through to victory by four wickets. Cairns' last hurrah saw him take nine wickets for the match. It was a Herculean display that belied his 15 years as a test cricketer.

NEW ZEALAND

M.H.Richardson	c Vaughan b Giles	73	lbw b Giles	49
S.P.Fleming*	c Thorpe b Flintoff	117	lbw b Flintoff	45
S.B.Styris	c sub (B.M.Shafayat) b Giles	108	(4) c Jones b Harmison	39
N.J.Astle	b Harmison	15	(5) lbw b Flintoff	0
C.D.McMillan	lbw b Harmison	0	(6) lbw b Harmison	30
J.D.P.Oram	c Strauss b Saggers	14	(8) c Flintoff b Harmison	0
C.L.Cairns	c Thorpe b Saggers	12	(9) b Giles	1
B.B.McCullum†	c Hoggard b Harmison	21	(3) c Flintoff b Giles	4
J.E.C.Franklin	not out	4	(7) c Jones b Flintoff	17
K.D.Mills	c Jones b Hoggard	0	c Harmison b Giles	8
C.S.Martin	c Vaughan b Hoggard	2	not out	0
Extras	(b 2, lb 14, nb 2)	18	(b 1, lb 21, nb 3)	25
TOTAL	**(121 overs)**	**384**	**(81 overs)**	**218**

ENGLAND

M.E.Trescothick	c Styris b Franklin	63	c & b Franklin	9
A.J.Strauss	c McCullum b Cairns	0	lbw b Cairns	6
M.A.Butcher	c Styris b Franklin	5	lbw b Cairns	59
M.P.Vaughan*	lbw b Cairns	61	lbw b Cairns	10
G.P.Thorpe	c McCullum b Franklin	45	not out	104
A.Flintoff	lbw b Cairns	54	c sub (H.J.H. Marshall) b Cairns	5
M.J.Hoggard	c Styris b Franklin	5		
G.O.Jones†	lbw b Styris	22	(7) c Oram b Franklin	27
A.F.Giles	not out	45	(8) not out	36
M.J.Saggers	b Cairns	0		
S.J.Harmison	b Cairns	0		
Extras	(b 2, lb 5, nb 12)	19	(b 4, lb 16, nb 8)	28
TOTAL	**(85.3 overs)**	**319**	**(71.3 overs) (6 wkts)**	**284**

Bowling	O	M	R	W	O	M	R	W		Fall of Wickets			
ENGLAND											NZ	E	NZ	E
Hoggard	25	6	85	2	6	2	25	0			*1st*	*1st*	*2nd*	*2nd*
Harmison	32	9	80	3	25	7	51	3	1st	163	1	94	12
Flintoff	14	2	48	1	20	3	60	3	2nd	225	18	106	16
Saggers	22	5	80	2	6	2	14	0	3rd	272	128	126	46
Giles	27	6	70	2	24	6	46	4	4th	272	140	134	134
Vaughan	1	0	5	0					5th	308	221	185	214
NEW ZEALAND									6th	331	244	198	-
Martin	1.5	0	1	0					7th	366	255	198	-
Cairns	23.3	5	79	5	25	2	108	4	8th	377	295	208	-
Franklin	26.1	4	104	4	17	2	59	2	9th	382	301	210	-
Mills	6	2	31	0					10th	384	319	218	-
Oram	15	0	47	0	14.3	1	50	0					
Styris	11	1	45	1	14	1	43	0					
McMillan	2	1	5	0									
Richardson					1	0	4	0					

Playing in his last test at his county ground of Trent Bridge, Chris Cairns was seen in this pose frequently as five of the nine wickets he captured were given out lbw.

MILESTONES

- Kyle Mills (227) made his test debut.

- Graham Thorpe became the 10th England batsman to score 6000 test runs.

- Scott Styris scored his 1000th test run in his 15th test.

- It was England's ninth victory in their last 13 tests.

- It was England's first clean-sweep of a series of three or more tests since 1978, also against New Zealand.

- In an injury-blighted career, Chris Cairns played 62 tests and scored 3320 runs at 33.35 with five centuries and 22 fifties. He captured 218 wickets at 29.46 and took five wickets in an innings 13 times. When he retired he had the test record of 87 sixes.

AVERAGES

New Zealand

BATTING	M	I	NO	Runs	HS	Ave
M.H. Richardson	3	6	0	369	101	61.50
S.P. Fleming	3	6	0	308	117	51.33
M.H.W. Papps	1	2	0	86	86	43.00
B.B. McCullum	3	6	0	200	96	33.33
J.D.P. Oram	3	6	1	160	67	32.00
S.B. Styris	3	6	0	191	108	31.83
C.L. Cairns	3	6	0	160	82	26.66
N.J. Astle	3	6	0	138	64	23.00
J.E.C. Franklin	1	2	1	21	17	21.00
D.L. Vettori	2	3	0	42	35	14.00
D.R. Tuffey	2	4	1	29	14*	9.66
C.D. McMillan	2	4	0	36	30	9.00
K.D. Mills	1	2	0	8	8	4.00
C.S. Martin	3	6	3	10	7	3.33

BOWLING	O	M	R	W	Ave
J.E.C. Franklin	43.1	6	163	6	27.16
C.L. Cairns	97.3	15	379	12	31.58
S.B. Styris	69.3	12	224	6	37.33
D.L. Vettori	69	8	205	4	51.25
C.S. Martin	80.5	18	314	6	52.33
D.R. Tuffey	66.1	14	246	3	82.00
J.D.P. Oram	74.3	13	212	2	106.00
M.H. Richardson	1	0	4	0	-
C.D. McMillan	2	1	5	0	-
K.D. Mills	6	2	31	0	-

England

BATTING	M	I	NO	Runs	HS	Ave
N. Hussain	1	2	1	137	103*	137.00
G.P. Thorpe	3	5	2	237	104*	79.00
M.E. Trescothick	3	6	1	322	132	64.40
A.F. Giles	3	4	2	113	45*	56.50
A. Flintoff	3	4	0	216	94	54.00
G.O. Jones	3	4	0	195	100	48.75
A.J. Strauss	3	6	0	273	112	45.50
M.P. Vaughan	2	3	0	84	61	28.00
M.A. Butcher	3	6	1	105	59	21.00
M.J. Hoggard	3	3	0	24	15	8.00
S.P. Jones	1	1	0	4	4	4.00
S.J. Harmison	3	3	2	0	0*	0.00
M.J. Saggers	2	2	0	0	0	0.00

BOWLING	O	M	R	W	Ave
S.J. Harmison	169.2	44	464	21	22.09
A. Flintoff	104.5	24	291	10	29.10
A.F. Giles	114	21	302	9	33.55
S.P. Jones	46	13	146	4	36.50
M.J. Hoggard	109	28	385	9	42.77
M.J. Saggers	63	16	185	4	46.25
M.E. Trescothick	2	0	3	0	-
M.P. Vaughan	3	0	8	0	-

2004/05 New Zealand in Bangladesh

Under coach Dav Whatmore, Bangladesh had been showing signs of improvement. Prior to the first test Habibul Bashar, the captain and best batsman and the only player to have appeared in all 30 previous tests, broke his thumb and was out for the series.

314 BANGLADESH v NEW ZEALAND *(First Test)*

at Bangabandhu National Stadium, Dhaka on 19, 20, 21, 22 October, 2004
Toss : Bangladesh. Umpires : M.R. Benson & D.J. Harper
New Zealand won by an innings and 99 runs

In ideal conditions, where the wicket was shaved of grass, Bangladesh had no hesitation in batting first. Losing their first three wickets for five runs shattered their fragile confidence and set the tone for the rest of the series. When wickets fell, they fell in clumps. A gutsy partnership of 115 between Mohammad Ashraful and Rajin Saleh halted the calamitous beginning. Their dismissals saw runs dry up and the day ended 165-6.

The second day saw James Franklin dismiss Manjural Islam Rana and Mohammad Rafique with the last two balls of his 14th over. Tapash Baisya misjudged the line of the first ball of the 15th over and was bowled, thus giving Franklin a hat-trick.

James Franklin became the second New Zealand bowler to take a test hat-trick. Stephen Fleming shows obvious delight.

New Zealand's reply to 177 faltered at 139-5 with only Mathew Sinclair (76) exhibiting sound technique against the two left-arm spinners. Rafique and Manjural threatened to bowl Bangladesh back into contention but McCullum resurrected New Zealand's innings, batting 340 minutes and going on to score his maiden test century.

The last five wickets added 263. McCullum finished with a scintillating 143, the last five wickets stretching New Zealand's total to 402, despite Rafique capturing six wickets.

New Zealand capitalised on their lead of 225 with Daniel Vettori thriving on the inability of the local batsmen to counter his variety of slow left-arm variations of pace, flight and line as he captured his first five-wicket bag in 22 tests. With Vettori assisted by Paul Wiseman's sharp-turning off-spin victory was achieved with five sessions to spare.

BANGLADESH					
Hannan Sarkar	c Fleming b Oram	0	(3) c & b Vettori		1
Javed Omar	b Franklin	1	c McCullum b Vettori		14
Nafis Iqbal	c McCullum b Oram	1	(1) run out		49
Rajin Saleh	c Oram b Franklin	41	c McCullum b Vettori		0
Mohammad Ashraful	c Astle b Vettori	67	c Styris b Vettori		26
Alok Kapali	c McCullum b Vettori	14	c McCullum b Wiseman		0
Khaled Mashud*†	not out	23	c Styris b Wiseman		2
Manjural Islam	c McCullum b Franklin	16	c Richardson b Vettori		1
Mohammad Rafique	c Styris b Franklin	0	c Fleming b Wiseman		24
Tapash Baisya	b Franklin	0	(11) not out		0
Tareq Aziz	c Astle b Oram	0	(10) lbw b Vettori		0
Extras	(lb 7, w 1, nb 6)	14	(b 6, nb 3)		9
TOTAL	(98.5 overs)	**177**	(54.5 overs)		**126**

NEW ZEALAND		
M.H.Richardson	c Mashud b Rafique	15
M.S.Sinclair	lbw b Rafique	76
S.P.Fleming*	c Mashud b Manjural	29
S.B.Styris	c Saleh b Manjural	2
N.J.Astle	c Manjural b Rafique	11
J.D.P.Oram	c Manjural b Rafique	23
B.B.McCullum†	c Kapali b Rafique	143
D.L.Vettori	c Nafis b Manjural	23
J.E.C.Franklin	c Saleh b Baisya	23
P.J.Wiseman	b Rafique	28
I.G.Butler	not out	15
Extras	(b 3, lb 5, w 4, nb 2)	14
TOTAL	(145.1 overs)	**402**

Bowling	O	M	R	W	O	M	R	W	Fall of Wickets	B	NZ	B
NEW ZEALAND										*1st*	*1st*	*2nd*
Oram	22.5	9	36	3	7	4	6	0	1st	0	34	27
Franklin	17	7	28	5	5	1	14	0	2nd	5	97	33
Styris	2	1	4	0					3rd	5	99	41
Butler	12	3	34	0	4	1	8	0	4th	120	122	87
Vettori	29	15	26	2	22	13	28	6	5th	124	139	88
Wiseman	16	5	42	0	16.5	1	64	3	6th	136	223	92
BANGLADESH									7th	165	294	101
Baisya	28	4	112	1					8th	165	351	112
Aziz	12	1	59	0					9th	165	371	122
Rafique	59.1	18	122	6					10th	177	402	126
Manjural	42	12	84	3								
Saleh	1	0	4	0								
Kapali	2	0	6	0								
Ashraful	1	0	7	0								

MILESTONES

- It was New Zealand's 55th test win.

- James Franklin became the second New Zealander to claim a hat-trick after Peter Petherick did so against Pakistan in Lahore in 1976/77 (test 120). Franklin also had his first five-wicket bag.

- Paul Wiseman took his 50th test wicket in his 20th test.

315 BANGLADESH v NEW ZEALAND *(Second Test)*

at M.A. Aziz Stadium, Chittagong on 26, 27, 28, 29 October, 2004
Toss : New Zealand. Umpires : M.R. Benson & D.J. Harper
New Zealand won by an innings and 101 runs

All eight New Zealand batsmen passed double figures as the team amassed 545-6 before tea on the second day, on a low-bouncing, slow-paced, subcontinental pitch.

After the demise of both openers Stephen Fleming and Scott Styris added 204 at better than a run a minute. Styris, from an indifferent beginning where he was dropped by the keeper and survived two confident appeals for lbw, took 87 balls to hit his first boundary. After that his on-side play flourished as he made 89.

It was to be a notable record-breaking game for Fleming who scored his second double-century (202) and became the highest run scorer for his country as well as the most capped player. Hamish Marshall, in his second test, was dropped first ball before resolutely advancing to his first test fifty.

New Zealand's opening attack of Jacob Oram and James Franklin was used for only five overs each before giving away to the spinning duo of Daniel Vettori and Paul Wiseman, who spun Bangladesh out for 182. Following on 363 runs in arrears it was a repetition of the first innings, with Vettori capturing six wickets for the second time in the match. It was the ninth time that he had taken five wickets in an innings.

Bangladesh started the fourth day at 210-8. Mohammad Rafique advanced his overnight score by one before he was out for 31. The other overnight batsman, Tapash Baisya, lashed out and in 19 minutes added all of the 45 runs added for the last wicket before McCullum stumped him for 66. This gave New Zealand victory by an innings and 101 runs.

NEW ZEALAND		
M.H.Richardson	c Mushfiqur b Enamul	28
M.S.Sinclair	b Rafique	23
S.P.Fleming*	c Mushfiqur b Saleh	202
S.B.Styris	c & b Rafique	89
N.J.Astle	lbw b Rafique	39
H.J.H.Marshall	c Baisya b Enamul	69
J.D.P.Oram	not out	38
B.B.McCullum†	not out	17
D.L.Vettori		
J.E.C.Franklin		
P.J.Wiseman		
Extras	(b 9, lb 11, w 2, nb 18)	40
TOTAL	(152 overs) (6 wkts dec)	**545**

BANGLADESH				
Nafis Iqbal	c Styris b Vettori	13	b Wiseman	9
Javed Omar	c Sinclair b Wiseman	58	c & b Franklin	1
Aftab Ahmed	lbw b Vettori	20	b Vettori	28
Rajin Saleh	c Sinclair b Wiseman	2	c Sinclair b Vettori	35
Mohammad Ashraful	c Astle b Wiseman	0	c Styris b Vettori	0
Alok Kapali	c Fleming b Vettori	13	c Astle b Wiseman	13
Khaled Mashud*†	lbw b Vettori	18	b Oram	51
Mushfiqur Rahman	c McCullum b Franklin	15	b Vettori	20
Mohammad Rafique	c Wiseman b Vettori	32	c Sinclair b Vettori	31
Tapash Baisya	c Sinclair b Vettori	0	st McCullum b Vettori	66
Enamul Haque	not out	0	not out	0
Extras	(b 4, lb 2, w 2, nb 3)	11	(b 4, lb 3, w 10)	8
TOTAL	(71.2 overs)	**182**	(70.2 overs)	**262**

Bowling	O	M	R	W	O	M	R	W		Fall of Wickets		
BANGLADESH										NZ	B	B
Baisya	17	0	82	0						1st	1st	2nd
Mushfiqur	15	1	68	0					1st	49	34	9
Rafique	55	12	130	3					2nd	61	66	25
Enamul	42	4	142	2					3rd	265	82	47
Saleh	19	0	81	1					4th	364	82	51
Ashraful	1	0	5	0					5th	447	108	74
Kapali	3	0	17	0					6th	517	128	123
NEW ZEALAND									7th	-	142	161
Oram	5	0	20	0	10	4	33	1	8th	-	181	183
Franklin	5	0	17	1	8	3	16	1	9th	-	182	217
Vettori	32.2	12	70	6	28.2	9	100	6	10th	-	182	262
Wiseman	27	5	68	3	24	4	106	2				
Astle	2	1	1	0								

Daniel Vettori had taken only 16 wickets in his previous nine tests but took 20 in the series against Bangladesh.

MILESTONES

- It was New Zealand's 56th test win.

- Stephen Fleming became New Zealand's most capped player in his 87th test, overtaking Sir Richard Hadlee.

- Fleming passed Martin Crowe's New Zealand record aggregate of 5444 runs.

- Daniel Vettori captured six wickets in an innings for the third successive time. It was his second 10-wicket match.

- Tapash Baisya made the fastest fifty for Bangladesh, taking 36 balls.

- It was the 18th time in 32 tests that Bangladesh had lost by an innings.

2004/05 New Zealand in Australia

In a graphic illustration of the non-stop nature of international cricket New Zealand were playing the first of two tests in Australia 11 days after playing in Bangladesh. Australia had lost the fourth test in Mumbai, India, and were playing New Zealand 13 days later in Brisbane.

316 AUSTRALIA v NEW ZEALAND *(First Test)*

at Brisbane Cricket Ground on 18, 19, 20, 21 November, 2004
Toss : New Zealand. Umpires : Aleem Dar & S.A. Bucknor
Australia won by an innings and 156 runs

The harsh reality of playing on a hard, fast pitch against Australia quickly erased the comfortable challenges posed in Bangladesh to a distant memory. Accurate, probing deliveries threatened the bat's edge, as well as the body, and boundary balls were rare. Mathew Sinclair was the mainstay of the first half of the first innings, scoring 69, before he was fifth out at 138. By stumps Shane Warne had made his presence felt before Jacob Oram, 63, and Daniel Vettori, 13, guided their side to 250-7.

Oram partially answered the question of "Who replaces Chris Cairns?" by steering his side to a further 103 before they were all out for 353. When Chris Martin came to the crease Oram was 10 runs short of his century. By skilful manipulation he reached an inspiring hundred and then hit three sixes to reach 126. He scored all 36 runs added for the last wicket. At the end of the second day the game appeared to be an even contest as Australia were 197-4.

The game and the series slipped away as Australia rediscovered their relentless mode as Michael Clarke, playing his first test in Australia, lived up to the critics' high praise by crafting 126 and with the effervescent Adam Gilchrist, also a century-maker, they plundered 216 runs in quick time. Unfortunately Craig McMillan and Gilchrist became involved in a heated argument about the merits of batsmen walking. It was to simmer on for the remainder of the second test.

Just when it looked as though Australia's lead would be restricted to about 130, when four wickets fell for 33, Jason Gillespie and Glenn McGrath embarked into foreign territory as both players scored maiden test fifties. Their partnership of 114 gave Australia a first innings lead of 232 and appeared to drain New Zealand of all their fighting spirit. They capitulated in 165 minutes for 76, thus giving Australia victory by an innings and 156 runs.

Jacob Oram was on 90 when Chris Martin joined him but got through to 126, scoring all 36 runs added for the last wicket.

NEW ZEALAND

Batsman	Dismissal 1st	Score	Dismissal 2nd	Score
M.H.Richardson	c Ponting b Kasprowicz	19	c Gilchrist b McGrath	4
M.S.Sinclair	c Ponting b Gillespie	69	lbw b McGrath	0
S.P.Fleming*	c Warne b Kasprowicz	0	c Langer b McGrath	11
S.B.Styris	c Gilchrist b Kasprowicz	27	lbw b Warne	7
N.J.Astle	run out	19	c Warne b Kasprowicz	17
C.D.McMillan	c Gilchrist b Warne	23	lbw b Gillespie	9
J.D.P.Oram	not out	126	c Hayden b Warne	8
B.B.McCullum†	st Gilchrist b Warne	10	c Gilchrist b Gillespie	8
D.L.Vettori	c Warne b Kasprowicz	21	c Hayden b Warne	2
K.D.Mills	c Hayden b Warne	29	not out	4
C.S.Martin	c Ponting b Warne	0	lbw b Warne	0
Extras	(b 1, lb 2, w 3, nb 4)	10	(lb 2, nb 4)	6
TOTAL	(117.3 overs)	**353**	(36.2 overs)	**76**

AUSTRALIA

Batsman	Dismissal	Score
J.L.Langer	lbw b Vettori	34
M.L.Hayden	lbw b Mills	8
R.T.Ponting*	c Astle b Martin	51
D.R.Martyn	c McMillan b Martin	70
D.S.Lehmann	c McCullum b Vettori	8
M.J.Clarke	b Vettori	141
A.C.Gilchrist†	c Styris b Martin	126
S.K.Warne	lbw b Vettori	10
J.N.Gillespie	not out	54
M.S.Kasprowicz	c Mills b Martin	5
G.D.McGrath	c Astle b Martin	61
Extras	(b 1, lb 7, w 1, nb 8)	17
TOTAL	(153.5 overs)	**585**

Bowling

AUSTRALIA	O	M	R	W	O	M	R	W
McGrath	27	4	67	0	8	1	19	3
Gillespie	29	7	84	1	10	5	19	2
Kasprowicz	28	5	90	4	8	2	21	1
Warne	29.3	3	97	4	10.2	3	15	4
Lehmann	4	0	12	0				

NEW ZEALAND	O	M	R	W
Martin	39.5	7	152	5
Mills	26	8	99	1
Styris	8	1	33	0
Oram	25	4	116	0
Vettori	50	9	154	4
McMillan	5	1	23	0

Fall of Wickets

	NZ 1st	A 1st	NZ 2nd
1st	26	16	6
2nd	26	85	7
3rd	77	109	19
4th	138	128	42
5th	138	222	44
6th	180	438	55
7th	206	450	69
8th	264	464	72
9th	317	471	72
10th	353	585	76

MILESTONES

- Michael Clarke made his first test century in Australia. He became the third player to score a century for his country in his first test both home and away.

- Glenn McGrath's 61 was the highest score made by a number eleven batsman for Australia.

- New Zealand's total of 76 was their lowest against Australia since 1945/46 (test 15).

317 AUSTRALIA v NEW ZEALAND (*Second Test*)

at Adelaide Oval on 26, 27, 28, 29, 30 November, 2004
Toss : Australia. Umpires : S.A. Bucknor & D.R. Shepherd
Australia won by 213 runs

Australia got off to a flying start when Justin Langer struck four boundaries off James Franklin's second over as the bowler erred badly by over-pitching the ball. On an excellent batting strip Matthew Hayden and Langer were totally at ease and for the 13th time they opened with a century stand.

In extremely hot conditions Langer's fitness and the running between the wickets of the home side were exceptional. After he had completed his century Langer repeated his assault of Franklin, hitting another four boundaries off his second over with the second new ball, to finish the day 144 not out.

Langer inevitably reached his double-century and, with five other batsmen scoring in excess of 50, Australia was able to declare at 575-8 with Daniel Vettori and Paul Wiseman claiming all eight wickets between them. New Zealand's reply of 251 was dominated by an elegant innings of 86 by Stephen Fleming, who shared a determined union worth 73 runs with Nathan Astle.

Unlike their New Zealand counterparts, who went wicketless, the Australian pace attack claimed nine. Ricky Ponting did not enforce the follow-on and Australia ended the third day at 57-0, with neither Hayden nor Langer appearing as aggressive as on the first day.

Various reasons were given for Ponting continuing to bat until declaring after lunch on the fourth day at 139-2, scored at a rate of 2.4 runs per over. Perhaps he wanted to physically and mentally grind down New Zealand as Australia had a further three tests to play against them in March.

At the conclusion of the game Ponting said, "We wanted to keep them in the field as long as we could so that they had no momentum." How right he was. New Zealand lost their first four wickets for 34 and only a bright episode, where Brendon McCullum used his feet effectively to reach Shane Warne on the full, displayed spirit and class.

The skill of the Australian bowlers, described by Fleming as "three Richard Hadlees and the greatest leg-spinner of all" won the day and New Zealand lost the game by 213 runs and the series 2-0.

AUSTRALIA

J.L.Langer	c Oram b Vettori	215	lbw b Wiseman		46
M.L.Hayden	c & b Wiseman	70	c McCullum b Vettori		54
R.T.Ponting*	st McCullum b Vettori	68	not out		26
D.R.Martyn	c Fleming b Wiseman	7	not out		6
D.S.Lehmann	b Wiseman	81			
M.J.Clarke	lbw b Vettori	7			
A.C.Gilchrist†	c & b Vettori	50			
S.K.Warne	not out	53			
J.N.Gillespie	c Richardson b Vettori	12			
M.S.Kasprowicz					
G.D.McGrath					
Extras	(b 4, lb 4, nb 4)	12	(lb 6, nb 1)		7
TOTAL	(155.2 overs) (8 wkts dec)	**575**	(56 overs) (2 wkts dec)		**139**

NEW ZEALAND

M.H.Richardson	b Kasprowicz	9	c Langer b Kasprowicz		16
M.S.Sinclair	c Warne b Gillespie	0	lbw b Gillespie		2
S.P.Fleming*	c Gilchrist b McGrath	83	b McGrath		3
P.J.Wiseman	lbw b Kasprowicz	11	(10) not out		15
N.J.Astle	c Langer b McGrath	52	c Langer b Lehmann		38
J.D.P.Oram	c Gilchrist b Gillespie	12	c Gilchrist b McGrath		40
B.B.McCullum†	lbw b Gillespie	10	lbw b Gillespie		36
D.L.Vettori	lbw b McGrath	20	c Gillespie b Lehmann		59
J.E.C.Franklin	lbw b Warne	7	c Gilchrist b Kasprowicz		13
S.B.Styris	c Clarke b McGrath	28	(4) c Clarke b Warne		8
C.S.Martin	not out	2	c Ponting b Warne		2
Extras	(b 3, lb 5, nb 9)	17	(b 1, lb 12, nb 5)		18
TOTAL	(88.1 overs)	**251**	(82.3 overs)		**250**

Bowling	O	M	R	W	O	M	R	W	Fall of Wickets				
NEW ZEALAND										A	NZ	A	NZ
Martin	27	4	118	0	6	1	11	0		1st	1st	2nd	2nd
Franklin	17	2	102	0	5	0	18	0	1st	137	2	93	11
Oram	24	7	55	0	5	1	17	0	2nd	240	44	119	18
Vettori	55.2	10	152	5	18	2	35	1	3rd	261	80	-	34
Wiseman	32	7	140	3	22	3	52	1	4th	445	153	-	34
AUSTRALIA									5th	457	178	-	97
McGrath	20.1	3	66	4	12	4	32	2	6th	465	183	-	150
Gillespie	19	4	37	3	16	5	41	2	7th	543	190	-	160
Warne	28	5	65	1	27.3	6	79	2	8th	575	213	-	206
Kasprowicz	16	3	66	2	14	4	39	2	9th	-	242	-	243
Lehmann	5	2	9	0	13	0	46	2	10th	-	251	-	250

MILESTONES

- Justin Langer and Matthew Hayden took their combined opening partnership record beyond 4000 runs with their 13th century stand.

- Shane Warne captured his 550th test wicket.

- Mark Richardson, who made his test debut at 29, retired aged 33. In 38 tests he scored 2776 runs at 44.77 with four centuries and 19 fifties.

Daniel Vettori scored 59 off 78 balls in New Zealand's second innings. Adam Gilchrist (helmet) and Shane Warne watch proceedings.

2004/05 Australia in New Zealand

318 **NEW ZEALAND v AUSTRALIA** *(First Test)*

at Jade Stadium, Christchurch on 10, 11, 12, 13 March, 2005
Toss : Australia. Umpires : Aleem Dar & D.R. Shepherd
Australia won by 9 wickets

For the first time since taking over as captain Ricky Ponting sent the opposing side in to bat. At the end of the first day he might have thought that his decision had backfired as New Zealand were well placed at 265-3. Craig Cumming, making his test debut, naturally struggled for survival against a relentless attack, but gradually developed the confidence to play shots of quality, scoring 74.

The diminutive, curly-topped Hamish Marshall's maiden test century was a polished affair that flourished late in the day. He and Nathan Astle attacked the second new ball leaving Marshall (103) and Astle (29) unbeaten.

The second day began with Marshall scoring 43 off the first 40 balls bowled with shots of classical precision. His partnership with Astle was worth 131 when he departed at 330-4. Glenn McGrath claimed the remaining six wickets and restricted New Zealand to 433.

Australia began the third day at 141-3 and New Zealand were buoyed when the sixth wicket fell at 201. The match was approaching the halfway stage and New Zealand was on an even par or slightly ahead of their all-conquering opponents. In 30 overs between lunch and tea a tenacious Simon Katich aided the irrepressible genius of Adam Gilchrist in adding 133.

New Zealand's momentum was swatted away as Gilchrist reached his 14th test hundred off 105 balls and, with Katich also scoring a century, 212 were added in three hours and three minutes. The last four wickets fell for 29 runs, mainly

to the long-suffering Daniel Vettori who finished with five wickets, and New Zealand had a lead of one run.

Australia's supreme confidence had been restored and Shane Warne bamboozled the batsmen by bowling round the wicket into deep footmarks and swept them aside in 50 overs for 131, snaring five wickets. New Zealand lost seven batsmen adjudged lbw.

Justin Langer and Ponting were merciless in hammering the target of 133 at a rate of 4.35 runs per over and restored Australia's psychological dominance, which had been absent for the first half of the game.

NEW ZEALAND					
C.D.Cumming	c Gillespie b Kasprowicz	74	lbw b Gillespie		7
S.P.Fleming*	lbw b Warne	18	lbw b McGrath		17
H.J.H.Marshall	b Warne	146	b Warne		22
L.Vincent	lbw b Clarke	27	lbw b Gillespie		4
N.J.Astle	lbw b McGrath	74	b Kasprowicz		21
C.D.McMillan	c Gilchrist b McGrath	13	c Katich b Warne		5
B.B.McCullum†	c Langer b McGrath	29	lbw b Gillespie		24
D.L.Vettori	not out	24	lbw b Warne		23
J.E.C.Franklin	lbw b McGrath	0	not out		5
I.E.O'Brien	c Gilchrist b McGrath	5	lbw b Warne		0
C.S.Martin	c Gilchrist b McGrath	1	lbw b Warne		0
Extras	(b 4, lb 14, w 2, nb 2)	22	(b 1, lb 1, nb 1)		3
TOTAL	(141 overs)	**433**	(50 overs)		**131**

AUSTRALIA					
J.L.Langer	b Franklin	23	not out		72
M.L.Hayden	c Astle b O'Brien	35	c Cumming b Vettori		15
R.T.Ponting*	c McCullum b Martin	46	not out		47
D.R.Martyn	lbw b Vettori	32			
J.N.Gillespie	c Cumming b Vettori	12			
M.J.Clarke	c McCullum b Franklin	8			
S.M.Katich	c Vincent b Astle	118			
A.C.Gilchrist†	c O'Brien b Vettori	121			
S.K.Warne	c Astle b Vettori	2			
M.S.Kasprowicz	not out	13			
G.D.McGrath	lbw b Vettori	0			
Extras	(b 2, lb 22, w 3, nb 4)	22	(nb 1)		1
TOTAL	(123.2 overs)	**432**	(31.3 overs) (1 wkt)		**135**

Bowling										Fall of Wickets				
AUSTRALIA	O	M	R	W	O	M	R	W			NZ	A	NZ	A
											1st	1st	2nd	2nd
McGrath	42	9	115	6	14	7	19	1		1st	56	48	20	25
Gillespie	29	5	87	0	12	2	38	3		2nd	153	75	30	-
Kasprowicz	25	6	85	1	10	3	33	1		3rd	199	140	34	-
Warne	40	6	112	2	14	3	39	5		4th	330	147	71	-
Clarke	5	0	16	1						5th	355	160	78	-
NEW ZEALAND										6th	388	201	87	-
Martin	29	6	104	1	8	0	27	0		7th	403	413	121	-
Franklin	26	5	102	2	5	1	26	0		8th	403	418	127	-
O'Brien	14	3	73	1	5	0	27	0		9th	415	426	131	-
Vettori	40.2	13	106	5	13.3	0	55	1		10th	433	432	131	-
Astle	14	6	32	1										

Hamish Marshall scored an accomplished and exciting 146 against the world's best attack. It was an innings that reeked of class.

MILESTONES

- Craig Cumming (228) and Iain O'Brien (229) made their test debuts.

- Glenn McGrath took his 26th five-wicket bag in tests.

- Daniel Vettori took his 12th five-wicket bag in tests.

- Shane Warne took his 29th five-wicket bag in tests and his 1000th first-class wicket.

- Seven New Zealand batsmen were dismissed lbw in the second innings. This equalled the test record set at Durham in 2003 when Zimbabwe had seven batsmen dismissed in that fashion.

319 NEW ZEALAND v AUSTRALIA *(Second Test)*

at Basin Reserve, Wellington on 18, 19, 20, 21, 22 March, 2005
Toss : New Zealand. Umpires : D.R. Shepherd & R.E. Koertzen
Match drawn

Wellington's frequently maligned weather failed to produce the strong winds that were forecast. In place were drizzle and sea fog that rolled in over the five days. Rain and fog prevented play on the first day.

Stephen Fleming, gambling that the pitch may have sweated under the covers, asked Australia to bat first on an extended second day. Australia had reached tea at 174-4 as Damien Martyn and Simon Katich both batted aggressively. When Katich departed Adam Gilchrist took his place and the tempo increased as 163 runs were added in the last session, with Martyn being 106 and Gilchrist 45 at stumps.

The carnage continued at the start of the third day and when Martyn departed, for his highest test score of 165, the pair had added a record 256 in 46 overs, a worthy rate in a one-day game, but remarkable for two batsmen in a test match. Gilchrist's brilliant innings ended after he had scored 162 off 146 balls, which included five sixes and 22 fours. Shane Warne added to New Zealand's misery, bludgeoning 50 off 37 deliveries, enabling Australia to declare at 570-8.

New Zealand began the task of batting for the remaining three hours in the day in the worst possible way, with Fleming being lbw to Glenn McGrath without playing a shot for 0. Lou Vincent showed a return to form and was 36 not out when the day ended with New Zealand 122-4.

Rain interrupted play throughout the fourth day and prevented any chance of Australia furthering their cause when New Zealand crashed to be out for 244 and were asked to follow on 326 runs in arrears.

Gloomy skies hinted at salvation on the fifth day but not before McGrath dismissed Fleming lbw for the third time in three innings. Drizzle and fog restricted the day's play to 17.2 overs with New Zealand struggling at 48-3. The weather was a blessed relief for New Zealand.

AUSTRALIA		
J.L.Langer	c McCullum b Vettori	46
M.L.Hayden	c Vincent b Franklin	61
R.T.Ponting*	lbw b Vettori	9
D.R.Martyn	c McCullum b O'Brien	165
M.J.Clarke	c Fleming b Astle	8
S.M.Katich	c McCullum b Franklin	35
A.C.Gilchrist†	c & b Franklin	162
S.K.Warne	not out	50
J.N.Gillespie	b Franklin	2
M.S.Kasprowicz	not out	2
G.D.McGrath		
Extras	(b 4, lb 8, w 2, nb 16)	30
TOTAL	(140 overs) (8 wkts dec)	**570**

NEW ZEALAND					
C.D.Cumming	b Kasprowicz	37	not out		10
S.P.Fleming*	lbw b McGrath	0	lbw b McGrath		1
H.J.H.Marshall	c Gillespie b McGrath	18	lbw b McGrath		0
L.Vincent	c Gilchrist b Kasprowicz	63	b Kasprowicz		24
N.J.Astle	c Warne b Clarke	9	not out		4
J.E.C.Franklin	c Gilchrist b Kasprowicz	26			
C.D.McMillan	b Warne	20			
B.B.McCullum†	c Clarke b Warne	3			
D.L.Vettori	c Martyn b Warne	45			
I.E.O'Brien	b Gillespie	5			
C.S.Martin	not out	0			
Extras	(b 4, lb 8, w 1, nb 5)	18	(b 3, lb 5, nb 1)		9
TOTAL	(81.1 overs)	**244**	(17.2 overs) (3 wkts)		**48**

Bowling	O	M	R	W	O	M	R	W		Fall of Wickets		
NEW ZEALAND										A	NZ	NZ
										1st	1st	2nd
Martin	28	6	123	0					1st	82	9	3
Franklin	28	4	128	4					2nd	100	55	3
O'Brien	24	4	97	1					3rd	146	78	37
Vettori	47	5	170	2					4th	163	108	-
Astle	13	2	40	1					5th	247	166	-
AUSTRALIA									6th	503	180	-
McGrath	14	3	50	2	6	3	10	2	7th	557	184	-
Gillespie	20	4	63	1	5	2	5	0	8th	559	201	-
Kasprowicz	16	2	42	3	3	0	11	1	9th	-	212	-
Warne	28.1	7	69	3	3.2	0	14	0	10th	-	244	-
Clarke	3	1	8	1								

James Franklin took 4-128 in Australia's mammoth total of 570-8d in the second test at Wellington.

MILESTONES

- Damien Martyn and Adam Gilchrist added 256, a record for the sixth wicket between Australia and New Zealand.

- Adam Gilchrist passed Ian Healy's total of 4356 runs in 86 fewer innings to become Australia's most prolific scoring wicketkeeper.

- Adam Gilchrist became the fifth Australian to score three hundreds in consecutive innings. The others were Sir Donald Bradman (1948), Arthur Morris (1947), Jack Fingleton (1936), on his way to scoring four consecutive centuries, and Charlie Macartney (1926).

320 NEW ZEALAND v AUSTRALIA *(Third Test)*

at Eden Park, Auckland on 26, 27, 28, 29 March, 2005
Toss : New Zealand. Umpires : R.E. Koertzen & J.W. Lloyds
Australia won by 9 wickets

The debut of James Marshall, Hamish Marshall's identical twin, was the chief talking point on a slow day's play. After the loss of Craig Cumming for five, the twins were virtually indistinguishable when batting together. Spectators and commentators relied on the fact that James was wearing a forearm guard and Hamish did not.

Stephen Fleming relished moving down the order to number four and produced his only fifty in the series. Together with Hamish Marshall, who was batting with maturity, 126 runs were gradually accrued for the third wicket. The metronomic pinpoint accuracy of Glenn McGrath conceded only 49 runs from 34 overs and only a forthright 41 from Daniel Vettori carried New Zealand through to 292.

The first stanza of Australia's innings was dominated by Ricky Ponting who put lie to the idea that the nature of the pitch was to blame for New Zealand's stodgy batting by caressing and stroking his 21st test century at a rate of a-run-a-ball.

New Zealand bowled themselves back into the game, led by James Franklin, when Australia reached 297-7. For the third time in the series Adam Gilchrist stole the momentum away from the home side, batting at his flamboyant best to score 60 not out of the 83 runs added for the last three wickets.

Franklin, with a classical left-armer's action, smooth and rhythmical, deserved his six wickets, though occasionally he was astray in his line and length. Australia's lead of 91 was hardly emphatic but when McGrath undid both openers before stumps on the third day, it looked decidedly useful.

At 23-4 it required a brief cameo of aggression from Lou Vincent and some old-fashioned grit from Nathan Astle to give the scoreboard some form of decency. Daniel Vettori continued his consistent batting sequence of the series, which read 24 not out, 23, 45, 41 not out and 65, to take New Zealand through to 245. McGrath and Shane Warne could not be denied and they each ended with four wickets in the innings and seven each in the game.

The forecast for the fifth day was for showers so Australia set about winning the game in the 33 overs left on the fourth day. The floodlights of Eden Park were turned on and, in spite of Fleming's stalling tactics, Justin Langer and Ponting batted imperially, adding 148 in 113 minutes, to give Australia victory by nine wickets and a one-sided series win by 2-0.

MILESTONES

* James Marshall (230) made his test debut. He was the identical twin brother of Hamish (213). They were the second set of twins to play test cricket after Steve and Mark Waugh of Australia.

NEW ZEALAND

C.D.Cumming	lbw b Gillespie	5	lbw b McGrath		0
J.A.H.Marshall	c Hayden b McGrath	29	c Langer b McGrath		3
H.J.H.Marshall	c Ponting b Warne	76	c Gilchrist b McGrath		7
S.P.Fleming*	b Kasprowicz	65	c & b Gillespie		3
N.J.Astle	c Langer b McGrath	19	c Katich b Warne		69
L.Vincent	b Gillespie	2	run out		40
B.B.McCullum†	c Gilchrist b McGrath	25	lbw b Warne		0
D.L.Vettori	not out	41	c McGrath b Warne		65
J.E.C.Franklin	c Katich b Warne	3	c Ponting b Warne		23
P.J.Wiseman	c Gillespie b Warne	8	b McGrath		23
C.S.Martin	c Clarke b Kasprowicz	0	not out		4
Extras	(b 4, lb 13, nb 2)	19	(b 1, lb 14, nb 2)		17
TOTAL	(116.2 overs)	**292**	(69.2 overs)		**254**

AUSTRALIA

J.L.Langer	b Franklin	6	not out	59
M.L.Hayden	lbw b Franklin	38	run out	9
R.T.Ponting*	c McCullum b Astle	105	not out	86
D.R.Martyn	b Wiseman	38		
M.J.Clarke	run out	22		
J.N.Gillespie	c McCullum b Martin	35		
S.M.Katich	c Wiseman b Franklin	35		
A.C.Gilchrist†	not out	60		
S.K.Warne	c Fleming b Franklin	1		
M.S.Kasprowicz	b Franklin	23		
G.D.McGrath	c McCullum b Franklin	0		
Extras	(b 4, lb 7, nb 9)	20	(lb 10, nb 2)	12
TOTAL	(118.1 overs)	**383**	(29.3 overs) (1 wkt)	**166**

Bowling	O	M	R	W	O	M	R	W		Fall of Wickets			
AUSTRALIA										NZ	A	NZ	A
										1st	1st	2nd	2nd
McGrath	34	20	49	3	16.2	5	40	4	1st	15	8	0	18
Gillespie	25	8	64	2	16	4	63	1	2nd	53	84	9	-
Kasprowicz	30.2	7	89	2	14	2	59	0	3rd	179	187	15	-
Warne	23	4	63	3	23	5	77	4	4th	183	215	23	-
Ponting	4	1	10	0					5th	194	226	93	-
NEW ZEALAND									6th	228	297	93	-
Martin	21	4	92	1	8	1	51	0	7th	247	297	174	-
Franklin	26.1	3	119	6	7	0	40	0	8th	262	303	220	-
Astle	21	7	50	1	7	0	33	0	9th	288	377	227	-
Vettori	19	4	47	0	4	0	19	0	10th	292	383	254	-
Wiseman	31	7	64	1	3.3	0	13	0					

The Marshall twins captured running between the wickets during their partnership of 38 in the third test. James is in the foreground.

AVERAGES

New Zealand

BATTING	M	I	NO	Runs	HS	Ave
D.L. Vettori	3	5	2	198	65	66.00
H.J.H. Marshall	3	6	0	269	146	44.83
N.J. Astle	3	6	1	196	74	39.20
L. Vincent	3	6	0	160	63	26.66
C.D. Cumming	3	6	1	133	74	26.60
S.P. Fleming	3	6	0	104	65	17.33
B.B. McCullum	3	5	0	81	29	16.20
J.A.H. Marshall	1	2	0	32	29	16.00
P.J. Wiseman	1	2	0	31	23	15.50
J.E.C. Franklin	3	5	1	57	26	14.25
C.D. McMillan	2	3	0	38	20	12.66
I.E. O'Brien	2	3	0	10	5	3.33
C.S. Martin	3	5	2	5	4*	1.66

BOWLING	O	M	R	W	Ave
J.E.C. Franklin	92.1	13	415	12	34.58
D.L. Vettori	123.5	22	397	8	49.62
N.J. Astle	55	15	155	3	51.66
P.J. Wiseman	34.3	7	77	1	77.00
I.E. O'Brien	43	7	197	2	98.50
C.S. Martin	94	17	397	2	198.50

Australia

BATTING	M	I	NO	Runs	HS	Ave
A.C. Gilchrist	3	3	1	343	162	171.50
R.T. Ponting	3	5	2	293	105	97.66
D.R. Martyn	3	3	0	235	165	78.33
J.L. Langer	3	5	2	206	72*	68.66
S.M. Katich	3	3	0	188	118	62.66
M.S. Kasprowicz	3	3	2	38	23	38.00
M.L. Hayden	3	5	0	158	61	31.60
S.K. Warne	3	3	1	53	50*	26.50
J.N. Gillespie	3	3	0	49	35	16.33
M.J. Clarke	3	3	0	38	22	12.66
G.D. McGrath	3	2	0	0	0	0.00

BOWLING	O	M	R	W	Ave
M.J. Clarke	8	1	24	2	12.00
G.D. McGrath	126.2	47	283	18	15.72
S.K. Warne	131.3	25	374	17	22.00
M.S. Kasprowicz	98.2	20	319	8	39.87
J.N. Gillespie	107	25	320	7	45.71
R.T. Ponting	4	1	10	0	-

2004/05 Sri Lanka in New Zealand

Sri Lanka's tour of New Zealand had been cut short after a tsunami devastated large parts of Sri Lanka on Boxing Day 2004. After the first one-day international the Sri Lankan players had returned home. The two tests were rescheduled for April 2005. Both sides were without their top spinners. Muttiah Muralitharan had not yet recovered from surgery on his shoulder and Daniel Vettori had a back injury.

321 **NEW ZEALAND v SRI LANKA** *(First Test)*
at McLean Park, Napier on 4, 5, 6, 7, 8 April, 2005
Toss : New Zealand. Umpires : S.A. Bucknor & D.B. Hair
Match drawn

On a shirt-front wicket the Marshall twins, James and Hamish, blossomed to add 107 in 139 minutes for the second wicket before James was dismissed after scoring his first test fifty. Nathan Astle made the most of the excellent batting conditions to begin a partnership that was eventually to add 125 for the fourth wicket with Hamish Marshall, who progressed to his second test century of the season, being 133 at stumps while Astle was on 37 and the team well positioned at 267-3.

Mahela Jayawardene dropped Brendon McCullum on six after Hamish Marshall (160) and Lou Vincent (0) were quickly disposed of on the second morning. Astle and McCullum formed an alliance that took the score through to 446 before Astle departed for 114. McCullum failed by one run to score his second test century but James Franklin reached his first test fifty. New Zealand finished with 561.

Just how good the pitch was for batting was borne out when Sri Lanka reached 407 before losing their fourth wicket, with both the captain, Marvan Atapattu, and vice-captain, Jayawardene, scoring centuries. Chris Martin took four of the first five wickets and Franklin captured four of the last five. Sri Lanka lost their last six wickets for 46 runs.

New Zealand batted after tea on the fourth day with a lead of 63 and a draw looking certain. Lasith Malinga, a fast, right-arm round-arm slinger, created some concern with his toe-crushing yorkers and reverse swing to capture his first five-wicket haul and take nine wickets in the game. Vincent and Stephen Fleming defiantly denied the visitors and the game ended in a draw.

NEW ZEALAND

C.D.Cumming	lbw b Vaas	12	lbw b Malinga	16
J.A.H.Marshall	c Samaraweera b Chandana	52	lbw b Jayasuriya	39
H.J.H.Marshall	c Vaas b Malinga	160	lbw b Malinga	6
S.P.Fleming*	b Malinga	16	(5) c Kulasekara b Malinga	41
N.J.Astle	c Jayasuriya b Vaas	114	(6) run out	19
L.Vincent	c Dilshan b Kulasekara	0	(7) b Chandana	52
B.B.McCullum†	lbw b Malinga	99	(8) c Samaraweera b Jayasuriya	7
J.E.C.Franklin	c Malinga b Herath	55	(9) b Malinga	7
K.D.Mills	b Malinga	4	(10) c Jayasuriya b Herath	22
P.J.Wiseman	c Atapattu b Herath	27	(4) lbw b Malinga	0
C.S.Martin	not out	1	not out	4
Extras	(b 5, lb 4, w 2, nb 10)	21	(b 6, lb 7, w 2, nb 10)	25
TOTAL	**(159.1 overs)**	**561**	**(92.4 overs)**	**238**

SRI LANKA

M.S.Atapattu*	c Fleming b Astle	127	not out	2
S.T.Jayasuriya	lbw b Martin	48	not out	5
K.C.Sangakkara†	b Martin	5		
D.P.M.D.Jayawardene	c McCullum b Franklin	141		
T.T.Samaraweera	c Fleming b Martin	88		
T.M.Dilshan	c Vincent b Martin	28		
W.P.U.J.C.Vaas	c Astle b Wiseman	17		
U.D.U.Chandana	c Martin b Franklin	19		
H.M.R.K.B.Herath	b Franklin	0		
K.M.D.N.Kulasekara	c Fleming b Franklin	0		
S.L.Malinga	not out	0		
Extras	(b 1, lb 6, w 6, nb 12)	25		0
TOTAL	**(148.1 overs)**	**498**	**(1.3 overs) (0 wkts)**	**7**

Bowling										Fall of Wickets				
SRI LANKA	O	M	R	W	O	M	R	W			NZ	SL	NZ	SL
											1st	1st	2nd	2nd
Vaas	33	5	125	2	17	4	38	0		1st	35	95	51	-
Malinga	34	5	130	4	24.4	4	80	5		2nd	142	101	64	-
Kulasekara	25	7	70	1	11	2	19	0		3rd	187	285	69	-
Herath	30.1	5	91	2	11	4	29	1		4th	312	407	85	-
Chandana	33	4	123	1	7	2	12	1		5th	317	452	115	-
Jayasuriya	3	1	8	0	21	8	41	2		6th	446	463	128	-
Dilshan	1	0	5	0						7th	487	488	148	-
Samaraweera					1	0	6	0		8th	497	491	181	-
NEW ZEALAND										9th	540	497	222	-
Martin	37	9	132	4	1	0	1	0		10th	561	498	238	-
Franklin	32.1	8	126	4	0.3	0	6	0						
Wiseman	38	7	128	1										
Mills	23	6	59	0										
Astle	18	6	46	1										

MILESTONES

• It was the first test in Napier for 10 years.

• Hamish Marshall's 160 was his highest first-class score.

• Nathan Astle became the third New Zealand batsman to score 10 test centuries after Martin Crowe (17) and John Wright (12).

• Marvan Atapattu scored his 16th test hundred, which meant he had scored a century against each of the other nine test playing countries.

• Atapattu and Mahela Jayawardene established a record of 184 for the third wicket against New Zealand.

• New Zealand's total of 561 was their sixth-highest in tests.

James Marshall scored 52 and 39 in the first test. Kumar Sangakkara is the Sri Lankan wicketkeeper.

322 NEW ZEALAND v SRI LANKA *(Second Test)*

at Basin Reserve, Wellington on 11, 12, 13, 14 April, 2005
Toss : New Zealand. Umpires : D.B. Hair & S.A. Bucknor
New Zealand won by an innings and 38 runs

For the third time in five tests at the Basin Reserve Chris Martin captured five wickets in an innings and all before lunch on the first day, when he captured the first six wickets to fall on a green pitch conducive to accurate seam bowling.

At 86-7 Thilan Samaraweera and Upul Chandana restored a little dignity to the Sri Lankan scoreboard by doubling the score. Chandana batted aggressively for 41 before becoming the first of Astle's three wickets. Samaraweera diligently defied the attack for over four hours, being last out for 73.

Following a solid start of 61 from the openers, the Marshall twins were dismissed by Chaminda Vaas with the score at 70. Lou Vincent batted obdurately, keeping his aggressive nature well in check, to end the second day on 80 not out, with his captain, Stephen Fleming, passing 50 for the first time in 11 innings, being 60 not out and the total at 253-4.

In ice-cold conditions Vaas emulated Martin by claiming the first six New Zealand wickets to fall. Vincent reached his century off 223 deliveries before embarking on a counter-attack with the lower order batsmen. He added a further 124

at a-run-a-ball pace and he was involved in three consecutive record partnerships for New Zealand against Sri Lanka.

Sri Lanka were dismissed towards the end of the fourth day, with the longest innings being played by nightwatchman Mohamed Maharoof who stayed for 153 minutes. Three other batsmen scored in excess of 30 but there were no big partnerships. New Zealand won by an innings and 38 runs.

SRI LANKA

M.S.Atapattu*	c Vincent b Martin	0	(2) c Fleming b Franklin	16
S.T.Jayasuriya	c Astle b Martin	22	(1) c Vincent b Martin	2
K.C.Sangakkara†	c Marshall J.A.H. b Martin	16	(4) b Franklin	45
D.P.M.D.Jayawardene	lbw b Martin	1	(5) c McCullum b Franklin	13
T.T.Samaraweera	lbw b Astle	73	(6) c Fleming b Astle	17
T.M.Dilshan	c McCullum b Martin	9	(7) b Astle	73
S.Kalavitigoda	c Vincent b Martin	7	(8) c McCullum b Mills	1
W.P.U.J.C.Vaas	b Franklin	5	(9) b Franklin	38
U.D.U.Chandana	lbw b Astle	41	(10) b Astle	8
M.F.Maharoof	c sub (J.M.How) b Astle	12	(3) c Astle b Mills	36
S.L.Malinga	not out	4	not out	0
Extras	(b 4, lb 5, w 1, nb 11)	21	(b 4, lb 10, w 2, nb 8)	24
TOTAL	**(65.1 overs)**	**211**	**(92.5 overs)**	**273**

NEW ZEALAND

C.D.Cumming	lbw b Vaas	47
J.A.H.Marshall	lbw b Vaas	28
H.J.H.Marshall	c Jayawardene b Vaas	6
L.Vincent	run out	224
N.J.Astle	c Kalavitigoda b Vaas	0
S.P.Fleming*	c Kalavitigoda b Vaas	88
B.B.McCullum†	c & b Vaas	0
J.E.C.Franklin	lbw b Malinga	15
K.D.Mills	c Jayawardene b Malinga	31
P.J.Wiseman	not out	32
C.S.Martin	not out	4
Extras	(b 11, lb 23, w 1, nb 12)	47
TOTAL	**(146 overs) (9 wkts dec)**	**522**

Bowling	O	M	R	W	O	M	R	W	Fall of Wickets			
NEW ZEALAND										SL	NZ	SL
										1st	1st	2nd
Martin	20	7	54	6	18	4	50	1	1st	0	61	6
Franklin	11	1	51	1	23.5	4	71	4	2nd	34	70	47
Mills	20	6	50	0	11	4	34	2	3rd	36	153	95
Astle	12.1	2	35	3	13	4	27	3	4th	41	153	117
Wiseman	2	0	12	0	26	7	75	0	5th	60	294	137
Vincent					1	0	2	0	6th	80	294	164
SRI LANKA									7th	86	342	177
Vaas	40	12	108	6					8th	175	440	255
Malinga	34	2	124	2					9th	200	499	267
Maharoof	28	10	96	0					10th	211	-	273
Jayawardene	6	2	14	0								
Chandana	28	4	97	0								
Jayasuriya	9	2	34	0								
Dilshan	1	0	15	0								

MILESTONES

- It was New Zealand's 57th test victory.

- Chris Martin, in his fifth test at the Basin Reserve, took five wickets in an innings for the third time to equal the ground record held by Sir Richard Hadlee.

- Lou Vincent scored his third test hundred and became the 10th New Zealander to score a test double-century.

- Vincent and James Franklin created a seventh wicket record of 48 for New Zealand against Sri Lanka.

- Vincent and Kyle Mills created an eighth wicket record of 98 for New Zealand against Sri Lanka.

- Vincent and Paul Wiseman created a ninth wicket record of 59 for New Zealand against Sri Lanka.

- Nathan Astle, playing in his 71st test, achieved his best bowling figures in each innings.

Lou Vincent shared in three record partnerships and became the tenth New Zealander to score a test double century.

2005/06 New Zealand in Zimbabwe

New Zealand visited Namibia and Zimbabwe in August and September. It was a tour marked by political controversy in New Zealand. The government asked New Zealand Cricket not to undertake the tour due to the political situation in Zimbabwe but NZC said they were obliged to go as they were contracted to the ICC to do so.

323 ZIMBABWE v NEW ZEALAND *(First Test)*

at Harare Sports Club, Harare on 7, 8 August, 2005
Toss : Zimbabwe. Umpires : M.R. Benson & D.B. Hair
New Zealand won by an innings and 294 runs

The youthful Zimbabwean captain, Tatenda Taibu, won the toss and elected to field and for 2½ hours his three main bowlers all had success as New Zealand limped to 113-5. Brendon McCullum joined Stephen Fleming and the game was transformed as McCullum raced to fifty off 40 balls, as 120 were added, before Fleming went for 73 just on tea.

The tempo of the innings intensified as McCullum hammered the bowling to bring up his second test century in 94 balls. Daniel Vettori raced through to the fastest test century for New Zealand, from 82 balls, but was very fortunate. On 67 he played a ball from Heath Streak onto his stumps. The leg bail flipped up only to land on top of the stump at right angles to it and keep its balance. He was thus not out. In the session after tea New Zealand scored 219 and were able to declare at 452-9, scored at 5.07 runs per over.

Zimbabwe's batting was deplorable and they were dismissed in 29.4 overs. The pace of Shane Bond, playing his first test for 26 months, perturbed without destroying. It was James Franklin, swinging the ball into the right-hand batsmen, who captured three wickets in four balls, with the third ball called for over-striding, to leave Zimbabwe 11-4.

Chris Martin grabbed three wickets in 10 overs and Zimbabwe followed on shortly after lunch when they were

dismissed for 59. Their second innings was a slight improvement as Hamilton Masakadza made 42 but they were still wiped aside for 99. Their loss by an innings and 294 runs was their heaviest in test cricket.

NEW ZEALAND		
J.A.H.Marshall	c Taibu b Mahwire	5
L.Vincent	c Carlisle b Mahwire	13
H.J.H.Marshall	lbw b Mpofu	20
S.P.Fleming*	c Carlisle b Mpofu	73
N.J.Astle	c Taylor b Streak	23
S.B.Styris	run out	7
B.B.McCullum†	c Cremer b Mahwire	111
D.L.Vettori	b Streak	127
J.E.C.Franklin	b Cremer	13
S.E.Bond	not out	41
C.S.Martin	not out	4
Extras	(b 3, lb 5, w 2, nb 5)	15
TOTAL	**(89 overs) (9 wkts dec)**	**452**

ZIMBABWE				
N.R.Ferreira	c McCullum b Franklin	5	c Fleming b Franklin	16
B.R.M.Taylor	run out	10	c Vettori b Franklin	0
D.D.Ebrahim	lbw b Franklin	0	b Martin	8
H.Masakadza	lbw b Franklin	0	c & b Vettori	42
C.B.Wishart	b Bond	0	c Fleming b Bond	5
S.V.Carlisle	not out	20	c Fleming b Bond	0
T.Taibu*†	lbw b Martin	5	c Fleming b Martin	4
H.H.Streak	c McCullum b Martin	0	lbw b Vettori	3
N.B.Mahwire	lbw b Martin	4	not out	4
A.G.Cremer	c Martin b Vettori	1	c Marshall J.A.H. b Vettori	3
C.B.Mpofu	st McCullum b Vettori	0	st McCullum b Vettori	0
Extras	(b 4, lb 2, w 1, nb 7)	14	(lb 8, nb 6)	14
TOTAL	**(29.4 overs)**	**59**	**(49.5 overs)**	**99**

Bowling ZIMBABWE	O	M	R	W	O	M	R	W
Streak	23.4	5	102	2				
Mahwire	26	4	115	3				
Mpofu	16.2	1	100	2				
Cremer	22	0	113	1				
Taylor	1	0	14	0				
NEW ZEALAND								
Bond	5	1	11	1	11	8	10	2
Franklin	5	0	11	3	10	3	19	2
Martin	10	1	21	3	8	5	16	2
Styris	7	4	9	0	2	0	3	0
Vettori	2.4	2	1	2	13.5	4	28	4
Astle					5	0	15	0

Fall of Wickets	NZ 1st	Z 1st	Z 2nd
1st	21	9	5
2nd	24	9	14
3rd	63	10	53
4th	104	11	76
5th	113	28	80
6th	233	46	84
7th	309	46	90
8th	369	51	90
9th	432	53	99
10th	-	59	99

MILESTONES

- It was New Zealand's 58th test victory.

- It was New Zealand's biggest winning margin.

- Daniel Vettori took 82 balls for his century, the fastest of the 194 that had been made for New Zealand to date. The previous record was held by Bruce Taylor (83 balls) against West Indies at Eden Park in 1968/69 (test 84).

- Vettori took his 200th wicket in his 63rd test.

- New Zealand made 452 runs on the first day, the most they had ever made on the opening day of a test.

- Zimbabwe became only the second test side to be dismissed twice in one day. The other was India against England at Manchester in 1962.

- Christopher Mpofu became the third player to be stumped twice on the same day of a test. The others were Bobby Peel, for England against Australia in 1894/95, and Ivan Barrow for West Indies against Australia in 1930/31.

Brendon McCullum's daring strokeplay saw him make his second test hundred off 94 balls.

324 ZIMBABWE v NEW ZEALAND *(Second Test)*

at Queen's Sports Club, Bulawayo on 15, 16, 17 August, 2005
Toss : Zimbabwe. Umpires : M.R. Benson & D.B. Hair
New Zealand won by an innings and 46 runs

Even though the Queen's Sports Club has a well-deserved reputation as being consistently one of the best batting strips in the world it did not prevent Shane Bond from capturing a wicket in each of his first three overs and taking five of the first six wickets to fall by the time 74 runs had been scored.

The diminutive Tatenda Taibu displayed courage and classical shots in reaching 76 before he essayed a hook at a Bond bouncer and brought about his own demise. He added 88 with Blessing Mahwire, taking Zimbabwe to 231. In reply New Zealand lost the Marshalls before stumps to be 48-2.

In idyllic conditions New Zealand scored 406 on the second day for the loss of five wickets. Those who batted all got a start and looked comfortable but only Nathan Astle applied himself sufficiently, making his 11th test hundred, though he was rather more sedate than normal.

From an overnight situation of 454-7, with Astle 116 not out, New Zealand lost their remaining three wickets inside 11 overs. The wily veteran Heath Streak claimed two more wickets to finish with four in the innings and terminate New Zealand's innings at 484, giving them a lead of 253.

So long as 19-year-old Brendan Taylor was at the crease Zimbabwe's second innings looked more settled and accomplished. In his 186-minute stay, for a worthwhile 77, two top order batsmen were run out, which aided New Zealand's cause greatly. With the end in sight Mahwire attacked boisterously hitting two sixes and eight fours, to record the fastest half-century for Zimbabwe, off 34 balls.

Bond took 10 wickets in the match for the first time in his career as New Zealand won by an innings and 46 runs. The two tests, which had been scheduled to last ten days, lasted for only five. Any thoughts of a return tour were quashed when the New Zealand government announced that it would not issue visas to a team from Zimbabwe.

Shane Bond was rewarded for an outstanding performance of pace bowling, claiming 10 wickets for 99 runs in the match.

ZIMBABWE

D.D.Ebrahim	lbw b Bond	0	c Styris b Bond		2
B.R.M.Taylor	c McCullum b Bond	37	c Vettori b Bond		77
S.V.Carlisle	lbw b Bond	1	run out		10
H.Masakadza	c Martin b Bond	0	b Vettori		28
C.B.Wishart	c Astle b Franklin	30	run out		0
T.Taibu*†	c Vettori b Bond	76	lbw b Vettori		25
H.H.Streak	c McCullum b Bond	0	c McCullum b Bond		2
K.M.Dabengwa	b Martin	17	c McCullum b Bond		4
N.B.Mahwire	c Astle b Vettori	42	not out		50
A.G.Cremer	not out	7	lbw b Vettori		1
C.B.Mpofu	c Marshall J.A.H. b Vettori	7	run out		3
Extras	(lb 4, nb 10)	14	(lb 2, nb 3)		5
TOTAL	(79 overs)	**231**	(61.1 overs)		**207**

NEW ZEALAND

J.A.H.Marshall	c Carlisle b Streak	10
L.Vincent	b Streak	92
H.J.H.Marshall	run out	13
S.P.Fleming*	c Taibu b Mahwire	65
N.J.Astle	b Streak	128
S.B.Styris	c Taibu b Mahwire	45
B.B.McCullum†	c Taylor b Dabengwa	24
D.L.Vettori	c Taibu b Dabengwa	48
J.E.C.Franklin	lbw b Streak	19
S.E.Bond	b Mahwire	8
C.S.Martin	not out	0
Extras	(b 6, lb 6, w 2, nb 18)	32
TOTAL	(111.1 overs)	**484**

Bowling	O	M	R	W	O	M	R	W
NEW ZEALAND								
Bond	17	5	51	6	14	1	48	4
Franklin	12	3	43	1	10	3	24	0
Martin	13	4	42	1	12	2	47	0
Styris	4	2	9	0	3	0	20	0
Vettori	27	9	56	2	22.1	8	66	3
Astle	6	2	26	0				
ZIMBABWE								
Streak	22	6	73	4				
Mahwire	25.1	2	121	3				
Mpofu	15	1	80	0				
Cremer	24	1	111	0				
Dabengwa	25	2	87	2				

Fall of Wickets	Z	NZ	Z
	1st	1st	2nd
1st	0	34	4
2nd	3	48	19
3rd	7	185	69
4th	65	205	69
5th	74	292	146
6th	74	346	146
7th	123	439	153
8th	211	475	164
9th	217	484	173
10th	231	484	207

MILESTONES

- New Zealand had their 59th test win.

- Shane Bond took 6-51, his best analysis at first-class level.

- Bond took 10 wickets in a game for the first time in his first-class career.

- Stephen Fleming became the first New Zealander to pass 6000 test runs. He did so in his 96th test.

2005/06 West Indies in New Zealand

325 **NEW ZEALAND v WEST INDIES** *(First Test)*

at Eden Park, Auckland on 9, 10, 11, 12, 13 March, 2006
Toss : West Indies. Umpires : D.J. Harper & R.E. Koertzen
New Zealand won by 27 runs

An intriguing match ensued over five days, mainly because the batting of both sides lacked conviction and class, with Scott Styris, Brendon McCullum, Chris Gayle and Daren Ganga excepted. It was an even contest in which both sides lost 20 wickets, where the final margin was 27 runs and where West Indies faced nine balls more in the game than did New Zealand.

New Zealand came into the test having played 22 consecutive one-day internationals in the previous seven months and loose shots contributed to New Zealand's stumbling to 96-4. Nathan Astle had not made the transformation back to test cricket mode as he hit 10 boundaries in scoring 51 off 57 balls.

In an even contest Scott Styris' unbeaten 103 was a major contribution to New Zealand's narrow victory by 27 runs.

It was left to Scott Styris to shepherd the lower order through to a reasonable score of 275 as he mixed caution with aggression in compiling his fifth test century and his second at Eden Park. At the close West Indies were 51-3 and Styris had again figured prominently by claiming two wickets.

The player tipped to be the successor to Brian Lara, Ramnaresh Sarwan, aided by the quality all-rounder Dwayne Bravo batted sensibly to bring their team to within 18 runs of New Zealand's total. After playing two years of one-day internationals Ian Bradshaw was making his test debut and claimed three early wickets as inept batting, in good conditions, saw New Zealand in the perilous situation of 146-7, a lead of only 164 at the halfway stage of the match.

Two partnerships involving Brendon McCullum, who spent over three hours making 74, rallied New Zealand's hopes. Firstly, 64 runs were scored with Daniel Vettori, and then another 62 were added with Shane Bond, which saw the home side dismissed for 272.

West Indies was left the target of 291, the highest innings total of the match. When the third day ended they had reduced that to 243 and still had all their wickets intact.

Play did not begin until 1 pm on the fourth day because of rain and Chris Gayle and Daren Ganga reached 100 with few problems encountered, as an elusive away test win appeared likely. Gayle struck Vettori for a huge six and the ball was lost. A replacement ball was bounced on the concrete to age it. At 148 Astle removed Gayle for 82.

Sarwan retired when he was struck by Bond on the back of his helmet and Lara was bowled behind his legs, first ball. Bond was bowling at a lively pace and was making the replacement ball reverse swing, and wickets began to tumble. It re-emphasised his worth to New Zealand in test cricket. From a dominant position of 148-0 West Indies squandered their chance and the fourth day ended at 246-8.

The coup de grâce was delivered early on the last day when Bond captured his fifth wicket and New Zealand had victory by 27 runs.

MILESTONES

- It was New Zealand's 60th test win.

- Peter Fulton (231) and Jamie How (232) made their test debuts.

- It was 50 years to the day since New Zealand had their first ever test victory (test 45) on the same ground, against the same opponents.

- Chris Martin made his fourth test pair, equalling the record held by Bhagwat Chandrashekar (India), Mervyn Dillon and Courtney Walsh (West Indies) and Marvan Atapattu (Sri Lanka).

NEW ZEALAND

H.J.H.Marshall	c Edwards b Taylor	11	c Ganga b Bradshaw		1
J.M.How	run out	11	c Ramdin b Bradshaw		37
P.G.Fulton	c Ganga b Bradshaw	17	b Edwards		28
S.P.Fleming*	c Ramdin b Bradshaw	14	lbw b Bradshaw		33
N.J.Astle	c Ramdin b Smith	51	(7) run out		13
S.B.Styris	not out	103	(5) c Bradshaw b Edwards		5
B.B.McCullum†	b Smith	19	(8) c Bravo b Gayle		74
D.L.Vettori	c Gayle b Smith	6	(9) c sub (D.S.Smith) b Gayle		33
J.E.C.Franklin	c sub (R.S.Morton) b Gayle	14	(6) b Gayle		20
S.E.Bond	b Gayle	3	not out		18
C.S.Martin	c Ramdin b Bradshaw	0	b Gayle		0
Extras	(b 4, lb 2, w 9, nb 11)	26	(lb 3, w 2, nb 5)		10
TOTAL	(69.1 overs)	275	(103.1 overs)		272

WEST INDIES

C.H.Gayle	c McCullum b Styris	25	c Fleming b Astle		82
D.Ganga	c How b Martin	20	c How b Astle		95
I.D.R.Bradshaw	c How b Styris	0	(9) c Fleming b Vettori		10
R.R.Sarwan	c Franklin b Bond	62	(3) c Styris b Bond		4
B.C.Lara	c sub (C.Cachopa) b Bond	5	(4) b Bond		0
S.Chanderpaul*	c McCullum b Franklin	13	(5) c Fulton b Vettori		15
D.J.Bravo	c Bond b Martin	59	(6) lbw b Bond		17
D.R.Smith	c McCullum b Martin	38	(7) c Fleming b Bond		0
D.Ramdin†	c & b Vettori	9	(8) c Franklin b Vettori		15
F.H.Edwards	c McCullum b Vettori	1	(11) not out		2
J.E.Taylor	not out	4	(10) b Bond		13
Extras	(lb 7, w 1, nb 13)	21	(b 1, lb 3, w 1, nb 5)		10
TOTAL	(71.2 overs)	257	(102.3 overs)		263

Bowling	O	M	R	W	O	M	R	W	Fall of Wickets	NZ	WI	NZ	WI
WEST INDIES										1st	1st	2nd	2nd
Edwards	15	1	76	0	21	3	65	2	1st	23	47	11	148
Bradshaw	23.1	3	73	3	34	10	83	3	2nd	31	48	66	157
Taylor	8	2	39	1	1	0	6	0	3rd	54	49	73	182
Smith	18	2	71	3	17	6	44	0	4th	69	60	88	211
Gayle	5	0	10	2	30.1	5	71	4	5th	140	90	118	216
NEW ZEALAND									6th	170	179	143	218
Bond	19	4	57	2	27.3	7	69	5	7th	199	237	146	221
Franklin	21	4	83	1	14	1	46	0	8th	240	248	210	246
Martin	17	1	80	3	16	5	39	0	9th	261	252	272	251
Styris	7	1	23	2					10th	275	257	272	263
Vettori	7.2	3	7	2	35	11	92	3					
Astle					10	4	13	2					

326 NEW ZEALAND v WEST INDIES *(Second Test)*

at Basin Reserve, Wellington on 17, 18, 19, 20, March, 2006
Toss : West Indies. Umpires : D.J. Harper & M.R. Benson
New Zealand won by 10 wickets

Shivnarine Chanderpaul did not hesitate to bat when he won the toss, knowing that the hero of the first test, Shane Bond, was suffering from a virus and had been replaced at the last moment by Kyle Mills. Both openers, Chris Gayle and Daren Ganga, and one of the greatest-ever batsmen, Brian Lara, had been dismissed by the time the score was 49. Runako Morton, whose career had been badly disrupted by off-the-field incidents, was playing in his third test at the age of 27.

He utilised the dire situation to advance his claims to more test appearances by scoring 63 in 173 minutes, with 50 of his runs coming from 11 fours and a six. Rain interfered with play after James Franklin, moving the ball both ways, had snared his third five-wicket haul. The visitors ended at 182-8.

The end came quickly on the second day when Mills mopped up the innings to finish with his best test figures of 3-53. Even though New Zealand lost both openers with the score at two, an accomplished partnership between Stephen Fleming and Peter Fulton added 165. This enabled their opponent's total to be overhauled for the loss of just three wickets.

Nathan Astle was the senior partner of a well-performing tail that took the total to 372. Fidel Edwards swung the ball at a lively pace to capture five wickets, while Darren Powell banged the ball in short to achieve his four wickets.

Chris Gayle looked a world-class player as he reached a colourful 63. Lara failed for the fourth time, to give him seven runs off 23 balls for the series. Rain stopped play at 118-4 and delayed play on the fourth day.

Eventually the fast-medium trio of Franklin, Chris Martin and Mills continued to dominate the test and between them they captured 17 of the 20 wickets to fall. Mills again had his best return, 3-29. New Zealand required fewer than nine overs to score the winning runs, winning by 10 wickets.

WEST INDIES

C.H.Gayle	c McCullum b Franklin	30	lbw b Vettori		68
D.Ganga	c McCullum b Mills	15	c McCullum b Martin		23
R.S.Morton	lbw b Franklin	63	c Fleming b Franklin		7
B.C.Lara	c Fleming b Franklin	1	c Marshall b Astle		1
S.Chanderpaul*	c Fleming b Martin	8	c Fleming b Mills		36
D.J.Bravo	lbw b Franklin	9	c Astle b Martin		7
D.Ramdin†	b Franklin	2	b Vettori		7
R.N.Lewis	c Fleming b Martin	22	c Astle b Mills		40
I.D.R.Bradshaw	not out	20	c Styris b Franklin		2
D.B.L.Powell	c How b Mills	16	c How b Mills		7
F.H.Edwards	c Fleming b Mills	0	not out		0
Extras	(b 2, lb 1, nb 3)	6	(w 6, nb 11)		17
TOTAL	(61.4 overs)	192	(90.5 overs)		215

NEW ZEALAND

H.J.H.Marshall	c Chanderpaul b Bradshaw	3	not out		23
J.M.How	b Edwards	0	not out		9
P.G.Fulton	c Ramdin b Powell	75			
S.P.Fleming*	c Bravo b Edwards	97			
N.J.Astle	c Ramdin b Powell	65			
S.B.Styris	c Morton b Powell	8			
B.B.McCullum†	c Ramdin b Powell	23			
D.L.Vettori	c Chanderpaul b Edwards	42			
J.E.C.Franklin	not out	28			
K.D.Mills	c Ramdin b Edwards	10			
C.S.Martin	b Edwards	0			
Extras	(lb 4, w 2, nb 15)	21	(nb 5)		5
TOTAL	(106.3 overs)	372	(8.1 overs) (0 wkts)		37

Bowling	O	M	R	W	O	M	R	W	Fall of Wickets	WI	NZ	WI	NZ
NEW ZEALAND										1st	1st	2nd	2nd
Martin	14	1	66	2	27	8	65	2					
Franklin	20	7	53	5	21	8	64	2	1st	43	3	54	-
Mills	19.4	7	53	3	9.5	2	29	3	2nd	45	3	75	-
Vettori	5	2	13	0	20	4	40	2	3rd	49	168	84	-
Astle	3	2	4	0	13	4	17	1	4th	80	207	113	-
WEST INDIES									5th	102	219	129	-
Edwards	15.3	2	65	5					6th	108	246	156	-
Bradshaw	19	2	97	1	4	0	16	0	7th	142	332	163	-
Powell	24	7	83	4	4.1	1	21	0	8th	165	335	189	-
Gayle	18	4	46	0					9th	186	372	210	-
Lewis	29	8	70	0					10th	192	372	215	-
Morton	1	0	7	0									

MILESTONES

• It was New Zealand's 61st test win.

• New Zealand had a record fifth successive test victory.

• It was the first time that New Zealand had won three consecutive series.

• It was New Zealand's third successive series victory over West Indies.

• It was West Indies' 12th consecutive away defeat.

• Stephen Fleming held six catches in the test. He became the first player to do so on three occasions.

Umpire Daryl Harper watches Kyle Mills bowl. Mills had a successful
game, claiming three wickets in each innings.

WEST INDIES		
C.H.Gayle	c Fulton b Martin	30
D.Ganga	b Bond	38
B.C.Lara	b Astle	83
R.S.Morton	not out	70
S.Chanderpaul*	run out	2
D.J.Bravo	not out	22
D.R.Smith		
D.Ramdin†		
I.D.R.Bradshaw		
D.B..Powell		
F.H.Edwards		
Extras	(lb 3, nb 8)	11
TOTAL	(78.1 overs) (4 wkts)	**256**

NEW ZEALAND		
H.J.H.Marshall		
J.M.How		
P.G.Fulton		
S.P.Fleming*		
N.J.Astle		
S.B.Styris		
B.B.McCullum†		
D.L.Vettori		
J.E.C.Franklin		
S.E.Bond		
C.S.Martin		

Bowling NEW ZEALAND	O	M	R	W		Fall of Wickets WI
						1st
Bond	18	2	87	1		
Franklin	15	1	66	0	1st	37
Martin	10	2	39	1	2nd	111
Astle	14	5	23	1	3rd	171
Styris	13.1	5	27	0	4th	189
Vettori	8	4	11	0	5th	-
					6th	-
					7th	-
					8th	-
					9th	-
					10th	-

327 **NEW ZEALAND v WEST INDIES** *(Third Test)*
at McLean Park, Napier on 25, 26, 27, 28, 29 March, 2006
Toss : New Zealand. Umpires : M.R. Benson & I.L. Howell
Match drawn

The inclement weather that had dogged the West Indian tour
struck with full force in the area with the best record for
sunshine in the country, Hawke's Bay.

Heavy rain fell in the region prior to the test and West
Indies were sent in to bat late on the first afternoon, facing
27.3 overs before darkness terminated play with the score at
95-1, Daren Ganga 31 and a circumspect Brian Lara on 28.

There was time for another 50.4 overs on the second day,
in which time the few spectators there were given the
opportunity to see the genius of Lara. In difficult conditions
he imperially stroked 24442 from one James Franklin over.
His innings was terminated at 83 when a ball from Nathan
Astle cannoned off his boot and onto his stump. Rain stopped
play and prevented any continuation on the saturated field for
the three remaining days.

MILESTONES

• Stephen Fleming captained New Zealand for the 75th time
in tests. This put him ahead of Clive Lloyd (West Indies)
and behind only Allan Border (Australia) with 93.

Stephen Fleming was playing his 75th test as captain of New Zealand.

AVERAGES

New Zealand

BATTING	M	I	NO	Runs	HS	Ave
S.B. Styris	3	3	1	116	103*	58.00
S.P. Fleming	3	3	0	144	97	48.00
N.J. Astle	3	3	0	129	65	43.00
P.G. Fulton	3	3	0	120	75	40.00
B.B. McCullum	3	3	0	116	74	38.66
J.E.C. Franklin	3	3	1	62	28*	31.00
D.L. Vettori	3	3	0	81	42	27.00
S.E. Bond	2	2	1	21	18*	21.00
J.M. How	3	4	1	57	37	19.00
H.J.H. Marshall	3	4	1	38	23*	12.66
K.D. Mills	1	1	0	10	10	10.00
C.S. Martin	3	3	0	0	0	0.00

BOWLING	O	M	R	W	Ave
K.D. Mills	29.3	9	82	6	13.66
N.J. Astle	40	15	57	4	14.25
D.L. Vettori	75.2	24	163	7	23.28
S.B. Styris	20.1	6	50	2	25.00
S.E. Bond	64.3	13	213	8	26.62
C.S. Martin	84	17	289	8	36.12
J.E.C. Franklin	91	21	312	8	39.00

West Indies

BATTING	M	I	NO	Runs	HS	Ave
R.S. Morton	2	3	1	140	70*	70.00
C.H. Gayle	3	5	0	235	82	47.00
D. Ganga	3	5	0	191	95	38.20
R.R. Sarwan	1	2	0	66	62	33.00
R.N. Lewis	1	2	0	62	40	31.00
D.J. Bravo	3	5	1	114	59	28.50
D.R. Smith	2	2	0	38	38	19.00
B.C. Lara	3	5	0	90	83	18.00
J.E. Taylor	1	2	1	17	13	17.00
S. Chanderpaul	3	5	0	74	36	14.80
D.B.L. Powell	2	2	0	23	16	11.50
I.D.R. Bradshaw	3	4	1	32	20*	10.66
D. Ramdin	3	4	0	33	15	8.25
F.H. Edwards	3	4	2	3	2*	1.50

BOWLING	O	M	R	W	Ave
C.H. Gayle	53.1	9	127	6	21.16
D.B.L. Powell	28.1	8	104	4	26.00
F.H. Edwards	51.3	6	206	7	29.42
D.R. Smith	35	8	115	3	38.33
I.D.R. Bradshaw	80.1	15	269	7	38.42
J.E. Taylor	9	2	45	1	45.00
R.S. Morton	1	0	7	0	-
R.N. Lewis	29	8	70	0	-

The New Zealand team that played the third test at Napier. Back row (from left): Dayle Shackel (physiotherapist), Lindsay Crocker (manager), Jamie How, Shane Bond, Peter Fulton, Hamish Marshall, Brendon McCullum, John Bracewell (coach), Bob Carter (assistant coach). Front row: Steve Jackson (trainer), James Franklin, Chris Martin, Daniel Vettori, Stephen Fleming (captain), Nathan Astle, Scott Styris, Michael Henstock (media liaison officer).

2005/06 New Zealand in South Africa

New Zealand's tour to South Africa was rearranged because of the Super Series in Australia. The one-day internationals were played in October and November and a series of three tests was played in April and May, a time when South Africans and New Zealanders usually think of rugby.

328   SOUTH AFRICA v NEW ZEALAND *(First Test)*

at SuperSport Park, Centurion on 15, 16, 17, 18, 19 April, 2006
Toss : South Africa. Umpires : M.R. Benson & D.J. Harper
South Africa won by 128 runs

With two of the three venues favouring fast bowling it was a killer-blow when Shane Bond injured a knee and flew home prior to the first test. That left South Africa holding a pair of fast aces in Makhaya Ntini and Dale Steyn, to which New Zealand had no response.

New Zealand's weakened attack did well, restricting South Africa to 266-8 on the first day and removing the last two wickets for 10 runs, with James Franklin and Kyle Mills each capturing four wickets.

Ntini and Steyn exploited the favourable bounce and movement offered by the pitch to have New Zealand floundering at 85-6. At this moment of crisis Jacob Oram, who had battled injury for the last 18 months, struggled manfully, survived and showed great tenacity to reach his third century and highest test score of 133, while partnering the indomitable Daniel Vettori to add 183 for the seventh wicket. The last three players stayed for another hour with Oram, while 50 vital extra runs were added to give New Zealand a lead of 51.

New Zealand captured three wickets before the deficit was eradicated as multi-talented sports player A.B. de Villiers, who could have played either golf or tennis professionally, scored a boundary-laden 97 of the 197 runs added while he was at the crease. Once again the underrated visiting bowlers performed above expectation and New Zealand were left 249 for victory.

On a rain-shortened fourth day New Zealand were swept away on what one South African critic described as "a chronically inconsistent pitch" and another as "a frighteningly fearful strip of dirt". All Ntini and Steyn had to do was to bowl accurately and the pitch would do the rest. New Zealand lost their sixth wicket at 26 and limped to stumps at 98-7, with Hamish Marshall batting courageously for 165 minutes throughout the carnage.

He took several balls on the body, suffering injuries that prevented him from playing in the next two tests. For the second time in the game Ntini captured five wickets in the innings, with his bowling colleague Steyn collecting his first five-wicket bag. South Africa won by 128 runs.

SOUTH AFRICA

G.C.Smith*	lbw b Franklin	45	lbw b Martin	7
H.H.Gibbs	b Mills	6	c Styris b Franklin	2
H.H.Dippenaar	c Fulton b Mills	52	c Fleming b Oram	16
J.H.Kallis	b Franklin	38	c Vettori b Styris	62
A.G.Prince	c Styris b Mills	9	c McCullum b Franklin	11
A.B.de Villiers	b Franklin	27	c Franklin b Oram	97
M.V.Boucher†	c Fleming b Martin	18	b Mills	21
S.M.Pollock	c Styris b Mills	24	lbw b Vettori	10
N.Boje	lbw b Franklin	23	c McCullum b Astle	31
D.W.Steyn	c Mills b Martin	13	not out	7
M.Ntini	not out	1	lbw b Vettori	16
Extras	(b 6, lb 4, w 3, nb 7)	20	(b 12, lb 2, nb 5)	19
TOTAL	(95.4 overs)	**276**	(98.1 overs)	**299**

NEW ZEALAND

H.J.H.Marshall	b Ntini	6	c Boucher b Ntini	25
P.G.Fulton	c Boucher b Pollock	14	c Boucher b Ntini	4
S.P.Fleming*	c & b Ntini	0	(4) c Kallis b Steyn	6
S.B.Styris	c Gibbs b Ntini	17	(5) c Boucher b Steyn	2
N.J.Astle	c Boucher b Steyn	4	(6) c de Villiers b Ntini	2
J.D.P.Oram	c Pollock b Steyn	133	(7) b Ntini	2
B.B.McCullum†	c Boje b Kallis	31	(8) c Dippenaar b Steyn	33
D.L.Vettori	c Prince b Ntini	81	(9) c Boucher b Steyn	38
J.E.C.Franklin	c Boucher b Ntini	8	(10) not out	0
K.D.Mills	c Boje b Pollock	12	(3) c Dippenaar b Ntini	0
C.S.Martin	not out	1	b Steyn	0
Extras	(lb 12, nb 8)	20	(lb 2, nb 6)	8
TOTAL	(71.4 overs)	**327**	(36 overs)	**120**

Bowling

NEW ZEALAND	O	M	R	W	O	M	R	W
Mills	18	7	43	4	21	5	57	1
Franklin	18	3	75	4	14	2	60	2
Martin	22.4	4	66	2	24	6	64	1
Oram	14	7	27	0	17	3	44	2
Vettori	18	2	44	0	15.1	0	42	2
Astle	5	2	11	0	5	1	15	1
Styris					2	0	3	1
SOUTH AFRICA								
Ntini	19	2	94	5	14	3	51	5
Steyn	18.4	1	95	2	17	4	47	5
Pollock	15	4	45	2	5	1	20	0
Kallis	9	1	41	1				
Boje	7	0	29	0				
Smith	3	1	11	0				

Fall of Wickets

	SA	NZ	SA	NZ
	1st	1st	2nd	2nd
1st	16	8	8	5
2nd	95	12	19	5
3rd	119	32	42	17
4th	130	38	73	23
5th	177	45	140	26
6th	197	89	194	28
7th	229	272	205	73
8th	233	280	270	119
9th	274	322	276	119
10th	276	327	299	120

For the first time in test cricket, three players made their 100th appearance in the same game. From left, Jacques Kallis, Stephen Fleming and Shaun Pollock.

MILESTONES

- Stephen Fleming became the first New Zealander to appear in 100 tests.

- Jacques Kallis and Shaun Pollock played their 100th tests for South Africa.

- Daniel Vettori scored his 2000th test run to add to his 200 wickets thus joining Sir Richard Hadlee and Chris Cairns as the only New Zealanders to complete this double.

- Makhaya Ntini captured 10 wickets in a game for the fourth time, a South African record.

329 **SOUTH AFRICA v NEW ZEALAND** *(Second Test)*

at Cape Town on 27, 28, 29, 30 April, 1 May, 2006
Toss : South Africa. Umpires : M.R. Benson & E.A.R. de Silva
Match drawn

The groundsman at Cape Town had been criticised for his pitch earlier in the extended season when Australia beat South Africa by seven wickets inside three days. He ensured that this pitch would last for eternity.

The dominant feature of the game was the weather, which proved what a folly it was to play cricket at this time of the year. At the start of the second day the groundsman was racing around the outfield on a hovercraft in an attempt to disperse the wintery dew.

Graeme Smith became the first South African captain since 1927 to field first after winning the toss at Newlands. When the third wicket fell at 82 he could have felt that it was a well-justified decision but, when the declaration was made one hour into the third day with New Zealand having made their highest score in South Africa of 593-8 declared, his team had spent 165 overs in the field proving otherwise.

Stephen Fleming was New Zealand's hero. He remained focused for 9½ hours to score 262, his third test double-century. Throughout his marathon performance the tempo of his innings didn't fluctuate nor did his shot production diminish, as graceful drives off the front foot, savage cuts and occasionally lofted shots over square-leg resonated continually.

He and James Franklin shared a record partnership of 256 for the eighth wicket, with Franklin batting with aplomb to score his first test century. Part-time bowler Ashwell Prince dismissed Fleming. At the end of the second day Franklin was on 93 so New Zealand batted for an hour on the third day while Franklin reached his century. Jeetan Patel made an accomplished 27 not out, to torture South Africa a little more.

On a pitch completely devoid of pace, bounce or spin South Africa always appeared likely to reach their first target, which was 394 to avoid the follow-on, which they did for the loss of only five wickets. Hashim Amla, a devout

Muslim of Indian descent, playing in his first test for 15 months, resurrected his flagging test career, which to date had produced only 62 runs from six innings.

He emulated Fleming in style, stance and focus in batting for 385 minutes for his maiden test century of 149. Prince reached his fourth century and was instrumental in the last five South African wickets adding a further 151. New Zealand enjoyed batting practice as the game ended, as it had threatened to do for the last four days, in a draw.

NEW ZEALAND					
M.H.W.Papps	b Nel	22	c Prince b Steyn		20
P.G.Fulton	c Boucher b Steyn	36	c Kallis b Ntini		11
S.P.Fleming*	b Prince	262			
S.B.Styris	c Dippenaar b Ntini	11	(3) not out		54
N.J.Astle	lbw b Ntini	50	(4) c Smith b Kallis		14
J.D.P.Oram	run out	13	(5) not out		8
B.B.McCullum†	lbw b Ntini	5			
D.L.Vettori	c Nel b Ntini	11			
J.E.C.Franklin	not out	122			
J.S.Patel	not out	27			
C.S.Martin					
Extras	(b 3, lb 15, w 1, nb 15)	34	(b 1, lb 9, nb 4)		14
TOTAL	(165 overs) (8 wkts dec)	**593**	(37 overs) (3 wkts)		**121**

SOUTH AFRICA		
G.C.Smith*	c & b Patel	25
H.H.Dippenaar	b Patel	47
H.M.Amla	lbw b Vettori	149
J.H.Kallis	c Martin b Oram	71
A.G.Prince	not out	108
A.B.de Villiers	c Papps b Patel	13
M.V.Boucher†	c Fleming b Franklin	33
N.Boje	lbw b Franklin	0
A.Nel	lbw b Franklin	12
D.W.Steyn	st McCullum b Vettori	13
M.Ntini	run out	11
Extras	(b 15, lb 10, nb 5)	30
TOTAL	(188 overs)	**512**

Bowling	O	M	R	W	O	M	R	W
SOUTH AFRICA								
Ntini	43	5	162	4	8	2	25	1
Steyn	31	4	114	1	9	3	26	1
Nel	27	3	98	1	10	2	41	0
Kallis	15	4	45	0	5	3	5	1
Boje	29	4	89	0	5	1	14	0
Smith	17	2	61	0				
Amla	1	0	4	0				
Prince	2	0	2	1				
NEW ZEALAND								
Martin	20	7	62	0				
Franklin	33	5	95	3				
Vettori	63	10	147	2				
Patel	42	8	117	3				
Styris	10	2	33	0				
Oram	18	10	24	1				
Astle	2	0	9	0				

Fall of Wickets	NZ 1st	SA 1st	NZ 2nd
1st	50	36	34
2nd	62	108	41
3rd	82	252	81
4th	188	344	-
5th	237	361	-
6th	259	435	-
7th	279	435	-
8th	535	462	-
9th	-	495	-
10th	-	512	-

MILESTONES

- Jeetan Patel (233) made his test debut.

- Stephen Fleming became the first New Zealander to score three test double-centuries.

- Fleming and James Franklin shared a partnership of 256, the best for any wicket for New Zealand against South Africa.

- New Zealand's 593 was its highest score in South Africa and its fourth-highest ever.

- James Franklin became only the fourth player to have taken a hat-trick and made a century in test cricket. The others were Johnny Briggs (England) and Wasim Akram and Abdul Razzaq (Pakistan).

By scoring 122 not out, James Franklin became only the fourth player in the history of test cricket to make a century as well as claim a hat-trick.

330 **SOUTH AFRICA v NEW ZEALAND** *(Third Test)*

at The Wanderers, Johannesburg on 5, 6, 7 May, 2006
Toss : South Africa. Umpires : E.A.R. de Silva & D.B. Hair
South Africa won by 4 wickets

By May winter had arrived in the Highveld so there was difficulty preparing the pitch. It took twice the normal time, with the last two days' preparation taking place under an artificially heated tent.

The player who had tormented New Zealand most, Makhaya Ntini, thrived on a pitch conducive to his pace and bounce as he captured five wickets in an innings for the third time in five innings. Asked to bat first the New Zealand scoreboard made frightening reading when Jamie How, Michael Papps and Scott Styris were all dismissed by the time the score was 2 and only Stephen Fleming, drawing on

his vast experience, managed to survive the appalling conditions.

New Zealand's total of 119 was overtaken by South Africa before the end of the first day when they finished at 133-4. A stunning partnership between the two left-hand batsmen Graeme Smith (60) and Hashim Amla (56) added 98 for the second wicket.

Apart from a swashbuckling 32 not out by Shaun Pollock these three were the only South African players to reach double figures as the home team lost their last eight wickets for 53 runs. Chris Martin and James Franklin made batting far from enjoyable.

New Zealand's second turn at bat was notable for greater application and production of runs via the generosity of the South African fieldsmen who dropped three catches off Ntini. When stumps were drawn New Zealand were 214-6 which meant that 26 wickets had fallen in two days.

Daniel Vettori showed great courage in getting behind each delivery and defiantly ground out 60 runs. Dale Steyn, whose pace unsettled the majority of the batsmen, finished with four wickets, giving him 16 in the series, four behind Ntini's 20.

Smith reached a half-century for the second time in the game to lead his team to a four wicket victory and the series win 2-0. During their extended season South Africa had played nine tests and 23 one-day internationals in six months.

NEW ZEALAND					
M.H.W.Papps	b Ntini	0	c Hall b Kallis		15
J.M.How	c de Villiers b Steyn	0	lbw b Steyn		4
S.P.Fleming*	c Boucher b Ntini	46	c de Villiers b Kallis		37
S.B.Styris	c de Villiers b Ntini	0	c & b Steyn		42
N.J.Astle	c Kallis b Steyn	20	c Boucher b Steyn		45
J.D.P.Oram	lbw b Pollock	18	c Dippenaar b Steyn		27
B.B.McCullum†	c & b Ntini	0	c Boucher b Pollock		5
D.L.Vettori	lbw b Steyn	2	c de Villiers b Hall		60
J.E.C.Franklin	c Boucher b Hall	19	b Pollock		19
K.D.Mills	not out	0	not out		0
C.S.Martin	c Smith b Ntini	1	c Amla b Hall		0
Extras	(lb 9, w 1, nb 3)	13	(b 5, lb 17, w 3, nb 4)		29
TOTAL	**(44 overs)**	**119**	**(78.5 overs)**		**283**

SOUTH AFRICA					
G.C.Smith*	c McCullum b Franklin	63	c McCullum b Franklin		68
H.H.Dippenaar	b Martin	0	c McCullum b Martin		37
H.M.Amla	c Papps b Styris	56	b Mills		28
J.H.Kallis	b Martin	9	c How b Mills		13
A.G.Prince	c McCullum b Martin	4	not out		43
A.B.de Villiers	c Styris b Franklin	2	b Franklin		5
M.V.Boucher†	lbw b Franklin	0	b Franklin		6
S.M.Pollock	not out	32	not out		6
A.J.Hall	lbw b Martin	5			
D.W.Steyn	b Martin	2			
M.Ntini	c McCullum b Mills	8			
Extras	(nb 5)	5	(b 4, lb 5, w 2, nb 3)		14
TOTAL	**(44 overs)**	**186**	**(47.3 overs) (6 wkts)**		**220**

Bowling	O	M	R	W	O	M	R	W
SOUTH AFRICA								
Ntini	16	7	35	5	17	4	44	0
Steyn	12	3	43	3	22	3	91	4
Hall	9	2	21	1	12.5	1	50	2
Pollock	7	2	11	1	13	3	36	2
Kallis					14	1	40	2
NEW ZEALAND								
Martin	15	2	37	5	17	1	64	1
Franklin	13	2	87	3	13.3	0	67	3
Oram	4	0	20	0	2	0	8	0
Mills	8	0	30	1	11	3	49	2
Astle	2	0	11	0				
Styris	2	1	1	1	3	0	12	0
Vettori					1	0	11	0

Fall of Wickets	NZ	SA	NZ	SA
	1st	1st	2nd	2nd
1st	0	1	9	69
2nd	0	99	40	130
3rd	2	131	82	156
4th	57	131	158	167
5th	78	139	177	180
6th	78	139	190	202
7th	82	139	239	-
8th	118	145	283	-
9th	118	161	283	-
10th	119	186	283	-

Brendon McCullum had a trying time behind the stumps because of the indifferent nature of the pitch. He claimed five catches in the course of the game.

AVERAGES

New Zealand

BATTING	M	I	NO	Runs	HS	Ave
S.P. Fleming	3	5	0	351	262	70.20
J.E.C. Franklin	3	5	2	168	122*	56.00
J.D.P. Oram	3	6	1	201	133	40.20
D.L. Vettori	3	5	0	192	81	38.40
S.B. Styris	3	6	1	126	54*	25.20
N.J. Astle	3	6	0	135	50	22.50
P.G. Fulton	2	4	0	65	36	16.25
H.J.H. Marshall	1	2	0	31	25	15.50
B.B. McCullum	3	5	0	74	33	14.80
M.H.W. Papps	2	4	0	57	22	14.25
K.D. Mills	2	4	2	12	12	6.00
J.M. How	1	2	0	4	4	2.00
C.S. Martin	3	4	1	2	1*	0.66
J.S. Patel	1	1	1	27	27*	-

BOWLING	O	M	R	W	Ave
K.D. Mills	58	15	179	8	22.37
S.B. Styris	17	3	49	2	24.50
J.E.C. Franklin	91.3	12	384	15	25.60
C.S. Martin	98.4	20	293	9	32.55
J.S. Patel	42	8	117	3	39.00
J.D.P. Oram	55	20	123	3	41.00
N.J. Astle	14	3	46	1	46.00
D.L. Vettori	97.1	12	244	4	61.00

South Africa

BATTING	M	I	NO	Runs	HS	Ave
H.M. Amla	2	3	0	233	149	77.66
A.G. Prince	3	5	2	175	108*	58.33
G.C. Smith	3	5	0	208	68	41.60
J.H. Kallis	3	5	0	193	71	38.60
S.M. Pollock	2	4	2	72	32*	36.00
H.H. Dippenaar	3	5	0	152	52	30.40
A.B. de Villiers	3	5	0	144	97	28.80
N. Boje	2	3	0	54	31	18.00
M.V. Boucher	3	5	0	78	33	15.60
M. Ntini	3	4	1	36	16	12.00
A. Nel	1	1	0	12	12	12.00
D.W. Steyn	3	4	1	35	13	11.66
A.J. Hall	1	1	0	5	5	5.00
H.H. Gibbs	1	2	0	8	6	4.00

BOWLING	O	M	R	W	Ave
A.G. Prince	2	0	2	1	2.00
M. Ntini	117	23	411	20	20.55
S.M. Pollock	40	10	112	5	22.40
A.J. Hall	21.5	3	71	3	23.66
D.W. Steyn	109.4	18	416	16	26.00
J.H. Kallis	43	9	131	4	32.75
A. Nel	37	5	139	1	139.00
H.M. Amla	1	0	4	0	-
G.C. Smith	20	3	72	0	-
N. Boje	41	5	132	0	-

MILESTONES

- Jacques Kallis became the second player in test cricket to score 8000 runs and take 200 wickets. The first was Sir Garfield Sobers.

- Chris Martin claimed his seventh five-wicket bag.

2006/07 Sri Lanka in New Zealand

331   **NEW ZEALAND v SRI LANKA** *(First Test)*

at Jade Stadium, Christchurch on 7, 8, 9 December, 2006
Toss : Sri Lanka. Umpires : S.J.A. Taufel & B.G. Jerling
New Zealand won by 5 wickets

Sri Lanka's captain, Mahela Jayawardene, completely misread the conditions of a juicy, well-grassed and less than rock-hard pitch when he decided to bat first.

The four New Zealand pace bowlers all revelled in the helpful conditions. Shane Bond's pace accounted for the first three wickets in his first six overs before James Franklin captured the next three wickets. Chris Martin and Jacob Oram finished off the lower order with two wickets apiece.

Sharp catching made it an impressive all-round team performance by the home side. Craig Cumming and Mathew Sinclair coped with the conditions better than the visitors, in adding 70 for the second wicket, to leave New Zealand, chasing 154, in a sound position of 85-2 at stumps.

The New Zealand score was taken to 106-2 before the now to be expected collapse occurred and four wickets fell in the space of seven runs. The experience of Stephen Fleming and the innovative skills of Daniel Vettori added 75 and took New Zealand to a first innings lead of 52.

Sri Lanka lost five wickets before edging in front. Bond again created havoc amongst the batsmen apart from Kumar Sangakkara who exhibited a cast-iron defence augmented by shots, particularly the cut, of exquisite excellence.

His one-man resistance continued on the third day when he took his overnight score of 63 to an unbeaten 100 as he added 71 runs with Lasith Malinga and Muralitharan. The innings ended in a bizarre fashion when Muralitharan left his crease after running from the non-striker's end for a single to complete Sangakkara's 11th test century.

The return came to Brendon McCullum who broke the stumps with Muralitharan walking up the track to congratulate his partner. It was the third run-out of the innings.

New Zealand's task of reaching 119 was aided considerably when Cumming was twice caught off no-balls. They reached 58-0 but then four wickets tumbled for 10 runs. The game finished in a flurry with McCullum hitting 14 off nine balls.

SRI LANKA

Batsman	dismissal	R	dismissal	R
W.U.Tharanga	c How b Franklin	33	c Fleming b Bond	24
S.T.Jayasuriya	c Fleming b Bond	5	run out	10
K.C.Sangakkara	c Sinclair b Bond	4	not out	100
D.P.M.D.Jayawardene*	c Franklin b Bond	8	c Fleming b Franklin	0
C.K.Kapugedera	lbw b Franklin	37	c Oram b Bond	1
L.P.C.Silva	b Franklin	0	c Vettori b Bond	0
H.A.P.W.Jayawardene†	c How b Martin	7	run out	11
W.P.J.U.C.Vaas	c McCullum b Oram	4	c McCullum b Oram	0
M.F.Maharoof	c Fleming b Oram	15	c McCullum b Bond	7
S.L.Malinga	not out	7	c McCullum b Franklin	0
M.Muralitharan	c Astle b Martin	14	run out	8
Extras	(lb 13, w 1, nb 6)	20	(lb 5, nb 4)	9
TOTAL	**(52.4 overs)**	**154**	**(53.1 overs)**	**170**

NEW ZEALAND

Batsman	dismissal	R	dismissal	R
C.D.Cumming	b Muralitharan	43	c Jayawardene H.A.P.W. b Vaas	43
J.M.How	lbw b Malinga	0	lbw b Muralitharan	11
M.S.Sinclair	c Jayawardene H.A.P.W. b Vaas	36	c Sangakkara b Muralitharan	4
S.P.Fleming*	c Kapugedera b Maharoof	48	lbw b Vaas	0
N.J.Astle	lbw b Muralitharan	2	lbw b Muralitharan	24
J.D.P.Oram	c Silva b Vaas	1	not out	12
B.B.McCullum†	b Vaas	0	not out	14
D.L.Vettori	c Jayawardene D.P.M.D. b Malinga	63		
J.E.C.Franklin	lbw b Muralitharan	0		
S.E.Bond	lbw b Muralitharan	1		
C.S.Martin	not out	0		
Extras	(lb 5, nb 7)	12	(b 1, lb 1, w 5, nb 4)	11
TOTAL	**(85.4 overs)**	**206**	**(33 overs) (5 wkts)**	**119**

Bowling NEW ZEALAND	O	M	R	W	O	M	R	W
Bond	13	2	43	3	19.1	5	63	4
Martin	16.4	2	37	2	11	2	38	0
Franklin	12	0	30	3	13	1	34	2
Oram	10	5	30	2	7	1	19	1
Astle	1	0	1	0	1	0	1	0
Vettori					2	0	10	0
SRI LANKA								
Vaas	18	4	49	3	12	3	33	2
Malinga	19.4	2	43	2	4	1	35	0
Maharoof	14	3	44	1	3	0	15	0
Muralitharan	34	7	65	4	14	5	34	3

Fall of Wickets

	SL 1st	NZ 1st	SL 2nd	NZ 2nd
1st	11	3	18	58
2nd	17	73	44	66
3rd	37	106	45	66
4th	87	108	46	68
5th	87	113	46	103
6th	106	113	74	-
7th	110	188	80	-
8th	121	190	99	-
9th	132	206	143	-
10th	154	206	170	-

In icy conditions Craig Cumming was one of the few batsmen to score runs in both innings of the match. He made 43 in each innings.

MILESTONES

- It was New Zealand's 62nd test win and their first test victory at Christchurch for 12 years.

- Chris Martin, playing his 32nd test, became the 11th New Zealand bowler to claim 100 test wickets.

- Kumar Sangakkara scored 100 out of Sri Lanka's 170, the second-lowest completed test innings to include a century. The lowest total was New Zealand's 159 against England in 1963 (test 60) when John Reid scored 100.

332 NEW ZEALAND v SRI LANKA *(Second Test)*

at Prime Finance Basin Reserve, Wellington on 15, 16, 17, 18 December, 2006
Toss : Sri Lanka. Umpires : S.J.A. Taufel & B.G. Jerling
Sri Lanka won by 217 runs

Learning from the first test Mahela Jayawardene had no hesitation about batting first. When he was the third batsman dismissed at 41, after a lively opening burst by Chris Martin, he would have thought that his nightmares were returning.

For the second time in six days Kumar Sangakkara was in a class of his own, displaying a wonderful repertoire of shots. Chamara Silva, with a pair on his test debut, ably assisted him to add 121 for the fifth wicket. Sangakkara cruised to his second unbeaten century, 156 not out, in consecutive tests.

In favourable batting conditions New Zealand ended the first day at 66-4, in reply to Sri Lanka's 268, after a fearsome bombardment from Lasith Malinga, whose round-arm slingers threatened toes and heads from his unusual catapult action.

In overcast conditions Brendon McCullum was the only batsman to combat Malinga's barrage and he had bruises to his hand, heel and shoulder to prove his bravery. Muralitharan so bamboozled the batsmen that Jacob Oram, James Franklin and Shane Bond fell consecutively lbw. With a substantial lead of 138 Sri Lanka ended the second day at 225-5 with Silva and Prasanna Jayawardene looking totally at ease.

Silva could not be contained as he used his feet effectively to drive with a commanding flourish, while working the ball off his hips with contempt. Daniel Vettori's accuracy, control of length and variation of pace saw him claim the last three wickets off four balls and finish with seven wickets in the innings to become the first slow-bowler to capture 10 wickets in a test match at the Basin Reserve.

Chasing 502 New Zealand reached a respectable 286 thanks to Vettori's 51, while Muralitharan joined Vettori in claiming 10 wickets in the game.

There were 10 lbws in the 17 wickets that Muralitharan captured in the two tests, which illustrated that the local batsmen never solved his "doosra". It was to be 333 days before New Zealand played their next test.

MILESTONES

- Daniel Vettori took 10-180, the first time in 46 tests at the Basin Reserve that a spinner had taken 10 wickets in a match. Muttiah Muralitharan repeated the feat with 10-118.

- Chamara Silva became the first batsman to score a pair in his first test and make a century in his next.

- It was to be Stephen Fleming's 80th and last test as captain. He had 28 wins, 27 losses and 25 draws.

- Both sides used two wicketkeepers during the game. Mathew Sinclair and Brendon McCullum for New Zealand; Prasanna Jayawardene and Kumar Sangakkara for Sri Lanka. All four wicketkeepers took a catch.

SRI LANKA

Batsman	First innings	Runs	Second innings	Runs
W.U.Tharanga	c McCullum b Martin	7	lbw b Martin	20
S.T.Jayasuriya	c Fleming b Martin	0	c Fleming b Vettori	31
K.C.Sangakkara†	not out	156	c Franklin b Bond	8
D.P.M.D.Jayawardene*	b Martin	0	c Sinclair b Vettori	31
C.K.Kapugedera	c Sinclair b Oram	5	b Vettori	27
L.P.C.Silva	c Fleming b Franklin	61	not out	152
H.A.P.W.Jayawardene†	lbw b Vettori	25	c sub (S.M.Mills) b Martin	37
W.P.J.U.C.Vaas	c McCullum b Bond	0	c McCullum b Vettori	47
M.F.Maharoof	c McCullum b Vettori	4	lbw b Vettori	1
S.L.Malinga	c Sinclair b Vettori	0	lbw b Vettori	0
M.Muralitharan	c & b Bond	0	st McCullum b Vettori	0
Extras	(b 1, lb 1, nb 8)	10	(lb 7, nb 4)	11
TOTAL	**(65 overs)**	**268**	**(109.3 overs)**	**365**

NEW ZEALAND

Batsman	First innings	Runs	Second innings	Runs
C.D.Cumming	b Maharoof	13	c Sangakkara b Muralitharan	20
J.M.How	lbw b Malinga	26	lbw b Malinga	33
M.S.Sinclair	b Malinga	6	c Jayawardene D.P.M.D. b Muralitharan	37
S.P.Fleming*	c Jayawardene H.A.P.W. b Malinga	0	c Sangakkara b Malinga	27
N.J.Astle	lbw b Malinga	17	lbw b Muralitharan	9
B.B.McCullum†	b Muralitharan	43	b Muralitharan	17
D.L.Vettori	b Malinga	0	(3) lbw b Muralitharan	51
J.D.P.Oram	lbw b Muralitharan	1	(7) lbw b Vaas	4
J.E.C.Franklin	lbw b Muralitharan	1	c Silva b Muralitharan	44
S.E.Bond	lbw b Muralitharan	8	c Sangakkara b Maharoof	6
C.S.Martin	not out	0	not out	4
Extras	(b 7, lb 6, nb 2)	15	(b 9, lb 7, w 11, nb 7)	34
TOTAL	**(39.1 overs)**	**130**	**(85.1 overs)**	**286**

Bowling	O	M	R	W	O	M	R	W
NEW ZEALAND								
Bond	16	1	85	2	19	3	67	1
Martin	13	2	50	3	23	1	98	2
Franklin	12	2	46	1	25	8	63	0
Oram	3	0	10	1				
Vettori	14	1	53	3	42.3	6	130	7
Astle	7	2	22	0				
SRI LANKA								
Vaas	4	0	8	0	18	2	64	1
Malinga	18	4	68	5	16	1	62	2
Maharoof	5	2	10	1	11	1	47	1
Muralitharan	12.1	3	31	4	34.1	9	87	6
Jayasuriya					6	3	10	0

Fall of Wickets	SL 1st	NZ 1st	SL 2nd	NZ 2nd
1st	0	30	44	56
2nd	27	40	62	60
3rd	41	40	62	115
4th	81	66	100	139
5th	202	75	168	156
6th	239	85	262	161
7th	240	90	350	163
8th	251	98	356	259
9th	259	116	365	278
10th	268	130	365	286

The ever-improving Jamie How looked as though he might be part of the solution to New Zealand's on-going problem with their opening batsmen. Further to his credit was his ability to field expertly in any position.

2007/08 New Zealand in South Africa

A non-stop diet of one-day cricket for the previous year, the retirement of several vastly experienced test players, the replacement of Stephen Fleming as captain by Daniel Vettori, two warm-up games of an ordinary nature and two test pitches with sub-standard surfaces looked like a recipe for an absolute disaster, and so it turned out.

333 **SOUTH AFRICA v NEW ZEALAND** *(First Test)*
at Wanderers Stadium, Johannesburg on 8, 9, 10, 11 November, 2007
Toss : South Africa. Umpires : M.R. Benson & D.J. Harper
South Africa won by 358 runs

New Zealand's attack performed admirably on the first day, supported by smart fielding and reliable catching, dismissing the home side for 226 an hour after tea on the first day. Craig Cumming and Michael Papps became the seventh different opening partnership in New Zealand's last 10 tests but both were gone before stumps with the score at 40-2.

The pace and outswing of Dale Steyn and the combative aggression of Makhaya Ntini tore through the under-prepared visiting batsmen within 42 overs, giving South Africa a lead of 108. In the remaining 55 overs Hashim Amla and Jacques Kallis extended this to 287 for the loss of two wickets. Both batsmen steadily advanced towards their centuries.

The partnership flourished, reaching a record 320 runs for the third wicket, before Kallis was dismissed for 186. Amla, who had resurrected his test career 19 months earlier against New Zealand at Newlands, again showed his fondness for their bowling, being 176 not out after 8½ hours of watchful, correct batting.

During the day New Zealand used four substitute fieldsmen and coach John Bracewell was next in line. The declaration, made at 422-3, challenged New Zealand to make 531 and allowed South Africa time to bowl 91 overs. Neither target was reached as New Zealand capitulated to be all out with 40 overs remaining and still 358 runs in arrears.

After the test the South African captain, Graeme Smith, was outspoken about the poor quality of South African test pitches, particularly the insidious presence of variable bounce.

SOUTH AFRICA

G.C.Smith*	b Martin	1	(2) b Martin	9
H.H.Gibbs	c Fleming b Martin	63	(1) c Papps b Bond	8
H.M.Amla	c McCullum b Bond	12	not out	176
J.H.Kallis	c McCullum b O'Brien	29	c McCullum b Oram	186
A.G.Prince	c Fleming b Bond	1	not out	25
A.B.de Villiers	c Oram b Bond	33		
M.V.Boucher†	c Papps b Vettori	43		
A.Nel	c McCullum b Bond	15		
P.L.Harris	lbw b Vettori	3		
D.W.Steyn	c McCullum b Martin	13		
M.Ntini	not out	0		
Extras	(lb 6, w 1, nb 6)	13	(b 9, lb 7, w 1, nb 1)	18
TOTAL	(74.3 overs)	**226**	(126 overs) (3 wkts dec)	**422**

NEW ZEALAND

C.D.Cumming	lbw b Steyn	12	c Smith b Steyn	7
M.H.W.Papps	c de Villiers b Ntini	2	(7) c de Villiers b Kallis	5
S.P.Fleming	c de Villiers b Ntini	40	(2) c Smith b Nel	17
S.E.Bond	b Steyn	1	absent hurt	
S.B.Styris	c Smith b Kallis	11	(3) c Boucher b Steyn	16
L.R.P.L.Taylor	c Gibbs b Kallis	15	(4) c Kallis b Nel	4
J.D.P.Oram	c Kallis b Steyn	1	(6) c Nel b Harris	40
B.B.McCullum†	lbw b Steyn	9	(5) c Gibbs b Steyn	26
D.L.Vettori*	c Harris b Ntini	7	(8) not out	46
I.E.O'Brien	not out	14	(9) c Amla b Steyn	0
C.S.Martin	c Harris b Steyn	0	(10) b Steyn	0
Extras	(lb 5, nb 1)	6	(b 7, lb 1, w 2, nb 1)	11
TOTAL	(41.3 overs)	**118**	(51 overs)	**172**

Bowling	O	M	R	W	O	M	R	W		Fall of Wickets			
NEW ZEALAND										SA	NZ	SA	NZ
										1st	*1st*	*2nd*	*2nd*
Bond	17	1	73	4	16	1	60	1					
Martin	17.3	3	67	3	24	6	55	1	1st	1	16	8	12
Oram	12	3	31	0	16.4	2	49	1	2nd	20	40	20	34
O'Brien	10	4	23	1	23	5	91	0	3rd	73	54	350	39
Vettori	18	6	26	2	37	3	116	0	4th	92	64	-	60
Styris					6	2	25	0	5th	141	83	-	90
Taylor					3.2	0	10	0	6th	162	84	-	109
SOUTH AFRICA									7th	182	88	-	154
Steyn	14.3	3	34	5	17	1	59	5	8th	195	102	-	170
Ntini	14	3	47	3	13	0	42	0	9th	219	118	-	172
Nel	9	1	21	0	12	1	37	2	10th	226	118	-	-
Kallis	4	0	11	2	3	0	15	1					
Harris					6	2	11	1					

MILESTONES

- Daniel Vettori became the 26th captain of New Zealand. He was playing his 74th test match.

- Ross Taylor (234) made his test debut.

- Hashim Amla and Jacques Kallis put on 320, a record partnership for the third wicket for South Africa against New Zealand.

- New Zealand's loss by 358 runs was its heaviest defeat in test cricket, in terms of runs.

- Similarly, it was South Africa's biggest victory.

- Dale Steyn took his first bag of 10 wickets in a game and had five wickets in each innings.

Daniel Vettori, who became New Zealand's 26th test captain, had every right to look pensive as his under-prepared team was beaten comprehensively.

334 **SOUTH AFRICA v NEW ZEALAND** *(Second Test)*

at SuperSport Park, Centurion on 16, 17, 18 November, 2007
Toss : New Zealand. Umpires : M.R. Benson & D.J. Harper
South Africa won by an innings and 59 runs

Shane Bond flew back to New Zealand with an abdominal strain while Jacob Oram had a hamstring strain.

Winning the toss and batting first, New Zealand's batsmen were guilty of poor shot selection and execution that saw them taken from the field shortly after tea because of bad light at 187-8. Craig Cumming, who saw New Zealand reach 101 for the loss of two wickets, was struck and felled by a fiery delivery from Dale Steyn.

He was operated on that night for a depressed fracture of the cheekbone and broken jaw. Cumming, a diabetic, was kept in the intensive ward for the evening for observation. He took no further part in the tour.

Martin bowled both South African openers with the score at 31-2 before Jacques Kallis and Hashim Amla again humbled their opponents, this time adding 220. Mark Gillespie was rewarded for a resolute spell of right-arm fast-medium bowling, taking five wickets on debut.

Mark Gillespie became the fifth New Zealand bowler to take five wickets on his test debut.

This was not only instrumental in dismissing South Africa for 383 but also for stalling their progress when New Zealand were, in boxing parlance, down and out. A slogging partnership between André Nel and Steyn saw 51 added for the ninth wicket off 11 overs.

New Zealand were again putty in the hands of Steyn, who took 6-49 and demolished the visitors in 34.3 overs. Apart from a brief encounter worth 60 between Stephen Fleming, who scored his team's only half-century in the two tests, and Scott Styris none of the batting was of test quality.

The game was completed within three days. South Africa won by an innings and 59, thus winning the series 2-0.

NEW ZEALAND

Batsman	1st dismissal	1st	2nd dismissal	2nd
C.D.Cumming	retired hurt	48	absent hurt	
M.H.W.Papps	c Gibbs b Ntini	9	lbw b Steyn	1
L.Vincent	c Harris b Steyn	33	(1) lbw b Steyn	4
S.P.Fleming	c Prince b Kallis	43	(3) lbw b Steyn	54
S.B.Styris	lbw b Steyn	3	(4) c de Villiers b Kallis	29
L.R.P.L.Taylor	c Prince b Nel	17	(5) run out	8
B.B.McCullum†	c de Villiers b Nel	13	(6) c Smith b Steyn	21
D.L.Vettori*	not out	17	(7) c de Villiers b Ntini	8
M.R.Gillespie	lbw b Steyn	0	(8) c Kallis b Steyn	0
I.E.O'Brien	c Gibbs b Steyn	0	(9) b Steyn	0
C.S.Martin	c Kallis b Ntini	0	(10) not out	0
Extras	(lb 2, nb 3)	5	(b 1, lb 9, nb 1)	11
TOTAL	(56.4 overs)	188	(34.3 overs)	136

SOUTH AFRICA

Batsman	Dismissal	Runs
G.C.Smith*	b Martin	2
H.H.Gibbs	b Martin	25
H.M.Amla	c Papps b O'Brien	103
J.H.Kallis	lbw b Gillespie	131
A.G.Prince	c sub (J.M.How) b Gillespie	13
A.B.de Villiers	c McCullum b Gillespie	33
M.V.Boucher†	b Gillespie	1
P.L.Harris	c McCullum b Gillespie	0
A.Nel	lbw b Vettori	25
D.W.Steyn	c Papps b O'Brien	25
M.Ntini	not out	0
Extras	(b 6, lb 4, w 2, nb 13)	25
TOTAL	(97.3 overs)	383

Bowling	O	M	R	W	O	M	R	W
SOUTH AFRICA								
Steyn	14	5	42	4	10.3	1	49	6
Ntini	15.4	4	52	2	12	4	39	1
Kallis	11	2	35	1	5	2	18	1
Nel	13	3	42	2	7	2	20	0
Harris	3	0	15	0				
NEW ZEALAND								
Martin	22	6	81	2				
Gillespie	30	7	136	5				
O'Brien	21.3	6	78	2				
Vettori	20	2	61	1				
Styris	4	0	17	0				

Fall of Wickets	NZ 1st	SA 1st	NZ 2nd
1st	26	2	4
2nd	88	31	9
3rd	105	251	69
4th	147	282	78
5th	165	312	117
6th	184	325	128
7th	187	332	128
8th	187	332	136
9th	188	383	136
10th	-	383	-

MILESTONES

- Mark Gillespie (235) made his test debut.

- Jacques Kallis and Hashim Amla became the fourth pair in test history to share three consecutive stands of over 150. Their partnerships were 170 against Pakistan in October and 320 and 220 against New Zealand.

- Dale Steyn became the first South African bowler to take 10 wickets in a game twice in one test series.

- Mark Gillespie became the fifth New Zealand bowler to take five wickets on test debut. The others were Fen Creswell (1949), Alec Moir (1950/51), Bruce Taylor (1964/65) and Paul Wiseman (1997/98).

- New Zealand were still to win a series against South Africa.

2007/08 Bangladesh in New Zealand

The University Oval in Dunedin became the 95th test venue. In the six weeks leading up to the game the ground and its condition made more headlines than any of the players. The Kakanui clay pitch was a drier surface that was not overly bouncy or conducive to seam bowling.

335 NEW ZEALAND v BANGLADESH *(First Test)*

at University Oval, Dunedin on 4, 5, 6 January, 2008
Toss : New Zealand. Umpires : P.D. Parker & N.J. Llong
New Zealand won by 9 wickets

Tamim Iqbal, making his test debut, was severe on Kyle Mills and dispatched loose balls to the boundary with the panache of a veteran. The inability of the visitors' batsmen to concentrate for more than an hour was apparent as wickets fell more by bad batting than by excellent bowling. They were dismissed after 46.1 overs for a disappointing 137.

There was time on the first day for Matthew Bell, who had last opened for New Zealand against Australia at Bellerive Oval in 2002, to make a substantial score in his comeback test for New Zealand.

From his overnight score of 74 not out he reached his second test century off 175 balls and cast off his normally undemonstrative demeanour with a series of exuberant leaps. Jacob Oram converted his overnight score of 17 into his fourth test century, adding 139 with Bell.

The last four wickets fell for 37 runs to a lively spell of right-arm, fast-medium bowling by Mashrafe bin Mortaza. Chris Martin, in his 49th test innings, reached double figures for the first time and played a cover drive for four that will undoubtedly be the batting highlight of his career.

Facing a deficit of 218, Tamim and fellow debutant Zunaed Siddique created a new record opening partnership of 161 scored at an Australian-like pace of 3.66 runs per over. When the partnership was broken the remaining nine wickets became a replay of the first innings, with batsmen coming and going, and they were toppled for 93 runs. Daniel Vettori rounded off a good all-round game, taking four wickets and leading New Zealand to their first victory under his captaincy.

Matthew Bell scored 107 in his comeback test, having last played for New Zealand 45 tests previously.

BANGLADESH

Batsman	1st innings		2nd innings	
Tamim Iqbal	c Fulton b Martin	53	b Mills	84
Zunaed Siddique	c Fleming b Martin	1	c Fleming b Martin	74
Habibul Bashar	c McCullum b Martin	23	c Sinclair b Oram	11
Mohammad Ashraful*	lbw b Martin	0	c Cumming b O'Brien	23
Shahriar Nafees	b Vettori	16	lbw b Vettori	28
Aftab Ahmed	b Oram	0	c Bell b O'Brien	0
Mushfiqur Rahim†	c Bell b Mills	7	lbw b Vettori	6
Mashrafe bin Mortaza	b Oram	22	c McCullum b Vettori	10
Shahadat Hossain	c McCullum b Oram	0	(10) lbw b Vettori	0
Enamul Haque	not out	2	(9) not out	6
Sajedul Islam	c McCullum b Mills	4	c McCullum b Martin	1
Extras	(b 1, lb 2, w 3, nb 3)	9	(lb 4, nb 7)	11
TOTAL	**(46.1 overs)**	**137**	**(83.1 overs)**	**254**

NEW ZEALAND

Batsman	1st innings		2nd innings	
C.D.Cumming	lbw b Sajedul	1	(2) lbw b Mortaza	4
M.D.Bell	lbw b Ashraful	107	(1) not out	20
P.G.Fulton	b Shahadat	14	not out	15
S.P.Fleming	c Mushfiqur b Sajedul	14		
M.S.Sinclair	lbw b Mortaza	29		
J.D.P.Oram	b Mortaza	117		
B.B.McCullum†	c Zunaed b Ashraful	7		
D.L.Vettori*	c Enamul b Shahadat	32		
K.D.Mills	c Mushfiqur b Mortaza	0		
I.E.O'Brien	c Mushfiqur b Mortaza	5		
C.S.Martin	not out	12		
Extras	(b 4, lb 10, w 2, nb 3)	19		
TOTAL	**(91 overs)**	**357**	**(8.1 overs) (1 wkt)**	**39**

Bowling								
NEW ZEALAND	O	M	R	W	O	M	R	W
Martin	13	1	64	4	20.1	6	56	2
Mills	7.1	1	29	2	12	1	54	1
Oram	13	4	23	3	12	5	21	1
O'Brien	7	2	10	0	15	2	49	2
Vettori	6	2	8	1	24	6	70	4
BANGLADESH								
Shahadat	18	0	95	2	1	0	6	0
Sajedul	19	2	71	2	3	1	13	0
Mortaza	23	3	74	4	4	0	14	1
Enamul	22	4	57	0				
Ashraful	9	0	46	2	0.1	0	6	0

Fall of Wickets		B	NZ	B	NZ
		1st	1st	2nd	2nd
1st		5	5	161	13
2nd		43	31	167	-
3rd		47	58	179	-
4th		82	121	205	-
5th		98	260	205	-
6th		100	270	222	-
7th		129	320	232	-
8th		129	320	252	-
9th		133	340	252	-
10th		137	357	254	-

MILESTONES

- It was New Zealand's 63rd test win.

- It was Bangladesh's 50th test match, and 44th loss.

- University Oval became the 95th test venue and the seventh in New Zealand.

- Tamin Iqbal and Zunaed Siddique put on 161, a record first wicket partnership for Bangladesh against all countries.

336 NEW ZEALAND v BANGLADESH *(Second Test)*

at Allied Prime Basin Reserve, Wellington on 12, 13, 14 January, 2008
Toss : New Zealand. Umpires : P.D. Parker & N.J. Llong
New Zealand won by an innings and 137 runs

The pitch at the Basin Reserve was, as to be expected, fast with good carry and ideal for test cricket. Once again the five-day match was almost assured of an early finish when Bangladesh's first innings was completed in under 200 minutes.

For the fourth time in the eight tests he had played at the Basin Reserve Chris Martin captured five wickets in an innings. His success in the first innings, with his pace, bounce and movement off the seam into the right-hand batsmen, was an interrogation of the highest class. Iain O'Brien enjoyed playing on his home ground, even though he was given the task of bowling into a strong breeze.

Stephen Fleming, who publicly said that he was determined to score a test hundred on the ground where he had played 16 tests, was 39 not out at stumps and well positioned to carry out his wish.

The second day began with Mathew Sinclair being dropped

three times in making 47. For the rest of the New Zealand innings of 393, dropped catches were more frequent than ambulance sirens are around the ground. Fleming's wish did not come true, even though he was given an easy life, on 61, before departing 13 runs short of his desire.

Daniel Vettori, in the midst of having an excellent run as a test batsman, scored 94 at better than a-run-a-ball pace. Although there was time for only 22 overs to be bowled at the end of the second day all four New Zealand bowlers took a wicket as Bangladesh disintegrated to be 51-5.

Because of a broken thumb, Tamim Iqbal did not bat and Bangladesh lost their last four wickets for 62. New Zealand won by an innings and 137. It had been a lacklustre series of only moderate cricket. New Zealand won the series 2-0.

Under the gaze of his captain, Daniel Vettori, Iain O'Brien appeared to revel in bowling into a strong breeze.

BANGLADESH

Tamim Iqbal	c Sinclair b Mills	15	absent hurt		
Zunaed Siddique	c Bell b Martin	13	c McCullum b Mills		2
Habibul Bashar	c McCullum b Martin	1	lbw b Martin		25
Mohammad Ashraful*	c McCullum b O'Brien	35	c Fleming b Mills		1
Shahriar Nafees	c Fulton b O'Brien	6	(1) c Bell b Martin		12
Aftab Ahmed	not out	25	(5) c Fleming b O'Brien		5
Mushfiqur Rahim†	lbw b Martin	8	(6) c Bell b Oram		0
Shakib Al Hasan	c Fulton b Martin	5	(7) not out		41
Shahadat Hossain	c McCullum b O'Brien	1	(8) c McCullum b O'Brien		5
Sajedul Islam	c Fleming b Martin	6	(9) run out		3
Mashrafe bin Mortaza	c Bell b Vettori	15	(10) c Mills b Oram		6
Extras	(b 2, lb 11)	13	(b 2, w 5, nb 6)		13
TOTAL	**(45.3 overs)**	**143**	**(47 overs)**		**113**

NEW ZEALAND

C.D.Cumming	lbw b Shakib	42
M.D.Bell	c Mushfiqur b Sajedul	1
P.G.Fulton	lbw b Mortaza	22
S.P.Fleming	c Aftab b Shakib	87
M.S.Sinclair	c Mushfiqur b Shahadat	47
J.D.P.Oram	c Mushfiqur b Shahadat	1
B.B.McCullum†	c Shakib b Shahadat	40
D.L.Vettori*	c & b Aftab	94
K.D.Mills	b Mortaza	4
I.E.O'Brien	b Aftab	4
C.S.Martin	not out	0
Extras	(b 5, lb 23, w 10, nb 13)	51
TOTAL	**(103.2 overs)**	**393**

Bowling NEW ZEALAND	O	M	R	W	O	M	R	W	Fall of Wickets			
										B	NZ	B
										1st	*1st*	*2nd*
Martin	16	3	65	5	13	1	35	2	1st	17	2	10
Mills	9	3	19	1	11	4	29	2	2nd	18	35	14
O'Brien	15	7	34	3	11	2	23	2	3rd	49	118	30
Oram	3	2	2	0	11	3	21	2	4th	68	214	44
Vettori	2.3	0	10	1	1	0	3	0	5th	71	216	45
BANGLADESH									6th	86	244	56
Mortaza	29	5	100	2					7th	110	323	79
Sajedul	14	1	91	1					8th	111	362	83
Shahadat	27	4	83	3					9th	122	390	113
Aftab	12.2	4	31	2					10th	143	393	-
Shakib	19	7	44	2								
Ashraful	2	0	16	0								

MILESTONES

- It was New Zealand's 64th test win.

- Daniel Vettori passed 4000 first-class runs and captured his 400th first-class wicket.

- Habibul Bashar passed 3000 runs in test cricket, the first Bangladesh batsman to do so.

- Chris Martin, playing in his 37th test, became the sixth-highest wicket-taker for New Zealand. He passed Ewen Chatfield's tally of 123 wickets in 43 tests.

2007/08 England in New Zealand

Both sides went into the first encounter unprepared for the demands of test cricket, having played little first-class cricket in the last four months.

337 **NEW ZEALAND v ENGLAND** *(First Test)*
at Seddon Park, Hamilton on 5, 6, 7, 8, 9 March, 2008
Toss : New Zealand. Umpires : S.J. Davis & D.J Harper
New Zealand won by 189 runs

On a pitch that was hard, but devoid of bounce, Steve Harmison and Matthew Hoggard bowled one bad ball an over. Jamie How's bat got straighter as the game progressed and his forward defensive shot was transformed into sublime straight drives to the boundary.

On a slow pitch Stephen Fleming's timing was a thing of beauty. There had been much conjecture about Ross Taylor's inability to curb his aggressive tendencies and play straight. He silenced all critics by exercising discretion and batting as a perfect model from the MCC's coaching manual.

Towards the end of the day Brendon McCullum enlivened proceedings with 51 runs off 55 balls and New Zealand ended at 282-6 with Taylor 54 not out. Alastair Cook distinguished himself with three stunning catches.

Joyous stroke play by Daniel Vettori and Taylor delighted the large crowd from the outset of the second day. Ryan Sidebottom, so parsimonious on the first day, was attacked with drives, cuts and pulls as 148 were swiftly added. Taylor reached his first test century off 185 balls while Vettori's 88 ensured New Zealand a handsome total of 470.

England's reply took 173 overs and almost strangled the life out of the game. Six of the visiting batsmen batted for over two hours but the run-rate hovered at two runs per over. Had they matched New Zealand's run rate of 3.39 they would have ended with a lead of 116 instead of a deficit of 122.

The New Zealand bowlers collectively bowled accurately and in good channels on a batsmen's wicket, none more so than Jeetan Patel.

When the England innings ended after lunch on the fourth day the test looked doomed to be a draw. How and Fleming stroked their way effortlessly to 99 before the game was revitalised as six wickets fell in 14 overs. Ryan Sidebottom accomplished the hat-trick, capturing Fleming, Mathew Sinclair and Jacob Oram. New Zealand ended the day, where 12 wickets had fallen, at 147-8.

For the fifth successive day conditions were perfect. Vettori immediately attacked and 30 runs were added before he declared, leaving England a target of 300 to score on a benign pitch off 81 overs.

Kyle Mills decided the outcome of the test before lunch with a stunning spell of four wickets off 25 balls with the new ball. Later, with the old ball, Chris Martin snaffled three wickets, while Ian Bell was undefeated on 54 as England were all out for 110, having been routed by 189 runs.

NEW ZEALAND					
J.M.How	c Collingwood b Panesar	92	c Hoggard b Sidebottom	39
M.D.Bell	c Cook b Harmison	19	c Ambrose b Sidebottom	0
S.P.Fleming	c Cook b Sidebottom	41	c Cook b Sidebottom	66
M.S.Sinclair	c & b Collingwood	8	c Cook b Sidebottom	2
L.R.P.L.Taylor	c & b Pietersen	120	(6) c & b Panesar	6
J.D.P.Oram	c Cook b Hoggard	10	(7) lbw b Sidebottom	0
B.B.McCullum†	c Ambrose b Sidebottom	51	(5) c Strauss b Panesar	0
D.L.Vettori*	c Strauss b Collingwood	88	c Cook b Sidebottom	35
K.D.Mills	not out	25	lbw b Panesar	11
J.S.Patel	c Strauss b Sidebottom	5	not out	13
C.S.Martin	b Sidebottom	0	not out	0
Extras	(b 1, lb 6, w 1, nb 3)	11	(lb 5)	5
TOTAL	(138.3 overs)	**470**	(55 overs) (9 wkts dec)	**177**

ENGLAND					
A.N.Cook	c sub (N.K.W.Horsley) b Martin	38	c McCullum b Mills	13
M.P.Vaughan*	c McCullum b Patel	63	lbw b Mills	9
M.J.Hoggard	c Fleming b Martin	2	(9) c McCullum b Martin	4
A.J.Strauss	b Vettori	43	(3) c McCullum b Mills	2
K.P.Pietersen	c & b Vettori	42	(4) lbw b Mills	6
I.R.Bell	b Mills	25	(5) not out	54
P.D.Collingwood	lbw b Oram	66	(6) b Vettori	2
T.R.Ambrose†	c Fleming b Patel	55	(7) b Martin	0
R.J.Sidebottom	not out	3	(8) c McCullum b Martin	0
S.J.Harmison	c Fleming b Patel	0	c Fleming b Patel	1
M.S.Panesar	lbw b Mills	0	c McCullum b Oram	8
Extras	(b 4, lb 1, nb 6)	11	(b 4, nb 7)	11
TOTAL	(173.1 overs)	**348**	(55 overs)	**110**

Bowling	O	M	R	W	O	M	R	W	Fall of Wickets				
ENGLAND										NZ	E	NZ	E
										1st	*1st*	*2nd*	*2nd*
Sidebottom	34.3	8	90	4	17	4	49	6	1st	44	84	1	19
Hoggard	26	2	122	1	12	3	29	0	2nd	108	86	99	24
Harmison	23	3	97	1	4	0	24	0	3rd	129	130	109	25
Panesar	37	10	101	1	16	2	50	3	4th	176	159	110	30
Collingwood	15	2	42	2	6	1	20	0	5th	191	203	115	59
Pietersen	3	1	11	1					6th	277	245	115	60
NEW ZEALAND									7th	425	335	119	60
Martin	32	15	60	2	13	4	33	3	8th	451	347	141	67
Mills	21.1	6	61	2	13	4	16	4	9th	470	347	173	77
Patel	43	14	107	3	11	2	39	1	10th	470	348	-	110
Oram	21	9	27	1	4	2	2	1					
Vettori	56	17	88	2	14	6	16	1					

Playing in his third test, Ross Taylor displayed the fortitude and concentration of a quality test batsman in making 120 off 235 balls.

MILESTONES

- It was New Zealand's 65th test victory.
- It was New Zealand's eighth win over England in 89 games. England had won 41.
- Ross Taylor, playing in his third test, scored his first test hundred.
- Ryan Sidebottom claimed a hat-trick, the second against New Zealand in tests. He became the 11th England player to take a test hat-trick and had match figures of 10-139.
- Brendon McCullum held five catches in England's second innings.

338 NEW ZEALAND v ENGLAND *(Second Test)*

at Allied Prime Basin Reserve, Wellington on 13, 14, 15, 16, 17 March, 2008
Toss : New Zealand. Umpires : S.J. Davis & R.E. Koertzen
England won by 126 runs

On a hard, fast pitch New Zealand asked England to bat first. Throughout the game the quicker bowlers were able to make the new ball swing when overcast conditions prevailed and the ball seamed for most of the game.

Michael Vaughan and Alastair Cook survived until lunch with the score at 79-0. Within two overs after lunch Jacob Oram dismissed both of them and completed an intelligent spell of 14 overs that contained seven maidens and conceded only eight runs. Three more wickets fell in the session to have England in a perilous state of 158-5 at tea.

The most adaptable England batsman, Paul Collingwood, played a supportive role as Tim Ambrose, who moved to England from New South Wales when he was 17, set about the bowlers from the outset of his innings. Together the pair added 135 in the session as Ambrose took advantage of short, wide bowling and cut and pulled to his heart's content. England ended the day at 291-5.

Starting the second day on 97 Ambrose reached his well-merited first test century. England toppled to 342 with Mark Gillespie enhancing his bowling figures by claiming the last three wickets in two overs.

The recent confidence of the New Zealand top order batting was absent when James Anderson, who had played for Auckland during the first test, nicked out three early wickets before Stephen Fleming and Ross Taylor, both dropped in the slips, added 71.

In the final two hours New Zealand were dismantled by inappropriate batting, losing seven wickets for 98 runs. Daniel Vettori passed 50 for the seventh time in 11 tests, a remarkable performance batting at eight or nine.

England's lead of 144 was extended under perfect conditions where the gates of the ground were closed with 9500 comfortably enclosed. Even though the pitch was excellent for batting only Cook and Collingwood passed 50.

For the second time in the game Collingwood exhibited the skills of a truly professional batsman, this time guiding the lower order through to 277-9 before he was out.

When New Zealand began their second innings they required 438 runs from 171 overs. As the highest successful run chase in a test in New Zealand was 324-5, against Pakistan in 1994, it was a daunting challenge. Six batsmen scored over 29 but the necessary ingredient – a large century – was not forthcoming.

England's cause was assisted when New Zealand were 242-6 with Oram and Brendon McCullum staging a recovery. The players were taken from the field because of bad light only to return and be confronted by Ryan Sidebottom with the new ball. Oram perished in the slips groping for it.

Vettori left at the end of the first over of the fifth day. The forlorn task was extended by swashbuckling McCullum who was the last man out, caught in front of the vocal "Barmy Army". Despite dropping five catches and missing a stumping England deserved to win by 126 runs and square the series.

ENGLAND

A.N.Cook	c McCullum b Oram	44	c Fleming b Mills		60
M.P.Vaughan*	b Oram	32	c McCullum b Mills		13
A.J.Strauss	c Sinclair b Mills	8	lbw b Oram		44
K.P.Pietersen	b Gillespie	31	run out		17
I.R.Bell	c McCullum b Martin	11	c Sinclair b Oram		41
P.D.Collingwood	lbw b Gillespie	65	lbw b Gillespie		59
T.R.Ambrose†	c Taylor b Mills	102	b Oram		5
S.C.J.Broad	b Oram	1	c McCullum b Martin		16
R.J.Sidebottom	c Bell b Gillespie	14	c How b Martin		0
M.S.Panesar	c McCullum b Gillespie	6	c Taylor b Martin		10
J.M.Anderson	not out	0	not out		12
Extras	(b 5, lb 15, nb 8)	28	(b 6, lb 5, nb 5)		16
TOTAL	**(107 overs)**	**342**	**(97.4 overs)**		**293**

NEW ZEALAND

J.M.How	c Strauss b Anderson	7	c Bell b Sidebottom		8
M.D.Bell	b Anderson	0	c Ambrose b Broad		29
S.P.Fleming	c Pietersen b Anderson	34	b Broad		31
M.S.Sinclair	c Ambrose b Anderson	9	c Bell b Anderson		39
L.R.P.L.Taylor	c Ambrose b Anderson	53	lbw b Sidebottom		55
J.D.P.Oram	lbw b Sidebottom	8	c Pietersen b Sidebottom		30
B.B.McCullum†	c Strauss b Broad	25	c Sidebottom b Panesar		85
D.L.Vettori*	not out	50	c Cook b Sidebottom		0
K.D.Mills	c Bell b Collingwood	1	lbw b Sidebottom		13
M.R.Gillespie	b Collingwood	0	c Ambrose b Anderson		9
C.S.Martin	b Collingwood	1	not out		0
Extras	(lb 8, w 1, nb 1)	10	(b 1, lb 10, w 1)		12
TOTAL	**(57.5 overs)**	**198**	**(100.3 overs)**		**311**

Bowling	O	M	R	W	O	M	R	W
NEW ZEALAND								
Martin	20	1	80	1	24.4	4	77	2
Mills	30	4	86	2	23	5	59	2
Gillespie	20	2	79	4	15	1	63	2
Oram	29	11	46	3	9	4	44	3
Vettori	8	0	31	0	15	2	39	0
ENGLAND								
Sidebottom	17	3	36	1	31	10	105	5
Anderson	20	4	73	5	15	2	57	2
Broad	12	0	56	1	23	6	62	2
Collingwood	7.5	1	23	3	9	2	20	0
Panesar	1	0	2	0	21.3	1	53	1
Pietersen					1	0	3	0

Fall of Wickets	E 1st	NZ 1st	E 2nd	NZ 2nd
1st	79	4	21	18
2nd	82	9	127	69
3rd	94	31	129	70
4th	126	102	160	151
5th	136	113	219	173
6th	300	113	231	242
7th	305	165	259	246
8th	335	176	260	270
9th	342	180	277	311
10th	342	198	293	311

MILESTONES

- Alastair Cook became the youngest England batsman to score 2000 runs in test cricket, aged 23 years and 79 days.
- Chris Martin, playing in his 39th test, became the fifth-highest wicket-taker for New Zealand. He went past Lance Cairns' tally of 130 wickets in 43 tests.

This aerial photograph shows the record crowds that basked in ideal conditions for four of the five days at the Basin Reserve.

339 **NEW ZEALAND v ENGLAND** *(Third Test)*
at McLean Park, Napier on 22, 23, 24, 25, 26 March, 2008
Toss : England. Umpires : D.J. Harper & R.E. Koertzen
England won by 121 runs

As Jacob Oram and Kyle Mills were injured the new ball was entrusted to 19-year-old Tim Southee. After 39 balls England were 4-3 with Southee having two wickets and Chris Martin one. England struggled throughout and it was only Kevin Pietersen who held them together, with 129, before he fell to Southee with the third delivery of the second new ball.

The second morning saw Southee claim two more victims to end with five wickets. Chasing 253 New Zealand were comfortably placed at lunch at 93-1, thanks to an innings as stunning as any that Stephen Fleming had played. He reached 50 off 53 balls as he caressed four fours and one six with precise placement.

The game was transformed when Ryan Sidebottom and Stuart Broad wiped away nine batsmen for 75 runs. Sidebottom bowled a good length, cutting and swinging the ball late either way. He also made it lift disconcertingly to return his best test, and first-class, analysis of 7-47. 21-year-old Broad ably supported him.

From a position of strength many of the home batsmen squandered their wickets on an excellent batting surface to trail England by 85, which had increased to 176 at the end of the day when England had eight second innings wickets intact.

On the third day England took full advantage of the excellent conditions and Andrew Strauss and Ian Bell both scored hundreds as they combined to add 187 for the fourth wicket. This formed the bulk of the 325 added in the day for the loss of only three wickets.

With his test place in jeopardy Strauss accumulated runs for eight hours, making 177 of England's mammoth 467, before they declared with seven wickets down. This left New Zealand 553 runs to score in 168 overs.

Matthew Bell and Fleming took the score to 146-1 at tea before bad shots saw four wickets fall for 25 runs inside 20 overs. The day ended at 222-5 with Ross Taylor and Brendon McCullum batting proficiently.

The fifth day began with Taylor completing his third half-century of the series. Monty Panesar's accuracy and occasional sharp turn from a wearing pitch saw him return his best test analysis of 6-126 but not before Southee, who had been relegated in favour of Jeetan Patel, mauled him savagely.

With Chris Martin as his partner he lashed out, hitting nine sixes and four fours as 84 runs were added for the 10th wicket. Southee scored New Zealand's fastest test half-century. England won by 121 runs and took the series 2-1.

Tim Southee took five wickets on debut and also hit the fastest fifty for New Zealand in a test.

ENGLAND

A.N.Cook	b Martin	2	c McCullum b Patel	37
M.P.Vaughan*	lbw b Southee	2	c McCullum b Martin	4
A.J.Strauss	c How b Southee	0	c Bell b Patel	177
K.P.Pietersen	c How b Southee	129	c Taylor b Vettori	34
I.R.Bell	c & b Elliott	9	c Sinclair b Vettori	110
P.D.Collingwood	c Elliott b Patel	30	c & b Vettori	22
T.R.Ambrose†	c Taylor b Patel	11	c & b Vettori	31
S.C.J.Broad	c McCullum b Southee	42	not out	31
R.J.Sidebottom	c Bell b Southee	14	not out	12
M.S.Panesar	b Martin	1		
J.M.Anderson	not out	0		
Extras	(lb 9, w 3, nb 1)	13	(lb 3, w 1, nb 5)	9
TOTAL	(96.1 overs)	**253**	(131.5 overs) (7 wkts dec)	**467**

NEW ZEALAND

J.M.How	c Strauss b Sidebottom	44	lbw b Panesar	11
M.D.Bell	lbw b Sidebottom	0	c Broad b Panesar	69
S.P.Fleming	c Collingwood b Sidebottom	59	c Ambrose b Panesar	66
M.S.Sinclair	c Broad b Sidebottom	7	c Ambrose b Broad	6
L.R.P.L.Taylor	c Ambrose b Broad	2	c Collingwood b Panesar	74
G.D.Elliott	c Ambrose b Sidebottom	6	c Bell b Broad	4
B.B.McCullum†	b Sidebottom	9	b Panesar	42
D.L.Vettori*	c Cook b Sidebottom	14	c Ambrose b Anderson	43
T.G.Southee	c Pietersen b Broad	5	(10) not out	77
J.S.Patel	c Panesar b Broad	4	(9) c Broad b Panesar	18
C.S.Martin	not out	4	b Sidebottom	5
Extras	(lb 13, w 1)	14	(b 6, lb 5, w 4, nb 1)	16
TOTAL	(48.4 overs)	**168**	(118.5 overs)	**431**

Bowling	O	M	R	W	O	M	R	W
NEW ZEALAND								
Martin	26	6	74	2	18	2	60	1
Southee	23.1	8	55	5	24	5	84	0
Elliott	10	2	27	1	14	1	58	0
Vettori	19	6	51	0	45	6	158	4
Patel	18	3	37	2	30.5	4	104	2
ENGLAND								
Sidebottom	21.4	6	47	7	19.5	3	83	1
Anderson	7	1	54	0	17	2	99	1
Broad	17	3	54	3	32	10	78	2
Panesar	1	1	0	0	46	7	126	6
Collingwood	2	2	0	0	2	0	20	0
Pietersen					2	0	14	0

Fall of Wickets	E 1st	NZ 1st	E 2nd	NZ 2nd
1st	4	1	5	48
2nd	4	103	77	147
3rd	4	116	140	156
4th	36	119	327	160
5th	125	119	361	172
6th	147	137	424	276
7th	208	138	425	281
8th	240	152	-	329
9th	253	164	-	347
10th	253	168	-	431

AVERAGES

New Zealand

BATTING	*M*	*I*	*NO*	*Runs*	*HS*	*Ave*
T.G. Southee	1	2	1	82	77*	82.00
L.R.P.L. Taylor	3	6	0	310	120	51.66
S.P. Fleming	3	6	0	297	66	49.50
D.L. Vettori	3	6	1	230	88	46.00
B.B. McCullum	3	6	0	212	85	35.33
J.M. How	3	6	0	201	92	33.50
M.D. Bell	3	6	0	117	69	19.50
K.D. Mills	2	4	1	50	25*	16.66
J.S. Patel	2	4	1	40	18	13.33
J.D.P. Oram	2	4	0	48	30	12.00
M.S. Sinclair	3	6	0	71	39	11.83
G.D. Elliott	1	2	0	10	6	5.00
M.R. Gillespie	1	2	0	9	9	4.50
C.S. Martin	3	6	3	10	5	3.33

BOWLING	*O*	*M*	*R*	*W*	*Ave*
J.D.P. Oram	74	31	119	8	14.87
K.D. Mills	87.1	19	222	10	22.20
M.R. Gillespie	35	3	142	6	23.66
T.G. Southee	47.1	13	139	5	27.80
C.S. Martin	133.4	32	384	11	34.90
J.S. Patel	102.5	23	287	8	35.87
D.L. Vettori	157	37	383	7	54.71
G.D. Elliott	24	3	85	1	85.00

England

BATTING	*M*	*I*	*NO*	*Runs*	*HS*	*Ave*
I.R. Bell	3	6	1	250	110	50.00
A.J. Strauss	3	6	0	274	177	45.66
K.P. Pietersen	3	6	0	259	129	43.16
P.D. Collingwood	3	6	0	244	66	40.66
T.R. Ambrose	3	6	0	204	102	34.00
A.N. Cook	3	6	0	194	60	32.33
S.C.J. Broad	2	4	1	90	42	30.00
M.P. Vaughan	3	6	0	123	63	20.50
R.J. Sidebottom	3	6	2	43	14	10.75
M.S. Panesar	3	5	0	25	10	5.00
M.J. Hoggard	1	2	0	6	4	3.00
S.J. Harmison	1	2	0	1	1	0.50
J.M. Anderson	2	3	3	12	12*	-

BOWLING	*O*	*M*	*R*	*W*	*Ave*
R.J. Sidebottom	141	34	410	24	17.08
P.D. Collingwood	41.5	8	125	5	25.00
K.P. Pietersen	6	1	28	1	28.00
M.S. Panesar	122.3	31	332	11	30.18
S.C.J .Broad	84	19	250	8	31.25
J.M. Anderson	59	9	283	8	35.37
S.J. Harmison	27	3	121	1	121.00
M.J. Hoggard	38	5	151	1	151.00

MILESTONES

- Grant Elliott (236) and Tim Southee (237) made their test debuts.

- Stephen Fleming passed 7000 test runs.

- Tim Southee became the sixth and youngest New Zealand bowler to take five wickets in an innings on debut. The others being Fen Creswell (1949), Alec Moir (1950/51), Bruce Taylor (1964/65), Paul Wiseman (1997/98) and Mark Gillespie (2007/08).

- Stephen Fleming played his last test. In a career covering 14 years he played 111 tests scoring 7172 runs at 40.06. He made nine centuries and 46 fifties.

- Tim Southee scored New Zealand's fastest test half-century off 29 balls, beating Ian Smith's record of 34 balls.

- Southee hit nine sixes in his innings. Nathan Astle hit 11 in his 222 against England in 2001/02.

- Ryan Sidebottom ended the three match series with 24 wickets, a record for England in New Zealand.

The Statistics
of New Zealand Test Cricket

10 January 1930 to 26 March 2008

The Players

ADAMS Andre Ryan
b Auckland 17/7/1975
Right-hand batsman, right-arm fast-medium bowler
2001/02

ALABASTER John Chaloner
b Invercargill 11/7/1930
Right-hand batsman, right-arm leg-break bowler
1955/56-1971/72

ALLCOTT Cyril Francis Walter
b Lower Moutere 7/10/1896, d Auckland 19/11/1973
Left-hand batsman, left-arm medium-pace bowler
1929/30-1931/32

ALLOTT Geoffrey Ian
b 24/12/1971 Christchurch
Right-hand batsman, left-arm fast-medium bowler
1995/96-1999

ANDERSON Robert Wickham
b 2/10/1948 Christchurch
Right-hand batsman, right-arm leg-break bowler
1976/77-1978

ANDERSON William McDougall
b 8/10/1919 Westport, d 21/12/1979 Christchurch
Left-hand batsman, right-arm leg-break bowler
1945/46

ANDREWS Bryan
b 4/4/1945 Christchurch
Right-hand batsman, right-arm fast-medium bowler
1973/74

ASTLE Nathan John
b 15/9/1971 Christchurch
Right-hand batsman, right-arm medium-pace bowler
1995/96-2006/07

BADCOCK Frederick Theodore
b 9/8/1897 Abbottabad, India, d 19/9/1982 Perth, Australia
Right-hand batsman, right-arm medium-pace bowler
1929/30-1932/33

BARBER Richard Trevor
b 3/6/1925 Otaki
Right-hand batsman, wicketkeeper
1955/56

BARTLETT Gary Alex
b 3/2/1941 Blenheim
Right-hand batsman, right-arm fast bowler
1961/62-1967/68

BARTON Paul Thomas
b 9/10/1935 Wellington
Right-hand batsman, slow left-arm bowler
1961/62-1962/63

BEARD Donald Derek
b 14/1/1920 Palmerston North, d 15/7/1982 Lancaster, England
Right-hand batsman, right-arm medium-pace bowler
1951/52-1955/56

BECK John Edward Francis
b 1/8/1934 Wellington, d 23/4/2000 Waikanae
Left-hand batsman
1953/54-1955/56

BELL Matthew David
b 25/2/1977 Dunedin
Right-hand batsman
1998/99-2007/08

BELL William
b 5/9/1931 Dunedin, d 23/7/2002 Auckland
Right-hand batsman, right-arm leg-break bowler
1953/54

BILBY Grahame Paul
b 7/5/1941 Wellington
Right-hand batsman
1965/66

BLAIN Tony Elston
b 17/2/1962 Nelson
Right-hand batsman, wicketkeeper
1986-1993/94

BLAIR Robert William
b 23/6/1932 Petone
Right-hand batsman, right-arm fast-medium bowler
1952/53-1963/64

BLUNT Roger Charles
b 3/11/1900 Durham, England, d 22/6/1966 London, England
Right-hand batsman, right-arm leg-break bowler
1929/30-1931/32

BOLTON Bruce Alfred
b 31/5/1935 Christchurch
Right-hand batsman, right-arm leg-break bowler
1958/59

BOND Shane Edward
b 7/6/1975 Christchurch
Right-hand batsman, right-arm fast bowler
2001/02-2007/08

BOOCK Stephen Lewis
b 20/9/1951 Dunedin
Right-hand batsman, slow left-arm bowler
1977/78-1988/89

BRACEWELL Brendon Paul
b 14/9/1959 Auckland
Right-hand batsman, right-arm fast-medium bowler
1978-1984/85

BRACEWELL John Garry
b 15/4/1958 Auckland
Right-hand batsman, right-arm off-break bowler
1980/81-1990

BRADBURN Grant Eric
b 26/5/1966 Hamilton
Right-hand batsman, right-arm off-break bowler
1990/91-2000/01

BRADBURN Wynne Pennell
b 24/11/1938 Thames
Right-hand batsman, right-arm slow-medium bowler
1963/64

BROWN Vaughan Raymond
b 3/11/1959 Christchurch
Left-hand batsman, right-arm off-break bowler
1985/86

BURGESS Mark Gordon
b 17/7/1944 Auckland
Right-hand batsman, right-arm off-break bowler
1967/68-1980/81

BURKE Cecil
b 22/3/1914 Auckland, d 4/8/1997 Auckland
Right-hand batsman, right-arm leg-break bowler
1945/46

BURTT Thomas Browning
b 22/1/1915 Christchurch, d 24/5/1988 Christchurch
Right-hand batsman, slow left-arm bowler
1946/47-1952/53

BUTLER Ian Gareth
b 24/11/1981 Auckland
Right-hand batsman, right-arm fast bowler
2001/02-2004/05

BUTTERFIELD Leonard Arthur
b 29/8/1913 Christchurch, d 5/7/1999 Christchurch
Right-hand batsman, right-arm medium-pace bowler
1945/46

CAIRNS Bernard Lance
b 10/10/1949 Picton
Right-hand batsman, right-arm medium-pace bowler
1973/74-1985/86

CAIRNS Christopher Lance
b 13/6/1970 Picton
Right-hand batsman, right-arm fast-medium bowler
1989/90-2004

CAMERON Francis James
b 1/6/1932 Dunedin
Right-hand batsman, right-arm fast-medium bowler
1961/62-1965

CAVE Henry Butler
b 10/10/1922 Wanganui, d 15/9/1989 Wanganui
Right-hand batsman, right-arm medium-pace bowler
1949-1958

CHAPPLE Murray Ernest
b 25/7/1930 Christchurch, d 31/7/1985 Hamilton
Right-hand batsman, slow left-arm bowler
1952/53-1965/66

CHATFIELD Ewen John
b 3/7/1950 Dannevirke
Right-hand batsman, right-arm medium-pace bowler
1974/75-1988/89

CLEVERLEY Donald Charles
b 23/12/1909 Oamaru, d 16/2/2004 Southport, Australia
Left-hand batsman, right-arm fast-medium bowler
1931/32-1945/46

COLLINGE Richard Owen
b 2/4/1946 Wellington
Right-hand batsman, left-arm fast-medium bowler
1964/65-1978

COLQUHOUN Ian Alexander
b 8/6/1924 Wellington, d 26/2/2005 Paraparaumu Beach
Right-hand batsman, wicketkeeper
1954/55

CONEY Jeremy Vernon
b 21/6/1952 Wellington
Right-hand batsman, right-arm slow-medium bowler
1973/74-1986/87

CONGDON Bevan Ernest
b 11/2/1938 Motueka
Right-hand batsman, right-arm medium-pace bowler
1964/65-1978

COWIE John
b 30/3/1912 Auckland, d 3/6/1994 Lower Hutt
Right-hand batsman, right-arm fast-medium bowler
1937-1949

CRESSWELL George Fenwick
b 22/3/1915 Wanganui, d 10/1/1966 Blenheim
Left-hand batsman, right-arm medium-pace bowler
1949-1950/51

CROMB Ian Burns
b 25/6/1905 Christchurch, d 6/3/1984 Christchurch
Right-hand batsman, right-arm medium-pace bowler
1931-1931/32

CROWE Jeffrey John
b 14/9/1958 Auckland
Right-hand batsman
1982/83-1989/90

CROWE Martin David
b 22/9/1962 Auckland
Right-hand batsman, right-arm medium-pace bowler
1981/82-1995/96

CUMMING Craig Derek
b 31/8/1975 Timaru
Right-hand batsman, right-arm medium-pace bowler
2004/05-2007/08

CUNIS Robert Smith
b 5/1/1941 Whangarei
Right-hand batsman, right-arm fast-medium bowler
1963/64-1971/72

D'ARCY John William
b 23/4/1936 Christchurch
Right-hand batsman
1958

DE GROEN Richard Paul
b 5/8/1962 Otorohanga
Right-hand batsman, right-arm medium-pace bowler
1993/94-1994/95

DAVIS Heath Te-Ihi-O-Te-Rangi
b 30/11/1971 Lower Hutt
Right-hand batsman, right-arm fast bowler
1994-1997/98

DEMPSTER Charles Stewart
b 15/11/1903 Wellington, d 12/2/1974 Wellington
Right-hand batsman
1929/30-1932/33

DEMPSTER Eric William
b 25/1/1925 Wellington
Left-hand batsman, slow left-arm bowler
1952/53-1953/54

DICK Arthur Edward
b 10/10/1936 Middlemarch
Right-hand batsman, wicketkeeper
1961/62-1965

DICKINSON George Ritchie
b 11/3/1903 Dunedin, d 17/3/1978 Lower Hutt
Right-hand batsman, right-arm fast bowler
1929/30-1931/32

DONNELLY Martin Paterson
b 17/10/1917 Ngaruawahia, d 22/10/1999 Sydney
Left-hand batsman, slow left-arm bowler
1937-1949

DOULL Simon Blair
b 6/8/1969 Pukekohe
Right-hand batsman, right-arm fast-medium bowler
1992/93-1999/00

DOWLING Graham Thorne
b 4/3/1937 Christchurch
Right-hand batsman
1961/62-1971/72

DRUM Christopher James
b 10/7/1974 Auckland
Right-hand batsman, right-arm fast-medium bowler
2000/01-2001/02

DUNNING John Angus
b 6/2/1903 Omaha, d 24/6/1971 Adelaide, Australia
Right-hand batsman, right-arm medium-pace bowler
1932/33-1937

EDGAR Bruce Adrian
b 23/11/1956 Wellington
Left-hand batsman, wicketkeeper
1978-1986

EDWARDS Graham Neil
b 27/5/1955 Nelson
Right-hand batsman, wicketkeeper
1976/77-1980/81

ELLIOTT Grant David
b 21/3/1979 Johannesburg, South Africa
Right-hand batsman, right-arm medium-pace bowler
2007/08

EMERY Raymond William George
b 28/3/1915 Auckland, d 18/12/1982 Auckland
Right-hand batsman, right-arm medium-pace bowler
1951/52

FISHER Frederick Eric
b 28/7/1924 Johnsonville, d 19/6/1996 Palmerston North
Right-hand batsman, left-arm medium-pace bowler
1952/53

FLEMING Stephen Paul
b 1/4/1973 Christchurch
Left-hand batsman
1993/94-2007/08

FOLEY Henry
b 28/1/1906 Wellington, d 16/10/1948 Brisbane
Left-hand batsman
1929/30

FRANKLIN James Edward Charles
b 7/11/1980 Wellington
Left-hand batsman, left-arm fast-medium bowler
2000/01-2006/07

FRANKLIN Trevor John
b 18/3/1962 Auckland
Right-hand batsman, right-arm medium-pace bowler
1983-1990/91

FREEMAN Douglas Linford
b 8/9/1914 Sydney, d 31/5/1994 Sydney
Right-hand batsman, right-arm leg-break bowler
1932/33

FULTON Peter Gordon
b 1/2/1979 Christchurch
Right-hand batsman, right-arm medium-pace bowler
2005/06-2007/08

GALLICHAN Norman
b 3/6/1906 Palmerston North, d 25/3/1969 Taupo
Right-hand batsman, slow left-arm bowler
1937

GEDYE Sidney Graham
b 2/5/1929 Auckland
Right-hand batsman
1963/64-1964/65

GERMON Lee Kenneth
b 4/11/1968 Christchurch
Right-hand batsman, wicketkeeper
1995/96-1996/97

GILLESPIE Mark Raymond
b 17/10/1979 Wanganui
Right-hand batsman, right-arm fast-medium bowler
2007/08

GILLESPIE Stuart Ross
b 2/3/1957
Right-hand batsman, right-arm fast-medium bowler
1985/86

GRAY Evan John
b 18/11/1954 Wellington
Right-hand batsman, slow left-arm bowler
1983-1988/89

GREATBATCH Mark John
b 11/12/1963
Left-hand batsman
1987/88-1996/97

GUILLEN Simpson Clairmonte
b 24/9/1924 Port of Spain, Trinidad
Right-hand batsman, wicketkeeper
1955/56

GUY John William
b 29/8/1934 Nelson
Left-hand batsman
1955/56-1961/62

HADLEE Dayle Robert
b 6/1/1948 Christchurch
Right-hand batsman, right-arm medium-pace bowler
1969-1977/78

HADLEE Richard John
b 3/7/1951 Christchurch
Left-hand batsman, right-arm fast-medium bowler
1972/73-1990

HADLEE Walter Arnold
b 4/6/1915 Lincoln, d 29/9/2006 Christchurch
Right-hand batsman
1937-1950/51

HARFORD Noel Sherwin
b 30/8/1930 Winton, d 30/3/1981 Auckland
Right-hand batsman, right-arm medium-pace bowler
1955/56-1958

HARFORD Roy Ivan
b 30/5/1936 London, England
Left-hand batsman, wicketkeeper
1967/68

HARRIS Chris Zinzan
b 20/11/1969 Christchurch
Left-hand batsman, right-arm medium-pace bowler
1992/93-2001/02

HARRIS Parke Gerald Zinzan
b 18/7/1927 Christchurch, d 1/12/1991 Christchurch
Right-hand batsman, right-arm off-break bowler
1955/56-1964/65

HARRIS Roger Meredith
b 27/7/1933 Auckland
Right-hand batsman, right-arm medium-pace bowler
1958/59

HART Matthew Norman
b 16/5/1972 Hamilton
Left-hand batsman, slow left-arm bowler
1993/94-1995/96

HART Robert Garry
b 2/12/1974 Hamilton
Right-hand batsman, wicketkeeper
2001/02-2003/04

HARTLAND Blair Robert
b 22/10/1966 Christchurch
Right-hand batsman
1991/92-1994

HASLAM Mark James
b 26/9/1972 Bury, England
Left-hand batsman, slow left-arm bowler
1992/93-1995/96

HASTINGS Brian Frederick
b 23/3/1940 Wellington
Right-hand batsman
1968/69-1975/76

HAYES John Arthur
b 11/1/1927 Auckland, d 25/12/2007 Auckland
Right-hand batsman, right-arm fast bowler
1950/51-1958

HENDERSON Matthew
b 2/8/1895 Auckland, d 17/6/1970 Wellington
Left-hand batsman, left-arm fast-medium bowler
1929/30

HORNE Matthew Jeffery
b 5/12/1970 Auckland
Right-hand batsman, right-arm medium-pace bowler
1996/97-2002/03

HORNE Philip Andrew
b 21/1/1960 Upper Hutt
Left-hand batsman
1986/87-1990/91

HOUGH Kenneth William
b 24/10/1928 Sydney
Right-hand batsman, right-arm medium-pace bowler
1958/59

HOW Jamie Michael
b 19/5/1981 New Plymouth
Right-hand batsman, right-arm off-break bowler
2005/06-2007/08

HOWARTH Geoffrey Philip
b 29/3/1951 Auckland
Right-hand batsman, right-arm off-break bowler
1974/75-1984/85

HOWARTH Hedley John
b 25/12/1943 Auckland
Left-hand batsman, slow left-arm bowler
1969-1976/77

JAMES Kenneth Cecil
b 12/3/1904 Wellington, d 21/8/1976 Palmerston North
Right-hand batsman, wicketkeeper
1929/30-1932/33

JARVIS Terrence Wayne
b 29/7/1944 Auckland
Right-hand batsman
1964/65-1972/73

JONES Andrew Howard
b 9/5/1959 Wellington
Right-hand batsman, right-arm off-break bowler
1986/87-1994/95

JONES Richard Andrew
b 22/10/1973 Auckland
Right-hand batsman
2003/04

KENNEDY Robert John
b 3/6/1972 Dunedin
Right-hand batsman, right-arm fast-medium bowler
1995/96

KERR John Lambert
b 28/12/1910 Dannevirke, d 27/5/2007 Christchurch
Right-hand batsman
1931-1937

KUGGELEIJN Christopher Mary
b 10/5/1956 Auckland
Right-hand batsman, right-arm off-break bowler
1988/89

LARSEN Gavin Rolf
b 27/9/1962 Wellington
Right-hand batsman, right-arm medium-pace bowler
1994-1995/96

LATHAM Rodney Terry
b 12/6/1961 Christchurch
Right-hand batsman, right-arm medium-pace bowler
1991/92-1992/93

LEES Warren Kenneth
b 19/3/1952 Dunedin
Right-hand batsman, wicketkeeper
1976/77-1983

LEGGAT Ian Bruce
b 7/6/1930 Invercargill
Right-hand batsman, right-arm medium-pace bowler
1953/54

LEGGAT John Gordon
b 27/5/1926 Wellington, d 9/3/1973 Christchurch
Right-hand batsman
1951/52-1955/56

LISSETTE Allen Fisher
b 6/11/1919 Morrinsville, d 24/1/1973 Hamilton
Right-hand batsman, slow left-arm bowler
1955/56

LOVERIDGE Greg Riaka
b 15/1/1975 Palmerston North
Right-hand batsman, right-arm leg-break bowler
1995/96

LOWRY Thomas Coleman
b 17/2/1898 Fernhill, d 20/7/1976 Hastings
Right-hand batsman, right-arm off-break bowler, wicketkeeper
1929/30-1931

McCULLUM Brendon Barrie
b 27/9/1981 Dunedin
Right-hand batsman, wicketkeeper
2003/04-2007/08

McEWAN Paul Ernest
b 19/12/1953 Christchurch
Right-hand batsman, right-arm medium-pace bowler
1979/80-1984/85

MacGIBBON Anthony Roy
b 28/8/1924 Christchurch
Right-hand batsman, right-arm fast-medium bowler
1950/51-1958

McGIRR Herbert Mendelson
b 5/11/1891 Wellington, d 14/4/1964 Nelson
Right-hand batsman, right-arm fast-medium bowler
1929/30

McGREGOR Spencer Noel
b 18/12/1931 Dunedin, d 21/11/2007 Christchurch
Right-hand batsman
1954/55-1964/65

McLEOD Edwin George
b 14/10/1900 Auckland, d 14/9/1989 Wellington
Left-hand batsman, right-arm leg-break bowler
1929/30

McMAHON Trevor George
b 8/11/1929 Wellington
Right-hand batsman, wicketkeeper
1955/56

McMILLAN Craig Douglas
b 13/9/1976 Christchurch
Right-hand batsman, right-arm medium-pace bowler
1997/98-2004/05

McRAE Donald Alexander Noel
b 25/12/1912 Christchurch, d 10/8/1986 Christchurch
Left-hand batsman, left-arm medium-pace bowler
1945/46

MARSHALL Hamish John Hamilton
b 15/2/1979 Warkworth
Right-hand batsman, right-arm medium-pace bowler
2000/01-2005/06

MARSHALL James Andrew Hamilton
b 15/2/1979 Warkworth
Right-hand batsman, right-arm medium-pace bowler
2004/05-2005/06

MARTIN Christopher Stewart
b 10/12/1974 Christchurch
Right-hand batsman, right-arm fast-medium bowler
2000/01-2007/08

MASON Michael James
b 27/8/1974 Carterton
Right-hand batsman, right-arm fast-medium bowler
2003/04

MATHESON Alexander Malcolm
b 27/2/1906 Omaha, d 31/12/1985 Auckland
Right-hand batsman, right-arm fast-medium bowler
1929/30-1931

MEALE Trevor
b 11/11/1928 Auckland
Left-hand batsman
1958

MERRITT William Edward
b 18/8/1908 Sumner, d 9/6/1977 Christchurch
Right-hand batsman, right-arm leg-break bowler
1929/30-1931

MEULI Edgar Milton
b 20/2/1926 Hawera, d 15/4/2007 Auckland
Right-hand batsman, right-arm leg-break bowler
1952/53

MILBURN Barry Douglas
b 24/11/1943 Dunedin
Right-hand batsman, wicketkeeper
1968/69

MILLER Lawrence Somerville Martin
b 31/3/1923 New Plymouth, d 17/12/1996 Kapiti
Left-hand batsman, left-arm slow-medium bowler
1952/53-1958

MILLS John Ernest
b 3/9/1905 Dunedin, d 11/12/1972 Hamilton
Left-hand batsman
1929/30-1932/33

MILLS Kyle David
b 15/3/1979 Auckland
Right-hand batsman, right-arm fast-medium bowler
2004-2007/08

MOIR Alexander McKenzie
b 17/7/1919 Dunedin, d 17/6/2000 Dunedin
Right-hand batsman, right-arm leg-break bowler
1950/51-1958/59

MOLONEY Denis Andrew Robert
b 11/8/1910 Dunedin, d 15/7/1942 El Alamein, Egypt
Right-hand batsman, right-arm leg-break bowler
1937

MOONEY Francis Leonard Hugh
b 26/5/1921 Wellington, d 8/3/2004 Wellington
Right-hand batsman, wicketkeeper
1949-1953/54

MORGAN Ross Winston
12/2/1941 Auckland
Right-hand batsman, right-arm off-break bowler
1964/65-1971/72

MORRISON Bruce Donald
b 17/12/1933 Lower Hutt
Left-hand batsman, right-arm medium-pace bowler
1962/63

MORRISON Daniel Kyle
b 3/2/1966 Auckland
Right-hand batsman, right-arm fast-medium bowler
1987/88-1996/97

MORRISON John Francis MacLean
b 27/8/1947 Wellington
Right-hand batsman, slow left-arm bowler
1973/74-1981/82

MOTZ Richard Charles
b 12/1/1940 Christchurch, d 29/4/2007 Christchurch
Right-hand batsman, right-arm fast-medium bowler
1961/62-1969

MURRAY Bruce Alexander Grenfell
b 18/9/1940 Wellington
Right-hand batsman, right-arm leg-break bowler
1967/68-1970/71

MURRAY Darrin James
b 4/9/1967 Christchurch
Right-hand batsman
1994/95

NASH Dion Joseph
b 20/11/1971 Auckland
Right-hand batsman, right-arm fast-medium bowler
1992/93-2001/02

NEWMAN Jack
b 3/7/1902 Brightwater, d 23/9/1996 Nelson
Right-hand batsman, left-arm medium-pace bowler
1931/32-1932/33

O'BRIEN Iain Edward
b 10/7/1976 Lower Hutt
Right-hand batsman, right-arm medium-pace bowler
2004/05-2007/08

O'CONNOR Shayne Barry
b 15/11/1973 Hastings
Left-hand batsman, left-arm fast-medium bowler
1997/98-2001/02

O'SULLIVAN David Robert
b 16/11/1944 Palmerston North
Right-hand batsman, slow left-arm bowler
1972/73-1976/77

ORAM Jacob David Philip
b 28/7/1978 Palmerston North
Left-hand batsman, right-arm medium-pace bowler
2002/03-2007/08

OVERTON Guy William Fitzroy
b 8/6/1919 Dunedin, d 7/9/1993 Winton
Left-hand batsman, right-arm fast-medium bowler
1953/54

OWENS Michael Barry
b 11/11/1969 Christchurch
Right-hand batsman, right-arm fast-medium bowler
1992/93-1994

PAGE Milford Laurenson
b 8/5/1902 Lyttelton, d 13/2/1987 Christchurch
Right-hand batsman, right-arm off-break bowler
1929/30-1937

PAPPS Michael Hugh William
b 2/7/1979 Christchurch
Right-hand batsman
2003/04-2007/08

PARKER John Morton
b 21/2/1951 Dannevirke
Right-hand batsman, wicketkeeper
1972/73-1980/81

PARKER Norman Murray
b 28/8/1948 Dannevirke
Right-hand batsman, right-arm leg-break bowler
1976/77

PARORE Adam Craig
b 23/1/1971 Auckland
Right-hand batsman, wicketkeeper
1990-2001/02

PATEL Dipak Narshibhai
b 25/10/1958 Nairobi, Kenya
Right-hand batsman, right-arm off-break bowler
1986/87-1996/97

PATEL Jeetan Shashi
b 7/5/1980 Wellington
Right-hand batsman, right-arm off-break bowler
2005/06-2007/08

PETHERICK Peter James
b 25/9/1942 Ranfurly
Right-hand batsman, right-arm off-break bowler
1976/77

PETRIE Eric Charlton
b 22/5/1927 Ngaruawahia, d 14/8/2004 Omokoroa
Right-hand batsman, wicketkeeper
1955/56-1965/66

PLAYLE William Rodger
b 1/12/1938 Palmerston North
Right-hand batsman
1958-1962/63

POCOCK Blair Andrew
b 18/6/1971 Auckland
Right-hand batsman
1993/94-1997/98

POLLARD Victor
b 7/9/1945 Burnley, England
Right-hand batsman, right-arm off-break bowler
1964/65-1973

POORE Matt Beresford
b 1/6/1930 Christchurch
Right-hand batsman, right-arm off-break bowler
1952/53-1955/56

PRIEST Mark Wellings
b 12/8/1961 Greymouth
Left-hand batsman, slow left-arm bowler
1990-1997/98

PRINGLE Christopher
b 26/1/1968 Auckland
Right-hand batsman, right-arm fast-medium bowler
1990/91-1994/95

PUNA Narotam
b 28/10/1929 Surat, India, d 7/6/1996 Hamilton
Right-hand batsman, right-arm off-break bowler
1965/66

RABONE Geoffrey Osborne
b 6/11/1921 Gore, d 19/1/2006 Auckland
Right-hand batsman, right-arm off-break bowler
1949-1954/55

REDMOND Rodney Ernest
b 29/12/1944 Whangarei
Left-hand batsman, slow left-arm bowler
1972/73

REID John Fulton
b 3/3/1956 Auckland
Left-hand batsman, right-arm leg-break bowler, wicketkeeper
1978/79-1985/86

REID John Richard
b 3/6/1928 Auckland
Right-hand batsman, right-arm fast-medium bowler, wicketkeeper
1949-1965

RICHARDSON Mark Hunter
b 11/6/1971 Hastings
Left-hand batsman, slow left-arm bowler
2000/01-2004/05

ROBERTS Andrew Duncan Glenn
b 6/5/1947 Te Aroha, d 26/10/1989 Wellington
Right-hand batsman, right-arm medium-pace bowler
1975/76-1976/77

ROBERTS Albert William
b 20/8/1909 Christchurch, d 13/5/1978 Christchurch
Right-hand batsman, right-arm medium-pace bowler
1929/30-1937

ROBERTSON Gary Keith
b 15/7/1960 New Plymouth
Right-hand batsman, right-arm fast-medium bowler
1985/86

ROWE Charles Gordon
b 30/6/1915 Glasgow, Scotland, d 9/6/1995 Palmerston North
Right-hand batsman
1945/46

RUTHERFORD Kenneth Robert
b 26/10/1965 Dunedin
Right-hand batsman, right-arm medium-pace bowler
1984/85-1994/95

SCOTT Roy Hamilton
b 6/3/1917 Clyde, d 5/8/2005 Christchurch
Right-hand batsman, right-arm medium-pace bowler
1946/47

SCOTT Verdun John
b 31/7/1916 Auckland, d 2/8/1980 Auckland
Right-hand batsman, right-arm medium-pace bowler
1945/46-1951/52

SEWELL David Graham
b 20/10/1977 Christchurch
Right-hand batsman, left-arm fast-medium bowler
1997/98

SHRIMPTON Michael John Froud
b 23/6/1940 Feilding
Right-hand batsman, right-arm leg-break bowler
1962/63-1973/74

SINCLAIR Barry Whitley
b 23/10/1936 Wellington
Right-hand batsman
1962/63-1967/68

SINCLAIR Ian McKay
b 1/6/1933 Rangiora
Left-hand batsman, right-arm off-break bowler
1955/56

SINCLAIR Mathew Stuart
b 9/11/1975 Katherine, Australia
Right-hand batsman
1999/00-2007/08

SMITH Frank Brunton
b 13/3/1922 Rangiora, d 6/7/1997 Christchurch
Right-hand batsman
1946/47-1951/52

SMITH Horace Dennis
b 8/1/1913 Toowoomba, Australia, d 25/1/1986 Christchurch
Right-hand batsman, right-arm fast-medium bowler
1932/33

SMITH Ian David Stockley
b 28/2/1957 Nelson
Right-hand batsman, wicketkeeper
1980/81-1991/92

SNEDDEN Colin Alexander
b 7/1/1918 Auckland
Right-hand batsman, right-arm off-break bowler
1946/47

SNEDDEN Martin Colin
b 23/11/1958 Auckland
Left-hand batsman, right-arm fast-medium bowler
1980/81-1990

SOUTHEE Timothy Grant
b 11/12/1988 Whangarei
Right-hand batsman, right-arm fast-medium bowler
2007/08

SPARLING John Trevor
b 24/7/1938 Auckland
Right-hand batsman, right-arm off-break bowler
1958-1963/64

SPEARMAN Craig Murray
b 4/7/1972 Auckland
Right-hand batsman
1995/96-2000/01

STEAD Gary Raymond
b 9/1/1972 Christchurch
Right-hand batsman, right-arm leg-break bowler
1998/99-1999/00

STIRLING Derek Alexander
b 5/10/1961 Upper Hutt
Right-hand batsman, right-arm fast-medium bowler
1984/85-1986

STYRIS Scott Bernard
b 10/7/1975 Brisbane, Australia
Right-hand batsman, right-arm medium-pace bowler
2001/02-2007/08

SU'A Murphy Logo
b 7/11/1966 Wanganui
Left-hand batsman, left-arm fast-medium bowler
1991/92-1994/95

SUTCLIFFE Bert
b 17/11/1923 Auckland, d 20/4/2001 Auckland
Left-hand batsman, slow left-arm bowler
1946/47-1965

TAYLOR Bruce Richard
b 12/7/1943 Timaru
Left-hand batsman, right-arm fast-medium bowler
1964/65-1973

TAYLOR Donald Dougald
b 2/3/1923 Auckland, d 5/12/1980 Auckland
Right-hand batsman, right-arm leg-break bowler
1946/47-1955/56

TAYLOR Luteru Ross Poutoa Lote
b 8/3/1984 Lower Hutt
Right-hand batsman, right-arm off-break bowler
2007/08

THOMSON Keith
b 26/2/1941 Methven
Right-hand batsman
1967/68

THOMSON Shane Alexander
b 27/1/1969 Hamilton
Right-hand batsman, right-arm off-break bowler
1989/90-1995/96

TINDILL Eric William Thomas
b 18/12/1910 Nelson
Left-hand batsman, wicketkeeper
1937-1946/47

TROUP Gary Bertram
b 3/10/1952 Taumarunui
Right-hand batsman, left-arm fast-medium bowler
1976/77-1985/86

TRUSCOTT Peter Bennetts
b 14/8/1941 Pahiatua
Right-hand batsman
1964/65

TUFFEY Daryl Raymond
b 11/6/1978 Milton
Right-hand batsman, right-arm fast-medium bowler
1999/00-2004

TURNER Glenn Maitland
b 26/5/1947 Dunedin
Right-hand batsman
1968/69-1982/83

TWOSE Roger Graham
b 17/4/1968 Torquay, England
Left-hand batsman, right-arm medium-pace bowler
1995/96-1999

VANCE Robert Howard
b 31/3/1955 Wellington
Right-hand batsman
1987/88-1989/90

VAUGHAN Justin Thomas Caldwell
b 30/8/1967 Hereford, England
Left-hand batsman, right-arm medium-pace bowler
1992/93-1996/97

VETTORI Daniel Luca
b 27/1/1979 Auckland
Left-hand batsman, slow left-arm bowler
1996/97-2007/08

VINCENT Lou
b 11/11/1978 Warkworth
Right-hand batsman, wicketkeeper
2001/02-2007/08

VIVIAN Graham Ellery
b 28/2/1946 Auckland
Left-hand batsman, right-arm leg-break bowler
1964/65-1971/72

VIVIAN Henry Gifford
b 4/11/1912 Auckland, d 12/8/1983 Auckland
Left-hand batsman, slow left-arm bowler
1931-1937

WADSWORTH Kenneth John
b 30/11/1946 Nelson, d 19/8/1976 Nelson
Right-hand batsman, wicketkeeper
1969-1975/76

WALKER Brooke Graeme Keith
b 25/3/1977 Auckland
Right-hand batsman, right-arm leg-break bowler
2000/01-2001/02

WALLACE Walter Mervyn
b 19/12/1916 Auckland, d 21/3/2008 Auckland
Right-hand batsman
1937-1952/53

WALMSLEY Kerry Peter
b 23/8/1973 Dunedin
Right-hand batsman, right-arm fast-medium bowler
1994/95-2000/01

WARD John Thomas
b 11/3/1937 Timaru
Right-hand batsman, wicketkeeper
1963/64-1967/68

WATSON William
b 31/8/1965 Auckland
Right-hand batsman, right-arm fast-medium bowler
1986-1993/94

WATT Leslie
b 17/9/1924 Waitati, d 15/11/1996 Dunedin
Right-hand batsman
1954/55

WEBB Murray George
b 22/6/1947 Invercargill
Right-hand batsman, right-arm fast bowler
1970/71-1973/74

WEBB Peter Neil
b 14/7/1957 Auckland
Right-hand batsman, wicketkeeper
1979/80

WEIR Gordon Lindsay
b 2/6/1908 Auckland, d 31/10/2003 Auckland
Right-hand batsman, right-arm medium-pace bowler
1929/30-1937

WHITE David John
b 26/6/1961 Gisborne
Right-hand batsman, right-arm off-break bowler
1990/91

WHITELAW Paul Erskine
b 10/2/1910 Auckland, d 28/8/1988 Auckland
Right-hand batsman
1932/33

WISEMAN Paul John
b 4/5/1970 Auckland
Right-hand batsman, right-arm off-break bowler
1997/98-2004/05

WRIGHT John Geoffrey
b 5/7/1954 Darfield
Left-hand batsman, right-arm medium-pace bowler
1977/78-1992/93

YOUNG Bryan Andrew
b 3/11/1964 Whangarei
Right-hand batsman, wicketkeeper
1993/94-1998/99

YUILE Bryan William
b 29/10/1941 Palmerston North
Right-hand batsman, slow left-arm bowler
1962/63-1969/70

The Umpires

	tests		tests
Bowden B.F.	46	McHarg R.L.	3
Dunne R.S.	39	King C.E.	3
Aldridge B.L.	26	Butler W.	2
Goodall F.R.	24	Forrester J.T.	2
Woodward S.J.	24	Brown J.M.A.	2
Cowie D.B.	22	Tonkinson S.B.	2
Martin W.T.	15	Currie R.G.	2
Copps D.E.A.	13	Clark L.G.	2
Gardiner W.R.C.	9	Dumbleton D.P.	2
Shortt R.W.R.	9	Watkin E.A.	2
MacKintosh E.C.A.	8	Page W.P.	1
Hastie J.B.R.	7	Burgess T.	1
Hill A.L.	7	Torrance R.C.	1
Cave K.	6	Gourlay H.W.	1
Monteith R.L.	6	Montgomery O.R.	1
Quested D.M.	5	Brook E.G.	1
Pengelly M.F.	4	Vine B.	1
Harris J.C.	4	Jelley A.E.	1
Morris G.C.	4	Tindill E.W.T.	1
Cobcroft L.T.	3	Johnston L.C.	1
McLellan J.	3	Burns D.C.	1
Pearce T.M.	3	Cassie H.B.	1
Cowie J.	3	Bricknell B.A.	1
Gwynne W.J.C.	3	Higginson I.C.	1
Kinsella D.A.	3		

Black Cap Numbers

1	F.T. Badcock	67	I.B. Leggat	133	A.D.G. Roberts	199	G.R. Loveridge
2	R.C. Blunt	68	I.A. Colquhoun	134	R.W. Anderson	200	D.L. Vettori
3	C.S. Dempster	69	S.N. McGregor	135	W.K. Lees	201	M.J. Horne
4	G.R. Dickinson	70	L. Watt	136	P.J. Petherick	202	S.B. O'Connor
5	H. Foley	71	J.C. Alabaster	137	N.M. Parker	203	D.G. Sewell
6	M. Henderson	72	P.G.Z. Harris	138	G.B. Troup	204	C.D. McMillan
7	K.C. James	73	T.G. McMahon	139	G.N. Edwards	205	P.J. Wiseman
8	T.C. Lowry	74	N.S. Harford	140	S.L. Boock	206	M.D. Bell
9	W.E. Merritt	75	E.C. Petrie	141	J.G. Wright	207	G.R. Stead
10	M.L. Page	76	J.W. Guy	142	B.P. Bracewell	208	M.S. Sinclair
11	A.W. Roberts	77	A.F. Lissette	143	B.A. Edgar	209	D.R. Tuffey
12	E.G. McLeod	78	S.C. Guillen	144	J.F. Reid	210	M.H. Richardson
13	J.E. Mills	79	I.M. Sinclair	145	P.N. Webb	211	C.S. Martin
14	G.L. Weir	80	R.T. Barber	146	P.E. McEwan	212	B.G.K. Walker
15	C.F.W. Allcott	81	J.W. D'Arcy	147	J.G. Bracewell	213	H.J.H. Marshall
16	H.M. McGirr	82	T. Meale	148	I.D.S. Smith	214	J.E.C. Franklin
17	A.M. Matheson	83	W.R. Playle	149	M.C. Snedden	215	C.J. Drum
18	I.B. Cromb	84	J.T. Sparling	150	M.D. Crowe	216	S.E. Bond
19	J.L. Kerr	85	B.A. Bolton	151	J.J .Crowe	217	L. Vincent
20	H.G. Vivian	86	R.M. Harris	152	E.J. Gray	218	I.G. Butler
21	D.C. Cleverley	87	K.W. Hough	153	T.J. Franklin	219	A.R. Adams
22	J. Newman	88	G.A. Bartlett	154	D.A. Stirling	220	R.G. Hart
23	D.L. Freeman	89	P.T. Barton	155	K.R. Rutherford	221	S.B.Styris
24	H.D. Smith	90	F.J. Cameron	156	V.R. Brown	222	J.D.P. Oram
25	P.E. Whitelaw	91	A.E. Dick	157	S.R. Gillespie	223	R.A. Jones
26	J.A. Dunning	92	R.C. Motz	158	G.K. Robertson	224	B.B. McCullum
27	J. Cowie	93	G.T. Dowling	159	W. Watson	225	M.H.W. Papps
28	M.P. Donnelly	94	B.W. Sinclair	160	T.E. Blain	226	M.J. Mason
29	W.A. Hadlee	95	B.W. Yuile	161	D.N. Patel	227	K.D. Mills
30	DA.R. Moloney	96	B.D. Morrison	162	P.A. Horne	228	C.D. Cumming
31	E.W.T. Tindill	97	M.J.F. Shrimpton	163	A.H. Jones	229	I.E. O'Brien
32	W.M. Wallace	98	S.G. Gedye	164	D.K. Morrison	230	J.A.H. Marshall
33	N. Gallichan	99	J.T. Ward	165	M.J. Greatbatch	231	P.G. Fulton
34	W.M. Anderson	100	W.P. Bradburn	166	R.H. Vance	232	J.M. How
35	C. Burke	101	R.S. Cunis	167	C.M. Kuggeleijn	233	J.S. Patel
36	L.A. Butterfield	102	R.O. Collinge	168	C.L. Cairns	234	L.R.P.L. Taylor
37	D.A.N. McRae	103	B.E. Congdon	169	S.A. Thomson	235	M.R. Gillespie
38	C.G. Rowe	104	R.W. Morgan	170	M.W. Priest	236	G.D. Elliott
39	V.J. Scott	105	P.B. Truscott	171	A.C. Parore	237	T.G. Southee
40	T.B. Burtt	106	T.W. Jarvis	172	G.E. Bradburn		
41	R.H. Scott	107	V. Pollard	173	C. Pringle		
42	F.B. Smith	108	B.R. Taylor	174	D.J. White		
43	C.A. Snedden	109	G.E. Vivian	175	B.R. Hartland		
44	B. Sutcliffe	110	G.P. Bilby	176	M.L. Su'a		
45	D.D. Taylor	111	N. Puna	177	R.T. Latham		
46	H.B. Cave	112	M.G. Burgess	178	S.B. Doull		
47	F.L.H. Mooney	113	R.I. Harford	179	M.J. Haslam		
48	G.O. Rabone	114	B.A.G. Murray	180	D.J. Nash		
49	J.R. Reid	115	K. Thomson	181	C.Z. Harris		
50	G.F. Cresswell	116	B.F. Hastings	182	M.B. Owens		
51	J.A. Hayes	117	B.D. Milburn	183	J.T.C. Vaughan		
52	A.R. MacGibbon	118	G.M. Turner	184	B.A. Pocock		
53	A.M. Moir	119	D.R. Hadlee	185	R.P. de Groen		
54	D.D. Beard	120	H.J. Howarth	186	B.A. Young		
55	R.W.G. Emery	121	K.J. Wadsworth	187	M.N. Hart		
56	J.G. Leggat	122	M.G. Webb	188	S.P. Fleming		
57	R.W. Blair	123	R.J. Hadlee	189	H.T. Davis		
58	F.E. Fisher	124	J.M. Parker	190	G.R. Larsen		
59	E.M. Meuli	125	D.R. O'Sullivan	191	D.J. Murray		
60	L.S.M. Miller	126	R.E. Redmond	192	K.P. Walmsley		
61	M.E. Chapple	127	B. Andrews	193	L.K. Germon		
62	E.W. Dempster	128	J.F.M. Morrison	194	R.G. Twose		
63	M.B. Poore	129	J.V. Coney	195	C.M. Spearman		
64	G.W.F. Overton	130	B.L. Cairns	196	N.J. Astle		
65	J.E.F. Beck	131	E.J. Chatfield	197	G.I. Allott		
66	W. Bell	132	G.P. Howarth	198	R.J. Kennedy		

Ground Records

Results by Grounds

In New Zealand	P	W	L	D
Eden Park, Auckland	47	9	15	23
Jade Stadium, Christchurch	40	8	16	16
Basin Reserve, Wellington	48	14	16	18
Carisbrook, Dunedin	10	3	4	3
McLean Park, Napier	6	—	2	4
Seddon Park, Hamilton	14	6	2	6
University Oval, Dunedin	1	1	—	—
Total	**166**	**41**	**55**	**70**

In England	P	W	L	D
Lord's, London	14	1	6	7
Oval, London	9	1	4	4
Headingley, Leeds	6	1	4	1
Trent Bridge, Nottingham	8	1	5	2
Old Trafford, Manchester	6	—	2	4
Egbaston, Birmingham	4	—	4	—
Total	**47**	**4**	**25**	**18**

In South Africa	P	W	L	D
Kingsmead, Durban	3	—	3	—
Ellis Park, Johannesburg	2	—	2	—
New Wanderers, Johannesburg	6	1	3	2
Newlands, Cape Town	4	1	1	2
St George's Park, Port Elizabeth	3	1	2	—
Goodyear Park, Bloemfontein	1	—	1	—
SuperSport Park, Centurion	2	—	2	—
Total	**21**	**3**	**14**	**4**

In Pakistan	P	W	L	D
National Stadium, Karachi	6	—	3	3
Bagh-e-Jinnah, Lahore	1	—	1	—
Dacca Stadium, Dacca	2	—	—	2
Niaz Stadium, Hyderabad	2	—	2	—
Rawalpindi Club Ground	1	—	1	—
Lahore (Gaddafi) Stadium	7	2	4	1
Iqbal Stadium, Faisalabad	1	—	1	—
Rawalpindi Cricket Stadium	1	—	1	—
Total	**21**	**2**	**13**	**6**

In India	P	W	L	D
Brabourne Stadium, Bombay	3	—	2	1
Wankhede Stadium, Bombay	2	1	1	—
Fateh Maidan, (Lal Bahadur Stadium) Hyderabad	3	—	1	2
Feroz Shah Kotla, Delhi	2	—	1	1
Eden Gardens, Calcutta	2	—	—	2
Corporation Stadium, Madras	2	—	1	1
Chepauk, (Chidambaram Stadium) Madras	2	—	1	1
VCA Ground, Nagpur	1	1	—	—
Green Park, Kanpur	2	—	1	1
Chinnaswamy Stadium, Bangalore	2	—	2	—
Barabati Stadium, Cuttack	1	—	—	1
Punjab C.A. Stadium, Mohali	2	—	—	2
Sardar Patel Stadium, Ahmedabad	2	—	—	2
Total	**26**	**2**	**10**	**14**

In West Indies	P	W	L	D
Queen's Park Oval, Port of Spain	3	—	—	3
Sabina Park, Kingston	2	—	1	1
Kensington Park, Bridgetown	4	1	2	1
Bourda, Georgetown	2	—	—	2
St Johns Recreation Ground, Antigua	1	—	—	1
Queen's Park, Grenada	1	—	—	1
Total	**13**	**1**	**3**	**9**

In Australia	P	W	L	D
Melbourne Cricket Ground	3	—	1	2
Sydney Cricket Ground	2	—	1	1
Adelaide Oval	3	—	2	1
WACA Ground, Perth	6	1	2	3
Woolloongabba, Brisbane	7	1	5	1
Bellerive Oval, Hobart	3	—	1	2
Total	**24**	**2**	**12**	**10**

In Sri Lanka	P	W	L	D
Kandy, Asgiriya Stadium	2	1	—	1
Sinhalese Sports Club Ground, Colombo	3	—	2	1
Colombo C.C. Ground, Colombo	2	1	—	1
Tyrone Fernando Stadium, Moratuwa	1	—	—	1
R. Premadasa Stadium, Colombo	1	1	—	—
Galle International Stadium	1	—	1	—
P. Saravanamuttu Stadium	1	—	—	1
Total	**11**	**3**	**3**	**5**

In Zimbabwe	P	W	L	D
Bulawayo Athletic Club	1	—	—	1
Harare Sports Club, Harare	4	3	—	1
Queens Sports Club, Bulawayo	3	2	—	1
Total	**8**	**5**	**—**	**3**

In Bangladesh	P	W	L	D
National Stadium, Dhaka	1	1	—	—
Chittagong Stadium	1	1	—	—
Total	**2**	**2**	**—**	**—**

Team Records

Summary of Results

	Played	Won	Lost	Drawn
v England	91	8	43	40
v Australia	46	7	22	17
v South Africa	35	4	20	11
v West Indies	35	9	10	16
v India	44	9	14	21
v Pakistan	45	6	21	18
v Sri Lanka	24	9	5	10
v Zimbabwe	13	7	—	6
v Bangladesh	6	6	—	—
Total	**339**	**65**	**135**	**139**

Highest Totals

For

671-4	v Sri Lanka	Wellington	1990/91
630-6d	v India	Mohali	2003/04
595	v South Africa	Auckland	2003/04
593-8d	v South Africa	Cape Town	2005/06
586-7d	v Sri Lanka	Dunedin	1996/97
563	v Pakistan	Hamilton	2003/04
561	v Sri Lanka	Napier	2004/05
553-7d	v Australia	Brisbane	1985/86
551-9d	v England	Lord's	1973
545-6d	v Bangladesh	Chittagong	2004/05

Against

660-5d	by West Indies	Wellington	1994/95
643	by Pakistan	Lahore	2001/02
621-5d	by South Africa	Auckland	1998/99
616-5d	by Pakistan	Auckland	1988/89
607-6d	by Australia	Brisbane	1993/94
593-6d	by England	Auckland	1974/75
585	by Australia	Brisbane	2004/05
583-7d	by India	Ahmedabad	1999/00
580-9d	by England	Christchurch	1991/92
575-8d	by Australia	Adelaide	2004/05

Lowest Totals

For

26	v England	Auckland	1954/55
42	v Australia	Wellington	1945/46
47	v England	Lord's	1958
54	v Australia	Wellington	1945/46
65	v England	Christchurch	1970/71
67	v England	Leeds	1958
67	v England	Lord's	1978
70	v Pakistan	Dacca	1955/56
73	v Pakistan	Lahore	2001/02
74	v West Indies	Dunedin	1955/56

Against

59	by Zimbabwe	Harare	2005/06
64	by England	Wellington	1977/78
77	by West Indies	Auckland	1955/56
81	by India	Wellington	1975/76
82	by England	Christchurch	1983/84
83	by India	Mohali	1999/00
88	by India	Bombay	1964/65
89	by India	Hyderabad	1969/70
93	by Sri Lanka	Wellington	1982/83
93	by England	Christchurch	1983/84

Individual Records

Centuries

299	Crowe M.D. v Sri Lanka at Wellington	1990/91
274*	Fleming S.P. v Sri Lanka at Colombo	2002/03
267*	Young B.A. v Sri Lanka at Dunedin	1996/97
262	Fleming S.P. v South Africa at Cape Town	2005/06
259	Turner G.M. v West Indies at Georgetown	1971/72
239	Dowling G.T. v India at Christchurch	1967/68
230*	Sutcliffe B. v India at New Delhi	1955/56
224	Vincent L. v Sri Lanka at Wellington	2004/05
223*	Turner G.M. v West Indies at Kingston	1971/72
222	Astle N.J. v England at Christchurch	2001/02
214	Sinclair M.S. v West Indies at Wellington	1999/00
206	Donnelly M.P. v England at Lord's	1949
204*	Sinclair M.S. v Pakistan at Christchurch	2000/01
202	Fleming S.P. v Bangladesh at Chittagong	2004/05
192	Fleming S.P. v Pakistan at Hamilton	2003/04
188	Crowe M.D. v West Indies at Georgetown	1984/85
188	Crowe M.D. v Australia at Brisbane	1985/86
186	Jones A.H. v Sri Lanka at Wellington	1990/91
185	Wright J.G. v India at Christchurch	1989/90
182	Jarvis T.W. v West Indies at Georgetown	1971/72
180	Reid J.F. v Sri Lanka at Colombo	1983/84
176	Congdon B.E. v England at Nottingham	1973
175	Congdon B.E. v England at Lord's	1973
174*	Coney J.V. v England at Wellington	1983/84
174*	Fleming S.P. v Sri Lanka at Colombo	1997/98
174	Crowe M.D. v Pakistan at Wellington	1988/89
173	Smith I.D.S. v India at Auckland	1989/90
170*	Jones A.H. v India at Auckland	1989/90
170	Styris S.B. v South Africa at Auckland	2003/04
166*	Congdon B.E. v West Indies at Port of Spain	1971/72
161	Edgar B.A. v Australia at Auckland	1981/82
160	Marshall H.J.H. v Sri Lanka at Napier	2004/05
158*	Reid J.F. v Pakistan at Auckland	1984/85
158	Cairns C.L. v South Africa at Auckland	2003/04
157	Horne M.J. v Zimbabwe at Auckland	1997/98
156*	Astle N.J. v Australia at Perth	2001/02
152	Lees W.K. v Pakistan at Karachi	1976/77
151*	Sutcliffe B. v India at Calcutta	1964/65
151*	Hadlee R.J. v Sri Lanka at Colombo	1986/87
150	Jones A.H. v Australia at Adelaide	1987/88
150	Sinclair M.S. v South Africa at Port Elizabeth	2000/01
148	Reid J.F. v Pakistan at Wellington	1984/85
147	Howarth G.P. v West Indies at Christchurch	1979/80
146*	Greatbatch M.J. v Australia at Perth	1989/90
146	Marshall H.J.H. v Australia at Christchurch	2004/05
145	Richardson M.H. v India at Mohali	2003/04
143	Dowling G.T. v India at Dunedin	1967/68
143	Crowe M.D. v England at Wellington	1987/88
143	Jones A.H. v England at Wellington	1991/92
143	Jones A.H. v Australia at Perth	1993/94
143	Richardson M.H. v Bangladesh at Hamilton	2001/02
143	McCullum B.B. v Bangladesh at Dhaka	2004/05
142	Reid J.R. v South Africa at Johannesburg	1961/62
142	Crowe M.D. v England at Lord's	1994
142	McMillan C.D. v Sri Lanka at Colombo	1997/98
142	McMillan C.D. v Zimbabwe at Wellington	2000/01
141	Wright J.G. v Australia at Christchurch	1981/82
141	Astle N.J. v Zimbabwe at Wellington	2000/01
140	Crowe M.D. v Zimbabwe at Harare	1992/93
139	McMillan C.D. v Zimbabwe at Wellington	1997/98
138	Sinclair B.W. v South Africa at Auckland	1963/64
138	Wright J.G. v West Indies at Wellington	1986/87
137*	Sutcliffe B. v India at Hyderabad	1955/56
137*	Howarth G.P. v India at Wellington	1980/81
137*	Vettori D.L. v Pakistan at Hamilton	2003/04

Score	Batsman	Match	Season
137	Crowe M.D. v Australia at Christchurch		1985/86
137	Crowe M.D. v Australia at Adelaide		1987/88
136	Dempster C.S. v England at Wellington		1929/30
135	Reid J.R. v South Africa at Cape Town		1953/54
133	Greatbatch M.J. v Pakistan at Hamilton		1992/93
133	Horne M.J. v Australia at Hobart		1997/98
133	Oram J.D.P. v South Africa at Centurion		2005/06
132	Congdon B.E. v Australia at Wellington		1973/74
130	Sinclair B.W. v Pakistan at Lahore		1964/65
130	Wright J.G. v England at Auckland		1983/84
130	Fleming S.P. v West Indies at Bridgetown		2001/02
129	Dowling G.T. v India at Bombay		1964/65
129	Edgar B.A. v Pakistan at Christchurch		1978/79
129	Fleming S.P. v England at Auckland		1996/97
128	Reid J.R. v Pakistan at Karachi		1964/65
128	Crowe J.J. v England at Auckland		1983/84
128	Astle N.J. v Zimbabwe at Bulawayo		2005/06
127	Edgar B.A. v West Indies at Auckland		1979/80
127	Vettori D.L. v Zimbabwe at Harare		2005/06
126*	Oram J.D.P. v Australia at Brisbane		2004/05
126	Congdon B.E. v West Indies at Bridgetown		1971/72
126	Cairns C.L. v India at Hamilton		1998/99
125	Astle N.J. v West Indies at Bridgetown		1995/96
124	Taylor B.R. v West Indies at Auckland		1967/68
124	Cairns C.L. v Zimbabwe at Harare		2000/01
123*	Reid J.F. v India at Christchurch		1980/81
123	Howarth G.P. v England at Lord's		1978
122*	Franklin J.E.C. v South Africa at Cape Town		2005/06
122	Howarth G.P. v England at Auckland		1977/78
122	Jones A.H. v Sri Lanka at Hamilton		1990/91
121	Parker J.M. v England at Auckland		1974/75
120*	Crowe J.J. v Sri Lanka at Colombo		1986/87
120*	Thomson S.A. v Pakistan at Christchurch		1993/94
120	Dempster C.S. v England at Lord's		1931
120	Reid J.R. v India at Calcutta		1955/56
120	Young B.A. v Pakistan at Christchurch		1993/94
120	Cairns C.L. v Zimbabwe at Auckland		1995/96
120	Taylor L.R.P.L. v England at Hamilton		2007/08
119*	Reid J.R. v India at Delhi		1955/56
119*	Burgess M.G. v Pakistan at Dacca		1969/70
119*	Oram J.D.P. v South Africa at Hamilton		2003/04
119	Wright J.G. v England at The Oval		1986
119	Crowe M.D. v West Indies at Wellington		1986/87
119	Latham R.T. v Zimbabwe at Bulawayo		1992/93
119	Styris S.B. v India at Mohali		2003/04
117*	Hastings B.F. v West Indies at Christchurch		1968/69
117*	Wright J.G. v Australia at Wellington		1989/90
117	Mills J.E. v England at Wellington		1929/30
117	Morrison J.F.M. v Australia at Sydney		1973/74
117	Turner G.M. v India at Christchurch		1975/76
117	Fleming S.P. v England at Nottingham		2004
117	Oram J.D.P. v Bangladesh at Dunedin		2007/08
116	Hadlee W.A. v England at Christchurch		1946/47
116	Sutcliffe B. v England at Christchurch		1950/51
116	Pollard V. v England at Nottingham		1973
116	Wright J.G. v England at Wellington		1991/92
115	Crowe M.D. v England at Manchester		1994
114	Sinclair B.W. v England at Auckland		1965/66
114	Howarth G.P. v Pakistan at Napier		1978/79
114	Astle N.J. v Zimbabwe at Auckland		1997/98
114	Astle N.J. v Sri Lanka at Napier		2004/05
113*	Smith I.D.S. v England at Auckland		1983/84
113*	Wright J.G. v India at Napier		1989/90
113	Turner G.M. v India at Kanpur		1976/77
113	Crowe M.D. v India at Auckland		1989/90
112	Crowe J.J. v West Indies at Kingston		1984/85
112	Spearman C.M. v Zimbabwe at Auckland		1995/96
111*	Coney J.V. v Pakistan at Dunedin		1984/85
111	McGregor S.N. v Pakistan at Lahore		1955/56
111	Burgess M.G. v Pakistan at Lahore		1976/77
111	McCullum B.B. v Zimbabwe at Harare		2005/06
110*	Turner G.M. v Australia at Christchurch		1973/74
110	Turner G.M. v Pakistan at Dacca		1969/70
110	Hastings B.F. v Pakistan at Auckland		1972/73
110	Wright J.G. v India at Auckland		1980/81
110	Bracewell J.G. v England at Nottingham		1986
110	Horne M.J. v Zimbabwe at Bulawayo		2000/01
110	Parore A.C. v Australia at Perth		2001/02
109	Barton P.T. v South Africa at Port Elizabeth		1961/62
109	Cairns C.L. v Australia at Wellington		1999/00
108*	Crowe M.D. v Pakistan at Lahore		1990/91
108	Parker J.M. v Australia at Sydney		1973/74
108	Reid J.F. v Australia at Brisbane		1985/86
108	Styris S.B. v England at Nottingham		2004
107*	Congdon B.E. v Australia at Christchurch		1976/77
107*	Greatbatch M.J. v England at Auckland		1987/88
107*	Rutherford K.R. v England at Wellington		1987/88
107*	McMillan C.D. v England at Manchester		1999
107	Rabone G.O. v South Africa at Durban		1953/54
107	Redmond R.E. v Pakistan at Auckland		1972/73
107	Wright J.G. v Pakistan at Karachi		1984/85
107	Crowe M.D. v Sri Lanka at Colombo		1992/93
107	Styris S.B. v West Indies at St George's		2001/02
107	Bell M.D. v Bangladesh at Dunedin		2007/08
106	Reid J.F. v Pakistan at Hyderabad		1984/85
106	Crowe M.D. v England at Lord's		1986
106	Richardson M.H. v Pakistan at Hamilton		2000/01
106	McMillan C.D. v Bangladesh at Hamilton		2001/02
106	Vincent L. v India at Mohali		2003/04
105*	Pollard V. v England at Lord's		1973
105	Taylor B.R. v India at Calcutta		1964/65
105	Hastings B.F. v West Indies at Bridgetown		1971/72
105	Burgess M.G. v England at Lord's		1973
105	Rutherford K.R. v Sri Lanka at Moratuwa		1992/93
105	Bell M.D. v Pakistan at Hamilton		2000/01
105	Fleming S.P. v Australia at Perth		2001/02
104	Page M.L. v England at Lord's		1931
104	Congdon B.E. v England at Christchurch		1965/66
104	Burgess M.G. v England at Auckland		1970/71
104	Parker J.M. v India at Bombay		1976/77
104	Crowe M.D. v West Indies at Auckland		1986/87
104	Vincent L. v Australia at Perth		2001/02]
103*	Styris S.B. v West Indies at Auckland		2005/06
103	Hadlee R.J. v West Indies at Christchurch		1979/80
103	Wright J.G. v England at Auckland		1987/88
103	Astle N.J. v West Indies at St John's		1995/96
103	Astle N.J. v India at Ahmedabad		2003/04
102*	Astle N.J. v England at Auckland		1996/97
102	Guy J.W. v India at Hyderabad		1955/56
102	Howarth G.P. v England at Auckland		1977/78
102	Rutherford K.R. v Australia at Christchurch		1992/93
101*	Coney J.V. v Australia at Wellington		1985/86
101	Sutcliffe B. v England at Manchester		1949
101	Harris P.G.Z. v South Africa at Cape Town		1961/62
101	Burgess M.G. v West Indies at Kingston		1971/72
101	Hastings B.F. v Australia at Wellington		1973/74
101	Turner G.M. v Australia at Christchurch		1973/74
101	Franklin T.J. v England at Lord's		1990
101	Wright J.G. v Sri Lanka at Hamilton		1990/91
101	Astle N.J. v England at Manchester		1999
101	Richardson M.H. v England at Lord's		2004
100*	Jones A.H. v Sri Lanka at Hamilton		1990/91
100*	Parore A.C. v West Indies at Christchurch		1994/95
100*	McMillan C.D. v India at Mohali		2003/04
100	Vivian H.G. v South Africa at Wellington		1931/32
100	Reid J.R. v England at Christchurch		1962/63
100	Crowe M.D. v England at Wellington		1983/84
100	Horne M.J. v England at Lord's		1999

Ten Wickets in a Match

15-123	Hadlee R.J. v Australia at Brisbane	1985/86
12-149	Vettori D.L. v Australia at Auckland	1999/00
12-170	Vettori D.L. v Bangladesh at Chittagong	2004/05
11-58	Hadlee R.J. v India at Wellington	1975/76
11-102	Hadlee R.J. v West Indies at Dunedin	1979/80
11-152	Pringle C. v Pakistan at Faisalabad	1990/91
11-155	Hadlee R.J. v Australia at Perth	1985/86
11-169	Nash D.J. v England at Lord's	1994
11-180	Martin C.S. v South Africa at Auckland	2003/04
10-88	Hadlee R.J. v India at Bombay	1988/89
10-99	Bond S.E. v Zimbabwe at Bulawayo	2005/06
10-100	Hadlee R.J. v England at Wellington	1977/78
10-100	Cairns C.L. v West Indies at Hamilton	1999/00
10-102	Hadlee R.J. v Sri Lanka at Colombo	1983/84
10-106	Bracewell J.G. v Australia at Auckland	1985/86
10-124	Chatfield E.J. v West Indies at Port of Spain	1984/85
10-140	Cowie J. v England at Manchester	1937
10-140	Hadlee R.J. v England at Nottingham	1986
10-144	Cairns B.L. v England at Leeds	1983
10-166	Troup G.B. v West Indies at Auckland	1979/80
10-176	Hadlee R.J. v Australia at Melbourne	1987/88
10-183	Vettori D.L. v Sri Lanka at Wellington	2006/07

Five Wickets in an Innings

9-52	Hadlee R.J. v Australia at Brisbane	1985/86
7-23	Hadlee R.J. v India at Wellington	1975/76
7-27	Cairns C.L. v West Indies at Hamilton	1999/00
7-52	Pringle C. v Pakistan at Faisalabad	1990/91
7-53	Cairns C.L. v Bangladesh at Hamilton	2001/02
7-65	Doull S.B. v India at Wellington	1998/99
7-74	Taylor B.R. v West Indies at Bridgetown	1971/72
7-74	Cairns B.L. v England at Leeds	1983
7-87	Boock S.L. v Pakistan at Hyderabad	1984/85
7-87	Vettori D.L. v Australia at Auckland	1999/00
7-89	Morrison D.K. v Australia at Wellington	1992/93
7-116	Hadlee R.J. v Australia at Christchurch	1985/86
7-130	Vettori D.L. v Sri Lanka at Wellington	2006/07
7-143	Cairns C.L. v England at Wellington	1983/84
6-26	Hadlee R.J. v England at Wellington	1977/78
6-27	Nash D.J. v India at Mohali	1999/00
6-28	Vettori D.L. v Bangladesh at Dhaka	2004/05
6-32	Bracewell J.G. v Australia at Auckland	1985/86
6-37	Morrison D.K. v Australia at Auckland	1992/93
6-38	Bartlett G.A. v India at Christchurch	1967/68
6-40	Cowie J. v Australia at Wellington	1945/46
6-46	Butler I.G. v Pakistan at Wellington	2003/04
6-49	Hadlee R.J. v India at Bombay	1988/89
6-50	Hadlee R.J. v West Indies at Christchurch	1986/87
6-50	Patel D.N. v Zimbabwe at Harare	1992/93
6-51	Hadlee R.J. v Pakistan at Dunedin	1984/85
6-51	Bracewell J.G. v India at Bombay	1988/89
6-51	Bond S.E. v Zimbabwe at Bulawayo	2005/06
6-52	Cairns C.L. v England at Auckland	1991/92
6-53	Hadlee R.J. v England at The Oval	1983
6-54	Tuffey D.R. v England at Auckland	2001/02
6-54	Martin C.S. v Sri Lanka at Wellington	2004/05
6-57	Hadlee R.J. v Australia at Melbourne	1980/81
6-60	Reid J.R. v South Africa at Dunedin	1963/64
6-63	Motz R.C. v India at Christchurch	1967/68
6-63	Collinge R.O. v India at Christchurch	1975/76
6-64	Vettori D.L. v Sri Lanka at Colombo	1997/98
6-67	Cowie J. v England at Manchester	1937
6-68	Rabone G.O. v South Africa at Cape Town	1953/54
6-68	Hadlee R.J. v West Indies at Dunedin	1979/80
6-69	Motz R.C. v West Indies at Wellington	1968/69
6-69	Morrison D.K. v West Indies at Christchurch	1994/95
6-70	Vettori D.L. v Bangladesh at Chittagong	2004/05

6-71	Hadlee R.J. v Australia at Brisbane	1985/86
6-73	Chatfield E.J. v West Indies at Port of Spain	1984/85
6-76	Cunis R.S. v England at Auckland	1970/71
6-76	Nash D.J. v England at Lord's	1994
6-76	Martin C.S. v South Africa at Auckland	2003/04
6-77	Cairns C.L. v England at Lord's	1999
6-78	Watson W. v Pakistan at Lahore	1990/91
6-80	Hadlee R.J. v England at Lord's	1986
6-80	Hadlee R.J. v England at Nottingham	1986
6-83	Cowie J. v England at Christchurch	1946/47
6-85	Cairns B.L. v West Indies at Christchurch	1979/80
6-85	Bracewell J.G. v Australia at Wellington	1989/90
6-87	Vettori D.L. v Australia at Perth	2001/02
6-90	Hadlee R.J. v Australia at Perth	1985/86
6-95	Troup G.B. v West Indies at Auckland	1979/80
6-100	Hadlee R.J. v Australia at Christchurch	1981/82
6-100	Vettori D.L. v Bangladesh at Chittagong	2004/05
6-105	Hadlee R.J. v West Indies at Auckland	1986/87
6-113	Patel D.N. v Zimbabwe at Bulawayo	1992/93
6-119	Franklin J.E.C v Australia at Auckland	2004/05
6-127	Vettori D.L. v India at Kanpur	1999/00
6-155	Moir A.M. v England at Christchurch	1950/51
6-162	Burtt T.B. v England at Manchester	1949
6-168	Cresswell G.F. v England at The Oval	1949
5-26	Taylor B.R. v India at Bombay	1964/65
5-28	Hadlee R.J. v England at Christchurch	1983/84
5-28	Boock S.L. v Sri Lanka at Kandy	1983/84
5-28	Franklin J.E.C v Bangladesh at Dhaka	2004/05
5-29	Hadlee R.J. v Sri Lanka at Colombo	1983/84
5-31	Cairns C.L. v England at The Oval	1999
5-31	Cairns C.L. v Zimbabwe at Bulawayo	2000/01
5-33	Cairns B.L. v India at Wellington	1980/81
5-34	Cameron F.J. v Pakistan at Auckland	1964/65
5-34	Howarth H.J. v India at Nagpur	1969/70
5-34	Hadlee R.J. v West Indies at Dunedin	1979/80
5-37	Martin C.S. v South Africa at Johannesburg	2005/06
5-39	Hadlee R.J. v Australia at Wellington	1989/90
5-41	Taylor B.R. v West Indies at Port of Spain	1971/72
5-41	Morrison D.K. v Pakistan at Hamilton	1992/93
5-44	Cairns C.L. v West Indies at Wellington	1999/00
5-46	Doull S.B. v Pakistan at Lahore	1996/97
5-47	Hadlee R.J. v India at Christchurch	1980/81
5-48	Cameron F.J. v South Africa at Cape Town	1961/62
5-50	Cairns C.L. v Zimbabwe at Harare	1997/98
5-51	O'Connor S.B. v Australia at Hamilton	1999/00
5-53	Hadlee R.J. v England at Birmingham	1990
5-53	Franklin J.E.C. v West Indies at Wellington	2005/06
5-55	Cairns B.L. v India at Madras	1976/77
5-55	Martin C.S. v South Africa at Wellington	2003/04
5-55	Southee T.G. v England at Napier	2007/08
5-58	Doull S.B. v Sri Lanka at Dunedin	1996/97
5-61	Morrison D.K. v West Indies at St Johns	1995/96
5-62	Moir A.M. v England at Auckland	1954/55
5-62	Hadlee R.J. v Pakistan at Christchurch	1978/79
5-62	Cairns C.L. v Sri Lanka at Colombo	1997/98
5-62	Vettori D.L. v Australia at Auckland	1999/00
5-63	Hadlee R.J. v Australia at Auckland	1981/82
5-63	Chatfield E.J. v Sri Lanka at Colombo	1983/84
5-63	Davis H.T. v Sri Lanka at Hamilton	1996/97
5-64	MacGibbon A.R. v England at Birmingham	1958
5-65	Congdon B.E. v India at Auckland	1975/76
5-65	Hadlee R.J. v Australia at Sydney	1985/86
5-65	Hadlee R.J. v Australia at Perth	1985/86
5-65	Hadlee R.J. v India at Bangalore	1988/89
5-65	Martin C.S. v Bangladesh at Wellington	2007/08
5-66	Doull S.B. v Pakistan at Auckland	1993/94
5-67	Boock S.L. v England at Auckland	1977/78
5-67	Hadlee R.J. v Australia at Melbourne	1987/88

5-68	Snedden M.C. v West Indies at Christchurch	1986/87
5-68	Hadlee R.J. v Australia at Adelaide	1987/88
5-69	Burtt T.B. v West Indies at Christchurch	1951/52
5-69	Morrison D.K. v England at Christchurch	1987/88
5-69	Bond S.E. v West Indies at Auckland	2005/06
5-71	Martin C.S. v Zimbabwe at Wellington	2000/01
5-73	Hadlee R.J. v Sri Lanka at Colombo	1983/84
5-73	Su'a M.L. v Pakistan at Hamilton	1992/93
5-73	Doull S.B. v South Africa at Durban	1994/95
5-74	Collinge R.O. v England at Leeds	1973
5-75	Bracewell J.G. v India at Auckland	1980/81
5-75	Morrison D.K. v India at Christchurch	1989/90
5-75	Cairns C.L. v Sri Lanka at Auckland	1990/91
5-75	Doull S.B. v England at Wellington	1996/97
5-77	Hart M.N. v South Africa at Johannesburg	1994/95
5-78	Bond S.E. v West Indies at Bridgetown	2001/02
5-79	Cairns C.L. v England at Nottingham	2004
5-80	Howarth H.J. v Pakistan at Karachi	1969/70
5-82	Collinge R.O. v Australia at Auckland	1973/74
5-82	Wiseman P.J. v Sri Lanka at Colombo	1997/98
5-83	Cameron F.J. v South Africa at Johannesburg	1961/62
5-84	Hadlee R.J. v England at Lord's	1978
5-84	Vettori D.L. v Sri Lanka at Hamilton	1996/97
5-85	Su'a M.L. v Zimbabwe at Harare	1992/93
5-86	Taylor B.R. v India at Calcutta	1964/65
5-86	Motz R.C. v India at Dunedin	1967/68
5-87	Cairns B.L. v Australia at Brisbane	1980/81
5-87	Hadlee R.J. v Australia at Perth	1980/81
5-87	Tuffey D.R. v Pakistan at Hamilton	2003/04
5-90	Wiseman P.J. v Zimabwe at Bulawayo	2000/01
5-93	Hadlee R.J. v England at Lord's	1983
5-93	Patel D.N. v Australia at Auckland	1992/93
5-93	Nash D.J. v England at Lord's	1994
5-95	Chatfield E.J. v England at Leeds	1983
5-97	Burtt T.B. v England at Leeds	1949
5-98	Morrison D.K. v India at Napier	1989/90
5-104	Hadlee R.J. v Pakistan at Auckland	1978/79
5-104	Bond S.E. v West Indies at St George's	2001/02
5-104	Martin C.S. v South Africa at Auckland	2003/04
5-106	Vettori D.L. v Australia at Christchurch	2004/05
5-108	Motz R.C. v England at Birmingham	1965
5-109	Hadlee R.J. v Australia at Melbourne	1987/88
5-113	Motz R.C. v West Indies at Christchurch	1968/69
5-117	Boock S.L. v Pakistan at Wellington	1984/85
5-121	Hadlee R.J. v Pakistan at Lahore	1976/77
5-127	Cowie J. v England at Leeds	1949
5-136	Gillespie M.R. v South Africa at Centurion	2007/08
5-137	Cairns C.L. v Pakistan at Rawalpindi	1996/97
5-138	Vettori D.L. v Australia at Hobart	2001/02
5-145	Morrison D.K. v India at Auckland	1989/90
5-146	Cairns C.L. v Australia at Brisbane	2001/02
5-148	O'Sullivan D.R. v Australia at Adelaide	1973/74
5-152	Martin C.S. v Australia at Brisbane	2004/05
5-152	Vettori D.L. v Australia at Adelaide	2004/05
5-153	Morrison D.K. v Sri Lanka at Wellington	1990/91

Hat-tricks

Petherick P.J. v Pakistan at Lahore		1976/77
Franklin J.E.C. v Bangladesh at Dhaka		2004/05

All Round Performances

Rabone G.O. 56 and 6-68 & 1-16 v South Africa at Cape Town	1953/54
Taylor B.R. 105 & 0* and 5-86 v India at Calcutta	1964/65
Congdon B.E. 54 & 54 and 5-65 v India at Auckland	1975/76
Hadlee R.J. 54* & 5 and 5-104 & 0-8 v Pakistan at Auckland	1978/79
Hadlee R.J. 51 & 17 and 5-34 & 6-68 v West Indies at Dunedin	1979/80
Hadlee R.J. 84 & 11 and 6-53 & 2-99 v England at The Oval	1983
Cairns B.L. 3 & 64 and 7-143 v England at Wellington	1983/84
Hadlee R.J. 99 and 3-16 & 5-28 v England at Christchurch	1983/84
Hadlee R.J. 54 and 9-52 & 6-71 v Australia at Brisbane	1985/86
Hadlee R.J. 68 and 6-80 & 4-60 v England at Nottingham	1986
Bracewell J.G. 52 & 32 and 2-81 & 6-51 v India at Bombay	1988/89
Patel D.N. 6 & 58* and 2-81 & 6-50 v Zimbabwe at Harare	1992/93
Nash D.J. 56 and 6-76 & 5-93 v England at Lord's	1994
Cairns C.L. 12 & 71* and 5-50 & 0-44 v Zimbabwe at Harare	1997/98
Cairns C.L. 11 & 80 and 5-31 & 1-50 v England at The Oval	1999
Cairns C.L. 72 and 3-73 & 7-27 v West Indies at Hamilton	1999/00
Cairns C.L. 61 & 43 and 5-146 & 1-29 v Australia at Brisbane	2001/02
Vettori D.L. 20 & 59 and 5-152 & 1-35 v Australia at Adelaide	2004/05
Vettori D.L. 0 & 51 and 3-53 & 7-130 v Sri Lanka at Wellington	2006/07
Southee T.G. 5 & 77* and 5-55 & 0-84 v England at Napier	2007/08

Most Dismissals in an Innings by a Wicketkeeper

7	Smith I.D.S. v Sri Lanka at Hamilton *(all caught)*	1990/91
5	Harford R.I. v India at Wellington *(all caught)*	1967/68
5	Wadsworth K.J. v Pakistan at Auckland *(all caught)*	1972/73
5	Lees W.K. v Sri Lanka at Wellington *(all caught)*	1982/83
5	Smith I.D.S. v England at Auckland *(4ct 1st)*	1983/84
5	Smith I.D.S. v Sri Lanka at Auckland *(all caught)*	1990/91
5	Parore A.C. v England at Auckland *(all caught)*	1991/92
5	Parore A.C. v Sri Lanka at Colombo *(4ct 1st)*	1992/93
5	Parore A.C. v Zimbabwe at Harare *(all caught)*	2000/01
5	Parore A.C. v Pakistan at Auckland *(all caught)*	2000/01
5	McCullum B.B. v England at Hamilton *(all caught)*	2007/08

Most Dismissals in a Match by a Wicketkeeper

8	Lees W.K. v Sri Lanka at Wellington *(all caught)*	1982/83
8	Smith I.D.S. v Sri Lanka at Hamilton *(all caught)*	1990/91
7	Dick A.E. v South Africa at Durban *(6ct 1st)*	1961/62
7	Harford R.I. v India at Wellington *(all caught)*	1967/68
7	Smith I.D.S. v India at Wellington *(all caught)*	1980/81
7	Smith I.D.S. v England at Leeds *(all caught)*	1983
7	Parore A.C. v Pakistan at Auckland *(all caught)*	2000/01
7	Parore A.C. v Pakistan at Hamilton *(all caught)*	2000/01

Most Catches in an Innings by a Fielder

5	Fleming S.P. v Zimbabwe at Harare	1997/98
4	Crowe J.J. v West Indies at Bridgetown	1984/85
4	Crowe M.D. v West Indies at Kingston	1984/85
4	Fleming S.P. v Australia at Brisbane	1997/98
4	Fleming S.P. v Zimbawe at Harare	2005/06
4	Fleming S.P. v West Indies at Wellington	2005/06

Most Catches in a Match by a Fielder

7	Fleming S.P. v Zimbabwe at Harare	1997/98
6	Young B.A. v Pakistan at Auckland	1993/94
6	Fleming S.P. v Australia at Brisbane	1997/98
6	Fleming S.P. v West Indies at Wellington	2005/06
5	Harris C.Z. v Zimbabwe at Bulawayo	1997/98
5	Fleming S.P. v India at Wellington	1998/99
5	Sinclair M.S. v Bangladesh at Chittagong	2004/05

Record Partnerhips

For

1st	387	Turner G.M. & Jarvis T.W. v West Indies	Georgetown	1971/72
2nd	241	Wright J.G. & Jones A.H. v England	Wellington	1991/92
3rd	467	Jones A.H. & Crowe M.D. v Sri Lanka	Wellington	1990/91
4th	243	Horne M.J. & Astle N.J. v Zimbabwe	Auckland	1997/98
5th	222	Astle N.J. & McMillan C.D. v Zimbabwe	Wellington	2000/01
6th	246*	Crowe J.J. & Hadlee R.J. v Sri Lanka	Colombo	1986/87
7th	225	Cairns C.L. & Oram J.D.P. v South Africa	Auckland	2003/04
8th	256	Fleming S.P. & Franklin J.E.C. v South Africa	Cape Town	2005/06
9th	136	Smith I.D.S. & Snedden M.C. v India	Auckland	1989/90
10th	151	Hastings B.F. & Collinge R.O. v Pakistan	Auckland	1972/73

Against

1st	413	Mankad M.H. & Roy P. for India	Madras	1955/56
2nd	369	Edrich J.H. & Barrington K.F. for England	Leeds	1965
3rd	330	Amla H.M. & Kallis J.H. for South Africa	Johannesburg	2007/08
4th	350	Mushtaq Mohammad & Asif Iqbal for Pakistan	Dunedin	1972/73
5th	281	Javed Miandad & Asif Iqbal for Pakistan	Lahore	1976/77
6th	281	Thorpe G.P. & Flintoff A. for England	Christchurch	2001/02
7th	308	Waqar Hassan & Imtiaz Ahmed for Pakistan	Lahore	1955/56
8th	246	Ames L.E.G. & Allen G.O.B. for England	Lord's	1931
9th	163*	Cowdrey M.C. & Smith A.C. for England	Wellington	1962/63
10th	114	Gillespie J.N. & McGrath G.D. for Australia	Brisbane	2004/05

Youngest Players

18 years 10 days	Vettori D.L. v England at Wellington	1996/97
18 years 197 days	Freeman D.L. v England at Christchurch	1932/33
18 years 267 days	Vivian H.G. v England at The Oval	1931
18 years 295 days	Collinge R.O. v Pakistan at Wellington	1964/65
18 years 316 days	Bracewell B.P. v England at The Oval	1978
19 years 5 days	Vivian G.E. v India at Calcutta	1964/65
19 years 102 days	Southee T.G. v England at Napier	2007/08
19 years 145 days	Beck J.E.F. v South Africa at Johannesburg	1953/54
19 years 154 days	Rutherford K.R. v West Indies at Port of Spain	1984/85
19 years 157 days	Crowe M.D. v Australia at Wellington	1981/82
19 years 163 days	Parore A.C. v England at Birmingham	1990
19 years 164 days	Cairns C.L. v Australia at Perth	1989/90
19 years 173 days	Pollard V. India at Madras	1964/65
19 years 186 days	Playle W.R. v England at Birmingham	1958
19 years 252 days	Donnelly M.P. v England at Lord's	1937
19 years 340 days	Sewell D.G. v Zimbabwe at Bulawayo	1997/98
19 years 344 days	Sparling J.T. v England at Leeds	1958

Oldest Players *(age on last day of final test)*

41 years 294 days	Alabaster J.C. v West Indies at Port of Spain	1971/72
41 years 196 days	Sutcliffe B. v England at Birmingham	1965
40 years 198 days	Congdon B.E. v England at Lord's	1978

Averages

Batting and Fielding

	M	Inns	NO	Runs	HS	Ave	100	50	ct	st
A.R. Adams	1	2	0	18	11	9.00	-	-	1	-
J.C. Alabaster	21	34	6	272	34	9.71	-	-	7	-
C.F.W. Allcott	6	7	2	113	33	22.60	-	-	3	-
G.I. Allott	10	15	7	27	8*	3.37	-	-	2	-
R.W. Anderson	9	18	0	423	92	23.50	-	3	1	-
W.M. Anderson	1	2	0	5	4	2.50	-	-	1	-
B. Andrews	2	3	2	22	17	22.00	-	-	1	-
N.J. Astle	81	137	10	4702	222	37.02	11	24	70	-
F.T. Badcock	7	9	2	137	64	19.57	-	2	1	-
R.T. Barber	1	2	0	17	12	8.50	-	-	1	-
G.A. Bartlett	10	18	1	263	40	15.47	-	-	8	-
P.T. Barton	7	14	0	285	109	20.35	1	1	4	-
D.D. Beard	4	7	2	101	31	20.20	-	-	2	-
J.E.F. Beck	8	15	0	394	99	26.26	-	3	-	-
M.D. Bell	18	32	2	729	107	24.30	2	3	19	-
W. Bell	2	3	3	21	21*	-	-	-	1	-
G.P. Bilby	2	4	0	55	28	13.75	-	-	3	-
T.E. Blain	11	20	3	456	78	26.82	-	2	19	2
R.W. Blair	19	34	6	189	64*	6.75	-	1	5	-
R.C. Blunt	9	13	1	330	96	27.50	-	1	5	-
B.A. Bolton	2	3	0	59	33	19.66	-	-	1	-
S.E.Bond	17	18	7	139	41*	12.63	-	-	6	-
S.L. Boock	30	41	8	207	37	6.27	-	-	14	-
B.P. Bracewell	6	12	2	24	8	2.40	-	-	1	-
J.G. Bracewell	41	60	11	1001	110	20.42	1	4	31	-
G.E. Bradburn	7	10	2	105	30*	13.12	-	-	6	-
W.P. Bradburn	2	4	0	62	32	15.50	-	-	2	-
V.R. Brown	2	3	1	51	36*	25.50	-	-	3	-
M.G. Burgess	50	92	6	2684	119*	31.20	5	14	34	-
C. Burke	1	2	0	4	3	2.00	-	-	-	-
T.B. Burtt	10	15	3	252	42	21.00	-	-	2	-
I.G. Butler	8	10	2	76	26	9.50	-	-	4	-
L.A. Butterfield	1	2	0	0	0	0.00	-	-	-	-
B.L. Cairns	43	65	8	928	64	16.28	-	2	30	-
C.L. Cairns	62	104	5	3320	158	33.53	5	22	14	-
F.J. Cameron	19	30	20	116	27*	11.60	-	-	2	-
H.B. Cave	19	31	5	229	22*	8.80	-	-	8	-
M.E. Chapple	14	27	1	497	76	19.11	-	3	10	-
E.J. Chatfield	43	54	33	180	21*	8.57	-	-	7	-
D.C. Cleverley	2	4	3	19	10*	19.00	-	-	-	-
R.O. Collinge	35	50	13	533	68*	14.40	-	2	10	-
I.A. Colquhoun	2	4	2	1	1*	0.50	-	-	4	-
J.V. Coney	52	85	14	2668	174*	37.57	3	16	64	-
B.E. Congdon	61	114	7	3448	176	32.22	7	19	44	-
J. Cowie	9	13	4	90	45	10.00	-	-	3	-
G.F. Cresswell	3	5	3	14	12*	7.00	-	-	-	-
I.B. Cromb	5	8	2	123	51*	20.50	-	1	1	-
J.J. Crowe	39	65	4	1601	128	26.24	3	6	41	-
M.D. Crowe	77	131	11	5444	299	45.36	17	18	71	-
C.D. Cumming	11	19	2	441	74	25.94	-	1	3	-
R.S. Cunis	20	31	8	295	51	12.82	-	1	1	-
J.W. D'Arcy	5	10	0	136	33	13.60	-	-	2	-
H.T. Davis	5	7	4	20	8*	6.66	-	-	4	-
R.P. de Groen	5	10	4	45	26	7.50	-	-	-	-
C.S. Dempster	10	15	4	723	136	65.72	2	5	2	-
E.W. Dempster	5	8	2	106	47	17.66	-	-	1	-
A.E. Dick	17	30	4	370	50*	14.23	-	1	47	4
G.R. Dickinson	3	5	0	31	11	6.20	-	-	3	-
M.P. Donnelly	7	12	1	582	206	52.90	1	4	7	-
S.B. Doull	32	50	11	570	46	14.61	-	-	16	-
G.T. Dowling	39	77	3	2306	239	31.16	3	11	23	-
C.J. Drum	5	5	2	10	4	3.33	-	-	4	-
J.A. Dunning	4	6	1	38	19	7.60	-	-	2	-
B.A. Edgar	39	68	4	1958	161	30.59	3	12	14	-

	M	Inns	NO	Runs	HS	Ave	100	50	ct	st
G.N. Edwards	8	15	0	377	55	25.13	-	3	7	-
G.D. Elliott	1	2	0	10	6	5.00	-	-	2	-
R.W.G. Emery	2	4	0	46	28	11.50	-	-	-	-
F.E. Fisher	1	2	0	23	14	11.50	-	-	-	-
S.P. Fleming	111	189	10	7172	274*	40.06	9	46	172	-
H. Foley	1	2	0	4	2	2.00	-	-	-	-
J.E.C. Franklin	21	28	5	505	122*	21.95	1	1	8	-
T.J. Franklin	21	37	1	828	101	23.00	1	4	8	-
D.L. Freeman	2	2	0	2	1	1.00	-	-	-	-
P.G. Fulton	7	10	1	236	75	26.22	-	1	6	-
N. Gallichan	1	2	0	32	30	16.00	-	-	-	-
S.G. Gedye	4	8	0	193	55	24.12	-	2	-	-
L.K. Germon	12	21	3	382	55	21.22	-	1	27	2
M.R. Gillespie	2	4	0	9	9	2.25	-	-	-	-
S.R. Gillespie	1	1	0	28	28	28.00	-	-	-	-
E.J. Gray	10	16	0	248	50	15.50	-	1	6	-
M.J. Greatbatch	41	71	5	2021	146*	30.62	3	10	27	-
S.C. Guillen	3	6	0	98	41	16.33	-	-	4	1
J.W. Guy	12	23	2	440	102	20.95	1	3	2	-
D.R. Hadlee	26	42	5	530	56	14.32	-	1	8	-
R.J. Hadlee	86	134	19	3124	151*	27.16	2	15	39	-
W.A. Hadlee	11	19	1	543	116	30.16	1	2	6	-
N.S. Harford	8	15	0	229	93	15.26	-	2	-	-
R.I. Harford	3	5	2	7	6	2.33	-	-	11	-
C.Z. Harris	23	42	4	777	71	20.44	-	5	14	-
P.G.Z. Harris	9	18	1	378	101	22.23	1	1	6	-
R.M. Harris	2	3	0	31	13	10.33	-	-	-	-
M.N. Hart	14	24	4	353	45	17.65	-	-	9	-
R.G. Hart	11	19	3	260	57*	16.25	-	1	29	1
B.R. Hartland	9	18	0	303	52	16.83	-	1	5	-
M.J. Haslam	4	2	1	4	3	4.00	-	-	2	-
B.F. Hastings	31	56	6	1510	117*	30.20	4	7	23	-
J.A. Hayes	15	22	7	73	19	4.86	-	-	3	-
M. Henderson	1	2	1	8	6	8.00	-	-	1	-
M.J. Horne	35	65	2	1788	157	28.38	4	5	17	-
P.A. Horne	4	7	0	71	27	10.14	-	-	3	-
K.W. Hough	2	3	2	62	31*	62.00	-	-	1	-
J.M. How	9	16	1	332	92	22.13	-	1	11	-
G.P. Howarth	47	83	5	2531	147	32.44	6	11	29	-
H.J. Howarth	30	42	18	291	61	12.12	-	1	33	-
K.C. James	11	13	2	52	14	4.72	-	-	11	5
T.W. Jarvis	13	22	1	625	182	29.76	1	2	3	-
A.H. Jones	39	74	8	2922	186	44.27	7	11	25	-
R.A. Jones	1	2	0	23	16	11.50	-	-	-	-
R.J. Kennedy	4	5	1	28	22	7.00	-	-	2	-
J.L. Kerr	7	12	1	212	59	19.27	-	1	4	-
C.M. Kuggeleijn	2	4	0	7	7	1.75	-	-	1	-
G.R. Larsen	8	13	4	127	26*	14.11	-	-	5	-
R.T. Latham	4	7	0	219	119	31.28	1	-	5	-
W.K. Lees	21	37	4	778	152	23.57	1	1	52	7
J.G. Leggat	9	18	2	351	61	21.93	-	2	-	-
I.B. Leggatt	1	1	0	0	0	0.00	-	-	2	-
A.F. Lissette	2	4	2	2	1*	1.00	-	-	1	-
G.R. Loveridge	1	1	1	4	4*	-	-	-	-	-
T.C. Lowry	7	8	0	223	80	27.87	-	2	8	-
A.R. MacGibbon	26	46	5	814	66	19.85	-	3	13	-
H.J.H. Marshall	13	19	2	652	160	38.35	2	2	1	-
J.A.H. Marshall	5	7	0	166	52	23.71	-	1	3	-
C.S. Martin	40	56	27	74	12*	2.55	-	-	9	-
M.J. Mason	1	2	0	3	3	1.50	-	-	-	-
A.M. Matheson	2	1	0	7	7	7.00	-	-	2	-
B.B. McCullum	32	51	3	1485	143	30.93	2	8	95	6
P.E. McEwan	4	7	1	96	40*	16.00	-	-	5	-
H.M. McGirr	2	1	0	51	51	51.00	-	1	-	-

	M	Inns	NO	Runs	HS	Ave	100	50	ct	st
S.N. McGregor	25	47	2	892	111	19.82	1	3	9	-
E.G. McLeod	1	2	1	18	16	18.00	-	-	-	-
T.G. McMahon	5	7	4	7	4*	2.33	-	-	7	1
C.D. McMillan	55	91	10	3116	142	38.46	6	19	22	-
D.A.N. McRae	1	2	0	8	8	4.00	-	-	-	-
T. Meale	2	4	0	21	10	5.25	-	-	-	-
W.E. Merritt	6	8	1	73	19	10.42	-	-	2	-
E.M. Meuli	1	2	0	38	23	19.00	-	-	-	-
B.D. Milburn	3	3	2	8	4*	8.00	-	-	6	2
L.S.M. Miller	13	25	0	346	47	13.84	-	-	1	-
J.E. Mills	7	10	1	241	117	26.77	1	-	1	-
K.D. Mills	11	18	4	174	31	12.42	-	-	3	-
A.M. Moir	17	30	8	327	41*	14.86	-	-	2	-
D.A.R. Moloney	3	6	0	156	64	26.00	-	1	3	-
F.L.H. Mooney	14	22	2	343	46	17.15	-	-	22	8
R.W. Morgan	20	34	1	734	97	22.24	-	5	12	-
B.D. Morrison	1	2	0	10	10	5.00	-	-	1	-
D.K. Morrison	48	71	26	379	42	8.42	-	-	14	-
J.F.M. Morrison	17	29	0	656	117	22.62	1	3	9	-
R.C. Motz	32	56	3	612	60	11.54	-	3	9	-
B.A.G. Murray	13	26	1	598	90	23.92	-	5	21	-
D.J. Murray	8	16	1	303	52	20.20	-	1	6	-
D.J. Nash	32	45	14	729	89*	23.51	-	4	13	-
J. Newman	3	4	0	33	19	8.25	-	-	-	-
I.E. O'Brien	6	9	1	33	14*	4.12	-	-	1	-
S.B. O'Connor	19	27	9	105	20	5.83	-	-	6	-
D.R. O'Sullivan	11	21	4	158	23*	9.29	-	-	2	-
J.D.P. Oram	27	47	8	1428	133	36.61	4	4	14	-
G.W.F. Overton	3	6	1	8	3*	1.60	-	-	1	-
M.B. Owens	8	12	6	16	8*	2.66	-	-	3	-
M.L. Page	14	20	0	492	104	24.60	1	2	6	-
M.H.W. Papps	8	16	1	246	86	16.40	-	2	11	-
J.M. Parker	36	63	2	1498	121	24.55	3	5	30	-
N.M. Parker	3	6	0	89	40	14.83	-	-	2	-
A.C. Parore	78	128	19	2865	110	26.28	2	14	197	7
D.N. Patel	37	66	8	1200	99	20.68	-	5	15	-
J.S. Patel	3	5	2	67	27*	22.33	-	-	1	-
P.J. Petherick	6	11	4	34	13	4.85	-	-	4	-
E.C. Petrie	14	25	5	258	55	12.90	-	1	25	-
W.R. Playle	8	15	0	151	65	10.06	-	1	4	-
B.A. Pocock	15	29	0	665	85	22.93	-	6	5	-
V. Pollard	32	59	7	1266	116	24.34	2	7	19	-
M.B. Poore	14	24	1	355	45	15.43	-	-	1	-
M.W. Priest	3	4	0	56	26	14.00	-	-	-	-
C. Pringle	14	21	4	175	30	10.29	-	-	3	-
N. Puna	3	5	3	31	18*	15.50	-	-	1	-
G.O. Rabone	12	20	2	562	107	31.22	1	2	5	-
R.E. Redmond	1	2	0	163	107	81.50	1	1	-	-
J.F. Reid	19	31	3	1296	180	46.28	6	2	9	-
J.R. Reid	58	108	5	3428	142	33.28	6	22	43	1
M.H. Richardson	38	65	3	2776	145	44.77	4	19	26	-
A.D.G. Roberts	7	12	1	254	84*	23.09	-	1	4	-
A.W. Roberts	5	10	1	248	66*	27.55	-	3	4	-
G.K. Robertson	1	1	0	12	12	12.00	-	-	-	-
C.G. Rowe	1	2	0	0	0	0.00	-	-	1	-
K.R. Rutherford	56	99	8	2465	107*	27.08	3	18	32	-
R.H. Scott	1	1	0	18	18	18.00	-	-	-	-
V.J. Scott	10	17	1	458	84	28.62	-	3	7	-
D.G. Sewell	1	1	1	1	1*	-	-	-	-	-
M.J.F. Shrimpton	10	19	0	265	46	13.94	-	-	2	-
B.W. Sinclair	21	40	1	1148	138	29.43	3	3	8	-
I.M. Sinclair	2	4	1	25	18*	8.33	-	-	1	-
M.S. Sinclair	32	54	5	1595	214	32.55	3	4	31	-
F.B. Smith	4	6	1	237	96	47.40	-	2	1	-
H.D. Smith	1	1	0	4	4	4.00	-	-	-	-
I.D.S. Smith	63	88	17	1815	173	25.56	2	6	168	8
C.A. Snedden	1	0	0	0	0	-	-	-	-	-
M.C. Snedden	25	30	8	327	33*	14.86	-	-	7	-
T.G. Southee	1	2	1	82	77*	82.00	-	1	-	-

	M	Inns	NO	Runs	HS	Ave	100	50	ct	st
J.T. Sparling	11	20	2	229	50	12.72	-	1	3	-
C.M. Spearman	19	37	2	922	112	26.34	1	3	21	-
G.R. Stead	5	8	0	278	78	34.75	-	2	2	-
D.A. Stirling	6	9	2	108	26	15.42	-	-	1	-
S.B. Styris	29	48	4	1586	170	36.04	5	6	23	-
M.L. Su'a	13	18	5	165	44	12.69	-	-	8	-
B. Sutcliffe	42	76	8	2727	230*	40.10	5	15	20	-
B.R. Taylor	30	50	6	898	124	20.40	2	2	10	-
D.D. Taylor	3	5	0	159	77	31.80	-	1	2	-
L.R.P.L. Taylor	5	10	0	354	120	35.40	1	3	4	-
K. Thomson	2	4	1	94	69	31.33	-	1	-	-
S.A. Thomson	19	35	4	958	120*	30.90	1	5	7	-
E.W.T. Tindill	5	9	1	73	37*	9.12	-	-	6	1
G.B. Troup	15	18	6	55	13*	4.58	-	-	2	-
P.B. Truscott	1	2	0	29	26	14.50	-	-	1	-
D.R. Tuffey	22	30	7	263	35	11.43	-	-	12	-
G.M. Turner	41	73	6	2991	259	44.64	7	14	42	-
R.G. Twose	16	27	2	628	94	25.12	-	6	5	-
R.H. Vance	4	7	0	207	68	29.57	-	1	-	-
J.T.C. Vaughan	6	12	1	201	44	18.27	-	-	4	-
D.L. Vettori	79	115	18	2676	137*	27.58	2	16	39	-
L. Vincent	23	40	1	1332	224	34.15	3	9	19	-
G.E. Vivian	5	6	0	110	43	18.33	-	-	3	-
H.G. Vivian	7	10	0	421	100	42.10	1	5	4	-
K.J. Wadsworth	33	51	4	1010	80	21.48	-	5	92	4
B.G.K. Walker	5	8	2	118	27*	19.66	-	-	4	-
W.M. Wallace	13	21	0	439	66	20.90	-	5	5	-
K.P. Walmsley	3	5	0	13	5	2.60	-	-	-	-
J.T. Ward	8	12	6	75	35*	12.50	-	-	16	1
W. Watson	15	18	6	60	11	5.00	-	-	4	-
L. Watt	1	2	0	2	2	1.00	-	-	-	-
M.G. Webb	3	2	0	12	12	6.00	-	-	-	-
P.N. Webb	2	3	0	11	5	3.66	-	-	2	-
G.L. Weir	11	16	2	416	74*	29.71	-	3	3	-
D.J. White	2	4	0	31	18	7.75	-	-	-	-
P.E. Whitelaw	2	4	2	64	30	32.00	-	-	-	-
P.J. Wiseman	25	34	8	366	36	14.07	-	-	11	-
J.G. Wright	82	148	7	5334	185	37.82	12	23	38	-
B.A. Young	35	68	4	2034	267*	31.78	2	12	54	-
B.W. Yuile	17	33	6	481	64	17.81	-	1	12	-

Bowling

	Balls	Runs	Wkts	Ave	Best	5W	10W
A.R. Adams	190	105	6	17.50	3-44	-	-
J.C. Alabaster	3992	1863	49	38.02	4-46	-	-
C.F.W. Allcott	1206	541	6	90.16	2-102	-	-
G.I. Allott	2023	1111	19	58.47	4-74	-	-
R.W. Anderson							
W.M. Anderson							
B. Andrews	256	154	2	77.00	2-40	-	-
N.J. Astle	5688	2143	51	42.01	3-27	-	-
F.T. Badcock	1608	610	16	38.12	4-80	-	-
R.T. Barber							
G.A. Bartlett	1768	792	24	33.00	6-38	1	-
P.T. Barton							
D.D. Beard	806	302	9	33.55	3-22	-	-
J.E.F. Beck							
M.D. Bell							
W. Bell	491	235	2	117.50	1-54	-	-
G.P. Bilby							
T.E. Blain							
R.W. Blair	3525	1515	43	35.23	4-85	-	-
R.C. Blunt	936	472	12	39.33	3-17	-	-
B.A. Bolton							
S.E. Bond	3079	1769	79	22.39	6-51	4	1
S.L. Boock	6598	2564	74	34.64	7-87	4	-
B.P. Bracewell	1036	585	14	41.78	3-110	-	-
J.G. Bracewell	8403	3653	102	35.81	6-32	4	1

	Balls	Runs	Wkts	Ave	Best	5W	10W
G.E. Bradburn	868	460	6	76.66	3-134	-	-
W.P. Bradburn							
V.R. Brown	342	176	1	176.00	1-17	-	-
M.G. Burgess	498	212	6	35.33	3-23	-	-
C. Burke	66	30	2	15.00	2-30	-	-
T.B. Burtt	2593	1170	33	35.45	6-162	3	-
I.G. Butler	1368	884	24	36.83	6-46	1	-
L.A. Butterfield	78	24	0	-	-	-	-
B.L. Cairns	10628	4279	130	32.91	7-74	6	1
C.L. Cairns	11698	6410	218	29.40	7-27	13	1
F.J. Cameron	4570	1849	62	29.82	5-34	3	-
H.B. Cave	4074	1467	34	43.14	4-21	-	-
M.E. Chapple	248	84	1	84.00	1-24	-	-
E.J. Chatfield	10360	3958	123	32.17	6-73	3	1
D.C. Cleverley	222	130	0	-	-	-	-
R.O. Collinge	7689	3393	116	29.25	6-63	3	-
I.A. Colquhoun							
J.V. Coney	2835	966	27	35.77	3-28	-	-
B.E. Congdon	5620	2154	59	36.50	5-65	1	-
J. Cowie	2028	969	45	21.53	6-40	4	1
G.F. Cresswell	650	292	13	22.46	6-168	1	-
I.B. Cromb	960	442	8	55.25	3-113	-	-
J.J. Crowe	18	9	0	-	-	-	-
M.D. Crowe	1377	676	14	48.28	2-25	-	-
C.D. Cumming							
R.S. Cunis	4250	1887	51	37.00	6-76	1	-
J.W. D'Arcy							
H.T. Davis	1010	499	17	29.35	5-63	1	-
R.P. de Groen	1060	505	11	45.90	3-40	-	-
C.S. Dempster	5	10	0	-	-	-	-
E.W. Dempster	544	219	2	109.50	1-24	-	-
A.E. Dick							
G.R. Dickinson	451	245	8	30.62	3-66	-	-
M.P. Donnelly	30	20	0	-	-	-	-
S.B. Doull	6053	2872	98	29.30	7-65	6	-
G.T. Dowling	36	19	1	19.00	1-19	-	-
C.J. Drum	806	482	16	30.12	3-36	-	-
J.A. Dunning	830	493	5	98.60	2-35	-	-
B.A. Edgar	18	3	0	-	-	-	-
G.N. Edwards							
G.D. Elliott	144	85	1	85.00	1-27	-	-
R.W.G. Emery	46	52	2	26.00	2-52	-	-
F.E. Fisher	204	78	1	78.00	1-78	-	-
S.P. Fleming							
H. Foley							
J.E.C. Franklin	3577	2143	76	28.19	6-119	3	-
T.J. Franklin							
D.L. Freeman	240	169	1	169.00	1-91	-	-
P.G. Fulton							
N. Gallichan	264	113	3	37.66	3-99	-	-
S.G. Gedye							
L.K. Germon							
M.R. Gillespie	390	278	11	25.27	5-136	1	-
S.R. Gillespie	162	79	1	79.00	1-79	-	-
E.J. Gray	2076	886	17	52.11	3-73	-	-
M.J. Greatbatch	6	0	0	-	-	-	-
S.C. Guillen							
J.W. Guy							
D.R. Hadlee	4883	2389	71	33.64	4-30	-	-
R.J. Hadlee	21918	9611	431	22.29	9-52	36	9
W.A. Hadlee							
N.S. Harford							
R.I. Harford							
C.Z. Harris	2560	1170	16	73.12	2-16	-	-
P.G.Z. Harris	42	14	0	-	-	-	-
R.M. Harris							
M.N. Hart	3086	1438	29	49.58	5-77	1	-
R.G. Hart							
B.R. Hartland							
M.J. Haslam	493	245	2	122.50	1-33	-	-
B.F. Hastings	22	9	0	-	-	-	-
J.A. Hayes	2675	1217	30	40.56	4-36	-	-
M. Henderson	90	64	2	32.00	2-38	-	-
M.J. Horne	66	26	0	-	-	-	-
P.A. Horne							
K.W. Hough	462	175	6	29.16	3-79	-	-
J.M. How							
G.P. Howarth	614	271	3	90.33	1-13	-	-
H.J. Howarth	8833	3178	86	36.95	5-34	2	-
K.C. James							
T.W. Jarvis	12	3	0	-	-	-	-
A.H. Jones	328	194	1	194.00	1-40	-	-
R.A. Jones							
R.J. Kennedy	636	380	6	63.33	3-28	-	-
J.L. Kerr							
C.M. Kuggeleijn	97	67	1	67.00	1-50	-	-
G.R. Larsen	1967	689	24	28.70	3-57	-	-
R.T. Latham	18	6	0	-	-	-	-
W.K. Lees	5	4	0	-	-	-	-
J.G. Leggat							
I.B. Leggatt	24	6	0	-	-	-	-
A.F. Lissette	288	124	3	41.33	2-73	-	-
G.R. Loveridge							
T.C. Lowry	12	5	0	-	-	-	-
A.R. MacGibbon	5659	2160	70	30.85	5-64	1	-
H.J.H. Marshall	6	4	0	-	-	-	-
J.A.H. Marshall							
C.S. Martin	7744	4443	136	32.66	6-54	8	1
M.J. Mason	132	105	0	-	-	-	-
A.M. Matheson	282	136	2	68.00	2-7	-	-
B.B. McCullum							
P.E. McEwan	36	13	0	-	-	-	-
H.M. McGirr	180	115	1	115.00	1-65	-	-
S.N. McGregor							
E.G. McLeod	12	5	0	-	-	-	-
T.G. McMahon							
C.D. McMillan	2502	1257	28	44.89	3-48	-	-
D.A.N. McRae	84	44	0	-	-	-	-
T. Meale							
W.E. Merritt	936	617	12	51.41	4-104	-	-
E.M. Meuli							
B.D. Milburn							
L.S.M. Miller	2	1	0	-	-	-	-
J.E. Mills							
K.D. Mills	1799	887	33	26.87	4-16	-	-
A.M. Moir	2650	1418	28	50.64	6-155	2	-
D.A.R. Moloney	12	9	0	-	-	-	-
F.L.H. Mooney	8	0	0	-	-	-	-
R.W. Morgan	1114	609	5	121.80	1-16	-	-
B.D. Morrison	186	129	2	64.50	2-129	-	-
D.K. Morrison	10064	5549	160	34.68	7-89	10	-
J.F.M. Morrison	264	71	2	35.50	2-52	-	-
R.C. Motz	7034	3148	100	31.48	6-63	5	-
B.A.G. Murray	6	0	1	0.00	1-0	-	-
D.J. Murray							
D.J. Nash	6196	2649	93	28.48	6-27	3	1
J. Newman	425	254	2	127.00	2-76	-	-
I.E. O'Brien	873	505	12	42.08	3-34	-	-
S.B. O'Connor	3667	1724	53	32.52	5-51	1	-
D.R. O'Sullivan	2744	1221	18	67.83	5-148	1	-
J.D.P. Oram	4226	1717	57	30.12	4-41	-	-
G.W.F. Overton	729	258	9	28.66	3-65	-	-
M.B. Owens	1074	585	17	34.41	4-99	-	-
M.L. Page	379	231	5	46.20	2-21	-	-
M.H.W. Papps							
J.M. Parker	40	24	1	24.00	1-24	-	-
N.M. Parker							
A.C. Parore							

	Balls	Runs	Wkts	Ave	Best	5W	10W
D.N. Patel	6594	3154	75	42.05	6-50	3	-
J.S. Patel	869	404	11	36.72	3-107	-	-
P.J. Petherick	1305	685	16	42.81	3-90	-	-
E.C. Petrie							
W.R. Playle							
B.A. Pocock	24	20	0	-	-	-	-
V. Pollard	4421	1853	40	46.32	3-3	-	-
M.B. Poore	788	367	9	40.77	2-28	-	-
M.W. Priest	377	158	3	52.66	2-42	-	-
C. Pringle	2985	1389	30	46.30	7-52	1	1
N. Puna	480	240	4	60.00	2-40	-	-
G.O. Rabone	1385	635	16	39.68	6-68	1	-
R.E. Redmond							
J.F. Reid	18	7	0	-	-	-	-
J.R. Reid	7725	2835	85	33.35	6-60	1	-
M.H. Richardson	66	21	1	21.00	1-16	-	-
A.D.G. Roberts	440	182	4	45.50	1-12	-	-
A.W. Roberts	459	209	7	29.85	4-101	-	-
G.K. Robertson	144	91	1	91.00	1-91	-	-
C.G. Rowe							
K.R. Rutherford	256	161	1	161.00	1-38	-	-
R.H. Scott	138	74	1	74.00	1-74	-	-
V.J. Scott	18	14	0	-	-	-	-
D.G. Sewell	138	90	0	-	-	-	-
M.J.F. Shrimpton	257	158	5	31.60	3-35	-	-
B.W. Sinclair	60	32	2	16.00	2-32	-	-
I.M. Sinclair	233	120	1	120.00	1-79	-	-
M.S. Sinclair	24	13	0	-	-	-	-
F.B. Smith							
H.D. Smith	120	113	1	113.00	1-113	-	-
I.D.S. Smith	18	5	0	-	-	-	-
C.A. Snedden	96	46	0	-	-	-	-
M.C. Snedden	4775	2199	58	37.91	5-68	1	-
T.G. Southee	283	139	5	27.80	5-55	1	-
J.T. Sparling	708	327	5	65.40	1-9	-	-
C.M. Spearman							
G.R. Stead	6	1	0	-	-	-	-
D.A. Stirling	902	601	13	46.23	4-88	-	-
S.B. Styris	1960	1015	20	50.75	3-28	-	-
M.L. Su'a	2843	1377	36	38.25	5-73	2	-
B. Sutcliffe	538	344	4	86.00	2-38	-	-
B.R. Taylor	6334	2953	111	26.60	7-74	4	-
D.D. Taylor							
L.R.P.L. Taylor	20	10	0	-	-	-	-
K. Thomson	21	9	1	9.00	1-9	-	-
S.A. Thomson	1990	953	19	50.15	3-63	-	-
E.W.T. Tindill							
G.B. Troup	3183	1454	39	37.28	6-95	1	1
P.B. Truscott							
D.R. Tuffey	4110	2057	66	31.16	6-54	2	-
G.M. Turner	12	5	0	-	-	-	-
R.G. Twose	193	130	3	43.33	2-36	-	-
R.H. Vance							
J.T.C. Vaughan	1040	450	11	40.90	4-27	-	-
D.L. Vettori	19016	8417	244	34.49	7-87	13	3
L. Vincent	6	2	0	-	-	-	-
G.E. Vivian	198	107	1	107.00	1-14	-	-
H.G. Vivian	1311	633	17	37.23	4-58	-	-
K.J. Wadsworth							
B.G.K. Walker	669	399	5	79.80	2-92	-	-
W.M. Wallace	6	5	0	-	-	-	-
K.P. Walmsley	774	391	9	43.44	3-70	-	-
J.T. Ward							
W. Watson	3486	1387	40	34.67	6-78	1	-
L. Watt							
M.G. Webb	732	471	4	117.75	2-114	-	-
P.N. Webb							
G.L. Weir	342	209	7	29.85	3-38	-	-
D.J. White	3	5	0	-	-	-	-

	Balls	Runs	Wkts	Ave	Best	5W	10W
P.E. Whitelaw							
P.J. Wiseman	5660	2903	61	47.59	5-82	2	-
J.G. Wright	30	5	0	-	-	-	-
B.A. Young							
B.W. Yuile	2897	1213	34	35.67	4-43	-	-

Most Matches

Fleming S.P.	111
Hadlee R.J.	86
Wright J.G.	82
Astle N.J.	81
Vettori D.L.	79
Parore A.C.	78
Crowe M.D.	77
Smith I.D.S.	63
Cairns C.L.	62
Congdon B.E.	61
Reid J.R.	58
Rutherford K.R.	56
McMillan C.D.	55
Coney J.V.	52
Burgess M.G.	50

Most Runs

Fleming S.P.	7172
Crowe M.D.	5444
Wright J.G.	5334
Astle N.J.	4702
Congdon B.E.	3448
Reid J.R.	3428
Cairns C.L.	3320
Hadlee R.J.	3124
McMillan C.D.	3116
Turner G.M.	2991
Jones A.H.	2922
Parore A.C.	2865
Richardson M.H.	2776
Sutcliffe B.	2727
Burgess M.G.	2684
Vettori D.L.	2676
Coney J.V.	2668
Howarth G.P.	2531
Rutherford K.R.	2465
Dowling G.T.	2306
Young B.A.	2034
Greatbatch M.J.	2021

Most Wickets

Hadlee R.J.	431
Vettori D.L.	244
Cairns C.L.	218
Morrison D.K.	160
Martin C.S.	136
Cairns B.L.	130
Chatfield E.J.	123
Collinge R.O.	116
Taylor B.R.	111
Bracewell J.G.	102
Motz R.C.	100

Most Catches

Fleming S.P.	172
Crowe M.D.	71
Astle N.J.	70
Coney J.V.	64
Young B.A.	54
Congdon B.E.	43
Turner G.M.	42
Reid J.R.	41
Crowe J.J.	41

Most Wicketkeeping Dismissals

	ct	st	total
Parore A.C.	194	7	201
Smith I.D.S.	168	8	176
McCullum B.B.	95	6	101
Wadsworth K.J.	92	4	96
Lees W.K.	52	7	59
Dick A.E.	47	4	51

Bibliography

Altham, HS & Swanton, EW. *A History of Cricket*, George Allen & Unwin, London, 1947.

Arlott, J. *A History of Cricket 1890-1965*, Arthur Barker Ltd, London, 1965.

Brittenden, RT. *A Cricket Century*, Papanui Press, Christchurch, 1981.

Fine, M & Smarrini, G. *The Encyclopedia of International Cricketers*, Bas Publishing, 2006.

McConnell, L. *The First Fifty: New Zealand cricket test victories 1956 to 2002*, HarperSports, Auckland, 2002.

McConnell, L & Smith, I. *The Shell New Zealand Cricket Enclyclopedia*, Moa Beckett, Auckland, 1993.

Neely, DO, King, RP & Payne, FK. *Men in White*, Moa Publications, Auckland, 1986.

Reese, TW. *New Zealand Cricket: 1841-1914*, Simpson and Williams, Christchurch, 1927.

Reese, TW. *New Zealand Cricket: 1914-1946*, Whitcombe and Tombs, Christchurch, 1936.

Roberts, EL. *Test Cricket Cavalcade: 1877-1946*, Edward Arnold, 1947.

Swanton, EW & Woodcock, J. *Barclays World of Cricket*, Collins Publishers, 1980.

Annual Publications

Payne, FK & Smith, I. *New Zealand Cricket Almanack (1983-2007)*, Moa Publications.

Cricket Almanack of New Zealand (1948-1982), Arthur Carman Sporting Publications.

DB Cricket Annual (1972-1985), Moa Publications.

Radio New Zealand Sport Cricket Annual (1985-1993), Moa Publications.

Wisden Cricketers' Almanack (1864-2007), John Wisden.

Periodicals

The Wisden Cricketer (UK)

Wisden Cricket Monthly (UK)

Internet

www.cricinfo.com

Photographic Credits

Don Neely: 1, 11, 12, 16, 17, 18, 19, 23 (right), 24, 25, 26, 27, 28, 30, 31, 33, 38, 39, 41, 42, 43, 44, 45, 46, 47, 48, 49 (left & right), 50 (left & right), 51 (left & right), 52 (left & right), 55, 56, 59, 60 (top), 61, 62, 63, 64 (right), 68, 79 (right), 82, 85 (left & right), 87, 88, 89, 90, 93 (right), 94, 95, 96, 98, 99, 106, 108, 113, 114, 115, 119, 126, 127, 128, 131, 133, 137, 138, 139, 140, 143 (left & right), 144, 146, 148, 149, 154, 156, 157, 158, 160, 164, 165, 167, 169 (left & right), 170, 172 (left & right), 174, 175, 176, 177, 180, 185, 186, 191, 192, 193, 194, 195, 197, 198, 201, 202, 205, 206, 207, 208, 212, 213, 214, 215, 216, 217, 218, 219, 221, 222, 226, 228, 238, 239, 240, 243, 244, 246, 258, 267, 268, 271, 272, 277, 278, 279, 284, 290 (right), 300, 301, 302, 315, 317, 319, 320, 328, 343.

Getty Images: 32, 78, 81, 129, 159, 229, 303, 305, 306, 307, 309, 310, 311, 314, 318, 322, 324, 325, 327, 329, 332, 334, 336, 337, 338, 340, 342, 344, 345, 346, 348, 349, 350, 351, 352, 354, 355, 356, 358, 359, 360, 361, 363, 364, 365, 366, 368, 369, 370, 371, 372, 373, 375, 376, 377, 378, 380, 381, 382, 385, 386, 389, 390, 391, 393, 394, 395, 396, 397, 398, 400, 401, 402, 404, 405, 407, 408, 409, 410, 411, 412, 413, 414, 415, 418, 419, 420, 421, 422, 424 (left), 426, 428, 429, 430, 431, 432, 433, 434, 435, 436, 438 (right).

John Blackwell: 187, 224, 230, 231, 232, 234, 241, 247, 249, 250, 252, 253, 257, 261, 263, 265, 266, 269, 273, 274 276, 281, 283, 286, 288, 291, 294, 295, 296, 297.

Fairfax Media: 58 (top & bottom), 70, 72, 77, 100, 104, 111, 112, 117, 118, 121, 123, 142, 150, 162, 163, 178, 189, 199, 204, 251, 287, 290 (left), 293, 298, 326, 331.

Photosport: 308, 335, 339, 384, 388, 416, 424 (right).

Patrick Eagar: 152, 153, 181, 183, 184, 210.

New Zealand Cricket: 107, 120, 161, 213. 256, 275, 292, 313, 392, 425

Sport and General: 23 (left), 35, 36.

Bert Sutcliffe: 60 (bottom), 64 (left), 65.

John R. Reid: 93 (left), 103 (left), 109.

Brian Hastings: 125, 132, 135.

New Zealand Herald: 74, 75,

New Zealand Cricket Museum: 79 (left), 316.

John Knight: 236 (left & right), 254.

Terry Baines: 321, 330.

Walter Hadlee: 34.

Henry Cooper: 67.

Canterbury Museum: 71.

John Sparling: 83.

Graham Dowling: 103 (right).

Weekly News: 124.

Hedley Howarth: 134.

Ken Kelly: 209.

Bruce Edgar: 225.

K. Gopinathan: 260.

Sean Neely: 264.

Craig McMillan: 399.

Marc Weakley: 438 (left).

Every effort has been made to trace all copyright holders of photographs published in this book. Please send any correspondence regarding copyright to the publisher.